For Reference

Not to be taken from this room

A CONCISE ENCYCLOPEDIA OF THE UNITED NATIONS

A Concise Encyclopedia
of the United Nations

edited by

HELMUT VOLGER

Second Revised Edition

MARTINUS
NIJHOFF
PUBLISHERS

LEIDEN • BOSTON
2010

Library of Congress Cataloging-in-Publication Data

Lexikon der Vereinten Nationen. English
  A concise encyclopedia of the United Nations / edited by Helmut Volger.—2nd, Rev. ed.
    p. cm.
  Includes index.
  ISBN 978-90-04-18004-8 (hardback : alk. paper)
   1. United Nations—Encyclopedias. 2. International law—Encyclopedias.
  3. International cooperation—Encyclopedias. 4. International relations—Encyclopedias.
  I. Volger, Helmut. II. Title.

    KZ4968.L4913 2010
    341.2303—dc22
                                                                    2009048272

This is the English version of: *Lexikon der Vereinten Nationen.*
© 2000 Oldenbourg Wissenschaftsverlag GmbH

Printed on acid-free paper

ISBN 978 90 04 18004 8

Mixed Sources
Product group from well-managed forests
and other controlled sources
www.fsc.org   Cert no. SGS-COC-006767
©1996 Forest Stewardship Council
FSC

PRINTED BY A-D DRUK BV - ZEIST, THE NETHERLANDS

Contents

IX

X

Introduction

When I had finished the editorial work for the German "Lexikon der Vereinten Nationen", conceived of as a one-volume encyclopedia for all those interested in the United Nations and published in 2000, I developed the idea of publishing an English edition of the book.

In this project I was supported by the group of authors who contributed to the "Lexikon". They translated their articles into English and encouraged me with suggestions and good wishes.

When the English edition, "A Concise Encyclopedia of the United Nations", came out in 2002, it was greeted with the same interest among the UN-related readership as its German predecessor, and was appreciated as reference literature for high school and college students as well as for UN diplomats and journalists.

Four years after its publication, the publishing house told me that the first edition had sold out and asked if I would be willing to prepare a second edition together with the contributing authors. I agreed to the suggestion.

When I asked the contributing authors whether they would be willing to update and revise their contributions for the second edition, I was glad to learn that the majority was ready to take up that work. Since not all contributing authors were in a position to revise completely their original entries or to revise them at all, I developed a compromise solution aimed at doing justice to all authors and their respective capacity to revise their contributions. I offered the authors three alternatives: they could completely revise their entries; they could write an updating "addendum" to the original entry of the first edition, to be printed together in the second edition; or they could leave it to another author to write an "addendum" to the original entry.

The authors made use of all three alternatives, with the revised texts forming the majority of the entries. In other words, if the reader finds an entry followed by an "addendum", then the original entry has been retained from the first edition written in 2001, with the "addendum" written in 2008 for the second edition. If the reader finds an entry without "addendum", this entry has been revised by the author for the second edition in 2008.

The views expressed in the contributions of the encyclopedia are the personal opinions of the authors which need not to be the standpoint of the institutions they are associated with.

I want to express my thanks and appreciation to the two native-speaking copy-editors James Arbuckle and Anthony McDermott who carried out the copy-editorial work with great care, stylistic sensitivity and inspiration. This English edition owes much to their work.

For good advice and encouragement during the making of the book, I would like to extend special thanks to Professor Klaus Hüfner, Dr. Axel Wüstenhagen and Dr. Norman Weiß, as well as to my wife Anna Volger for her support in the editorial work and during the layout.

My cordial thanks goes to all contributing authors whose interest and engagement have made it possible to publish the second edition of the "Concise Encyclopedia of the United Nations".

It is my hope that this English edition will promote the international exchange of ideas on the United Nations, and will win the UN some new friends and supporters. The United Nations deserves it.

Helmut Volger

How to use this book

All statements in this book are based on the latest available data as of 31 December 2008, unless otherwise indicated. In some cases, current statistics or facts may not have been available, whereas in others more recent developments could be taken into account.

References in an entry to other entries of the encyclopedia are indicated by an arrow before the word or group of words, for example "... the permanent members of the → Security Council ...".

Since UN documents are cited in most of the entries, a brief introduction to the UN document number system is provided in the annex of the book to help the reader to locate the documents cited. The annex also contains information on the institutions and organizations to which to address inquiries concerning UN documents. Further information can be found in the contributions "Documentation System" and "Internet, Websites of the UN System in the".

The bibliographies at the end of each entry containing references and further reading are organized in alphabetical sequence by name of the author.

In the Internet addresses at the bottom of the entries and in the annex of the encyclopedia the element "http://" is omitted to save printing space. If the addresses begin with "www." for WorldWideWeb, for example, "www.un.org" stands for the complete address "http://www.un.org". If the addresses contain other elements in place of "www.", then the complete Internet address is given, e.g. "http://documents.un.org" for the website of the Official Document System of the United Nations.

Abbreviations used in the encyclopedia are to be found in the list of "Abbreviations".

Entries are referenced in the index in the annex by page number. The titles of the entries are printed in bold type, followed by the corresponding page numbers, also in bold type. The index is intended as a primary source of reference – additional cross-references will be found within the text cited.

Abbreviations

AASL	Annals of Air and Space Law
ACABQ	Adminstrative and Budgetary Committee
ACC	Adminstrative Committee on Coordination
ACP states	African, Caribbean and Pazific states being members of the Lomé Agreement with the EC
AJIL	American Journal of International Law
AOSIS	Alliance Of Small Island States
APZ	Aus Politik und Zeitgeschichte, Supplement to the Weekly "Das Parlament"
Art(s).	Article(s)
ASIL Proc.	Proceedings of the annual meetings of the American Society of International Law
AULRev.	American University Law Review
AVR	Archiv des Völkerrechts
BGBl.	Bundesgesetzblatt (German: Federal Statute Book of the FRG)
BrooklJIL	Brooklyn Journal of International Law
Bull.	Bulletin
BWC	Convention on the Prohibition of the Development, Production and Stockpiling of Bacteriological (Biological) and Toxic Weapons and on their Destruction
BYIL	The British Year Book of International Law
Calif. W Int'l. LJ	California Western International Law Journal
Can. YIL	Canadian Yearbook of International Law
CARICOM	Caribbean Community
CAT	Committee Against Torture
CBD	Convention on Biological Diversity
CBM	Confidence Building Measure
CCD	Conference of the Committee on Disarmament
CD	Committee on Disarmament (1979-1983); Conference on Disarmament (1983-)
CEB	UN System's Chief Executives Board for Coordination
CEDAW	Committee on the Elimination of the Discrimination against Women
CERD	Committee on the Elimination of Racial Discrimination
cf.	confer (Latin: compare)
CFE	Treaty on Conventional Forces in Europe (1990)
CFE 1A	Follow-on Agreement to CFE Treaty (1992)
CFSP	Common Foreign and Security Policy (of the EU)
CHR	Common on Human Rights
CIS	Commonwealth of Independent States
CLCS	Commission on the Limits of the Continental Shelf
COCOM	Coordination Committee for East-West-Trade Policy
ColJTransL	Columbia Journal of Transnational Law
COPOUS	Committee on the Peaceful Uses of Outer Space
CPC	Committee for Programme and Coordination
CPIUN	Convention on Priviliges and Immunities of the United Nations
CRC	Committee on the Rights of the Child
CSBM	Confidence and Security Building Measures
CSCE	Conference on Security and Co-operation in Europe
CSD	Commission on Sustainable Development
CSW	Commission on the Status of Women
CTBT	Comprehensive Nuclear-Test Ban Treaty (1986)
CTBTO (Vienna)	Comprehensive Nuclear-Test Ban Treaty Organization

CWC	Convention on the Prohibition of Development, Production, Stockpiling and Use of Chemical Weapons and on their Destruction
Den. J Int'l. L&Pol.	Denver Journal of International Law and Policy
DESA	Department of Economic and Social Affairs
DFS	Department of Field Services
DGACM	Department for General Assembly and Conference Management
DGVN	Deutsche Gesellschaft für die Vereinten Nationen (German Association for the United Nations)
Diss.	Dissertation
DM	Department of Management
Doc.	Document
DPA	Department of Political Affairs
DPI	Department of Public Information
DPKO	Department of Peacekeeping Operations
Dt.Ges.f.VR	Deutsche Gesellschaft für Völkerrecht (German Association for International Law)
E10	the ten elected members of the Security Council
EA	Europa-Archiv (Journal)
ECA	Economic Commission for Africa
ECE	Economic Commission for Europe
ECLAC	Economic Commission for Latin America and the Caribbean
ECOSOC	Economic and Social Council
EC	European Community
ECR	Reports of the Court of Justice of the European Communities (European Court Reports)
ed(s).	editor(s)
edn.	edition
EES	Group of Eastern European States
EFTA	European Free Trade Association
e.g.	exempli gratia (Latin: for example)
EJIL	European Journal of International Law
EHRC	European Human Rights Commission
EmoryILRev.	Emory International Law Revue
ENDC	Eighteen-Nations Conference on Disarmament
EOSG	Excutive Office of the Secretary-General
EPIL	Bernhardt, R. et al. (eds.): Encyclopedia of Public International Law, Amsterdam et al. 1981ff.
ESCWA	Economic and Social Commission for Western Asia
et al.	et alii (Latin: and others)
et seq.	et sequentes (Latin: and the following)
ETS	European Treaty Series
EU	European Union
EuGRZ	Europäische Grundrechte-Zeitschrift
f(f).	following page(s)
FAO	Food and Agricultural Organization
FOSS	Forum Of Small States
Fs.	Festschrift (presentation anthology)
FW	Die Friedens-Warte (Journal)
FY	fiscal year
G7	Group of 7 (the seven leading industrial nations of the world)
G15	Group of 15
G77	Group of 77 (organization of the developing countries of the world)
GA	General Assembly
GAFS	Group of African States
GAOR	General Assembly Official Records

GASS	Group of Asian States
GATT	General Agreement on Tariffs and Trades
GEF	Global Environment Facility
GG	Grundgesetz (Basic Law/Constitution of the FRG)
GRULAC	Group of Latin American and Caribbean States
GYIL	German Yearbook of International Law
Harv. Int'l. LJ	Harvard International Law Journal
HarvardIRev.	Harvard International Revue
Harv. LRev.	Harvard Law Review
HDR	Human Development Report
HLCM	High-level Committee on Management
HLCP	High-level Committee on Programmes
HRC	Human Rights Council
HRJ	Human Rights Journal
HRLJ	Human Rights Law Journal
HRQ	Human Rights Quarterly
HSFK	Hessische Stiftung Friedens- und Konfliktforschung
HuV-I	Humanitäres Völkerrecht, Information (Journal)
IA	International Affairs (Journal), (Cambridge)
IAEA	International Atomic Energy Agency (in Vienna)
ibid.	ibidem (Latin: in the same place (article or passage))
IBRD	International Bank for Reconstruction and Development
ICAO	International Civil Aviation Organization
ICC	International Criminal Court
ICJ	International Court of Justice
ICJ Pleadings	International Court of Justice. Pleadings, Oral Arguments, Documents
ICJ Reports	International Court of Justice. Reports of Judgements, Advisory Opinions and Orders
ICJ Review	Review of the International Commission of Jurists
ICJ Yearbook	Yearbook of the International Court of Justice
ICLQ	International and Comparative Law Quarterly
ICSID	International Centre on the Settlement of Investment Disputes
IDA	International Development Association
IDS	Institute of Development Studies
i.e.	id est (Latin: that is (to say), in other words)
IFAD	International Fund for Agricultural Development
IFC	International Finance Corporation
IJ	International Journal
ILC	International Law Commission
ILCYB	Yearbook of the International Law Commission
ILM	International Legal Materials
ILO	International Labour Organization
ILQ	International Law Quarterly
ILR	International Law Reports
IMF	International Monetary Fund
IMO	International Maritime Organization
INF	Intermediate Nuclear Forces (Treaty 1987)
INSTRAW	International Research and Training Institute for the Advancement of Women
IO	International Organization (Journal)
IP	Internationale Politik (Berlin) (Journal), formerly EA = Europa Archiv
IPCC	Intergovernmental Panel on Climate Change
IPG	Internationale Politik und Gesellschaft (Journal)

ITLOS	International Tribunal for the Law of the Sea
ITU	International Telecommunication Union
JA	Juristische Arbeitsblätter (Journal)
JCC	Joint Coordination Committee
JIR	Jahrbuch für Internationales Recht (Yearbook for International Law)
JIU	Joint Inspection Unit
JPR	Journal of Peace Research
JSL	Journal of Space Law
JWTL	Journal of World Trade Law – from 1988 Journal of World Trade
LDCs	least developed countries
Lit.	literature
LJIL	Leiden Journal of International Law
LLDCs	land-locked developing countries
LNTS	League of Nations Treaty Series
loc. cit.	loco citato (Latin: in the place cited
LOSC	United Nations Convention on the Law of the Sea
LoyLAInt & CompLJ	Loyola of Los Angeles International and Comparative Law Journal
MDG(s)	Millennium Development Goal(s)
MIGA	Multilateral Investment Guarantee Agency
MLR	Modern Law Review
MTCR	Missile Technology Control Regime
NAM	Non-Aligned Movement
NEPAD	New Partnership for Africa's Development
Neth. QHR	Netherlands Quarterly of Human Rights
NGO(s)	non-governmental organization(s)
NIEO	New International Economic Order
NILR	Netherlands International Law Review
Nordic JIL	Nordic Journal of International Law
NPT	Non-Proliferation Treaty (1968)
NYIL	Netherlands Yearbook of International Law
NYUJ of Int'l. L&Pol.	New York University Journal of International Law and Politics
OAS	Organization of American States
OAU	Organization of African Unity
OCHA	Office for the Coordination of Humanitarian Affairs
ODA	Office for Disarmament Affairs
OECD	Organization for Economic Cooperation and Development, former OEEC
OHCHR	Office of the UN High Commissioner for Human Rights
OHRM	Office of Human Resources Management
OIC	Organization of the Islamic Conference
OIOS	Office of Internal Oversight Services
OLA	Office of Legal Affairs
op. cit.	opere citato (Latin: in the work cited)
OPEC	Organization of Petroleum Exporting Countries
OPCW	Organization for Chemical Disarmament (in The Hague)
OSCE	Organization for Security and Cooperation in Europe
p(p).	page(s)
P5	the five permanent members of the Security Council
p.a.	per annum (Latin: yearly)
para(s).	paragraph(s)
PBC	Peacebuilding Commission
Plen.	Plenary
PLO	Palestine Liberation Organization
PVS	Politische Vierteljahresschrift (Journal)
RdC	Receuil des Cours de l'Académie de Droit International

XVI

Res.	Resolution
resp.	respectively
RIAA	Reports of International Arbitral Awards
RIDP	Revue Internationale de droit pénale
RISA	Revue International des Sciences Administratives
s.a.	sine anno (Latin: without date)
SALT I	Strategic Arms Limitation Treaty I of 1972
SALT II	Strategic Arms Limitation Treaty II of 1979
SC	Security Council
SCOR	Security Council Official Records
sess.	session
S+F	Vierteljahresschrift für Sicherheit und Frieden (Journal)
SG	Secretary-General
SGA	Special General Assembly
START I	Strategic Arms Reduction Treaty of 1991
START II	Strategic Arms Reduction Treaty of 1993
Supp(l).	Supplement
SWAPO	South West Africa People's Organization
TDB	Trade and Development Board
TEU	Treaty of the European Union
Tex. Int'l. LJ	Texas International Law Journal
TWQ	Third World Quarterly
UNAT	United Nations Administrative Tribunal
UNCED	United Nations Conference on Environment and Development
UNCHS	United Nations Centre for Human Settlements
UNCITRAL	United Nations Commission on International Trade Law
UNCIVPOL	United Nations Civilian Police
UNCLOS	United Nations Convention on the Law of the Sea
UNCTAD	United Nations Conference on Trade and Development
UN Doc.	United Nations Document
UNDP	United Nations Development Programme
UNDG	United Nations Development Group
UNDYB	United Nations Disarmament Yearbook
UNEP	United Nations Environment Programme
UNESCO	United Nations Educational, Scientific and Cultural Organization
UNFCCC	United Nations Framework Convention on Climate Change
UNFPA	United Nations Population Fund
UN-HABITAT	United Nations Human Settlements Programme
UNHCR	United Nations High Commissioner for Refugees
UNICEF	United Nations Children's Fund
UNIDIR	United Nations Institute for Disarmament Research
UNIDO	United Nations Industrial Development Organization
UNIFEM	United Nations Development Fund for Women
UNITAR	United Nations Institute for Training and Research
UNOG	United Nations Office at Geneva
UNON	United Nations Office at Nairobi
UNOPS	United Nations Office for Project Services
UNOV	United Nations Office at Vienna
UNRISD	United Nations Research Institute for Social Development
UNRWA	United Nations Relief and Works Agency for Palestine Refugees in the Near East
UNTS	United Nations Treaty Series
UNU	United Nations University
UNV	United Nations Volunteers
UNWTO	United Nations World Tourism Organization

UNYB	Yearbook of the United Nations
UPU	Universal Postal Union
US Digest	Digest of United States Practice in International Law
VCLT	Vienna Convention on the Law of Treaties
viz	videlicet (Latin: namely)
v(s).	versus (Latin: against, in opposition, esp. in a lawsuit)
VN	Vereinte Nationen (Journal)
vol(s).	volume(s)
WEOG	Western European and Other States Group
WFC	World Food Council
WFP	World Food Programme
WFUNA	World Federation of United Nations Associations
WHO	World Health Organization
WIPO	World Intellectual Property Organization
WMO	World Meteorological Organization
WQ	The Washington Quarterly
WSIS	World Summit on Information Society
WTO	World Trade Organization
Yale J Int'l. L	Yale Journal of International Law
YBWA	Yearbook of World Affairs
YILC	Yearbook of the International Law Commission
ZaöRV	Zeitschrift für ausländisches öffentliches Recht und Völkerrecht
ZfP	Zeitschrift für Politik
ZLW	Zeitschrift für Luft- und Weltraumrecht
ZÖR	Zeitschrift für Öffentliches Recht
ZPol	Zeitschrift für Politikwissenschaft
ZRP	Zeitschrift für Rechtspolitik

Africa as Topic in the UN

From the outset the process of → decolonization was of overall importance with regard to Africa in the organs of the United Nations. After the majority of African countries had gained their independence in the early sixties, Africa played an increasingly important role for the → specialized agencies and other UN bodies dealing with development issues (→ Development Cooperation of the UN), such as UNECA, → UNCTAD, → UNDP, → WHO, → FAO, → ILO, → UNIDO, → UNICEF, → UNESCO, → UNEP. But it was not until the 80s that Africa became a special topic for the UN, as for the first time a whole continent was a subject for the UN.

The development crisis in the eighties

This special commitment was induced by the African development crisis which then became more and more obvious. The "lost development decade" left deep marks in Africa. The collapse of commodity prices during this period hit the continent particularly hard, especially as in most African countries exports are based on just a few commodities (monocultures).

Therefore, most countries became extremely over-indebted, despite comparatively high Official Development Assistance (ODA) flows to Africa as bilateral and multilateral aid. Corrupt elites and conflicts that were escalated by East-West rivalry increased the economic drain. Furthermore, a vicious circle ensued between the overexploitation of resources and natural disasters. The modernization achievements of the 60s and 70s were destroyed. Impoverishment and social decline became rampant. States could no longer fulfill their core obligations for the welfare of their peoples. Some states even collapsed.

The response of the → IMF and the World Bank (→ World Bank, World Bank Group) to this development crisis was to impose Structural Adjustment Programmes (SAPs). However, their impact was as if thirst was being quenched with seawater. The first generation of SAPs in particular deepened the slump. Devaluations and liberalization of exchange rates as part of SAPs increased the oversupply of commodities on world markets, and accelerated the erosion of commodity prices. At the same time imports became more expensive. As a result, SAP-funding sometimes was not even enough to pay for essential imports. Therefore, debt and debt service could not be reduced as intended by SAPs, but were in fact further increased. The economic austerity measures led to demand compression of public as well as private households. This virtually destroyed the achievements of the first phase of industrialization in the field of import substitution.

The Programme of Action for Africa UNPAAERD

The United Nations tried to reverse this economic and social degradation in Africa with its "United Nations Programme of Action for the Economic Recovery and Development of Africa" (UNPAAERD), adopted by the 13th Special Session of the UN → General Assembly on 1 June 1986 (UN Doc. A/S-13/16).

UNPAAERD was a framework for the development actors in Africa including the international donor community. It was prompted by the famine which ravaged large parts of Africa in 1983/84, which had in turn resulted from the drought caused by the El-NinoPhenomenon. This phenomenon had then occurred for the first time simultaneously north (Sahel and Horn of Africa) and south (Zambia, Zimbabwe and Mozambique) of the equator. All over the world, solidarity actions in support of the African peoples involved pop stars, athletes and the media. In Germany the Public Broadcasting Network ARD organized a special "Africa Day". The 13th Special Assembly of the UN was accompanied by fundraising events, such as a concert and the "world race against the time", produced by Bob Geldof.

UNPAAERD, and its base document prepared by the African governments (entitled "Africa's submission to the special session of the United Nation General Assembly on Africa's economic and social crisis"), avoided an assessment of economic structures and of their conformity with markets, as had been the focus of the SAPs of IMF and World Bank. They simply estimated the financial flows required to meet given sectoral economic growth targets. The resulting financial gap for the whole continent to be filled by ODA was four times greater than had been estimated by the World Bank.

During the first five years of the programme, Africa's share of global ODA flows rose from 35% in 1985 to 37% in 1987. Therefore the target set by UNPAAERD to fill the annual ODA gap estimated at 9 billion US dollars was almost met. But otherwise the results were distressing. Some examples may highlight the failure, which at the same time required considerable sacrifices (UN Doc. A/45/591 of 8 October 1990 and A/RES/46/151). The ratio between budget revenues and Gross Domestic Product (GDP) for the whole of Africa was increased from 22% in 1986 to 24% in 1989, and public deficits were reduced from 7% to 5% of GDP. But this led to a cut of average incomes in the civil service by 50%. The expenditures for health and education were down by 50% and 25% respectively. Enrolment in primary education fell from 80% to 70%. One third of the pupils in primary schools dropped out within the first two years. The savings rate stagnated at 16%, despite an increase in real interest rates; in 1980 the savings rate had been as high as 24%. The investment rate dropped from 24% to 19%. The rate of food self-sufficiency in Africa decreased from 92% in 1980 to 85% in 1990. In the five-year period of the programme the number of the very poor increased from 270 to 335 million, which is 52% of the total African population. The number of unemployed went up as well, from 100 to 130 million.

The dependency of most African countries on the export of commodities grew during the programme period. In four out of five countries the ratio of commodity exports to total exports is above 80%. Finally, debts leaped up from 212 billion US dollars in 1986 to 272 billion US dollars in 1990, which corresponds to 110% of GDP (in Latin America the ratio was less than 50%).

The "New Agenda" for Africa: UNNADAF

Despite these sobering results, the UN General Assembly adopted a new ten-year special programme on 18 December 1991, the "United Nations New Agenda for the Development of Africa in the 90s" (UNNADAF). The main target of this programme was a 6% annual rate of economic growth for the whole of Africa. Human development through health and education became the focus of development. The promotion of peace was put center stage and pressure was mounted on African governments to enhance democratization (→ Democratization and the UN), improve good governance and accelerate market-friendly reforms for the benefit of private investment.

A midterm-review was carried out in 1996 (UN Doc. A/51228 and Add.1 and UN Doc. A/AC.25/5), which still drew a bleak picture. But it also identified first signs of a turn in the trend. It was established that only a few countries remained with negative per capita economic growth. On the other hand, only seven countries achieved the annual GDP growth target of at least 6%. The overall economic growth rate in Africa increased from 0.7% 1993 to 2.3% in 1995.

The decrease of overall ODA to Africa from 25 billion US dollars in 1992 to 21 billion US dollars in 1991 was deplored. Simultaneously debts grew by 50 billion US dollars, to 332 billion US dollars in 1995. The ratio of debts to multilateral institutions reached almost one third of all debts. Despite numerous negotiations in the Paris Club to reduce debt, the debt-service ratio with exports for all Africa rose above 30%.

2

The efforts to push regional economic integration forwards received a positive mark. On 3 June 1991 the treaty for the establishment of an African Economic Union was signed in Abuja, the capital of Nigeria, which entered into force in 1994 after two thirds of the African countries had ratified the agreement. In the same year the "Preferential Trade Area of Eastern and Southern Africa" (PTA) was expanded into the "Common Market of Eastern and Southern Africa" (COMESA), and the "Southern African Development Coordination Conference" (SADCC) became the "Southern African Development Community" (SADC). Furthermore, the tasks of the "Economic Community of West African States" (ECOWAS) were extended. Two further communities complete the picture: the "Economic Community of Central African States" as well as the "Arab Maghreb Union".

Parallel to the midterm review of the UNNADAF the then UN Secretary-General (→ Secretary-General) Boutros Boutros-Ghali declared a "Special Initiative on Africa" (SIA) of the UN. In order to increase synergistic effects, the aim of this initiative was to further strengthen the "UN Inter-Agency Task Force" (UNIATF) into a solid co-operation of all specialized agencies of the UN. This seemed so attractive for the World Bank, which in the 80s had installed a competing "Special Programme for Africa" (SPA), that it decided to become associated with the UNIATF and to finance the bulk of costs of this cooperation.

The relevance of UNPAAERD and UNNADAF lies less in the development of programmes or on the level of projects, but on the level of conceptualization and of policies. Recent initiatives have ensured the continuation of commitments to Africa by governments and by the UN. Even more important is the impact on reform policies. Today the political frameworks and socio-economic structures in Africa have essentially changed compared to the 70s, and up to the mid-80s. Reforms with a market orientation were mainly enforced by the SAPs of IMF and World Bank. But the reform of the reform, i.e. to provide the SAPs with a human face, is the result of the special programmes of the UN for Africa.

Konrad Melchers

Lit.: *Melchers, K.:* Freiwillige und unfreiwillige „Politikreformen". Die 13. Sondergeneralversammlung der Vereinten Nationen, in: VN 34 (1986), 90-94: *Melchers, K.:* Hehre Ziele, klares Scheitern. Die Schlußbilanz des Aktionsprogramms der Vereinten Nationen für Afrika (UNPAAERD), in VN 40 (1992), 81-87; *The United Nations Systemwide Special Initiative on Africa (UNSIA):* One Year Later. June 1997, published on the internet (www.unsia. org/unsi-arep98.htm); ongoing reports and articles in the journal "Africa Recovery" (www.un.org/ecosocdev/geninfo/afrec).

Addendum

In the new millennium the UN efforts to keep Africa on the UN agenda, to analyze progress and failures in the efforts of the African states as well as of the ODA donor countries and of the UN institutions in the endeavor to improve the socio-economic situation and the living conditions of the African people, and to develop more efficient forms of cooperation continued and were even put on a higher level.

New Partnership for Africa's Development (NEPAD) 2002

In a critical evaluation of the results of the UNNADAF, the Assembly of the Heads of State and Government of the Organization of African Unity decided at its Lusaka conference in July 2001 to establish the "New African Initiative" (AHG/Decl. 1 (XXXVII), renamed a year later by the OAU's successor organization African Union (AU) in New Partnership for Africa's Development (NEPAD) as the new strategy and framework for the development of Africa (ASS/AU/Decl. 1 (I)).

The main targets of NEPAD are poverty eradication, the reversal of Africa's increasing marginalization in the globalization process and the integration of the plementing economic reforms, above all with the democratic instrument of the voluntarily agreed-on peer review. That is, all in all, a silver lining on the horizon.

Helmut Volger

Lit.: *Souare, I.A.:* Africa in the United Nations system 1945-2005, London 2006; *United Nations - General Assembly:* Independent evaluation of the implementation of the United Nations New Agenda for the Development of Africa, UN Doc. A/AC.251/9 of 14 June 2002; *United Nations - General Assembly:* Independent evaluation of the United Nations New Agenda for the Development of Africa in the 1990s. Report of the Secretary-General, UN Doc. A/57/156 of 2 July 2002; *United Nations - General Assembly:* Africa's development needs: state of implementation of various commitments, challenges and the way forward. Report of the Secretary-General, UN Doc. A/63/130 of 15 July 2008; *United Nations - General Assembly:* Political declaration on Africa's development needs, UN Doc. A/RES/63/1 of 22 September 2008; *United Nations Office of the Special Adviser on Africa:* Human Security in Africa, New York December 2005; *United Nations Office of the Special Adviser on Africa:* Peace Consolidation in Africa – Challenges and Opportunities, New York December 2005; *Wilson, Z.:* The United Nations and democracy in Africa, London 2006.

Internet: New Partnership for Africa's Development (NEPAD): www.nepad.org; Homepage of the Special Adviser on Africa (information on NEPAD): www.un.org/africa/osaa/nepad.html; Homepage of the UN Economic Commission on Africa: www.un-eca.org; Homepage of the African Union: www.africa-union.org.

Agenda for Development

The → General Assembly requested the UN Secretary-General (→ Secretary-General) by Resolution 47/181 of 22 December 1992 to submit a report on an "Agenda for Development", as a complementary document to the → "Agenda for Peace" submitted in summer 1992, which had apparently neglected the aspects of development policy. Obviously, not only the Western in-

dustrialized countries, but also the UN Secretariat (→ Secretariat) had initially thought of leaving the leading role in development policy to the Bretton Woods institutions, i.e. to the World Bank (→ World Bank, World Bank Group) and to the → IMF, as well as to the World Trade Organization WTO (→ WTO/GATT) – a form of division of labor which had been rejected by the Group of 77 (→ Group of 77 and the UN).

Long Process of Production

The production of this report would take much longer than for the "Agenda for Peace". As the Secretary-General had already emphasized in the first agenda, he had received many ideas and suggestions from governments, regional organizations and → non-governmental organizations (→ NGOs), as well as from institutions and individuals from many states. But, the production of his second agenda would last nearly 17 months. This resulted not only from the fact that the Secretary-General was now confronted with a far more complex issue, which finally made the "Agenda for Development" much longer, but was due as well to the larger number of relevant actors in development politics to be consulted within the → UN system, and to the fact that the General Assembly on behalf of all member states had requested the agenda.

Initially, the Secretary-General was to submit his "Agenda for Development" to the 48th regular session of the General Assembly in 1993. The Agenda was to make suggestions to strengthen the role of the UN in the development sector (→ Development Cooperation of the UN System), as well as proposals concerning the future relation of the UN with the Bretton Woods institutions. Instead of the requested report, the Secretary-General submitted an interim report (UN Doc. A/48/689) at the end of November 1993, in which he, on the one hand, briefly described the subject areas of his second Agenda. On the other, he discussed the answers of member states, who had responded to his verbal note of

The efforts to push regional economic integration forwards received a positive mark. On 3 June 1991 the treaty for the establishment of an African Economic Union was signed in Abuja, the capital of Nigeria, which entered into force in 1994 after two thirds of the African countries had ratified the agreement. In the same year the "Preferential Trade Area of Eastern and Southern Africa" (PTA) was expanded into the "Common Market of Eastern and Southern Africa" (COMESA), and the "Southern African Development Coordination Conference" (SADCC) became the "Southern African Development Community" (SADC). Furthermore, the tasks of the "Economic Community of West African States" (ECOWAS) were extended. Two further communities complete the picture: the "Economic Community of Central African States" as well as the "Arab Maghreb Union".

Parallel to the midterm review of the UNNADAF the then UN Secretary-General (→ Secretary-General) Boutros Boutros-Ghali declared a "Special Initiative on Africa" (SIA) of the UN. In order to increase synergistic effects, the aim of this initiative was to further strengthen the "UN Inter-Agency Task Force" (UNIATF) into a solid co-operation of all specialized agencies of the UN. This seemed so attractive for the World Bank, which in the 80s had installed a competing "Special Programme for Africa" (SPA), that it decided to become associated with the UNIATF and to finance the bulk of costs of this co-operation.

The relevance of UNPAAERD and UNNADAF lies less in the development of programmes or on the level of projects, but on the level of conceptualization and of policies. Recent initiatives have ensured the continuation of commitments to Africa by governments and by the UN. Even more important is the impact on reform policies. Today the political frameworks and socio-economic structures in Africa have essentially changed compared to the 70s, and up to the mid-80s. Reforms with a market orientation were mainly enforced by the SAPs of IMF and World Bank. But the reform of the reform, i.e. to provide the SAPs with a human face, is the result of the special programmes of the UN for Africa.

Konrad Melchers

Lit.: *Melchers, K.:* Freiwillige und unfreiwillige „Politikreformen". Die 13. Sondergeneralversammlung der Vereinten Nationen, in: VN 34 (1986), 90-94: *Melchers, K.:* Hehre Ziele, klares Scheitern. Die Schlußbilanz des Aktionsprogramms der Vereinten Nationen für Afrika (UNPAAERD), in VN 40 (1992), 81-87; *The United Nations Systemwide Special Initiative on Africa (UNSIA):* One Year Later. June 1997, published on the internet (www.unsia. org/unsi-arep98.htm); ongoing reports and articles in the journal "Africa Recovery" (www.un.org/ecosocdev/geninfo/afrec).

Addendum

In the new millennium the UN efforts to keep Africa on the UN agenda, to analyze progress and failures in the efforts of the African states as well as of the ODA donor countries and of the UN institutions in the endeavor to improve the socio-economic situation and the living conditions of the African people, and to develop more efficient forms of cooperation continued and were even put on a higher level.

New Partnership for Africa's Development (NEPAD) 2002

In a critical evaluation of the results of the UNNADAF, the Assembly of the Heads of State and Government of the Organization of African Unity decided at its Lusaka conference in July 2001 to establish the "New African Initiative" (AHG/Decl. 1 (XXXVII), renamed a year later by the OAU's successor organization African Union (AU) in New Partnership for Africa's Development (NEPAD) as the new strategy and framework for the development of Africa (ASS/AU/Decl. 1 (I)).

The main targets of NEPAD are poverty eradication, the reversal of Africa's increasing marginalization in the globalization process and the integration of the continent into the global economy. As necessary preconditions, peace and security shall be promoted as well as democratic systems in the African countries together with sound political, economic and corporate governance, supported by improved regional co-operation and integration.

In contrast to earlier initiatives of the African states putting often the blame primarily on the structures of the world economic system, the declaration of the establishment of NEPAD in 2001 emphasizes the main responsibility of the African states for the development of Africa: "We ... reaffirm that the Revival and Development of Africa are primarily the responsibility of our Governments and Peoples. Consequently, we are determined to establish the conducive political, economic and social environment and create the required economic transformation in our countries ..." (AHG/Decl. 1 (XXXVII), para. 3)

In order to underline the commitment to democratic structures and to common responsibility, the African states also adopted the *Declaration on Democracy, Political, Economic and Corporate Governance* (AHG/235 (XXXVIII) Annex I) and established – on a voluntary basis – the *African Peer Review Mechanism (APRM)* (AHG/235 (XXXVIII) Annex II). The APR process entails periodic reviews of the policies and practices of participating countries to monitor progress being made towards mutually agreed goals in four focus areas, namely democracy and political governance, economic governance, corporate governance, and socio-economic development. As of June 2008, 29 African countries had voluntarily acceded to APRM (cf. www.un.org/africa/osaa/nepad.html.)

All in all, NEPAD constitutes in fact a new understanding of responsibility, new priorities and political mechanisms in Africa.

The United Nations welcomed the African NEPAD initiative and endorsed it explicitly. To support Africa in its effort to develop new concepts and to gather political support among the UN member states for NEPAD, the UN Secretary-General submitted in 2002 an evaluative report on the United Nations New Agenda for Development of Africa (UNNADAF) in the 1990s written by a panel of eminent personalities (UN Doc. A/AC.251/9 of 14 June 2002), supplemented by a report by the Secretary-General on the same issue (UN Doc. A/57/156 of 2 July 2002). The latter emphasized in his report that the evaluation report had highlighted that "the overriding reliance on liberalization, privatization and market reforms in Africa" had shown its limits (ibid., para. 6).

The General Assembly explicitly decided in November 2002 to bring its old programme UNNADAF to a close and to accept NEPAD as "the framework within which the international community, including the United Nations, should concentrate its efforts for Africa's development." (UN Doc. A/RES/57/7 of 4 November 2002, para. 4)

The Assembly underlined in its resolution the preconditions for any success of NEPAD, namely the readiness of the donor countries to make concrete efforts towards reaching the target of 0.7 per cent of their GNP as ODA to developing countries (ibid., para. 16), to implement in particular the commitments on ODA to the least developed countries (LDCs) made at the Third UN Conference on the LDCs in Brussels 2001 (UN Doc. A/CONF.191/11 of 20 May 2001), to find a durable solution to the problem of external indebtedness of the heavily indebted poor countries in Africa (A/RES/57/7, para. 16), and to grant an improved market access for African exports within the framework of the Doha round negotiations of the World Trade Organization (→ WTO) (ibid., para. 18).

Because one of the causes of the relative failure of earlier UN Africa initiatives had been the insufficient co-ordination of the respective UN activities, Secretary-General Annan established in 2003 the *Office of the Special Adviser on Africa* with the main purposes
- to act as focal point for NEPAD with the UN Secretariat;

- to support the General Assembly and ECOSOC in their deliberations on Africa;
- to co-ordinate the interdepartmental task force on African affairs, "to ensure a coherent and integrated approach for United Nations support for Africa".

To provide him with the necessary authority the Special Adviser is directly accountable to the Secretary-General (UN Doc. ST/SGB/2003/6 of 23 April 2003).

The General Assembly kept NEPAD on its agenda in debating in subsequent years an implementation report with regard to NEPAD and by adopting a respective resolution.

In 2008 the General Assembly decided to give NEPAD a higher political priority in gathering a high-level meeting on Africa's development needs as part of the General Assembly session in September 2008. The meeting was prepared by a report of the Secretary-General for the high-level meeting, striking a provisional balance of the progress made so far with regard to the UN efforts to support Africa's development (UN Doc. A/63/130 of 15 July 2008).

The report contains a mixed balance: while some progress has been made with regard to the poverty eradication, African economies are still far from reaching the planned GNP growth rates (ibid., para. 19). With regard to the Millennium Development Goals in general the report states only a slow rate of progress (ibid., para. 20). The development assistance from the donor countries through bilateral and multilateral channels is still far from being satisfactory and far away from the 0.7% target (ibid., para. 51ff).

There is an urgent need to reform multilateral assistance with regard to the heavily indebted countries (ibid., para. 57ff.) and, last but not least, the improved market access for developing countries remains a key-factor for the success of African development efforts (ibid., para. 59ff.).

If one considers the situation from a positive perspective, one could argue that the GA high-level meeting 2008 has drawn the attention of the world public again to the needs of Africa, since the heads of state and government assembled in New York explicitly reaffirmed in the concluding resolution of the meeting (A/RES/63/1), given the rank of a "political declaration", the special needs of Africa and the commitment of the UN member states to support Africa in the implementation of NEPAD and expressed their concern about the insufficient progress with regard to the increase of the development assistance and apparent lack of progress in promoting Africa's international trade in the Doha round of the WTO.

If one regards the situation, on the other hand, from a realistic standpoint one has to state that progress with regard to Africa in 2008 is still very slow; or, to draw on the words of GA President D'Escoto Brockman at the high-level meeting, "It is time to move from promises to concrete action." (UN Doc. A/63/PV.3 of 22 September 2008, 3)

Secretary-General Ban Ki-moon expressed the difficult situation also very frankly at the high-level meeting: "No one is more alarmed than the members of the General Assembly at the current trends, which indicate that no African country will achieve all the Goals [the Millennium Development Goals – MDGs, H.V.] by 2015. But I am convinced that, through concerted action by African governments and their development partners, the MDGs remain achievable in Africa ..."

It remains to be seen if the increased public awareness of the African problems within the UN, promoted through the better coordination achieved by the Office of the Special Adviser and the annual debates in the General Assembly about NEPAD, will result in more concrete projects and more development assistance in general.

Without doubt NEPAD has promoted Africa's realization of its own responsibilities and tasks, has strengthened Africa's own efforts in regional co-operation and in the mutual support in improving democratic structures and implementing economic reforms, above all with the democratic instrument of the voluntarily agreed-on peer review. That is, all in all, a silver lining on the horizon.

Helmut Volger

Lit.: *Souare, I.A.:* Africa in the United Nations system 1945-2005, London 2006; *United Nations - General Assembly:* Independent evaluation of the implementation of the United Nations New Agenda for the Development of Africa, UN Doc. A/AC.251/9 of 14 June 2002; *United Nations - General Assembly:* Independent evaluation of the United Nations New Agenda for the Development of Africa in the 1990s. Report of the Secretary-General, UN Doc. A/57/156 of 2 July 2002; *United Nations - General Assembly:* Africa's development needs: state of implementation of various commitments, challenges and the way forward. Report of the Secretary-General, UN Doc. A/63/130 of 15 July 2008; *United Nations - General Assembly:* Political declaration on Africa's development needs, UN Doc. A/RES/63/1 of 22 September 2008; *United Nations Office of the Special Adviser on Africa:* Human Security in Africa, New York December 2005; *United Nations Office of the Special Adviser on Africa:* Peace Consolidation in Africa – Challenges and Opportunities, New York December 2005; *Wilson, Z.:* The United Nations and democracy in Africa, London 2006.

Internet: New Partnership for Africa's Development (NEPAD): www.nepad.org; Homepage of the Special Adviser on Africa (information on NEPAD): www.un.org/africa/osaa/nepad.html; Homepage of the UN Economic Commission on Africa: www.uneca.org; Homepage of the African Union: www.africa-union.org.

Agenda for Development

The → General Assembly requested the UN Secretary-General (→ Secretary-General) by Resolution 47/181 of 22 December 1992 to submit a report on an "Agenda for Development", as a complementary document to the → "Agenda for Peace" submitted in summer 1992, which had apparently neglected the aspects of development policy. Obviously, not only the Western in-

dustrialized countries, but also the UN Secretariat (→ Secretariat) had initially thought of leaving the leading role in development policy to the Bretton Woods institutions, i.e. to the World Bank (→ World Bank, World Bank Group) and to the → IMF, as well as to the World Trade Organization WTO (→ WTO/GATT) – a form of division of labor which had been rejected by the Group of 77 (→ Group of 77 and the UN).

Long Process of Production

The production of this report would take much longer than for the "Agenda for Peace". As the Secretary-General had already emphasized in the first agenda, he had received many ideas and suggestions from governments, regional organizations and → non-governmental organizations (→ NGOs), as well as from institutions and individuals from many states. But, the production of his second agenda would last nearly 17 months. This resulted not only from the fact that the Secretary-General was now confronted with a far more complex issue, which finally made the "Agenda for Development" much longer, but was due as well to the larger number of relevant actors in development politics to be consulted within the → UN system, and to the fact that the General Assembly on behalf of all member states had requested the agenda.

Initially, the Secretary-General was to submit his "Agenda for Development" to the 48th regular session of the General Assembly in 1993. The Agenda was to make suggestions to strengthen the role of the UN in the development sector (→ Development Cooperation of the UN System), as well as proposals concerning the future relation of the UN with the Bretton Woods institutions. Instead of the requested report, the Secretary-General submitted an interim report (UN Doc. A/48/689) at the end of November 1993, in which he, on the one hand, briefly described the subject areas of his second Agenda. On the other, he discussed the answers of member states, who had responded to his verbal note of

20 May 1993 in which he asked for their opinions about the agenda in progress. The General Assembly took note of this interim report on 21 December 1993 (UN Doc. A/RES/48/166) and accepted that the final "Agenda for Development" would be submitted in the first half of 1994. It invited the President of the General Assembly "to promote, as early as possible in 1994, in an open-ended format, broad-based discussions and an exchange of views on an agenda for development."

There was remarkably little response to this request of the Secretary-General. The total number of 30 states responding was a very low return, even taking into account that Belgium spoke for the EU and Finland for the Nordic states.

The Agenda for Development

On 6 May 1994, UN Secretary-General Boutros Boutros-Ghali presented in his "Agenda for Development" (UN Doc. A/48/935) a new and seemingly visionary concept of a universal "culture of development" oriented towards people and their needs. The agenda closely links peace, economy, environment, social justice and democracy as the five main dimensions of development (cf. part II of the agenda). "Whether this vision is fulfilled or not will be measured by what this living generation of the world's peoples and their leaders make or fail to make of the United Nations." (para. 237).

The above mentioned five dimensions of development are seen as a continuum, as:

- without peace human resources cannot be used effectively;
- without economic growth (as the "engine to development"), there cannot be any sustainable, broad-based improvement to material welfare;
- without environmental protection, the basic needs of human survival are eroded;
- without social justice, growing imbalance threatens society; and
- without free political participation, development remains fragile and permanently endangered.

Boutros-Ghali's concept of a *"social market economy"* implies that "the market" alone is not able to secure sustained and lasting economic growth: "Finding the right blend of government direction of the economy and encouragement of private initiative is perhaps the most pressing challenge of economic development. This is not only a problem for developing or transitional economies. In the search for the difficult path which lies between dirigisme and laissez-faire, all countries are involved. Major market economies, with recurrent recession and persistent high rates of unemployment, are also facing this challenge." (para. 50)

In part III , the UN Secretary-General considered the whole variety of actors in the development sector and further explained, with regard to the UN world conferences in the 90s (→ World Conferences), the process through which the United Nations could interlink these actors in the different dimensions of development. He further discussed the work of the → specialized agencies including the Bretton Woods institutions, demanding "second thoughts" about the existing division of labor: "The Bretton Woods institutions, as specialized agencies, are an integral part of the United Nations system. They are important sources of development finance and policy advice. They are increasingly active in technical assistance, which has the potential of creating overlap with the central funding role of UNDP, and in areas where competence exists in other specialized agencies. Special attention needs to be given to considering how these institutions and other organizations of the system could collaborate more closely on the basis of their respective areas of comparative strength. More systematic use of capital assistance from the Bretton Woods institutions in a coordinated, complementary and mutually reinforcing manner with technical assistance funding provided through UNDP and the specialized agencies is warranted in operational activities." (para. 229)

The UN Secretary-General not only pointed out the "unique" world-wide net of UNDP country offices (→ UNDP), but also recommended to further strengthen the system of the UNDP resident coordinators on the spot. Furthermore, he advocated a stronger position of the Economic and Social Council (→ ECOSOC), whose coordination measures should not only encompass governments and intergovernmental institutions, but should also take into account the work of the numerous non-governmental actors in the development cooperation.

Boutros Boutros-Ghali noted, that there was a "steady proliferation of subsidiary bodies" (para. 227), that showed less and less policy coherence (→ Principal Organs, Subsidiary Organs, Treaty Bodies). As reasons for the "lack of cohesion and focus within the system" he mentioned the lack of clear political guidance by the General Assembly on the one hand, and the lack of "effective policy coordination and control" by the ECOSOC on the other hand (→ Coordination in the UN System).

The UN Secretary-General understood his report as a first step to "revitalize the vision of development" (para. 9). His attempt to create a comprehensive *"culture of development"* and to synthesize it with the existing → UN system did not get the expected response. His report was, on the contrary, criticized as being too academic, containing no concrete suggestions as did the → "Agenda for Peace". Direct criticism was only expressed rudimentally in a few points, for example with regard to the statement that the five permanent members of the Security Council account for 86 percent of world-wide arms supplies (para. 32), as well as to the demand for an international economic policy coordination by the Group of Seven industrialized countries in integrating the more important developing countries (para. 59).

Further Consultations

At the beginning of June 1994, the report was discussed in a series of "World Hearings on Development", which were convened by the President of the General Assembly in New York. This constituted a novelty in the procedure of the General Assembly; it resulted in an open dialogue between experts, former heads of states and governments, media representatives and members of the → permanent missions of the member states of the UN. The President of the General Assembly summarized and published the results (UN Doc. A/49/320).

Summary of the World Hearings on Development

On the one hand, this summarizing report moved within the framework of the analytic system set up by Boutros Boutros-Ghali, on the other, criticism was brought much more pointed: neither the UN, nor the Group of Seven states, nor the Bretton Woods institutions, were regarded as being suited to master the challenges of the international economic order (para. 79). Apart from the proposal to appoint a Deputy Secretary-General for economic affairs, the suggestion was made to set up an *Economic and Social Security Council*, in presenting different organizational patterns up to an development council, composed of the representatives of Group of Seven, Group of 77 (→ Group of 77 and the UN) and OPEC (paras. 81-91). This illustrates how skeptically the previous work of the ECOSOC was examined in the hearing.

Also discussed was the merger of some of the autonomous → specialized agencies; altogether, they should fall under the jurisdiction of the UN Secretary-General (paras. 103, 104). Moreover, varying opinions about improving the cooperation between the UN and the Bretton Woods institutions were expressed during the hearing.

In July 1994, the ECOSOC also examined in its annual session period the "Agenda for Development". The Secretary-General was asked to integrate the respective statements made during the ECOSOC debate, and summarized by the President of ECOSOC (UN Doc.

E/1994/109), in his report, *An Agenda for Development: Recommendations.* That report (UN Doc. A/49/665 of 11 November 1994) was submitted to the 49th regular session of the General Assembly in November 1994.

Agenda for Development: Recommendations

Boutros Boutros-Ghali emphasized three goals in these recommendations:
1. To strengthen and revitalize the international cooperation for development in general, to overcome the "fatigue of the donors";
2. To establish a stronger, more efficient and more coherent multilateral system for supporting development; and
3. To increase the efficiency of the UN proper and of the UN system as a whole.

The Secretary-General noted with regret that the donors made decreasing efforts to reach the goal of 0.7%, by which the member states were to donate 0.7% of their GNP for official development assistance (ODA). He suggested new interim goals for increasing the ODA. He further mentioned the debt problem, and called for a general cancellation of the debts of the least developed and poorest countries. He also suggested that the General Assembly should convene an international conference on the financing of development, in close consultation with the Bretton Woods institutions, the regional development banks, and the Development Assistance Committee (DAC) of the OECD.

His recommendations for reaching the second goal (No. 38-61) concerned (a) the General Assembly, (b) the ECOSOC, (c) the Bretton Woods institutions and (d) the sectoral and technical agencies within the UN System:

The General Assembly, as the primary political forum, should concentrate on finding "gaps and inconsistencies" and on working on "norms, standards and rules" concerning the management of global interdependence in the world economy.

The ECOSOC should be reorganized to become the center of an effective multilateral development system:
- the Council should deliberate and decide upon the full range of development issues while including all specialized agencies;
- it should serve as a unifying governing entity for the assessment and review of the multilateral development assistance; and
- the Council should identify potential or emerging humanitarian emergencies and work out coordinated initiatives.

To meet these demands, the UN Secretary-General suggested two institutional and organizational changes of the ECOSOC:
- to strengthen the ECOSOC by an expanded bureau meeting inter-sessionally, which is able to act rapidly if needed;
- to establish a council of international development advisors to support the General Assembly and the ECOSOC: "This council would issue an independent annual or biennial independent report, analyze key issues concerning the global economy and their impact on development, and inform international opinion." (para. 48)

Boutros Boutros-Ghali further suggested closer co-operation between the Bretton Woods institutions and the United Nations. On the one hand, he named specific fields of cooperation; on the other, he suggested reviving the Liaison Committee between the United Nations and the Bretton Woods institutions (para. 56).

Although these suggestions were formulated rather cautiously and diplomatically, they were too far-reaching for some member states, especially the USA. All in all, the outcome of the discussions was unsatisfactory for the developing countries. But the Group of 77 did not give up. On 19 December 1994, the General Assembly agreed with Resolution A/RES/49/126 on setting up an *ad hoc open-ended working group* for all member states, to work out an "action-oriented, comprehensive agenda for development" (para. 1).

Strenuous Working Process

The working group of the General Assembly held three meetings in 1995, which took five weeks in total. But by fall 1995 they had managed to produce only an interim report, in which it was stated that the Agenda could not yet be finished. Accordingly, the mandate of the working group was extended for one year. However, during the subsequent meetings in 1996 still no agreement was reached.

The controversies between the industrialized and the developing countries, that were already obvious in 1995, led to a hardening of positions in 1996. The discussion about institutional matters and subsequent measures revived the old differences of the 60s. While the Group of 77 wanted above all to strengthen the competencies of the General Assembly and of → UNCTAD, in which they had a clear majority, the EU and the USA insisted on a strict division of functions. The United Nations should keep on dealing with the "soft" matters (environment, social issues and → human rights), and the WTO, the IMF and the World Bank group should deal with the "hard" economic issues. Despite numerous compromises, made by taking over formulations from different programmes of actions of the world conferences in the 90s, no consensus could be reached, so that the General Assembly agreed on 16 September 1996 that the working group should end its task "as soon as possible".

Adoption of the Agenda in June 1997

In the first half of 1997, thanks to an increased overall pressure for reforms (→ Reform of the UN) to which the new Secretary-General, Kofi Annan, had to react, all controversial questions could be resolved by further compromises. The General Assembly adopted the "Agenda for Development", without formal voting, as an annex to Resolution 51/240 on 20 June 1997. It had taken nearly five years until the General Assembly was able to agree on the wording. Nevertheless, it did not reach its goal to create an action-oriented, comprehensive programme for the multilateral cooperation for development within the UN system.

The "Agenda for Development" of the General Assembly consists of three parts: I. Setting and Objectives; II. Policy Framework, including Means of Implementation; III. Institutional Issues and Follow-up. It claims to create a new *framework for international cooperation*, to define the role of the United Nations and to set out the development priorities and a time-frame for implementation (para. 42). In contrast to the "Agenda for Development" of Boutros Boutros-Ghali, which is not directly referred to, part I contains his basic ideas without a corresponding analytic consistency.

Thus, part II also seems rather to be a catalogue of the demands taken over from the programmes of action of the world conferences in the 1990s.

Part III also has very little content. Apart from noncommittal phrases concerning the obvious necessities, this part only provides that, according to the principle of hope, reforms are necessary, but that there is no consensus on how and when, nor on what kind of reforms are to be realized.

However, consensus had been reached on a multi-dimensional, comprehensive and integrated development approach: there is a necessity to revitalize the system of international cooperation for development. The General Assembly "should exert greater policy leadership on development issues" (para. 245). ECOSOC should continue "to strengthen its role as central mechanism for coordination" of the UN system (para. 251). These and similar formulations dominate the text, enriched by a number of practical, organizational suggestions. But, all in all, the Agenda is dominated by diplomatically formulated compromises of the type of "persuasion", which can be supported by all member states.

Striking the Balance

After five years of work, the UN organs did not succeed in formulating suggestions for the reform of the UN system which would lead to greater competences of the United Nations concerning development issues, and which would integrate the G-7/8-states and the Bretton Woods institutions more effectively in the work of the United Nations.

There is a lack of practical political will to launch the necessary reforms in the economic and social sector, which would also make a revision of the Charter ($\rightarrow$ Charter of the UN) inevitable. Notwithstanding, problems and necessities were recognized, but the overall critique of the "Agenda for Development" by Boutros-Ghali in 1994, that the agenda was not action-oriented and lacked concrete suggestions, turned out to be a boomerang. Thanks to thorough and diplomatic adept preparations devised by Secretary-General Kofi Annan, who used skillfully a kind of "millennium impetus", in September 2000 the "Millennium Summit" of the $\rightarrow$ General Assembly adopted an eight-part "United Nations Millennium Declaration" (UN Doc. A/RES/55/2) which contains a number of concrete development goals, called "Millennium Development Goals", to be reached by the year 2015. Kofi Annan succeeded not only in operationalizing selected economic and social development goals, but also in committing the member states to reach those targets within a given time period. The "Millennium Development Goals" were reaffirmed in the final document of the UN World Summit 2005, the "2005 World Summit Outcome" (UN Doc. A/RES/60/1, 16 September 2005, para. 17ff.).

Most probably not all targets will be reached by all member states concerned, but an annual road-map indicates which progress has been made so far and allows necessary corrections (cf. for example the "Millennium Development Goals Report 2007", *United Nations* 2007).

Klaus Hüfner

Lit.: *Martens, J.:* The Development Agenda after the 2005 Millennium+5 Summit (Briefing Paper prepared by the Friedrich-Ebert-Stiftung and the Global Policy Forum), Berlin 2005; *Martens, J.:* Kompendium der Gemeinplätze. Die Agenda für Entwicklung: Chronologie eines gescheiterten Verhandlungsprozesses, in: VN 46 (1998), 47-52; *United Nations - General Assembly:* An Agenda for Development. Report of the Secretary-General, 6 May 1994 (UN Doc. A/48/935); *United Nations - General Assembly:* Agenda for Development. Note by the President of the General Assembly, 22 August 1994, UN Doc. A/49/320 with Annex (Open-Ended and Broad-Based Consultations on the Agenda for Development); *United Nations - General Assembly:* An Agenda for Development: Recommendations. Report of the Secretary-General, 11 November 1994, UN Doc. A/49/665; *United Nations - General Assembly:* Resolution 49/126: An Agenda for Development, 19 December 1994, UN Doc. A/RES/49/126; *United Nations - General Assembly*: Resolution 51/240: Agenda for Development. Annex: Agenda for Development. New York: United Nations, 20 June 1997, UN Doc. A/RES/51/240; *United Nations - General Assembly:* United Nations Millennium Declaration. Resolution adopted by the General Assembly, 8 September 2000, UN Doc. A/RES/55/2; *United Nations:* The Millennium Development Goals Report 2007, New York 2007.

Agenda for Peace

After the end of the Cold War (1989), the successful operations in Namibia (UN Transition Assistance Group, UNTAG, 1989-90) and in Kuwait (1991 coalition campaign, led by the USA, with UN Security Council authorization ($\rightarrow$ Security Council), followed by the UN Iraq Kuwait Observation Mission, UNIKOM, on the Iraqi-Kuwait border, and the deployment of the UN Special Commission, UNSCOM, to find and destroy weapons of mass destruction, as well as humanitarian operations in Iraq to assist the Kurdish and other refugees) led to exaggerated expectations that the United Nations might in future be able to act more on its own in maintaining international peace and security ($\rightarrow$

Peacekeeping; → Peacekeeping Operations).

At that time it was not possible to foresee that some of the major UN operations which followed, such as the administration of a referendum in Western Sahara (MINURSO, from 1991), the UN Transitional Administration in Cambodia (UNAMIC and UNTAC, 1991-94), and the UN Protection Force in former Yugoslavia (UNPROFOR from 1992, later split into UNCRO in Croatia, UNPROFOR in Bosnia-Herzegovina, and UNPREDEP in Macedonia), were to prove partial failures. In the optimistic mood after the end of the Cold War, many UN staff members overlooked the fact that the UN is ultimately not an actor *per se* (and was never intended to be), but rather serves as a stage for the member states, and is dependent on their national interests and their political will – as further developments in the nineties would prove this.

A remarkable document of this optimistic "atmosphere of departure" is the report to the Security Council by UN Secretary-General Boutros Boutros-Ghali (→ Secretary-General) in 1992, subsequently published as "Agenda for Peace" (UN Doc. A/47/277-S/24111, 17 June 1992). The Council had asked the Secretary-General to report on possibilities for international intervention in conflicts. Although often misinterpreted as a definition of different types of intervention (the terms used by Boutros Boutros-Ghali are still used in discussions about peace operations to this day), it is really a model chronology of the development of a conflict.

Phases of conflicts and of international action following the Agenda for Peace by Secretary-General Boutros Boutros-Ghali, 1992

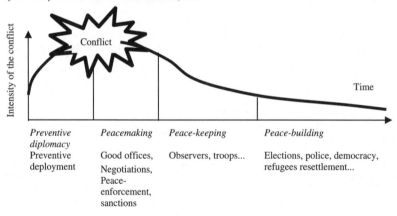

According to this model, the international community could intervene in a conflict,

- before a crisis escalates into (armed) conflict (→ "preventive diplomacy"),
- to terminate the fighting during a conflict ("peace-making"),
- to secure a truce or an armistice after the conflict ("peacekeeping"), and
- to consolidate an armistice into a lasting peace ("post-conflict peace-building").

In all four phases the possible means range from diplomatic negotiations and good offices to the deployment of military forces. Therefore – and logically – Boutros-Ghali included the "preventive deployment" of troops in the prevention phase, just as he did fact-finding missions or confidence-building measures. He also listed the deployment of military forces to pressure the parties to end the fighting ("peace enforcement") among the possible forms of intervention in the peace-making phase. Some found this confusing, as "peace-making" is usually used in a more narrow sense to mean diplomatic efforts such as good offices alone. Indeed, in his 1995 "Supplement" to the Agenda Boutros Boutros-Ghali listed "enforcement" and → sanctions as categories of their own, thus abandoning his own chronological model of 1992

On the whole, one has to credit Boutros-Ghali with introducing the "peace-building" phase in this model, and with emphasizing the importance of peace consolidation. Especially in internal conflicts and civil wars – resulting from ethnic tensions or from other causes – the establishment and consolidation of new structures is of decisive importance.

This ranges from the establishment of a new civil administration, including a proper police force ("community policing", → UNCIVPOL), a reliable judiciary, and a prison system respecting → human rights, through the holding of elections to the re-integration of former fighters and refugees into the civil society. All of these tasks, however, are long-term challenges: according to US experience in Latin America, for example, it can take anything from five years upwards to establish a new, reliable police force. To maintain the political will of the international community – and the countries involved – to adhere to these tasks is probably the most decisive factor for the success (or failure) of these missions.

Despite the good intentions behind the "Agenda for Peace" and other ideas (including the establishment of rapidly deployable UN forces), some of these far-reaching ideas eventually proved unrealistic. Most member states – notably the P-5 – proved highly reluctant to strengthen any ability of the UN to act more autonomously as an organization. The often cumbersome UN administration had proved adequate for the direction and support of smaller, more traditional peacekeeping missions such as the deployment of lightly armed "blue helmets" or military → observers to supervise troop disengagements and armistice agreements (→ Peacekeeping Forces). It was not capable, however, of exercising command of larger forces in more complex military operations. In a fashion similar to the sixties, when the failure of the Congo operation (ONUC 1960-64) led to a down-scaling of UN missions, after the missions in former Yugoslavia (1992-95) and Somalia (UNOSOM I and II, 1992-95), subsequent UN peacekeeping operations were generally smaller, more manageable tasks.

Between 1989 and 1994, UN peacekeeping operations had increased from some 10,000 to 80,000 troops. This size could not be maintained for long and was consequently reduced to 30,000 in 1996 and 12,000 in 1999. Since then, UN peacekeeping operations have increased again. In 2008, there were 16 UN peacekeeping operations worldwide, totaling 107,876 personnel, of whom 82,230 were military and police, coming from 119 countries.

In the face of the increasing organizational, strategic, financial and political problems connected with the peacekeeping operations, Boutros-Ghali's successor Kofi Annan initiated significant reforms to improve the preparation and management of UN missions. Some of these reforms are based on a report on UN peacekeeping operations which had been commissioned by Kofi Annan and submitted to the Security Council and the → General Assembly on 21 August 2000 (UN Doc. A/55/305-S/2000/809). The comprehensive review by a panel of experts under Lakhdar Brahimi (Algeria) attempts to examine some of the shortcomings of earlier peacekeeping operations.

Looking back to the "Agenda for Peace", its most important achievement was to emphasize the peace-building phase, which eventually led to the establishment of a new UN Peacebuilding Commission.

Based on the preparatory work of an expert panel, the High-level Panel on Threats, Challenges and Change, which submitted a report on the shared responsibility for global security (UN Doc. A/59/565), Kofi Annan suggested in his reform report "In Larger Freedom: Towards development, security, and human rights for all" of 21 March 2005 (UN Doc. A/59/2005), the creation of a UN Peacebuilding Commission.

This suggestion was approved by the UN World Summit in September 2005 in the "2005 World Summit Outcome" document and the Peacebuilding Commission was established by resolutions from the Security Council (UN Doc. S/RES/1645) and the General Assembly (UN Doc. A/RES/60/180) on 20 December 2005 and began work in 2006 as a new intergovernmental advisory body to support peace efforts in countries emerging from conflict. It brings together the relevant actors (including donors), marshals resources, and advises on strategy for post-conflict peacebuilding and recovery action. A Peacebuilding Fund (launched on 11 October 2006, with a target of 250 million US dollars) and a Peacebuilding Support Office (with sections on policy planning, support, and financing) were also established in 2006.

Annan's successor Ban Ki-moon took up in some way the conceptual work of Boutros-Ghali in his "Agenda for Peace" when he motivated DPKO to work out a text with basic terminological, conceptual and political guidelines for UN peacekeeping operations, a text which was presented to the public in March 2008, titled "United Nations Peacekeeping Operations: Principles and Guidelines." (*United Nations* 2008). Like Boutros-Ghali in his "Agenda" DPKO attempts in this text to define the different forms of peacekeeping operations, its purposes, objectives and preconditions.

The United Nations is only likely to have success in maintaining or restoring peace if it does its work on a reliable material, political and conceptual basis.

Erwin A. Schmidl

Lit.: *Johansen, R.:* The Future of United Nations Peacekeeping and Enforcement: A Framework for Policymaking, in: Global Governance 2 (1996), 299-333; *Otunnu, O. A./Doyle, M. (eds.):* Peacemaking and Peacekeeping for the Next Century, Lanham/USA 1998; *Schmidl, E.A./Wimmer, J.:* Friedenserhaltende Operationen, Vienna 1998; *United Nations:* Security Council Concludes Debate on Maintenance of Peace and Security and Post-Conflict Peace-Building, UN Press Release SC/6617, 23 December 1998; *United Nations - Department of Peacekeeping Operations:* Multidisciplinary Peacekeeping: Lessons From Recent Experience, New York 1999; *United Nations:* Report of the Panel on United Nations Peace Operations, UN Doc. A/55/305-S/2000/809, 21 August 2000; *United Nations - Department of Peacekeeping Operations:* United Nations Peacekeeping Operations: Principles and Guidelines, New York 2008, www. un.org/Depts/dpko/ dpko/selectedPSDG/ index.html.

Internet: Homepage of UN Headquarters, Department of Peacekeeping Operations: www.un.org/Depts/dpko/dpko; Homepage of the Peacebuilding Commission: www.un. org/peace/peacebuilding.

Aggression, Definition of

I. Public International Law Norms Regarding the Prohibition of Aggression

The determination by the United Nations → Security Council of a threat or a breach of the peace or an act of aggression is the prerequisite for → sanctions under chapter VII of the *United Nations Charter* (Art. 39) (→ Charter of the UN) . An act of aggression that qualifies as an armed attack, also gives the victim the right to individual or collective self-defence (Art. 51 UN Charter). The aggression is therefore a central notion in the scope of the international prohibition of the use of force (→ Use of Force, Prohibition of). The prohibition of aggression is a peremptory norm of general international law and as such an obligation *erga omnes* which arises towards the international community as a whole, if it involves a gross or systematic failure by the responsible state (Arts. 40 and 41 of the Articles on the "Responsibility of States for Internationally Wrongful Acts", UN Doc. A/RES/56/83, 12 December 2001, Annex, corrected by UN Doc. A/56/49 (Vol.1)/Corr.4). In consequence thereof, any state may demand of the responsible state to refrain from waging a war of aggression.

In addition, the persons responsible for the German acts of aggression during World War II were held criminally responsible by the Nuremberg war crimes tribunal (Art. 6 (a) Statute of the International Military Tribunal); the same is true for the Tokyo War Crimes Tribunal. On the other hand, aggression is not included as a criminal offence in the statutes of the International Criminal Tribunals for Yugoslavia and Rwanda, established by the UN Security Council. According to its *Rome Statute* (UNTS 2187, No. 38544; UN Doc. A/CONF. 183/9) the *International Criminal Court* (→ ICC – International Criminal Court) has jurisdiction over acts of aggression, but so far there has been no agreement on the necessary definition, nor on the authority of the Security Council in proceedings before the court. Therefore no legally binding definition yet exists. Before acts of aggression could be indicted at the ICC, such a definition must be included in the *Rome Statute* by a treaty amendment – which is not at the moment very likely (cf. *Baek* 2006 and *Politi/Nesi* 2004, there in particular *Kaul* 2004).

By contrast, the *Draft Code of Crimes against the Peace and Security of Mankind* (UN Doc. A/51/10, para. 50) of the International Law Commission (→ ILC) (1996) contains a statutory definition of aggression. However, this draft code is not regarded as having much chance to become legally binding as an international treaty.

II. The Resolution of the General Assembly Concerning the Definition of Aggression

History

Efforts to define a concept of aggression date back to the period between the World Wars and were mainly initiated by the Soviet Union. The Litvinov-Definition, named after the Soviet foreign minister of that time, enumerated exhaustively the possible acts of aggression. According to the priority principle, the state who committed such an act first, was the aggressor. After World War II, the Soviet Union submitted in 1950 new drafts that were subsequently discussed in special committees of the → General Assembly in the following period, but these discussions were without issue. The western states (for their proposals see *Bothe* 1975; *Bruha* 1980) looked upon this plan with great skepticism and objected in particular to over rigid rules.

Content

Only the 4th special committee on the question of defining aggression, established in 1967, was able to draft a generally acceptable definition, which was adopted as General Assembly Resolution 3314 (XXIX) "Definition of Aggression" on 14 December 1974 in a consensus procedure, but accompanied by numerous interpretative declarations

(*Bruha* 1980). The resolution calls upon all states to refrain from all acts of aggression and recommends that the Security Council take account of the definition as guidance in determining the existence of an act of aggression according to Article 39 of the UN Charter. The eight articles of the Annex of the resolution define aggression as follows:

According to Article 1 aggression "is the use of armed force by a State against the sovereignty, territorial integrity or political independence of another State". Thus an aggression requires military action of a state or substantial involvement of a state in comparable actions of armed bands. Non-state actors as such cannot carry out acts of aggression. A non-exhaustive (see Art. 4) *enumeration of acts of aggression* is contained in Article 3:

(a) "The invasion or attack by the armed forces of a State on the territory of anther State, or any military occupation, however temporary, resulting from such invasion or attack, or any annexation by the use of force of the territory of another State or part thereof;

(b) Bombardment by the armed forces of a State against the territory of another State or the use of any weapons by a State against the territory of another State;

(c) The blockade of the ports or coasts of a State by the armed forces of another State;

(d) An attack by the armed forces of a State on the land, sea or air forces, or marine and air fleets of another State;

(e) The use of armed forces of one State which are within the territory of another State with the agreement of the receiving State, in contravention of the conditions provided for in the agreement or any extension of their presence in such territory beyond the termination of the agreement;

(f) The action of a State in allowing its territory, which it has placed at the disposal of another State, to be used by that other State for perpetrating an act of aggression against a third State;

(g) The sending by or on behalf of a State of armed bands, groups, irregulars or mercenaries, which carry out acts of armed force against another State of such gravity as to amount to the acts listed above, or its substantial involvement therein."

An aggression therefore always contains a violation of the prohibition of the use of force enshrined in Article 2 (4) of the UN Charter, but is narrower than this prohibition. Aggression always requires the use of armed force; neither its threat nor other coercive measures suffice. Furthermore, in comparison to the definition of the prohibition of the use of force in the "Declaration on Principles of International Law concerning Friendly Relations and Co-operation among States in accordance with the Charter of the United Nations", the so-called "Friendly Relations Declaration" (UN Doc. A/RES/2625 (XXV) of 24 October 1970), much higher standards are required for encroachments of irregular troops in Article 3 (g) of the "Definition of Aggression". The aggression is consequently described in paragraph 5 of the preamble as the most serious and dangerous form of illegal use of force. However, the notion of aggression is wider than the one of armed attack used in Article 51 UN Charter, because the latter is not applicable to attacks on merchant fleets (also for an aggression an attack on individual ships is not sufficient, *Ferencz* 1992). Article 5 (2) of the "Definition of Aggression" therefore rightly describes only a war of aggression, but not every act of aggression, as an international crime (*Broms* 1977; *Dinstein* 2005).

Violations of the prohibition of aggression can not be justified on any grounds, and according to the *Stimson*-doctrine, the benefits resulting from such an act shall not be recognized as lawful (Art. 5 (3)). The right of peoples under colonial or racist regimes or other forms of alien domination to fight for self-determination (→ Self-Determination, Right of), freedom and independence and to seek and receive support to that end of other states remains unaffected. It was left open, whether the struggle for freedom could include the use of armed force. *The state who first uses armed force shall be regarded prima facie as the aggressor*; but in the light of all relevant factual circumstances a different conclusion is possible (Art. 2).

Legal and Actual Relevance

According to Article 13 UN Charter resolutions of the General Assembly are *recommendations* that do not bind as such the member states or the organs of the United Nations (→ Resolution, Declaration, Decision). However, this view does not grasp the full significance of resolutions for public international law (see generally *Fastenrath* 1993). *They can reflect the agreement between states regarding the content of treaty provisions* that has to be taken into account by their interpretation according to Article 31 (3) a of the Vienna Convention of the Law of Treaties (→ Treaties, Law of). Furthermore, *by adopting resolutions states can pronounce their opinio juris*, which is one element in the creation of *customary international law*. At least, resolutions can reflect existing customary law (→ International Law and the UN). Also the ICJ (→ ICJ – International Court of Justice) referred in this very cautious way to the definition of aggression of the General Assembly in its (1986) judgment Nicaragua v. United States of America (I.C.J. Reports 1986, 14) and similarly in the judgment Congo v. Uganda, 2005 (I.C.J. Reports 2005).

However, *Resolution 3314 (XXIX)* itself *reduces* its *legal importance* by declaring itself to be amendable, and by explicitly allowing the Security Council to take a divergent decision in particular cases. But also its *practical importance* is *small*. The Security Council avoids, even in clear cases like the Iraqi invasion of Kuwait, the determination of aggression (see resolutions 660, 662, 674 (1990). Instead it employs the notions of

a threat to or breach of the peace, which are sufficient to impose → sanctions. Even if resolutions do declare the existence of an aggression, they do not refer to Resolution 3314 (XXIX) of the General Assembly (cf. resolutions A/RES/ 573 (1985), A/RES/602 (1987) and A/RES/611 (1988)). With few exceptions, reference has not yet been made to this resolution in the debates of the Security Council (*Bruha* 1980). The ICJ as well avoids the determination of an act of aggression even in cases which appear to be textbook examples, such as the invasion of Ugandan forces into large parts of Congo's territory. The Court only made use of the definition of aggression contained in the resolution in the negative in order to deny the prerequisites of acts of aggression (Nicaragua v. United States, 1986; Congo v. Uganda, 2005).

Accordingly the aggression and its definition is neither legally nor politically decisive for actions of the Security Council. However, to invoke the right of self-defence, the existence of an aggression is not sufficient; the decisive notion of an armed attack remains undefined.

III. The definition of Aggression in International Criminal Law

Criminal provisions have to focus naturally on possible actions of individual persons, and could not take up a whole complex of factual events like an aggression. The ILC therefore provides, in Article 16 of the *Draft Code of Crimes against the Peace and Security of Mankind* (1996), and closely following the Statute of the Nuremberg International Military Tribunal, that: "An individual who, as leader or organizer, actively participates in or orders the *planning, preparation, initiation or waging of aggression committed by a State* shall be responsible for a crime of aggression." [emphasis through italics added by author] The act of aggression itself is not defined. In its commentary on the draft, the ILC does not however refer to the notion of aggression in Art. 39 of the UN Charter and the resolution 3314 (XXIX), or to the narrower notion of armed attack in Article 51 of the UN Charter, but to the broader one of the prohibition of the use of force contained in Article 2 (4) UN Charter (§ 5 of the ILC Commentary to Art. 16, UN Doc. A/51/ 10, p. 43). It is not very likely that an international crime of aggression, formulated in this form, will reach universal agreement, as the negotiations on the Statute of the International Criminal Court have shown (*Kaul* 1998, *Stahn* 1998).

Ulrich Fastenrath

Lit.: *Baek, B.S.:* The Definition and Jurisdiction of the Crime of Aggression and the International Criminal Court, Cornell Law School LL.M. Paper Series, No. 19, 2006 (http://lsr.nellco.org/cornell/lps/papers/19); *Bothe, M.:* Die Erklärung der Generalversammlung der Vereinten Nationen über die Definition der Aggression, JIR 18 (1975), 127-145; *Broms, B.:* The Definition of Aggression, in: RdC 154 (1977 I), 299-399; *Dinstein, Y.:* War, Aggression and Self-Defence, 4th edn., Cambridge 2005; *Fastenrath, U.:* Relative Normativity in International Law, in: EJIL 4 (1993), 305-340; *Ferencz, B.B.:* Aggression, in: EPIL, Vol. I, Amsterdam 1992, 58-65; *Kaul, H.-P.:* Durchbruch in Rom – Der Vertrag über den Internationalen Strafgerichtshof, in: VN 46 (1998), 125-130; *Kaul, H.-P.:* The crime of aggression: Definitional options for the way forward, in: Politi, M./Nesi, G. (eds.): The International Criminal Court and the Crime of Aggression, Burlington/USA 2004, 97-108; *Kress, C.:* The Crime of Aggression before the First Review of the ICC Statute, in: LJIL 20 (2007), 851-865; *Meron, T.:* Defining Aggression for the International Criminal Court, in: Transnat'lLR 25 (2001), 1-15; *Politi, M./Nesi, G. (eds.):* The International Criminal Court and the Crime of Aggression, Burlington/USA 2004; *Röling, B.V.A.:* Die Definition der Aggression, in: Delbrück, J./Ipsen, K./Rauschning, D. (eds.): Recht im Dienst des Friedens, Fs. Menzel, Berlin 1976, 387-404; *Schwebel, S.M.:* Aggression, Intervention and Self-Defence in Modern International Law, in: RdC 136 (1972 II), 411-497; *Stahn, C.:* Zwischen Weltfrieden und materieller Gerechtigkeit – die Gerichtsbarkeit des Ständigen Internationalen Gerichtshofs, in: EuGRZ 25 (1998), 577-591; *Steins, M.S.:* The Security Council, the International Criminal Court, and the Crime of Aggression: How Exclusive is the Security Council's Power to Determine Aggression?, in: IndianaICLR 16 (2005), 1-36; *Stone, J.:* Aggression and World Order, London 1958; *Verosta, S.:* Die Definition des Angriffs und die Staatenpraxis, in: Tittel, J. (ed.): Multitudo legum ius unum, Vol. 1, Fs. Wengler, Berlin 1973, 693-704; *Weisbord, N.:* Prosecuting Aggression, in: HarvILJ 49 (2008), 161-220.

Budget

I. Introduction

There exists no unified, comprehensive budget of the United Nations. It must be differentiated between (a) the *regular budget* of the Organization, predominantly financed through assessments of the member states, (b) *obligatory contributions for special accounts to finance the → peace-keeping operations* of the UN (only two smaller peace-keeping operations are financed through the regular budget of the UN: UNTSO since June 1948 in the Middle East and UNMOGIP since January 1949 in Kashmir, and (c) the budgets of the special organs and programmes of the UN (→ UN System) whose activities are financed by voluntary contributions of the members of the United Nations and/or → specialized agencies. In the following, only the *regular budget* will be analyzed.

II. Charter Provisions

According to Article 17, para. 1 of the UN Charter (→ Charter of the UN) the → General Assembly considers and approves the budget of the Organization. Article 17, para. 2, stipulates that the expenses of the Organization are borne by the UN member states as apportioned by the General Assembly. Article 18, para. 2, of the Charter provides that decisions of the General Assembly on important questions which include budgetary questions shall be made by a two-thirds majority of the members present and voting. Article 19 of the Charter states that: "A Member of the United Nations which is in arrears in the payment of its financial contributions to the Organization shall have no vote in the General

Assembly if the amount of its arrears equals or exceeds the amount of the contributions due from it for the preceding two full years".

Articles 17, paras 1 and 2, 18, para 2, and 19 of the UN Charter form the *general financial constitution* of the United Nations. Also to be taken in consideration is Article 97 of the Charter in which the → Secretary-General is designed as the "chief administrative officer of the Organization". In this capacity he is also responsible for the preparation, submission and implementation of the budget as well as for the financial management of the Organization.

Details of the budget process of the Organization are mainly to be found in the rules 152-160 of the *Rules of Procedure of the General Assembly* (→ Rules of Procedure) as well as in the *Financial Regulations and Rules of the UN* (the current version of the Financial Regulations being adopted by the General Assembly on 20 December 2002 with Decision 57/573 and published in the Secretary-General's bulletin of 9 May 2003, UN Doc. ST/SGB/2003/7). The Rules 155-157 and 158-160 of the Rules of Procedure of the GA (UN Doc. A/520/Rev. 17) refer to the appointment, composition and functions of the *Advisory Committee on Administrative and Budgetary Questions* (ACABQ) and the *Committee on Contributions*.

III. Budget Process

In the following, reference will be made only to the budgetary procedure introduced since 1988. It consists of two sequential parts: in off-budget years, for the first time applied in 1988, the Secretary-General submits a budgetary outline in August containing his estimates of resources required for the following biennium, programme priorities, and the rate of growth of the budget. This budget outline which also contains information about the estimated amount of the contingency fund for meeting expenses for any unforeseen activities is then debated in the *Committee on Programme and Co-ordination (CPC)* and the *Advisory Committee on Administra-*

tive and Budgetary Questions (ACABQ) before being presented to the *Fifth Committee* of the General Assembly (→ Committees, System of) responsible for budgetary matters. The General Assembly finally approves the budget outline on the basis of the recommendations of the Fifth Committee.

During these negotiations in the off-budget year the CPC is, without doubt, the first and most important hurdle which can only be overcome by consensus. Not only the 34 member states of the CPC but also other UN member states can participate in these negotiations as observers with the right to speak. The second hurdle is the ACABQ which consists of 16 governmental experts; it discusses in detail the financial implications of the proposed budget outline with the UN Secretariat (→ Secretariat); it does not meet in public and decides its conclusions by consensus. The third hurdle is the *Fifth Committee*; as an organ of the General Assembly all member states can participate in its consultations. Here – on the basis of the recommendations of the CPC and the ACABQ – both the political aspects as well as the financial implications of the budget outline are discussed with the aim of achieving the highest degree of unanimity before the recommendation is submitted to the plenum of the General Assembly for final action.

The *second stage of the biennial budgeting process* takes place in the year of the approval of the budget (uneven year: "budget year", for the first time in 1989), whereby the procedure of the single institutional hurdles is identical to that of the first stage. On the basis of the budget outline approved by the General Assembly in the preceding year, the Secretary-General submits a draft of the concrete programme budget to which, first of all, the CPC comments with regard to its interrelationship with the six-year medium-term plan, but also to the intended plan of foreseen posts and to the approved budget outline. Based on the recommendations of the CPC, the ACABQ then makes concrete recommendations concerning the allocation of resources including single proposals for savings. Then, the draft budget is debated in the Fifth Committee taking into due account the recommendations of the CPC and ACABQ. Finally, the General Assembly approves the programme budget on the basis of the recommendations of the Fifth Committee. The first programme budget according to the new budgetary process was approved by consensus at the 44th General Assembly in December 1989 for the biennium 1990-1991. This principle of consensus has been applied for 18 years. In December 2007, only the United States voted in the General Assembly against the adoption of the budget resolution, thus breaking this principle. This move might complicate future work (cf. *Swart* 2008).

The details of the programme planning process, about the programme aspects of the budget as well as about the procedures for monitoring its implementation and about the methods of evaluation are decided by the General Assembly in the "Regulations and Rules Governing Programme Planning ...", the current version being adopted by the General Assembly with resolution 53/207 of 18 December 1998 and issued in a Bulletin of the Secretary-General of 19 April 2000 (*United Nations* 2000, UN Doc. ST/SGB/2000/8).

The "Regulations" provide the legislative directives governing respectively the planning, programming, monitoring and evaluation of the budgeting and the implementation of the budget.

IV. The Regular UN Budget 2008-09

The programme budget of the UN for the biennium 2008-2009 consists of 14 Parts which are divided into 35 Chapters. It was approved by the 62nd General Assembly in December 2007. Appropriations totaled 4.171 billion US dollars.

The largest expenditure items are Part I (Overall Policy-making, Direction and Co-ordination as well as General Assembly Affairs and Conference Services) with 718.560 million US dollars

(= 17.23%), Part II (Political Affairs, Disarmament, Peacekeeping Operations) with 626.07 million US dollars (= 15%), and Part VIII (Management and Central Support Services) with 540.200 million US dollars (= 12.95%). The most important area of activity is without doubt the International and Regional Co-operation for Development (Parts IV and V) which together amount to 875.600 million US dollars (= 20.99%). Also the "transitory" item, which expands the budget, is substantial: the staff assessment in Part XIV amounts to 461.370 million US dollars (= 11.06%). This taxation of the staff salaries had to be introduced, because the United States, also host country of the UN, does not offer its citizens belonging to the UN staff tax exemption. This is, however, neither a tax in a narrow sense nor a real income, because in the budget this item can be found both in the expenditure and the revenue section.

In addition, the UN receives income from rental of premises and reimbursement for services provided for the specialized agencies, which are expected to amount to 47.95 million US dollars for the biennium 2008-2009. Furthermore, 1.73 million US dollars are expected from services to the public.

Without doubt, the assessed obligatory contributions from the member states, calculated on the basis of an assessment scale, are the most important income source. For 2008-2009 this expected income amounts to about 3.76 billion US dollars.

V. Scale of Assessments

The criteria for the apportionment among the members of the expenses of the UN are not mentioned explicitly in the Charter. For this purpose a *Committee on Contributions* was set up by the General Assembly; its 18 members are selected by the General Assembly upon recommendation of the Fifth Committee on the basis of broad geographical representation, personal qualification and experience for a period of three years.

Since 1946, the Committee on Contributions continuously developed and re-

fined the system of contributions in annual meetings which, however, at no time fully satisfied the member states. Due to methodological difficulties as well as divergent political interests only "compromises on limited time" are to be expected. The supplementary elements, which were either introduced into the system or varied, are:
- the fixing of the ceiling and floor rate;
- the length of the base period;
- the scheme of limits for increases and decreases of contributions;
- the introduction of special allowances; and
- the taking into account of specific economic difficulties.

The most important criterion for the determination of the individual assessment rate of the member states to the regular budget of the UN is the "capacity to pay", since 1993 calculated on the basis of the gross national income (in the past, net national product was the standard). All other factors sooner or later taken into account have a correcting influence in order to avoid abnormal results. Immediately after the founding of the United Nations the per capita income, war-related economic distortions and the amount of hard currencies (US dollars and gold) were taken into account. Whereas the criterion of war-related economic losses which was included in the original mandate lost already importance during the 1950s, the high levels of external debt which led to reductions became relevant during the 1980s.

The scale of assessments is established by the following individual steps: the starting point is the statistical calculation of the gross national income (GNI) of all member states measured in national currencies, related to the statistical base period. Its length has a significant influence on the size of the estimated GNI and thus on the assessment. Originally, this base period was one year; in 1953, it was fixed at three years. In 1978, the base period was extended to seven years, and between 1981 and 1994, to ten years. This happened because of the demands of the oil-producing countries which claimed

that the consideration of only the "fat" years was unjustified; supported by the majority of the Group of 77 in the General Assembly ($\rightarrow$ Group of 77 and the UN) they were in the position to successfully implement this change. After the collapse of the socialist countries and the foundation of many, newly independent states the demand for a drastic reduction of the base period was raised. This demand was justified by the fact that in the case of the majority of these new states a "recalculation" for a period of the last ten years had to be based on a number of arbitrary assumptions. Also the fact that these countries were in a rather bad economic situation plays an important role, resulting from a "big bang" transformation from centrally planned economies to market-orientated systems. For the first time, the base period was reduced to 7.5 years (= average of the periods 1985-92 and 1986-92) for the years 1995-97 and to 6 years for the years 1998-2000. The current scale of assessments is based on the average of the results of using base periods of three and six years. Also, the next step in order to reach a common denominator, namely the conversion of the GNIs expressed in national currencies in US dollars, is connected with several problems. Normally, average market exchange rates to the US dollar are applied, as calculated by the International Monetary Fund ($\rightarrow$ IMF) and published in the International Finance Statistics. Thereby, it is assumed that those exchange rates reflect differences in the purchase power under market-economic conditions. Because of the above mentioned difficulties of measurement it was not surprising that the Committee on Contributions has been asked from the beginning of its work to develop appropriate methods to correct the calculated national income figures in order to reach a higher degree of "contribution justice". It was not surprising that member states protested against their assessed contributions which seemed too high for them; therefore, they demanded adjustment mechanisms, such as, e.g., reductions because of ex-

21

tremely low per capita income or high levels of external debt. Other states argued against these adjustment mechanisms, because reductions on the one side would necessarily lead towards additional increases for other member states ("zero-sum game").

Basically, it must be assumed that all states follow two targets in the determination of their assessment rates: on the one hand, they would like to be classified at the lowest possible rate of the assessment scale, on the other, they favor a very slow increase, if at all, of the total volume of the regular budget which then leads to a desired low national contribution in US dollars as a result of the multiplication of the national assessment rate with the adopted volume of the regular UN budget.

From the technical point of view, the reduction due to low per capita income levels is calculated in the following way: first of all, a certain threshold level must be statistically determined in order to identify the member states with a low per capita income. The following reduction formula for the low per capita income adjustment has been developed:

$$\frac{\text{threshold level income} . / . \text{per capita income}}{\text{threshold level income}} \times \text{favoring factor ("gradient")}$$

Since 1948, the data used for threshold level incomes on the one hand and for gradients on the other were politically determined whereby the large majority of the developing countries in the General Assembly was primarily interested in profiting as much as possible from the reduction formula. Between 1995 and 1997 a threshold level of 3,200 US dollars and a gradient of 85% were applied. Because of the pressure of the EU and the United States a reduction of the gradient to 80% has been applied since the period 1998-2000. The present threshold level is 5,684 US dollars.

The application of the reduction formula leads to a redistribution, whereby the countries with a per capita income

below the threshold per capita income level benefit from it. The lower the per capita income is, the higher is the reduction. The closer the per capita income approaches the threshold level, the smaller will be the reduction.

Besides this deduction for member states with low per capita incomes also an adjustment factor is used since 1986-1988 taking into account high levels of external debt, the debt-burden adjustment. Over the years, several ad hoc adaptations of the assessment scale were undertaken. For 2008-2009, an adjustment has been undertaken for member states with a per capita income below 10,725 US dollars. This adjustment has been related to 12.5% of the total official and private external debt which has been deducted from the national income. It has been assumed that these foreign debts will be, on the average, repaid within a period of eight years.

After having calculated the GNIs of the member states, expressed in US dollars, and having taken into account the reduction factors, the next step in determining the assessment scale is affected by the upper limit (ceiling) and the minimum (floor) scale. At present, the ceiling rate is fixed at 22.00% and the floor rate of 0.001%. Taking into account the concept of the capacity to pay, the ceiling rate of the United States stood originally at 49.89%, based upon data for the years 1938-40. From the beginning, the United States insisted on a reduction of this ceiling rate with the argument that it would not be in the interest of the Organization that one single state bears such a heavy burden, thereby leading to a high dependence of the UN. Under heavy political pressure the United States succeeded in reducing its first assessment rate to 39.89% and later, in 1954, to 33.33%. Further reductions followed in 1957 to 30.00%, and in 1972, based upon a unilateral decision by the US Congress, to 25.00%. The ceiling rate of 25.00%, beginning in 1973, could be adopted by the General Assembly without major political disputes due to the admission of the two German states to the UN; they contributed a total of 8.32 percentage points which could easily compensate the difference of 5 percentage points caused by the United States. During the second half of the 1990s, the United States demanded a further reduction of its assessment rate to 22 and 20%. In December 2000, after long and tough negotiations a compromise was reached in the General Assembly: as from 2001 the ceiling has been reduced to 22% (UN Doc. A/RES/55/5B-F of 23 December 2000).

Originally, the floor rate was fixed at 0.04%. This rate was kept for almost 30 years in order to guarantee a "minimum of self-commitment". It was reduced since 1974 to 0.02% and since 1978 to 0.01%. This minimum contribution rate has been extremely low in absolute terms (in 1995: 140,000 US dollars); however, related to the capacity to pay of the least developed countries, this rate has been often above their actual national income which meant that they paid, in relative terms, more than the United States. As from 1998, the floor rate has been reduced to 0.001% in order to correct this (which meant in absolute terms 18,290 US dollars in 2008).

For the 12 largest contributors, the scale of assessments for 2001, 2004-2006, 2007 - 2009 is the following:

Member State	2001	2004-2006	2007-2009
United States	22.000 (1)	22.000 (1)	22.000 (1)
Japan	19.629 (2)	19.468 (2)	16.624 (2)
Germany	9.825 (3)	8.662 (3)	8.577 (3)
France	6.503 (4)	6.030 (5)	6.301 (5)
United Kingdom	5.568 (5)	6.127 (4)	6.642 (4)
Italy	5.094 (6)	4.885 (6)	5.079 (6)
Canada	2.573 (7)	2.813 (7)	2.977 (7)
Spain	2.534 (8)	2.520 (8)	2.968 (8)
Netherlands	1.748 (9)	1.690 (12)	1.873 (12)
Republic of Korea	1.728 (10)	1.796 (11)	2.173 (11)
Australia	1.636 (11)	1.592 (-)	1.787 (-)
China	1.541 (12)	2.053 (9)	2.667 (9)
Mexico	1.093 (-)	1.883 (10)	2.257 (10)
	80.379	79.927	80.138

These 12 member states pay about 80% of the total assessed contributions during the period 2007-2009. China is on 9th position with more than 2.6%, whereas Russia holds the 15th position (1.2%). Altogether, 17 member states contribute more than one percent to the regular budget (= 86.514%). 54 of the 192 member states pay the floor rate of 0.001%; they contribute a total 0.054% to the regular budget. The share of the EU member states continued to increase, from 35.37% in 1997 to 37.128% in 2002 and to 38.857% in 2009; among them, Germany is the largest contributor with 8.577%.

VI. Outlook

The table included above does not say anything about the "payment morale" of the member states. As of 31 January 2008, only 36 of the 192 member states had met their obligations and paid their contributions to the regular budget for 2008 in full and on time. These have included for many years the Nordic countries, Canada, Ireland, Luxembourg, New Zealand, Kuwait and South Africa; as of 31 December 2007, only 140 of the 192 member states had paid their assessed contributions to the regular UN budget for 2007 and for prior years in full; the United States had obligations towards the Organization of 392.7 million US dollars (= 92% of all arrears). Germany normally pays 50 percent of its dues in January and the other half in June of the year.

All changes in the scale of assessments mentioned above are primarily the result of the political pressure from the EU and the United States. Whether and when the United States will pay its arrears remains an open question. The financial crisis (→ Financial Crises) and the negative nominal growth of the regular budget have crippled the Organization and endangered its mandates and programmes. The requisites for the creation of a stable, sustainable financing mechanism in the service of the goals and principles of the United Nations are still missing.

The dramatic financial situation of the UN is mainly due to the non- or late payment of its dues by the United States – a member state which, although having the ability to pay, continues to demonstrate its unwillingness to pay, thus being primarily responsible for the bad image of the UN as compared to regional governmental organizations. As Secretary-General Ban Ki-moon put it frankly in his report "Improving the financial situation of the United Nations" (UN Doc. A/63/514) in October 2008: "The financial position of the United Nations remains fragile ... The only way to overcome the problem and to ensure a more stable financial base for the work of the United Nations is for Member States to meet their financial obligations to the Organization in a fuller and more timely fashion."

Klaus Hüfner

Lit.: *Global Policy Forum/Friedrich-Ebert Foundation:* The Challenges of UN Finance. Meeting on 22 March 2006 in New York, www.globalpolicy.org/un-finance/general-articles/27324.html; *Hüfner, K.:* Die Finanzierung des VN-Systems, Bonn 2006 (DGVN-Texte 53); *Hüfner, K.:* Finanzierung. In: Volger, H. (ed.): Grundlagen und Strukturen der Vereinten Nationen, Munich 2007, 417-437; *Koch, L.:* Haushaltsgestaltung nach Vorgabe des US-Kongresses, in: VN 46 (1998), 35; *Koschorreck, W.:* Beitragsfestsetzung weder gerecht noch transparent, in : VN 46 (1998), 33-35; *Koschorreck, W.:* Ted Turner als Deus ex machina, in: VN 49 (2001), 65-67; *Laurenti, J.:* Financing the United Nations (International Relations Studies of the Academic Council on the United Nations System), New Haven 2001; *Laurenti, J.:* Financing, in: Weiss, T.G./Daws, S. (eds): The Oxford Handbook on the United Nations, Oxford 2007, 675-700; *Lehmann, V./McClellan, A.:* Financing the United Nations (Dialogue on Globalization - Fact Sheet - FES New York), New York 2006, http://library.fes.de/pdf-files/iez/global/50425.pdf; *Swart, L.:* Why Was the UN Budget Approved by Vote and not by Consensus? UN Reform Watch No. 30, 29 January 2008, published by the Center for UN Reform Education, www. centerforunreform. org; *United Nations Association of the USA:* Crisis and Reform in United Nations Financing, New York 1997; *United Nations:*

Regulations and Rules Governing Programme Planning, the Programme Aspects of the Budget, the Monitoring of Implementation and the Methods of Evaluation. Secretary-General's Bulletin, 19 April 2000, UN Doc. ST/ SGB/2000/8 (quoted as: United Nations 2000); *United Nations - General Assembly:* Report of the Committee on Contributions. Sixty-seventh session (11-29 June 2007). New York 2007 (UN Doc. A/62/11); *United Nation - General Assembly:* Report of the Committee on Contributions. Sixty-eighth session (9-27 June 2008), New York 2008 (UN Doc. A/63/11); *United Nation – General Assembly:* Improving the financial situation of the United Nations. Report of the Secretary-General, 31 October 2008, UN Doc. A/63/514.

Internet: *1) within the UN system:* a) information about the work of the Fifth Committee of the General Assembly: www.un. org/ga/63/fifth (replace the 63 with the number of the respective session); *b) information about the ACABQ:* www.un.org/ga/acabq/index.asp; the CPC: www.un.org/ga/cpc/; *c) press releases about the work of ACABQ, CPC and the budget in general:* UN search machine www.un.org/search/ under the search words budget, ACABQ and CPC; *2) website on UN finances of the Global Policy Forum:* www.globalpolicy. org/finance/index.htm.

Charter of Economic Rights and Duties of States

This Charter was first proposed in 1972 by the former Mexican President Echevarria, at UNCTAD III in Chile (→ UNCTAD). The Charter of Economic Rights and Duties of States (UN Doc. A/RES/3281 (XXIX)) was then adopted by the 29th regular session of the UN General Assembly (→ General Assembly) on 12 December 1974 with a large majority from the developing countries (whose interests were met best by the Charter), against the votes of the Western industrialized countries.

The content and the tendency of the Charter is largely in agreement with the decisions of the 6th special session of the General Assembly relating to commodities and development in May 1974, (→ International Economic Relations, NIEO) which were meant to indicate the necessity to restructure the world economy according to the principles of equality, sovereignty and international co-operation. On 1 May 1974 the General Assembly adopted in consensus the Declaration on the Establishment of a New International Economic Order, as a proclamation of principles (UN Doc. A/RES/3201 (S-VI)) and a corresponding Programme of Action (A/RES/3202 (S-VI)).

The Charter, composed of 34 articles, is structured in four chapters: Fundamentals of International Economic Relations (Chapter I, lit a-o); Economic Rights and Duties of States (Chapter II, Art. 1-28); Common Responsibilities Towards International Community (Chapter III, Art 29, 30); Final Provisions (Chapter IV, Art. 31-34) and contains *four central concepts*:

First: It emphasizes the principle of sovereignty (→ Sovereignty), territorial integrity, political independence and sovereign equality of all states. (Chapter 1 a-o)

Second: It accentuates those rights that comprise state sovereignty, regarded as inalienable: the right to choose the economic, political, social, and cultural system (Chapter II, Art. 1), the right of sovereignty over the national resources, and of control over foreign property and transnational companies, including the right of nationalization and regulation of compensatory payments for nationalized products and goods. (Chapter II, Art. 2 a-c)

Third: It calls for far-reaching equality in international economical relations. This includes the rejection of any form of discrimination (Chapter II, Art 4), the right to participate in the advances and development in science and technology (Chapter II, Art. 13) and the duty to collaborate in promoting, expanding and liberalizing world trade and in improving the welfare and the living standards of all peoples, especially of developing countries. (Chapter II, Art. 14). And finally it demands equal participation in the leading institutions of world economy, such as the World Bank (→ World

Bank, World Bank Group) and the International Monetary Fund (→ IMF).

The *fourth group* of principles states the demands of the charter in concrete terms. This includes, in addition to the duty of concluding long-term multilateral commodity agreements (Chapter II, Art. 6), the requirement to increase trade with the socialist countries (Chapter II, Art. 20) and to promote and expand the trade relations and economic cooperation between the developing countries. (Chapter II, Art. 21 and 23)

Further it includes those articles authorizing the raw material producing countries to form raw material cartels (Chapter II, Art. 5), the demand for non-reciprocal preferences (not based on mutuality) in the international trade in favor of developing countries (Chapter II, Art. 26) and finally the duty of the states to work jointly for the adjustment of the export prices of the developing countries in relation to their import prices (price indexation). (Chapter II, Art. 28).

Not all of the regulations prescribed in the Charter are equally important or of equal validity with regard to the time factor. A critical appreciation of the intended adjustments must account for the politicizing of the debate about a new design of the world economy. This becomes especially clear if one compares the basic principles of the Charter with its recommendations for concrete measures. Whereas the articles containing the essential rights of the developing countries open with the formula "all states have the right ...", those articles of the fourth group containing the principles postulating bilateral actions and cooperation start with the words "all states should ..." or "all states have the duty to ..."

There are further incompatibilities in the declaration of intent laid down in the charter, as for example the charter recommends on the one hand the formation of commodity cartels, while it recommends on the other hand the conclusion of commodity agreements and agreements on commodity programmes. As well, the charter demands on the one hand a reform and an adjustment of the international economic order, but on the other hand clings in principle to the traditional principles of international division of labor in obliging all states "to contribute to the balanced expansion of the world economy". (Chapter IV, Art. 31)

In a word, the often-proclaimed restructuring of the world economy, as described in the charter, has been in fact more the expression of common declarations of intent and tendencies, rather than a sign that there has been clarity about concrete measures to achieve a restructuring, and to codify settlements at the time when the charter was adopted. This situation is basically unchanged today, and there is still no clarity about measures to restructure world economy.

Mir A. Ferdowsi

Lit.: *Jonas, R./Tietzel, M. (eds.) :* Die Neuordnung der Weltwirtschaft, Bonn-Bad Godesberg 1976; *Lake, D.A.:* Power and the Third World: Toward a Realistic Political Economy of North-South-Relations, in: International Studies Quarterly, 31 (1987), 217-234; *Petersmann, E.-U.:* International Economic Order, in: Bernhardt, R. (ed.), EPIL 8 (1985), 336-343; *Somjee, A.H.:* Development Theory: Critiques and Explorations, Basingstoke 1991.

Addendum

Over the last decades, the Charter of Economic Rights has largely lost its relevance. After the breakdown of socialism at the end of the 1980's, market liberalization, privatization and the doctrine of free trade have gained momentum world-wide. The establishment of the WTO (→ WTO, GATT) in 1994 marked a turning point. The number of MNCs increased rapidly. Simultaneously the economic dependence of developing countries on Foreign Direct Investment has grown. This involves a tendency of a race to the bottom in terms of human rights and environmental protection.

In order to address this challenge the multilateral organizations have attempted to deal with the increasing ethical problems in revised versions of their basic texts and guidelines: the → ILO revised the Tripartite Declaration on Multinational Enterprises and Social Policy in 2001 (*ILO* 2001) and again in 2006 (*ILO* 2006), the OECD revised the "Guidelines for Multinational Enterprises" in 2000 with respect to ethical aspects, human rights and environmental protection (*OECD* 2000).

Within the system of the United Nations the *UN Global Compact* was founded by the Secretary General in 2000 as a voluntary pact by which enterprises declare to the United Nations that they are committed to aligning their operations and strategies with ten universally accepted principles in the areas of human rights, labor, the environment and anti-corruption, as established by the United Nations (cf. UN Global Compact Annual Review 2007).

As well, the Subcommission on the Promotion and Protection of Human Rights of the UN Commission on Human Rights worked on and eventually adopted "Norms on the Responsibilities of Transnational Corporations and Other Business Enterprises with Regard to Human Rights" in August 2003 (UN Doc. E/CN.4/Sub.2/2003/12/Rev.2), but these norms have up to now not moved beyond draft status.

Moreover, on the request of the Commission on Human Rights in its resolution 2005/69 (UN Doc. E/CN.4/RES/ 2005/69 of 20 April 2005), the UN Secretary-General in July 2005 appointed John Ruggie to be Special Representative of the Secretary-General on the issue of human rights and transnational corporations and other business enterprises. The UN Human Rights Council, which in 2006 replaced the Commission on Human Rights, renewed the mandate of the Special Representative in June 2008 by resolution 8/7 (UN Doc. A/HRC/RES/8/7 of 18 June 2008).

In other words, the international organizations are battling to establish at the least a rather general, but commonly accepted set of ethical rules, giving the rapidly developing and changing world economy a kind of orientation. The basic aim which the United Nations tried in vain to achieve in 1974 with the Charter remains still to be solved: creating more equality of living and working conditions for the people of the different nations within the world economy. It involves the willingness of the rich nations to share their resources with the poor nations to a larger extent than now

Antje Hennings

Lit.: *I. Documents/Basic Texts International Labour Office (ILO):* Tripartite Declaration of Principles Concerning Multinational Enterprises and Social Policy, as amended in November 2000, Geneva 2001; *International Labour Office (ILO):* Tripartite Declaration of Principles Concerning Multinational Enterprises and Social Policy, as amended in March 2006, Geneva 2006, www.ilo.org/public/english/employment/multi/download/declaration2006.pdf; *Organisation for Economic Co-operation and Development (OECD):* The OECD Guidelines for Multinational Enterprises, Revision 2000, Paris 2000, www.oecd.org/dataoecd/56/36/1922428.pdf; *UN Commission on Human Rights – Subcommission on the Promotion and Protection of Human Rights:* Norms on the Responsibilities of Transnational Corporations and Other Business Enterprises with Regard to Human Rights, UN Doc. E/CN.4/Sub.2/2003/12/Rev.2, 13 August 2003; *United Nations Global Compact Office:* UN Global Compact Annual Review 2007 Leaders Summit, New York 2007;
II. Secondary Literature: Addo, M.K. (ed.): Human Rights Standards and the Responsibility of Transnational Corporations, The Hague 1999; *Jägers, N.:* Corporate Human Rights Obligations: In Search of Accountability, Antwerp 2002; *Joseph, S.:* Taming the Leviathans: Multinational Enterprises and Human Rights, in: Netherlands International Law Review 46 (1999), 171-203; *Kinley, D./Tadaki, J.:* From Talk to Walk: The Emergence of Human Rights Responsibilites for Corporations at International Law, in: Va.J Int'l.L 4 (2004), 931-1023; *Ratner, S.R.:* Corporations and Human Rights: A Theory of Legal Responsibility, in: Yale Law Journal 111 (2001), 443-545.

Internet: Homepage of UNCTAD (information on the economic North-South relations): www.unctad.org; cf. also: www.ilo.org; www.oecd.org; www.unhchr.org; www.unglobalcompact.org.

Charter of the UN

The Charter is the international founding treaty for the Organization of the community of states, which was named according to the wish of its founding members as the "United Nations". The Charter was signed at the conclusion of the founding conference in San Francisco, on 26 June 1945. This conference was initiated at the end of World War II by the original 50 member states (Poland subsequently joined, and became the 51st founder state). The Charter came into force on 24 October 1945 (→ History of the Foundation of the UN). The Charter has indefinite validity. Contrary to the Covenant of the → League of Nations, which was part of the peace treaties concluded at the end of World War I, the contractual basis of the UN was completed and passed independently of the peace treaty settlements enacted after 1945.

The Charter is not only the multilateral basis of contract for the establishment of the United Nations, but also at the same time the basic constitutional document of the Organization, in which its purposes and objectives as well as its working principles and rules of procedure are prescribed. Since the Charter also contains the crucial provisions for the institutional composition and the division of competencies between the different UN organs (→ Principal Organs, Subsidiary Organs, Treaty Bodies), it is at the same time the binding organizational statute of the UN. In the course of the universal extension of membership (→ Membership and Representation of States; → Universality) and the related worldwide recognition of the principles of law established therein, the Charter has become the basis of current universal international law (*Verdross/Simma* 1984, 72).

The Charter consists of a preamble and 111 articles, which are divided into 19 chapters. The Statute of the International Court of Justice (→ ICJ), which is designated according to Article 92 of the Charter as the main judicial body of the UN, is part of the Charter.

The creators of the UN have endowed the founding treaty and constitutional document with great durability. While the Charter can be altered or revised on the base of Article 108 or Article 109, these changes or revisions to the Charter, however, in principle require a two-thirds vote of the members of the → General Assembly, and need to be ratified afterwards by two thirds of the UN members, including all permanent members of the → Security Council in accordance with their constitutional law. Thus efforts to change or to adjust the Charter in accordance with conditions of the international system which may have altered since the time of its origin, have some serious obstacles to overcome.

I. Amendments and Revision of the UN Charter

Over the course of the development of the UN (→ History of the UN) the Charter has only been marginally changed. The amendments have so far mainly concerned the number of members in the Security Council and in the Social and Economic Council (→ ECOSOC), and are referred to in Article 23, 27, 61, and 109. With respect to the increased number of members on 17 December 1963 according to Resolution 1991A and B (XVIII) of the General Assembly the number of non-permanent members of the Security Council was raised from the original six to ten (Art. 23) and accordingly the quorum for decisions in this crucial body was raised to nine members (Art. 27 (2) and (3)); the number of members in the ECOSOC was raised from 18 to 27 (Art. 61). Both modifications came into force on 31 August 1965. In another Resolution 2101 (XX) of 20 December 1965, Article 109 (1) was also adjusted in accordance with the increased number of members in the Security Council (nine instead of formerly seven members). At the instigation of the member states from the Third World, the number of members in the ECOSOC was raised again by a resolution of the General Assembly (Resolution 2847 (XXVI)) on 20 December 1971, from 27 to 54 members. That second modification of Art. 61 came into force on 24 September 1973. The changes of the years 1963/1965 and 1971/1973 remain to date the only formal amendments to the Charter. They illustrate the particular continuity, but at the same time inflexibility, of the founding treaty and constitutional document of the Organization. All other attempts for a contractual revision of the Charter within the scope of a → reform of the UN have remained up to now without results.

I.1. The Reform Debate in 2004/2005

In the course of the sustained discussions on reforming the UN, which began in the late 1990s, the issue of a revision of the Charter was also addressed. It was argued that at least some of the more fundamental measures required related amendments of the Charter.

In recent years, deliberations on a reform of the UN and concomitant questions of revising the Charter gathered momentum. Especially in connection with the events commemorating the sixtieth anniversary of the foundation of the UN in 2005 and at the same time to follow-up the outcome of the Millennium Summit (2000), pertinent efforts by interested member states, UN officials, and different expert groups increased.

The High-level Panel on Threats, Challenges and Change, appointed by the then Secretary-General Kofi Annan in 2003, in its report "A More Secure World: Our Shared Responsibility" (UN Doc. A/59/565), published in December 2004, dealt also with the prospects of the Charter. The experts point out that their recommendations on Security Council reform (the respective alternative models A and B) would require the amendment of Article 23 of the Charter. Moreover, the Panel suggests only "modest" changes to the Charter: Article 53 and 107 (references to enemy states) are regarded as outdated and should be revised, the Trusteeship Council (Chapter XIII) should be deleted, likewise the Military Staff Committee (Art. 47) as should be all references to this body in Article 26, 45 and 46. Basically, the Panel took the view "that the Charter as a whole continues to provide a sound legal and policy basis for the organization of collective security" (para. 301).

In his salient reform report "In larger freedom: towards development, security and human rights for all" (UN Doc. A/59/2005), published 21 March 2005, Secretary-General Annan addressed also the topic "Updating the Charter". Annan, for the most part, endorsed the recommendations of the High Level Panel mentioned above. He is also convinced that the principles of the Charter remain fully valid and that "the Charter itself, in the main, continues to provide a solid foundation for all our work." (para. 216) With regard to concrete changes of the Charter Annan suggests the elimination of the anachronistic "enemy" clauses in Article 53 and 107 and to delete Chapter XIII, The Trusteeship Council (para. 217 and 218). In addition, Article 47 on "The Military Staff Committee" should be deleted as well as all references to this in the Articles 26, 45 and 46 (para. 219).

In view of the recommendations and proposals suggested for amending the Charter it was interesting to see how the World Summit gathered at United Nations Headquarters in New York from 14 to 16 September 2005 (as a follow-up summit meeting to the United Nations 2000 Millennium Summit) would handle that matter. The so-called "Outcome Document" of the Summit (UN Doc. A/RES60/1 of 16 September 2005), deals in its final three paragraphs (176, 177, and 178) with the revision of the Charter. Recognizing that the Trusteeship Council has no remaining functions, the Document stated that it should be deleted (Chapter XIII and references to the Council in Chapter XII). In regard to the outdated enemy clauses, the Document contains the following convoluted provision: "Taking into account General Assembly resolution 50/52 of 11 December 1995 and recalling the related discussions conducted in the General Assembly, bearing in mind the pro-

found cause for the founding of the United Nations and looking to our common future, we resolve to delete references to 'enemy states' in Articles 53, 77 and 107 of the Charter." (para. 177) At this point the Outcome Document refers to a previous resolution of the General Assembly, in which the General Assembly in 1995 unanimously declared that the enemy clauses have become "obsolete" (A/RES/50/52 of 11 December 1995, p. 3). With reference to the Military Staff Committee (Art. 47 UN Charter) the Outcome Document does not speak of a clear-cut deletion of that body, but refers to the discretion of the Security Council: "We request the Security Council to consider the composition, mandate and working methods of the Military Staff Committee." (para. 178).

In consideration of the fact that the Outcome Document of September 2005 advocated only modest changes to the Charter and that the efforts of interested member state groups for the extension of the Security Council did not lead to formal resolutions amending the related provisions of the Charter up to now, the issue of a revision of the charter still is what it has been for a long time, an unfinished business.

I.2. Informal Revisions

Besides the rather remote possibility of a formal alteration of the Charter, the UN also provides for informal or de facto revisions of its statute. These are realized either by a basic declaratory act of the General Assembly, through which the political goals or procedures of the Organization are substantiated or specified; or by a de facto change of the statute, which can also result from an interpretation of the Charter on the base of a long standing implementation practice. Examples of these somewhat controversial changes in the interpretation of the Charter are the → "Uniting for Peace Resolution" 377 (V) of the General Assembly of 3 November 1950, or the voting practice of the Security Council, where an abstention of a permanent member of the Council counts as approval in the sense of Article 27 (3) of the Charter (and not as constituting a veto) (→ Veto, Right of Veto). Another example is the mandating of → peace-keeping operations, which are not explicitly mentioned in the Charter (→ Peacekeeping; → Peacekeeping Forces).

II. Purposes and Principles

A timeless validity can unquestionably be attributed to the purposes and principles of the UN as established in the Charter, which are prominent in the preamble and in the first chapter (Art. 1 and Art. 2). They are further elaborated in the subsequent articles of the Charter.

II.1. Purposes

The major purposes and basic principles of the UN are mentioned already in the preamble, which only became an integral part of the Charter at the founding conference in San Francisco. These are further elaborated in Article 1 (purposes) and Article 2 (principles). There exists a close relationship between the purposes and principles, which are not clearly distinguished from one another. Guiding principles are the declared determination "to save succeeding generations from the scourge of war", "to reaffirm faith in fundamental human rights, in the dignity and worth of the human person" and "to establish conditions under which justice and respect for the obligations arising from treaties and other sources of international law can be maintained, and to promote social progress and better standards of life in larger freedom". In order to achieve these ambitious goals the UN is obliged to unite its strength "to maintain international peace and security". Armed force shall only be used in the common interest. Moreover, international machinery shall be employed "for the promotion of the economic and social advancement of all peoples".

These introductory declarations of intent, which are part of the preamble, already point to the main objectives of the UN: The UN was first of all founded as a global organization for peace, whose mandate for maintaining international

peace and security was immediately related to other tasks such as the promotion of the economic and social advancement of peoples and nations. Accordingly, in the proclamations of intent in the preamble introducing the Charter, the goal-defining mandate for maintaining international peace and security is not established in an unconditional and abstract way. Rather it is related to a series of other tasks or self-obligations of the members, through which the bases and premises of a life in peace within the community of nations and societies shall be created.

This qualified peace mission, which is already mentioned in the preamble, is further elaborated in the first article of the Charter. The prescribed list of goals includes four points:

First of all (Art. 1 para. 1) maintaining international peace and security appears as the principal purpose and universal mission. This objective shall be achieved in two ways: international disputes or situations which might lead to a breach of peace, shall be solved or removed in the first place by peaceful means and in conformity with the principles of justice and international law; threats to the peace, acts of aggression and other breaches of the peace, however, shall be encountered with "effective collective measures".

In para. 2 members are obliged to develop friendly relations among nations and "to take other appropriate measures to strengthen universal peace".

In para. 3 the UN and its members are called upon "to achieve international cooperation in solving international problems of an economic, social, cultural or humanitarian character, and in promoting and encouraging respect for human rights and for fundamental freedoms for all without distinction as to race, sex, language or religion".

According to para. 4 the UN shall "be a centre for harmonizing the actions of nations in the attainment of these common ends".

Both in the wording of the preamble and the proclaimed objectives of Article 1 the principal purpose of maintaining peace is described in two ways, without, however, further defining the meaning of the term "peace" (→ Peace, Peace Concept, Threat to Peace).

On the one hand, the objectives aim at maintaining or restoring peace in the sense that wars and the use of military violence are prevented or called to a halt. Apart from the induction of a thus understood "negative" peace (the absence of war and violence) the Charter, on the other hand, also contains objectives, that are connected to the advancement of "positive" peace processes (development of friendly relations among nations, solution of international problems, respect for human rights).

Though it is beyond doubt that the creators of the Charter saw the main objective of the UN in its mandate to maintain international peace and security and to that end they postulated a series of other goals and tasks as a means to achieve this main objective.

However it is also true that, in view of the long standing practices of the Organization, the targets for the achievement of a comprehensive international cooperation as prescribed in Article 1 para. 3 are also extremely important independent objectives in their own right.

II.2. Principles

The principles, which are placed on a list of seven items under Article 2, are in many ways interrelated with the purposes stated in Article 1. The catalogue of principles can be summarized as follows:

The Organization is based on the principle of the sovereign equality of all its members.

All members are called upon to fulfill in good faith the obligations assumed by them in accordance with the Charter.

All members are called upon to settle their international disputes by peaceful means in such a manner that international peace and security, and justice, are not endangered.

All members are called upon to refrain in their international relations from the threat or use of force.

The fifth principle provides for the duty of assistance of all members vis-à-vis the Organization.

The sixth principle obliges the UN and its bodies to exert their influence also on non-members in order to ensure in the interest of international peace and security the recognition of the UN principles.

Finally, another principle prohibits any intervention in the domestic affairs of a state with the exception of the application of enforcement measures under Chapter VII (→ Intervention, Prohibition of).

The list of guidelines for action in Article 2 contains a series of rules for behavior that have already been part of the customary international law before the Charter entered into force (e.g. para. 1, 2) (cf. *Randelzhofer* 1995, 996). Furthermore, the catalogue of principles also provides rules, through which international law is further advanced.

The most important one is the general prohibition on the threat or use of force established in Article 2 para. 4. In accordance with this rule of conduct, relating to international law, the member states of the UN are obliged to refrain in their international relations from any threat or use of force against the territorial integrity or political independence of any state, or in any other manner inconsistent with the purposes of the UN. With this prohibition of force (that already applies to the threat of force) the outlawing of war, which has been in place since the inter-war time (Briand-Kellogg Pact of 1928), was extended toward a more comprehensive prohibition of force.

In the history of the UN, the General Assembly has confirmed and elucidated, with the help of several resolutions, this fundamental statutory norm for the maintenance of peace as a central function of the Organization and its members. Resolution 2625 (XXV) of 24 October 1970 ("Declaration on Principles of International Law concerning Friendly Relations and Cooperation among States in accordance with the Charter of the United Nations") gained particular relevance in this respect.

The Charter provides for three exceptions from the general prohibition of the use of force:

first, measures against former enemy states, although the respective regulations (Art. 53 and 107) became obsolete with the accession of all former enemy states to the UN (→ Enemy State Clauses);

second, enforcement measures ordered by the Security Council which may include the application of military force;

third, measures of individual and collective self-defense against an armed attack in accordance with Article 51.

Closely related to the general prohibition of force is the standardized prohibition of interfering with the domestic affairs of other states as prescribed in Article 2 (7). The application of enforcement measures according to Chapter VII (in the case of threats to the peace, breaches of the peace, and acts of aggression) is the only explicit exemption from this rule. The principle of Article 2 (7) has presented certain problems of interpretation, since in the case of a too rigid reading, tensions or contradictions with respect to other principles prescribed in the Charter may occur. For example, the resolute engagement of the Organization for the sake of protecting → human rights can be met with resistance by the states in question who, in turn, may invoke the rule of non-intervention. In addition, with the outbreak of civil wars and other events of the domestic application of violence, the external environment is often affected as well (i.e. through boundary-crossing refugee movements).

The violent domestic conflicts that emerged at an increasing rate during recent years (e.g. Somalia, Bosnia-Herzegovina, Kosovo, Afghanistan, Iraq, Darfur), have reinforced the doubts of the community of states as to whether these conflicts can still be essentially regarded as internal affairs, especially since they may entail massive threats to international peace.

These potential dilemmas resulting from the adherence to the purposes and principles of the Charter can be overcome, in accordance with the provisions of the Charter, by the Security Council declaring in the case of a serious domestic conflict situation (e.g. in the case of a severe violation of human rights) the existence of a threat to international peace and security, which then can justify an intervention.

A milestone in this development concerning the Charter interpretation was the Security Council Resolution 688 of 5 April 1991 on the base of which, after the second Gulf War, emergency measures were ordered to help the suppressed Kurdish (and Shiite) civilian population in Iraq without the consent of the Iraqi government, although at that time the massive violation of human rights did not lead to any decision in favor of explicit enforcement measures against Iraq (*Parsons* 1995, 66-68, 70, 73; *Pape* 1997, 163-183).

Manfred Knapp

Lit.: *Cot, J.-P./Pellet, A. (eds.):* La Charte des Nations Unies. Commentaire article par article, 3rd edn., Paris/Bruxelles 2005; *Goodrich, L.M./Hambro, E./Simmons, A.P.:* Charter of the United Nations. Commentary and Documents, 3rd and rev. edn., New York/London 1969; *Knapp, M.:* 50 Jahre Vereinte Nationen: Rückblick und Ausblick im Spiegel der Jubiläumsliteratur, in: ZPol 7 (1997), 423-481; *Ministry of Foreign Affairs and Trade, New Zealand (ed.):* United Nations Handbook 2007/2008, 45th edn., Wellington 2007; *Pape, M.:* Humanitäre Intervention. Zur Bedeutung der Menschenrechte in den Vereinten Nationen, Baden-Baden 1997; *Parsons, A.:* From Cold War to Hot Peace. UN Interventions 1947-1995, London 1995; *Randelzhofer, A.:* Purposes and Principles of the United Nations, in: Wolfrum, R. (ed.): United Nations: Law, Policies and Practice, Munich/Dordrecht., Vol. 2, 1995, 994-1002; *Rittberger, V./Mogler, M./Zangl, B.:* Vereinte Nationen und Weltordnung. Zivilisierung der internationalen Politik? Opladen 1997; *Simma, B. (ed.):* The Charter of the United Nations. A Commentary, 2 Vols., 2nd edn., Oxford 2002; *Unser, G.:* Die UNO. Aufgaben, Strukturen, Politik, 7th edn., Munich 2004; *Verdross, A./Simma, B.:*

Universelles Völkerrecht. Theorie und Praxis, 3rd edn., Berlin 1984; *Varwick, J./Zimmermann, A. (eds.):* Die Reform der Vereinten Nationen – Bilanz und Perspektiven, Berlin 2006; *Volger, H.:* Die Vereinten Nationen, Munich/Vienna 1994; *Volger, H. (ed.):* Grundlagen und Strukturen der Vereinten Nationen, Munich/Vienna 2007; *Volger, H.:* Geschichte der Vereinten Nationen, 2nd enlarged and rev. edn., Munich/Vienna 2008; *Wolfrum, R.(ed.):* United Nations: Law, Policies and Practice, 2 vols., new, rev. English edn., Munich/Dordrecht 1995.

Collective Security

"Si vis pacem, para bellum – If you want peace, prepare for war" – this recommendation, formulated by Flavius Vegetius Renatus in the 4th century after Christ, was considered for centuries as a proven basic rule of military theory and security policy. It was implemented by maintaining effective armaments, and above all by military alliances and pacts which complemented domestic military and political security. That the states had a right to war *(ius ad bellum)* was one of the non-controversial principal preconditions of international relations for many centuries. The right to war has been, in the four centuries since the Thirty Years' War, a result of the principle of national → sovereignty, which has since 1648 been one of the fundamental characteristics of the modern system of states, as it is of developing classical international law.

Historical Background

Notwithstanding this right to war for the enforcement of self interests, there were early efforts to civilize war and warfare, by establishing rules *(ius in bello)*.

The Hague Peace Conferences of 1899 and 1907 were significant steps towards this goal. While they succeeded in establishing the first foundations of international → humanitarian law, the efforts to establish international disarmament conventions and permanent arbitration organs were unsuccessful due to the states' insistence on their sovereignty.

Long before these initiatives, attempts had already been made to organize security collectively. The first important designs for a collective security system were contained in the writings of *William Penn* ("Essay towards the Present and Future Peace of Europe" 1693), *Abbé S. Pierre* ("Projet pour rendre la paix perpétuelle en Europe" 1713) and *Immanuel Kant* ("Zum ewigen Frieden" (E. "Perpetual Peace") 1795. For all their differences in the details, these proposals have a number of central elements in common: the idea that an order of international law and peace is necessary, yet which does not question the right to war of the individual states, but limits it; a system of institutions with whose assistance the states endeavor jointly to maintain international peace and security, be it by preventing or de-escalating conflicts through an international arbitration court or be it through collective action against aggression and other forms of unjust use of force. Security was to be safeguarded not only against attacks from the outside, but also against illegal use of force inside the security system.

The first attempts at a practical implementation of such ideas can be found already in the 19th century in the framework of the "European Concert", which was however based on the concept of a balance of power. This concept puts its trust in the maintenance of international security in the context of an intensifying system of consultations, conferences and congresses; above all in the mechanics of changing coalitions among the members, which were designed to maintain the power equilibrium. In this connection war was considered a legitimate means.

It was the First World War, in particular, which shattered the trust in the viability of the balance-of-power concept, and gave fresh impetus to those movements which advocated an alternative security concept. Such movements had emerged during the war in the United Kingdom and the USA, whereby the British League of Nations and the

American League to Enforce Peace were of great importance.

A core element of this alternative concept was the establishment of an international organization. Under its roof international security was to be safeguarded through the creation of institutions with specific responsibilities, and by establishing a conference system of the "European Concert", in the form of periodic meetings of the representatives of the states.

Complementary elements were the prohibition of the threat or the application of force among states (→ Use of Force, Prohibition of), the setting up of binding rules and mechanisms for the → peaceful settlement of disputes and collective enforcement measures → Sanctions), for the case that the efforts for a peaceful settlement were not successful.

The concept of the labile balance of power, which required continuous adjustment, was replaced by the concept of a preponderance of collectively acting states which would deter aggressors, with superior strength if necessary.

The concept was thus based on a number of assumptions, *inter alia*, that the member states of such an organization would consider themselves responsible for the international security, even when their own interests were not directly affected by a conflict. Another assumption was that the collective power of the community of states would be great enough in any case to stand up to every aggressor, even a great power. To make this more credible, disarmament measures, reducing the armament of the individual states to the minimum necessary for defense purposes, were envisaged. Both assumptions soon turned out to be wrong.

Further preconditions for the proper functioning of this system of collective security were the → universality of the system, in particular the participation of all great powers, a high degree of international solidarity, the impartiality of the international organization, and, above all, the readiness of the states to surrender essential components of their sovereignty.

The League of Nations

The most important elements of the different proposals for an international security system were incorporated in the Covenant of the → League of Nations, which became an integral part of the Paris Peace Treaties.

In addition to a partial prohibition on war the Covenant contained initial elements of a system of collective security, without the term proper being used. While Article 8 postulated the internationally controlled reduction of national armaments "to the lowest point consistent with national safety and the enforcement by common action of international obligations" as a fundamental requirement for the maintenance of peace, the members undertook in Aricle 10 "to respect and preserve as against external aggression the territorial integrity and existing political independence of all Members of the League."

Essential elements of international → peacekeeping and peaceful settlement of disputes were contained Articles 12, 13 and 15. The members thereby oblige themselves to settle disputes only by peaceful means (Art. 12). This goal led to the establishment of a Permanent Court of International Justice (Art. 14), as well as to procedures for mandatory mediation through the Council of the League (Art. 15). In case that a Member of the League should begin a war in violation of this obligation, it should be considered "to have committed an act of war against all other Members of the League" (Art. 16) and would thereby result in collective economic, financial and military sanctions. In such a situation, the Council was to recommend to the governments of the member states "what effective military, naval or air force the Members of the League shall severally contribute to the armed forces to be used to protect the covenants of the League." Similar regulations were contained Article 17, in the case of conflicts between a member state of the League and a non-member state.

As history proved, the League of Nations was not able to fulfill the expectations placed upon it.

Neither was it able to intervene successfully as a mediator in a number of regional conflicts (Manchuria, Abyssinia, Gran Chaco), nor was it able to prevent the outbreak of the Second World War.

The causes thereof lay in unfavorable conditions, as well as in serious flaws in the security system. To the former factors belonged the complete absence of the USA and the temporary, absence of other great powers (Germany, Japan, the USSR), as well as the lack of an international status quo on whose maintenance there was agreement among the great powers. To the latter factors belonged first of all the only limited prohibition of the use of force. Furthermore the planned reductions of armaments were not implemented, and the determination of breaches of the peace turned out to be difficult because of a lack of clarity. Centrally coordinated decision-making mechanisms were lacking when sanctions were to be applied. The system of non-military sanctions proved to be not fully developed enough, and especially the fact that participation in sanctions was not obligatory, but was left to the discretion of the member states, caused great problems. As the efforts to overcome the existing deficits also failed – the Briand-Kellog-Pact of 27 August 1928 with its comprehensive prohibition of the use of force was not integrated into the Covenant – the failure of the League of Nations was a foregone conclusion.

The United Nations

Despite these bad experiences, the allied powers oriented themselves after the Second World War at the concept of collective security when they established a new security system in the framework of the United Nations. The basic idea of a collective and cooperative peace order is emphasized in the preamble of the UN Charter, when it underlines the determination of the peoples "to unite our strength to maintain international peace and security". Consequently the catalogue of purposes in Article 1 begins with a statement that it is necessary for maintaining international peace and security "to take effective collective measures". The obligation to collective action is also prescribed in the principles for acting in Article 2. Thus Article 2 (5) obliges the member states to give "the United Nations every assistance in any action it takes in accordance with the present Charter". Accordingly they shall not give assistance to states against which the United Nations is taking preventive or enforcement action.

The "collective measures" for the maintenance of international peace and security in the stricter sense are embedded in a complex of more far-reaching measures. These measures range from the establishment of "friendly relations among nations based on respect for the principle of equal rights and self-determination of peoples" to the promotion of international cooperation in solving international problems of an economic, social, cultural or humanitarian character. These measures, too, are an integral part of the system of collective security (Art. 1 (2) and (3)), insofar as they aim to abolish the root causes of potential conflicts by intensifying international cooperation. Although measures of this kind had already been established in the in the League of Nations, the UN Charter goes far beyond the Covenant.

The catalogue of purposes and principles of the United Nations, as described in the Charter, also sets unmistakable limits on the competence of the world organization, and thereby also on the system of collective security. The limit is formed by "matters which are essentially within the domestic jurisdiction of any state" (Art. 2 (7)); exempt from this principle are only mandatory measures according to chapter VII. The Charter is in accordance with this emphasis of the principle of sovereignty when it stipulates that "international peace and security" are the main fields of work of the United Nations. Intra-state conflicts and severe human rights violations (→ Human Rights, Protection of) were excluded thereby from the competence of the world organization by the architects of the UN.

In the face of the inhuman policies of totalitarian regimes against whom the allied nations had gone to war, such a restriction of the system of collective security may be considered astonishing. On the other hand, this reflects the force of the principle of sovereignty in general, which was in 1945 still quite vigorously protected, especially by the great powers.

The central element of the system of collective security in the stricter sense is formed by the prohibition of the use of force prescribed in Article 2 (4), which is also valid in its comprehensive formulation, in respect of non-member states. The only exception, according to Article 51, is "the inherent right of individual or collective self defence", but only until the Security Council "has taken measures necessary to maintain international peace and security". The exercise of that right of self-defence may thus be in practice only of short duration, until the Security Council meets its "primary responsibility for the maintenance of international peace and security" (Art. 24 (1)). If this is not the case – be it that the Security Council does not want to intervene, be it that it is prevented from doing so through the veto of one or more of its permanent members –, then the right of self defense can become a permanent state. The lack of a Charter obligation of the Security Council to intervene, as well as the risk that the use of the veto could prevent the council from intervention, implied from the beginning the inherent danger in the Charter that the universal prohibition of the use of force would not function, and that the individual and collective self defense would become a permanent state. Thus it was only logical that the member states would prepare themselves for such situations, a development which was to be detrimental to the system of the collective security within the framework of the United Nations.

Unlike the Covenant of the League of Nations, the UN Charter has clearly defined decision-making competence: as already mentioned, the primary responsibility for the maintenance of international peace and security lies with the Security Council. To be able to react to peace threatening situations rapidly and effectively, each member of the Security Council is to be represented at all times at the seat of the organization (Art. 28 (1)). The Security Council has a monopoly in determining whether there exists a threat to the peace, and deciding upon the measures to be taken. The implementing decisions, however, require an affirmative vote of nine members, including the concurring votes of all permanent members (Art. 27 (3)) of the Security Council. The basic consensus of the permanent members is thus the basic precondition for the functioning of the entire system. If this basic consensus is lost – as happened soon after the outbreak of the East-West-conflict, this will lead to the complete incapacity of the Council to act in conflicts where the interest of the great powers and their allies are at stake.

In this situation it was necessary to seek a means to maintain the capacity of the UN security system to act, at least to a limited extent. One of these means was the resolution "Uniting for Peace" (UN Doc. A/RES/3777 (V)), adopted by the General Assembly on 3 November 1950 in order to circumvent a Soviet veto against further actions of the United Nations in the war on the Korean peninsula. The resolution authorizes the General Assembly to act in crisis situations where there appear to be threats to the peace, and when the Security Council cannot act because of a the threat or the fact of a veto. In such cases, the General Assembly may recommend to the member states appropriate "collective measures", including "the use of armed force where necessary to maintain or restore international peace and security." The attempt to expand the capacity to act of the General Assembly in this way gave rise to large number of legal and political problems: the resolution was only partly in accordance with the UN Charter. The Charter gives the General Assembly the right to "discuss" all questions relating to the maintenance of international peace and security and to make "recommendations" with regard to these questions to the conflict parties or to the Security Council (Art. 11), provided that the Council is not then dealing with the dispute (Art. 12). But this right to make recommendations was restricted in the Charter to peaceful measures. No less problematic was the fact that the resolution would in the long run erode the prominent position of the Security Council and its permanent members.

A further measure for maintaining a limited capacity to act was the implementation of → peacekeeping operations where the aim was not – as in the Korean War – to enforce peace but only to keep the peace. The instrument of → peacekeeping was developed on the basis of the Uniting for Peace Resolution in 1956, on the occasion of the Suez Crisis in Egypt. It found repeated use during the East-West conflict and, after the Cold War was used more frequently and in new differentiated ways.

The basic principle of the universal prohibition of the use of force in the UN Charter corresponds with the central importance of the principle of the peaceful settlement of disputes. The appropriate measures are dealt with in detail in Chapter VI of the Charter. In the first place, they provide various means for the resolution of disputes by agreement, offering in Article 33 a number of suitable procedures – "negotiation, enquiry, mediation, conciliation, arbitration, judicial settlement, resort to regional agencies or arrangements, or other peaceful means of their own choice." If the settlement is not achieved or fails, the Security Council can recommend "appropriate procedures or methods of adjustment", including the invocation of the International Court of Justice (Art. 36). If this recommendation leads to no settlement, too, the conflict parties are required to refer the matter to the Security Council (Art. 37).

But the system of the United Nations Charter is not limited to the peaceful settlements of disputes. Already the preamble of the Charter speaks of the acceptance of principles and the institutions of methods which ensure "that armed force shall not be used, save in the common interest". The procedures for settlement of disputes by collective enforcement are prescribed in Chapter VII of the Charter. These are applied when the Security Council is of the opinion that a "threat to the peace, breach of the peace or act of aggression" exists (Art. 39). In this case the council can call upon the conflict parties "to comply which such provisional measures as it deems necessary or desirable", leaving the rights and claims of the conflict parties untouched. (Art. 40)

If the conflict parties do not comply with this demand, the council can decide on measures under Article 41 and 42. While Article 41 contains a catalogue of non-military enforcement measures, *inter alia* the interruption of economic relations and of rail, sea, air transport, Article 42 provides for military measures by air, see or land forces. The graduation and gradual escalation of measures in the dispute settlement illustrates that for the UN the prohibition of the use of force has a high priority, and that the use of armed force enters into consideration only when all other possibilities have been exhausted.

For the use of armed force the Charter provides different options:
- the use of national armed forces which were made available to the Security Council by a special agreement (Art. 43): As up to now no such special agreements have been concluded, this option has remained so far without significance. The same is true for the Military Staff Committee, which was intended by the Charter to advise and assist the Security Council in military questions (Art. 47);
- the authorization of member states to carry out the decisions of the council (Art. 48): This option has proved valuable in the Kuwait Crisis, but has given rise to some problems at the same time.

Moreover this option exists only if there are states who are willing to act on behalf of the Security Council;

- the utilization of regional arrangements or agencies through the Security Council "for enforcement action under its authority" (Art. 53): This option was chosen by the UN in different conflicts, it can however be easily blocked by the lack of consent of any the permanent members of the Security Council, as it was the case in the Kosovo. A further problem lies in the fact that in only a few regions in the world there are regional organizations with the competence to act effectively in conflict resolution.

As none of the three options will necessarily ensure "prompt and effective action by the United Nations", as Article 24 of the Charter requires, a number of other possibilities have been discussed since the end of the East-West conflict, which are intended to make available to the Security Council rapidly deployable military units, which will be able to ensure compliance with cease fire agreements or the implementation of humanitarian actions, acting in conjunction with armed force if necessary. The former Secretary-General Boutros Boutros-Ghali suggested the establishment of peace enforcement units, whereas Sir Brian Urquhart suggested the establishment of a kind of standing UN force of volunteers. Up to now this discussion has only resulted in an agreement on stand-by forces, of which the Security Council can make use in case of need, with the consent of the states concerned, which it is not sure to get. On the whole the lack of rapidly deployable forces is a further weakness of the UN security system.

Evaluation

An evaluation of the UN system of collective security comes to an ambiguous conclusion: on the one hand the system of the United Nations has a markedly clearer profile than that of the League of Nations. It contains a general prohibition of the use of force, the centralization of the decision-making structures in the Security Council, and the universality of the member states. On the other hand the history of the United Nations so far has shown that there still exist deficits in the system, and difficulties in its practical implementation:

- The complete system loses its effectiveness where a basic consensus of the permanent members of the Council is lacking.
- There is a tendency of the permanent members toward selective action, oriented at criteria of political opportunity;
- There is insufficient protection for third states effected by economic sanctions;
- There are insufficient instruments for the implementation of military enforcement measures;
- A concept of security which is predominantly oriented at international conflicts will render intervention in internal conflicts, with severe human rights violations, extremely difficult.

These deficits restricted the capacity to act of the UN security system during the East-West-Conflict to such an extent that it lived only a shadow existence beside the two great military alliances. It was neither able to intervene in the great conflicts of that time as mediator nor to curb the armament race. After the end of the East-West conflict it seemed for a short time as if the re-discovered basic consensus of the great powers would have a positive effect on the UN's capacity to act, and would enable it to overcome the weaknesses in the system through appropriate reform measures. The course of the reform debate so far has dampened these hopes to a large extent. The basic consensus of the great powers begins to become fragile again, and there is no solid consensus for reforms in sight. Furthermore the inadequate representational composition of the Security Council does not reflect the changes which the international system has undergone in the second half of the 20th century, and erodes the legitimacy of the entire UN system. If in the new century no breakthrough is reached, the danger can not be excluded that the UN may suffer the same destiny as its predecessor, the League of Nations. The consequences would be no less catastrophic. For in the face of the economic problems intensifying in the decades to come, increasing social disparities and weapon systems of increasing destructive force, humanity needs more than ever in its history an efficient system of collective security for maintaining international peace.

Peter J. Opitz

Lit.: *Beyerlin, U.:* Kollektive Sicherheit, in: Seidl-Hohenveldern, I. (ed.): Lexikon des Rechts: Völkerrecht, Berlin 1992, 171-173; *Bindschedler, R.L.:* Grundfragen der kollektiven Sicherheit, in: Schätzel, W./Schlochauer, H.-J. (eds.): Rechtsfragen der internationalen Organisationen, Fs. H. Wehberg, Frankfurt (am Main) 1956, 67–88; *Bourquin, M. (ed.):* Collective Security: A Record of the Seventh and Eighth International Studies Conference, Paris 1934 - London 1935, (Paris International Institute of Intellectual Cooperation) 1936; *Delbrück, J.:* Collective Security, in: Bernhard, R. (ed.): EPIL III, Amsterdam 1982, 104 – 114; *Doehring, K.:* Collective Security, in: Wolfrum, R. (ed.): United Nations: Law, Policies and Practice, Vol.1, Munich/ Dordrecht 1995, 110-115; *Flynn, G./Scheffer, D. C.:* Limited Collective Security, in: Foreign Affairs 80 (1990), 77–101; *Joffe, J.:* Collective security and the future of Europe: failed dreams and dead ends, in: Survival, Spring 1992, 36–50; *Kant, I.:* Zum Ewigen Frieden. Ein philosophischer Entwurf, in: Kant, I.: Kleine Schriften zur Geschichtsphilosophie, Ethik und Politik, edited by K. Vorländer, Hamburg 1973, 115-169; *Kimminich, O.:* Was heißt kollektive Sicherheit? in: S+F 2 (1984), 5–12; *MacNair, A. D.:* Collective Security: an inaugural lecture, Cambridge 1936; *Meesen, K. M.:* Sovereignty, in: Wolfrum, R. (ed.): United Nations: Law, Policies and Practice, Vol.2, Munich/Dordrecht 1995, 1193-1201; *Menk, Th. M.:* Gewalt für den Frieden. Die Idee der kollektiven Sicherheit und die Pathognomie des Krieges im 20. Jahrhundert, Berlin 1992; *Meyn, K.-U.:* Das Konzept der kollektiven Sicherheit, in: Schwarz, K.D. (ed.): Sicherheitspolitik, 3rd edn., Bad Honnef 1981, 111–129; *Roberts, A./Kingsbury, B. (ed.):* United Nations, Divided World, 2nd edn., Oxford 1993; *Scheuner, U.:* Die kollektive Sicherheit des Friedens im gegenwärtigen Völkerrecht, Berichte der Deutschen Gesellschaft für Völkerrecht, Vol. 2, (1958), 1–34; *Scheuner, U.:* Kollektive Sicherheit, in: Schlochhauer, H.J. (ed.): Wörterbuch des Völkerrechts, Vol. 2, Berlin 1958, 242–251.

Addendum

In recent years, the system of *collective security* as established by the UN Charter has been the subject of intense discussions. These discussions have dealt in particular with two aspects of international security: the first being the increasing number of threats to security and their interrelation, the second aspect being the responsibility of the international community for the protection of populations against massive crimes against humanity and war crimes, in cases where the own state fails to protect its population.

The second aspect, the responsibility to protect populations, was for the first time discussed with higher priority when the Canadian government established – against the background of the events in Somalia, Bosnia and Kosovo – an expert commission in September 2000, the "International Commission on Intervention and State Sovereignty", tasked to discuss the question whether a humanitarian intervention by the international community was justified in cases where states did not protect their populations from gross and systematic violations of human rights. The Commission submitted its report "The Responsibility to Protect" in December 2001. As the title of the report indicates, the commission puts forward the thesis of the international responsibility to protect: "Where a population is suffering serious harm, as a result of internal war, insurgency, repression or state failure, and the state in question is unwilling or unable to halt or avert it, the principle of non-intervention yields to the international responsibility to protect it." (*International Commission on Intervention and State Sovereignty* 2001, XI, Synopsis, B).

The *High-level Panel on Threats, Challenges and Change*, convened by

Secretary-General Kofi Annan in 2004, took up those issues in its report "A more secure world: Our shared responsibility" (UN Doc. A/59/565 of 2 December 2004), and analyzed several elements of collective security in order to make recommendations on how to deal with today's challenges and threats.

The Panel members argue that since the establishment of the United Nations, the world has changed drastically, one of the most prominent examples being the events of September 11 2001, which have shown that international terrorism poses a threat to all states. The Panel concludes that "today, more than ever before, threats are interrelated and a threat to one is a threat to all. The mutual vulnerability of weak and strong has never been clearer" (*United Nations* 2004, para. 17), thus broadening the traditional understanding of security to include the concept of human security by adding a larger range of threats (for example diseases, poverty, environmental pollution). According to the Panel members, the case for collective security rests on three pillars: "Today's threats recognize no national boundaries, are connected, and must be addressed at the global and regional as well as the national levels" (ibid., Synopsis). This expansion changes the "classic" definition of the breach of peace (cf. *Fassbender* 2005). The Panel members call for a "credible collective security system", characterized by three elements: effectiveness, efficiency, and equity (*United Nations* 2004, para. 31ff.).

Concerning the use of force, they deal with the question whether a state can act under Article 51 "not just pre-emptively (against an imminent or proximate threat) but preventively (against a non-imminent or non-proximate one)" (ibid., para. 189), which might be, for example, the case with terrorists armed with nuclear weapons. The panel refers with this text passage obviously to the argumentation of the US administration with regard to the Iraq intervention in 2003, which claimed to act in a kind of preventive self-defense. The Panel rejects unilateral actions in such a situation:

"The ... answer is that if there are good arguments for preventive military action, with good evidence to support them, they should be put to the Security Council, which can authorize such action if it chooses to." (ibid., para. 190). Only the Security Council should deal with the question whether and when action in self-defense is legitimate, since "in a world full of perceived potential threats, the risk to the global order and the norm of non-intervention on which it continues to be based is simply too great for the legality of unilateral preventive action as distinct from collectively endorsed action to be accepted. Allowing one to so act is to allow all." (ibid., para. 191) The Panel calls for improvements to the Security Council's work instead of looking for alternatives to the Council as source of authority: "The Security Council is fully empowered under Chapter VII of the Charter of the United Nations to address the full range of security threats with which States are concerned. The task is not to find alternatives to the Security Council as a source of authority but to make the Council work better than it has." (ibid., para. 198)

The Panel analyzes and endorses the above mentioned *new aspect of collective security*, the emerging norm of the *collective international responsibility to protect populations* in cases of internal conflicts, mass atrocities and genocide within states. In situations where a government is unable or unwilling to protect its citizens, the international community should take up responsibility by peaceful means, i.e. mediation. As a last resort, the Security Council may authorize a humanitarian intervention.

For the system of collective security to function effectively in those situations, the Panel points out that decisions must be based on legality and legitimacy. Decisions by the Security Council on the authorization of the use of force should take into account at least five *criteria*: (1) *seriousness of threat*, (2) *proper purpose*, making sure "that the primary purpose of the proposed military action is to halt or to avert the threat in question, whatever other purposes or motives may be involved", (3) *last resort*, meaning that "all non-military options for meeting the threat have been explored, with reasonable grounds for believing that other measures will not succeed", (4) *proportional means*, and (5) *balance of consequences*, meaning that the consequences of action should not be worse than the consequences of inaction. (ibid., para. 207)

In March 2005, Secretary-General Kofi Annan took up the Panel's recommendations in his reform report "In larger freedom: towards development, security and human rights for all" (UN Doc. A/59/2005 of 21 March 2005). In this report, he stresses that states must not only take into account the needs of their own citizens, but also the needs of others, calling for the "imperative of collective action" (*United Nations* 2005a, Part I C). In detail, he describes his vision of collective security, supporting the Panel's suggestions and calling for "a new security consensus, the first article of which must be that all are entitled to freedom from fear, and that whatever threatens one threatens all." (ibid., para. 81)

During the World Summit in September 2005, the UN member states discussed the concept of collective security based on the understanding of interrelated threats as outlined in the report of the High-level Panel and in the reform report of the Secretary-General, and supported explicitly this concept: "We ... affirm our commitment to work towards a security consensus based on the recognition that many threats are interlinked, that development, peace, security and human rights are mutually reinforcing, that no state can best protect itself alone by acting entirely alone, and that all states need an effective and efficient collective security system pursuant to the purposes and principles of the Charter" (UN Doc. A/RES/60/1, para. 72, quoted as: *United Nations* 2005b).

Furthermore, they underlined the importance of the responsibility of the individual states and of the international community to protect populations from genocide and war crimes: "Each individual State has the responsibility to protect its populations from genocide, war crimes, ethnic cleansing and crimes against humanity. The international community, through the United Nations, also has the responsibility to use appropriate diplomatic, humanitarian and other peaceful means, in accordance with Chapters VI and VIII of the Charter, to help to protect populations from genocide, war crimes, ethnic cleansing and crimes against humanity. In this context, we are prepared to take collective action, in a timely and decisive manner, through the Security Council, in accordance with the Charter, including Chapter VII, on a case-by-case basis and in cooperation with relevant regional organizations as appropriate, should peaceful means be inadequate and national authorities are manifestly failing to protect their populations from genocide, war crimes, ethnic cleansing and crimes against humanity." (ibid., para. 138 and 139).

The Security Council reaffirmed in early 2006 this responsibility to protect in its resolution on the protection of civilians in armed conflict of 28 April 2006 (UN Doc. S/RES/1674), referring explicitly to the relevant paragraphs on this topic in the World Summit Outcome Document: "*The Security Council ... Reaffirms* the provisions of paragraphs 138 and 139 of the 2005 World Outcome Document regarding the responsibility to protect populations from genocide, war crimes, ethnic cleansing and crimes against humanity" (*United Nations* 2006, para. 4).

The topic continues to be discussed during country-related debates, such as Darfur, but the Council has not yet considered how the norm can be put into practice effectively. In October 2007, UN Secretary-General Ban Ki-moon stressed in his United Nations Day message that he planned to work with member states and civil society to translate the concept of the responsibility to protect into practice "so as to ensure timely action when populations face genocide, ethnic cleansing or crimes against humanity" (UN Press Release SG/SM/ 11203, 3 October 2007).

With regard to the concept of collective security, the United Nations has reacted to the developments and challenges of the last decades, and has brought forward new and useful concepts for its interpretation, which need to be further discussed to be put into practice in a broadest possible consensus of the international community.

Irene Weinz

Lit.: *Evans, G.:* The responsibility to protect, in: Foreign Affairs 81 (2002), 6, 99-110; *Fassbender, B.:* UN Reform and Collective Security. Global Issue Papers No 17, April 2005, www.boell.de/downloads/ global/GIP17_ENG_UN-Reform_Sicherheit .pdf; *International Commission on Intervention and State Sovereignty:* The Responsibility to Protect. Report, Ottawa 2001; *Kaldor, M.:* Human security: reflections on globalization and intervention, Cambridge et al. 2007; *Ozgercin, K.:* Collective Security and the United Nations: The Work of the High-Level Panel on Threats, Challenges and Change. FES-Briefing Paper, New York, September 2004, http://library.fes.de/pdf-files/iez/ global/50102.pdf; *Ozgercin, K./ Steinhilber, J.:* Towards a More Secure World? The Work of the High-Level Panel on Threats, Challenges and Change. FES-Briefing Paper, New York, January 2005, http://library.fes.de/pdf-files/iez/global/5010o. pdf; *Stahn, C.:* Responsibility to protect: political rhetoric or emerging legal norm? In: AJIL 101 (2007), 99-120; *Thakur, R.:* The United Nations, peace and security: from collective security to the responsibility to protect, Cambridge et al. 2006; *United Nations Association Canada:* The Responsibility to Protect: Moving the Agenda Forward. Report by United Nations Association Canada, March 2007, www.reformtheun.org /index.php/eupdate/3087; *United Nations - General Assembly:* A More Secure World: Our Shared Responsibility. Report of the High-level Panel on Threats, Challenges and Change, 2 December 2004, UN Doc. A/59/565 (quoted as: United Nations 2004); *United Nations - General Assembly:* In Larger Freedom. Towards Development, Security and Human Rights for All. Report of the Secretary-General, 21 March 2005, UN Doc. A/59/2005 (quoted as: United Nations 2005a); *United Nations - General Assembly:*

2005 World Summit Outcome, 16 September 2005, UN Doc. A/RES/60/1 (quoted as: United Nations 2005b); *United Nations - Security Council:* Resolution on the protection of civilians in armed conflict, 28 April 2006, UN Doc. S/RES/1674; *United Nations Press Release:* Secretary-General expresses determination "to ensure we make progress on pressing issues of our time, step by step", in message for United Nations Day, 24 October 2006, SG/SM/ 11203.

Internet: www.responsibilitytoprotect.org; www.reformtheun.org; www.un-global security.org.

Committees, System of

All communal principal organs of the United Nations, that is, the → General Assembly, the → Security Council, the Economic and Social Council (→ ECOSOC), and the Trusteeship Council (→ Principal Organs, Subsidiary Organs, Treaty Bodies), have established committees. Article 7 (2) of the UN Charter authorizes them to do so, in enabling them to establish "such subsidiary organs as may be found necessary in accordance with the present Charter."

Articles 22 and 29 repeat this general principle in particular relation to the General Assembly and the Security Council, respectively. Article 68 authorizes ECOSOC to "set up commissions". These committees have been established to relieve the principal organs from the time-consuming expert detail work and the organizational and financial planning, and to prepare for debates on reports, draft resolutions or other items on the agenda of the principal organs, which is generally quite voluminous, as the agenda of the General Assembly comprises usually more than 150 items. In this way the principal organs save time for the discussion of principles, and for taking important decisions.

As the principal organs of the United Nations have used these provisions of the Charter for the establishment of "subsidiary organs" not only to establish the usual network of main and procedural committees for the organization of their work, but also to establish a multitude of thematic committees and commissions, which have often consolidated themselves in the course of the time and have become "special organs", "programmes" or "funds" of the principal organs, this article deals only with those committees which have a direct relation to the work of the principal organs. Information about the other kinds of "subsidiary organs" can be found in the articles on the → UN system, → coordination in the UN system and in the articles on the principal organs.

In general it is difficult to make any clear distinction and to give a precise functional description because of the extreme complexity of the UN system, and the interdependence of organizational and political aspects which play an important role in the establishment of organs within the framework of international organizations.

I. Committees of the General Assembly

The Rules of Procedure of the General Assembly (→ Rules of Procedure) provided originally for seven main committees (Rule 98) and two procedural committees (Rules 155-160). At its 47th regular session the General Assembly decided to merge two of the main committees, so that there have been since then six main committees.

Committees of the General Assembly meet in principle in open session. The right to exclude the public is limited according to Rule 60 of the Rules of Procedure to situations in which, in the opinion of the committee, the exclusion is called for by exceptional circumstances.

The committees are to discuss their specific topics in a smaller circle, to review individual proposals and to work out draft resolution texts for the General Assembly. The committees of the General Assembly can be divided into four groups: the *main committees*, the *procedural committees*, the *standing committees* and the *ad hoc committees* or *ad hoc working groups*

1. Main Committees

Every member state has the right to be represented on each main committee ("committee of the whole"). The main committees deal with most of the items of the agenda, from the first discussion to the preparation of the draft resolutions which are later submitted to the plenary of the General Assembly for voting. Those items on the agenda not allocated to one of the main committees are dealt with in the plenary sessions of the assembly. Since the main committees convene parallel to the plenary, assess the various standpoints and find out if there are sufficient majorities for the projects discussed, they exercise a selective function. Although decisions in the main committees are taken according to the majority principle, which is also valid for the decision to submit a draft resolution, etc. to the plenary, it has become accepted usage that only those motions are put to vote in the main committee for which the two-thirds majority is already assured, since here decisions are taken in the General Assembly with a two-thirds majority (Rule 83 of the Rules of Procedure). Only very seldom are there significant changes in the voting behavior between main committees and plenary.

Until 1993 the committee structure of the main committees was as follows: First Committee (Political and Security, including the Regulation of Armaments), Special Political Committee, Second Committee (Economic and Financial), Third Committee (Social, Humanitarian and Cultural), Fourth Committee (Trusteeship, including Non-Self-Governing Territories), Fifth Committee (Administrative and Budgetary), and Sixth Committee (Legal). The Special Political Committee dealt with selected political issues assigned by the General Assembly, *inter alia* in particular with respect to the Palestine conflict, and apartheid.

With Resolution 47/233 of 17 August 1993, the General Assembly decided to amend Rule 98 of the Rules of Procedure so that the *main committees* were reduced from the original seven to six and are as follows (the relevant document symbols for their documents are indicated in brackets):

- *Disarmament and International Security Committee (First Committee)* (A/C.1/sess./-): The First Committee is concerned with the issues of disarmament and international security, sometimes in agreement, but sometimes also dissenting from the work of the Security Council.

- *Economic and Financial Committee (Second Committee)* (A/C.2/sess./-). The Second Committee is dedicated to the economic problems of the member countries, of underdevelopment, population growth, world food problems, world trade relations and international debt.

- *Social, Humanitarian and Cultural Committee (Third Committee)* (A/C.3/ sess./-): The Third Committee is concerned with racial discrimination, fundamental human rights and with the work of the United Nations High Commissioner for Refugees (→ UNHCR).

- *Special Political and Decolonization Committee (Fourth Committee)* (A/C.4/sess./-): The Fourth Committee deals with those political topics that are not dealt with in the first committee, for example the whole spectrum of peacekeeping operations.

- *Administrative and Budgetary Committee (Fifth Committee)* (A/C.5/sess./-).: The Fifth Committee deals with the organizational matters of the United Nations, advises on the financial reports and on the reports of the board of auditors, discusses the budget plan and regulates administrative cooperation in the budgeting procedure.

- *Legal Committee (Sixth Committee)* (A/C.6/sess./-): The Sixth Committee plays an important role in the progressive development of international law within the framework of the UN (→ International Law and the UN). In this connection, the International Law Commission (→ ILC) provides important preparatory work for the Sixth Committee. When discussing the reports of the ILC and of other UN organs which deal with the drafting of international agreements, the Sixth Committee comments on every item of the drafts. Thus it plays a decisive role in the final drafting of the conventions.

2. Procedural Committees

There are two procedural committees which are important for the organization of the sessions of the General Assembly: the first is the *Credential Committee*. Its nine members are chosen upon the recommendation of the retiring or the provisional president of the General Assembly at the beginning of each session. The committee ensures that the credentials of the delegates from the member states are in order. The second more important procedural committee is the 28-member *General Committee* which consists of the president of the General Assembly, the 21 vice presidents and the chairmen of the main committees. Its task is the coordination and steering of the work of the plenary and the main committees, and in establishing the agenda for the General Assembly.

3. Standing Committees

A third group is comprised of the *standing committees*. In contrast to the main and the procedural committees, the standing committees do not meet only during the regular sessions of the General Assembly. They consist of experts and support mainly the work of the Fifth Committee: The *Advisory Committee on Administrative and Budgetary Questions (ACABQ)*, established by the General Assembly in 1946 (UN Doc. A/RES/14 (I) of 13 February 1946), deals prior to the Fifth Committee with the planning of the budget, while the *Committee on Contributions* established by the same resolution in 1946 deals with the means of allocation of member's contributions and the treatment of defaulting payers among the member states. The members of the standing committees are elected by the General Assembly for three years, in contrast to the above-mentioned committees which are elected only for a one-session period.

4. Ad Hoc Committees and Working Groups

Additionally, the General Assembly has established in its history so far a large number of *ad hoc* committees and working groups for certain, clearly defined tasks. To this group belong the reform working groups which have dealt or still deal with the elaboration of reform proposals (→ Reform of the UN), namely for the financial field, the structure of the Security Council, the → Agenda for Peace, → Agenda for Development, economic and social questions and UN reform in general.

II. Committees of ECOSOC

A similar network of committees has developed around the ECOSOC plenary, which assists ECOSOC in the exercise of its tasks (carrying out investigations, writing reports, coordinating the activities of the specialized agencies as well as the relations with the non-governmental organizations (→ NGOs):

1) two *sessional committees* for economic and social questions;

2) six *standing committees*, among them:

a) the *Committee for Programme and Coordination (CPC)*, which plays an important role in the planning and coordination of work in the whole UN system, and which has, since the end of the 1980s, gained *de facto* an even more important role in the budgeting procedure (→ Budget) as result of massive pressure by the USA, generated by their withholding parts of their assessed contributions to the budget (→ Financial Crises), when the General Assembly decided that a consensus instead of a majority vote is required in the CPC in the budgeting procedure; and

b) the *Committee on Non-Governmental Organizations* (→ NGOs);

3) five *Regional Economic Commissions* (→ Economic Commissions, Regional);

4) nine *functional commissions:* the Statistical Commission, the Commission on Population and Development, the Commission for Social Development, the Commission on the Status of Women (→ Women and the UN), the Commission on Narcotic Drugs, the Commission on Crime Prevention and Criminal Justice and the Commission on Sustainable Development, the Commission on Science and Technology for Development, and the United Nations Forum on Forests;

5) a special committee for coordination with the UN system (→ Coordination in the UN System), the *United Nations Chief Executives Board for Coordination (CEB)*, until 2001 called *Administrative Committee on Coordination (ACC)*, where the executive heads of 28 UN organizations, including UN funds, programmes and → specialized agencies, as well as the IAEA, the IMF, the World Bank and the WTO, meet twice annually under the chairmanship of the UN Secretary-General, in order to deal with the problems of coordinating and harmonizing the policies and activities of the different elements of the → UN system, in particular with regard to coordination among the UN principal organs and their subsidiary organs on the one hand, and the more or less autonomous specialized agencies in the UN system, on the other. In its work the CEB is supported by two subsidiary organs established by the CEB, the *High-level Committee on Management (HLCM)* and the *High-level Committee on Programmes (HLCP)*.

III. Committees of the Security Council

The Security Council has so far been relatively reluctant in establishing committees. This might be due to the small number of its members (fifteen), which less frequently necessitates the delegation of tasks to smaller groups.

45

To the committees of the Security Council belong:

1) The Military Staff Committee

According to Article 47 of the UN Charter the Military Staff Committee (MSC) is composed of the military staff chiefs of the permanent members of the Security Council. It was intended by the founders of the UN as an advisory organ for the Council on military questions. Although it meets every two weeks for short, formal sessions, is has remained without any military and political significance: On the one hand the originally planned concept of making larger units of national armed forces "available to the Security Council" for the "maintenance of international peace and security ... in accordance with special ... agreements" (Art. 43 UN Charter) has never been put into practice, so that the Military Staff Committee became obsolete in this regard (cf. also Art. 44 and 45). On the other, the "permanent five" have made no use of this organ to coordinate their planning with respect to ongoing or planned peacekeeping missions; they prefer to do so on their own or to operate in this regard only in the framework of regional military or political alliances (→ Regionalization).

2) Standing Committees

a) The *Committee of Experts on Rules of Procedure*, which has been not active for a long time;

b) the *Committee on the Admission of New Members*, which examines the applications of new members for admission;

c) the *Committee on Council Meetings away from Headquarters*, which has been established for meetings away from New York (which took place in 1972, 1973, and 1990).

3) Ad Hoc Committees and Special Commissions

For particular purposes the Security Council establishes – mostly for a limited period of time – ad hoc committees or special committees:

a) Sanctions Committees

For monitoring sanctions imposed by the Security Council, the Council has established a number of sanctions committees (11 committees as of 31 December 2008), which comprise all members of the Council and meet in closed session (information: www. un.org/Docs/sc/committees/).

b) Ad Hoc Working Groups

The Security Council has established, *inter alia*, ad hoc informal working groups on the Council's documentation and other procedural questions, on the effectiveness of UN sanctions, on conflict prevention and resolution in Africa, on children and armed conflict, and on → peacekeeping operations. One of these informal working groups has received in recent years some public attention as one of the instruments of incremental Security Council reform: the Security Council Informal Working Group on Documentation and Other Procedural Questions. It was established in June 1993 to enhance and streamline ways and means whereby the Security Council addresses issues related to its documentation and other procedural questions. It makes recommendations, proposals and suggestions to the members of the Council. On 19 July 2006, for example, the Security Council approved a Note by the President of the Security Council (UN Doc. S/2006/507) with a view to enhancing the efficiency and transparency of the Council's work, as well as its interaction and dialogue with non-Council members, a paper which had been prepared by the Informal Working Group and which confirmed explicitly already practiced informal reform measures of the Security Council with regard to the information and participation of non-Council members, Secretariat officials and NGOs.

IV. Evaluation

Since the foundation of the United Nations its highly complex structure has attracted criticism and provoked reform proposals. Without doubt, the system of committees with regard to all principal organs of the United Nations belongs to one of the main issues of this criticism.

Taken over from national parliamentary systems the device to prepare the work of the main organs in a network of organizational and thematic committees has a great practical value and follows a functional logic. The problem within the UN system lies in the great number of committees and the weaknesses in the division of labor between committees and main organs. The most prominent example is the Main Committees of the General Assembly. Most topics dealt with in the General Assembly are discussed first in one of the Main Committees, which presents its recommendations, usually in the form of draft resolutions and decisions, to a plenary meeting of the Assembly for its consideration There the topic is discussed again and decided on.

That is without doubt redundant and duplicative work, but a large majority of states rejects any reform proposals in this regard, as they appreciate in this duplicative procedure the double occasion to take the floor in the General Assembly, first in the Main Committee and then in the debate in the plenary.

But if you judge this time-consuming procedure in the General Assembly from its results, it works quite well: the General Assembly has adopted dozens of international conventions in the fields of human rights and environmental protection and has initiated a series of remarkable world conferences, just to quote two results of a long list of achievements in the history of the General Assembly. Apparently, the complex committee system is necessary in order to achieve a sustainable political consensus among the member states.

And to be fair, the United Nations constantly discusses its own intricate committee system and looks for incremental reform steps: thus several Main Committees have introduced in recent years interactive dialogues, involving Secretariat officials, representatives from specialized agencies, external experts and NGOs (cf. *United Nations* 2004, Annex IV).

The same is true for the abundance of committees in the realm of the Security Council and ECOSOC: Some of them just produce papers without great political significance; others like the Commission on Sustainable Development promote important political debates.

Reforms with regard to the committee system should therefore not endeavor to abolish them, but should invent ways and means of better integrating the results of their work into the debates and decisions in the principal organs of the UN.

Helmut Volger

Lit.: *Lindemann, B./Hesse-Kreindler, D.:* Committees, System of, in: Wolfrum, R. (ed.): United Nations. Law, Policies, Practice, Vol. 1, Munich/Dordrecht 1995, 129-137; *Luck, E.:* Prospects for Reform: Principal Organs, in: Weiss, T.G./Daws, S. (eds): The Oxford Handbook on the United Nations, Oxford 2007, 653-674; *Peterson, M.J.:* General Assembly, in: Weiss, T.G./ Daws, S. (eds): The Oxford Handbook on the United Nations, Oxford 2007, 97-116; *Fitschen, T.:* Article 21, in: Simma, B. (ed.): The Charter of the United Nations. A Commentary, 2nd edn., Vol. I, Oxford 2002, 399-420; *United Nations - General Assembly:* Historical and analytical note on the practices and working methods of the Main Committees. Note by the Secretariat, 10 March 2004, UN Doc. A/58/CRP.5.

Internet: 1) General Assembly: a) homepage of Main Committees: www.un.org/ ga/maincommittees.shtml; b) other GA committees: www.un.org/ga/committees.shtml; 2) committees and working groups of the Security Council: www.un.org/Docs/sc/ unsc_structure.html; 3) committees and commissions of ECOSOC: www.un.org/ ecosoc/about/subsidiary.shtml.

Common Heritage of Mankind

The expression "Common Heritage of Mankind" describes initiatives of the UN and its member states to protect cultural and natural properties of territories not under the sovereignty of nation states, and the environment in general. The basic principle is to protect regions and assets that have value for all states, either philosophically in an idealistic sense or practically through the common use of resources. Furthermore, this manner of dealing with cultural and natural assets and the environment aims at safeguarding the interests of future generations.

One of the most important steps for the protection of the common heritage of mankind was initiated by → UNESCO, when it adopted the *Convention Concerning the Protection of the World Cultural and Natural Heritage* in November 1972 at its 17th General Conference (UNTS Vol. 1037, No. 15511). This convention established the *World Heritage List*.

The expression "common heritage of mankind" was coined in the context of UN codifications aimed at protecting regions outside the reach of national jurisdictions. The concept of the common use of outer space (→ Space Law) had already been acknowledged in 1959 and in 1963 in two resolutions of the → General Assembly. These two resolutions paved the way for the adoption of the *Outer Space Treaty* (Treaty on Principles Governing the Activities of States on the Exploration and Use of Outer Space, including the Moon and Other Celestial Bodies, UNTS Vol. 610, No. 8843, 205). The Outer Space Treaty demanded, among other things, international cooperation for the exploration of outer space, its common and peaceful use and the avoidance of harmful impacts on the environment.

Similarly, the United Nations has focused on the use of the sea. Developments at the end of the sixties indicated that unilateral military use and economic exploitation of the oceans would endanger their quality as a common good of mankind. To counter these developments, the General Assembly declared in a resolution, the so-called Sea-Bed Principles Declaration (UN Doc. A/RES/2749 (XXV) of 17 December 1970), the sea-bed to be part of the common heritage of mankind. This resolution demanded that the sea-bed and its natural resources be exploited only for the benefit of all mankind, and

that allowances be made for the interests of developing nations.

In 1982 the United Nations Convention on the Law of the Sea (*UNCLOS*), which incorporated these claims, specified the resources to be protected and concluded that these definitions were immutable (→ Law of the Sea).

With special emphasis on the common ground of the heritage of mankind, developing countries demand that industrialized countries support them in their initiatives to protect the common heritage with a transfer of technology to them. This claim finally resulted in an agreement, in the Convention on the Law of the Sea, on technology transfer and the equal participation of all states parties in the exploitation of the sea. However, due to the ongoing resistance from industrialized countries, as of present an agreement has not been reached on overall principles, nor on concrete steps to implement a transfer of technology to developing nations.

Although the Antarctic Treaty (UNTS Vol. 402, No. 5778), adopted in 1959, is not a case where the concept of the common heritage of mankind is applied, it states the interests of mankind in general. The principles of cooperation, non-acquisition and non-militarization are implemented to a lesser degree, as compared to other regions not under the → sovereignty of nation states.

The decisive event that finally led to a general convention for the protection of cultural and natural heritages was the construction of the Aswan dam in Egypt. After the governments of Egypt and Sudan had informed UNESCO about the danger the construction of the dam posed to the temples in Abu Simbel, UNESCO started an international fundraising campaign. Donations from more than 50 countries made it possible to disassemble the whole temple site and reconstruct it at a higher level on the river bank. As a result of the international efforts to save the temples of Abu Simbel, the concept of closer cooperation between nation states for the protection of cultural and natural properties took shape. The idea of the mutuality of the world heritage and of the environment as a common good of mankind was finally taken up and further developed in the Convention Concerning the Protection of the World Cultural and Natural Heritage (UNTS Vol. 1037, No. 15511), adopted by the General Conference of UNESCO in 1972.

This Convention – in which at present more than 150 states participate – specifies the duties of the *World Heritage Committee*, makes financing suggestions and defines criteria for the *World Heritage List*.

The World Heritage Committee is in charge of implementing the Convention's basic principles. It convenes annually to decide the placement of cultural and natural property on the World Heritage List. The Committee is responsible for budgeting and distributing funds to specific projects. It also decides which property becomes part of the *List of World Heritage in Danger*. The purpose of this particular list is to draw the attention of the world community to the endangered object in order to obtain additional financial support for its protection.

The first step in placing a cultural or natural site on the World Heritage List is its nomination through the country in which it is located. The criteria for becoming a recognized cultural property, which is considered part of the common heritage of mankind, is for a building or monument to represent an important exchange of human values, to be an expression of human creativity or to reflect special attributes of a given culture. Protection as a natural property requires that the site be a location representing an extraordinary event or a part of a process in the development of the earth, an example of special natural phenomena, or to be the home of endangered animals or plants.

Since 1992 the UNESCO *World Heritage Center* has supported the work of the *World Heritage Committee*. The World Heritage Center was established to advance and to supervise the everyday implementation of the convention. It cooperates with all organizations that are part of the system to protect the common heritage of mankind, and has administrative authority over the budget. The budget is composed of obligatory payments from the states parties to the convention and voluntary contributions. The annual budget is approximately three million US dollars.

The *World Heritage Committee*, whose 21 members are elected by the general assembly of the states parties to the convention, perceives the protection of the common heritage of mankind as a continuing process which is to emphasize the mutuality of the heritage and its preservation for future generations. Unfortunately, these aims are not easy to achieve. The number of properties on the *World Heritage List* has increased to 690 by the year 2000. Due to the limited budget, difficulties in implementing measures to preserve the cultural and natural heritage are increasing. The concept of protecting culture and nature as common goods of mankind is also neglected when a signatory state does not fulfill its obligations. The neglect of a nation state may result in properties of the World Heritage List being located on their territory being removed from the list.

Out of a total of 529 cultural, 138 natural and 23 mixed properties on the World Heritage List in the year 2000 24 properties are located in Germany. These include the domes in Aachen, Speyer and Cologne, the Wieskirche, the castles in Potsdam and, since 1998, the classic Weimar. Other well-known sites are the Great Barrier Reef in Australia, the Great Wall in China, the pyramid fields from Giza to Dahshar in Egypt, the Acropolis in Athens, Greece, the Taj Mahal in India, the Tower of London in the United Kingdom and the Statue of Liberty in New York, USA.

In contrast to cultural and natural sites, which are under the sovereignty of a nation state, the protection of the environment ($\rightarrow$ Environmental Protection) is perceived as a global challenge that cannot by dealt with by national initiatives alone. Therefore the international community is seeking guidelines for dealing with the environment and its resources. This search began with the first conference on the environment in Stockholm in 1972. Since then, the practice of utilizing multilateral agreements to protect the environment was intensified in the 1990s in the form of several → world conferences. Although the phrase "common heritage of mankind" was not used in this context, the final documents of these world conferences often mirror the same basic ideas.

With the codification of rules for the use and the protection of the environment in multilateral treaties, the principle of the mutuality of the heritage of mankind has become part of international customary law (→ International Law, and the UN; → Environmental Law, International). This is true primarily for the protection of territories that are not under the jurisdiction of a nation state, and to a lesser extent for the protection of the environment and of cultural and natural properties. Due to the fact that the implementation of the rules rests with national governments it consists mainly of general obligations rather than specific duties.

With respect to territories that are not under the jurisdiction of a nation state, the principles of non-acquisition, non-occupation and non-militarization, concern for the environment when exploiting natural resources and the idea of fair distribution with special consideration to developing countries, are generally accepted.

Gregor Kolk

Lit.: *Fitschen, T.:* Common Heritage of Mankind, in: Wolfrum, R. (ed.): United Nations: Law, Policies and Practice, Vol. 1, Munich/Dordrecht 1995, 149-159; *Gehlhoff, W.:* Krise und Wandel in der UNESCO, in: EA, No. 19 (1992), 557-565; *Wolfrum, R.:* Common Heritage of Mankind, in: Bernhardt, R. (ed.): EPIL, Vol. 11, Amsterdam 1989, 65-69.

Addendum

1. Since 2000, the common heritage concept has continued to influence ever more diverse and more specific areas of international law. In this process of mainstreaming the concept, treaties protecting the cultural diversity have been particularly important. In 2003 and 2005 respectively, states adopted the UNESCO Conventions on *the Safeguarding of the Intangible Cultural Heritage* (2003) and on the *Protection and Promotion of the Diversity of Cultural Expressions* (2005), which seek to protect cultural diversity and human creativity from processes of globalization and social transformation (conventions available at http://portal.unesco. org, link: Legal Instruments, link: Conventions). Both of these have attracted a considerable number of ratifications (85 and 73 respectively) and have highlighted the importance of 'cultural diversity' as part of the common heritage of humanity.

Another UNESCO Convention, on the *Protection of the Underwater Cultural Heritage* (2001) (available ibid.), has given rise to much more controversy. It applies to "all traces of human existence having a cultural, historical or archaeological character" (such as ships, artifacts or cargo) that have been underwater for 100 years or more, and with respect to them, derogates from the regular rules of salvage and finds. This derogation is seen as over-ambitious by some countries, which are also concerned that the convention does not properly recognize the sovereign immunity of sunken ships. Opposed by major maritime nations, the Convention has so far been ratified by 15 states only and has yet to enter into force.

2. While the common heritage concept has continued to branch out, some of its aspects have been put into question, even in traditional areas of application such as the law of the sea (→ Law of the Sea) or outer space (→ Space Law). For example, states seem to consider the potential commercial uses of outer space more favourably than they used to. In its resolution 1/2002, adopted at its conference in New Delhi , the International Law Association (reproduced in ILA (ed.): Report of the

Seventieth Conference, New Delhi 2002) expressly stated "that the common heritage of mankind concept has developed today as also allowing the commercial uses of outer space for the benefit of mankind" and suggested a more liberal international regime for the exploitation of moon resources than that set up by Article 11 of the "Agreement Governing the Activities of States on the Moon and Other Celestial Bodies, in short "Moon Treaty" (UN Doc. A/RES/34/58, 5 December 1979; UNTS 1363, No. 23002).

As far as the law of the sea is concerned, states have not contested the basic principle pursuant to which the seabed and ocean floor beyond the limits of national jurisdiction and their resources are the common heritage of mankind laid down in Article 136 of the United Nations Convention on the Law of the Sea (in short Law of the Sea Convention – LOSC), UNTS 1833, No. 31363). However, lured by ocean bed oil and gas deposits, some of them have begun to test the geographical limits of the common heritage area by claiming extended zones of national jurisdiction. In this respect, Russia's claim to an extended continental shelf in the Arctic waters (proffered by the spectacular planting of the Russian flag in August 2007) certainly has been the most spectacular example in point. Yet other countries have made or announced an intention to make claims to large portions of the seabed around Antarctica; whether these can be brought in line with the 1959 Antarctic Treaty (UNTS 402, No. 5778) and the Law of the Sea Convention is subject to much debate. While respecting the legal principle laid down in Article 136 LOSC, these claims, if successful before the UN's Continental Shelf Commission, would reduce the geographical application of the common heritage principle considerably. In addition, there has been new debate about the substantive scope of that principle: Under the Law of the Sea Convention, the International Seabed Authority (cf. www.isa.org.jm/en/home), established as the cornerstone

of the international exploitation regime, controls mineral-related activities on the international seabed. Yet, scientific progress has shown that in addition to minerals, the deep seabed may also hold extremely valuable genetic resources. Whether these should be covered by the common heritage regime or be subject to the more liberal regime of the freedom of the high seas is an open question of immense relevance, both practical and conceptual.

3. Since 2000, the World Heritage Committee, established under the 1972 World Heritage Convention, has further expanded the list of world heritage sites. At present (April 2008), that list covers 851 properties (660 cultural, 166 natural, 25 mixed), 32 of which are located in Germany. Since it believed them to be threatened by city development projects, the World Heritage Committee decided to place two of the German sites (the Cologne Cathedral – now restored – and the Elbe River Valley) on the list of 'world heritage in danger'. The ensuing litigation in German courts has highlighted the difficulties of securing the effective implementation of the 1972 Convention. Leaving aside problems created by Germany's federal structure, it is worth noting that according to a decision of the German Federal Constitutional Court rendered in 2007 (Bundesverfassungsgericht 2 BvR 695/07), the inclusion in the World Heritage List does not prevent states or sub-state authorities from modifying protected sites; rather, the Court stressed that even the 1972 Convention "fully respect[ed] the sovereignty of the States on whose territory the cultural and natural heritage ... is situated" [translated from German by the author]

Christian J. Tams

Lit.: *Brunnée, J:* Common Areas, Common Heritage, and Common Concern, in: Bodansky, D./Brunée, J./Hey, E. (eds.): The Oxford Handbook of International Environmental Law, Oxford 2007, 550-573; *Dromgoole, S.:* The protection of the underwater cultural heritage: national perspectives in light of the UNESCO Convention 2001, 2nd edn., Leiden 2006; *Fastenrath, U.:* Der Schutz des Weltkulturerbes in Deutschland: zur innerstaatlichen Wirkung von völkerrechtlichen Verträgen ohne Vertragsgesetz (Verwaltungsabkommen i.S.d. Art. 59 Abs. 2 GG), in: Die öffentliche Verwaltung 59 (2006), 1017-1027; *Grob, J.:* Antarctica's Frozen territorial Claims: a Meltdown Proposal, in: Boston College International and Comparative Law Review 30 (2007), 461-484; *Hobe, S.:* Was bleibt vom gemeinsamen Erbe der Menschheit?, in: Dicke, K. et al. (eds.):: Weltinnenrecht. Liber amicorum Jost Delbrück, Berlin 2005, 329-346; *Leary, D.K.:* International law and the genetic resources of the deep sea, Leiden 2007; *O'Keefe, R.:* World Cultural Heritage: Obligations to the International Community as a Whole? in: ICLQ 53 (2004) 189-209; *Porras, D.A.:* The "Common Heritage" of Outer Space : Equal Benefits for Most of Mankind, in: Calif. W Int'l. LJ 37 (2006), 143-176; *Schlinkert, J.C.:* Lebendige folkloristische Ausdrucksweisen traditioneller Gemeinschaften, Berlin 2007; *Scovazzi, T.:* Mining, Protection of the Environment, Scientific Research and Bioprospecting: Some Considerations on the Role of the International Sea-Bed Authority, in: The International Journal of Marine and Coastal Law 19 (2004), 383-409.

Internet: Homepage of the World Heritage Committee with the World Heritage List: www.unesco.org/whc/heritage.htm; UN Office of Legal Affairs, Division for Ocean Affairs and the Law of the Sea: http://untreaty.un.org/ola/div_doalos. aspx?section=doalog.

Control Mechanisms in the UN, External and Internal

I. Introduction

The *control and monitoring* of the work of the → Secretariat of the UN and its special funds and programmes takes place at different levels, whereby the applied, politically and/or professionally determined criteria of evaluation can differ considerably. It can be undertaken through either *inter-governmental* or *inter-institutional bodies*. In this context, it is difficult to clearly define the borders between *external* and *internal control*. On the one hand, close mechanisms of co-operation exist, such as, e.g., between external and internal auditors, on the other hand institutions exist, which,

besides the UN institutions, also include the → specialized agencies as objects of investigations. To that extent, it would be more appropriate to differentiate between *inter-* and *intra-institutional control*.

Objects of control could be the input or output side or also the transformation processes from inputs to outputs. Here, the principle of economic rationality is implicitly assumed, which means that given targets (outputs) should be realized through a minimum of inputs or a maximum of outputs at given inputs. In the following, the most important *organs of control* are briefly characterized. Afterwards, a description of the networking of these organs follows. Finally, their work will be evaluated.

II. The Advisory Committee on Administrative and Budgetary Questions (ACABQ)

The ACABQ was set up as a subsidiary organ (→ Principal Organs, Subsidiary Organs, Treaty Bodies) at the first session of the → General Assembly by resolution 14A (I) of 1946 which defined the following tasks:

- to examine the programme budget estimates submitted by the → Secretary-General, the special accounts for → peacekeeping operations and the administrative budgets of the special funds and programmes;
- to advise the General Assembly on all administrative and budgetary matters;
- to examine on behalf of the → General Assembly the administrative budgets of the → specialized agencies of the UN;
- to consider the reports of the auditors on the accounts of the UN and its specialized agencies. (UN Doc. A/RES/ 14A (I) of 13 February 1946)

The ACABQ is an expert body. Since 1978 its membership stands at 16, most being diplomats from the → permanent missions of the member states at the UN Headquarters in New York. The ACABQ members are elected for a period of three years by the Fifth Committee of the General Assembly (→ Committees, System of) in a secret ballot and appointed by the General Assembly; immediate re-election is possible. Personal qualifications and experience are necessary, whereby at least three of the members are to be recognized financial experts who may not retire simultaneously. The members are elected on the basis of a broad geographical representation.

The fact that the Group of Western European and Other States is represented by five experts, indicates, however, that the regional distribution is more closely linked to the (obligatory) assessments to the regular → budget of the UN than to the geographical representation (cf. *Münch* 1996, 46-47).

The ACABQ meets for two (sometimes also three) periods per year in New York for about eight months. The members meet in private (closed) sessions.

III. The Board of Auditors

This *Board of Auditors* was also established by the first General Assembly in December 1946 (UN Doc. A/RES/74 (I) of 7 December 1946) to serve as external auditors. It is composed of three members to be elected by the General Assembly from the Auditors-General (or officers holding equivalent titles) of the member states. The 55th General Assembly extended the term of Board members from three years to a non-consecutive term of six years from 1 July 2002 (UN Doc. A/RES/55/248 of 12 April 2001).

The Board is "completely independent and solely responsible for the execution of its work" (Financial Regulations and Rules of the United Nations, 9 May 2003, UN Doc. ST/SGB/2003/7, Regulation 7.6). The ACABQ may, however, request the Board "to perform certain specific examinations" (ibid., Regulation 7.7). According to the Financial Regulations of the UN the Board is responsible for the audit of the financial statement and the efficient functioning of the administration (ibid., Regulation 7.5). To be audited are the accounts of the Secretariat of the UN, the → International Court of Justice as well as the

UN funds and programmes, such as, inter alia, → UNICEF, → UNDP, → UNEP, → UNHCR, → UNRWA. The specialized agencies of the UN have their own external auditors.

At present, the Board is composed of the Auditors-General of China, France, and South Africa. Each member must provide an audit staff of up to 50 professionals for four months a year. In addition, they delegate each a full-time *Director of External Audit* as a permanent representative to the UN Headquarters in New York.

The three Board members meet only twice or three times a year in order to adopt reports of the Board or to discuss some general problems. The on-going co-ordination of audit and the preparation of the Board decisions is undertaken by the three Directors of External Audit, supported by a secretariat of the Board.

The *external audit* by the Board covers the *financial statements* as well as the *financial operations*. In the case of the financial statements the Board must hand over a positive audit opinion, i.e. to approve the regularity of the annual closing of accounts by a respective number of sample audits. The Board can also express a qualified audit opinion which is meant to be a warning-signal for the → Secretariat as well as for the body of the affected institutions to remedy grievances.

The audit of the financial operations covers increasingly also the efficient use of resources; since 1991, between two to three cross-cutting audits of thematic focuses are also undertaken. The Board produces about 22 reports over a two-year cycle to the General Assembly. These reports are available to the public and can be accessed through its website (www.un.org/auditors/board/reports. shtml).

The → Group of 77 criticized the unequal regional distribution in the membership and demanded an increase in membership from three to five, but without success.

IV. The Joint Inspection Unit (JIU)

The *Joint Inspection Unit* (JIU) has been created as the result of the first major → financial crisis of UN during the 1960s, after disputes about the financing of the → peace-keeping operation in the Congo (ONUC). Following a French initiative, the General Assembly established the JIU in 1966 which began to work in 1968 (UN Doc. A/RES/2150 (XXI) of 4 November 1966). Its mandate has been several times extended until the General Assembly approved the Statute in 1976 (UN Doc. A/RES/ 31/192 of 22 December 1976), establishing a subsidiary organ of the General Assembly according to Article 22 of the → Charter of the UN. Besides the UN (and its funds and programmes), the → IAEA and eleven specialized agencies (with the exception of the Bretton Woods institutions and IFAD) accepted the JIU Statute.

Insofar, the Joint Inspection Unit (www.unjiu.org/) is a subsidiary organ of the legislative bodies of all the institutions mentioned above; its expenditures are shared by the participating institutions. The budget for the biennium 2006-2007 amounted to 11.1 million US dollars, of which 93.7% were for staff costs. The largest shares are borne by the UN (24.2%) and its special funds and programmes, UNDP (20.4%), WFP (11.5%), UNICEF (9.4%) and the → World Health Organization (10.7%).

The Unit consists of eleven inspectors, appointed for a term of five years that can be renewed once. The appointment follows a rather complex consultation mechanism which includes the Presidents of the General Assembly and → ECOSOC as well as the Secretary-General in his function as Chairman of the UN System's *Chief Executives Board for Coordination (CEB)*. The Inspectors have the status of officials of the UN, but are not considered to be staff members under the supervision of the Secretary-General; they serve in their personal capacity and are legally independent: "The Inspectors shall discharge their duties in full independ-

ence." (Statute of the JIU, UN Doc. A/RES/31/192, Art. 7). They are assisted by an Executive Secretary and 19 other staff members, nine of them research officers.

The Unit's tasks are:
- to undertake independent *inspections, evaluations* and *investigations* aimed at improving management and greater co-ordination within the UN system (Art. 5, 1-3 JIU Statute), and
- to make *proposals to increase the efficiency* of the financial operations (Art. 5, 5 JIU Statute).

The Unit prepares internally agreed reports on selected issues concerning organization and management, personnel, budgeting, planning and evaluation, which are transmitted via the heads of the inspected organizations to their legislative bodies, requiring a response within three to six months (Art. 11, 4 JIU Statute). By the end of 2007, a total of 372 reports had been produced (www.unjiu.org/en/reports.htm).

During the course of its hitherto 42 years of existence, the Unit has been often criticized. Its number of eleven Inspectors is regarded of being too small in order to gain a sufficient broad coverage which includes the whole UN system. Also, the study of *Wündisch* (1999) shows that, despite the often raised criticism, the Unit continues to be composed to a large extent of former diplomats with an extremely high age of entrance on the average rather than of experts who fulfill the qualifications as demanded in the JIU Statute. Also criticized have been the quality of the reports, and the low average output per Inspector (a maximum of one report a year), but at the same time under criticism have been the enormous time-lags taken by the UN institutions concerned in their responses as well as the extremely limited intervention possibilities of the Inspectors as they are defined by the JIU Statute.

V. The Office of Internal Oversight Services (OIOS)

This *Office of Internal Oversight Services – OIOS* (www.un.org/Depts/oios/)

has been created upon pressure from the main contributors, especially the United States, by the General Assembly in 1994 (UN Doc. A/RES/48/218B). The Office is headed by an Under-Secretary-General, who is not appointed by the → Secretary-General autonomously, because the appointment requires the approval of the General Assembly; he is appointed for one fixed term of five years, without any possibility of renewal, and is independent in the execution of his programme of work. For the first time in the → history of the UN an effective internal oversight system has been created which fulfills in an independent and concentrated way the functions of internal audit, monitoring, inspection, evaluation and investigation vis-à-vis the General Assembly and its Fifth Committee (cf. resolution 48/218B, para. 5 a).

The competence of the Office covers *all UN activities under the Secretary-General's authority,* the five regional commissions as well as the specialized funds and programmes, such as → UNDP, → UNEP, → UNICEF, → UNHCR, but not the specialized agencies of the UN.

Besides the functions mentioned above, the Office has an Investigation Section which verifies reports from staff members of the Secretariat who discovered cases of corruption, mismanagement and wastage. This Section can be reached by all staff members via a "hot line" around the clock. All contacts are treated confidentially.

The current OIOS report, containing information about the Office's activities from the 1 July 2006 to 30 June 2007 (UN Doc. A/62/281 (Part I) of 17 August 2007), provides some insight into the increase of efficiency and economic benefit gained by the work of OIOS. During the reporting period, the Office issued 268 oversight reports which included 1,792 recommendations to improve internal controls, accountability mechanisms, and organizational efficiency and effectiveness. Through the recommendations, OIOS identified a to-tal of 27.8 million US dollars in cost savings (ibid., 1).

Since 1995, OIOS has identified potential savings and recoveries in the UN organization of some 436 million US dollars, of which 204 million US dollars were recovered and saved (as of 31 December 2007, source: www.un.org/ Depts/oios/pages/highlights. html).

Several reports of the United States Government Accountability Office have examined the work of OIOS and have underlined the fact that the work of OIOS would be of great importance for the United Nations in its efforts "to make progress in its reform agenda and achieve lasting results." (*GAO* 2005a, 1; cf. also *GAO* 2005b)

In many cases OIOS has provided UN institutions and offices with arguments to fight for an increase of budgetary resources, for instance in the case of the Office of the High Commissioner for Human Rights – OHCHR, where in 2003 the members of the Fifth Committee reacted with promises to improve the financial situation of the OHCHR (cf. United Nations Press Release GA/ AB/3554, 4 March 2003) when they were informed about the growing disparity between scarce resources and the increasing workload of OHCHR through an OIOS management review of OHCHR (UN Doc. A/57/488 of 21 October 2002).

Moreover the OIOS has contributed through its investigations towards detecting cases of fraud, embezzlement, theft of UN-owned equipment and other illicit activities within the UN and has given recommendations to deter further illicit practices. This is important for the UN image in view of the constant and often polemical criticism by Western member states, in particular the USA, of the UN's management practices, even if OIOS reports are used by US newspapers in their lopsided coverage to give their readers the impression of extensive waste and corruption in the UN system (cf. *Thalif Deen*, UN Image Being Tarnished by Lopsided Coverage, Inter-Press Service, 7 December 1997).

To increase its efficiency, OIOS has recently started investigations of its own work, the methods of work in its Investigation Division (*Grimstad* 2007) as well as its "work culture" (*Girodo* 2007).

VI. Network of the Organs of Control

All organs of control are interrelated through a network. In the following, some of the decision-making and co-ordination processes will be described.

All proposals of budgetary and administrative relevance of the Secretary-General are addressed via the *ACABQ* to the *Fifth Committee* of the General Assembly if no other expert bodies, such as, e.g., the Committee on Contributions, are interposed. The *Board of Auditors* also reports to the *Fifth Committee* of the General Assembly. In addition, *ACABQ* examines the cost implications of resolution drafts of the other Main Committees of the General Assembly; this committee is also empowered by the General Assembly to allow rearrangements between the different items of the budget upon request by the Secretary-General. Finally, the *ACABQ* is also involved in determining the division of labor among the three members of the *Boards of Auditors* and the activities of the *JIU* whose reports are accompanied by opinions of the ACABQ to the General Assembly.

Close co-operation clusters exist between the *Board of Auditors* and *OIOS* created in 1994 as a result of the tasks of external and internal audit. Beyond the mutual exchange of examination results, regular meetings take place in order to co-ordinate the activities of both bodies. In addition, the Board can, whenever necessary, submit opinions related to the reports of the *OIOS*. Finally, *OIOS* is audited by the Board, being part of the UN Secretariat.

The Board also works closely together with the internal auditors of the special funds and programmes and organizes regular meetings with the JIU.

The external auditors co-ordinate their work in *a Panel of External Auditors of the United Nation's Specialized Agencies*.

VII. Balance Sheet

The demand for co-ordination is extremely high – not only in the UN domain between external control undertaken by the Board of Auditors and internal control through the Office of Internal Oversight Services, but also between the OIOS and the Joint Inspection Unit. Common to all three organs is the primacy of professional control and guaranteed independence. By comparison, the Advisory Committee on Administrative and Budgetary Questions, although originally intended to be an expert body, is more to be seen as an external political organ of control, which is – together with the Committee for Programme and Co-ordination (CPC; cf. → UN system) – placed before the Fifth Committee in the decision-making process.

Extremely high is the demand for co-ordination within the UN system (→ Coordination in the UN System). Here the JIU has competences which are, however, clearly limited due to the JIU Statute and the small number of Inspectors. The same is true in the case of the ACABQ which, although having the mandate to examine the administrative budgets of the specialized agencies, has not exercised this right since the early 1970s because of the unwillingness of the specialized agencies to co-operate. Especially problematic is the fact that, in the case of the majority of the specialized agencies, the functions of internal audit, evaluation and inspection have neither been put together in institutional-organizational terms nor have attained the degree of independence which has been reached in the UN through the creation of OIOS. This situation is depicted in detail in a report of JIU on the oversight in the UN system (*JIU* 2006), which compares the oversight regulations of the UN with those of the specialized agencies.

There seems to exist no consensus among the (groups of) states how and to what extent control mechanisms are necessary. But the options are clear: either a basic revision of the JIU Statute towards a mandate such as OIOS and a corresponding organizational concentration of the functions for an efficient internal inspection system within the secretariats of the specialized agencies, or an abolition of the JIU and its replacement through the OIOS model to be set up within the individual specialized agencies.

Klaus Hüfner

Lit.: *Kaltenbach, E.:* Die externe Finanzkontrolle der Vereinten Nationen. Zur Arbeit des Rates der Rechnungsprüfer, in: VN 45 (1997) 168-172; *Münch, W.:* Inspektionen, Evaluierung und Untersuchungen. Zur Tätigkeit der Gemeinsamen Inspektionsgruppe (JIU) der Vereinten Nationen, in: VN 45 (1997), 172-176; *Münch, W.:* Experten für den Interessenausgleich. Aufgaben und Arbeitsweise des Beratenden Ausschusses für Verwaltungs- und Haushaltsfragen (ACABQ), in: VN 44 (1996), 45-50; *Office of Internal Oversight Services:* A Culture Review of the Investigation Division of OIOS. Consultant's Report Submitted to the Office of Internal Oversight Services by Michel Girodo, 13 July 2007, www.hrw.org /pub/2008/un/Culture.Review.OIOS.Inv.Div. pdf; *Office of Internal Oversight Services:* Review of the OIOS Investigation Division, United Nations. Final Report, submitted by Erling Grimstad, 26 June 2007, www.hrw. org/pub/2008/un/External.ReviewOIOS.pdf (quoted as: Grimstad 2007); *Paschke, K.T.:* Innenrevision in den Vereinten Nationen – eine neue Erfahrung, in: VN 44 (1996), 41-45; *United Nations - General Assembly:* Report of of on the activities of the Office of Internal Oversight Services for the period from 1 July 2006 to 30 June 2007, 17 August 2007 (UN Doc. A/62/281 Part I); *United Nations - General Assembly:* Report of the Joint Inspection Unit for 2007 and Programme of work for 2008, New York 2008 (UN Doc. A/62/34/Add.1); *United Nations:* Oversight Lacunae in the United Nations System. Prepared by the Joint Inspection Unit (JIU/REP/2006/2), Geneva 2006, also: UN Doc. A/60/860/Add. 1, 25 May 2006, www.unjiu.org/data/reports/2006/en2006_2. pdf), quoted as: JIU 2006); *United States Government Accountability Office:* Sustained Oversight Is Needed for Reforms to Achieve Lasting Results, 2 March 2005, Washington, GAO-05-392T (quoted as:

GAO 2005a); *United States Government Accountability Office:* United Nations – Preliminary Oberservations on Internal Oversight and Procurement Practices, 31 October 2005, Washington, GAO-06-226T (quoted as: GAO 2005b); *Wündisch, M.:* Die United Nations Joint Inspection Unit als Instrument zur Einführung organisatorischer Rationalität in internationalen Organisationen, Frankfurt (Main) 1999.

Internet: ACABQ: www.un.org./docs/ acabq; Board of Auditors: www.un.org/ auditors/board; Joint Inspection Unit: www. unjiu. org; Office of International Oversight Services: www.un.org/depts/oios.

Coordination in the UN System

The → UN system, which has been designed as an association of loosely connected organizations, requires considerable co-ordination efforts to limit overlapping, duplication and friction. The → Secretary-General has realistically described the situation in his reform proposals of 1997 (→ Reform of the UN): "The Charter provides that the United Nations should draw in its work on a decentralized system of specialized agencies. Each of these agencies was established by a separate treaty among Governments and each is directly accountable to its own governing bodies. The United Nations authority over their policies and activities is limited, under the Charter, to making 'recommendations' for their 'coordination' ".

There are historical, political and technical reasons for the fragmentation of the UN system:

Some → specialized agencies are older than the United Nations (for instance the → ITU and → UPU); their full integration would have been difficult for constitutional reasons. Consequently, Article 57 of the Charter (→ Charter of the UN) merely stipulates that the existing specialized agencies shall be brought "into relationship" with the United Nations.

If the United Nations were to founder, which judged by the experience of the → League of Nations could not be ruled out from the start, the work of the tech-

57

nical agencies should not be adversely affected (*Childers/Urquhart* 1994, 40).

The division of the system into independent units enables all states to measure out its membership (→ Membership and Representation of States) in accordance with its own priorities.

During the Cold War and the North-South Conflict the fragmentation helped separate "political" and "technical" problems. The blocs of states could deal with political controversies in the → General Assembly and → Security Council without jeopardizing the necessary collaboration in the various technical fields.

Establishing new organizations allowed a flexible response – as the examples of → UNCTAD and IDA show – to the demands of groups of states, especially developing countries (→ Group of 77 and the UN; → Non-Aligned Movement and the UN).

The different mandates and the geographical location of the specialized agencies require a high degree of independence. Full integration of all sectorial, thematic and regional functions into a single hierarchical structure under central leadership and control would have created an even more unwieldy bureaucratic monster.

According to *Dicke* this pluralism is a strength of the UN system (→ UN System), since it ensures "for multiplicity of political styles and political programmes, specialization of techniques and a less heavy and slow structure". Furthermore, the research of organizations has given "sufficient evidence that the way of decentralization taken by the UN, is more adequate to the dezentralized character of the international system than a centralized 'world organization' or international government could be" (*Dicke* op. cit., 388).

Critics, by contrast, claim that the specialized agencies have extended their programmes beyond their original mandate, and propose to redefine the responsibilities and priorities of each of the components of the UN system. In his 1997 reform programme "Renewing the United Nations: A Programme for Re-

form" (UN Doc. A/51/950 of 14 July 1997) the Secretary-General suggested the establishment of a Special Commission, at the ministerial level, to review the Charter and the treaties from which the specialized agencies derive their mandates with the objective of examining how the weakness of the decentralized system can best be corrected while preserving its advantages. This proposal has not yet been taken up by the states community, since it is to be expected that it will meet with resistance even within member states. *Childers/Urquhart* observe that it has been possible for the diplomats of member-governments at the UN itself to call for greater coherence, while their own sectorial delegates to the specialized agencies have taken the diametrically opposite line championed by the agency heads (*Childers/Urquhart* 1994, 41).

The coordination in the UN system takes place at three different levels – within member states, between member states, and between organizations.

1. Coordination within Member States (Intra-State Coordination)

The responsibility for international organizations within member states rests with government departments and is usually exercised by the ministerial bureaucracy. The United Nations has not yet succeeded in being recognized as an independent field of politics, as is the case with European politics. Therefore, participation in the world body usually takes place within the context of specific fields of work, such as foreign policy, → human rights, transports, drugs, health and nuclear policies, and is, thus subject to the pertinent pressures and conditions. To the extent that the fields of work of international organizations coincide with the areas of competence of governmental departments, the latter will also determine who is nationally responsible for a specific international organization. That is to say, the health department will be responsible for the → WHO, the agriculture department for the → FAO, and the foreign office for the General Assembly and the Security

Council. Often, inter-ministerial committees or central coordination bodies are being established to ensure uniform policies vis-à-vis the UN within a country.

Experience shows, though, that the coordination between the government departments involved often does not function properly, and that coherence vis-à-vis the outside is still insufficient in most member states. According to *Paschke* it is not unusual that a member state loudly demands economies without any compromises throughout the UN system, while the representatives of the same country in a specialized agency may argue in favor of considerable budgetary increases (*Paschke* 1996, 42). A lack of coordination also exists between governments and ministerial bureaucracy, on the one hand, and non-governmental organizations (→ NGOs), on the other, even though the increased involvement of the latter is seen as a means to put the national UN policies on a broader basis. *Childers/Urquhart* consider policy coordination within member states the "Achilles Heel" of the UN system, since the system itself cannot overcome the lack of coherent national positions (*Childers/Urquhart* 1994, 140-141).

2. Coordination between Member States (Inter-Governmental Coordination)

Coordination between member states takes place in the governing bodies of the individual organizations, in which diplomats and civil servants represent the interests of their countries. Within the UN system only the General Assembly has no restrictions as to subject matters; that is to say, it can in principle place any problem on its agenda upon request of its members. The responsibility of the corresponding governing organs of the specialized agencies, by contrast, is confined to the sectors for which they have been given mandates. The exceptions are specific organs of the United Nations which, in addition, perform limited system-wide functions, such as the *Economic and Social Council (→ ECOSOC)*, the *Committee for Programme and Co-ordination (CPC)*, the *Advisory Committee on Administrative and Budgetary Questions (ACABQ)*, the *Committee on Contributions*, the *Joint Inspection Unit (JIU)*, the *Fifth Committee* and the *International Civil Service Commission (ICSC)* (→ Committees, System of).

The Charter entrusts the *Economic and Social Council (ECOSOC)* with the coordination between the United Nations and the specialized agencies. Article 63 (1) empowers the Council to enter into agreements with the specialized agencies, thus defining the terms of their relations with the United Nations. All specialized agencies have concluded such agreements, in which they undertake to coordinate their activities, exchange information, provide reports to the *ECOSOC*, and consult on administrative, personnel and financial matters. Furthermore, Article 63 (2) gives *ECOSOC* the – arguably insubstantial – right to coordinate the activities of the specialized agencies through "consultation" and "recommendations". It is generally considered that the *ECOSOC* has been unable to exercise its system-wide coordination role effectively because of a lack of the necessary political and legal prerequisites. The *ECOSOC* has no authority to issue directives but can, at best, make "recommendations" to the specialized agencies, whose independent governing bodies will decide on their implementation. Recommendations of the *ECOSOC* have, from the start, little chance of success, since the membership and specific interests of the specialized agencies often differ from those of the respective organs of the United Nations. The Secretary-General, in his reform programme, has consequently pointed out that the efforts within the → Secretariat to enhance conceptual and institutional coherence should be paralleled at the intergovernmental level. He suggests to rethink the role of the *ECOSOC* and to provide it, if need be, with greater authority through Charter revision for policy management and coordination.

59

The *CPC*, established as a joint subsidiary organ of the *ECOSOC* and the General Assembly, reviews the programmes of the United Nations and its associated relief agencies, programmes and funds, recommends priorities and develops evaluation procedures. Its position within the budgetary process (→ Budget) of the United Nations was considerably strengthened in 1986 in favour of the major contributors. The Committee is also to consider, sector by sector, the programmes of the agencies and to recommend to them guidelines to strengthen programme coherence and coordination within the system. Since 1991, the *ECOSOC* has been receiving from the *ACC* and through the *CPC* annual reports on the programmes and resources of the specialized agencies. There is no evidence, however, that these reports have resulted in any more programme coherence, nor have they achieved better coordination.

The *ACABQ*, which was established in 1946 by the General Assembly as a standing committee, does not only advise the Fifth Committee in all administrative and financial matters relating to the United Nations and its subsidiary organs, but has also system-wide functions. According to Article 17 (3) of the Charter, the General Assembly – assisted by the *ACABQ* – examines the administrative budgets of the specialized agencies with the undefined aim of making "recommendations" to them. The *ACABQ* meets regularly at the different headquarters duty stations, to be briefed by the specialized agencies about budgetary and administrative questions. In addition, it receives annually from the *ACC* statistical information concerning the budgetary and financial situation of all organizations within the UN system. Consideration of these reports seems to be a mere formality without any visible impact on the budgetary performance of the specialized agencies.

The second standing committee of the General Assembly, the *Committee on Contributions*, also has system-wide functions. It may advise a specialized agency on its scale of contributions, if requested by this agency to do so. Most specialized agencies are utilizing this offer insofar as they submit the scale of contribution promulgated by the General Assembly (→ Financial Crises) to their own governing bodies for approval, after having made the necessary adjustments to reflect their sometimes differing membership.

The *Joint Inspection Unit (JIU)*, which consists of eleven independent inspectors with wide experience in financial and administrative matters, was established by the General Assembly in 1966 in order to ensure that the UN system undertakes its activities in the most economical manner and that optimum use is made of the resources available. The effectiveness of the JIU is somewhat controversial, since it lacks the necessary authority, and opinions of the quality of its reports vary widely (→ Control Mechanisms of the UN; Internal and External).

Coordination in the area of personnel has progressed farthest and takes place within the framework of the *Common System* (→ Personnel). The relationship agreements between the specialized agencies and the United Nations stipulate the objective of establishing a uniform international civil service through common personnel standards, methods and arrangements.

In 1975, the *International Civil Service Commission (ICSC)* was founded as the central organ for the regulation and coordination of conditions of employment for the personnel of the whole UN system. Recommendations, which concern the essential conditions such as the salaries of the Professional Staff, must be submitted by the *ICSC* to the General Assembly for approval, which in these cases performs legislative functions for the whole UN system. Such recommendations are first reviewed by the Fifth Committee and, as concerns their financial implications, by the *ACABQ*. For other matters, the *ICSC* has the authority to take decisions of its own which are binding on those organizations that have accepted its statute.

Criticism has been voiced that the Common System lumps all organizations indiscriminately together, and does not pay due regard to the variety of their tasks, programmes and methods of work. The General Assembly has repeatedly prevented organizations from going their own way (e.g. → *ILO*, → *ITU* and → *WIPO*), and has consistently emphasized that the integrity of the Common System, and coherence of conditions of employment, must be maintained. The Common System also includes a Pension Fund, and two Administrative Tribunals for legal action by the staff against administrative decisions – one at the United Nations in New York (*UNAT*) and one at the *ILO* in Geneva (*ILOAT*). The *ACC* has established a Consultative Committee on Personnel and Administrative Questions (*CCAQ/PER*), which collectively represents the participating organizations within the Common System and before the *ICSC*. Staff representatives, too, have their system-wide umbrella organizations (*FICSA* and *CCISUA*) to represent their interests within the Common System.

On the one hand, it is recognized that the → universality of its membership is the most important strength of the United Nations, while, on the other, it is evident that the large number of sovereign member states renders the decision-taking process in the governing bodies more difficult. For this reason a variety of inter-governmental groupings and informal decision-making processes have evolved, which foster the early reconciliation of diverging interests (→ Groups and Groupings in the UN). The informal decision-making processes include drafting and contact groups as well as "friends of the chair" which, for instance, assist in the negotiation of draft resolutions by seeking common ground for bridging the diverging positions, and arriving at a basis for a generally acceptable compromise. The decision-making capacity of governing bodies would have been severely hampered without these flexible negotiation mechanisms because of the diverging na-

tional interests, the overloaded agendas and the increased membership.

An important role in the inter-governmental coordination is played by groupings of member states reflecting common political, economic or geographical interests, with sometimes overlapping membership. The five → Regional Groups usually decide on the filling of offices, or the election of members in the main and subsidiary organs (→ Principal Organs, Subsidiary Organs, Treaty Bodies). In the Non-Aligned Movement and in the "Group of 77," developing countries have given themselves instruments to further their political, economic and social interests, and to take advantage of their negotiating capacity in all important questions. During the Cold War and the North-South Conflict in the seventies and eighties, the "Group of 77" exercised considerable influence and could achieve some successes since it enjoyed (with the support of socialist states) an "automatic majority" in the General Assembly. Due to the changed international situation its influence has, however, diminished, and a new pragmatism is also recognizable within this grouping.

There is no equivalent on the part of the industrialized countries to the Non-Aligned Movement and the "Group of 77". Political coordination takes place among like-minded states or countries within the same geographical region (for instance, Nordic States). The European Union (→ European Union, CFSP at the UN) takes increasingly uniform positions in the United Nations and also presents them with one voice in the governing bodies. All industrialized countries contributing more than 1% to the budget of the United Nations work together in the informal "Geneva Group" (→ Geneva Group), and their combined financial shares gives their positions special weight. The focus of this Group, however, is mainly on questions of administrative efficiency, cost control, budgetary performance and human resources management. It does not put up an externally united front, however, but relies on its members to reflect the agreed positions in the respective governing bodies, either individually or through any of the other groupings.

Overall, the inter-governmental coordination mainly serves the purpose of reconciling diverging interests and national positions of member states. An effective coordination of the activities of the various components of the UN system is hardly possible without cooperation between the governing bodies of the individual organizations, which currently does not exist.

3. Coordination between Organizations (Inter-Agency Coordination)

Coordination between the Secretariats of the United Nations and the specialized agencies, even though it has been provided for in the related agreements, takes place on a voluntary basis since each organization – under the supervision of its own governing body – has full authority over its programmes and funds. The specialized agencies, as a rule, defend their independence vehemently, and collaboration will only be pursued where it is in the interest of all parties concerned. While overlapping is almost excluded in the narrowly defined technical fields such as atomic energy, intellectual property and civil aviation, there is competition for mandates and funds in the broad sector of economic and social development. At the same time, the UN system shows gaps, for instance, in the energy and technology sectors. The 1997 reform programme of the Secretary-General, therefore, concludes that a much greater degree of concerted will and coordinated action is required throughout the system as a whole, if the objectives of the United Nations are to be fully realized.

The main coordinating body within the UN system at the level of the Secretariats is the *Administrative Committee on Coordination (ACC)*, which was established in 1946 by a resolution of the *ECOSOC*. It consists of the Secretary-General of the United Nations as chairman and the directors general of the specialized agencies, the other independent organizations and the associated relief agencies, programmes and funds. The World Bank (→ World Bank, World Bank Group) and the International Monetary Fund (→ IMF) are also members. The *ACC* is supposed to monitor the implementation of the relationship agreements, coordinate the programmes approved by the governing bodies of the various organizations and, more generally, promote collaboration within the UN system.

Since the Committee only meets twice a year for two days each, it serves in the first instance as a forum for the exchange of views between the Secretary-General and the Directors-General as well as for the preparation of statements on acute issues and for giving directives to its sub-committees. The Secretary-General, as chairman, has the position of a "first among equals" (*primus inter pares*); and the largely independent Directors General, who as elected officials are only answerable to their own governing bodies, will in case of a conflict between system-wide and organization-specific interests – understandably – heed the latter. Critics have, therefore, exaggeratedly compared his position to that of a conductor to whom the orchestra pays minimum heed (*Childers/Urquhart* 1994, 32). The members of the *ACC* are called upon to maintain a continuous dialogue in order to identify possibilities for collaboration in the planning phase, and to respond more quickly to changing circumstances.

The Secretary-General, in his 1997 reform programme, stated the objective of strengthening the capacity of the *ACC* in order to adapt the UN system as a whole to the new challenges, and to rationalize the division of labor within existing structures. There is general agreement among the members of the *ACC* that the UN systems must show a much higher degree of unity of purpose and coherence of action. The ACC establishes, therefore, priorities for joint action in concrete situations or on specific issues, such as peace and development in Africa, to which each organization contributes in accordance with its own functional competence. For specific tasks, such as the promotion of → human rights, or the reduction of poverty, partnerships are to be formed between the various UN organizations and non-governmental organizations. Specific problems are to be addressed by all organizations that have the necessary capacity and competence, agreeing jointly on the actions to be taken under the leadership of a "lead agency". One priority item for joint efforts in inter-agency coordination is the follow-up on the measures adopted at major UN conferences.

An *Organizational Committee (OC)* assists the *ACC* with its work and in steering its sub-committees. In addition, there are sub-committees for administrative questions (*CCAQ*), programme and operational questions (*CCPOQ*), sustainable development (*IACSD*) and women issues (*IACWGE*), which in turn have their own subsidiary structures. The *ACC* and *OC* receive administrative support from an organizational unit in the UN Secretariat, the Office of Inter-Agency Affairs which, in addition, is expected to promote consultations and a continuous exchange of information within the UN system. Some of the sub-committees have their own small secretariats, mostly located in Geneva.

The so-called *Resident Coordinators* play a special role within the framework for coordination at the country level. All premises of the United Nations, including the Information Offices and the associated relief agencies, programmes and funds, will be accommodated in one "UN House" and, under the leadership of the Resident Coordinator, are to represent the United Nations in a unified manner to the outside world. The specialized agencies have been called upon to participate in the unified country representation. This should ensure that the various activities of the UN system at the country level are closely linked with each other as well as with national priorities, and that country development programmes receive better support. The Resident Coordinators are also responsible for following-up, in consultation with the governments concerned, the measures agreed upon at major international conferences. The system of unified country representation through the Resident Coordinators is being financed and managed by the → *UNDP*. The objective of the new Staff College for the UN in Turin is also the promotion of coherence and coordination in the UN system, by means of inter-disciplinary and inter-sectoral training courses.

Overall, the awareness of the necessity for a better division of labor in the UN system has increased, and coordination efforts have been intensified at all levels. However, coordination is not an end in itself, but serves different purposes such as standardization, rationalization and determination of priorities. Coordination within the UN system is subject to marked limitations which are inherent in the system. All coordination efforts, even if pursued with the greatest energy, will at best meet with limited success, because it is impossible to form a monolith from a deliberately fragmented shape.

4. Delivering as One

The high degree of differentiation of the UN System in its mandates and structures has remained unabated, and there have been no serious attempts by member states to increase the unity of purpose and coherence of work through a comprehensive review of the various components. The World Summit of 2005 did not fail to recognize the need for better coordination and identified in its outcome document a number of steps that need to be taken in order to strengthen the work of the UN System, including the following:

- A review of all mandates older than five years originating from resolutions of the General Assembly and other organs;
- Coordinating the representation of member states on the governing boards of the various development and humanitarian agencies so as to ensure that they pursue a coherent policy in assigning mandates and allocating resources throughout the system;

- Ensuring that the main horizontal policy themes, such as sustainable development, human rights and gender, are taken into account in decision-making throughout the United Nations;
- Implementing current reforms aimed at a more effective, efficient, coherent, coordinated and better-performing United Nations country presence with a strengthened role for the senior resident official;
- Exploring the possibility of a more coherent institutional framework to address the need for better integration of environmental activities in the broader sustainable development, including a more integrated structure, building on existing institutions and internationally agreed instruments, as well as the treaty bodies and the specialized agencies. (*United Nations* 2005)

These and other steps that were identified in the outcome document do not go, in essence, beyond a declaration of support for stronger system-wide coherence. There is almost a note of resignation in the statement which pays tribute to the diversity of the UN System: "We recognize that the United Nations brings together a unique wealth of expertise and resources on global issues. We commend the extensive experience and expertise of the various development-related organizations, agencies, funds and programmes of the United Nations system in their diverse and complementary fields of activity and their important contributions to the achievement of the Millennium Development Goals and the other development objectives established by various United Nations conferences." (*United Nations* 2005, para. 168). In spite of various declarations, there is no political will to tackle seriously the issues of fragmented structures, overlapping mandates, scattered resources and insufficient intra-state and inter-governmental coordination in any fundamental way.

However, in operational activities at the country level more progress has been made. The impetus came from a High-level Panel on United Nations System-wide Coherence in the areas of development, humanitarian assistance and the environment, which the outgoing Secretary-General, Kofi Annan, had established in 2006 in response to a request made in the outcome document of the 2005 World Summit (UN Doc. A/RES/60/1 of 16 September 2005, para. 168 and 169). The Panel included three serving prime ministers (from Pakistan, Mozambique and Norway) as well as other high-ranking holders of government offices in member states (including the current Prime Minister of the UK, Gordon Brown, then Chancellor of the Exchequer). The Panel's report, entitled "Delivering as one", which was presented on 20 November 2006 (UN Doc. A/61/583), recommended in the area of development "One United Nations" at the country level that has full country ownership, and is supported by a strengthened and more consolidated funding structure to substantially increase the effectiveness of United Nations interventions. The proposals encompass a framework for a unified and coherent United Nations structure at country level to be matched by more coherent governance, funding and management arrangements.

Since then "Once Country" programmes are being developed in countries, wherever possible, by Country Teams under the leadership of UNDP and within a United Nations Development Assistance Framework (UNDAF). This constitutes the collective response of all UN organizations operating within a specific country to the priorities of the national development plans and the Millennium Development Goals.

The main coordinating body within the UN System at the level of the Secretariats, the *Administrative Committee on Coordination (ACC)*, was renamed *Chief Executive Board for Coordination (CEB)* and its subsidiary machinery was restructured in 2000-2001. It brings together on a regular basis the executive heads of the organizations of the United Nations system, under the chairmanship of the Secretary-General of the United Nations to further coordination and cooperation on a whole range of substantive and management issues facing United Nations system organizations. In addition to its regular reviews of contemporary political issues and major concerns facing the UN system, CEB approves policy statements on behalf of the UN system as a whole on the basis of recommendations from bodies reporting to it.

The support structure that had been established for the old ACC has been revamped. CEB is now supported by two high-level committees (usually at the level of deputy secretaries/directors-general) – one responsible for substantive programme areas (*High-level Committee on Programmes – HLCP*) and the other for the strategic management of the organizations (*High-level Committee on Management – HLCM*). The numerous sub-committees and working groups dealing with specific subject-matters such as human resources management, financial matters, IT, security and others have been formally dissolved in an attempt to streamline the coordinating machinery. However, the dissolved sub-committees have meanwhile reappeared in the form of '*Networks*' – there is a "Finance and Budget Network" for instance – since there is a genuine need for collaboration among the professionals of the various substantive areas. (cf. for details about the current inter-agency coordination machinery: www.unsystem ceb.org)

The latest addition is a *United Nations Evaluation Group (UNEG)* which is the professional consultative framework for development of evaluation policies, standards and methodologies and the promotion of transparency, accountability and learning in the UN System. It is currently engaged in performing an independent evaluation of the initiatives by UN Country Teams to "Deliver as One", to which member states attach high importance.

All in all, these changes appear to be more cosmetic than substantive and do not signify a leap in inter-agency coordination. The CEB continues to meet twice a year for a few days which are devoted to the exchange of views on relevant developments and endorsing papers submitted by the subsidiary machinery. Its members represent the interests of their own organizations, and the Secretary-General of the UN, who chairs the meetings, does not have any specific competences except his authority as Chief Administrative Officer of the largest organization of the UN System.

Dieter Göthel

Lit.: *Childers, E./Urquhart, B.:* Renewing the United Nations System, Uppsala 1994; *Dicke, K.:* Effizienz und Effektivität internationaler Organisationen, Berlin 1994; *Dicke, K.;* Decentralization, in: Wolfrum, R. (ed.): United Nations: Law, Policies and Practice, Vol. 1, Munich/Dordrecht 1995, 380-389; *Göthel, D.:* Die Vereinten Nationen: Eine Innenansicht, Bonn 1995; *Renninger, J.P.:* Can the Common System be Maintained? UNITAR, New York 1986; *Puchala, D.J./Coate, R.:* The Challenge of Relevance: The United Nations in a Changing World Environment, Hanover 1989; *Tassin, J.:* Administrative Coordination in the United Nations Family, in: Cooker, C. de (ed.): International Administration, The Hague 1990; *United Nations:* Renewing the United Nations: A Programme for Reform. Report of the Secretary-General, UN Doc. A/51/950, 14 July 1997; *United Nations - General Assembly:* 2005 World Summit Outcome. Resolution adopted by the General Assembly, UN Doc. A/RES/60/1, 16 September 2005 (quoted as United Nations 2005); *United Nations - General Assembly:* Delivering as one. Report of the High-level Panel on United Nations System-wide Coherence in the areas of development, humanitarian assistance and the environment, 20 November 2006, UN Doc. A/61/583; *United Nations - General Assembly:* Recommendations contained in the report of the High-level Panel on United Nations System-wide Coherence in the areas of development, humanitarian assistance and the environment. Report of the Secretary-General, 3 April 2007, UN Doc. A/61/836.

Internet: Homepage of the ACC: http://ceb.unsystem.org; Website of the Department of Economic and Social Affairs on policy coordination: www.un.org/esa/coordination/dpcb.htm; Homepage of the United Nations System Chief Executives Board for Coordination (CEB): http://unsystemceb.org;

Homepage of the United Nations Evaluation Group (UNEG): www.uneval.org.

CSD – Commission on Sustainable Development

The Commission on Sustainable Development (CSD) was established in 1992 at the "Earth Summit", the UN Conference on Environment and Development (UNCED) in Rio de Janeiro.

"Agenda 21", as the "Programme of Action on Sustainable Development" agreed in Rio was called, stated the rationale for the CSD this way: "In order to ensure the effective follow-up of the Conference, as well as to enhance international cooperation and rationalize the intergovernmental decision-making capacity for the integration of environment and development issues and to examine the progress in the implementation of Agenda 21 at the national, regional and international levels, a high-level Commission on Sustainable Development should be established in accordance with Article 68 of the Charter of the United Nations." (Agenda 21, chapter 38, para. 11) The 47th regular session of the General Assembly in 1992 decided to establish the CSD (UN Doc. A/RES/47/191 of 22 December 1992).

In formal terms, the CSD is one of the nine functional commissions of the Economic and Social Council (→ ECOSOC), not to be confused with the Commission on Social Development. Its main *task* is to monitor the *national and international implementation of the decisions of Agenda 21 concerning environment and development*, and to formulate recommendations for further implementation by governments and the UN.

When the UN secretariat was restructured after the Rio conference, a new Department for Policy Coordination and Sustainable Development (DPCSD) was set up. DPCSD was merged in 1997 – on the basis of General Assembly Resolution 50/227 of 24 May 1996 – with the Department of Economic and Social Information and Policy Analysis and the Department of Development Support and Management Services into the new Department of Economic and Social Affairs (DESA), headed currently (2008) by Under-Secretary-General Sha Zukang. One branch of DESA is the *Division for Sustainable Development* (www.un.org/esa/sustdev/) that functions as the CSD secretariat.

The CSD meets once a year at the UN Headquarters in New York, usually in April or May. It is clearly impossible to come even close to dealing with the whole of Agenda 21's 40 chapters. Therefore the Commission focuses on a few selected issues, agreed in a 15-year programme of work at the World Summit for Sustainable Development (WSSD) in Johannesburg in 2002 (UN Commission on Sustainable Development, Report on the eleventh session 2003, UN Doc. E/CN.17/2003/6). Every CSD session includes a two-three day High-level Segment where Ministers (usually those responsible for the environment or the session's key theme) participate.

The CSD has 53 members (13 from Africa, 11 from Asia, 10 from Latin America and the Caribbean, 6 from Eastern Europe, 13 from West Europe and other states). The members are elected for three-year terms. However, any other state can participate as an observer (→ Observer Status); except for the right to have representatives elected to official functions, they enjoy the same privileges as the members. The Chair is elected for one year, at the end of each session so that he or she can assume responsibility for the whole year of preparations.

Usually the CSD decides by consensus, the main players being the EU and the G77, while the participation of the United States is taking place on a rather low level. The consensus culture of the CSD collapsed completely at the CSD-15 in 2007. The main theme of energy is a highly controversial theme anyway, but this was exacerbated by the chairman from an OPEC country (Qatar) and additional politicization by a number of countries in the run-up to the Bali Climate Conference. On top of that came the nomination of Zimbabwe by the African group as chair for CSD-16 which was strongly opposed by the EU and many other countries. CSD-15 ended with no agreement on a negotiated text, and for the first time there was a vote on the next chair: Zimbabwe's environment minister Nhema was only narrowly elected (cf. documents of CSD-15: www. un.org/esa/sustdev/documents/docs_csd15 .htm).

Apart from this spectacular event, the CSD has slowly become increasingly less relevant in the context of the many fora where sustainable development issues are negotiated on the global level. The CSD of course cannot issue binding decisions, and its decisions and initiatives only rarely break new ground. However, to avoid becoming irrelevant it needs to be innovative and not merely repeat agreed language. The reason is not only the consensus principle, but also the fact that most delegations are in fact composed primarily, if not exclusively, of officials from the New York permanent missions rather than of experts on the issues they are discussing. The observation that the CSD has so little impact occasionally prompted CSD chairs to try to change this state of affairs. In 1999 New Zealand's environment minister Simon Upton, as CSD chair, tried to breathe some life into the boring ritual of endless prepared ministerial speeches, by interactive dialogues between ministers and even so-called major groups (non-governmental actors as defined in Agenda 21). Initiatives like this generally can help, but the underlying problem is the lack of commitment, if so few officials committed to the issues are participating and so many professional diplomats, who participate in this commission as they might in any other UN commission.

Another basic problem of the CSD's setup is that in many nations it is considered primarily a domain of the environment ministers, while many of the issues discussed at the CSD actually are beyond their competence: agriculture, energy, trade, forests, etc. Thus the CSD

sometimes is essentially a commission where environment ministers urge their colleagues in other ministries to do something, which is not a very promising endeavor when these other ministers have not been part of the deliberations.

The CSD differs from other UN commissions also by giving non-governmental actors (→ NGOs) more participatory rights, a legacy from Rio. Agenda 21 has established nine so-called major groups (business and industry, children and youth, farmers, indigenous people, local authorities, NGOs, scientific and technological community, women, workers and trade unions) which have been established as key groups to implement the Rio decisions. These participatory rights are also a feature of other intergovernmental processes established in Rio or its follow-up. Even if this may have little influence over the actual content of its decisions, it at least provides the CSD with more attention outside the confines of the UN headquarters than most other UN commissions.

Jürgen Maier

Internet: Homepage of CSD: www.un.org/ esa/sustdev/csd/csd.htm; www.forum-ue.de/ 16.0.html; www.iisd.ca/process/sustdevt.htm.

Decolonization

750 million people were living in non-sovereign states (→ Sovereignty) when the UN was founded in 1945. If decolonization is defined as the achievement of independence of formerly non-self governing territories, this process has today nearly been completed.

The UN was not a major player in this development, although the UN Charter (→ Charter of the UN) laid down a basic principle of international law for decolonization with the right of self-determination of peoples (Art. 1 and 55 UN Charter) (→ Self-Determination, Right of). The UN Charter created the UN Trusteeship System (Art. 75-91 UN Charter) to realize this goal (→ Trustee-

ship Council). The Trusteeship System applied to
- territories held under mandates established by the → League of Nations after the First World War;
- territories detached from "enemy states" (cf. → Enemy State Clauses) as a result of the Second World War;
- territories voluntarily placed under the Trusteeship System by states responsible for their administration.

However, only the territories of the first and second group were included in the international Trusteeship System, altogether 11 territories. Due to this restriction, the Trusteeship Council could not play a major role in the process of decolonization.

All territories falling under the Trusteeship System have either become independent or voluntarily associated themselves with a state (*United Nations 2000*, 275ff.)

The victorious powers and former colonial powers opposed the inclusion of all the other "dependent territories" under the Trusteeship System. The majority of colonies were thus covered by only two Articles within the UN Charter (Chapter XI).

Article 73 required the colonial powers "to ensure, with due respect for the culture of the peoples concerned, their political, economic, social, and educational advancement, their just treatment, and their protection against abuses" and "to develop self-government, to take due account of the political aspirations of the peoples, and to assist them in the progressive development of their free political institutions". Article 73 also required that those powers having or assuming such responsibilities should "transmit regularly to the Secretary-General for information purposes, subject to such limitation as security and constitutional considerations may require, statistical and other information of a technical nature relating to economic, social, and educational conditions in the territories for which they are respectively responsible other than those territories to which Chapters XII and XIII apply".

Nevertheless, the UN stated explicitly during the seventies that decolonization was to be a focal point of their activities. One of the Main Committees of the General Assembly (→ Committees, System of), the Fourth Committee, was devoted until 1993 exclusively to the problems of decolonization, in 1993 the General Assembly decided to merge the Special Political Committee with the Fourth Committee, which since then has the name "Special Political and Decolonization Committee", i.e. has still decolonization as one of its main fields of activity.

The UN influenced the process as a rule not directly, but perhaps more importantly by the process of "decolonization with resolutions". In this connection a prominent role was played by the → General Assembly, which asked the community of nations several times to translate the right of self-determination and decolonization into action without conditions. The UN has thus been a forum for the concept of self-determination and for the newly evolving states. In this process General Assembly Resolution 1514 (XV), adopted on 14 December 1960, has been a milestone: The "Declaration on the Granting of Independence to Colonial Countries and Peoples" led in 1961 to the establishment of a Special Committee, the *Special Committee on the Situation with Regard to the Implementation of the Declaration on the Granting of Independence to Colonial Countries and Peoples*, commonly referred to as the *Special Committee of 24 on Decolonization.*

In some cases (for example Somalia or Indonesia), the UN played an active role in the process of a peaceful decolonization.

But the UN had no influence on whether the decolonization was effected by a war of liberation or by negotiations: "The UN was only brought into play when a peaceful decolonization failed as in the former Congo; the UN was called in when some part of the world caught fire – but they could rarely put out the fire, because those who were responsible for the fire in the first place denied the UN adequate means to fight it" (*Nuscheler* 1981, 197).

The first phase of decolonization had already been finished when the UN was founded. North and South America were already independent. Only the second phase, the decolonization of Africa and Asia, took place after the creation of the UN (cf. → History of the UN).

At present (March 2001), the Special Committee of 24 on Decolonization is concerned with 17 remaining territories listed as non-self-governing territories by the General Assembly (mostly small island states).

To mention two prominent examples of the territories on the list: the decolonization of the Western Sahara and of East Timor is taking place at present under strong involvement of the UN in the form of two peacekeeping missions (the United Nations Mission for the Referendum in Western Sahara MINURSO and the United Nations Transitional Administration in East Timor (UNTAET); cf. → Peacekeeping), but are still marked by severe conflicts among the concerned conflict partners.

The collapse of the former Soviet Union, and the creation of the Commonwealth of Independent States (CIS) occurred outside the UN system, which limited in practice the term "colony" to overseas territories.

Decolonization has brought major changes to the UN: at the end of the most important phase of decolonization (about the year 1975), the UN counted 144 member states (→ Membership and Representation of States). In the General Assembly the states of Africa, Asia and Latin America now held the majority. This group of countries initiated in the General Assembly new topics and fields of activity for the UN (cf. → Group of 77 and the UN; → Non-Aligned Movement and the UN). In the seventies an intense discussion of the economic dimension of self-determination, and an extended concept of sovereignty, which included the problems of economic dependence, were direct results of these changes (→ International Economic Re-

lations and New International Economic Order (NIEO); → North-South Relations and the UN).

The United Nations still keeps the problems of decolonization on its agenda: It declared in 1988 (UN Doc A/RES/43/47 of 22 November 1988) the decade 1990-2000 to the "International Decade for the Eradication of Colonialism" and declared in 2001 the decade 2001-2010 to the "Second International Decade for the Eradication of Colonialism" (UN Doc A/RES/55/146 of 6 March 2001). With reference to the work of the Special Committee of 24 on Decolonization and the remaining non-self-governing territories the UN Secretary-General Kofi Annan stated at the opening of the 2001 session of the latter: "The activities of the Committee ensure that the issue of decolonization remains firmly on the agenda of the Organization. We have yet to see full implementation of the objectives of the 1960 Declaration on the Granting of Independence to Colonial Countries and Peoples."

Heike Henn

Lit.: *El-Ayouty, Y.:* The United Nations and Decolonization: the Role of Afro-Asia, The Hague 1971; *El-Ayouty, Y.:* Der historische Imperativ der Entkolonialisierung, in: VN 33 (1985), 170-173; *Bleckmann, A.:* Decolonization, in: Bernhardt, R. (ed.): EPIL 10 (1987), 75-79; *Kunig, P.:* Decolonization, in: Wolfrum, R. (ed.): United Nations: Law, Policies and Practice, Vol. 1, Munich/Dordrecht 1995, 390-397; *Nuscheler, F.:* Die Entkolonialisiserungsbilanz der Vereinten Nationen, in: VN 29 (1981), 195-199; *Schümperli, W.:* Die Vereinten Nationen und die Dekolonisation, Berne 1970; *United Nations - Department of Public Information:* Basic Facts About the United Nations, DPI/2155, New York 2000.

Addendum

As is pointed out in the above entry on decolonization many state or potential state representatives were most concerned to end colonialism (decolonization) both by agreeing a suitable United Nations Charter and building appropriate

Third World groupings to help ensure the colonial demise. Hedley Bull argues (*Bull/Watson* 1984, 220-223) that the revolt against the West (the dominators) by the South (the dominated) comprised a struggle for equal sovereignty with the West; against colonialism; for racial equality; for economic justice and finally for cultural liberation. He goes on to suggest (*Bull/Watson* 1984, 224-228), that the subsequent collapse old Western-dominated order was brought about by five factors: the psychological or spiritual awakening of non-Western peoples; the weakening of the will of Western powers to maintain their dominant position; the impact of the Bolshevik revolution and the rise of the Soviet Union as a major power; the existence of a more general equilibrium of power; and finally the transformation of the legal and moral climate of international relations brought about by Third World groupings (the Afro-Asian movement; the Non-Aligned and the Group of 77).

The Fourth Committee of the GA (since 1993: Special Political and De-colonization Committee) produced ten draft resolutions on decolonization and a further 14 on other Fourth Committee issues. They were adopted in plenary in December 2006. These included a draft resolution by which the Assembly would request the administering Powers to transmit or continue to transmit the information prescribed in Article 73(e) of the Charter (UN Doc. A/RES/61/122). France, Israel, United Kingdom and United States were the only four states to abstain. The report on the "Implementation of the Declaration on the Granting of Independence to Colonial Countries and Peoples" of 6 October 2006 (UN Doc. A/61/415) suggested six draft resolutions and a decision. These included draft resolutions on Western Sahara, New Caledonia, Tokelau, and together American Samoa, Anguilla, Bermuda, British Virgin Islands, Cayman Islands, Guam, Montserrat, Pitcairn, Saint Helena, Turks and Caicos Islands and the United States Virgin Islands. This latter draft was passed by 173 to 4 against including Israel and

United States. The draft decision was on Gibraltar.

The range of material relating to de-colonization and discussed elsewhere in the UN remains large. Many other General Assembly resolutions are often involved. General Assembly resolution 61/127 (adopted without a vote) on Tokelau, for instance, recalls that New Zealand and Tokelau signed a document in November 2003 entitled "Joint statement of the principles of partnership", setting out in writing, for the first time, the rights and obligations of the two partner countries. The resolution rightly noted that "Tokelau has wider significance for the United Nations as it seeks to complete its work on decolonization." The February 2006 referendum on these issues failed by a narrow margin to produce the two-thirds majority of the valid votes cast. This project, nevertheless, may well pay dividends in the future for Tokelau and other island territories. The referendum package has been maintained.

The difficult process of finding an answer to a range of decolonization problems can be examined in the context of the Western Sahara. General Assembly resolution A/RES/61/125 of 14 December 2006 on Western Sahara was passed by a recorded vote of 70 in favor to none against with 91 abstentions. (The year before a resolution on the same topic had been adopted by consensus.) Germany and the United Kingdom voted for with Algeria, one of the main contenders. Morocco, the other, abstained with Egypt, France, Israel, Spain and United States.

One further issue is the Falkland Islands (Malvinas) dispute. The Special Committee on Decolonization, in a resolution passed in June 2007 (UN Doc. A/AC.109/2007/L.8), expressed regret that implementation of General Assembly resolutions aimed at peacefully ending the dispute had not yet begun. The issue, of course for Argentina, revolves around the question of its territorial integrity and not that of self-determination.

Decolonization remains a challenging and important issue in the United Nations.

Sally Morphet

Lit: *Bull, H./Watson, A. (eds.):* The Expansion of International Society, Oxford 1984.

Internet: 1) Homepage of the Special Political and Decolonization Committee (Fourth Committee) of the UN General Assembly: www.un.org/ga/56/fourth; 2) Website of the United Nations on decolonization (information on history, the Special Committee of 24, the Trusteeship System and Council and documents on decolonization: www.un.org/Depts/dpi/decolonization/main. htm; list of non-self-governing territories: www.un.org/Depts/dpi/decolonization/ trust3.htm.

Democratization and the UN

Since the end of the socialist bloc under the leadership of the Soviet Union, the concept of democratization appears to have won virtually universal support and acceptance as a political programme. In a technically and procedurally restrained way the term is often used – against traditions of extremely one-sided, authoritarian balances of power – to refer to the political and organizational initiation and preparation, implementation and control of a general, equal and secret vote for competing candidates or parties at the national and communal level. In a more generalized functional sense, the concept of democratization refers to processes of institution building (for example, an independent judiciary system, a controlled police apparatus, independent and responsible mass media), and certain changes in the value commitments internalized by the inhabitants of the countries concerned (increased tolerance of pluralism and commitment to democratic procedures). Such changes take a number of years, if not decades to become effective.

A relatively new phenomenon is that the UN has been asked to provide technical assistance for democratization efforts, about 70 times since the end of the eighties.

Another dimension of the current debate about democratization is that there are the conflict-prone links and interdependencies between democratization processes at the local and national level on the one hand, and the global level of humanity as a whole, on the other.

This article outlines major trends and benchmarks in the development of the debate about democratization in the UN context since 1945. Seen from a general social science perspective, these developments in recent decades are not a novel phenomenon, but the contemporary version of a belated socio-political adaptation to the barely perceived and little understood secular dynamics of integration of world society, or the capitalist world system, respectively.

1) From the Founding of the UNO (1945) to the Climax of the Vietnam War (1972)

The terms democracy or democratization were never employed in the Charter of the United Nations Organization ($\rightarrow$ Charter of the UN). At those times these terms were too precise, too controversial, and too American to be declared as a shared long-term programmatic vision, let alone a common characterization of the aspirations of the 51 small and big states of the anti-fascist war alliance. Nevertheless, the terms and concepts used and the procedural rules set forth in the Charter of the UN clearly reflect central ideological premises of the philosophy of the enlightenment and parliamentary democracy. Typically, the respect for human rights and basic freedoms for all, without distinction of race, gender, language and religion is not only referred to, but are to be furthered and enhanced (cf. as examples Articles 1 and 2 of the Charter). Similarly, the principle of the sovereign equality of member states is interpreted in parallel to the concept of equal rights of enfranchised citizens, and is procedurally translated into the active and passive voting rights of member states of the organization (1 citizen/1 state = 1 vote).

In principle, the overall political competence is accorded to the → General Assembly of the member states/citizens as the highest legitimate sovereign, in particular, the competence to deliberate on the budget and, finally, to enact it with a qualified majority.

The criteria for the individual budget contributions (→ Budget) of the member states are set by the collective sovereign, the General Assembly. The Charter provides that the political weight of the vote of member states – big or small, poor or rich – is equal, with the collective sovereign deciding on the criteria affecting the assessment scale of contributions, essentially criteria of absolute and relative economic performance and power. Formally, all political decisions in the → UN system require a (qualified) majority of votes of the member states duly participating in the various bodies (→ Voting Right and Decision-Making Procedures). This majority principle is a pervasive organizational and procedural characteristic of all → specialized agencies and all programmes of the UN system. Prominent exceptions to the rule are the → Security Council with the veto right (→ Veto, Right of Veto) of the five major World War II allies, and the Bretton Woods institutions, which weigh the votes according to the very unequal capital-shares held by the member states (→ World Bank, World Bank Group; → IMF). The qualified majority needed for valid decisions of the Security Council requires nine votes (seven before its enlargement from 12 to 15 member states in 1965), provided that none of the five permanent members casts a veto. In the case of the Bretton Woods institutions, the principle of linking the political weight of the votes of member states to their ownership of capital-shares held implies that the handful of the economically most powerful member states commands a blocking minority, or even the majority of votes.

It is important to remember that for quite a number of years subsequent to the founding of the UN system:

- there was no contemporary body of universally accepted principles of (let alone conventions on) human rights and basic freedoms, beyond the more or less diffuse bourgeois and socialist lines of interpretation and articulation of these values in the western tradition;
- very large parts of the South were colonies and protectorates of Western/European empires; the Charter only mentioned them in a rather summary way in the perspective of enhancing their welfare on the way to self-government (but not → decolonization).

After 1947, however, all parts of the world rapidly became involved in the dynamics of the East-West confrontation which was part and parcel of the series of crises, upheavals and wars of the decolonization movement which rapidly gained in worldwide momentum. This led very quickly to a pronounced marginalization of the UN system because the main protagonists of the East-West confrontation shifted the bulk of their political attention and efforts to the creation of and increasing support for regional, bloc-based political, military and economic alliances.

Still, the UN and its specialized organizations remained to serve as a much appreciated stage for symbolic politics: for the – initially – minority of socialist and young Third World countries to present and fight for their minority positions, for the West (and especially, the USA) because it was still in command of the majority of votes (with the support of the Latin American countries until the end of the 50s, the so-called American rubber-stamp machine).

In addition, it had become evident that the administrations of the various bodies of the UN system had acquired technical competence in a wide array of issues and domains of international cooperation, in combination with a procedural and logistical infrastructure for the mobilization of multilateral expertise, negotiations and diplomacy.

The patient, conflict-ridden and protracted efforts to spell out and specify → human rights proved to be a very important domain of work, from the first step (1948) of the Universal Declaration of Human Rights (→ Human Rights, Universal Declaration of), hardly noticed at the time of its proclamation, to the International Covenants on Civil and Political Rights (CCPR) and on Economic, Social and Cultural Rights (CESCR) in 1966 and a large number of other, specific human rights conventions (→ Human Rights Conventions, CCPR; → Human Rights Conventions, CESCR; → Human Rights Conventions and their Measures of Implementation; → Human Rights, Protection of).

Another important field of work of the UN system, rapidly becoming ever more complex in the 1950s, was the emergence of a scientific-statistical competence to describe and analyze a multitude of functionally specific, yet interdependent world problems and the creation of administrative capacities to handle corresponding projects of technical assistance and cooperation (→ Development Cooperation of the UN System).

The admission of a large number of decolonized young states to the UN and to the specialized agencies between 1959 and 1965 (→ Membership and Representation of States) led structurally to a "new" UN system, with a majority of states and votes belonging to the South. Thus, the question arose to what extent the North (more particularly, the West, or, parts of the West) would be willing to accept the priorities of the South, at least in those domains of development policies not directly linked to wars and major political crises.

Many liberal Western political scientists and (international) lawyers believed (or, hoped, together with many of their colleagues from the South) that the West would have to respond favorably to that challenge, since the very rules of the democratic North were at stake. Very soon, however, it became evident that such expectations would constantly and consistently be frustrated: *de facto*, the West (under the leadership of the hegemonic power) would rescind all majority mechanisms in international (treaty) law, though the respective pro-

visions were never formally changed or declared obsolete. Thus, the provisions of qualified majorities voting on the regular → budget of the UN and the specialized organizations (thereby approving enlarged and diversified programs and measures to be financed via the assessment scale for compulsory financial contributions) were *de facto* changed to a mandatory regime of "consensus", thereby establishing and procedurally covering up the financial veto power of a handful of big contributor states.

In a similar way, the debates of the late fifties/early sixties about world taxes or world duties to finance UN development activities (in a sense functional equivalents for scales based on economic criteria to determine the compulsory budget contributions) were soon blocked and declared impractical by the donor community. The reticence of the rich states to accept any binding rules and commitments concerning the financing of world public goods and services was politically sold by administering the sweet pill of promises of voluntary contributions (preferably, not in the form of (lost) subsidies via the normal UN system, but as repayable loans at preferential conditions via the International Development Agency (IDA) of the World Bank).

The rapidly increasing involvement of the USA in the Vietnam War after 1965 did much to enhance and radicalize the position of the hegemonic power on these issues and options. In spite of the critical distance of most of the other western states towards the US policies in the Vietnam War and in development policies at large, they shared most of the basic premises of the hegemonic power (the least so being the Scandinavian countries, the Netherlands and Canada).

2) From the Oil Crisis to the End of the Socialist Bloc (1989)

With regard to the UN system and its role in world politics the "political macro-climate" of the 1970s was a continuation of the lines of conflict and the configuration of political forces as they had evolved by the second half of the 1960s: the South offensively claimed (but did not achieve) a restructuring of North-South relations in the form of a New International Economic Order (NIEO), enhanced by the success of OPEC policies (→ North-South Relations and the UN; → International Economic Relations and New International Economic Order (NIEO)). The Western industrialized countries continued to follow their defensive policies of very restricted cooperation, with the self-esteem of the USA seriously shaken by the internal strife related to the Vietnam War and its humiliating end (1973/1975).

The "political macro-climate" deteriorated seriously in the last phase of East-West confrontation and the reinvigorated arms race during the first half of the 1980s. Part of the reassertion of the hegemonic position of the USA under President Reagan was a marked shift of US policies vis-à-vis the UN system, consisting of a generalized downgrading of support for the UN system, essentially continuing up to the present (→ UN Policy, USA). While the other Western countries did not join the USA in its radical realignment of their policies, they were not willing to compensate for the disastrous financial effects of the American policy on the UN system in particular and on development cooperation in general.

After 1985, Gorbachev's policies of *glasnost* and *perestroika* in the USSR, to be followed by the transformation of Eastern Europe, held out the promise of improving the effectiveness of the UN system rapidly and in a sustainable way (→ UN Policy, Russia). On the surface, this is what happened in many instances and in a fair number of domains, but in structural and strategic terms the patterns and intensity of multilateral cooperation within the UN system remained unchanged.

I used the image of the "political macro-climate" consciously and deliberately: it exists and is of utmost importance if we refer to the figurations of power, interests, and commitments of major social actors organized at the state level.

But "political micro-climates" relevant for international relations also exist, and may eventually become more important in the future. I refer to qualitative changes in the political publics during the last two or three decades, most visible (and analyzed) in Western industrialized countries but in the meantime fairly well established in many countries of the South and the East. These new actors are variously called "civil society", "new social movements", or "non-governmental organizations" (→ NGOs), and refer to associations and organizations which have emerged in respectable numbers besides traditional (mass) organizations committed to the public good and public welfare such as political parties, trade unions and churches. While the membership in the traditional organizations and the participation in public elections have markedly declined during the last decades in many countries with well-established democratic regimes, the NGOs have begun to play an important role as the representatives of critical and competent, active minorities of the general public.

There seems to exist good empirical evidence for the importance of such NGOs for the rational articulation of responses to world societal problems, even in so-called well-established democracies. This is particularly evident for the controlling function of the NGOs vis-à-vis the administrations, the executive level, and the political parties, especially with regard to the danger of opportunistic manipulation of popular fears and hopes of the general voting public.

3) Since 1990: The Booming of Neo-liberal Globalization and the Hopes for the Emergence of Civilized Constraints

There no longer exists a Rome or Mecca of orthodox criticism of the liberal paradigm of market economy and democracy. But, there always was and still is a critical potential of reflectivity and self-criticism as a constitutive part of the liberal-bourgeois conception of social order, a potential which has, historically, repeatedly brought about a taming of some of the socially destructive dynamics of capitalism. And in a long-term perspective of social processes, the UN system can rightly be interpreted as a first step of institutionalization of such a self-reflexive political system for humanity as a whole.

Since 1990 the yearly → Human Development Reports (HDRs) of the United Nations Development Programme (→ UNDP) emerged as a respected intellectual source of constructive criticism vis-à-vis the contemporary globalization push (→ Globalization), and the reaction and intervention needs and chances at the national and international level. In the meantime, more than 120 countries have followed the same methodology and prepared more than 260 national human development reports.

From the start and up to the present the main analytic thrust of the HDRs was the construction of summary statistics to empirically characterize the quality of life, the freedom of choice and chances of social participation of human beings in a worldwide perspective, in a more valid way than hitherto possible by using the statistic gross national product per capita. Thus, the analytic focus is on the degree and change over time of inequality in different domains of human living conditions, together with issues of their limited and basic social control and regulation by changes in framework conditions on the national and international level and by certain interventions and transfers. The basic preoccupation of the HDRs is in the first place to cognitively realize the existence of glaring inequalities and disparities and secondly to devise and invent social strategies which eventually would allow the still persisting trends towards deterioration and polarization to be stopped.

On the basis of World Bank data – which has been very much improved over the last 20 years to better measure the incidence of poverty and absolute poverty – it is estimated that, in 1960 the richest 20 % of the world population had a yearly income 30 times as large as that of the poorest 20 %, while by 1997,

this gap had increased to 74 times (this last estimate being based on studies on the income and living conditions of households, which are today available for a large number of countries).

As a basis for their recommendations and suggestions, the HDRs regularly synthesize and develop technical studies of the specialized UN organizations and programs as well as relevant academic studies and discussions. Formally, the HDRs are not accepted by governments and, therefore, do not have the status of legitimated political programs. In a sense, these yearly reports on poverty and richness are social-science-based complements to the individual state reports submitted regularly in the context of the conventions on political, economic, social and cultural human rights.

Here we shall summarize a few of the reform suggestions primarily related to the level of the UN system which are more or less extensively discussed in a number of HDRs:

(a) Changes in the international financial structure: abolition of the IMF in its present form, because its mandate is too narrow (lack of sensitivity for welfare dimensions) and its decision structures are grossly undemocratic (excessive political weight of a handful of rich states). Instead, a World Central Bank should be established with enhanced capacities for monetary intervention and effective control mechanisms of the banking system;

(b) A revision of the existing World Trade Organization (→ WTO/GATT), which currently is too narrowly focussed on liberalization policies; its mandate should be widened to include global competition and anti-trust policies, including the competence to devise and monitor the effectiveness of codes of conduct regarding the observance of environmental and labor standards (→ Environmental Protection; → Environmental Law, International);

(c) An International Criminal Court (→ ICC) with a widened mandate for the prosecution of violations of human rights. The goal should be to hold individuals responsible for gross violations

75

of human rights (beyond war crimes and crimes against humanity, no matter whether they act on behalf of governments and public administrations or belong to the business community);

(d) A World Investment Trust, financed by redistributive world rates and taxes, with the primary objectives to help support education and health systems, to improve international → humanitarian assistance and disaster relief, to better combat organized crime and to further hitherto under-financed fields of research and development. As sources of finance, among others, the following taxes were suggested: a world tax of about 0.05 US dollars on a liter of crude oil (or the equivalent of other fossil fuels); a world tax of 0.05% on international capital transfers ("Tobin Tax"), a yearly property tax of 1% on the assets of the world's most prosperous individuals (the assets of the most prosperous 200 individuals grew from 440 billion to 1,042 billion US dollars between 1994 and 1998, thus exceeding the yearly income of 41% of humanity). The annual budget of this trust should amount to about 260 billion US dollars, an annual budget about 26 times as large as the present annual budget of the UN system as a whole and about twice as large as that of the EU.

An extended and reformed UN system (→ Reform of the UN) with a restructured Security Council (replacing the present veto of the Permanent Five by some sort of a qualified majority), a strengthened Economic and Social Council (→ ECOSOC) and, besides the General Assembly of member states, a second chamber with representatives of international NGOs.

All these are medium or even long-term perspectives of institutional change for which, however, first steps should be initiated, if necessary, provisionally and voluntarily by a limited number of states. From the wide range of suggestions for such first limited steps we can refer to the plea to strengthen the juridical advocacy and political consulting support (through UNDP and NGOs) for individual or groups of developing countries to counter the overwhelming technical expertise of the European Union and the USA in international negotiations on new regimes of all sorts.

All these propositions presuppose that the political elites of at least some countries of the center and the periphery (including, of course, the respective oppositions) agree to take first steps. We also have to face, however, the reality of the deplorable decay of American UN policies and the lack of serious compensating European initiatives (cf. → European Union, Common Security and Foreign Policy at the UN). In a sense, then, the Human Development Reports could also – realistically, or pessimistically – be interpreted to be nothing other than the self-assuring whistling of a small band of optimists in the rapidly growing dark woods of the current global beggar-thy-neighbor-liberalization.

Jens Naumann

Lit.: *a) Documents: United Nations:* Reports of the UN Secretary-General on the Support by the United Nations System for the Efforts of Governments to Promote and Consolidate New or Restored Democracies: UN Doc. A/50/332 (7 August 1995); A/51/ 512 (18 October 1996; A/51/761 (20 December 1996), reprinted as "Agenda for Democratization"; A/52/513 (21 October 1997; A/53/554 (29 October 1998); A/54/ 492 (22 October 1999); A/55/489 (13 October 2000); A/56/499 (23 October 2001); *b) Secondary Literature: Boutros-Ghali, B.:* Unvanquished, London/New York 1999; *Elias, N.:* Wandlungen der Wir-Ich-Balance, in: *Elias, N. (ed.):* Die Gesellschaft der Individuen, Frankfurt (Main) 1987, 207-315; *UNDP:* Human Development Report, Oxford, annually since 1990; *Wallerstein, I.:* Unthinking Social Science. The Limits of Nineteenth-Century Paradigms, Cambridge 1991.

Addendum

The cautious perspective Jens Naumann took in 2001 in the above entry for the first edition with regard to the potential for democratizing effects within the UN system is still valid in 2008. A few structures have been modified in the direction of more democratic participation, but in other, often more important fields, the resistance of the economically and politically powerful states has delayed necessary democratic reforms.

1) Progress in the Field of Human Rights and International Criminal Law

Important progress has been achieved with regard to the protection of human rights worldwide: with the establishment of the → Human Rights Council as a subsidiary organ of the General Assembly in 2006 (UN Doc. A/RES/ 60/251 of 15 March 2006), which replaced the rather ineffective Commission on Human Rights (→ Human Rights Council), which had been a functional commission of the → ECOSOC, for not only the political weight of the central UN human rights organ was upvalued, but with the establishment of the Universal Peer Review as a basic mechanism of the Council, i.e. the human rights review of all UN member states at certain intervals, a very effective democratizing effect has been introduced into the human rights protection system of the UN: instead of dealing only with the human rights balance sheets of a few countries with bad reputation, all countries are reviewed, including those which had never been so far on the agenda of its predecessor, the Commission on Human Rights. Together with the increasing efforts made by the Office of the UN High Commissioner for Human Rights (→ Human Rights, United Nations High Commissioner for) to give the member states practical advice for the improvement of their national human rights institutions this could – in the long run – turn UN human rights protection from putting public pressure only on those with extremely bad human rights records to a common effort of all nations to improve human rights protection, thus improving the prospects for a worldwide acceptance and implementation of human rights standards as prerequisite for functioning democratic institutions.

Furthermore an encouraging development in international law gaining gradually wider acceptance among academic experts and in international politics might contribute to a further improvement in the protection of human rights: the "responsibility to protect". Under the impact of the failure of the UN to prevent the massacres of Srebrenica and Rwanda an initiative developed within the United Nations to formulate a new principle of international law, restricting the Charter principle of non-intervention (Art. 2 (7)) in certain cases. On a Canadian initiative an international commission developed in a report submitted in 2001 the principle of the "responsibility to protect": if a state is unwilling or unable to protect groups of its population from massive and systematic human rights violations with genocidal character and thus fails to fulfill its responsibility to protect its population, then the international community has the responsibility to protect this group of people and the obligation to take appropriate measures including – if necessary – enforcement measures under Chapter VII of the UN Charter.

This principle of international responsibility was explicitly supported by the High-level Panel on Threats, Challenges and Change in its report "A more secure world: our shared responsibility" submitted in December 2004 (UN Doc. A/59/565, para. 203), affirmed by Secretary-General Kofi Annan in his reform report of March 2005 "In larger freedom: towards development, security and human rights for all" (UN Doc. A/59/ 2005, para. 135) and eventually expressly re-affirmed by the UN member states in the concluding document of the UN World Summit 2005, the "2005 World Summit Outcome" of 16 September 2005 (UN Doc. A/RES/60/1, para. 138). In particular the endorsement of the principle through the World Summit constitutes a broad acceptance of the new principle which might help to strengthen the human rights protection capacity of the UN, even if it can only be effective in terms of protection when the UN member states are willing to act. But all in all, the principle marks significant progress as it emphasizes the common responsibility of all states and puts into proportion to some extent the significance of national → sovereignty, not least because many states had failed to fulfill their state responsibility.

Human rights protection will also benefit from the fact that the International Criminal Court (→ ICC) (UN Doc. A/CONF.183/9 of 17 July 1998; UNTS Vol. 2187, No. 38544), established in 1998 through a diplomatic conference in Rome, has begun to work in 2003. Its trials concerning crimes against humanity and massive war crimes will without doubt have a deterring effect on potential high-ranking perpetrators worldwide, since with the statute of the ICC the principle has been established that the criminal responsibility of people does not depend on their political position, be it in the official capacity as a head of state, a member of government or parliament or military commander. That person is not exempted from criminal responsibility under the Statute of the ICC (Arts. 27 and 28). That is indeed a ground-breaking step of progress aimed at deterring warlords and rival politicians in conflict-ridden states from human rights violations, since they must take into account that they might be tried before the ICC later on. This might restrain the use of force in intra-state conflicts and, it is to be hoped, foster the use of non-violent methods in political conflicts.

2) No Progress in Disarmament: Weapons for War-lords and Regional Hegemonic Actors

In another field influencing the manner political conflicts are dealt with in many states, disarmament and arms control, respectively – involving the disarmament of nuclear weapons, the reduction of conventional weapons production and the control of the trade in small arms – progress has been slow over the years. Here not only the influence of the great military powers and their security concepts prevail, but also the interests of regional lead powers such as India and Pakistan. In this area the limits of the influence and persuasive power of the UN are clearly visible. In contrast to the hopes of the UN founding fathers, the UN is still not able to exercise an effective influence on the disarmament process, which has not made real progress for a number of years; disarmament is still negotiated bilaterally or in small regional groupings. The still very large quantities of weapon stockpiles worldwide tend to further regional hegemonic political tendencies; thus the UN must attempt to exert more influence in this field, as it was able to do in the 1980s.

3) Democratic Participation in World Trade: Still No Real Progress

The hopes of many developing states that the ongoing Doha negotiations within the framework of the World Trade Organization (→ WTO/GATT) would bring them improved access to the world markets and thus more democratic structures in the sense of more equality of chances to benefit from its own economic resources have not come true so far: the different groups of countries stay still in their "camps" of political and economic interests, with the industrialized countries being by far in a better negotiating position.

The same is true of the world financial system which has shown recently its volatility and absence of any state control and regulation in a large sector of this global system, the so-called "off-shore banking system", being also "off-shore" in control terms. It is not astonishing that these economically hazardous structures could develop, since the institutions in charge of the supervision of this field, the IMF and the World Bank, have since their foundation after World War II been dominated by the large industrialized countries due to the weighted voting system on the basis of size of a country's deposits in the two financial institutions. Attempts to change this undemocratic system by giving poorer countries more influence through voting power have so far led only to marginal reforms of this system. Perhaps the total failure of the two institutions to prevent the present problems of the world finance system will also lead to some reforms in this regard; at least these institutions have lost much of their political reputation gained through their role in the multilateral development assistance efforts with the UN system.

4) Improving the Situation of the Many through the MDGs: Only Slow Progress

Optimistic UN officials and supporters of the UN in the member states hoped – with some justification – that the set of clearly defined Millennium Development Goals (MDGs) (UN Doc. A/56/236 of 6 September 2001) – developed in the context of the Millennium Declaration (UN Doc. A/RES/55/2 of 8 September 2000) adopted at the Millennium Summit of the General Assembly in September 2000 and re-affirmed in the concluding resolution of the UN World Summit 2005 (UN Doc. A/RES/60/1 of 16 September 2005) – would lead to co-ordinated and sustainable efforts from the donor countries to reach the goals by 2015 and to achieve partial successes already on the way. Without doubt the MDGs have focused the world's attention again on the most urgent global problems and have motivated many politicians to make new promises and NGOs in the donor countries to develop new initiatives. But the progress achieved so far with regard to most MDGs is too small in relation to the problems. Without better access of the developing countries to the world markets and more voluntary contributions of the donor countries to UN programmes UN → development co-operation will not achieve enough to alleviate the problems. Without sufficient "human development" as it has been convincingly outlined in the HDRs the enjoyment of political rights as well as of other human rights is not possible since the physical well-being of the people is the basis of the enjoyment.

5) Electoral Assistance: a Silver Lining on the Horizon

In spite of the great number of unresolved socio-economic problems many UN member states are still fighting with, remarkable and increasing efforts towards the strengthening of democratic institutions and procedures have taken place in many developing countries: a growing number of UN member states have made use of the assistance of the United Nations in the organization of democratic elections (→ Electoral Assistance), supplemented by UN advice for building up public administration structures and appropriate judicial institutions. From being in the beginning just one element of complex multi-dimensional peacekeeping operations (→ Peacekeeping Operations), electoral assistance has developed into an independent branch of UN activities, organized by a subdivision of the Department of Political Affairs in the UN → Secretariat. Perhaps the United Nations is at its best when the UN acts as a helpful and neutral expert organization asked for help by its member countries.

6) No Progress towards More Participation in the UN Principal Organs through Structural Reforms

So far I have discussed the progress and failures of the United Nations in promoting democratic structures within the international political and economic system and within individual member countries.

One might argue that some of the failures in UN efforts might be due to the fact that the principal organs of the UN themselves are not structured – to a sufficient degree – according to democratic principles and thus neglect often the interests of the majority of member states since the industrialized countries dominate the Security Council and enjoy a decisive influence in the General Assembly and in ECOSOC through their budgetary power, i.e. by making the largest financial contributions.

What can be done in this situation? A "realistic" politician would argue that without this peculiar distribution of power within the UN the large industrial countries are not willing to accept the UN as instrument of political decision-making; the USA has repeatedly demonstrated this attitude when the UN made decisions being interpreted by the USA as contrary to their own interests (cf. → UN Policy, USA). Following this line of argument only management reforms increasing the efficiency through changing the power structures can be attempted in the United Nations with some chance of success.

A politician with "functionalist" conviction would argue that the UN has in its history always adapted to changing political circumstances with changes of its structures and that even the great powers have accepted these changes after initial resistance, for example to the increase of membership in the Security Council and the ECOSOC or to the active role of the Secretary-General in international conflicts.

Such a change is also necessary in the present phase of international politics to enable the UN to cope with the global challenges. But so far the influential UN actors, in particular the P5 of the Security Council, have not accepted this political insight. They fear a reduction of their own political status, above all France, the United Kingdom and Russia, when the other member states obtain more influence in the Security Council. But without broader participation of all member countries in the search for answers to problems such as climate change or terrorism the solutions developed in the UN organs will not be effective because the majority of the member states will in this case simply not implement the solutions. This is a lesson the P5 and G8 countries, respectively, will have to learn.

From this perspective the recent failures in the attempt to reform the structures of the General Assembly, the Security Council and ECOSOC in 2005 and the following years are disappointing, since they have prevented a broader participation of the member states, more transparency of the decision-making process and the necessary concentration on

the essential issues at stake in the case of the General Assembly, even if some first tiny reform measures have been decided upon and implemented in recent years with regard to the General Assembly and ECOSOC.

The positive aspect in these failed reform attempts lies in the fact that much political dynamic and public attention has been created in the reform process which will in the long run probably have beneficial effects on the UN system, leading to incremental mini-reforms, while being small enough not to provoke the resistance of the powerful nations.

The reform impact has at least had two concrete results, which do not concern the principal organs indirectly, rather than directly: the World Summit 2005 decided to establish the UN Peacebuilding Commission, which was subsequently set up as a common subsidiary organ of the Security Council and the General Assembly (UN Doc. A/RES/60/180 and S/RES/1645 (2005) of 20 December 2005) with the goal of improving the cooperation of UN organs in the phase of peacebuilding in conflict regions. The summit also decided – as already mentioned above – to establish the UN Human Rights Council (A/RES/60/1, para. 157-160; cf. also: A/RES/60/251), replacing the discredited Commission on Human Rights. Both examples prove that the UN is capable of reform, but only on a small scale.

7) Progress through the Backdoor: Democratic Participation through the NGOs?

Whereas the reform of the decision-making structures of the UN Principal Organs (→ Principal Organs, Subsidiary Organs, Treaty Bodies) in recent years has not been successful, informal reform measures have taken place without being much noticed by the public: reforms concerning the role of the NGOs. This progress is somehow surprising, since an attempt to reform the official ways and means of NGO participation with the help of a report of an expert group, the so-called "Cardoso Report", named after the group's chairman, had not been successful in this regard. When the group submitted its report in June 2004 (*United Nations* 2004a), UN Doc. A/58/817), Secretary-General Kof Annan supplemented and supported the report by his own report which he submitted to the General Assembly in September 2004 (*United Nations* 2004b, UN Doc. A/59/354). Both reports advocated a simplified, unbureaucratically organized accreditation procedure for NGOs through a committee of the General Assembly instead of an ECOSOC committee. Moreover, the "Cardoso Report" called for interactive sessions of NGOs with member state delegates in the context of General Assembly meetings, but outside the formal meeting format. Kofi Annan even advocated in his report opening NGOs' access to formal General Assembly meetings, starting with an accreditation of NGOs to the Main Committees.

When the General Assembly discussed in October 2004 the SG's report, the majority of states reacted somewhat reservedly to the reform concepts; no reform decisions were taken by the Assembly. Consequently the Outcome Document of the World Summit 2005 did not contain any reform decisions in this direction; the Assembly only appreciated the positive contributions of the NGOs and welcomed the informal interactive Assembly hearing with NGOs that had taken place in the forefront of the World Summit (cf. report of the hearing: UN Doc. A/60/331 of 2 July 2005)

Thus, while the recent official reform attempts have not been successful, the NGOs have been rather successful in establishing a number of informal channels to give advice and acquire influence, in particular with regard to the Security Council, where the briefing of and meeting with NGOs has become informal routine and has in the meantime been confirmed by a Presidential Note of 19 July 2006 (UN Doc. S/2006/507). This is an astonishing development in the direction of more informal democratic participation and more transpar-

ency with regard to the Council. The increased briefing and participation possibilities concern not only NGOs, but also non-member states of the Council. In the course of this development, the Council has increased its number of orientation and thematic debates open to all UN member states as audience, in some cases even provided the opportunity to make oral statements (cf. UN Doc. S/2006/507, para. 26ff.) – without doubt an increase in democratic quality, even if these formats are all informal and are not codified in the Council's Rules of Procedure, which the P5 would not accept.

With regard to the General Assembly the number of informal interactive debates of the Assembly with NGOs in the Main Committees and in the Plenary – in so-called "thematic debates" – have increased recently (cf. for example the report of the Secretary-General A/62/208 of 2 December 2007; see also: www.un.org/ga/president/62/Thematic-Debates/thematicdebates.shtml), even if the official participation of NGOs in the regular sessions is not to be expected in the near future, because many member states, in particular from the Third World seem to fear the possible downgrading thereby of the role of the member state delegations in the Assembly.

The preparatory process of the World Summit 2005 as well as the debates in the newly-established Human Rights Council demonstrate, however, that even without this right of participation in the formal sessions of the General Assembly, the NGOs exert a considerable influence within the UN system through informal and official channels.

The UN organs benefit considerably from their work through information and expert advice as well as with regard to the implementation of UN decisions and programmes by making use of the grassroots work of the NGOs in the member states.

In this regard the attitude of some UN officials and many member states to put the NGOs together with the so-called "private sector", i.e. business firms and/or their organizations, and other so-called "civil society organizations" should be considered critically, as they all have different interests, judicial constructions and different qualities of legitimation with respect to the number of organization members, election processes and the question of how representative their demands are. Obviously Secretary-General Kofi Annan wanted to increase with the concept of the "Global Compact" (cf. www.unglobalcompact.org) the efficiency of implementing UN labor and human rights standards by integrating, on a voluntary basis, private commercial enterprises, but, on a general political level, the different groupings should be considered separately and integrated in different ways into the UN decision-making process.

8) The debate about a parliamentary level of the UN

Throughout the history of the United Nations and in particular around the World Summit 2005 the question has been discussed by the member states whether the United Nations needs an additional parliamentary organ, a parliament consisting of representatives elected in the member states for this purpose. Those advocating such an institution criticize the fact that the General Assembly of the UN consists of delegates who are, by and large, appointed by the state governments and receive their instructions from the latter. They argue that elected representatives would possess a greater democratic legitimation.

This argumentation leaves out completely the political reality: a precondition for such a parliament would be that in all member states there are democratic structures – a condition seldom satisfactorily fulfilled. It is difficult to conceive how such a large parliament should reach a consensus and difficult to understand why such an organ could reach more democratic quality in its decisions than the General Assembly comprising the delegates of parliamentarily elected governments. Furthermore it would raise the question: what decision-making powers such a parliament would enjoy in relation to the General Assembly and to the Security Council: should the latter hand over powers to the parliament?

Moreover the costs of such a large parliamentary assembly, in particular for holding the worldwide elections, would be extremely high, and this against the background of the bankrupt UN. And, what is most important, such a UN parliament would require an amendment of the UN Charter and it is difficult to imagine that the permanent members of the Council, whose consent is necessary for every Charter amendment, would agree to such a far-reaching change of the UN structures.

Improving the quality of the work of the UN requires more financial resources and more political support for the UN from the member states, not the burden of an additional UN parliament. UN politics should be discussed more intensely in the national parliaments. That would improve the situation of the UN in general and its capacity to solve the urgent global problems considerably.

9) Summary

The balance sheet of the UN with regard to its impact on democratization in its member countries as well as to its own structures contains some failures and some progress. The UN has been able to strengthen in recent years to some extent the democratic structures in the states of the world through advice and assistance and through establishing a new institution, the International Criminal Court, supplemented by new developments in international law strengthening the common responsibility of the states. The UN itself has improved its democratic quality to some extent by informal reforms, even if the amount of openness to inputs from the member states could and should be increased. But at least the UN has accepted the challenge, as the interactive debates of the Security Council and informal hearings of the General Assembly in recent years have shown.

Helmut Volger

Lit.: *1) Documents: International Commission on Intervention and State Sovereignty: The Responsibility to Protect.* Report, Ottawa 2001; *United Nations Diplomatic Conference of Plenipotentiaries on the Establishment of an International Criminal Court:* Rome Statute of the International Criminal Court, 17 July 1998, UN Doc. A/CONF. 183/9, UNTS Vol. 2187, No. 38544; *United Nations - General Assembly:* United Nations Millennium Declaration, 8 September 2000, UN Doc. A/RES/55/2; *United Nations - General Assembly:* We the Peoples: Civil Society, the United Nations and Global Governance. Report of the Panel of Eminent Persons on United Nations-Civil Society Relations, UN Doc. A/58/117 of 11 July 2004, known as "Cardoso Report" (quoted as: United Nations 2004a); *United Nations - General Assembly:* Report of the Secretary-General in response to the report of the Panel of Eminent Persons on United Nations-Civil Society Relations, UN Doc. A/ 59/354 of 13 September 2004 (quoted as: United Nations 2004b); *United Nations - General Assembly:* A more secure world: our shared responsibility. Report of the High-level Panel on Threats, Challenges and Change, 2 December 2004, UN Doc. A/59/565; *United Nations - General Assembly:* In larger freedom: towards development, security and human rights for all. Report of the Secretary-General, 21 March 2005, UN Doc. A/59/ 2005; *United Nations - General Assembly:* Informal interactive hearings of the General Assembly with representatives of non-governmental organizations, civil society organizations and the private sector. Note by the President of the General Assembly, 2 July 2005, UN Doc. A/60/331; *United Nations – General Assembly:* 2005 World Summit Outcome, 16 September 2005, UN Doc A/RES/60/1;
2) Secondary Literature: Annan, K.A.: Democracy as an International Issue, in: Global Governance 8 (2002), 135-137; *Fox, G.H.:* Democratization, in: Malone, D.M. (ed.): The UN Security Council. From the Cold War to the 21st Century, Boulder/Col. 2004, 69-84; *Hulton, S.C.:* Council Working Methods and Procedures, in: Malone, D.M. (ed.): The UN Security Council. From the Cold War to the 21st Century, Boulder/Col. 2004, 237-251; *Knight, W.A.:* Democracy and Good Governance, in: Weiss, T.G./ Daws, S. (eds.): The Oxford Handbook on the United Nations, Oxford 2007, 620-633; *Paul, J.:* Working with Nongovernmental Organizations, in: Malone, D.M. (ed.): The UN Security Council. From the Cold War to the 21st Century, Boulder/Col. 2004, 373-387; *Peterson, M.J.:* The General Assembly, New York 2006.

Internet: Human Development Reports: www.undp.org/hdro.

Depository Libraries

In order to disseminate information about the United Nations worldwide and to offer the general public access to UN documents (→ Documentation System) and publications (→ Publications of the UN), the United Nations supports a network of currently over 400 libraries in more than 140 countries that are officially designated depository libraries.

These libraries maintain collections of official UN documentation and publications and may receive newly issued UN materials on a regular basis. For various reasons, many depository libraries have discontinued receipt of UN documents in print format and now rely on online access to UN documentation via the *United Nations Official Document System* (http://documents.un.org). A directory of UN depository libraries can be found at www.un.org/Depts/dhl/deplib/index.html.

A country's national library, as well as its parliamentary library (if open to the public), receive the deposit free of charge, whereas other libraries pay a lump sum that help defray the cost of maintaining the depository library system. Libraries receive either a partial deposit that comprises UN publications, the official records, and the documents of the regional commissions (in Europe the Economic Commission for Europe) (→ Economic Commissions, Regional), or a full deposit that includes, in addition to the above, all UN documents in general distribution, e.g. letters, reports and meeting records.

Depository libraries are responsible for organizing their UN documents collections according to established best practices, for assigning competent staff to their care, and for providing the public with free and unrestricted access to them. Library users who are unable to visit a depository library in person are entitled to receive UN documents and publications free of charge through inter-library loan or document delivery services.

Depository libraries offer access to important tools for documents research (→ Documentation System), e.g. the *Indexes to proceedings* or the *Yearbook of the United Nations*, as well as expert research assistance with an ever-increasing variety of online databases, catalogues and electronic repositories of UN documents and publications, including the *United Nations Official Document System (ODS):* http://documents.un.org.

A network of United Nations information centres and services (→ Public Information of the UN) complements the depository library system. While these are primarily in charge of informing the public about the activities of the UN, they typically maintain small libraries with collections of current UN materials and may have access to a wide array of online databases and research tools that are relevant for UN documents research.

UN information centers and services are located around the world – a directory can be found at www.un.org/aroundworld/unics/english/directory.htm. Contact information for UN information centres in Brussels, Geneva and Vienna is included in the directory of depository libraries in the annex.

The International Court of Justice (→ ICJ) and the → specialized agencies, e.g. the World Bank (→ World Bank/World Bank Group), → UNESCO or the World Health Organization (→ WHO), disseminate their documentation and publications independently from the UN. However, many UN depository libraries also collect documents and publications of the ICJ and of the specialized agencies. *Depolib,* a searchable and browseable (by country, UN agency, library name) database hosted by the World Bank, provides references to depository libraries of the entire UN system.

Ramona Kohrs

Lit.: *United Nations – Secretariat:* Instructions for depository libraries receiving United Nations material, UN Doc. ST/LIB/13/Rev.5 of 5 March 1995.
Internet: United Nations Depository Libraries homepage: www.un.org/Depts/dhl/deplib/index.html; Depolib: Depository Libraries of the United Nations System: www.worldbank.org, use path Index → Depository Libraries.

Deutscher Bundestag (German Federal Parliament), Positions of the German Parties towards the UN

The Federal Republic of Germany's accession to the United Nations in 1973 did little to increase the attention paid to the world organization in the domestic political arena. This situation did not alter until the major changes to the international order at the end of the eighties, which brought reunification for Germany and enhanced enormously the UN's standing as a force for peace.

Following these changes, all the parties represented in the Bundestag set out their basic policy positions on the UN in parliamentary motions and in the context of election campaigns during the nineties. The parties are in agreement that the United Nations must be institutionally strengthened by means of reforms, to allow it to take action in central areas of policy. A comparison of the policies of the different parties shows that, although they agree on numerous points, there are marked differences in the policy fields of "deployment of troops abroad and international peacekeeping", as well as "reform" and "finances".

Social Democratic Party of Germany (SPD)

The SPD has lent strong and active support to the reform of the UN (→ Reform of the UN), in order to build it into an effective global system of → collective security. Nevertheless, at the end of the eighties, the SPD categorically rejected the idea of German participation in any deployments abroad that were not of a purely humanitarian nature. The political conviction held within the SPD was that, due to the burdens of German history, restraint was called for as regards military deployments. From a legal point of view, the Social Democrats believed that the deployment of armed units abroad was not permissible under the Basic (Constitutional) Law. Yet, in the course of debates, the party was obliged by degrees to modify its original stance. Following the ruling by the Federal Constitutional Court that deployments abroad were indeed compatible with the Basic (Constitutional) Law, i.e. the German Federal Constitution, the SPD does now support participation in peace-enforcing measures as an ultima ratio (→ Peacekeeping; → Peacekeeping Operations), where other means of combating breaches of the peace (→ Peace, Peace Concept, Threat to Peace) and grave human rights violations (→ Human Rights) have failed.

Since the UN lacks the necessary instruments and resources for robust or military peace enforcement, the SPD holds that NATO should be involved to a greater extent in crisis management. But the Social Democrats insist that deployments be supported by a UN mandate, because this is required under international law and because they wish to maintain the UN's monopoly on the use of force. They see NATO air attacks on rump Yugoslavia in the spring of 1999, which were supported by the SPD-led government, as an exception.

The parliamentary group of the SPD in the Bundestag emphasized the need for reform of the United Nations in its parliamentary motions from a very early stage. It believes that enlargement of the → Security Council to include Germany, Japan and certain countries in the Third World would increase the UN's legitimacy, whilst restricting the right of veto (→ Veto, Right of Veto) would increase its effectiveness. The SPD is also convinced of the necessity of structural reforms in the area of development (→ Development Cooperation and the UN System) and environment (→ Environmental Protection). It believes this

should include enhancing the status of the Economic and Social Council (→ ECOSOC), exploiting the UNDP's potential for management and coordination and strengthening the financial position through compliance with the demand for 0.7 % of GDP to be made available for development assistance. In view of the ongoing budgetary consolidation, it remains to be seen whether the improvement of multilateral cooperation within the UN framework announced by the Red-Green Federal Government will lead to an increase in voluntary contributions.

Christian Democratic Union (CDU)/ Christian Social Union (CSU)

Following the outbreak of the second Gulf War, the CDU/CSU swiftly revised its stance on the question of Bundeswehr deployments abroad, deciding that the Basic (Constitutional) Law does not prevent Bundeswehr participation in peacekeeping missions. It believes that Germany's unconditional accession to the UN requires that it enjoys all rights and fulfils all obligations. Germany's contribution within the framework of the NATO and WEU military alliances is given clear priority by the CDU/CSU over strengthening the UN in the area of peace policy. The CDU/CSU disputes the UN's monopoly on the use of force (→ Use of Force, Prohibition of) and emphasizes the right to individual and collective self-defence (Art. 51 UN Charter). It sees a UN mandate for Bundeswehr deployments abroad as desirable, but not essential, as it wishes to avoid any dependence on Russia and China, both of whom have a right of veto as permanent members of the Security Council. The fact that, in taking this stance, the CDU/CSU has "shifted the right to use force from the UN back to the individual states and alliances of states to a considerable extent" (*Löwe* 1994, 4), is in line with its basic realpolitik attitude, which gives sovereign states precedence over international organizations and views systems of collective defense as more effective than systems of collective security.

The CDU/CSU believes that the UN is in need of reform, but questions the Organization's capacity to achieve reform. The work of the CDU/CSU-led ministries under the last government indicated a somewhat skeptical attitude towards the UN. Federal Chancellor Kohl did not really support the efforts made by the FDP-led Federal Foreign Office to achieve enlargement of the Security Council and permanent member status for Germany. The Christian Democrat Minister of Defence rejected the idea of a German contribution to the stand-by arrangements for UN peacekeeping missions which the Federal Foreign Office hoped would boost the German candidacy for a permanent seat. The Finance Minister pursued a policy of zero growth, believing that reforms should not cost anything and giving priority to enhancing the organization's efficiency by cutting back bureaucracy. Despite the commitment to increase expenditure on state development aid to 0.7 % of GDP, the voluntary contributions were reduced more and more, falling to 0.26 % of GDP by the end of that term of office.

Alliance 90/The Greens

The Greens see the UN as an important frame of reference for their concepts of foreign policy. They would like to see the UN's role as a force for peace reinforced, through crisis prevention, traditional peacekeeping and a long-term "civilization" of international politics. By opposing the widening of the range of tasks and of the areas of deployment of the Bundeswehr, the Greens hoped to counteract the militarization of German foreign policy which they feared might occur. They also saw a danger of the Security Council developing into an instrument of Western hegemonic interests. The fact that the UN was founded expressly in order to bring about an end to the 20th century tradition of warfare and that, in contrast to the → League of Nations, it was equipped with a general

ban on the use of force (→ Use of Force, Prohibition of) and with powers to take action, if necessary by means of coercion, against aggressors, played no role. The war in Bosnia-Herzegovina showed the difficulties of a refusal to distinguish between legitimate force and illegal force. In view of the helplessness of rigorous pacifism in the face of atrocities, some parts of the parliamentary group of the Greens altered their stance on the use of force. These politicians now believe that grave violations of human rights must be responded to, also, by military means if there is no other alternative, but that the UN's monopoly on the use of force must be preserved at all costs. Like the SPD, Alliance 90/The Greens does not regard the air attacks on rump Yugoslavia carried out by NATO without a UN mandate as setting a precedent.

The Greens believe that institutional reform should aim to enhance the status of and to introduce a greater degree of democracy to the UN (→ Democratization and the UN). The Greens call for permanent seats for underrepresented regions in the Security Council, but reject the idea of a permanent seat for Germany. They believe the right of veto should be abolished. In the area of economic and social policy, the Greens want to see corrections to the asymmetrical decision-making structures (→ Voting Right and Decision-Making Procedures) to allow the countries of the Southern hemisphere to participate on an equal basis. In addition, the Greens would like to see an enhancement of the status of → ECOSOC, allowing it to function as a democratic council for economic, social and environmental affairs.

In order to solve the UN's financial crisis (→ Financial Crises), the Greens are proposing a move away from the policy of no real growth, with the introduction of independent financing sources (→ Budget).

Free Democratic Party (FDP)

Unlike its then coalition partner, the CDU/CSU, the FDP initially took a very restrictive stance, both politically and legally, on Bundeswehr deployments abroad. In 1989, it supported participation by German soldiers only in UN peacekeeping measures. In legal terms, it believed an amendment to the Basic (Constitutional) Law was necessary for Bundeswehr deployments. In line with this belief, the FDP, like the SPD, instituted proceedings before the Federal Constitutional Court when Bundeswehr pilots took part in AWACS reconnaissance flights over the former Yugoslavia.

But a shift in opinion occurred within the FDP and its stance gradually moved closer to that of the CDU/CSU. First, the events of the Gulf War persuaded it of the necessity of combat missions, albeit only where a UN mandate existed. Later, it adopted the same position as the CDU/CSU, in a joint draft amendment to the Basic (Constitutional) Law, which stated that combat missions were acceptable also without a UN mandate.

After initial hesitation by the then Federal Government, the FDP-led Federal Foreign Office made a permanent German seat in the Security Council to the centrepiece of its efforts towards UN reform. Foreign Minister Klaus Kinkel justified this position by pointing out that Germany, in its capacity as third largest contributor, had a right to be involved in decision-making. This issue overshadowed other reform aims. The FDP was unable to halt the continual reduction in the level of German resources channeled to the UN, but was able to successfully resist the attempt by the Finance Ministry to avoid paying in full the assessed contributions.

Party of Democratic Socialism (PDS)

The PDS has the most restrictive position of all the parties with regard to Bundeswehr deployments abroad. Even after the above-mentioned ruling by the Federal Constitutional Court, the PDS continues to rule out any deployment of German forces abroad, even in a case where the North Atlantic Treaty obliges contracting parties to assist each other, including the use of armed force. It believes that the Bundeswehr should restrict itself to the defence tasks within Germany's own borders. It criticizes any Bundeswehr deployments going beyond this restriction as "militarization of foreign policy". In its programme for the 1994 Bundestag elections, the PDS called for "a ban on Bundeswehr deployments outside the borders of the Federal Republic of Germany". The Security Council is viewed by the PDS as the extended arm of the great powers and is automatically suspected of being an agent of "global interventionism". The PDS does not accept that there is either a legal obligation or a political necessity to make available troops to the UN for its peacekeeping missions. Requests by the UN → Secretary-General to the German government have obviously failed to change the stance of the PDS, which is willing to accept the renationalization of German foreign and defense policy. The PDS thus even goes so far as to print election campaign posters showing UN peacekeeping troops (→ Peacekeeping Forces) with the slogan "make peace without weapons!", suggesting that it is the UN which is the primary source of violence in international relations.

The PDS believes that UN reform should involve abolishing the distinction between permanent and non-permanent members of the Security Council, creating an environmental affairs council, making resolutions adopted by the General Assembly legally binding and safeguarding the UN's financial basis via reductions in the armaments budgets.

Summary

All the parties represented in the Bundestag present a UN-friendly image at the declarative level. One reason for this is that the aims and demands listed in the motions submitted by the parties are formulated on such an abstract level as to prevent parliamentary evaluation, or an assessment of their political feasibility. The lists of the aims and demands seldom take the form of concrete calls for action. The aims set out by the governing parties in their electoral programmes can be assessed in the light of the actions actually taken whilst in office. This also applies to the newly-elected Red-Green coalition, which generated great expectations of constructive UN engagement through its coalition agreement and other declarations of intent. It remains to be seen whether the constraints of budgetary consolidation will allow these self-proclaimed objectives to be achieved. If the coalition fails to set a good example at least in some fields, this will lead to grave disappointment and will provoke sharp criticism from → NGOs, the parliamentary opposition and the general public.

Wolfgang Ehrhart

Lit.: Friedenspolitische Positionen der Parteien. Gegenüberstellung der Wahlprogrammaussagen, in: Wissenschaft und Frieden, No. 1/1994, Dossier No.16; *Hoffmann, O.:* Deutsche Blauhelme bei UN-Missionen. Politische Hintergründe und rechtliche Aspekte, in: Koch, E. (ed.): Die Blauhelme. Im Einsatz für den Frieden. Stellungnahmen der Parteien des Deutschen Bundestages zum Thema UNO-Einsätze der Bundeswehr, Frankfurt (Main) 1991, 240-255; *Löwe, V.:* Unendliche Geschichte, notwendiger Streit. Die Auseinandersetzung um deutsche Blauhelme, in: VN 42 (1994), 1-7; *Philippi, N.:* Bundeswehr-Auslandseinsätze als außen- und sicherheitspolitisches Problem des geeinten Deutschland, Frankfurt (Main) 1997; *SPD:* Protokoll vom Außerordentlichen Parteitag Bonn 16.-17. November 1992, Bonn 1992.

Addendum

In the new millennium the German parties represented in the Bundestag more or less continued to retain their positions towards the United Nations as described for the decade earlier in the preceding entry. They even arrived slowly at more positions in common than had been the case in the 1990s.

Common Platform

The parties SPD, Alliance 90/The Greens, CDU/CSU have demonstrated a large field of commonalities in their positions towards the United Nations expressed in the plenary debates dealing with parliamentary consent to the prolongation of the deployment of Bundeswehr units in UN peacekeeping missions or with the reform of the UN Security Council and other UN topics, positions shared also to some extent by the FDP.

With the exception of the Left Party (Partei Die Linke) which rejects any participation of Bundeswehr contingents in UN peacekeeping missions, the other parties agree on German participation in UN peacekeeping. They all, also, demand a reform of the UN Security Council, support strengthened UN development cooperation, and affirm the need to further develop the UN climate protection system and UN human rights protection.

Alliance 90/The Greens

The Alliance 90/The Greens (Bündnis 90/Die Grünen) changed its former UN position step-by-step while it was coalition partner of the SPD from 1998 until 2005 in the Schröder/Fischer government. Its initial fundamental criticism of any German participation in UN peacekeeping missions and UN mandated NATO peacekeeping missions, which parts of their parliamentary group showed in spite of their general consent given in the coalition agreement of 1998 (cf. *SPD - Bündnis 90/Die Grünen* 1998, 45) gave way after fierce debate within the party institutions to pragmatic consent to participation on the basis of a UN mission mandate or UN authorization of a NATO mission.

While in government the Greens kept their strong interest in UN human rights protection and supported this field of UN activity, among others by establishing a German Institute for Human Rights in Berlin. Moreover they advocated the increased support of UN development cooperation and UN environmental protection.

On the issue of Security Council reform, Foreign Minister Fischer of the Greens turned from a rather indifferent stance towards a German permanent seat – considering an additional European permanent seat as the better solution – to an outspoken candidate for a German seat on the occasion of the UN Millennium Summit in 2000 and made the German ambassador in New York work actively and with self-confidence for the German claim.

After returning to the opposition benches in the Bundestag in 2005, the Greens gave up the claim in their official statements. In a decision of their party conference in 2008 they demanded only that the composition of the Security Council be made fairer through the participation of the African, Latin American and Asian states. Europe is not mentioned at all (*Bündnis 90/Die Grünen* 2008, 2). With regard to UN-mandated peacekeeping mission they retain, however, the position of consent also as opposition party.

Social Democratic Party of Germany (SPD)

While the centre and the conservative wing of the SPD as well as Chancellor Schröder had supported the German participation already in the 1990s, the left wing of the SPD had some trouble during the time in government in agreeing to military deployment, but with the exception of a few members of parliament they finally made their peace with such a role for Germany, still fearing Germany could develop into a hegemonic power. In 2002 the party signaled its consent to this stance in a decision of the party conference on the government programme for 2002 and subsequent years, agreeing to a deployment of German soldiers in peacekeeping missions when legitimized by UN mandate and consent of the Bundestag (*SPD* 2002, 11).

With regard to his position towards the US-British coalition war in Iraq

2003, the SPD supported Chancellor Schröder's position strongly, as his rejection of a military solution to the Iraq conflict mirrored the mood of broad circles of the party members and of the majority of the German population.

During his chancellorship, Gerhard Schröder even developed a stronger liking for environmental issues and supported Environment Minister Jürgen Trittin (Alliance 90/The Greens) in his fight for a strong common European position for strengthening the UN environmental protection, for example at the Johannesburg UN Conference 2002, against the heavy opposition of the USA.

With regard to UN development cooperation, the SPD was in the new millennium rhetorically an advocate of increasing ODA and of granting developing countries more access to world markets (cf. *SPD* 2002, 13), but in practice the Chancellor and the SPD ministers in his cabinet, in particular the Minister for Economic Cooperation and Development, Heidemarie Wieczorek-Zeul (SPD), did not fight very convincingly for these goals in the international negotiations and failed to increase Germany's UN voluntary contributions in this field. The resources were even cut (cf. *Hüfner* 2008).

When the SPD formed a coalition government with the CDU/CSU in 2005, it retained its political position with regard to the United Nations in general, benefiting from the fact that Chancellor Merkel is the proponent of the UN-supporting wing in the CDU. This co-incidence of political standpoints found its expression in the coalition agreement of 2005, where CDU/CSU and SPD advocate an effective multilateralism, the deployment of German troops within the framework of the UN Charter and a UN reform making it fit for future challenges, including the reform of the Security Council.

Under the impact of the failed attempt to obtain a Security Council permanent seat in summer 2005, the SPD returned in the coalition agreement again to the more cautious stance of being ready to take over a permanent seat for Germany, but of striving in the long run for a permanent seat for Europe (*CDU/CSU - SPD* 2005, 158).

*Christian Democratic Union (CDU)/
Christian Social Union (CSU)*

While the CDU/CSU assumed during the chairmanship of Kohl for long years a somewhat indifferent attitude towards the United Nations in fields such as development assistance and Security Council reform, the exception was environmental issues where Kohl developed, due to the increasing concerns in the German population, a defined interest in elaborating his own position, then the CDU/CSU developed – when Merkel, who had been from 1994 to 1998 Environment Minister under Chancellor Kohl and had taken part in UN environment conferences in this capacity, took over the CDU chair in 1998 – a stronger interest in UN politics. This positional change found, for example, its expression in the readiness to take part in a joint declaration of the Bundestag on UN reform and UN policy in 2001 (cf. plenary protocol 14/177 of Deutscher Bundestag, 22 June 2001, 17468ff.), being tabled and adopted by CDU/CSU, SPD, FDP and Alliance 90/The Greens, but also in public statements of Merkel on important occasions. At the Munich Security Conference 2002 she advocated a reformed and effective United Nations as a central institution in world politics, supported a German permanent seat in the Security Council, because in her opinion a seat for the EU would have no realistic chance for the near future, and welcomed the development of international law through the United Nations, explicitly mentioning the new concept of the "responsibility to protect" (*CDU* 2002, 5), a remarkable well-informed and UN-supporting attitude for a CDU politician at that point of time.

But Merkel's UN policy met some resistance among the more conservative circles within the CDU which were initially even more influential, as can be seen for example in the guidelines for foreign policy adopted by the party conference of the CDU in December 2001. In this paper the CDU criticizes the UN for not having fulfilled expectations. Without reform the UN would lose its significance. Demanding a German permanent seat is regarded as a mistake, since Germany – according to the CDU's guidelines – was no global actor with the necessary resources, connections and strategic interests (*CDU* 2001, 25f.). With regard to UN development cooperation, the CDU guidelines assert a clearly neo-liberal position – in contrast to the position of the Chancellor – advocating naively open markets as best form of development assistance and omitting any reference to the increase of ODA and other UN projects in this regard.

When the CDU/CSU formed the government with the SPD in 2005, Merkel's approachment to UN-supporting positions continued: in the presentation of her government programme the Chancellor reaffirmed her position as expressed in the above-mentioned statement, affirming the United Nations as the central forum for resolving conflicts, the need for reforms, the readiness to take over a permanent seat in the Security Council as first step to a seat for the European Union, and assured the implementation of the UN goal of increasing the ODA in steps to 0.7 per cent in 2015 (*CDU* 2005, 18).

Now also the majority of the party supported her UN policy, this support being expressed, for example, in the decision of the CDU party conference of 2006 on principles for the foreign policy (*CDU* 2006, 15). The decision asserts that the United Nations has the greatest legitimacy to tackle global problems and that Germany should strive for strengthening the strength and efficiency of the UN.

Free Democratic Party (FDP)

Being an opposition party in the Bundestag since 1998 the FDP has turned in this time from an outspoken supporter of the United Nations under Foreign Minister Klaus Kinkel in the early and mid-nineties to an idealizing critic far removed from reality. Thus the FDP Executive Committee considered in a decision of April 2003 the military intervention of the US coalition troops flatly and simply as setback for the UN – notwithstanding the fact that the majority of the Security Council members had courageously withstood US pressures to agree to a draft resolution which would have authorized explicitly the military intervention. UN reform should and could in their opinion only be achieved in close alliance with the USA, a fact which the Schröder government had to their minds not adequately taken care of. Moving away from Kinkel's claim for a permanent seat in the Security Council for Germany the text makes a claim for a seat for the EU.

Also in subsequent years this mixture of naive UN reform concepts and overdrawn criticism continued, expressed for example in a decision of the FDP Presiding Committee of September 2005: in this paper, the FDP demands the strengthening of the UN's capacity for conflict prevention, crisis management, post-conflict peace-building, and global governance, without outlining any concrete concepts and measures to reach these ambitious goals. The FDP warns in the text of an over-estimation of the ODA-GNP quota as benchmark for development assistance and is against financial transfers to developing countries which would only lead to dependence and would impede development. Instead good governance and self-reliance of the developing countries should be promoted as preconditions for any development progress (cf. *FDP* 2005, 4). The role of unfair structures on the world markets is completely omitted in the paper as well as the massive poverty and nutrition problems and the heavy indebtedness of many developing countries. It is, in fact, a document of pure neo-liberalist thinking, a backlash in the party's political concepts.

In the same attitude of simple-minded neo-liberal and idealistic thinking, the FDP parliamentary group in the Bundestag advocates in an undated Internet statement [accessed in 2008, H.V.] a reform of the General Assembly and its subsidiary organs, speaking in this context naively of strengthening the mechanisms for decision-making and implementation, as if the General Assembly would have any significant decision and implementation capacity at all. It advocates also independent resources for UN peacekeeping missions without indicating where these resources should come from.

How far the FDP has moved away from its positions in the 1990s can be concluded from the fact that in January 2006 the outspoken critic and polemic UN "basher", the US UN Ambassador John Bolton spoke on the invitation of the FDP in Berlin. Bolton, who had – in the conviction of the majority of ambassadors of the UN member states the main responsibility for the meager results of the UN World Summit 2005 – had been invited – as FDP Chairman Westerwelle said in his statement – as an important step to improve German-American relations (cf. *FDP* 2006). This invitation demonstrates that the FDP has indeed returned to old neo-liberal positions being similar to those of the Bush administration, which considered while in office UN reform only under the aspect of management reform and of increasing the capacity of the UN to fight against terrorism and to safeguard the interests off industrialized countries on the world markets.

The Left Party (Die Linke), formerly Party of Democratic Socialism (PDS)

The most naive position is however assumed by the party, The Left (Die Linke). In their public statements and papers the party representatives depict the UN without any detailed knowledge as a powerful international state organization which is able to implement article for article the goals of the UN Charter.

Deutscher Bundestag (German Federal Parliament), Positions of the German Parties towards the UN

In its election platform 2009 put on its Internet website (http://die-linke.de/wahlen/positionen/themen_az/uz/uno/) the party lists a catalogue of demands which sound completely unrealistic and naive: in order to strengthen the UN politically and financially the member states should hand over more resources and political competences to the United Nations. In the field of peace-keeping NATO should be strictly subordinated to the UN. The UN should be reformed in such a way that it would be able to develop common economic, social and ecological strategies for the development of all peoples; the UN should be given the competence to ensure the implementation of the commitments of the member states; the assessed contributions to the UN should be increased and all UN institutions should be democratized, and, above all, the permanent seats in the Security Council should be abolished. In fact, this amounts to a naive catalogue of nice ideas far removed from the political reality of what is feasible in a world of nation states.

In the Bundestag debates about the deployment of Bundeswehr units in UN peacekeeping mission The Left always disagreed with the deployment of Bundeswehr units in the framework of UN missions or UN-mandated NATO forces such as ISAF (cf. for example Deutscher Bundestag plenary protocols 16/74 and 16/119, regarding the prolongation of the participation of German military units in Darfur/Sudan (UN Advance Mission UNAMIS) in December 2006 and in Afghanistan (International Security Assistance Force ISAF) in October 2007, respectively).

This party thus remains in a kind of fundamental opposition with regard to the German role in the United Nations, viewing the UN in a polemical distortion as an instrument of alleged hegemonic US foreign policy, a gross simplification of the UN situation, neglecting above all the role of the other UN member states, and obviously influenced by the stubborn ideological thinking patterns of the communist wing within the party.

Summary

Summing up, it can be said that the large parties SPD and CDU/CSU as well as the smaller Alliance 90/The Greens have developed and continue to develop constructive UN policies, while the FDP has partly moved away from UN-supporting positions to a more naive concept of independent nation states competing with equal opportunities for the resources of the world. The Left Party can simply not be taken seriously with its UN position, as its documents show, lacking any knowledge of the UN and any concrete suggestions taking into account the UN structures and competences. It considers the UN from a predominantly ideologically determined perspective.

Compared with previous decades the preconditions for a constructive German UN policy have improved as the two large parties as well as the Greens have integrated the UN into their political programmes as important field of foreign policy.

Helmut Volger

Lit.: *I. Documents: Bündnis 90/Die Grünen:* Eines für Alle: Das Grüne Wahlprogramm 2005, Berlin 2005; *Bündnis 90/Die Grünen:* Frieden bewegen – Grüne Friedens- und Sicherheitspolitik. Beschluss der 28. Ordentlichen Bundesdelegiertenkonferenz, Erfurt, 14-16 November 2008 (quoted as: Bündnis 90/Die Grünen 2008); *Christlich Demokratische Union Deutschlands (CDU):* Leitsätze für eine aktive Außen- und Sicherheitspolitik. Beschlüsse des 14. Parteitages der CDU Deutschlands, Dresden, 2-4 December 2001 (quoted as: CDU 2001); *Christlich Demokratische Union Deutschlands (CDU):* Vier Koordinaten einer deutschen Außen- und Sicherheitspolitik. Rede der Partei- und Fraktionsvorsitzenden Dr. Angela Merkel, auf der XLI. Münchner Konferenz für Sicherheitspolitik, 12.02.2002 (quoted as: CDU 2002); *Christlich Demokratische Union Deutschlands (CDU):* Deutschlands Verantwortung und Interessen in Europa und der Welt wahrnehmen. Beschluss des 20. Pareiages der CDU Deutschlands, Dresden, 27-28 November 2006 (quoted as: CDU 2006): *Deutscher Bundestag:* Regierungserklärung der Bundeskanzlerin Dr. Angela Merkel, in: Plenarprotokoll 16/4, 30 November 2005 (quoted as: CDU 2005); *CDU/CSU - SPD:* Gemeinsam für Deutschland. Mit Mut und Menschlichkeit. Koalitionsvertrag von CDU, CSU und SPD, Berlin, 11 November 2005 (quoted as: CDU/CSU - SPD 2005); *Freie Demokratische Partei (FDP):* Kontinuität, Prinzipien und neue Herausforderungen für liberale Außenpolitik. Beschluss des Präsidiums der FDP, Berlin, 6 September 2005 (quoted as: FDP 2005); *Freie Demokratische Partei (FDP) - Portal Liberal:* Bolton auf FDP-Forum: Veränderung der UNO drängt. Pressemitteilung v. 13.01.2006, www.liberale.de (quoted as: FDP 2006); *Freie Demokratische Partei (Internetportal der FDP-Bundestagsfraktion):* Thema Vereinte Nationen, www.fdp-fraktion.de [accessed 30.12.2008] (quoted as: FDP 2008); *Sozialdemokratische Partei Deutschlands – Bündnis 90/Die Grünen:* Aufbruch und Erneuerung – Deutschlands Weg im 21. Jahrhundert. Koalitionsvereinbarung zwischen der Sozialdemokratischen Partei Deutschlands und Bündnis 90/Die Grünen, Bonn, 20 October 1998 (quoted as: SPD - Bündnis 90/Die Grünen 1998); *Sozialdemokratische Partei Deutschlands (SPD):* Erneuerung und Zusammenhalt – Wir in Deutschland. Regierungsprogramm 2002-2006. Beschluss des Bundesparteitags, Berlin, 2 June 2002 (quoted as: SPD 2002); *II. Secondary Literature: Hüfner, K.:* Peanuts für die UNO. Das deutsche Finanzengagement seit 1960, Frankfurt (Main) 2008.

Internet: *Homepages of the parties represented in the Bundestag:* a) Christian Democratic Union (CDU): www.cdu.de; b) Christian Social Union (CSU): www. csu.de; c) Free Democratic Party (FDP): www.fdp. de; d) Alliance 90/The Greens (Bündnis 90/Die Grünen): www.gruene.de; e) Party of the Democratic Socialism (PDS): www.pds-online.de; f) Social Democratic Party of Germany (SPD): www.spd.de.

Deutscher Bundestag (German Federal Parliament), Subcommittee on the United Nations

The German Bundestag decided only relatively recently to establish a separate committee to deal with the policies of the United Nations (UN). It was not until eighteen years after the accession of the Federal Republic of Germany to the United Nations that it was agreed in the parliamentary groups and the Committee on Foreign Affairs, which is the only Bundestag committee exclusively concerned with the United Nations, to set up a Subcommittee on the United Nations.

Only after some years of persistent work by committed Members of the Bundestag, particularly the untiring efforts of Social Democratic Member Helga Timm, was it possible to reach a consensus in the Committee on Foreign Affairs favoring such a subcommittee. Whereas in the preceding years Parliament had dealt with the subject of the United Nations in a rather "businesslike and listless" manner (*Skupnik* 1980), at the beginning of the 12th legislative term (1990-1994) it was determined to attach greater importance, in organizational and substantive terms, to UN policies and, by establishing the subcommittee, to ensure institutionalized interaction between the Subcommittee and the Government. In view of the radical upheaval in global politics in 1989/1990 and the resultant enhanced status of the United Nations, which heralded new foreign policy challenges, parliamentarians no longer wanted to leave German UN policy to the Government. The German Bundestag therefore created a *"Subcommittee on the United Nations/International Organizations"* on 6 September 1991.

1. Establishment and Status of the Subcommittee

In accordance with the Rules of Procedure of the German Bundestag, the committees may set up subcommittees to deal, over and above day-to-day politics, with specific subjects in greater depth and over an extended period of time. The Committee on Foreign Affairs has frequently made use of this possibility. As a rule, the related decision is taken at the beginning of every new legislative term. It is dependent on the coordination of political interests and a consensus between the majority supporting the Government and the minority forming the opposition, for it is not possible to set up a subcommittee if a third of the committee members expressly disagree.

The term "subcommittee" indicates that the body concerned is subordinate to the main committee both as regards its establishment and its accountability. Like the other subcommittees, the United Nations Subcommittee works for the Committee on Foreign Affairs, to which it reports on its activities; as a rule, this takes place in the form of an annual report to the main committee by the chairman of the Subcommittee. Normally almost all the members of a subcommittee serve on the parent main committee. However, the members of the subcommittees set up by the Committee on Foreign Affairs usually come from various other committees. Thus the United Nations Subcommittee comprises members of the Committee on Foreign Affairs, the Committee on Economic Cooperation and the Defence Committee; however, the chairman has always been a member of the Committee on Foreign Affairs.

2. Work Programme and Functions

Whereas the specialized committees consider only those aspects of the programmes and activities of the United Nations which fall within their terms of reference, the parliamentary deliberations of the United Nations Subcommittee are intended to transcend departmental boundaries and can in principle cover all the fields of work of the United Nations as well as those of other global organizations belonging to the UN family.

The work programme of the United Nations Subcommittee is conceived less on a sectoral basis than in terms of tasks cutting across a wide variety of fields. This enables the Subcommittee to combine various thematic strands, which are split up by the committees because of the subject matter involved, and to place them in the context of the UN system.

Issues transcending departmental boundaries, such as strengthening and reforming the United Nations, can be systematically addressed by the Subcommittee without the deliberations being confined to one specific field.

The work programme of the United Nations Subcommittee is determined by its function, which has a dual perspective, facing both inwards and outwards, as it were. Looking inwards, the Subcommittee follows the Government's United Nations policy using parliamentary means. However, it also offers specialist circles, which comprise mainly non-governmental organizations ($\rightarrow$ NGOs), UN institutions and academics, an opportunity to exert influence on parliamentary work by inviting their representatives and experts to meetings, holding hearings or conducting an exchange of information in other ways. Looking outwards, the Subcommittee seeks to take action in establishing and maintaining parliamentary contacts with the United Nations and its specialized agencies and by participating in international parliamentary initiatives aimed at strengthening the United Nations. It also has the task of ensuring more active involvement of German politics in the international discussion on reform of the United Nations ($\rightarrow$ Reform of the UN).

In addition to deliberating on items referred to it by the plenary, the United Nations Subcommittee is mainly concerned with the policy dialogue on topical and fundamental questions regarding UN policies. Since Parliament's legislation in the foreign policy field plays only a minor role, special importance attaches to the right of the Committee on Foreign Affairs to take up an issue on its own initiative in the main committee and its subcommittees. As far as the United Nations Subcommittee is concerned, this means that it can decide its own agenda; agreement with the Committee on Foreign Affairs is not required. As a rule, the Subcommittee asks the Federal Government for a report on the relevant item on the agenda. Subsequently more detailed questions are put to the representative of the Federal Foreign Office or of other ministries, and the members of the United Nations Subcommittee discuss the matter. The meetings of the United Nations Subcommittee are usually non-public; meetings can, however, be open to the public, if the Subcommittee so decides.

Control, information and participation in the Federal Government's policies are the most important functions which the Subcommittee aims to achieve through a policy dialogue. Through the reports of the Federal Government and the questions put to experts, the members of the United Nations Subcommittee ensure a continuous flow of information on topics on which their political interest focuses. Information procurement is one of the decisive factors on which an ability to take political action, and thus also to control the Government, hinges. This control primarily consists of checking the Government's action against the yardstick of its own declared goals (control of the political direction); it also includes the economic use of appropriate and effective means to achieve these goals (efficiency control).

Since the distinguishing feature of a parliamentary democracy is not the dualism of Parliament and Government but the opposition between the Government and the parliamentary majority, on the one hand, and the parliamentary minority, on the other, the representatives of the opposition on the United Nations Subcommittee naturally take a greater interest in the control of the Government. They therefore make more extensive use of the Subcommittee as an instrument with which to obtain information and ask critical questions; conversely, their colleagues from the governing parliamentary groups make sure that when votes are taken on concurrent motions the coalition is able to bring its majority to bear. However, the opposition does not concentrate exclusively on expressing criticism, it also seeks to influence the positions of the Federal Government and, with the limited means at its disposal, to help shape German UN policy. One way of doing this is to sound out joint positions in the Subcommittee and include them in cross-party motions, as was the case, for example, with the motion on UN peace policy in Western Sahara.

3. Thematic Focus

During the 12th and 13th legislative terms (1990-94 and 1994-98) of the German Bundestag, the United Nations Subcommittee completed a wide-ranging working programme. The committee meetings focused on current trouble spots where the United Nations was and is active in the field of peace policy, on the issue of reforming and strengthening the UN, the financial crisis, UN world conferences and the Federal Government's UN policy.

Following the end of the East-West conflict the United Nations gained in importance in the field of international → peacekeeping, but this only lasted for a few years. After the failure of some peacekeeping measures (→ Peacekeeping Operations), the number of such measures fell in the mid-1990s almost as fast as it had increased in the first half of the decade. In the 13th legislative term (1994-98) peacekeeping measures therefore appeared less frequently on the agenda of the United Nations Subcommittee than in the 12th legislative term (1990-94). The Subcommittee devoted special attention to a few trouble spots; in addition to Cyprus and Central Africa, these included, above all, the conflicts in Western Sahara and in the Balkans. At the beginning of the 1990s, foreign policy discussion focused on the question of Germany's commitment with respect to UN missions. The dispute was not about the deployment of German citizens on humanitarian or police missions beyond NATO's borders, which had already occurred before German reunification, e.g. in Namibia and Central America; the divisive issue was whether the participation of armed Bundeswehr units in peacekeeping measures or coercive military measures was compatible with the Basic Law, the German

95

constitution. The debate was not only between the conservative-liberal Government and the opposition parties, the Social Democrats and Alliance 90/The Greens, but also within the government and opposition camps. The bills to clarify the constitutional conformity of out-of-area deployment of the Bundeswehr introduced by the SPD opposition (Sub-committee Document 12/2893) and the ruling coalition (Sub-committee Document 12/4107) did not even reach the United Nations Subcommittee. Since there was no political agreement, the legal situation was finally clarified by the Federal Constitutional Court in its ruling of 12 July 1994, according to which the decision on out-of-area deployment is primarily a political question. However, legal questions will still have to be answered in future as well, because, on the one hand, Parliament will guard its right to take a decision and, on the other, it will continue to be confronted with the question whether deployment is in conformity with the international law in force.

From the outset the United Nations Subcommittee has sought to support the Budget Committee in controlling financial expenditure. However, in this connection its influence is very limited. The United Nations Subcommittee can participate only indirectly, either through the proposals for amendments put forward by the rapporteurs, or through an opinion expressed by the Committee on Foreign Affairs. Though it succeeded in 1998 in reducing the drastic cuts affecting the United Nations Development Programme ($\rightarrow$ UNDP), it was, despite the backing of the Federal Foreign Office, unable to gain support for its request that a single payment be made to settle the GDR's remaining contribution arrears ($\rightarrow$ UN Policy, GDR).

One of the most important areas of the Subcommittee's work is reform of the United Nations, which is an ongoing political task. On 9 November 1992 the Subcommittee held a public hearing on the topic "Reform of the United Nations". All the experts agreed that, on account of the increasing number of tasks to be performed by the United Nations and the latter's difficult financial situation, radical reforms were urgently required. These included an overhaul of the composition of the $\rightarrow$ Security Council. The experts rated the work of the Economic and Social Council ($\rightarrow$ ECOSOC) as unsatisfactory and, to improve payment behavior, called for $\rightarrow$ sanctions such as more consistently depriving the countries concerned of the right to vote in the General Assembly, as well as charging interest on outstanding contributions ($\rightarrow$ Financial Crises). In the human rights field, new standards were, in the experts' view, less important than the enforcement of existing standards ($\rightarrow$ Human Rights, Protection of). The experts called for the Federal Government to coordinate UN policy more efficiently at national level, both among the ministries and between the Government and Parliament, and recommended even closer coordination in the context of the EU ($\rightarrow$ European Union, CFSP at the UN). From the results of the hearing and the information it provided, the Subcommittee gained numerous new ideas for its work.

The parties represented in the Bundestag drew up motions of their own to present their positions and deepen the discussion on renewal of the United Nations. Following the motion entitled "Reform of the United Nations" (Sub-committee Document 12/1719) introduced by the SPD opposition in 1991, the ruling coalition set forth its views in two motions (Sub-committee Documents 12/3702 and 12/3703) at the end of 1992; Alliance 90/The Greens and the PDS later followed suit with motions of their own (Sub-committee Documents 12/5728 and 12/4568 respectively). Whereas the need to reform and strengthen the UN was undisputed, the priorities and the main focus of the overhaul were perceived differently. This was also the reason why the attempt to bring about a joint motion introduced by the ruling coalition and the SPD opposition failed (cf. $\rightarrow$ Deutscher

Bundestag, UN Policies of the Parties). In subsequent years the Subcommittee time and again considered individual questions regarding reform of the United Nations, above all to adjusting the Security Council to changes in the international system, enhancing the UN's operational capabilities in the peace-keeping field and dealing with the UN's financial crisis. The Subcommittee discussed the ability of the Economic and Social Council to function, and the need for reform of specific specialized agencies and programmes.

Another central aim of the Subcommittee was to improve enforcement of international law (→ International Law and the UN). As a result, the International Court of Justice (→ ICJ), the International Criminal Tribunals for the Former Yugoslavia and for Rwanda and the setting up of an → International Tribunal for the Law of the Sea in Hamburg were the subject of its parliamentary deliberations on several occasions. The Subcommittee proposed recognition of the ICJ's obligatory jurisdiction and, on a visit to The Hague, saw for itself the valuable work being done by the Tribunal for the Former Yugoslavia. Moreover, the Subcommittee supported the setting up of a permanent International Criminal Court (→ ICC) actively advocated by the Federal Government.

The official trips made by the United Nations Subcommittee served to provide first-hand information and to establish the Subcommittee's own network of contacts in the foreign policy field. On their visits to New York the members of the Subcommittee were received by Secretaries-General Boutros Boutros-Ghali and Kofi Annan (→ Secretary-General). In addition to visiting UN institutions in New York, Geneva, Vienna and Nairobi, the Subcommittee has also traveled to Sweden to obtain information on the training of peacekeepers (→ Peacekeeping Forces; Peacekeeping Operations). In 1994 Subcommittee members visited the Western Sahara and conferred with both parties to the conflict about resolving it; in this connection, they used all the means at their disposal to bring about the release of prisoners.

On various occasions the Subcommittee has discussed the Federal Government's personnel policy with respect to the United Nations (→ Personnel). In the Subcommittee the Federal Government has been asked several times to establish adequate representation of Germany in the United Nations in terms of staff, to improve income and pension conditions as well as measures for the advancement of young staff, and to ensure inter-ministerial coordination of these matters. The Association of German Staff in International Organizations (VDBIO) had time and again drawn the Subcommittee's attention to problems regarding German personnel policy. In response to the VDBIO's criticism, the SPD opposition urged the Federal Government in a detailed inquiry to disclose the proportion of German staff in the United Nations and its → specialized agencies (Sub-committee Document 13/4067). The fact that meetings of State Secretaries were arranged at the Federal Chancellery to coordinate personnel policy shows that these efforts were partially successful.

4. Conclusions

It is not least thanks to the activities of the United Nations Subcommittee that the United Nations is no longer a topic neglected by the German Bundestag. Generating initiatives and serving as a catalyst, it has helped ensure that in the 1990s considerably more plenary debates were held on the United Nations than in the preceding decades. On several occasions it invited other committees to attend joint meetings – quite a rare occurrence in the Bundestag – in order to speed up the parliamentary progress on specific matters relating to UN policy. The Subcommittee's work has achieved a number of visible results, e.g. increasing the German contribution to the Centre for Human Rights (→ Human Rights, United Nations High Commissioner for), preventing Germany from leaving → UNIDO, helping bring about the release of prisoners in Western Sahara and reducing the size of cuts in voluntary contributions to UN institutions (→ Budget).

Nevertheless the Subcommittee was able to exert only limited influence within Parliament and on the UN policies of the conservative-liberal Federal Government. In debates on UN matters in the plenary which had an impact on public opinion the members of the Subcommittee often played only a subordinate role as speakers. The Council of Elders mostly placed these items so far down the agenda that there was from the outset little chance of their producing a response among the public (→ Public Opinion and the UN). Moreover, the Subcommittee was unable to gain acceptance for its cross-party proposal that a celebration be held in the German Bundestag to mark the 50th anniversary of the United Nations. The Government, too, was disinterested, as Chancellor Kohl's decision not to attend the central celebration in New York showed. Finally, the reduction in the number of members of the Subcommittee, which it had to accept at the beginning of the 13th legislative term (1994-98), was disappointing.

It should be pointed out that there are structural limits on the Subcommittee's work. It is a deliberative body, not a decision-making body. Its views on motions are merely recommendations, and it does not have the right to initiate legislation. It can act as a single political player to only a limited extent, since it cannot escape the rules of political competition between the parliamentary majority and the opposition. Moreover, the radius of action of a subcommittee is smaller than that of the main committee. For instance, deliberations on a motion tabled by the Federal Government on deployment of the Bundeswehr abroad take place in the Committee on Foreign Affairs, and the United Nations Subcommittee is not involved at all. Its subordinate character is also noticeable in another way: ministers or the Secretary-General of the United Nations speak before the main committee, not the Subcommittee.

The fact that the United Nations Subcommittee has been set up again in the 14th legislative term is a mark of success for the Subcommittee and for the cause of the United Nations in the German Bundestag. That its official name is now only "Subcommittee on the United Nations" and the additional title "International Organizations" has been deleted, does not mean a loss of competence; rather, it indicates that the Subcommittee now concentrates on the United Nations system (→ UN System).

To increase its influence within Parliament and outside it, it will have to strengthen its cooperation with non-governmental organizations (→ NGOs) and specialist circles. The Subcommittee could make greater use of the fact that in the last few years a growing number of German NGOs have taken an active interest in the work of the United Nations. Holding more hearings and more frequent public meetings with invited representatives of UN institutions, NGOs and the media, reporting regularly on its work and setting clear priorities in its work programme, could be considered. However, the NGOs, too, should address their requests and concerns more specifically to the United Nations Subcommittee; distributing position papers and catalogues of demands is not sufficient. More effective interaction between NGOs and the United Nations Subcommittee can only benefit German UN policies. The present Federal Government composed of the SPD and Alliance 90/The Greens has announced that it will promote the United Nations more than has been the case hitherto. It remains to be seen whether this will give the United Nations Subcommittee an opportunity to strengthen its parliamentary influence.

Eberhard Brecht / Wolfgang Ehrhart

Lit.: *Ehrhart, W.:* UN-Politik: nicht mehr allein der Exekutive überlassen. Der neue Unterausschuß „Vereinte Nationen/Weltweite

Organisationen" des Deutschen Bundestages, in: VN 41 (1993), 132-137; *Ehrhart, W.*: Deutscher Bundestag: Vorschläge zur UN-Reform, in: VN 41 (1993), 205-206; *Ehrhart, W.*: Bericht über die UN-Politik im Deutschen Bundestag, in: VN 44 (1996) 156-158; *Ehrhart W.*: Deutscher Bundestag: Große Anfrage zur Reform der Vereinten Nationen, in: VN 45 (1997), 185-187; *Ehrhart W.*: Nicht im Rampenlicht, aber wirkungsvoll. Der Unterausschuß „Vereinte Nationen/Internationale Organisationen" des Deutschen Bundestages nach zwei Legislaturperioden, in: VN 46 (1998), 131-135; *Hüfner, K.*: Deutsche VN-Politik im Bundestag, in: DGVN (ed.): 20 Jahre deutsche Mitgliedschaft in den VN auf dem Prüfstand, Bonn 1994, 37-47; *Jung, K.*: Deutscher Bundestag: UN-Politik der Bundesregierung unter der Lupe, in: VN 37 (1989), 126-127; *Münzing, E./Pilz, V.*: Der Auswärtige Ausschuß des Deutschen Bundestages: Aufgaben, Organisation und Arbeitsweise, in: Zeitschrift für Parlamentsfragen, No. 4/1998, 575-604; *Skupnik, W.*: UNO: notwendig, nützlich und ziemlich unbeachtet. Die Vereinten Nationen als Thema des 8. Deutschen Bundestages, in: VN 28 (1980), 131-136; *Unser, G.*: Die UNO. Aufgaben und Strukturen der Vereinten Nationen, 6th rev. edn., Munich 1997.

Addendum

1. The Common Declaration of 2001

In the 14th legislative term (1998-2002) the United Nations Subcommittee of the German Federal Parliament (Bundestag) succeeded in achieving a most significant hallmark in its work. As a kind of farewell present the long-standing chairman of the Subcommittee, Dr. Eberhard Brecht, who gave up his mandate as member of parliament to take up his new office as mayor of a German town in summer 2001, laid in tedious and skillful preparatory work – with the support of the working group for foreign policy of the SPD parliamentary group in the German Bundestag – the foundation for a substantial common declaration of the parliamentary groups of the CDU/CSU, the SPD, the FDP and the Alliance 90/ The Greens, which after a highly interesting debate was adopted with the votes of the four above-

mentioned parliamentary groups (text: Bundestag printed paper 14/5855, cf. also: Bundestag stenographic record 14/177 of 22 June 2001).

In welcoming the results of the UN Millennium Summit of September 2000 and in affirming an active role for Germany in the United Nations, the declaration established a number of benchmarks which still form the evaluative basis of the German UN policy: the German Federal Government was asked among other things to safeguard a binding coordination of all government departments in order to reach a unified German UN policy in the different organs of the UN family, to submit a biennial report on the UN policy of the government starting in 2001, to strive for an expansion of the United Nations through a parliamentary dimension and for the supply of regular and extensive information of the national parliaments about the current UN issues and to let the NGOs take part as already practiced in the decision-making processes of German UN policy.

In addition to this general catalogue of benchmarks, the declaration defined a number of specific goals to be striven for by German UN policy in the different fields of UN activity – international law, peacekeeping, reform of the UN Security Council, economic and social issues, and environment. It amounted to one of the most detailed and progressive outlines of national UN policy goals ever adopted by a national parliament, which can in many points still serve as the political guideline for UN policy.

This declaration proved that a small subcommittee is capable of working out substantial and meaningful political programmes, even if their implementation is dependent on other political factors outside of its influence such as budgetary questions, political opportunity and strategy, support by other UN member states and many more. Such a subcommittee can obviously not make policy, but it can be a benchmark tester for political concepts and of their implementation, provided it can have at its disposal committed members and a dedicated chairman such as Eberhard Brecht.

2. The Biennial Reports

Following the parliamentary request contained in the 2001 declaration the German Federal Government submitted in June 2002 its first report on the Cooperation between Germany and the United Nations – covering the year 2001, followed in December 2004 by the second report covering the years 2002 and 2003, in December 2006 by the third report covering the years 2004 and 2005 and in July 2008 by the fourth report covering the years 2006 and 2007 and including now also the international financial organizations ($\rightarrow$ IWF and $\rightarrow$ World Bank). Prepared by the Federal Foreign Office as department in charge in an editorial function, supplemented by contributions from other government departments and finalized in continual political contacts with the Chairman of the Subcommittee, the reports turned out to be collections of substantial information on the different aspects of German UN policy, being of great importance for academic research, but – most regrettably – seldom used as a basis for parliamentary debates on UN policy and even more seldom as a starting point for an article in a journal or newspaper.

One reason might be that – since the report is written by government officials – it lacks a certain critical distance. Perhaps Germany should copy the US model of asking the Federal Court of Audit (Bundesrechnungshof) or the UN model to ask a scientific endowment or a high-level panel of experts to write such a report. In this case the report would without doubt also contain critical observations and evaluative remarks.

3. The Debate about the Parliamentary Dimension of the UN

The Subcommittee experienced in early 2005 a higher valuation of its political standing – at least temporarily: in reaction to the so-called "Cardoso-Report"

submitted in June 2004 to the UN General Assembly by a panel of eminent persons on the topic of the relations between the United Nations and civil society, which contained among others some suggestions concerning the improvement of the cooperation between the United Nations and national parliaments, the German Bundestag adopted in September 2004 a motion of the parliamentary groups of the SPD, CDU/CSU, Alliance 90/The Greens, and the FDP to develop their own concept for the participation of parliaments within the $\rightarrow$ UN system (cf. German Bundestag: a) printed paper 15/3711 of 22 September 2004; b) stenographic record 15/126, 23 September 2004, 11494B). On the basis of this decision the Presidium of the German Bundestag asked the Subcommittee in November 2004 in a formal letter to work out their proposal with the participation of members of the German delegation to the Inter-Parliamentary Union (IPU) and to submit the proposal to the plenary of the Bundestag.

In dealing with this request the Subcommittee held two public hearings in February and March 2005 with academic experts, and representatives of the IPU and NGO representatives ($\rightarrow$ NGOs), respectively, and worked out on the basis of these hearings a report with proposals, which was subsequently adopted unanimously in the Committee on Foreign Relations in May 2005. This resulted in a motion of the parliamentary groups of the SPD and Alliance 90/The Greens on parliamentary participation in the $\rightarrow$ UN system, which was adopted with the votes of the members present of the SPD and Alliance 90/The Greens parliamentary groups, with the CDU/ CSU and FDP abstaining (cf. Bundestag printed paper 15/6590 of 15 June 2005 and Bundestag stenographic record 15/181 of 16 June 2005).

4. Recognizing the Role of the Subcommittee – No Real Progress?

While the analysis of the concept for the participation of the national parliaments in the UN system is left out here, because the entry deals with the role of the Subcommittee, the decision of the German Bundestag is remarkable with respect to the role of the United Nations Subcommittee and to the role of its parent committee, the Committee on Foreign Relations: the Bundestag stated in the decision that the parliamentary control of and participation in the German UN policy would not be sufficiently transparent and would lack systematic procedures. The fact that the Committee on Foreign Relations and its subcommittees "United Nations" and "Globalization and External Economic Policy" dealt with UN policy as part of German foreign policy and German global policy and that the other Committees of the German Bundestag were free in their decision as to whether and how far they took up UN matters falling into their respective sphere of competence would not suffice to ensure a consistent and transparent parliamentary control and participation.

The Bundestag decision appreciated explicitly the role of the United Nations Subcommittee in improving the information of the German Bundestag on UN issues and underlined in this respect the importance of the biennial reports of the Federal Government on the cooperation between Germany and the UN.

The decision noted that – in reaction to a request resolved by the Committee on Foreign Relations in March 2004 – the Federal Government informs since then the Committee on Foreign Relations in writing about the planned conferences of the UN and other international organizations and their themes, and submits written reports on the course and results of the conferences.

The Bundestag recommended the institutionalization in a durable manner of the way the Committee on Foreign Relations deals with UN issues and global issues and the organization also in this context of the way other Bundestag committees deal in a supplementary manner with the UN issues.

The Bundestag recommended that the competent Bundestag committees should arrange an annual public UN and global governance hearing, with the invitation of high-level representatives of the UN and other international organizations, in particular IMF, World Bank, → ILO and →WTO.

The request of the Presidium of the Bundestag, the public hearings in early 2005 and the Bundestag decision of June 2005 have strengthened to some extent the position of the Subcommittee, since its role in ensuring sufficient information of the Bundestag was made visible and since the Bundestag called for a systematic institutionalization of the manner the parliament deals with UN matters within the Committee on Foreign Relations.

But, regrettably, the conservative and bureaucratic forces within the German Bundestag and the Federal Government proved to be stronger. Until now (December 2008) no such procedure has been established and laid down in the rules of procedure of the Committee on Foreign Relations and in the rules of procedure of the competent government departments. Also the recommendation to hold annual public hearings has not been put into practice so far.

Thus – without established procedures for the parliamentary handling of UN issues – the Subcommittee is still dependent in its work on the interest of parliamentary groups in the Bundestag to deal more intensely with UN matters and to make use of the United Nations Subcommittee as in the above-mentioned case on an *ad hoc* basis.

6. Evaluation and Prospects

Without doubt the United Nations Subcommittee has established itself since its foundation in 1991 as a source of reliable information on UN matters for the German Bundestag and – to some extent – as instrument of political control, but only to a small extent as an instrument to start a public debate on the goals of UN policy.

In this connection the procedure established in 2004 to get reports on the course and results of all UN-related conferences has without doubt strengthened to some degree the control function of the Subcommittee towards the Federal Foreign Office and other Government Departments; but the control effect is relatively small, as effective control could only be achieved if the Subcommittee would get often enough the opportunity to present its findings in a plenary debate of the Bundestag.

It would be advisable – if one compares the way UN policy is handled in Germany with the procedures for example in the USA or Switzerland – to hold at least a general plenary debate on UN policy in the German Bundestag shortly before the parliamentary summer recess, where the Bundestag could submit the Federal Government a catalogue of concepts and goals to be taken into account by the UN delegation of the Federal Government in the general debate of the UN → General Assembly starting annually in September.

The Subcommittee should make use of the opportunity provided by the Bundestag decision of June 2005 to initiate and prepare together with other subcommittees and/or committees of the Bundestag annual public hearings on the UN: that would increase the public awareness of the German UN policy and strengthen also the standing of the Subcommittee.

The Subcommittee should also attempt to develop its working relations with the media – the 2005 public hearings, for example, were almost neglected by the mass media.

If the Subcommittee does not fight for a larger role, it will remain a diligent information collector and focal point for academic researchers and high-level visitors from the UN. That is not enough if it is measured against the justified demand of the Bundestag in its 2005 decision for a transparent and effective parliamentary control of and participation in German UN policy.

Helmut Volger

Lit.: *Zöpel, C.:* Die Vereinten Nationen und die Parlamente. Zur Mitwirkung des Bundestags an der deutschen UN Politik, in: VN 53 (2005), 97-99; *Zöpel, C.:* Die Vereinten Nationen und die Parlamente (II). Zu einer parlamentarischen Dimension der UN, in: VN 53 (2005), 145-148.

Internet: *Homepage of the Subcommittee on the UN:* www.bundestag.de/ausschuesse/a03/a03_vn/index.html.

Development Concepts, Development Research

Introduction

Development debates in the → UN system have always reflected a multitude of development perspectives, definitions and theories. The reason is the large number of member states, the growing number of civil-society organizations and business representatives in recent decades, the diversity of and disparities among countries, as well as the fact that governments are not unitary actors and government delegations often have to represent the concerns of various national constituencies.

Moreover, debates within UN system forums are, for the most part, relatively fair. They afford opportunities for an effective voice to all member states and concerned non-state parties. Put differently, they are marked by competitive deliberations, and a pluralism of ideas and priorities. The result is development concepts that mix various analytical and policy approaches but possess a most intriguing and important main property: the search for balance – a balance between the national and the international, private and public, economic and social and environmental, and the short and the longer-term.

This entry will trace UN system debates on development over the past six decades. It will proceed in three stages. I will, first, distinguish and describe in broad-brush strokes five historical periods of development thinking in the UN system. At the second stage, I will discuss to what extent and when the UN system debates have not only reflected prevalent thinking that existed in the world but been shaped also by new and innovative thinking that emerged from within the organization. At the concluding third stage, I will summarize the main findings and speculate on the question of the future: what might be the next large development topics on which UN system deliberations might focus.

Because of the complexity of the issue I will limit my remarks to a description of the outcomes of various thought and negotiation processes and not attempt an analysis of the precise origin of each input. To the extent that I attempt such an attribution, I will do so at a highly aggregate level, referring to such possible sources as for example, the "developing countries", "industrial countries", or "NGOs". (Supporting references to relevant documents, reports and studies are listed at the end of the article, in the section on 'Literature' (= Lit.))

I. UN System Development Concepts:
An Historical Overview

The focus of UN system deliberations on development over the past six decades has changed. This change has not, or at least, not so much meant a change in the development concept but rather a broadening of its definition. And this widening of the conceptual lens reflects the growing complexity of the development opportunities and constraints that presented themselves over time. Initially, development was seen as developing countries "catching up" with industrial countries. Then the international context came into focus, notably with the debate on a new international economic order (→ International Economic Relations and New International Economic Order (NIEO)). This debate was subsequently complemented by a renewed emphasis on national level policy initiatives in the economic, social and environmental fields. From there, the debates went back to the international level to explore and emphasize the role of the private sector, including that of integrating markets into development. And finally, in recent times, we see that

UN system development debates increasingly recognize the blurring of the divide between the domestic policy spheres and the international context. Policy interdependence among countries and the linked issue of the provision of global public goods such as climate stability, energy security, or controlling communicable diseases are coming to the fore.

In more detail, the conceptual evolution of UN system development debates can be depicted as follows.

1. Development as a Process of the
South "Catching Up" with the North

The early discussions about development within the UN system – as well as elsewhere in the world – were primarily about the group of countries that became known as "developing countries". The defining criterion of these countries was then a population growth rate of above 2 %. By now, this criterion has been replaced by that of poverty, notably poverty in income terms.

Consequently, the discussion about development had a strong focus on aid, taking the Marshall Plan, the US programme for the reconstruction of European and other war-torn countries, as a model. It was also in the UN that the proposal for a 0.7 % aid target was born. Aid, consisting of the transfer of both financial resources (to close the developing countries' financial gaps) and technical expertise (to support national capacity building), was then perceived as an initiative that would take as its guiding framework the national policy priorities of the recipient country. In fact, there was a strong emphasis on national policy-making sovereignty. One reason for that was the then emerging East-West confrontation and system rivalry; another was that many recipient countries had just gained their political independence and were jealously guarding that newly-won freedom.

In fact, it was precisely this East-West divide that gave multilateralism, aid dispensed through the UN system, a particular role at that time. Multilateral aid served as a bridge-building device

103

between East and West, since both blocs typically supported UN system aid such as UNDP-financed programmes.

Thus, the UN system's development activities had a Southern focus, were largely guided by national policy priorities and were of an operational rather than a norm-setting nature.

The "other" economic, social and environmental activities of the system – many of which we would, today, probably place into the development category – were of just the opposite type. Deliberations on these issues were often limited to non-committal exchanges of views and experiences, with bloc members emphasizing the value of their respective economic system. They certainly had little impact on the system's operational activities. More binding agreements typically concerned *between-country* issues, for example international traffic rules, such as, the use of the high seas (→ IMO) or setting technical and procedural standards for international aviation (→ ICAO).

2. An Added Emphasis on a New International Economic Order – and Basic Needs

Until the 1980s, both the then "socialist" and the then "market-oriented" economies had a "strong" state. Planning played a role in both systems, and development in particular was perceived as a state-led process. Hence, it is not surprising that the late 1970s saw the notion of a more planned international economy – a new international economic order (NIEO) – emerge. The argument was that an adverse international system – e.g. falling commodity prices or the patenting of critical technology – could easily thwart the results of national development efforts in developing countries. The proposal, therefore, was to adopt global policy measures, such as a stabilization fund for commodity prices to ensure more predictability and reliability in the South's export earnings, and hence, a more stable context for its development strategies.

The NIEO debate surged at a time when economic liberalization had begun to settle in. The Bretton Woods system of fixed exchange rates had collapsed in 1973. Trade liberalization and enhanced access of developing countries to Northern markets, notably the US market, was being promoted both for economic as well as political, i.e. alliance-building, reasons. And developing countries had taken on a mounting volume of external debt, tempted by the relatively "easy" availability of credit in the wake of the oil crises of the early 1970s. Dependent on a limited range of export products, indebted developing countries increased their production of these crops to be able to meet their debt servicing obligations. Yet, they soon realized that the harder they worked, and the more they produced, the more they drove the prices of their exports down and the more expensive their debt became. Other adverse factors, which added to progressive emergence of the external debt crisis in the 1980s, were high interest rates and technological advances which limited the demand for developing-country exports, notably for primary commodities.

Understandably, the developing countries were concerned about these trends; and understandably they called for a more conducive international environment, a debate which received analytical backing within the UN system through the work of → UNCTAD, the United Nations Conference on Trade and Development, and the Economic Commission for Latin America and the Caribbean. Developing countries found some support for their claims among a number of industrial-country policy-makers and thinkers. A testimony to that understanding is, for example, the so-called *Brandt Commission Report* (Independent Commission on International Development Issues 1980) (→ Independent Commissions, Reports of).

Yet, on the whole there was strong opposition to the NIEO proposals among industrial countries. Initially, the call for a NIEO was countered by industrial countries who pointed out that the developing countries themselves had the primary responsibility for making development work within their countries and that they had not exercised that responsibility fully. Critics pointed to the pervasiveness of avoidable poverty, i.e. poverty that could have been reduced, had there been the requisite political will to do so.

The "basic needs" approach was put forward often as an alternative to the NIEO proposals to demonstrate that even without the suggested systemic reforms, economy poverty could be alleviated. The "basic needs" approach was a first attempt of being "prescriptive" – commenting on *behind-the-border* policy choices that countries had made, or ought to make. It was the beginning of policy conditionality that became a dominant feature of the subsequent period of development thinking and strategizing.

3. Getting the Economic Fundamentals Right – and Making Development More People-Centred and Sustainable

As the external debt crisis of the 1980s began to surface more clearly, conditionality became an increasingly debated and practiced policy instrument. The "theory" – espoused within the UN system, primarily by the International Monetary Fund ($\rightarrow$ IMF) and the World Bank – was that in order to grow and develop countries had to adjust their economies and follow a set of "good economic policies", including in particular, fiscal prudence, a sustainable debt burden, privatization and economic liberalization. To achieve these goals, cuts in public spending were a key ingredient of the stabilization and structural adjustment programmes typically prescribed.

In many instances rising poverty levels were the consequence, a policy outcome that stood in stark contrast to the basic-needs concern that had been emphasized by industrial countries during the NIEO phase. Interestingly, the impetus to putting a "more human face" on structural adjustment programmes came from members of the academic community

who had been involved in formulating the basic-needs concept (*Cornia, Jolly* and *Stewart* 1988); and importantly, it was from the realm of the UN proper, and in particular $\rightarrow$ UNICEF, the United Nations Children's Fund, that this work was promoted.

The stabilization and structural adjustment programmes (SAPs) met with considerable opposition in developing countries and caused a great deal of social pain. While the second- and third-generation programmes were more concerned than earlier ones with cushioning the social costs of adjustment, they remained firm on the issue of policy conditionality. In fact they did this so effectively, that by now conditionality is hardly any longer a contentious issue. Many more issues than just the economic fundamentals have by now become subject to international conditionality. Just think of the issue of "good governance", including the demands for transparency and accountability, or more recently, the call for enhanced financial regulation and banking supervision. Today's processes of market integration and globalization would virtually be unthinkable without the "ground-breaking" efforts of the SAPs.

Social and environmental issues have in many respects benefited from the growing acceptance by nation states of global policy expectations and conditionalities introduced through the SAPs. Women's issues and environmental issues had been receiving attention within the UN system since the early 1970s. The Stockholm Conference on the Environment and Human Settlements was held in 1972 (cf. $\rightarrow$ UNEP); and the first Conference on Women and Development took place in Mexico City in 1975 (cf. $\rightarrow$ Women and the UN). These issues were in many instances sponsored by non-governmental organizations, such as women's groups or environmental advocates. These groups early on realized that if they joined forces across borders and lobbied governments internationally, they stood a better chance of being heard than when struggling individually, behind national borders.

But many of these social concerns – and the environmental concerns, too, – remained for a long time just "further", "additional" items on the development agenda, adjuncts to primarily growth-oriented development strategies. It was only in 1990 that UNDP's *Human Development Report* (→ Human Development Reports) began to change that situation. The Report, in a way, placed development thinking back on its feet. It argued that policy outcomes such as balanced budgets or low inflation rates are only means towards the end of human development – a widening of human choices for all.

The Report also did away with the traditional focus of development on the South. Its Human Development Index (HDI) ranked all countries, industrial and developing, according to their achievements in terms of human development. This ranking deviated in a number of instances quite significantly from the ranking of countries according to their level of income, e.g. their gross national product (GNP) per capita. The Report thus promoted a globalization of the social dimensions of development. It also gave a significant impetus to re-adjusting the balance between economic and social concerns, clearly reminding the international community that income expansion and wealth are not the sum total of human life. Rather, the success criterion ought to be whether, at the end of the day, people are better off – all people, not just a shrinking group of a privileged few.

What the *Human Development Report* did for the social aspects of development, the 1992 United Nations Conference on the Environment and Development, the so-called Earth Summit, did for the environment: it made sustainability a major requirement of development – inspired and guided by the trail-blazing report of the Commission on Sustainable Development, also often referred to as the "Brundtland Commission" after its chair, Gro Harlem Brundtland of Norway. This report introduced into the international debate the concept of sustainable development.

In fact, the 1990s saw a flurry of major international conferences (→ World Conferences), which all served to strengthen the policy focus on growth plus sustainable, human development. The first summit ever within the UN context was the Children's Summit convened under UNICEF auspices in 1990. It was followed by the 1993 UN Conference on Human Rights and the 1994 Conference on Population and Development, as well as the 1995 World Summit on Social Development and the 1995 Conference on Women and Development.

Thus, UN system debates in the 1990s largely helped universalize notions of "good" economic, social and environmental principles. While the economic concerns were primarily negotiated through the Bretton Woods institutions, such as the IMF and the World Bank, the social and environmental issues were discussed and promoted primarily within the context of the other parts of the UN system, especially the UN General Assembly. By this time, however, the Bretton Woods organizations had taken many of the social and environmental concerns "on board" and accordingly adjusted their policy recommendations. Conversely, other parts of the UN system moved their thinking closer to that of the Bretton Woods institutions.

4. Rebalancing the role of markets and states – and recognizing the new forms of volatility and the risks that globalization brings along

The wave of privatization and economic liberalization that emerged in the 1980s in industrial countries, notably the United Kingdom and the United States and spread, funneled by SAPs, through most, if not all parts of the world did not stop at national borders. In the late 1990s and early 2000s it also reached the international cooperation domain. The focus of international cooperation debates increasingly turned to other issues, for example, the role of the private sector in development. How to organize and manage public-private partnerships became a prominent concern in many UN system agencies as did issues of corporate social responsibility and voluntary private regulation. The debates on this last issue took on a visible form with the creation of the UN Global Compact initiative. The Compact invites private firms voluntarily to commit themselves to ten principles of good corporate global citizenship.

New thinking about the role of the private sector and of markets in development, however, affected not only how development strategies were conceived, but also the functioning of UN system entities. More and more activities were outsourced and contracted out to non-profit organizations, often also organized with public and private participation – as global public-private partnerships. To mention but two examples of perhaps by now more than 100 such arrangements, sponsored by or operating with support of UN system agencies, reference can be made to the Global Fund to fight AIDS, Tuberculosis and Malaria and the Prototype Carbon Fund.

The trend towards combining market, individual state, intergovernmental, and civil-society forces in support of development continues. Markets and market-based policy approaches are being explored and used for environmental purposes. The "purchase" by the Global Environment Facility (GEF) of global environmental services from developing countries against payment of compensatory finance (incremental costs) to providing developing countries as well as the Clean Development Mechanism (CDM) and Joint Implementation (JI) scheme launched to facilitate inter-nation greenhouse gas emissions trading under the Kyoto Protocol are cases in point ($\rightarrow$ Environmental Protection).

More recently, studies have also emerged on "inclusive markets": analyses of successful practices that private firms could seek to replicate in order to make their products fit price-wise and unit-wise better into the limited financial envelop of poor households. Juxta-posed to these analyses are, however, other studies such as various issues of the *World Economic and Social Survey* (WESS) prepared by the UN's department of Economic and Social Affairs that draw attention to and suggest policy approaches for dealing with the new risks and insecurities that "more markets", economic openness and globalization bring along, calling for new roles of government to cushion those.

5. More Conditionality, Targeting and Coordination – As Well Greater Calls for National Ownership

Forums of the UN proper like the UN $\rightarrow$ General Assembly still discuss in rather broad and general terms development issues in connection with their deliberation of publications like the WESS. But in many other forums, notably in the legislative bodies with operational mandates, the development notion has often vanished. For example, although the *Human Development Report* continues to appear ($\rightarrow$ Human Development Reports), the *Millennium Development Goals* have now moved to the center stage of UN system development debates; the discussions are often back to considering "isolated" issues – education, health, water, sanitation, poverty reduction – each defined as a quantified target to be attained by a set date. Monitoring and evaluating progress towards these goals has become a major pre-occupation of the analytical work conducted in many parts of the system. And intriguingly, the more intensified the monitoring and evaluation efforts become, the more the policy ownership of developing countries is also being discussed.

Yet, at the same time, the UN system agencies also express growing concern about "delivering as one" so as to reduce the transaction costs involved in assistance delivery – without, however, offering a systematic discussion on how the proposed approaches of targeting, monitoring, and delivering as one in a harmonized and coordinated way, on the one hand, could possibly be reconciled with more country ownership, on the other.

In fact, the limits of national policy ownership, and thus, national policy-making → sovereignty are being pointed out in ever clearer terms as concepts such as those of "failed states" or "responsibility to protect" signal and closer links are being seen between the security of all, global security and development, or the lack thereof, in developing countries.

6. Deepening Policy Interdependence and the Recognition of Global Public Goods

The turn towards increased policy conditionality in UN system development debates is no doubt a response to the growing unease among many countries and population groups with respect to globalization, processes such as market integration, the shrinking of time and space as well as the growing number of global challenges the world is confronting, including the threats of climate change, international terrorism and the global financial crisis of 2008. There is growing recognition that greater economic openness has deepened the policy interdependence among countries and led to a globalization of public goods like public health, peace and security, financial stability, and efficient and well-functioning market regimes. Under conditions of economic openness these goods (things, conditions) cannot be adequately provided through domestic policy initiatives alone. Their availability requires cross-border cooperation – national-level policy harmonization and the management of (un)desirable cross-border spillovers. Hence, the debate is shifting from "Whither globalization?" to "How best to manage globalization?"

As on previous occasions, it has been the UN proper, in particular the UNDP, that has moved the debate forward, suggesting that today's crises are an expression of a serious under-supply of public goods. The main challenge is not that → globalization has gone too far but that governments have not gone far enough: they still try to solve problems through domestic action only – "going it alone" – when international cooperation is needed. Cooperation must not mean creating a bloated system of international organizations. First and foremost it ought to mean achieving democratically formed international consensus on behind-the-border policy harmonization – for example, a consensus on reducing certain pollutants or on certain banking standards and practices of banking supervision.

II. Conclusion: From a Statist Notion of Development in the South to a Multi-actor Concept of Global Development – on to Which Next Notion of Development?

The *main findings* emerging from the foregoing debate can perhaps be summarized in four points.

First, the debate about development in the UN system during the past six decades thus mirrors an interesting trend. It reflects how the world during this time has moved from being a community of relatively closed *nation states* focused in its development debates, on aid to poorer countries and on *inter-national relations* to one that is marked by growing *economic openness and globalization* broadening the notion of development, from one that pertains primarily to poorer countries to one that often concerns all countries, rich and poor.

Second, the debate also shows that even as reflected in UN system debates, development is no longer the concern of governments or inter-governmental agencies alone. It is conceptualized as a multi-actor concern.

Third, the evolution of UN system development thinking is marked by a search for balance. Various political "factions" have had their particular niches within the UN system. The more economistic, neo-liberal views on development traditionally had their homes more in the Bretton Woods institutions; and the more socially oriented, egalitarian perspectives had theirs within the UN proper, especially within the General Assembly and ECOSOC context or within such agencies as UNDP or

UNICEF. If one were to include in this review narrower topics, such as population or labor, the latter – i.e. the egalitarian – group of agencies would probably also include the United Nations Populations Fund (→ UNFPA) or such agencies as the International Labour Organization (→ ILO) or the World Health Organization (→ WHO) – in short, more or less all the non-Bretton Woods agencies. These differences in policy orientation between the various parts of the system no doubt reflect underlying differences in voting patterns on the various governing bodies of different agencies. By now, however, these differences have become blurred and seem to be vanishing. Today, policy differences exist more *between* different groups of actors, notably between governments and civil society as well as business, than among governments themselves.

And fourth, UN development debates have not only been reflective of various external theories that member state delegations and other partners brought with them. Rather, on several occasions the secretariats of UN system agencies have been innovative and presented novel development perspectives and research work and helped reshape ongoing debates.

The *challenges* that the development debate in the UN system now faces are also several. A first challenge is not to allow the new agenda, the GPG agenda, to drown the aid agenda. There is a need to adequately address each on its own merits.

A second is for the UN system agencies, in particular their secretariats, to become more pro-active in thinking systematically through global incentive policies that could reduce the risk of free-riding and collective inaction in respect of providing GPGs like climate stability. No government has a strong enough self-interest in assuming that role, but they all would benefit from well functioning cooperation. Under conditions of openness of national borders, problems must be resolved effectively lest they continue to roam the international public domain. Effective international cooperation thus is more important now than ever before.

Third, the decision-making patterns of UN system forums have to be rethought to accommodate the new world powers, recognize that many development initiatives today require multi-actor inputs, and that democracy cannot stop at national borders. But of course, a balance will have to be found between participation and effectiveness for decision-making, which may have to vary between different issue areas.

In addition, perhaps the time has come for more than piecemeal reforms of the structure and functioning of the UN system. Maybe, a more fundamental review would be in order in particular to reflect the broadened concept of development, including the dual but intertwined challenge of GPG provision and supporting poorer countries in their national development efforts. However, this may call for research and debates about the UN system's development role outside the UN system, at world leadership level, and broad-based consultation of all stakeholders.

Inge Kaul

Lit.: *Brandt, W. et. al.:* Der Brandt-Report: Das Überleben sichern. Gemeinsame Interessen der Industrie- und Entwicklungsländer. Bericht der Nord-Süd-Kommission, Frankfurt (Main) 1980; *Cornia, G./Jolly, R./Stewart, F.:* Adjustment with a Human Face: Protecting the Vulnerable and Promoting Growth, New York 1988; *Emmerij, L. et al.:* The United Nations: A History of Ideas and their Future, Bloomington 2006; *International Labour Organization:* Employment, Growth and Basic Needs: A One-World Problem, New York 1977; *Kaul, I. et al. (eds.):* Providing Global Public Goods: Managing Globalization, New York/Oxford 2003; *Kaul, I./Conceição, P. (eds.):* The New Public Finance: Responding to Global Challenges, New York/Oxford 2006; *Newman, E. et al. (eds.):* Multilateralism Under Challenge? Power, International order, and Structural Change, Tokyo 2006; *United Nations:* Millennium Development Goals at www.un.org/millenniumgoals/; *United Nations:* World Economic and Social Survey, New York 1948-2008; *United Nations Development Programme:* Creating Value for

All: Strategies for Doing Business with the Poor, New York 2008; *United Nations Development Programme:* Human Development Reports 1990-2008/2009, New York 1990-2008, http://hdr.undp.org/; *United Nations - General Assembly:* Report of the United Nations Conference on the Human Environment. (UN Doc. A/CONF.48/141/ Rev.1, Stockholm 1972; reprinted in: ILM 31(1992), 849-873; *United Nations - General Assembly:* World Social Situation, UN Doc. A/RES/31/84, 13 December 1976; *United Nations - General Assembly:* Restructuring of the Economic and Social Sectors of the United Nations System, UN Doc. A/RES/32/197, 20 December 1977; *United Nations - General Assembly:* World Social Situation, UN Doc. A/RES/34/152, 17 December 1979; *United Nations - General Assembly:* Global Negotiations Relating to International Economic Co-operation for Development, UN Doc. A/RES/34/138, 14 December 1979; *United Nations - General Assembly:* Agenda 21. Adopted by the UN Conference on Environment and Development, UN Doc A/CONF.151/26/Rev.1, Vol. 1, Rio de Janeiro, Brazil 1992; *United Nations - General Assembly:* Vienna Declaration and Programme of Action, UN Doc. A/CONF.157/23 of 12 July 1993, Vienna 1993; *United Nations - General Assembly:* Report of the International Conference on Population and Development, UN Doc. A/CONF.171/13/Rev.1, Cairo 1994; *United Nations - General Assembly:* Report of the World Summit for Social Development, UN Doc. A/CONF.166/9, Copenhagen 1995; *United Nations - General Assembly:* Report of the Fourth World Conference on Women, UN Doc. A/CONF.177/20/Rev.1, Beijing 1995; *United Nations - General Assembly:* A More Secure World: Our Shared Responsibility. Report of the High-level Panel on Threats, Challenges and Change, UN Doc. A/59/565 of 2 December 2004; *United Nations Intellectual History Project:* at www. unhistory.org/; *Weiss, T.G./Daws, S. (eds.):* The Oxford Handbook on the United Nations, Oxford 2007.

Development Cooperation of the UN System

Introduction

This entry presents an overview of the historical evolution of the UN system's international development cooperation (→ UN system), focusing in particular,

110

on the operational side – as opposed to the norm- and standard-setting side – of this system.

The analysis shows UN system development cooperation – like other multilateral efforts and much of bilateral development cooperation – began as an assistance or aid effort. Yet by now, two strands of development cooperation have emerged: aid continues to be one strand; and international operational initiatives aimed at meeting global challenges – global public goods provision – are the second strand.

Also, whereas UN system operational development cooperation in its beginnings was strongly country-driven, based on nations' policymaking sovereignty, it has now become more conditionality-focused.

A key reason for the aforementioned trends is the growing interdependence among countries, or as some analysts put it, the present process of → globalization. Globalization calls for more behind-the-border policy harmonization; and it calls for more decisive management of cross-border spillovers like pollution or communicable diseases. Both in turn require greater reliance on conditionality – a more focused, results-oriented approach to international cooperation.

A further fundamental change in UN system development cooperation has been its transformation from an essentially intergovernmental process to a multi-actor process characterized by increasing public-private partnering and the use of markets and market-based instruments in promoting global public policy concerns.

In more detail, the shifts in UN system development cooperation were as follows.

UN System Development Cooperation: The Two Main Strands

One important role – if not *the* most important role – of the UN system's different agencies and bodies is to facilitate exchange of policy experiences among member states so as to forge a better understanding for international norm and standard setting. Just think of conventions such as the *Universal Declaration on Human Rights* (→ Human Rights, Universal Declaration of) or treaties such as the *Montreal Protocol* on the reduction of ozone-depleting substances (→ Environmental Protection), the decisions taken within the framework of the International Monetary Fund (→ IMF) on the surveillance of financial markets or the many resolutions passed within the context of the International Labour Organization (→ ILO) on labor rights and standards, to mention but a few examples. Through these types of inter-governmental policy agreements a considerable amount of international development cooperation has been and is being achieved.

However, there is a second main strand of international development cooperation on which this entry will primarily focus. That is what I will call the operational side of international development cooperation. This operational side involves *joint follow-up activities*, such as the provision of multilateral development assistance or the creation of other joint facilities, such as the establishment of a dispute settlement mechanism within the World Trade Organization (WTO; → WTO/GATT).

The Origins of UN System Operational Activities for Development

In 1948, the UN → General Assembly requested the → Secretary-General to organize teams of experts, through the UN proper or through the system's → specialized agencies, to assist developing countries in building capacities to help themselves. Given the strong demand for this initial programme and its early successes, the Economic and Social Council (→ ECOSOC) of the UN General Assembly in 1949 decided to establish an *Expanded Programme of Technical Assistance for Economic Development of Under-developed Countries* (EPTA). EPTA was a truly system-wide initiative. Besides an inter-governmental legislative body, the Technical Assistance Committee, the *Programme*

also had an inter-agency supervisory board, the Technical Assistance Board.

However, it soon became evident that "good advice" alone would not suffice. Developing countries also had critical financial gaps. While the World Bank was there to help meet some of these needs, the General Assembly felt it would also be useful to set up another special fund to help create conditions that would render other capital assistance more effective. In 1957 the General Assembly thus created a *Special United Nations Fund for Economic Development* (SUNFED), which became operational in 1959. Six years later, in 1965, EPTA and SUNFED were merged to create → UNDP, the United Nations Development Programme.

The original UNDP was the UN system's country-office network and central funding agency for *technical assistance*. The substantive responsibility for its programmes and projects rested in large measure with the system's specialized agencies, such as the Food and Agriculture Organization (→ FAO), the International Civil Aviation Agency (→ ICAO) or the World Health Organization (→ WHO).

Early Principles of 'Good' Development Cooperation

Clearly, development assistance constitutes an international activity that reaches behind recipient countries' national borders from the outside. From the very beginning of UN system assistance, this has been perceived as a sensitive matter. After all, the recipient countries had typically just won their political independence and aspired to becoming sovereign nations with their own policy-making power. In establishing EPTA in 1949, ECOSOC thus laid down explicit principles to guide the delivery of assistance programmes and projects. For example, it stipulated that assistance was to be rendered only upon the request of the developing countries and free of any considerations of a political nature.

These basic requirements underpinned the emerging notion of "multilateral" –

as opposed to "bilateral" – assistance. UN system operational activities for development were expected to be neutral and disinterested, aimed at supporting countries in achieving their respective national objectives. UN system assistance was also expected to be universal and to reach out to qualifying countries anywhere, whether they were part of the then "East" or "West" or non-aligned. The World Bank (→ World Bank, World Bank Group) and the IMF were somewhat of an exception to this rule, given their weighted, more "Western"-biased decision-making format.

Accordingly, UN system assistance was delivered primarily based on the recipient country's own development programme, as a tripartite arrangement, including the government, UNDP as the funding agency and the specialized agencies as the executing technical body. Because of its neutrality and universality, UN system assistance during the cold-war era served an important purpose as a bridge between the rival power blocs. It could tread where neither "East" or "West" could go. Not surprisingly, the vanishing of the "East"-"West" divide led – at least temporarily – to a serious slump in the funding for UN system assistance programmes.

The 1980s-90s: A Period of Change

The UN system of operational activities had remained rather stable until the mid-1980s. No doubt, the earlier periods had witnessed ups and downs in funding. But the basic original pattern of assistance had prevailed throughout: project-based assistance guided by the recipient country's national development objectives. This pattern began to change in the late 1980s. Seven trends are worth mentioning:

A first change was brought about by the *growing management capacities in developing countries* which encouraged many governments to pursue more "government execution" – in a way, competing with UN system agency execution, which had until then be taken for granted. Of course, some governments continued to rely on the advice of UN

system agencies to assist them in project implementation. Yet, it now was governments – rather than international organizations – which were increasingly in charge of assistance projects.

A second factor that broke into the hitherto firm tripartism of UN system development cooperation was the worldwide policy shift towards *economic liberalization and privatization.* The UN system specialized agencies were increasingly expected to compete with other service providers – private businesses as well as non-governmental organizations (→ NGOs) – for project execution. This opened the door to a much wider range of policy advice than developing countries had been receiving until then; and it unleashed a rapid growth in the number of new actors – notably, nonprofit-organizations often organized as public-private partnerships – entering the operational international cooperation domain. By now, the number of these new service providers may well be close to the one-thousand mark.

Third, it became increasingly evident that, besides sector-based developments, overall development depends on the proper management of a number of *cross-cutting issues* – e.g. the environment, gender equality, human rights, governance and technology. UNDP, which until then had been primarily a funding agency, now took on a number of these cross-sectoral issues as its substantive domains.

Fourth, UNDP's move towards assuming a substantive role of its own, however, came at a price: the organization lost much of its central funding role. Donors increasingly placed their contributions directly to the substantive issues and projects – and agencies – they wished to support. This also had an impact on developing countries. UN system development cooperation became *more centralized* and developing countries' policymaking → sovereignty constrained.

The World Bank went through a similar change process as UNDP, viz. from being primarily a lending organization to becoming a development organization. This change was encouraged by the enhanced access of a growing number of developing countries to financial markets, and consequently, their growing reliance on *private finance*. The Bank in response increased its grant-making capacity, leading to a blurring of lines between its mandate and that of other UN system entities, notably that of UNDP, and furthering reinforcing the trend towards more centralized development cooperation, relying on global funds and programmes.

Fifth, governments in both industrial and developing countries have, during the recent past, increasingly noticed that their country's national development depends not only on domestic policy action but also on concerted action by other countries. For example, the risk of global warming can only be averted if all countries – or at least all major energy consumers – agree to change their energy policies and practices. A similar argument can be made in respect to the ozone layer. Looking at health, a disease-free world in today's age of interdependence requires cross-border cooperation, lest infectious diseases travel and threaten human security. Or take the case of financial stability. Unless financial markets function well everywhere, there is a risk that a crisis could occur, and in its wake affect other countries. This lesson emerged from many earlier crisis events; and it is once again emerging from the financial crisis of 2008.

Obviously, many public goods have "gone global": deepening policy interdependence among countries has turned from national public goods into *global public goods (GPGs)*. Their adequate provision today requires international cooperation to achieve requisite behind-the-border policy convergence and actual policy results. In fact, a growing volume of development cooperation funds are now going to such global-public-goods concerns as financial stability, market efficiency, health, environmental sustainability or peace. According to some estimates, every fourth dollar of official development assistance (ODA) serves global purposes. This is no longer aid in the traditional sense (helping the poor), but rather an investment in the future of the international community as a whole.

Sixth, and closely linked to the previous point, is the growing emphasis on such cooperation measures as conditionality, targeting, monitoring, reporting and surveillance. Underlying these measures is *a changed principle of national policymaking sovereignty*. The principle of a nation's "exclusive policymaking sovereignty" within its territory is giving way to a principle of globally "responsive policymaking sovereignty" – the country's commitment to help foster global opportunities (e.g. the formation of an efficient and fair multilateral trade regime) and to avert global constraints like the risk of global warming. "Responsive policymaking sovereignty" has replaced the founding multilateral aid principle of country sovereignty in determining aid and other development cooperation priorities. The reason is linked to the fact that a part of international development cooperation today is geared towards the provision of GPGs. It is more a "trade" in global public goods and services than aid – e.g. compensation for maintaining forestry resources rather than using them for logging purposes. Or, aid is provided for global efficiency – rather than equity – purposes. A case in point would be to assist developing countries in strengthening financial regulation rather than waiting for a next financial crisis to occur and meeting its (mostly more expensive) costs.

Seventh, as the sophistication of markets and governments increased, not only did public-private partnerships spread but new and innovative financing instruments in support of international cooperation were developed, which also entered UN system cooperation initiatives.

These new tools were, in part, designed to create incentives for private actors to contribute to global development efforts. Examples are the issuing of bonds against commitments by donor countries of future aid payments, practiced by the International Finance Facility for immunization (IFFim), and the tool of differential patenting, employed by the Medicines for Malaria Venture (MMV).

Also, the creation of new markets has been explored and tested, notably in the area of fostering the reduction of greenhouse gas emissions.

Efforts have also been undertaken to facilitate the access for poor countries to international insurance markets. An already functioning case is the weather insurance for Ethiopia facilitated by the → World Food Programme.

Public-private partnerships were often created in order to facilitate the development and use of these new instruments – a factor that also contributed to the rise in their number.

Conclusion and Outlook

Thus, as we enter the 21st century, many features of the overall system of international cooperation have changed in a fundamental way; and so too have the basic characteristics of the UN system of development cooperation.

International cooperation now is composed of two main strands: GPG provision has been added to foreign aid; and in many instances international cooperation now involves besides (inter-)governmental actors also non-state actors. It often is a multi-actor process, relying on an expanding gamut of policy tools and financing instruments based on public-private partnering.

Moreover, international cooperation now often struggles for the right balance between globalization and centralization, on the one hand, and local context-specificity and national ownership, on the other.

Most important during the coming years would be fully to recognize that the reality of international cooperation has outpaced many of our concepts of international cooperation. A new international cooperation understanding and architecture will need to be constructed, if the global challenges confronting humankind are to be met – effectively, efficiently, and equitably.

At the centre of a new international cooperation theory and practice would need to be the realization that under conditions of openness of borders and policy interdependence among countries national interests will often best be served not by "going it alone" but by engaging in successful, adequately incentivized and results-oriented international cooperation.

Inge Kaul

Lit.: *Ahrens, H. (ed.):* Development cooperation – Evaluation and new approaches, Berlin 2005; *Andersson, G-B.:* In pursuit of Global Public Goods, in: D+C Development and Cooperation 33 (2006), 186-189; *Carbone, M.:* Supporting or resisting global public goods? The policy dimension of a contested concept, in: Global Governance 13 (2007), 179-198; *Easterly, W. (ed.):* Reinventing Foreign Aid. Cambridge, Mass. 2008. *Kaul, I. et al. (eds.):* Global Public Goods; Managing Globalization. New York 2003 (excerpts available at www. globalpublicgoods.org); *Kaul, I. /Conceição, P. (eds.):* The New Public Finance; Responding to Global Challenges. New York 2006 (excerpts available at www. thenewpublicfinance.org); *Nelson, P.:* Human rights, the Millennium Developmemt Goals, and the future of development cooperation, in: World Development 35 (2007), 2041-2055; *Reisen, H.:* Innovative Approaches to Funding the Millennium Development Goals; Paris 2004 (available at www.oecd.org/document/; *Stokke, O. (ed.):* Foreign Aid Toward the Year 2000: Experiences and Challenges, London 1996; *Stokke, O.:* Towards a new development cooperation paradigm? Introduction, in: Forum for Development Studies 33 (2006), 203-213; *United Nations - Department of Economic and Social Affairs:* Funding for United Nations development cooperation. Challenges and options, New York 2005, also accessible at: www.un.org/esa/coordination; *United Nations Development Programme:* Generation: Portrait of the United Nations Development Programme, New York 1985; *United Nations Development Programme:* Evaluation of the Third Global Cooperation Programme, New York 2008, also accessible at www.un.org/esa/coordination; *United Nations - General Assembly:* A More Secure World: Our Shared Responsibility. Report of the High-level Panel on Threats, Challenges and Change, UN Doc. A/59/565 of 2 December 2004; *United Nations - General Assembly:* Delivering as One. Report of the High-level Panel on System-wide Coherence in the areas of development, humanitarian assistance and the environment, UN Doc. A/61/583 of 20 November 2006; *Wieczorek-Zeul, H.:* Global Public Goods and development policy, in: D+C Development and Co-operation 31 (2004), 100-1003; *Zoellick, R.B.:* Modernizing Multilateralism and Markets. Speech to the Opening Plenary of the 2008 Annual Meetings. Washington 2008. (available at www. worldbank.org/, click at Office of the President-Statements).

Internet: For further information and references, see also www.un.org/, the UN's website, which also offers links to the funds and programmes as well as specialized agencies of the UN system.

Disarmament

Since the end of the 19th century *disarmament* has been a goal of those macro theories of international relations which are interested in cooperation and of the activities of the societal peace movements both of the workers and of the middle classes. During the 20th century disarmament has become a policy area of states, international organizations and regimes that have been influenced by non-governmental actors (→ NGOs). In the 20th century the concepts of *disarmament* and *arms control* have often been used jointly in official documents.

In 1961, the United States established an independent Arms Control and Disarmament Agency (ACDA). However, in 1999 when ACDA was abolished and merged with the State Department, a new bureau on 'arms control' was set up and the term 'disarmament' dropped.

According to the *Encyclopedia Britannica* (15th edn., 1998, Vol. 4, 120) in international relations *disarmament* refers to four different conceptions:

(1) the penal destruction or reduction of the armament of a country defeated in war;
(2) bilateral disarmament agreements applying to specific geographic areas;
(3) the complete abolition of all armaments; and

(4) the reduction and limitation of national armament by general international agreement.

This last is the most frequent current use of the term. Accordingly (15th edn., 1998, Vol. 1, 572) arms control is defined as "any international limitation of the development, testing, production, deployment, or use of weapons that, at the same time, accept the inevitability of the continued existence of national military establishments. Implied in arms control is some form of collaboration between generally antagonistic states in areas of military policy. In a broader sense, 'arms control' embraces the related notion of disarmament. ... By the century's end the term 'arms control' had come to denote any disarmament or arms-limitation agreement".

In contrast to this definition in the Encyclopedia Britannica, this author refers to disarmament in a wider sense as a generic term for all political efforts aimed at a complete elimination, negation as well as reduction of military potentials, i.e. of weapons systems, of industrial and technological capacities and manpower, as well as of the control and steering of armament processes (arms control), of confidence building and crisis prevention and for the limitation of military options.

Disarmament policy may be defined as the *institutional conditions, processes, contents and consequences of political activities* as well as the total of all unilaterally arranged binding *measures* that aim at an *elimination, limitation, reduction, or removal of military arms, at a reduction of military manpower and the control of research and production capacities for military means.* A comprehensive disarmament strategy refers to the means for achieving national, international and common security, for the prevention of wars, for the implementation of principles for the non-use of force, of preventing options and for supporting international cooperation and peace. *Disarmament policy* is both a topic of domestic and foreign policy as well as of international relations, but primarily an object of the scientific efforts of international relations and peace research.

Disarmament as a goal of international politics has been closely linked to the development of international order that is being determined by the world-views or macro theories of the observer and analyst. From the vantage point of the *pessimists* (Machiavelli, Hobbes, Waltz) both the goal as well as the institutional framework have been an illusion, i.e. for realists power has been the central category of international politics and military alliances have been the primary means for creating and maintaining stability as well as for the realization of national and alliance interests. For the *optimists* (e.g. Immanuel Kant, Woodrow Wilson) the creation of a 'league of nations' has been the framework and disarmament has been a means for the creation of a peaceful world order, while for *pragmatists* (Hugo Grotius) disarmament has been both a goal and means of a cooperative and common security policy.

In 1945, the architects of the post-war order – Roosevelt, Churchill and Stalin – set up a new institutional framework for disarmament with the creation of the United Nations. The UN Charter (→ Charter of the UN), as approved on 26 June 1945, distinguished among three supplementary security systems:

(a) a universal system of collective security contained in Chapters VI on pacific settlement of disputes (Art. 33 to Art. 38) and in Chapter VII on "Action with respect to threats to the peace, breaches of the peace and acts of aggression" (Art. 39 to 50);

(b) "regional arrangements or agencies for dealing" with regional security issues in Chapter VIII (Art. 52 to 54); and

(c) a provision referring to the "inherent right of individual or collective self-defence" contained in Article 51 appended to Chapter VII.

While the first two systems were to deal primarily with threats from within, among member states, the third system was specifically oriented against an outside threat. These two systems were to perform two functions:

a) peaceful settlement of disputes and

b) peace enforcement and,

c) later on, a third function was added by the UN General Assembly, dealing with peace-keeping operations.

But neither in its preamble, nor in its purposes (Art. 1) and principles (Art. 2), did the UN Charter specifically mention "disarmament", arms regulation or arms reduction.

Rather it refers to this issue as an agenda item that the General Assembly (Art. 11, Sec. 1) may "consider the general principles of co-operation in the maintenance of international peace and security, including the principles governing disarmament and the regulation of armaments, and may make recommendations with regard to such principles to the members or to the Security Council or to both."

According to Article 26 UN Charter, the Security Council shall be responsible "for formulating, with the assistance of the Military Staff Committee ... plans ... for the establishment of a system for the regulation of armaments" with the specific goal "to promote the establishment and maintenance of international peace and security with the least diversion for armaments of the world's human and economic resources". According to Article 47, the Military Staff Committee is to advise the Security Council *inter alia* on "the regulation of armaments, and possible disarmament". The final document of the first Special Session of the General Assembly devoted to disarmament (1978) called on all states "to abandon the use of force in international relations and to seek security in disarmament" (Final Document of the Tenth Special Session of the General Assembly, 30 June 1978, UN Doc. A/S-10/2, I: Introduction).

As a consequence of the emerging fundamental systemic and power conflict of the two new superpowers during the East-West Conflict especially in its two cold war phases (1946-1963, 1980-1986), this new collective security system with teeth was blocked from the outset and the exception became the rule: security by collective self-defense guaranteed by rival military alliances. Even Roosevelt's subdued Wilsonianism once again succumbed to Hobbesian pessimism in the foreign and defense policy of the USA itself.

A *comprehensive disarmament strategy* comprised at least four conceptual components: *disarmament, arms control, crisis management* and *confidence building measures* (cf. Table 1, p. 134). The terms *"disarmament"* and *"arms control"* are used interchangeably. While the United Nations and the peace research community gave preference to "disarmament", the Western strategic studies community uses "arms control".

Disarmament has been discussed in relationship to three related concepts of arms control, crisis management, and confidence- and security-building measures. Prior to 1989, disarmament measures were referred to as: "necessary means toward establishing a global collective security system. However, to become effective they have to be supplemented by measures to achieve strategic stability (arms control) between the major military rivals and political stability (conflict solution, crisis prevention, and crisis control) in those areas of the world where the Cold War has been fought with military means and caused its greatest death tolls." (*Brauch* 1990, 107)

Originally, *arms control* denoted rules for limiting arms competition with three major goals: enhancing stability, limiting damage and reducing costs. Arms control included measures intended to "(a) freeze, limit, reduce or abolish certain categories of weapons; (b) prevent certain military activities; (c) regulate the deployment of armed forces; (d) proscribe transfers of some military important items; (e) reduce the risk of accidental war; (f) constrain or prohibit the use of certain weapons or methods of war; and (g) build up confidence among states through greater openness in military matters" (*Goldblat* 1994, 3).

During the East-West conflict *Williams* (1976) distinguished between two schools on the prevention, control and management of crisis as a political strategy for war prevention focusing either "on peaceful resolution of confrontations" or using it "as an exercise of winning".

For the post-Cold War era, in his report *"Agenda for Peace"* (UN Doc. A/47/277-S/24111, 17 June 1992), produced at the request of the Security Council, Secretary-General Boutros-Ghali defined "preventive diplomacy" as "action to prevent disputes from arising between parties, to prevent existing disputes from escalation into conflicts and to limit the spread of the latter when they occur" (ibid., para. 20).

During the Cold War, confidence- (and security-) building measures (CBMs and CSBMs) were a political tool both in bilateral US - Soviet relations and in the multilateral context of the Conference on Security and Cooperation in Europe (CSCE, since 1994: OSCE) to reduce the likelihood of a nuclear war by accident, misperception and a conventional surprise attack in Europe. Since the end of the East-West conflict, CBMs have been considered as tools of preventive diplomacy for conflict avoidance and post-conflict peace-building.

Table 1 distinguishes these four pillars of a comprehensive disarmament strategy with respect to policy, systemic and action goals, objects to be achieved, its regional and substantial scope, the prevailing procedures and the achievements during the six major phases of the East-West Conflict (1946-1989) and in the post Cold War period since 1990. No global disarmament agreement was reached during the First (1946-1963) and the Second (1980-1987) Cold War, but during the first détente (1969-1974) the BWC and, during the second détente (1987-1989), the INF treaties were signed. Disarmament required a certain relaxation of tensions and contributed towards détente. With the end of the East-West conflict major bilateral (START I and II) regional (CFE 1, CFE 1A, Open Skies, Vienna Document 1990, 1992) and global (Chemical Weapons Convention 1993, CTBT 1996) confidence building, arms control and disarmament agreements became possible. Disarmament benefited from the global transformation but it was not its cause.

The Role of Disarmament in the Different Phases of World Policy

During the Cold War (1946-1989), disarmament was a political goal that was primarily a topic of speeches as part of the ideological competition in a bipolar world (e.g. proposals by Khrushchev, McCloy-Zorin agreement) and whose realization appeared to be unlikely. From the vantage point of the dominant realists the "security dilemma" required high defense expenditures in order to maintain the stability of the overall system and thus world peace.

With the end of the East-West conflict, disarmament has become a legitimate political goal, and the → collective security system an effective means, as long as they did not conflict with the goals of the only remaining super power. Since 1990, the refusal of states to make those means and structures available for such a collective security system as were needed for the performance of its tasks, and the institutional self-interest by the military alliances, as well as the persistence of realist or Hobbesian thinking and of the system of collective self-defense, have paralyzed the world order debate since 1990.

Since 2001, with the shift of US President George W. Bush towards a unilateral national security strategy, with the withdrawal from the Anti-Ballistic Missile (ABM) Treaty (www.state.gov/www /global/arms/treaties/abm/abm2.html) in 2002, and in March 2003 with the launch of a war against Iraq, this multilateral collective security system has been further weakened. Russia has announced its withdrawal from the Intermediate-Range Nuclear Forces (INF) Treaty (www.armscontrol.org/documents /inf), on 12 December 2007 it suspended its implementation of the Conventional Armed Forces in Europe (CFE) Treaty (www.osce.org/documents/doclib/1990/

11/13752en.pdf) and it announced that it would not participate in treaty data exchanges and notifications, as well as inspections (cf. Arms Control Association, Fact Sheet on CFE, February 2008, www.armscontrol.org/factsheets/%252 Fcfeback2). With its active military role in the Georgia conflict in August 2008 Russia has further weakened the prospects for solutions in a collective security framework (cf. Georgian Conflict Clouds Future Arms Pacts, Arms Control Association, Fact sheet on CFE, September 2008). All these developments have prevented the creation of a security architecture in which means and legitimacy are in accordance with each other.

In the 21st century, disarmament policy should increasingly involve the new global challenges – population growth and environmental crises – that cannot be solved within the categories of a realist security dilemma, but that require a new conceptual thinking which analyses disarmament not just in the categories of national security, but also includes elements of "human security" in the context of a survival dilemma.

In 2003 the Commission on Human Security, established in January 2001 through the initiative of the government of Japan in response to the Millennium Report of the Secretary-General "We the people: the role of the United Nations in the twenty-first century" (UN Doc. A/54/2000 of 27 March 2000), where Annan had urged the UN member states in view of the new security challenges "to think creatively and to adapt our traditional approaches to better meet the needs of our new era" (ibid., para. 197), elaborated the concept of human security in its report "Human Security Now" (*Commission on Human Security* 2003). Disarmament research should thus no longer focus exclusively on a reduction of violence, but should address questions of survival. This will require a change in the functions of disarmament, i.e. disarmament must sustain multilateral problem solutions by reducing the means for violent outcomes, by constraining their use and their proliferation, and thus also the means for an early solution of global challenges. The Report of the High-level Panel on Threats, Challenges and Change, "A more secure world: our shared responsibility" (UN Doc. A/59/565, 2 December 2004), submitted to the General Assembly in December 2004, introduced this comprehensive concept of security in the UN debate. The new security concept was then taken up in the reform report of Secretary-General Kofi Annan of March 2005 "In larger freedom: towards development, security and human rights for all" (UN Doc. A/59/2005, 21 March 2005) and in the final document of the UN world summit in September 2005, the "2005 World Summit Outcome" (UN Doc. A/RES/60/1 of 16 September 2005).

UN Institutions in the Field of Disarmament

Since 1945, the United Nations has provided an institutional machinery to perform these major disarmament functions: a) communication (with governments, NGOs and experts); b) initiation of and c) conduct of negotiations.

The verification and implementation of agreements are not carried out by the UN but by special treaty-implementing bodies, such as the International Atomic Energy Agency (→ IAEA), the Organisation for Chemical Disarmament (OPCW) in The Hague (www.opcw.org) and the future Organisation for a Comprehensive Test Ban (CTBO) in Vienna. After the Gulf War, in 1991, UNSCOM was set up to enforce a ceasefire agreement against violators (www.un.org/Depts/unscom/). On 17 December 1999 the Security Council replaced UNSCOM by the *United Nations Monitoring, Verification and Inspection Commission* (UNMOVIC); cf. UN Doc. S/RES/1284 (1999). UN Secretary-General Kofi Annan appointed Hans Blix (Sweden) as its Executive Chairman (1 March 2000 to 30 June 2003) who was succeeded by Mr. Demetrius Perricos as Acting Executive Chairman. After its inspectors were withdrawn from Iraq

in March 2003, UNMOVIC continued to operate outside of Iraq. On 29 June 2007, the Security Council terminated the mandate of UNMOVIC (www.unmovic.org/).

The Main Platforms for the UN Disarmament Debate

In January 1946, in its first resolution, the General Assembly established the *Atomic Energy Commission* to deal with nuclear weapons (UN Doc. A/RES/1 (I) of 24 January 1946) and in 1947, the *Commission for Conventional Armaments* was created by a decision of the Security Council (UN Doc. S/RES/18 (1947) of 13 February 1947). In 1952, the Assembly consolidated both Commissions into a single *Disarmament Commission* (UN Doc. A/RES/502 (VI) of 11 January 1952), which remained the major disarmament body until 1957. It was enlarged twice in 1957 (UN Doc. A/RES/1150 (XII) of 19 November 1957) and 1958 (UN Doc. A/RES/1252 D (XIII) of 4 November 1958), but it held only two further sessions, in 1960 and 1965.

Since 1959, when the Assembly called for "general and complete disarmament under effective international control", the UN has pursued two parallel approaches to disarmament. Concurrently, agreements on partial disarmament measures were pursued. In 1959, beside the UN Disarmament Commission the *Ten-Nation Committee on Disarmament* was established by agreement of the Foreign Ministers of France, the USSR, the United Kingdom and the United States with equal participation from the West and the East. The four nations declared in a communiqué on the occasion of the foundation of the Committee that setting up the new committee should in no way diminish or encroach upon UN responsibility in this field (UN Doc. DC/144 of 7 September 1959).

In 1961, its negotiating function was reorganized in bilateral negotiations of the USA with the USSR with the establishment of the *Eighteen-Nations Conference on Disarmament* by adding

119

eight non-aligned members – the UN General Assembly could do nothing but approve this modification of a negotiating forum outside the UN with resolution 1722 (XVI) of 20 December 1961 – in the hope that the rest of the UN member states would eventually have a benefit from the negotiations results. In 1969, the negotiating body was renamed the *Conference of the Committee on Disarmament (CCD)* and its membership expanded to 26 – again approved by the General Assembly (UN Doc. A/RES/2602 B (XXIV) of 16 December 1969), then further to 31 nations in 1975 on the basis of an agreement reached in the CCD in 1974 as endorsed by the General Assembly in its resolution 3261 (UN Doc. A/RES/3261 B (XXIX) of 9 December 1974). In this phase the main focus of the disarmament negotiations was obviously outside the UN bodies in the Geneva negotiating forum with changing names and changing size, depending on the agreement of the super-powers.

The Final Document of the first special session of the General Assembly devoted to disarmament (23 May to 30 June 1978), was composed of four sections: *Introduction, Declaration, Programme of Action* and *Machinery*, and set out goals, principles and priorities for the disarmament field (UN Doc. A/S-10/2, 30 June 1978).

With respect to machinery, the Final Document stated that the General Assembly (assisted by its First Committee) should remain the chief and permanent deliberative organ of the United Nations on disarmament (ibid., para. 115), it re-established the *Disarmament Commission* (ibid., para. 118), which meets annually for about four weeks in May/June and reports to the General Assembly.

The CCD was renamed as the *Committee on Disarmament* (1979-1983) and subsequently the *Conference on Disarmament* (since 1983). Its membership was increased to 40 states and according to the explicit mandate of the UN General Assembly it was to remain the "single multilateral negotiating body on disarmament" (A/RES/38/183 I of

20 December 1983, preamble). Furthermore, it abolished the co-chairmanship of the US and USSR. In 1996, the CD membership increased first to 61, and in 1999 to 66 member states.

In 1979, the CD agreed on a permanent decalogue of ten areas: "(1) Nuclear weapons in all aspects; (2) chemical weapons; (3) other weapons of mass destruction; (4) conventional weapons; (5) reduction of military budgets; (6) reduction of armed forces; (7) disarmament and development; (8) disarmament and international security; (9) collateral measures; confidence-building measures; effective verification methods in relation to appropriate disarmament measures acceptable to all parties concerned; (10) comprehensive programme of disarmament leading to general and complete disarmament under effective international control." (Committee on Disarmament: Agenda and program of work, 12 April 1979, UN Doc. CD/12)

Due to a deterioration of the international climate, the *Programme of Action* of 1978 remained largely unimplemented. The second special session of the General Assembly devoted to disarmament (7 June to 10 July 1982) expressed regret that "at its twelfth special session it has not been able to adopt a document on the Comprehensive Programme of Disarmament and on a number of other items on its agenda. ..." (the Report of the Ad Hoc Committee of the Twelfth Special Session – UN Doc A/S-12/32 of 9 July 1982, para 62 with the exception of the expansion of the UN disarmament fellowship programme, and the launching of the World Disarmament Campaign (renamed the UN Disarmament Information Programme in 1992). Instead of adopting a final declaration and plan of action, the General Assembly only "approved the report of the Ad Hoc Committee of the Twelfth Special Session as the Concluding Document ..." (UN Doc. A/S-12/24), a complete diplomatic defeat.

Despite the improved climate in US - Soviet relations but due to regional disputes, during the third special session (31 May to 25 June 1988) the member states again failed to adopt by consensus a final document (cf. UN Doc. A/S-15/6), and failed as well to activate multilateral arms control efforts.

The institutional machinery for dealing with disarmament issues was set up by the UN Charter and by subsequent decisions of the General Assembly and the Security Council. Since the 1950s, the Assembly with its subsidiary bodies (First Committee, Disarmament Commission) has exercised the main initiative and has been the main deliberative organ to facilitate both ongoing negotiations and the implementation of agreements.

In 1980, the *United Nations Institute for Disarmament Research (→ UNIDIR)* was established in Geneva (www.unidir. org/html/en/home.html) to undertake independent research on disarmament in close cooperation with the UN Secretariat in New York. Furthermore, three UN regional centres for peace and disarmament were set up for Africa in Lomé (1986), for Latin America and the Caribbean in Lima (1987) and for Asia and the Pacific in Kathmandu (1988). (On UNIDIR, see also below).

The Role of the Principal Organs in the UN Disarmament Debate

During the East-West conflict, the General Assembly was primarily limited to declaratory politics. According to J. Goldblat, most of its over 1,000 resolutions in the first 48 years "have had little effect on national policies or on the course of arms control negotiations. There are several reasons for this failure. In the first place, the accelerated proliferation of resolutions, especially in the 1980s, considerably reduced their value. ... Such documents cannot play the role originally assigned to UN resolutions, that of serving as a sounding board for governmental proposals. ... As a result, the other important role of the General Assembly, that of providing guidance for arms control talks has been weakened." (*Goldblat* 1994, 26)

Since the 1950s, the role of the Security Council on disarmament issues has been limited. In 1968, the Council

adopted a resolution offering immediate assistance to non-nuclear members of the Non-Proliferation Treaty if they were to become the victims of nuclear threats or aggression. In several treaties, the Council was given a role in responding to complaints of treaty violations.

Since the end of the East-West conflict, in the so-called ceasefire resolution (UN Doc. S/RES/687 (1991) of 3 April 1991) the Security Council entrusted the UN Special Commission on Iraq (UNSCOM) with the implementation of the destruction of Iraq's weapons of mass destruction. In the final statement of the Summit Meeting of the Security Council on the level of heads of state and of government, held on 31 January 1992 the Security Council members "underline the need for all Member States to fulfil their obligations in relation to arms control and disarmament; to prevent the proliferation in all its aspects of all weapons of mass destruction ... The members of the Council commit themselves to working to prevent the spread of technology related to the research for or production of weapons of mass destruction." (UN Doc. S/23500 of 31 January 1992) In resolution 1172 (1998) the Council unanimously condemned the nuclear tests by India and Pakistan.

Within the United Nations Secretariat, on 1 January 1983, the *Centre for Disarmament* was upgraded to the *Department for Disarmament Affairs*. In 1992 it was again downgraded to an *Office for Disarmament Affairs*, but in January 1998, the General Assembly re-established the *Department for Disarmament Affairs (DDA)*)as a result of the programme for reform submitted by the Secretary-General in his report "Renewing the United Nations: A Program for Reform (UN Doc. A/51/950) in July 1997 and approved by the General Assembly with GA resolution 52/12 (UN Doc. A/RES/52/12 A of 12 November 1997 and A/RES/52/12 B of 19 December 1997).

In 2007 under the new Secretary-General Ban Ki-moon, the Department of Disarmament Affairs became the

121

United Nations Office for Disarmament Affairs (UNODA) (www.un.org/disarmament/index.shtml). In July 2007 Ban Ki-moon appointed Sergio de Queiroz Duarte (Brazil) as the High Representative for Disarmament Affairs at the Under-Secretary-General level, who heads UNODA.

The United Nations Office for Disarmament Affairs (UNODA) is structured in five branches:

a) *Conference on Disarmament Secretariat & Conference Support Branch* (Geneva): provides organizational and substantive servicing to the Conference on Disarmament;

b) the *Weapons of Mass Destruction Branch (WMD):* provides substantive support in the area of the disarmament of nuclear, chemical and biological weapons, supports and participates in multilateral efforts to strengthen the non-proliferation of WMD and cooperates in this connection with relevant intergovernmental organizations and → specialized agencies of the United Nations system (IAEA, OPCW, CTBTO PrepCom);

c) the *Conventional Arms (including Practical Disarmament Measures) Branch:* focuses its efforts in the conventional field of promoting transparency and confidence-building, curbing the flow of small arms in regions of tension, and developing measures of practical disarmament;

d) the *Regional Disarmament Branch:* provides substantive support and advice to member states, to regional and sub-regional organizations on disarmament and related security matters and oversees and coordinates the activities of the three Regional Centres for Peace and Disarmament in Africa, Asia and Latin America;

e) the *Information and Outreach Branch:* organizes special events and programmes in the field of disarmament, produces UNODA publications (such as the Disarmament Yearbook and the ODA Occasional Papers), and maintains databases for specialized areas (such as the Register of Conventional Arms, the *Status of Multilateral Arms Regulation and Disarmament Agreements*, including the Mine-Ban Convention (http://disarmament.un.org/Treaty Status.nsf), the Resolutions of the General Assembly (with regard to disarmament (http://disarmament.un.org/vote. nsf) on the website of the UNODA Documents Library (www.un.org/disarmament/HomePage/library.shtml), a specialized archive that provides quick and direct access to United Nations disarmament-related documents in one convenient location starting from the 56th General Assembly Session.

The General Assembly and the Advisory Board on Disarmament Studies (since 1978), since 1999 called Advisory Board on Disarmament Matters and provided with a new mandate (GA decision 54/418 of 1 December 1999), initiated a multitude of studies. Some even succeeded in promoting specific measures, for example the studies on the Non-Proliferation Treaty NPT (1967), on the Biological Weapons Convention BWC (1969), on Napalm (1971), on standardized military budgets (since 1974), on CBMs (1981), verification (1990) and conventional arms transfers (1991), and recently on small arms (1997, 1999). Recent occasional papers dealt with nuclear doctrine (1999), missile development and its impact on global security (1999), a conceptual approach on arms control and disarmament (2000), on the "Revolution in Military Affairs" (2001).

In its discussions the Advisory Board focused *inter alia* on biological weapons and the BWT convention, small arms and light weapons, weapons of mass destruction and terrorism (February 2002); preparedness of public health systems to deal with bio-terrorism, nuclear security and safety, and disarmament and development (July 2002); on compliance, verification and enforcement of multilateral treaties, disarmament and human security, and rising military expenditures (July 2003); on disarmament and reconciliation in conflict prevention (February 2004), and on its contribution to the work of the Secretary-General's High-level Panel on

Threats, Challenges and Change, and on export controls (July 2004), on nuclear fuel cycle, fissile material control, small arms and light weapons (February 2005); on challenges and opportunities at the regional level in the areas of weapons of mass destruction and conventional arms (July 2005). In February 2006 it reviewed the disarmament field in light of decisions taken at the World Summit of the General Assembly (September 2005), and measures to prevent the proliferation of weapon systems to non-state actors (February 2006); and in June 2006 it discussed building an international security system. In July 2007 the Board reviewed ways to advance the disarmament agenda and emerging weapons technologies, including outer space aspects. During its meetings in February and July 2008 the Board discussed issues of energy security and environment; and emerging weapons technologies, including outer space aspects (UN Doc. A/62/309).

Since 1980, the *United Nations Institute for Disarmament Research (UNIDIR)* has become the major interface between the United Nations and the academic community, with the goals to assist "ongoing negotiations on disarmament" and to stimulate "new initiatives for new negotiations". Since 1996, UNIDIR has published reports and books on diverse armament issues, among other things on tactical nuclear weapons, on fissile material stocks, on small arms and their control, on illicit trafficking in firearms, on a world free of weapons of mass destruction, on non-offensive defense, on nuclear weapon free zones, on the transfer of sensitive technologies and future control regimes.

Prior to 1995, UNIDIR published reports on issues such as the NPT, CW, conventional disarmament in Europe, verification, bilateral and multilateral negotiations, nuclear test ban, on confidence-building measures, arms transfers, the security in Europe and in third world countries, on non-military aspects of security, on non-offensive defence, on economic aspects of disarmament and on economic adjustment after the

Cold War. From 1988-1997, the UNIDIR Newsletter and since 1998 the bilingual Disarmament Forum and two UNIDIR Repertories of Disarmament Research (1982, 1990) have facilitated the communication within the disarmament research community. Between 2000 and 2008, UNIDIR published some 70 books and reports and in its quarterly Disarmament Forum since 1988 it focused on a broad spectrum of disarmament topics (see at: www. unidir. ch/html/en/publications.php).

Besides UNIDIR, → *UNESCO's Division on Human Rights and Peace* has been another major partner of the peace research community organizing conferences on peace and disarmament education, facilitating communication among researchers and, since 1980, publishing the *UNESCO Yearbook on Peace and Conflict Studies*. In 2000, one focus was its trans-disciplinary project "Towards a Culture of Peace" that continues with the "International Decade for a Culture of Peace and Non-violence for the Children of the World (2001-2010)", another its global quest for tolerance programme and a recent publication is on new approaches and methods of conflict resolution.

Disarmament successes were dependent on the overall East-West relations. During the first (1946-1963) and second (1980-1987) Cold Wars no global disarmament agreements were adopted. Disarmament required a relaxation of tensions and contributed towards détente. With the end of the East-West conflict major bilateral (START I and II) regional (CFE 1, CFE 1A, Open Skies, Vienna Document 1990, 1992) and global (Chemical Weapons Convention) confidence-building, arms control and disarmament agreements became possible. Disarmament thus benefited from the global transformation.

Several major global disarmament treaties were achieved within the United Nations framework: the *Biological Weapons Convention* (1972) (UNTS Vol. 1015, No. 14860), the *Convention on Certain Conventional Weapons* (1981) (UNTS Vol. 1342, No. 22495), and the *Chemical Weapons Convention* (1993) (UNTS Vol. 1974, No. 33757). The most significant global arms control agreement has been the *Non-Proliferation Treaty* of 1968 (UNTS Vol. 729, No. 10485), which was extended permanently in 1995. Less significant have been the Environmental Modification Convention (ENMOD) of 1977 and the Moon Treaty of 1979. A major nuclear arms control treaty was the *Comprehensive Nuclear Test Ban Treaty* of 1996 (UN Doc. A/50/1027; and C.N.429.2002 of 6 May 2002); this however has so far not entered into force, because the US Senate did not ratify it in 1999, even though the Russian Duma did so in 2000.

While the contextual change since 1989 was instrumental for the signing of several significant arms control and real disarmament agreements, it also put new issues on the disarmament and arms control agenda: to contain the horizontal and vertical proliferation and new sources of political instability. Between 1990 and 1993, several major nuclear arms control and disarmament agreements were signed by the USA and the Soviet Union (or Russian Federation): the START I Treaty (31 July 1991) and the START II Treaty (3 January 1993). In May 1991, the INF Treaty was fully implemented. Between 1990 and 1992, before the wars in former Yugoslavia (Bosnia, Kosovo) escalated, on the multilateral level in Europe the following disarmament and CSBM agreements were signed:

- the *Conventional Forces in Europe (CFE) Treaty* of November 1990 among the then 22 members of NATO and the WTO that was supplemented by a Final Protocol of the 29 parties to the treaty on 5 June 1992;
- the *Vienna Document of 1990 on Confidence and Security Building Measures (CSBM)* of 34 CSCE states;
- the *Open Skies Treaty* of 24 March 1992 of 25 CSCE states;
- the Vienna Document of [March] 1992 on CSBM of then 48 CSCE states;

- the Final Act on the Negotiations on Manpower Strength of the Conventional Forces in Europe (CFE IA Treaty) of 10 July 1992 of 29 CSCE states.

In addition, the reciprocal unilateral announcements of President George Bush on 27 September 1991, and Michail Gorbachev's speech of 4 October 1991 promising to withdraw all land-based short-range nuclear missiles and artillery, were implemented by mid-1992. Thus, elements of a gradualist strategy complemented traditional arms control by negotiations. Without any treaty, all American chemical weapons were withdrawn from Germany by September 1990. By end of June 1992, all Soviet tactical nuclear weapons had also been transferred to Russia from the other CIS member states. Thus, a nuclear disengagement or a nuclear weapon-free zone has been achieved in Europe from the Baltic through Central Europe to the Balkans.

Nevertheless, the weapons innovation process – at least in the West – continues unabated. Since 1990, the public focus has shifted to horizontal proliferation issues: ABC weapons, ballistic missiles and dual-use technologies as well as to the "brain drain" of weapons experts from the CIS to Third World countries. While the "horizontal proliferation" of ABC weapons and missiles is addressed, the proliferation of conventional weapons continues without any major national constraints – at least for the major arms exporters. In 1992, the General Assembly established a *"Register of Conventional Arms"* (UN Doc. A/RES/ 46/36L of 6 December 1991) as a means to enhance confidence and transparency in military activities of states that does neither aim nor will it be able to curb these transfers.

Disarmament required détente among the conflict parties while arms control efforts (SALT I) supported détente among the superpowers. During the East-West Conflict only one global disarmament agreement was adopted with the B-Weapons Convention of 1972, and only after the end of the Cold War the chemical weapons convention was approved in 1992 (and entered into force in April 1997). Most bilateral (START I, START II) and regional disarmament agreements (CFE, CFE 1A) became possible after the end of the East-West Conflict in 1990.

Many global, regional and bilateral arms control agreements were signed during the period of limited détente (1963-1968): the Outer Space treaty, the Non-proliferation treaty and during the first (1959-1974 or 1979 respectively) and second détente (1987-1989) (cf. Table 2, p. 135). The global turn since fall of 1989 permitted the adoption of several disarmament treaties on the global level (CWC of 1993), in Europe (CFE-1 (1990) and CFE-1A (1992) treaty), between the USA and USSR (or since 1992 with Russia, Ukraine, Belarus) the START I (1991) and START II (1993) treaties, and regional arms control treaties (Open Sky, Vienna Documents on 1990, 1992 and 1994). However, these disarmament efforts excluded conventional arms exports (horizontal proliferation), and the weapons innovation process (vertical proliferation).

Despite the improved global climate, the momentum of the disarmament efforts has slowed since the first, and even more during the second Clinton Administration and during the first and second Bush jr. Administrations. The most important arms export countries, were not ready to forego any major exports after the significant reduction of their production capacities. While the overall volume of major conventional weapons declined between 1987 and 1994, the volume rose again until 1997/1998 and after a drop until 2002 the total volume increased until 2006. SIPRI (2008, 293-294) noted a long-term upward trend in transfers that began in 2003-2004 that were 7% higher than in 2002-2006. Again, the five largest suppliers: the USA (31%), Russia (25%), Germany (10%), France (9%) and the UK (4%) accounted for about 80% of all deliveries. In 2006, the estimated value of the international arms trade was 45.6 billion US dollars, where

the US exports amounted to 14 billion US dollars, Russia 6.5 billion US dollars, France 5.1 billion US dollars, UK 3.8 billion US dollars and Israel 3 billion US dollars. This trend seems to be further on the rise, as the US Department of Defence approved the sale and transfer of weapons amounting to 32 billion US dollars between January and August 2008 alone that will be exported to countries in the Middle East and North Africa, Latin America, Europe and Canada (Source: *Eric Lipton*: White House drives rapid rise in weapons sales, in: *International Herald Tribune*, 15 September 2008; 1, 7). According to estimates by the US Congressional Research Service the US share of world arms exports increased from 40% in 2000 to 52% in 2006; Russia ranked second 2006 with 21% of the world arms export share and the United Kingdom third with 12% (*Congressional Research Service* 2007, 10).

As the danger of a nuclear war diminished, the public pressure for further disarmament measures declined, as did the scientific interest in disarmament issues. With the resurgence of the "old thinking" in the categories of the security dilemma, disarmament remains still a task both for international but also for foreign and domestic policies. Despite the new global disorder since the end of the East-West Conflict (1990), for the first time there is an opportunity to realize the two definitive articles of Kant's eternal peace: a) a democratic system of rule and b) a system of collective security.

With the third wave of democratization, a third attempt was made to test elements of a collective security concept at both the global and regional levels. In Europe, the war in former Yugoslavia has demonstrated the limitations for the actions and for the problem-solving capacities of the UN and the OSCE. So far the third opportunity since 1919 to realize a system of collective security has been insufficiently used.

The preference for an eastward-enlargement of NATO, instead of extending the OSCE and of the use of NATO forces (IFOR, SFOR) instead of UN blue helmets in Bosnia-Herzegovina, hardly offers prospects for establishing a collective security system. Since 1990, too often too much has been expected from the Security Council with regard to maintaining peace and security.

Until 2001, the means and instruments for an effective preventive diplomacy, for peace-keeping and peace-building were lacking, and since then they have developed at a slow pace.

A division of labor between the global and regional systems of collective security (Arab League, OAS, OAU/AU and OSCE) so far exists only in an embryonic state. These four regional organizations have been able to contribute little to the solutions to the problems because the effective means to deal with these challenges are lacking. The weakening of the collective security system created by the UN Charter has been further deepened during the administration of George W. Bush (2001-2008) when the UN Security Council was only considered useful as long as it endorsed US strategic interests, e.g. in the "war on terror" against Al Qaida and the Taliban in Afghanistan. However, small and medium-sized countries succeeded in the UN Security Council to table their human security and humanitarian agenda (protection of civilians, children and women in war), as these successfully did against the veto of the permanent members of the Security Council (or the consensus requirement of the CD) by negotiating and implementing the *Convention on the Prohibition of the Use, Stockpiling, Production and Transfer of Anti-Personnel Mines and on Their Destruction* outside the United Nations because the major powers blocked any progress in this matter on the UN level. The convention, commonly called Ottawa Convention or Mine Ban Treaty, was signed in 1997 and entered into force on 1 March 1999. The same proceeding was chosen in the case of the Convention on Cluster Munitions (CCM), which was approved on 30 May 2008 by 107 countries in Dublin.

The disarmament successes of the early 1990s were a direct consequence of the global turn of events of 1989 and 1990. Since the Cold War both the imagination and the will among major actors to initiate major new disarmament initiatives has been lacking. From 1997 until 2008, the multilateral disarmament efforts of the CD have been stalemated by disputes among the US, Russia and China on negotiations on a fissile material treaty, on nuclear disarmament, on plans for ballistic missile defence and efforts pertaining to limitations of the militarization of outer space.

Since 1997, due to the linkage between the US interest in negotiations on a *Fissile Material Cut-off Treaty (FMCT)* and the Russian and Chinese insistence on negotiations for a treaty against the militarization of outer space that was opposed by the US, the major disarmament body of the United Nations with 65 member states and 30-40 observers has been blocked, as no agreement could be reached on a work programme on substantial disarmament negotiations.

At the top of the arms control agenda of NATO states has been the non-proliferation of weapons of mass destruction and of missiles. In January 1993, with the signing of the CWC and in May 1995 with the permanent extension of the NPT a major goal was achieved.

As a supplement to the three existing disarmament regimes (NPT, BWC, CWC) a group of selected and potential supply countries have adopted rules and procedures outside the UN framework for nuclear questions in the London Suppliers Club, for Biological and Chemical Weapons and for dual-use technologies in the Australian Group (prior to the CWC), and for missile launchers in the Missile Technology Control Regime (MTCR).

For the export of militarily sensitive technologies, in April 1996 the CoCom Guidelines have been replaced by the Wassenaar Arrangement for Export Controls for conventional weapons, for dual-use goods and technologies that have concentrated at four states: Iran, Iraq, Libya and North Korea.

While all these measures have focused at horizontal proliferation, vertical proliferation issues have to a large extent been ignored, even though the NPT Review Conferences (1995, 2000, and 2005) recognized the problem. Both at the international and at the national level, this area should become an object of controls. But this will require improved obligations for information exchange, for international surveys and for effective sanctions against violators. Nuclear weapons states have been committed to the goal of nuclear disarmament, but despite bilateral or unilateral reductions, none of them has fulfilled their obligations under article VI of the NPT.

The seventh NPT Review Conference of 2 to 27 May 2005 was a total failure, partly due to the US policy that opposed any reference to the final declaration of the previous Review Conference in 2000. Many non-aligned countries were highly frustrated, and the members of the "New Agenda Coalition" in 2000 (Egypt, Brazil, Ireland, Mexico, New Zealand, Sweden, South Africa) were not diplomatically active in 2005. This failure benefited both Iran and North Korea that were not bound by new obligations (*Müller* 2005).

With the INF (1987), START I (1991) and START II (1993) treaties, this obligation has so far only been implemented by the USA and the former USSR and its successor states with nuclear weapons on their territory (Russia, Ukraine, Belarus and Kazakhstan), while France, Great Britain and China have not been obliged by treaties to reduce their nuclear arsenals.

An important goal with regard to a stop for the development of new nuclear weapons has been the *Comprehensive Test Ban Treaty* that was opened for signature on 24 September 1996. As of July 2008, a total of 178 countries had signed the CTBT and 144 states have ratified it. On 13 October 1999, the US Congress rejected its ratification while the Russian Duma ratified it in spring

2000. The US administration of George W. Bush refused to ask the Senate to reconsider the CTBT but said it would observe the moratorium, announced on 2 October 1992 by President Bush Sr.

Nuclear Weapon Free Zones have been created by the treaties of Tlatelolco for Latin America (1967), of Rarotonga for the South Pacific (1985). As early as 1971, the ASEAN states have declared their region as a zone of peace, liberty and neutrality (ZOPFAN). On 15 December 1995, the heads of state and governments of ten states in South-East Asia signed a treaty on the creation of a nuclear weapon free zone whereby they also consulted with the four nuclear weapon states (USA, China, France and Great Britain). After 35 years, in Africa the so-called Pelindaba Treaty for a nuclear weapons free zone was approved on 13 June 1995 and signed by the heads of state on 11 April 1996 in Cairo. As of September 2008, the Treaty of Pelindaba has not yet entered into force, but 51 countries have now signed and 26 have ratified it.

A special case is the territory of the five new states in Germany that have become a *quasi* nuclear weapon-free zone in the Treaty on the Final Settlement with respect to Germany (2+4 Treaty) of 12 September 1990, whose Article 5.3 requires that "foreign armed forces and nuclear weapons or their carriers will not be stationed in that part of Germany or deployed there".

Additional proposals for a *Central Asian Nuclear Weapons Free Zone (CANWFZ)*, for a Central European NWFZ and for a Southern Hemisphere NWFZ have been tabled. By September 2008, all five Central Asian countries (Turkmenistan, Uzbekistan, Kyrgyzstan, Kazakhstan and Tajikistan have signed the Central Asian Nuclear Weapons Free Zone (CANWFZ), but only the first three have ratified it in 2007 and 2008. Additional proposals for a Central European NWFZ and for a Southern Hemisphere NWFZ have been discussed. Proposals for nuclear weapon free zones in the Middle East, in South and North Asia have not produced results.

On 27 April 1997, the *Chemical Weapons Convention CWC* entered into force. Until September 2008, the CWC has been signed by 165 states and 184 have ratified it. From the date of the entry into force of the CWC in 1997 it was initially envisioned to take another 10 to 15 years until humankind would be free of chemical weapons. The CWC has entered new territory because it not only calls for a comprehensive prohibition of the development, production, deployment and use of these weapons, but it also requires international controls in chemical industry and it regulates the grey area towards toxicological and pharmaceutical uses that are permitted.

The CWC created a stringent international verification regime to oversee states parties' compliance with treaty obligations, and it established in The Hague the *Organisation for the Prohibition of Chemical Weapons (OPCW)* that conducted, by March 2000, a total of 561 inspections in 31 states parties. Thereby it confirmed inactivation of all 60 chemical weapon production facilities that had been declared under the terms of the convention.

Between May 1997 and September 2008, two review conferences of the CWC have taken place in 2003 and 2008 in The Hague. The First Review Conference (2003) reviewed the operation of the CWC and assessed the current process of destruction of declared arsenals. It also re-examined the provisions of the Convention relating to verification in the chemical industry. The Conference provided strategic guidance for the next phase of the implementation of the CWC. The Second Review Conference (2008) reaffirmed the provisions of the CWC and the work of the Organization for the Prohibition of the Chemical Weapons (OPCW), to achieve universality, complete the destruction of chemical weapons, further strengthen verification measures to ensure non-proliferation, provide assistance and protection, and promote the uses of chemistry for peaceful purposes (cf. OPCW Conference Report, RC-2/4, 18 April 2008, www.opcw.org).

The *Biological Weapons Convention (BWC)* of 10 April 1972 that entered into force on 26 March 1975 counted in September 2008 162 states parties and 13 signatories.

The Sixth Review Conference of the BWC in Geneva (20 November to 8 December 2006) succeeded in comprehensively reviewing the Convention, adopting a final document by consensus. It also decided on specific and concrete measures to strengthen the implementation of the Convention. The states parties adopted a detailed plan for promoting universal adherence, and decided to update and streamline the procedures for submission and distribution of the Confidence-Building Measures (CBMs). They also adopted a comprehensive inter-sessional programme spanning from 2007 to 2010. In a significant development, the Conference agreed to establish an Implementation Support Unit (ISU) to assist states parties in implementing the Convention.

In the treaty regimes for ABC weapons, nuclear, chemical and biological basic research represents a grey area for which national self-controls of science and politics are required in order to prevent the development of even more cruel weapons, or to counter efforts to undermine existing treaty regimes.

While the ABM Treaty of 1972 has survived the final phase of the East-West Conflict despite the persistent efforts of the Reagan Administration to reinterpret it, since the early 1990s, pressures by proponents of a territorial defense by ground-based missile defense systems in the USA have increased. On 13 December 2001, US President George W. Bush announced the unilateral US withdrawal from the ABM Treaty, as it prevented US development of defenses against possible terrorist or "rogue-state" ballistic missile attacks. The US withdrawal took effect 13 June 2002.

Both the USA and Russia signed an additional protocol at the Summit in September 1997 related to the Treaty.

The Russian Duma ratified START II on 14 April 2000 by a vote of 228 to 131 with a caveat that would allow the president to abrogate all arms control treaties if the US pulled out of the ABM Treaty and deployed a missile defense system. The Russian Federation Council voted 126 to 18 for the treaty on 19 April 2000, and it was signed by Putin on 4 May 2000.

On 14 June 2002, a day after the US withdrew from the ABM Treaty, Russia announced that it would no longer be bound by its START II commitments. On 24 May 2002, the USA and Russia had agreed on the *Strategic Offensive Reductions Treaty* (SORT), which requires the United States and Russia to reduce their deployed strategic arsenals to 1,700-2,200 warheads apiece by December 31, 2012. This replaced START II's requirement for both parties to deploy no more than 3,000-3,500 warheads by December 2007. Key START II provisions, e.g. the prohibition against deploying multiple independently targetable reentry vehicles (MIRVs) on intercontinental ballistic missiles (ICBMs), were excluded in the SORT agreement.

The revival of the efforts for a *limitation on conventional arms exports* among the five permanent members of the Security Council (which supply about 80 % of the conventional arms) failed due to a lack of political interest. After initial efforts in the early 1990s by the permanent members of the Security Council to limit arms exports, these talks were not pursued further as components of a conflict prevention strategy. With crises in the weapons procurement sectors as background, export interests prevailed over arms control efforts. However, these opportunistic and economically determined policies are fundamentally in conflict with the goal of conflict prevention. These policies may lead to constraints in conflicts, and may limit the flexibility for foreign policy decisions.

So far the receptiveness of the states towards "micro disarmament" for conventional weapons has remained limited. In October 1995, after a massive campaign by the International Committee of the Red Cross, only a conditional prohibition of the use and proliferation of laser blinding weapons could be adopted, while research and development of such weapons, e.g. for blinding optical systems, remains permitted.

In 1995, a review of the *Convention on Certain Conventional Weapons (CCW)* produced an Amended Protocol II, strengthening restrictions on certain uses, types (self-destroying and detectable) and transfers of anti-personnel landmines. Without a global campaign against Anti-personal mines these weapons would not have become an object of international efforts to prohibit them. In response, a group of states negotiated an agreement on a total ban on all anti-personnel landmines *(Convention on the Prohibition of the Use, Stockpiling, Production and Transfer of Anti-personnel Mines on Their Destruction or Mine-Ban Convention)* which opened for signature on 3 December 1997 in Ottawa, Canada and was signed by 133 states. On 1 March 1999 this treaty entered into force, and by 1 June 2008 156 states had ratified it, and two countries had signed it. However, major powers, such as the United States, Russia, and China are not signatories, and only few countries in regions of tension, namely the Middle East and South Asia, have participated. Millions of mines are planted in the ground of some 70 some countries and global APL stockpiles may total more than 170 million mines. The US administration of George W. Bush announced on 27 February 2004 that the United States would not join the Ottawa Convention. In September 2008 China, Russia, the USA, India, Pakistan, North and South Korea, Egypt, Syria, Lebanon and Israel had not joined this treaty. This Convention has spurred the campaign to reduce needless human suffering by increasing resources for mine clearance, mine awareness and mine assistance. It has been proposed that the CD negotiate a ban on mines transfers, a measure which a number of states that have not adhered to the Mine-Ban Convention would find acceptable. But due to its continued paralysis for over a decade the CD since 1997 has been unable to agree on a work programme.

The proliferation of small arms and light weapons (SALW) was first raised in a 1995 General Assembly resolution (UN Doc. A/RES/50/70 B). In his Millennium Report (2000), Secretary-General Kofi Annan focused on small arms most of which are traded illicitly. Controlling the proliferation of illicit weapons is a necessary first step towards the non-proliferation of small arms. A UN Conference on the "Illicit Trade in Small Arms and Light Weapons in All Its Aspects" took place from 9-20 July 2001, when the participating states adopted a Programme of Action (PoA) to Prevent, Combat, and Eradicate the Illicit Trade in SALW. The Secretary-General submitted a study on the feasibility of restricting the manufacture and trade of small arms to manufacturers and dealers authorized by states. Within the UN system, an internal mechanism was put in place in 1998 to coordinate small arms control activities throughout the system with the DDA as the focal point, to set priorities, to encourage public advocacy of efforts to address small arms issues, to increase the UN's ability to assist countries that seek such help, and to advance the UN's broader disarmament goals.

Two biennial meetings were held in July 2003 and from 26 June to 7 July 2006. The Office of Disarmament Affairs (ODA) supported the group of governmental experts to study the feasibility of an international instrument on SALW and the Open-Ended Working Group to Negotiate an International Instrument to Enable States to Identify and Trace Illicit SALW. Due to the CD's decade long paralysis, no negotiations could be launched in this framework.

In 1996, at the suggestion of the GA a group of "interested States in practical disarmament measures" was set up to examine, and wherever possible, support concrete projects of practical disarmament to assist those states that face problems from post-conflict or post-tur-

moil situations (demobilization, reintegration of former combatants into civil society, weapons collection programmes). In 1998, Kofi Annan created a *Trust Fund for the Consolidation of Peace through Practical Disarmament Measures*, which supported projects such as that in Albania, where the population is encouraged to surrender weapons in exchange for community development incentives.

On 17 November of 2000, the Secretary-General speaking exclusively on disarmament issues and on the role of the academia stressed: "[we] must, in the broadest sense, agree on a new vision of human security for the post-cold war world. ... Some see a future characterized by the continued presence of nuclear weapons and other weapons of mass destruction. ... I would like to present an alternative vision. ... Earlier this year, the nuclear-weapon States made an 'unequivocal commitment' to 'accomplish the total elimination of all nuclear weapons'. ... I want only to suggest that with proper monitoring and enforcement, legally binding international regimes can have their intended effect. ... Disarmament is not self-sustaining. ... What is missing is the will to use that machinery. ... An overwhelming emphasis on military security, at the expense of economic and social security, can be short-sighted and destabilizing. Security is not simply a prerequisite for disarmament: disarmament itself can build confidence and enhance security by reducing the frequency, intensity, and duration of serious conflicts."

Secretary-General Kofi Annan points to the severe difficulties disarmament diplomacy is confronted with in the early 21st century: The 1990s have been a turning point with regard to disarmament. Following the major breakthroughs and significant achievements immediately after the turn (November 1990 to January 1993) during the Bush Administration, a significant slowdown occurred during the first Clinton Administration, which was followed (since 1997) by a paralysis during the second Clinton Administration. This was partly due to uncooperative legislatures, the (Republican-controlled) US Congress and the Russian Duma, but also to a dearth of diplomatic initiatives (including by EU countries). These factors were exacerbated by increasing controversies in the CD on US policy positions (unwillingness to address further nuclear disarmament) and weapons programmes (missile defense, outer space), as well as further controversies between the US on the one side and China, Russia and many developing countries on the other. The 2008 SIPRI Yearbook noted that "world military expenditure in 2007 is estimated to have been 1229 billion US dollar, a real-terms increase over 2006 of 6.0 %. Over the 10-year period 1998-2007, world military expenditure has increased by 45 % in real terms. Military spending in 2007 corresponded to 2.5 % of world gross domestic product (GDP) and 202 US dollar per capita" (*SIPRI* 2008, 175). Of this total, the US alone spent in 2007 (in constant 2005 prices) 547 billion or 45 % of the world total or 1799 per person. By 2007 US military spending "was higher than at any point since the end of World War II" (ibid., 179). From 2001 to 2007, "US military expenditure increased by 85 % in nominal terms and by 59 % in real terms according to SIPRI data." In the 2008 budget, the Bush administration requested a total budget authority for national defence of 645.6 billion US dollar and an additional emergency supplemental request of 93.4 billion US dollar for FY 2007 for the global war on terror.

According to the SIPRI Yearbook 2008, Russia's military spending in 2007 amounted to an estimated 35.4 billion US dollar, or 3 % of the world share. Military expenditure in US dollar terms for Russia amounted to an estimated 78.8 billion, or slightly more than 14 % of the US total. One of the highest increases in military spending since 2003 occurred in Georgia whose military expenditure increased more than tenfold in real terms from "a low point of 0.6 per cent of GDP in 2000 to 5.2 % in 2006" (*SIPRI* 2008, 189) what was officially

justified with Georgia's "aim of NATO membership." On 12 September 2008, Novosti News, reported that the Russian budget spending on state defense orders would amount to 46.8 billion US dollars in 2009, compared with 30 billion US dollars in 2007 and 43 billion US dollars in 2008. (http://en.rian.ru/russia/20080912/116752099.html).

With the end of the Cold War, the threat as a legitimation for arms competition has disappeared. The US National Security Strategies of 2002 and 2006 indicated a shift from a "threat-based" to a "capability-based" military posture. Nevertheless the old thinking has not been overcome, nor have the interests of the national security state whose adherents have promoted the old recipes for new challenges.

Nineteen years after the end of the Cold War, there has been no peace dividend, global military spending in real terms has been higher in 2008 than in 1988, and, since 1997, the Conference on Disarmament has been blocked due to the inability of the USA, Russia and China to agree on a work programme. Instead, members of the Human Security Network have taken the lead in disarmament negotiations outside the CD that has so far resulted in the only two major disarmament agreements during the past decade, in the convention banning anti-personnel landmines (1997) and the Convention against Cluster Munitions that was adopted on 30 May 2008 in Dublin during the Irish Presidency of the Human Security Network. While the narrow Hobbesian worldview has prevailed in the USA during the two Bush Administrations, the Georgian crisis of August 2008 has strengthened the position of the hardliners in Russia, too, who have called for major increases in Russian military expenditure as well.

However, the global challenges of the 21st century may be increasingly of a non-military nature, and may not be solved with military means. Since the year 1992, there has been an increasing politicization and since 2000 an initial securitization of issues of global environmental change, of water, desertification and climate change (*Brauch* 2002, 2008, 2009, 2010).

The goal of a scientific discipline that is linked to the goal of peace, has to accept the challenges and contribute to the creation of a "survival society" in the 21st century by thinking ahead, to gradually replace the "risk society" of the late 20th century, and to replace the security dilemma with a survival dilemma that requires co-operative problem solutions in multilateral international organizations and regimes.

In September 2008, after a major increase in military expenditure and arms exports, both in the USA, and in the rest of the world, the world has not become more peaceful and safer. Bosnia-Herzegovina and Kosovo – despite its declaration of independence – remain Western protectorates and highly dependent on EU spending and military presence. The war on terror against the Taliban in Afghanistan remains inconclusive and Iraq's humanitarian crisis with several million refugees has not been resolved.

While the Hobbesian security worldview relies on military power, on high military expenditures for armed forces and military equipment, security perspective in the tradition of Hugo Grotius has shifted public attention to another 'soft' security challenge that cannot be resolved with military means; the foreseeable security impact of global climate change may lead to domestic food riots, forced migration, small-scale conflict and an increasing competition over energy, water and food (*Brauch* 2008). This new challenge cannot be solved with Hobbesian military rationales. It requires a new thinking that must address the environmental dimension of human security (*Brauch* 2008). During 2007 and 2008, the British and the German governments have tabled the international security dimension of climate change in the UN Security Council (April 2007) and the European Council (June 2007) to which the European Council and Commission have responded in March 2008 in a joint policy paper that may be reflected in the revised European Security Strategy of 2008.

During its Presidency of the Human Security network, Greece addressed the human security aspects of climate change. These positions fundamentally differ from the focus on the national security dimension of climate change that has prevailed since 2007 in the US environmental security debate. The controversy and debate of these two worldviews on security will continue during the next decade. Both point to different policy strategies, policy priorities and allocation of public resources.

The multilateral Grotian perspective requires progress on disarmament and arms control to shift the focus to the new non-military threats, challenges, vulnerabilities and risks that can neither be solved from a Hobbesian perspective nor with military means. They require a shift of public resources from arms to a progressing decarbonization of the energy economy. Thus, arms control and disarmament become important tools in support of such a proactive new security policy that addresses these non-military threats posed by global environmental change.

Nicholas Stern (2006) has reminded us, that the costs for coping with the consequences of climate change will rise, the later we address these challenges. Proactive cooperative and multilateral strategies are needed that require mutual trust while the Hobbesian fear is based on distrust on the motives and behavior of the other. Thus, overcoming the deadlock in the disarmament talks of the past decade is a precondition for being able to fundamentally shift focus and allocation of resources to the new non-military security challenges posed by the consequences of global environmental change (*Brauch* et al. 2008).

Hans Günter Brauch

Lit.: *Boutros-Ghali, B.:* An Agenda for Peace 1995 with the New Supplement and Related UN Documents, New York 1995; *Brauch, H.G.:* Paradigma und Praxis: Die Vereinten Nationen und die Abrüstung (1945-2000), in: VN 44 (1996), 167-174; *Brauch, H.G./Graaf, H.J. v.d. et al. (eds.):* Controlling the Development and Spread of

Military Technology, Amsterdam 1992; *Brauch, H.G./Graaf, H.J.v.d. et al.:* Militärtechnikfolgenabschätzung und Präventive Rüstungskontrolle. Institutionen, Verfahren und Instrumente, Münster/Hamburg 1996; *Brauch, H.G./Mesjasz, C./Møller, B.:* Controlling weapons in the quest for peace: Nonoffensive defence, arms control, disarmament, and conversion, in: Alger, C.F. (ed.): The Future of the United Nations System: Potential for the Twenty-first Century, Tokyo et al. 1998, 15-53; *Brauch, H.G.:* "Conceptualising the environmental dimension of human security in the UN", in: ISSJ, 2008 supplement, 19-48; *Brauch, H.G. et al.:* Globalisation and environmental challenges: reconceptualising security in the 21st century, Heidelberg et al. 2008; *Brauch, H.G. et al.:* Facing global environmental change: environmental, human, energy, food, health and water security concepts Heidelberg et al. 2008; *Brauch, H.G. et al.:* Coping with global environmental change, disasters and security Heidelberg et al. (in preparation); *Congressional Research Service:* Conventional Arms Transfers to Developing Nations, 1999-2006, Washington, 26 September 2007, RL34187; *Daalder, I.:* Cooperative Arms Control: A New Agenda for the Post-Cold War Era, College Park, MD 1992; *Goldblat, J.:* Arms Control. A Guide to Negotiations and Agreements, Oslo/London 1994; *Liebert, W./Scheffran, J. (eds.):* Against Proliferation Towards General Disarmament, Münster 1995; *Müller, H.:* "Ein Scherbenhaufen", in: VN 51 (2005), 148-151; *OPCW – Conference of the States Parties:* Report of the Second Review Conference, 7-18 April 2008, RC-2/4, www.opcw.org; *SIPRI:* SIPRI Yearbook 2001. Armaments, Disarmament and International Security, Oxford/New York 2001; *SIPRI:* SIPRI Yearbook 2008. Armaments, Disarmament and International Security, Oxford/New York 2008; *Stern, N.:* The Economics of Climate Change – The Stern Review Cambridge/New York 2006.

Internet: United Nations Office for Disarmament Affairs: www.un.org/disarmament/; Preparatory Commission for the Comprehensive Nuclear-Test Ban Treaty Organization: www.ctbto.org; Organization for the Prohibition of Chemical Weapons: www.opcw.org.

Table 1: Four related pillars of a comprehensive disarmament strategy

Concepts: Policy & Goals	Disarmament	Arms Control	Crisis Management	Confidence Building Measures
Policy goals	Peace and international collective security	War prevention	Prevention of escalation into conflict or war	Positive climate for détente, disarmament, peace-building
Systemic goals	Rule of international law	Enhancement of strategic stability	Code of conduct, cooperation	Cooperation to prevent a surprise attack
Action goals	Limitation, regulation, reduction, elimination, destruction	Damage limitation if deterrence has failed	Improvement of communication (societal, political)	Openness, transparency, predictability
Objects	Armaments, military industry, manpower, bases	Armaments, manpower, budgets, arms transfers	Prevention of crises and of spill-over into war	Information, verification, communication, constraints
Regional scope	Global (UN), regional, subregional, bilateral and trilateral	Global (UN), regional, subregional, bilateral and trilateral	Bilateral among nuclear powers, regional among conventional weapons states	Global UN study on CBMs, regional and bilateral agreements on CBMs
Substance	Weapons industry, manpower, base closure	Nuclear and conventional weapons industry	Crisis communication, accident prevention	Counter surprise attack and horizontal escalation
Procedures	Unilateral, gradualist, by treaty	Unilateral, gradualist, by treaty	Unilateral and mutual compromise	Unilateral and gradualist, political agreement (treaty)

Table 2: Disarmament Negotiations and Results of Arms Control and Disarmament Efforts (1945-2000)

Concepts and phases	Disarmament	Arms Control	Crisis Management	Confidence Building Measures. Humanitarian Law
Capitulation	Demilitarisation of Germany and Japan in 1945	These concepts did not yet exist		
Cold War (1946-1962)	N: Baruch plan; Disarmament Commission (DC), 10 Nations Disarmament Committee	O: Antarctica Treaty (1959)	N: none O: none	N: none O: none
Limited Détente (1963-68)	N: Eighteen Nations Disarmament Committee (ENDC)	B: Ltd Test Ban T. ('63) R: Tlatelolco Treaty (1967) G: Outer Space T. ('67); Non-proliferation T. ('68)	B: Hot Wire (direct communication link between US and USSR) 1963	N: none O: none
Global and regional détente in Europe (1969-1979)	N: Conference Committee on Disarmament (CCD) until 1978; then DC O: Biol. Weapons Conv ('72)	R: Final Act of Helsinki (1975) N: Belgrade Follow-up (1978)		G: Geneva protocols (1977-79) on Mines, Napalm R: Final Act of Helsinki (1975) N: Belgrade Follow-up of SCCE (1978)
Bilateral Détente: US-USSR (1969-1974)		B: SALT I: Interim Treaty and ABM-Treaty (1972)	B: Improved direct communication link between US and USSR (1971), B: Agreement on Nuclear Accidents (1972) B: Nuclear War (1972)	
Increasing US - USSR Tensions (1974-	N: CCD until 1978; then DC	B: SALT II Treaty not ratified (1979)		
Cold War 2 (1980-1986)	N, B: INF, START G: CCD since 1984	N, G: CD since 1984 O, R: Raratonga NWFZ (1996) N, B: INF, START		G: Conv. on Certain Conventional Weapons (1981) N: Madrid Follow-up of CSCE (1980-1983) R: Stockholm Agreement (1986)
Détente 2 (1987-1989)	N, G: CD (Chemical weapons) N, B: INF (1987)	B: INF Treaty (1987)	B: US-Soviet Centres for the Reduct. of Nucl. Risks ('87)	N: Vienna Follow-up of CSCE (1987-1989)
Global Turn ('89-'90)	N, G: CD; N, R: CFE (1990)	R: CFE (1990)		R: Vienna Document 1990
Post-Cold War period (1991-1996): Progress	B: START I (1991); START (1993) G: CWC (1993)	R: CFE 1A (1992) R: NWFZ in Africa (1995), in South East Asia ('96) B: START I ('91); START II ('93)		G: UN Arms Register (1993 -) G: Geneva Protocol on Laser Blending Weapons (1995) R: CSCE Vienna Documents of '92; Budapest Decl. ('94); Lisbon Document ('96)
Post-Cold War period (1997-): Paralysis	G: Ottawa Anti-Personnel Mine Treaty (1997)			R: OSCE: Istanbul Declaration (1999).

B: Bilateral; G: Global; N: Negotiations; NWFZ: Nuclear-Weapon-Free Zone; O: Outcome; R: Regional; T: Treaty

135

Documentation System

Introduction

Those seriously concerned with questions and issues in the area of international relations and its treatment by the United Nations will want to gain access to the documentation and the publications issued by the UN. The complexity of the UN's system of documentation should not be underestimated: it reflects the hierarchical and highly differentiated organizational structure of the United Nations system.

However, by following a systematic research strategy and by making use of the manifold reference works and research tools, the required information, documents or publications can usually be identified. The purpose of this article is not to add another highly structured documents guide to those that already exist, e.g. *United Nations documentation: research guide* (www.un.org/Depts/dhl/resguide/), prepared by the Dag Hammarskjöld Library, or the *Brief guide to United Nations documents*, compiled by Ilona Stölken-Fitschen (see *Wolfrum* 1995, 1505). Rather, the article is to convey an understanding of the UN documentation system as gained in several years of working directly with these materials in the reference service for UN documentation of the Dag Hammarskjöld Library.

The article will present the most important reference works covering the UN, provide definitions and document identifiers, describe different categories of documents as well as a variety of research tools, and identify options for gaining access to UN documentation. It concludes with a list of Internet addresses for selected UN documents collections found online.

1. General Reference Works about the United Nations

Since when is Belize a member state of the United Nations? What was the United Nations' role in the Korean War? Who drafted the Universal Declaration of Human Rights? Which UN organs are charged with the issue of environ-

mental protection? Answers to these and many other questions can be found in key reference works about the United Nations, which span the gamut from general introductions to detailed handbooks and records of activities to document indices.

The United Nations today, formerly published as *Basic facts about the United Nations,* a thematically organized guide published by the United Nations, gives a first glimpse into the creation, structure, and the scope of activities of the UN. More detailed information and essential data for further research can be found in several handbooks. The various editions (last published in 1986) of Everyone's *United Nations* give a synopsis of main events in the history of the United Nations and indicate the fora (main organs, specialized agencies, UN conferences, etc.) that dealt with a certain issue or conflict or that elaborated a convention, declaration or programme of action. The *Encyclopedia of the United Nations and international agreements,* compiled by Edmund Jan Osmanczyk and Anthony Mango, the publication in hand, or also the handbook *United Nations: law, policies and practice,* edited by Rüdiger Wolfrum, furnish comprehensive information about the areas of work of the United Nations and the organs that are engaged in those fields. The *Yearbook of the United Nations* (http://unyearbook.un.org) reports in even more detail about the activities of the organization during a particular year. It contains numerous document references and reproduces the texts of key resolutions. The various *Indexes to proceedings* (cf. below 4. *Tools for UN documents research*) provide references to the primary literature, i.e. the documents themselves.

Information regarding the creation, the mandates and the composition or membership of the numerous UN bodies (main and subsidiary organs, special programmes, committees, commissions, specialized agencies) can be easily obtained from the *Handbook of the United Nations,* published annually by the New Zealand Ministry of Foreign Affairs and

Trade, or from *Die Vereinten Nationen und ihre Sonderorganisationen*, an in-depth guide compiled by Klaus Hüfner.

Another excellent source of information is the *United Nations Internet site* (www.un.org) that was launched in 1995 (→ Internet, Websites of the UN System in the).

In addition to the UN homepage, the Global Policy Forum (www.globalpolicy.org), the United Nations Association of the USA (www. unausa.org) or the multilingual web site of the Regional United Nations Information Centre in Brussels (www.unric.org/) are good starting-places for exploring both the structure of the organization as well as current areas of activity and issues of concern to the UN.

With its *United Nations System Pathfinder* www.un.org/Depts/dhl/pathfind/frame/start.htm) the Dag Hammarskjöld Library offers thematic access to fundamental reference works and publications of the United Nations system. The *Pathfinder* identifies major reports and studies, handbooks, bibliographies and documents indices, as well as compilations of treaties and statistics in subject areas of particular interest to persons engaged in United Nations research: international security and peacekeeping operations, economic and social development, environmental protection, human rights, and world trade.

Further information about the work of the organizations within the UN system can be retrieved at the web site "Official Web Site Locator for the United Nations System of Organizations": www.unsystem.org.

In order to keep up-to-date with ongoing UN activities, the quarterly journal UN Chronicle (www.un.org/Pubs/chronicle/) and the press releases posted on the UN homepage (www.un.org/News/) deliver both the latest news stories as well as news analysis. The UN Foundation produces UNWire (www.smartbrief. com/un_wire) that provides a synthesis and aggregation of major news stories about UN-related issues. A useful compilation of working papers, draft resolutions etc. concerning the reform of the United Nations, together with resources on UN reform from governments and civil society as well as press coverage can be found on the web site of ReformtheUN.org (www.reformtheun.org), a project of the World Federalist Movement – Institute for Global Policy (WFM-IGP). The website of the Security Council Report (www.securitycouncilreport.org), a non-profit organization in affiliation with the Columbia University's Center on International Organization, provides regular reports on the Council's existing and prospective agenda, as well as reports on membership in, elections of, and working methods of the Council. Lastly, there is UN Pulse (www.un.org/Depts/dhl/unpulse), a blog maintained by the Dag Hammarskjöld Library that informs about and links to just-released UN publications and reports of vital interest to the UN community.

2. United Nations Issuances

Essentially, United Nations issuances can be grouped into two major categories: *official documents*, including the *official records*, and *sales publications*. Official UN documents are texts presented for deliberation to one or several UN organ(s) under one or several agenda item(s). In the upper part of the title page called the masthead they bear the emblem or logo and the name of the organ in question as well as one (occasionally several) *document symbol(s)* that allow for precise identification of a document. The official records are always identified as such on the title page. Sales publications are identified by so-called *sales numbers*.

The unofficial United Nations *press releases* do not form part of the official UN issuances in the strictest sense; however, because of their currency and their great informational value they should not be overlooked. They are identified with one (or several) *press release symbols*.

Document Symbols, Sales Numbers, and Press Release Symbols

A *document symbol* consists of a sequence of numbers and letters that form distinctive elements separated by slashes. These elements may denote, among others, the organ to which the document was presented, the session or year, the type of document and any modifications to the original text. Following this model, resolution 30 of the 53rd session of the General Assembly (GA) is identified with the document symbol A/RES/53/30, the summary record of the 2nd meeting of the Economic and Social Council (ECOSOC) during the year 1998 with the document symbol E/1998/SR.2, and the 318th document prepared for the Security Council (SC) in 1998 with the document symbol S/1998/318. A detailed overview of the system of UN document symbols with numerous examples can be found in the *United Nations documentation: research guide* (www.un.org/Depts/dhl/resguide/symbol.htm). At its creation, every UN organ is assigned a specific document series symbol, and all documents prepared for or presented to that body are issued under the series symbol assigned to it.

Several reference tools have been issued to help with the identification of these series symbols:
- United Nations document series symbols, 1946-1977, UN Doc. ST/LIB/SER.B/5/Rev.3, UN Sales No. 79.I.3
- United Nations document series symbols, 1978-1984, UN Doc. ST/LIB/SER.B/Rev.3/Add.1, UN Sales No. 85.I.21
- United Nations document series symbols, 1946-1996, UN Doc. ST/LIB/SER.B/5/Rev.5, UN Sales No. 98.I.6

A *sales number* consists of 4 elements indicating the language and year of publication, the subject category or UN issuing agency, and a sequential number, for example: E.08.II.C.2, World economic situation and prospects 2008, the 2nd title published in 2008 in subject category II.C "World economy" in the English language. The *United Nations documentation: research guide* includes a listing of the sales categories at www.un.org/Depts/dhl/resguide/symbol1.htm.

A *press release symbol* is composed of 2 or 3 elements (numbers and letters) and indicates either a topic or the UN body that is reported on, and a sequential number, for example: HR/CN/875, a press release reporting about a meeting of the Commission on Human Rights. Again, a listing of series in which press releases can appear is included in the *United Nations documentation: research guide* at www.un.org/Depts/dhl/resguide/press1.htm.

3. Document Types and Categories

In order to work effectively with UN documents and to perform focused research for relevant information it is helpful to familiarize oneself with the most important types and categories of documents, their purpose or function, their content and their patterns of issuance or publication. Should someone want to get an idea of UN activities in the area of women's advancement the best place to start would be the reports of those UN bodies with a corresponding mandate. Reactions by UN member states to nuclear testing carried out by India and Pakistan in May 1998 are reflected in member states' letters and recorded in the respective delegates' statements to the ($\rightarrow$ Security Council). The collective will of the states represented in the UN as expressed in the resolutions and decisions of UN organs ($\rightarrow$ Resolutions/Declarations/Decisions) is also of great interest. The following overview should make orientation in the complex system of UN documentation easier.

Journal of the United Nations/Bulletin of Meetings in the Palais des Nations at Geneva

The daily *Journal* or *Bulletin* contains details about meetings of UN bodies that are scheduled for a particular day. It indicates the questions and topics to be discussed along with any relevant documentation that was prepared for the meeting (most commonly reports and draft resolutions). The part "Summary of official meetings" presents a brief roundup of meetings held the previous day and may include references to resolutions that were adopted or record other important actions taken, e.g. elections or nominations. All references to UN texts are provided with Internet links to the electronic full text version (pdf) in the ODS database (http://documents.un.org).

The recent (English) issue of the Journal can be accessed at www.un.org/ Docs/journal/En/lateste.pdf; back issues of the Journal can be accessed at www.un. org/ga/search/journal.asp.

Agenda

The *agenda* specifies all questions and issues to be deliberated by a UN organ at a particular session or meeting. Often annotations with background information and document references for the individual agenda items are provided. Whereas the GA, ECOSOC and their subsidiary and specialized organs work with one agenda containing all agenda items for the whole duration of their session, a separate agenda is issued for each meeting of the SC in the document series S/Agenda/.

The process of setting up the agenda for the General Assembly passes through several stages and may take approximately six months from the initial preliminary list until the adoption of the final agenda by the General Assembly. The annotated preliminary list of agenda items is an essential tool in preparing for sessions of the General Assembly: it provides a brief historical overview of how the various issues were treated at previous sessions of the General Assembly, including references to the most important documents (reports and resolutions), and it indicates key documents expected for the upcoming session. In addition, it contains lists of the presidents and vice-presidents of the General Assembly (from 1946 onwards), of the officers of the main committees (from the 20th session onwards), of the nonpermanent members of the Security Council (from 1946 onwards), of the members of the Economic and Social Council (from 1946 onwards), as well as a current list of UN member states. The final decision about the composition of the agenda is taken in the General Committee of the General Assembly. Its report discloses which agenda items that had been proposed for inclusion in the agenda were rejected and which ones were deferred to sessions in the future.

Reports

Reports form an essential part of all conference and session documentation, as they often contain information that will serve as the basis for debate and negotiations.

The *resolutions* adopted by both main and subsidiary organs of the UN often contain a section mandating the → Secretary-General to furnish *reports* on issues and topics on their respective agendas. In particular, the Secretary-General's report on the work of the Organization, always issued as Supplement No. 1 to the official records of the General Assembly, and the reports about conflict situations and the progress of UN peace-keeping operations, draw special attention. Reports by the Secretary-General may contain important recommendations, such as the proposals regarding the reform of the organization submitted to the General Assembly in mid-1997 or those to the Security Council on the establishment of new peace-keeping operations.

The *main committees* of the General Assembly (→ Committees, System of) each elaborate one report for every agenda item assigned to them. These reports contain a summary of the discussions, the texts of the final versions of draft resolutions and draft decisions, as well as the voting results in committee in those cases when a recorded vote was requested.

All *subsidiary* and *special UN organs* (→ Principal Organs/Subsidiary Organs/Treaty Bodies) along with those UN organs responsible for the implementation of human rights instruments (→ Human Rights, Protection of) are required *to report regularly on their ac-*

tivities to the superior body. These reports contain the resolutions, decisions, and other recommendations adopted by the respective bodies and are issued as *supplements to the official records of the main organs.* The Security Council, the Economic and Social Council and the → International Court of Justice (ICJ) are required to report to the General Assembly; consequently, their reports are issued as supplements to the official records of the GA.

In addition to the reports of the various UN bodies, the following types of reports deserve special mention:

Both the → *International Law Commission (ILC)* and the → *Commission on Human Rights* as well as its successor body, the *Human Rights Council,* appoint *special rapporteurs* with the mandate to study specific questions in the field of international law or human rights or to investigate the situation of human rights in specific countries.

The *states parties to human rights covenants and conventions* (→ Human Rights Conventions and their Measures of Implementation) are under the obligation to regularly furnish information regarding the implementation of treaty provisions to the respective competent treaty bodies in the form of initial and periodic *reports.*

The *reports of conferences* called for by the General Assembly or by the Economic and Social Council (→ World Conferences) usually contain the texts of declarations, programmes of action or treaties that were negotiated at the respective events.

Document symbols for the types of reports mentioned in this section as well as for other kinds of reports can be easily identified with the help of the *United Nations Info Quest (UN-I-QUE)* database (http://www.un.org/Depts/dhl/ unique).

Letters

Essentially, letters can be grouped into two categories: *letters by member states* and *letters by the Secretary-General.* Letters sent by member states usually serve the purpose to inform the UN organ that they are directed to about the member state's position on certain questions. However, they may transmit important documents, such as treaties or the final documents agreed upon at summit meetings of intergovernmental organizations (e.g. the African Union, Organization of the Islamic Conference), or they may contain reports by international commissions not belonging to the UN system. Thus, the text of the Dayton Agreement was furnished to the GA and the SC in an annex to a letter by the United States (UN Doc. A/50/790-S/1995/999); the report of the International Commission on Intervention and State Sovereignty was transmitted by a letter from Canada (UN Doc. A/57/303). Chiefly, the letters by the Secretary-General are concerned with personnel movements and other administrative questions relating to the → peacekeeping operations, but may also provide the SC with up-to-date information about current developments in areas of crisis, e.g. Kofi Annan's letter dated 24 June 2005 about the urgent humanitarian needs of the people of Sudan (UN Doc. S/2005/413).

Resolutions and Decisions

Resolutions and decisions, as well as the presidential statements of the Security Council reflect the official position of a UN organ or they express its collective will. They are issued in a variety of formats.

Resolutions of the General Assembly and the Security Council, as well as the presidential statements of the Security Council first come out as individual documents in document series A/RES/, S/RES/ and S/PRST/. At a later date they are issued as an unofficial compilation in form of a press release that also provides the voting results. Finally, several months later, they are published collectively in their final, official form as a supplement to or as part of the official records.

Up-to-date lists of recently adopted resolutions are included in *United Nations documentation: research guide:* check www.un.org/Depts/dhl/resguide/gares1.htm for General Assembly resolutions and www.un.org/Depts/dhl/resguide/scact.htm for Security Council actions.

Decisions of the General Assembly and of the Security Council are not issued as individual documents and are therefore only available in the compilations.

Resolutions and decisions of the Economic and Social Council come out exclusively in form of compilations: the preliminary version in document series E/INF/ and the final, official version as a supplement to the official records.

The resolutions and decisions of all subsidiary and special UN organs, with some exceptions, form a part of the reports to their respective superior bodies. According to this practice, the resolutions and decisions adopted by the Human Rights Council are included in its report to the GA (e.g. UN Doc. A/62/53).

The texts of treaties and declarations represent an interesting phenomenon. Occasionally, texts of draft resolutions are presented to the GA recommending to it the adoption of certain agreements or declarations. These texts usually have to pass through the full hierarchy of UN bodies and are passed on from subsidiary to superior body as part of their reports or in form of resolutions. The so-called "Declaration on Human Rights Defenders" that was drafted by a working group established by the Commission on Human Rights, is an example to illustrate this case: 1. report of the working group to the Commission on Human Rights containing the draft text of the declaration (UN Doc. E/CN.4/1998/98); 2. resolution 1998/7 by the Commission on Human Rights; 3. resolution 1998/33 by ECOSOC; 4. resolution 53/144 by the GA (UN Doc. A/RES/53/144).

A listing of all texts of treaties and declarations adopted by the GA since 1946 can be found *in United Nations documentation: research guide* (www. un.org/Depts/dhl/resguide/resins.htm).

Preliminary voting records for resolutions and decisions are provided in the press releases covering individual meetings of the General Assembly and the Security Council, in the resolution compilations that are issued for the GA and the SC as press releases, in the voting charts that are annexed to the *Indexes to proceedings* (GA and SC), as well as in the voting records database of *UNBISnet*, the Dag Hammarskjöld Library's public web catalogue (http://unbisnet. un.org) and the "voting information" file of *UNBIS Plus on CD-ROM*. Official voting records are exclusively contained in the meeting records.

Meeting Records

Meeting records contain the speeches and statements made by delegates at official meetings of UN bodies, as well as the official voting records for resolutions and decisions. Most important of all are the speeches delivered by heads of state at the General Assembly's general debate, the forum for world leaders to present their nations' foreign policy priorities. The *United Nations Info Quest (UN-I-QUE)* database contains listings of these preeminent statements for all member states.

The General Assembly, the First Committee of the GA and the Security Council are entitled to full *meeting records (procès verbaux* or *verbatim records)*. These can be identified in the document symbol by the element "/PV.".

The Second to Sixth Committees of the GA and the Economic and Social Council receive summary records, indicated with the element "/SR." in the document symbol. Only very few subsidiary and special organs and treaty bodies are entitled to summary records; for all other UN bodies and most UN conferences, no meeting records are prepared.

In this case, only the press releases and the reports inform about the negotiations and their outcome. The SC has often been criticized for its lack of transparency as negotiations are usually held in informal closed meetings for which no meeting records are produced. The meeting records of the main organs and of some of the subsidiary organs are reissued as official records with a delay of several years.

Press Releases

Despite their unofficial character, United Nations press releases are valued chiefly for their topicality. They report daily on meetings of the most important UN bodies, provide background information for upcoming sessions (background press releases) and summaries at the conclusion of sessions (round-up press releases). They replace temporarily the official reports and meeting records that are issued with ever-increasing delays because of budget cuts and staff reductions. The resolutions adopted by the GA and the resolutions and presidential statements of the SC are first issued as compilations in the form of press releases, again long before the official compilations come out. Furthermore, press releases are the only source of information for the texts of speeches or statements made by the Secretary-General at events not organized by the United Nations or for biographical data about high-level UN officials and the permanent representatives of the member states.

4. Tools for United Nations Documents Research

To facilitate the identification and retrieval of UN documents and publications, a variety of document indices and databases are at the researcher's disposal.

The *Indexes to proceedings* cover the deliberations of the General Assembly, of the Security Council and of the Economic and Social Council, respectively, during a particular session or year. They consist of two parts: a *subject index* listing all documents (reports, letters, draft resolutions and decisions, meeting records and final resolutions and decisions) by subject, and an *index to speeches* with references to meeting records listed separately under the names of countries or organizations, by name of speaker and by subject. In addition, the *Indexes to proceedings* of the GA and the SC are furnished with a voting chart.

The *United Nations documents index* (published from 1998 until 2006) and its

precursors UNDOC, UNDI and UNDEX provide subject access to the full spectrum of documents issued by the numerous UN bodies. The Dag Hammarskjöld Library has discontinued this index.

UNBIS Plus on CD-ROM includes various databases of the Dag Hammarskjöld Library: a bibliographic database of UN documents issued since 1979, an index to speeches, a "voting information" file containing the voting records for resolutions, a database of the documentation series, as well as the full text in English of resolutions adopted by the GA, the SC and ECOSOC. References and documents can be retrieved with the aid of a user-friendly search mechanism using a broad range of search criteria (e.g. full text search in the resolutions file). The Dag Hammarskjöld Library discontinued producing updates to *UNBIS Plus on CD-ROM* in 2005.

UNBISnet (http://unbisnet.un.org) is the Dag Hammarskjöld Library's public online catalogue. In addition to a bibliographic database containing records for all United Nations documents issued since 1979, selected materials from the → specialized agencies, and books, journals and other materials held by the library, users may search in special databases for voting records and speech records. The search can be constructed by using multiple criteria and can be limited to specific document types, such as reports, resolutions or meeting records. Records contain links to the electronic full text version (pdf) on ODS whenever available.

United Nations Info Quest (UN-I-QUE) (http://lib-unique.un.org/lib/unique.nsf) provides access to document symbols and sales numbers of frequently requested types of UN documents. Among others, the reports produced by UN bodies and the special rapporteurs, the speeches made during the general debate of the GA, a listing of major documents on UN reform (→ Reform of the UN), or the key documents relating to the → peacekeeping operations are included in this database. *UN-I-QUE* contains complete listings that may go all the way back to 1946 and is updated daily by the Dag Hammarskjöld Library.

The *United Nations Official Documents System (ODS)* and (to a much lesser degree) the *United Nations Homepage* (see below) offer limited search options, but they have the advantage of permitting full text searches in the documents that are stored.

The following indices can be used to specifically identify UN resolutions:

- *Index to resolutions* of the General Assembly, 1946-1970. 2 vols., UN Doc. ST/LIB/SER.H/1, UN Sales No. 72.I.3 (pt. 1) and 72.I.14 (pt. 2)
- *Index to resolutions* of the Security Council, 1946-1996, UN Doc. ST/LIB/SER.H/5/Rev.1, UN Sales No. 98.I.4
- *Tables of vetoed draft resolutions* in the United Nations Security Council, 1946-1993, [London]: International and Commonwealth Section, Research and Analysis Dept., Foreign and Commonwealth Office, 1994
- *Index to resolutions of the Economic and Social Council*, 1946-1970, UN Doc. ST/LIB/SER.H/4, UN Sales No. 81.I.16

5. Access to UN Documents

Having successfully completed one's research for the documentation, various possibilities exist to gain access to the actual documents and publications of the UN.

They can be consulted in depository libraries, the United Nations Library in Geneva and the United Nations Information Centres (see listing in annex), or they can be purchased from the UN Sales Offices in Geneva and New York:

United Nations Sales Office and Bookshop
Palais des Nations
CH-1211 Geneva 10
Tel.: +41 (22) 917-2613/14
Fax: +41 (22) 917-0027
E-mail: unpubli@unog.ch

United Nations Publications
2 United Nations Plaza
New York, NY 10017
USA
Tel.: +1 212-963-8302
Fax: +1 212-963-3489
E-mail: publications@un.org

The *United Nations Official Documents System (ODS)* offers the largest collection of UN documents in electronic form in all official languages with approximately one and a half million files (100,000 files are added every year) and is freely accessible at http://publications.un.org. The ODS consists mainly of two databases: a nearly complete collection of UN documents issued since 1993, and a collection of all resolutions and decisions adopted by the main UN organs since 1946. The Dag Hammarskjöld's digitization programme strives to continually expand the coverage of ODS for earlier years, esp. for the documentation of the Security Council. Search options on the ODS are limited and sometimes not user-friendly and other research tools, such as UNBISnet or UN Info Quest, may be more helpful in identifying specific documents. On the other hand, ODS offers researchers the ability to perform full text searches in all six official languages of the UN.

Apart from the *Official Document System,* a significant number of UN documents have been made available on the *United Nations Internet site* (www.un. org) and the Internet sites of UN programmes and funds.

The following list provides the Internet addresses for selected documents collections (current as of 1 July 2008):

Secretary-General's reports:
   www.un.org/documents/secretariat.htm
Secretary-General's speeches:
   www.un.org/apps/news/infocus/sgspeeches
UN Documentation Center (GA, SC, ECOSOC, UN Journal):
   www.un.org/documents/
UN press releases:
   www.un.org/apps/pressreleases
Yearbook of the United Nations:
   http://unyearbook.un.org
Reports of global conferences and GA special sessions:
   www.un.org/events/index.html
UN reform:
   www.un.org/reform/
Peacekeeping operations:

www.un.org/Depts/dpko/dpko (open web site for specific mission, click "UN Documents")

Millennium Development Goals (MDGs):
www.un.org/millenniumgoals/documents.html

Palestine question (UNISPAL):
http://unispal.un.org/unispal.nsf

Disarmament:
http://disarmament.un.org (follow links to "Conference on Disarmament" and "Disarmament Commission")

International Court of Justice (ICJ):
www.icj-cij.org

International Law Commission:
www.un.org/law/ilc

International Criminal Court:
www.un.org/law/icc

UNCITRAL:
www.uncitral.org/uncitral/en/commission_working_groups.html

Law of the sea:
www.un.org/Depts/los/index.htm

Human Rights:
www.ohchr.org/en/HRBodies/pages/humanrightsbodies.aspx

Refugees:
www.refworld.org

Sustainable development:
www.un.org/esa/sustdev/documents/docs.htm

Social development:
www.un.org/esa/socdev/csd/

Women's issues:
www.un.org/womenwatch/directory (follow link "UN Intergovernmental Bodies")

Climate change:
http://unfccc.int/documentation/items/2643.php
www.ipcc.ch/

Drug control:
www.unodc.org/unodc/en/commissions/CND/index.html

UNCTAD:
www.unctad.org/en/pub/pudoc.htm

UNDP/UNFPA:
www.undp.org/execbrd/

UNEP:
www.unep.org/resources/gov

UNICEF:
www.unicef.org/about/execboard/index_25993.html

World Food Programme (WFP):
www.wfp.org (open "Executive Board" section, click on "Documents")

Humanitarian assistance:
www.reliefweb.int (especially the "Policy & Issues" section)

Economic Commission for Europe (ECE):
www.unece.org/meetings/meetings.htm

UN documents in German:
www.un.org/Depts/german/

Ramona Kohrs

Lit.: *Stölken-Fitschen I.:* Brief guide to United Nations documents, in: Wolfrum, R. (ed.): United Nations: law, policies and practice, 2 vols., Munich/Dordrecht 1995, Vol. 2, 1505-1517; *United Nations:* United Nations Documentation: A Brief Guide, New York 1994, UN Doc. ST/LIB/34/Rev.2 and UN Doc. ST/LIB/34/Rev.2/Corr.1 and Corr.2 of 10 January 1995 and 12 January 1995, respectively.

Internet: United Nations documentation: research guide: www.un.org/Depts/dhl/resguide

Economic Commissions, Regional

Developments and overview

Economic and social questions are clearly reflected in the institutions of the United Nations. This is in contrast to the structure of the → League of Nations, and is due to the historical experience which has led to an increased awareness of the importance of these issues for international peace and security (→ Charter of the UN, Goals and Principles of the UN). The Economic and Social Council (→ ECOSOC) most clearly manifests this development. However, the → UN system provides only a very limited regional sub-structure.

Therefore, ECOSOC viewed with some skepticism the first steps to create such structures with a view to the needs of post-World War II reconstruction in Europe and Asia and the Far East. However the → General Assembly recommended to ECOSOC that two regional economic commissions should be set up (UN Doc. A/RES/46 (I) of 11 December 1946), one for Europe and one for Asia and the Far East. ECOSOC followed the recommendation and established both commissions: Economic Commission for Europe (ECE), founded on 28 March 1947 by UN Doc. E/RES/36 (IV); and Economic Commission for Asia and the Far East (ECAFE), founded on 28 March 1947 by E/RES/37 (IV)). In 1951 ECOSOC bestowed permanent status on the originally temporary commissions (E/RES/414 (XIII) of 18 September 1951).

Later on it created three additional commissions: the Economic Commission for Latin America (ECLA), founded on 5 March 1948 by ECOSOC Res. 106 (VI), renamed Economic Commission for Latin America and the Caribbean (ECLAC) on 27 July 1984 (E/RES/1984/67); the Economic Commission for Africa (ECA), founded on 29 April 1958 by E/RES/671 (XXV); and the Economic Commission for Western Asia (ECWA), founded on 9 August 1973 by E/RES/1818 (LV), renamed the Economic and Social Commission for Western Asia (ESCWA) on 26 July 1985 by E/RES/1985/69.

Members of these regional economic commissions are the UN member states of the respective regions, often in company with other UN member states, which join them either as full members or as observers (→ Observer Status). The objectives of these regional commissions are only vaguely stated, generally providing only that the commissions should strengthen economic cooperation in the region. Generally, the main organ is a general assembly of the Economic Commission, while the everyday work is dealt with by committees and commissions. In addition, they have their own, usually well-equipped secretariats. They are financed by the general → budget of the UN; in addition, they have certain financial means for different projects. Under the UN system, the Regional Commissions are subsidiary organs under Article 7 (2) of the UN-Charter (→ Principal Organs, Subsidiary Organs, Treaty Bodies). They are under the supervision of and report to ECOSOC.

In the economic and social fields of the UN, to which ECOSOC and other organizations, e.g. → UNDP, belong, the regional economic commissions fulfill planning and coordination tasks as well as keeping statistical records, but are also concerned with monitoring and implementing development projects.

Some commissions are in close contact with regional security structures and organizations dealing with economic integration and development banks.

The commissions so far played their role without much discussion, although ECOSOC attempted several times to reform the regional commissions, for instance in 1998 with resolution E/RES/1998/46 of 31 July 1998, Annex III, where ECOSOC defined the present role of the regional commissions in the UN system.

In the recent comprehensive reform efforts within the UN system, they were hardly mentioned. Thus, Secretary-General Kofi Annan in his famous 2005 report "In larger freedom" did not explicitly mention the commissions, but only briefly addressed the issue of "regional infrastructure and institutions" (UN Doc. A/59/2005, para. 69).

In the context of the implementation of the Millennium Development Goals (MDGs) the commissions have been given a certain role in monitoring and supporting the implementation of the MDGs in their respective region. They have submitted regional MDG reports, for instance the Economic Commission for Africa the report "Assessing Progress in Africa towards the Millennium Development Goals Report 2008" (UN Doc. E/ECA/COE/27/10 of 6 March 2008).

The regional commissions have also presented their views on the debate about more coherence in the economic and social activities of the United Nations, inter alia, in two papers on the reform of the environmental institutional framework of the UN and on the regional dimension of development (*Regional Commissions* 2006a and 2006b, accessible at: www.un.org/regionalcommissions/).

145

Economic Commission for Africa (ECA)

ECA plays a major role in the regional development and development planning, and maintains close ties to the Organization of African Unity (OAU, now the African Union/AU). ECA, which has 53 state members is headquartered in Addis Ababa (Ethiopia) and has several branch offices. Nowadays it is mainly concerned with the promotion of regional economic integration and with meeting Africa's special needs and emerging global challenges.

Economic Commission for Asia and the Pacific (ESCAP)

Originally, only China, India, the Philippines and Thailand, as well as Australia and the superpowers belonged to ESCAP, but today all Asian states, and the former Soviet Republics in this region, are also members.

Due to considerable cultural and political divergences, the commission encountered some difficulties, and at first functioned as a kind of research institution. Today, the Commission, which has its headquarters in Bangkok, has 62 members, nine of them are not members of the United Nations (American Samoa, Cook Islands, French Polynesia, Guam, Hong Kong, Macao, New Caledonia, Niue, Northern Mariana Islands). ESCAP is very active in the area of poverty reduction, managing globalization and in tackling emerging social issues.

The Economic Commission for Europe (ECE)

The ECE, of which the USA and Canada and, more recently, Israel (on a temporary basis), have become members, was originally created for rebuilding Europe after the Second World War. However with the outbreak of the Cold War, it had to cede this role to the OECD. The membership structure, which did not run along the boundary lines of the two political blocs and was therefore originally not adequate for the original purpose, was later just the basis for great successes. The ECE was for a long time the only forum for regional, non-partisan cooperation, and was especially successful in promoting cooperation in traffic and transportation policies, as well as elaborating common initiatives in → environmental protection.

Cooperation of the states around the Mediterranean Sea also falls within the scope of activities of the ECE, which is situated in Geneva and today counts 56 member states.

Economic Commission for Latin America and the Caribbean (ECLAC)

Among the 44 Members of ECLAC with its headquarter in Santiago de Chile are all Northern, Central, and South American states, but also a number of European states, namely France, Germany, the Netherlands, Portugal, Spain, Italy, the United Kingdom, as well as Canada, the United States, Japan and South Korea. The Commission also includes in its membership eight non-independent territories in the Caribbean. Its relationship with the Organization of American States (OAS) is unclear. The strong focus on economic and development policies within ECLAC has led to the creation of a new theory – the *Cepalismo* (named after the acronym of the Spanish translation of its name (CEPAL – Comisión Económica para América Latina y el Caribe) – which links statements concerning the global economy and development policy issues, and which has greatly influenced the policy in developing countries, and in the United Nations as a whole. This theory, which was put forward *inter alia*, by Raúl Prebisch, takes up elements of the Marxist world trade theory and further expands on them. It views the developed states as being at the center of the international system while the developing states are on its periphery, and the concept postulates that an integration of developing states into the system will jeopardize the interests and development of the central states. The presupposition that prices for natural resources will have a tendency to fall, and that developing states will therefore have falling export revenues, is of great significance for this theory. However, today, such theory no longer plays a significant role in the work of the Commission.

Economic and Social Commission for Western Asia (ESCWA)

Thirteen states in the Gulf Area and North Africa, as well as Palestine (in the form of the Palestinian Authority), are members of ESCWA, which has its headquarters in Beirut, Lebanon. Its work is also influenced by the conflict in the Middle East.

Evaluation

Today, the Economic Commissions play a relatively limited role. In the field of economic support, they often trail regional development banks. With regard to cooperation in economic and trade issues, regional economic and free-trade areas (e.g. Andean Pact, APEC, ASEAN, Mercosur and SADCC) are far more significant today. Within the UN system the general topic "development" still lies mainly in the hands of UNDP. Economic issues between the North and the South are mainly dealt with by → UNCTAD, and in part, by → UNIDO, while the latter is in turn becoming overshadowed by WTO (→ WTO/GATT).

Within their limited scope, the economic commissions have often found areas of concern specific to the region and the institutions. Sometimes, they have found their calling in helping to settle regional conflicts.

The fact that the regional commissions have recently established their own Internet website www.un.org/regionalcommissions/about.html, where all relevant UN documents and background texts can be accessed might be considered as a sign that the role of the regional commission could gain some importance in the future with regard to regionalization and cooperation efforts in the UN.

Peter Tobias Stoll

Lit.: *Berthelot, Y. (ed.):* Unity and diversity in development ideas: perspectives from the UN regional commissions, Bloomington et al. 2004; *Berthelot, Y.:* Regional and global

UN entities: a constructive exchange of ideas, in: Forum for Development Studies 32 (2005), 127-150; *Szasz, P.C./Willisch, J.:* Regional Commissions of the United Nations, in : Bernhardt, R. (ed.): EPIL, Vol. 6, Amsterdam 1983, 296-301; *Stoll, T.:* Economic Commissions, Regional, in: Wolfrum, R. (ed.): United Nations: Law, Policies and Practice, Vol. 1., Munich/Dordrecht 1995, 434-450; *United Nations - Economic and Social Council:* Regional Cooperation in the economic, social and related fields. Report of the Secretary-General, 20 June 2008, UN Doc. E/2008/15; *United Nations Regional Commissions:* Towards a more coherent framework for the UN System's Environmental Activities. Views and Role of the Regional Commissions, New York, May 2006 (quoted as: UN Regional Commissions 2006a); *United Nations Regional Commissions:* Note on the Regional Dimension of Development with the UN, New York, 15 June 2006 (quoted as: UN Regional Commissions 2006b).

Internet: *ECA:* www. uneca. org/;
ECE: www.unece.org;
ECLAC: www. eclac.org;
ESCAP: www.unescap.org;
ESCWA: www.escwa.un.org/;
common homepage of the regional commissions: www. un.org/ regionalcommissions/ about.html.

ECOSOC – Economic and Social Council

The Economic and Social Council (ECOSOC) is one of the six principal organs of the UN (→ Principal Organs, Subsidiary Organs, Treaty Bodies), as laid down in the → Charter of the UN.

Since 1971 the Council consists of 54 members (originally it was made up of 18 and, from 1965 to 1970, of 27 members). Every year 18 members of the Council are elected by the UN → General Assembly for a term of three years. Retiring members are eligible for immediate re-election. Each member of the Council has one vote; decisions are made by a simple majority of the members present and voting. Activities of the Council are conducted under the authority of the General Assembly (Art. 60).

The Council can furnish information to the → Security Council of the UN, assists the Security Council upon its request (Art. 65) and performs all functions allocated by the General Assembly (Art. 66).

It is the *purpose* of ECOSOC to discuss, promote and coordinate the economic, social, cultural and humanitarian activities of the UN. In accordance with Article 62 and 64 UN Charter, ECOSOC can conduct or initiate studies and reports with respect to international economic, social, cultural, educational, health, and related matters. The Council can make recommendations to the General Assembly and to the → specialized agencies concerned in promoting respect for and observance of → human rights and fundamental freedoms. The Council is requested to elaborate agreements as well as draft conventions for international cooperation in these fields. ECOSOC can enter into agreements with international specialized agencies, defining the terms on which the agency concerned shall be brought into relationship with the UN (Articles 57 and 63). Such agreements are subject to approval by the General Assembly.

ECOSOC is requested to contribute to the establishment of peaceful relations between the peoples of the world based, on respect for the principles of equal rights and self-determination of peoples (→ Self-Determination, Right of). In accordance with the Charter of the UN, ECOSOC is to draft and to submit strategies and concepts as well as rules and principles for cooperation, and to coordinate effectively the activities of the UN – including the specialized agencies – in the above mentioned fields.

In performing these tasks and functions, ECOSOC established a number of subsidiary organs in accordance with Article 68 of the Charter. The Council adopted its own Rules of Procedure which – *inter alia* – include the procedure of electing the President, the Vice-Presidents and the Rapporteur, as well as the methods of organizing the work of the Council (Art. 72 UN-Charter).

The *subsidiary organs/bodies of the Council* can be classified as follows:
- *Sessional Committees*;

- *Ad-Hoc Committees;*
- *Permanent Committees*, which are established permanently for important tasks (for instance the Committee for Programme and Coordination (→ Budget), the Committee for Natural Resources, the Committee for Non-Governmental Organizations (→ NGOs);
- *Regional Economic Commissions* (ECE – Economic Commission for Europe; ESCWA – Economic and Social Commission for Western Asia; ECA – Economic Commission for Africa; ESCAP – Economic and Social Commission for Asia and the Pacific; ECLAC – Economic Commission for Latin America and the Caribbean; → Economic Commissions, Regional);
- *Functional Commissions* (for instance the Commission for the Status of Women (→ Women and the UN);
- *Expert Committees* (for instance the Committee for Development Planning, the Committee for Economic, Social and Cultural Rights).

The number of subsidiary organs of ECOSOC as well as other additional intergovernmental bodies in the economic, social, humanitarian and ecological fields increased considerably in the course of the 60s and 70s of the last century. This development reflected the emergence of new challenges in international relations, which required global and regional solutions. Simultaneously the impact of developing countries on the content of the activities and priorities of the UN became stronger and stronger. Rightfully this group of states requested a stronger concentration on urgent issues of eradicating underdevelopment, poverty and misery, as well as the group's unequal position in the international economy. New challenges have been developing as a result of the disastrous consequences of destroying the human environment by the expansion of the economies and of the capital in the developed countries, and also as result of the consequences of the underdevelopment of the majority of the Asian, African and Latin American states (→ Environmental Protection; →

Humanitarian Assistance). On the other hand, the expansion in the number of organs and institutions of the UN system dealing with such issues did not lead to increased efficiency of the UN in this field, especially of that principal organ – ECOSOC, which was and still is in charge of elaborating concepts and creating favorable international conditions for sustainable solutions.

There exists more or less a general consensus that, up to now, ECOSOC has not been in a position to realize its tasks and functions in accordance with the Charter of the UN. One of the reasons for this is the existence of a large number of organs and institutions, and the inability of ECOSOC to provide the political guidance and to manage the coordination of these bodies (→ Coordination in the UN System). The decisive reason for the failure of ECOSOC is obviously the lack of political will of the member states of the UN to end the dominance of the international finance organizations, such as the World Bank (→ World Bank, World Bank Group) and the International Monetary Fund (→ IMF).

In the meantime a number of proposals exist for revitalizing ECOSOC and enabling it to play a central role in solving existing economic, social, humanitarian and ecological problems of our world. Some of these proposals really tackle the crucial problem which has to be solved: strengthening the authority of ECOSOC with regard to the international finance organizations, increasing its competence, and determining its priorities as well as establishing an international framework which enables a sustainable economic, social and ecological development and a just international economic order (→ International Economic Relations and New International Economic Order (NIEO)).

Proposals have been made to transform ECOSOC into a "World Security Council", or to establish a "Security Council for Development". Other considerations are not as far-reaching. It has been recommended that ECOSOC should concentrate on fundamental political issues in promoting international, social and ecological cooperation, and not on operational activities. In order to increase the continuity and efficiency of ECOSOC, it has been proposed to establish an "Enlarged Bureau" or an "Executive Committee of ECOSOC" which should meet between the sessions of ECOSOC. Finally it has been suggested that ECOSOC be divided into an Economic Council and a Social Council.

Some of these proposals could be realized within the framework of the existing Charter of the UN, which still offers considerable scope for reform (→ Reform of the UN). Other proposals require a revision of the Charter. As far as a revision of the Charter is concerned, many member states – especially the permanent members of the Security Council – hesitate to agree or have even rejected outright any revision of the existing Charter. In accordance with Article 108 of the Charter an amendment of the Charter requires a two-thirds majority of the members of the General Assembly of the UN, including all the permanent members of the Security Council.

Any step forward in strengthening ECOSOC entails very sensitive political decisions. The divergent political positions of the member states concerning the role of states in the development of international economic, monetary and financial relations involve either promoting further deregulation or strengthening the role of states, elaborating and agreeing upon norms, principles and mechanism on the basis of international law.

In view of the dominant role of transnational corporations in the field of international economic relations, as well as the dominance of neo-liberal theories and concepts on the policies of the leading industrial nations, the chances for fundamental reforms of ECOSOC and of strengthening ECOSOC seem to be limited. The tendency to restrict considerations of international security to the military field and to underrate or ignore economic, ecological and social security as essential elements of international security enhance this development. There-

149

fore reforms concerning ECOSOC will probably be limited to rationalizing the existing structures and improving the methods of work of ECOSOC.

In this direction the General Assembly of the UN adopted *inter alia* A/RES/50/227 of 1 July 1996 and A/RES/52/12 B of 19 December 1997 giving orientations and taking decisions in this direction. A process of reorganization and rationalization within the → Secretariat and ECOSOC is on the way. Commissions and committees have been merged, the number of members of subsidiary organs has been reduced, the duration and frequency of meetings has been decreased, and names of subsidiary organs have been changed. These "technical and organizational" changes have been linked with political issues, as they have often been connected with the determination of new priorities, as well as eliminating, or giving a new image to, subsidiary organs of ECOSOC.

Wolfgang Spröte

Lit.: *1. UN Documents: United Nations:* Report of the Economic and Social Council for the Year 1998, GAOR Fifty-third session, Suppl. No 3; UN Doc. A/53/3, New York 1998; *United Nations:* Proposed Basic Programme of Work of the Council for 1998 and 1999; *United Nations:* Restructuring and Revitalization of the United Nations in the Economic. Social and Related Fields, UN Doc. E/1999/1, 2 February 1999: *2. Secondary Literature: Albrecht, U./Volger, H. (eds.):* Lexikon der internationalen Politik, Munich/Vienna 1997; *Hüfner, K. (ed.):* Die Reform der Vereinten Nationen, Opladen 1994; *Hüfner, K.:* Die Vereinten Nationen und ihre Sonderorganisationen, Teil 1: Die Haupt- und Spezialorgane, DGVN-Texte 40, 2nd edn., Bonn 1995.

Addendum

Also in the new millennium the attempts to reform the ungovernable ECOSOC continued. The reform proposals still faced the same problems Wolfgang Spröte has outlined in the preceding entry: strengthening ECOSOC's competences in order to improve its ability to play an important role as a "clearing house" in debating and preparing decisions on the urgent global economic, social, humanitarian and ecological problems only makes sense and is only supported by influential UN members in the same measure that changes are agreed on with respect to the international economic, financial and social global framework. Because changes on this level – for example with regard to the UN system of environmental protection or to the international economic order where the → WTO member states still search for viable compromises in the Doha round of negotiations – are still lacking, the economically strong UN member states, above all the industrialized countries, are not ready to provide ECOSOC with more competences for coordination with regard to the large number of subsidiary UN bodies and of the organizations connected with ECOSOC through relationship agreements.

This became apparent when the High-level Panel on Threats, Challenges and Change which had been tasked by UN → Secretary-General Kofi Annan in 2003 to evaluate the present → UN system and to develop proposals for the reform of the existing UN institutions submitted its report in December 2004 "A more secure world: our shared responsibility" (UN Doc. A/59/565 of 2 December 2004).

With regard to ECOSOC, the panel of experienced national politicians and long-standing UN officials strikes in its report a sober but realistic balance in considering the institutional fragmentation and lack of coordination as a consequent result of the provisions of the UN Charter itself in "allowing for the creation of → specialized agencies independent of the principal United Nations organs". Recognizing this basic construction feature, the panelists conclude rightly in their report that it would not be "realistic to aim for the Economic and Social Council to become the centre of the world's decision-making on matters of trade and finance, or to direct the programmes of the specialized agencies or the international financial institutions." (ibid., para. 274)

Seldom before has the basic structural problem of ECOSOC been depicted so clearly as leaving no room for illusions about reform. The panelists as experienced politicians know that the leading nations will not agree to let the WTO, the Bretton Woods institutions IMF and World Bank as well as the specialized agencies hand over any significant competences to ECOSOC.

But if that is so, what is then the role of ECOSOC? The panelists see the role of ECOSOC not in attempting in vain to coordinate in terms of organization, finances and oversight, but in a "normative and analytical leadership" (ibid., para. 276) with regard to looking for solutions for the economic and social threats to peace. In this context the panelists welcome the exchange of ideas between ECOSOC and the Security Council through meetings of their Presidents.

With regard to UN development cooperation ECOSOC could according to the panelists fulfill two functions:
- it can provide a forum where the states measure their commitments to achieving key development objectives such as the Millennium Development Goals – a kind of benchmarking institution – (para. 277);
- it can provide an effective forum for substantial development cooperation, above all through a small executive committee which should, in interaction with UN principal organs, agencies and programmes, survey the implementation of UN development cooperation and through the efficient use of the annual meetings of ECOSOC with the Bretton Woods institutions (para. 278).

In his reform report of March 2005 "In larger freedom: towards development, security and human rights for all" (UN Doc. A/59/2005) Secretary-General Kofi Annan welcomed the suggestions of the panel and added some elements to the suggestions: for the benchmarking function with regard to the implementation of the development goals, having emerged from the → world conferences and summits ECOSOC should hold annual ministerial level assessments of progress towards agreed development goals. (ibid., para. 175)

To monitor the coherent implementation of development activities of the different actors ECOSOC should transform the high-level segment of the Council meeting biannually into a high-level development cooperation forum. (ibid., para. 176)

Annan added two important proposals, providing ECOSOC with new functions: ECOSOC should with regard to economic and social challenges, threats, crises, and natural disasters convene timely meetings to promote coordinated responses to the crises and disasters (ibid., para. 177). And in order to institutionalize the post-conflict peacebuilding of the UN Annan suggested the establishment of a Peacebuilding Commission, composed of members of the Security Council, of members of ECOSOC, leading troop contributors and major donors of development aid. (ibid., para. 114ff.)

The UN World Summit in September 2005 followed in its concluding resolution, the "2005 World Summit Outcome" document (UN Doc. A/RES/60/1 of 16 September 2005), with regard to ECOSOC the suggestions of the High-Level Panel and of Kofi Annan.

They decided that ECOSOC should
- hold "a biennial high-level Development Cooperation Forum to review trends in international development cooperation ... [and to, H.V.] promote greater coherence among the development activities of the different development partners ..." (ibid., para. 156b);
- hold "annual ministerial-level substantive reviews to assess progress" to ensure the follow-up of the major UN conferences (ibid., para 156c);
- support "international efforts aimed at addressing humanitarian emergencies, including natural disasters, in order to promote an improved, coordinated response" from the UN (ibid., para. 156d).

Moreover the World Summit decided to establish the Peacebuilding Commission (ibid., paras. 97-105) suggested in Annan's report (A/59/2005, para. 114ff.).

In December 2005, the General Assembly and the Security Council established in concurrent resolutions (UN Doc. A/RES/60/180 and S/RES/1645 (2005) of 20 December 2005) the *Peacebuilding Commission.*

It consists of seven members of the → Security Council, including permanent members, seven members of ECOSOC, elected from the regional groups, the five top assessed contributors to UN budgets (→ Budget) and of voluntary contributions to UN funds, programmes and agencies, and the five top contributors of military personnel and civilian police to UN missions (→ Peacekeeping Forces; → Peacekeeping Operations).

This decision has without doubt strengthened ECOSOC, as it now participates on a concrete level in peace-building efforts together with the Security Council, the big donors and troop-contributing countries.

Another decision of the World Summit has weakened the role of ECOSOC in the field of → human rights: the summit decided to replace the *Commission on Human Rights*, a subsidiary organ of ECOSOC, with a new organ, the → *Human Rights Council*, established as subsidiary organ of the General Assembly. The decision was put into practice in spring 2006: on 15 March 2006 the General Assembly decided to establish the new Human Rights Council of 47 member states elected directly and individually by secret ballot by the majority of members of the → General Assembly (→ Principal Organs, Subsidiary Organs, Treaty Bodies). In the same resolution the General Assembly recommended that ECOSOC request the Commission on Human Rights to conclude its work at its 62nd session and that ECOSOC abolishes the Commission in June 2006. ECOSOC followed this request of the General Assembly in adopting on 22 March 2006 ECOSOC Resolution 2006/2 which abolished the Commission with effect of 16 June 2006.

Without doubt the annual human rights debates within the Commission on Human Rights, with the criticism of its Subcommission and its Special Rapporteurs of massive human rights violations in UN member states had guaranteed ECOSOC a certain amount of public attention, in particular as in many cases ECOSOC had to deal with the reports and decisions of the Commission. But in the course of the years the Commission had attracted increasing criticism because of its growing trend towards bloc voting resulting often in impeding discussions about and investigations of human rights situations in states with bad human rights records.

Many UN experts hope that the abolition of the Commission on Human Rights as a subsidiary organ of ECOSOC might help ECOSOC to focus on its role as coordinator and analytical forum for → development cooperation and → humanitarian assistance (cf. *Rosenthal* 2007, 146).

All in all, the World Summit 2005 did not address some of the major historical weaknesses of ECOSOC originating from the provisions of the UN Charter (→ Charter of the UN): the ambiguous relationship with the General Assembly with much overlap and duplication of work, the non-binding nature of its decisions and the weak position towards the specialized agencies.

It is not clear whether the renewed call for overall coordination in the activities of UN funds, programmes and agencies in order to achieve greater coherence and to avoid overlap and duplication will be any more successful than previous attempts, since ECOSOC has still no decision competence.

This is all the more the case as the different groups of member states, above all the Group of 77 on the one hand and the industrialized states on the other, disagree on the interpretation of the role given to the Council by the World Summit Document. While the former see its task as providing guidance for objectives and strategies in UN development projects, the latter put the emphasis on the improvement of organizational coherence and avoidance of duplication (cf. *Martinetti* 2006, 4).

The annual meetings of ECOSOC with the Bretton Woods institutions, however, constitute a step in the right direction, having started with concrete results in the preparation phase of the Monterrey UN Conference 2002 and having continued annually since then (cf. *United Nations* 2008a), the *Annual Ministerial Review* and the biennial *Development Cooperation Forum* of ECOSOC, the latter two originating from the resolution of the World Summit 2005: the *Annual Ministerial Review (AMR)* consisting of a general debate and roundtable discussions with high-level officials and leading experts from academia and NGOs representatives attempts to assess progress or lack thereof with regard to a particular aspect of development efforts, e.g. education or sustainable development). Additionally a number of countries present on a voluntary basis national presentations.

The *Development Cooperation Forum (DCF)* serves as a platform for sharing experiences and lessons learned where donor countries and recipient nations can discuss their experiences and problems with regard to managing and coordinating development aid in practice. NGOs can contribute their experiences.

Both forms (AMR and DCF) seem to have an eminent practical approach to the issues at stake, a positive contrast to many fruitless programmatic debates in ECOSOC in the past (cf. *United Nations* 2008b).

Even if the decisions are taken elsewhere in the national cabinets, or in the Geneva Group of the big donors, or in the IMF and World Bank, ECOSOC seems to offer in its present structure more chances for common learning processes of donor and recipient countries and of the officials in the secretariats of WTO and the international financial institutions.

If the non-governmental organizations (→ NGOs) with consultative status which are registered at ECOSOC and have defined rights of taking part in the sessions of ECOSOC and its subsidiary organs and whose fight for more participation rights has not been very successful in recent years do, it is to be hoped, improve their status, then ECOSOC will without doubt benefit from it. Its work deserves more attention and public debate.

Helmut Volger

Lit.: *Akram, M.:* Working Paper on Implementation of the 2005 World Summit decisions regarding Economic and Social Council. Working Paper from Ambassador Munir Akram, Permanent Representative of Pakistan, President of ECOSOC, October 2005, www.globalpolicy.org/socecon/un/reform/20 05/10implement.pdf; *Martinetti, I.:* A Strengthened United Nations' Economic and Social Council. Agreement on draft resolution still delayed, in: U.N. Reform Watch No. 20, 26 October 2006, www.centerforunreform.org; *Rosenthal, G.:* The Economic and Social Council of the United Nations. An Issues Paper (Friedrich-Ebert-Stiftung Occasional Papers No. 15), New York 2005; *Rosenthal, G.:* Economic and Social Council, in: Weiss, T.G./Daws, S. (eds.): The Oxford Handbook on the United Nations, Oxford 2007, 136-148; *United Nations - ECOSOC:* Summary by the President of the Economic and Social Council of the high-level special meeting of the Council with the Bretton Woods institutions, the World Trade Organization and the United Nations Conference on Trade and Development (New York, 14 April 2008), UN Doc. A/63/80-E/2008/67 of 19 May 2008 (quoted as: United Nations 2008a) *United Nations – ECOSOC:* Economic and Social Council Opens High-Level-Segment of Substantive Session, UN Press Release ECOSOC/6346, 30 June 2008 (quoted as United Nations 2008b).

Internet: *ECOSOC Dokumente:* www.un. org/ecosoc.

Electoral Assistance

I. Forms of Electoral Assistance

1. Election Observation

Election observation is one of four forms of electoral assistance provided by democratic governments, transnational organizations and non-governmental organizations (→ NGOs) to former colonies on their way to independence, as well as to newly establishing democracies. The international observers are in charge of different tasks: they observe the pre-election phase, the election campaign, the registration and identification of the voters, the drawing of electoral district lines and the registration of candidates and political parties (*long-term observation*). Furthermore they observe the main event: the election day itself, meaning the voting and the counting of the votes (*short-term observation*). Observers should not interfere in the election process as such, even in the case where they may recognize irregularities or clear violations of the law. Instead of interfering, they should bring the irregularities to the attention of the local election officials or the public.

2. Other Forms of Electoral Assistance

Beside this rather passive form of election observation, there exist three other – less used – forms of *electoral assistance:*

Material and personal support to conduct the election: In this case assistance is given to formulate the election law, technical equipment like ballots and ballot boxes is provided, and local staff in charge of the election process is educated.

Conduct of election: the strictest way of international intervention in a national election. In this case an external organization conducts and is in charge of the whole election process.

Monitoring of the election: Here the international observers are actively helping in conducting the election. Furthermore they have the authority to interfere in the case of irregularities (*Mair* 1994, 4-5).

II. Electoral Assistance of the United Nations

1. Electoral Assistance in UN History

Beginning with the end of the East-West confrontation, observation of elections has emerged as an important task in support of democratic transition and universal human rights. In contrast to the widespread and frequent usage of election observation missions, this instrument of supporting democracy has not been investigated systematically in the academic community. This is documented by a lack of publications analyzing observation missions. So far the observation of elections is judged more as art than as science (*Gabler* 1993, 7).

The character of observation missions has changed rapidly, beginning with the first mission in 1948 in Korea, up to the current common forms. In the phase of → decolonization in the late fifties and the early sixties, election assistance was only provided to those trust areas (→ Trusteeship Council) on their way to independence, in which power was to be handed over from the colonial masters to the people by the free expression of their will. These kinds of intervention in the internal affairs of a country were consistent with international law, because the mission was not conducted in a sovereign state. The mandate was given either by the → General Assembly of the UN or by the Trusteeship Council. In this period the British Commonwealth played the most active part, accompanying the elections in its areas of influence.

Beginning with the wave of democratization in the late eighties in Africa, the second generation of election observation began. For the first time observation missions were conducted in sovereign states like Namibia, Nicaragua and later in the East European states.

The first step before taking over an international mandate in sovereign states is the voluntary invitation of international observers by the government. Further preconditions of the UN before providing assistance are: a clear international dimension of the election and the possibility to observe the whole election process without limits, beginning with the voter registration over the election campaign up to the announcement of the results.

One of the most successful cases of electoral assistance was the UN Mission to Namibia (1 April 1989 to 1 April 1990), including military elements as well as civilian elements (*Szasz* 1993). In contrast to this positive example, the mission in Kenya (December 1992) serves as a negative example, of how not to conduct electoral assistance. The Commonwealth observers were accused of being biased and having their own political interests, because they did not react to various complaints of national and international NGO observers (*Geisler* 1993).

Under observation are those elections, whose legitimacy is questioned and which therefore need a "stamp of quality" awarded by neutral observers. Normally these are the first elections after the declaration of independence, after a civil war or after the transition from an authoritarian to a democratic political system (*Engel/Mehler* 1994, 29).

Together with the wave of democratization in Eastern Europe the number of requests for election assistance rose strongly. As a result the UN delegated the organization of the missions to regional divisions of the UN like the Organization of American States (OAS), the Organization of African Unity (OAU) and the OSCE. Furthermore the European Council and several → NGOs, like the US-American National Democratic Institute for International Affairs (NDI) and the International Human Rights Law Group, as well as churches and trade unions, are involved in observation missions.

Thus the electoral assistance given to the East European transformation countries is organized by the Office for Democratic Institutions and Human Rights (ODIHR). ODIHR, situated in Warsaw, was established in 1990 as a division of the Organization for Security and Cooperation in Europe (OSCE). The missions organized by ODIHR consist of preparatory seminars and long-term as well as short-term election observation.

2. *Structures of the UN Electoral Assistance*

As the United Nations received since the late 1980s an increasing number of requests for electoral assistance from UN member states, it re-organized its electoral assistance in 1991/1992. In 1991, the General Assembly commissioned the UN Secretary-General to designate a focal point for the coordination of electoral assistance; the Secretary-General designed the Under-Secretary-General for Political Affairs as *Focal Point for Electoral Assistance Activities*. In April 1992, pursuant to General Assembly Resolution 46/137 of 9 March 1992, the *United Nations Electoral Assistance Division (EAD)* was established to assist the Focal Point in carrying out his functions. Major activities of EAD include: evaluating government requests for electoral assistance, conducting needs assessment missions, cooperating with other UN system agencies in the design of electoral assistance project activities and in developing the electoral components of → peacekeeping operations. Furthermore EAD provides logistical and advisory support to international observer groups, maintains a roster of electoral experts and organizes conferences and training courses.

3. *Forms of UN Electoral Assistance*

There are two main forms of UN electoral assistance: standard electoral assistance activities and major electoral missions which are usually conducted within the context of comprehensive peacekeeping operations:

a) *Standard Electoral Assistance Activities*

Since the establishment of the EAD in 1992 the UN has provided various forms of electoral assistance to over 70 member states. As a rule the assistance takes the form of relatively small-scale, technical assistance activities that do not require a specific mandate from the General Assembly or the → Security Council.

The following standard types of assistance activities are used, often adapted and modified to suit the needs of the requesting country:

Coordination and support of international observers: the EAD establishes a small secretariat in the requesting country in cooperation with → UNDP to

155

help coordinate and provide logistical support to international election observers (e.g. sponsored by member states, intergovernmental and non-governmental organizations).

Technical assistance: Technical assistance is the most frequently requested type of electoral assistance and covers a broad range of assistance activities in assisting the national election authorities in administering elections among others in such areas as electoral planning, voter registration, election budgeting, training of election officials.

Support for national election monitors: This means to support the activities of the local civil society to monitor elections on a non-partisan basis by providing training courses and advisory assistance.

Limited observation ("follow and report"): In special cases a small UN observer team may be sent to a country to follow the final phase of an electoral process and issue an internal report to the UN Secretary-General on its conduct.

b) Major Electoral Missions

Major electoral missions require a mandate from the General Assembly or the Security Council and are regarded exceptional activities of the Organization. They are normally a central element of a comprehensive peacekeeping mission that includes an electoral component. In the context of major missions the UN provides three types of electoral assistance:

- *organization and conduct of an electoral process*;
- *supervision of an electoral process;* and
- *verification of an electoral process.*

4. Objectives of Election Observation

The objectives of election observation are ambitious and manifold. On the one side, the people involved in the election process should be supported psychologically. On the other, any kind of manipulation during the voting and the counting process should be identified, the public is to be informed about the fairness of the process and, in the case of profound disputes about the results of the election, observers should mediate. To meet the listed objectives of an observation mission, competent and well-instructed national and international observers are a very important precondition. Good language skills, as well as knowledge about the country, and about its current political situation are required. Pre-existing contacts within the country and good health are assets (*Mair* 1994, 29). During their mission the observers are coordinated by the organization in charge of the mission.

5. Course of Election Observation

Before their deployment, observers should be informed about the current situation in the deployment area, and provided with material such as the election law, and information about the candidates. The observers should begin their deployment by talking to representatives of all political parties and the media, to get an impression of the course of the pre-election campaign. The main objective of *short-term election observation* – the most common form of observation – is to assess the election day. Therefore observers have to verify whether the ballot boxes are sealed, the polling stations are appropriately equipped, no agitation is taking place within the polling station and that no one is prevented from entering the polling station. At the close of the polls, observers should be present to ascertain that the procedures for closing are followed, and they should stay to observe the count. The mission ends with the announcement of the results. Directly after the election, the observers send first information about the election process to the central coordination committee for their preliminary assessment. There are several handbooks providing guidelines for the conduct of duties during the mission, as well as for the writing of the final examination (*Europarat* 1992; *ODIHR* 1999; *Garber* 1984). A detailed assessment is given in the final examination after the election.

The final assessment of the election is the most important and most sensitive part of the observation. The two adjectives "free and fair" should summarize the whole course of the election. An election is called "free", if – despite some acceptable exemptions – all citizens having the right to vote were really in the position to vote. An election is called "fair", if all voters had the same number of votes, no political party or group was excluded from the election in a discriminatory manner and all groups involved in the election had the same possibility to campaign (*Engel et al.* 1996, 39). One often quoted problem with the final assessment is that the complex election process with all its single steps has to be summarized and judged by the observers with two words. This leads to conflicts, because the reality in the newly establishing democracies cannot be described by black and white criteria. *Garber* (1993, 8) assumes instead that most of the elections in the transition period have to be judged as "grey". Taking these arguments seriously it is common to find a compromise for the final assessment, which takes the specific situation of the country into consideration. Furthermore there exists no clear definition up to which point an election could be still judged as "free and fair". Many of the observers have therefore criticized the manner of final overall assessments. They argue for a more differentiated conclusion, and may dispute the simplistic declaration of the formula: "The election has been conducted free and fair".

III. Significance of Election Observation

One of the main problems of election observation is its lack of clearly defined consequences in the case of irregularities or of an undemocratic course of the election. Even though World Bank and International Monetary Fund (since 1989) as well as the Organization for Economic Co-operation and Development (OECD since 1992) do link the provision of development assistance with the willingness of a country to establish a democratic political system,

they do not always apply those criteria uniformly. In case of doubt one tends to declare an election "free and fair", rather than to exclude the country from development assistance.

Another problem of election observation is a direct result of its success. The UN is not able to conduct all observation missions they are asked for. The UN has to reject many of the requests.

Election observation will only serve as an efficient instrument to assist the democratization process, if it is carried out carefully and the request for assistance will be rejected if the necessary preconditions are not met. One such precondition for efficient mission planning is an early invitation from the host government. Furthermore the host country must guarantee that the observers can operate without restrictions, and that they will be secure. And, finally, the publication of the results within the country has to be ensured. If one of the listed conditions is not fulfilled, it will be important to rethink the decision and in some cases even to cancel the election observation. Observations which are able to judge and assess the election only to a limited extent, would reduce the stamp of quality "free and fair" to that of a carte blanche.

Short-term election observation is mainly criticized because it is too much concentrated on the election day, even though manipulations are rather uncommon on that day. Much more important is the undemocratic behavior in the pre-election phase. It has occurred, for example in Kenya, that one part of the voters was not registered, or in other cases candidates of the opposition were not allowed to campaign or were prevented from campaigning. Therefore it is useful to combine *short-term observation* with some *long-term observers*. Sometimes the number of international observers is so limited, that it is not possible to ensure an observation which covers the whole country. In this case only a part of the election can be reported, or international observers will have to co-operate with national observers. A last point of critique mentions the political bias or self-interest of the international organizations. They may be so interested in fostering democracy and helping those governments to succeed, that they may be less willing to take complaints seriously. In the case of Ghana (November 1992), for example, the final assessment of the central observation committee was given even before the closing of the polling stations. (*Geisler* 1993, 619)

As the former → Secretary-General of the UN, Boutros Boutros-Ghali, pointed out in his → Agenda for Peace (1992), there is a clear link between democratic practices and a peaceful political system. Taking this into consideration, the promotion of democracy is one of the most important global goals. *McGoy/ Garber/Pastor* (1991) see the implementation of elections as one important element of the promotion of democracy. In this context the failure of an election can be seen as a threat to national and international peace. Against this background one cannot deny the importance of election observation missions as a tool of international politics. They are an appropriate and relatively cheap form of conflict prevention. But one has to keep in mind that it has to be accompanied by additional tools, like the observation of the following elections, which can bear much better witness to the democratic consolidation process, than perhaps might that first democratic election.

Simone Schwanitz

Lit.: *Beigbeder, Y.:* International Monitoring of Plebiscites, Referenda and National Elections. Self-determination and Transition to Democracy, Dordrecht et al. 1994; *Council of Europe:* Handbook for observers of elections, Strasbourg 1992; *Engel, U./Hofmeier, R./Kohnert, D. et al. (eds.):* Wahlbeobachtung in Afrika: Erfahrungen deutscher Wahlbeobachter, Analysen und Lehren für die Zukunft (= Arbeiten aus dem Institut für Afrika-Kunde 90), 2nd rev. and expanded edn., Hamburg 1996; *Garber, L.:* Eher Kunst als Wissenschaft, in: Der Überblick 29 (1993), 5-8; *Garber, L.:* Guidelines for International Election Observation, edited by the International Human Rights Law Group, Washington D.C. 1984; *Geisler, G.:* Fair? What Has Fairness Got to Do with It? Vagaries of Election Observations and Democratic Standards, in: JMAS, No. 4/1993, 613-637; *McCoy, J./Garber, L./ Pastor, R.:* Pollwatching and Peacemaking, in: Journal of Democracy, No. 4/1991, 102-114; *Mair, S.:* International election observation: One form of democratization assistance. Political and institutional considerations on Germany's contribution, Ebenhausen 1994; *OSCE-ODIHR (ed.):* The ODIHR Election Observation Handbook, 4th edn., Warsaw 1999; Internet source: www. osce.org/odihr/ documents/guidelines/election_handbook/ index.htm; *(no author indicated):* Rußland: Wahlen '95, in: Osteuropa, No. 5/1996, 430-529; *Szasz, P.:* Vorbild oder Sonderfall? Lehren aus der UN-Mission für Namibia, in: Der Überblick 29 (1993), 19-23; *(no author indicated):* Themenschwerpunkt: Wahlbeobachtung, in: Der Überblick 29, No. 1/1993.

Addendum

The demand for electoral assistance has remained high in the years of the new millennium: on average, about 20 official requests for electoral assistance were made per year by UN member states. Since it began to provide electoral assistance in 1991, the United Nations has received 406 requests from 107 UN member states (figures as of August 2007).

Over the years, a number of trends has emerged in UN electoral assistance:

(1) initial skepticism that such assistance might encroach on national → sovereignty has gradually diminished;

(2) requests to organize or observe elections have decreased substantially; technical advice and assistance to electoral authorities and other institutions is the norm;

(3) the complexity of requests, including for technological innovations, is increasing;

(4) a growing number of projects are focused on local elections, which can be more complex and more costly than national elections.

There is an increasing realization among those providing electoral assistance that building capacity to organize fair and credible elections may require assistance over a sustained period. And, even more important, successful elections require not only transparent technical operations, but also the commitment of the political actors to create the appropriate environment to ensure acceptance of results and government formation in a peaceful atmosphere (cf. *United Nations* 2007, 2).

In order to provide the intergovernmental organizations and → NGOs taking part in electoral assistance with common guidelines for their work a number of intergovernmental organizations, among them the UN, the African Union, the European Commission, and the Organization of American States, and non-governmental organizations, among them the Carter Center, the Electoral Reform International Services, and the European Network of Election Monitoring Organizations, have adopted in October 2005 a *Declaration of Principles for International Election Observation* and a *Code of Conduct for International Election Observers* (*United Nations et al.* 2005).

Electoral assistance will without doubt remain for many years an important task for UN organizations, as a part of helping to establish broader processes and institutions of democratic governance, but the UN should take into account the political, cultural and historical context in which the elections take place. The assistance should have the goal of helping the states to develop their own democratic institutions and values.

Helmut Volger

Lit: *Ellis, A. et al.*: Effective Electoral Assistance – Moving from Event-Based Support to Process Support. Conference report and conclusions (International Institute for Democracy and Electoral Assistance), Stockholm 2006; *UNDP:* UNDP and Electoral Assistance – Ten Years of Experience, New York 2001; *UNDP - Evaluation Office:* Electoral Assistance (UNDP Essentials No. 14), December 2003; *United Nations et al.:* Declaration of Principles for International Election Observation and Code of Conduct for International Election Observers, New York, October 2005, www.un.org/Depts/dpa/declar-principles-05.pdf; *United Nations* - *General Assembly:* Strengthening the role of the United Nations in enhancing the effectiveness of the principle of periodic and genuine elections and the promotion of democratization. Report of the Secretary-General, 23 August 2007, UN Doc. A/62/293.

Internet: a) *Homepage of the Electoral Assistance Division in the UN Secretariat:* www.un.org/Depts/dpa/ead/index.shtml; *Website of the Office for Democratic Institutions and Human Rights of the OSCE on election assistance and observation:* www. osce.org/odihr-elections/.

Enemy State Clauses

The United Nations was initially an alliance of the World War II victors. Articles 53 (1) 2, 53 (2) and 107 of the UN Charter (→ Charter of the UN), known as the "enemy state clauses," highlight this aspect. Article 53 (2) defines an "enemy state" as "any state which during the Second World War has been an enemy of any signatory of the present Charter". This applied to Germany, Japan and Italy, as well as Bulgaria, Finland, Rumania, Hungary and probably even Thailand. Austria and Korea were *not* considered "enemy states" for having been annexed by Germany and Japan, respectively, in violation of international law (*Ress/Bröhmer* 2002, Index No. 59 ff.; *Blumenwitz* 1995, 91). It is highly controversial whether UN membership (→ Membership and Representation of States), which was granted to Thailand in 1946 and the two Germanies in 1973, precludes a state's enemy status. The strict wording of Article 53 (2) of the Charter backs this assumption. Yet, this was disputed in the case of Germany as a whole, especially as far as Article 107 was concerned, and it was argued that the respective rights had only been waived vis-à-vis the two German states which in 1973 had become members to the UN (*Ress/Bröhmer* 2002, Index No. 65, 80). If signatories retained their "enemy state" status, other member states, which have contractual obligations toward *all* UN signatories, could formally be classed as allied "enemy states". As a conse-

159

quence, the clause could no longer differentiate between "enemy states" and others. Furthermore, Article 4 of the Charter requires of states to be "peace-loving" prior to UN admission. Membership is thus inconsistent with an "enemy state" tag. Creating distinct classes of UN member states also undermines the "principle of the sovereign equality of *all* of its Members," which is enshrined in Article 2 (1) of the Charter (*Blumenwitz* 1995, 93; *Ress/Bröhmer* 2002, Index No. 65). Articles 53 and 107 of the Charter would be exceptions to this fundamental principle. This remains to be justified.

The "enemy state clauses" were meant to exclude *temporarily* the states that were defeated in World War II, notably Germany, Japan and their allies, from the peacekeeping system (→ Peacekeeping) of the UN Charter. Whereas military interventions by regional alliances or agencies generally require the consent of the → Security Council, measures undertaken against enemy states "provided for pursuant to Article 107 or in regional arrangements directed against renewal of aggressive policy on the part of any such state" (Art. 53 [1] UNC) require no such approval. This is, however, solely a procedural rule that does not abrogate the general prohibition of the use of force (→ Use of Force, Prohibition of). The latter is *ius cogens* (Art. 53 of the Vienna Convention on the Law of Treaties; → Treaties, Law of) and, cannot, therefore, be amended by international agreements (*Heberlein* 1991, 91f.; *Ress/Bröhmer* 2002, Index No. 42). Article 107 of the Charter determines that nothing in the Charter "shall invalidate or preclude action in relation to any state which during the Second World War has been an enemy of any signatory to the present Charter, taken or authorized as a result of that war by the Governments having responsibility for such action." Unlike Article 53 (2) of the Charter, which applies to all member states involved in the "anti-enemy coalition," Article 107 pertains only to the main victorious powers of World War II

(the four Allied Powers and China were considered to "have responsibility" in relation to Germany and Japan respectively). (*Ress* 2002, Index No. 15f.) Against this historical backdrop, the provision is limited to actions taking place "as a result" of World War II. The Soviet Union held that Article 107 of the Charter restricts the powers of the Security Council; the Western Allied Powers, however, rejected this interpretation (*Ghebali* 2005, 2185f.; *Ress Bröhmer* 2002, Index No. 49).

The "enemy state clauses" never gained practical importance, even though the Soviet Union repeatedly (for the last time in 1968) threatened to use them (*Ghebali*, ibid.). Once the "enemy states" were granted UN Membership, the clauses became irrelevant – not necessarily as a matter of law, but of fact. Article 107 of the Charter no longer applied to Germany when the "Two plus Four Treaty," which surrendered the remaining Allied rights and responsibilities to the German government, was signed on 12 September 1990 (*Heberlein* 1991, 100 ff.; *Ress/Bröhmer* 2002, Index No. 80; *Ress* 2002, Index No. 11). In earlier treaties, the Allies affirmed that the principles of Article 2 of the Charter apply to Germany, but never formally renounced their special rights vis-à-vis "enemy states". This implies that the enemy status and UN Membership had to be brought into line somehow. The "enemy state clauses" could be either disregarded because of enduring non-application (*desuetudo*) or considered obsolete because of their transitory nature. A political and legal anachronism (*Ghebali* 2005, 2188), the "enemy state clauses" are likely to fall victims to the next revision of the Charter. In the meantime, these provisions will be nothing but reminders of early UN history.

Jörn Axel Kämmerer

Lit.: *Blumenwitz, D.:* Feindstaatenklauseln – Die Rechtsordnung der Sieger, Munich 1972; *Blumenwitz, D.:* Enemy State Clause in the United Nations Charter, in: EPIL II (1995), 90-95; *Ghebali, V.Y.:* Article 107, in:

Cot, J.-P./Pellet, A. (eds.): La Charte des Nations Unies. Commentaire article par article, 3rd edn., Paris 2005, 2181-2189; *Heberlein, H.:* Geltungsbeendigung der Feindstaatenklauseln – ein äußerer Aspekt der deutschen Einheit, in: AVR 29 (1991), 85-103; *Ress, G./Bröhmer, J.:* Article 53, in: Simma, B. (ed.): The Charter of the United Nations. A Commentary, 2nd edn., Vol. I, Oxford 2002, 854-890; *Ress, G.:* Article 107, in: Simma, B. (ed.): The Charter of the United Nations. A Commentary, 2nd edn., Vol. II, Oxford 2002, 1330-1340.

Environmental Law, International

I. Introduction

Since the UN Conference on Environment and Development, Rio de Janeiro, 3-14 June 1992 (→ Environmental Protection) at the latest, states must be aware that severe global environmental problems, such as climate change, the marine living resources threatened with extinction, the degradation of tropical forests and the growing desertification, are endangering our whole ecosystem. Despite the states' increasing efforts at the international level, these problems have not yet been sufficiently solved.

It was only within the last 30 years that international environmental law developed to a separate realm of international public law. It comprises all norms of international law to which states and international organizations dealing with environmental affairs are bound. Among these norms are in particular international treaties, international customary law and general principles of law. The so-called "soft law" is not part of international environmental law, as it cannot impose legally binding obligations on states to behave in a certain way. Anyhow, quite often "soft law" lays the ground for international treaty-making and can indicate developing international customary law.

II. Development of International Environmental Law

The mass of genuine international environmental treaties were enacted only in the last 35 years, although a few relevant treaties date from the late 19th century. Another important step in the development of international environmental law was the famous arbitral award in the Trail Smelter case of 1941 (RIAA, Vol. 3 (1949), 1903) which settled a dispute between the US and Canada concerning transboundary air pollution. It established a fundamental rule for solving problems concerning transboundary environmental conflicts arising between neighboring states. Pursuant to this rule a state must not engage in, or permit, any activity on its territory which causes or is likely to cause significant harm to the environment across the border. Today, this rule is part of international customary law. Nevertheless, in 1945 states were not really aware of the endangerment of human beings and nature by activities causing environmental harm, whether transboundary or global in character. This is reflected by the silence of the UN Charter as regards the environment. The few international agreements made in the first 25 years after the end of the Second World War in the field of the law of the sea and the law of fresh water resources focused on water utilization rather than water protection.

The almost universal *United Nations Conference on the Human Environment*, held in Stockholm from 5 to 16 June 1972 (cf. report of the conference UN Doc. A/CONF.48/14/Rev.1, 3-5), dealt for the first time with the whole complex of environmental pollution and considered the possibilities to achieve an ever closer intergovernmental environmental cooperation. The "Stockholm Declaration" (UN Doc. A/CONF.48/14/Rev.1; ILM 11 (1972), 1416), which is part of "soft law", reflects the readiness of states to cooperate with each other and their awareness that environmental protection and development are closely interrelated. It contains 26 important "principles" of international environmental protection, some of which have come to be accepted as customary international law. Thus, Principle 21 reiterates the "no-harm rule" established in the Trail Smelter case, and extends its application to the areas beyond the limits of national jurisdiction. Still in 1972 the United Nations Environment Programme (→ UNEP) was established (UN Doc. A/RES/2997 (XXVII). In its now 36 years of existence it has earned considerable praise, despite the severe internal structural problems it yet faces. In the period from 1972 to 1992 many multilateral agreements were concluded which cover a wide range of cross-border environmental problems (cf. below III.).

The *United Nations Conference on Environment and Development) (UNCED),* which was held in Rio de Janeiro from 3 to 14 June 1992 (cf. report UN Doc. A/CONF.151/26/Rev.4 (Vol. I)), had to be successful, because there was urgent need to redress the global environmental injuries which had by that time grown significantly, such as the increasing warming up of climate, as well as the phenomena of desertification and over-exploitation of natural and living resources by land and sea.

Although UNCED was not the breakthrough as originally hoped, it finally brought some important if partial success: The Framework Convention on Climate Change (UNTS 1771, No. 30822; ILM 31 (1992), 849) and the United Nations Convention on Biological Diversity (UNTS 1760, No. 30619; ILM 31 (1992), 818), which both had been negotiated and adopted before, were signed by more than 150 states in Rio. In addition, three legally non-binding instruments were adopted there: the Declaration of the UN Conference on Environment and Development (the so-called "Rio Declaration") (UN Doc. A/CONF.151/26/Rev.1 (Vol. I), Annex I; ILM 31 (1992), 874), which embraced new concepts of international environmental law like "common but differentiated responsibilities", the "polluter pays" principle, or the "precautionary" principle; the "Non-Legally Binding Authoritative Statement of Principles for a Global Consensus on the Management, Conservation and Sustainable Development of All Types of Forests" (UN Doc. A/CONF.151/26/

Rev.1 (Vol. I), Annex III; ILM 31 (1992), 881); and "Agenda 21" (UN Doc. A/CONF.151/26/Rev.1 (Vol. I), Annex II), designed to promote the implementation of the Rio commitments. Moreover, UNCED finally established the concept of "sustainable development" in international environmental relations.

This concept, famously defined by the "Brundtland Commission" in its 1987 Report "Our Common Future" as "development that meets the needs of the present without compromising the ability of future generations to meet their own needs", de facto binds all relevant actors in international environmental relations to pursue a policy which comprehends development and environmental protection as equivalent integral components of an undivided task; furthermore, it calls upon states to have care for the wellbeing of future generations.

The broad catalogue of measures proposed by "Agenda 21", as well as the establishment of the *United Nations Commission on Sustainable Development* (→ CSD – Commission on Sustainable Development) (UN Doc. E/RES/1993, para. 207), nourished hopes for a dynamic post-Rio process. However, in June 1997 the UN General Assembly, in its New York special session ("Rio + 5") for reviewing the states' efforts thus far undertaken, finally reached rather negative conclusions (cf. Assessment of Progress Made Since the United Nations Conference on Environment and Development, 27 June 1997, UN Doc. A/S-19/29, Annex II). Nevertheless, it could point to a few important new instruments, such as the 1994 Convention to Combat Desertification in Those Countries Experiencing Drought and/or Desertification, Particularly in Africa (UNTS 1954, No. 33480; ILM 33 (1994), 1328), the 1995 Agreement on the Conservation and Management of Straddling Fish Stocks and Highly Migratory Fish Stocks (UNTS 2167, No. 37924; ILM 34 (1995), 1542), and the 1996 Protocol to the 1972 London Dumping Convention (IMO Doc.

LC/SM 1/6 of 14 November 1996; ILM 36 (1997), 7).

The "implementation gap" perceived after the Rio Conference was to be addressed by the international community at the World Summit on Sustainable Development, held in Johannesburg, South Africa, from 26 August to 4 September 2002 (cf. UN Doc. A/CONF.199/20). The goal of this Summit was to reinvigorate the implementation of the Rio outcomes. However, considerable differences emerged between the participants in the preparatory process as to how this aim could be achieved: While some states were prepared to commit to new binding obligations, others, primarily the USA, advocated the promotion of voluntary "public private partnerships" for sustainable development involving governments, international organizations, and relevant stakeholders, arguing that new binding law would only face the same fate as the Rio commitments. At Johannesburg, about 220 partnerships were officially announced. The CSD Partnerships Database as of January 2008 (http://webapps01.un.org/dsd/partnerships/public/welcome.do) listed 334 partnerships. However, it is not clear how many of these partnerships are actually new or only old projects that have been relabeled; moreover, the CSD as the institution designated to promote and facilitate partnerships has not been able to establish an effective monitoring system so far.

Traditional "Type I" outcomes of the Johannesburg Summit are the "Political Declaration" and the "Johannesburg Plan of Implementation" (UN Doc. A/CONF.199/20, Annex), both legally non-binding. The Political Declaration reaffirms the commitment to Agenda 21 and the Rio Declaration. The Plan of Implementation for the most part also restates previous commitments. It essentially consolidates the results of the "Millennium Declaration" (2000), the Monterrey International Conference on Financing for Development (2003), and the Doha Ministerial Conference.

While the environment might not have had a very good summit at Johan-nesburg, at least it can be said that the World Summit on Sustainable Development did not fall behind the progress made at Rio.

The 2005 High-level Plenary Meeting of the United Nations General Assembly (the "2005 World Summit"), although not focusing primarily on the environment, added a new dimension to the official environmental protection discourse by identifying environmental degradation as a "soft threat" to human security (cf. UN Doc. A/RES/60/1 of 16 September 2005, para. 48ff.). This security dimension of environmental degradation was confirmed when the UN Security Council, in April 2007, held a debate on the impact of climate change on international peace and security (UN Doc. S/PV.5663 of 17 April 2007).

III. Today's International Treaty Practice

1. International Watercourses

While in the past states bordering on international watercourses were mainly interested in solving questions concerning water utilization, today their relevant treaty practice reflects the understanding that there is a close interdependence between utilization and ecological protection of watercourses. Consequently, many rivers such as the Rhine, the Moselle, the Elbe, the Oder, the Danube, the Zambezi, and the Mekong, as well as many lakes, such as the Lake Constance and the Great Lakes, are subjected to a contractual regime of an environmentally sound utilization of international watercourses. Under the 1997 Convention on the Law of the Non-navigational Uses of International Watercourses (UN Doc. A/51/229, Annex; ILM 36 (1997), 700), which is based on the respective 1994 Draft Rules of the International Law Commission (→ ILC) (YBILC 1994, Vol. II, Part 2), every state bordering on an international watercourse is entitled to utilize an international watercourse in an equitable and reasonable manner, but in doing so is obliged to take all appropriate measures to prevent causing significant harm to other watercourse states.

Furthermore, the Convention establishes rules as to the protection and preservation of ecosystems and the marine environment, and regarding the prevention of pollution and of the introduction of alien or new species. This framework convention has not yet entered into force, but it reflects in large parts customary international law and has influenced subsequent watercourse agreements.

The 1992 Convention on the Protection and Use of Transboundary Watercourses and International Lakes (UNTS 1936, No. 33207; ILM 31 (1992), 1312), adopted under the auspices of the UN-ECE and including two Protocols, also partly reflects the ILC Draft Rules, but contains more detailed and comprehensive environmental provisions than the 1997 Watercourses Convention, thus further developing the international law in this field. A 2003 amendment to this convention, which has not yet entered into force, will allow countries from outside the UNECE region to accede to it.

2. Seas and their Resources

A large number of universal and regional agreements provide for a rather dense network of international rules protecting the seas from pollution caused by the discharge of harmful substances from ships, land-based sources and by the air, as well as from the dumping of wastes and oil leaking out from damaged tankers. There are also many agreements aimed at hindering any over-exploitation of marine living resources. As those agreements are oriented towards utilization rather than conservation of the resources concerned, they do not fully reach that goal. The 1982 UN Convention on the Law of the Sea (UNCLOS) (UNTS 1833, No. 31363; ILM 21 (1982), 1261), whose Part XII deals with the protection and preservation of the marine environment, tried to strike the balance between these traditionally antagonist interests (arts. 192, 193), but it did not really succeed ($\rightarrow$ Law of the Sea) . With its set of mostly procedural framework rules aimed at es-

tablishing a comprehensive regime for the protection of the marine environment and the conservation of marine living resources, UNCLOS strongly influenced relevant universal and regional agreements. Important universal agreements relating to marine pollution are the 1972 London Convention on the Prevention of Marine Pollution by Dumping of Wastes and other Matter (UNTS 1046, No. 15749) with its 1996 Protocol (ILM 36 (1997), 7), the 1973 International Convention for the Prevention of Pollution from Ships, as modified by the 1978 Protocol (MARPOL 73/78) (UNTS 1593, No. 22484; ILM 17 (1978), 546), and the 1990 International Convention on Oil Pollution Preparedness, Response and Co-operation (ILM 30 (1991), 733) with its 2000 Protocol (IMO doc. HNSOP RC/CONF/11/Rev 1). Universal agreements concerning marine resources are the 1946 International Convention for the Regulation of Whaling (UNTS 161, No. 2124) and the 1995 Straddling and Highly Migratory Fish Stocks Agreement (UNTS 2167, No. 37924; ILM 34 (1995), 1547), which implements the relevant UNCLOS provisions. There are also a number of significant regional agreements like the 1991 Protocol on Environmental Protection to the 1959 Antarctic Treaty (ILM 30 (1991), 1461), the 1980 Convention on the Conservation of Antarctic Marine Living Resources (UNTS 1329, No. 22301; ILM 19 (1980), 841), the 1992 Convention on the Protection of the Marine Environment of the Baltic Sea Area (EC Official Journal No. L 73/20, 16 March 1994), the 1992 Convention on the Protection of the Black Sea Against Pollution (UNTS 1764, No. 30674; ILM 32 (1993), 1110), the 1992 Convention for the Protection of the Marine Environment of the North-East Atlantic (OSPAR Convention) (ILM 32 (1993), 1069), and the 2003 Framework Convention for the Protection of the Marine Environment of the Caspian Sea (www.caspianenvironment.org/NewSite/ConventionFrameworkConventionText.htm), as well as the agreements concluded within the framework of the UNEP Regional Seas Programme, like the 1976 Barcelona Convention for the Protection of the Mediterranean Sea against Pollution (UNTS 1102, No. 16908; ILM 15 (1976), 290), as amended on 10 June 1995 (Law of the Sea Bulletin, No. 31 (1996), 65), with a number of Protocols related thereto.

3. Air; Ozone Layer; Climate

The 1979 Convention on Long-Range Transboundary Air Pollution (UNTS 1302, No. 21623; ILM 18 (1979), 1442), adopted under the auspices of the UNECE, was a reaction to the phenomenon that certain pollutants were transported by the air for long distances („acid rain"). This framework convention was complemented by a number of protocols containing specific obligations to reduce certain kinds of air pollution emissions: the 1985 Helsinki Protocol on the Reduction of Sulphur Emissions or their Transboundary Fluxes (UNTS 1480, No. 25247;ILM 27 (1988), 707); the 1988 Sofia Protocol Concerning the Control of Emissions of Nitrogen Oxides or Their Transboundary Fluxes (ILM 28 (1989), 212); the 1991 Geneva Protocol Concerning the Control of Emissions of Volatile Organic Compounds (VOC) or Their Transboundary Fluxes (UNTS 2001, No. 34322; ILM 31 (1992), 573); the 1994 Oslo Protocol on Further Reduction of Sulphur Emissions (UNTS 2177, No. 21623; ILM 33 (1994), 1542); the two 1998 Arhus Protocols on Persistent Organic Pollutants (POPs) (UNTS 2322, No. 21623; ILM 37 (1998), 505) and on Heavy Metals (UNTS 2322, No. 21623; Dutch Tractatenblad 1998, No. 287), and the 1999 Gothenburg Protocol to Abate Acidification, Eutrophication and Ground-Level Ozone (available at: www.unece. org/env/lrtap/multi_h1.htm).

In the early 1970s, it was discovered that the emission of certain anthropogenic gases, particularly chlorofluorocarbons (CFCs), lead to the very rapid depletion of the stratospheric ozone layer. This phenomenon induced states to agree upon the 1985 Vienna Convention for the Protection of the Ozone Layer (UNTS 1513, No. 26164; ILM 26 (1987), 1529). Only two years later this framework convention was followed by the 1987 Montreal Protocol on Substances that Deplete the Ozone Layer.) (UNTS No. 26369; ILM 26 (1987), 1550). This protocol, as amended in 1990, 1992, 1997, and 1999 (UNTS 2297, No. 26369), imposes on states parties the duty to provide for a step by step reduction and eventual abolishment of both production and consumption of substances known as "ozone killers". Its adoption has been rightly considered as one of the greatest moments so far in the international struggle to achieve an effective global environmental protection.

By signing the Framework Convention on Climate Change (FCCC) (see above II.) during UNCED in 1992, the state community responded to the massive increase in emissions, mainly by the industrialized states, of carbon dioxide and methane. The greenhouse effect resulting from these emissions seriously impairs the balance of our whole ecosystem. However, the Framework Convention neither imposed concrete obligations to reduce emissions to certain levels nor determined any time-limits for reaching the goal of preventing "dangerous anthropogenic interference with the climate system". It was up to the Third Conference of the Parties to the FCCC (COP 3), held in Kyoto in 1997, to adopt a protocol bringing about quantified emission limitation and clear-cut reduction obligations. The Kyoto Protocol (UNTS No. 30822; ILM 37 (1998), 32) provides that the industrialized states have to reduce their overall emissions "by at least 5 percent below 1990 levels in the commitment period 2008 to 2012". In early 2001 it became evident that the USA would object the ratification of the Kyoto Protocol. However, after the ratification by Russia, the Protocol entered into force in February 2005.

The Protocol contains a number of mechanisms to provide flexibility in the implementation of the emission reduction obligations, such as joint implementation, emissions trading, and the Clean Development Mechanism. The modalities and procedures for using these mechanisms were negotiated in the 2001 Marrakesh Accords and formally adopted at the eleventh Conference of the Parties to the FCCC and the first Conference of the Parties serving as the Meeting of the Parties to the Kyoto Protocol (COP/MOP 1), held in Montreal in 2005.

There were doubts from the outset whether the measures provided for in the Kyoto Protocol were adequate for sufficiently redressing climate change with all its fatal ecological effects. In 2005, first preparations for negotiating obligations under the second commitment period of the Kyoto Protocol commenced. However, COP/MOP 2, held in Nairobi in 2006, did not yield any tangible results. COP/MOP 3, held in Bali, Indonesia, from 3-14 December 2007, agreed on the "Bali Roadmap" which sets the agenda for the negotiation, by December 2009, of an agreement on post-2012 commitments.

4. Flora and Fauna; Biological Diversity; Soils and Forests

The endeavors of states for conserving flora and fauna date back to the 19th century. However, the most important instruments were developed only in the 1970s. Among them are: the 1971 Ramsar Convention on Wetlands of International Importance especially as Waterfowl Habitat (UNTS 996, No. 14583; ILM 11 (1972), 963); the 1972 Paris Convention for the Protection of the World Cultural and Natural Heritage (UNTS 1037, No. 15511; ILM 11 (1972), 1358); the 1973 Washington Convention on International Trade in Endangered Species of Wild Fauna and Flora (CITES) (UNTS 993, No. 14537; ILM 12 (1973), 1085); the 1979 Bonn Convention on the Conservation of Migratory Species of Wild Animals (UNTS 1651, No. 28395; ILM 19 (1980), 15); and the 1979 Berne Convention on the Conservation of European Wildlife and Natural Habitats (UNTS 1284, No. 21159). What these

instruments have in common is that they aim to strike a balance between the sovereignty of the state, on whose territory valuable wildlife and natural habitats are located, and the interest of the community of states in species conservation. Their rules reflect the idea that the custodial state should manage and care for those species as a kind of trustee. But they do not offer sufficient economic incentives for custodial states to provide for adequate species conservation. Moreover, despite the impressive number of agreements adopted, they have not achieved to halt the rapid extinction of plants and animals.

The 1992 Convention on Biological Diversity (see above II.) effects a compromise between the sovereign right to use genetic resources and the obligation to conserve them by means of a system offering mutual incentives: Industrialized states are obliged to support developing countries by means of financial and technological transfer, thereby giving a clear incentive for the latter to engage in species conservation. On the other hand, access of industrialized states to genetic resources in developing countries is guaranteed under the Convention. But the latter are entitled to a fair and equitable share of the benefits arising from biotechnologies based upon these genetic resources. In order to specify further the rules on access and benefit sharing, the Sixth Conference of the Parties to the CBD adopted the 2002 Bonn Guidelines on Access to Genetic Resources and Fair and Equitable Sharing of Benefits Arising out of their Utilization (COP 6 Decision VI/24). The Bonn Guidelines had been developed by the Ad Hoc Open-ended Working Group on Access and Benefit Sharing, which is entrusted with the elaboration, by 2010, of an international Access and Benefit Sharing Regime. In 2000, the Cartagena Protocol on Biosafety to the Convention on Biological Diversity was established (UNTS 2253, No. 30619; ILM 39 (2000), 1027). Its aim is to protect the environment from risks posed by the transboundary transport of living modified organisms (LMOs) created by modern biotechnology via an advance informed agreement procedure. The 2001 International Treaty on Plant Genetic Resources for Food and Agriculture (available at: www.planttreaty. org), elaborated under the auspices of the FAO, has as its objective the conservation and sustainable use of plant genetic resources as well as the sharing of the benefits arising out of their use, while being in harmony with the Convention on Biological Diversity.

A comprehensive system of forest protection is still missing in international environmental law. However, the 1994 Geneva International Tropical Timber Agreement (UNTS 1955, No. 33484; ILM 33 (1994), 1014) gives at least a clue for developing a regime of sustainable use of forests. Whether states will ever succeed in establishing an international instrument providing for an overall protection of forests along the lines of the Rio Forest Principles (see above II.) is an open question.

As to the protection of soils, which is also closely connected with conservation of biological diversity, only few isolated rules of international law exist, such as the 1991 Convention on the Protection of the Alps (UNTS 1917, No. 32724; ILM 31 (1992), 767), and, in particular, the 1994 Convention to Combat Desertification in Those Countries Experiencing Drought and/or Desertification (UNTS 1954, No. 33480) (see above II.). The latter aims at preventing land degradation in arid, semi-arid and dry sub-humid areas, especially in Africa. It urges the affected countries and regions to take own initiatives in this respect ("bottom up" approach). Industrialized states commit themselves to mobilize the financial means needed for taking those initiatives.

5. Wastes and Hazardous Substances

The 1989 Basel Convention on the Control of Transboundary Movements of Hazardous Wastes and Their Disposal (UNTS 1673, No. 28911; ILM 28 (1989), 657) provides for an adequate control of transboundary movements of hazardous wastes. By means of intro-

ducing a system of prior informed consent, both the importing and exporting states are held responsible under this Convention to provide for an environmentally sound disposal of wastes. An amendment to the Convention that was adopted by the Third Conference of the Parties in 1995 (not yet in force) bans trade in hazardous wastes between primarily OECD countries and non-OECD countries. In 1999, the Fifth Conference of the Parties to the Basel Convention adopted the Protocol on Liability and Compensation for Damage Resulting from Transboundary Movements of Hazardous Wastes and Their Disposal (UN Doc. UNEP/CHW.1/WG/1/9/2). The 1991 Bamako Convention on the Ban of the Import into Africa and the Control of Transboundary Movement and Management of Hazardous Wastes within Africa (UNTS 2101, No. 36508; ILM 30 (1991), 773) follows the lines of the 1989 Basel Convention. It prohibits exports of hazardous wastes from non-OAU states into Africa.

There are two international treaties designed to control industrial chemicals and pesticides: the 1998 Rotterdam Convention on the Prior Informed Consent Procedure for Certain Hazardous Chemicals and Pesticides in International Trade (UNTS 2244, No. 39973; ILM 38 (1999), 1) and the 2001 Stockholm Convention on Persistent Organic Pollutants (POPs) (UNTS 2322, No. 40214; ILM 40 (2001), 532) which imposes worldwide controls on 12 POPs.

6. Procedural Environmental Obligations

There are a number of treaties regulating procedural obligations like environmental impact assessments, early notification, and access to information. Among them are the 1986 Vienna Convention on Early Notification of a Nuclear Accident (ILM 25 (1986), 1370), the 1991 Espoo Convention on Environmental Impact Assessment in a Transboundary Context (UNTS 1989, No. 34028; ILM 30 (1991), 802), the 1992 Helsinki Convention on the Transboundary Effects of Industrial Accidents (UNTS 2105, No. 36605; ILM 31 (1992), 1330), and the 1998 Aarhus Convention on Access to Information, Public Participation in Decision-Making and Access to Justice in Environmental Matters (UNTS 2161, No. 37770; ILM 38 (1999), 517). The latter agreement, established within the framework of the ECE, represents an innovative instrument that creates far-reaching intrastate procedural environmental obligations.

IV. Work of the International Law Commission Relating to International Environmental Law

In recent years, the International Law Commission ($\rightarrow$ ILC) has produced a number of drafts that have a bearing on international environmental law. The 2001 ILC "Draft Articles on Responsibility of States for Internationally Wrongful Acts" (UN Doc. A/RES/56/83, Annex), which deal with the responsibility of states for all acts and omissions in breach of an international obligation, provide parameters for state responsibility which also apply in cases of international environmental litigation. In 2006, the ILC adopted the "Draft Principles on the Allocation of Loss in the Case of Transboundary Harm Arising out of Hazardous Activities" (UN Doc. A/61/10), dealing with liability for damage caused by hazardous activities not prohibited by international law. Like the 2001 "Draft Articles on Prevention of Transboundary Harm from Hazardous Activities" (UN Doc. A/56/10), these Draft Principles emanated from the ILC topic "international liability for injurious consequences arising out of acts not prohibited by international law", which had been subdivided into the two aspects "prevention" and "liability" in 1997. Also in 2006, the ILC adopted on first reading the "Draft Articles on the Law of Transboundary Aquifers", the second reading of which will take place in 2008. These Draft Articles form part of the ILC topic "shared natural resources", which the ILC has been working on since 2002.

V. Means of Enforcing International Environmental Law

To the traditional ways and means of law enforcement belongs in particular bringing suit against a state being in breach of international law before an international court, but also imposing a reprisal on that state. However, hitherto states were rather reluctant to make use of law enforcement measures in international environmental relations. Only few specifically environmental disputes were settled either by arbitration (Trail Smelter (1941), Lac Lanoux (1957), Gut Dam (1968)), or by the International Court of Justice (Gabcikovo-Nagymaros (1997), Pulp Mills on the River Uruguay (pending)). Some modern multilateral environmental agreements, in particular the 1987 Montreal Protocol, as modified in 1990 and 1992 (see above III.), contain not only traditional dispute settlement clauses, but also provisions establishing procedures of compliance control and compliance assistance which are cooperative rather than repressive in character. These new procedures are aimed at responding to compliance deficits in a non-adversarial, cooperative manner. Thus, under certain circumstances the non-complying state can count on being supported by the other states parties by means of capacity-building, as well as transfer of technology and finance.

The compliance control mechanism of the Kyoto Protocol (see above III.), established by the 2001 Marrakesh Accords, forms a certain contrast to this trend, as it does not only rely on facilitative forms of ensuring compliance. Its Compliance Committee is divided into a Facilitative Branch and an Enforcement Branch, which can for example enjoin sanctions in the form of reductions of future emission allowances on states which fail to reach their emission targets.

This approach however is due *inter alia* to the fact that under the current Kyoto Protocol regime, only developed countries are submitted to binding emission reduction obligations; thus, in this case non-compliance generally does not result from lack of capacity, but from lack of political will.

Ulrich Beyerlin / Jenny Grote

Lit.: *Beyerlin, U.:* Umweltvölkerrecht, Munich 2000; *Beyerlin, U./Marauhn, T.:* Law-Making and Law-Enforcement in International Environmental Law after the 1992 Rio Conference, Berlin 1997; *Beyerlin, U./ Stoll, P.T./Wolfrum, R. (eds.):* Ensuring Compliance with Multilateral Environmental Agreements: A Dialogue between Practitioners and Academia, Leiden 2006; *Birnie, P.W./Boyle, A.E.:* International Law and the Environment, Oxford 2002; *Bodansky, D./Brunnée, J./Hey, E. (eds.):* The Oxford Handbook of International Environmental Law, Oxford 2007; *Brown Weiss, E.:* In Fairness to Future Generations: International Law, Common Patrimony and Intergenerational Equity, Tokyo 1989; *Kiss, A./Shelton, D.:* Guide to International Environmental Law, Leiden 2007; *Kiss, A./Shelton, D.:* International Environmental Law, Ardsley/ New York 2004; *Louka, E.:* International Environmental Law: Fairness, Effectiveness, and World Order, Cambridge 2006; *Nanda, V.P./Pring, G.:* International Environmental Law and Policy for the 21st Century, Ardsley/New York 2003; *Sands, P.:* Principles of International Environmental Law, 2nd edn., Cambridge 2003; *Wolfrum, W. (ed.):* Enforcing Environmental Standards: Economic Mechanisms as Viable Means? Berlin 1996; *World Commission on Environment and Development:* Our Common Future, Oxford 1987.

Internet: *Website of the United Nations Environment Programme:* www.unep.org; *Website of the CSD Partnerships for Sustainable Development:* www.un.org/esa/ sustdev/partnerships/partnerships.htm; *Website of the World Conservation Union:* www.iucn.org; *UNFCCC Homepage:* http://unfccc.int; *Earth Negotiations Bulletin:* www.iisd.ca/voltoc.html.

Environmental Protection

Today, environmental problems have increasingly global origins, either because they are by nature global, such as climate change, or because they result from pressures of a globalized economy on the environment, for instance defor-estation. The need for global action is obvious, but unlike economic institutions so far it has been impossible to develop a comprehensive system of international environmental governance that includes effective compliance and enforcement mechanisms.

After the first UN Conference on the Environment 1972 in Stockholm (→ World Conferences), attended by exactly two prime ministers, environmental issues for the first time took center stage in international politics with the historic *United Nations Conference on Environment and Development (UNCED)* in 1992 in Rio de Janeiro (UN Doc. A/CONF.151/). Attended by more heads of state and government than any other conference before, the "Earth Summit" after the end of the Cold War established new conventions and broke new ground for the participation of non-governmental organizations (→ NGOs) in the → UN system.

The conference approved "Agenda 21" (UN Doc. A/CONF. 151/26, Vols. I-III), a voluminous blueprint for sustainable development for the 21st century. Its 40 chapters were the most comprehensive document ever approved by the international community on environment and development issues – but it was not a legally binding document.

At the follow-bup conferences in 1997 (Special Session of the General Assembly in New York, www.un.org/esa/ earthsummit/index.html) and 2002 (World Summit on Sustainable Development, Johannesburg, UN Doc. A/ CONF.199/, www.un.org/events/wssd/), serious implementation deficits were obvious and were criticized by most participants, governments and non-governmental observers alike. Despite the far-reaching ambitions of "Agenda 21", the political ambitions of governments to really tackle the fundamental changes necessary for making development more sustainable were receding quickly in the years after Rio.

As economic globalization was advancing rapidly, the need for political regulation of this process became obvious. While environmental issues gained increasing prominence in national politics all over the globe, in international policy-making progress was mainly made in the context of the foundation of the World Trade Organization ($\rightarrow$ WTO/GATT) (1995) and its far-reaching set of instruments. The WTO agreements are sufficiently comprehensive to regulate not only liberalized trade, but essentially the globalized economy. The WTO was established deliberately outside the United Nations, and unlike UN organizations and conventions, it has far-reaching mechanisms to enforce its treaties, including effective sanctions. For the implementation of Agenda 21 and the Rio conventions, the environmental indifference of the newly-established WTO was a serious setback, just as it was a setback for the UN as a whole that the WTO was established outside the $\rightarrow$ UN system.

It became increasingly obvious that some provisions in WTO treaties are in potential contradiction to UN conventions, in particular environmental conventions aiming at changing industrial production. For instance, if Kyoto Protocol signatories try to limit carbon dioxide emissions, producers in non-signatories may enjoy competitive advantages, and could prompt Kyoto signatories to impose carbon taxes for such products. This has been proposed many times in the EU, but also in the USA for the case that the USA joins a Kyoto successor agreement without emission limits for China. Such carbon taxes for imported goods would be almost impossible without clashing with WTO obligations not to discriminate between products on the basis of how they have been produced. Another politically controversial example is the negotiations in the conference of parties of the Convention on Biological Diversity about access and benefit sharing, aiming at a legally binding protocol at the CBD's COP-10 in Nagoya 2010. Under such a regime, countries would be obliged to grant patents on inventions using biological resources only if the country of origin of these resources is specified and that country would then be remunerated

with a share of the profits from that patent. WTO law (the TRIPs agreement), however, requires granting such patents without such conditions.

It is an open question which treaty in the end prevails. One problem is that the membership of the WTO, of course, does not always overlap with the membership of UN multilateral environmental agreements. For instance, if a WTO member state does not ratify the Montreal Protocol for the Protection of the Ozone Layer, it could theoretically challenge trade restrictions in ozone-depleting fluorochlorocarbons in the WTO. If in such a case one conflicting party has not ratified, the answer looks simple. Only a treaty that all sides have signed can apply.

In case all parties have signed the treaties, we have a conflict where the environment tends to be on the losing side. According to the Vienna Convention on the Law of Treaties of 23 May 1969 (UN Doc. A/CONF.39/27) in such a case of conflicting international agreements the most recent one prevails ($\rightarrow$ Treaties, Law of). This is often the case for the relatively recent WTO agreements, and important players such as the USA insist in environmental negotiations on "WTO saving clauses", thus making sure WTO law prevails even over more recent environmental agreements. This was the case, for instance, during the negotiations for a legally binding protocol on biological safety within the Convention on Biological Diversity.

This protocol, known as the Cartagena Protocol, regulates the transboundary movement of genetically modified organisms – clearly an intersection of trade and environment. However, WTO decisions more frequently affect national environmental policies rather than international agreements. European environmental laws and regulations have been challenged repeatedly in the WTO by the USA or Canada, for instance the restrictive EU policies on genetically modified organisms (GMOs), on hormone treatment of beef, on asbestos, etc.

At the same time, the WTO's jurisdiction has been gradually moving from a narrow interpretation of trade agreements to giving greater weight to environmental considerations. Certainly, there remain major obstacles such as the WTO's prohibition of different treatment of physically "like" products according to their production methods, or the role of the *Precautionary Principle* established at the Rio Summit.

The *Precautionary Principle* is in direct contradiction to the principles of the WTO. According to the *Precautionary Principle*, products such as genetically modified organisms or hormones in meat production whose potential risks and dangers cannot be satisfactorily ruled out by scientific means should be treated with caution as long as these questions remain, while WTO law puts the obligation exactly the other way round: the EU has to prove that beef hormones are harmful, or it may not ban them.

However, with environmental problems becoming considerably more urgent, the situation has shifted in the last years. As economic globalization is progressing, it has come under considerable political pressure around the world. The feeling that there are more losers than winners from this process has gained ground, and as a consequence the WTO has been stalemated since the failed Ministerial Conference in Cancún in 2003.

In particular, climate change has become one of the most important topics in international affairs. When US President Bush announced in early 2001, shortly after taking office, that the US would not ratify the Kyoto Protocol and that the protocol as a consequence was obsolete, he galvanized the great majority of the rest of the world into a defiant position to enforce the Kyoto protocol anyway. After years of uncertainty, Russia's ratification let the Protocol enter into force in February 2005, more than seven years after the Kyoto Conference where it had been agreed. This was a key test for the international community whether it can survive deliberate attempts by a major player to derail parts of the environmental agenda. The Protocol is binding international law, but essentially without sanctions – so it is another question how many signatories will have fulfilled their commitments in 2012.

Since then, climate has dramatically moved up the scale of international politics. G8 Summits have been focusing on climate since the Gleneagles Summit in 2005. Germany's environment minister Sigmar Gabriel aptly said at the UN Climate Conference in Nairobi in 2006 that climate negotiations are now becoming like the arms control talks in the 1980s: the key to the results no longer lie with the responsible ministers but with presidents and prime ministers.

It is also no longer true that the environment is an issue that primarily interests northern, industrial countries, while southern developing countries are more preoccupied with development. Indira Gandhi's speech at the Stockholm Conference in 1972 echoed strong sentiments among the developing countries when she said: "Are not poverty and need the greatest polluters? ... How can we speak to those who live in villages and slums about keeping oceans, rivers and air clean when their own lives are contaminated at the source? The environment cannot be improved in conditions of poverty." (*Indira Gandhi* 1972) More and more countries now realize that poverty cannot be alleviated in conditions of eroding and collapsing ecosystems.

Development without taking environmental issues into account is simply no longer possible. This is primarily a result of the skyrocketing prices for fossil fuels and other raw materials, but also due to the fact that the impact of climate change becomes visible not only with hurricanes and floods but also with impacts on agricultural productivity. Overexploitation of natural resources, from timber to fisheries, has also confronted developing country economies with serious problems that need to be addressed.

The fragmented institutional setup of the international environmental negotiations is also becoming increasingly difficult to manage. At the Bali climate conference in 2007, for the first time there was also a finance ministers' meeting talking exclusively about climate change, reflecting the fact that the impacts of climate change are no longer just a sectoral issue for environment ministers. However, this does not – yet, at least – mean that finance ministers work hand-in-hand with their colleagues in the environment departments to solve the problem.

The Convention on Biological Diversity (CBD) also encountered problems resulting from the different responsibilities of its main players (www. cbd.int). Brazil, one of the main actors at the CBD, is instrumental in reaching a "grand deal" between northern proposals to expand protected areas and southern demands to obtain more royalties from the use of biological resources. Yet when Brazil's foreign minister, who is in charge of the CBD as well as the WTO, puts a proposal on the table calling for an amendment to the WTO's TRIPs agreement that patents on biological inventions can only be granted when the disclosure of the origin of the biological resources becomes mandatory, European environment ministers may agree – but TRIPs is beyond their responsibility. Not even their national trade ministries would be able to agree to such a proposal since the responsibility for trade lies with the EU Commission. But why should an EU trade commissioner agree to such a proposal? Speeding up the CBD negotiations is not his problem. The increasing prominence of environmental problems is not only a challenge to the UN's institutional structures, it is just as much a challenge to national governments and their decision-making procedures.

Compared with the political prominence of environmental issues, its structural setup in the United Nations becomes more and more anachronistic. G8 summits focus on climate, yet UNEP (→ UNEP – United Nations Environment Programme) is only a minor suborganization of the UN. Proposals to upgrade UNEP to a full specialized agency (→ Specialized Agencies) or to create a new World Environment Organization or United Nations Environment Organization, have been put on the table many times, but progress towards such a stronger UN environment organization is extremely slow.

What has clearly helped is the strong voice of scientific expertise that has become a political factor, at least in the climate negotiations. The *Intergovernmenal Panel on Climate Change (IPCC)* has managed to steer clear of political interference and confront the governments of the world with its stark findings in its Fourth Assessment Report (www.ipcc.ch/pdf/assessment-report/ar4/syr/ar4_syr.pdf), released in 2007, urging faster and stronger action. This has clearly had a strong impact and may have been one of the key factors leading the critical climate conference in Bali (COP-13) in December 2007 to success (cf. http://unfccc.int/meetings/cop_13/items/4049.php). There are now proposals to establish similar panels in the Convention on Biological Diversity and in the debates about UNEP reform.

Another weak point is the precarious funding of global environmental institutions. Despite all calls for more harmonization, the number of usually not so large funding lines and institutions created by donor governments continues to proliferate, thereby further increasing the problem of fragmentation. UNEP depends on voluntary contributions and co-operation projects for its operations. The example of the *Global Environment Facility (GEF)* amply demonstrates that without sufficient resources and an efficient management of these resources, the performance of the UN system in addressing environmental problems will be disappointing.

The GEF (www.gefweb.org/), the financial instrument of the Rio conventions, managed to collect only 2 billion US dollars for the three-year period 1994-96. At Rio, the industrial nations had promised three times this amount.

The money was also tied to the condition that the GEF would have a complicated administrative structure, with the World Bank, UNEP and UNDP as agencies implementing its projects and programs. Since then, it has had to struggle more and more to get even this small amount, and the GEF has become such a slow and inefficient bureaucracy that the average time for a decision over projects has now reached five years. In 2006, 32 donor countries pledged 3.1 billion US dollars to fund operations between 2006 and 2010.

The need for reform in the UN system is probably greater in the environmental field than in most other fields because the need for action is rapidly increasing. However, only stronger political influence for environmental institutions and higher priority for environmental policies at the national level will ultimately create enough political momentum among governments to take the necessary steps.

Jürgen Maier

Lit.: *Agarwal, A./Narain, S./Sharma, A. (eds.):* Global Environmental Negotiations 1: Green Politics, New Delhi 1999; *Agarwal, A./Narain, S./Sharma, A./Imchen, A. (eds.):* Global Environmental Negotiations 2: Poles Apart, New Delhi 2001; *Chasek, P.S.:* Earth Negotiations – Analyzing thirty years of environmental diplomacy, Tokyo 2001; *Forum Umwelt & Entwicklung:* Umwelt, Entwicklung und Globalisierung. Eine Bilanz 10 Jahre nach Rio, Bonn 2002; *Gandhi, I:* "Life is One and the World is One". Prime Minister Indira Gandhi Speaks to the Plenary. Speech at the Stockholm Conference on the Human Environment Reprinted in Environment, Stockholm: Centre for Economic and Social Information at the United Nations European Headquarters, Geneva, 1972; *Ministry of Environment Sweden:* Stockholm thirty years on – Progress achieved and challenges ahead in international environmental co-operation, Stockholm 2002; *Oberthür, S./Ott, H.E.:* The Kyoto Protocol – International Climate Policy for the 21st Century, Berlin/Heidelberg 1999; *Schmidt, F.:* Die Architektonik globaler Umweltpolitik. Neueste Beiträge zu ihrer Reform, Berlin 2003.

Internet: 1) *Homepage of UNEP:* www.unep.org; 2) *Environment and Human Settlements Division of the UN Economic Commission for Europe:* www.unece.org/env/welcome.html; 3) *Website of the Global Policy Forum on environmental policy and the UN system:* www.globalpolicy.org/socecon/envronmt/index.htm; 4) *Earth Negotiations Bulletins des International Institute for Sustainable Development:* www.iisd.ca.

European Union, Common Foreign and Security Policy at the UN

The current fifteen member states of the European Union (EU) strive for coordination, harmonization and eventual unification of their foreign and security policies by their *Common Foreign and Security Policy (CFSP)*. This CFSP is the continuation of the *European Political Cooperation (EPC)*, which was initiated by the then-six member states of the European Community (EC) in 1970.

1. From EPC to CFSP

The EPC consisted of an intergovernmental system of co-operation in foreign policy. It developed initially outside the founding treaty of the EC on the basis of informal intergovernmental arrangements. In 1974 the EC member states established the supreme body of the EPC, the European Council of Heads of State and Government which, too, was legally located outside the EC Treaty. The so-called "London Declaration" signed by the foreign ministers of the EC member states in 1981 created a written procedural basis for the work of the EPC. A contractual foundation was not laid until 1986 in the context of the *Single European Act (SEA)*.

In 1992 the EPC was extended by a common security policy to form the Common Foreign and Security Policy (CFSP), and additionally became part of the so-called *"Maastricht Treaty"*, the *Treaty on European Union* (TEU, Art. 11-28).

The CFSP is one of the three "pillars" of the EU, alongside the EC and the Co-operation in Justice and Home Affairs (CJHA) in the well-known image of the

173

"EU-Temple". At the same time according to the TEU the aforementioned European Council became the supreme body of the entire EU.

The CFSP is based on the oftentimes very diverse pre-conditions, traditions, and interests of the foreign and security policies of the individual EU member states.

Unlike the EC and parts of the CJHA, the CFSP is therefore not intended to act integratively, but to remain strictly intergovernmental without any restrictions of the sovereignty of the EU member states. Unanimity of the member states is the essential principle of the CFSP and all its branches as well as, more specifically, of all decisions and actions that emanate from the CFSP. In sum, without consensus among the member states, there cannot take place any CFSP.

This inevitable necessity of consensus sometimes leads to a selective or rather indistinct CFSP, or one that is based on a low common level. The Treaty of Amsterdam of 1997 amended the existing TEU by some procedures that are intended to improve the accomplishment of consensus by making its denial more difficult. The fundamental principle of consensus, however, has not been influenced by this. The organs and procedures of the EPC/CFSP continue to correspond to their intergovernmental style.

Those organs are the European Council, the Council of Foreign Ministers, the Political Committee of high-ranking senior officials of the foreign ministries, and a special communications system among the foreign ministries (COREU). The political leadership of the CFSP is within the hands of the respective presidency of the EU. Since 1999 a special High Representative for the CFSP – sometimes referred to as "Mr. CFSP" – has personified a distinct and permanent CFSP, i.e. one that is independent of the biannually rotating EU presidency. On this basis the procedures of the CFSP include consultations among the governments of the EU member states, among their embassies in third states, and among their delegations to international organizations.

Not only in structural terms, but also with regard to its contents, CFSP still strongly corresponds with the purely foreign-policy former EPC. The common security policy of the EU – which consists of eleven NATO members plus four neutral member states – does not comprise a common defense policy.

The CFSP regards itself as a policy of politically conditioned military interventions outside the territory of the EU and NATO; those interventions, however, are not to be executed by the EU itself, but rather by the Western European Union (WEU). The WEU consists of 27 states with different membership status. Its ten full members are simultaneously members of NATO and the EU. Additionally, the CFSP is designed to promote a so-called "European Security Identity" within NATO.

2. CFSP as Part of the Practical Foreign Policy of the EU

As the CFSP consists primarily of a foreign policy objective, it is realized first and foremost by a common opinion-building process in the form of many of its typical common declarations, as well as statements of the EU member states regarding questions of international politics. Additionally and more concretely, CFSP is carried out with the most ease wherever an internal pool of commonality can be found. This is particularly the case in political areas which are closely related to the common economy sustaining the EU. Advantageous preconditions for the CFSP also exist as far as relations and exchanges among the group of states of the EU and other groups of states are concerned, e.g. the relations of the EU to the countries abutting the Mediterranean Sea or the Association of South-East Asian Nations (ASEAN).

Further, advantageous preconditions exist for the CFSP, too, whenever the economic opportunities of the EU can be utilized. This is also true for the co-operation in development and foreign affairs with the so-called ACP countries, the states on the former colonial territories of EU members in Africa, the Caribbean, and the Pacific. In this case, however, the former colonial powers within the EU naturally dominate those common interests.

Altogether, thanks to both the commonality of the EU member states in basic interests and the long history of interaction among the EU member states in foreign affairs, the CFSP has reached a considerable measure of consistency within the framework of its opportunities in foreign affairs. It is quite obvious, however, that reaching consensus within today's CFSP, as with the former EPC, becomes increasingly complicated with each expansion of the EU.

The CFSP's potential in those areas of common foreign policy which are primarily a function of power politics, as is the case in the development of a common security policy, remains considerably limited. In these areas, national interests of individual member states of the EU oftentimes outweigh the desire for EU commonality.

This became obvious in the Iraq crises in 1991 and 1998, and in the attempts of the EU to become engaged in the Israeli-Palestinian conflict, as well as in the case of the Algerian domestic conflict. Other examples of a low level of CFSP effectiveness, due to certain power-political constellations and national interests, can be found in the EU's policy towards Iran and the silent liquidation of an EU human rights policy towards China (→ UN Policy, China), in which case common economic interests eventually turned out to be stronger than the interest in implementing common values (→ Human Rights, Protection of).

So far, the most severe test of the CFSP in its security policy part has been the conflict in the former Yugoslavia, starting with the conflict in Bosnia and followed by the Kosovo war. In the former case the CFSP was characterized by far-reaching differences in foreign and power political interests among the EU Members, until the conflict was finally terminated by the Dayton Peace Agreement mediated by the United States in 1995.

During the Kosovo war, the EU member states renounced a distinct, singular European policy in favor of the action of NATO. During a critical stage of NATO's conduct of the war, however, the EU member states developed – on the grounds of a German initiative – a common policy that facilitated the ending of the war. Yet, in both cases, the EU was not a power-political factor in the light of the power-political role of the USA and its leadership of NATO.

3. The Importance of CFSP in the UN

Within the UN, the effect of the CFSP is somewhat less noticeable than outside, but also here any CFSP activity still moves within the same boundaries of its opportunities as described above. Its weight in the UN is determined – as in all other international organizations – to a large extent by the considerable financial contributions of the EU members to the world organization (→ Budget).

The main operational part of the CFSP within the UN – and reflective of the importance of the UN even more than in other international organizations – consists of permanent consultations among the representatives of EU countries that aim at coordinating or unifying their UN policies. Through these consultations, the more comprehensive direct CFSP consultations among the governments of the EU Members are completed and implemented on the spot in operational UN policies. These consultations are highly valuable for the development of EU commonality, especially under the specific conditions of the permanent conference diplomacy in the UN.

However, similar to the developments in individual EU member states, a common UN policy as such or even of a piece has yet to evolve within the CFSP. To date, only political co-ordination or standardization towards the political problems arising within the UN has evolved.

Remarkable, however, was the aforementioned European step during the

Kosovo war. This step not only broke the deadlock within NATO's crisis management that was one-dimensionally based on the use of force; but it also led NATO's crisis management – which under US-American guidance had deliberately bypassed the UN in a severe violation of international law as laid down in the UN Charter (→ Charter of the UN) – back to the UN, without which a solution of the conflict would have been impossible.

4. The Three Levels of CFSP in the UN

In particular, the CFSP materializes in the UN on three different levels: in the → General Assembly in New York, in the → specialized agencies for economic, humanitarian, scientific, and technical affairs, above all in Geneva, Nairobi, Paris, and Rome, and in the UN Security Council in New York (→ Security Council). The characteristics of CFSP in these cases are the following:

(1) In the UN General Assembly the common voting behavior among the individual EU member states has become increasingly consistent over the years. In 1998, EU members voted unanimously in 95% of the votes on all resolutions (→ Resolution, Declaration, Decision) – including not only those with simple majority voting but also those adopted in consensus. EU unanimity was reached in 80% of those resolutions with simple majority voting.

(2) In the specialized agencies of the UN for economic and humanitarian affairs, in which the agenda topics are more specific and complex and the interests of the states more diverse, additional explanatory statements in connection with the unanimous EU voting are occasionally given by individual member states. On both levels the common action of the EU member states in the UN as well as in other international organizations is especially effective whenever – based on common EU basic values and conceptions – not only the representation of common interests, but rather the improvement of international co-operation as such is the political objective. Examples include the → reform

of the UN and the human rights policy (→ Human Rights, Protection of), notwithstanding the quoted example of China. A similar situation for CFSP can be found in the Organization for Security and Co-operation in Europe (OSCE) which perceives itself as a regional organization of the UN.

(3) In the UN Security Council things are a little bit different due to its specific power-political orientation, and because of the specific position of France (→ UN Policy, France) and the United Kingdom (→ UN Policy, United Kingdom) as two of the Council's five permanent members. In New York, France and the UK, like all EU members, participate in CFSP consultations about the topics discussed in the Security Council. However, the actual operative pre-discussions for the sessions of the Security Council usually take place less in the formal EU framework, but more frequently in informal settings with representatives of the USA (→ UN Policy, USA), Germany (→ UN Policy, Germany), France, the UK, and Russia (→ UN Policy, Russia).

The clear and general condition for the CFSP within the UN remains that both France and the UK perceive their position as Permanent Members of the Security Council from a strictly national point of view, but under no circumstances as European positions. The idea to create a single common seat for all EU Members in the Security Council, one concept that has been considered in the EU for quite some time, has never had a chance to be realized.

During the decades of the Cold War, the EPC/CFSP was shaped inside and outside of the UN by the bipolar global system as well as by the common policy of the western bloc led by the USA. Since the end of the Cold War, there have been increasing signs that the EU Europeans are willing to play a more independent, common European role in world politics by means of the CFSP. These signs range from the Treaty of Maastricht (1992) via the Treaty of Amsterdam (1997) to the EU summit in Cologne in June 1999, where this desire was articulated strongly – before the background of a minor European role in the Kosovo war.

This desire, however, is contrasted by the actual policy of the EU member states, for instance illustrated by the aforementioned role of the eleven EU countries, that are simultaneously NATO members, during the Kosovo war, and also by the role of the EU members within the UN Security Council. While the concept of a European Union acting commonly in power politics may be an attractive one, the path to its realization, if at all achievable, might be long and troublesome.

Hans Arnold

Lit.: *Arnold, H.:* Europa neu denken - Warum und wie weiter Einigung?, Bonn 1999; *Auswärtiges Amt (ed.):* Gemeinsame Außen- und Sicherheitspolitik der Europäischen Union (GASP). Dokumentation, 10th edn., Bonn 1995; *Borkenhagen, F.:* Europa braucht GASP, Bonn 1993; *Dembinski, M.:* Langer Anlauf - kurzer Sprung - Die Aussenpolitik der Europäischen Union nach der Reform von Amsterdam, HSFK-Report 7/1997, Frankfurt (Main) 1997; *Leurdijk, D. A.:* Gemeinschaft und Gemeinsamkeiten. Die EG und die Vereinten Nationen, in: VN 39 (1991), 157-162; *Regelsberger, E.:* Gemeinsame Außen- und Sicherheitspolitik, in: Weidenfeld, W./Wessels, W. (eds.): Europa von A - Z, 6th edn., Bonn 1997, 221-228; *Stadler, K.-D.:* Die Europäische Gemeinschaft in den Vereinten Nationen, Baden-Baden 1993.

Addendum

With the accession to the European Union of Poland, the Czech Republic, Hungary, Slovakia, Estonia, Latvia, Lithuania, Slovenia, Cyprus and Malta (2004) as well as of Romania and Bulgaria (2007) the EU plays an ever increasing role at the United Nations. Nowadays, member states of the European Union are spread over three → regional groups in the UN (Western Group, Eastern Group and Asian group due to Cyprus) and the EU block can exercise 27 votes in plenary organs.

Apart from these developments directly connected with the increased size of the Union, one can also identify improvement in its status at various UN bodies, the coverage of more policy fields and an intensification of internal coordination on UN matters.

While not being a member of the United Nations, the European Community was admitted as a full member to the → FAO (1991) and the Codex Alimentarius (2006), a subsidiary body of the FAO and the WHO. In early 2008, the newly established Peacebuilding Commission, a subsidiary organ of the → Security Council and the → General Assembly, invited the European Community to attend all its meetings in the capacity of an institutional donor. Membership in a given UN body has the consequence that a sole Community position is presented by the European Commission on matters covered by Community competence (such as agriculture, fisheries, trade, development), and common positions that also cover domains falling under member states competence, either by the Commission or the Presidency, depending on the thrust of the matter. The European Community is also a member of various treaty bodies established by important UN Conventions, in particular in the environmental field, next to its member states. Moreover, the European Community can participate in treaty negotiations on an equal footing with states (exercising all procedural rights except the right to vote) in many special agencies from the rank of an observer to the organization. Examples are the negotiation of the cultural diversity convention (2006) under the auspices of → UNESCO or the tobacco framework convention (2004) under the auspices of the → WHO. Full participants' rights are also regularly granted to the European Community at UN → world conferences since the aftermath of the Rio Summit on sustainable development. Finally, the European Community makes good use of its → observer status in the General Assembly (granted in 1974) and the main committees thereof.

177

The policy fields, on which the EU intervenes at the United Nations, have also been considerably extended. In the first pillar, the European Community takes the floor, next to the traditional issues such as international trade and development, more and more on the external dimension of internal Community policies, such as internal market, environment, public health, or transport. In the second pillar, the gradual establishment of the EU's security and defence policy (ESDP) since 1999 and the launch of the EU's first military missions since 2001 enabled the European Union to emphasize this field also with respect to the United Nations. Based on the Joint EU-EU Declaration on Cooperation in Crisis Management of September 2003, the EU and the UN nowadays hold regularly consultations on this sensitive policy field. In the third pillar (justice and home affairs), the EU also adopts regularly common positions that are communicated to relevant UN bodies. One may cite as an example EU statements on issues of counterterrorism and close cooperation with the UN sanctions committees.

Finally, it can be noted that internal UN coordination in the EU has further been strengthened in the last decade. The Council of Ministers has established a working group in Brussels specialized in UN matters (CONUN) which meets once a month with representatives of capitals to discuss all matters of UN policy relevant for coordination. Coordination meetings in New York and Geneva have reached the peak of intensity. Moreover, ex-post information and ex-ante coordination takes also place for matters on the agenda of the → Security Council since 2001. In particular, the non-permanent elected EU member states to the Council use their two years term to bring about closer collaboration in the EU framework to the benefit of those EU member states which are not sitting in the Council. The increased role of the EU can also be read from occasional invitations issued to the CFSP High Representative to make direct interventions in the discussions of the →

Security Council as of 2004. On the other hand, it cannot be denied that internal EU coordination reaches its limits where underlying policy disagreements between member states sustain. This can be the case for ad hoc issues such as the Iraqi war in 2003, or for long-standing difficult dossiers such as disarmament questions or the Middle East Peace Process. However, in general, EU cohesion on matters dealt with in the UN has nowadays reached an average of over 90 %, and the EU was also able to reach a common line for the UN reform in 2005 (with the notable exception of the reform of the Security Council).

Frank Hoffmeister

Lit.: *European Commission:* The Enlarging European Union at the United Nations: Making Multilateralism Matter, Luxembourg 2004; *Laatikainen, K.V./Smith, K.E. (eds.):* The European Union at the United Nations: intersecting multilateralism, Basington, 2006; *Wouters, J./Hoffmeister, F./Ruys, T. (eds.):* The United Nations and the European Union: An ever stronger Partnership, The Hague 2006; *Rasch, M.B.:* The European Union at the United Nations – The Functioning and Coherence of EU External Representation in a State-centric environment, Leiden 2008.

Internet: EU@UN-Website (Information on the EU's CFSP and the UN): www.europa-eu-un.org.

FAO – Food and Agriculture Organization

Foundation

This specialized agency (→ Specialized Agencies), with its seat in Rome, was founded on 16 October 1945 at a state conference in Quebec, as permanent forum for international cooperation in the agricultural field. According to the Agreement of 12 December 1946 (UNTS Vol. 1 II, No. 10), it became a specialized agency of the UN.

In essence, FAO has replaced the International Agricultural Institute, which was founded in 1905 and dissolved into FAO in 1948. The number of member states has risen from the original 42 to

180 in 2001. In November 1991 the European Union became the only regional organization in the FAO.

Purposes and Tasks

The Preamble of the FAO Constitution (UNYB 1946-47, 693-702) prescribes the following purpose: "raising levels of nutrition and standards of living of the peoples under their respective jurisdictions; securing improvements in the efficiency of the production and distribution of all food and agricultural products; bettering the condition of rural populations; and thus contributing towards an expanding world economy" and – since an amendment to the FAO Constitution in 1965 – "ensuring humanity's freedom from hunger".

According to Article I of the FAO Constitution, FAO should fulfill the following functions. FAO "shall collect, analyse, interpret and disseminate information relating to nutrition, food and agriculture", whereby the term "agriculture" and its derivatives "include fisheries, marine products, forestry and primary forestry products". It "shall promote and, where appropriate, shall recommend national and international action" with respect to research, education, administration and public awareness relating to nutrition, food and agriculture. In addition, FAO shall promote "the conservation of natural resources, the adoption of improved methods of agricultural production; the improvement of the processing, marketing and distribution of food and agricultural products; the adoption of policies for the provision of adequate national and international agricultural credit", and "the adoption of international policies with respect to agricultural commodity arrangements". If member states wish, FAO can also provide technical assistance.

Structure

The three governing bodies of FAO are the *Conference* of the member states, the *Council* and the *Director-General*. The Conference meets in regular sessions once in every two years, and each member state has one vote. The Conference determines the policy of the organization, approves the budget, and makes recommendations to members and international organizations on any matter pertaining to the objectives of FAO. Moreover, the Conference elects the Council, which consists of 49 member states elected according to a regional ratio. This executive body meets between the regular sessions of the Conference under an independent Chairman and makes all important decisions with the support of eight committees.

The Director-General is equipped with considerable powers, and is appointed by the Conference for a term of six years (since 1977 he is eligible for reappointment). In 1993, the present Director-General Jacques Diouf replaced his predecessor Edouard Saouma, who strongly influenced the organization during his three terms in office.

Programmes and Budget

The work of FAO is divided in two areas. The first area, the Regular Programme, covers internal operations, including support of field operations, advice to governments on policy and planning, and a wide range of development projects. Its regular biennium budget for 2000-2001 was 650 million US dollars, which is financed through contributions of the member states; the contributions are calculated according to the member states' gross national product. In cooperation with the World Bank, FAO also manages an investment programme to ensure the funding of development projects. In recent years, the second area, the so-called Field Programmes, has become increasingly important. These field projects are usually undertaken in cooperation with national governments and other specialized agencies and UN programmes such as → UNDP, → WHO, → UNESCO, → UNEP. The Field Programmes' funding in 1999 was 77% derived from national trust funds; 9% from UNDP; 13% through FAO's Technical Cooperation Programme and 1% through its Special Programme for Food Security.

Historical Development

In the post-war time after World War II, FAO was mainly involved in technical assistance for the reconstruction of agricultural production. Today, it is the biggest development organization with an emphasis on emergency relief via its field programme (→ Development Co-operation of the UN System). Significant events in its history include: the World Hunger Campaign in 1960; the establishment of the World Food Programme in 1961 (→ WFP); the World Food Summit of 1974 including the foundation of the World Food Council (→ WFC); the development of the Global Information and Early Warning System; and in cooperation with WHO the development of the Codex Alimentarus, which serves to protect consumers and establishes criteria for product quality; the Special Programme for Food Security which has been in operation since 1994; and the World Food Summit of 1996. The Special Programme for Food Security wants to cut the present number of malnourished people in the world by half, by the year 2015. The Programme operates in 64 countries and its biennium budget for 2000-2001 is 10 million US dollars. The next World Food Summit will be held in November 2001.

Evaluation

Since the foundation of FAO 50 years ago, the world and thereby the functions of FAO have changed considerably. During the 1950s and 1960s, all development assistance was dominated by economic and foreign policy goals. Then, with the food crisis of the 1970s, the focus shifted to development policies, and hence to more field assistance. Since the beginning of the 1990s, the direct provision of aid through individual states has been decreasing and to a large extent has been taken over by multilateral organizations.

The necessity of emergency relief has increased enormously in the last few years, peaking in 1994 when more than 35% of all food aid was going to emergencies versus only 10% in the 1970s.

This development can be attributed to the ending of the Cold War, as well as the increasing problems triggered by overpopulation and natural disasters. Political instability, for example in the East European states and in the states of the former Soviet Union, inhibits permanent access to food. In addition, population growth is highest in states which receive the largest portion of total development aid and where most people suffer from hunger. According to official UN statistical data, Africa's share of the world population will rise to 20% by 2050, double its present share. Another factor is the increase in emergencies through natural disasters as well as through inter- and intra-state conflicts.

The constant broadening of FAO's functions creates financial and organizational problems for the organization. Arguments over responsibilities between the WFP and FAO are steadily increasing, which stems from the fact that FAO now performs many of the functions which were originally handled by WFP, such as emergency relief and field programmes. FAO has recognized the need for reform and has undergone significant restructuring to decentralize operations, streamline procedures and reduce costs. Savings of 50 million US dollars a year have been realized so far. Reforms encompass a change in priorities such as the transfer of staff from headquarters to the field, the increased use of experts from developing countries, and the broadening of links between the private sector and non-governmental organizations (→ NGOs). FAO is also attempting to better define its own programmes and will partially retreat from emergency assistance (→ Humanitarian Assistance).

Barbara Hofner

Lit.: *Abbott, J.C.:* Politics and poverty - a critique of the Food and Agriculture Organization, London 1991; *Food and Agriculture Organization:* FAO: the first 40 years, Rome 1985; *Food and Agriculture Organization:* Sustainable development and the environment: FAO policies and actions, Stockholm 1972 – Rio 1992, Rome 1992; *Food and Ag-*

riculture Organization: Elements for Policy Inclusion in a Draft Policy Document and Plan of Action on Universal Food Security, Document CL 108/12 for the 108th session of the FAO Council, Rome 1995; *Food and Agriculture Organization:* Food, Agriculture and Food Security: The Global Dimension. Historical development, present situation, future prospects, Document WFS 96/Tech/ 1b for the FAO World Food Conference, Rome 1995; *Food and Agriculture Organization:* World Food Report (annually); *Schütz, H.-J.:* FAO – Food and Agricultural Organization, in: Wolfrum, R. (ed.): United Nations: Law, Policies and Practice, Vol. 1, Munich/Dordrecht 1995, 499-521; *Talbot, R.B.:* Historical dictionary of the international food agencies: FAO, WFP, WFC, IFAD, Metuchen/NY 1994; *Uvin, P.:* The International Organization of Hunger, London 1994.

Addendum

In 2005, the World Summit first took stock of the progress made towards achieving the Millennium Development Goals (MDGs) established at the UN Millennium Summit 2000 (UN General Assembly resolution 55/2 of 8 September 2000) to be reached by the year 2015. The results were modest, however, a first step of rethinking traditional development aid has been taken by stipulating individual country strategies to fight hunger. This opened the doors to approaches considering, for example, land redistribution. Nevertheless, binding agreements concerning enhanced development aid are still missing.

Reform

The reform of the FAO continues to focus on structural adjustments and decentralization as it was recommended, for instance, in the report of the Independent External Evaluation of the FAO submitted to the FAO Council in September 2007 (*FAO 2007*).

One of the main points is to downsize the budget while enhancing the efficiency of the programmes and of the FAO departments and divisions. However, downsizing could not be continued after 2000/2001. In 2004/2005 the budget rose about 155.5 million US dol-

lars to a total of 749.1 million U.S. dollars, and increased again to 765.7 million US dollars in 2006/2007. The FAO justified the raise with personnel increases in field offices due to the decentralization and with inflation. Therefore, the efficiency gains of 38.6 million US dollars were absorbed by rising costs.

Two recent reform proposals appear to be rather promising: The reduction of the absolute number of FAO departments to eight is the most recent structural reform implemented within the budget of 2006/2007 in order to achieve the efficiency and accountability goals.

The other recent reform proposal was put forth in FAO's *State of the Food and Agriculture* report 2006. There, the FAO suggested a radical shift from traditional food aid to, where possible, the distribution of cash and food coupons as well as contracting local food suppliers for delivering food aid. Along with the proposed information and monitoring improvements, the reform offers a thoughtful solution to current problems. However, the implementation has yet to be decided upon by the member states.

Overall, the crucial aspect for the performance of the FAO is its funding by voluntary contributions, which the US as one the main contributors has significantly cut back since 2001. Principally affected is the emergency relief programme, where US donations diminished from 28 million US dollars in 2004 to 4 million in 2007.

Millennium Development Goal No. 1 – Taking Stock

FAO's flagship initiative is to cut the number of undernourished people by half from 823 million people in 1990 to 412 million in 2015 in order to achieve Millennium Development Goal No. 1 (MDG 1) by the year 2015. Half way to 2015, only slow and uneven progress regarding the eradication of hunger has been achieved, while overall, hunger is on the rise in the developing world. In 2007, 854 million people faced hunger, 31 million more than in 1990. While some countries, such as China, achieved MDG 1 already in 2000 due to exceptional economic growth, only modest success has been achieved in the Caribbean and in South America. The rising number of hungry in Central America, the Near East and in Central, South and East Africa raises concerns for the achievability of MDG 1, with almost half of those countries unlikely to meet MDG 1 by 2015. Overall, the most crucial issue remains the continuous underfinancing of the FAO – so far unaddressed in the reform debate.

Friederike Hoffmann

Lit.: *Barrett , C. B./Maxwell D. G.:* Food Aid After Fifty Years: Recasting Its Role, London 2; *Food and Agricultural Organization:* FAO Reform – A vision for the twenty-first century, FAO Doc. C 2005/INF/19, Rome 2005; *Food and Agricultural Organization:* The State of Food Insecurity in the World 2006: Eradicating world hunger – taking stock 10 years after the World Food Summit, Rome 2006; *Food and Agricultural Organization:* The Director General's Revised Programme of Work and Budget 2006-07, Document C 2005/3, Rome 2005; *Food and Agricultural Organization:* The State of Food and Agriculture 2006 (FAO Agriculture Series No. 37), Rome 2006; *Food and Agricultural Organization:* The Challenge of Renewal. Report of the Independent External Evaluation of the Food and Agriculture Organization, September 2007, Rome 2007, FAO Doc. C 2007/7A.1-Rev.1 (quoted as: FAO 2007); *Giesbert, L.:* Millennium Development Goals – zu hohe Ziele fuer Afrika? GIGA Institut fuer Afrikastudien, Hamburg 2007; *Martens, J.:* Armutszeugnis. Die Millenniumsentwicklungsziele der Vereinten Nationen. Halbzeitbilanz – Defizite – Perspektiven, Global Policy Forum Europe, Juli 2007; *Loewe, M.:* Die Millennium Development Goals: Hintergrund, Bedeutung und Bewertung aus Sicht der deutschen Entwicklungszusammenarbeit, DIE Discussion Paper No. 12, Bonn 2005; *Rosegrant, M. W. et al.:* Agriculture and Achieving the Millennium Development Goals, IFPRI und Weltbank, Rome 2006, www.ifpri.org/pubs/cp/ agmdg.asp; *United Nations - General Assembly*: In larger freedom: towards development, security and human rights for all. Report of the Secretary-General, UN Doc. A/59/2005, 21 March 2005; *United Nations*: The Millennium Development Goals Report 2007, New York 2007; *United Nations - General Assembly:* World Summit Outcome 2005, UN Doc. A/RES/60/1, 16 September 2005. **Internet:** Homepage of FAO: www. fao.org.

Financial Crises

I. Introduction

The debates around the adequate volume of the → budget of the UN, the payment for international civil servants (→ Personnel), the calculation of the percentages of the scale of assessments to be paid by the individual member states are as old as the Organization itself. The painful bargain to reach compromises to balance diverging interests is well known in both cases, in securing the necessary financial means as well as in allocating these resources for alternative ends.

The situation for the continuing existence of an organization becomes dangerous as soon as individual members of the UN are, although able to pay, no longer willing to pay, thereby deliberately violating their legal obligations concerning their membership. This behavior of applying the economic lever of a "financial veto" leads especially in the case of members with high assessment rates to a dangerous risk to the existence of the Organization.

The UN experienced three financial crises in its history in the course of which the third one is still going on today. In the following passages, those three financial crises will be briefly described and in a summary evaluated.

II. The First Financial Crisis: The Debate Around the Financing of Peacekeeping Operations in 1956/57

During the course of financing the first UN Emergency Force (UNEF I))in order to solve the Suez conflict (→ Peacekeeping operations), there were three different groups of payment withholders:

(a) member states which interpreted the UNEF Resolution of the → General Assembly on the basis of the "Uniting for Peace"- Resolution 337 (V) of 3 November 1950 as a break with the provisions of the → Charter of the UN. To this group belonged the USSR and its allied eastern bloc states. In their opinion a military deployment should only take place on the basis of Article 42 of the Charter. In this regard, only the → Security Council was authorized, in accordance with Article 43 of the Charter, to come to a special agreement with the member states.

(b) member states which, although recognizing the competence of the General Assembly to act also in questions of world peace and international security, however disapproved of the financing regulation of collective responsibility decided by the General Assembly in connection with UNEF I according to Article 17, para. 2 of the Charter. To those members belonged, among others, the Arab and the Latin American states;

(c) member states which, because of their economic situation and lack of convertible currencies, were not in the position to pay their obligatory shares to the relatively high costs which were involved in the execution of the peace-keeping operations.

Accordingly, there was also a range of alternative concepts of finance:
- The USSR, as well as the Arab states, demanded a financing scheme according to the originator principle whereby solely the aggressors should be made liable to pay the costs. In the case of UNEF I, France, the United Kingdom and Israel were meant;
- China suggested dividing the costs amongst all of the states which were involved in the conflict;
- France demanded a financing scheme based solely on voluntary contributions;
- The Latin American states insisted on an assessment of cost allocation according to the scale of assessments, whereby the developing countries should receive substantial reductions;
- Spain demanded that the major share of the costs for peace-keeping operations should be divided amongst the permanent members of the Security Council ("P-5").

It became clear that these alternative finance proposals were directed against the General Assembly's resolution to allocate the costs amongst all of the member states according to the scale of assessments for the regular UN budget (cf. *UNYB* 1957, 50-52).

The only concrete reaction to these proposals was the General Assembly's resolution of February 1957 to finance the increase of the costs framework by 6.5 million US dollars solely through voluntary contributions (UN Doc. A/RES/1090 (XI), 27 February 1957). Repeated appeals addressed by the → Secretary-General and the General Assembly to the main contributors to the regular UN budget to close the increasing financial gap through voluntary contributions remained, however, without success.

However, the financial situation began to threaten the very existence of the Organization when the UN intervened in the Congo conflict on 14 July 1960. The costs of ONUC were several times higher than those for UNEF I. Although ONUC was deployed by the Security Council with the consent of the USSR, it retained its dues for the same reasons as in the case of UNEF I, claiming that solely the Security Council was authorized to decide upon the financing of peace-keeping operations. Moreover, France, at that time the fourth largest contributor to the regular budget, also refused to participate in the financing of this peace-keeping operation (cf. *UNYB* 1960, 120ff.).

Only through the high amount of voluntary contributions made by the United States (→ United States, UN policy of), did the Secretary-General succeed in keeping the financing gap within limits. However, no consensus was attained as to a new financing mechanism; instead, the General Assembly decided at the end of 1960 once more to apportion the costs of 139 million US dollars for UNEF I and ONUC for 1961 to all member states according to the scale of assessments (UN Doc. A/RES/1583 (XV), 20 December 1960). This implied a pre-programmed increase of the deficit which amounted to 85 million US dollars at the end of 1961 (as a comparison: the assessments for the regular UN budget 1961 came to a total of 69.4 million US dollars).

In view of these circumstances, the General Assembly authorized the Secretary-General to issue 200 million US dollars worth of United Nations bonds at 2%; total subscriptions amounted to about 170 million US dollars, of which the United States had a share of about 45%. A financial collapse of the United Nations could be for the time being prevented; also, the obligatory contributions of the developing countries could be reduced to 20% of their assessments to the regular UN budget.

Since no consensus could be reached about the future financing of UN peace-keeping operations, the General Assembly agreed on 20 December 1961 with resolution 1731 (XVI) to ask the → International Court of Justice for an advisory opinion on the issue of applicability of Article 17, para. 2 of the UN Charter regarding expenditures for UN peace-keeping operations.

The International Court of Justice clearly stated in its advisory opinion (Certain expenses of the United Nations *(Article 17, paragraph 2, of the Charter)*, Advisory Opinion of 20 July 1963; *ICJ Reports* 1962, 151) that
- the General Assembly had the sole competence in budget matters; to these also belong those expenditures which arise by the execution of peace-keeping operations;
- according to Articles 11 and 14 of the Charter the General Assembly is empowered to recommend measures which had as their goal the maintenance of world peace and international security unless it was a matter of military enforcement actions.

After long debates (cf. *UNYB* 1962, 541-555), the 17th General Assembly endorsed the advisory opinion of the International Court of Justice on 19 December 1962 with 75 votes in favour, 18 votes against and 44 abstentions (UN Doc. A/RES/1854 (XVII)). In agreement with the advisory opinion, the General Assembly recognized at the same time that the scale of assessments for the UN peace-keeping operations did not have to be necessarily identical to that for the regular budget. Since those member states, which refused to contribute, insisted on maintaining their previous positions, again a special committee was appointed to find a solution as quickly as possible, because the cumulative debts for both peace-keeping operations had reached a total of 142 million US dollars by the end of 1962 (as a comparison: the assessments for the regular UN budget amounted to 82.1 million US dollars). Moreover, the United States had threatened to limit its contributions to its assessed obligatory share of 32.02% (previously, the United States had paid about 50% of the costs for both peace-keeping operations).

This culmination of the first financial crisis was without doubt reached in the year 1964, when before the beginning of the 19th General Assembly a majority under the leadership of the United States threatened to apply Article 19 of the Charter in the case of the USSR. This article provides that a member state shall have no vote in the General Assembly, "if the amount of its arrears equals or exceeds the amount of the contributions due from it for the preceding two full years".

The USSR thereupon threatened with its immediate withdrawal from the Organization in the case that Article 19 of the Charter should be applied. This consequence was, however, contrary to the interests of the United States; as a result, a unique procedure was agreed upon in order to escape this legal dilemma. Open voting was renounced, and a consultation procedure was endeavored by which the delegates of the member states whispered their votes in the ear of the President of the General Assembly who then revealed the results. A further special committee for peace-keeping operations was set up which reached an agreement about the non-application of Article 19 of the Charter for UNEF I and ONUC so that for the 20th General Assembly in autumn 1965 the competence to pass resolutions could be re-attained (cf. *UNYB* 1964, 1-58).

As a reaction to this, the United States made an announcement which became of major importance for the third financial crisis. In a kind of anticipating, non-liability clause, the US representative retained likewise the right to claim exceptions from the basic principle of collective responsibility if compelling reasons should arise.

Although the political crisis could be mastered in this manner, a basic consensus about future peace-keeping operations could not be reached during the following years. The United Nations only avoided a financial bankruptcy due to the fact that ONUC expired in 1964 so that the heaviest financial burden had fallen away since then.

At the end of October 1973 the Security Council passed a resolution to set up a second United Nations Emergency Force (UNEF II) within 24 hours. The conditions implied that on the one hand no permanent member of the Security Council be allowed to participate in the action and on the other hand the sole responsibility rested upon the Security Council. The → Secretary-General was obliged to report continuously to the Security Council about the progress of this peace-keeping operation as well as consulting it for all decisions to be made.

With regard to the financing of UNEF II there was from the beginning a consensus that all the costs should be regarded as expenses of the Organization according to Article 17, para. 2 of the Charter – a regulation which had still sparked off violent controversies in the cases of UNEF I and ONUC. The USSR as well as France abandoned their otherwise vehemently defended positions.

After the collective responsibility for UNEF II had been declared in the Security Council, the General Assembly decided on 11 December 1973 to open a special account outside the regular budget for all the expenses arising in connection with UNEF II (UN Doc. A/RES/3101 (XXVIII).

This amount should, however, not be raised by all member states on the basis of the scale of assessments for the regular → budget. Instead a so-called Four-Class Financing Model was adopted which, although based on the scale of assessments, then undertook certain distinctions. The amount of the financial burdens or relieves between the groups resulted from the offsetting of the respective groups' amounts to each other, whereby the permanent members of the Security Council were assessed the highest and the least developed countries the lowest. The following groups were formed:

- *Group A: The permanent members of the Security Council:* in this group, the five permanent members were assessed with their assessments to the regular budget. Moreover, they met the amount of the difference which arouse from the minimum assessments of the developing countries in Groups C and D, which was divided among them in pro rata proportions to their assessments.
- *Group B: The economically developed states:* to this group belonged all of the Western industrialized states as well as some of the Eastern Block states and South Africa. At the beginning it consisted of (with the exception of the permanent members of the Security Council) the 23 economically most developed countries, which were assessed according the scale of assessments for the regular budget.
- *Group C: The developing countries:* this group consisted of the highest number of the then total of 135 member states (82 in 1973). Their compulsory contributions to the UN peace-keeping operations were assessed with 20 percent of their respective assessments to the regular budget.
- *Group D: The least developed states:* this group of the poorest countries ("least developed countries") consisted in 1973 of 25 member states. They had to pay only 10 % of their minimum rate of 0.01 % to the regular UN budget.

185

This new financing model was a compromise between the capacity to pay of the member states, based on the scale of assessments to the regular budget, and taking into account the economic difficulties of the developing countries on the one hand, and special responsibility of the five permanent members of the Security Council for the maintenance of world peace and international security on the other. The basic concept of this model remained valid until 1995.

Decisive for this compromise was the departure of the USSR from the originator principle as the only acceptable basis for the financing of UN peace-keeping operations. However, it was not until 1987 that the USSR proclaimed itself prepared to settle its debts in installments. This began just when the United States for the first time retained its contributions for UN peace-keeping operations.

III. The Second Financial Crisis: The United States Demands Zero Growth

For the regular UN budget for 1982-83 the United States demanded *zero real growth*, i.e. the budget should only increase by the amount of the rate of inflation. For the UN budget 1984-85 the Reagan Administration even demanded *zero nominal growth*, i.e. the volume of the budget should be "frozen" at the level of 1982-83. In the case of non-observance, the United States threatened to correspondingly reduce or delay their payments.

However, the majority of the General Assembly approved in 1981 against the votes of the United States, the United Kingdom, the Federal Republic of Germany and Japan the regular UN budget for 1982-83 which provided for an increase of 12% (a zero real growth would have amounted to a nominal increase of 1-2%). As a reaction, the US Congress decided to retain certain amounts for UN programmes which the United States did not politically support. In order to increase its pressure the US Administration announced the postponement of its obligatory contributions until the fourth quarter of the year (thus appropriating its UN assessment for each calendar year as part of the US fiscal year, which begins on 1 October) – a decision which has not been changed until today. After withdrawing from → UNESCO in 1984 the US Administration also intended to revise the → Charter by introducing a system of weighted voting on budget issues.

During the second half of the 1980s the overdue obligatory contributions of the United States rose drastically from 35% at first (1985) to just under 80% of the overdue assessed contributions of all member states. The operational capacity of the United Nations was thereby extremely jeopardized.

In order to emerge from this crisis, based upon an initiative of Japan (→ Japan, UN policy of) a group consisting of 18 high ranking experts (G-18) was commissioned in 1985 to examine the administrative and financial efficiency of the United Nations. The G-18 proposed a procedure "which would associate with the preparation of the medium-term plan and the programme budget and which would better facilitate broad agreement among Member States in budgetary matters". The 41st General Assembly adopted on 19 December 1986 a new budgetary procedure which enabled the main contributors a de facto right to veto (→ Veto, Right of Veto) by increasing the number of members in the Committee for Programme and Co-ordination (CPC) and introducing the consensus procedure. This concession vis-à-vis the United States and other (western and eastern) main contributors meant a "de facto" revision of the Charter: by the consensus procedure in the CPC, the Plenum of the General Assembly was virtually deprived of an important classical parliamentary function in which according to Article 18, para. 2 of the Charter decisions about budgetary questions are to be made by a two-third majority of the members present and voting, whereby each member has one vote.

IV. The Third Financial Crisis: The United States Continues Not to Pay its Obligatory Contributions

The expected readiness of the United States to meet after this compromise its obligations, i.e. even if not promptly and fully within four weeks after ratification by the Secretary-General, then at least to pay fully its obligatory contributions to the regular budget within the budget year of the UN, was, however, never fulfilled. Thereby, the second financial crisis during the 1980s proceeded almost without interruption into the third financial crisis during 1990s (cf. for the details: *US Congressional Research Service* 2008, 24ff.).

Although the Bush Administration (and later the Clinton Administration) promised to fully support the work of the Organization in view of the new challenges facing the United Nations, this was not manifested in the financing behavior of the United States. The United States did indeed pay its complete obligatory contributions in the years 1991 and 1992, but still behind schedule, i.e. during the last quarter. Apart from this, it did not reduce its mountain of debts from earlier years although the paying off of these arrears in five annual installments was promised.

In 1995, the United States suggested a radical re-organization and reduction in size of the United Nations as well as the privatization of certain functions such as, e.g., public information. The US payments to the United Nations should be made dependent upon "UN reforms" (→ Reform of the UN) which was the equivalent of economic blackmail of the Organization. Moreover, the United States declared in a unilateral act that due to a law passed by the US Congress it would, as from October 1995, contribute a maximum of 25 % to the costs of UN peace-keeping operations, although due to the agreement of 1973 the permanent members of the Security Council would take an additional obligation, which in the case of the United States corresponded to about six additional percentage points.

In 1997, the new Secretary-General, Kofi Annan, proposed that a Revolving Credit Fund be established, at the level of up to one billion US dollars, through voluntary contributions or other means that member states may wish to suggest. Such a fund should allow the Secretary-General to finance, as recourse, newly arising overdue payments of the member states. He also suggested that any unspent funds from the regular budget should be utilized as a "down payment". Neither proposal was accepted by the member states. They were neither willing to offer additional resources to fill the gap caused by the non-payers, especially the United States, nor ready to change the existing provisions and to renounce potential surpluses of the budget.

In 1997, the Clinton Administration negotiated a deal with the US Congress: an aggregate amount of 926 million US dollars in arrears was acknowledged and the payment of 819 million US dollars authorized (this figure resulted from the deduction of an controversial 107 million US dollar credit owed by the UN to the United States for outstanding peace-keeping reimbursements). This bill contained 38 conditions which, *inter alia*, included: no tax or fee on any US national; no external borrowing by the UN; no interest fees or other arrears penalties.

In December 1997, when the 52nd General Assembly adopted the scale of assessments for 1998-2000 (UN Doc. A/RES/52/215A-D of 22 December 1997), it ignored the US demand to lower the ceiling from 25 to 22 % and stated that it would consider reviewing this issue, depending on whether the United States would pay back its arrears, including disputed amounts.

In October 1998, the Clinton Administration and the US Congress reached an agreement that permitted the payment of a sum to the UN which was sufficient to save the United States from loosing its voting right in 1999 under Article 19 of the Charter.

The negotiations about the scale of assessments for 2001-2003 started already in the middle of 2000. The United States

187

insisted on a reduction from 25 to 22%, beginning in 2001, the second year of the UN budget for 2000-2001, as well as on its unilateral decision of 1995 to pay only a maximum of 25% for peace-keeping operations as from 1996. After long and tough negotiations the 55th General Assembly reached with resolution A/RES/55/5B-F an agreement on 23 December 2000: the maximum rate of assessment to be paid by the United States was fixed at 22%. For the budget year 2001 a compromise could be reached through a voluntary donation by CNN founder Ted Turner who offered a one-time 34 million US dollars to make up the regular budget shortfall of 3 percentage points that resulted from the reduction of the ceiling from 25 to 22%.

The General Assembly also adopted on the same day new regulations for the financing of peace-keeping operations through resolution A/RES/55/235: Instead of the four former groups A-D, a total of ten levels of contributions was introduced. The financing scheme continues to be based on the scale of assessments for the regular UN budget. Reductions from the rate paid according to the assessment scale for the regular budget are tied to per capita income; those with per capita incomes between 500 and 9600 US dollars are allocated among levels C to J based on a sliding income scale. The permanent members of the UN Security Council form a separate level A; all discounts resulting from adjustments in levels C through J shall be borne on a pro rata basis by them, whereas the industrialized countries (level B) continue to pay 100% of their shares to the regular UN budget. In the levels C through J the discounts range from 7.5 to 90%. This new scheme offers a higher degree of flexibility as compared to the former mechanism of 1973.

V. Outlook

The history of the United Nations could be well written in terms of financial crisis management: since the beginning of its existence the Organization suffered under tremendous problems of financing

its activities. Despite the compromise mentioned above, the United Nations did not receive a cent from the United States until the end of March 2001. Moreover, the December 2000 arrangements reduce the US obligation only in phases; presently, the United States are supposed to pay more that 25% of the costs for peace-keeping operations. Furthermore, the United States will pay its dues for the calendar year, if at all, not before October which continues to make life extremely difficult for the UN. The United States will also continue to combine its payments with specific conditions concerning the budget size and its components. Under these conditions, there is no reason to assume that the United States will change its role towards a constructive leadership in the UN. Under these circumstances, there is no reason to belief that the third financial crisis is yet over. In other words, the "financial position of the United Nations remains fragile", as Secretary-General Ban Ki-moon formulated it in his report on the financial situation of the UN of 31 October 2008. Unpaid assessed contributions are heavily concentrated: As of 29 February 2008 the United States owed for prior years 393 million US dollars (= 92% of total debts to the UN) and for 2008 453 million – a total of 846 million US dollars. In addition, the total amount outstanding for peacekeeping operations at the end of 2007 was over 2.7 billion US dollars of which 1.08 billion was owed by the United States (= 40%).

Klaus Hüfner

Lit.: *Global Policy Forum/Friedrich-Ebert Foundation:* The Challenges of UN Finance. Meeting on 22 March 2006 in New York, www-globapolicy.org/finance/docs/ 2006/03 22challenges.htm; *Hüfner, K.:* Die Finanzierung des VN-Systems, 1971-2003/2005, Bonn 2006 (DGVN-Texte 53); *Koschorreck, W.:* 52. Financial Crisis, in: Wolfrum, R. (ed.): United Nations: Law, Policies and Practice. Vol. 1, Munich 1995, 523-531; *Koschorreck, W.:* Ted Turner als Deus ex machina, in: VN 49 (2001), 65-67; *International Court of Justice:* Certain expenses of the United Nations (Article 17, paragraph 2, of the Charter), Advisory Opinion of 20 July 1962, in: ICJ Reports 1962, 151; *Laurenti, J.:* Financing the United Nations (International Relations Studies of the Academic Council on the United Nations System), New Haven 2001; *Laurenti, J.:* Financing, in: Weiss, T.G./Daws, S. (eds.): The Oxford Handbook on the United Nations, Oxford 2007, 675-700; *Lehmann, V./McClellan, A.:* Financing the United Nations (Dialogue on Globalization - Fact Sheet - FES New York), New York 2006, http://library.fes.de/pdf-files/iez/global/50425.pdf; *Schlesinger, T.:* Financing and Financial Crisis, in: Cede, F./Sucharipa-Behrmann, L. (eds.): The United Nations: Law and Practice, The Hague et al. 2001, 289-302; *United Nations Association of the USA:* Crisis and Reform in United Nations Financing, New York 1997; *United Nations - General Assembly:* Improving the financial situation of the United Nations. Report of the Secretary-General, 31 October 2008, UN Doc. A/63/514; *US Congressional Research Service:* United Nations System Funding: Congressional Issues. CRS Report for Congress RL33611, Updated 1 February 2008, Washington 2008.

Internet: *1) within the UN system: a) information about the work of the Fifth Committee of the General Assembly:* www.un.org/ga/63/fifth (replace the 63 with the number of the respective session); *b) press releases about the UN finances:* UN search machine www.un.org/search/ under the search words UN finances, budget, ACABQ and CPC; *2) website on UN finances of the Global Policy Forum:* www.globalpolicy.org/finance/index.htm.

General Assembly

I. Founding History and Competence

The Allied plans for a new World Organization (→ History of the Foundation of the UN) were clearly dominated by the superpower-controlled → Security Council. At the Founding Conference in San Francisco, the less powerful states applied themselves successfully to attempts to give the General Assembly more power and autonomy, and to place it as a co-ordination organ at the center of the → UN system. In questions relating to peace (→ Peace, Peace Concept, Threat to Peace) and security, however, the General Assembly remained subordinated to the Security Council.

The General Assembly is one of the six principal organs of the UN, and the only one in which all member states (→ Membership, Representation of States) have a seat and a right to vote (→ Principal Organs, Subsidiary Organs, Treaty Bodies). Each country may send up to five delegates, but has only one vote. The regular annual sessions of the General Assembly – for which a respective President is elected – begin every third Thursday in September and end as a rule just before Christmas. In recent times, sessions were often resumed in the next year and sometimes they continued until just before the opening of the new session. In addition, the UN Charter (→ Charter of the UN) allows the Secretary-General to convoke, at short notice (Art. 20), a Special Session of the General Assembly. This may be in response to requests either of the Security Council, or of the majority of the UN member states. UN practice has made it clear that the right to veto (→ Veto, Right of Veto) according to Article 27 (3) does not extend to such a request of the Security Council for a Special Session. To the present, nineteen Special Sessions of the General Assembly have taken place, e.g. on → disarmament (1978, 1982 and 1988), international economic cooperation (1975, 1980 and 1990) or the drug problem (1990 and 1998). Moreover, as provided in GA Resolution 377 A (V) of 3 November 1950 (→ Uniting for Peace Resolution), the General Assembly, when confronted by an immanent threat to peace, and in the event that the Security Council is unable to act because of a lack of unanimity of its permanent members, i.e. a veto, may decide to discuss the matter with a view to making appropriate recommendations for collective coercive measures (→ Sanctions) to the member states. Additionally the resolution allows outside the session period of the General Assembly to summon an Emergency Special Session of the General Assembly within 24 hours, either at the request of the majority of the members of the General Assembly or at the request of the Security Council. As this calling for such an Emergency Special Session is a procedural resolution (Art. 27 (2) UN Charter), such a resolution of the Council is not subject to a veto of the permanent members.

To the present, there have been ten Emergency Special Sessions of the General Assembly. They dealt with, *inter alia*, the Korean War (1950-1953), the Suez Crisis (1956), the Soviet invasion in Afghanistan (1980) and the settlement policy of Israel in the Occupied Territories (1997).

All member states are represented in the six Main Committees of the General Assembly (→ Committees, System of). Around these Main Committees, a complex committee system has developed, a system comprising procedural committees, standing committees and subsidiary and ad hoc bodies, in which a large part of the practical work is done. According to the Charter the General Assembly is to coordinate the ensemble of the UN organs (→ Coordination in the UN System; → UN System) through its directly subordinated body, the Economic and Social Council (→ ECOSOC). In reality, the General Assembly exerts only a limited influence on the → specialized agencies, which have become more and more numerous over the years.

According to Articles 11 to 14 of the UN Charter, the General Assembly has advisory, control, and electoral functions. For important decisions, such as decisions concerning the maintenance of international peace and security, the election of the non-permanent members of the Security Council and the admission of new members, a two-thirds majority of the members present and voting is required. In procedural questions and less important matters, a simple majority of the members present and voting suffices (→ Voting Right and Decision-Making Procedures).

With the exception of disputes with which the Security Council is already seized, the General Assembly may discuss all questions and matters within the scope of the Charter and may make recommendations to the member states (Art. 10 UN Charter). Additionally, the General Assembly is entitled to deal with "the general principles of cooperation in the maintenance of international peace and security, including the principles governing disarmament and the regulation of armaments" (Art. 11 (1) UN Charter). It may call the attention of the Security Council to peace-threatening situations (Art. 11 (3) UN Charter) and may even make statements in cases where the Security Council is blocked by a veto. In any legal question, the General Assembly may ask the International Court of Justice (→ ICJ) to give an advisory opinion (Art. 96 (1) UN Charter). The General Assembly controls and surveys the activities of the → Secretariat. The Trusteeship Council, responsible for the dependent territories, operates under the authority of the General Assembly. Together with the competence for promoting international cooperation in the fields of politics, law, economy, social services and culture according to Chapters IX and X of the Charter, these Charter provisions open a large space of action for the General Assembly.

The General Assembly elects members of other UN bodies, above all of the ECOSOC, as well as the non-permanent members of the Security Council and the Trusteeship Council, it elects the Secretary General upon the recommendation of the Security Council (Art. 97 UN Charter) and it elects the judges of the International Court of Justice together with the Security Council in two separate votes. It decides on the admission of new members to the UN upon the recommendation of the Security Council. It receives and considers the annual and special reports of the Security Council, Secretary General, ECOSOC and the Trusteeship Council. It considers and approves the → budget of the UN and it determines the member states' contributions. With the Security Council it shares the authority to draft amendments to the Charter and to summon a conference for revising the Charter (Art. 108 and 109 UN Charter).

II. Peacekeeping and Crisis Management

In the first years, the General Assembly developed many more activities in peacekeeping and crisis management than the founders had intended or expected. A first culminating point was the occupation with the Palestine Question, which was solved in November 1947, when the General Assembly decided, in a resolution with two-thirds majority, upon a division of the country. Since the General Assembly was not able to implement its decision on the spot, it rather contributed to the aggravation of the Near-East Conflict.

The General Assembly took over joint responsibility, too, for the situation on the Korean peninsula. When the Security Council was blocked by a Soviet veto, the General Assembly adopted the "Uniting for peace" Resolution on 3 November 1950 (UN Doc. A/RES/377 (V)). This made it possible to bypass the Security Council and to legitimize the military UN operations in Korea. Again in the Suez Crisis in autumn 1956 (establishment of the peacekeeping force UNEF I (→ Peacekeeping; → Peacekeeping Forces) by the General Assembly) and in the Congo Crisis of 1960-1962, the "Uniting for peace" Resolution" was made use of (→ Uniting for Peace Resolution). Later Emergency Special Sessions, where the majority of the members blamed for example the attitude of Israel and the USA in the Middle-East Conflict, were criticized by the Western countries as mere propaganda events. In this context, the session of 1980 was an exception, when Soviet invasion in Afghanistan was condemned. After the end of the Cold War, the General Assembly stepped back behind the Security Council in peacekeeping issues. Today, it is given only a small part in the Middle-East peace process, because it is considered in the opinion of the USA, that it takes too much the side of the Palestinians.

III. Decolonization and Racial Discrimination

Through the Trusteeship Council, the General Assembly was linked strongly with the process of the dissolution of the colonial empires (→ Decolonization). It dealt very early with racial discrimination in South Africa; first with the discrimination against Indian inhabitants, later on increasingly with the discrimination against the black majority of the population, who were suffering under the Apartheid policy. A milestone was set by the General Assembly on 14 December 1960 with the adoption of the "Declaration on the Granting of Independence for Colonial Countries and Peoples" (A/RES/1514 (XV)). Subsequently, the majority called for the termination of all colonial dependent relationship as soon as possible. In the conflict concerning South Africa, the General Assembly decided to impose sanctions, ranging from arms embargoes over economic sanctions to the prohibition of segregated sport events. When the General Assembly achieved free and equal elections in Namibia (1989) and South Africa (1994), it had indeed reached considerable success. The admission of Palau marked the end of the phase of decolonization, but not the end of the fight against racial, ethnic or religious discrimination.

IV. Development Assistance and Economic Cooperation

With the help of ECOSOC, the General Assembly endeavored to coordinate and intensify the activities of the different UN organs in the field of development assistance of the UN (→ Development Cooperation of the UN System). Since 1961, it proclaimed four "Development Decades" one after another, held several Special Sessions of the General Assembly dealing with this issue and created a huge number of new organizations, such as the United Nations Conference for Trade and Development → UNCTAD, the UN Development Programme → UNDP, the UN Industrial Organization → UNIDO. Furthermore it organized a series of → world conferences dealing with the problems of → environmental protection, population, nourishment, science, technology, etc.

The striving of the developing countries for a global economic balancing of interests culminated in the 1970s in demanding a new international economic order (→ International Economic Relations and New International Economic Order (NIEO)). The industrialized states made certain concessions, but pursued, under the leadership of the United States, an alternative, liberal strategy of opening the developing countries for international competition and for their increased integration into the world market. This strategy has succeeded in the 1990s to a large degree, which has in turn lead to a decreasing influence of the General Assembly in this question. As the → "Agenda for Development" of 1992 clearly demonstrates, the General Assembly will remain nevertheless a forum for the development dialogue on the global level.

V. Human Rights and the Development of International Law

Since the establishment of the Commission on Human Rights (→ Human Rights, Commission on) in 1946 and the adoption of the Universal Declaration on Human Rights (→ Human Rights, Universal Declaration of) on 10 December 1948, the General Assembly has played an important role in the codification and the progressive development of → human rights. Meanwhile, the rights formulated in 1948 were concretized – often in reaction to pressure from and within the forum of the General Assembly – in the form of more than twenty pacts, conventions and declarations. In the course of this development, the UN has created a legally binding standard of human rights and has established bodies for their monitoring (→ Human Rights, Protection of).

Of central significance are the International Covenant on Civil and Political Rights (→ Human Rights Conventions, CCPR) and the International Covenant on Economic, Social and Cultural Rights (→ Human Rights Conventions, CESCR), which were adopted unanimously in December 1966 by the General Assembly, and which entered into force in 1976. Afterwards, efforts concentrated on protecting the rights of women and children and on the fight against torture (→ Human Rights Conventions and their Measures of Implementation; → Human Rights Conventions, CEDAW; → Human Rights Conventions, CRC; → Human Rights Conventions, CAT). Nevertheless, the dispute over the universality of human rights, and over the balance between civil and political rights on the one and the economic rights on the other side, has been escalating recently. Vehement discussions are to be expected on the question whether there is a "third generation" of human rights, rights to peace, development and a healthy environment and whether – besides individuals – states and peoples may appeal to them, too.

Although the General Assembly – according to the Charter – may only make recommendations, a majority of the member states regards its decisions and declarations (→ Resolution, Declaration, Decision) as appropriate instruments for accelerating the development of international law (→ International Law and the UN). Resolutions as such cannot create international law, but may help to prepare the formation and shaping of new international law, and may constitute elements or steps of the commonly accepted process of the development of international law. Hence, the content of numerous multilateral agreements, negotiated within the framework of the United Nations, was pre-shaped by recommendations and decisions of the General Assembly. A prominent example in this context is the "work of the century", the international law of the sea (→ Law of the Sea), which was negotiated during the Third UN Conference on the Law of the Sea, lasting from 1973 till 1982. In recent times, progress has been achieved in the fields of → humanitarian law and of the persecution of war crimes (→ ICC).

Within the scope of its competence, the General Assembly worked also towards the introduction and accomplishment of disarmament negotiations. In the context of the Cold War, however, most of the more than 1000 resolutions dealing with the issue of disarmament had unfortunately as little consequences as the proposals and plans of the Geneva Conference on Disarmament, which had been established by the General Assembly. Still, the General Assembly was able to make a contribution to the conclusion of the Limited Test Ban Treaty for Atomic Weapons (1963) and the Non-Proliferation Treaty (1968).

In 1972, an Agreement on the Development, Production and Stockpiling of Biological and Toxicological Weapons (Biological Weapon Convention) was negotiated within the United Nations system, which entered into force in 1975. After the end of the Cold War, an agreement on a Convention on the Development, Production and Stockpiling of Chemical Weapons and the unlimited extension of the Non-Proliferation Treaty (1995) was achieved *inter alia*. Many of the initiatives realized in the meantime had been advanced first at three Special Sessions of the General Assembly on disarmament affairs in 1978, 1982 and 1988. Although at present its engagement in disarmament affairs is stagnating, the General Assembly will continue urging a multilateral development of international law in the disarmament sector.

VI. Position and Importance of the General Assembly

According to Article 10 of the UN Charter, the competence of the General Assembly includes any questions and any matters, "within the scope of the present Charter or relating to the powers and functions of any organs provided for in the present Charter." Hence, the range of competence of the General Assembly goes as far as the range of competence of the United Nations as such, whereas all other organs may be only take action in certain areas of the competence of the United Nations. The resolutions of the General Assembly, however, which go beyond the internal organization of the UN are just recommendations, that is, they have no binding legal quality for the addressee. Insofar, the real power of the General Assembly is limited. This can be seen very clearly in its relation to the Security Council. The Council is subject to the authority of the General Assembly only inasmuch as it must report on its activities to the Assembly on a yearly basis. However, it is highly significant that the General Assembly has not discussed these reports for many years, but merely takes note of them. Moreover, decisions concerning international peace and security are taken exclusively in the Security Council; the competence of the General Assembly is limited to discussing the problems and on making recommendations.

In the context of the discussion about the → reform of the UN the General Assembly has therefore submitted suggestions for the strengthening of its competence. Corresponding suggestions of a "Working Group for the Strengthening of the United Nations System" (UN Doc. A/51/24), which was established in 1995, were discussed at great length by the General Assembly in November 1997. In its report, the working group calls for greater transparency of the work of the Security Council, which could be guaranteed by submitting the monthly working programme of the Council to the General Assembly. Besides, an institutionalized dialogue between the two forums should be established, for example by consultations between the Security Council and the Presidency of the General Assembly, respectively a smaller committee of members of the General Assembly. Concerning the election of the Secretary General, the Council should keep its right to nominate the candidate, and a more active role of the General Assembly in this matter could be established by the possibility to make recommendations for potential candidates. The limitation of the term of office of the Secretary-General is also under discussion. But, of course, even the realization of these suggestions would not change very much the limited influence of the General Assembly in the UN system.

The importance of the General Assembly, however, cannot be measured by judicial criteria alone. The background of its political impact as a *communication forum* has to be taken into account. It provides not only opportunities for member states to present their own foreign and economic policy, but enables every government to contact other governments and to discuss bilateral and multilateral questions. This is of special importance for smaller states, which cannot afford a diplomatic representation in every capital (→ Permanent Missions).

Moreover, as a world conference convening periodically, the General Assembly provides the framework for discussing questions of international politics and economy, and contributes to the search for consensual approaches to the solution of the problems. Hence, the General Assembly contributes considerably to the setting of the agenda of international cooperation: with its discussion of global political events and its statements in the form of resolutions, the General Assembly exerts moral pressure on the governments of member states and therefore achieves a certain power control. For this reason, the General Assembly should be capable, in spite of all difficulties, of influencing the "process of civilization" (*Elias* 1980) as a *global negotiation forum* and as *meta-state coordination agency*.

Jürgen Heideking

Lit.: *Dicke, K.:* Zwischen weltpolitischer Analyse, politischem Meinungskampf und Ritual der Staatengleichheit. Die Generaldebatte der 41. Generalversammlung, in: VN 36 (1988), 1-7; *Elias, N.:* Über den Prozess der Zivilisation, Frankfurt (Main) 1980; *Fischer, F.:* Rituale, Resolutionen und Frustrationen. Die internationale Verhandlungsmaschinerie, in: VN 31 (1983), 114-118; *Luard, E.:* A History of the United Nations: Vol. 1: The Years of Western Domination, 1945-

1955; Vol. 2: The Age of Decolonization, 1955-1965, London 1982/1989; *Marín-Bosch, M.:* How Nations Vote in the General Assembly of the United Nations, in: IO 41 (1987), 705-724; *McWhinney, E.:* United Nations Law Making, New York 1984; *Opitz, P.J./Rittberger, V. (eds.):* Forum der Welt: 40 Jahre Vereinte Nationen, Munich 1986; *Peterson, M.J.:* The General Assembly in World Politics, Boston 1986; *Reisman, M.:* The Constitutional Crisis in the United Nations, in: AJIL 87 (1993), 83-100; *Tomuschat, C.:* General Assembly, in: Wolfrum, R. (ed.): United Nations: Law, Policies and Practice, Vol. 1, Munich/Dordrecht 1995, 548-557; *Vallat, F.:* General Assembly, in: Bernhardt, R. (ed.): EPIL 5 (1983), 323-329.

Addendum

Problems and Criticism

Having experienced its peak of importance in the 1970s and 1980s, when it had been the centre of the global debates on disarmament, development and the international economic order, since the beginning of the 1990s the General Assembly (GA) has increasingly become less important, whereas the → Security Council has been able to use its capabilities better since the end of the Cold War.

Even more to the point, the General Assembly suffered a massive loss of global credit, since the industrial countries of the North successfully blocked any meaningful reform of the world trade and world finance systems attempted in subsidiary organs of the General Assembly, above all in the United Nations Conference on Trade and Development → UNCTAD. Thus the states of the Third World eventually turned away from the General Assembly with regard to the socio-economic issues and placed their hopes in their participation in the Bretton Woods institutions: The most serious questions of utmost importance for the future of mankind thus are today no longer covered essentially by the General Assembly, but by other UN organs or international institutions: for instance, problems of economic and social development are discussed by the → IMF, → World Bank and WTO (→ WTO/GATT) or even by exclusive informal bodies like the G7/8 and the G20, where the majority of the UN member states is either not represented – in the case of the G7/8 group – or only represented by some larger G-77 states (→ Group of 77 and the UN) – in the case of the G-20.

If the General Assembly wants to regain its capacity to play the central role stipulated by the → Charter of the UN, it must adapt its structures and particularly its working methods to meet current and future challenges, as both are highly ineffective and more attuned to the symbolic demonstration of political weight than to the efficient search for workable consensus solutions for global problems. Unfortunately even in this crucial question of reform (→ Reform of the UN), this sole universal body seems to be for most UN member states only of secondary importance – or at least it receives less attention than it should – in contrast to the Security Council, where the majority of the member states wants to exercise political influence.

The reasons for the decreasing influence of the General Assembly in almost every field of the work of the UN are mainly the inefficiency and unwieldiness of its functioning. These are caused to a large extent by the political vanity of the member states – everybody wants to be seen and heard in the General Assembly, regarded by many as the red carpet of international diplomacy – and also by the legally non-binding character of its resolutions. The fact that the resolutions will have only a symbolic meaning and will not be implemented in reality, leads often to political "show business" and "diplomatic boxing matches", i.e. too often time is wasted with repeated reports and pointless debates on petty issues.

The criticisms of the work of the General Assembly are all too common nowadays: inability to address key issues, formal rituals constraining the workflow, far too many agenda topics (mostly without relevance except for the government which has put them on the agenda and fights for their retention there), endless production of papers (mostly never read again) and toothless resolutions (mostly never implemented). Nowhere are the symptoms of this diagnosis better heard or seen than in the ritualistic General Debate: unless the speaker is the leader of a major power or the like, attendance is embarrassingly poor, even though there is intense competition between governments to speak on certain days or in a special order. After all, for many countries of the world or rather their governments, the General Debate is the only opportunity to speak to the world and to be heard by the world – or at least in theory.

National or group egotism and specific political and/or economic interests determine the positions each delegation adopts in the General Assembly. However, a crucial factor for its functioning is a certain culture of consensus which is an essential precondition for the fruitful co-operation of more than 190 member states. Finding a consensus takes its time, and – more seriously – usually the outcome is beyond dispute.

Ever since the creation of the UN, the Organization has been confronted by criticism and various calls for reform. At least three categories of reform processses within the UN can be discussed: the increase in productivity (rules of procedures, working methods, management), structural changes (membership of a body, creation of new ones, or a privilege such as the power to use the veto), and making fundamental progress with respect to normative principles (aims and principles, development of international law, e.g. the discussion of the principle of non-intervention versus the assertion of the "responsibility to protect").

Substantive structural change is extremely difficult to achieve in so far as an amendment of the Charter of the UN would be required: Article 108 states that amendments come into force by a vote of two-thirds of the members of the GA and must be ratified by two-thirds of the members of the UN including the five permanent members of the Security Council. Because of this very demanding barrier, the usual approach to reforming the UN is somewhat incremental, also known as "muddling through". This means that apart from few substantive and structural reforms there have been a great number of modifications in practices and policies within the → UN system along the way.

Even though the considerable increase in the number of member states (→ Membership and Representation) since the 1960s changed the agenda and the political rules of the General Assembly fundamentally, the body never was confronted by serious demands for structural modifications. Except the extensive creation of new subsidiary bodies and institutions (e.g. UNCTAD, → UNEP, → UNIDO), there has never been a substantial reform of the body itself. The overdue change of the General Assembly is conceivable only through step-by-step modest and concrete reform measures.

While efforts for greater efficiency have always been a recurring topic, concrete proposals were marginally implemented. After nearly two decades of debate, the idea of reform in order to make the main body more effective, efficient, and relevant, is well-established under the somehow strange metaphor of "revitalization" of the General Assembly (cf. the GA resolutions on this topic A/RES/46/77, 47/233, 48/264, 55/285, 58/126, 58/316, 59/313, 60/286 and 62/278). The focus is not on a rapid structural change, but mainly on an informal evolution of working methods.

"Revitalization of the General Assembly"

For the "Revitalization of the work of the General Assembly" three clusters have been used in the discussions of the body itself (cf. Report of the Ad Hoc Working Group on the Revitalization of the General Assembly, UN Doc. A/60/999, 5 September 2006):

1. *Enhancing the role and authority of the General Assembly.*

2. *The role of the General Assembly in the election of the → Secretary-General (SG).*

3. *Improving the working methods of the General Assembly.*

Add 1: The politically most crucial point is the relationship between General Assembly and Security Council; there is a clear antagonism between North and South on the question of primacy. Many delegations expressed their uneasiness with the Security Council's encroachment on functions and issues they consider to be part of the duties assigned to the Assembly by the Charter of the UN. Furthermore, a potential normative or even legislative function of the General Assembly is increasingly postulated by GA member states, but remains highly controversial. Finally, the catchphrase of "democratization of the body" is in vogue but remains rather vague (→ Democratization and the UN).

Improving the implementation of resolutions adopted by the General Assembly is a popular demand, yet nobody so far has been able to explain how this demand should be implemented. More realistic are the proposals for more thematically focused debates ("streamlining the agenda": clustering, bi- or triennialization, and elimination of agenda items) and as well new forms of interactive discussions which should make the agenda both shorter and more concentrated on priority issues. Promising are, as well, the recommendations for strengthening the Presidency of the General Assembly. Additionally, the suggested improvement of the public visibility of the General Assembly's work through enhanced contact of its Presidents with representatives of the media and of → NGOs is highly desirable.

Add 2: Being in fact a special case of cluster 1, this point could be a touchstone of the GA "revitalization" eventually. The General Assembly on several occasions has stressed the need for improved transparency, inclusiveness, interaction with the official SG candidates, regional rotation and gender equality. The body has laid claim to a more influential role for its President in the finding of potential SG candidates and tried to establish criteria for the candidates' qualifications, but so far in vain.

Add 3: Next to the already mentioned streamlining and rationalizing of the agenda a thorough reduction and consolidation of documentation and the improving of proceedings (dates, promptness, rules of procedure, voting) are recommended by the Working Group in its report. A very important field of action would be the improvement in the exchange of information and in the mechanisms of coordination among the Main Committees ($\rightarrow$ Committees, System of) and in relation to other bodies, as well as to the specialized agencies, plus the harmonizing of their respective working methods.

Recommendations like these constantly face the obstacle that every practice seen as dispensable or even destructive by one delegation is seen as being of paramount and vital importance by another. "Debates in the GA are often repetitive, resulting in the adoption of equally repetitive resolutions without having an effective mechanism to assess their implementation. Ironically, efforts to revitalize the GA have suffered from some of the same problems" (*Swart* 2008, 21).

But in fact, there are some examples of successful implementations:
- The position of the President of the General Assembly has been strengthened and his competence been extended; e.g. he can now set a main topic for each session and initiate discussions.
- The President of the General Assembly, the chairmen of main committees and so on are to be elected three months before the next session.
- Agenda items have been reduced; some have even been eliminated or at least adjourned; the setting of thematic blocs corresponding to main problems and goals is made possible; interactive debates can replace the usual series of monologues.

- The inundation of paper has been at least reduced by various arrangements (e.g. a maximum number of pages).

The process of "revitalization" of the General Assembly will take much more time. Unfortunately, no international body is capable of working better and more efficiently than its members do at home as well as in international organizations. But the attempt to improve – slowly, but steadily – the quality of the work of the General Assembly is worth trying. The better it works, the more attention and respect it will gain in world public opinion and both are the foundation for its political impact on world politics.

Reinhard Wesel

Lit.: *Franda, M.F.:* The United Nations in the Twenty-first Century. Management and Reform Processes in a Troubled Organization, Lanham/USA 2006; *Krasno, J.E. (ed.):* The United Nations: Confronting the Challenges of a Global Society, Boulder 2004; *Peterson, M.J.:* The UN General Assembly, London/New York 2006; *Peterson, M.J.:* General Assembly, in: Weiss, T.G./Daws, S. (eds.): The Oxford Handbook on the United Nations, Oxford 2007, 97-116; *Smith, C.B.:* Politics and Process at the United Nations. The Global Dance, Boulder/London 2006; *Smouts, M.-C.:* The General Assembly. Grandeur and Decadence, in: Taylor, P./Groom, A.J.R. (eds.): The United Nations at the Millennium. The Principal Organs, London 2000, 21-60; *Swart, L.:* Revitalization of the Work of the General Assembly, in: Freiesleben, J.v./Swart, L. et al.: Managing Change at the United Nations, New York 2008, 21-36 (*download*: www.centerforunreform.org/node/308); *United Nations – General Assembly:* Report of the Ad Hoc Working Group on the Revitalization of the General Assembly, 5 September 2006, UN Doc. A/60/999.

Internet: *Website of the UN General Assembly:* www.un.org/ga *Homepage of the GA President:* www.un.org/ga/president/62/issues/rga.shtml; *Information on GA reform on the homepages of NGOs*: www.globalpolicy.org/reform/topics/gaindex.htm; www.reformtheun.org/index.php/issues/1741?theme=alt4 (GA revitalization); www.centerforunreform.org/node/34 (GA revitalization).

Geneva Group

The "Geneva Group" is an informal grouping of the largest budgetary contributors to the United Nations. It has no formal charter or rules of procedure. Its members are those UN member states which contribute more than 1 % of the regular budget of certain → specialized agencies such as → FAO, → ILO, → UNESCO and → WHO, and which are pluralistic democracies on the western model. Current members are Australia, Belgium, Canada, France, Germany, Italy, Japan, the Netherlands, the Russian Federation (the Soviet Union joined in 1991; its obligations thereafter assumed by the Russian Federation), Spain, Sweden, the United Kingdom and the US, as well as Switzerland.

The Geneva Group was founded in 1964 at the initiative of the USA and the United Kingdom, at a time when the membership of the UN (→ Membership and Representation of States) had increased dramatically, as had the regular budgets (from the original 76 members to 113 states in 1963) (→ Budget).

These developments made closer cooperation seem imperative to the larger contributors in order to limit the increase in assessed contributions and thus the financial burden of the Geneva Group members, and to ensure that the funds available were used in the most efficient way possible. The Geneva Group meets twice a year for a wide-ranging exchange of opinion on fundamental issues relating to the UN budgets, programmes, finances and administration. One meeting, traditionally held in Geneva in the spring, concentrates on issues relating to the specialized agencies and UN funds and programmes; at the autumn meeting in New York, UN Secretariat matters (→ Secretariat) are discussed.

The principal objectives include:
- Drawing up common guidelines prior to the budgetary debates, which include not just the growth rate of the budgets but also priority-setting for programmes, evaluating the results of the work of the UN specialized agencies and general administrative questions.
- Compensating for late or outstanding contributions to the relevant budgets whilst avoiding borrowing and/or additional contributions.
- Preserving and strengthening the common standardized pay, employment and personnel systems (→ Personnel) of the United Nations and its specialized agencies ("common system") while avoiding exceptions and special arrangements for individual organizations.

The Geneva Group is organized at the following three levels:
- The level of the Directors-General for UN Affairs in the members' Foreign Ministries (the Consultative Level Meeting, CLM). The above-mentioned annual meetings in Geneva and New York are held at this level;
- The Geneva Group General (GGG) at the level of Ambassadors to the UN specialized agencies in Geneva;
- Local Geneva Groups at all United Nations offices, whereby each UN specialized agency or subsidiary organization has a Geneva Group which meets at least once a year, frequently more often.

Given the informal character of the Geneva Group, none of the above-named levels has an official mandate.

In the view of the Geneva Group members, the consultation process developed in this framework has proven to be a successful form of cooperation. Since the mid-80s, the budgets of all specialized agencies and of the United Nations itself have been constrained to zero real growth; given the continued existence of budgetary difficulties for all major contributors the elaboration of common guidelines for financial and budgetary issues has recently taken on greater significance (→ Financial Crises).

The budgetary management of the organizations has also become more transparent, at least for the Geneva Group. The heads of the specialized agencies, together with the G77 (→ Group of 77 and the UN) at first severely criticized the Geneva Group as a "club of the rich". They considered its policies diametrically opposed to the postulate of sovereign equality of the member states in the official organs of the specialized agencies ("one state one vote"), but this has now given way to a sober assessment of reality. When it comes down to it, the Geneva Group today contributes over 83 % of their budgets (originally it was only 66 %), and for peacekeeping measures the percentage is considerably higher.

Günther Altenburg

Addendum

Also in the new millennium the Geneva Group has retained its political and economic weight as the informal "club" of the large UN payers with regard to the regular budgets of the UN organizations as well as to voluntary contributions. According to their own public statements, the Geneva Group only coordinates the positions of the group members with regard to financial matters, UN personnel, management, oversight and accountability within the UN system. However, the Geneva Group means more. In this group the influential UN member states coordinate their UN policies, with regard to the choice of UN top positions and UN reform in general. The fact that the Geneva Group not only convenes quite often at the level of budget experts, but also twice a year (in spring in Geneva and in autumn in New York) at the level of the Directors-General for UN Affairs in the members' Foreign Ministries is ample proof of the political weight of this coordination mechanism. They defined for example in advance the criteria for the reforms of the World Summit 2005, as a US Department of State official frankly admitted in a testimony before the House of Representatives International Relations Committee in May 2005: "... we have met with the group of major UN contributors ... the Geneva Group ... We agreed that it is essential that whatever set of reforms the UN considers later this year, matters of management, administration, personnel, accountability, transparency, and oversight must be included." (Mark Lagon, Testimony before the U.S. House International Relations Committee, 19 May 2005). They have often priority over UN organs in evaluating reform proposals. When → Secretary-General Kofi Annan developed his proposals for administrative reform in his reform report "Investing in the United Nations: for a stronger Organization worldwide" in March 2006 (UN Doc. A/60/692), he sent in April 2006 his Deputy Secretary-General Mark Malloch Brown to Geneva to meet the members of the Geneva Group to "speak on UN reform" (Noon Briefing of the Spokesman of the UN Secretary-General, 21 April 2006); remarkable is the wording "on UN reform". Using the generalizing formulation instead of specifying "on administrative reform measures" the people in the Secretariat reveal that they know about the decision-making potential of the Geneva Group. The General Assembly had the opportunity to discuss the reform proposals not before July 2006, a clear order of priority.

The problem with the Geneva Group lies not so much in the fact that the "big payers" coordinate their UN policies – other groups of UN states, such as the Group of 77, do the same – but in two features of this particular coordination:

a) the Geneva Group members coordinate their UN policies in general without publicly admitting it; they insist on the pure budgetary and administrative character of the coordination implicitly knowing that money and administrative structures are powerful instruments of influencing political decision-making;

b) the decisions of the Geneva Group are taken without any participation of NGOs and any reports and critical comments of the media.

The NGOs and the media concentrate on the G8 meetings, where questions of world economy, including the WTO, are decided, but they neglect the Geneva Group, where important decisions on UN development assistance, environmental protection and other fields of UN activities are to a large extent taken, long before they reach the agenda of the respective UN organ for decision.

The decision-making processes in the Geneva Group should attract more public attention and provoke more public discussion, this we should learn from the example of the reform debate of the year 2005.

Helmut Volger

Lit.: *Hüfner, K.:* Die Finanzierung des VN-Systems 1971 – 2003/2005 (DGVN-Texte 53), Berlin 2006, 64-66; *Lagon, M.:* Testimony before the House International Relations Committee – Management Reform of the UN, 19 May 2005, US Department of State, quoted after: www.globalpolicy.org/ reform/topics/manage/2005/0519congress.htm; *Masset, J.-P.:* Une non-institution: le groupe de Genève, in: Société française pour le droit internationale (ed.): Les organisations internationales contemporaines, Paris 1988, 205-219.

German Translation Section

By → General Assembly Resolution 3355 (XXIX) of 18 December 1974 sponsored by the then three German-speaking member states (Austria, German Democratic Republic and Federal Republic of Germany), a small German Translation Section was created, fully integrated into the UN → Secretariat, financed by a Trust Fund (now fed by Austria and Germany with contributions by Liechtenstein and Switzerland). As of 1 July 1975 all resolutions of the → Security Council and the → General Assembly (including conventions or charters annexed to them), which are also published in an annual volume as part of the Official Records, the annual reports of the → Secretary General on the work of the Organization as well as outcome documents of major UN conferences and other important documents (such as the → Rules of Procedure of the General Assembly and the Security Council) are officially translated into German and published in the same form as in the six → official languages.

A list of all UN documents so far translated into German, including important resolutions adopted before 1 July 1975 and available in the form of German translation manuscripts, can be retrieved from the German Section's website (www.un.org/Depts/german).

A selection of these documents translated into German, including recent resolutions, is also available for downloading. The German Section was the first Secretariat translation service to establish a website, allowing the publication of German translations of topical UN documents electronically, and thus making them sooner available to a larger public.

Printed UN documents in the German language can be consulted at the official UN Depository Libraries and may be ordered at bookshops or at the Sales Section of the United Nations Headquarters at New York and of the Offices at Geneva and Vienna (→ Publications; Internet: https://unp.un.org/). Important resolutions are reprinted regularly in the journal "Vereinte Nationen", published by the German UN association "Deutsche Gesellschaft für die Vereinten Nationen", as well as in the journal "Internationale Politik", published by the Deutsche Gesellschaft für Auswärtige Politik (German Council on Foreign Relations).

The German Translation Section maintains a terminology database, called DETERM, which is publicly accessible on the Internet. This database (in English, German, French, and Spanish) contains organizational names, acronyms, conventions, declarations and other terms frequently used in the United Nations system and is based on the "Dreisprachenliste" a United Nations sales publication published in 1986 (Trilingual Compendium of United Nations Terminology; Compendium trilingue de terminologie des Nations Unies; vol. I-IV, 1665 p., US dollar 75, UN Sales No. E/F/G86.I.20). Translation-related inquiries may be directed to the German Translation Section at 001-212-963 2097 (phone), 001-212-963 2577 (fax) or by e-mail to deutsch@un.org.

Following the example of the Arabic language, whose similar small translation unit was established in the year of Austria's accession to membership in the United Nations (1955), and was transformed into an official translation service, 18 years later, in the year of accession of the then two German states (1973), the German Translation Section was equally intended to be the preliminary stage for a full-fledged official language service. At that time, the necessary majority in the → General Assembly seemed to be ensured, and though the overall translation costs would have increased by ten times, they would have remained more or less the same for the German-speaking countries with their approximate 10% share of the regular → budget. Since no further initiatives were forthcoming, the German Translation Section retained its status as an official UN translation service for certain documents, without German having become an official language.

The practical value of UN documents translated into German is however less an operative one for use in meetings, correspondence etc., where only official languages may be used and where all relevant documents, the wording of which is often closely interrelated, must be completely available. However, important UN documents can now be quoted in one and the same version in all German-speaking countries. And, as the "Explanatory Memorandum" of the three sponsors of that resolution puts it, the German language versions "would facilitate to a large degree the respective work of government and administrative as well as parliamentary bodies and further the work of political and scientific institutions". Moreover, the memorandum continued, this "would broaden the general awareness of the objectives, tasks and activities of the United Nations, promote international understanding and thus contribute to the realization of the aims of the Charter". (UN Doc. A/9705, 16 August 1974)

Ruprecht Paqué

Lit.: *Ammon, U.*: Die internationale Stellung der deutschen Sprache, Berlin/New York 1991; *Paqué, R.*: Deutsch im Rahmen der Vereinten Nationen? (Stiftung Wissenschaft und Politik Ebenhausen, SWP-AZ 1094 of December 1972), Ebenhausen 1972; *Paqué, R.*: Deutsche Sprachentscheidungen im politischen Umfeld der Vereinten Nationen, in: Multilingua 2 (1983), No. 1 and No. 4; *Paqué, R.*: Vielsprachigkeit, Mehrsprachigkeit, Einsprachigkeit – Zu den Sprachen der Vereinten Nationen und zur Resolution 50/11 der Generalversammlung über ,Multilingualism', in: VN 45 (1997), 61-68; *Scharf, K./Böhm, B.*: Arbeitgeber Internationale Organisation. Als Übersetzer bei den Vereinten Nationen, in: Kurz, I./Moisl, A. (eds.): Berufsbilder für Übersetzer und Dolmetscher, 2nd, revised and expanded edn., Vienna 2002, 71-79.

Internet: *Homepage of the German Translation Section:* www.un.org/Depts/german; *List of translations:* www.un.org/depts/german/gts/gts0.pdf; *DETERM terminology database:* http://unhq-appspub-01.un.org/dgaacs/gts_term.nsf.

Globalization

1. Introduction

Due to modern information technologies and media of communication, but also due to the liberalization of capital, goods and movement of persons, our big world is becoming small. Globalization can be understood as the "extension and accelerator of an ongoing process of transnationalisation" (*Sur* 1997, 429), or as a process of intensifying worldwide social relations (*Messner* 1998, 31). The psychological effects on the citizens of the emerging "global village" are considerable, due to the fundamental changes in values which accompany globalization. There are warnings of an impending danger to democracy and welfare, an exclusion of low-income groups, further of loss of jobs, ecological destruction, a weakening of policy-power and a marginalization of the developing countries (today about 85% of the world population are living in low-income countries) – a sort of a "globalization-trap" (*Martin/Schumann* 1996), or a "globalization-shock" (*Messner/Voruba* 1998, 4).

At the same time over-regional economic crises, environmental disasters and worldwide terrorist attacks reflect the fact that the world population is linked more closely than ever.

In two respects the process of globalization is of importance to the United Nations:

- On the one hand, the UN has itself participated actively in topics with global range during recent decades (see below section 2). Thus, the United Nations may be seen as actively participating in the globalization processes.
- On the other hand, globalization confronts the UN itself with new challenges. As *Rubens Ricupero*, Secretary General of the UNCTAD, emphasized in the "Trade and Development Report 1997" (→ UNCTAD), the hope exists that global competition would lead to greater equality of incomes and standards of living on a world-wide scale; *de facto*, however, both the gaps between incomes in the North and the South and those within individual countries have been widening since the early 80s. Today the wealthier 20% of the world's population consume 86% of all items, whereas the poorest 20 % consume only about 1.3%.

The relatively slow liberalization of those markets where developing countries actually have comparative commercial advantages (e.g. agriculture, textiles) is contributing to the striking "asymmetry" of the globalization process.

While the UN member states' capacity for leadership and action is decreasing, *Kratochwil* (1997, 76) speaks of a "disappearance of the public", and of states being more and more "price takers instead of price makers", parts of the civil society are becoming stronger, and demand a say in the framework of the UN (see below section 3). Apart from the response to such structural challenges, the UN has to tackle a number of new substantial tasks. With a view to the UN's distinctive aim of securing international peace and security, it will be particularly important to avoid negative side effects of globalization, and to resolve upcoming distributive conflicts (see below section 5).

2. The UN in the Context of Globalization

In his speech to the 53rd General Assembly (→ General Assembly) on 22 September 1998, the German Minister of Foreign Affairs Klaus Kinkel emphasized that the "age of globalization" is the "age of the United Nations" (UN Doc. A/53/PV.9, 16). He outlined that only here, in the framework of the UN, can all states of the world meet, and that only here may be found common responses to global questions of the present and of the future.

Indeed, the UN views itself – pursuant to Article 1 (4) of the UN Charter (→ Charter of the UN) – as a "centre", in which all states of the world cooperate with a view to achieving common goals such as → peacekeeping, development cooperation (→ Development Cooperation of the UN System) and human rights protection (→ Human Rights, Protection of).

Some UN bodies have from the very beginning of their existence been participating actively in the development of a "world law" within a "world order". For example, the UN General Assembly, although not being a "world parliament" because its resolutions (→ Resolution, Declaration, Decision) are merely recommendations, has doubtless contributed to the emergence of a sort of 'collective consciousness', not least by the proclamation of world commemoration days and world decades (e.g. 10th of December: Human Rights Day; 1997-2006: First Decade of the UN on the Eradication of Poverty).

The International Law Commission (→ ILC), established in 1947, to give another example, is developing rules of a global scope, for instance for the establishment of an international criminal court (→ ICC). In case of conflicts between UN member states, the UN main body of justice, the International Court of Justice (→ ICJ) in The Hague, is entitled to pronounce judgments; by giving legal opinions it may also contribute to the development of globally applicable international law (→ International Law and the UN).

The decision of 17 July 1998 to establish an International Criminal Court (UN Doc. A/CONF. 183/9) was a substantial step toward an UN-promoted world order under the rule of the law. The creation of this court, like the two Ad hoc Tribunals for the punishment of war crimes in former Yugoslavia and in Rwanda, can be seen as the breakthrough of a concept – promoted also by the UN – to establish globally valid legal rules based on the direct criminal responsibility of individuals for acts committed by them.

In addition, GATT, like the World Trade Organization (WTO) in Geneva, has made substantial contributions to globalization – at least in the economic field – by promoting a world-wide opening of markets. However, WTO officials usually stress that WTO/GATT (→ WTO, GATT) is not responsible for globalization as such. To the contrary, they underline that WTO is supposed to ensure that the globalization process takes place within a "rule based system" (see *Warren Lavorel*, in: ASIL 1997, 20).

It is a further merit of the UN that → environmental protection and → human rights have been made global topics. Today, no state is able to legitimize domestic violations of human rights by reference to the principle of the noninterference (→ Intervention, Prohibition of). Even if individual actors, i.e. individuals or groups, still do not possess rights and obligations under international law, "the system as a whole increasingly permeates state boundaries for the sake of protection of individual and group rights" (*Simma/Paulus* 1998, 27). Human Rights are indivisible, regardless of national and regional specificities, and they apply to all human beings in the world, as was corroborated by the Declaration on the Universality of Human Rights of the Vienna World Conference on Human Rights ("Vienna Declaration and Action Program", 12 Ju-

ly 1993, UN Doc A/CONF.157/23). This was further manifested by the appointment, on 20 December 1993, of a High Commissioner on Human Rights, who is responsible for the promotion of human rights world-wide (→ Human Rights, United Nations High Commissioner for) (UN Doc. A/RES/48/141, 20 December 1993).

The solution of ecological problems has highest priority for the UN as well. Only a global approach to regulation will bring to a halt the increasing environmental pollution and destruction, secure a life in human dignity for future generations and allow a peaceful regulation of distribution problems (such as the acute shortage of water in more than 80 countries).

3. The Inclusion of the Civil Society in the Work of the UN

In the context of globalization our world is not only moving toward world economy but also toward world civilization. Often the activities of → NGOs, as of Amnesty International, Greenpeace, the International Committee of Red Cross, World Wildlife Fund and others, initiate newly binding rules and promote new forms of global policy and transnational cooperation. Also NGOs may exercise civilian pressure, e.g. the campaign by North-American NGOs to prohibit antipersonnel mines, led to the successful signing of a convention (→ Disarmament) by several UN member states at the end of 1997.

One important function of the UN may be seen in assuming the role of a mediator between state players and civil society. For so long as the East-West conflict prevailed, NGOs had few possibilities to influence the work of the UN. Relations between the United Nations and NGOs, however, intensified in the 1990s due also to the intense cooperation of NGOs on major → world conferences, e.g. on environment and development in Rio 1992, on human rights in Vienna 1993, on population and development in Cairo 1994 as well as on social development in Copenhagen 1995, and on women in Peking

1995. In the → "Agenda for Development" the → Secretary-General underlined that the number and importance of NGOs had risen extraordinarily during the decade past, and meanwhile the networks of NGOs extend over the whole world (Agenda for Development 1994, para. 147).

De facto, NGOs today represent important partners for cooperation with the UN. The influence of NGOs on the fields of activity of the world organization is growing constantly. Representatives of civil society become more and more involved in global managing processes, which are often referred to as "global governance". The importance of NGOs was recognized by the revision of resolution 1296 (XLIV) of the Economic and Social Council (→ ECOSOC) of 23 May 1968. After three years of negotiations with ECOSOC, Resolution 1996/ 31, entitled "Consultative Relations between the United Nations and Non-Governmental Organization", was adopted on 25 July 1996, thus improving the possibilities for cooperation with NGOs in the UN system. NGOs now are accorded consultative status more easily, and they may participate on a wide basis in world conferences and pertinent follow-up conferences.

As far as questions of economic globalization are concerned, NGOs become more often than in the past important "contact points" for the UN. For example, in 1998 a new NGO alliance, the "International NGO Committee on Human Rights in Trade and Investment" was created. It seeks to give recognition to the fact that processes accompanying economic globalization, in particular trade and financial liberalization, indebtedness regimes and structural adjustment programs, may violate economic, social and cultural human rights.

The task to incorporate the most important "global players", the transnational enterprises, into UN-efforts for a globalization process to be compatible with social and development needs, remains largely unresolved. Enterprises represent an important part of civil society (in 1998 there were already 51 enterprises and only 49 states forming the 100 largest entities of the world, see Bulletin German Federal Government No. 64, p. 813, 23 Sept. 1998). In order to create more transparency and altogether more reliable basic conditions for a world economy, Germany suggested the establishment of a global "public private partnership" between UN member states, international financial organizations and enterprises.

4. Remarks

As the influence of UN member states on transnational processes of globalization is reduced, and traditional instruments seem no longer appropriate for action on the global level, there might occur a chance to strengthen the network of international institutions, acting in the paramount public interest, as well multilateral instruments on UN level.

However, it seems to be questionable whether the UN will in fact seize this opportunity. It has been stated that, in the course of globalization, not only was the General Assembly marginalized and the → Security Council avoided in critical situations, but there was seen as well a weakening of international conference diplomacy (*Sur* 1997, 429; see the reply of *Alston* 1997, 437ff.). Powerful actors are still able to delay the solution of global problems, as the negotiations on climate protection show. In addition, there is a tendency to keep the treatment of explosive social questions out of the influential World Bank Group (→ World Bank, World Bank Group), dominated by Western states, as well as out of the World Trade Organization WTO and to leave them, consequently, as direct national responsibilities. Together with the financial pressure, which has for years been placed on the UN by the most powerful contributors (→ Financial Crises; → Budget; → UN Policy, USA), one may get the impression that industrialized nations are less concerned about a socially and developmentally compatible transnationalization process, than about a strategically favorable position in the global competition.

Western industrialized nations see the main problems of globalization in some areas, such as corruption, drug fighting, terrorism, organized crime, money laundering, proliferation of weapons of mass-destruction, unhindered access to markets, stable investment conditions, as political fields whose regulation exceeds their national capacities. They therefore urge the inclusion of these areas on the agenda of the UN. Some initial successes have been achieved in the disarmament sector. In addition, the UN's efforts in the fight against drugs, organized crime and terrorism were intensified; the fight against corruption became a main objective of World Bank and IWF.

In contrast to this, humanitarian issues, which are of central interest to the majority of the world's population, and which include malnutrition, homelessness, absolute poverty, refugee-movements, the collapse of social and health systems in the Third World, as well as the solution of indebtedness problems, are pushed increasingly into the background (→ Humanitarian Assistance; → UNCTAD). Despite continuing neediness of the poor, multilateral development assistance, and World Bank credits for education and health, have been reduced. There is the illusion that these problems could be handled by market-driven solutions. The opposite is demonstrated, however, by both the UNCTAD "Trade and Development Report" 1997 and the → UNDP "Human Developments Reports" 1997 and 1998 (→ Human Development Reports). These made clear that nobody can count seriously anymore on "trickle down effects" which have served in past years to justify speedy economic liberalization.

5. Global Challenges

One of the major challenges facing the UN consists in aligning economic globalization with credible norms of international justice, social equality, thus serving the interests of future generations. Globalization cannot be left to market forces, it must be ruled politically, framed institutionally and covered by international law. It could be based on an ethics of world-wide solidarity, as already reflected in the late eighties' context of the "Right of Development" (→ Human Rights).

The implementation of human rights, as well as the enforcement of social standards and environmental regulations, ought to be a principal aim not only of international trade, but also of global investment and financial policy (see the title of a resolution by the UN Sub-commission on Prevention of Discrimination and Protection of Minorities from 20 August 1998: "Human Rights as the Primary Objective of Trade, Investment and Financial Policy", UN Doc. E/CN.4/Sub.2/RES/1998/12).

Furthermore, the ecological consequences of globalization should not be ignored any longer. The logic of global markets encourages an externalization of costs. Sustainable development and sufficient food production will not be possible without a drastic increase in development aid and the cancellation of a huge amount of debts.

These are well known claims of development policy (→ Development Cooperation of the UN System; → Development Concepts, Development Research,), however, in view of the globalization-conditioned gap now widening between North and South, their rapid implementation is more urgent than ever. Otherwise, the benefits forecasted by all of those involved in the globalization process will not be realized. Worse, social conflicts or riots, possibly endangering international security, cannot be excluded.

The Millennium Summit of the highest ranking UN representatives and heads of government of all regions convened by UN Secretary Kofi Annan in the year 2000 on the occasion of the new millennium, contained a chance to decide on rules for a fairer distribution of growth and development. In fact the summit adopted a Millennium Declaration (A/RES/55/2, 8 September 2000) aiming at an improvement of the social problems within 15 years, but it remains to be seen whether the declaration is fol-

205

lowed by concrete implementation measures.

The "Global Compact" between the United Nations and economic stakeholders on common values and principles, which UN Secretary-General *Kofi Annan* suggested in early 1999 and which has started its work in the meantime, is perhaps also a viable means to support the dialogue so urgently needed between North and South. For globalization must not exhaust itself in economic global management but must include a new dimension of ethics.

Sabine von Schorlemer

Lit.: *1. Documents: The Commission on Global Governance:* Our Global Neighbourhood, Cambridge 1995; *UNDPI (ed.):* The Vienna Declaration and Action Programme, Adopted 25 June 1993 by the World Conference on Human Rights, UN Doc. A/CONF. 157/23, 12 July 1993; *2. Secondary Literature: Alston, P.:* The Myopia of the Handmaidens: International Lawyers and Globalization, in: EJIL 8 (1997), 435-438; *Henkel, H.-O.:* Globalisierung der Wirtschaft: eine Herausforderung für die internationale Gemeinschaft. Liberale Bedingungen für Welthandel und Auslandsinvestitionen als Ziel für das 21. Jahrhundert, in: VN 43 (1995), 193-196; *Kratochwil, F.V.:* Globalization and the Disappearance of "Publics", in: Jin-Young Chung (ed.): Global Governance. The Role of International Institutions in the Changing World, Seoul 1997, 71-123; *Martin, H.P./Schumann, H.:* Die Globalisierungsfalle. Der Angriff auf Demokratie und Wohlstand, 8th edn., Reinbek/Hamburg 1996; *Messner, D.:* Die Transformation von Staat und Politik im Globalisierungsprozeß, in: epd-Entwicklungspolitik 13 (1998), 31-40; *Messner, D.:* Globalisierung, Global Governance und Entwicklungspolitik, in: IPG, Bd. 1 (1999), 5-18; *Messner, D./Nuscheler, F.:* Globale Trends, Globalisierung und Global Governance, in: Stiftung Entwicklung und Frieden (ed.): Globale Trends 1998, Frankfurt, 27-40; *Messner, D./Vobruba, G.:* Die sozialen Dimensionen der Globalisierung. INEF-Report No. 28, Duisburg 1998; *Nunnenkamp, P.:* Schreckgespenst Globalisierung. Chancen und Risiken für den Standort Deutschland, in: IP 53 (1998), No. 5, 15-24; *Simma, B./Paulus, A.L.:* The „International Community": Facing the Challenge of Globalization, in: EJIL 9 (1998), 266-277; *Sur, S.:* The State between Fragmentation and Globalization, in: EJIL 8 (1997), 421-434.

Addendum

The „Great Global Transformation"

At present, the global system is going through a rapid process of profound transormation. The most pertinent changes refer to four fundamental trends (*Weiss/Daws* 2007, 4-11):

a) *New threats:* Cross-border linkages and technological innovations have drastically deepened (asymmetrical) interdependencies between states and policy areas. The universal model of industrialization overstretches the carrying capacities of global ecosystems. Poverty, violations of human rights, pandemics, terrorism, organized crime and failure of states are threats to security and prosperity everywhere.

b) *New actors:* Nation states have to spar with a proliferation of actors in transnational spaces, such as international organizations, media, parliamentarians, civil society, expert communities, and business interests. The substantial contributions of non-state actors to global problem-solving can best be mobilized through horizontal networking, not by hierarchical control.

c) *New sovereignty:* In a significant reformulation of state sovereignty human rights have been introduced as legitimate concerns of the international community. In 2005, the UN General Assembly adopted a new principle ("responsibility to protect"), which calls for outside intervention (in the last resort by the use of force) if a government is unable or unwilling to protect its own population against humanitarian crisis (*United Nations* 2005, para. 139).

d) *New power constellation:* The brief unipolar constellation after the end of the Cold War is being replaced by a new multipolar system, even though U.S. preponderance in the military field will endure for some time. The rise of emerging powers, especially in Asia (China, India), will bring an end to Western dominance which began with the industrial revolution 250 years ago. It remains to be seen if the "great global transformation" will lead to "turbulent" multipolarity or to stable arrangements of cooperative multilateralism.

UN and Global Governance

The United Nations continues to play an ambiguous role in the globalization process. While it provides an indispensable forum for dialogue, joint learning and collective action in selected policy fields, the world organization has not (yet) become the strategic centre for global governance (*Kennedy* 2006). Member states make use of it as it suits their (short-term) national priorities, but are not willing to invest the political and financial resources needed for UN leadership in meeting global challenges. After the upswing of multilateralism in the 1990s, national prerogatives have again become the key agenda of state actors.

Main factors of the present stalemate are:
- The terrorist attacks of 9/11 (2001) have strengthened the unipolar orientation of US foreign policies. The ensuing war against Iraq without UN mandate has paralyzed intergovernmental consensus-building in the UN.
- Primary concerns for state security have squeezed political spaces for non-state actors in the UN. Calls for increased participation of parliaments, civil society and business have been sidelined by member states.
- Industrialized countries are not willing to grant the UN a coordinating role in international economic policies. They rather opt for new variants of club governance under the umbrella of the G8 (*Fues* 2007). This has deepened the North-South divide in global politics.

All states should reconsider their reservations towards the UN. Increasing threats to human survival and global stability can only be dealt with effectively, if the world organization is transformed into the strategic centre of a democratic global governance system.

Thomas Fues

Lit.: *Fues, T.:* Global Governance beyond the G8: Reform Prospects for the Summit Architecture, in: IPG, 2/2007, 11–24; *Kennedy, P.:* The Parliament of Man: The United Nations and the Quest for World Government, London 2006; *United Nations - General Assembly:* 2005 World Summit Outcome, UN Doc. A/RES/60/1, 16 September 2005; *Weiss, T.G./Daws, S.:* World Politics: Continuity and Change since 1945, in: Weiss, T.G./Daws, S. (eds.): The Oxford Handbook on the United Nations, Oxford 2007, 3-38.

Internet: *a) Information on globalization and references on the website of the Global Policy Forum:* www.globalpolicy.org/globalization.html; *b) information on the Millennium Summit and the Millennium Declaration:* www.un.org/millennium/index.html; *c) Millennium Development Goals:* www.un.org/millenniumgoals/index.shtml; *d) Global Compact:* www.unglobalcompact.org.

Group of 77 and the UN

The Group of 77 – comprising today 133 states – was founded on 12 May 1964 during the first UN Conference on Trade and Development (→ UNCTAD), when 75 developing countries from Africa, Asia and Latin America united to the so-called "Group of 75". At the end of the conference, however, they had grown to a "Group of 77" as South Korea, South Vietnam and Kenya joined the group, and New Zealand left the group (the 77 states: from Latin America and the Caribbean: 21; from Africa: 32; from Asia and the Near East: 22; and from Europe: Cyprus and Yugoslavia).

Their goals are described in the "Joint Declaration of the Seventy-Seven Developing Countries made at the Conclusion of the United Nations Conference on Trade and Development" of 15 June 1964 as follows:

"The developing countries regard their own unity, the unity of the seventy-five, as the outstanding feature of this conference. This unity is sprung out of the fact that facing the basic problems of development they have a common interest in a new policy for international trade and development. They believe that it is this unity that has given clarity and coherence to the discussions of this Conference ... This unity is also an instrument for enlarging the area of cooperative endeavor in the international field and for securing mutually beneficent relationships with the rest of the world ... The seventy-five developing countries, on the occasion of this declaration, pledge themselves to maintain, foster and strengthen this unity in the future." (Joint Declaration of the Seventy-Five Developing Countries ..., Geneva, 15 June 1964, para. 7).

The Group of 77 has no formal institutions, but has a chairman who acts as a spokesman and coordinates the work. Since 1974 this position has gained in importance due to the rapidly increasing amount of work. The office of the chairman rotates every year between the three regions Africa, Asia and Latin America and the Caribbean. The coordinator country is formally announced after informal consultations based on the degree of identification with the work of the group and on the ability to serve this task for one year. It has become a custom that the formal determination of the coordinator is carried out by the meeting of the Foreign Ministers of the Group of 77 at the beginning of the regular sessions of the → General Assembly of the UN.

The group began its work in the early seventies in all important areas of the → UN system as a kind of "trade union of the poor", and the main organ of the Third World for articulating and developing their own common economical interests, as well as representing these interests in negotiations with the industrialized countries. At first the Group of 77 established a "Group of 24" in 1972 which was to represent the interests of the Group of 77 at the International Monetary Fund (→ IMF) and at the World Bank (→ World Bank, World Bank Group). Two years later the Group of 77 formed a "Group of 30" on 8 March 1974, with 10 countries representing each of the three regions. But to

make the work of this group more efficient, it was replaced by a "Group of 6" in March of the same year. It was this group that worked out the draft of the "Declaration and Programme of Action on the Establishment of a New International Economic Order" (→ International Economic Relations and New International Economic Order (NIEO)) and the → "Charter of Economic Rights and Duties of States". In March 1975 the "Group of 27" was established, which functions since then as steering committee of the Group of 77. Beside being present at the main seat of UNCTAD in Geneva, the Group of 77 has established itself also officially at the → UNIDO in Vienna, the UN Headquarters in New York, → FAO in Rome , → UNESCO in Paris, → IAEA in Vienna and → UNEP in Nairobi and also at almost every international conference of the UN since 1975 (→ World Conferences).

The main accent of the work of the Group of 77 lies still today in the framework of UNCTAD. To prepare the UNCTAD conferences and to fine-tune their negotiating positions the member states meet shortly before the opening of the conferences. To point out only two final landmark declarations, which gave important impulses to the policy of the developing countries in relation to the industry states in the framework of the North-South Dialogue, out of the many declarations developed at the Group of 77 meetings, which defined the objectives and positions of the Third World countries (cf. *Sauvant* 1981):

(1) The *"Charter of Algiers"* on the economic rights of the Third World of 25 October 1967, at the Conference of Algiers for preparing UNCTAD II in New Delhi 1968:

It was not only one of the first political documents of the developing countries containing demands towards the industrialized states of the West and the East as well as demands towards the developing countries themselves. Moreover it underlined the belief in themselves and in their own future. The content and spirit of the charter are marked not least by the warning of the Algerian president Houari Boumedienne, who in his opening speech called on the developing countries to prepare for a resolute fight against foreign exploitation in order to achieve a radical change in the circumstances dominating the world at that time. In his opinion they could reach this change if they aimed at two goals:

-    "that our peoples must get the full control over the own natural resources again, which are often exploited in their name and often against them" and

-    "that the contribution the industrialized countries are asked for with a view to speeding up the development of the poorer countries, should considered anew, it should be regarded as a small part of reparation of the debt the Western powers have taken upon them, while they were exploiting these countries in a detestable manner, some for centuries, others for decades." (cited after *Timmler* 1967, 728; English translation by the author).

He underlined the willingness of the members to abandon declamatory declarations about common miseries, and to examine instead in a constructive manner what solutions there might be for the abolition of these miseries, and to determine which common positions the member states have to adopt in order to press for these solutions. The Algerian foreign minister Abdelaziz Bouteflika pointed out the importance of the charter for the Group of the 77. He said: "The charter ... opens without any doubt a new page in the history of international economic relations. Beside the hope the charter has awakened in Africa and Asia, it is an invitation to the well-off states to begin the necessary structural change and to declare the readiness to take part along with us in the most profitable fight of our century that our peoples ... undertake every day: the fight against underdevelopment "(cited after *Timmler* 1967, 733; English translation by the author).

(2) The *"Arusha Programme for Self-Reliance and Framework for Negotiations"* of 16 February 1979:

It was developed within the framework of the "Arusha Conference" for the preparation of the negotiation terms and strategy of UNCTAD V in Manila in 1979. In the Arusha Programme it was forcefully confirmed that UNCTAD should be the key instrument for international negotiations over trade and development, in particular for their efforts to establish a new international economic order, in order to prevent that the complex interlinked problems of trade, industry, currency and finance are randomly debated in different fora, sometimes with contradictory goals and strategies.

To strengthen the negotiating power of the Group of 77, and to effect changes to the existing international economic order, the programme of action underlines the determination of the developing countries to work together, even if only in recognition of the fact that they are forced to do so.

The necessity of close cooperation between the developing countries as key issue was established by the Tanzanian president Julius K. Nyerere in his opening speech. He said: "We have all in common that we as nations stand in a relation of dependence with the developed world, not in a relation of interdependence. Every national economy has developed as a by-product of and a supplier for the development in the industrialized North and is oriented outwards. We are not those who determine our own destiny for the main part. This makes us ashamed, but we must admit that we are appendages, half-colonies at best and no sovereign states ... We, the Third World, demand now that the systems which make the rich richer and the poor poorer must be changed, in order to keep pace with other changes in the world – the end of colonialism, the progress of technology and the new awareness of human equality and human dignity ... For it is the aim to complete the liberation of the states of the Third World from domination from the outside. This is the basic idea of the new international economic order. And unity is our instrument – our only instrument – for liberation" (*Nyerere* 1979, 194ff.).

In spite of these programmatic objectives and appeals to common interests, the practical work of the Group of the 77 was marked by strongly diverging direct interests and positions of many of the members. Beside cultural, ideological and political differences there were the differences in the economic development, especially between the Latin American group and the African group. Therefore the decisions of the Group of 77 mostly had to be made as "package deals" to reach a consensus (*Hagemann* 1987, 100).

However, since the beginning of the 90s, three developments have contributed to the fact that the members of the Group of 77 themselves deviated even from this tradition on the occasion of the preparation of UNCTAD IX in Midrand/South Africa 1996. Firstly, the socialist countries fell out of line after the end of the East-West conflict. They even became competitors of the states of the South. Secondly, the WTO (→ WTO, GATT) had in the meantime become universal, whose members included some of the hitherto most important actors of the Group of 77: beside the South-East Asian "tiger states" some newly industrialized countries in Latin-America, plus India, were now members. The third fact was the different development paths of the member states of the Group of 77.

These developments led to the fact that the members of the Group of 77 did not meet any longer in the framework of a general conference to coordinate their positions, as they did in the past, but met only in their regional groups. Although all three regional groups confirmed a far-reaching mandate for the UNCTAD-IX negotiations in keeping with the founding resolution of 1964, the three regional groups developed very different problem analyses.

The Latin American states passed on the 23 January 1996 the "Declaration of Caracas" in which they evaluated → globalization and liberalization as positively as the structural adjustment programmes. The only contentious points for them were the debt problem and the situation of the LDCs.

The Asian countries emphasized in their "Final Document of Amman", adopted on 24 January 1996, the risks of globalization and liberalization, especially the marginalization of LDCs, the growing protectionism of the industrialized countries and the insufficient debt reductions. They demanded a larger freedom of movement for work migrants and compensation payments to the losers of the Uruguay talks.

The African governments established their position in the "Declaration of Addis Ababa" of 16 February 1996. In view of the particularly difficult situation of the continent they demanded firstly more debt reductions, also with regard to multilateral debts, compensations for the erosion of the trade preferences, the implementation of a diversification fund for African commodities, the observance of payment obligations to the "Common Fund" and the liberalization of personal migration.

Not least the reforms initiated at UNCTAD IX in Midrand/South Africa in 1996 point to the fact that the previous main task of the Group of 77, namely to strengthen the negotiating power of the developing countries as group in trade and development issues, has become obsolete and that the group is in search of new tasks.

Mir A. Ferdowsi

Lit.: *Geldart, C./Lyon, P.:* The Group of 77 – a perspective view, in: IA 57 (1981), 79-101; *Hagemann, H.:* Der Einfluß der Gruppe 77 auf die Entscheidungen der Vereinten Nationen, Münster 1987; *Mortimer, R. A.:* The Third World Coalition in International Politics, New York 1980; *Nyerere, J.:* Eröffnungsrede bei der Arusha-Konferenz der „Gruppe der 77", published in: EA, No. 8/1979, D 194-199; *Raghavan, Ch.:* Ergebnisse des Arusha-Treffens der Gruppe der 77. Dialog und Konfrontation für die neue Weltwirtschaftsordnung, in: E+Z 20 (1979), No. 4, 4-5; *Sauvant, K.P.:* The Group of 77: Evolution, Structure, Organization, New York 1981; *Sauvant, K.P.:* „Gruppe der 77" – Gewerkschaft der Dritten Welt, in: VN 29

(1981), 189-195; *Sauvant, K.P. (ed.):* The Collected Documents of the Group of 77, New York 1981ff., since 1989 together with J.W. Müller; *Timmler, M.:* Algier: das erste Regierungstreffen der ganzen Welt, in: Außenpolitik 18 (1967), 725-734; *Williams, M.:* Third World Cooperation. The Group of 77 in UNCTAD, London et al. 1991.

Addendum

The Group of 77 now composed of 130 countries has been particularly engaged with UNCTAD, since 1996 especially UNCTAD IX as well the WTO and movement and lack of movement in the Doha Round negotiations of WTO.

A new book on UNCTAD (*Taylor/ Smith* 2007) suggests that it was at UNCTAD VII in Geneva (1987, 74) that the new secretary-general introduced, for the first time in UNCTAD's history and before the end of the Cold War, the notion that the market should play the key role in development. Behind this was a United States threat to abolish UNCTAD.

UNCTAD VIII was held in Cartagena in 1992. There the main function of UNCTAD was corralled and limited to analysis, consensus building on some trade related issues, and technical assistance.

As the authors note UNCTAD IX in Midrand 1996 (*Taylor/Smith* 2007, 91) under South Africa's chairmanship, continued and extended the move away from questioning the overall global situation and how this structurally affected development, and towards the more "pragmatic" position of making economies in the South as attractive as possible to foreign investors. UNCTAD had been transformed from being a radical critique of global capitalism to an apparatus of global economic governance (*Taylor/Smith* 2007, 92). This onslaught provided more fuel to the different views of the African, Asian and Latin American groups of countries and those within them which make up the Group of 77.

The relationship of the World Trade Organization (set up January 1995) to certain members of the Group of 77 was also divisive. As Donna Lee notes (*Lee* 2006, 53) recent studies show that Southern activism in the WTO is largely restricted to the upper-income level developing countries and the middle powers. Most developing countries, and especially the less developed countries, are seldom involved in the key decisions and seldom consulted during the deliberative process despite their involvement in certain alliances.

Nevertheless as noted above other Southern developing countries have been increasingly active (*Lee* 2006, 53): they authored almost half of the submissions for both the Ministerial Declarations at both Seattle and Doha. Southern delegations have also enhanced their delegation's skills besides establishing the G20+ that has actively opposed the majors on agriculture and the Singapore Issues – investment, competition, government procurement and trade facilitation. But as Lee states (*Lee* 2006, 54) the G20+ have not been able to enjoy significant influence on issues of key interest to them.

G77 Ministers for Foreign Affairs always meet in September/October in New York to discuss their preoccupations. At their 30th annual meeting in September 2006, they stressed the importance of the implementation of the Outcome of the Second South Summit held in Doha, Qatar, in June 2005 (cf. *The Group of 77*, Ministerial Statement, New York 2006, para. 2). They expressed serious concern over the suspension of negotiations which jeopardized the development promises of the Doha Round for developing countries and called upon the developed countries to demonstrate flexibility and political will necessary for breaking the current impasse in the negotiations (ibid., para. 4). They also drew attention to the urgent need for comprehensive reform of the international financial architecture towards enhancing the voice and participation of developing countries (ibid., para. 6).

The Group of 77 is trying to adapt to new realities as well as showing concern over long-standing problems of the developing countries.

Sally Morphet

Lit.: *The Group of 77:* Ministerial Statement – Thirtieth Annual meeting of Ministers for Foreign Affairs of the Group of 77, United Nations Headquarters, New York, 22 September 2006, www.g77.org/ammfa/30/ conclusion.html; *Lee, D.:* South Africa in the World Trade Organisation, in: Lee, D./Taylor, I./Williams, P.D. (eds.): The New Multilateralism in South African Diplomacy (Studies in Diplomacy and International Relations), Houndmills/Basingstoke 2006, 51-77; *Taylor, I./Smith, K.:* The United Nations Conference on Trade and Development (UNCTAD) (Global Institutions Series), London/New York 2007.

Internet: Homepage of the Group of 77: www.g77.org; major declarations and programmes of action of the Group of 77: www.g77.org/doc/docs.html.

Groups and Groupings in the UN

1. General

The day-to-day business of the United Nations is very much influenced by groups of states, which have combined to formulate group interests, and to attempt to impose their positions in the organizations and programmes. The → Charter of the UN does not provide for such groups. However, the fact that the UN now encompasses some 192 states makes it necessary for states to form interest groups. Without informal discussions, it would be nearly impossible to keep on top of negotiations and procedural matters (*Peterson* 1989). This practical reason for the existence of numerous groups within the → UN system was long augmented by a bipolar division into blocs defined by the Cold War, and by the prosperity gap between the developed North and the less developed South (*von Schorlemer* 1995) (→ North-South-Relations and the UN). Today the Eastern and Western blocs are of diminishing significance (*Kim/ Russett* 1996), even if – especially in the

economic and social field of the Second and Third Committees – prominent representatives of individual groups still seem to act along bloc lines (→ Committees, System of).

2. Group Diversity

The most institutionalized group formation is the system of regional groups (→ Regional Groups in the UN), currently five in number. The regional groups include all 192 member states (as of June 2008), with the exception of Kiribati (and, to a certain extent, Israel and the USA). Also of significance for UN practice are regional sub-groups such as the Caribbean Community (CARICOM), the Alliance of Small Island States (AOSIS), the Arab Group, the Rio Group, the Central American Group, the Nordic States and the five African sub-groups of Eastern, Western, Central, Southern and Northern Africa. Almost all negotiations are conducted among major political groupings such as the Non-Aligned Movement (NAM) (→ Non-Aligned Movement and the UN), the Group of 77 (G77) (→ Group of 77 and the UN), and now also the JCC, the Joint Coordination Committee of these two groupings, on which China also sits. There are also numerous "Groups of Friends", whose work concentrates on a particular topic. A UN office-holder is frequently linked to the group ("Friends of the President for ...", "Friends of the Secretary-General on ..."). Also significant are the ad-hoc groups created to achieve specific negotiating objectives. These are entirely informal, but are instrumental in the negotiating process (*Peterson* 1989).

Not to be confused with the above groupings are political associations and regional alliances such as ASEAN, the Organization of the Islamic Conference (OIC), the Arab League and the European Union (EU). The European Union in particular seeks to present joint positions wherever possible as part of its Common Foreign and Security Policy CFSP (→ European Union, Common Foreign and Security Policy at the UN). It has now become a significant UN player. A number of states, especially from Western and Eastern Europe, now associate themselves with the joint statements of the EU states. Others use these statements as a guide for formulating their own, often identical positions.

3. Major Political Groupings

The major political groupings include the Group of 77 with its 130 members. China is associated with this group. The Non-Aligned Movement can boast 118 members (and 15 observers) as of June 2008. While the Group of 77 concentrates on economic and social issues, the Non-Aligned Movement looks at all matters, predominantly political ones. Within the → Security Council the non-aligned members form a "caucus". A joint coordination committee (JCC), on which China also sits, takes decisions on common positions shared by the two groups. Both movements recruit members from the ranks of the developing countries, including states such as Singapore, Brazil, Chile and Uruguay. Some European states (such as Sweden) have more contact with non-aligned states than others.

4. Regional Groups and Sub-Groups

The → regional groups comprise 53 African states (GAFS), 53 Asian states (GASS), 33 Latin American/Caribbean states (GRULAC), 21 Eastern European states (EES) and 28 Western European and Other states (WEOG) and primarily serve to prepare election decisions to important UN bodies. Regional sub-groups act as consultation groups and are of their nature smaller: the Caribbean Community (CARICOM) has 15 members, the Alliance of Small Island States (AOSIS) has 43 (including 4 observers), the Arab Group 21, the Rio Group 12 (Latin American states plus one representative each from Central America and the Caribbean), the Central American Group including Belize has 6, and the Nordic States 5.

5. "Groups of Friends"

In order to help the → Secretariat, and in particular the → Secretary-General,

to resolve regional conflicts under discussion by the Security Council, it has long been the practice to form so-called "Groups of Friends of the Secretary-General", in which those states interested in or necessary for the resolving of the conflict (should) participate (cf. *Prantl* 2006, 70-86). Since the end of the Cold War, the formation of Friends and other groups has "exploded" (Whitfield 2004), amongst them: Friends of / Contact Group on Angola, Burundi, Central African Republic, DRC, UN Mission in Ethiopia and Eritrea, the Great Lakes Region, Guinea-Bissau, Liberia, Mozambique, Namibia, Sierra Leone, Somalia, Sudan, Western Sahara (in Africa), Colombia, El Salvador, Guatemala, Haiti, Venezuela (all in the Americas), Afghanistan, Cambodia, East Timor, Myanmar (in Asia), Cyprus, Kosovo, Former Yugoslavia, Georgia, Tajikistan (in Europe/the Former USSR), Egypt, Iraq, Lebanon (in the Middle East). 14 of these groups do still operate, not including institutional advisory groups (as of December 2006).

Groups of Friends meet intensively during the conflict in question and include the country in which the conflict is located. Draft resolutions (→ Resolution, Declaration, Decision) are frequently drawn up by such groups. Whether a state may join a group of friends is up to the responsible coordinator with the consent of the group members. An example of a Group of Friends which changed its composition is the Group of Friends for Afghanistan, or the original and the New Group of Friends for Georgia. Groups of Friends are not exclusive in nature. Key to success of a Group of Friends is composition (responsible leadership, small size, mixture of regional and influential states).

6. Ad Hoc Groups

Ad hoc groups – also known as "informal" or "temporary" groups – come into their own at major multilateral conferences. The negotiations in the framework of the Third UN Conference on the Law of the Sea (→ Law of the Sea) are repeatedly cited as the first example of the formation of this type of group, variously described as working groups, editorial committees, "Friends of the President" or named after their interests (*Evensen* 1986). In 1998, the States Conference to establish an International Criminal Court in Rome was successfully guided by the "group of like-minded states" (→ ICC). It has however been correctly stated that such practices have long been a feature of negotiations of the → General Assembly (*Peterson* 1989). A somewhat informal and special alliance is the so-called Group of 4 (Brazil, Germany, India and Japan), established in 2003 and with the shared aim of promoting Security Council reform in both membership categories in the ongoing reform process (→ Security Council).

7. Political Associations and Regional Alliances

International and supranational organizations such as CARICOM, the Commonwealth Secretariat, the EU, the Arab League, the AU and OIC have → observer status at the UN. They, too, are a source of considerable group activity. The most active is no doubt the European Union, which endeavors to present a uniform front within the organization wherever possible. Its members coordinate their positions closely with one another. EU positions exert considerable influence on associated states and others in the Eastern and Western European area (see section 2 above). These "building blocks of a new world order" (*Genscher* 1990) are, however, more independent players than institutions which are defined by their work in the UN, and are thus to be distinguished from the rest of the groupings.

8. Other Groups

Other groups worth mentioning include the Barton Group, which examines First Committee issues (all 27 West European and Other states (WEOG), coordinated by Canada) and the Vinci Group, which discusses Second Committee issues (OECD members, the Holy See,

Malta, the Czech Republic, Poland, Mexico, South Korea). The Group of 20 (G20) serves as an informal forum for the international finance system as represented by the twenty most significant and emerging markets economies (P5 (see below), Japan, Germany, Italy, Spain, Canada, Mexico, India, South Korea, Brazil, Australia, Russian Federation, Turkey, Indonesia, Saudi-Arabia, South Africa, Argentine). The Group of 15 (G15) is a platform for the major developing countries to discuss topics of South-South cooperation and North-South dialogue. Its members are Algeria, Argentina, Brazil, Chile, Egypt, India, Indonesia, Jamaica, Kenya, Malaysia, Mexico, Nigeria, Peru, Senegal, Sri Lanka, Venezuela and Zimbabwe. One particularly notable institution is the Forum of Small States (FOSS), chaired by Singapore. FOSS, which meets at irregular intervals, is open to any UN member state which has a population of not more than 10 million. The fact that 91 countries have now (as of June 2008) joined the group is evidence of its attractiveness. FOSS is designed to improve the electoral chances of smaller states and those states which turn to FOSS for support.

9. Organization

Following standard New York practice, meetings of the various groupings are arranged by their chairpersons and then posted with the Secretariat (however, this does not apply for Groups of Friends and ad hoc groups). The Secretariat announces these events in the official UN journal under the rubric "meetings other than meetings of United Nations bodies", giving the venue and time. The meetings can take place at expert, Ambassador, or – in rare cases if circumstances permit – at ministerial level. Joint sessions (for example of African and Arab groups) are also common. In many cases the groups meet as working groups (e.g. African Group/ Economic Experts, African Group/Third Committee, G77/Second Committee, G77/Fifth Committee). The groups usually elect coordinators who are respon-

sible for constantly monitoring particular topics.

10. Major Powers and Other Important Players

The five permanent members (P5) of the
Security Council are somewhat ambivalent as regards the various groupings.
They have to date been regarded as a
"natural" group of their own (*Aust*
1991), especially when common P5 interests demand or indicate solidarity between them. Within the Security Council, the "E10" (elected ten) may be identified as representing the interests of the
non permanent membership of the Council. The United States ($\rightarrow$ UN Policy,
USA) often seems naturally to oppose
the larger groupings of developing
countries (NAM, G77), for whom China
often speaks ($\rightarrow$ UN Policy, China) (see
its above mentioned participation in the
JCC). The United States, the Russian
Federation ($\rightarrow$ UN Policy, Russia) and
China participate with restraint in the
regional groups to which they belong.
The P5 states usually present a common
front when issues that affect their position and privileges in the Security Council are involved. On the other hand, initiatives by the Non-Aligned Movement
often attack the privileges of the P5 indirectly (e.g. A/RES/51/193 of 17 December 1996 on the Report of the Security Council to the General Assembly
sponsored by Colombia and Egypt).
France and the United Kingdom participate in the CFSP of the EU and inform
their EU partners of events in the Security Council on a weekly basis. Their
special position and interests make it
sometimes harder for common EU positions to be agreed. In addition to the P5
states, the following also play a special
role in the UN group system: Germany
(especially in the EU, WEOG), Egypt,
Cuba, India, Pakistan, South Africa (especially in the Non-Aligned Movement), Mexico, Singapore (especially in
the Group of 77) as well as Japan ($\rightarrow$
UN Policy, Japan) and Brazil (member
of the Group of 77 and NAM observer).

11. Functions

In addition to their function of influencing negotiations and working methods
(see above), the existing groupings do
justice to the basic political requirements of the UN member states. On the
one hand they arise from the quest for
allies and alliances. On the other, it can
also be advantageous to allow one's
own positions to overlap with those of
the group. After all, being part of a
group, and appointing coordinators,
means that the workload is divided. The
existing group structures can however
also mean that – particularly in the larger groupings – only minimal common
ground can be found, making it rather
more difficult rather than easier to negotiate with third parties. Coordinators can
also "hijack" groups with their specialist
knowledge. Large groups are seldom in
a position to coordinate detailed practical steps in advance. The situation is
further worsened by the fact that groups
such as the NAM are still trying to define themselves under the altered global
conditions. In addition to positions that
cut through each other and other inconsistencies (cf. *Bennigsen* 1991), rivalries
between the leading group members
cannot be overlooked. Nevertheless, the
numerous groups remain indispensable
to the smaller states as they enable them
to articulate their own interests more
simply, and stand a chance of seeing
them implemented.

Ingo Winkelmann

Lit.: *Aust, A.:* The procedure and the practice of the Security Council today, in: Dupuy, R.-J. (ed.): Le développement du rôle
du conseil de sécurité, The Hague 1995;
365-374; *Ball, M.:* Bloc Voting in the General Assembly, in: IO 45 (1991), 3-31; *Behn-
am, A.:* The Group System, in: Boisard,
M.A./Chossudovsky, E.M. (eds.): The
United Nations System at Geneva, Geneva
1991, 234-43; *Bennigsen S.:* Block- und
Gruppenbildung, in: Wolfrum, R. (ed.):
Handbuch der Vereinten Nationen, 2nd edn.,
Munich 1991, 62-70; *Evensen, J.:* Working
methods and Procedures in the Third United
Nations Conference on the Law of the Sea,
in: Recueil des Cours 199 (1986 IV), 415-
520; *Genscher, H.D.:* Regionale Zusammen-

schlüsse – Bausteine einer neuen Weltordnung, in: VN 28 (1980), 175-178; *Kim, S.Y./ Russett, B.:* The new politics of voting alignments in the United Nations General Assembly, in: IO 50 (1996), 629-652; *Peterson, M.J.:* „Freunde des Präsidenten" und andere Helfer – Informelle Verhandlungspraktiken in der Generalversammlung der Vereinten Nationen, in: VN 37 (1989), 121-125; *Prantl, J.:* The UN Security Council and Informal Groups of States: Complementing or Competing for Governance? Oxford 2006; *Schorlemer, S. von:* Blocs and Groups of States, in: Wolfrum, R.: (ed.): United Nations: Law, Policies and Practice, Vol. 1, Munich/Dordrecht 1995, 69-77; *Whitfield, T.:* Groups of Friends, in: Malone, D. (ed.): The UN Security Council, London 2004, 311-324; *Whitfield, T.:* Friends indeed? United Nations, Groups of Friends, and the Resolution of Conflict, Washington, D.C. 2007; *Winkelmann, I.:* European Union and EU Member States' interests in the United Nations: cooperation and representation, in: ZaöRV 60 (2000), 413-445.

History of the Foundation of the UN

In essence the concept of creating a system of → collective security to safeguard the peace and to prevent breaches of peace goes back to the alliance of states against Germany, Italy and Japan in the Second World War. Although the → League of Nations – which had been equipped with too few powers and which had not been able to prevent breaches of international law in the form of acts of aggression and war actions in major international conflicts – still existed, the states of the Anti-Axis Powers Coalition showed little inclination to continue the League of Nations after the end of the Second World War.

A new organization was to express the hope for a new "world order" in which world peace should be protected better and more effectively than had been the case so far. Furthermore, the new organization was to differ in an important point from the League of Nations: it was to include the USA, whose absence from the League of Nations on the grounds of its disapproval by the US Senate had decisively weakened that organization. That meant that the new organization had from the very beginning to take the interests of US foreign policy into account, so that there would be sufficient chances of obtaining the approval of the founding agreement in the US Senate.

US President Roosevelt was already at an early point of time, i.e. before the USA entered the war after Japan's attack on Pearl Harbour on 7 December 1941, convinced that it would be necessary to create a world organization for keeping world peace. He pleaded for the concept of a world organization under the leadership of the two great powers, USA and the United Kingdom of Great Britain (cf. *Russell/Muther* 1958, 96).

1. First Outlines of an International Organization: The Atlantic Charter of August 1941

With the intention of coordinating his own concepts of the post-war world order – including the planned world organization – with those of Churchill, President Roosevelt invited Churchill to a meeting on board a warship in the Atlantic near the coast of Newfoundland.

At that time the concepts of both statesmen differed considerably, in particular with regard to the new world organization. Churchill wanted to establish an international organization after the model of the League of Nations, supplemented by the principle of regional representation of states. Roosevelt however advocated an organization with an explicit leadership of the USA and of the United Kingdom, which was to control the disarmament of the former enemy states, the Axis powers and their allies, with the help of a strong British-American military force. Churchill wanted to mention the establishment of an international security organization in the final declaration of the meeting. Roosevelt was against it. He was of the opinion that the US Congress and public opinion in the USA were not ready – at that time, and with influential isolationist trends still being strong – to accept such a concept.

In the final declaration of the meeting of the two statesmen of 14 August 1941, called the "Atlantic Charter", Roosevelt had prevailed to a large extent over Churchill. The planned world organization is mentioned only in one subordinate clause. In the Atlantic Charter Roosevelt and Churchill define common goals of the national foreign policies of their countries. They speak out against any attempts at territorial expansion, and against "territorial changes that do not accord with the freely expressed wishes of the peoples concerned." They speak out in favor of the right of all peoples to choose the form of government under which they will live, and they wish to see restored the sovereign rights and the self-government to those peoples who have been forcibly deprived of them. As for world economy, they plead for access of all states on equal terms to the trade and the raw materials of the world, and for collaboration with the objective of securing improved labor standards, economic progress and social security. Finally they advocate the abandonment of the use of force in foreign politics and disarmament: "... they believe that all of the nations of the world, for realistic as well as spiritual reasons, must come to the abandonment of the use of force. Since no future peace can be maintained if land, sea or air armaments continue to be employed by nations which threaten, or may threaten, aggression outside of their frontiers, they believe, pending the establishment of a wider and permanent system of general security, that the disarmament of such nations is essential." (*US Department of State* Bulletin, August 16, 1941, 125; reprinted in: *UNYB* 1946-47, 2).

Although Roosevelt and Churchill define in the Atlantic Charter the principles of the future world organization, they mention the organization – for the above-mentioned reason – only in the subordinate clause above quoted, namely in its function to create a system of general security.

Stalin had not been invited to the meeting of Roosevelt and Churchill, although the German attack on the USSR in June 1941 and the British-Soviet agreement on a common military action against Germany from July 1941 had changed the constellations in world politics decisively (*McNeill* 1953).

2. The Declaration By United Nations of 1 January 1942

After the USA and the United Kingdom had declared war on Japan on 8 December 1941, in reaction to the Japanese assault on Pearl Harbour, and Germany and Italy had answered this with their declaration of war on the USA, the latter was now interested in a broad coalition of states in a military and political alliance, in order to create a safe foundation for the war against the Axis powers. After a meeting of Roosevelt and Churchill on 22 December 1941 in Washington, where this issue was discussed, such a political alliance was formed in the "Declaration By United Nations," in which the signatory states explicitly approved the Atlantic Charter, and declared that they intended to work together for the defense of freedom, independence and human rights in the fight against Germany, Japan, Italy and their allies. The 26 signatory states were the USA, the United Kingdom, the USSR, China, Australia, Belgium, Canada, Costa Rica, Czechoslovakia, Cuba, the Dominican Republic, El Salvador, Greece, Guatemala, Haiti, Honduras, India, Luxemburg, New Zealand, the Netherlands, Nicaragua, Norway, Panama, Poland, South Africa and Yugoslavia. In the course of the war a further 21 states entered the alliance: Mexico, the Philippines and Ethiopia in 1942, Iraq, Brazil, Bolivia, Iran, Colombia in 1943, Liberia and France in 1944, Ecuador, Peru, Chile, Paraguay, Venezuela, Uruguay, Turkey, Egypt, Saudi-Arabia, Lebanon and Syria in 1945. (cf. *US Department of State* 1942, 1; reprinted in: *UNYB* 1946-47, 1)

The signatory states of the Washington declaration of 1 January 1942 called themselves "United Nations", a name which – following the explicit desire of President Roosevelt – was transferred later to the planned world organization. With regard to its programmatic content, the declaration did not contain any concrete hints about the prospective post-war order; on the contrary, the USA tried to prevent the early discussion of concrete details, which were controversial, in order to keep the war alliance stable.

3. The Concepts of the Great Powers 1942/43: Dual Hegemony or Alliance of Four

Originally President Roosevelt had proceeded on the assumption that the post-war order could be determined by the two great powers, the USA and the United Kingdom alone. Later on he was ready to include the USSR and China, but he remained of the opinion that the control of world policy should lie in the hands of a few powerful states, and that the other states should disarm completely. In this way the former enemy states which Roosevelt regarded as the only genuine danger for international peace would be prevented from again becoming a threat to peace, and the smaller states could then go about their business in peace (cf. *Luard* 1982, 19f.). Roosevelt proposed such a concept of the world organization to Molotov when he visited Washington in May 1942. The Soviet Union for its part did not at that point reveal what ideas it had in mind for the post war world order.

Churchill had no confidence in Roosevelt's idea that the new international organization should be based on the cooperation of the "Big Four": he had doubts that China, being at that time still under Japanese occupation, could really take over the role envisaged for it, and, above all, he anticipated difficulties in the cooperation with the Soviet Union. Moreover he recognized the weak point in each system of → collective security, which also Roosevelt's concept possessed: the problem of finding sufficient commitment for the defense of states suffering aggression, especially among those member states of the alliance which are far away from the conflict area, and whose security is therefore not directly affected (cf. *Luard* 1982, 19). Churchill saw the interests of the United Kingdom as being located principally in Europe, and advocated a greater role for regional organizations within the international organization to be established.

Thus Churchill suggested during a visit in Washington in May 1943 that – under the roof of a "world council" of the USA, the UK and the USSR – three regional councils should be established, one for the Western hemisphere, one for Europe and one for the Far East. The regional councils should be provided with far-reaching powers, with their own armed forces which would be able to enforce their decisions and to prevent renewed aggressions, and war preparations. The great powers should be represented in more than one of the councils, preferably with the USA in all three regional councils. Should the regional councils fail in the settlement of disputes, the matter would be referred to the world council (cf. *Luard* 1982, 21).

At this time, in spring 1943, Roosevelt seemed to follow concepts similar to those of Churchill: on 10 April 1943, in a newspaper article written by Forest Davies, but published with the President's approval in the "Saturday Evening Post". Davies proposed the establishment of two security commissions: one, including the United States, the United Kingdom and the USSR, looking after the affairs in Europe, another, including China, for Asia. These countries would have a monopoly of armed force, and there would be no need for international forces or international bases. The smaller nations should disarm (cf. *Luard* 1982, 7).

Roosevelt's concept of a monopoly of armed force of the great powers received skeptical reactions in the foreign offices of the USA and the UK. They did not believe that France or other West European countries could be kept in a state of disarmament in the long run, and they also rejected the regional structure of the world organization. In summer 1943 President Roosevelt himself moved away from the regional concept, while Churchill still held to this concept.

Roosevelt was at that time strongly interested in concrete decisions on the world organization, whereby it was clear for him that the initiative should lie with the great powers. According to Roosevelt's concept, the four great powers should agree on a declaration about the principles of the post-war order in general, then the "Big Three" (USA, UK, USSR) should proceed to negotiate a protocol on the basic structures of the world organization they had in mind. After Roosevelt had come to an agreement on this concept with Churchill, the United States elaborated together with the United Kingdom at a conference in Quebec in August 1943 a draft declaration on the outlines of the future world organization, which they hoped the Soviet Union and China would also endorse. In this proposed declaration the four governments recognized "the necessity of establishing at the earliest practicable date a general international organization, based on the principle of the sovereign equality of all nations and open to membership by all nations, large and small for the maintenance of international peace and security." (quotation from *Luard* 1982, 22).

4. The Consensus of the Four: The Moscow Declaration of the Four Powers of 30 October 1943

Roosevelt's policy of emphasizing the common points was successful at the Moscow conference of the foreign ministers in October 1943: the United Kingdom gave up its regional concept, and declared its consent to include China in the circle of the four powers responsible for international peace. The Soviet Union also agreed to this. The draft declaration worked out at the conference of Quebec was accepted by the Soviet Union. It only amended the text by inserting "peace-loving" between "all" and "states", to ensure that former enemy states would not automatically qualify for membership of the new world organization.

The "Declaration of Four Nations on General Security" was signed by the foreign ministers of the USA, the USSR and the United Kingdom and by the ambassadors of the Republic of China of 30 October 1943. In paragraph 4 of the declaration the signatories declared "that they recognize the necessity of establishing at the earliest practicable date a general international organization, based on the principle of sovereign equality of all peace-loving states and open to membership by all such states, large and small, for the maintenance of international peace and security" (*UNYB* 1946-47, 3; *Goodrich/Hambro/Simmons* 1949, 571f.).

Before the discussion about the details of the organization could begin, the Big Three had to clarify some basic problems. At the conference of the three allies in Teheran in November 1943, Roosevelt described to Stalin his concept of the "Four Policemen", who should take over the primary responsibility, if not even the exclusive responsibility, for international peace after the war. Therefore the world organization should consist of three organs: first there should be an assembly of all nations of the world, meeting in different places throughout the world, to discuss international problems and to make recommendations. Next there should be an executive committee consisting of the four great powers, together with representatives of other groups of countries, to deal mainly with non-military problems, food, health and economics. It would have only the power to make recommendations, including recommendations for the peaceful settlements of disputes. Finally there should be the organ of the "Four Policemen" the main enforcement body, with the power to deal with any threat to the peace in any sudden emergency. (cf. *Luard* 1982, 24)

Stalin objected that such a concentration of power among the Big Four would meet resistance from the smaller states. Moreover China would not have sufficient power after the war to be a generally acceptable member of a body having enforcement powers in Europe.

He proposed a system more similar to that favored by Churchill: a committee for Europe, including the United Kingdom, the USSR, the USA and perhaps one other state, together with a similar committee for the Far East. But Roosevelt doubted whether the US Congress would agree to the United States becoming a member of a primarily European body which could involve the commitment of US troops. Eventually Stalin appeared to endorse Roosevelt's view that a single world wide organization might be better than one divided on regional lines.

After this agreement in principle the three great powers began, as they had agreed in Moscow, to elaborate a more detailed and comprehensive document on the post-war organization. To be more precise, the United States began the work since the British Foreign Secretary Eden was of the opinion that the USA should take the initiative in this process. The USSR, having obviously no definite views of its own at this stage, did not object. The result was that throughout the discussions which followed, until the UN Charter had been formulated, the United States took the initiative and formulated proposals to which the others only reacted. So it is small wonder that the UN Charter, as it finally emerged, was only a slightly modified version of the original US proposal (cf. *Luard* 1982, 24).

5. First Contours of the new World Organization the "Outline Plan" of the USA

Thus the State Department of the USA developed in December 1943 the so-called "Outline Plan", a relatively detailed plan for the new world organization, which it submitted to the President as an attachment to a memorandum on 29 December 1943, and which Roosevelt approved in principle in February 1944. The plan had the title "Plan for the Establishment of an International Organization for the Maintenance of International Peace and Security" (*US Department of State* 1950, 576ff.). This plan contains in principle already all

structural features of the later Charter of the United Nations (→ Charter of the UN): the primary functions of the international organization shall be first "to establish and maintain peace and security, by force if necessary" and second "to foster cooperative effort among the nations for the progressive improvement of the general welfare" (Outline Plan, chapter I). The organization shall serve the following purposes: it shall "prevent the use of force or of threats to use of force in international relations except by authority of the international organization itself". The organization shall "settle disputes between nations likely to lead to a breach of the peace"; it shall "strengthen and develop the rule of law in international relations", "facilitate the adjustment of conditions likely to impair the security or undermine the general welfare of peace-loving nations", and "promote through international cooperative effort the political, economic and social advancement on nations and peoples." (chapter I, paras. 1-5)

The organization should have the following organs: an *Executive Council*, a *General Assembly* and an *International Court of Justice*. While all members of the organization should be represented on the General Assembly, representation on the Executive Council was to be limited (Outline Plan, chapter III).

It should consist of the permanent members USA, United Kingdom, USSR and China, together with six other members which should be elected for limited periods. The elected members of the Council should be elected by a two-thirds vote of the General Assembly. The Executive Council should investigate, either on its own initiative or at the request of member states, any situation which is likely to impair the security or to lead to a breach of the peace. It should have the right to make recommendations to the states concerned to prescribe the terms of dispute settlements, and to institute measures for the enforcement of its decisions, "to determine the existence of a threat or act of aggression and ... to institute measures to repress such threat or act." (chapter

III, para. 3) Decisions of the Executive Council in these matters should require unanimity of all permanent members (alternatively a three-fourths vote of the permanent members).

The General Assembly should meet once annually, but "may be convened in special session on its own initiative or on the initiative of the Executive Council" (chapter IV). The General Assembly should refer to the Executive Council all peace-threatening situations which its members might have brought to its attention, as the Executive Council alone has the competence for deciding on the necessary measures. Moreover the General Assembly "should initiate studies and make recommendations concerning (a) the interpretation and revision of rules of international Law and (b) the promotion of international cooperation" (chapter IV, para. 3). It should admit, by a two-thirds vote, other nations to membership in the international organization.

The International Court of Justice should have the right to render at the request of the Executive Council an advisory opinion on the legal aspects of any questions the Council refers to it.

All in all the Outline Plan contains in essence the characteristic features of the later United Nations: a Council with permanent and non-permanent members, responsible for measures of peace-keeping, a General Assembly with the competence to admit new members and to make recommendations, but without competence to act in matters of international peace and security, and, last but not least, an International Court with the competence to give its advisory opinion on international conflicts at the request of the council.

6. First Preliminary Consensus on the Structures: The "Tentative Proposals"

The US administration discussed the Outline Plan with the congressional leaders, and then with the United Kingdom and Russia. As a result the US government worked out a revised version of the Outline Plan: the so-called "Unit-

ed States Tentative Proposals for a General International Organization" (*US Department of State* 1950, 595ff.). The proposals where transmitted to the other powers on 18 July 1944. They differed from the Outline Plan mainly in two points: in favor of France the number of permanent members of the Executive Council was increased from four to five, and with regard to reservations in the United Kingdom and Latin America, regional arrangements and organizations were allowed in the framework of the security system.

The "Tentative Proposals" found, apart from some reservations in principle, the approval of the other three states (the UK, the USSR and China), so that the American proposals served also as basis for a conference which the four states agreed to hold at Dumbarton Oaks, near Washington, in August 1944 to work out a concrete common draft for the charter of the future world organization. Because of the poor state of Sino-Soviet relations – the Soviet Union was still officially in alliance with Japan, while China was at war with Japan – it was agreed that the two powers should not be present together at the conference: the Soviet Union would take part in the first part of the conference and China in the second.

7. Draft of the Charter of the United Nations: The Conversations of the Four Powers in Dumbarton Oaks in Summer 1944

In fact the Dumbarton Oaks Conversations from 21 August till 9 October 1944 accomplished the great achievement to work out a complete draft of the Charter of the United Nations, which later became, with only a few modifications, the final version of the Charter (cf. *Goodrich/Hambro* 1949, 572ff.). The American Delegation was headed by Edward Stettinius from the State Department, the British delegation by the British ambassador in Washington Alexander Cadogan and the Soviet delegation by Andrej Gromyko, the Soviet ambassador in Washington. The US proposals were quickly accepted as basis for the further negotiations. The other conference delegations had no interest in questioning the general structure which the Tentative Proposals described. But in a few important points the concept of the Tentative Proposals was expanded at Dumbarton Oaks (cf. Luard 1982, 27ff.). For example, the USA had proposed in the Tentative Proposals that the Charter should oblige the member states to use various bilateral procedures for a peaceful settlement of disputes. If this failed they would be obliged to refer the disputes to the Executive Council. At Dumbarton Oaks it was agreed that the Security Council could then, as the Soviet Union demanded, call on the conflict parties to reach a settlement, or even recommend procedures or methods of adjustment. With regard to the composition of the council, it was agreed to offer France a permanent seat on the council. The Council should consist altogether of five permanent and six non-permanent members. In contrast to the Council of the League of Nations, it should meet in permanent session, thus the member states of the Security Council would be obliged to be permanently represented at the headquarters of the organization.

With regard to the voting procedure of the General Assembly, the American proposal contained a weighted voting right in decisions with respect to the budget, similar to the voting right in the World Bank organs, i.e. each member state should have voting power in proportion to its contribution to the expenses of the organization. This was unacceptable to the others, as it would have given a large proportion of the votes to the United States. Eventually there was a general agreement that a simple majority would apply for most questions of the General Assembly, with a two-thirds majority needed only for "important decisions", including budgetary matters and recommendations with respect to the maintenance of international peace and security.

Concerning the election of the Secretary-General, the USA had proposed to have the election by the Assembly with the concurrence of the Council, thus leaving the initiative with the Assembly. But the USSR – supported by the others – thought that the Security Council should recommend a candidate, by its own majority, to the General Assembly, which the Assembly would elect then in a second step. This solution was finally accepted. As this example illustrates, the USSR was pursuing a policy of concentrating authority in the Security Council, where it would hold a veto.

The United Kingdom and China both wanted to upgrade the role of the Secretary-General and suggested giving to him the power to bring before the Council any matter which he considered a threat to the peace. The USA and the USSR accepted this proposal, and this provision later became the well-known Article 99 of the Charter.

No agreement was reached only on two important questions: the right of veto in the Council, and the scope of membership. The USSR insisted on being able to exercise its veto even in conflicts or alleged breaches of peace when it was itself involved. The other three states were of the opinion that in this case the concerned power should be unable to vote and thus also be unable use its veto, with the exception that even in such cases the concerned power would retain its vote and its right of the veto, when the Council came to take decisions on enforcement measures. Although Roosevelt sent a personal message to Stalin on this matter, no agreement was reached in this matter. The second controversial issue was membership. Gromyko demanded that all sixteen Soviet Republics should be admitted as separate members of the organization. This demand was rejected by the other powers, but the Soviet Union held firmly to it. At that point it was agreed to shelve the matter temporarily.

The first conference phase with the Russians took over five weeks (from August 21 to September 29), the Chinese phase lasted just over one week (from September 29 to October 7). This was partly because they were considered less important, and partly because they agreed to most of the proposals of the other powers without discussion.

On 9 October 1944 the "Proposals for the Establishment of a General International Organization" were published (*US Department of State* 1945, 5-16; *Great Britain Foreign Office* 1944; *UNYB* 1946-47, 4-9). They formed the basis for the founding conference of the United Nations in San Francisco, whose convening was agreed on at the summit conference of the Big Three in Yalta in February 1945.

8. Agreement in Yalta on the Disputed Points in the Draft Charter

The unresolved conflicts of Dumbarton Oaks were discussed again at the summit conference at Yalta in February 1945 and were solved by compromise: Roosevelt and Churchill agreed to the admission of the Soviet Republics Byelorussia and Ukraine as full members to the Organization, with voting rights in the General Assembly. Stalin for his part agreed to a modified voting formula in the Security Council. This formula provided that the Security Council would reach decisions with the affirmative votes of seven members, including the concurring votes of the five permanent members in non-procedural matters. In cases of peaceful settlements of disputes and of settlements through regional arrangements, permanent members should abstain when they were themselves involved (cf. *US Department of State Bulletin*, 18 February 1945, 213-216; *Great Britain - Foreign Office*: Report of the Crimea Conference, 11 February 1945 (H.M. Stationery Office, Misc. No. 5 (1945), Cmd. 6598), London 1945; UNYB 1946-47, 9-10).

The Big Three decided to go ahead with the establishment of the new organization as soon as possible, that is to establish it if possible before the war was ended. One of the reasons was doubtless Roosevelt's conviction that public opinion in the USA might be more willing to agree to the membership in the new organization if the war was not finished. Roosevelt told the US

Congress: "This time we shall not make the mistake of waiting until the end of the war to set up the machinery of peace. This time, as we fight together to get the war over quickly, we work together to keep it from happening again." (*Luard* 1983, 36). It was decided to convene the conference for the foundation of the United Nations on 24 April 1945 in San Francisco.

The USA, the United Kingdom and the USSR invited China and France to take over the sponsorship for the conference together with them. China accepted, but France rejected the invitation because the Big Three did not accept its demand to consider France's proposals for modifications of the Dumbarton Oaks Proposals as an equitable negotiation basis for the founding conference (cf. *Luard* 1982, 39). The result was that France did not become one of the sponsoring powers.

The sponsoring powers invited all states which had signed the Declaration by United Nations of 1 January 1942, and had declared war against Germany or Japan, altogether forty-five states, with the exception of Poland, whose right of representation was disputed between the Soviet Union and the Western Allies, which could be clarified only after the closing of the conference (cf. *UNYB* 1946-47, 12). The Soviet Union wanted that the Lublin Committee, being politically close to the USSR, should represent Poland at the conference, whereas the Western powers wanted to ensure the participation of Poland's government-in-exile in London, the latter being politically close to the West.

9. The Charter of the United Nations Is Created: The San Francisco Conference 1945

Shortly before the Conference was due to begin, President Roosevelt died on 12 April 1945. As Roosevelt had been so intensively concerned with the drafting of the preliminary versions of the Charter and had pleaded for support for the new organization in the US Congress and in the public opinion of the

USA, there was concern in many states that the change in the presidential office in the USA might weaken the impetus for the foundation of the World Organization. But the new President Harry S. Truman declared shortly after formally taking office that the Conference would be held as planned, and that the US support for the project was undiminished (cf. *Luard* 1982, 39f.).

On 24 April 1945 the Conference opened at the opera house in San Francisco, with forty-six participating states. The US Secretary of States Stettinius was in the chair of the opening meeting. After a short battle between the USA and the USSR, which was to be symptomatic of the future course of the conference, the question of the presidency of the conference was decided by compromise. The USSR had demanded that the presidency should be held in rotation by each of the four sponsoring powers USA, USSR, UK and China. The USA did not agree, but eventually a compromise proposed by the British Foreign Secretary Eden was accepted. The presidency of the public sessions was to rotate among the four sponsoring powers, while in the steering in the executive committee, and in the informal meetings of the four presidents themselves, Stettinius was to be in the chair (cf. *UNYB* 1946-47, 13).

The next controversy arose with the regard to the question of inviting further participants to the Conference: before the Conference the four powers had agreed to invite Byelorussia and the Ukraine. The Latin American states opposed this invitation for tactical reasons, as they wanted Argentina to be invited. Argentina did not belong to the signatories of the Declaration by United Nations and therefore had not been invited. But as it had been admitted recently to the Organization of American States, the other Latin American States felt responsible for its admission to the Conference (cf. *Luard* 1982, 42). In this situation the USSR saw a chance for the participation of Poland, or better of the Lublin Committee, by making a "package deal" linking the participation of

Argentina and Poland. Eventually the Conference agreed in a resolution on 27 April to delay the invitation to Poland until a Polish government was formed, which would be recognized by the four sponsoring powers (cf. *UNYB* 1946-47, 12-13; *Luard* 1982, 41-42). In another resolution of 30 April the Conference invited Byelorussia, the Ukraine and Argentina to take part in the Conference, on 5 June Denmark, which had just been liberated from German occupation, was invited to the Conference (cf. *UNYB* 1946-47, 13). Thus a total of 50 nations attended.

Very early at the Conference a decision was made which was to be of decisive importance for the cause of the Conference, and for the final text of the Charter. At a meeting of the heads of delegations on 27 April it was agreed that the agenda would be the Dumbarton Oaks Proposals, as supplemented by the Yalta Conference and by the Chinese proposals agreed to by the sponsoring governments, as well as the comments thereon submitted by the participating countries (cf. *UNYB* 1946-47, 14). This procedure represented a great advantage to the sponsoring countries, because it meant in effect that the two-thirds majority was required to change the proposals of the great powers.

In other words, because the discussion took the Dumbarton Oaks Proposals as the basis for discussion instead of starting at zero, the Charter of the United Nations developed more or less as a variation of the ideas of the Dumbarton Oaks Conversations.

On the other hand, it is hardly conceivable that the great powers would have accepted a completely new conception of the world organization, deviating considerably from their concepts developed at Dumbarton Oaks.

The four sponsoring governments themselves submitted jointly to the Conference on 5 May 1945 a series of amendments to the Dumbarton Oaks Proposals, thus giving an even more precise outline of their concept of the UN Charter (text: *UNYB* 1946-47, 14-17).

9.1 The Security Council and its Responsibilities

It is small wonder that the most intensive discussions at San Francisco concerned the core element of the Charter, the Security Council. At Yalta the Big Three had agreed on a formula which was fiercely criticized at San Francisco by the other nations: the formula provided that procedural questions including the decision to place a matter on the agenda, could be reached by a vote of seven members of the Council whereby the concurring votes of the permanent members were not needed, i.e. without a right of veto. The veto would, however, normally apply to all subsequent decisions of the Council, being non-procedural questions, i.e. the votes of all permanent members had to be among the seven affirmative votes. Moreover, as was the agreement at Yalta, a permanent member who was a party to a dispute could not veto any decision to institute peaceful settlement procedures relating to that dispute. The effect of that formula seemed obviously to be that no permanent member could use the veto to prevent any question involving a permanent member from being discussed by the Council, but it might be used to prevent enforcement action from being taken against such a member.

As already mentioned, the other states criticized this veto formula at San Francisco. It was regarded as unclear and imprecise, and it was feared that in practice it might still enable the permanent members to prevent a subject from being discussed at all.

The five great powers, now including France, did not wish to yield this veto power. On the contrary, the USSR seemed even to retreat from the Yalta formula, which had provided that no permanent member could by its veto prevent a matter from being discussed. The Soviet delegate demanded now that the permanent members should be able to use the veto on the question of whether or not a matter was a procedural nature, i.e. a double right of veto. The Western powers tried to overcome the

problem by sending Harry Hopkins, President Truman's special envoy, to Moscow to negotiate the question directly with Stalin on 6 June 1945. In this negotiation Stalin conceded a little: he regarded the question as trivial and accepted the Western position that the veto could not be used to prevent all discussion.

But the joint four-power statement of the sponsoring powers of 7 June 1945, which France joined one day later, meant in practice to take over the Soviet position. The statement contained the provision that the decision regarding the preliminary question as to whether or not a matter is procedural had to be taken by a vote including the concurring vote of the permanent members, i.e. the voting procedure with the right to veto. In other words, the veto did also apply to the decision whether or not a matter was procedural. That meant that in all cases where no permanent member was involved as a conflict party, the permanent members could prevent by their veto even decisions on the peaceful settlement of the disputes. The great powers made clear that they would not be willing to assume any obligation to act with regard to decisions of the council on non-procedural matters, if these were to be taken without the veto right of the permanent members: "In view of the primary responsibilities of the permanent members, they could not be expected ... to assume the obligation to act in so serious a matter as the maintenance of international peace and security in consequence of the decision in which they had not concurred." (*UNYB* 1946-47, 24-25)

This interpretation of the right of veto by the Big Five was pushed through at San Francisco in spite of all the criticism of other Conference members. In the following decades this veto formula was the reason that in many international conflicts the Security Council could block even the discussion of peaceful settlement measures through the veto of its permanent members (cf. *Luard* 1982, 47f.).

There was criticism as well at the Conference of the provision in the Dumbarton Oaks Proposals that the permanent members of the Council should be able to veto amendments to the Charter. The Big Five however rejected all criticism of the other Conference members. The only concession they made was to agree to a Charter article (Art. 109) which provides for the possibility to summon a special conference to review the Charter, if a two-thirds majority of the General Assembly and of the Security Council, here without right of veto, demands it. But here again the amendments to the Charter recommended by a two-thirds vote of the conference shall only take effect when ratified "in accordance with their respective constitutional processes by two thirds of the members of the United Nations including all the permanent members of the Security Council", i.e. at this point the permanent members can make use of their veto right.

There were also controversies at the Conference concerning the composition of the Security Council with respect to the permanent members, but also with regard to the number and the distribution of the non-permanent seats. The Latin American States, for example, wanted a permanent seat for a Latin American state, or at least three non-permanent seats for their continent. India demanded that, with regard to the distribution of non-permanent seats, special account should be taken of population size and economic resources. Liberia wanted an alphabetical rotation among the non-permanent members, so that small states would have an equal chance of election with the large ones. The Netherlands wanted a special role specified for the middle powers in the Council. None of these proposals was adopted (cf. *Luard* 1982, 50ff.).

But at least a small step was taken to meet the concern of the Netherlands by including a provision in Article 23 of the Charter to the effect that, in electing members of the Council, the General Assembly should pay special regard "to the contribution of members of the United nations to the maintenance of international peace and security and to the other purposes of the organization, and also to equitable geographical distribution". (Art. 23 (1))

This could be taken to imply paying some regard to size in electing members of the Council, though it has not often been interpreted in this sense by the regional groups (→ Regional Groups in the UN), which make the determining decisions before the elections proper.

9.2. The Powers of the General Assembly

Complementary to the efforts of the smaller and medium-sized powers to reduce the great power domination in the Security Council, these nations also made efforts to enhance the role of the General Assembly: in the security field the Assembly had been given under the Dumbarton Oaks Proposals virtually no powers at all. It could establish general principles of cooperation in maintaining the peace, but any questions on which action was necessary were to be referred to the Security Council. The General Assembly had no competence to make any arrangements or agreements relating to the maintenance of international peace and security on its own initiative. It was here, above all, that the delegates at San Francisco demanded changes, as they wanted to ensure that the Assembly would at least have some concurrent powers for the maintenance of international peace and security.

Eventually and rather hesitatingly, the Big Five gave a little: on a proposal of the USA, the relevant provision of the Dumbarton Oaks Proposals was modified, declaring now that the General Assembly could not only "consider the general principles of cooperation in the maintenance of international peace and security" (Art. 11 (1)), but also discuss any questions relating to it and "make recommendations with regard to any such questions to the state or states concerned or to the Security Council or to both" (Art. 11 (2)). If such a question makes action necessary it shall be referred by the Assembly to the Security

Council, either before or after discussion. Furthermore, the General Assembly is entitled to call the attention of the Security Council "to situations which are likely to endanger international peace and security". (Art. 11 (3))

This competence of the General Assembly, however, is restricted by an important condition: as soon and as far as the Security Council deals with a dispute or situation in the exercise of its functions assigned to it by the Charter, the General Assembly is not allowed to make any recommendations with regard to that dispute or situation unless the Security Council explicitly so requests (Art. 12 (1)). The Big Five insisted on this condition to prevent a weakening of the authority of the Security Council. Nevertheless the concession of the Big Five was an important expansion of the powers of the General Assembly with regard to → peacekeeping.

But the smaller powers wanted wider powers for the General Assembly: New Zealand and Australia demanded that the General Assembly should have the right to discuss any question it wanted. The great powers were rather reserved on this question, above all the Soviet Union was strongly opposed to this demand. After some intensive negotiations in smaller circles, *inter alia* in meetings between Stettinius, Gromyko and the Australian Foreign Minister Evatt, a compromise was worked out, which the USSR eventually accepted after the USA had again intervened directly in Moscow. The newly inserted Article 10 of the Charter provided that the General Assembly could discuss "any matters within in the scope of the present Charter". But this competence of Article 10 is also restricted by the condition of Article 12, concerning the matters under consideration by the Council.

Without doubt the insertion of Article 10 strengthened the position of the General Assembly in relation to the Security Council, by giving the Assembly at least a competence in peacekeeping and all other international matters, as long as the Security Council was not concerned with the matter. The competence of the Assembly is limited, however, to statements on international problems and conflicts, for example in the form of recommendations to all conflict partners and, in the case of acts of aggression, in the form of a political and moral condemnation of the aggressor, or as recommendation to the Security Council to take sanctions in order to react to a threat to the peace.

Also, with regard to the admission of new members, the other states tried to reduce the influence of the permanent members of the Council. There were efforts at the Conference to replace the Dumbarton Oaks provision that the admission through the General Assembly could only take place upon recommendation of the Security Council by a provision in the Charter that the admission was decided only by the General Assembly, excluding the right of veto of the great powers. Since the great powers were of the same opinion of this question, the proposal for change did not succeed.

The proposal to elect the Secretary-General directly through the General Assembly, i.e. without a previous recommendation by the Security Council, giving the great powers the possibility of making use of their right to veto, aimed in the same direction. This proposal did also not succeed because of the resistance of the Big Five (cf. *Luard* 1982, 64f.).

All in all, the San Francisco Conference only achieved a small expansion of the powers of the General Assembly. The dominant position of the Security Council, connected with a weaker position of the Assembly, as it was contained in the Dumbarton Oaks Proposals, was taken over in the Charter.

9.3. The Secretary-General: Powers and Mode of Election

There was less controversy at San Francisco about the position and function of the Secretary-General. He was to be the chief administrative officer of the organization, he was to perform secretarial and organizational functions for all organs of the UN and he was to report an-

227

nually on the activities of the organization to the Assembly.

There was also agreement on the Dumbarton Oaks proposal to give the Secretary-General the right to bring "to the attention of the Security Council any matter which in his opinion may threaten the maintenance of international peace and security" (Art. 99). As the history of the United Nations showed in the next decades, this right under Article 99 would become an important basis for the gradual expansion of the role of the Secretary-General within the system of the United Nations; this all the more so when the Security Council was blocked in its capacity to act through the controversies among the great powers during the Cold War.

There was controversy, however, about the term of office of the Secretary-General and his re-election. The USSR proposed a two-year term of office and wanted to exclude a direct re-election. The same provision would apply for four Deputy Secretaries-General. All should be nationals of the five major powers and each depute would expect to become Secretary-General eventually. The effect would be that within a decade a national of each of the great powers would serve as Secretary-General. The other great powers wanted a term of office extended to three years; and, though they were also willing to have the deputies appointed, they were not of the opinion that they should be nationals of the great powers.

The Conference decided eventually against determining any term of office for the Secretary-General; the first regular session of the Assembly eventually decided by resolution on a five-year term with the possibility of re-election for further five years. (UN Doc. A/RES/11 (I) of 1 February 1946). The Conference decided also against electing Deputy Secretaries-General. It was of the opinion that this would reduce the independence of the Secretary-General, who should be free to appoint his own senior staff (cf. *Luard* 1982, 65f.).

The controversy about the Deputies is an example of the fact that, in spite of the dominance of the great powers in the preparation phase and during the preparation conference, and in spite of their power to prevent through their veto the entering into force of the Charter, the great powers were not able to push their concept through in each case, if they met the resistance of a great number of participating states. In these cases they had to conclude compromises and had even to give surrender some of their goals.

9.4. The International Court of Justice

There was quite some discussion about the competence of the International Court of Justice. The proposal from a number of Conference delegations that every UN member should accept the compulsory jurisdiction of the Court was rejected by both the USSR and the USA. The compromise proposal by New Zealand, whereby every state would accept the compulsory jurisdiction of the Court but would have the opportunity to make general and uniform reservations, was also rejected by the two states. Both states made it clear that if the proposal were adopted, even in its compromise form, they would not ratify the statute of the International Court. The result was that the majority of states which had formally favored compulsory jurisdiction relinquished their standpoint and accepted that of the two great powers.

The provision which was provided in the Statute of the Court concerning its competence was thus that the states could either refer all cases to the Court *ad hoc* when they decided to do so, or they could declare that they recognize the jurisdiction as compulsory *ipso facto* (Art. 36 of the Statute of the International Court of Justice). Furthermore the states parties to treaties and conventions could provide in the treaties for the competence of the Court.

The other point of controversy concerned the question how the judgments of the Court were to be enforced. There was agreement that the Charter should impose a general obligation on all members to comply with the Court decisions.

China proposed additionally that the Charter should provide that, if a party failed to comply with the judgment of the Court, the Security Council should be entitled to take action to give effect to the judgment. Norway wanted to change the discretionary provision of the Chinese proposal for an obligation of the Security Council to take such measures. The USA, the USSR and the United Kingdom were against both proposals. But the overwhelming majority of Conference states was in favor of such a provision in the Charter and eventually pushed through a formulation close to the Chinese proposal: "If a party to a case fails to perform the obligations incumbent upon it under a judgment rendered by the Court, the other party may have recourse to the Security Council, which may, if it deems necessary, make recommendations or decide upon measures to be taken to give effect to the judgment." (Art. 94 (2) UN Charter)

The great powers agreed at San Francisco that the reservation "if it [the Security Council] deems necessary" should be interpreted in such a way that this reservation would justify the Council in calling for enforcement action only if peace and security were threatened. That means they considered the provision in Article 94 (2) not to be an expansion of the powers of the Council. For in a case of a threat to peace the Council had already under Chapter VI and VII of the Charter far-reaching powers with regard to the peaceful settlement of disputes or enforcement measures in case of threats to the peace, breach of the peace or military aggression.

10. The UN Charter – A Compromise?

If one compares the results of the San Francisco Conference with the Dumbarton Oaks Proposals, it becomes obvious that on a number of points there were controversies between the Big Five and the majority of the other Conference states, so that a number of smaller changes were made in the original draft. But none of these modifications change the

basic structures of the organization and the powers of its principle organs in a decisive way: it remained at San Francisco in its essentials the organization which the USA, the USSR, the United Kingdom and China had outlined it in Dumbarton Oaks.

Although many participating states had different ideas about a world organization, they have yielded to the great powers on many points, because without the membership of the latter the foundation of a world organization for peacekeeping would have made hardly any sense. The structure of the United Nations reflects this history of its foundation very clearly. The United Nations is an organization where the great powers exercise the dominating influence and where they can prevent – above all in the peacekeeping field – any action of which they do not approve.

Many participating states at San Francisco hoped that the great powers would support the world organization just because of their own influential position, and would thus enable the organization to handle international conflicts successfully.

Other states feared that just the opposite would happen, namely that the influence of the great powers in international conflicts would make the United Nations completely unable to act effectively in such crises.

The Charter of the United Nations was, at the time when it was written, the maximum of what could be reached as compromise between the great powers on the one hand and the medium-size and smaller states on the other, with regard to the powers of an international organization.

The history of the United Nations in the following decades proved that the provisions of the Charter contained enough flexibility on the one hand, and standards of international law on the other, to offer the states of the world sufficient chances for effective crisis prevention, settlement of conflicts and means for effective international cooperation, notwithstanding the fact that the states in many situations made no use of the possibilities inherent in the UN Charter.

11. The Birthday of the United Nations 24 October 1945

On 24 June 1945 the Charter of the United Nations was unanimously adopted by the plenary of the San Francisco Conference, and one day later the Charter was signed by the participating states. The founding members of the United Nations numbered 51 states. Poland had not been able to participate for reasons previously mentioned, but signed later on, and is counted among the founding members. After the requisite number of states had ratified the Charter, the Charter entered into force on 24 October 1945 (*UNYB* 1946-47, 33-34). This foundation day is celebrated annually (since 1972), according to a resolution of the General Assembly, as "United Nations Day".

In the beginning of 1946, the General Assembly of the United Nations and the Security Council began their work. The history of the foundation of the United Nations was finished; the history of the United Nations had begun.

Helmut Volger

Lit.: *I. Documents:*
1. Atlantic Charter etc: U.S. Department of State: Postwar Foreign Policy Preparation, 1939-1945, Publication 3580, Washington 1950;

2. Dumbarton Oaks Proposals: Great Britain - Foreign Office: Dumbarton Oaks conversations on world organisation, 21st August - 7th October 1944. Statement of tentative proposals (H.M. Stationary Office, Misc. No. 4 (1944), Cmd. 6560), London 1944; *Great Britain - Foreign Office:* A commentary on the Dumbarton Oaks Proposals for the Establishment of a General International Organisation (H.M. Stationary Office, Misc. No. 6 (1944), Cmd. 6571), London 1944; *U.S. Department of State:* Dumbarton Oaks Documents on International Organization (Department of State Publication 2192, Conference Series 56), Washington (Govt. Printing Office) 1944; reprinted in: Yearbook of the United Nations 1946-47, Lake Success/New York 1947, 4-9; *U.S. Department of State:* Dumbarton Oaks documents together with chart and questions and answers (revised) (Department of State Publication 2257, Conference Series 60), Washington (Govt. Printing Office) 1945; *U.S. Department of State:* The United Nations: Dumbarton Oaks Proposals for a General International Organization, to be subject of the United Nations Conference at San Francisco, April 25, 1945 (Department of State Publication 2297, Conference Series 66), Washington (Govt. Printing Office) 1945;

3. United Nations Conference on International Organization, San Francisco, 1945: United Nations: United Nations Conference on International Organization, San Francisco 1945, 18 vols., 1945-1954; *U.S. Department of State:* The United Nations Conference on International Organization, San Francisco, California, April 25-June 26, 1945. Selected Documents (Department of State Publication 2490, Conference Series 83), Washington (Govt. Printing Office) 1946;

II. Secondary Literature: Dean, V.M.: The four cornerstones of pace: The aims and achievements of the United Nations Conferences at Dumbarton Oaks, Yalta, Mexico City, San Francisco, New York 1946; *Goodrich, L.M.:* From League of Nations to United Nations, in: IO 1 (1947), 3-21; *Goodrich, L.M./Hambro, E./Simmons, A.P.:* Charter of the United Nations. Commentary and Documents, 3rd edn., New York 1969; *Grewe, W.G.:* History of the United Nations, in: Simma, B. (ed.): The Charter of the United Nations. A Commentary, Munich/Oxford 1994, 1-23; *Grewe, W.G./Khan, D.-E.:* Drafting History, in: Simma, B. (ed.): The Charter of the United Nations. A Commentary, 2ed. edn., Vol. I, Oxford 2002, 1-12; *Hilderbrand, R.C.:* Dumbarton Oaks: The Origins of the United Nations and the Search for Postwar Security, Chapel Hill (USA) 1990; *Hoopes, T./Brinkley, D.:* FDR and the Creation of the U.N., New Haven (USA) 1997; *Kelsen, H.:* The Old and the New League: The Covenant and the Dumbarton Oaks Proposals, in: AJIL 39 (1945), 45-83; *Luard, E.:* A History of the United Nations, Vol. 1: 1945-1955, London 1982; *Luck, E.:* UN Security Council – Practice and Promise, London/New York 2006, 2-15; *Russell, R.B./Muther, J.E.:* A History of the United Nations Charter. The Role of the United States 1940-1945, Washington, D.C. 1958; *United Nations Information Office:* United Nations Conference on International Organizations: The story of the Conference in San Francisco, New York 1945; *Volger, H.:* Geschichte der Vereinten Nationen, 2nd rev. edn., Munich/Vienna 2008; *Weber, H.:* History of the United Nations, in: Wolfrum, R. (ed.): United Nations: Law, Policies and Practice, Vol. 1, Munich/Dordrecht 1995, 572-580..

History of the UN

The history of the United Nations since its foundation in 1945 reflects very clearly the prevailing state of international relations, in particular in the changes in the attitude of the governments and of the public in the member states towards the world organization. This history reflects the capability and incapability, respectively, of state governments to prevent wars, to settle disputes peacefully and to cooperate in a constructive manner.

I. The United Nations 1945-1954: Passing the First Test for the World Organization

Quite soon after its foundation, the UN was affected considerably in its working capacities by the increasing confrontation between the USA and the USSR. Since February 1946, the USSR made frequent use of its right of veto ($\rightarrow$ Veto, Right of Veto) as a Permanent Member of the Security Council. It blocked for example the adoption of resolutions ($\rightarrow$ Resolution, Declaration, Decision) concerning the Greek civil war in the years 1946 and 1947, the Berlin Blockade and the Korean War. Furthermore it prevented the admission of many new members ($\rightarrow$ Membership and Representation of States) through its veto, because the Western states blocked the admission of East European states to the $\rightarrow$ Security Council and the $\rightarrow$ General Assembly. Consequently only those states were admitted to the UN which were considered by both sides, the USSR and the Western states, to be "neutral" states: Thailand, Iceland and Afghanistan in 1946, Yemen and Pakistan in 1947, Burma in 1948 and Israel in 1949. About twenty other states remained on the waiting list for admission. This state of affairs lasted till 1955, when both sides reached an agreement about the further procedure for admitting new members.

Nevertheless, the conflict situation between the superpowers did not lead to a complete blockage of the work of the UN. There were international conflicts where both superpowers cooperated in the Security Council. This was the case with regard to the conflicts in the Iranian Azerbaijan and in Palestine. In both cases the USSR did not use its veto right, although in the former conflict the USSR was a direct party to the conflict, and considerable pressure was exerted on it to withdraw from Azerbaijan (which it finally did).

In the remaining conflicts where the USSR made use of its veto, it turned out that the UN was able to find other means of promoting the resolution of the conflict. In the case of the Greek civil war the Western states used for the first time a mechanism which was subsequently to be used more often: instead of turning to the Security Council when it was clearly blocked by the veto of the USSR, they turned to the General Assembly, whose resolutions cannot be vetoed. In the Greek conflict the General Assembly decided to set up a committee of inquiry for fact-finding, another instrument which was to become characteristic of the UN activities when dealing with international conflicts.

In the case of the Berlin Blockade, which was placed on the agenda of the Security Council at the request of the Western states at the end of September 1948, the USSR was able to prevent the passing of any Council resolutions. Nevertheless the UN became the scene of a number of mediating activities in the following months: for example, the six non-permanent members of the Security Council established – with the consent of the Four Allies – a committee with the task of developing concepts for the solution of the contentious currency issue. At the request of the US UN-delegate Jessup, UN $\rightarrow$ Secretary-General Trygve Lie acted as mediator in establishing negotiation contacts with Soviet Deputy Foreign Minister Vyshinsky, via their respective UN Secretariat senior staff members Sobolev (USSR) and Feller (USA). Both mediating initiatives, however, were unsuccessful.

But, when US President Truman decided on 31 January 1949 to answer an indirect offer of negotiations (which Stalin had made some weeks before in an interview with a US news agency) with a signal of his willingness to have talks, the USA chose deliberately the UN for their secret talks with the USSR. The US UN-delegate Jessup met repeatedly the Soviet UN-delegate Malik, and it was they who negotiated the termination of the Berlin Blockade (cf. *Acheson* 1969, 268f.). In the Berlin conflict, the UN finally passed its test as an instrument for the settlement of disputes, in spite of the fact that the Security Council was at that time blocked by the Soviet veto.

The most important test the United Nations had to pass in its first decade came during the Korean War. It had to react to the military aggression of North Korea against South Korea. In the first phase of the conflict the Security Council was also able to take measures against the aggressor, since the USSR did not take part in the sessions of the Council from January to August 1950 (in protest against the refusal of the Council majority to admit the People's Republic of China to the UN in the place of the Republic of China [Taiwan]). In the absence of the USSR, the Council condemned North Korea as the aggressor and called upon the UN member states in a resolution of 27 June 1950 to supply South Korea with the necessary means to repel the attack and to restore international peace and security in this area (UN Doc. S/RES/83 (1950) of 27 June 1970). Subsequently fifteen states decided to dispatch national troop contingents for the military support of South Korea. A further resolution recommended placing all troops under a United Nations command and flag, with a US supreme command. After China joined North Korea, the conflict developed more and more into a large-scale war. In this situation some UN members warned the UN to make

use of the newly-created instrument of the General Assembly, the "Uniting for Peace" resolution ($\rightarrow$ Uniting for Peace Resolution), which the General Assembly had passed after the return of the USSR to the Security Council in August 1950, when the Soviet Union blocked all resolutions concerning the Korean War. In the Uniting for Peace Resolution of 3 November 1950 (UN Doc. A/RES/377 (V)) the General Assembly claimed the right to convene within twenty-four hours an emergency session of the General Assembly in cases of clear breaches of peace or situations where peace is in imminent danger, if the Security Council remains passive and fails to act, and to make recommendations for collective measures, including the use of armed forces. The critics of this resolution saw in this makeshift procedure a considerable risk of conflict escalation, in particular in the case of the Korean Conflict.

However, the great powers were not very interested in settling the dispute with the help of the UN: the truce negotiations which led in 1953 to the end of the war were held only between the parties to the conflict, without the participation of the UN.

The Korean War was a decisive event in the history of the UN: it was the first time that a multinational armed force came to help a state which had been attacked by an aggressor on the grounds of an explicit mandate of the Security Council, which is in fact one of the main tasks of the UN as system of $\rightarrow$ collective security. But in its further history the UN did not often use this possibility, which is provided by Chapter VII of the Charter – with the notable exceptions of the Congo Conflict 1960/1961, and in the Gulf War 1990/1991. This approach is seen to entail great risks, as had been proven by the Korean Conflict: this was the first conflict where there was the possibility that both superpowers could clash on the battlefield. This risk of superpower confrontation, which the right of the veto of the permanent members would normally prevent, could only develop in that case because of the temporary withdrawal of the USSR from the Security Council in 1950, and because the General Assembly then assumed the political initiative, through its recommendations based on the Uniting for Peace Resolution.

Although the balance sheet of the UN in → peacekeeping was quite mixed in its first decade, it did succeed in establishing a breakthrough in the field of → human rights with the adoption of the "Universal Declaration of Human Rights" (UN Doc. A/RES/217 (III), 10 December 1948) (→ Human Rights, Universal Declaration of), which underlines the universal character and validity of all human rights, and enumerates all important human rights. Although the Universal Declaration as a mere recommendation of the General Assembly in the form of a "declaration" does not have any legally binding force, it turned out to be of decisive influence on the human rights debate in many states in the following decades. Parallel to the work on the Universal Declaration, the Commission on Human Rights of ECOSOC began its work in 1946, which since then examined the human rights situation in the UN Member states by means of state reports, and by deciding to assign special rapporteurs to report on the human rights situations at issue. Additionally, the Commission examined – in a non-public procedure - the complaints of individuals and non-governmental organizations about systematic violations of human rights, with the help of its Subcommission on the Promotion and Protection of Human Rights (formerly the Subcommission on Prevention of Discrimination and Protection of Minorities). (→ Human Rights, Protection of) (In 2006 the Commission on Human Rights was replaced through Resolution 60/251 of the General Assembly by the → Human Rights Council, subsidiary organ of the General Assembly)

Furthermore, the UN created a system of subsidiary organs and programmes respectively (→ Principal Organs, Subsidiary Organs, Treaty Bodies) for social and humanitarian purposes, such as the United Nations Children's Fund (→ UNICEF) in 1946, the United Nations High Commissioner for Refugees (→ UNHCR) in 1949 and, in the same year, the Expanded Programme of Technical Assistance for Economic Development of Underdeveloped Countries (EPTA), which was later merged in 1966 with the Special Fund founded in 1959, the United Nations Development Programme (→ UNDP). Already at this early stage the newly-founded group of subsidiary organs suffered from a scarcity of financial funds, caused by the lack of willingness of the Western industrial states to channel their Official Development Assistance through multilateral organizations within the framework of the United Nations (→ Development Cooperation of the UN System).

If one takes the difficult situation of the UN at the outset into account, particularly that arising from the East-West confrontation, it must be acknowledged that the UN has not only experienced some failures in its first decade, but has also been successful in some instances, above all in peacekeeping and in the protection of human rights, while achieving much less in the economic and social areas.

II. The United Nations 1955-1970:
New Majorities, New Possibilities,
New Challenges

In 1955 the aforementioned agreement between the USA and the USSR on the admission of candidates for membership led to an increase in membership from hitherto 60 members to 76. The phase of → decolonization which now commenced led in the next decades to a rapid further increase of membership. In 1960 the UN had 100 members, in 1965 118, in 1970 127. Also the composition of the membership with regard to the geographic regions changed profoundly. From the 127 member states in 1970, 42 came from Africa, 29 from Asia, 3 from Oceania, 26 from America and 27 from Europe. This far-reaching change in the membership structure had consequences for the decision-making processes in the UN, which resulted in amendments to

233

the Charter increasing the number of non-permanent members in the Security Council – from 6 to 10 – and the number of members in ECOSOC – first from 18 to 27, then later on from 27 to the present 54. But, above all, the atmosphere in the debates of the General Assembly changed significantly: the topics of decolonization and international economic order (→ International Economic Relations and New International Economic Order (NIEO)) gained more weight in the discussions.

In fact the UN deserves praise for its achievements, in so far as its institutions have accompanied and promoted the most difficult process of decolonization. Thus the member states from the Third World used their increasing percentage of votes in the General Assembly to push through the foundation of further UN institutions for multilateral development assistance, and that of the United Nations Conference on Trade and Development (→ UNCTAD). From the latter they expected an improvement of their situation in world trade, as they saw only small chances for negotiations in the hitherto existing UN organizations in this field – the World Bank (→ World Bank, World Bank Group) and the International Monetary Fund (→ IMF) – because of the large predominance of Western votes in these institutions, the votes being distributed proportionately according to the respective capital contribution. In this field the conflict lines for the coming decades were clearly visible on the horizon.

In the area of peacekeeping this period of time was marked by three major international crises, in two of which the UN was able to act as successful mediator (in the Suez conflict and in the Cuba crisis), while it took on too much in the third case (in the Congo conflict).

The most important test for the future of the UN proved to be the Suez conflict in 1956. The UN succeeded in remaining capable of acting although two permanent members of the Security Council – the UK and France – were direct parties to the conflict. The veto blockade of both states in the Council was

overcome because the USA exerted considerable pressure on both to agree to a mediated settlement and – even more – because the USA and the USSR agreed to the "detour" to convene an emergency session of the General Assembly on the basis of the Uniting for Peace Resolution. The General Assembly gave UN Secretary-General Hammarskjöld the authority to implement the proposal of the Canadian UN delegate Lester Pearson: namely to set up a lightly armed UN force with the task of monitoring the truce negotiated shortly before. In contrast to the hitherto established peace-observing missions this was the first UN peacekeeping force (→ Peacekeeping Forces). This decision of the General Assembly constituted a further (informal) development of the Charter, whereby such UN troops which would not implement military sanctions according to Chapter VII, but should merely monitor a truce with the consent of the conflict parties, were not provided for. Today the UN peacekeeping forces are doubtless the most important instrument of the UN, even though the world community often expects too much from them.

The mission of the UN peacekeeping forces in the Congo from 1960 to 1963 revealed for the first time the limits for the use of peacekeeping forces, the problems which they may encounter when they depart from the strict practice of monitoring a truce, but intervene directly in a conflict with military means. This is particularly the case if the situation is an internal (domestic) conflict, as the UN may then risk losing its reputation as a neutral force, and subsequently its position as mediator between the conflict parties.

One of the most important achievements the UN was able to accomplish was in the Cuban crisis, the most dangerous crisis in world politics until then, since it implied the risk of a nuclear war between the USA and the USSR. At the height of the confrontation, when the Soviet ships were on the way to Cuba and US President Kennedy had defined a quarantine zone around Cuba, which the Soviet ships were forbidden to enter, UN Secretary-General U Thant was able to stop the escalation mechanism by two identical letters to Khrushchev and Kennedy, which he wrote on 24 October 1962, and in which he asked them for a limited standstill and further letters of 25 October, in which he asked them again to avoid further confrontations. In his answering letter Khrushchev agreed with U Thant with regard to the view of the risks of the situation and told him that he had ordered the Soviet ships to stay outside the quarantine zone, this measure being however only temporary. President Kennedy assured U Thant in his reply that the US ships would try to avoid any confrontation with the ships of the USSR, as long as the Soviet ships remained outside the quarantine zone. But he insisted on immediate negotiations about the withdrawal of the Soviet missiles from Cuba. With these two letters from Khrushchev and Kennedy, the escalation was stopped, and time was gained for negotiations. Subsequently, a direct exchange of letters between Kennedy and Khrushchev between the 26th and the 28th of October 1962 led to an agreement to settle the conflict. On the 29th of October the US government told the press and the public that the US had come to an agreement with the USSR on the settlement of the missile crisis and that the US would cease its quarantine on 30 October (cf. *U Thant* 1978, 460ff.; *U.S. Department of State* 1966, 437).

In the management of the Cuban crisis the United Nations played a decisive role. The initiative of U Thant helped to avoid direct confrontation, gave the two conflict parties the necessary time to look for other solutions and allowed them to leave their former political positions without loss of face, in order to come to an agreement on the settlement of the conflict.

In the field of human rights, the UN extended its protective system. In 1966 the UN passed the International Covenants on Civil and Political Rights and on Economic, Social and Cultural Rights (→ Human Rights Conventions,

CCPR; → Human Rights Conventions, CESCR) which were legally binding for all signatories and entered into force in 1976. In addition to these basic human rights conventions, the UN passed in the following decades a large number of conventions and resolutions for the protection of specific groups of persons and of specific human rights, creating treaty bodies to monitor the implementation of the conventions and to receive complaints about violations of human rights (→ Human Rights Conventions and their Measures of Implementation). Thus a differentiated system for the protection of human rights was created which has its basis in collecting information, above all from → NGOs, about violations of human rights and in conducting hearings – partly non-public, partly public hearings – with states about the above-mentioned human rights complaints. This system proved to be effective for an international procedure with sovereign states as actors (cf. *Tomuschat* 1988).

In this phase of deep-rooted change in world politics through decolonization, the UN proved to be flexible, and able to exert some pressure. It integrated a large number of new members and created new institutions for the solution of the economic and social problems, established a set of instruments for the protection of human rights and made decisive contributions to the settlement of severe international crises (e.g. Suez, Cuba).To sum up, the United Nations passed its tests in this period.

III. The United Nations 1971-1986: Disappointed Hopes of the Third World and Crises in Peacekeeping and in Financing the Organization

Within the United Nations the seventies were the decade of great hopes for the Third World states. These states felt in a strong position, particularly after the People's Republic of China had replaced the Republic of China (Taiwan) in October 1971 upon the decision of the General Assembly (UN Doc. A/RES/2758 (XXVI)) to restore "all its rights to the People's Republic of China and to recognize the representatives of its Government as the only legitimate representatives of China in the UN", since the new Chinese member state presented itself in the UN, in its position as a permanent member of the Security Council, also as a spokesman for the Third World.

In this period of time the work of the UN focused on the attempts of the Third World to reform the international economic order. Relying on their voting power of about hundred member states, the Third World states tried to effect a far-reaching structural change of the international economic order through decisions of the General Assembly and of UNCTAD conferences. Thus a special session of the General Assembly in 1974 adopted by consensus a "Declaration on the Establishment of a New International Economic Order" (UN Doc. A/RES/3201 (S-VI), 1 May 1974). It was supplemented by a "Charter of Economic Rights and Duties of States" (UN Doc. A/RES/3281 (XXIX), 12 December 1974), which was adopted as a resolution by the General Assembly (→ Charter of the Economic Rights and Duties).

The main items of the New International Economic Order were fair price relations for the Third World, the gradual abolition of tariffs and non-tariff trade barriers in order to make the access of the Third World states to the markets of the Western industrial countries easier, as well as an increase in the official development assistance of the whole international community. As the documents on the reform of the world economy had been adopted by consensus of all member states – including the industrialized countries of the West –, the Third World states were optimistic that they would succeed in implementing the reform steps without delay. But in the subsequent conferences of UNCTAD and in the negotiations in the World Bank, the International Monetary Fund and in the General Agreement on Tariffs and Trades (GATT) (→ WTO/GATT), the Third World states did not

succeed in achieving substantial structural changes to the world trade system. This was due to the tough resistance of the Western industrialized states, which were diplomatically flexible, but stubborn in terms of material concessions towards the Third World states. The 1983 UNCTAD conference in Belgrade signaled – in the opinion of many conference observers – the failure of the attempt of the Third World to establish a New International Economic Order, a failure with devastating consequences for the living conditions of the majority of people in most states of the Third World. With this failure the United Nations failed – and this is still true today – in an important dimension of its work, the reform of the international economic order.

Also in the area of peacekeeping the UN found itself in the seventies and eighties in a severe crisis. It maintained its presence in the Near East and on Cyprus with a number of peacekeeping missions, but in both regions it was not able to prevent renewed fighting. Furthermore, it failed during this period to make any helpful contributions either to the settlement of newly arising conflicts in Nicaragua, Western Sahara, Cambodia and Afghanistan, or to the intensifying war between Iran and Iraq. The main problem for UN peacekeeping lay in the fact that the parties to the conflicts as well as the great powers paid little attention to the recommendations and suggested solutions from the UN. Thus the UN Secretary-General spoke in his annual report to the 38th General Assembly in 1983 of a process of "erosion of multilateralism and internationalism". He complained about the tendency of the great powers to interfere in regional conflicts by supplying arms: "On some occasions this process has gone so far that regional conflicts have been perceived as being wars by proxy among more powerful nations. In situations of this kind, the deliberative organs of the United Nations tend to be bypassed or excluded or, worse yet, to be used solely as a forum for polemical exchanges." (UN Doc. A/38/1, 12 September 1983, 1)

This crisis in UN peacekeeping grew into a general crisis of the United Nations, as a result of the refusal of the USA during the presidency of President Reagan to pay its assessed contributions to the UN since the mid-eighties ($\to$ UN Policy, USA). The refusal of the USA was motivated by its annoyance over voting defeats in the General Assembly and over Security Council resolutions, where the USA saw itself in a position of being forced to use its veto to prevent sanctions against South Africa and Southern Rhodesia, as well as outspoken criticism in Council resolutions concerning the policy of Israel towards its neighboring states and the Palestine people. On top of that irritation there were the criticisms from politicians in the USA of the way the administrative apparatus of the UN was working inefficiently and wasting money. In 1983 the USA announced its withdrawal from UNESCO, to come into effect at the end of 1984, referring to the lack of reforms in its official State Department letter of December 1984 confirming the withdrawal (reprinted in: US Department of State Bulletin, February 1985). In December 1984 the United Kingdom followed the example of the USA, by declaring its withdrawal from UNESCO for the end of 1985. (Both countries later rejoined UNESCO, the UK in 1997, the USA in 2003.)

More grave than the consequences of the US withdrawal from UNESCO were the consequences of its refusal to pay its assessed contributions in full and on time which it was obliged to pay according to the UN Charter ($\to$ Budget). In reaction to growing criticism in the US Congress concerning the principle of equal votes, which does not take into account the weight of the respective contribution of the member states to the UN budget, in the organs of the UN, the Congress passed a law, the so-called Kassebaum Amendment, which prescribed a five percent reduction of the US contribution to the regular UN budget, until the UN agreed to introduce a weighted voting system. This unilateral reduction of its contribution led quickly to arrears of the USA of several hundred million dollars. These US arrears were accompanied and aggravated by payment arrears of the USSR and many other East European states, as well as of many small states ($\to$ Financial Crises). In order to save the solvency of the United Nations the majority of UN member states agreed at the end of 1986 in the General Assembly to the following compromise with the USA (UN Doc. A/RES/41/213, 19 December 1986): the principle of equal voting was preserved also in budgetary matters – in principle, but *de facto* the UN introduced a right of veto of the large payers, as the abovementioned resolution provides that the decisions on the budget in the competent committees ($\to$ Committees, System of) are to be taken by consensus. Thereby at least the absolute bankruptcy of the UN was avoided.

In this phase of its history the United Nations had been confronted with failures and symptoms of crises in many of its fields of work, which shattered the existential basis of the world organization and made it quite plain which essential preconditions have to be fulfilled by the states of the world if the UN shall keep its efficiency and its effectiveness. The UN can only help to settle international conflicts and to solve economic and social problems if all parties involved do agree to it and are willing to look for a consensus within the frame work of the UN.

*IV. The United Nations 1987-1999:
New Chances, But also New
Problems*

*1. The Rapprochement of the USA and
the USSR towards the UN*

Until the end of the eighties the UN did not have many possibilities – in particular in peacekeeping and the settlement of disputes, since the decisive organ, the Security Council, was still much restricted in its work by the lack of co-operation of the two superpowers USA and USSR. Certainly a limited form of cooperation between the two had developed after the Cuba crisis in the phase of détente policy, in particular in the fields of disarmament and European détente – the CSCE process, but this cooperation was nevertheless often interrupted by crises. Thus the Security Council was not able to act effectively in the Afghanistan conflict nor in the Gulf War between Iran and Iraq, because, in both conflicts, both superpowers were to some extent involved: in the Afghanistan conflict the USSR as aggressor and the USA as arms supplier for the Afghan rebel groups, in the Iran-Iraq war both powers were arms suppliers.

Only when a radical change in the UN policy of the USSR took place in 1987 within the context of Gorbachev's new concept of foreign policy, which was answered – after some hesitation – by a gradual rapprochement of the USA towards the UN, the United Nations faced a new, more positive situation leading to a profound change of the working basis for the UN.

The change of course of the USSR was documented first in a Pravda article of 17 September 1987 written by Gorbachev with the title "Reality and Safeguards for a Secure World – Proposals for a More Efficient UN System". Gorbachev suggested the upgrading of the role of the UN Security Council by holding sessions of the Security Council on the level of the foreign ministers. He also suggested that the five permanent members should take over a guarantee role for peace and security in their respective regions. Furthermore, he demanded the expansion of the role of the UN peacekeeping forces in stabilizing peace, and in preventing international conflicts. Gorbachev expressed the new UN policy of the USSR most explicitly in his speech at the UN General Assembly on 7 December 1988. He suggested monitoring the truce in Afghanistan through UN peacekeeping forces, and that a UN Afghanistan conference be convened. He pleaded for strengthening the UN, and underlined the new chances lying ahead for the United Nations in all fields of work within its scope of com-

petence: international problems concerning military politics, world economy, science and technology, ecology and → humanitarian assistance (cf. UN Doc. A/43/PV.72, 8 December 1988). Moreover the UN diplomats of the USSR asserted the willingness to pay the arrears of the USSR to the regular UN budget and the peacekeeping budget.

After initial reluctance the US government gave a cautiously positive answer to the Soviet offer for cooperation in the UN. The first sign for this new cooperation within the UN was the adoption of Security Council resolution 598 in July 1987 which called on Iraq and Iran to obey a cease fire immediately, to end all military activities and to withdraw their troops to the internationally recognized borders. The next steps of superpower cooperation were the signing of the Afghanistan agreement in Geneva in April 1988, and the conclusion of the truce agreement between Iran and Iraq. In both cases it was decided to make use of UN → observers and UN peacekeeping forces respectively. Furthermore, the UN diplomats of the USA and of the USSR developed common initiatives for the settlement of the conflicts in Angola, Namibia, Cambodia and Western Sahara.

Nevertheless US President Reagan remained reserved towards the concept of cooperation with the USSR in the UN. He reacted rather coolly to Gorbachev's offer for cooperation which he made in his speech at the General Assembly on 7 December 1988. In a speech he gave on the same day in Washington President Reagan underlined his cautiousness: "We [Gorbachev and Reagan, H.V.] ... reviewed progress in arms control, resolution of regional conflicts, and our bilateral relationship ... But we also recognized that fundamental differences between our countries remain in many areas ... [W]e have proved with our policy of peace through strength that when we are strong, peace and freedom will prevail." (Daily Telegraph, December 8, 1988)

The more profound change, of course, in the US foreign policy with regard to the UN took place with the change of US presidency from Reagan to Bush. The fact that Bush took a more positive view of the UN found its expression in his speech at the General Assembly in September 1989: "The United Nations can do great things. No, the United Nations is not perfect ... But it is a vital forum where the nations of the world try to replace conflict with consensus and it must remain a forum of peace." (UN Doc. A/44/PV.4, 25 September 1989; cf. also: U.S. Department of State 1990, 11f.) He stated that the UN was moving closer to that ideal and it would have the support of the USA in this striving.

But the promising announcements of President Bush were not followed by deeds, neither in his term of office nor in that of his successor Clinton. Both presidents proved to be either incapable of or unwilling to bring the US Congress to a change in its policy of payment refusal. Thus the USA pays until today its assessed contributions only in part and with considerable delay, and refuses to pay some of its arrears: as of 30 November 2001 the arrears of the USA for the regular UN budget amounted to 265 million US dollars; the arrears for the peacekeeping budget amounted to 790 million US dollars; the US debts in the two budget categories amount to 75% and 3%, respectively, of the total amount owed to the United Nations by the member states (Source: statistical data compiled by the Global Policy Forum on the basis of UN statistical data).

Also with regard to UN peacekeeping, the US government backed partly off from its former position of positive involvement. One reason was that the US Congress and the American public reacted with disappointment at the course of the peacekeeping missions in Somalia and Yugoslavia, a disappointment which was further intensified by a polemical media campaign by the Republican Party in the USA.

This renewed accent on unilateralism and backing off from multilateralism found its most significant expression in a secret document of the Clinton admin-

istration on foreign policy, the so-called "Presidential Decision Directive 25" (PDD 25) establishing "U.S. Policy on Reforming Multilateral Peace Operations", signed by Clinton on 3 May, 1994. The administration released two days later an unclassified summarizing text on PDD 25, after the press had written about PDD 25. In PDD 25 the Clinton administration underlines the priority of national security policy over multilateral peace operations: "When our interests dictate, the U.S. must be willing and able to fight and win wars, unilaterally whenever necessary ... UN peace operations cannot substitute for this requirement. Circumstances will arise, however, when multilateral action best serves U.S. interests in preserving or restoring peace." (Key Elements of PDD 25, published in: *U.S. Department of State* 1994)

The attitude of the USA in the Kosovo conflict in 1999 showed again that the USA tends often to push through its own concept of foreign policy instead of cooperating with Russia and China in the Security Council, because this would have meant in this case most probably some changes in the US concept of an air strike. This stubborn attitude led to unnecessary tensions between Russia and the USA which were neither very favorable towards the settlement of the crisis, nor very supportive of the international system as a whole, as the situation implied a considerable risk of escalation.

In such conflict situations, where military interventions are at stake, resolutions of the Security Council are indispensable just because they require the agreement of all five Permanent Members of the Council. Military Interventions can only make sense in the long run if they are based on a solid consensus of the great powers as they require a broad moral legitimization and a clear legal basis in international law.

Not only the US withdrawal to more unilateralism, but also exhaustion and failures brought the UN peacekeepers to a point where they held back from exaggerated great expectations and tried to reduce their workload from the maximum of the desirable to the doable. The first success stories in peacekeeping and in the dispute settlement at the beginning of the nineties had led to great expectations in the world public. The constructive cooperation of the great powers since 1988 made it possible for the UN to make its contribution to solving a number of international conflicts or at least to approaching a peaceful solution to some extent in, for example, South Africa, Namibia, Angola, Cambodia, and Nicaragua. But the peacekeeping missions in these conflict areas were much more ambitious, complex and costly than other missions before, as the mandates provided not only the monitoring of truce agreements, but also the use of peacekeeping forces for the protection of humanitarian assistance for civil war refugees, for the safe-guarding of protection zones for ethnic minorities threatened by genocide, and/or the reconstruction of democratic structures, including the preparation of general elections and election monitoring (→ Electoral Assistance) in the conflict areas, as it was the case in Cambodia. At the same time the number of peacekeeping missions increased, yet this was not accompanied by an appropriate willingness of the member states to finance the additional costs, so that the permanent financial crisis of the UN was merely aggravated.

In the mid-1990s, the number peacekeeping forces deployed in UN missions considerably decreased (from about 60.000 in 1995 to about 14.000 in 1998; source: DPKO website www.un.org/Depts/dpko/dpko) and disillusionment set in with regard to the ambitious goals of the missions. The balance sheet for the peacekeeping missions in the nineties made clear – on the one hand – that the UN risked losing a large part of its reputation and peacekeeping potential if it undertook peacekeeping missions in states with civil wars (e.g. Somalia and Bosnia-Herzegovina) without sufficient support and consent, respectively, of the conflict parties, in order to protect measures of humanitarian assistance or to prevent genocide. On the other hand the extent of the violations of human rights seemed to call urgently for their presence in the area – a conflict difficult to solve or resolve.

2. Seeking Solutions for the Global Problems: The World Conferences of the 1990s

Whereas the UN had to face repeated defeats in the seventies and eighties in its striving to relieve the increasing social, economic, ecological and humanitarian problems in many member states – above all in the Third World, because the industrialized countries offered tough resistance against the expensive aid programmes as well as against the demand for a restructuring of the international economic order, the UN tried now – in the nineties – to find solutions to the increasingly urgent global problems by means of well-prepared → world conferences: in 1992 the UN organized the UN Conference on Environment and Development in Rio de Janeiro, in 1993 the World Conference on Human Rights in Vienna, in 1994 the International Conference on Population and Development, in 1995 the World Summit for Social Development in Copenhagen and the Fourth World Conference on Women in Beijing, in 1996 Habitat II, the Second United Nations Conference on Human Settlements, and the World Food Summit in Rome, and in 1998 the United Nations Diplomatic Conference of Plenipotentiaries on the Establishment of an International Criminal Court.

This series of ambitious conferences have notched up successes as well as defeats. A great success of all conferences lies in the large-scale participation of the non-governmental organizations (→ NGOs), in the marked presence of top politicians of the member states at the conferences and in the widespread media coverage (cf. *UNDPI:* The World Conferences, New York 1997). Thereby the global problems discussed at the conferences were made known to the broad public, which became aware of the urgency and global quality of the problems (→ Public Opinion and the UN; → Globalization). But it has to be considered as a failure that the conferences on social issues could not reach politically binding pledges of the solvent states to provide the UN organizations working in this field with additional financial resources. However, one could at least start a negotiating process about how all the states can solve the global problems in a joint action by balancing their respective interests – a partial success. Also, with regard to legally binding agreements, the world conferences could claim only partial success: as a rule the conferences resulted in declarations of intent and programmes of action.

The positive exceptions from the rule were the UN Conference on Environment and Development (UNCED) in Rio de Janeiro 1992, the World Conference on Human Rights in 1993 in Vienna and the Conference on the Establishment of an International Criminal Court in Rome in 1998.

In Rio, UNCED adopted at least two legally-binding framework conventions on climate change and on biological diversity, which need however to be supplemented with precise decisions at further conferences for their implementation (→ Environmental Protection; → Environmental Law, International).

It was a success as well that the human rights conference in Vienna could ward off in its final conference document, the Vienna Declaration and Programme of Action (UN Doc. A/CONF. 157/24 (Part I), Chapter III) the attempt by a number of member states to restrict the principle of universality with regard to human rights and – a further success – that the UN General Assembly created in December 1993 – in reaction to a respective passage in the final declaration of the Vienna conference – the post of a UN High Commissioner for Human Rights with UN Doc. A/RES/48/141, 20 December 1993 (→ Human Rights, United Nations High Commissioner for).

A marked success for human rights was also the adoption of the Rome Stat-

ute of the International Criminal Court at the respective diplomatic conference of plenipotentiaries in 1998 (UN Doc. A/CONF.183/9, 7 July 1989), which provides for the establishment of an International Criminal Court (→ ICC) for the punishment of war crimes, genocide and crimes against humanity. The Rome Statute came into force after the ratification of 60 state parties in 2002 and the International Criminal Court began its work in The Hague.

Apart from these items of success in the fields of international environmental law, and of the protection of human rights, the United Nations had not been able to make significant contributions to the solution of the global problems in this period, because of the continuing disagreement within the UN and lack of willingness of many member states to transfer further elements of their national → sovereignty to an international organization, and to accept reductions of the national GNP in favor of a sustainable growth and a more just distribution of resources.

3. The Reform Debate 1992-1997

The improved capacity to act as well as the increasing global problems since the eighties intensified the continual reform debate (→ Reform of the UN) in the nineties which ran parallel to the debate about the solution of the global problems. This debate about UN reform had its climax between 1992 and 1997.

The starting point and first point of crystallization of this debate was the meeting of heads of government and heads of state respectively of the Security Council members on 31 January 1992. On this occasion the Council gave the Secretary-General the assignment to work out recommendations for the improvement of UN peacekeeping. Boutros-Ghali presented this study, the "Agenda for Peace" (UN Doc. DPI/1247), to the Council in June 1992 (→ Agenda for Peace). The study on peacekeeping was later supplemented by studies of the Secretary-General on disarmament – "New Dimensions of Arms Regulation and Disarmament"

241

(UN Doc. A/C.1/47/7, 27 October 1992) and on development assistance – "Agenda for Development" (UN Doc. A/48/935, 6 May 1994) (→ Agenda for Development). The three studies led to an intense conceptual debate on → preventive diplomacy, peacekeeping and multilateral development assistance (→ Development Cooperation of the UN System), but they did not bring concrete results for the practical everyday work of the UN – probably, because the concepts of the studies were still too abstract and too demanding for the majority of states.

Parallel to this debate on the reform of UN peacekeeping and of the multilateral development assistance, the UN began a debate on far-reaching, structural reforms, above all about the enlargement of the Security Council with new permanent members and about the restructuring of → ECOSOC and a re-appraisal of its tasks.

Initially one could get the impression that the General Assembly would be able to agree on a reform concept for the 50th anniversary of its foundation in October 1995. When this proved not to be the case, many reform supporters hoped that Kofi Annan, who took up his office in 1997, would bring new energy in the reform debate. But in his talks with UN ambassadors behind the scenes he quickly found that key member states, the Permanent Five (the USA, Russia, China, France and the UK) were reluctant with regard to structural reforms of the principal organs, in particular of the Security Council. They were much more interested in management reforms of the UN → Secretariat, whereas the developing countries were eager to have the Security Council reformed.

That is why Annan decided in this situation to confine himself to the doable in the reform: he organized the Secretariat in a new manner by creating four core groups comprising all the departments of the Secretariat, UN funds, programmes and specialized agencies working in the respective main field of UN activity and coordinated by a monthly meeting of the "executive com-

mittees". He started practicing a "team style" leadership with weekly "cabinet" meetings of the most important Secretariat staff people.

While these reform measures made good sense, the job cuts implemented by Boutros-Ghali and Annan tended to erode the positive developments: the massive job reductions caused by the financial crisis of the UN affected the substance of the world organization, working with a very small staff compared with its multitude of tasks, a problem still existing in the UN Secretariat.

If one tries to draw a conclusion from a critical review of UN history for the reform debate, it could be the following. Formal amendments to the Charter as they are suggested for the Security Council and ECOSOC are difficult to realize, and were seldom really necessary in UN history. The UN has time and again found practical solutions under the threshold of Charter revisions in reaction to crisis situations. When the Security Council was blocked by the veto of the great powers, it was decided to transfer the decisions to the General Assembly; when truces in conflict areas had to be safeguarded, UN peacekeeping forces were "invented"; in both cases this was achieved without formal amendments to the Charter.

V. The United Nations in the New Millennium: New Goals, New Concepts, Old Obstacles

1. New Development Initiative

Secretary-General Kofi Annan saw the chance to make use of the beginning of the new millennium for starting an initiative to define the development goals of the United Nations in a more comprehensive way connected with a concrete programme of work. He found the support of a number of UN member states and started preparing a high-level meeting of the General Assembly in September 2000, the "Millennium Summit". In the preparatory phase of the conference Kofi Annan submitted in March 2000 a ground-breaking report titled "We the peoples: The role of the United Nations in the 21st century" (UN

Doc. A/54/2000), in which he presented a comprehensive outline of the global challenges confronting the world community and of the tasks for the United Nations.

He asserted that the United Nations would have to adapt to the challenges of the new era in order to reach the objectives of the UN Charter: peace, prosperity and social justice. He demanded that the UN should serve increasingly as "catalyst for collective action" (ibid., para. 360), in particular to improve the fortunes of developing countries. The management of risks and threats affecting all the world peoples could and should only be handled multilaterally. He concluded his report in setting up a number of concrete development goals for the next fifteen years, among others to halve by 2015 the number of poor people worldwide and the number of people unable to reach or to afford safe drinking water.

The UN Millennium Summit in September 2000 followed in fact Annan's demands and adopted the "United Nations Millennium Declaration" (UN Doc A/RES/55/2, 8 September 2000). The UN member states recognized in the Declaration that developing countries face special difficulties in responding to the globalization challenges and therefore should be helped by the other nations. They affirmed the principle of "shared responsibility" for managing worldwide economic and social development as well as threats to international peace and security. They explicitly affirmed a number of development goals to be reached by the year 2015, the so-called *Millennium Development Goals (MDGs)*. With the Millennium Summit, Annan succeeded in making the situation of developing countries and multilateral development assistance again a priority issue on the global agenda, after the topic had nearly vanished from the public awareness in the 1990s.

The issue was taken up again at the UN Conference on Financing for Development in Monterrey in March 2002 where the developed states re-affirmed their commitments with regard to increasing their official development assistance (ODA) – but only at a rather slow pace of increase – and at the Millennium+5 Summit, the UN World Summit in September 2005, where a first balance sheet was drawn up concerning the implementation of the MDGs, showing progress in some goals, but still deficits with regard to many others (see the final document of the summit with the title "2005 World Summit Outcome", UN Doc. A/RES/60/1, 16 September 2005). But all in all, the UN had managed to draw again the attention of politicians and the world public to this important issue again – concrete measures are not the strength of the UN, it is the states which have to implement their promises in this respect.

In a field closely connected with multilateral development assistance, namely the reform of the international economic order and the international financial system, the United Nations has not been able to achieve very much. In the negotiations of the Doha Round of the World Trade Organization WTO no consensus has so far been achieved with regard to an improved access of the developing countries to the world markets, in particular through the reduction of import barriers of the European Union, the USA and Japan. Also in the IMF and the World Bank the developing countries have still not succeeded in increasing their voting rights through a reform of the existing system depending on the money deposited in both financial institutions.

At least some positive development has taken place in recent years: the Bretton Woods institutions cooperate more closely with the UN institutions working in the field of development cooperation and with the respective NGOs. This readiness for improved cooperation is illustrated by the annual spring meetings of the Bretton Woods institutions with the other UN institutions and the UN member states within the framework of ECOSOC.

2. Progress in Human Rights Protection

In the new millennium the UN managed to effect a few small improvements with regard to human rights protection which might, however, prove important in the long run: the General Assembly approved a staff increase in the Office of the High Commissioner for Human Rights in Geneva; human rights aspects were increasingly integrated into the planning of peacekeeping missions; a human rights advisory service was provided in many countries in their efforts to improve their national human rights protection; and the treaty bodies of the different human rights conventions began a debate on the coordination and reform of the respective reporting and monitoring systems. Moreover the trials at the two International Criminal Tribunals for Yugoslavia and Rwanda began to have a deterrent effect with regard to crimes in civil wars.

In this context the United Nations strengthened human rights protection by affirming at the above-mentioned World Summit 2005 in the final document, the "2005 World Summit Outcome Document" (UN Doc, A/RES/60/1, 16 September 2005), the "responsibility to protect", i.e. the common responsibility of the UN member states to protect the basic human rights of peoples or ethnic groups of people when the host state is not able or not willing to protect them against massive violations of human rights, comprising genocidal actions, war crimes and crimes against humanity. The international community has in these cases the responsibility to "use appropriate diplomatic, humanitarian and other peaceful means" and "collective action, in a timely and decisive manner, through the Security Council, in accordance with the Charter, including Chapter VII, ... should peaceful means be inadequate ..." (ibid., paras. 138-139).

This new principle was welcomed by UN human rights institutions, NGOs and experts of international law, even if the practical implementation through the UN member states remains to be seen.

3. Peacekeeping: Too Many Tasks?

The overstretch of peacekeeping capacities in the first half of the 1990s revealing severe deficits in the planning and implementation process of the peacekeeping missions motivated Secretary-General Kofi Annan, having ample experience in this matter as former head of the respective Secretariat department (DPKO), to assign to a high-level panel the task of sketching a concept for comprehensive reform of UN peacekeeping. After the group chaired by Lakhdar Brahimi had submitted its reform report in 2000, Annan succeeded in rallying sufficient support in the General Assembly to put through a large number of the reform proposals, providing UN peacekeeping with more staff, better and planning procedures and logistic infrastructure and better information about troops and equipment being available for peacekeeping missions in potential troop-contributing countries. This being an important improvement, the improved peacekeeping capacities have in subsequent years been again overstretched again as the UN Security Council has agreed since 2004 to an increasing extent to establish new large-scale peacekeeping missions, so that as of 31 December 2008 more than 110,000 UN personnel (uniformed and civilian personnel) were serving in 16 UN peacekeeping operations (source: DPKO website).

Even if one has to admit that in all these cases the basic human rights of the people in need are at risk and must be protected, critics warn that UN peacekeeping is again overstretching its own resources and that the complex mandates, comprising military, political, administrative and judicial aspects, are too ambitious, endangering often the credibility and prospects for success. The UN cannot and should not stabilize every failing state. This is the task of the respective regional states and their organizations.

4. Slow Progress in Environmental Protection

Also in the new millennium the rhetorical commitment of nations to the protection of the environment could only at a very slow pace be implemented in the form of UN conventions and protocols. The Johannesburg Summit on Sustainable Development 2002 as well as the diverse conferences within the system of the UN Framework Convention on Climate Change and of the Kyoto Protocol in the new millennium revealed that the industrialized countries as well as the developing countries are reluctant to commit themselves to new protection measures, the latter fearing that the introduction of such protection mechanisms would increase their production expenses and do damage to their competitive situation on the world markets. Without doubt the industrialized countries would make progress in this field much easier if they would increase developmental resources granted to the developing countries in connection with the implementation of UN environmental standards. In this field the United Nations has in the new millennium fought continuously for progress, but so far only with moderate success.

5. Structural Reforms Not Necessary?

In the new millennium as in the decade before, the debate about the necessity for and the extent of UN reforms continued, in particular since the last reform attempt in 1997 concerning the Security Council had been without success.

Prepared by the reports of several high-level panels dealing with global security, development assistance and the role of civil society, Secretary-General Kofi Annan submitted in March 2005 – as preparation for the World Summit in September – a report containing a comprehensive concept of UN reform. In the report titled "In larger freedom: towards development security and human rights for all" (UN Doc. A/59/2005, 21 March 2005) he outlined the concept of the United Nations as an institution where the different groups of states would cooperate in the attempt to solves the global problems with regard to development, security, human rights and protection of the environment. He emphasized his conviction that because of the interdependency of the problem fields it would be in the interest of all nations to cooperate even if, at first glance, a problem seemed not to affect a group of states.

With regard to the principal organs of the United Nations he advocated a rationalization and streamlining of the work of the General Assembly, an upgrading of the ECOSOC to a high-level forum for development cooperation, the substitution of the commission on human rights by a new body, the Human Rights Council as subsidiary organ of the General Assembly, and a reform of the composition of the Security Council, presenting two competing models, one with additional permanent and nonpermanent seats and another only with additional non-permanent seats, but of an new category, namely with a renewable four-year term of office.

The subsequent informal consultations of the General Assembly from April to August 2005 revealed that the hope of the Secretary-General that the member states would accept the reform package as such without discussing every detail did not materialize, since the member states did not follow his conviction that the reform concept would give every group enough advantages in compensation for the sacrifices made elsewhere. Particularly the Security Council reform revealed to be the main bone of contention: the member states did not succeed in finding a consensus between three different draft resolutions developed by three groups of states.

Accordingly the World Summit produced rather meager results: no reform of the Security Council, no concrete commitment to the reform of the General Assembly and of ECOSOC, but at least the decision to establish the Human Rights Council and, as a new institution, the Peacebuilding Commission as common advisory organ of the General Assembly and the Security Council.

But it is debatable whether this should be considered as failure of the UN or not. It can be argued that the United Nations does not need such structural reforms concerning the composition of its organs. In the case of the Security Council any enlargement would impair the efficiency of the Council since more members would need more time to reach a consensus. Such a reform might be even considered as superfluous as the informal changes in the working methods of the Council since the mid-1990s have resulted in more transparency towards the member states outside the Council and towards the media and the public and have given troop-contributing countries, experts and NGOs more influence in the deliberations of the Council.

With regard to the Council as well as with regard to the other UN organs and their problems in the different fields of work, the causes lie not so much in the structures of the UN, which are flexible and effective enough, the causes lie more in the disagreement of the member states and in their lack of willingness to implement the necessary political and economic measures in a multilateral framework. Always when the state governments were ready in the past to act in a multilateral framework as global community, the UN was able to fulfill the tasks given it by the Charter in a very effective manner.

Helmut Volger

Lit.: *Acheson, D.:* Present At The Creation. My Years in the State Department, New York 1969; *Finkelstein, L.S. (ed):* Politics in the United Nations System, Durham/London 1988; *Gorbachev, M.:* Speech at the 43rd General Assembly of the United Nations on 7 December 1988, published in: UN Doc. A/43/PV.72 (1988); *Luard, E.:* A History of the United Nations, Vol. 1: 1945-1955, London 1982, Vol. 2: 1955-1965, London 1989; *Malone, D. (ed.):* The UN Security Council: From the Cold War to the 21st Century, Boulder/London 2004; *Roberts, A./Kingsbury, B. (eds.):* United Nations – Divided World. The UN's Roles in International Relations, 2nd rev. and expanded edn., Oxford et al. 1993; *Taylor, P./Groom, A.J.R. (eds):* Global Issues in the United Nations' Framework, Basingstoke 1989; *Taylor, P./Groom, A.J.R. (eds):* The United Nations at the Millennium. The Principal Organs, London/New York 2000; *United Nations - Department of Public Information:* The World Conferences. Developing Priorities for the 21st Century, New York 1997; *United Nations - General Assembly:* We the peoples: the role of the United Nations in the 21st century. Report of the Secretary-General, 27 March 2000, UN Doc. A/54/2000; *United Nations - General Assembly:* United Nations Millennium Declaration, 8 September 2000, UN Doc. A/RES/55/2; *United Nations - General Assembly:* In larger freedom: towards development security and human rights for all. Report of the Secretary-General, 21 March 2005, UN Doc. A/59/2005; *United Nations - General Assembly:* 2005 World Summit Outcome, 16 September 2005, UN Doc. A/RES/60/1; *U.S. Department of State:* American Foreign Policy. Current Documents 1962, Vol. I, Washington, D.C. 1966; *U.S. Department of State:* American Foreign Policy. Current Documents 1989, Publication 9815, Washington, D.C. 1990, 11-15; *U.S. Department of State:* Clinton Administration Policy on Reforming Multilateral Peace Operations (PDD 25), U.S. Department of State Publication No. 10161, released by the Bureau of International Organization Affairs May 1994; *Volger, H.:* Geschichte der Vereinten Nationen, 2nd rev. edn., Munich/Vienna 2008; *Weiss, T.G./Daws, S. (eds.):* The Oxford Handbook on the United Nations, Oxford et al. 2007.

Host State Agreements

Host state agreements deal with questions resulting from the fact that the UN and its → specialized agencies possess no territory of their own, but have established seats in different states. Host state agreements are marked by the contrast that, while organizations will seek for the performance of their tasks as much freedom from local constraints as possible, their host states will seek to limit to the largest extent the effects of the "guest's" presence on their territorial sovereignty. In contrast to diplomatic relations between states, there is no reciprocity. The host state's benefit from the concession of a seat for an organization is seen to be in potential revenues and the gain in reputation.

By the means of very differing host state agreement the organizations are granted those rights, privileges and immunities they require for fulfilling their statutory tasks. Moreover, the rights of the member states (see for example → Permanent Missions) and observers (→ Observer Status) are subject to regulation.

Attempts to codify the general issue of the relationship between host state and the international organization have been without much success. The *Convention on Privileges and Immunities of the United Nations (CPIUN)* of 13 February 1946 (UNTS Vol. 1, No. 4) contains only a very general legal framework for this relationship; moreover it has not yet been ratified by the host state Switzerland. The *Vienna Convention on the Representation of States in Their Relations with International Organizations of a Universal Character* of 14 March 1975 (UN Doc. A/CONF.67/16, reprinted in AJIL 69 (1975), 730) was not ratified by the relevant host states and has not entered into force yet because of an insufficient number of ratifications so far. Therefore the International Law Commission → ILC decided in 1992 not to commence the following project that was supposed to deal with substantial relations between host states and organizations. This was generally considered a victory for the states' claim of → sovereignty, in that after all the nation-states continue to play the dominant role in international relations (*Muller* 1995).

The most important UN host state agreement is the Agreement regarding the Headquarters of the United Nations, between the United Nations and the United States of America of 26 June 1947 (UNTS Vol. 11, No. 147) which determines technical issues. This host state agreement provides for example for the preservation of law and order inside the headquarters, as well as the maintenance of security jointly through organs of the Organization and those of the host state. Furthermore, police protection for the headquarters by the host state is regulated, as well as the transit of UN employees, and the representatives of member states and other organizations, to and from headquarters, supply and management services are described, and the right to operate broadcasting equipment is provided. The host state agreement vests the international organization with a private-law legal personality. In the case of the UN this is as prescribed in Article 104 of the UN Charter: "The Organization shall enjoy in the territory of each of its Members such legal capacity as necessary for the exercise of its functions and the fulfillment of its purposes."

This general provision is made concrete by the above-mentioned general agreement on privileges and immunities as well as by bilateral host state and other agreements. Thereby the UN is in particular empowered to conclude private-law contracts, to acquire, hold and dispose of property, and to be a party to a legal proceeding. The Organization and its property are generally not subject to any legal proceeding, but enjoy immunity. The premises of the UN, the archive and the documents are inviolable and are precluded from search, seizure or any other interference with the sovereignty of the Organization. Additionally, the UN is exempt from taxes.

Beside the UN itself, the permanent employees have privileges and immunities which are enjoyed independent of the respective citizenship. Regarding their official acts they are granted jurisdictional immunity and immunity from other legal proceedings. This immunity can be waived by the organization, if it does not affect its ability to function. Employees enjoy personal inviolability and are entitled to free travel to and from the Organization's headquarters. This provision in particular has repeatedly evoked tensions between the UN and the USA, as the official travel of UN employees who were citizens of socialist states was periodically restricted by the USA. UN employees are exempt from several taxes and other fiscal levies on their wages. Similar privileges and immunities are also granted to experts working on behalf of the organization and to members of delegations that participate in seminars or conferences sponsored by organs of the UN.

The relations between the UN and the host state are subject of a special UN committee, the *Committee on Relations with the Host Country*, consisting of 19 members elected by the General Assembly, that discusses the respective problems, adopts recommendations and reports annually to the General Assembly on unsolved problems – interference in the activities of UN agencies, restrictions on freedom of travel, denial of entry visas for member state officials taking part in UN conferences, parking and health insurance, so for example in the Report of the Committee on Relations with the Host Country 2007 (UN Doc. A/62/26, 1 November 2007) –, noted by the General Assembly annually in a routine resolution – for example in 2007 in UN Doc. A/RES/62/72 of 6 December 2007. The Office of Legal Affairs provides secretariat services to the Committee and deals with legal questions arising out of the Headquarters Agreement with the United States of America and out of the other agreements with host governments.

Hans-Joachim Heintze

Lit.: *Gerster, M.:* Art. 105, in: Simma, B. (ed.): The Charter of the United Nations. A Commentary, 2nd edn., Vol. II, Oxford 2002, 1314-1325; *Hug, D.:* Die Rechtsstellung der in der Schweiz niedergelassenen internationalen Organisationen, Berne 1984; *Muller, A.S.:* International Organizations and their Host States, The Hague 1995; *Reisman, W.M.:* The Arafat Visa Affair: Exceeding the Bounds of Host State Discretion, in: AJIL 1989, 519 ff.; *Seidl-Hohenveldern, I./ Loibl, G.:* Das Recht der internationalen Organisationen einschließlich der supranationalen Gemeinschaften, Vienna 1991; *Shore, J.L.:* The PLO Observer Mission Dispute: An Argument for US Compliance with the UN Headquarters Agreement, Fordham International Law Journal 1989, 751ff.

Internet: On the homepage of the United Nations refer to: www.un.org/News/Press/archives.htm and search for the key-word "host country".

Human Development Reports

1. Background

Since 1990 the United Nations Development Programme (→ UNDP) has published the *Human Development Report* (HDR) each year. The report immediately took its place among the leading → world reports. It does not focus on a specific area (such as "agriculture" or "trade"), but considers a different overarching theme each year.

The Human Development Report places the emphasis on man or "human development". It sees itself as complementing or contrasting with other world reports that deal primarily with economic aspects of development. The first few editions in particular were therefore seen as a criticism of the World Development Reports published by the World Bank (→ World Bank/World Bank Group) and its growth-oriented policy. Against this background, various new indices introduced by the Human Development Report endeavour to take account of the "human development" paradigm.

As UNDP did not attract any serious attention in Germany and other industrialized countries until the Human Development Report appeared, the organization's image is largely determined by the report, which should not, however, be equated with UNDP and its policy; in fact, it has been sharply criticized by UNDP's own Executive Board on various occasions.

The Human Development Report appears in more than a dozen languages (including German) and is launched in more than 100 countries annually. (February 2007). The teams were led by Mahbub ul Haq, – its main initiator, and Inge Kaul from 1990 through 1994; by Mahbub ul Haq and Sakiko Fukuda-Parr in 1995, by Richard Jolly and Sakiko Fukuda-Parr from 1996 through 2000, and by Sakiko Fukuda-Parr with Nancy Birdsall from 2001 through 2003. In 2004, after 10 years as the Lead Author Sakiko Fukuda-Parr was followed by Kevin Watkins, current Director of the Human Development Report Office and Lead Author of the HDR. An independent team of advisers and background papers commissioned for the HDR also play an important part in the preparation of the various reports.

As a complement to the Human Development Report, country-related reports, known as *National Human Development Reports* (NHDRs), were drawn up in the first half of the 1990s. These national reports are edited national teams. Since 1996 efforts in this respect have been stepped up significantly, with the result that more than 540 national and sub-national HDRs have been produced so far by 135 countries, in addition to 31 regional reports. (February 2007) Besides the global Human Development Reports and the NHDRs, four regional reports, each covering a certain group of countries, have appeared.

2. Conception and Criticism of the HDR

Mahbub ul Haq describes the orientation of the HDR as follows: "The basic purpose of development is to enlarge people's choices. In principle, these choices can be infinite and can change over time. People often value achievements that do not show up at all, or not immediately, in income or growth figures: greater access to knowledge, better nutrition and health services, more secure livelihoods, security against crime and physical violence, satisfying leisure hours, political and cultural freedoms and sense of participation in community activities. The objective of development is to create an enabling environment for people to enjoy long, healthy and creative lives." (*Mahbub ul Haq*, in: http://hdr.undp.org/hd/)

According to this approach a relatively simple definition explains the idea underlying the concept of "human development": "Human development is a process of enlarging people's choices.

Enlarging people's choices is achieved by expanding human capabilities and functionings." (HDR 1998, 17)

At all levels of development, the definition continues, the three essential capabilities for "human development" are: (1) a long and healthy life, (2) education and (3) access to the resources needed for a decent standard of living; if these basic capabilities are not achieved, many choices are simply not available and many opportunities remain inaccessible; such other dimensions and global concerns as "sustainability", "justice" and "human rights" are similarly very important. The concept also seeks to cover certain aspects that are difficult to quantify, such as "self-respect", "empowerment" and "a sense of belonging to a community", since they play a major role in people's creativity and productivity.

The concept of "human development" is linked to two important contentions: firstly, although economic growth is an important means of expanding choices and people's well-being, it is not enough on its own and must not be seen as an end in itself, but has an instrumental function; secondly, "human development" as a goal is not automatically achieved in the classical industrialized countries when incomes reach a high level. The question that is always of crucial importance is whether resources are being appropriately used for "human development".

Since its first edition the Human Development Report has therefore included a set of indicators and indices which are intended as a corrective to the conventional growth indicator GNP or GDP (gross national product or gross domestic product) in that they provide information on the state of "human development". The most important new yardstick formed by the Human Development Report has been the *Human Development Index* (HDI) (see below). Although the HDI has made a decisive contribution to the dissemination and appearance of the report, it often comes in for some severe criticism.

While the first Human Development Report in 1990 placed the emphasis on the basic idea of "human development" and on the depiction and interpretation of the HDI, subsequent reports linked the concept to a given focal area. Some of the reports referred to the → *world conferences* that took place in the 1990s and in the new millennium (thus the 1994 HDR referred to the World Summit for Social Development held in Copenhagen in 1995, the 1995 HDR to the World Conference on Women held in Beijing in 1995, the 2003 HDR corresponded to the United Nations Millennium Declaration of 2000).

Past reports have considered the following issues:

1990: Concept and Measurement of Human Development
1991: Financing Human Development
1992: Global Dimensions of Human Development
1993: People's Participation
1994: New Dimensions of Human Security
1995: Gender and Human Development
1996: Economic Growth and Human Development
1997: Human Development to Eradicate Poverty
1998: Consumption for Human Development
1999: Globalization with a Human Face
2000: Human Rights and Human Development
2001: Making New Technologies Work for Human Development
2002: Deepening Democracy in a Fragmented World
2003: Millennium Development Goals: A Compact Among Nations to End Human Poverty
2004: Cultural Liberty in Today's Diverse World
2005: International cooperation at a crossroads: Aid, trade and security in an unequal world
2006: Beyond scarcity: Power, poverty and the global water crisis
2007/2008: Fighting climate change: Human solidarity in a divided world

Various statements and recommendations made in the reports have been the focus of considerable interest in the international debate on development. The theses that have attracted attention, some of which were being discussed in the context of development policy even before the first Human Development Report was published, include the following:

- economic growth is not an end in itself but a means of achieving "human development" (HDR 1990);
- global disparities are enormous: the richest fifth of the population now receives 150 times the income of the poorest fifth;
- market access restrictions (including the prevention of the migration of labour) and unequal partnerships cost the developing countries some US$ 500bn (HDR 1992);
- at least 20% of official development aid should be spent on "human priorities" (health, primary education, environmental protection and limiting population growth); the proportion calculated by the Human Development Report, on the other hand, is only 6.5% (HDR 1993);
- the 1997 Human Development Report assumed that absolute poverty (which affects some 1.3 billion people) can be eradicated in the first and second decades of the 21st century given the necessary political will;
- a "20:20 compact" would ensure minimum standards in "human development"; this would require industrialized countries to make 20% of their development aid budgets and developing countries 20% of their national budgets available for basic social services (HDR 1994);
- globalization, even if not a new phenomenon, is due to increasingly competitive markets, outpacing the governance of markets and the repercussions on people can be severe (HDR 1999);
- cultural freedoms, policies more cognizant of group differences, multiculturalism and inclusion without coercion to assimilate are the basis of sus-

tainable development. Culture is not a determent to political and economic progress, but a contingent constraint. (HDR 2004)

- extreme inequality among countries and within countries are one of the main barriers to human development and are a powerful brake on progress towards the MDGs. (HDR 2005);

During the political and academic debate many of the statements referred to above and many of the figures shown in Human Development Reports have been criticized, described as unbalanced or even, in some cases, classified as untrustworthy. *Wilson* (2006) criticizes the HDR of 2000 and 2002 (both on democracy, human rights and good governance) for their "relentless inexplicitness" and their claming for "universal (and therefore self-justified) values." The point of the debate on economic growth as an "end" or a "means", for example, has often been disputed. *Ravallion* (1997) argues that the main problem for the world's poor is not that there is too little high-quality growth, as the Human Development Report would have it, but too little growth of a perfectly normal quality. Where the figures are concerned, various factors have resulted in the Human Development Report often being attacked or rejected. Thus the sum of 500 billion US dollars lost to the developing countries is frequently dismissed as an incredible figure (see, for example, *Boer/Koekkoek* 1993); some governments also claim that the Human Development Report underestimates the proportion of development aid spent on "human development". In addition, the whole conceptual and theoretical foundation of the concept of "human development" or certain central aspects of it are questioned (→ Development Concepts, Development Research) (see *Tandon* 1996). *Nuscheler* (1998), for example, accused the concept of claiming originality as a development theory when it was no more than a *mixtum compositum* of set pieces from the discourse on development policy.

3. The HDI and Other Indices

Each year the Human Development Report presents extensive statistical material on some 175 countries (developing and industrialized), providing information on the level of "human development" that has been achieved. These data pivot on the Human Development Index, which is often considered to be the decisive innovation generated by the Human Development Report. The report emphasizes that the HDI too is unable to reflect "human development" in its entirety, because the underlying concept is far more broadly based, and that many important dimensions of "human development" are ultimately non-quantifiable ("sustainability", for instance) or methodologically incompatible and cannot therefore be included in the HDI. Therefore the index could be considered as an approach to establish a method of measurement of the complex and – in its entirety unmeasurable – concept of "human development".

The HDI seeks to represent a country's overall achievements in three basic *dimensions* of "human development" by initially applying one *indicator* in each case:

- life expectancy at birth;
- educational attainment on the basis of a weighted combination of the adult literacy rate and combined primary, secondary and tertiary enrolment;
- satisfaction of basic needs/income measured by reference to real GDP based on purchasing power parity (PPP$) within fixed margins.

These three indicators are combined to form the HDI, which theoretically produces a value between 0 and 1. As an aid to interpretation the Human Development Report uses a system of three main categories: countries with a high (> 0.800), medium (0.500-0.799) and low (< 0.500) level of "human development".

In the 2006 HDR the first three of a total of 177 places in the international ranking were taken by Norway (HDI: 0,965), Iceland (0,960) and Australia (0,957), the last three places by Mali

251

(0,338), Sierra Leone (0,335) and Niger (0,311). The last 22 places were completely occupied by sub-Saharan African states.

A comparison of countries with the aid of HDI tables and income-related overviews reveals a number of disparities. Such oil-rich countries as Kuwait, the United Arab Emirates and Qatar, for example, rank very low in the HDI measurement, while the former socialist countries are ranked higher because of relatively high life expectancy and good educational attainment by international standards.

Other indices used by the Human Development Report are a *Human Poverty Index* (HPI), which is designed differently for poverty in developing countries (HPI-1) and poverty in industrialized countries (HPI-2), a *Gender-related Development Index* (GDI) and a *Gender Empowerment Measure* (GEM). A *Human Freedom Index* (HFI) respectively a Political Freedom Index (PFI) used in the 1991 and 1992 Human Development Reports has since been abandoned. (For a comparison of HDI, GDI, HPI-1 and HPI-2 see Table 1, p. 254)

Views on the HDI and the other indices in the development debate differ. The new approach has often been received very positively and welcomed; the index is, moreover, frequently used in statistics alongside GNP or GDP. In some areas of the academic debate, however, the HDI is criticized and even completely rejected by some; this is especially true of economists and statisticians (see *Noorbakhsh* 1998 and *Boer/ Koekkoek* 1993). Various commentators also refer to older indices (such as the *Physical Quality of Life Index*, or PQLI, dating back to 1977) which they claim were once similarly informative.

Among the criticisms voiced in the past is that the HDI unjustifiably attaches the same importance to the three dimensions it covers, that the sources and quality of data sometimes pose problems and that the results give a distorted picture of the facts. The Human Development Report has reacted to the criticism of the HDI by undertaking

various adjustments and reforms. This has not, however, convinced opponents of the HDI, who have fundamental doubts about the wisdom of aggregated indices. The Human Development Report has responded to the strong resistance from politicians and the academic community's criticism of the HDI by abandoning the attempt to introduce an index to cover political aspects. The efforts originally made to include the environmental dimension in the HDI were similarly dropped because of hitherto unresolved methodological problems.

4. Assessment

Since it first appeared, the Human Development Report has provided some important and innovative impulses. It has attracted considerable public and political attention throughout the world and even proved relevant to the domestic policies of some countries. The Human Development Index has made a decisive contribution to the report's dissemination and success, as it provides an access to cross-national comparisons and to national development trends. Although the report has been unable in many respects to overtake the World Bank's World Development Report, it has established itself as an important corrective complement to it.

The Human Development Report not only stimulates the international development debate: it is especially to the report's credit that it has helped to change the image of development by also referring to shortcomings in "human development" that are specific to industrialized countries and by making recommendations.

In its first few years in particular the Human Development Report came under considerable political pressure in UNDP's Executive Board and other fora. It does not, moreover, have the same relationship to UNDP as the World Development Report has to the World Bank. Despite these factors, the Human Development Report has succeeded in developing and maintaining a clear profile.

The Human Development Report undoubtedly has its weaknesses. They are largely due to a very broad conceptual approach and to the occasionally unsatisfactory quality of the data in the HDI and its structural shortcomings as an aggregated index. Various "teething troubles" – especially those suffered by the HDI – have been overcome. However, the Human Development Report continues to be a target for political and academic attack. As a world report that takes an across-the-board view, it is essential for precisely this reason.

Stephan Klingebiel

The update of the article was assisted by
Marius Hildebrand

Lit.: *Boer, L./Koekkoek, A.:* Human Development Report: Fad or Fixture?, in: Development Policy Review 11 (1993), 427-438; *Klingebiel, S.:* Entwicklungsindikatoren in der politischen und wissenschaftlichen Diskussion. (INEF Report No 2), Duisburg 1992; *Noorbakhsh, F.:* A Modified Human Development Index, in: World Development 26 (1998), 517-528; *Nuscheler, F.:* Old Wine in New Skins. Some Critical Comments on the UNDP Reports, in: Messner, D. (ed.): New Perspectives of International and German Development Policy (INEF Report No 33), Duisburg 1998, 25-35; *Ravallion, M.:* Good and Bad Growth. The Human Development Reports, in: World Development 25 (1997), 631-638; *Tandon, Y.:* Naiv oder bewusst verschleiernd: der Human Development Report 1996, in: epd-Entwicklungspolitik (1996), No 21, d1-d8; *Wilson Z.:* Human Development Report: "Universally valued by the people of the world over", in: The United Nations and Democracy in Africa: Labyrinths of Legitimacy, New York 2006, 47-73.

Internet: Human Development Reports: http://www.undp.org/hdro.

Table 1: HDI, GDI, HPI-1 and HPI-2 – same components, different measuring methods

	Longevity	*Knowledge*	*Decent standard of living*	*Participation or exclusion*
HDI	Life expectancy at birth	1. Adult literacy rate 2. Combined enrolment ratio	Adjusted per capita income in PPP$	
GDI	Female and male life expectancy at birth	1. Female and male literacy rate 2. Female and male combined enrolment ratio	Female and male earned income share	
HPI-1	Percentage of people not expected to survive to age 40	Illiteracy rate	Deprivation in economic provisioning, measured by: 1. Percentage of people without access to water and health services 2. Percentage of underweight children under five	
HPI-2	Percentage of people not expected to survive to age 60	Functional illiteracy rate[a]	Percentage of people living below the income poverty line (50% of median disposable income)	Long-term unemployment rate (12 months or more)

[a] Based on level 1 prose literacy according to the results of the OECD International Adult Literacy Survey; source: HDR 1998

254

Human Rights

I. Introduction

Human rights are rights which are enjoyed by all human beings, on the basis that they are human. Human rights derive not from the state but from the individual itself. As such they cannot be granted by the state, however, the state is bound to guarantee them. As a result the state must always, in the performance of its duties, pay respect to human rights and to liberty.

This understanding of human rights is – on the domestic level – clearly expressed in the first draft of the Grundgesetz (German Basic (Constitutional) Law) 1948 in Article 1 para. 1: "The state exists for the sake of man, not man for the sake of the state."

Human rights, as we understand them today, are public international law norms. This, however, was not always the case. For centuries the treatment of a state's own nationals was considered a purely domestic matter and thus not subject to external interference. During the period of the constitutional state system, individuals were granted basic rights by their sovereign. It is only recently, indeed since the Second World War, that human rights entered the realm of international law.

II. Historical Development

Our knowledge of the history of civilization tells us that law has been an integral part of the civilized world for more than four thousand years. We have proof of criminal sanctions for offences and of formal requirements for legal transactions (e.g. Codex Hammurabi, 17th century B.C.). Our knowledge does not, however, provide evidence of human rights laws as we understand them today. There is certainly evidence of rules requiring the protection of particular groups, but we find no reference to a principle which as of right demands respect for and protection of the rights and dignity of every human being.

In the past, rights were accorded to people on the basis of their social standing. The introduction of the concept of civil liberties was based on such thinking, and did not immediately develop into the notion of individual freedoms. This theory is illustrated well in the history of England, where the concept of civil liberties was first introduced by way of the Magna Carta (1215). The Carta granted certain civil liberties to English barons in order to reach a compromise on the distribution of powers between the king and his nobles. It was not until the constitutional change of the 17th century that these class-oriented liberties were developed into individual freedoms.

In 1628 the Petition of Rights granted every Englishman certain individual rights, such as protection against arbitrary detention and against the levying of excessive taxes. Fifty years later, the Habeas Corpus Act (1679) provided the English parliament with an effective guarantee for the personal freedom of the individual. A further ten years passed until the English government recognized in the Bill of Rights (1689) that every Englishman had certain rights which were inviolable, i.e. in which could not be interfered without the consent of the parliament.

It was the Age of Enlightenment which eventually saw the individual beginning to acquire rights simply because of his existence as a human being. After the reformation of the theory of the state, which rendered the pre-modern state and its class system meaningless, the individual became simply a subject without rights vis-à-vis his state. It therefore became necessary to develop a new system of rights. Notwithstanding, it was not the convincing philosophies of the Enlightenment which enforced a change. Towards the end of the 18th century a combination of various different factors led to a clear turning point in the development of individual rights.

With the acceleration of the Industrial Revolution in Europe came a dynamic economic process which rearranged the class system, and led to a significant rise in social standing for the ordinary citizen. At the same time, this economic process itself had to be protected from non-economic or political factors. Consequently, the first civil liberties to be proclaimed were rights such as the right to private property and protection against arbitrary detention. Alongside these rights came the right to religious freedom, a right which had faced substantial difficulties in previous centuries.

These rights were not granted only to the bourgeoisie. Thus, the notion developed during the Age of Enlightenment, that every person must be recognized as a legal person and as such every person has rights vis-à-vis the state, took effect. This development, combined with the struggle of the American colonies to secure independence from Great Britain, led to the first declaration of human rights in the Virginia Bill of Rights (1776): "All men are by nature equally free and independent and have certain inherent rights, of which, when they enter into a state of society, they cannot by any compact deprive or divest their posterity."

The meaning is clear: these inherent rights are not derived from the state. On the contrary, these innate and inalienable rights form the foundation of the state and of society. They fall outside the competence of the legislature.

Further, the Bill of Rights guarantees more specifically, "the enjoyment of life, and liberty, with the means of acquiring, and possessing, property and pursuing and obtaining happiness and safety."

By the second half of the 19th century, following the ups and downs of revolution and restoration, most of Europe had established constitutional states, devoted to the rule of law. States now guaranteed human rights to an extent that was previously unknown. This being said, states did not always implement the claims fully, in particular the principles of the French Declaration of Human Rights (1789). Another problem was that these claims were not fulfilled equally for all people without distinction, as regards for example the voting right for women.

Not even after World War I was the community of states ready to make human rights a comprehensive topic of international law. The nation state with the rule of law was still considered to be the competent protector of human rights and fundamental freedoms. However, the years to follow were to prove that a further development with regard to human rights was indeed required in order to fight off the threat of totalitarianism. The very first attempts to internationalize areas of human rights laws, such as for example the protection of minorities (→ Minorities, Protection of) by the → League of Nations, and to make them a matter of international concern were, however, of little success.

The atrocities committed by the Nazi regime in Germany marked a signal defeat for the notion of human rights. These events proved that human rights had still not reached the status of common values. After the defeat of the national-socialist dictatorship of Germany and the end of the Second World War, the concept of inalienable human rights belonging to every human being had to be promoted in a substantial and sustainable way, and plans were indeed underway to do so. Measures to implement respect for and protection of human rights were to be put into place after victory over Germany. US President F. Roosevelt, in his "State of the Union" message of January 1941, established some essential social and political objectives which were described as the Four-Freedoms Doctrine. The Four Freedoms were freedom of speech, freedom of religion, freedom from want, and freedom from fear of physical aggression. In August 1941 he and Winston Churchill confirmed the British and the US devotion to the fundamental freedoms of mankind, and included the aforementioned doctrine in the Atlantic Charter (→ History of the Foundation of the UN).

In the following years, models for a universal organization of states were developed. The aim of the organization was to be to secure peace and to ensure respect for human rights. Human rights were no longer considered a domestic matter. They were removed from the "domaine réservé" and were now considered a matter of urgent international concern.

The internationalization of human rights laws led to state responsibility, vis-à-vis other members of the international community, for internal human rights breaches. The practical implementation of the respect for human rights in international law has since been of a dual nature, consisting of standard setting and monitoring (→ Human Rights, Protection of).

III. The Creation of International Human Rights Law

1. The United Nations

Human rights are accorded an important position in the Charter of the United Nations (→ Charter of the UN), and their universality is described in the preamble, and accentuated in the body of the Charter (Art 1 (3) and Art 55 (c)). The goals of the organization are defined in Article 1, among them to promote and encourage respect for human rights and fundamental freedoms for all, without distinction as to race, sex, language or religion.

In fulfillment of this obligation the UN immediately began work on a document aimed at safeguarding human rights with the result that only three years after the founding of the organization, the Universal Declaration of Human Rights (UDHR) was passed as a Declaration (→ Resolution, Declaration, Decision) of the → General Assembly (→ Human Rights, Universal Declaration of) in 1948.

This achievement is all the more remarkable if one considers the conflicting positions of the member states which manifested themselves during the debates. The USA, the United Kingdom and France all advocated the same principles of parliamentary democracy. Since their constitutions served as examples for Central and Latin America, for these countries the production of a human rights declaration meant nothing more than establishing national principles on the international level. The USSR, on the other hand, rejected human rights because of their fundamental contradiction to their concept of Marxism which understood human rights law as nothing more than instruments to be used in overcoming capitalism. Moreover, the doctrine of the four freedoms conflicted with the totalitarian demands of Stalinism. Additionally, some Asian states had developed their own principles for regulating the relationship between the individual and the community which were equally incompatible with Western ideas.

The UDHR seeks to reconcile both positions in dealing with civil and political freedoms as well as with economic, social and cultural rights. Nevertheless, the declaration was not adopted under unanimous consensus, but with the communist states, South Africa and Saudi Arabia all abstaining.

Due to the increasing confrontation between the East and the West Blocs, the conclusion of a binding international convention on human rights slipped further and further out of reach. The international human rights covenants (The International Covenant on Civil and Political Rights – CCPR – and the International Covenant on Economic, Social and Cultural Rights – CESCR) were, after extensive and lengthy debate, eventually concluded in 1966, whereupon another ten years passed before they were eventually ratified and entered into force (→ Human Rights Conventions, CCPR; → Human Rights Conventions, CESCR).

The two covenants are not only legally binding, but additionally they establish control mechanisms. Their propagation is worldwide, with 163 and 159 states parties respectively (as of 1 December 2008). The efficacy of their control mechanisms should be assessed with regard to international law, and taking into account the heterogeneity of the international community. It must be borne in mind that international control mechanisms effect a direct clash with the → sovereignty of states, and that not all states are equally ready to compromise their sovereignty. In this connection, fundamental political positions, expediency considerations and trust in the independence and impartiality of the control authority are all factors which must be taken into account.

To evaluate the efficiency of the control mechanisms fairly requires that one keeps in mind the number and differing nature of the states parties. In Europe, the 47 states parties to the European Human Rights Convention have already had to accept differences in legal systems and moral ideals between the member states. This problem is magnified with regard to the two covenants, each of which has three times as many states parties, originating from very different cultures and legal backgrounds. Irrespective of the need for universal acceptance of human rights, governments must be given some discretion in order to take national moral ideals into consideration.

In this respect, the control mechanisms in place for the protection of human rights appear not to be so inefficient after all (→ Human Rights Conventions and their Measures of Implementation). In addition, we must not forget the specific guarantees and the individual control mechanisms laid down in other human rights conventions (e.g. → CAT, → CERD, → CEDAW, → CRC). Both, guarantees and mechanisms further increased after the millennium (Convention on the Rights of Persons with Disabilities, Optional Protocol CAT, Optional Protocol CEDAW, Optional Protocol CESCR).

The Commission on Human Rights, subsidiary organ of the Economic and Social Council, was replaced by the Human Rights Council in 2006, established as subsidiary organ of the General Assembly with resolution A/RES/ 60/251. The Council's new monitoring procedure, the Universal Periodic Review (UPR) is mandatory for all UN member states (A/RES/60/251, para. 5 lit. e). The UPR started in 2008 and the first cycle will be completed in 2011. Time will show whether it is an effective mechanism for the protection and the promotion of human rights in all member states. International human rights law and practice is, therefore, a vivid area.

2. Regional Systems

To date, the international human rights system is supplemented by three regional systems; in Africa (The African Union with the African Charter on Human and People's Rights), in America (The Organization of American States with the American Declaration on the Rights and Duties of Man and the American Human Rights Convention) and in Europe.

A detailed analysis of these instruments falls outside the scope of this article; however, a brief overview of the system of protection of human rights under the auspices of the Council of Europe will be presented.

The Council of Europe is an international organization which seeks to achieve a greater unity between its members for the purpose of safeguarding and realizing the ideals and principles which are their common heritage and for the purpose of facilitating their economic and social progress.

The European Convention for the Protection of Human Rights and Fundamental Freedoms (ECHR) adopted on 4 November 1950 is to date binding for all 47 member states of the Council of Europe. The ECHR was the first public international law treaty to provide a legally binding catalogue of human rights and fundamental freedoms and to set up a judicial control mechanism. Since 1950 there has been a continuous need for restructuring in order to maintain and improve the efficiency of the machinery of protection, mainly in view of the growing membership of the Council of Europe. On 4 November 1998 the 11th Protocol to the ECHR came into force, fundamentally reforming its control mechanism by replacing the existing European Commission and Court of Human Rights by a new permanent Court, whose sole task it is to apply and interpret the standards of the ECHR.

IV. Problem Areas

1. The Universality of Human Rights

The universal nature of human rights has been debated since the onset of the human rights era, which began with the adoption of the UDHR without the unanimous consent of the UN General Assembly. The adoption of the UDHR in this manner set the tone of non-consensus which still continues today, with arguments being raised against the universality of human rights, not least at the World Conference on Human Rights in June 1993 (→ World Conferences). Despite these objections, however, the concluding remarks of the conference declare that human rights are indeed universal (*United Nations* 1993, Part I, para. 1).

Those arguments which deny the universal character of human rights are based on the assertion that human rights are a typically Western idea. Human rights and their philosophical foundations are thus understood as the result of the particular historical development of Europe and of parts of North America. The concept of human rights therefore would stem from a specific cultural context. As such this concept could not be transferred to other cultures which are based on entirely different values and historical developments. Opponents of universal human rights condemn the "American way of life" and the well-known consequences of over-emphasizing the individual. Critiques accentuate the numerous drawbacks of Western societies such as the negative consequences of hedonism, drug abuse, crime and isolation. Behind the claim for universality, it is argued, hides Western cultural imperialism and the propagation of Western values.

A further argument against universality maintains that a country's economic development should take precedence over the protection of certain human rights since only an authoritarian regime is able to guarantee effective economic growth. This line of argumentation emphasizes that, contrary to the position in the West, in some cultures the commu-nity is of greater importance than the individual, that each person has duties which enjoy at least the same degree of importance as – if not a higher degree than – individual rights.

Conversely, there are also many arguments supporting the universality of human rights. The three main arguments in favor are:

(a) Human Dignity

Whilst human rights and human dignity are not identical, human rights are founded on human dignity. Both are inviolable and are not at the disposal of the state. This principle has been articulated very clearly in the wording of Article 1 of the German Basic Law.

Similar affirmations are contained within the constitutions of numerous states. Dignity is an intrinsic value of every person, derived simply from their existence as a human being. It is the fundamental, and perhaps the only, point where all people are equal.

(b) Confirmation

The assertion that human dignity is not a matter with which the state may interfere, but is at the same time the basis for all state action, has been continuously verified since its introduction in 1948. Throughout this time, all UN member states (→ Membership and Representation of States) have taken regard of the UDHR and devoted themselves to its principles. Whilst it is noted that an assertion is not proven true simply through repetition, it is true that law can be created through state practice and through the long-term conviction that a principle is binding. (Customary law, cf. Art. 38 para. 1 lit. b ICJ Statute)

Additionally, more and more areas of human rights law have been codified in international treaties, such as the aforementioned International Human Rights Covenants, the Convention on the Elimination of all Forms of Racial Discrimination, the Convention Against Torture and Other Cruel, Inhuman or Degrading Treatment or Punishment, the Convention on the Rights of the Child and the Convention on the Elimination of all

Forms of Discrimination Against Women.

It must not be forgotten, however, that treaties have binding effect only for those states who are parties to them. Therefore, it is important to note the varying number of states parties to each treaty.

Nevertheless, certain standards in the field of human rights are to be respected even by those states which have not bound themselves by the respective treaty. Since World War II, certain human rights guarantees have evolved into customary international law, some even attaining the status of *ius cogens* (→ International Law and the UN). This is true, for example, for the prohibition of genocide and of slavery, the prohibition of torture and of arbitrary detention, the prohibition of racial discrimination and for denial of justice. These are basic guarantees, derived from human dignity, which demand respect for human life.

(c) Modernization

Another view which supports universality considers human rights law to be a reaction to a socio-economic modernization process. According to this view, human rights law offers a solution to the problem created by the fact that the human species is vulnerable, a problem which becomes all the more evident in radical or extreme situations. Humans are confronted with such situations all over the world and for this reason require the protection of human rights law. Thus the particulars of the historical formation and outward manifestation of human rights does not contradict the universality of its aims, that is to guarantee human liberty.

It is noteworthy that it is often non-democratic regimes which rely on non-western cultural traditions in order to prevent their people from enjoying their human rights. Their arguments are aimed more at stabilizing their power than protecting their cultural identity.

2. The Right to Development

The right to development is the right of every person or group to "equal access to the means of personal and collective advancement and fulfillment in a climate of respect for the values of civilizations and cultures, both national and world-wide" (first stated in the UNESCO Declaration on Racial Prejudice 1978, Art. 3) (→ UNESCO). The right to development is a principle of public international law and a human right with both an individual and a collective dimension.

The Declaration on the Right to Development of 4 December 1986 expresses that all human rights have equal standing and do not form a hierarchy. The Declaration sought to end the discussion on the three generations of human rights (first: civil and political rights; second: economic, social and cultural rights; third: right to development, right to environment, etc.). The concluding remarks of the World Conference on Human Rights (1993) confirmed this view (cf. *United Nations* 1993, Part I, para. 5ff.), thus gaining the support of those states who had been reluctant during the 1986 Declaration. Prior to Vienna the UN Conference on Environment and Development in Rio de Janeiro (1992) showed a broad consensus amongst states that the right to development is a norm of customary international law.

Nevertheless, the discussion continues as to whether the right to development should really be considered an enforceable human right or whether it falls outside this category. Western critics maintain that political demands for a more just international community and for a new international economic order are misplaced as demands for human rights. On the other hand, it has been submitted that the right to development is nothing more than a conglomerate of already established human rights. However, it is exactly this "multiple nature" of the right to development that blocks its acceptance as a binding norm, since in this respect it lacks the requisite clarity and unambiguous quality. As far as the realization of long-term policy aims is concerned, there are no legal claims that could ever be judicially enforced.

The right to development brings public international law together with economic issues. Classical international law did not favor any particular economic system: Soviet-style socialism was as acceptable as Western capitalism. Nowadays, public international law gets increasingly more value-oriented and therefore tends to influence economic structures. Areas such as the donation of aid or the recognition of states on the one hand and the criteria of government, transparency, the rule of law, democracy, minority protection and respect for human rights on the other, are often regarded as being inter-linked.

3. Enforcement and Promotion of Human Rights

Alongside the setting of human rights standards and the monitoring of their observance, active measures are required in order to implement the established guarantees. This is a task primarily for states. Their domestic legal systems must provide the individual with protection against both arbitrary official acts and against powerful private actors. Thus, the legislature holds primary responsibility for bringing municipal law into line with international standards. Additionally, both the executive and the judiciary are obliged to apply human rights standards within the national legal system.

With regard to TNCs as especially powerful private actors, the last decade has witnessed developments that aim at making them respect human rights. The Global Compact was launched by then Secretary-General Kofi Annan in July 2000. It is a policy initiative for enterprises and corporations that are committed to aligning their operations and strategies with ten universally accepted principles in the areas of human rights, labor, environment and anti-corruption. At present, the GC is accepted by more than 4700 corporate participants and stakeholders from over 120 countries (cf. figures on the GC website www.un-globalcompact.org, as of 1 December 2008). The codex of human rights norms for the Global Compact, the

"United Nations Norms on the Responsibilities of Transnational Corporations and Other Business Enterprises with Regard to Human Rights" (UN Doc. E/CN.4/Sub.2/2003/12/Rev.2) (2003), were developed by the former Sub-commission on the Promotion and Protection of Human Rights, the independent expert body of the Human Rights Commission in 2003. These norms bring together standards which have been laid down in various international documents, declarations and legal instruments (like the Universal Declaration on Human Rights, the Convention on the Rights of the Child, the ILO Declaration on Basic Principles and Rights on Labour and the Rio Declaration on the Environment and Development) as well as in non-binding instruments (like the OECD Guidelines for multi-national Corporations and the Global Compact). Thus, these norms do not create new obligations. But they result from a formal and complete discussion which took place within the framework of the United Nations. Governments, enterprises, workers' unions and NGOs were involved. It is to be hoped that these norms may gain importance as soft law.

In 2005, the Secretary-General created the post of a "Special Representative of the Secretary-General on the issue of human rights and transnational corporations and other business enterprises" at the request of the Commission on Human Rights (UN Doc. E/CN.4/RES/2005/69). The mandate, formulated in the resolution of the Commission, requires the Special Representative to "identify and clarify", to "research" and "elaborate upon", and to "compile" materials – in short, to provide a comprehensive mapping of current international standards and practices regarding business and human rights. The mandate also invites the incumbent to submit his/her "views and recommendations" for consideration by the Commission. This mandate was extended pursuant to Human Rights Council Decision 1/102. The first report of the Special Representative was discussed before the Human

Rights Council (on its 4th session in March 2007, cf. UN Doc. A/HRC/4/35).

In addition to the imperative task of respecting human rights obligations within a state's own territory, it can also be necessary for states to take an active stance in implementing respect for human rights in foreign territories. If human rights abuses reach a level of severity that threatens international peace and security, then states are entitled to take collective measures (→ Sanctions) in accordance with Chapter VII of the UN Charter in order to bring the abuses to an end. Taking the international law prohibition on the use of force (→ Use of Force, Prohibition of) into consideration, it is highly doubtful whether states individually (individually in this sense refers to a state or a group of states which are acting without prior → Security Council authorization according to Chapter VII of the UN Charter) may use armed force in order to put an end to gross and systematic human rights abuses. If one looks at the actual incidents of "humanitarian intervention" which have taken place since 1948 it is not difficult to show that the intervening powers were not acting primarily to protect human rights but that they acted far more out of political interests.

Following a report of the International Commission on Intervention and State Sovereignty (ICISS) in December 2001, the so-called "responsibility to protect" (R2P) has been discussed as an evolving concept about the duties of governments to prevent and end unconscionable acts of violence against the people of the world.

In 2005, the Outcome Document of the UN World Summit (UN Doc. A/RES/60/1, 16 September 2005) declared that the international community has a responsibility to protect the world's populations from genocide, massive human rights abuses and other humanitarian crises (ibid., para. 138 and 139). This responsibility to prevent, react to and rebuild following such crises rests first and foremost with each individual state. The international community shares a collective responsibility to respond only when states manifestly fail to protect their populations. This response should consist of first peaceful, and then, if necessary, coercive, including forceful, steps to protect civilians.

It is highly disputed whether extraterritorial military and other law enforcement activities are bound by international human rights law. Most prominently, the US administration tried to throw off its obligations in Guantánamo Bay. These obligations emanated from national constitutional law, and from international human rights law as well as from international humanitarian law. Constitutional and human rights law deal with *habeas corpus* rights in general, whereas humanitarian law offers special protection in situations of armed conflict. As extraterritoriality did not allow any deviation with regard to this obligation, the US administration invented a special status of "enemy combatants" which was wrongly meant to fall out of the scope of protection of international humanitarian law.

Human rights treaties protect individuals who are under a party's jurisdiction (cf. Art. 2 para. 1 CCPR). A party has jurisdiction if it exercises effective control over a territory and the peoples.

The Bankovic decision (European Court of Human Rights, 12 December 2001) applied restrictively the concept of extraterritorial application of human rights obligations referring to the notion of effective control which, in the Court's view, was lacking in this case.

In general, effective control seems to be a criterion well accepted by the international community. It also constitutes well-established case law of the European Court of Human Rights and is the position of the UN Human Rights Committee.

This principle could be applied to multinational forces when they have effective military control over a territory.

Another tool useful in promoting respect for human rights is the conditioning of international humanitarian aid (→ Humanitarian Assistance). Increasingly, donor states are entitled to suspend aid if the receiving state does not pay sufficient regard to certain criteria, such as the respect for human rights, the rule of law or democratic governance.

4. Perspectives

Since the adoption of the UDHR in the aftermath of World War II, the area of human rights law has seen significant developments, to the extent that the fundamental structure of classical public international law has been altered. This development has been the work of international organizations, highly-motivated experts in science and politics and of non-governmental organizations (→ NGOs).

More than 60 years have passed since the adoption of the UDHR, in which period many binding international human rights laws have been established. The extensive setting of human rights standards has been complemented with a continuously increasing system of control and monitoring mechanisms. States are no longer the only potential perpetrators of human rights violations, as the individual has now entered the realm of responsibility. The conclusion of the Statute for the International Criminal Court in Rome 1998 (UN Doc. A/CONF.183/9, 17 July 1998), which entered into force in 2002, has been an enormous step forward in implementing world-wide individual responsibility for human rights violations (→ ICC – International Criminal Court).

It now remains to be seen whether the long-term advantages of such a system will outweigh the initial fears over loss of sovereignty which have manifested themselves during the initial stages.

Norman Weiß

Lit.: *Alston, P.:* The United Nations and Human Rights – A Critical Appraisal, 2nd edn., Oxford, publication date: January 2010; *Donnelly, J.:* Universal Human Rights in Theory and Practice, 2nd edn., Ithaca 2002; *Haratsch, A.:* Die Geschichte der Menschenrechte, 3rd edn., Potsdam 2006; *International Commission on Intervention and State Sovereignty:* The Responsibility to Protect. Report of the International Commission on Intervention and State Sovereignty, Ottawa 2001; *Klein, E.:* Menschenrechte, Stille Revolution des Völkerrechts, Baden-Baden 1997; *Klein, E./Menke, C. (eds):* Universalität – Schutzmechanismen – Diskriminierungsverbote, Berlin 2008; *Lauren, P.G.:* The Evolution of International Human Rights - Visions Seen, Philadelphia 1998; *Mahoney, K.E./Mahoney, P. (eds.):* Human Rights in the 21st Century: A Global Challenge, Dordrecht et al. 1993; *Menke, C./Pollmann, A.:* Philosophie der Menschenrechte, Hamburg 2007; *Nowak, M.:* Introduction to the International Human Rights Regime, Leiden/Boston 2003; *Odendahl, G.:* Das Recht auf Entwicklung, Aachen 1997; *Robertson, A.H./Merrills, J.G.:* Human Rights in the World, 4th ed, Oxford/New York 1996; *Strauß, E.:* Die Entstehungsgeschichte der Allgemeinen Erklärung der Menschenrechte, in: MenschenRechtsMagazin, Vol. 2, Themenheft 50 Jahre AEMR, (1997), 13-21; *United Nations:* The Vienna Declaration and Programme of Action, Adopted 25 June 1993 by the World Conference on Human Rights, UN Doc. A/CONF. 157/23, published by UN-DPI New York 1993; *United Nations - Commission on Human Rights - Sub-commission on the Promotion and Protection of Human Rights:* Economic, Social and Cultural Rights. Norms on the responsibilities of transnational corporations and other business enterprises with regard to human rights, UN Doc. E/CN.4/Sub.2/2003/12/Rev.2, 26 August 2003; *Weiß, N.:* Menschenrechtsschutz, in: Volger, H. (ed.): Grundlagen und Strukturen der Vereinten Nationen, Munich/Vienna 2007, 163 – 187.

Internet: comprehensive information is provided on the homepage of the Office of the UN High Commissioner for Human Rights: www.ohchr.org; NGO information on human rights: Homepage of Human Rights Watch: www.hrw.org.

Human Rights, Protection of

Ever since the end of the Second World War, promoting the respect for, and observance of, → human rights and fundamental freedoms everywhere in the world has been a major concern of the international community. The United Nations has made a significant contribution to the promoting and protection of human rights, and its achievements in the area of standard-setting are without precedent. The full, truly universal and complete implementation of these standards, set forth in documents of different legal quality, is the challenge now faced by the family of nations.

(a) The Scope of Human Rights

The Charter of the United Nations (→ Charter of the UN) makes repeated reference to human rights and fundamental freedoms. In the present context, two of them shall be quoted. The preamble states:

> *"We the peoples of the United Nations determined ... to reaffirm faith in fundamental human rights, in the dignity and worth of the human person, in the equal rights of men and women and of nations large and small ... ."*

The purposes of the United Nations are listed in Article 1 of the Charter, of which the third paragraph reads:

> *"To achieve international cooperation in solving international problems of an economic, social, cultural, or humanitarian character, and in promoting and encouraging respect for human rights and for fundamental freedoms for all without distinction as to race, sex, language, or religion."*

The Charter of the United Nations does not further define the content of human rights. The framers of the Charter left this task to the Organization itself and it was decided that for this purpose an International Bill of Human Rights should be drawn up. What finally emerged was the Universal Declaration of Human Rights (1948) (→ Human Rights, Universal Declaration of), the International Covenant on Economic, Social and Cultural Rights (1966) (→ Human Rights, CECSR), the International Covenant on Civil and Political Rights (→ Human Rights, CCPR) and two Optional Protocols thereto, providing for the right of individual petition (1966), and aiming at the abolition of the death penalty (1989), which together form the five constituent parts of the International Bill of Human Rights. These texts can be considered the authoritative interpretation of the human rights clauses of the Charter of the United Nations.

While the human rights provisions of the Charter of the United Nations should be read in conjunction with the International Bill of Human Rights, the Charter provisions themselves shed considerable light on the scope of human rights in connection with the system of promotion and protection established by the United Nations. As the Charter puts it, the promotion and encouragement of respect for human rights and fundamental freedoms is an undertaking to be carried out *for all.*

For too long human rights were, by and large, the attributes of privileged people. They represented an exclusive notion. Most people of colored skin, female sex, non-Christian faith, or foreign stock were excluded from and deprived of the enjoyment of many human rights. As a matter of principle, the Charter brings all human beings within the scope of human rights and this notion is reinforced by later international instruments, in particular the Universal Declaration of Human Rights. *Ratione personae* human rights are universal (→ Universality) or all-inclusive.

A second characteristic of the Charter provisions on human rights is the emphasis on equality or non-discrimination, which is reflected in the words *"without distinction as to race, sex, language, or religion."* This notion of equality or non-discrimination is closely connected with the concept of universality inasmuch as they mutually reinforce each other. The prevention and the elimination of discrimination has become a major objective in United Nations activities in the field of human rights. Numerous instruments were drawn up and a good number of supervisory mechanisms were devised with a view to combating discrimination, with particular emphasis on discrimination in the field of race, religion, and sex.

Thirdly, human rights are placed by the Charter in a system of *international cooperation.* This implies that national borders put no limits to human rights but that by their nature human rights represent transboundary values. The notion of international cooperation implies also that human rights are a matter of legitimate international concern and that whenever and wherever human rights are in serious jeopardy, the international community is entitled to raise such issues. And not least, international cooperation entails an obligation on the part of states to fulfill in good faith the undertakings they have assumed on the basis of the Charter of the United Nations and other relevant international instruments.

(b) Categories of Human Rights

Human rights can be classified into various categories. The most current distinction is that between *civil and political rights* on the one hand, and *economic, social and cultural rights* on the other. The Universal Declaration of Human Rights comprises these two major categories of human rights in one document. However, when the other component parts of the International Bill of Human Rights were elaborated, it was decided to split these two categories of human rights into two separate documents, an International Covenant on Civil and Political Rights, and an International Covenant on Economic, Social and Cultural Rights. The rationale for this division was that the two sets of rights differed in nature – one category of rights was subject to immediate application, whereas the other category required progressive realization – and therefore different implementation measures were called for.

It is, however, questionable whether a clear distinction can be made between civil and political rights and economic, social and cultural rights. At least there should be no misunderstanding that both Covenants entail legal undertakings on the part of states parties. The preambles of both Covenants underline the conceptual interdependence of both categories of human rights by explicitly recognizing that, in accordance with the Universal Declaration of Human Rights, the ideal of free human beings enjoying freedom from fear and want can only be achieved if conditions are created whereby everyone may enjoy their economic, social and cultural rights as well as their civil and political rights. Moreover, many United Nations pronouncements emphasize the *indivisibility and interdependence of all human rights.* Thus, for example, the Declaration on the Rights to Development (1986) states:

> *"All human rights and fundamental freedoms are indivisible and interdependent; equal attention and urgent consideration should be given to the implementation, promotion and protection of civil, political, economic, social and cultural rights."* (UN Doc. A/RES/41/128, 4 December 1986)

In the present context the broad range of human rights will not be spelled out in detail. By way of general indication it should be mentioned that among the civil and political rights are counted: the rights pertaining to the life, integrity, liberty and security of the human person; the rights with respect to the administration of justice; the right to privacy; the rights to freedom of religion or belief and to freedom of opinion and expression; freedom of movement, the right to assembly and association; and the right to political participation. Economic, social and cultural rights include: the right to work; trade union freedoms; the right to an adequate standard of living, including food, clothing and housing; the right to health care; the right to education; and the right to take part in cultural life.

All these rights are contained in the Universal Declaration of Human Rights, and are further defined in the subsequent component parts of the International Bill of Human Rights and in a number of more specific international instruments. They all confirm the notion already included in the Charter of the United Nations and reaffirmed in the Universal Declaration that all persons are entitled to these rights, without distinction of any kind, such as race, color, sex, language, religion, political or other opinion, national or social origin, property, birth or other status. The significance and scope of this *principle of non-*

265

discrimination is further highlighted by the provision contained in the Universal Declaration of Human Rights that all persons are equal before the law and are entitled without any discrimination to equal protection of the law.

Another distinction frequently referred to is that of *individual and collective rights*. In the International Bill of Human Rights many human rights are formulated in a way that makes the individual human being the main beneficiary: "Everyone has the right ..."

Some human rights combine individual and collective aspects. For instance, freedom to manifest religion or belief can be exercised either individually or in community with others. With regard to other human rights, the collective aspects prevail. This applies for instance to the rights of the family and trade union freedoms. But there are also rights which by their very nature and their subject matter are rights of large collectivities. Cases in point are the rights of minorities, (→ Minorities, Protection of), compromising considerable numbers of persons with common ethnic, religious or linguistic ties, as well as peoples' rights. The latter include the right to self-determination (→ Self-Determination, Right of), the right to development, the right to peace and security, and the right to a healthy environment (→ Environmental Protection). The right of peoples to self-determination is enshrined in Article 1 of both Covenants and reaffirmed by the World Conference on Human Rights in the Vienna Declaration and Programme of Action (1993); the right to development is spelled out in the Declaration on the Right to Development and is also reaffirmed in the Vienna Declaration and Programme of Action (UN Doc. A/CONF.157/23, 12 July 1993). It should be noted that human rights and peoples' rights are recognized in their dialectic relationship in the African Charter on Human and Peoples' Rights (1981). This document was the first human rights treaty to contain an enumeration of the rights of peoples.

(c) Human Rights in Relation to Peace and Development

Among the purposes of the United Nations, outlined in Article 1 of the Charter, the promotion and encouragement of human rights and fundamental freedoms rank prominently together with the maintenance of international peace and security, the development of friendly relations among nations based on respect for the principle of equal rights and self-determination of peoples, and the achievement of international co-operation in solving international problems of an economic, social, cultural or humanitarian character. It is against this background that human rights should be viewed in relation to peace and development.

The → Human Rights Committee, established under the International Covenant on Civil and Political Rights, drew attention to the close link between human rights, in particular the right to life, and the prevention of war. The committee stated that "... war and other acts of mass violence continue to be a scourge of humanity and take the lives of thousands of innocent human beings every year". The Committee further observed: "Every effort they (i.e., the States Parties) make to avert the danger of war, especially thermo-nuclear war, and to strengthen international peace and security would constitute the most important condition and guarantee for the safeguarding of the right to life". (UN Human Rights Committee, General Comment 6 (16), 30 July 1982, The right to life (Art. 6), 16th session, 1982, para. 2; text in compilation of General Comments adopted by human rights treaty bodies, UN Doc. HRI/GEN/1/Rev.9 (Vol. I), 176-178).

At the same time there are more dimensions to the relationship between human rights and peace, as was set out by the UN → Secretary-General in his → "Agenda for Peace" (1992). Peace (→ Peace, Peace Concept, Threat to Peace) is an essential pre-condition for the realization of human rights and fundamental freedoms. Whenever peaceful relations between human beings, groups of persons, peoples and nations are threatened, human rights tend to be jeopardized. Wars and armed conflicts cause *per se* flagrant and massive violations of human rights. On the other hand, under certain circumstances involving persistent patterns of gross violations of human rights, action in favor of human rights may in itself result in disturbing peaceful relations. Many liberation struggles are human rights struggles and by implication this notion is well reflected in the preamble of the Universal Declaration of Human Rights:

"Whereas it is essential, if man is not to be compelled to have recourse, as a last resort, to rebellion against tyranny and oppression, that human rights should be protected by the rule of law."

Therefore, no peace can be sustained without justice and without respect for human rights."

Article 55 of the Charter of the United Nations spells out areas of international economic and social cooperation which, on the basis of Article 56 of the Charter, require joint and separate action by the Organization and its members. Among these areas of international cooperation are, in the words of Article 55, the promotion of:

"a. higher standards of living, full employment, and conditions of economic and social progress and development;

b. solutions of international economic, social, health and related problems, and international cultural and educational co-operation; and

c. universal respect for, and observance of, human rights and fundamental freedoms for all without distinction as to race, sex, language, or religion."

Over the years the United Nations membership has sought to relate human rights to major global issues, in efforts to find solutions for human rights concerns affecting the millions of deprived, dispossessed, discriminated against, and marginalized. The approach, which is reflected in the Proclamation of Teheran

(1968) and many subsequent documents, is also known as the *structural approach*. This approach proposes:
- to link human rights to major world-wide patterns and issues;
- to identify the root causes of human rights violations;
- to assess human rights in the light of concrete contexts and situations;
- to recognize the diversity of political and social systems, cultural and religious pluriformity, and different levels of development.

The structural approach to human rights is also clearly reflected in the Declaration on the Right to Development. This declaration places due emphasis on the central position of the human person in the development process and makes an important contribution to the conceptual link between rights and development. At the same time, the Declaration can serve as a guide to national and international development policies. If taken seriously, the Declaration may be instrumental in:
- strengthening the relevance of human rights in the development process;
- recognizing the centrality of the human person and the human factor in development efforts;
- providing a sound political, legal, social and moral basis and rationale for development cooperation;
- serving as a yardstick in the development and human rights dialogue between developed and developing nations.

In this connection the World Conference on Human Rights stated in the Vienna Declaration and Programme of Action that, while development facilitates the enjoyment of all human rights, the lack of development may not be invoked to justify the abridgement of internationally recognized human rights. The universal nature of these rights is beyond question.

(d) Inventory of Human Rights Instruments

Probably the greatest accomplishment of the United Nations system in the field of human rights is the creation of a body of international human rights law as the product of many years of international legislative work. The main foundation of this international *corpus juris* is the International Bill of Human Rights with its five constituent parts. The Compilation of International Human Rights Instruments (Volume 1, Universal Instruments) published by the United Nations in 2002, lists no less than 94 texts of international conventions, declarations and other documents.

In an inventory of human rights instruments, various categories can be distinguished, viz.:
- general and special instruments;
- global and regional instruments;
- legally binding instruments (treaties) and other instruments.

General instruments usually comprise a wide range of human rights. Although these instruments are not part of the formal constitutions of international organizations and institutions, they are of a constitutional order in a broader sense and give content to the rule of law in the framework of the United Nations or of regional structures of international cooperation. The most prominent of these general instruments are:
- The Universal Declaration of Human Rights (1948)
- The International Covenants on Human Rights (1966)
- The European Convention for the Protection of Human Rights and Fundamental Freedoms (1950)
- The European Social Charter (1961)
- The American Declaration of the Rights and Duties of Men (1948)
- The American Convention on Human Rights (1969)
- The African Charter on Human and Peoples' Rights (1981)
- The Arab Charter of Human Rights (1994).

As far as the *special* instruments are concerned, the above-mentioned United Nations Compilation of International Human Rights Instruments makes a classification into the following categories:
- The Right of Self-Determination
- Rights of Indigenous Peoples and Minorities

- Prevention of Discrimination
- Rights of Women
- Rights of the Child
- Rights of Older Persons
- Rights of Persons with Disabilities
- Human rights in the administration of justice: protection of persons subjected to detention or imprisonment
- Social Welfare, Progress and Development
- Promotion and Protection of Human Rights
- Marriage
- Right to Health
- Right to Work and Fair Conditions of Employment
- Freedom of Association
- Slavery, Slavery-like Practices and Forced Labor
- Rights of Migrants
- Nationality, Statelessness, Asylum and Refugees
- War Crimes and Crimes against Humanity, including Genocide
- Humanitarian Law ($\rightarrow$ Humanitarian Law)

It is noticeable that in connection with the scope and content of special instruments, three objectives are of a particularly prominent nature, namely the elimination of discrimination, the protection of vulnerable persons and groups, and the fight against large-scale evil practices. Instruments with a view to combating racism and racial discrimination, discrimination against women, discrimination based on religion or belief, discrimination in employment, occupation and remuneration, and discrimination in education all rank high on the agenda. Refugees, women, children, workers, detainees and prisoners, the disabled, indigenous people, migrant workers and their families, all form categories of persons whose rights and interests need special protection. Genocide, torture, enforced disappearances, slavery and other forms of human exploitation are evil practices that fall within the area of international crimes and crimes against humanity. Legal instruments have been drawn up specifically to combat these grave abuses.

The second major distinction made above concerns instruments elaborated by organizations of global vocation, such as the United Nations, the International Labour Organization ($\to$ ILO), or the United Nations Educational, Scientific and Cultural Organization ($\to$ UNESCO) and instruments emerging from *regional* institutions or structures. As far as the latter are concerned, the Council of Europe, the Organization of American States, the Organization of African Unity and the League of Arab States have been active in developing comprehensive human rights standards. Equally, the participating states in the Organization on Security and Cooperation in Europe (OSCE) have reached in the East-West context a far-ranging consensus on human rights principles and their elaboration, as part of their efforts to ensure the effective exercise of human rights and fundamental freedoms and to facilitate contacts and communication between people. Initial fears that regional instruments may constitute a threat to the integrity and validity of global instruments have largely faded away. The view now prevails, after many years of experience with the coexistence of global and regional instruments, that they are complementary and that they mutually reinforce each other.

Another distinction concerns *legally binding* instruments (treaties) and *other* instruments. It is undeniable that human rights standards, when enshrined in a treaty reinforced with implementation provisions, gain a good deal of authority. This is particularly true for treaties that are the result of solid preparation and that have been widely ratified on the basis of a firm commitment to compliance undertaken by states. Many of these human rights treaties have established supervisory mechanisms, including reporting systems which aim to give concrete expression to the accountability of the states parties to these treaties.

However, certain standard-setting initiatives – following the example of the Universal Declaration of Human Rights and subsequent international instruments other than treaties – tend to give preference to the non-treaty form, by way of declarations, bodies of principles, codes of ethics, guidelines, etc. Such instruments do not require ratification (which often cause long delays in the entry into force of a treaty instrument) and address themselves, at least at the level of the United Nations, to all the members of the United Nations and, as the case may be, to other actors of society at national and international levels. These other instruments represent not only important political commitments by states, but they are also ground rules for the conduct of international relations and, particularly in the field of human rights, ground rules for the conduct of domestic policies.

(e) Supervisory Procedures

International implementation procedures in the field of human rights serve a number of joint or separate purposes. Some procedures may help states concerned to devise better national policies aimed at the realization of human rights. Such procedures have an *advisory function*. There are also procedures that may trigger off international action with a view to rendering material or other forms of assistance to states. These procedures have an *assistance function*. Again, other procedures which focus on non-compliance with international standards have as their main purpose the correction of a human rights situation or certain aspects thereof. These procedures are characterized by their *corrective function*. But there are also procedures which serve to provide relief or remedies to victimized persons or groups. These procedures have therefore a *relief or remedy function*. Most of these procedures have in common that they may prevent certain situations from deteriorating or certain evils from being (again) inflicted upon persons or groups. This may be called the *preventive function* of international control procedures. Much of the effectiveness of these procedures depends on the quality and the expertise of the control mechanisms and on the degree of political will on the part of the states concerned to cooperate

269

in good faith with the mechanisms of international supervision.

The type of supervisory procedure most commonly applied and accepted is the *reporting system*. This system was introduced by the ILO on the basis of its original Constitution, and expanded by amendments to it. The reporting system can be considered a *regular supervisory system*. It is mainly non-contentious in nature and based on the method of constructive dialogue. Committees of independent experts, established under the respective international human rights treaties and often referred to as "treaty bodies", are functioning as control mechanisms in order to review and asses progress made and difficulties encountered with respect to the implementation of these treaties by the states parties. The reporting system progressively found its way into a number of important human rights treaties, in particular:

- The International Covenant on Economic, Social and Cultural Rights;
- The International Covenant on Civil and Political Rights;
- The International Convention on the Elimination of All Forms of Racial Discrimination (→ Human Rights Conventions, CERD);
- The Convention on the Elimination of All Forms of Discrimination against Women (→ Human Rights Conventions, CEDAW);
- The Convention against Torture and Other Cruel, Inhuman or Degrading Treatment or Punishment (→ Human Rights Conventions, CAT) and the Optional Protocol thereto on Prevention;
- The Convention on the Rights of the Child (→ Human Rights Conventions, CRC) and the Optional Protocols thereto on the Sale of Children, Child Prostitution and Child Pornography, and on the Involvement of Children in Armed Conflict;
- The International Convention on the Protection of the Rights of All Migrant Workers and Members of Their Families (→ Human Rights Conventions, CMW);
- The Convention on the Rights of Persons with Disabilities;
- The International Convention for the Protection of All Persons from Enforced Disappearance.

From the reporting procedures provided for in human rights treaties should be distinguished the *Universal Periodic Review* (UPR) which applies to all states members of the United Nations. The United Nations General Assembly, in its resolution 60/251 of 15 March 2006 creating the Human Rights Council to replace the former Commission on Human Rights requested the Council to "undertake a universal periodic review (UPR), based on objective and reliable information, of the fulfilment by each State of its human rights obligations and commitments in a manner which ensures universality of coverage and equal treatment with respect to all States; the review shall be a cooperative mechanism, based on an interactive dialogue, with the full involvement of the country concerned and with consideration given to its capacity-building needs; such a mechanism shall complement and not duplicate the work of treaty bodies."

In its resolution 5/1, Annex I of 18 June 2007 the Human Rights Council set out the terms of the new universal periodic review mechanism, including the basis of the review, the principles and objectives, the periodicity of the review, the process and modalities of the review, the outcome of the review and the follow-up. The periodicity of the review for the first cycle is four years. This implies the examination of 48 States per year. The review is based on information based on a report prepared by the state concerned, and additionally on a compilation prepared by the Office of the High Commissioner for Human Rights of information contained in reports of treaty bodies and special procedures, as well as on additional, credible and reliable information from other sources, notably civil society organizations. The outcome of the review leads to recommendations and their follow-up.

From the *regular supervisory proced-ures* should be distinguished the *special procedures*. Such special procedures deal with a particular human rights situation prevailing in a country of territory and causing special concern to responsible members of the international community. This type of special procedures is often referred to as the *"country approach"*. The special procedures may also apply to certain practices affecting large numbers of people in many countries or territories and giving rise to widespread international concern. These special procedures represent the *"thematic approach"*.

Some special procedures are set in motion by petitions or complaints lodged under legal instruments. They are usually referred to as *"communications"* by these instruments and are either available to individuals or groups of individuals regarding alleged violations of rights by the state party, or to states parties claiming that another state party is not fulfilling its obligations under the relevant instruments, or to both. A common feature of most of these complaints is their *quasi-judicial character* with respect to the principles of due process of law. This implies that the supervisory body gives the opportunity to all parties to present written and – as the case may be – oral evidence and information in support of their respective positions, and that the principle *audiatur et altera pars* is duly respected. It also implies that the supervisory body, if it is unable to reach a friendly settlement, will express an opinion whether a breach of the convention has been incurred by the state party concerned or whether the state party has failed to give effect to any of its obligations under the convention. The various complaints procedures provided for in a number of global and regional human rights conventions have by and large these quasi-judicial features in common. Reference is made in this respect to the complaints procedures which find their basis in the Constitution of the ILO, in the International Covenant on Civil and Political Rights and the Optional Protocol thereto, in the International Convention on the Elimination of All Forms of Racial Discrimination, in the Convention Against Torture and Other Cruel, Inhuman or Degrading Treatment or Punishment, in the Convention on the Elimination of All Forms of Discrimination against Women and the Optional Protocol thereto, in the Optional Protocol to the Convention on the Rights of Persons with Disabilities, in the International Convention for the Protection of All Persons from Enforced Disappearance, in the European Convention for the Protection of Human Rights and Fundamental Freedoms, in the American Convention on Human Rights and in the African Charter on Human and Peoples' Rights. The World Conference on Human Rights (1993) has recommended that where such complaints procedures are optional, states parties to human rights treaties should consider accepting all the available optional procedures.

In addition to the special procedures of a quasi-judicial character, a whole series of other special procedures have come into being as a result of other recommendations made and decisions taken by policy organs of the United Nations, notably the former Commission on Human Rights and its successor the Human Rights Council created by General Assembly resolution 60/251 of 15 March 2006. The institution of these special procedures is a response to widespread and strongly felt concerns on the part of large sectors of the United Nations membership.

Thus, the Commission on Human Rights established in 1967 the Ad Hoc Working Group of Experts on Southern Africa, whose mandate was renewed many times until it was terminated in 1995 in view of the establishment of a united, non-racial and democratic government in South Africa. Over the years many other country situations and territories have been the subject of investigation and monitoring by Special Rapporteurs or Working Groups because such situations appeared to reveal a consistent pattern of gross violations of human rights. The findings of those

271

Special Rapporteurs or Working Groups provided the basis for pronouncements and recommendations by United Nations policy organs. The current list of country-specific procedures (as of April 2009) relates to Burundi, Cambodia, Haiti, Democratic People's Republic of Korea, Myanmar, Palestinian territories occupied since 1967, Somalia, and Sudan.

While these procedures focus on a *country* or a *territory*, the practice also developed of concentrating on certain phenomena that affect large numbers of people in many countries and therefore cause widespread concern. This practice is reflected in the so-called *thematic approach*.

Thus, in 1980 a Working Group was created by the Commission on Human Rights to examine questions relevant to enforced or involuntary disappearances of persons. In later years, other thematic mechanisms were created dealing with the integrity of human life and the human person and having in common that they monitor and report on flagrant practices in many countries and that in urgent cases of imminent threat they intercede on a humanitarian basis with a view to obtaining immediate attention and relief. To this category of thematic mechanisms belong, in addition to the Working Group on Enforced or Involuntary Disappearances, the Special Rapporteur on Extrajudicial, Summary or Arbitrary Executions, the Special Rapporteur on Torture and Other Cruel, Inhuman or Degrading Treatment or Punishment, and the Working Group on Arbitrary Detention. But also other phenomena and practices causing serious and widespread concern led to the creation of additional thematic monitoring devices and procedures. They deal respectively with contemporary forms of racism, racial discrimination and xenophobia; freedom of opinion and expression; impact of armed conflict on children; independence of judges and lawyers; internally displaced persons; human rights defenders; mercenaries; freedom of religion or belief; sale of children, child prostitution and child porno-

graphy; toxic wastes, and violence against women, its causes and consequences, rights of indigenous people, and rights of migrants. The promotion and protection of economic and social rights are also the subject of thematic special procedures: the right to education, the right to housing, the right to food, the right to health, and human rights and extreme poverty. New special procedures mandates include: trafficking in persons, minority issues, and the promotion and protection of human rights while countering terrorism.

The Human Rights Council maintained the system of special procedures and brought them in its resolution 5/1, Annex II, of 18 June 2006 under its closer control by setting out detailed rules for the selection and appointment of mandate-holders and by adopting in its resolution 5/2 a Code of Conduct for Special Procedures Mandate-holders. The independence and expertise of the mandate-holders, their investigations, their accessibility to civil society organizations and their capacity to deal with urgent cases and situations make them a vital component of the human rights protection system.

Finally, in addition to regular and special procedures, a distinction can be made between *treaty-based control mechanisms* and *charter-based control mechanisms*. In principle, control mechanisms provided for in treaties are only operative with respect to states parties to these legal instruments. The states ratifying these treaties *ipso facto* accept to cooperate in good faith with these control mechanisms. The terms of reference of the supervisory organs are defined in the treaties. These control procedures and mechanisms are clearly founded on legal basis. As general rule, the treaty-based control mechanisms have a permanent character. The charter-based control mechanisms and procedures owe their existence to a decision, usually in the form of a resolution, of a policy organ which is a representative body reflecting the membership of the organization. The legal basis of these mechanisms and procedures is the constitution of the organization or, in the case of the United Nations, its Charter.

It is clear that there is a great variety in implementation tools and mechanisms. Many types of procedures coexist: regular procedures and special procedures; (quasi-) judicial and political procedures; country procedures and thematic procedures; treaty-based and charter-based procedures. Moreover, these various types of procedures also coexist between and within the framework of the United Nations, its → specialized agencies, and regional organizations (→ Regionalization). In many instances, these coexisting procedures and mechanisms may be dealing with the same right or the same set of rights, with the same situations or even with the same cases. In order to maintain consistency in the interpretation of standards and in the assessment of facts and information, and with a view to avoiding duplication and confusion, there is much need for co-ordination between the various coexisting procedures and mechanisms. This co-ordination should be a constant concern of the Office of the UN High Commissioner for Human Rights (→ Human Rights, United Nations High Commissioner for), other international human rights secretariats and of the control mechanisms themselves, notably the chairpersons of all the treaty bodies.

A very important role is played in the international system of protection and promotion of human rights by non-governmental organizations (→ NGOs). Among the many other tasks non-governmental organizations undertake, they act as sources of information which greatly contribute to the effective functioning of all human rights supervisory procedures and control mechanisms.

It should be understood that international supervisory procedures and control mechanisms can never be considered as substitutes for national mechanisms and national measures with the aim of giving effect to human rights standards. Human rights have to be implemented first and foremost at national and local levels. The primary responsibility of states to realize human rights is vis-à-vis the people who live under the jurisdiction of these states. However, with the internationalization of human rights and with the recognition that the protection and promotion of human rights does not fall within the exclusive domain of states, the international community can take a legitimate interest in the compliance with internationally recognized standards of each and every state or of any other actor exercising effective power.

Consequently, although international control procedures are no substitute for means and methods of national implementation of human rights, international procedures have an important subsidiary or complementary role to play.

(f) Assessment

The United Nations has developed over the years an impressive legal framework for the promotion and protection of human rights, comprising an extensive network of standards as well as treaty-based and charter-based supervisory mechanisms. The methods of dialogue, fact-finding and follow-up control applied by these supervisory mechanisms have progressively become more refined, more specific and more geared towards effective implementation. At the same time it is an agonizing experience that the means and methods employed by the UN human rights machinery prove to be of limited impact in situations of armed conflict, violence and other types of emergencies when human life is in grave jeopardy. In such situations comprehensive strategies of peace-making, peace-keeping and peace-building (→ Peacekeeping) are required and the → Security Council has to face heavy responsibilities. In recent years the Security Council has become more sensitive to human rights and humanitarian law concerns as an integral part of the peace and security agenda. The establishment by the Security Council of *ad hoc* international criminal tribunals for the former Yugoslavia and for Rwanda in 1993 and 1994 are clear proof of this new tendency and the role assigned to the Security Council in the

Statute of the International Criminal Court (→ ICC) confirms this trend.

A significant trend is the recognition in the outcome document of the 2005 World Summit of the Responsibility to Protect when populations are threatened by genocide, war crimes, ethnic cleansing and crimes against humanity (General Assembly resolution A/RES/60/1, 16 September 2005, paras. 138-140). This implies that when a state manifestly fails to protect its population from such widespread and gross violations of human rights and humanitarian law, the international community may take collective action, through the Security Council, for the protection of such populations against these grave abuses (cf. the report of the *International Commission on Intervention and State Sovereignty* 2001 "The Responsibility to Protect"). However, the implementation of this concept is still in its infant stage.

Too long human rights remained a marginal matter in the structure and the operations of the United Nations. However, the creation in 1993 by the General Assembly of the post of a United Nations High Commissioner for Human Rights gave the human rights programme an increased political and moral weight and offers more room for initiatives and dynamic action.

This applies in particular to the role the High Commissioner has assumed in the prevention of human rights violations, in securing a human rights presence in the field – either in the form of a self-contained structure or as a part of larger United Nations operations – and in conducting a human rights diplomacy in the form of high-level dialogue with Governments.

The establishment of the High Commissioner's Office also contributed to advancing and integrating human rights in the broader United Nations system and allowed for focused action with regard to the human rights of women and children, minorities and indigenous people.

However, an essential weakness of the UN human rights programme remains the scarce resources attributed to this programme. In this respect it is worth noting that the 2005 World Summit resolved strengthening the Office of the UN High Commissioner for Human Rights, *inter alia* by the doubling of its regular budget resources over a period of the next five years (General Assembly resolution A/RES/60/1, para. 124).

A recent development of considerable interest for the protection of human rights through the United Nations system is the upgrading of the main human rights policy organ from a functional commission of the ECOSOC to a subsidiary organ of the General Assembly: the new Human Rights Council. Like its predecessor the Human Rights Council is composed of states members of the United Nations and is therefore a political body. As a quasi-permanent body with several regular sessions per year and with facilities to meet in special sessions to deal with urgent situations, it has the potentials to address more effectively gross and systematic violations of human rights and to play an early warning role if escalation of human rights violations is imminent, provided it is sensitive to the voices and concerns of the human rights victims.

The effectiveness of the Council's protection function will depend to a great extent on the manner it will preserve the independence and impartiality of the *special procedures* which is essential to their operations and which appears to be challenged by a part of the membership of the Council.

The credibility of the Council will further depend on the working of the *universal periodic review mechanism* which in its early phase gave rise to concerns because of lack of constructive cooperation on the part of some of the reviewed states.

The Council will have to prove its role as a protector of human rights by strengthening the procedures that operate under its authority, notably in securing proper follow-up monitoring.

The test will be that the Council, in fruitful cooperation with OHCHR, relies more firmly on the findings and recommendations of independent expertise and that it gives credit to the input of NGO's and other organs of civil society.

Theo van Boven

Lit.: *Danieli, Y./Stamatopoulou E./Dias, C.:* The Universal Declaration of Human Rights Fifty Years and Beyond, New York 1998; *Evans, G./Sahnoun, M.:* The responsibility to protect, in: Foreign Affairs 81 (2002), 99-110; *Hilpold, P.:* The duty to protect and the reform of the United Nations : a new step in the development of international law? In: Max Planck Yearbook of United Nations Law 10 (2006), 35-69; *International Commission on Intervention and State Sovereignty:* The Responsibility to Protect, Ottawa 2001, (www.iciss. gc.ca); *Mertus, J.A.:* The United Nations and Human Rights: A Guide for the New Era, London 2005; *Ramcharan, B.G.:* The Principle of Legality in International Human Rights Institutions: Selected Legal Opinions, The Hague 1997; *Ramcharan, B.G. (ed.):* Human Rights Protection in the Field, Leiden 2006; *Ramcharan, B.G.:* Human Rights – Norm and Machinery, in: Weiss, T.G./Daws, S. (eds.): The Oxford Handbook on the United Nations, Oxford 2007, 439-462; *Robinson, M.:* A Voice for Human Rights, Philadelphia 2006; *Stahn, C.:* Responsibility to protect: political rhetoric or emerging legal norm? In: AJIL 101 (2007), 99-120; *Steiner, H.J./Alston, P.:* International Human Rights in Context, Law, Politics, Morals, 2nd edn., Oxford 2000; *Thakur, R.:* The United Nations, peace and security: from collective security to the responsibility to protect, Cambridge et al. 2006; *Tomuschat, Ch.:* Human Rights: between Idealism and Realism, Oxford 2003; *United Nations:* Human Rights, A Compilation of International Instruments, Vol. 1 (First and Second Part), Universal Instruments, New York 2002; *Welsh, J./Thielking, C.J. /Mac Farlane, S.N.:* The responsibility to protect: assessing the report of the International Commission on Intervention and State Sovereignty, in: IJ 57 (2002), 489-512.

Internet: general and detailed information on the protection of human rights within the United Nations system: www.ohchr.org.

Human Rights, United Nations High Commissioner for

In its Charter (→ Charter of the UN) the United Nations gave itself two main tasks: the maintenance of international peace, and the promotion and protection of human rights (→ Human Rights, Protection of). The mandate in the field of human rights is laid down in the preamble of the Charter and is further detailed in Articles 1, 55, 56 and 68.

In 1946 the world organization established a secretariat for human rights in New York, known as "Division of Human Rights" until 1982 (cf. UN Doc. A/RES/34/47 of 23 November 1979, 35/194 of 15 December 1980, and A/DEC/37/237 of 21 December 1982), as "Centre for Human Rights from 1982 to 1997, and since then as *"Office of the United Nations High Commissioner for Human Rights"* (OHCHR).

The first director of the Division of Human Rights was the Canadian professor of international law John P. Humphrey, who held the office until 1966. His successors in this post and in the post of the director of the Centre, respectively, were the Belgian Marc Schreiber (1966-1977), the Dutchman Theo van Boven (1977-1982), the Austrian Kurt Herndl (1982-1987), the Swede Jan Martenson (1987-1992), the French Antoine Blanca (1992) and the Senegalese Ibrahima Fall (1993-1994).

The first High Commissioner for Human Rights was the Ecuadorian José Ayala Lasso (1994-1997). He was followed by the former Irish President Mary Robinson (1997-2002), the Brazilian Sergio Vieira de Mello (2002-2003), the Guyanan Acting High Commissioner Bertrand Ramcharan (2003-2004) and by the Canadian Louise Arbour (2004-2008) In September 2008 Navanethem Pillay of South Africa, took office as High Commissioner.

The Division of Human Rights had its seat at UN headquarters in New York until 1974, when it was moved by UN Secretary-General Pérez de Cuéllar to the Palais des Nations in Geneva (→ UN Office Geneva). As Theo van Boven, the third High Commissioner stated in a book contribution in 1992, "it was believed that the Secretary-General had an interest in relocating this sensitive part of the Secretariat, which for all political purposes was considered more of a liability than an asset, at a suitable distance from the political centre (*van Boven* 1992, 561).

In November 1998 the Office of the UN High Commissioner for Human Rights moved to the Palais Wilson in Geneva, which had been the first seat of the → League of Nations.

The High Commissioner keeps an office at UN headquarters in New York and seven regional offices throughout the world. Country offices are currently operating in Angola, Bolivia, Bosnia and Herzegovina, Burundi, Cambodia, Colombia, Democratic Republic of the Congo, Guatemala, Kosovo, Mexico, Nepal, in the Occupied Palestinian Territories [term used by the OHCHR)], the Russian Federation, Togo and Uganda. Former offices in Georgia, Serbia, Sierra Leone, South Africa and Tajikistan have been closed.

The Office of the High Commissioner is administratively a part of the UN Secretariat (→ Secretariat) and not an autonomous → specialized agency of the UN such as the International Labour Organization (→ ILO) or the World Health Organization → WHO). Thus, the High Commissioner is subordinate to the UN Secretary-General (→ Secretary-General), respectively to the Office of the Under-Secretary-General for Political Affairs, and is thereby subject to the resolutions (→ Resolution, Declaration, Decision) of the → Security Council, the → General Assembly, and the Economic and Social Council (→ ECOSOC).

1. Setting Standards

Out of the ruins of the Second World War a strong conviction arose that it was imperative to establish universally valid standards of human rights and freedoms. The UN Division of Human Rights under John Humphrey had the task to coordinate and assist in the elaboration of those standards by the Commission on Human Rights of the United Nations, which was established in 1946 as a subsidiary organ of ECOSOC by virtue of ECOSOC resolution E/RES/5 (1) of 16 February 1946

(→ Principal Organs, Subsidiary Organs, Treaty Bodies). The Commission held 62 regular sessions until its dissolution in June 2006 (ECOSOC decision E/DEC/2006/2 of 22 March 2006) and was replaced, pursuant to General Assembly Resolution A/RES/60/251 of 15 March 2006, by the → Human Rights Council, which opened its first session on 19 June 2006.

The Universal Declaration of Human Rights (→ Human Rights, Universal Declaration of) was the first result of the work of the Commission on Human Rights. It was jointly drafted by John Humphrey, together with the first Chairperson of the Commission on Human Rights, Eleanor Roosevelt, as well as the French delegate René Cassin and the Lebanese delegate Charles Malik.

The declaration was, of course, no legally binding international treaty. After its adoption followed many years of tough negotiations in order to ensure the codification of the norms. In 1965 the International Convention on the Elimination of All Forms of Racial Discrimination (→ Human Rights Conventions, CERD) was adopted by the General Assembly. A year later, in December 1966, the two International Covenants on Civil and Political Rights and on Economic, Social and Cultural Rights (→ Human Rights Conventions, CCPR; → Human Rights Conventions, CESCR) followed. Other Conventions are the Convention on the Elimination of all Forms of Discrimination Against Women 1979 (→ Human Rights Conventions, CEDAW), the Convention against Torture and Other Cruel, Inhuman and Degrading Treatment or Punishment 1984 (→ Human Rights Conventions, CAT), the Convention on the Rights of the Child (→ Human Rights Conventions, CRC) 1989, and the Convention on the Rights of All Migrant Workers and Members of their Families. On 13 December 2006 the General Assembly adopted the Convention on the Rights of Persons with Disabilities (UN Doc. A/RES/61/106), which has not yet entered into force.

Although many people consider codification to be completed, important declarations are still being elaborated and adopted by the General Assembly which some day may enter into force as optional protocols to the Covenants, thus for example, the Declaration on the Rights of Persons Belonging to National, Ethnic, Religious and Linguistic Minorities, adopted by the General Assembly on 18 December 1992 as resolution A/RES/47/135, the Draft Declaration on Population Transfer and the Implantation of Settlers, adopted by the Sub-Commission on Promotion and Protection of Human Rights in 1997 (UN Doc. E/CN.4/Sub.2/1997/23, and E/CN.4/Sub.2/RES/1997/29 of 28 August 1997), and the United Nations Declaration on the Rights of Indigenous Peoples (UN Doc. A/RES/61/295 of 13 September 2007).

2. Implementation Mechanisms

The standard-setting in human rights was accompanied by the establishment of monitoring organs and implementation mechanisms. The following expert committees, serviced by OHCHR, were established:

- in 1969 the Committee on the Elimination of Racial Discrimination (CERD);
- in 1976 the → Human Rights Committee;
- in 1980 the Committee on the Elimination of Discrimination Against Women (CEDAW);
- in 1985 the Committee on Economic, Social and Cultural Rights (CESCR);
- in 1987 the Committee Against Torture (CAT);
- in 1991 the Committee on the Rights of the Child (CRC); and
- in 2004 the Committee on Migrant Workers (CMW).

These treaty-monitoring bodies do not have universal jurisdiction, since each committee was established on the basis of a given treaty and thus derives its competence from it and only with respect to the contracting states. One committee, however, has almost universal reach: the Committee on the Rights of the Child with its 193 states parties (as of 31 December 2008), practically all sovereign states of the world with the exception of the non-contracting states USA and Somalia. The Human Rights Committee counts 163 states parties (as of 31 December 2008), among them the permanent members of the Security Council with the exception of the People's Republic of China, which signed the Covenant on Civil and Political Rights in 1998, but had not ratified it as of December 2008.

The committees are financed from the regular budget of the United Nations and are serviced logistically and materially by the UN Secretariat.

Besides the Commission, there existed from 1947 to 2006, as supporting organ, the Sub-Commission on Prevention of Discrimination and Protection of Minorities, whose name was changed by ECOSOC in 1999 into "Sub-Commission for the Promotion and Protection of Human Rights" and which conducted 58 sessions up to August 2006. Like the Commission on Human Rights, the Sub-Commission and its working groups held their meetings in Geneva. The Working Groups of the Sub-Commission on Indigenous Populations, on Minorities and on Communications have done important work, the former two in preparing declarations and in conducting thorough in-depth research on the situation of the groups they are concerned with, the latter in dealing with complaints of systematic violation of human rights in preparation of subsequent deliberations in the Sub-Commission and the Commission on Human Rights.

The Sub-Commission was abolished by the new Human Rights Council and replaced in 2007 by an expert advisory body, the *Human Rights Council Advisory Committee* (UN Doc. A/HRC/RES/5/1, 18 June 2007).

3. The Office of the High Commissioner for Human Rights

Since the early days of the Commission on Human Rights, many voices had advocated the establishment of the office of a high commissioner or ombudsman for human rights. This demand was rejected by numerous opponents for decades. Not without justification they feared that the suggested office would interfere in the internal affairs of sovereign states (→ Sovereignty) as soon as there emerged the suspicion that human rights were being violated. Such an interference, however, so ran their argumentation, would constitute a violation of Article 2 (7) of the UN Charter (→ Intervention, Prohibition of). In this context one has to admit that human rights were instrumentalized in the times of Cold War and are still used today as a political weapon to embarrass other states.

The idea of creating the office of a high commissioner for human rights originated from the first Director of the Division of Human Rights, John Humphrey. The General Assembly asked in Resolution 3221 (XXIX) of 6 November 1974 the Secretary-General to elaborate a report on this topic, which was submitted in 1975 (UN Doc. A/10235). Two further reports were produced in 1976 and 1977 (UN Doc. A/32/178 and A/32/179). However, no consensus could be reached. Only after the end of the Cold War could the Humphrey initiative prosper. It was taken up again at the Vienna World Conference on Human Rights and endorsed in Part II, paragraph 18 of the "Vienna Declaration and Programme of Action" (UN Doc. A/CONF.157/24, 25 June 1993): "The World Conference on Human Rights recommends to the General Assembly ... consideration of the question of the establishment of a High Commissioner for Human Rights for the promotion and protection of all human rights." Thereupon a committee of the General Assembly was entrusted with the task of formulating the terms of reference of the High Commissioner.

By resolution A/RES/48/141 of 20 December 1993 the General Assembly created the post of the UN High Commissioner for Human Rights at the Under-Secretary-General level, and on 14 February 1994 the General Assembly appointed, on recommendation of Secretary-General Boutros-Ghali, the Ambassador of Ecuador to the UN, José Ayala Lasso as the first High Commissioner for Human Rights. Ayala Lasso, former chairman of the committee which had drafted the pertinent resolution of the General Assembly, assumed the post on 5 April 1994, was appointed for a four-year term, with the prospect of reappointment for a second term of office. In March 1997, however, Ayala Lasso resigned from his post in order to return to Ecuador as foreign minister and negotiator for a treaty with Peru, so as to avert an impending armed conflict over a border dispute.

4. The Mandate of the High Commissioner for Human Rights

General Assembly resolution A/RES/48/141 defines the tasks and responsibilities of the High Commissioner. With more authority than the preceding Directors of the Centre of Human Rights, the High Commissioner is mandated to "coordinate the human rights promotion and protection activities throughout the United Nations system" (para. 3 (i)). It is obvious that this function requires a high degree of diplomatic skill from the office-holder. This requirement is made plain by the fact that the large number of → specialized agencies of the United Nations, special organs and programmes, which for many years had pursued and continue to pursue their own human rights activities would only reluctantly accept supervision by the new High Commissioner. In this context mention should be made of the International Labour Organization (→ ILO), the World Health Organization (→ WHO), the UN Organization for Education, Science and Culture (→ UNESCO), the UN Development Programme (→ UNDP), the Environmental Organization (→ UNEP), the World Organization for Children (→ UNICEF) and the UN High Commissioner for Refugees (→ UNHCR).

Therefore the High Commissioner began the necessary negotiations with these and other organizations, in order to conclude as soon as possible agreements, so-called "memoranda of understanding", intended to define the mutual relationship and avoid conflicts of competence.

According to para. 4 (f) of GA resolution 48/141, the High Commissioner shall "play an active role in removing the current obstacles ... to the full realization of all human rights". Even more important is para. 4 (g) of the resolution stipulating his obligation to engage in dialogue with states and pro-actively to develop initiatives for the protection of human rights.

As the High Commissioner has to interact with the different cultures of the world, the resolution emphasizes that the High Commissioner should be a person who is familiar with all relevant cultures and who can keep a neutral standpoint ("shall possess ... the general knowledge and understanding of diverse cultures necessary for impartial, objective, non-selective and effective performance" of his duties (para. 2 (a)).

5. The Activities of the High Commissioners since April 1994

When Ayala Lasso was appointed, the priorities of the office had yet to be defined: when, how and where should he act? The main task was to establish his authority and the credibility of his Office, vis-à-vis the member states and the different UN organs. He set himself the following goals: crisis management; preventive strategies; the right to development; support for the establishment of national human rights institutions; technical assistance to states requesting such help; universal ratification of human rights conventions; and the development of follow-up capacities, with the purpose of ensuring that the states implement the decisions and recommendations of the treaty bodies. Ayala Lasso launched an ambitious plan to expand the presence and visibility of his office by opening regional bureaus in all regions of the world. Some of these offices rendered good services in the area of technical assistance.

Of course no High Commissioner can be expected to solve the enormous problems of human rights in the world, in their towering extent and complexity. The main task should rather be to develop step by step a "culture of human rights", that people became aware of their rights and learn how to invoke them. In this connection the establishment of national human rights commissions or independent national institutions is of great importance, for human rights can be discussed in the UN office in Geneva, but they can be realized only on the ground, in Africa, Asia, Europe and the Americas.

A seasoned diplomat, Ayala Lasso excelled in quiet diplomacy, but he also conducted highly publicized missions, e.g. to Cuba.

Ayala Lasso endorsed the worldwide campaign for the abolition of capital punishment. He also set up geographic and thematic desks to provide logistical and substantive support to the Commission's Country and Thematic Rapporteurs.

The years in office of Mary Robinson are memorable for the organization of the World Conference against Racism, held in Durban, South Africa from 31 August to 8 September 2001. She deployed a media-effective presence, highlighted by her many missions to promote the ratification of human rights treaties, her success in persuading China to sign the International Covenant on Civil and Political Rights, and her successful doubling of the OHCHR budget. Her courage in condemning the denial of *habeas corpus* and indefinite detention of terror suspects in Guantanamo and elsewhere eventually caused her to lose her job in 2002.

High Commissioner Sergio Vieira de Mello assumed his responsibilities on 12 September 2002. He was a dynamic and invigorating High Commissioner, giving the office a high profile. In May 2003, shortly after the start of the US-led war in Iraq in March 2003, he was asked by Secretary-General Kofi Annan to take a four-months leave of absence from his position as High Commissioner in order to serve in Iraq as Special Representative of the Secretary-General. It was there that he was tragically killed

279

on 19 August 2003 in a terrorist attack on the UN Office in Baghdad.

Bertrand Ramcharan, Deputy High Commissioner for Human Rights since 1978, became Acting High Commissioner in May 2003, a post that he held until July 2004. A thorough human rights scholar with numerous academic publications and 30 years of experience in the United Nations system, Ramcharan proved to be an effective trouble-shooter and a good manager. He strongly supported staff activities and encouraged staff to publish in academic journals so as to give the OHCHR greater public visibility and acceptance. The OHCHR should be seen as a "center of excellence".

Louise Arbour was appointed in July 2004 on a four-year term, until 2008. She displayed remarkable initiative in supporting the new Human Rights Council, insisting on impartiality and non-discrimination. She demonstrated courage in criticizing also the major powers and introducing the practice of supporting human rights litigation by drafting "*amicus curiae*" briefs, most recently one submitted to the United States Supreme Court on the issue of Guantanamo detainees.

Louise Arbour also meaningfully supported the rights of migrant workers.

She took her broad mandate seriously and deployed her energy in support of the Millennium Development Goals and the abolition of extreme poverty. As she wrote in an op-ed article on Human Rights Day 10 December 2006, published in more than 30 newspapers worldwide: "All human rights – the right to speak, to vote, but also the rights to food, to work, to health care and housing – matter to the poor because destitution and exclusion are intertwined with discrimination, unequal access to resources and opportunities, and social and cultural stigmatization. A denial of rights makes it harder for the poor to participate in the labor market and have access to basic services and resources. In many societies they are prevented from enjoying their rights to education, health and housing simply because they cannot afford to do so. This, in turn, hampers their participation in public life, their ability to influence policies affecting them and to seek redress against injustice." (*Arbour* 2006)

Due to political pressures against her independence, Louise Arbour did not seek reelection when her first term expired in July 2008.

She was succeeded by Navanethem Pillay of South Africa, who took office in September 2008. She practiced law in Natal, where she defended many regime critics, including Nelson Mandela. She served as judge in the High Court of South Africa since 1995 and was appointed to the International Criminal Tribunal for Rwanda, where she served for eight years. In 2003 she was elected to the panel of judges of the International Criminal Court and resigned in 2008 in order to assume her responsibilities as UN High Commissioner for Human Rights.

Her new mandate has been characterized by a concern to enhance the credibility of the Office and to demonstrate, like Ayala Lasso before her, that all victims of human rights violations deserve our attention and compassion. Among others the promotion of women's rights, the rights of migrant workers and of indigenous populations figure prominently on her agenda.

6. Structure of OHCHR

Organizationally the Office was restructured into three branches in 1997: a "Research and Right to Development Branch", the "Activities and Programmes Branch", responsible for the advisory services and technical assistance projects, and the "Support Services Branch", responsible for planning, preparing and servicing of the meetings of the Commission on Human Rights, its Sub-Commission and of the committees established by human rights treaty bodies; this branch also integrated the activity of the former Communications Branch, where much of the legal work of the Office of the High Commissioner was concentrated.

OHCHR has been restructured several times since 1997, for example in 2000 the dismantled Communications Branch was partly reestablished in the form of the new Petitions Unit, responsible for processing all complaints addressed to the treaty bodies.

At present OHCHR has two Divisions: 1) the *Human Rights Procedures Division*, which encompasses the Treaties and Council Branch, and 2) the *Operations, Programmes and Research Division*, which encompasses the Research and Right to Development Branch and the Field Offices Branch. There is also a Programme Support and Management Services Branch.

7. Technical Cooperation

Besides standard-setting and monitoring activities, OHCHR has a vast programme of advisory services and technical assistance.

Components of the programme focus on the incorporation of international human rights standards in national laws and policies, on the building or strengthening of national institutions capable of promoting and protecting human rights and democracy under the rule of law, on the formulation of national plans of action for the promotion and protection of human rights, on human rights education and training; and on promoting a "culture of human rights". Such assistance takes the form of expert advisory services, training courses, workshops and seminars, fellowships, grants, provision of information and documentation, and assessment of domestic human rights needs.

Technical cooperation activities are seen by OHCHR as a complement to, but never a substitute for, the monitoring and investigative activities by the Human Rights Council and the seven human rights treaty bodies. The Programme is funded from the regular budget of the United Nations and from the United Nations Voluntary Fund for Technical Cooperation in the Field of Human Rights. The Voluntary Fund became operational in 1988 and is administered by a Board of Trustees.

8. Budget

One of the main problems of the Office of the High Commissioner has been its meager budget. While some UN organs are relatively well financed, others fulfill their tasks only with great difficulties. At the time Ayala Lasso took office, he counted on a staff of approximately 200 members and less than 40 million US dollars per annum, which were reduced by 2.6 million in view of the UN financial crisis. Of course, economy is a high UN priority, but it is hard to explain to people deprived of their rights that the OHCHR really cannot help them, because the necessary material means are insufficient. By contrast, two other UN organs with comparable scopes of duties have greater resources: the UN High Commissioner for Refugees (UNHCR) has a secretariat of about 5,000 staff members worldwide and has a budget of 1.4 billion US dollars per annum. The UN Development Programme (UNDP) operates with about 6,000 staff members and a budget of 2 billion US dollars.

The General Assembly has gradually recognized that the OHCHR must have greater financial support and that it cannot be exclusively financed from the regular UN budget ($\rightarrow$ Budget). The regular UN budget for OHCHR has thus been increased to 43 million US dollars per annum in 2006 and to 59.5 million US dollars in 2008, to which an additional 95.7 million came (in 2007) from voluntary contributions (*OHCHR* 2007, 146; *OHCHR Internet Homepage* 2008). Thanks to its annual appeals, OHCHR has been successful in obtaining funds from national governments as well as from private donations. With these voluntary contributions, OHCHR currently maintains seven trust funds: the general Trust Fund for the Activities of OHCHR, the Fund for Indigenous Populations, the Fund on Contemporary Forms of Slavery, the Fund for the Programme of Action for the Third Decade to Combat Racism and Racial Discrimination, the Fund for the Victims of Torture, the Fund for a Human Rights Education in Cambodia, and the Fund for Technical Cooperation.

At present the staff numbers some 300 at OHCHR headquarters and some 300 at the field offices. Continued expansion of the human rights secretariat is necessary and expected.

9. NGOs

The Office works closely with civil society and with non-governmental organizations (→ NGOs), fighting for human rights in all countries, members of small organizations as well as of larger networks such as Amnesty International, Equality Now, Human Rights Watch, International Commission of Jurists, International Federation of Human Rights Societies, the German Internationale Gesellschaft für Menschenrechte, PEN International and Lawyers for Human Rights. Without theses idealists the work of the Office of the High Commissioner would be much more difficult.

10. Success Stories

The activities of the Office as described above have fortunately resulted in many successes: thus, for instance, as a direct result of decisions of the Human Rights Committee, national legislation is amended, new administrative directives are issued, detained persons are released, persons sentenced to death have their sentences commuted, investigation into the fate of disappeared persons is conducted, persons guilty of extra-judicial executions and torture are tried and punished, compensation is paid to victims, aliens obtain residence permits or refugee status, etc.

Besides the codification of human rights in the form of international treaties, the decisions (case law) of the Human Rights Committee, the Committee Against Torture and the Committee on the Elimination of Racial Discrimination constitute the visible concretization of human rights. Such case law entails the interpretation of norms in a concrete case, the identification of an individual victim and the formulation of a concrete solution, thus constituting living law or

"law in action". Over the past thirty years significant jurisprudence has emerged, which is quoted by many national courts and international tribunals. The experience with the follow-up and the implementation of the decisions of the human rights treaty bodies gives reason for optimism.

Through their good offices and quiet diplomacy, the High Commissioners for Human Rights have been able to intercede on behalf of victims of human rights violations and have generally promoted a higher commitment by states to a "culture of human rights".

Evaluation

In the last six decades the United Nations has made considerable progress on the way to the universal recognition and enforcement of human rights norms. Decisive results have been achieved in codification and in the establishment of monitoring mechanisms. There is no doubt that millions of people can enjoy human rights today to an extent that they could not do before.

The Office of the High Commissioner for Human Rights possesses great areas for further development. But in order to realize these possibilities, the Office needs considerable additional financial resources. The fact that the High Commissioner receives such modest budgetary allocations, while states spend billions on armaments and wars, shows that the political will to promote human rights exists only to a limited extent. A further danger which should not be underestimated lies in the bureaucratization of human rights, and the emergence of what critics have called the "human rights industry". This is incompatible with the ideal of human rights and with the *raison d'être* of the Office, the *dignitas humana*.

Resolutions must not be allowed to become ends in themselves, conferences must not be degraded to rituals, where the practical recognition of human rights does not take place or is even not desired. Many observers also criticize that some UN organs, including the Commission on Human Rights and the new Human Rights Council apply double standards. Indeed, there seem to exist "politically correct" victims and those whose suffering may be safely ignored, e.g. the 370 million indigenous peoples of the world, who continue to suffer from the consequences of the assault on their cultures, their deprivation of their natural resources, not to speak of discrimination, marginalization, and extreme poverty. There are so-called "consensus victims" and those "unsung victims" who are denied their status as victims. Herein lies a further serious risk for the credibility and the effectiveness of the United Nations and, in particular of OHCHR.

Indeed, if a High Commissioner for Human Rights is inspired with his/her task, then he or she will put human dignity always at the center of the work of the Office and will stand up for all the rights of all people in all countries of the world. It is time to abandon the artificial hierarchy of human rights, neatly divided into first generation (civil and political), second generation (economic, social and cultural), and so-called third generation (peace, development, environment). As all High Commissioners have frequently said, all human rights are organically interrelated. A better approach to human rights would be to identify them in their functions as enabling rights, such as the human right to peace, over-arching rights, such as the right to equality, and end rights, such as the right to culture and identity, that is, the right to be just who we are.

Alfred de Zayas

Lit.: *1) Documents: United Nations:* Reports of the United Nations High Commissioner for Human Rights to the General Assembly 1994, 1995, 1996, 1997, 1998, 1999, 2000, 2001, 2002, 2003, 2004, 2005, 2006, 2007 (UN Docs. A/49/36, A/5O/36, A/51/36, A/52/36, A/53/36, A/54/36, A/55/36, A/56/36, A/57/36, A/58/36, A/59/36, A/60/36, A/61/36, A/62/36); Report of the United Nations High Commissioner on his mission to Rwanda 11-12 May 1994 (UN Doc. E/CN.4/S-3/3); *United Nations:* The Vienna Declaration and Programme of Action, Adopted 25 June 1993 by the World Conference on Human Rights, published by the UN Department of Public Information, New York 1993 (UN Doc. A/CONF.157/23); *United Nations Centre for Human Rights:* The High Commissioner for Human Rights, an Introduction, Notes of the United Nations High Commissioner for Human Rights, No. 1, HR/PUB/HCHR/96/1, 1996; *United Nations - Office of the High Commissioner for Human Rights:* Annual Appeals 2000, 2001, 2002, 2003, 2004, 2005, 2006, 2007; *United Nations - Office of the High Commissioner for Human Rights:* 2007 Report - Activities and Results, Geneva 2008; *2) Secondary Literature: Ayala Lasso, J.:* Defining the Mandate, in: Harvard LRev., Winter 1994/95, 38-41 and 78; *Ayala Lasso, J.:* Making human rights a reality in the twenty-first century, in: Emory ILRev. 10 (1996), 497-508; *Ayala Lasso, J.:* Foreword, in Ramcharan, B.G. (ed): UN High Commissioner for Human Rights, 2002; *Boven, T. van:* The Role of the United Nations Secretariat, in: Alston, P. (ed.): The United Nations and Human Rights. A Critical Appraisal, Oxford 1992, 549-579; *Clapham, A.:* Creating the High Commissioner for Human Rights: The Outside Story, in: EJIL 5 (1994), 556-568; *Clark, R.S.:* A United Nations High Commissioner for Human Rights, The Hague 1972; *Ermacora, F.:* Ein VN-Hochkommissar für Menschenrechte?, in: ÖZA 6 (1966), 259-265; *Hannum, H.:* Human rights in conflict resolution: the role of the Office of the High Commissioner for Human Rights in UN peacemaking and peacebuilding, in Human Rights Quarterly 28 (2006), 1-85; *Hobbins, A.J.:* Humphrey and The High Commissioner: The Genesis of the Office of the UN High Commissioner for Human Rights, in: Journal of the History of International Law 3 (2001), 38-74; *Howland, T.:* Mirage, magic, or mixed bag? The United Nations High Commissioner for Human Rights' Field Operations in Rwanda, in HRQ 21 (1999), 1-55; *Humphrey, J.P.:* Human Rights and the United Nations, a great adventure, Epping 1984; *Humphrey, J.P.:* No Distant Millennium. The International Law of Human Rights, UNESCO, Paris 1989; *Humphrey, J.P.:* A United Nations High Commissioner for Human Rights: the birth of an initiative, in: CanYIL 2 (1973), 220-225; *Kedzia, Z.:* The United Nations High Commissioner for Human Rights, in: Beyerlin, U. et al (eds.): Recht zwischen Umbruch und Bewahrung: Völkerrecht, Europarecht, Staatsrecht. Fs. R. Bernhardt, Berlin et al. 1995, 435-452; *Klein, E. (ed.):* The Institution of a Commissioner for Human

Rights and Minorities and the Prevention of Human Rights Violations (Colloquium, Potsdam, Germany, 14-15 December 1994), Potsdam 1995; *Lord, J.:* The United Nations High Commissioner for Human Rights: Challenges and Opportunities, in: LoyLA Int&CompLJ 17 (1995), 329-363; *Nanda, V.:* Global challenge of protecting human rights: promising new developments, in: Den. J Int'l. L&Pol. 34 (2006), 1-15; *Ramcharan, B.:* The United Nations High Commissioner for Human Rights. The Challenges of International Protection, The Hague 2002; *Ramcharan, B.:* A UN High Commissioner in Defence of Human Rights, Leiden 2005; *Ramcharan, B.:* Future of the UN High Commissioner for Human Rights, in Round Table. No. 378, Jan 2005, 97-111; *Ramcharan, B.:* Human Rights: Norms and Machinery, in: Weiss, T.G./Daws, S. (eds.): The Oxford Handbook on the United Nations, Oxford 2007, 439-462; *Tikhonov, A.:* UN High Commissioner for Human Rights, in Moscow Journal of International Law 1 (1995), 21-30; *de Zayas, A.:* The United Nations High Commissioner for Human Rights, in Bernhardt, R. (ed.): Encyclopaedia of Public International Law, Vol. IV, Amsterdam 2000, 1129-1132; *Proceedings of the Symposium on the United Nations High Commissioner for Human Rights:* the First 10 Years of the Office and the Next (17-18 February 2003), in: Columbia Human Rights Law Review 35 (2004).

Internet: Homepage of the Office of the UN High Commissioner for Human Rights (with graphic survey of the structure of the office, links to meeting reports and other documents, human rights conventions, press releases etc.): www.ohchr.org.

Human Rights, Universal Declaration of

The *Universal Declaration of Human Rights (UDHR)*, which was adopted by the United Nations → General Assembly on 10 December 1948 with 48 votes in favor, none against and 8 abstentions (UN Doc. A/RES/217 (III)), is considered one of the most important documents of the twentieth century. The Declaration has had a fundamental influence on the constitutions of numerous states, as well as on the further development of international law (→ International Law and the UN). This great

influence may tend to obscure the fact that the Declaration itself has been a stage in a more comprehensive intellectual and political process, whose origins date back to before the foundation of the United Nations (→ History of the Foundation of the UN), or even the beginning of the Second World War. Therefore the appreciation of the Declaration should also include those groups of people and committees who engaged themselves since the early 1920s – sometimes under difficult circumstances – not only for the revival of the concept of → human rights, but who also paved the way – and that was indeed something new – for the development of the international protection of human rights (→ Human Rights, Protection of), a way along which the Declaration was to become one of the most important milestones.

1. Initiatives for an International Protection of Human Rights

In the first half of the 20th century there were several distinct efforts to place the protection of human rights on the international agenda: A first initiative took place in the framework of two institutes of international law – the *Académie Diplomatique Internationale* and the *Institut de Droit International* –, where first and foremost two persons were engaged in particular: *André Mandelstam* and *Antoine Frangoulis*. Shocked by the severe infringements against minorities before and during the First World War, they had made it their duty to universalize the civil and human rights, which were fixed in the League of Nations treaties for the protection of minorities (→ League of Nations), thus to lay the foundation for an international system for the protection of human rights. Although immediate practical success did not occur, their drafts of human rights declarations were important preparatory works on the way to the universal protection of human rights.

A second initiative started in the mid-1930s. The background was first formed by the events in the fascist states and the streams of refugees leaving them, soon afterwards followed by the Second

World War. The leadership of this initiative was drawn from authors, journalists and Nobel Peace Prize winners. One of the activists of that movement was *Herbert George Wells* (1866-1946), whose international reputation rested on several well-known novels. Together with like-minded people he drew up the elements of the postwar order, and in this context he also developed a "Declaration of Rights", which he advocated worldwide in various articles, books and lecture tours.

The Second World War formed the background for the third initiative, as well. At its head stood a man who had not only the will, but the power as well, to raise the idea of human rights to the level of domestic politics, and soon to the level of the international politics, too: the American President *Franklin D. Roosevelt*. On 4 January 1941 Roosevelt proclaimed in his "State of the Union Address" his vision of a world order to come, which was based on "Four Freedoms": freedom of speech, freedom of belief, freedom from want and freedom from fear. In the autumn of 1941 the *"Four Freedoms"* found their expression in the *"Atlantic Charter"*, which in its turn became the basis for the *"Declaration By United Nations"*, which was signed by 26 states on 1 January 1942 (→ History of the Foundation of the UN). At the same time in the USA a huge number of organizations and law institutes began their work on declarations of human rights – *inter alia* the *American Law Institute* and the *Commission to Study the Organization of Peace*, to name just two of many.

2. The Protection of Human Rights in the Charter of United Nations

Although the demand for the international protection of human rights rapidly gained breadth and momentum in the USA, the topic of human rights played only a subordinate role at the conference at Dumbarton Oaks, where the negotiations of the superpowers concerning the draft of the Charter of the United Nations (→ Charter of the UN) in fall 1944 came to their final stage.

The reserve of the Roosevelt administration regarding the international protection of human rights had two sources. On the one hand there was concern that the assignment of the international protection of human rights to an international organization – which had yet to be created – would fail because of the opposition of the US Senate, and thus probably endanger the whole project. On the other hand there were strong reservations, from the Soviet Union, and from the United Kingdom, both of which feared interference of the new international organization in their colonial policies.

If human rights, however, eventually received more emphasis in the Charter than had been intended at Dumbarton Oaks, this was principally due to the success of two groups, which together can be considered as comprising a fourth initiative: a group of states of the South, which advocated a more positive appreciation of the need for international protection of human rights, as well as a group of American non-governmental organizations (→ NGOs), which exerted a similar pressure on the American delegation at the founding conference in San Francisco in 1945. The inclusion of the formulation "promoting and encouraging respect for human rights and for fundamental freedoms" in Article 1 (3) of the UN Charter, which was not intended in the proposals worked out in Dumbarton Oaks, as well as the establishment of a special commission for human rights issues (→ Human Rights, Commission on) at the Economic and Social Council (→ ECOSOC), can be ascribed to those NGOs. It was also this group of NGOs, which pressed for the elaboration of an "International Bill of Rights". These supplements were explicitly supported by states of the South, such as Brazil, the Dominican Republic, Nicaragua and India.

In a review of the stages along the way to the Universal Declaration of Human Rights, the following intermediate results can be recorded: Proposals for the creation of a system of international protection of human rights were

285

worked out in legal form for the first time at the end of the 1920s. The initiators of this process were at first not the old Western democracies, but private individuals – specialists in international law, writers, humanitarian organizations – as well as a number of smaller states of the South.

The starting impulses for these initiatives were – beside the crimes of the Third Reich – also the experiences of persecution of minorities, of racial discrimination, and of colonial repression. It took three more years till the draft of an "International Bill of Rights" was submitted. It had been worked out by the Commission on Human Rights, which had been established, in accordance with Article 68 of the UN Charter on 27 January 1946, by the United Nations (→ Human Rights, Commission on). Under the direction of Eleanor Roosevelt, the widow of the American President and Chairwoman of the Commission, the Commission had held its meetings first in New York, but later in Geneva and Paris. Among its members were persons of renown such as René Cassin from France, Carlos Romulo from the Philippians, André (Charles) Malik from the Lebanon, Vladimir M. Koretsky from the USSR and John P. Humphrey, head of the UN human rights department (→ Human Rights, United Nations High Commissioner for). The consultations extended far into 1948. This had different reasons: on the one hand the length of the consultations was due to the international environment in which they took place; on the other hand it was due to the political attitudes of the UN member states; and finally because of nature of the issue itself, human rights.

3. The International Environment
   Surrounding the Deliberations
   on the UDHR

As the commission commenced its consultations, the international horizons had already darkened noticeably. The former Anti-Hitler-Alliance, which had united in 1942 under the "Declaration By United Nations", and had called the United Nations into being in 1945, showed considerable signs of dissolution. With increasing clarity the contours of a coming conflict emerged, a conflict which was soon to encompass the entire world, and which would cause hundreds of wars and conflicts, with massive violations of human rights.

In March 1947 President Truman requested financial means from the US Congress for the stabilization of Greece and Turkey, and promised American aid, as he put it, for those free peoples, whose freedoms were threatened. At the end of the year (25 November-15 December 1947) the Conference of Foreign Ministers of the victorious powers in London was adjourned without agreement on the German question. And while the Western powers started to consolidate their occupation zones, the Soviet Union started make its East-European approaches safe, by concluding friendship treaties and pacts for mutual assistance. In Berlin the Soviet representative left the Allied Control Council, and on 26 June 1948 Moscow commenced the blockade of the German capital. In the meantime the positions in East Asia had also become entrenched. In China Stalin passed Manchuria – in violation of his responsibilities to the Republic of China – to the hands of the Chinese communists, thereby contributing essentially to their victory over the Kuomintang. On the Korean peninsula the elections which had been decided by the United Nations, could only be held in the South because of the resistance of the Soviet Union. These intensifying international tensions imposed strains not only on the deliberations of the Commission on Human Rights itself, but led to the fact that the Soviet Union insisted – after the deliberations had been finished in the commission – on deliberations not less detailed in the Third Committee of the General Assembly (→ Committees, System of). Only after 85 difficult sessions the Third Committee finally adopted the draft of the declaration on 6 December 1948, and passed it to the General Assembly.

In spite of these protracted consultations complete agreement could not be reached in the Third Committee: Several delegations abstained from their vote – beside the Soviet Union Belarus, the Ukraine, the CSSR, Poland and Yugoslavia, and Canada belonged to this group of seven abstentions. With the exception of Canada all those states abstained once more, together with Saudi Arabia and the South African Union, when on 10 December 1948 the motion was put to vote in the General Assembly. It was thereupon adopted with the overwhelming majority of 48 states voting in favor, none against and eight abstentions.

4. The Attitude of the Governments towards the Protection of Human Rights

Already during the negotiations on the UN Charter in Dumbarton Oaks, the superpowers had agreed that the protection of human rights should not be implemented at the expense of the sovereignty of states ($\rightarrow$ Sovereignty). Thus Article 2 (7) of the Charter specifies that the Charter does not authorize the United Nations "to intervene in matters which are essentially within the domestic jurisdiction of any state". This view of domestic jurisdiction was shared by the smaller and middle states. It was the common view that human rights were to be counted among the domestic affairs reserved to the states. Only France had advocated interventions by the $\rightarrow$ Security Council in cases of gross violations of human rights, however this concept was not accepted.

When Eleanor Roosevelt pleaded in the commission for a step-by-step procedure, by which a catalogue of principles would be adopted, that was to be followed by negotiations on a legally binding international agreement – with binding obligations of states and an internationally monitored examination procedure –, she was reacting not only to the cooling climate of international relations. It was also her thoroughly realistic assessment that the negotiations on such a treaty would take much more time than those concerning a non-binding "Universal Declaration", but above all it reflected her assessment of the uncertainty of the outcome, as states in the East, West and South alike would proceed with great care for the protection of their sovereignty. Last but not least, she was aware of significant opposition in the USA.

5. The Controversy about the Scope and the Value Basis of the Human Rights

The difficulties piled up here, too. Because if the declaration was to be "universal", i.e. acceptable for all states, religions and civilizations, the catalogue of rights could not be restricted only to the classical political freedom and defense rights connected with the Western philosophical concept and values of liberalism (cf. *Farer/Gaer* 1993, 250ff.). The delegations from the Western world only recognized those classical liberal rights as having human rights character. If the catalogue should go beyond those liberal rights and include social and economic rights – as delegates from the Communist states and the young states of the South demanded – then rejection by the West could not be excluded. But the front lines did not only run between the East and the West, objections were also made by some representatives from the South: Saudi-Arabia considered the right of freedom of worship incompatible with the Sharia, and the delegate from the People's Republic of China refused absolutely to accept the wording originally provided for Article 1, that all people were "free and equal by nature". To exclude this original formulation, perceived as too heavily marked by Western states, eventually agreement was reached on a formulation which stated that all human beings "are born free and equal in dignity and rights".

No less difficult than the determination of the scope of human rights was the decision on their roots, which means the problems of their underlying basis in terms of moral values. Thus neither the attribution of human rights to God nor to "nature" turned out to be productive of a consensus. The commission evaded this problem by being content on the whole with the statement, that all peoples of the UN had once again reaffirmed "their faith in fundamental human rights, in the dignity and worth of the human person". What contentious issue is involved in the issue of the value basis of human rights became obvious, in the beginning of the 90s, when the question of the universality of human rights moved into center of the discussion worldwide.

It has turned out, too, that the characterization of the status of the "Universal Declaration of Human Rights" was no less vague and ambiguous. Whereas the French version (the German version by the way follows the French version) declares it in a non-committal way as "l'idéal commune à attendre par toutes les peuples et toutes les nations", the English version spoke in a more concrete and active manner of a "common standard of achievement for all people and all nations".

6. The UDHR as a Compromise

With regard to this background, the final text of the Declaration proves to be a result of a difficult compromise. The statement in Article 1 which says that all human beings are born free and equal in dignity and rights, and the comprehensive ban on discrimination in Article 2, are followed by three groups of rights: a first group is formed by the classical liberal freedom rights in Articles 3 to 19, among them the right to life, liberty and security of the person; equality before the law; the right to seek asylum from persecution; the right to property and to freedom of thought, conscience and religion. A second group is formed by the Articles 20 and 21, which include the right to freedom of peaceful assembly and association, and the right to take part in the government of one's country, directly or through freely chosen representatives. Together with the principles of the rule of law, those articles form the basis for a democratic constitutional state. The Articles 22 to 27, as a third group, contain social, economic and cultural rights,

among them the right to social security, work and education. Together with the "freedom from fear and want," as stated in the Preamble, they refer back to two of the "four freedoms" enunciated by President Roosevelt. Of particular interest are the Articles 28 and 29. Whereas Article 28 states that "[e]veryone is entitled to a social and international order in which the rights and freedoms set forth in this Declaration can be fully realized", Article 29 points out that "[e]veryone has duties to the community", although significantly without detailing what duties are thereby referred to.

Among those three groups of rights mentioned above there is neither an order of precedence (difference in rank), nor a differentiation of rights, which – like the right to life – are considered as absolute, and others, which can be restricted under certain circumstances. The absence of such a differentiation is even more problematic, as the limit on restrictions by law provided in Article 29 – the "just requirements of morality, public order and the general welfare in a democratic society" – is rather vague and leaves much room for interpretation.

The final text met a great deal of international approval, but drew criticism, as well. Criticism was particularly directed against the non-committal and timid manner of the Declaration. This criticism is not unjustified. The Preamble in fact contains the remark that it is essential, "that human rights should be protected by the rule of law". But instead of addressing an unambiguous demand to the states, to safeguard this "rule of law" as soon as possible, and to account to the international community for the measures they take, one can only find the dull appeal to all peoples and all nations "that every individual and every organ of society, keeping this Declaration constantly in mind, shall strive by teaching and education to promote respect for these rights and freedoms and by progressive measures, national and international, to secure their universal and effective recognition and observance, both among the peoples of Member States themselves and among the peoples of territories under their jurisdiction". The last point was related to the still existing colonies. The British specialist in international law Hersch Lauterpacht probably related to this hesitation and freedom from obligation, as he observed that the Universal Declaration of Human Rights "has proved acceptable to all for the reason that it imposes obligations upon none" (*Lauterpacht* 1945).

7. The UDHR as a Foundation Stone of the Protection of Human Rights

Regardless of the criticism, however, it has to be recognized, that the "Declaration", although it is only a non-binding declaration relating to international law, and which therefore did not require ratification by the parliaments of the signatory states, nevertheless became the starting point – and probably the most important cause – for a huge number of developments, which led to a revaluation and worldwide dissemination of the concept of human rights.

These developments basically took place on three levels: On a first level numerous states integrated catalogues of human rights in their constitutions, *inter alia* in the Basic (Constitutional) Law of the Federal Republic of Germany, but above all in the constitutions of many developing countries. A second wave was formed by the former East-European allies of the Soviet Union at the beginning of the 90s, where many of them put catalogues of fundamental rights at the top of their new democratic constitutions.

A second level was formed by regional arrangements for the protection of human rights: The "European Convention for the Protection of Human Rights and Fundamental Freedoms" of 4 November 1950 (effective since 3 September 1953); the "American Convention on Human Rights" (UNTS Vol. 1144, No. 17955), which was adopted by the Organization of American States (OAS) on 22 November 1969; the Final Act of the Conference on Security and Coop-

eration in Europe (Helsinki-Agreement) of the year 1975; as well as the "African Charter on Human and Peoples' Rights" (Banjul-Charter) which was adopted on 27 June 1981 in the framework of the Organization of African Unity and entered into force on 21 October 1986 (UNTS Vol. 1520, No. 26363).

A third level is finally formed by the international and global conventions, declarations, protocols, etc., many of which were negotiated and concluded within the framework of the United Nations.

Peter J. Opitz

Lit.: *Burgers, J.H.:* The Road to San Francisco: The Revival of the Human Rights Idea in the Twentieth Century, in: HRQ 14 (1992), 447-477; *Dicke, K.:* "... das von allen Völkern und Nationen zu erreichende gemeinsame Ideal ..." Zum Politikprogramm der Allgemeinen Erklärung, in: VN 46 (1998), 191-194; *Farer, T.J./Gaer, F.:* The UN and Human Rights, in: Roberts, A./Kingsbury, B. (eds.): United Nations, Divided World. The UN's Roles in International Relations, 2nd edn., Oxford 1993, 240-296; *Humphrey, J.P.:* Human Rights and the United Nations: A Great Adventure, Epping 1984; *Lauterpacht, H.:* International Law and Human Rights, London 1950; *Lauterpacht, H.:* An International Bill of Rights of Man, New York 1945; *Maritain, J. (ed.):* Um die Erklärung der Menschenrechte, Zürich et al. 1951; *Morsink, J.:* World War Two and the Universal Declaration, in: HRQ 15 (1993), 357-405; *Opitz, P.J.:* Der internationale Menschenrechtsschutz im 20. Jahrhundert, Munich 1999; *Robinson, N.:* The Universal Declaration of Human Rights, its Origin, Significance and Interpretation, 2nd edn., New York 1958; *United Nations:* Human Rights: A Compilation of International Instruments of the United Nations; UN Doc. ST/HR/5, New York 1988.

Addendum

When the General Assembly adopted the Universal Declaration, it was regarded not as a statement of legal obligation, but rather as a common standard for all nation states to work toward. But in the course of time, in particular since the middle of the nineties, the relevance of the UDHR increased. As *Kirgis* observed in 2005: "Over the ensuing years, though, the Universal Declaration has increasingly been regarded within UN circles and elsewhere as a statement of rules and principles having the status of international law." (*Kirgis* 2005, 2)

The final document of the World Summit in 2005 underlines this increased relevance of the UDHR for human rights in general in formulating in paragraph 120: "We reaffirm the solemn commitment of our States to fulfil their obligations to promote universal respect for and the observance and protection of all human rights and fundamental freedoms for all in accordance with the Charter, the Universal Declaration of Human Rights and other instruments relating to human rights and international law. The universal nature of these rights and freedoms is beyond question." (UN Doc. A/RES/60/1, 16 September 2005, para. 120)

For Kirgis the authors of the 2005 World Summit Outcome Document recognized the legal quality of the UDHR: The Outcome Document "appears to recognize that the Declaration has legal significance (since it is among the instruments "relating to human rights and international law") rather than simply being a political statement of goals." (*Kirgis* 2005, 1)

Also remarkable is the ranking: The UDHR is named directly after the UN Charter as guiding principles for the protection of human rights, before the different human rights conventions.

This remarkable tendency of upgrading the UDHR is subsequently to be found in another important document with regard to human rights protection, the institution-building resolution of the newly established *Human Rights Council*. The *Commission on Human Rights* was replaced by the *Human Rights Council* who started work in June 2006. As set out in General Assembly resolution 60/251, the Human Rights Council reviewed the various control mechanisms and procedures introduced by its predecessor. For those mechanisms which were prolonged, or, such as the

Universal Periodic Review (UPR) of all members of the United Nations, newly introduced, the UDHR is serving as a major standard of reference: With regard to the complaint procedures established under the *Commission on Human Rights* which the *Human Rights Council* decided to keep in function, the Council defined as admissibility criteria for the complaints "It is not politically motivated and its object is consistent with the Charter of the United Nations, the Universal Declaration of Human Rights and other applicable instruments in the field of human rights law." (UN Doc. A/HRC/RES/5/1, 18 June 2007, para. 87a)

In nearly the same wording the Council defines in the Annex of resolution 5/1 as basis for the UPR: "The basis of the review is: (a) The Charter of the United Nations; (b) The Universal Declaration of Human Rights; (c) Human rights instruments to a which a State is a party; ..." (ibid., para. 1).

The ranking of the UDHR as admissibility criterion for the human rights complaints and as the basis of the of the UPR, in both cases placed directly after the UN Charter and before the human rights conventions, re-confirms the appreciation of the World Outcome Document and illustrates the high relevance and acceptance of the UDHR as basic document for the interpretation of human rights. The UDHR – although not being a human rights treaty – therefore can serve as a very useful instrument to promote "dignity and justice for all of us" as the official UN campaigning commemorating the declaration's 60th birthday claims.

Norman Weiß

Lit.: *Alfredsson, G./Eide, A. (eds.):* The Universal Declaration of Human Rights: A Common Standard of Achievement, The Hague et al. 1998; *Ehrensperger, E.:* Die Allgemeine Erklärung der Menschenrechte als Modellfall der Deliberation. Theorie, Dokumentation, Analyse, Baden-Baden 2006; *Glendon, M.A.:* A World Made New: Eleanor Roosevelt and the Universal Declaration of Human Rights, New York 2001; *Klein, E. (ed.):* MenschenRechtsMagazin: Themenheft 50 Jahre Allgemeine Erklärung der Menschenrechte, Potsdam 1997; *Kirgis, F.:* International Law Aspects of the 2005 World Summit Outcome Document, in: ASIL Insights, 4 October 2005, www.asil.org /insights/ 2005/10/ insights051004.html; *Korey, W.:* NGOs and the Universal Declaration of Human Rights, "A Curious Grapevine", New York 1998; *Morsink, J.:* The Universal Declaration of Human Rights: Origins, Drafting, and Intent, Philadelphia 1999.

Internet: Homepage of the Universal Declaration of Human Rights: www.ohchr.org/ EN/UDHR/Pages/60UDHRIntroduction.aspx

Human Rights Committee

I. Establishment and Composition

The Human Rights Committee, though provided for in the International Covenant on Civil and Political Rights (CCPR) (→ Human Rights Conventions, CCPR – International Covenant on Civil and Political Rights) as an international supervisory organ right from the beginning (Articles 28-45), changed in character during its long genesis. First envisaged was a body composed of nine members, tasked with fact-finding and conciliation, and against which findings access to the International Court of Justice (→ ICJ) should have been given. In the end, a different concept prevailed: the Committee consists of 18 members who need to be nationals of states parties. The fact that for the election of the members, among others, recognized competence in the field of human rights is required and that reference is made explicitly to the usefulness of the participation of some persons having legal experience, has had the result that the work of the Human Rights Committee has received a predominantly legal character This has proven to be quite beneficial to the reputation of the Committee, even though the Committee does not pass legally binding decisions.

Committee members are nominated by states parties and elected by secret ballot at a meeting of those states. Members are elected for a term of four years, and are eligible for re-election. The continuity of the Committee's work is safeguarded by electing nine of its members every two years. Members receive expense allowances.

The Human Rights Committee is not a subsidiary organ of the UN, but a supervisory organ that is based solely on the CCPR ("treaty body") (→ Principal Organs, Subsidiary Organs, Treaty Bodies). The work of the Committee is, however, institutionally linked with the UN human rights machinery (→ Human Rights, Protection of) through the Office of the High Commissioner for Human Rights (→ Human Rights, United Nations High Commissioner). Pursuant to Article 36 of the CCPR, the UN → Secretary-General provides the necessary staff and facilities for the effective performance of the functions of the Committee. The Committee meets at the Headquarters of the UN in New York City (→ UN Office New York), or at the Office in Geneva (→ UN Office Geneva); expenses are borne by the UN → budget. The initial meeting of the Committee took place on 21 March 1977.

According to Article 39 of the CCPR, the Human Rights Committee established its own Rules of Procedure (UN Doc. CCPR/C/3/Rev.8, 22 September 2005) as well as the offices of Chairperson, three Vice-Chairpersons and a Rapporteur (reporting annually to the → General Assembly of the UN). Together they are also referred to as the "Bureau". The officers are elected by the Committee for a term of two years and are eligible for re-election.

Committee members perform their duties in their personal capacity; they do not represent their states and therefore are not subject to instructions. They shall discharge their duties impartially. This requirement is scarcely reconcilable with the exercise of the official duties in an administrative function in one of the states parties. The Committee has emphasized its independence and impartiality through the adoption of "Guiding Principles" (1997).

Accordingly, a member of the Committee shall, for example, neither participate in the examination of the reports presented by his or her country, nor in the review of communications directed against his or her country (UN Doc. CCPR/C/61/GUI, para. 4, reprinted in: *United Nations* 1998*)*.

II. Functions

1. Reporting Procedure

The main task of the Committee is the continuous supervision of states parties' compliance with their obligations under the Covenant. Pursuant to Article 40, all states parties are obliged to submit periodic reports (every three to five years depending on the human rights situation in the state) to the Committee, the initial report being due within one year after entry into force of the Covenant for the state party concerned.

Country reports are to be prepared according to the Guidelines issued by the Committee (see UN Doc. CCPR/C/66/GUI/Rev.2, 26 February 2001). The reports should not only deal with the legal framework and norms for the implementation of the Covenant rights, but should also explain and exemplify the practical application of and the progress made in giving effect to the rights. The 2006 "Harmonized guidelines on reporting under the international human rights treaties, including guidelines on a common core document and treaty-specific documents" (UN Doc. HRI/MC/2006/3, 10 May 2006), that shall harmonize the reporting of the different human rights treaties, have not yet been implemented by the Committee. The Committee prepares the examination of the reports by a written List of Issues, sent to the state delegation in advance, which then – together with additional oral questions – is to be answered during public session by an often very high ranking delegation.

In the end of the scrutiny, the Chairman summarizes the most important results of the discussion, however, without anticipating the written "Concluding Observations" which are adopted and notified to the state by the Committee. These observations list the main posi-

tive and negative aspects of the report and contain – more or less detailed – recommendations addressed to the state. Such views on individual states only became possible after the changes in world politics at the beginning of the 1990s. Before that time, only by means of "General Comments," and in a quite generalizing manner, could attention be drawn to failure to comply with the Covenant obligations and difficulties occurring during the discussion of state reports, without targeting an individual state.

Although by virtue of the reporting procedure a dialogue with the states parties was established, and the Committee can give important assistance and encouragement, there are weighty deficiencies: A major problem is the lack of willingness of many states to comply with their reporting obligation. Some countries are far more than ten years in arrears with their reports, some states having not even submitted their initial report. In such cases, the Committee could until recently do not much more than request the report over and over again. Since the year 2001, by amendment of its Rules of Procedure (UN Doc. CCPR/C/3/Rev.8, new rule 70), the Committee has started to put pressure on these states by scheduling an actual examination date, even if no report is submitted. In such circumstances the Committee has to rely on all material available from different sources within and outside the United Nations. The Committee may even adopt provisional concluding observations which – after taking into account any comments by the state party, to which the observations have to be submitted first – may become final and be made public (ibid., Rule 70). Serious delays are also enumerated in the Annual Report to the General Assembly in a "red list" (headed by the negative example of Gambia with 22 years delay by July 2007). Another problem is that the reports, which are usually drafted by government officials, may often inadequately reflect the real situation in a given country. The Committee therefore has to rely upon information provided by other sources (→ specialized agencies; → NGOs; own knowledge) in order to enable a constructive dialogue with the state party concerned. Regularly only one day (six hours) is available for the oral discussion of the periodic report and one and a half day (nine hours) for the initial report. On average, the Committee examines four state reports per session.

Another important deficiency in the past was the fact that the Committee had not yet developed a follow-up procedure in order to maintain an ongoing discussion with states regarding the Committee's recommendations. The dialogue could only be taken up again on the occasion of the submission of the next periodic report. Since the year 2001, the Committee requests the state party to report back to the Committee within 12 months with regard to specific points of concern. In the year 2002 a "Special Rapporteur for follow-up on concluding observations" was appointed (cf. Report of the Human Rights Committee 2002, UN Doc. A/57/40, Vol. I and II). He examines the follow-up information and submits his findings to the Committee. The Committee discusses these findings and adopts formal recommendations. It will depend on the quality of the state's reply whether the timeframe for the submission of the next periodic report will be changed.

General Comment No. 30 (75) of the Human Rights Committee (UN Doc. CCPR/C/21/Rev.2/Add.12, 16 July 2002) gives a clear outline of the reporting obligations under Article 40 of the CCPR.

2. Inter-State Complaints

As of 31 July 2008, 48 states had accepted the competence of the Committee to receive and consider complaints ("communications") of other state parties which themselves have made the same declaration under Article 41 of the CCPR (cf. UN Doc. A/63/40 (Vol. I), 187-188). This complaints procedure is regulated precisely, placing the Committee in a position where it can help to find an amicable settlement of the dispute on the basis of the respect for the Covenant rights. Up to the present (as of 31 July 2008), this procedure has never been invoked.

3. Individual Complaints

The most adequate form of the protection of human rights is to accord to the victims of human rights violations themselves the possibility to complain of such violations. As a general agreement on such a complaints possibility could not be reached at the time of the negotiations on the CCPR, the individual complaints procedure was arranged in an Optional Protocol, which, however, entered into force at the same time as the CCPR. As of 27 May 2008, 111 states had ratified this (first) Optional Protocol, and thus accepted the competence of the Human Rights Committee to consider individual communications. As of 31 July 2008, more than 1,700 communications were registered and more than 400 cases are pending (cf. ibid., p. iv).

If a complaint ("communication") is declared admissible – a particularly important requirement is the exhaustion of domestic remedies (Art. 2 and 5 (2) of the Optional Protocol) – the Committee examines the communication in the light of all written information at hand, notably statements of the individual and of the defendant state, and decides whether a violation of Covenant rights has occurred. If this be the case, the Committee declares that a violation has been disclosed and requests the state concerned to provide reparation to the victim (based on Art. 2 (3) of the CCPR – "effective remedy"), such as immediate release from detention, commutation of a death sentence, or compensation.

Under this procedure, too, the Committee cannot take a legally binding decision, but can only provide its legal opinion ("view"). States parties to the Optional Protocol are nonetheless required to consider this legal opinion thoughtfully, and to notify the Committee why they do not want to comply with the opinion. Since 1990, the Human Rights Committee has formally established a follow-up procedure, enabling the Committee by way of a "Special Rapporteur for follow-up on views" to keep in touch with the state concerned, and to call for compliance and to remind it of the respective measures called for by the Committee (cf. Report of the Human Rights Committee 1990, UN Doc. A/45/40, Vol. I, paras. 636-639 and Vol. II, Annex XI). It is estimated that, in about 30 to 35% of the cases, states parties finally adopt the Committee's view; it is, however, very difficult to assess a clear success rate, as some Committee decisions will bear fruit only in the long run.

In order to avoid irreparable damage to the victim of the alleged violation, the Committee may – according to Rule 92 of the Rules of Procedure – ask the state party concerned to adopt interim measures until the Committee has decided upon the admissibility or merits of the case (e.g., in cases of imminent executions after dubious legal proceedings). Mostly, states have respected such requests, though there are regrettable exceptions. The Committee has hold that a state party to the Optional Protocol is legally obligated to comply with a request according to Rule 92 of its Rules.

The length of the procedure is also regrettable. Often the Committee can decide only four or five years after the petition was received, partly because the procedure is delayed by the parties concerned (complaining individual, state concerned) and to some extent because the personnel and time resources of the Committee are not sufficient. On average, the Committee is able to adopt final views on 15 to 20 individual complaints per session, not included the complaints that are declared inadmissible or will be discontinued for a variety of reasons.

4. Other Tasks

An important additional task of the Committee is the adoption of "General Comments". At first (until 1990) meant to substitute for the lacking possibility of making concluding observations on individual country reports, these Gen-

eral Comments have now acquired the function of describing the Committee's practice with regard to each of the Covenant provisions and of indicating possible deficits and misinterpretations of the CCPR to states parties, thereby giving them also guidance for future reporting. At the same time, some of the Comments contain statements on questions of principle, for example on the reservation and denunciation problem. Until the end of 2008, the Committee had adopted 32 General Comments (see the compilation contained in UN Doc. HRI/GEN/1/Rev.9 (Vol. I), 27 May 2008). The Committee is momentarily preparing its General Comment No. 33 on the obligations of states regarding the first optional protocol (cf. http://www2.ohchr.org/english/bodies/hrc/docs/CCPR.C.GC.33.pdf).

Further, the discussions of and statements on particular developments or drafts of other bodies (e.g. other human rights organs; → ILC) or on the improvement of its own methods of work, demand considerable time during each Committee session.

III. Organization of Work

The Human Rights Committee convenes three times a year for three weeks in New York or Geneva. Each session is prepared by a working group composed of Committee members meeting one week before the session. The meetings of the Committee are public, except for the consideration and adoption of views on individual complaints, and of the Concluding Observations on country reports.

Principally, the Committee convenes in plenary session. Experience shows more and more clearly that this procedure is inadequate to keep up with the growing work load of the Committee. The abundance of pending individual complaints and the backlog of not discussed state reports (despite the many delays in reporting) threaten the effectiveness of the Committee's work. Redress is needed to encounter this situation, e.g., through a "chamber system". Two other proposals recently discussed are the so called Unified Standing Treaty Body that would replace all treaty bodies, and a unified body dealing with individual communications of all relevant treaty bodies. The Committee is of the view that both propositions face insurmountable legal and political challenges, at least in the short and medium term.

Despite the composition of the Committee, reflecting the principal legal systems in the community of states (Art. 31 of the CCPR), major differences in interpreting the Covenant rights on the basis of different cultural approaches have seldom occurred since the end of the East-West confrontation. Yet the Committee is quite aware of the fact that the rights guaranteed have to stand the test of different situations and that rigidity in the interpretation of human rights must be avoided. However, the Committee has always adhered to its conviction that the Covenant rights demand universal respect, and must not be weakened by the states parties.

The success of the Committee's work is decisively dependent on the taking notice of its work in the contracting states. This means, *inter alia*, that the concluding observations, views and General Comments of the Committee need to be published in the official language of the states parties.

Eckart Klein

Lit.: *Boerefijn, I.:* The Reporting Procedure of the Covenant on Civil and Political Rights – Practice and Procedures of the Human Rights Committee, Antwerpen et al. 1999; *Deutsches Institut für Menschenrechte (ed.):* Die „General Comments" zu den VN-Menschenrechtsverträgen, Baden-Baden 2005; *Ghandhi, P.R.:* The Human Rights Committee and the Right of Individual Communication – Law and Practice, Aldershot 1998; *Klein, E. (ed.):* The Monitoring System of Human Rights Treaty Obligations, Berlin 1998; *Klein, E.:* General Comments, in: Ipsen, J./Schmidt-Jortzig, E. (eds.): Recht – Staat – Gemeinwohl, Fs. D. Rauschning, Cologne et al. 2001, 301-311; *McGoldrick, D.:* The Human Rights Committee, Oxford 1991; *Opsahl, T.:* The Human Rights Committee, in: Alston, P. (ed.): The United Na-

tions and Human Rights – A Critical Appraisal, Oxford 1992, 369-443; *Schäfer, B.:* Die Individualbeschwerde nach dem Fakultativprotokoll zum Zivilpakt. Ein Handbuch für die Praxis, 2nd edition, Berlin 2007; *Tomuschat, C.:* International Covenant on Civil and Political Rights, Human Rights Committee, in: Bernhardt, R. (ed.): EPIL, Vol. 2, Amsterdam et al. 1995, 1115–1119; *Tistounet, E.:* Rapport sur la nature, les fonctions et les activités du Comité de New York, Revue Universelle des Droits de l'Homme, Vol. 1 (1989), 50–61; *United Nations - General Assembly:* Report of the Human Rights Committee, Vol. I, New York 1998, UN Doc. A/53/40, Annex III : Guidelines for the exercise of their functions by members of the Human Rights Committee; *United Nations - International Covenant on Civil and Political Rights:* Consolidated guidelines for State reports under the International Covenant on Civil and Political Rights, 26 February 2001, UN Doc. CCPR/C/66/GUI/Rev.2; *United Nations - International Human Rights Instruments:* Harmonized guidelines on reporting under the international human rights treaties, including guidelines on a common core document and treaty-specific documents, 10 May 2006, UN Doc. HRI/MC/ 2006/3.

Internet: Homepage of the Human Rights Committee: www.ohchr.org/english/bodies/hrc/index.htm.

Human Rights Conventions and their Measures of Implementation

Traditionally the guarantee of → *human rights* had been the sole responsibility of the states, acting within their national legal systems. With the foundation of the UN, the concept came to the fore that maintaining international peace and security (→ Peacekeeping) and the protection of human rights (→ Human Rights, Protection of) are connected with each other, that massive infringements of human rights threaten peace (→ Peace, Peace Concept, Threat to Peace), and that states can influence the adherence to human rights through international human rights conventions. The → Charter of the UN assigned to the world organization the task of fostering respect for, and contributing to a realization of human rights (Art. 1 (3)

295

and Art. 55 lit. c UN Charter). Thus the Charter of the UN has established the preconditions for the *internationalization of human rights*. In this process of internationalization the latter have developed more and more through international treaties (→ Treaties, Law of) and the activities of the UN bodies (→ UN System; → Principal Organs, Subsidiary Organs, Treaty Bodies) to an international system of human rights.

The human rights conventions include the largest number of universally-designed treaties compared with other parts of international law (→ UNTS – United Nation Treaty Series).

The scope of human rights norms covers a wide area: There is hardly any social field which is not marked by human rights standards set up by international conventions. The following conventions deserve particular emphasis: the → Convention on the Prevention and Punishment of the Crime of Genocide of 9 December 1948, the International Convention on the Elimination of All Forms of Racial Discrimination of 21 December 1965 (→ Human Rights Conventions, CERD), the International Covenant on Civil and Political Rights of 16 December 1966 (→ Human Rights Conventions, CCPR), the International Covenant on Economic, Social and Cultural Rights of 16 December 1966 (→ Human Rights Conventions, CESCR), the Convention on the Elimination of All Forms of Discrimination against Women of 18 December 1979 (→ Human Rights Conventions, CEDAW), the Convention against Torture and Other Cruel, Inhuman or Degrading Treatment or Punishment of 10 December 1984 (→ Human Rights Conventions, CAT), and the Convention on the Rights of the Child of 20 November 1989 (→ Human Rights Conventions, CRC).

Considering the complex system of human rights conventions, and noting that in almost all fields of life international human rights standards have been established and that some human rights have been laid down several times, one will find the number of *regulations for their implementation* fairly low compared with the number of norms.

While the *process of enacting laws* in the area of human rights can be seen as completed, and a Convention on Enforced Disappearance has more recently been adopted (UN Doc. A/Res/61/177, Annex, 20 December 2006), the *implementation mechanisms* have to be organized more efficiently. The treaty bodies for implementation rely in their work on the support of the states concerned.

The *treaty bodies* of the above-mentioned conventions consist of independent experts. All members are elected by the state parties to each convention and can be re-elected. The Committee on Economic, Social and Cultural Rights (CESCR) constitutes an exception as it is not provided for in the Covenant on Economic, Social and Cultural Rights and is elected by ECOSOC. With the committees there exists a multitude of organs for treaty-monitoring whose functions often overlap as the material standards of the conventions coincide as well. This poses the question whether unifying the committees would be possible, thus leading perhaps to greater efficiency. First tentative ideas have been developed which propose a unified treaty-monitoring body to examine common state reports (Concept Paper on the High Commissioner's proposal for a unified standing treaty body, UN Doc. HRI/MC/2006/2 of 22 March 2006) to ensure a better implementation of human rights obligations by the state parties. Furthermore a unified treaty-monitoring body could result in greater efficiency and consistency in interpretation.

The conventions provide for procedures for the promotion and protection of human rights, for the prevention of infringements of human rights and for the monitoring of human rights situations in the states, through the *reporting procedure* and the *complaints procedure*. The reporting procedure is the most generally accepted one. The regular form of the *implementation procedures* is the obligatory *reporting procedure*, i.e. *state reports* are given to and discussed by expert committees. All conventions stipulate that one or two years after the entry into force of the treaty a state shall submit its initial report and after a time span ranging from two to five years with the different conventions its periodic reports on the implementation of the rights provided for in the treaties. These reports shall give a comprehensive insight in the human rights situation of the country concerned and shall inform about the implementing procedures. Reporting practices vary considerably. Only few states report extensively on their human rights situation and allow critical scrutiny. Most states report only with great delay and have no interest in delivering insights into their own human rights situation. The committees not only concentrate on the information given to them by the states, they also receive them from → NGOs. The reporting states are interested in presenting themselves to their best advantage to the committee and not being placed under the pressure to justify themselves.

In spite of initial opposition by some states, it is now accepted practice that after the reports are examined in a critical debate with the member state representatives and non-governmental organizations (NGOs) presenting their often conflicting views of the human rights situation, the committees formulate their concluding observations and recommendations. These are published in an annual report. The states are expected to follow the recommendations and give account of their implementation. As a result of the experiences in the committees, the expert members develop general comments and recommendations which are adopted by consensus and constitute the most important instrument for the interpretation of the different treaty provisions. The *Convention on the Prevention and Punishment of the Crime of Genocide* does not have its own implementation body. It has to refer to the competent bodies of the UN which, upon request by the state parties, can deal with the issue of what appro-

priate measures are to be taken in reaction to genocidal actions.

All the above-mentioned conventions dispose of an *obligatory reporting procedure* for the implementation of treaty obligations. These instruments are connected within the reporting procedure. The treaty-monitoring bodies can also demand reports which are focused on the observance of obligations whose infringements have been discovered in an individual complaints procedure.

The examination of the state reports is not prescribed in detail within the different human rights conventions; however, the examinations take place as public hearings. The publicity of the procedure has as result that the minutes of the sessions of the committees are made public, too. The examination of the reports in an examining body set up by the respective committee is realized through the right to question the representatives of the respective state, a right which needs no further authorization. By the same token the reporting states are not forced to deal with every question posed. With regard to the participation of the → specialized agencies of the UN in this examining procedure, the Committee on Economic, Social and Cultural Rights (CESCR) goes farthest by granting them the right to make general statements at the end of the report examination. The NGOs are free to supply the examination body with material concerning the state which is on the agenda for the examination of its report. Of course the NGOs can participate in the public sessions of the examination bodies. In addition, they make use of the possibility to speak privately with the experts of the examining bodies. In its rules of procedure the CESCR has also granted the NGOs the right to make written statements.

The *complaints procedures* provided for in some conventions, comprise the *inter-state complaint (or state-to-state complaint)* and the *complaint made by individuals*. Both procedures are only applied if the states have submitted specifically by formal declaration to those regulations. Some conventions provide for complaints procedures in the forms of inter-state complaints and individual complaints for states which made a declaration to that effect or ratified an optional protocol. The conventions use the relatively soft term "communication" for complaints, and claimants are referred to as "authors" and decisions as "views". This is to emphasize that these are not judgments with binding legal force.

The *inter-state complaint* is rarely used by the states – they are not interested in officially accusing each other. But the *individual complaints procedure*, i.e. the complaint of individuals concerning an alleged violation of human rights, is increasingly made use of.

The individual complaints procedure to the → Human Rights Committee of the CCPR is of most importance. The Convention Against Torture, which established the Committee Against Torture (CAT), allows for individual complaints under its Article 22. So far 61 states have recognized the individual complaints procedure. 318 complaints have reached the committee hitherto, most of which deal not with accusations of torture but violations of non-refoulement under Article 3 of the Convention. The International Convention on the Elimination of All Forms of Racial Discrimination which forms the framework for the Committee on the Elimination of Racial Discrimination (CERD) has until now only been active in 36 individual complaints cases. The International Covenant on Economic, Social and Cultural Rights has at its disposal the monitoring Committee on Economic, Social and Cultural Rights (CESCR). The Covenant does not provide for an individual complaints procedure, but an optional protocol modeled on the Optional Protocol of the → Covenant on Civil and Political Rights will be adopted soon. An Optional Protocol to the Convention on the Elimination of All Forms of Discrimination against Women for an individual complaints procedure has existed since 1999.

Investigation procedures are only provided for in Article 20 of the Convention Against Torture and Article 8 of the Optional Protocol of the Convention on the Elimination of All Forms of Discrimination against Women. The procedures in both conventions are obligatory, but states have the possibility to "opt out" on signature or ratification. This possibility has been used by 9 states according to Article 28 of the Convention Against Torture and 4 states according to Article 10 of the Optional Protocol to the Convention Against All Forms of Discrimination against Women. Investigation procedures are initiated ex-officio and only if the committee receives reliable information that torture is being systematically practiced, or that women are gravely and systematically being discriminated against The states concerned are asked to comment on the allegations. In cases where the allegations are confirmed, the committee may conduct confidential inquiries, also in the state itself, but only with the consent of the government concerned. Following the investigation, a confidential report is transmitted to the government in question. The committee may also publish summaries of such reports in its annual report.

Martina Haedrich

Lit.: *Alston, P. (ed.):* The United Nations and Human Rights, Oxford et al. 1992; *Alston P.:* The UN's Human Rights Record: From San Francisco to Vienna and Beyond, in: HRQ 16 (1994), 376-388; *Donnelly; J.:* The Social Construction of International Human Rights, in: Danne,T./Wheeler, N.J. (eds.): Human Rights in Global Politics, Cambridge 1999, 71-102; *Farer, T.J./Gaer, F.:* The UN and Human Rights: At the End of the Beginning, in: Roberts, A./Kingsbury, B. (eds.): United Nations, Divided World. The UN's Roles in International Relations, 2nd edn., Oxford et al. 1993, 240-296; *Haedrich, M.:* Von der Allgemeinen Erklärung der Menschenrechte zur internationalen Menschenrechtsordnung – ein Überblick, in: JA 31 (1999), 251-260; *Haedrich, M.:* Rassismusbekämpfung nach Völkerrecht und innerstaatliche Wirkungen in: JA 35 (2003), 899-905; *Hampson, F. O.:* An Overview of the Reform of the UN Human Rights Machinery, in: Human Rights Law Review 2007, 7-28; *Nowak, M.:* The Need for A World Court of Human Rights, in: Human Rights Law Review 7 (2007), 251-260; *Oberleitner, G.:* Menschenrechtsschutz durch Staatenberichte. Europäische Hochschulschriften, Reihe 2 Rechtswissenschaft, Bd. 2394, Frankfurt (Main) 1998; *O'Flaherty, M./O'Brien, C.:* Reform of the UN Human Rights Treaty Monitoring Bodies: A Critique of the Concept Paper of the High Commissioner's Proposal for a Unified Standing Treaty Body, in: Human Rights Law Review 7 (2007), 141-172; *Seidel, G.:* Handbuch der Grund- und Menschenrechte auf staatlicher, europäischer und universeller Ebene, Baden-Baden 1996; *Simma, B.:* Die internationale Kontrolle des UN-Paktes über wirtschaftliche, soziale und kulturelle Rechte, neue Entwicklungen. Fs. Bernhardt, Heidelberg 1994, 5.26; *Tomuschat, C.:* Human Rights, Petitions and Individual Complaints, in: Wolfrum, R. (ed.): United Nations: Law, Policies and Practice, Vol. 2, Munich/Dordrecht 1995, 619-627.

Internet: A compilation of all international human rights instruments including the treaties, the status of their ratification, reservations, etc., as well as comprehensive information on the work of the treaty bodies can be found on the homepage of the United Nations High Commissioner for Human Rights: www.ohchr.org.

Human Rights Conventions, CAT – Convention against Torture and Other Cruel, Inhuman or Degrading Treatment or Punishment

The prohibition of torture is already been laid down in the International Covenant on Civil and Political Rights ($\rightarrow$ Human Rights Conventions, CCPR), a fact to which the preamble of the *"Convention against Torture and Other Cruel, Inhuman or Degrading Treatment or Punishment"* – in short *"Torture Convention"* (UN Doc. A/RES/39/46, 10 December 1984; UNTS Vol. 1465, No. 24841), refers to explicitly.

But the Torture Convention includes obligations going beyond those in the precursor convention. The convention defines torture (in Art. 1, para. 1) as

"any act by which severe physical or mental pain or suffering is intentionally inflicted on a person for such purposes as obtaining from him or a third person a confession, punishing him for an act he or a third person has committed or is suspected of having committed, or intimidating or coercing him or a third person, or for any reason based on discrimination of any kind", when such pain or suffering is inflicted by a public official or other person acting in an official capacity. It does not include pain or suffering arising only from, inherent in or incidental to lawful sanctions (Art. 1, para. 1, 2nd sentence). This *restricting regulation* is a concession to the states of the Islam, whose criminal law includes cruel corporal punishment. However it remains doubtful whether such severe violations of human rights, and other related practices, can be justified by laws, culture and tradition.

The Convention obliges the contracting states to take effective measures within the framework of their national legislature to prevent acts of torture in any territory under their jurisdiction. It expressly prohibits that exceptional circumstances or orders from a superior or a public authority may be invoked as a justification of torture (Art. 2). Moreover the states are obliged to take precautions against the possibility that persons who are accused of torture escape by going abroad. Even without a demand for extradition they are to extradite the accused or to submit the case to its competent authorities for the purpose of prosecution – *aut dedere, aut indicare* – (Art. 5 II, 6-9). Thus the Convention is the only universal human rights treaty providing for universal jurisdiction. The Convention asks the contracting states to inform the law enforcement personnel about the prohibition against torture, and to organize the appropriate training for such persons (Art. 10). The Convention also expressly laid down the right of torture victims to obtain fair and adequate compensation and obliges the states to establish such provisions in their legal systems (Art. 14), and pronounces an absolute prohibition on invoking evidence which has been obtained through torture (Art. 15).

The states are required to compile *state reports* on the measures they have taken for implementing the Convention and to submit them to the *Committee Against Torture (CAT)* (Art. 19). Additionally, the states must respond to allegations of tortures and other maltreatment as these may arise. At present the Convention has 145 states parties (as of 15 December 2008).

The *Committee against Torture (CAT)* was established pursuant to Article 17, para. 1 of the Convention, and consists of 10 human rights experts, who serve in their personal capacity. They are elected by the states parties for a term of four years.

If the Committee receives reliable information which appears to contain well-founded indications of systematic torture, the Committee has the power to start its own inquiries, even if the state concerned does not cooperate with the Committee; the only consequence of non-cooperation is that the members of the Committee conducting the inquiry will be unable to visit the country concerned. The states parties of the Convention are bound to accept this investigation procedure unless they expressly declare that they do not accept this competence of the Committee under Article 20. So far only a handful states have not accepted the procedure; the majority has. Thus this investigation procedure goes beyond those of other human rights conventions (→ Human Rights Conventions and their Measures of Implementation).

The *procedure of examining the state reports,* which has been largely borrowed from the procedure of the *International Covenant on Civil and Political Rights,* constitutes a further development in that the Committee against Torture can give an assessment on each report in the form of "general comments", and that each state report is published. In this respect the activities of the → NGOs, who submit information to the Committee, are worthy of note. The Committee can also conduct confidential inquiries (Art. 20, par. 2), which take place in agreement with the contracting state concerned on its territory. However, this procedure according to Article 20 (2) can be expressly excluded at the ratification of the Torture Convention by a formal declaration of the state party under Article 28. Thus Article 28 has the function of an opting-out clause through which the member states can exclude the competence of the committee in its legal effect with respect to the other contracting states. So far nine states have made use of this possibility.

The instruments of *state complaints* (Art. 21), *individual complaints* (Art. 22) are provided in the Convention similar to the respective procedures in the International Covenant on Civil and Political Rights. So far 58 states have acknowledged the competence of the CAT under Article 21 and 63 states under Article 22 (as of 12 August 2008).

The right of carrying out oral proceedings and hearing witnesses within the framework of the individual's complaint procedure is an improvement, as compared to the International Covenant on Civil and Political Rights. The individual complaints procedure ends with the CAT the "adoption of views" by the Committee. While these are not formally binding on the state party, they have a similar status to the views adopted by the Human Rights Committee, which are formulated by that Committee as if they were a court decision and which have generally been given effect to by the state party concerned.

The majority of the individual complaints dealt with so far have been petitions of applicants for asylum, who claimed that they were not safe from torture in their home states (see for example the decisions of the 38th session, May 2007, UN Doc. CAT/C/38/D/249/2004; CAT/C/38/D/305/2006; CAT/C/8/D/270/2005).

Since 1992 a working group of the → Commission on *Human Rights* had endeavored to develop a *supplementary protocol to the convention,* according to which a controlling body with the right to visit prisons and detention centers shall be established.

In 2002 the General Assembly adopted the Optional Protocol to the Convention against Torture (UN Doc. A/RES/57/199, 18 December 2002, Annex). It entered into force in 2006 and has so far been ratified by 40 states (as of 15 December 2008). The Optional Protocol follows a preventive concept and provides for an international mechanism in the form of a Subcommittee on Prevention. It also obliges the states parties to establish internal visiting mechanisms through independent national visiting bodies. The visits are not limited to prisons, but also comprise police facilities as well as nursing homes. As a result of the visits these bodies shall report and give recommendations, e.g. on the conduct or education of the staff.

Martina Haedrich

Lit.: *Boulesbaa, A.:* The UN Convention on Torture and the prospects for enforcement, The Hague, 1999; *Byrnes, A.:* The Committee against Torture, in: Alston, P. (ed.): The United Nations and Human Rights. A Critical Appraisal, Oxford et al. 1992, 509-546; *Cassesse, A.:* A New Approach in Human Rights – the 1987 Convention for the Prevention of Torture, in: AJIL 83 (1989), 128-153; *Donnelly, J.:* The Emerging International Regime against Torture, in: NILR 33 (1986), 1-23; *Haedrich, M.:* Von der Allgemeinen Erklärung der Menschenrechte zur internationalen Menschenrechtsordnung – ein Überblick, in: JA 31 (1999), 251-260; *Karl, W.:* Besonderheiten der internationalen Kontrollverfahren zum Schutz der Menschenrechte, in: Aktuelle Probleme des Menschenrechtsschutzes. Berichte der Deutschen Gesellschaft für Völkerrecht, Bd. 33, Heidelberg 1994, 83-128; *Mahler, C.:* Das Fakultativprotokoll der Konvention gegen Folter und anderer grausame, unmenschliche oder erniedrigende Behandlung oder Strafe (CAT-OP), in: MenschenRechtsMagazin 2003, 183-186; *Nowak, M.:* The Implementation Functions of the UN Committee against Torture, Fs. Ermacora, Kehl et al. 1988, 493-526.
Internet:
www.ohchr.org/english/bodies/cat/index.htm

Human Rights Conventions, CCPR – International Covenant on Civil and Political Rights

I. Origins and General Description

The International Covenant on Civil and Political Rights (CCPR) (UNTS Vol. 999, No. 14668, 171) and its two Optional Protocols, together with the International Covenant on Economic, Social and Cultural Rights (CESCR) (→ Human Rights Conventions, CESCR), constitute the core of the legally binding human rights protection at the universal level (→ Human Rights, Protection of). Combined with the 1948 Universal Declaration of Human Rights (UDHR) (→ Human Rights, Universal Declaration of), these are generally referred to as the "International Bill of Rights".

With the adoption of the UDHR in 1948, at a time where an agreement on a legally binding human rights instrument (i.e. an international treaty) could not be reached, a definition of the notion of → human rights as contained in the → Charter of the United Nations (Preamble, Articles 1, 13, 55, 62, 68 and 76) was achieved, and thereby an essential field of tasks of the Organization was defined.

The fact that no legally binding instrument was adopted proved to be beneficial in the end, as it opened, for those states that were skeptical or even hostile towards a human rights concept on the international level, as such a concept would necessarily restrict state → sovereignty, the possibility to join the discussion on the issue. After this seemingly harmless first step was taken, the concept took on such force that opposition to setting up international standards for human rights could no longer be upheld. Rather, the controversy now turned towards the question, whether codification should embrace not only civil and political rights and freedoms, but also economic, social and cultural rights (this position was supported in particular by the socialist countries), or whether it was more appropriate to prepare two separate treaties. Within the UN Commission on Human Rights (→ Human Rights, Commission on), which was first charged with this task of translating the content of the UDHR into the form of an international treaty, the Western countries succeeded in getting through their "separation concept" (i.e. two treaties) in 1951.

The → General Assembly of the United Nations approved this course, but the further drafting of the treaties was referred to the General Assembly's Third Committee (Social, Humanitarian and Cultural Affairs) (→ Committees, System of), and it was requested that, to emphasize the common aim of the treaties, both treaties were to be submitted for adoption at the same time. In addition, it demanded that as many similar provisions as possible should be contained in both Covenants, among them the provision for the right to self-determination (in Art. 1 of both Covenants), to which was obviously attributed a basic function for both Covenants. This reflects the growing influence of the newly emerging independent states that were increasing in number as member states of the UN as the → decolonization process progressed. When finally, on 16 December 1966, the two Covenants were put to the vote, both were adopted unanimously by the General Assembly (UN Doc. A/RES/2200 A (XXI)).

It was almost 10 years until the CCPR would enter into force (23 March 1976), after the 35th instrument of ratification had been deposited. As of 31 December 2008, 163 states were parties to the Covenant. From the group of the more influential countries, only the People's Republic of China is not yet a state party of the Covenant,; it signed the Covenant on 5 October 1998, but has not ratified it up to now.

The CCPR starts with a preamble, expressly referring not only to the UN Charter and the UDHR, but also to economic, social and cultural rights as agreed upon in the parallel Covenant, the CESCR. The subsequent text of the Covenant is subdivided into five parts: Part I is solely devoted to the right of self-determination of peoples (Art. 1). Part II contains provisions for the implementation of the Covenant by the states parties (Arts. 2-5). Part III comprises the substantive rights (Arts. 6-27), followed by Part IV regulating the establishment and the terms of reference of the → Human Rights Committee (Arts. 28-45). Part V clarifies – in the sense of an interpretative rule – the relationship between the Covenant and the UN Charter: the provisions of the Charter and the responsibilities of the organs of the UN and its specialized agencies shall not be impaired, in regard to the matters dealt with in the CCPR (Art. 46), as well as the right of all peoples to enjoy and utilize their natural resources (Art. 47). Part VI contains final provisions.

Together with the CCPR, the General Assembly adopted the (first) Optional Protocol (UNTS Vol. 999, No. 14668, 302) authorizing the Human Rights Committee to receive and consider "communications" from individuals, in other words individual complaints, though the adoption was not unanimous (66 votes to 2 with 38 abstentions). However, after the deposition of the 10th instrument of ratification, the Optional Protocol would enter into force together with the CCPR on 23 March 1976. As of 31 December 2008, 111 states had ratified the Optional Protocol.

II. The Rights Guaranteed

The catalogue of rights guaranteed (Part III of the ICCPR) contains almost all classical liberal human rights and freedoms that are particularly in danger of violation, as historical experience through the centuries has shown.

Article 6 provides protection for the right to life; however, it does not contain a general prohibition of the death penalty. A second Optional Protocol of 15 December 1989 (UN Doc. A/RES/ 44/128, Annex; UNTS Vol. 1642, No. 14668), which pronounces such a prohibition, has become binding by ratification for only 70 states so far (as of 31 December 2008), amongst them 44 European states. Article 7 prohibits to be subjected to torture or cruel, inhuman or degrading treatment or punishment; Article 8 prohibits slavery, slave trade and forced or compulsory labor. Further articles provide: protection from arbitrary arrest or detention (Arts. 9 and 11); the right of detained persons to be treated with humanity and with respect for the inherent dignity of the human person (Art. 10); the right to liberty of movement and freedom to choose one's residence (Art. 12); the protection of aliens from arbitrary or unlawful expulsion (Art. 13); the right to a fair trial (Art. 14); the prohibition of retroactivity of the criminal law (Art. 15); the right to recognition as a person before the law (Art. 16); the right to freedom from arbitrary or unlawful interference with one's privacy, family, home or correspondence (Art. 17); the right to freedom of thought, conscience and religion (Art. 18); the right to freedom of opinion and expression (Art. 19); the right to peaceful assembly and freedom of association (Arts. 21 and 22); the right to marry and found a family (Art. 23); the protection of the children and their right to a name and nationality (Art. 24); the political rights of citizens, in particular to take part in the conduct of public affairs and to vote and to be elected (Art. 25); equality before the law, equal protection of the law and prohibition of discrimination and protection against discrimination on any ground such as race, color, sex, language, religion, political or other opinion, national or social origin, property, birth or other status (Arts. 26; 2 and 3). Finally, the Covenant provides also protection for the right of persons belonging to ethnic, religious or linguistic minorities "to enjoy their own culture, to profess and prac-

tise their own religion, or to use their own language" in community with other members of their group (Art. 27); a right which proved to be quite important in practice and has been rather seldom been provided for elsewhere in legally binding international agreements.

However, no agreement could be reached to transfer all the rights and freedoms of the UDHR into the CCPR. In particular the right to seek and to enjoy asylum (Art. 14 UDHR), the prohibition of arbitrary deprivation of one's nationality (Art. 15 UDHR), the right to own property (Art. 17 UDHR), the right to work and to free choice of employment (Art. 23 UDHR) were not incorporated into the Covenant. The idea that everyone has also duties to the community, as stipulated in Article 29 of the UDHR, is not generally taken up by the Covenant. However, the idea is hinted at in Article 19 (3) of the Covenant with regard to the freedom of expression, and the Preamble draws attention to this aspect, as well: "... the individual, having duties to other individuals and to the community to which he belongs, is under a responsibility to strive for the promotion and observance of the rights recognized in the present Covenant".

III. Scope and Limitations

For the practical application of human rights contained in a treaty, a clear formulation of their scope and of possible limitations is of decisive importance. In this respect, there is no clear structure within the Covenant. While some provisions are laid down rather detailed (e.g., Arts. 6, 8, 14 and 25), other formulations require considerable interpretation efforts (e.g., Art. 18 (1) with respect to the right to conscientious objection; Article 12 (4) regarding the definition of "own country", which to enter no one shall be arbitrarily hindered).

Numerous questions arise also with regard to admissible interferences (regulation of limitations). A general clause is contained in Article 5, prohibiting the interpretation of the Covenant as implying for any state any right to engage in the destruction of the rights recognized in the CCPR. Paragraph 2 of the same provision clarifies that the rights of the Covenant are only minimum guarantees and therefore cannot be utilized for restricting other human rights guarantees of greater extent in other human rights treaties. With regard to some rights, possible limitations are formulated relatively detailed (e.g., Arts. 6 (2), 12 (3), 19 (3), 21 or 22 (2)); in other cases only arbitrary or unlawful limitations are prohibited (e.g., Arts. 9 (1), 12 (4), or 17 (1)). In the latter cases and in cases where provisions require a "lawful" use of the right (e.g., Arts. 12 (1), 13 (1)), the exercise of the freedom is at risk of becoming dependent on national regulations and thereby becoming ineffective. However, with regard to this risk, the prohibition can be deduced from Article 2 (2) that the states parties must not make the rule (the freedom) to the exception and, vice versa, the exception (limitation) to the rule. On the grounds of this maxim it was established in jurisprudence, for example, that the almost total denial of the right "to leave any country, including his own" (Art. 12 (2)) and the corresponding practice upheld over decades by the former German Democratic Republic, based on the argument of protecting its "national security" (referring to Art. 12 (3)), was legally inadmissible under the Covenant. Some rights are formulated in absolute terms, thus they do not provide for any limitations (Arts. 7 and 16); as a direct emanation of the human dignity they are protected strictly and not amenable to restrictions in favor of other, albeit weighty, interests, such as public security. Formulated in absolute terms is also the prohibition of discrimination (Art. 26), which is, however, phrased in such a way that reasonable and objective differentiations do not constitute discrimination. Insofar the same problems arise as with the application of the general principle of equality in national law.

In the context of the Covenant, Article 20 expressly calls upon states parties to restrict freedom of opinion with the view of prohibiting by law all propaganda for war and advocacy of national, racial or religious hatred that constitutes incitement to discrimination, hostility or violence. Many states have declared a reservation especially to this provision, referring to the importance of freedom of expression.

Of great importance for securing the rights guaranteed is Article 4. According to this provision, states parties may contemporarily derogate from their obligations under the CCPR "in time of public emergency which threatens the life of the nation and the existence of which is officially proclaimed, ... provided that such measures are not inconsistent with their other obligations under international law", observe the principle of proportionateness and do not involve discrimination on the ground of race, sex, or religion. From some rights no derogation is permissible at all (e.g., the right to life; prohibition of torture; freedom of thought, conscience and religion). With regard to these rights, any restriction must follow the conditions provided for in the respective guarantees themselves; there is no additional restriction allowed in time of emergency. Although human rights first and foremost commit the state not to interfere with the rights of its people, Article 2 para 1 provides that states parties have to "respect and ensure" human rights. From this flows a positive obligation to ensure and protect the rights laid down in the Covenant. This might even lead to a duty to investigate and criminally prosecute human rights violations. Furthermore, Article 2 para. 3 lit. (a) contains the duty to compensate for human rights abuses.

The personal and territorial scope of the CCPR is regulated in Article 2 para 1. All individuals within in the state's territory and under its jurisdiction are protected by the Covenant. In its General Comment No. 31/80 of 29 March 2004 the Committee states that the rights must be protected and ensured to any person "within the power or effective control of that state party, even if not situated within [its] territory." According to a narrow interpretation of the wording of the relevant provisions, this is being contested by, inter alia, the United States and Belgium.

IV. Reservations

Numerous countries have made reservations to the CCPR and the Optional Protocols, thereby having limited the scope of their obligations. It is disputed, however, whether and what reservations are permissible and – in if not – what legal consequences may be drawn. Whereas the Second Optional Protocol (abolition of the death penalty: UN Doc. A/RES/44/128 of 15 December 1989; UNTS Vol. 1642, No. 14668) clearly sets limits to the admissibility of reservations, the other two treaties do not provide equivalent clauses. The general rules of public international law are thus applicable, as codified in the 1969 Vienna Convention on the Law of Treaties (UNTS Vol. 1155, No. 18232, 331; → Treaties, Law of). According to its Article 19, reservations incompatible with the object and purpose of the treaty are inadmissible. From this follows that the provision to which the reservation relates does not apply as between the two states to the extent of the reservation. The specific nature of human rights treaties, attributing rights particularly to human beings, has put into doubt the applicability of the general regime of reservations in this respect. The Human Rights Committee, in its General Comment on this issue (see General Comment No. 24 (52) of 4 November 1994, UN Doc. CCPR/C/21/Rev.1/Add.6), declared that all reservations incompatible with object and purpose are without legal effect. The competence of the Human Rights Committee to comment on this issue as well as the Committee's conclusion was contested by France, the United Kingdom and the USA. The debate, meanwhile also occupying the International Law Commission (→ ILC), is continuing.

V. State Succession and Denunciation

Interesting developments have also taken place with regard to the question, whether successor states automatically assume the obligations of the CCPR and its Optional Protocols. In any case, the Human Rights Committee has taken this position by perceiving the Covenant as a treaty quasi "embedded" within the peoples; i.e., Covenant rights once accorded to the population of a territory cannot get lost again by changes in international responsibility. The Committee has advocated this stance, e.g., with regard to the successor states of the former Soviet Union and Yugoslavia, but also with regard to the return of Hong Kong and Macao to the People's Republic of China in 1997 and 1999, respectively.

The CCPR and the Second Optional Protocol do not provide for denunciation or withdrawal – in contrast to the (first) Optional Protocol. According to the general law of treaties, denunciation or withdrawal is only permissible, if it was intended by the parties to the treaty or is implied by the nature of the treaty. Neither can be assumed in the present case. For these reasons, the → Secretary-General of the UN and the Human Rights Committee have declared inadmissible the denunciation of the CCPR by North Korea in 1997. The Committee additionally referred to its view that the protection of the rights under the Covenant devolves with territory (General Comment No. 26 (61) of 29 October 1997, para. 4, UN Doc. CCPR/C/21/Rev.1/Add.8/Rev.1). In the outcome, North Korea itself has accepted this view.

VI. Practical Implementation

The success of all human rights treaties finally depends upon the willingness of states to comply with their treaty obligations. Certain supervisory mechanisms involving international bodies can contribute to this end. In this sense the CCPR provides for the establishment of the Human Rights Committee. Since the Committee has commenced its work in

1977, it has, through its continuous work, significantly contributed to the fact that – despite all practical deficits – the CCPR has developed to the major instrument of human rights protection at the universal level.

Eckart Klein

Lit.: *Bair, J.:* The International Covenant on Civil and Political Rights and its (first) Optional Protocol: a Short Commentary Based on Views, General Comments and Concluding Observations by the Human Rights Committee, Frankfurt (Main) 2005; *Bossuyt, M.J.:* Guide to the "travaux préparatoires" of the International Covenant on Civil and Political Right, The Hague 1987; *Boyd, S.:* The United Nations Human Rights Covenants: Problems of Ratification and Implementation, in: Am. Soc. Int'l Proc. 62 (1968), 83-123; *Carlson, S.N./Gisvold, G.:* Practical Guide to the International Covenant on Civil and Political Rights, Ardsley 2003; *Cohen Jonathan, G.:* Human Rights Covenants, in: Bernhardt, R. (ed.): EPIL, Vol. 2, 1995, 915–922; *Gollwitzer, W.:* Menschenrechte im Strafverfahren: MRK und IPBPR. Kommentar, Berlin 2005; *Henkin, L. (ed.):* The International Bill of Rights – The Covenant on Civil and Political Rights, New York 1981; *Joseph, S./Schultz, J./Castan, M.:* The International Covenant on Civil and Political Rights – Cases, Materials and Commentary, 2nd edition, Oxford 2004; *Klein, E. (ed.):* The Duty to Protect and to Ensure Human Rights, Berlin 2000; *Klein, E. (ed.):* MenschenRechtsMagazin Themenheft 25 Jahre Internationale Menschenrechtspakte, Potsdam 2002; *Lorenz, D.:* Der territoriale Anwendungsbereich von Grund- und Menschenrechten – Zugleich ein Beitrag zum Individualschutz in bewaffneten Konflikten, Berlin 2005; *Nowak, M.:* UN Covenant on Civil and Political Rights, CCPR Commentary, 2nd ed., Kehl et al. 2005; *Partsch, K.J.:* Human Rights, Covenants and Their Implementation, in: Wolfrum, R. (ed.): United Nations: Law, Policies and Practice, Vol. 1, Munich/Dordrecht 1995, 592–602; *Ramcharan, B.G.:* Human Rights: Thirty Years after the Universal Declaration, The Hague 1979; *de Zayas,A./Möller, T./Opsahl,T.:* Application of the International Covenant on Civil and Political Rights under the Optional Protocol by the Human Rights Committee, in: GYIL 28 (1988), 9-64.

Internet: CCPR: http://www2.ohchr.org/english/law/ccpr.htm

Human Rights Conventions, CEDAW – Convention on the Elimination of All Forms of Discrimination Against Women

History of the Convention

The UN *Convention on the Elimination of All Forms of Discrimination against Women (CEDAW)* was drafted by the UN Commission on the Status of Women (CSW) and the Third Committee of the UN → General Assembly (GA) in the 1970s (UNTS Vol. 1249, No. 20378). On 18 December 1979, the General Assembly adopted the Convention (UN Doc. A/RES/34/180 of 18 December 1979). It entered into force on 3 September 1981.

As of 15 February 2008, 185 member states of the United Nations, through ratification or accession, are states parties to the Convention. The goal of universal ratification by the year 2000 as stipulated in the Beijing Platform for Action in 1995 (Report of the Fourth World Conference on Women, Bejing, 4 - 15 September 1995, UN Doc. A/CONF.177/20, Annex II, para. 230) was not achieved. As of February 2008, at least another seven ratifications or accessions are missing in order to reach that goal.

The Second UN World Conference on Human Rights (Vienna, 1993) as well as the Fourth UN World Conference on Women (Beijing, 1995) had called for a right to petition under CEDAW. On 6 October 1999, the General Assembly adopted an Optional Protocol to CEDAW (OP), which entered into force on 22 December 2000 (UN Doc. A/RES/54/4 of 6 October 1999; UNTS Vol. 2131, No. 20378). As of March 2008, ninety states parties to CEDAW were also states parties to the Optional Protocol. As the term "optional" indicates, a state party to the Convention is not legally bound to ratify the Optional Protocol.

The Convention is the most important and encompassing human rights instrument for women in international law. The treaty protects women against all forms of discrimination on the basis of sex and gender in all fields of their lives, and obligates states parties to guarantee them the full exercise and enjoyment of their human rights on an equal basis with men. Other human rights instruments also contain the norm of equality between women and men in the exercise and enjoyment of their → human rights and of the norm of non-discrimination on the ground of sex: the Charter of the United Nations (1945) (→ Charter of the UN) and the Universal Declaration of Human Rights (1948) (→ Human Rights, Universal Declaration of) prohibit discrimination based on sex and stipulate the principle of equal rights of men and women. The *International Covenant on Civil and Political Rights* (1966) and the *International Covenant on Economic, Social and Cultural Rights* (1966) (→ Human Rights Conventions, CCPR; → Human Rights Conventions, CESCR) make these norms legally binding in international law. The provisions of the Charter and the Universal Declaration are considered international customary law today. However, it is only the Convention that obliges states parties to focus specifically on the elimination of discrimination against women.

In the 1950s and 1960s, CSW and the International Labour Organization (→ ILO) formulated a series of women-specific international legal instruments with respect to a limited number of women's human rights in some areas of their lives, but none of these instruments had a monitoring body of independent experts attached to them.

In 1967, CSW submitted the Declaration on the Elimination of Discrimination against Women to the General Assembly for adoption, which took place on 7 November 1967 (UN Doc. A/RES/ 2263 (XXII)). As a declaration, however, it is not legally binding.

When CEDAW was formulated in the 1970s, elements of these more limited women-specific conventions and of the 1967 Declaration were integrated into it. The Convention contains a mixture of states parties' obligations that are of a "nondiscriminatory," a "protective" and a "corrective" nature.

Norms of the Convention

The Convention consists of a preamble and of 30 articles. The wording of the Preamble refers to the earlier human rights instruments for women. It links the full implementation of equal rights for men and women to a fundamental change in men's and women's attitudes, behavior and roles in all spheres of life, including the recognition of the fact that women's birthing and nursing capacities must not be a basis for discrimination and that the responsibility of both parents as well as of society as a whole in the upbringing of children is warranted in order to achieve equality between the sexes. The Preamble also calls for some equally fundamental general political requirements, which are considered necessary for the promotion of full equality between women and men in the exercise and enjoyment of their human rights. These include a new international economic order, the abolition of racism and apartheid as well as of foreign occupation and foreign rule, and universal and comprehensive disarmament. Most important, the Preamble postulates the equal participation of women with men as a necessary condition for the development of each country as well as for peace.

As of 2008, these ideas have found acceptance in the policies and practices of individual countries as well as of national and international institutions and agencies involved in development cooperation. They are also reflected in the 2000 Security Council Resolution 1325 on Women, Peace and Security (UN Doc. S/RES/1325 of 31 October 2000).

The Convention obliges states parties through obligations of conduct and results to pursue and achieve formal and

307

substantive equality of women and men. Some of the obligations require immediate recognition and implementation (Articles 9 and 15), while others tend to give states parties a smaller or wider margin of discretion in their implementation efforts, although a minimum of steps to respect, protect and fulfill the rights contained in the Convention will have to be taken in any case.

Substantive equality requires that women also be treated differently from men to protect their biological maternity or to accelerate the achievement of the *de facto* equal exercise and enjoyment of their human rights with men.

Articles 1-16 and 24 of the Convention, the so-called substantive articles, name and define legal and other measures, which states parties are obligated to pursue and implement.

The so-called procedural articles, Articles 17-22, formulate the rules regarding the reporting obligation of states parties to the Committee on the Elimination of Discrimination against Women (CEDAW Committee), which monitors the implementation of the Convention, as well as the Committee's composition and work. The remaining procedural articles, Articles 23 and 25-30, refer to the validity of already existing national legislation or international conventions, treaties or agreements, which may be more conducive to the achievement of equality between women and men; to regulations regarding the processes of ratification or accession; to the issue of reservations; to the handling of disputes between states parties regarding the interpretation or application of the Convention; and to the authenticity of the Convention's text in all UN languages.

The Convention covers all areas of women's lives and all forms of discrimination to which women are subjected, even though not all areas and forms are mentioned explicitly. Article 1 defines the elements of the legal offence of discrimination as "any distinction, exclusion or restriction made on the basis of sex which has the effect or purpose of impairing or nullifying the recognition, enjoyment or exercise by women, irrespective of their marital status, on a basis of equality of men and women, of human rights and fundamental freedoms in the political, economic, social, cultural, civil or any other field." Thus, by referring to both "purpose" and "effect," the Convention encompasses what today in a number of legal systems is known as direct and indirect discrimination. This is an important distinction. Many countries, in particular industrialized countries, can rightly claim that their female population no longer experiences direct discrimination in law or practice. The same cannot be said for an absence of indirect discrimination. Within the framework of European Union Directives, which can be understood as a regional implementation of the Convention, and the jurisprudence of the European Court of Justice (ECJ), indirect discrimination against women has been defined as existing, when apparently neutral provisions, criteria or practices disadvantage a substantially higher proportion of the members of one sex unless these provisions, criteria or practices are appropriate and necessary and can be justified by objective factors unrelated to sex.

It is also important to note that discrimination based on the marital status of a woman is explicitly mentioned as being forbidden. It can be found in nationality laws as well as laws and practices regulating education, employment, health care, economic and social rights and women's legal capacity. Equally important are states parties' obligations concerning women's rights in marriage and family relations, which women are to exercise and enjoy on an equal basis with men (Article 16). The Convention thus also stipulates states parties' obligation to safeguard the human rights of women in the private sphere.

While the term "gender" is not explicitly mentioned in the Convention, since at the time of the formulation of the Convention, it had not yet moved from social science research into a broader application, including its application in legal discourse, it can be read into Article 1 in conjunction with Article 5 (a). Discrimination based on gender, i.e. on the socially and culturally constructed meanings given to biological sex differences as well as to the power relations between men and women, is thus also prohibited by the Convention.

Article 2 including its subparagraphs (a-g), which is considered to be the core article of the Convention regarding states parties' obligations, enumerates a number of measures, including legal ones, which states parties must pursue in order to eliminate discrimination against women in law and practice. Thus, discriminatory provisions in law must be corrected. Discriminatory actions by the executive and legislative branches of government, as well as through the jurisprudence of the judiciary must be prohibited and sanctioned. Discriminatory acts against women by any person, private organization or enterprise are also prohibited. A state party is responsible for human rights violations of non-state actors, if it fails to prevent, correct or punish such discriminatory acts and to ensure compensation for such violations. States parties to the Convention must act in conformity with all provisions in Article 2 and pursue their obligations of conduct without delay. The elimination of discrimination against women is not dependent on the existence of a sufficient amount of human or financial resources and it cannot be derogated in times of crises.

Article 3 calls for legislative and other appropriate measures in all spheres of life, to ensure the full "development and advancement" of women. Because of this article, the Convention often was misunderstood as a mere development tool rather than a human rights instrument, which positions such development and advancement of women as a human rights claim. Article 24 stresses the obligation of states parties to adopt all necessary measures to guarantee the full realization of the rights recognized in the Convention. Both articles lend themselves to an interpretation of the Convention to cover such obligations not explicitly mentioned in the Convention's text as, for example, Security Council Resolution 1325 (2000), or the necessity to apply gender-mainstreaming in all legal, policy and programmatic efforts.

Article 4 (1) permits the application of temporary special measures solely in favor of women (e.g. the preference over equally qualified male competitors; or the establishment of numerical goals or quotas) in order to accelerate the achievement of de facto equality between women and men. In its General Recommendation No. 25 (www2.ohchr.org/english/bodies/cedaw/comments.htm), the CEDAW Committee voiced its opinion that the application of such measures may be, in fact, necessary since they are the most appropriate ones to accelerate the achievement of equality in practice. Article 4 (2) allows for women-specific measures aimed at protecting maternity. Neither of these measures in Article 4 is considered discriminatory.

Article 5 (a) is unique in that it recognizes the underlying root causes of women's discrimination, for example. Culturally and socially shaped attitudes and customs based on the alleged inferiority of women and the alleged superiority of men. This article obliges states parties to take all appropriate measures to modify such patterns of conduct and to eliminate existing role stereotypes of men and women, including the underlying prejudices and the resulting discriminatory practices against women. This article is supported by a similar obligation in Article 2 (f). Article 5 (2) is important in that it differentiates between biological motherhood and maternity as a social function. It also stipulates the common responsibility of men and women with respect to the upbringing of their children, thus allowing women to be recognized and empowered in roles additional to that of being a mother.

This provision is mirrored in the Preamble and in Article 11 (2)(c).

Articles 1-5 and 24 are so-called general or framework substantive articles. The obligations contained therein affect the implementation of all remaining specific substantive Articles 6-16. States parties are required to act on legal, policy and program levels. Thus, states parties must recognize and eliminate both forms of direct and indirect discrimination against women in the different areas of their lives under Articles 6-16. Apart from eliminating discriminatory legislation and introducing specific new legislation to guarantee equal opportunities or criminalize violence against women, states parties must examine whether the application of temporary special measures or protective measures is warranted. They must also create and protect such material conditions that advance and empower women and allow them to exercise and enjoy their human rights on an equal basis with men. All actions by states parties, organizations, enterprises and individuals must be examined as to whether they are permeated and justified by cultural stereotypes discriminating against women. If that is the case, such stereotypes must be abolished.

Article 6 carries the obligation for a state party to abolish all forms of trafficking in women and of their exploitation in prostitution. Articles 7 and 8 prohibit discrimination against women in political and public life at the national or international levels. General Recommendation No. 23 elucidates states parties' obligations under these articles. Article 9 grants women equal rights with men to acquire, change or retain their nationality and pass it on to their children. Articles 10 and 11 make states parties responsible for the elimination of all forms of discrimination in the spheres of education and employment. Article 12 guarantees women's equal access to health care and their appropriate treatment before, during and after pregnancy. General Recommendation No. 24 describes states parties' obliga-

tions under this article in more details. Article 13 prohibits discrimination against women in economic, social and cultural life, and Article 15 obliges states parties to ensure their equality with men before the law.

Article 14 focuses separately on states parties' obligations concerning the rights of women in rural environments. It was deemed necessary to include such a specific article, because the majority of the world's women live in such environments and suffer from multiple forms of discrimination as women and as members of rural, and sometimes even indigenous populations. The fact that states parties' obligations toward women living in rural areas are recognized in a separate article opens the way to interpreting the Convention as covering other forms of multiple discrimination, which women may experience simultaneously and that have a compounded negative impact on their lives. The Committee recognized such multiple forms of discrimination in its General Recommendations Nos. 15 (women and AIDS) and 18 (disabled women), although many more instances need to be acknowledged.

Article 16 covers states parties' obligations to ensure women's equal rights in all matters relating to marriage and family relations. These include the right to marry; to freely choose a spouse; to enjoy the same rights and responsibilities during marriage and its dissolution; the same rights as parents and guardians; the same rights to decide freely and responsibly on the number and spacing of children; the same rights to choose a family name, profession or occupation while married; and the same rights during marriage in respect of ownership, acquisition, management, administration, enjoyment and disposition of property. States parties are also obligated to prohibit child marriages, institute the same marriage age for women and men and to make marriage registration compulsory. General Recommendation No. 21 fully explains states parties' obligations and recognizes different forms of families, in which states parties will have to protect women's equal rights with men.

Reservations to the Convention

Article 28 allows a state party to formulate reservations at the time of ratification and accession. The reason for formulating such reservations is based on the fact that a state party wants to abstain from implementing specific provisions of the Convention at this point in time for a number of legal and political reasons. In practice, the Convention is weakened by too many reservations. Even though Article 28 (2) prohibits – in accordance with the Vienna Convention on the Law of Treaties (UNTS vol. 1155, No. 18232) – reservations, which are not compatible with the object and purpose of the Convention, this provision does not prevent a number of states parties from voicing very general and comprehensive reservations often based on religious grounds, or with reference to traditional customs and practices. Reservations to Article 16 (women's equal rights in marriage and family relations), often taken in tandem with reservations to parts of Article 2, or all provisions of Articles 2, considerably limit the effectiveness of the Convention for women in the respective state party and negate the very universality of the legal norms of the Convention.

Other states parties may object to these reservations (and a few do). However, up to now no state party ever initiated any negotiations with respect to reservations voiced by another state party, nor did any state party submitted this matter to arbitration, which states parties may do according to Article 29 (1), not least because states parties may, and in fact, do also voice a reservation against this procedure, thus abolishing their legal obligation to participate in the dispute settlement.

The Committee has criticized the nature and scope of reservations entered by many states parties in several statements and general recommendations, and has urged their withdrawal, or, at a minimum level, their formulation in more precise ways including the establishment of a timeframe for eliminating them. In particular, it has made clear that it sees reservations to Articles 2, 9 and 16, and possibly also to 7, as going against the object and purpose of the Convention.

On the other hand, the Committee is aware of the fact, that the very right to voice reservations permits some governments to ratify the Convention, and consequently submit to the scrutiny of the reporting system. Thus, a state party becomes accountable for the implementation of at least the non-reserved articles. The constructive dialogue with the Committee offers the prospect that the situation of women in this respective country may at least be improved in those areas covered by these articles. Experience has also shown that through this dialogue and the concluding observations by the Committee regarding the respective reservations of a state party relevant politicians as well as members in the judiciary and civil society may be strengthened to request and ultimately achieve the removal of such reservations.

Reservations are not permitted to the Optional Protocol to the Convention (Article 17, OP); however, according to Article 10 a state party may opt out of the inquiry procedure as contained in Articles 8 and 9 of the OP at the time of signature and ratification of the Protocol or accession thereto, thus accepting only the communication procedure.

General Recommendations Interpreting the Convention

At the time of the adoption of the Convention, certain forms of discrimination against women had not yet achieved a sufficient amount of public recognition at the international level. Thus, public and private forms of violence against women are not mentioned explicitly in the Convention. However, from a legal perspective, such forms of discrimination are included, because, according to Article 1, all forms of discrimination in any area of women's life are prohibited. The Committee has developed, as have the other UN human rights treaty bodies, a practice of interpreting the Convention through general recommendations (www2.ohchr.org/english/bodies/cedaw/comments.htm) on the basis of Article 21 (1) of the Convention. Thus, general recommendations Nos. 12, 14 and 19, as formulated by the Committee, proscribe the manifold forms of violence against women, including genital mutilation, in all spheres of their lives as a form of discrimination. These general recommendations clearly lay out the necessary legislative and other measures, which states parties are obliged to take in order to prevent such human rights violations against women, to assist victims, rehabilitate and compensate them and to punish and rehabilitate perpetrators. As of 2008, the Committee has interpreted the Convention and the obligations of states parties through 25 such general recommendations, which, though considered as "soft law" by international jurists, need to be taken into account by states parties when implementing the Convention and when reporting on such implementation.

Monitoring Procedures under the Convention: the Reporting Procedure

The Convention itself allows for two monitoring procedures: a reporting procedure under Article 18 and a state complaint procedure under Article 29. The latter has never been used with respect to the Convention.

Article 17 of the Convention determines that a monitoring Committee is established. Articles 19 to 22 regulate its mode of work with respect to the reporting procedure. Due to the rapid ratification of the Convention, the Committee started its first session in 1982 with the regular number of 23 experts. As of 2008, there were only three male experts in the CEDAW Committee. Since experts are nominated and elected by states parties to the Convention, these states parties are responsible for this gender imbalance. The same holds true

for a reverse gender imbalance in other UN human rights treaty bodies which, except for the Committee on the Rights of the Child (CRC), only have a small number of female experts. Experts are elected for a four-year term. Re-election is possible and ensures continuity in the work of the Committee. According to Article 17 (1), experts should be persons of "high moral standing and competence in the field covered by the Convention." Experts serve on the Committee in their personal capacity, i.e. independent of the policies of their respective governments. In the nomination and election process, states parties shall give consideration "to equitable geographical distribution and to the representation of the different forms of civilization as well as the principal legal systems." This goal, however, is not always achieved. The number of experts from different regions of the world varies. For example, in the 1980s, experts from socialist countries from different continents were in the majority, due to the fact that these countries had been among the first to ratify the Convention. After 1990, the political and economic transition processes in many of these countries interrupted the nomination of experts. As a result Eastern European countries did not send any experts to the Committee from 1995 until the end of 2002. Election of experts takes place every two years, and since the 1990s competition among nominees has increased sharply, requiring many lobbying efforts by the nominating states parties and the nominees to be successful. CEDAW experts are recruited from various professional fields (law, medicine, social sciences and the humanities). Some are government officials (diplomats, or governmental office holders for women's affairs or for equal opportunities affairs) or come from the judiciary; others head national or international non-governmental organizations, teach at universities or run their own law or medical practices. This broad spectrum of professions is necessary and beneficial to adequately cover the broad range of the Convention.

Reporting Process

A state party is obliged to submit a report to the Secretary-General of the United Nations for consideration by the Committee within one year after ratification or accession, and thereafter at least every four years, and subsequently whenever the Committee so requests (Art. 18). This reporting obligation is both an opportunity and a challenge for a state party. It is an opportunity in that a country can assess its implementation of the Convention by involving all parts and levels of government in a consciousness-raising, fact-finding and evaluation process, which should be the basis for legal and policy changes if needed. It is a challenge, since this process involves political will, which does not always exist and human, financial and technical resources, which are not always available.

Article 20 (1) of the Convention provides that the Committee "shall normally meet for a period of not more than two weeks annually." This provision for a restricted meeting time is due to an oversight. It remained included in the treaty's text after the nature of the monitoring body had been changed to its current format shortly before the adoption of the Convention. No other human rights treaty body is faced with such a restriction, which impeded the Committee's work for many years and often caused a backlog of reports. However, due to ongoing requests by the Committee over the years, it was gradually given more meeting time. In most recent years it was formally more or less on a par with other UN human rights treaty bodies in this respect, although it has still less time per state party than other treaty bodies. In 1995, the General Assembly agreed on an amendment of Article 20 (1), which, however, still awaits its entry into force, since it has to be accepted by two-thirds of all states parties (UN Doc. A/RES/50/202 of 22 December 1995). As of March 2008 acceptance

of this amendment stands at only 52 states parties. In recent years the Committee has been permitted, for a short time and on an exceptional basis, to work in two chambers rather than in plenary. This new format was instrumental in reducing the backlog of reports and gave opportunity for a more in-depth discussion of a state party's performance in implementing the Convention. Acceptance of this format, however, is contested both within the Committee and among states parties. The most recent decision by the GA authorizes the Committee to convene for three annual sessions of three weeks each, with a one-week pre-sessional working group for each session for an interim period effective from January 2010, pending the entry into force of the amendment (UN Doc. A/RES/62/218 of 22 December 2007). This resolution also authorizes the Working Group under the Optional Protocol to the Convention to meet in three annual sessions.

From 1982 until the end of 2007, the Division for the Advancement of Women (DAW) established in 1946, which also services CSW, serviced the CEDAW Committee. Locations were first, Vienna and later, New York. This administrative and geographical separation from the other human rights treaty bodies, which – since their inception – have been serviced by the then Centre for Human Rights and today by the Office of the High Commissioner for Human Rights (OHCHR) ($\rightarrow$ Human Rights, United Nations High Commissioner for) in Geneva, isolated the Committee and contributed to its lack of recognition as a human rights body until the 1990s. Within the framework of UN reform efforts, the then Secretary-General, Kofi Annan, decided in 2006 to move the Committee to Geneva. Since 2008 the OHCHR services the CEDAW Committee together with all other human rights treaty bodies. The Committee continues to convene for one session per year in New York.

Other reform goals were voiced by the former Secretary-General, e.g. to allow a state party to combine all its reports under the various human rights treaties into a unified report, and by the High Commissioner for Human Rights, Louise Arbour, i.e. to combine all treaty bodies into a unified body with fully paid experts who would meet all year. These proposals did not find acceptance among treaty bodies, non-governmental organizations and most states parties. The proposals, however, did generate a renewed and ongoing discussion as well as some decisions regarding the harmonization of the work of human rights treaty bodies. With all treaty bodies situated in Geneva, it has become easier to implement the proposal by the CEDAW Committee, to strive towards a "harmonized and integrated human rights treaty bodies system." (UN Doc. A/61/38, Report of the Committee on the Elimination of Discrimination against Women, 35th Session, 7-25 August 2006, Annex I). Various efforts at harmonizing working methods and reporting formats are under way. Regarding the format of reports, an expanded common core document is now the first part of any report a state party submits to any of the treaty bodies, while the respective treaty-specific document forms the second part. With this new arrangement, which still needs to be tested in practice, states parties, treaty bodies and the UN administration hope to shorten reports and avoid repetition. Treaty-specific reporting guidelines are currently being revised and work on human rights indicators is in progress. The introduction of such indicators could assist states parties in monitoring their progress and could also lead to shorter reports.

While scrutinizing states parties' reports, the Committee does not act as a court that can sanction a state party for not abiding by the Convention. Rather, experts and the state party's delegation engage in a so-called "constructive dialogue." Today, a pre-sessional working group of the Committee will send a list of questions based on a close reading of the report under discussion to the state

party prior to this dialogue, which the state party will have answered in writing before appearing in front of the Committee. This procedure is now valid for both initial and periodic reports to the Committee, and the meeting time of five hours allotted for the discussion of a state party's report now is the same for both types of reports, too.

In earlier years the discussion of the Committee with governmental representatives was summarized and published in a detailed report. Today, experts formulate and adopt so-called "concluding comments", which, since 2008 and due to harmonization of terminology with other human rights treaty bodies, are now called "concluding observations". In these statements the Committee voices praise and criticism concerning the implementation of the Convention, as well as recommendations for the improvement of the state party's performance. The United Nations publishes these statements in a brief report.

They are also available on the website of the servicing UN Secretariat, i.e. until 2007 on the website of DAW, and as of 2008, on the website of OHCHR, under the link "Treaty body document search": http://tb.ohchr.org/ default.aspx.

The respective state party is requested to publish and disseminate these concluding observations widely, discuss them in its national parliament and utilize them as the basis for its work for further implementing the Convention.

As of early 2008, two procedures that are pursued by some other human rights treaties bodies have been on the Committee's agenda for some time but are still waiting to be adopted and implemented. Due to its lack of working time, the Committee has not been able to develop a follow-up procedure for its concluding observations to states parties' reports. Nor has it been able to discuss a state party that never reported or did not report for a long time without a written report having been submitted. Unfortunately, many states parties do not follow the required reporting cycle of one year after the Convention's entry into force and thereafter every four years. For a variety of reasons – lack of political will, war and internal military conflicts, lack of human or financial resources – they are late in reporting and some do not report at all. The Committee has the possibility of "humiliating" such countries by pointing to their negligence in its annual report, which is submitted through the Economic and Social Council (→ ECOSOC) to the UN General Assembly according to Article 21 (1). In order to assist states parties which are overdue with their reports, the Committee has allowed them to combine reports. Both DAW and OHCHR can arrange seminars and technical assistance to provide encouragement and help.

Alternative Reports

Article 22 of the Convention allows UN → specialized agencies to be present during the discussion of states parties' reports and also submit their own reports, if the reports of states parties concern their spheres of work. The Committee has developed guidelines with respect to the kind of information it expects UN specialized agencies to provide and values highly their contribution. Most recently, UN specialized agencies have begun to coordinate their reports.

The Convention does not provide for a role of non-governmental organizations (→ NGOs), i.e. national or international women's associations and human rights organizations. Nevertheless, the Committee has developed a practice to accept written alternative or "shadow-reports" from such NGOs and also permits them to address orally both the pre-sessional working group and the plenary of the Committee before a state party's report will be discussed. This input has proven to be of great importance. It enables the Committee to evaluate the real situation of women's enjoyment of their human rights in the country concerned. The practice also makes possible a fruitful interaction between the Committee, the government representatives of the respective state party, and representa-

tives of its civil society. For NGOs the process of writing an alternative report on the implementation of the Convention is often just as important as the product itself. As a result of their work they often form coalitions and begin to lobby their governments to further implement the Convention and the concluding observations of the Committee.

The Second UN World Conference on Human Rights Vienna 1993 called for the creation of national human rights institutions (NHRIs) and the former UN Secretary-General, Kofi Annan, stressed the importance of such institutions for monitoring the implementation of UN human rights treaties at the national level. The CEDAW Committee appreciates highly the written and oral contributions by NHRIs both for the preparation of its lists of issues and questions in its pre-sessional working groups and its oral discussion of states parties' reports. Such contributions range from independent alternative reports to commentaries given to the respective state party. Some NHRIs refrain from producing their own reports and would rather facilitate national discussions with various stakeholders on the state party's implementation efforts. In its fortieth session in January 2008 the Committee issued a statement to define its working relationship with such NHRIs that are based on the Paris Principles (CEDAW Decision 40/II, UN Doc. E/CN.6/2008/CRP.1, Annex II).

Role of the Beijing Declaration and Platform for Action for the Monitoring Process

In 1995, at the Fourth UN World Conference on Women in Beijing, the Committee acquired the additional mandate to monitor states parties' implementation of the Beijing Platform for Action. It has done so since then on a regular basis and included the request for information from states parties on this issue in its reporting guidelines. This Platform – in contrast to the Convention – is not a legally binding instrument. However, the Committee, in various statements, has linked the Platform's twelve areas of concern, in which goals for women's equality with men and steps to achieve them are formulated, to the substantive articles of the Convention. Thus, a state party to the Convention should utilize the Platform in order to further implement the legal obligations it has accepted under the Convention. In this context it is important to note, that the Platform for Action is also explicitly concerned with the human rights situation of girls, which is covered by CEDAW as well as CRC, although girls are not explicitly mentioned in either of these treaties.

Monitoring Procedures under the Convention: Procedures under the Optional Protocol

During the process of formulating the Convention in the 1970s, there had been discussion about including additional monitoring procedures as contained in other human rights treaties or their optional protocols. However, there had been no consensus to include them in the Convention. In the 1990s, due to pressure exerted by the international women's movement and reinforced by UN member states in the declarations and action platforms of the various UN → World Conferences of the 1990s these proposals were discussed again. CSW, in less than four years, formulated an Optional Protocol (OP) to the Convention, which contains two additional monitoring procedures – a communication and an inquiry procedure. The UN General Assembly adopted the new treaty without a vote on 6 October 1999 with resolution 54/4, and the treaty came into force on 22 December 2000 (UNTS 2131, No. 20378).

The Communication Procedure

The communication procedure permits a woman or a group of women, to submit or have submitted on her or their behalf to the Committee for consideration, a communication about an alleged violation by the respective state party of her or their right(s) under the Convention

(Article 2, OP). A pre-condition for admissibility for the communication is the exhaustion of domestic remedies within the state, unless that process is "unreasonably prolonged or unlikely to bring effective relief." (Art. 4 (1)) A communication on behalf of another person or other persons can only be submitted with her or their consent, unless the author(s) of the submission can justify acting on her or their behalf without such consent (Art. 2). The communication has to be brought before the Committee in writing and "shall not be anonymous" (Art. 3). Five conditions make the communication inadmissible (Art. 4): the "same matter" has already been examined by the Committee or is at the same time under investigation by another international body; the subject matter is incompatible with the provisions of Convention; the communication is not sufficiently substantiated or manifestly ill-founded or, it is an abuse of the right to complain; and lastly, the facts that are the subject of the communication occurred prior to the entry into force of the Optional Protocol for the respective state party, "unless those facts continued after that date." (Art. 4 (2) a-e) These criteria for admissibility give room for interpretation. In deciding upon admissibility the Committee takes notice of such interpretations as formulated by other human rights treaty bodies and regional human rights courts.

According to Article 5 of the OP, the Committee, even before it has reached a decision on admissibility, can require "interim measures" from the state party concerned to protect the alleged victim(s) and "avoid possible irreparable damage." The state party also has to protect the complaining person or persons from "ill treatment or intimidation" as a consequence of communicating with the Committee (Art. 11).

After registering a communication the Committee will request information from the respective state party on the substance of the communication to which, in turn, the author(s) of the communication can reply. On this basis, the

Committee will decide on the admissibility and, either at the same time, or at a later point, on the merits of the communication. If the Committee finds a violation of a right under the Convention, it formulates its opinion in a view, which includes recommendations. These include changes in legislation, the creation of programs, the enforcement of legislation and payment of compensation to the victim(s). As of January 2008, the Committee registered 18 communications. It concluded 10 and discontinued one. The views of the Committee are documented on the respective websites and in its annual reports.

The Inquiry Procedure

The Optional Protocol also includes the right of the Committee to designate one or several experts to conduct an inquiry if it receives "reliable information indicating grave or systematic violations by a State Party of rights set forth in the Convention." (Art. 8) Grave violations would be such as those of a life-threatening nature. Systematic violations would have to show a pattern regarding acts or omission of acts by states parties that would lead to violations of specific rights. Such an inquiry may include a visit to the territory of the state party. The inquiry does not require the exhaustion of domestic remedies. A few states parties opted out of this procedure so far. As of March 2008, the Committee conducted only one inquiry concerning the murders of women in Ciudad Juárez at the Mexican-American border, which were characterized both as grave and systematic in their nature. The Committee concluded this inquiry in January 2005. The report is documented on the Committee's website of DAW. In pursuing the two procedures under the OP, the Committee again never acts as a court with binding decisions; it rather sees its function in assisting a state party to fulfill its obligations under the Convention.

Evaluation of Monitoring Procedures

While the reporting procedure allows the Committee to do an overall scrutiny of the implementation of the Convention by a state party, the communication procedure permits it to focus on alleged violations of the human rights of an individual woman or a group of women, including the opportunity to recommend specific redress for such violations. The inquiry procedure opens the possibility for the Committee to investigate specific areas of life-threatening or systematic patterns of violations of women's human rights. The Committee pursues follow-up procedures to monitor the implementation of its views under both procedures of the OP, which are mentioned in Articles 7 (5) and 9 of the treaty. Taken together, the three monitoring procedures allow for an effective evaluation of a state party's legal, policy and programmatic efforts regarding the respect for and the protection and fulfillment of the human rights of women.

Other Activities of the Committee

Apart from the mandate to formulate general recommendations, through which the Committee interprets the Convention, the Committee can also adopt suggestions and decisions. In the practice of the Committee "suggestions" include statements to UN world conferences; "decisions" refer to the Committee's working methods. "Suggestions", "decisions", and "general recommendations" are contained in the reports of the Committee and are available on the respective UN websites.

Evaluation of the impact of the Convention

Since 1979 the Convention and its Committee have been strengthened and through them women's exercise and enjoyment of their human rights have been strengthened, too in many parts of the world. No longer is the Committee marginalized among the UN human rights treaty bodies, and a number of UN specialized agencies, in particular the United Nations Development Fund for

Women (UNIFEM), integrated the empowerment of states parties and their civil societies regarding the implementation of the Convention into the objectives of their own work. The other human rights treaty bodies have been increasingly made alert to and aware of human rights violations against women and girls and pursue a policy of gender mainstreaming in their scrutiny of states parties' reports under their respective treaties. However, more needs to be done by states parties and other human rights treaty bodies to recognize that women are not simply one more "vulnerable group" to be placed next to other vulnerable groups as defined by ethnicity, race, age, disability, and other grounds. Women are approximately half of the world's population and they are always members of these groups. They may suffer discrimination both within and outside these groups, and, in fact, often suffer from multiple forms of discrimination based on their intersecting identities as women and as members of such groups. In addition, in most discriminatory contexts, the relationship between oppressor and victim is uniquely and universally intimate for women, in that the majority of women live with men in nuclear and extended families.

Reports by states parties as well as scholarly studies show that the impact of CEDAW on national legislative action, jurisprudence, government institutions, policies and programs is evident. On the other hand, political, economic and social processes at national and international levels in the framework of globalization, including wars, expulsion, voluntary or involuntary migration, the HIV/AIDS pandemic, natural disasters, and the re-emergence of old and new forms of nationalism, ethnic strife and religious fundamentalism continue to impede, endanger and annul the human rights of girls and women in practice.

Hanna Beate Schöpp-Schilling

Lit.: *Byrnes, A./Connors, J.:* Enforcing the Human Rights of Women: a Complaints Procedure for the Women's Convention, in:

BrooklJIL 21 (1996), 682-797; *König, D.:* Die Durchsetzung internationaler Menschenrechte. Neuere Entwicklungen am Beispiel des Übereinkommens der Vereinten Nationen zur Beseitigung jeder Form von Diskriminierung der Frau, in: Dicke, K. et al. (eds.): Weltinnenrecht. Liber amicorum Jost Delbrück, Berlin 2005, 401-427; *Schöpp-Schilling, H.B. (ed.)/Flinterman, C. (ass. ed.):* The Circle of Empowerment. Twenty-five Years of the UN Committee on the Elimination of Discrimination against Women, New York 2007; *Schöpp-Schilling, H.B.:* Das Übereinkommen zur Beseitigung jeder Form von Diskriminierung der Frau (CEDAW) und sein Vertragsausschuss nach 25 Jahren – Bilanz und Ausblick, in: Zimmermann, A./Giegerich,T. (eds.): Gender und Internationales Recht, Berlin 2007, 137-169; *Schöpp-Schilling, H.B.:* Treaty Body Reform: The Case of The Committee on the Elimination of Discrimination Against Women, in: Human Rights Law Review 7 (2007), 201-224; *Sokhi-Bulley, B.:* The Optional Protocol to CEDAW: First Steps, in: Human Rights Law Review 6 (2006), 143-159.

Internet: Homepage of CEDAW: www.unhchr.ch/html/menu2/6/cedw.htm; bibliographies for CEDAW: www.lawlib.utoronto.ca/diana/index.htm; www.iwrp.org/pdf/biblio.pdf.

Human Rights Convention, CERD – International Convention on the Elimination of All Forms of Racial Discrimination

The *"International Convention on the Elimination of All Forms of Racial Discrimination"* (UNTS Vol. 660, No. 9464), in short CERD, was adopted as A/RES/2106 A (XX) by the UN → General Assembly on 21 December 1965 and entered into force three years later in January 1969. At present CERD has 173 states parties (as of 31 December 2008).

In this Convention the term "racial discrimination" means "any distinction, exclusion, restriction or preference based on race, color, descent, or national or ethic origin" with has the purpose or effect that the recognition, enjoyment or exercise of, on equal footing, of → human rights and fundamental freedoms in the political, economical, social, cultural or any other field of public life is nullified or impaired (Art. 1 (1) CERD). The Convention is not applicable to distinctions, exclusions, restrictions or preferences that the contracting states make between citizens and non-citizens (Art. 1 (2) CERD), that means that foreigners can be treated differently.

The special quality of racial discrimination, which in comparison to the discrimination on other grounds, has negative consequences for the enjoyment of a large number of human rights, is met in the Convention by the setting up a list of all those rights whose enjoyment is particularly impaired by racial discrimination in Article 5 of the Convention. The list follows the enumeration of human rights in the Universal Declaration of Human Rights (→ Human Rights, Universal Declaration of) and connects the political and other civil rights with economic, social and cultural rights.

According to Article 2 CERD the states parties are obliged to pursue policies leading to an elimination of racial discrimination and contributing to improvement of understanding among all races. For that purpose several measures and means for the elimination of the racial discrimination are mentioned, such as the obligation to prevent actions or practices by public authorities which contradict the prohibition of racial discrimination, the obligation to prevent any support of followers of the racist doctrines and of their organizations as well as obligation to amend, rescind or nullify laws and regulations that have the effect of creating or perpetuating racial discrimination. In addition, measures are to be taken to ensure that racial discrimination cannot occur in the private, non-public sphere. The concrete measures which the states are to take are, however, to a great extent discretionary.

The above mentioned obligations apply principally in the territory of the states, but they also have extraterritorial implications. On the other hand, the obligation of the states to prevent, prohibit and eliminate segregation, apartheid and all similar practices refers expressly only to the territory of the states parties: "States Parties particularly condemn racial segregation and apartheid and undertake to prevent, prohibit and eradicate all practices of this nature in territories under their jurisdiction" (Art. 3). In order to give this latter obligation of the states also an extraterritorial effect, since it constitutes one of the few rights having an immediate legal effect and therefore being directly applicable in domestic affairs, in the interpretation of this article the preamble of the Convention is cited, which provides that the states are resolved "to build an international community free from all forms of racial segregation and racial discrimination". The General Assembly has expressly approved of this interpretation of Article 3 concerning the relations to the apartheid regime in South Africa.

For the *implementation* of the Convention the *Committee on the Elimination of Racial Discrimination (CERD)* has been established with 18 human rights experts (Art. 8 (1) CERD) who are elected by the contracting states for a term of four years (Art. 8 (5), lit. a). The Committee was established in 1970, six years earlier than the → Human Rights Committee for the International Covenant on Civil and Political Rights (→ Human Rights Conventions, CCPR).

The Committee is – formally considered – a body of the contracting states. But it has the special quality that its secretariat is provided by the UN → Secretary-General (Art. 10 (3) CERD), who must approve all formal decisions (time and place of the meetings, finances). The services of the secretariat are financed by the regular UN budget (→ Budget), while the expenses of the experts are provided from a special fund which receives contributions from the contracting states (Art. 8 (6) CERD). However, a large number of states do not currently meet their contribution obligations, therefore the Committee cannot completely fulfill its program of meetings presently.

The purpose of the CERD consists *firstly* in the examination of the periodic *state reports* (Art. 9(1) CERD).

Secondly it has the function to receive *inter-state complaints* (Art. 11 (1)). The inter-state complaint procedure of the convention is – as an exception among the UN conventions – obligatory. However, this feature has not strengthened this procedure, which is largely meaningless. None of the more than 170 states parties have used this yet. According to Article 11-13 CERD the Committee can carry out subsequently a dispute settlement procedure if the complaint cannot be adjusted by bilateral negotiations. When the Committee deals with such a matter (Art. 11 (3) CERD), it can state its opinion on the material content of the transmitted communication. This phase of the procedure is not concluded by a decision, but by a report of the committee. After the necessary information on the matter has been collected, a Conciliation Commission is appointed by the Chairman of the Committee in the next phase of the settlement procedure. The Commission is to make its "good offices" available to the states concerned and may submit recommendations at the end of its work as it may think proper for the amicable resolution of the dispute (Art. 13 (1) CERD). The Committee for its part has also the right to recommend a settlement for the dispute. Additionally it may request the states concerned to inform the Committee within three months whether they accept the recommendations for the settlement.

Thirdly the Committee has responsibility for the examination of *individual complaints* against states which have submitted by formal declaration to this complaints procedure (Art. 14 CERD). 49 states have stated their submission to this procedure, up to now. The number of individual complaints, since CERD started its work (so far 51, of which 22 have already been decided), is very low. To conclude the examination procedure,

the Committee is to submit "suggestions and recommendations ... to the State party concerned and to the petitioner" (Art. 14(7), lit. b CERD).

Fourthly the Committee has the task to examine the obligations of state parties with regard to Trust and Non-Self Governing Territories (→ Trusteeship Council) in matters related to the principles and objectives of the convention and to examine petitions from the inhabitants of those territories (Art. 15).

Furthermore, the Committee can submit general recommendations/ which mainly refer to the interpretation of the Convention. Thus the Committee has discussed racial discrimination in the criminal justice system in 2005 at its 66th and 67th sessions and adopted "General Recommendation XXXI on the prevention of racial discrimination in the administration and functioning of the criminal justice system" (UN Doc. A/60/18, 98-108). The comment contains indicators for discrimination in the criminal justice system as well as steps that need to be taken to prevent such discrimination. Furthermore, the Committee plans to adopt a General Comment on affirmative action.

Above all, in the CERD meetings the conventional forms of racial discrimination come up for discussion; the debates deal with the successes and failures in implementing the convention by monitoring legislative and administrative measures in the member states. However, at recent meetings the Committee also dealt with such issues as the prevention of genocide, the protection of non-citizens and discrimination based on descent. In 2008 the Committee held a thematic discussion on the relationship between racism and religion.

Martina Haedrich

Lit.: *Haedrich, M.:* Rassismusbekämpfung nach Völkerrecht und innerstaatliche Wirkungen, in: JA 35 (2003) 899-905; *McKean, W.:* Equality and Discrimination under International Law, Oxford 1983; *Meron, T.:* The Meaning and the Reach of the International Convention on the Elimination of all Forms of Racial Discrimination, in: AJIL 79 (1985), 283-318; *Partsch, K.-J.:* The Racial Discrimination Committee, in: Alston, P. (ed.): The United Nations and Human Rights. A Critical Appraisal, Oxford et al. 1992, 339-368; *Partsch, K.-J.:* Racial Discrimination, in Wolfrum, R. (ed.): United Nations: Law, Policies and Practice, Vol. 2, Munich/Dordrecht 1995, 1003-1011; *Thornberry, P.:* Confronting Racial Discrimination: A CERD Perspective, in: Human Rights Law Review 5/2 (2005), 239-269; *Weiß, N.:* Die Bekämpfung des Rassismus in Deutschland vor dem Hintergrund der Arbeit des CERD, in Klein, E./Volger, H. (eds.): Globale Problemlösungen in der Bewährungsprobe – Bilanz der Arbeit der Vereinten Nationen vor dem Millenniumsgipfel 2000, Potsdam 2001, 27-40; *Wolfrum, R.:* The Committee on the Elimination of Racial Discrimination, in: Max Planck UNYB Vol. 3, The Hague et al., 1999, 489-519; *Wolfrum, R.:* The Elimination of Racial Discrimination: Achievements and Challenges, in: Matsuura, K./Robinson, M. (eds.): United to Combat Racism, Paris 2001, 23-56.

Internet: Homepage of CERD: http://www2.ohchr.org/english/bodies/cerd/

Human Rights Conventions, CESCR – International Covenant on Economic, Social and Cultural Rights

I. Origins and Outline

Like the International Covenant on Civil and Political Rights (CCPR, → Human Rights Conventions, CCPR), the International Covenant on Economic, Social and Cultural Rights (CESCR) was drafted on the basis of the 1948 Universal Declaration of Human Rights (UDHR; → Human Rights, Universal Declaration of). At the time of drafting, no majority was given for a joint elaboration of the two types of human rights in one treaty. However, both Covenants were adopted simultaneously by the UN → General Assembly on 16 December 1966 (UN Doc. A/RES/2200A (XXI)). Three months after the 35th ratification, the CESCR entered into force on 3 January 1976 (UNTS Vol. 993, No. 14531). As of 31 December 2008, 160 states were party to the Covenant.

To emphasize the correlation of both Covenants, they were structured in a very similar manner. The Preamble refers to the UN Charter (→ Charter of the UN), the UDHR, and the civil and political rights of everyone. The Covenant is sub-divided into five parts: Part I covers the → right of self-determination of all peoples (Art. 1 CESCR). Part II contains general provisions (Arts. 2-5) that apply to all the provisions of Part III, where the substantive rights are listed (Arts. 6-15). Part IV outlines the international mechanism for supervision; Part V contains final provisions.

II. The Rights Guaranteed

The substantive rights are included in Part III and codified in the same sequence as the title of the Covenant suggests. First, the economic rights are stated, which are: the right to work (Art. 6); the right to the enjoyment of just and favorable conditions of work (Art. 7); the right to form and join trade unions, including the right to strike (Art. 8); and the right to social security, including social insurance (Art. 9). As in the CCPR, the right to own property is not mentioned; insofar the international protection of the latter rests on other sources of international law.

The following social rights were included in the catalogue of the Covenant: protection of and assistance for the family, including special assistance for mothers and children (Art. 10); the right to an adequate standard of living, including adequate food, clothing and housing (Art. 11); and the right to the highest attainable standard of physical and mental health (Art. 12). As cultural rights are enumerated in the Covenant the right to education (Art. 13) and the right to participate in cultural life and enjoy the benefits of scientific progress (Art. 15). For the progressive implementation of the right to education, those states parties not having introduced compulsory primary school education free of charge at the time of becoming a state party undertake, within two years, to work out and adopt a detailed plan of action to this end (Art. 14).

Differing from the classical liberal freedom rights which – in their defensive dimension with regard to the states – are respected by states through abstention from interference with these rights of the individual person, the rights protected by the CESCR require states to take action, sometimes connected with considerable financial implications. This explains why the rights guaranteed in the CESCR are formulated in such legal terms that they allow only in few cases direct recourse by individuals, but are articulated in terms obliging states parties to create the preconditions for the enjoyment of these rights. Nevertheless, even this obligation is not an absolute one. Article 2 (1) CESCR requires only that a state party "take steps, individually and through international assistance and cooperation, ... to the maximum of its available resources, with a view of achieving progressively the full realization of the rights ... by all appropriate means, including particularly the adoption of legislative measures". It is even left to developing countries whether they will guarantee economic rights to non-nationals: "Developing countries, with due regard to human rights and their national economy, may determine to what extent they would guarantee the economic rights recognized in the present Covenant to non-nationals." This provision might not only discourage foreign investors, but contradicts the basic concept of human rights. With regard to individual rights, the obligations for implementation are formulated more detailed. This is particularly valid for the realization of the right to primary education free of charge (Arts. 13 and 14), setting also a time frame for the implementation.

The rights contained in the CESCR cannot always be separated strictly from the rights guaranteed by the CCPR. This is additional argument for the necessity to deal with the rights of both Covenants together, despite all dogmatic differences. This holds true, for example,

for the right to enter into marriage "with the free consent of the intending spouses", which is guaranteed in both Covenants in similar terms (Art. 10 (1) CESCR; Art. 23 (3) CCPR). The right to form and join trade unions is also contained in both Covenants (Art. 8 CESCR; Art. 22 CCPR). In these cases the limiting possibilities – in so far as they are admissible at all – are formulated almost by the same wording. As for the rest, the CESCR contents itself with a quite general limitation clause (Art. 4); the possible limitations, as provided for by this provision, are to be considered by the state when adopting national legislation on, and implementing measures concerning, the rights protected. Article 3 (equal treatment of men and women), and Article 5 (interpretation principles), contain parallel provisions to the respective articles of the CCPR, and are formulated in almost the same words.

III. Reservations, State Succession and Denunciation

In the case of the CESCR numerous states parties have made reservations, on the admissibility of which the competent Committee has not yet commented. Also the question of state succession has not played an essential role up to now. So far, no state party has declared a denunciation of the CESCR; the Committee supported, however, the opinion of the → Human Rights Committee with regard to the denunciation of the CCPR by North Korea in 1997, in which the Human Rights Committee declared the denunciation inadmissible.

IV. Implementation and Supervision

The success of all human rights conventions depends mainly on the willingness of the states parties to fulfill their treaty obligations. An essential contribution to achieve this aim can be made by monitoring mechanisms with the participation of international organs: Pursuant to Article 16 CESCR, states parties are obliged to report on the measures which they have adopted and the progress made in achieving the observance of the rights recognized in the Covenant. First it was provided for that the Economic and Social Council of the UN ($\rightarrow$ ECOSOC) was to examine the states reports. However, this body soon proved to be too big for this task. Therefore, the task was delegated to a Sessional Working Group of 15 state delegates of the Council (and thus being subject to instruction); however, this solution also proved to be inadequate. Eventually, in 1985, ECOSOC adopted a reform which clearly orientated itself on the model of the Human Rights Committee. In 1987, the new *Committee on Economic, Social and Cultural Rights (CESCR)* (in short: Committee) commenced its work. The Committee consists of 18 members elected by ECOSOC (54 members) from a list of nominees submitted by the states parties for a term of four years, re-election is possible. The members serve in their personal capacity and as independent experts. From a legal point of view, the Committee is a subsidiary organ of ECOSOC (cf. Art. 68 of the UN Charter; $\rightarrow$ Principal Organs, Subsidiary Organs, Treaty Bodies). At the same time, however, its status is that of a treaty body; nevertheless, in comparison to other treaty bodies, especially the Human Rights Committee, the linkage to the UN is more explicit. The method of considering reports is almost the same as that of the Human Rights Committee. The discussions are prepared by a written List of Issues; additional oral questions are posed. Since the early 1990s, the Committee also adopts concluding observations, which not only identify the progress made, but also point out principle subjects of concern, and contain recommendations.

The Committee is confronted with problems similar to those facing the Human Rights Committee. In the beginning there were some differences in the manner in which these are handled. The Committee has, for example, repeatedly examined the situation in a country on the basis of the material available to the Committee (the main sources being in-formation provided by specialized agencies and $\rightarrow$ NGOs, for the NGO-Guidelines see UN Doc. E/2001/22, Annex V) and has issued "Concluding Observations", despite the fact that the concerned state party had not submitted its report. This is a form of absentia-procedure. By now, the HRC has adopted this in-absentia approach as well.

The Committee attempts as well to maintain a continuing dialogue with states beyond the examination of the reports (follow-up procedure).

The reporting procedure is still the only supervision mechanism available to the Committee. Attempts to create a kind of individual complaints procedure, comparable to the one provided for by the Optional Protocol to the ICCPR, have not succeeded so far, due to the resistance of states. Still, a draft has been presented at the end of 2007 (UN Doc. A/HRC/8/WG.4/2, 24 December 2007). The Optional Protocol is expected to be adopted by the General Assembly on 10 December 2008, the 60th anniversary of the Universal Declaration of Human Rights. It resembles the mechanisms of other individual complaint procedures.

A more general method to have effect on the states parties, to give them guidance for the implementation of the rights agreed upon and for their reporting obligations, is the adoption of "General Comments", e.g., on the nature of Covenant obligations, on the right to adequate housing, or on the domestic application of the Covenant. As of May 2008, the Committee had adopted 19 General Comments (see UN Doc. HRI/GEN/1/Rev.9 (Vol. I), 27 May 2008). Further General Comments (on article 2 para. 2, non-discrimination, and article 15, the right to participate in cultural life) are prepared at present.

Furthermore, since 1992 the Committee devotes one day per session to a general discussion of a particular right or aspect of the Covenant.

Since 1991 the Committee adopts statements to clarify and confirm its position with respect to major international developments and issues bearing upon the implementation of the Covenant.

Eckart Klein

Lit.: *Alston, P.:* The Committee on Economic, Social and Cultural Rights, in: Alston, P. (ed.): The United Nations and Human Rights. A Critical Appraisal, Oxford et al. 1992, 473-508; *Baderin, M.A./McCorquodale, R. (eds.):* Economic, Social and Cultural Rights in Action, Oxford 2007; *Craven, M.C.R.:* The International Covenant on Economic, Social and Cultural Rights, Oxford 1995; *Coomanns, F./Hoof, G.J.H. van (eds.):* The Right to Complain about Economic, Social and Cultural Rights, SIM Special No. 18, Utrecht 1995; *Eide, A./Krause, C./Rosas, A. (eds.):* Economic, Social and Cultural Rights, Dordrecht 1995; *Hoof, G.J.H. van:* The Legal Nature of Economic, Social and Cultural Rights: A Rebuttal of Some Traditional Views, in: Alston, P./Tomasevski, K. (eds.): The Right to Food, The Hague 1984, 97-110; *Matscher, F.:* Die Durchsetzung wirtschaftlicher und sozialer Menschenrechte, Kehl 1991; *Sepúlveda, M.M.:* The Nature of the Obligations under the International Covenent on Economic, Social and Cultural Rights, Antwerpen 2003; *Simma, B.:* The Examination of State Reports: International Covenant on Economic, Social and Cultural Rights, in: Klein, E. (ed.): The Monitoring System of Human Rights Treaty Obligations, Berlin 1998, 31-48; *United Nations - Committee on Economic, Social and Cultural Rights:* Report on the Twenty-Second, Twenty-Third and Twenty-Fourth Session, New York and Geneva 2001, UN Doc. E/2001/22-E/C.12/2000/21, Annex V: Nongovernmental organization participation in the activities of the Committee on Economic, Social and Cultural Rights; *United Nations - High Commissioner for Human Rights, Economic, Social and Cultural Rights:* Handbook for National Human Rights Institutions, New York 2005; *United Nations - Human Rights Council:* Revised Draft Optional Protocol to the International Covenant on Economic, Social and Cultural Rights, 24 December 2007, UN Doc. A/HRC/8/WG.4/2.

Internet: Homepage of the CESCR: http://www2.ohchr.org/english/bodies/cescr/index.htm.

Human Rights Conventions, Convention on the Prevention and Punishment of the Crime of Genocide

Through the *Convention on the Prevention and Punishment of the Crime of Genocide*, in short *Genocide Convention*, adopted by the UN General Assembly on 9 December 1948 as A/RES/260 A (III) (UNTS Vol. 78, No. 1021), all crimes of genocide are qualified as crimes under international law, no matter whether these measures are committed in time of peace or in time of war (Art. I Genocide Convention). The norms of the Genocide Convention have been acknowledged as important element of international customary law early on, for instance by the International Court of Justice (→ ICJ) in an advisory opinion of 28 May 1951 regarding the admissibility of reservations on the Genocide Convention (ICJ Reports 1951, 23). At present, the Genocide Convention has 140 states parties (as of 31 December 2008).

The Convention defines in Art. II as "genocide" the following acts "committed with intent to destroy, in whole or in part, a national, ethnical, racial or religious group, as such: (a) killing members of the group; (b) causing serious bodily or mental harm to members of the group; (c) deliberately inflicting on the group conditions of life calculated to bring about its physical destruction in whole or in part; (d) imposing measures intended to prevent births within the group; (e) forcibly transferring children of the group to another group." This definition is a central norm of International Criminal Law and has also been used in Art. 6 of the Statute of the International Criminal Court (called "Rome Statute", UN Doc. A/CONF.183/9, 17 July 1998). Punishable under the Convention is the act of committing genocide, the attempt to commit it, the conspiracy and the complicity to commit genocide, as well as the direct and public incitement to commit it (Art. III).

The state in the territory of which one of the criminal acts enumerated in Article III is committed is obliged to prosecute the criminal act, regardless of whether the criminal offences occur in time of peace or in time of war, and whether they are committed by "constitutionally responsible rulers, public officials or private individuals" (Art. IV).

However, the contracting states have established a jurisdiction for these acts only according to the principle of territoriality (Art. VI). The possibility to try the offenders by an international criminal tribunal, which "may have jurisdiction with respect to those Contracting Parties which shall have accepted its jurisdiction" as provided for in the same Article VI of the Convention, has not been established in the framework of this convention. Moreover, the Genocide Convention has not established own implementation organs or executive bodies at all. Rather Article VIII provides that the contracting parties may call upon "the competent organs of the United Nations to take such action under the Charter of the United Nations as they consider appropriate for the prevention and suppression of acts of genocide ..." (→ Principal Organs, Subsidiary Organs, Treaty Bodies; → Charter of the UN).

The latest judgment of the ICJ dealing with the application of the Genocide Convention of 26 February 2007 (Case Concerning the Application of the Convention on the Prevention and Punishment of the Crime of Genocide, Judgment, 26 February 2007, ICJ General List No. 91, available on the ICJ homepage, www.icj-cij.org/docket/files/91/13685.pdf) deals with proceedings filed by Bosnia-Herzegovina against Serbia and Montenegro. The Court decided that the crimes committed in Srebrenica constitute genocide, however the former Yugoslavia was not responsible for the crimes even though it had failed to prevent the massacre and had not prosecuted the culprits.

The international criminal jurisdiction for crimes of genocide has first been made possible by the UN Security Council in establishing the Ad-hoc Criminal Tribunal of the UN for the Former Yugoslavia in 1993 (UN Doc. S/RES/827 (1993), 25 May 1993), and for Rwanda in 1994 (UN Doc. S/RES/955 (1994), 8 November 1994). Article 4 of the statute of the Tribunal for Former Yugoslavia and Article 2 of the statute of the Tribunal for Rwanda give the two Tribunals, *inter alia*, the power to prosecute genocide.

Also the Rome Statute of the International Criminal Court (UN Doc. A/CONF.183/9, 17 July 1998), which was adopted at the UN Diplomatic Conference of Plenipotentiaries on the Establishment of an International Criminal Court in Rome on 17 July 1998 (→ ICC) and which entered into force in 2002, includes the crime of genocide (Art. 6 Rome Statute).

Martina Haedrich

Lit.: *Barth, B.:* Genozid. Völkermord im 20. Jahrhundert. Geschichten, Theorien, Kontroversen, Munich 2006; *Cassese, A.:* International Criminal Law, Oxford 2003; *Haedrich, M.:* Von der Allgemeinen Erklärung der Menschenrechte zur internationalen Menschenrechtsordnung – ein Überblick, in JA 31 (1999), 251-260; *Hübner, J.:* Das Verbrechen des Völkermords im internationalen und nationalen Recht, Frankfurt (Main) 2006; *Jescheck, H.-H.:* Genocide, in: Bernhardt, R. (ed.): EPIL, Vol. 8, 1985, 255-258; *Lattimer, M. (ed.):* Genocide and Human Rights, Aldershot, Hampshire 2007; *Robinson, N.:* The Genocide Convention. A Commentary, New York 1960; *Seidel, G.:* Handbuch der Grund- und Menschenrechte auf staatlicher, europäischer und universeller Ebene, Baden-Baden 1996; *Singh, N.:* The Development of International Law, in: Roberts, A./Kingsbury, B. (eds.): United Nations, Divided World. The UN's Roles in International Relations, 2nd edn., Oxford et al. 1993, 384-419 (in particular 393-395); *Tomuschat, C.:* Das Internationale Strafgesetzbuch der ILC, in EuGRZ 25 (1998), 3-7.

Internet: Text of the convention: http://www2.ohchr.org/english/law/genocide.htm; status of ratifications etc.: http://treaties.un.org, link: „Status of Treaties", link: "Chapter IV: Human Rights".

**Human Rights Conventions, CRC –
Convention on the Rights of the Child**

1. Origins

The *Convention on the Rights of the Child – CRC* (UN Doc. A/RES/44/25 of 20 November 1989; UNTS Vol. 1577, No. 27531) was carefully drafted over the course of 10 years from 1979 to 1989, starting with a Polish draft which led to the establishment of a working group of the United Nations Commission on Human Rights (→ Human Rights, Commission on) in 1979. The working group made up of members of the UN Commission on Human Rights, independent experts and representatives of → NGOs and was then charged with the drafting of the convention. This took place shortly before the proclamation of the International Year of the Child.

This initiative for drafting a convention on the rights of the child ran parallel to three other important developments: The first was the creation of the post of a special advisor to the United Nations for the monitoring of child prostitution, child pornography and child trafficking. The second was the enhanced endeavors of → UNICEF and → ILO to register with statistical means the infant victims of military conflicts, malnutrition and the lack of basic social services, to assess the number of economically active children. Finally, there was the move to reframe and focus ILO conventions with the aim to prevent at least the worst and most debasing forms of child labor, and to rehabilitate and to educate working children with the assistance of new development programmes (most prominently the International Programme for the Elimination of Child Labor, IPEC).

The reasons for this new activism are to be found in the advance of the concept of universal human rights (→ Human Rights), and their manifestation in international and regional covenants (→ Human Rights, Protection of; → Human Rights Conventions and their Measures of Implementation). Regarding children, the concept that childhood is a separate age, in need of special protection, has gained increasing recognition. It has also been acknowledged that children are especially exposed to the risks of violence and inequity, either in the form of labor in hazardous and degrading occupations (debt bondage, child prostitution etc.), or by denying them adequate wages, minimal workplace security etc., or by direct or indirect involvement in armed conflicts, or by police excesses. The awareness of these hazards to the young has been reinforced by campaigns led by national and international NGOs. They have appealed as well to consumers and governments in wealthy countries to ban sex tourism with children, or to boycott products made by child labor.

*1. Ratification and Reservations Made
by Individual Governments*

The Convention on the Rights of the Child stands out among all human rights covenants as the one having obtained the highest number of ratifications: After having been passed unanimously on 20 November 1989, it was signed at the earliest possible date (26 January 1990) by 61 states. Seven months later, on 2 September 1990, the required quorum of ratifications was secured to put the convention into force. At present, all members of the United Nations with the exception of Somalia and the United States, which has signed the convention in 1995, but not yet ratified it, have ratified. The signing of the Convention does oblige the parties to refrain from all activities which could undermine the objectives of the convention. Accession may be by ratification or by consent (without prior signing). Both procedures are legally binding in terms of the Convention rules. Parties of the Convention are expected to implement the regulations within a "reasonable" time frame, at the latest before the agreed handing over of the first country reports (two years after ratification or consent). The Convention differentiates between social, economic and cultural rights of children on the one hand, and civil or political rights on the other. The former shall be guaranteed by contracting states in terms of available resources, a formulation which leaves certain latitude. The objectives of the Convention may also be achieved by international cooperation, i.e. bilateral or multilateral aid. This constitutes a contractual innovation.

The nearly universal ratification of the Convention should not obscure the fact that a certain number of its objectives were to some extent jeopardized by more than sixty national declarations and reservations in signing or ratifying the text. Arab states referred to the continuing validity of the Islamic right (sharia), and to the limitation of freedom of opinion and of religion in countries where Islam is the state religion; poorer developing countries pointed to their more liberal practices of adoption; other professed reservations concerning the slower implementation of social rights for children (India), stricter parental guidance (South East Asia) or stricter family planning (China). Representatives of Western countries made reservations with regard to the further reaching European human rights protection of children through European human rights conventions, as well as with respect to the different treatment of minor and adult delinquents, and to the equal treatment of children of national and foreign origin prescribed by the Convention. Some Western governments (but also some governments of more developed Third World countries) objected to the clause restricting compulsory recruitment into the armed forces to persons above the age of 18 (instead of 15).

2. Content of the Convention

The Convention on the Rights of the Child is composed of two parts. The first part essentially extends the coverage of the usual civil rights to children (freedom of expression, religion and information, right to a name and nationality, to an intact family, non-discrimination, public care if parents are lost). The second part confers social, economic and cultural rights in the field of health care, social security, education and participation in cultural life. It also protects

children against paid and bonded labor, sexual exploitation, detention, torture and involvement in armed conflict. An important point of controversy during negotiations was the question of how the granting of these rights could be made binding, and how compliance would be measured. Informal agreement was reached to use the "National Performance Gaps" of the Human Development Report (→ Human Development Reports) as yardsticks, i.e. to measure shortfalls in educational attainment, child mortality etc. against the identified norms (and in accordance with the stage of development), and to treat a shortfall of 40% or more as an obvious case of official child neglect.

Two additional Optional Protocols to the Convention – adopted by the UN General Assembly with A/RES/54/263 on 25 May 2000 – are intended to prevent: (a) involvement of children in armed conflict and compulsory recruitment below the age of 18 years; and (b) to combat the sale of children, child prostitution and child pornography (*United Nations* 2000a and 2000b). The former protocol does not set a minimum age for voluntary recruitment; the latter will necessarily pursue its objectives through international cooperation. Both have been signed by 124 and 116 member countries, and ratified by 126 and 130 states parties, respectively, as of 31 December 2008.

3. Effects and Assessment

The main instrument for enforcing the Convention on the Rights of the Child was the establishment of the *Committee on the Rights of the Child*, which paralleled the entry into force of the Convention. The mandate of the Committee is to observe and encourage the conformity of national legislation with the Convention. The Committee is composed of ten independent international experts of "high moral standing", elected for a term of four years. The Committee is the addressee of reports which the states parties are to submit on the situation of children and national endeavors for implementing the Convention.

NGOs (→ NGOs) are requested to write parallel reports and to comment on the official reports. The Committee then debates the reports in the presence of representatives of the government in question, and makes recommendations, which governments are required to publish. The implementation of these recommendations is checked after five years. Nearly all members have forwarded country reports to the Committee, some of them quite self-critical. NGOs have presented parallel reports, most of them highly critical of government actions. Besides moral pressure, the Committee does not dispose of any sanctions, if we ignore development finance earmarked for implementing the Convention. Promoters of the Convention are however confident that the approach selected, that of constructive critique, is the right one.

The Commission has been able to identify some follow-up actions on the Convention which have led up to now less to an improvement in the conditions of children in member states, than to the setting-up of new administrative bodies for promoting child rights and preparing national action programmes as well as legislative reforms on a large scale (for the restriction of child labor, the elimination of child prostitution etc.). The latter have been implemented mainly in Latin America and South East Asia. Here and there, social services for children have improved, child commissioners or ombudsman have been installed and some additional states have developed distinct systems of youth justice. The content of the Convention has also been translated into national curricula and – in Nepal – children were consulted in the drafting of national reports.

A form of institutional follow-up to the Convention was the General Assembly Special Session on Children (2002), intended by the General Assembly as an end-decade review of the follow-up of the World Summit for Children (1990) which had adopted a "World Declaration on the Survival, Protection and Development of Children" together with a "Plan of Action"

for implementing the declaration (*United Nations* 1990, Annex) The special session was prepared by a report of the UN Secretary-General on the progress made in the implementation of the of the above-mentioned "World Declaration of 1990 "We the Children: End-decade review of the follow-up to the World Summit for Children" (*United Nations* 2001) This report listed achievements in the well-being of children during the 1990s, but highlighted also the "unfinished business" (widespread poverty, malnourishment, lack of school enrolment and recruitment of child soldiers).

The Special Session was the first event of the United Nations, where children acted as participants. The session ended with an agreement on a resolution titled "World Fit for Children" (UN Doc. A/RES/S-27/2, 10 May 2002), a text prepared by UNICEF, laying out a "plan of action" to bridge the gap between promises and achievements of the 1990s. The plan created time-bound targets for achieving the Millennium Development Goals directly related to children and for protecting children against exploitation and violence. It also sets countries the task of developing, by the end of 2003, national action plans to meet the targets (ibid., para. 59).

In this context the resolution underlines the comprehensive political significance of the human rights of the children:

"We, the Governments, participating in this special session, commit ourselves to implementing the Plan of Action through consideration of such measures as:

... Putting in place ... effective national legislation, policies and actions plans and allocating resources to fulfil and protect the rights and to secure the well-being of children;

... Enhancing widespread awareness and understanding of the rights of the child." (ibid., para. 31).

Joachim Betz

Lit.: *a) Documents: International Labour Office:* Child Labour. Targeting the Intolerable, Geneva 1996; *Ministry of Foreign Affairs of the Netherlands:* Children and Development, The Hague 1996; *UNICEF:* The Convention: Child Rights and UNICEF Experience and Country Level, Florence 1991; *UNICEF:* The State of the World's Children 2002: Leadership, New York 2001; *UNICEF:* Guide to the Optional Protocol on the Involvement of Children in Armed Conflict, New York 2003; *UNICEF/Inter-Parliamentary Union:* Child protection: A handbook for parliamentarians, New York 2004; *UNICEF:* Implementation Handbook for the Convention on the Rights of the Child, fully revised third edition, Geneva 2007; *United Nations - General Assembly:* Declaration and Plan of Action Adopted by World Leaders at the World Summit for Children, 30 September 1990, UN Doc. A/45/625 of 18 October 1990, Annex (quoted as: United Nations 1990); *United Nations:* Optional Protocol to the Convention on the Rights of the Child on the involvement of children in armed conflict, New York, 25 May 2000 (UN Doc. A/RES/263; UNTS Vol. 2173, No. 27531), (quoted as: United Nations 2000a); *United Nations:* Optional Protocol to the Convention on the Rights of the Child on the sale of children, child prostitution and child pornography, New York, 25 May 2000 (UN Doc. A/RES/54/263; UNTS Vol. 2171, No. 27531), (quoted as: United Nations 2000b); *United Nations - General Assembly:* We the Children: End-decade review of the follow-up to the World Summit for Children. Report of the Secretary-General, 4 May 2001, UN Doc. A/S-27/3 (quoted as: United Nations 2001); *United Nations – General Assembly:* A world fit for children, New York 11 October 2002 (UN Doc A/RES/S-27/2, 10 May 2002);
b) Secondary Literature: van Bueren, G.: The International Law on the Rights of the Child, Dordrecht 1998; *David, P.:* Enfants sans enfance, Paris; *Haspels, N./Jankanish, M. (eds.):* Action Against Child Labour, ILO, Geneva 2000; *Himes, J.R.:* The UN Convention on the Rights of the Child: Three essays on the challenge of implementation (UNICEF Innocenti Essay 5), Florence 1993; *Himes, J.R.:* Implementing the Convention on the Rights of the Child: Resource mobilization in low-income countries, Dordrecht/Florence 1995; *Petren, A./Himes, J.R. (eds.):* Children's Rights: Turning principles into practice, Stockholm 2000.

Internet: Homepage of the Committee on the Rights of the Child: http://www2. ohchr.org/english/bodies/crc/index.htm; website of UNICEF on the CRC: www.unicef.org/crc; Homepage of the Child Rights Information Network: www.crin.org.

Human Rights Council

After 60 years the *Commission on Human Rights*, established by ECOSOC resolution E/RES/5 (I) of 16 February 1946 as a subsidiary organ of → ECOSOC for the promotion and protection of human rights, was abolished with effect on 16 June 2006 by ECOSOC resolution E/RES/2006/2 of 22 March 2006 at the request of the General Assembly in resolution A/RES/60/251 of 15 March 2006.

With the same resolution the → General Assembly decided "to establish the Human Rights Council, based in Geneva, in replacement of the Commission on Human Rights, as a subsidiary organ of the General Assembly." Why did the General Assembly and ECOSOC, respectively, abolish the Commission on Human Rights and what are the structures, purposes and procedures of the successor organ, the Human Rights Council?

I. What Was the Commission on Human Rights?

The *Commission on Human Rights*, established in 1946 by ECOSOC on the basis of the requirement laid down in Article 68 of the UN Charter (→ Charter of the UN) that ECOSOC "shall set up commissions in economic and social fields and for the promotion of human rights", was the principal human rights body within the UN system.

Its work was serviced initially by the *Division for Human Rights* in the UN → Secretariat, upgraded in 1979 at the request of the General Assembly (UN Doc. A/RES/34/47, 23 November 1979) for a *"Centre for Human Rights"*, headed since 1983 by a Director with the rank of an Under-Secretary-General (cf. UN Doc. A/RES/37/237, 21 December 1982), and since 1994 headed by the newly-established High Commissioner for Human Rights (UN Doc. A/RES/41/141, 20 December 1993).

The Commission as a subsidiary body of ECOSOC was made up of 53 states elected for three-year terms by ECOSOC with a balance of representation of the UN's five → regional groups. The major roles of the Commission were standard-setting in the field of human rights and monitoring of compliance with human rights standards. The Commission was moreover for a long time the main forum for → NGOs to raise human rights concerns publicly and in discussions with states and to lobby for the creation of new human rights standards or for action in cases of human rights violations. NGOs accredited by ECOSOC could participate in the Commission's sessions and make oral and written statements.

1. Standard-Setting

With regard to standard-setting, the Commission had in fact a number of remarkable successes on its balance sheet: it drafted the Universal Declaration of Human Rights which was then adopted by the General Assembly in resolution A/RES/217A (III) on 10 December 1948, as well as the two basic international human rights conventions the "International Convention on Civil and Political Rights" and the "International Convention on Economic, Social and Cultural Rights" which were both adopted by the General Assembly in December 1966 and entered into force in 1976. Furthermore the commission also drafted the Convention against Genocide (adopted by the General Assembly in 1948), the Convention against Torture (adopted by the General Assembly in 1984) and the Convention on the Rights of the Child (adopted by the General Assembly in 1989).

2. Human Rights Protection

Due to its somewhat weak and unclear legal mandate for monitoring the compliance with human rights standards by UN member states, it took the Commission quite some time to develop a significant role in this regard. Initially the Commission even denied having any competence with regard to complaints about human rights violations when the Secretary-General of the United Nations asked the Commission what he should do with the large number of human rights complaints addressed to the United Nations. The Commission stated in its first session in 1947: "The Commission recognizes that it has no power to take any action in regard to any complaints concerning human rights." (cf. UN Doc. E/259 (Supp.), Official Records of the Economic and Social Council, Fourth session, Supplement No. 3).

Philip Alston assumes that the reasons for this astonishing indifference of the Commission towards human rights violations might be that the USA was worried about possible complaints alleging racial discrimination against its negro citizens, while the United Kingdom, France, Belgium, Portugal and other colonial powers feared complaints about conditions and practices in their colonies. The East European states might have been afraid of being criticized for political oppression in the predominantly Stalinist regimes (*Alston* 1992, 141).

Thus it is not by accident that the first significant attempts to develop a human rights protection system took place in the Commission when the UN membership had massively increased by a large number of states from Africa and Asia, former colonies which had recently gained their independence. The representatives of this group of states in the Commission were interested in developing an effective mechanism for dealing in the Commission with the human rights violations in the colonial states in Southern Africa, in particular in South Africa. Thus the Commission developed since the late 1960s two different procedures to deal with human rights complaints endorsed through respective resolutions of ECOSOC:

- the so-called *1503 procedure* (based on E/RES/1503 (XLVIII) of 27 May 1970). The Commission examined in this confidential procedure with the help of its Subcommission on the Prevention of Discrimination and Protection of Minorities the transmitted human rights complaints whether they found in countries massive and systematic human rights violations and – depending on the outcome of the investigation – decided to inform ECOSOC (and thus also the public) in its annual report that the country had been the subject of the 1503 procedure of the Commission, a kind of public blaming at the end of a highly confidential procedure.

- the so-called *1235 procedure* (based on E/RES/1235 (XLII) of 6 June 1967). The Commission could in this procedure decide – after checking the human rights complaints with the help of its above-mentioned Sub-Commission in the same way as in the 1503 procedure whether cases of massive and systematic human rights violations were to be found – to hold a public debate on the respective case and to study and investigate the respective situation further. The Commission made since the 1980s increasingly use of this latter possibility, the so-called "special procedures" and appointed an increasing number of special rapporteurs and independent experts with the task of examining the human rights situation in a certain country (cf. *Alston* 1992, 159ff.

Moreover the Commission started in the early eighties also to establish so-called "thematic procedures" or "thematic mandates"; it appointed special rapporteurs with the task of examining the situation with regard to a certain type of human rights violation, such as torture or enforced disappearance not only in one country, but in all countries where these problems had become known (cf. ibid., 173ff).

3. Evaluation of Its Work

While the merits of the Commission in human rights standard-setting are undisputed, the efficiency and credibility of its human rights protection were always a topic of critical debate, in particular, when since the mid-1970s the treaty bodies of the human rights conventions entering into force (→ Human Rights Conventions and their Measures of Implementation) began their work and could – due to their stronger competences stipulated in the conventions – deal at regular intervals publicly and more critically with the human rights behavior of their member states, since all the member states had to report on the implementation of their human rights obligations according to the respective convention.

The problem of the Commission was that it had no legal basis in a convention or in the UN Charter to check the human rights situation in every UN member country. It had to find in every case a majority for starting one of its procedures with regard to a certain country and had to prove that massive and systematic human rights violations had taken place in that country. It had also to find a majority for choosing the confidential (1503) or public (1235) procedure. So it is not astonishing that often the confidential procedure was taken.

Experts agree that both procedures were very slow, cumbersome and not very effective, but – since at that time there were no other UN human rights protection instruments – the best the United Nations could offer, producing some political pressure against a state violating human rights in the hope that the state would react with an improvement of its human rights situation.

The country and thematic rapporteurs being used since the late 1970s and the 1980s, respectively, proved to be more effective than the 1503 and the 1235 procedures since their detailed reports brought the countries at issue into much greater trouble than they had expected, in particular, since the NGOs provided the rapporteurs with ample material.

To judge the achievements of the Commission fairly one has to take into consideration that it developed its protection procedures without any definite legal basis provided by its founders. As a result it had to assemble in a very difficult procedure piece-by-piece of its protection competences as granted by its

331

member states, supported by ECOSOC and adopted by the General Assembly.

The increasing criticism against the Commission on Human Rights which eventually led to its abolition in 2006 is in my opinion somewhat unfair and out of proportion. First, the Commission could not be blamed for the fact that countries with bad human rights records became repeatedly members of the Commission as – within the usual election procedures – it was up to the regional groups to decide on the candidates for their group which were then elected, a procedure still practiced in most UN bodies. Second, the Commission depended in the choice of its human rights situations to be examined and discussed on Council majorities, and if a state to be examined succeeded in gaining the support of the Council members from his region for a number of reasons, it could not be put on the agenda. Third, the lack of effectiveness of its mechanisms was due to the fact that the General Assembly for many decades did not want to provide the Commission through an explicit authorization in form of a resolution with more competences.

One might get the impression that the criticism was intentionally exaggerated in the arena of the World Summit 2005 in the hope of obtaining a General Assembly mandate for the establishment of a new human rights body with more competences. The plan succeeded but it remains to be seen whether the better construction of the new human rights body will also lead to better results.

II. The Reform 2005/2006

The initiative for replacing the Commission on Human Rights by a new human rights organ was started in the Report of the High-Level Panel on Threats, Challenges and Change, submitted in December 2004 (UN Doc. A/59/565). In criticizing the Commission's "eroding credibility and professionalism" (ibid., para. 283) the panel recommends as a first measure expanding the membership of the Commission to "universal membership" (ibid., para. 285). In the longer term, the panel recommends the Commission should be replaced by "a 'Human Rights Council' that is no longer subsidiary to the Economic and Social Council, but a Charter body standing alongside it and the Security Council and reflecting in the process the weight given to human rights, alongside security and economic issues, in the Preamble of the Charter." (ibid., para. 291)

Secretary-General Kofi Annan repeated in his reform report of March 2005 "In larger freedom: towards development, security and human rights for all" (UN Doc. A/59/2005) the criticism with regard to the lack of credibility and professionalism of the Commission on Human Rights and made the suggestion of replacing the Commission with a smaller Human Rights Council, either as a principal organ of the United Nations or a subsidiary body of the General Assembly; its members should be elected directly by the General Assembly by a two-thirds majority of members present and voting. (ibid., para. 183)

IV. The Establishment of the Human Rights Council

The UN World Summit in September 2005 decided in its concluding resolution "2005 World Summit Outcome" (UN Doc. A/RES/60/1, 16 September 2005) to establish a Human Rights Council, but did not decide on its size, mandate or modalities. It requested the President of the General Assembly to conduct negotiations for this purpose.

Since the member states had problems agreeing on the membership of the Council with regard to size and membership criteria as well as to the voting procedure it took over six months of negotiations for the UN member states to work out the details. On 15 March 2006 the General Assembly adopted resolution A/RES/60/251 with 170 votes in favor, four against and three abstentions, which formally established the *Human Rights Council (HRC).*

According to the resolution, the Council elections were to be held on 9 May 2006 and the Council was to begin its work on 19 June 2006.

V. Structures and Tasks of the Human Rights Council

The *Human Rights Council*, seated in Geneva, is a subsidiary body of the General Assembly that reports directly to the Assembly (ibid., para. 1).

It is composed of 47 member states elected in a secret ballot by an absolute majority of the General Assembly (para. 7), taking into account the candidates' contribution to the promotion and protection of human rights and voluntary pledges and commitments (para. 8). After two consecutive terms council members are not eligible for immediate reelection (para. 7). Any council member that commits gross and systematic violations to human rights can be suspended by the General Assembly by a two-thirds majority (para. 8).

The Council is to meet regularly throughout the year and to hold no fewer than three sessions per year for a total duration of no less than ten weeks (para. 10). The Council shall apply the rules of procedure established for committees of the General Assembly (→ Committees, System of); for the participation and consultations with observers the arrangements and practices observed by the Commission of Human Rights shall be applied (para. 11).

The responsibilities of the Council are (as set out in the GA resolution):
- to promote universal respect for the protection of all human rights and fundamental freedoms for all (para. 2);
- to "address situations of violations of human rights, including gross and systematic violations, and make recommendations thereon" (para. 3); and
- to promote the effective coordination and the mainstreaming of human rights within the United Nations system (para. 3);

In its work the Council shall *inter alia* serve as forum for dialogue on thematic issues on all human rights (para. 5 lit. b), make recommendations to the General Assembly for the further development of international law in the field of human rights (para. 5 lit. c), submit an annual report to the General Assembly (para. 5 lit. j), and assume the role and responsibilities of the Commission on Human Rights relating to the work of the Office of the High Commissioner for Human Rights (para. 5 lit. g).

While these tasks are quite similar to that of its predecessor, the Council has a new task: to "undertake a universal periodic review, based on objective and reliable information, on the fulfillment by each State of its human rights obligations and commitments"; the review shall be "a cooperative mechanism, based on interactive dialogue, with the full involvement of the country concerned ..." (para. 5 lit. e).

With regard to the functions and procedures, the Council is to "assume, review and, where necessary, improve and rationalize all mandates, mechanisms, functions and responsibilities of the Commission on Human Rights in order to maintain a system of special procedures, expert advice and a complaint procedure ..." (para. 6).

VI. Reactions to the Establishment of the Human Rights Council (HRC)

Human rights experts and NGOs as well as human rights supportive UN member states welcomed the establishment of the Council. They hoped that
- its position as a subsidiary organ of the General Assembly would strengthen the political authority of the organ;
- the election through the General Assembly would reduce the number of members with bad human rights records;
- the longer meeting period would provide more time for thorough and comprehensive deliberations; and
- the Universal Periodic Review (UPR) mechanism would increase the chance to take all human rights violating states to account, also those which had avoided this so far because regional bloc voting in the Commission had prevented them from getting on the agenda; and at the same time the universality of the review would increase the credibility of the mechanism.

VII. First Experiences with the Council

The first three years of the Council work fulfilled some of the hopes of its supporters, but revealed also a number of problems and open questions.

It took the Council a whole year of intense debate with highly conflicting views to find a consensus on the further institution-building of the HRC within the framework provided by the founding resolution.

On 18 June 2007, the Council adopted resolution 5/1 (UN Doc. A/HRC/RES/5/1), which was later on explicitly endorsed by the General Assembly with resolution A/RES/62/219 of 22 December 2007.

The HRC resolution contained all the details about the UPR, the special procedures, the complaint procedure, the establishment of the Human Rights Council Advisory Committee, the agenda and the rules of procedure of the Council.

All in all, the resolution on the institution-building constituted a minimal compromise between two groups of the Council, the one engaging itself for a strong and efficient human rights organ with effective mechanisms and structures, and the other attempting skillfully to restrain competences and abolish mechanisms considered not to be in the interest of the respective states – or to put it more simply – the group of the human rights supporters versus the group of states considering human rights as means of intervention by the Western countries. In this regard the political conditions for the work of the HRC differ not much from those experienced by the Commission on Human Rights.

1. Elections, Membership and Voting Behavior

The Council proved – like many other newly-established UN organs – that political problems cannot be solved alone by reforming the structures: the elections so far have shown that indeed the number of states with problematic human rights records among the Council members decreased. But the voting behavior in the decisions of the Councils

sessions of the years 2006, 2007 and 2008 showed that here again the states tend to bloc-vote along political, regional and ideological lines. In this regard the situation has not much improved in comparison to the Commission on Human Rights. So the European Parliament criticized in January 2009 in a resolution on the development of the HRC (European Parliament Resolution P6_TA (2009)0021, 14 January 2009) "the growing division of the UNHRC into regional blocs", and maintained that "this 'bloc mentality' undermines the ability of the UNHRC to deal effectively, impartially and objectively with human rights violations around the world ...".

The smaller size of the Council in connection with the distribution of the seats in the regional groups resulted in a relative weakening of the position of the Council states belonging to the regional group of Western European and other States (WEOG), so that this group had to come to terms with a weaker standing in the Council.

2. Mandates and Procedures

The review of the existing country mandates and thematic mandates of the special procedures was battled over in the discussions of the Council more than perhaps had been expected. A number of Council members attempted to make the Council abolish some of the mandates. The Council majority did eventually not agree to these attempts, but in two cases country mandates (Cuba and Belarus) were not prolonged.

The thematic procedures have been maintained so far; but it became obvious in the Council debates that a number of Council member states try to exploit the use of the review process as an attempt to curtail the number of these procedures. Here the human rights supporting countries in the Council must pay attention to pre-empt these attempts.

The work of the special rapporteurs is in the Council much more a topic for discussion than was the case in the Commission: that can be regarded positively, as their findings thus attract more publicity, since not only the member states, but also the NGOs and national human rights institutions have more opportunity to take part in the discussions.

But on the other hand, the rapporteurs which enjoyed an important independence in their work might lose part of their political standing if they are too often and too tightly controlled by the Council.

3. The Human Rights Advisory Committee

The place and function of the Subcommission of the Commission on Human Rights which played an important role for the work of the Commission as a think-tank for new concepts, initiator for important studies and key institution in the 1503 complaint procedure has been given in the institution-building resolution of the HRC to the Human Rights Advisory Committee.

In comparison to its predecessor organ, the Subcommission of the Commission on Human Rights, the Advisory Committee enjoys fewer competences and less freedom of action. It functions also as think-tank, but only at the request of the Council; in contrast to its predecessor, it cannot take its own initiatives. The themes of its deliberations are restricted to the issues pertaining to the mandate of the Council; the Committee is not entitled to adopt resolutions or decisions and will be regulated by specific guidelines worked out by the Council (UN Doc. A/HRC/RES/5/1, para. 75ff.).

That is indeed a far remove from encouraging intellectual freedom and creativity in the way displayed by the members of the Subcommission who were a source of inspiration and incremental reform for the Commission on Human Rights, and, in a way, the creators of the evolving system of human rights protection mechanisms.

Obviously the majority of the Council members did not want to continue this tradition. The Advisory Committee in this legal framework will not be able to play a similar role for the Human Rights Council and the UN human rights system in general. In this regard the council reform has to be considered as a setback. (cf. *Abraham* 2007, 16ff.; see also *International Service for Human Rights* 2008a, 20f.).

4. The Relation to OHCHR

The council members not so enthusiastic about human rights attempt also to make use of the vague definition of the relationship between the High Commissioner for Human Rights and the Council in the founding resolution of the HRC – "... the Council shall assume the role and responsibilities of the Commission on Human Rights relating to the work of the Office of the United Nations High Commissioner for Human Rights as decided by the General Assembly in its resolution A/RES/48/141 of 20 December 2003" – for gaining control over the work of OHCHR.

At the sixth session of the HRC, a number of Council members, among them Russia and Pakistan, called for more accountability of OHCHR and for institutional checks and balances, and for the comments of the Council members to be reflected in the strategic planning of OHCHR – a clear attempt to micromanage the work of OHCHR, and to gain political control (cf. *International Service for Human Rights* 2008b, 3).

Neither the mandate of OHCR nor the mandate of HRC authorize such a claim, but the supporters of an active OHCHR should take care to reject these destructive attempts of subordinating OHCHR to the control of HRC.

5. The Complaints Procedure

The 1503 procedure of the Commission on Human Rights has been taken over – with some slight variations – for HRC in its institution-building resolution 5/1. For the complaint procedure the Advisory Committee has established two working groups, the Working Group on Communications and the Working Group on Situations, the first with the task of checking the admissibility of the communications concerning human rights violations, the second working group having the task of finding out whether consistent patterns of massive and reliably attested violations can be found and to make recommendations to the Council on the action to be taken (UN Doc. A/HRC/RES/5/1, para. 89ff.). Up to this point the procedure is confidential as was its predecessor procedure.

The Council decides then in closed session on further action, among others to request a state to provide further information, to appoint an independent expert to monitor the situation or to take up a public consideration of the case (ibid., para. 109). On the recommendation of the Advisory Committee the HRC can also decide to deal with the matter in public session, in particular in the case of lack of cooperation of the state concerned (ibid., para. 104).

This resembles for the most part the old 1503 procedure. Improvements are that in the new procedure the complainant is informed about the proceedings whereas in the old procedure only the state concerned was informed. Moreover, the complainant can request that his or her identity not be communicated to the state concerned.

It is also an improvement that the complaints procedure contains a time limit in saying that between receipt of the complaint and its consideration by the Council the period of time should not exceed twenty-four months. Regrettably the procedure does not contain any provision for interim measures of protection or remedies for the complainant.

Proposals to take the complaints procedure also as an early warning system for the Council by drawing its attention to emerging situations of massive human rights violations were not taken up; neither were proposals for sharing information gained in the 1503 procedure with the mandate holders of the special procedures or for introducing the information in the UPR.

All in all, it is fair to say that the complaints procedure has been preserved and even slightly improved.

6. The Universal Periodic Review (UPR)

The UPR is conducted by the entire Council sitting as a working group through an interactive dialogue with the concerned state (UN Doc. A/HRC/RES/5/1, para. 18). The Review is based on three documents: a national report, a compilation by OHCHR of the information contained in the reports of treaty bodies, special procedures and UN documents, and a summary prepared by OHCHR of information received from other stakeholders, including NGOs (ibid., para. 15). The Council, as the working group, then prepares a report which is later adopted as the outcome report in a plenary session of the Council. The report contains recommendations which are legally non-binding (ibid., para. 26ff.).

Observer states can participate in the review process and in the interactive dialogue with the concerned state. Other stakeholders such as national human rights institutions or NGOs can also attend the review but may not ask questions. During the consideration of the outcome report by the HRC plenary, however, NGOs will be allowed to make genral comments before the adoption of the outcome (ibid. para. 31).

The quality of the UPR will depend very much on the extent of the information the Council takes into consideration provided by NGOs, since the OHCHR material on the implementation of the treay obligations will not usually have a high informative value. Problems and human rights violations are more likely to be discovered through NGO material.

A big problem involved with the UPR is that in order to make the UPR with all UN member states within four years as prescribed in Resolution 5/1, the time available for the review of a certain state will be rather short.

Also the UPR is in danger of becoming the object of political running fights, as the European Parliament criticizes in its above-mentioned resolution of 2009, denouncing "the use of political alliances to shield certain States from scrutiny rather than to critically assess human rights conditions and protections" (European Parliament Resolution P6_TA (2009)0021, para. 23).

Thus is maybe that the UPR develops more or less as a symbolic exercise rather than an effective means of human rights protection but even in this case it will make clear explicitly that all UN member states are reviewed under the same human rights standards. This might be very useful for the acceptance of human rights standards world wide.

7. Evaluation

All in all, the great expectations with regard to the Human Rights Council have made place for sober realism and some disappointment. The improvements in the different human rights procedures and mechanisms of the Council in comparison with the Commission on Human Rights are minor and their value seems to be outweighed by the setbacks in other points. In particular the limited mandate of the Advisory Committee and the continuous attempts of a number of Council members to restrict the special procedures and to exert control over the work of OHCHR have to be considered as serious setbacks.

It is to be hoped that the HRC might develop over the years sufficient political will to counterbalance the forces within the Council attempting to reduce its effectiveness and that the Council is able to develop in small steps effective means to strengthen its own capacity of protecting human rights.

Helmut Volger

Lit.: *Abraham, M.:* Building the New Human Rights Council. Outcome and analysis of the institution-building year (Friedrich-Ebert-Stiftung: Dialogue on Globalization - Occasional Papers Geneva No. 33), Geneva 2007; *Alston, P.:* The Commission on Human Rights, in: Alston, P. (ed.): The United Nations and Human Rights. A Critical Appraisal, Oxford 1992, 126-210; *European Parliament:* European Parliament resolution of 14 January 2009 on the development of the UN Human Rights Council, including the role of the EU, P6_TA(2009)0021; *International Service for Human Rights:* Human Rights Monitor No. 65/2007, Geneva 2008 (quoted: International Service for Human Rights 2008a); *International Service for Human Rights:* Council Monitor: Human Rights Council, 8th Session, 2-18 June 2008 (quoted as: International Service for Human Rights 2008b); *Yeboah, N.:* The Establishment of the Human Rights Council, in: Center for UN Reform Education (ed.): Managing Change at the United Nations, New York 2008, 79-95.

Internet: Homepage of the Human Rights Council: http://www2.ohchr.org/english/bodies/hrcouncil.

Humanitarian Assistance

1. Definition

The *humanitarian assistance* process of the United Nations is a complex interaction of the *Office for the Coordination of Humanitarian Affairs (OCHA)* within the UN → Secretariat, the UN → Security Council, operational UN agencies and non-governmental organizations (→ NGOs), donor governments, the governments concerned and the affected populations.

Humanitarian assistance is understood to mean all aid and action designed to save lives, alleviate suffering and maintain and protect human dignity during and in the aftermath of emergencies. As humanitarian assistance is based on a humanitarian motivation and does not pursue political, economic or military objectives, it should be clearly distinguished from political, economic and military assistance. The terms "aid and action" are broadly defined, since they include the planning, preparation, implementation and evaluation of humanitarian relief operations as well as the permanent co-ordination between relief organizations and other UN departments. The guiding principles of UN humanitarian assistance are the principles of humanity, neutrality, and impartiality. The scope of UN humanitarian activity ranges from humanitarian crises resulting from war and violent conflict, to natural and technical disasters (e.g. Chernobyl). Since 1990, humanitarian assistance in the context of "complex emergencies" has become increasingly important. According to the OCHA, "complex emergencies" are humanitarian crises with multiple causes (political, military, economic, etc.) that require a broad and comprehensive assistance approach instead of separate interventions by different agencies and institutions. (cf. the definition in: *UN DHA 1997*)

The legal foundations for the humanitarian engagement of the United Nations are the UN Charter (→ Charter of the UN) and the Geneva Conventions of 1949, including its two Additional Protocols of 1977 (cf. → Humanitarian Law, International).

As part of the overall UN reform process, the international humanitarian community initiated a humanitarian reform process in 2005 with the objective of improving the timeliness, appropriateness and equity of crisis response. This process has significantly changed the humanitarian response structure and the funding mechanisms of the United Nations by establishing system-wide sectoral responsibilities for operational agencies, reshaping roles and responsibilities, modifying funding mechanisms and strengthening cooperation with non-governmental agencies (→ NGOs).

2. Institutions and Mechanisms

The humanitarian reform agenda initiated in 2005 has changed the humanitarian structures and mechanisms of the United Nations. Key UN actors are the *Office for the Coordination of Humanitarian Affairs (OCHA)*, the *UN Inter-Agency Standing Committee (IASC)*, UN operational agencies as well as Humanitarian Coordinators at country level.

The central coordination body for humanitarian assistance within the United Nations is the *Office for the Coordination of Humanitarian Affairs (OCHA)*. OCHA is one of the five departments of the → Secretariat (since 1998) led by the Under-Secretary General for Humanitarian Affairs who at the same time is the UN's *Emergency Relief Coordinator* and reports to the → Secretary-

General. Following the 1998 restructuring of the Secretariat (→ Reform of the UN) OCHA succeeded the Department of Humanitarian Affairs (DHA).

The OCHA focuses on three main activities: first, coordinating humanitarian operations (main activities) of UN operational agencies, second, elaborating and formulating humanitarian strategies and third, representing humanitarian issues in political bodies, notably the Security Council.

The coordination of humanitarian assistance is the core activity of the OCHA and aims to ensure coherent and coordinated operations of all UN agencies and actors involved in humanitarian operations (→ FAO, → WFP, → UNICEF, → UNHCR, → UNDP, and → WHO) during all stages of a relief operation from resource mobilization to final evaluation of interventions. At the country level, the Humanitarian Coordinator is responsible for ensuring coherence of relief efforts in the field. The OCHA supports the Humanitarian Coordinator in needs assessment, contingency planning and the formulation of humanitarian programmes. The Humanitarian Coordinator also often has the role of UN Resident Coordinator.

The OCHA's coordinating role is primarily performed through the *Inter Agency Standing Committee (IASC)* which comprises all humanitarian partners, the Red Cross Movement and NGOs and chaired by the OCHA. The IASC is the UN's primary inter-agency mechanism for coordinating humanitarian assistance. It develops humanitarian policies, agrees on a clear division of responsibility for the various aspects of humanitarian assistance, identifies and addresses gaps in response, and advocates effective application of humanitarian principles. In addition, the IASC takes joint decisions on humanitarian operations, plans and evaluates needs assessments, consolidated financial appeals, field operations and develops concepts and policies.

Through its second coordinating instrument, the *"Consolidated Inter-Agency Appeal Process"* (CAP), the OCHA coordinates the raising of funds and the planning and programming of humanitarian activities. With the CAPs, the OCHA coordinates the planning and formulation of country-based Annual Appeals, Common Humanitarian Action Plans (CHAPs) that serve as common, strategic planning tools as well as Flash Appeals for raising funds for rapid, life-saving needs within one week after an emergency. The resources mobilized with the help of CAPs are used for implementation by participating agencies, including UN relief organizations and programmes (WFP, UNHCR, UNDP, FAO, WHO, UNHCHR, → UN-Habitat, UNDCP, → UNFPA, → UNRWA, → UNESCO, → ILO, IOM, → UNV) and NGOs. By now, CAPs have also developed into the main tool for strategy development and programming of joint humanitarian operations.

The third instrument of coordination, administered and coordinated by the OCHA is the *Central Emergency Response Fund (CERF)*. Established in 2006, the Fund replaces the former Central Emergency Revolving Fund and allows the UN to react immediately after a crisis or disaster by making funding available for life-saving activities to eligible agencies such as UN and its funds, programmes, and → specialized agencies and the International Organization for Migration (IOM).

The CERF is intended to complement – not to replace – existing humanitarian funding mechanisms. The CERF provides seed funds to jump-start critical operations and life-saving programmes not yet funded through other sources. The Fund provides a grant facility of up to 450 million US dollars and loan facility of up to 50 million US dollars. Since March 2006, the grant component of the CERF has received pledges and contributions from 100 public and private donors of more than 1.1 billion US dollars. In the first months of 2008, 76 member states, one observer state and four private organizations have pledged 430.2 million US dollars. In 2007, the CERF committed 227.8 million US dollars to rapid response grants in 49 countries

and 123.1 million US dollars to underfunded emergencies in 23 countries. (figures according to www.ochaonline.org/cerf as of July 2008)

Within the UN humanitarian field, nearly all humanitarian operations are funded by voluntary contributions and not through the regular UN budget (→ Budget). Voluntary contributions are mainly received from member states of the United Nations making them an important player in all humanitarian operations of the UN. The ability of the UN system to respond rapidly and adequately to humanitarian crisis depends thus heavily on the timely availability of voluntary funding. Donor governments have increasingly been aware of their critical role in UN humanitarian assistance and have coordinated their responsibility in the "Good Humanitarian Donorship Initiative" that aims to set humanitarian financing standards for the donor community.

As part of its coordinating mandate, the OCHA plays a strong role in information management. As such, the OCHA provides up-to-date information on all emergencies and humanitarian operations through websites (for example 'www.reliefweb.int'), development of an early warning system and an *"Integrated Regional Information Network" (IRIN)*. Additionally, the OCHA manages a central roster of resources for rapid mobilization in emergency situations. The roster includes the full stock of relief organizations, relief experts and military and civil defense capacities.

In addition to coordinating relief operations, the OCHA is responsible for the UN "strategic coordination" of humanitarian affairs. As such, it facilitates the development of comprehensive UN strategies in humanitarian crises taking into account political, military and humanitarian considerations. This strategic coordination aims at insuring coherent approaches of different policy areas and thus includes all relevant actors such as governments and the military. The humanitarian reform process in 2005, through a comprehensive humanitarian response review, identified major gaps

339

in the humanitarian system that needed dedicated capacities, leadership and resources. As a response, the UN introduced the so called "humanitarian cluster approach" that aims to strengthen the overall humanitarian response capacity through sufficient global capacity, predictable leadership, better partnerships, strengthened accountability and strategic field-level coordination and prioritization. Predictable leadership and strengthened accountability was sought to be ensured by clarifying the division of labor among organizations, and better defining their roles and responsibilities within the different sectors of the response. The IASC has subsequently designated different agencies to lead the UN sectoral work – so-called clusters – in eleven areas of humanitarian activity during and after an emergency. The following agencies are responsible for the following sectors: FAO for agriculture, UNHCR and IOM for camp coordination after conflict, respectively after a disaster, UNDP for early recovery, UNICEF and Save the Children (UK) for education, UNHCR and the International Federation of Red Cross and Red Crescent Societies (IFRC) for emergency shelter after a conflict, respectively after a disaster, the OCHA, UNICEF and WFP for emergency telecommunications, WHO for health, WFP for logistics, UNICEF for nutrition, UNHCR, OHCHR and UNICEF for protection, including both internationally displaced people as well as civilians affected by conflict/disasters and UNICEF for water, sanitation and hygiene.

An Executive Committee for Humanitarian Affairs (UN-ECHA), composed of representatives of all relevant departments of the UN Secretariat, such as the Department for Peacekeeping Operations (→ Peacekeeping Operations) or the Department for Political Affairs and headed by the Emergency Relief Coordinator, ensures coherence of humanitarian aspects with other policy areas like military intervention. An example for this strategic coordination is the "strategic framework approach" for Af-

ghanistan. The OCHA also serves as headquarters of the International Strategy for Disaster Reduction (ISDR, previously *International Decade for Natural Disaster Reduction, ISDR*). Together with → UNEP, the OCHA works in the *Joint Environmental Unit,* focusing on environmental aspects of natural and technical disasters (→ Environmental Protection).

In the course of the implementation of humanitarian assistance the OCHA follows the *"Relief-to-Development Continuum"* aiming at a continuous process from humanitarian emergency situations to rehabilitation and reconstruction, and on to "normal" development (UN Doc. A/RES/46/182, 19 December 1991). In accordance with this principle, the UN approach to humanitarian assistance aims to ensure a smooth transition of emergency assistance to rehabilitation and reconstruction measures and long-term development cooperation.

The OCHA has about 1,585 staff (with international staff at 540 and local/ national staff 1,045 in 2008). In addition to its head office in New York the OCHA has offices in Geneva and Turin (the latter primarily concerned with operational aspects such as handling relief stocks) and regional support offices and Regional Disaster Response advisors in Africa, the Caribbean and Latin America, the Middle East, and Asia Pacific. In 2007, OCHA's total budget was 152.8 US dollars with 13.5 million US dollars received from the Regular Budget and 139.3 million US dollars received in voluntary donor contributions.

It is not only due to the location of the OCHA within the Secretariat that the Secretary-General plays a key role in humanitarian assistance: in January 2008, the new Secretary-General Ban Ki-moon stressed the importance of a continued reform of the humanitarian response system of the UN. Humanitarian assistance also played a key role in the UN reform process in 2005, the Secretary-General's Report "In Larger Freedom – Towards Security, Development and Human Rights for All" of March 2005 (*United Nations* 2005) and the Report of the Secretary-General's High-level Panel on System-wide Coherence: "Delivering As One" of November 2006 (*United Nations* 2006). Already during the UN reform in 1997/1998 Secretary-General Kofi Annan had boosted the importance of humanitarian issues in the course of far-reaching restructuring measures. Former Secretary-General Boutros-Ghali had also considered the importance of UN humanitarian assistance in his annual reports, especially in his → "Agenda for Development". Particularly the mainstreaming of humanitarian issues into other policy fields, above all → peacekeeping, post-war recovery and rehabilitation and development assistance of the UN (→ Development Cooperation of the UN System), had been emphasized by both Secretaries-General.

In addition to the OCHA and the operating agencies, the six main organs of the UN (→ Principal Organs, Subsidiary Organs, Treaty Bodies) have played an increasingly important role in humanitarian assistance in recent years. Since the early 1990s, the Security Council has passed several resolutions (→ Resolution, Declaration, Decision) dealing with humanitarian issues, including the initiation of UN humanitarian operations and the provision of security aspects during humanitarian missions. In many cases, particularly in Somalia and in the territory of former Yugoslavia, the Security Council favored military escorts for relief transports and relief personnel (*Weiss/ Collins* 1996).

In recent years, the → General Assembly has been actively concerned with humanitarian issues. In 1991 the Assembly passed Resolution 46/182, leading to the creation of DHA, IASC, Consolidated Inter-Agency Appeals and the Central Emergency Revolving Fund. Through its special programmes such as UNHCR and UNEP, the General Assembly can play a crucial role in the policy formulation and administration of the implementing agencies. One substantive focus of the General Assembly is to ensure a continuous transition process from emergency relief situations to reconstruction and development assistance ("Relief-to-Development-Continuum").

The Economic and Social Council (→ ECOSOC), which had discussed concrete humanitarian issues in its regular session in 1998 for the first time, has also stressed the importance of the OCHA and set objectives for future priority areas for humanitarian engagement. (cf. United Nations - General Assembly, Report of the Secretary-General on the work of the Organization, 27 August 1998, UN Doc. A/53/1, para. 125). Through its quasi-autonomous special programmes, such as UNDP and UNICEF, ECOSOC can become actively involved in humanitarian activities.

3. Historical Development

During its existence the role of humanitarian assistance has been shaped by political circumstances. The historical development of humanitarian assistance can be divided into four periods.

In the first phase, the Cold War period, the field of humanitarian assistance was of minor importance within the UN. Strongly limited by the principle of domestic state sovereignty, international humanitarian assistance could only become operational during and after natural disasters or conflicts between states. During that period, international humanitarian aid was only possible upon the request and goodwill of the respective government.

Places of humanitarian intervention in this period were concentrated mainly in the drought- stricken regions in Sub-Saharan Africa during the 1970s and 1980s, and in regions with a high number of refugees, as for example the Cambodian refugee camps in Thailand at the end of the 1970s. Since 1971, UN humanitarian assistance was coordinated by the *UN Disaster Relief Organization (UNDRO)*, whose task was to mobilize and coordinate international relief measures in response to natural disasters and to ensure coherence with the activities of international organizations and NGOs. Critical voices have been raised concerning UNDRO's engagement in too few emergencies and its not taking the leading role in major emergencies. Reasons for this low level of engagement can be found in UNDRO's unclear mandate, insufficient resources and the hesitation of the UN implementing agencies to be co-ordinated (*Henn/Klingebiel* 1993).

During the second period, from the end of the 1980s to the mid-1990s, the scope of UN humanitarian assistance broadened significantly. This allowed for a geographically and politically wider and by far greater humanitarian engagement, accompanied and marked by the general euphoria after the end of the Cold War. The beginning of the 1990s was marked by three processes: (1) the weakening of the principle of → sovereignty, (2) the end of the bipolar structure and (3) the rising number and growing extent of humanitarian crises resulting from armed conflicts (e.g. Iraq, Rwanda). This increased the UN's capacity to act, among its prime tasks, to maintain international peace and security and facilitate development.

The international community felt the need for an increasing responsibility to respond to the growing number of crises by military and humanitarian means. Following these changes the UN, for the first time, became active in unresolved intrastate conflicts (South Sudan, Ethiopia, Angola, later Somalia, Bosnia, Rwanda, Sierra Leone and others). These humanitarian operations had their legal basis in UN Security Council resolutions and followed the principle of "negotiated access": the safe access of relief organizations (UN agencies and NGOs) to the suffering population was negotiated by the political branch of the UN and the parties to the conflict. This approach also initiated a formal division of labor among the UN implementing agencies in the field based on their mandate and further led to close cooperation between the UN and NGOs. Those operations were led by either the Emergency Relief Coordinator or by one of the UN agencies. At the beginning of this second phase, especially during the humanitarian aid missions in

Northern Iraq, several problems became apparent: lack of comprehensive coordination, insufficient cooperation, and an approach that was based too much on experience with natural disasters, which was only partly applicable in complex emergencies. It soon became obvious that agencies were inadequately prepared for the type and extent of the crises that they faced (multiple causes, strong political agenda with ethnic and/or religious connotations). As an institutional response, the General Assembly established with Resolution A/RES/46/182 of 19 December 1991 the foundation for establishing the Department of Humanitarian Affairs, the Central Emergency Revolving Fund, the Consolidated Appeals and the Inter-Agency Standing Committee.

The third period, from 1994 until the early years of the 21st century, has been shaped by an increasing regulation and institutionalization of humanitarian assistance, on the one hand, and a decreasing optimism with regard to the impact of humanitarian assistance, being more and more replaced by a down-to-earth realism, on the other.

The major humanitarian relief operations of the UN in Somalia, Bosnia and Rwanda during the 1990s have shown that humanitarian assistance in complex emergencies and especially in war situations may be confronted by limits that make it difficult to carry out a humanitarian mandate and can even have counter-productive consequences. In conflict zones, humanitarian resources brought in by relief agencies can become a target of the conflict parties and can be misused for their material support. During the crisis in Rwanda in 1994, aid operations of the UN in Zaïrian refugee camps were strongly criticized. Contrary to the humanitarian goal pursued by the UN, Hutu extremists misused the aid to continue the armed fight against the new government of Rwanda.

The experiences in Rwanda, Somalia and Bosnia have turned initial optimism into the realization that humanitarian goals can only be reached under certain political, military and economic conditions. However, public pressure to engage in humanitarian crises remained high and humanitarian assistance has crystallized as an independent policy field within the United Nations.

In a fourth period, a so-called "new humanitarianism" has emerged during the early years of the new millennium. Crises such as that in Darfur in 2003-2004 have again demonstrated the inability of the international community to adequately respond to such crises and initiated a major shift in the approach of humanitarian assistance. Consequently, the protection of civilians has emerged as a key objective and guiding principle for all humanitarian work. Humanitarian assistance is thus no longer characterized by the sole objective of life-saving needs, but by the principles to protect civilians, prevent sexual and gender-based violence and uphold human rights. The UN's acceptance of the "responsibility to protect" principle has been captured in the World Summit Declaration in 2005 with implications that go well beyond the humanitarian system. Since then, critical changes have emerged in the area of peace-building and in the structure of UN integrated missions. Today, the UN's humanitarian assistance is thus part of a wider UN response system that focuses on sustainable peace-building and tries to establish integrated missions at country level to ensure coherence of political, security, development, human rights, rule of law, recovery and humanitarian efforts. The humanitarian reform process started in 2005 is a response to this major policy shift and the reflection of the system's shortcomings. This increasingly integrated approach to humanitarian assistance also calls for strengthened cooperation between UN actors operating in a post-crisis situation on the ground as well as for streamlined cooperation and structures at headquarters.

4. Key Issues and Challenges

Changes in the scope and nature of disasters and of conflicts continue to pose significant challenges to the UN humanitarian response system.

With regard to natural disasters, the last decade has seen a marked increase in the occurrence of disasters with increased losses of life, property and material damage. The rise of disasters associated with the effects of climate change is expected to augment risks and vulnerabilities of an increasing number of people. Given this expectation and calculating the human, financial and material costs of disaster effects, UN humanitarian assistance will need to invest more in disaster preparedness and reducing the risks of disaster. This will not only limit the devastating effects of disasters, but also accelerate the recovery process afterwards.

In recent UN humanitarian operations after large-scale disasters, such as the Indian Ocean tsunami in 2004, the earthquake in Pakistan in 2005, the cyclone in Bangladesh in 2007 and the cyclone Nargis in Myanmar in 2008, the positive effects of the humanitarian reform could be observed in the better coordination of actors through the cluster approach and their improved accountability. Challenges remain in the areas of joint needs assessments after a disaster to provide a common basis for planning and financing as well as adequate funding of identified priority gap areas.

Particularly since the humanitarian missions in Bosnia, the refugee crisis in Rwanda and the crisis in Darfur, the "political vacuum" in which humanitarian assistance operates has become a major challenge. During many crises (e.g. Rwanda, Bosnia, Liberia, Somalia, and Sudan) it became apparent that the international community, represented by the Security Council, had no common or an insufficient *political* interest in taking action, but felt obliged to show its responsibility and commitment by supporting humanitarian operations. Not only in Bosnia and Rwanda this has led to large scale humanitarian missions, compensating for a lack of political engagement. However, humanitarian aid as a substitute for political action cannot solve complex emergencies, but rather

343

leads to an unwanted politicization of humanitarian aid, thus contradicting the principles of neutrality and humanity. Some UN member states are not only criticized for lack of humanitarian engagement, but also for disguising political motives with the help of humanitarian assistance, and the use of humanitarian aid for "hidden agendas". Another challenge of complex emergencies is the lack of commitment for stronger preventive action by the international community. Member states have been reproached for supporting large scale humanitarian missions that are widely and effectively reported in the media rather than engaging in the prevention of conflicts and crises with less media attention, but presumably more impact. In crises such as Rwanda or Iraq, where government institutions were responsible for humanitarian crises by targeting certain population groups, the limits of UN humanitarian assistance became evident. As an interstate organization the UN still depends heavily on the cooperation of the member states. In crises where a population suffers from violent acts of the government a far-reaching engagement of the UN is not possible since this requires the consent of the respective government. The new paradigm of humanitarian assistance to protect civilians from violence, sexual exploitation and abuse is a commitment to human rights and the fact that humanitarian assistance, albeit impartial and neutral, cannot be neutral and impartial where human suffering is involved. However, implementing this protection approach in practice is posing severe challenges in regions where protection from government sources is required, as was the case in Darfur. Challenges that the UN is facing with regard to protection are adequate protection of civilians, defining protection mechanisms for humanitarian actors, establishing a culture of protection and defining minimum obligations. In future, the protection of civilians will remain the key challenge for humanitarian actors, and ways and mechanisms to successfully protect civilians with humanitarian means need to be found.

The large scale humanitarian crises during the 1990s have also proved that the approaches of international humanitarian assistance are partly inadequate and insufficiently adjusted to today's conflict and crisis pattern. Characteristics of most conflicts and crises today are the development of a war economy, a high number of civil casualties, ethnic and/or religious features of the conflict and a discrepancy of values between most conflict parties and humanitarian aid organizations. The danger that humanitarian assistance becomes part of the conflict cycle through its resources remains a risk in most conflicts. In some cases, aid may even prevent the settlement of the conflict through the unintended supply of the conflict parties with resources, such as food or other humanitarian goods. Although misuse of relief items has always been a problem, the extent and frequency of misuse by conflict parties has increased. By now, all humanitarian missions in complex emergencies have to be monitored regularly to ensure that humanitarian objectives are met and unintended impacts on the conflicts prevented. In the daily routine of humanitarian operations, however, those conceptual questions are often neglected. Generally during aid missions, operational details are concentrated upon at the expense of conceptual considerations.

The starting points for improvement could be the use of detailed and relevant analyses of the conflict parties, the political and economic conditions in the conflict region and the sensitization of aid personnel with regard to local and regional political power structures. The principles of "do no harm" should also guide all humanitarian actions.

The recent situations in Afghanistan and Iraq are also posing a set of new questions and challenges. What are the implications of providing protection in places where there is neither a functioning government nor a UN peacekeeping operation? With "traditional" peacekeeping operations being less the norm, what is it that partners need and UN humanitarian actors can cooperate with, especially in cases where armed forces are operating without a UN mandate? In some countries, cooperation with non-state armed groups is necessary in order to reach beneficiaries and to protect civilians. Careful negotiations with such groups are important conditions for any such engagement of UN humanitarian actors. The numerous challenges aid personnel have to face in the field have also led to increased sensitivity in that regard. This is especially visible in the field of security. The security and protection of aid workers and goods has not only been of crucial importance to the Security Council, but also to international law which pays increasing attention to these problems ($\rightarrow$ International Law and the UN). The emphasis on security issues is also demonstrated by military escort of humanitarian operations, which appear more normal and necessary nowadays. It can be argued that, on the one hand, this militarization of aid leads to a better protection of personnel and goods, but, on the other, it raises questions about the neutrality and humanitarian character of aid. A balanced relationship between civil humanitarian aid and military escorts is yet to be found.

Competition between relief organizations and resistance to coordination is often observed in the field and is still seen to prevent an efficient and comprehensive operation. The introduction of the humanitarian cluster approach is a positive step towards better coordination that needs to be continued. However, with the number and mandates of humanitarian actors increasing there continues to be a pressing need to work more closely with non-governmental organizations, government agencies, financial institutions as well as with private sector companies. Non-UN humanitarian actors, especially non-governmental organizations are crucial providers of humanitarian assistance and due to their institutional set up and funding often have different operating possibilities not available to the UN. At a global level, steps towards better partnerships with non-governmental organizations have been made, for example through the Global Humanitarian Platform in 2007. At country level, efforts are made to establish equitable partnerships with non-governmental organizations and use common planning and funding instruments for both UN and non-UN partners. The approach for pooled funding of humanitarian needs in the Democratic Republic of Congo is a successful example in this regard.

Over the last years, private sector companies have increased their engagement in humanitarian assistance in a variety of areas, for example through the provision of essential drugs or management services, such as financial management or expenditure tracking. The UN humanitarian actors are increasingly cooperating with private sector companies. In early 2008, the UN and private sector companies finalized joint Guiding Principles for Public-Private Collaboration in Humanitarian Action that will guide future cooperation ("The World Economic Forum (WEF) – OCHA Guiding Principles for Public-Private Collaboration in Humanitarian Action").

Timely and sufficient mobilization of financial resources is often a problem for humanitarian agencies. Nearly the entire budget for humanitarian action is financed through voluntary contributions from member states. In the past, donors were willing to provide financial assistance at the beginning of a crisis, but were rather hesitant to finance the long-term programmes for rehabilitation with limited media attention. The dependency on voluntary contributions and the irregular contributions by member states make it difficult to plan long-term, to maintain continuity, and to ensure a smooth transition from emergency to rehabilitation. These factors often contribute to permanent crisis situations without long term perspectives. Continuous financing would be desirable, so that countries in post-crisis situations are enabled to define a long-term, sustainable transition process. The

"Good Humanitarian Donorship Initiative" has contributed to an improvement of the situation. While in the past, financial procedures within donor institutions allowed either the financing of humanitarian or development needs, leaving out the crucial period of transition and recovery, some donor governments have also already started to adjust their financing regulations to allow the funding of transitional recovery activities that link development projects to humanitarian needs.

Whether humanitarian assistance becomes an effective instrument in humanitarian emergencies depends on a number of inter-dependent factors: first, only a clear political engagement of member states with a commitment to crisis prevention and recovery, and a joint engagement in the fields of peacemaking and peacekeeping can protect humanitarian assistance from being a replacement for political solutions; second, the ability of UN agencies to protect civilians from acts of war and violence and provide necessary assistance to beneficiaries is another major challenge that will determine whether humanitarian aid is successful; third, the capacity and the will of the UN to deal with and adjust to the special characteristics of modern conflicts and today's disasters, and to attempt to prevent conflicts and to prepare for disasters, will be of great importance; fourth, continuing the humanitarian reform process and adjusting it to new challenges if needed is critical for having the right structures and mechanisms in place to respond adequately to a humanitarian crisis; and finally, humanitarian assistance that is not linked to the broader efforts of peace-building, recovery and development will only be of short-term value. Embedding humanitarian assistance in longer term agendas from the beginning will help to ensure that humanitarian aid not only provides relief but contributes to stabilization, recovery and peace.

Gita Swamy Meier-Ewert

Lit.: *Duffield, M.:* Complex Emergencies and the Crisis of Developmentalism, in: IDS Bulletin 25 (1994), No. 4, 37-45; *Henn, H./ Klingebiel, S.:* Helfer im Kreuzfeuer. Humanitäre Hilfe in Kriegssituationen, in: Matthies, V. (ed.): Frieden durch Einmischung?, Bonn 1993, 105-121; *Sirleaf, E. J.:* From Disaster to Development, in: Cahill, K. (ed.): A Framework for Survival: Health, Human Rights and Humanitarian Assistance in Conflicts and Disasters, New York 1993, 299-307; *Overseas Development Institute (ODI):* Good Humanitarian Donorship: overcoming obstacles to improved collective performance (Humanitarian Policy Group Discussion Paper), London 2006, www.odi.org.uk/ hpg/papers/discussion_GHD.pdf; *Overseas Development Institute (ODI):* The currency of humanitarian reform (Humanitarian Policy Group Briefing Note), London 2005, www. odi.org.uk/hpg/papers/Humanitarian_reform. pdf; *United Nations:* Yearbook of the United Nations. Special Edition: UN Fiftieth Anniversary 1945-1995, New York 1995, 215-235; *United Nations:* Humanitarian Response Review, August 2005, New York/ Geneva 2005, www.reliefweb.int/library/ documents/2005/ocha-gen-02sep.pdf; *United Nations - General Assembly:* Report of the Secretary-General on the Work of the Organization 1998, UN Doc. A/53/1, 27 August 1998; *United Nations - General Assembly:* In larger freedom: towards security, development and human rights for all. Report of the Secretary-General, 21 March 2005, UN Doc. A/59/2005; *United Nations - General Assembly:* Delivering as one. Report of the High-level Panel on United Nations System-wide Coherence in the areas of development, humanitarian assistance and the environment, 20 November 2006, UN Doc. A/61/583; *United Nations - Office for the Coordination of Humanitarian Affairs:* OCHA Annual Report 2007, http://ochaonline. un.org/OCHA2007ar/; *United Nations Department of Humanitarian Affairs (DHA):* Humanitarian Report 1997: humanitarian coordination in complex emergencies and natural disasters, UN Doc. DHA/97/72, New York 1997, www.reliefweb.int/ocha_ol/pub/ humrep97/coord.html; *Weiss, T./Collins, C:* Humanitarian Challenges and Intervention, Colorado 1996.

Internet: UNOCHA homepage: www.un. org/ha/general.htm; Reliefweb homepage: www.reliefweb.int; Humanitarian Reform website: www.humanitarianreform.org; Good Humanitarian Donorship website: www.

goodhumanitariandonorship.org; UN IASC website: www.humanitarianinfo.org.

Humanitarian Law, International

International humanitarian law emerged after the Second World War in the framework of the law of armed conflicts. Since then, two categories of international humanitarian law have been distinguished: the original international law of armed conflict restricting the methods of warfare, and another body comprising rules for the protection of life and human dignity in times of war (*Coursier* 1955). Thus the international law of armed conflict contains a body of international legal rules that are applicable in times of armed conflict. They are "a minimum of humanity for inhumane situations" (*Sassòli* 1995, 218).

On the other hand, the core sector of international humanitarian law is more limited. It is made up of provisions dealing with the means and methods of warfare, the distinction between combatants and the civil population and the protection of specific groups of persons (civilians, internees, captives, wounded, sick and shipwrecked) and objects (hospitals, hospital ships and cultural goods). International humanitarian law decides on the legality of the use of force by states. Most rules cover the treatment of citizens of the opponent, and third states, by a party to the conflict.

Scope of Application

Before the Second World War, the application of the law of armed conflict commenced with a formal state of belligerence. Thereafter, the states effectively prevented formal declarations of war through the prohibition of the use of force (→ Use of Force, Prohibition of). Since international humanitarian law seeks however to extend protection to the civil population, insofar as possible in all conflicts, it no longer refers to a state of belligerence. Rather it is applicable in all armed conflicts. Hence, the actual presence of armed conflict is de-

cisive, and does not rest on the declaration of a state of belligerence by a state.

There has remained a need to distinguish between international armed conflict (involving states, international organizations like the United Nations, and peoples in national wars of liberation), and non-international armed conflict. The regulation of the latter was particularly difficult. This is now covered by Article 1 (1) of the Additional Protocol II of 8 June 1977 to the Geneva Conventions of 12 August 1949 (AP II), according to which a non-international conflict takes place on the territory of a contracting state between armed forces and insurgent armed forces or other armed groups serving a responsible command. The latter must exercise control over a part of the sovereign territory, and be capable of performing long-lasting, coordinated combat actions, and to apply AP II. Thus the scope of their application has become somewhat narrowed. On the other hand, the common Article 3 of the Geneva Conventions of 12 August 1948 (GC) is applicable in an essentially wider scope, as they cover all armed conflicts without international character. At the same time, the distinction between these conflicts and other violent acts, such as banditry and terrorism, is particularly difficult. In these cases international humanitarian law is not applicable, but the requirement for respect of human rights remains in effect.

Practice shows that there is an increasing overlap between international humanitarian law and the human rights instruments – in particular regarding the indefeasible human rights which may not be derogated (*Heintze* 1993) (→ Human Rights; → Human Rights Conventions and their Measures of Implementation). These intend an extension of protection of the civil population that is as comprehensive as possible.

International Regulation

In 1864 the first convention on the amelioration of the condition of wounded in armies in the field was enacted in Geneva. This was the starting point of the codification process of international humanitarian law which still continues today.

Fundamental steps up to the Second World War were the Declaration of St. Petersburg of 1868 aiming at the prohibition of the use of certain projectiles in times of war, and the two International Peace Conferences of 1899 and 1907 in The Hague. These led to agreements on the limitation of means and methods of warfare. Deserving special mention are the Hague Regulations on Land Warfare of 18 October 1907 (HRLW), the Convention for the Adaptation to Maritime Warfare of the Principles of the Geneva Conventions of 1864, as well as the Declaration on the prohibition of bullets that easily expand or flatten themselves in human bodies (Dum-Dum bullets). Since most rules were agreed on in The Hague, this body of law is often called "Hague Law", to be distinguished from the "Geneva Law" comprising the strict international humanitarian law as elaborated in Geneva.

After the shock of the Second World War, the International Committee of the Red Cross (ICRC) initiated in 1949 a diplomatic conference for the codification of international humanitarian law. There, the four Geneva Conventions were elaborated, which by October 2008 had been ratified by 194 states. These are thus the most important sources of international humanitarian law.

The First Geneva Convention aims at the amelioration of the conditions of the wounded and sick of armed forces in the field, the Second Convention serves the same object in regard to the naval forces, the Third Convention regulates the treatment of prisoners of war and the Fourth Convention provides for the protection of the civil population. Since almost all states are parties to the Geneva Conventions, they are of nearly universal scope.

It is important to note that all four contain a common Article 3, which establishes a minimum standard for the observance of fundamental human rights in non-international armed conflicts, as opposed to resistance.

Both Additional Protocols (APs) to the Geneva Conventions were agreed upon in the course of the Diplomatic Conference of 1974-1977. These confirm and modernize both the Hague and the Geneva Law, in that they deal with the status of national liberation movements and internal conflicts in international humanitarian law. AP I refers to international armed conflicts, and AP II to non-international. Since the APs confirm and modify both the Geneva and the Hague Law, this distinction is widely regarded as obsolete (*Risse* 1991, 180). Although the protocols have initially been subject to criticism by the Western super-powers – because of the ban on nuclear weapons which can be deduced from AP I – they have in the meantime (October 2008) been ratified by not less than 168 (AP I) and 164 (AP II) states respectively. Amongst them are the nuclear powers of Russia, China and Great Britain, however not the USA. Israel still cannot be found on the list of ratifying member states.

At the request of the 26th International Conference on the Red Cross and the Red Crescent movement in December 1995, the ICRC undertook a study on customary international humanitarian law. The main objective of the study was to fill some of the gaps in the treaty-based rules of international humanitarian law applicable in non-international armed conflicts which comprise the majority of armed conflicts in the world today. It took the ICRC ten years to complete the study on customary international law which was published in 2005 (*Henckaerts/Beck* 2005). It was compiled with the assistance of experts from more than 50 countries and state practice from 148 countries was analyzed.

The study concludes that many of the fundamental principles and rules of international humanitarian law are customary in nature and that most are applicable in both international and non-international armed conflicts (cf. *Henckaerts* 2005).

This opinion was also supported by the International Court of Justice (→

ICJ) in its Nicaragua judgment (Nicaragua v. United States of America, *ICJ Reports* 1986, 14).

Other agreements concern detailed questions and the protection of certain objects of legal protection. Here the Geneva Protocol for the Prohibition of the Use of Asphyxiating, Poisonous or Other Gases, and of Bacteriological Methods of Warfare of 17 June 1925 deserve attention, as well as the Convention on the Prohibition of the Development, Production and Stockpiling of Bacteriological (Biological) and Toxin weapons and their destruction of 10 April 1972, and the Convention on the Prohibition of Military or Any Hostile Use of Environmental Modification Techniques of 10 December 1976.

Also part of this body of law is the Hague Convention for the Protection of Cultural Property in the Event of Armed Conflict of 14 May 1954. The latter prohibits attacks against real estate and objects of cultural, historic and religious significance. The principles of this convention can be found also in Article 53 AP I. Since the Convention of 1954 is to be seen as a consequence of plundering in the Second World War, it is currently being revised in the light of the experiences of the war in former Yugoslavia (*Desch* 1998, 103).

Moreover, the Convention on Prohibitions or Restrictions on the Use of Certain Conventional Weapons Which May be Deemed to be Excessively Injurious or to Have Indiscriminate Effects of 10 October 1980 is of fundamental significance. It is a framework convention that is supplemented by three protocols (Protocol on Non-Detectable Fragments; Protocol on Prohibitions or Restrictions on the Use of Mines, Booby-Traps and Other Devices (supplemented on 3 May 1996, and extended to non-international conflicts) and the Protocol on Prohibitions or Restrictions on the Use of Incendiary Weapons. In order to be a contracting party of the convention, at least two protocols have to be ratified. On 13 October 1995 the convention was supplemented by Protocol IV on Blinding Laser Weapons. Additionally, the

Convention on the Prohibition of the Development, Production, Stockpiling and the Use of Chemical Weapons and on Their Destruction of 13 January 1993 is of great significance for international humanitarian law This convention represents the logical consequence of the prohibition of the use of these weapons by international humanitarian law in stipulating their controlled stock destruction. Thereby a "strengthening of the prohibition of weapons in the law of armed conflict" was reached (*Ipsen* 1998, 208).

Finally, there is the Convention on the Prohibition of the Use, Stockpiling, Production and Transfer of Anti-Personnel Mines and Their Destruction of 3 December 1997, which has enjoyed much public attention, and which obliges the contracting parties (at the beginning of 2001 already 100, amongst them Germany, France, Canada and Great Britain; missing are the mine-producing countries China, Russia and the USA) to destroy their stocks within a period of four years. The Convention prohibiting Anti-Personnel Mines is the first treaty prohibiting a widely used weapon.

Collectively, all of these treaties have an effect on → disarmament that renders them of high political importance, even though only the absolute prohibition of the use of chemical weapons belongs to international humanitarian law.

Fundamental Rules

The International Committee of the Red Cross considers itself the guardian of international humanitarian law (*Sandoz* 1998), and has elaborated its seven fundamental rules.

The *first rule* is the distinction between combatants and non-combatants. The definition of the combatant is included in the HRLW as well as Article 33 GC III and Article 43 AP I. Basically, combatants are members of the armed forces that are empowered to participate in military operations. In the case of capture they have the status of prisoners of war. Their punishment for taking part in lawful combat actions is prohibited. Non-combatants are mem-

349

bers of the armed forces that do not participate in combat actions. Moreover, civilians have no combatant status. Persons not engaged in or nor longer engaging in combatant actions, enjoy in all conflicts and without distinction respect for their life as well as for their physical and spiritual integrity (passive element), and their protection (active element). They are to be treated with humanity under all circumstances and without distinction. After the Second World War this rule of distinction was discussed, resulting in the extension of protection of the civil population from indiscriminate attacks. At the center of these discussions was the question to what extent collateral damage to the civilian population is to be accepted in the case of lawful attacks against combatants. The question emerges in particular in the application of mass destruction weapons, but increasingly in civil wars as well. The latter are commonly directed against the civil population as a method of warfare (*Fischer* 1998).

The *second rule* prohibits the killing and injuring of *opponents out of action*. According to Article 40 AP I, it is prohibited to order that there will be no survivors, to use this as threat to the opponent or to conduct hostilities with this goal.

According to the *third rule* there exists an obligation to rescue and nurse wounded and sick. This results from the common Article 3 (2) GC, from Part II of AP I, and from Part III of AP II. The rule includes respect for the emblems of protection (Red Cross and Red Crescent).

According to the *fourth rule* captured combatants and civilians enjoy rights in the opponent parties' sphere of power; for example, their life, dignity and their convictions are to be respected. It is not permitted to expose them to violence or repression. They are entitled to appropriate nutrition, drinking water, clothing and medical treatment as well as to a safe place of internment.

The *fifth rule* provides fundamental legal guarantees to persons under the control of an opponent. According to

these provisions, there exists no collective responsibility for actions that have not been committed by the specific person. Only punishments specified in law may be pronounced. Torture and inhumane treatment are prohibited. Innocence is presumed. Everyone has the right to an impartial and proper trial. These provisions are as prescribed in Article 75 (4) AP I and Article 6 (2) AP II.

The *sixth rule* points out the restrictions that international humanitarian law imposes regarding the methods and means of warfare. Weapons and methods which cause superfluous injuries are prohibited. The principle of proportionality has to do with the relationship between humanity and military necessity (HRLW Arts. 22 and 23 as well as Art. 35 (1) AP I). The *seventh rule* prohibits attacks on the civil population; attacks are to be directed solely against military objects. This also means that an attack against a military object is unlawful, if it results in civil losses that are not proportionately related to the expected, concrete and immediate military advantage (Art. 51 (5) lit. b AP I).

*Implementation of International
  Humanitarian Law*

In common with international public law, international humanitarian law has no comprehensive mechanism for its coercive implementation at its disposal. Nonetheless it is in the objective interest of the parties to the conflict to obey international humanitarian law. The reasons for this are in particular respect for public opinion, and an expectation of reciprocity of the parties to the conflict. Only those who obey international humanitarian law can expect that an opponent will also respect the rules of humanity in armed conflict. Moreover, the maintenance of discipline requires obedience to international humanitarian law, otherwise doubts as to the lawfulness of one's own actions will undermine the authority of the military leader. Furthermore, the fear of reprisals contributes to respect for international humanitarian law. (By means of reprisals an opponent violating the obligations of international law can be motivated to give up his unlawful behavior.)

Finally, the disciplinary and penal provisions of international humanitarian law are to be mentioned. Grave breaches are to be punished by penal law. Subsidiary to the national penal jurisdiction, an international penal jurisdiction is becoming more widely established. With the creation of the ad-hoc tribunals for former Yugoslavia and for Rwanda as well as the enactment of the Statute for a permanent International Criminal Court (→ ICC), patterned after the Nuremberg and Tokyo Trials, a fundamental change has taken place.

For the implementation of international humanitarian law, for the first time in history a permanent commission of inquiry has been created in 1991, in accordance with Article 90 AP I.

This commission is to inquire into any allegation of grave breaches of international humanitarian law. However, its inquiry in fact requires the consent of both parties to the conflict, and for this reason the commission has not been able so far to put its mandate into practice in an inquiry.

A specific instrument of the implementation of international humanitarian law is the dissemination of the rules of international humanitarian law. This tends to serve as an internal deterrent, preventing people from violating the norms of humanity. More and more often it turns out that the implementation mechanisms of human rights treaties are capable of contributing to the implementation of international humanitarian law.

One example are the decisions of the organs of the European Convention on Human Rights with regard to the actions of the Turkish military against the Kurds on Cyprus. These actions have been repeatedly characterized by the latter organs as violations of the minimum standards of human rights. Turkey has been called upon to adhere to these norms (*Reidy* 1998), but it remains to be seen what effect this may have. Last but not least, reference is to be made to the activities of specific implementation

bodies of UN human rights treaties. For example the Committee on the Rights of the Child, that was established according to the Convention on the Rights of the Child of 20 November 1989 (→ Human Rights Conventions, CRC), deals with the implementation of Article 39 of this treaty that requires compliance with international humanitarian law regarding the protection of the child in armed conflict.

Altogether it can be stated that the implementation mechanisms of international humanitarian law are now more frequently being put into practice.

Asymmetrical Warfare as Challenge to International Humanitarian Law

In contrast to this positive trend there is the challenge to international humanitarian law through asymmetrical wars: September 11 has been the starting point for intensive discussions about the phenomenon of asymmetrical warfare (cf. *Pfanner* 2005 with further literature). The parties to such conflicts are characterized by their inequality, disparate aims and the employment of dissimilar means and methods to pursue their tactics and strategies. Especially terrorists deliberately reject the traditional and legally regulated methods of warfare are and commit perfidious acts against civilians. The objective is to cause greater loss of human life and economic damage. They are also ready to use prohibited devices like chemical weapons and to act anywhere and at any time. The fundamental goal is to pound the military power of the adversary and to spread insecurity. Therefore the weaker parties try to strike so-called "soft targets", i.e. civilians. The application of international humanitarian law in asymmetrical war is complicated, because it rests on a balance of humanitarian and military interests. It is quite obvious that the asymmetrical war does not fit with the traditional concept of the international humanitarian law. Especially the military weaker party is tempted to use unlawful methods. However, international humanitarian law cannot be applied in all situations of an asymmetrical

351

war. Despite warlike components of the struggle against terrorism it cannot be considered as an armed conflict in the sense of the law of war.

This does not mean, however, that the asymmetrical wars "take place in a lawless international domain" (*Pfanner* 2005, 174). The benchmarks of international human rights law and international criminal law (Rome Statute) and the "elementary considerations of humanity" as laid down on Article 3 common to all four Geneva Conventions of 1949 constitute "universally binding rules for all, even unequal and asymmetrical, parties to any situation of armed violence" (ibid.). The state community should lay more emphasis on this common basis of humanitarian protection.

Hans-Joachim Heintze

Lit.: *Bruderlein, C.:* People's security as a new measure of global stability, in: International Review of the Red Cross 83 (2001), 353-366; *Chadwick, E.:* Self-Determination, Terrorism and the International Humanitarian Law of Armed Conflict, The Hague 1996; *Chesterman, S./Lenhardt, C. (eds.):* From Mercenaries to Market, Oxford 2007; *Coursier, H.:* Définition du droit humanitaire, in: Annuaire Français de Droit International 1955; *Desch, T.:* The Convention for the Protection of Cultural Property in the Event of Armed Conflict and its Revision, in: HuVI 11 (1998), 103-109; *Dörmann, K.:* Elements of War Crimes under the Rome Statute of the International Criminal Court – sources and commentary, Cambridge 2003; *Fischer, H./Oraá Oraá, J.:* International law in humanitarian assistance, European Commission Luxembourg 1998; *Fischer, H./ Kress, C./Lüder, S. (eds.):* International and National Prosecution of Crimes Under International Law, Berlin 2001; *Fleck, D. (ed.):* The Handbook of Humanitarian Law in Armed Conflicts, Oxford 1995; *Fleck, D. (ed.):* The Handbook of The Law of Visiting Forces, Oxford 2001; *Hasse, J./Müller, E./ Schneider, P. (eds.):* Humanitäres Völkerrecht. Politische, rechtliche und strafgerichtliche Dimensionen, Baden-Baden 2001; *Heintze, H.-J.:* Notstandsfeste Menschenrechte und bewaffneter Konflikt, in: HuV-I 6 (1993), 134-139; *Henckaerts, J.-M.:* Study on customary international humanitarian law: A contribution to the understanding and respect for the rule of law in armed conflict,

in: International Review of the Red Cross 87 (2005), 175-212; *Henckaerts, J.-M./Dos wald-Beck, L.:* Customary International Humanitarian Law, 2 vols., Cambridge 2005; *ICRC (ed.):* International humanitarian law and the challenges of contemporary armed conflicts. Reports and Documents, in: International Review of the Red Cross 89 (2007), 719-757; *ICRC (ed.):* Increasing respect for international humanitarian law in non-international armed conflicts, Geneva 2008; *Kalshoven, F./Zegveld, L.:* Constraints on the waging of war: an introduction to international humanitarian law, 3rd edn., Geneva 2001; *Kittichaisaree, K.:* International Criminal Law, Oxford 2001, *Kröning, V.:* Kosovo and International Humanitarian Law, in: HuV-I 1 (2000), 44-51; *Kwakwa, E.:* The International Law of Armed Conflict: Personal and Material Fields of Application, Dordrecht 1992; *Moir, L.:* The Historical Development of the Application of Humanitarian Law in Non-International Armed Conflicts to 1949, in: ICLQ 47 (1998), 337-361; *Pfanner, T.:* Asymmetrical warfare from the perspective of humanitarian law and humanitarian action, in: International Review of the Red Cross 87 (2005), 149-174; *Reidy, A.:* The approach of the European Commission and Court of Human Rights to international humanitarian law, in: International Review of the Red Cross 80 (1998), 513-529; *Risse, H.:* Humanitarian Law in Armed Conflicts, in: Wolfrum, R. (ed.): United Nations: Law, Policies and Practice, Munich/Dordrecht 1995, Vol. 1, 638-645; *Sandoz, Y.:* The International Committee of the Red Cross as guardian of international humanitarian law, Geneva 1998; *Sassòli, M.:* Kriegsvölkerrecht: eine Heuchelei, die die Inhumanität legalisiert, oder ein Minimum von Menschlichkeit für eine unmenschliche Situation, in: HuVI 8 (1995), 218-220; *Sassoli M./Bouvier, A.A.:* How Does Law Protect in War? Volumes I, II, 2nd edn., International Committee of the Red Cross, Geneva 2006; *Schindler, D./Toman, J. (eds.):* The Laws of Armed Conflicts: A Collection of Conventions, Resolutions, and Other Documents, Dordrecht/Geneva 1988; *Seibt, H.:* A Compendium of Case Studies of International Humanitarian Law, Geneva 1994; *Steinhoff, U.:* On the Ethics of War and Terrorism, Oxford 2007.

Internet: Information on the different aspects of international humanitarian law, including the text of the relevant conventions and the status of their ratifications: www.

icrc.org/eng/ihl and www.ruhr-uni-bochum.de/ifhv.

IAEA – International Atomic Energy Agency

The *International Atomic Energy Agency (IAEA)* is an independent international organization with headquarters in Vienna and a membership of 130 states (as of May 2001). Strictly speaking, the IAEA is not one of the → specialized agencies of the United Nations defined in Article 57 of the Charter (→ Charter of the UN) because the cooperation of the two organizations does not follow the procedure of Article 63 of the Charter. However, their legal relationship is close enough for the IAEA to identify itself sometimes as a "specialized agency within the United Nations system". (→ UN System)

The initiative for the IAEA's foundation was taken by the United States. On 8 December 1953, President Eisenhower proposed, in his "Atoms for Peace" speech before the → General Assembly, the establishment of an "international atomic energy agency ... under the aegis of the United Nations". After some preparatory work, the Conference on the Statute of the International Atomic Energy Agency, meeting at UN headquarters in New York, approved the statute of the new organization on 23 October 1956. The statute entered into force on 29 July 1957.

The pre-history of the IAEA goes back to 1945. Nuclear energy had become a major political problem with the two atomic bombs on Hiroshima and Nagasaki, at the latest. On 24 January 1946, the General Assembly unanimously approved Resolution 1 (I) establishing the *United Nations Atomic Energy Commission (UNAEC)*. The commission, however, quickly became a failure due to differences of opinion between the United States and the Soviet Union. In spring 1948, negotiations came to an end; in January 1952, UNAEC was dissolved officially.

According to its statute, the IAEA's objectives are in economic policy as well as in security policy. Article II declares that the Agency "shall seek to accelerate and enlarge the contribution of atomic energy to peace, health and prosperity throughout the world" and that it "shall ensure, so far as it is able, that assistance provided by it or at its request or under its supervision or control is not used in such a way as to further any military purpose". Among the agency's specific tasks are to encourage and to assist research and development of peaceful uses of nuclear energy and to establish appropriate standards of safety (Art. III A). The IAEA submits reports on its activities annually to the General Assembly and, when appropriate, to the Security Council, to the Economic and Social Council (→ ECOSOC) and other organs of the United Nations (Art. III B No. 4 and 5).

The IAEA's *internal organization* exhibits the threefold structure typical of international organizations. The *General Conference*, meeting in regular sessions once a year, is composed of representatives of all member states, each having one vote (Art. V A). The General Conference approves the agency's budget. Its rights include the right to suspend a member from the privileges and rights of membership (Art. V E). The agency's main policy-making organ is the *Board of Governors* (Art. VI F), generally meeting five times a year. Members of the Board are selected by a complicated procedure. First, the outgoing Board of Governors designates for membership on the Board the ten members "most advanced in the technology of atomic energy," plus the most advanced member in each of eight geographic areas listed in Article VI A 1, in which none of the "top ten" is located. These members of the Board hold office for one year. Second, the General Conference elects 22 additional members for a period of two years, following an elaborate model designed to yield equitable representation of the geographic areas (Art. VI A 2). Each member of the Board has one vote. The day-to-day

353

work of the organization is carried out by the *Secretariat* and *Staff* headed by the *Director-General* (Art. VII); currently, the number of staff members is roughly 2,000.

The IAEA's *financial system* is essentially based on two budgets: the *regular budget*, funded mainly by obligatory membership dues apportioned in accordance with the principles used in assessing contributions to the regular → budget of the United Nations (1999: 224.3 million US dollars), and the *operational budget*, funded by voluntary contributions to the *Technical Co-operation Fund* (1999: 73 million US dollars).

The IAEA's history has been defined by both *economic and security policy objectives*. In the civil sector, the objective to benefit from positive aspects of nuclear energy (generation of electricity, nuclear medicine, use of isotopes in agriculture) still plays a considerable role; since the 1970s, however, the risks of nuclear technology have become a second focus of the IAEA's work. Specific efforts have been made to develop international standards for the security of nuclear power plants, for the transport and disposal of radioactive waste and for the handling of and responsibility for nuclear accidents. Numerous international agreements have been established under the auspices of the IAEA, for example the *Convention on Early Notification of a Nuclear Accident* (after the Chernobyl accident) and the *Convention on Nuclear Safety* in the mid-90s.

The IAEA's most important task in the security policy sector is the verification of international agreements prohibiting the military use of nuclear energy, the most prominent such agreements being the *Treaty on the Non-Proliferation of Nuclear Weapons (NPT)*, which entered into force in 1970 and was extended indefinitely in 1995; it has been ratified by 187 states. (→ Disarmament)

To fulfill this task, the IAEA concludes *Safeguards Agreements* with the individual states and undertakes about 2,500 inspections per year. Nevertheless, complete surveillance is almost impossible. The most critical cases of

the past years involve North Korea and Iraq: both countries have been suspected or proven guilty of pursuing, programs of nuclear armament and of violating the obligations of international treaties or resolutions of the Security Council.

Concerning the future of the organization, one thing seems certain: the nuclear agenda will rather grow than shrink. The risks of nuclear weapons and nuclear power plants will remain; the latter may very well be aggravated through a rising demand for electricity, especially in developing countries, on the one hand, and the growing destruction of the planet's eco-system on the other.

Marc Schattenmann

Lit.: *Pelzer, N.:* IAEA – International Atomic Energy Agency, in: Wolfrum, R. (ed.): United Nations: Law, Policies and Practice, Vol. 1, Munich/Dordrecht 1995, 646-655; *Scheinman, L.:* The International Atomic Energy Agency and World Nuclear Order, Washington 1987; *Szasz, P. C.:* International Atomic Energy Agency, in: Bernhardt, R. (ed.): EPIL II (1995), 1015-1057.

Addendum

The cases of North Korea and Iraq have remained on the IAEA agenda also in the years after the millennium, complemented by the case of the Iran.

In the case of Iraq, the inspections of the IAEA together with the Security Council-mandated UNSCOM successfully discovered and eliminated most – if not all – of Iraq's chemical and biological weapon production facilities. In the months immediately preceding the war of 2003 the assessments of Iraq's weapon programs made by IAEA and UNSCOM inspectors were remarkably close to what since has been found, and far more accurate than the alleged armament situation of the Iraq that American and British government officials claimed in their public statements between autumn 2002 and March 2003 (cf. *Cirincione et al.* 2004, 7ff.). The search of US specialists after the Iraq war confirmed what most observers had assumed in advance and what IAEA and

UNSCOM inspections had indicated before the war: Iraq did not have any significant quantities of chemical, biological or nuclear weapons or long-range missiles. The main justification for launching the 2003 Iraq war was not true. As a number of scientific studies revealed in the years after the war, the US administration had systematically misled the American people and world public as to the nature of the threat and the need for military action.

Ironically the Iraq case, where the findings of the IAEA inspectors were dismissed contemptuously by US officials, proved in the end the value and significance of the IAEA inspection system: obviously this system had hindered Saddam Hussein from producing non-conventional weapons on a larger scale.

In the cases of North Korea and Iran, the IAEA attempts to make sure through its inspections that both states keep their obligations under terms of the Non-Proliferation Treaty, confirmed in international negotiations in recent years, namely not to produce nuclear weapons, which is important for the regional and global security situation and which helps avoid far-reaching economic and military sanctions which might be decided upon by the UN Security Council in case of a breach of the obligations. But in both cases the problems are not solved, as the states move between co-operation and resistance.

In these cases, too, the IAEA has again proved its value, in providing the facts on the nuclear facilities and their use as foundation for the debates and decisions.

It was in appreciation of this fact-finding work in the service of the fight for nuclear non-proliferation, that the Committee for the Nobel Peace Prize awarded the 2006 Prize to the IAEA and its Director-General Baradei.

Some NGOs, which agreed with this view of the non-proliferation work of the IAEA, criticized on the other hand the function of the IAEA in supporting its member states (146 as of February 2009) in the peaceful use of nuclear energy in power plants, which also be-longs to the tasks of the IAEA according to its statute (Art. III(1)).

But as long as states are not willing to do without nuclear energy it is valuable that the IAEA checks the safety of the facilities and prevents states from a clandestine use of nuclear material for weapon production. The IAEA alone cannot prevent states from violating their legal obligations in this regard, but it can provide the leading political powers with the necessary information to decide on measures to take in such a case. The history of the IAEA in recent years has proved that it is well equipped for this purpose and does not compromise in advocating adequate measures even if a world power like the USA does not agree with its findings and conclusions.

Helmut Volger

Lit: *Blix, H.:* The Role of the IAEA in the Development of International Law, in: Nordic JIL 58 (1989), 231-242; *Cirincione, J. et al.:* WMD in Iraq - Evidence and Implications (Carnegie Endowment for International Peace), Washington 2004; *Goldschmidt, P.:* The Increasing Risk of Nuclear Proliferation: Lessons Learned, in: IAEA Bulletin 45/2, December 2003, 24-27; *Kirgis, F.L.:* Iran and the Nuclear Non-Proliferation Treaty, in: ASIL Insights, Vol. 10, No. 13, 30 May 2006, www.asil.org/insights060530.cfm; *Mathews, J.T.:* WMD and the United Nations. Keynote Speech to the International Peace Academy 5 March 2004, accessible at: www.carnegieendowment.org/publications

Internet: Homepage of IAEA: www.iaea.org.

ICAO – International Civil Aviation Organization

The *International Civil Aviation Organization (ICAO)* was established by the *Convention on International Civil Aviation* signed in Chicago on 7 December 1944 (UNTS Vol. 15, No. 102), known as the "Chicago Convention". The Convention came into force on 4 April 1947 after ratification of the requisite number of 26 states. The ICAO is one of the → specialized agencies within the UN system (→ UN System). Its headquarters is located in Montreal. ICAO has currently 190 contracting states (as of 31 December 2008).

Aims and Objectives

The priority objective of the ICAO is to safeguard an orderly development of international civil aviation. Its scope of duties includes, on the one hand, the development of principles and of techniques of international civil aviation, and on the other, the promotion of the planning and development of international air transport.

Specifically the ICAO is to:
- ensure safe and orderly growth of international civil aviation;
- meet the needs of the peoples of the world for safe, regular, efficient and economical air transport;
- promote safety of flight in international air navigation;
- foster the design and use of aircraft for peaceful purposes;
- promote the development of airways, airports and air navigation facilities of international civil aviation;
- prevent economic waste caused by unreasonable competition;
- avoid discrimination between contracting states; and
- ensure the rights of contracting states are respected, and that every contracting state has an opportunity to operate international airlines (cf. ICAO Convention, Art. 44).

Structure and Organization

The supreme organ of the ICAO is the *Assembly*. It consists of all member states, each having one vote. The Assembly meets at least once every three years. It elects the ICAO *Council*, the executive organ, determines the general policy guidelines of the organization, approves the budget, and examines and monitors the entire work of the ICAO in the technical, economic and legal fields, which have not been specifically assigned to the Council (cf. Art. 49 ICAO Convention).

The *Council* as executive organ of the ICAO is composed of 36 member states

and is elected by the Assembly for a three-year term. In electing the members of the Council, the Assembly is required under the ICAO Convention to ensure that all the following groups of member states are adequately represented:
1) the states of chief importance in air transport;
2) the states not otherwise included which make the largest contribution to the provision of facilities for international civil air navigation; and
3) the states belonging neither to group 1 nor 2, whose presence will ensure that all major geographic areas of the world are represented on the Council. (Art. 50 ICAO Convention)

The main functions of the *Council* are of a legislative, administrative and judicial nature. It adopts international standards and recommended practices, i.e. specifications whose uniform application is recognized as necessary for the safety or regularity of international air navigation. The aim is the highest possible degree of uniformity in national regulations, procedures and organizations relating to aircraft personnel, airways and auxiliary services with the view to reaching a global concordance of national guidelines, recommendations and procedures. These ICAO Standards and Recommended Practices which the Council adopts are added as "Annexes" to the Convention. They relate for instance to personnel licensing, the meteorological service for air navigation, aeronautical charts, airworthiness of aircraft, aeronautical telecommunications, search and rescue, operation of aircraft, air traffic services and aircraft nationality and registration marks.

The Council may act as arbiter between ICAO member states on matters concerning aviation and implementation of the ICAO Convention.

The *President of the Council* is elected by the Council for a term of three years: he may be re-elected. The President convenes meetings of the Council and directs the work of the organization on behalf of the Council (Art. 51 (c)). He assumes a mediating role in international negotiations on aviation matters.

In discharging the functions assigned to them by the ICAO, the Convention Assembly and Council are assisted by seven subsidiary bodies, expert committees.

The ICAO *Secretariat* is headed by the *Secretary-General*, appointed by the Council. In addition to his office, which is responsible for the administration of financial matters, external relations, public information and regional affairs, the Secretariat consists of five main departments for air navigation, air transport, legal affairs, technical cooperation and administrative matters.

The ICAO has established regional offices to monitor the regional developments in civil aviation and the implementation of the decisions of the ICAO, to offer advice to the state members in the respective region and to formulate recommendations.

The ICAO works in close cooperation with other members of the UN system such as the → WMO, the → UPU, the → WHO and → IMO.

ICAO's Work on the Environment

The ICAO has dealt with environmental issues since the 1960s, when the growing number of jet aircraft caused severe noise problems for the people in the vicinity of the airports, and in the early 1970s the first ICAO noise standards were established. The environmental impact of international aviation exhaust emissions came later into the focus of the ICAO: it was in the year 1981 that ICAO Standards were adopted setting limits for the emission of smoke and gaseous pollutants from aircraft engines. In reaction to the increasing international debate about the greenhouse gases the ICAO adopted in 1993, in 1999 and again in 2004 more stringent limits on aircraft engine exhaust emissions. In September 2007, the ICAO Assembly eventually agreed in resolution A36-22 to establish a new "Group on International Aviation and Climate Change", whose purpose is to develop a plan of action for reducing the emissions (cf. *ICAO* News Release PIO 10/07, 28 September 2007). In the same year the

ICAO produced its first-ever Environmental Report (*ICAO* 2007b). The publication of the following triennial Environmental Reports will coincide with the ICAO Assemblies to come. The ICAO seems to have grasped the importance of this issue for its work, in the words of the ICAO Report 2007: "... the Organization was particularly active in the area of aircraft engine emissions and their impact on the environment, a reflection of the growing concern of the world community over climate change." (*ICAO* 2007a, 39)

Yet the majority in the ICAO Assembly apparently disagrees with the emissions trading approach suggested by the Conference of Parties of the UN Framework Convention on Climate Change (UNFCCC) and supported by the EU member states in the ICAO Assembly: "There was general agreement on the value of emissions trading, together with the reduction of emissions at source ... for controlling the impact of emissions on the environment. The Assembly, however, has difficulty reconciling the concept of common but differentiated responsibilities contained in the United Nations Framework Convention on Climate Change (UNFCCC) with the concept of non-discrimination contained in the Convention on International Civil Aviation. The majority of States considered that participation in an emission trading scheme should only be on the basis of mutual consent." (*ICAO* 2007a, 41; for the political background cf. *Porter/Ries* 2008)

The environment issue reveals once again the conflict over values and methods between the more technically oriented and in economic terms neo-liberally minded specialized agencies and the UN funds and programmes representing a stronger value orientation in terms of common responsibility and solidarity.

Recent Challenges

Beside the growing environmental concerns the ICAO has faced in recent years rapidly changing circumstances for its work such as globalization and transnationalization of markets and operations, commercialization of government service providers (e.g. air traffic control services), and the reaching of physical limits of infrastructure capacity. It remains to be seen whether the ICAO which has had so far a good balance sheet in terms of safeguarding reliable and safe air traffic will be in a position to find solutions also for these new challenges. Necessarily it will have to define indirect limits for the growth of air traffic through its standards in the interest of the safety even if the profits of the airlines might be reduced. More or less it will have to develop a master plan for a sustainable framework of international civil aviation – a genuine benchmark test for the quality of the work of the ICAO.

Helmut Volger

Lit.: *I. ICAO texts: ICAO:* Annual Report of the Council 2007, ICAO Doc. 9898, Berne 2007 (quoted as: ICAO 2007a); *ICAO:* ICAO Environmental Report 2007, Berne 2007 (quoted as: ICAO 2007b); *ICAO:* The Convention on International Aviation – Annexes 1 to 18. Information Brochure, Berne 2008; *II. Secondary Literature: Faller, E.:* ICAO – International Civil Aviation Organization, in: Wolfrum, R. (ed.): United Nations: Law, Policies and Practice, Vol. 1, Munich/Dordrecht 1995, 665-672; *Hailbronner, K.:* International Civil Aviation Organization, in: Bernhardt, R. (ed.): EPIL 5, Amsterdam et al. 1983, 68-71; *Milde, M.:* The Chicago Convention – After forty years, in: AASL 9 (1984), 119-131; *Porter, L.S./ Ries, D.K.:* International Civil Aviation Organization (ICAO). Reports on International Organizations of the American Society of International Law 2008, www.asil.org/rio/icao.html.

Internet: Homepage of ICAO: www.icao.int

ICC – International Criminal Court

1. Introduction

On 17 December 1997, in its Resolution 51/207, the General Assembly decided upon the convocation of a diplomatic conference in Rome for the establishment of a new criminal tribunal. Finally, on 17 July 1998, after intense delibera-

tions, 120 state representatives adopted the Statute of the *International Criminal Court,* headquartered in The Hague, with seven votes against (China, Iraq, Israel, Yemen, Qatar, Libya, and the United States of America) and 21 abstentions (UN Doc. A/CONF.183/9, 17 July 1998). The establishment of a permanent criminal jurisdiction may be seen as a milestone in international relations and offers several unique opportunities, among others:

- to promote respect for human rights and international humanitarian law for the benefit of victims;
- to improve the rule of law;
- to hold participants of armed conflicts personally responsible for their offences;
- to deter other persons from committing crimes in future conflicts; and
- to investigate the crimes committed in armed conflicts and therefore contribute to the reconciliation process in the country concerned.

2. Origins of the International Criminal Court

After World War II, the Allied Powers charged and convicted the main German and Japanese war criminals in the international military tribunals of Nuremberg and Tokyo, respectively, for crimes against peace, war crimes, and crimes against humanity.

Implicit in the Convention on the Prevention and Punishment of Genocide of 9 December 1948 (UNTS Vol.78, No. 1021, 277) was the establishment of an International Criminal Court. However, the court provided for in the convention was never founded. It was not until the establishment of the ad-hoc International Criminal Tribunal for the Prosecution of Persons Responsible for Serious Violations of International Humanitarian Law Committed in the Territory of the Former Yugoslavia (ICTY), established by Security Council Resolution 827 (1993) of 25 May 1993, and the International Criminal Tribunal for the Prosecution of Persons Responsible for Genocide and Other Serious Violations of International Humanitarian Law Committed in the Territory of Rwanda and Rwandan Citizens Responsible for Genocide and Other Such Violations Committed in the Territory of Neighboring States between 1 January and 31 December 1994 (ICTR), established by Security Council Resolution S/RES/955 (1994) of 8 November 1994, that for a second time – after the proceedings in Nuremberg and Tokyo – individuals were tried by an international court for grave violations of international law. As a result of the work of these courts, the world community became aware of the possibilities a permanent international criminal court with universal jurisdiction could offer.

UN efforts to develop a body of international criminal law on a treaty basis date back to the end of World War II. In 1947, the General Assembly mandated with resolution A/RES/177 (II) the International Law Commission (ILC) to summarize the principles of international law as recognized in the UN Charter and in the judgments of the Nuremberg Tribunal, and "to prepare a draft code of offences against the peace and security of mankind".

In December 1948 the General Assembly, with resolution A/RES/260B (III), invited the ILC "to study the desirability and possibility of establishing an international judicial organ for the trials of persons charged with genocide or crimes over which jurisdiction will be conferred upon that organ by international conventions," and requested the ILC, in carrying out that task, "to pay attention to the possibility of establishing a Criminal Chamber of the International Court of Justice". (→ ICJ – International Court of Justice)

In the following years the General Assembly, with resolution A/RES/489 (V) of 12 December 1950 and resolution A/RES/687 (VII) of 5 December 1952, entrusted two different committees with the task to explore the implications and consequences of establishing an international criminal court and developing a draft statute (cf. *ILC* 2005; see also *Graefrath* 1990, 67ff.)

In 1954, after discussing the report of the 1953 Committee on International Criminal Jurisdiction, which included draft statutes (UN Doc. A/2645), the General Assembly decided in resolution A/RES/898 (IX) of 14 December 1954 "to postpone consideration of an international criminal jurisdiction"; further work was repeatedly adjourned by the General Assembly in the following years (*Nanda* 1998, 414ff.; *Reichart* 1996, 124ff.).

It was only following the end of the East-West-Conflict and in response to atrocities in the former Yugoslavia and in Rwanda that public interest in a permanent criminal court began to grow. Again, the ILC played a prominent role: After having been asked by the General Assembly to address the question of establishing an international criminal court (UN Doc. A/RES/44/39, 4 December 1989), the ILC deliberated on this question from its 42nd session in 1990 until its 46th session in 1994. Having adopted the "ILC Draft Statute for an International Criminal Court" in 1994 (UN Doc. A/49/10 (SUPP)), the ILC concluded its subsequent work on the "Draft Code of Crimes Against Peace and Security of Mankind" (UN Doc. A/51/10, chapter II, para 30-50) two years later (*Berg* 1996, 221ff.; *Rudolf* 1996, 225 ff.).

Corresponding to General Assembly Resolution A/RES/51/207 of 17 December 1996, a Preparatory Committee on the Establishment of an International Criminal Court was created to submit a draft statute which would yield consensus (*Zimmermann* 1998, 48ff.; *Kaul* 1998, 125 f.). The Committee met for the first time from 25 March to 12 April 1996 to discuss the draft and to prepare a consolidated text of the convention. Two years later, the draft Statute on the Establishment of the International Criminal Court (UN Doc. A/CONF.183/2/Add. 1) was completed. Delegations from 160 countries, as well as 14 UN organizations and over 2000 non-governmental organizations (→ NGOs), the latter organized as the "NGO Coalition for an International Criminal Court

(CICC)", finally took part in the "United Nations Diplomatic Conference of Plenipotentiaries on the Establishment of an International Criminal Court" which met in Rome from 15 to 17 June 1998, convened on the basis of General Assembly resolution A/RES/52/160 of 15 December 1997 "with a view to finalizing and adopting a convention on the establishment of an international criminal court". The delegations were divided into two camps: one supported a strong and independent court (50-60 so-called "like-minded nations", among them the states of the European Union, Canada, Australia, Argentina, Brazil, Chile, and South Africa), while the remainder desired a far weaker court (e.g. the United States of America, Russia, Egypt, and Indonesia). In order to defend their sovereign rights, the latter group lobbied for making the functions of the Criminal Court conditional upon approval from the states concerned or the Security Council (cf. *Kaul* 1998, 126). Due in large part to the determination of the International Red Cross Committee (ICRC) and numerous NGOs, broad consent for the Rome Statute of the International Criminal Court was finally achieved.

3. Structure and Legal Effect of the Statute

In contrast to the international tribunals which were created on an *ad hoc* basis by virtue of a Security Council decision, the International Criminal Court is established on the basis of a special contractual agreement (Rome Statute of the International Criminal Court, adopted by the UN Diplomatic Conference of Plenipotentiaries on the Establishment of an International Criminal Court on 17 July 1998, UN Doc. A/CONF.183/ 9). According to its Statute the Criminal Court, which has an international legal identity, shall be brought "into relationship with the United Nations through an agreement" (Art. 2). The respective treaty between the Criminal Court and the United Nations was drafted by the Preparatory Committee and approved by the Assembly of States Parties before it

was signed by the President of the Criminal Court and the Secretary-General of the United Nations (Negotiated Relationship Agreement between the International Criminal Court and the United Nations. The Treaty entered into force upon signature on 4 October 2004 (ICC-ASP/3/Res.1, UN Doc. A/58/874, Annex).

The original suggestion to establish the court by amending the UN Charter was not effected at the founding conference, although this would have had the undoubted advantage of making the Criminal Court's statute binding for all UN member states (*Tomuschat* 1998, 336).

Moreover, in order to make the Criminal Court operational, the Criminal Court concluded a headquarters agreement with the host state, the Netherlands ("Headquarters Agreement between the International Criminal Court and the host State", approved by the Assembly of States Parties in its Fifth Session on 1 December 2006, and signed on 7 June 2007 by the President of the Criminal Court and the Foreign Minister of the Netherlands, ICC-ASP/5/32, Annex II). This agreement contains 58 provisions, mainly concerning privileges and immunities of the Criminal Court, its staff and other persons participating in the court proceedings (e.g. witnesses, victims, experts), as well as visa regulations and security and operational matters.

The whole Rome Statute is comprised of 13 parts and 128 articles. In its preamble, states parties affirm their determination "to put an end to impunity for the perpetrators" of grave crimes and "to contribute to the prevention of such crimes" (Preamble, para. 6). Important provisions of the Statute concern the catalogue of crimes within the jurisdiction of the Criminal Court (Art. 5-8, see *infra* 4), the "elements of crimes" (Art 9, see *infra* 6), and the jurisdiction of the Criminal Court (Art. 11ff.), but also the Criminal Court's composition and administration (Art. 34ff.), its criminal proceedings (Art. 53ff.), penalties (Art. 77ff.), the execution of sentences (Art.

103ff.), the necessary cooperation with the states parties, and the judicial assistance of the latter (Art. 86ff.). Every member state is able to withdraw from the Statute simply by notifying the UN Secretary-General. However, such action does not release it from duties originating from the Statute before the time of withdrawal (Art. 127). In order to allow the Criminal Court to pursue its work efficiently, a state would have to continue its collaboration in any ongoing preliminary proceedings.

Only seven years after the coming into force of the Rome Statute (i.e., in 2009) are states parties allowed to submit a text containing a proposed amendment. The Assembly of States Parties, in which each state has one representative, will then decide at its next meeting, by simple majority of those present and voting, whether to adopt the amendment directly or whether to convene a Review Conference. In each of these two cases, either a consensus or a two-thirds majority of states parties is required (Art. 121 (3)). In its sixth session in December 2007, the Assembly of States Parties decided that the first Review Conference should be convened in 2010, not only to discuss and adopt possible amendments to the Rome Statute, but also for a stocktaking process of international criminal justice (ICC-ASP/6/L.3/Rev.1).

Ratification by 60 states was necessary to put the Statute into effect (Art. 126); this occurred on 1 July 2002. As of 1 June 2008, 106 countries are states parties to the Rome Statute, with 30 of them from Africa, 13 from Asia, 16 from Eastern Europe, 22 from Latin America and the Caribbean, and 25 from Western Europe and other states.

4. Composition and Jurisdiction of the Criminal Court

After the adoption of the Rome Statute in 1998, another Preparatory Commission was established (Resolution F of the Final Act of the United Nations Diplomatic Conference of Plenipotentiaries on the establishment of an International Criminal Court, Rome on 17 July 1998,

UN Doc. A/CONF.183/10*)). Its mandate was, *inter alia*, to prepare proposals for practical arrangements for the establishment and operationalization of the Criminal Court, e.g. the relationship agreement with the UN, the headquarters agreement, the financial regulations and rules, the Agreement on Privileges and Immunities of the International Criminal Court (APIC), and a budget for the first financial year. Furthermore, the Preparatory Commission had to finalize the Rules of Procedure and Evidence, the Elements of Crimes, and to prepare the draft text of the rules of procedure of the Assembly of States Parties. The tenth and final session of the Preparatory Commission was held at the United Nations headquarters from 1 to 12 July 2002.

The Criminal Court is comprised of four categories of organs:

- the *Presidency* (i.e. the President and the First and Second Vice-President who are elected by an absolute majority of the judges) responsible for the proper administration of the Criminal Court, with the exception of the Office of the Prosecutor;
- the *Pre-Trial Division* (not less than six judges), the *Trial Division* (not less than six judges) and the *Appeals Division* (composed of the President and four other judges);
- the *Office of the Prosecutor*, headed by the Prosecutor who is elected by an absolute majority of the members of the Assembly of States Parties by secret ballot and is responsible for receiving referrals and any substantiated information on crimes within the jurisdiction of the Criminal Court; two Deputy Prosecutors assist the Prosecutor;
- the *Registry*, headed by the Registrar, who is elected by the judges by an absolute majority and by secret ballot, is responsible for the non-judicial aspects of administration and servicing of the Criminal Court and meets regularly with lawyers' associations and experts.

Other offices include the Office of Public Counsel for Victims and the Office

361

of Public Counsel for Defence, both of which fall under the Registry for administrative purposes, but function independently.

The judges, being independent in the performance of their duties, are required to serve on a full-time basis at the seat of the Criminal Court and to sit in Chambers which are responsible for conducting the proceedings of the Criminal Court at different stages.

The *Assembly of States Parties*, established by Article 112 of the Statute of Rome, is the body responsible for a variety of issues concerning the administration and management of the Criminal Court and is often described as "the legislative body" of the International Criminal Court. Among its duties, it adopts documents, decides the budget for the Criminal Court, elects judges, the Prosecutor and his/her deputies, and considers any question relating to non-cooperation of states. The Assembly of States Parties has a Bureau which meets as often as necessary, consisting of a President, two Vice-Presidents and 18 members elected for three-year terms.

The Criminal Court has jurisdiction only with respect to crimes committed after the introduction of the Rome Statute (Art. 11), provided that either a situation in which a crime appears to have been committed is referred to the Prosecutor by a state party or the Security Council (see *infra* 8) or the Prosecutor has personally instigated an investigation. In order for an individual to be brought before the court, there are three possibilities: (1) the state on the territory of which the crime has been committed (territorial link) or (2) the state of which the person accused is a national (nationality link) is a contracting party of the Statute or the state has accepted the jurisdiction of the Criminal Court by a declaration lodged with the Registrar (Art. 12) or (3) the Security Council has referred the situation to the Prosecutor. This means the Statute membership of a state on the territory of which a criminal may be found does not automatically result in the jurisdiction of the Criminal Court if neither the territorial nor the na-

tionality link exists. Thus, it could happen that the transfer of accused war criminals to The Hague is not possible, even if they are arrested in a member state of the Statute *(Kaul* 2002, 583, 612ff.).

The jurisdiction of the Criminal Court shall be complementary to national criminal jurisdictions (Art. 1; Art. 17 (1) (a)), i.e. the Criminal Court is to exercise criminal jurisdiction whenever criminal courts of sovereign states are "unwilling or unable" to carry out the investigation or prosecution. This means, generally and as a rule, offenders are to be sentenced by competent national courts. The Criminal Court determines, at its own discretion, if a national system has failed (i.e., is unwilling or unable to carry out the investigation or prosecution) and only then can it assume jurisdiction. As a result, some states improved their criminal law to avoid international jurisdiction by the Criminal Court (see, for example, the adoption of the German Code of Crimes against International Law of 26 June 2002; Federal Law Gazette *(Bundesgesetzblatt)* 2002, Part I., No. 42, 29 June 2002, pp. 2254-2260; in this context see *Schlunck* 1999, 27ff.).

If there appears to be a risk of parallel exercise of national and international criminal jurisdiction, a state may inform the Criminal Court that it is investigating or has investigated its nationals or other persons within its jurisdiction with respect to crimes which are investigated or are going to be investigated by the Prosecutor. At the request of that state, the Prosecutor shall defer to the state's investigation unless the Pre-Trial Chamber decides to authorize the investigation (Art. 18).

5. Prosecuted Crimes

The Criminal Court concentrates on the prosecution of the most serious, universally punishable "core crimes". Therefore, the crimes within the jurisdiction of the Criminal Court are not subject to any statute of limitations.

In becoming a member of the Statute – with reservations being explicitly ex-

cluded (Art. 120) –, states automatically accept the Criminal Court's jurisdiction regarding the following four crimes:
- genocide (Art. 6);
- crimes against humanity (Art. 7);
- war crimes (Art. 8);
- the crime of aggression (Art. 5 (2)).

The fact that crimes against humanity as well as genocide can be prosecuted, even when not committed in armed conflicts, proves to be of special importance for the development of international criminal law. Since experience shows that most of the recent massive violations of human rights occur in civil war situations, it is important that war crimes committed in non-international conflicts are included in the Statute, as well. With a view to the further development of human rights protection, progress was made in the fact that the enforced disappearance of persons is also classified as a crime against humanity. However, Article 7 (2) (i) Rome Statute provides that enforced disappearances may only be prosecuted by the Criminal Court if they have taken place over a "prolonged period of time", a point that has been criticized by experts. Yet further progress was made in that different forms of sexual acts (including rape, enforced prostitution, and enforced sterilization) were also classified as crimes against humanity. Even the highly controversial term "forced pregnancy" was mentioned as a possible crime against humanity, against the will of some abortion opponents.

The Rome Statute also contains elements corroborating the protection of children's rights. For example, it is now a war crime to conscript or enlist children under the age of fifteen years into armed forces or groups, or to use them to participate actively in hostilities (Art. 8 (2) (b) (xxvi)). With regard to children soldiers, Article 26 is also relevant as it excludes the Criminal Court's jurisdiction over persons who are "under the age of 18 at the time of the alleged commission of a crime", thus indirectly stressing the idea of possible social rehabilitation of adolescents.

It is regrettable, however, that the treatment of environmental crimes as elaborated upon in former ILC drafts does not fall into the competence of the Criminal Court (*Tomuschat* 1998, 340). With respect to nuclear powers, it should be noted that the definition of war crimes does not include any reference to nuclear weapons nor does the Statute include serious acts of international terrorism. However, it is also important to note that widespread or systematic terrorist attacks against civilian populations may qualify as crimes against humanity under Article 7 of the Rome Statute. Theoretically, it would be possible to discuss the likelihood of the inclusion of terrorist acts in the Statute on the occasion of the next Review Conference in 2009 or at a later date.

In so far as punishment for the crime of aggression is concerned, the Criminal Court shall exercise jurisdiction "once a provision is adopted" defining the crime and setting out the conditions under which it shall exercise jurisdiction. This means that the crime of aggression is, in principle, part of the jurisdiction of the Criminal Court; however, the precise elements, i.e. the definition of the individual's conduct, the leadership clause and the role of the Security Council must be determined first. This proves to be difficult (*O'Donovan* 2007, 507ff.; *Reisman* 2002, 181ff.), as the Informal Inter-sessional Meeting of the Special Working Group on the Crime of Aggression (held at the Liechtenstein Institute on Self-Determination, Woodrow Wilson School, Princeton University, from 11 to 14 June 2007) showed (ICC-ASP/6/SWGCA/INF.1, 25 July 2007; see also ICC-ASP/5/35, Report of the Working Group on the Crime of Aggression).

Especially the United States, but also the United Kingdom, China, Russia, and New Zealand raised the argument that soldiers are under legal obligation to execute orders in all possible situations. According to the Rome Statute, a soldier or other person may therefore claim to have been under the legal obligation to obey the orders of his/her government or superior (Art. 33 (1) (a) of the Statute). In this case, he/she is relieved of criminal responsibility.

6. The Role of the Elements of Crimes

Article 9 of the Rome Statute rules that the Elements of Crimes "shall assist the Court in the interpretation and application of articles 6, 7 and 8", i.e. the interpretation and application of genocide, crimes against humanity, and war crimes. Although most delegations at the time of the codification of the Statute – especially those from states with civil law traditions – were skeptical with regard to the usefulness of the Elements, they agreed to enter into negotiations about structure and content of the Elements in order to improve the chances for the Statute to be ratified by the United States (*Politi* 2002, 445ff.). On 30 June 2000, the Preparatory Commission for the International Criminal Court adopted by consensus the draft Elements of Crimes. The Chairman of the Preparatory Commission, *Philippe Kirsch*, described the negotiations on the Elements of Crimes as a "very useful exercise" as they provided the opportunity to resolve difficult legal problems and to develop a single coherent structure (*Philippe Kirsch*, Foreword, in: *Dörmann* 2002, xiii). The Elements are contained in the Annex to the Statute and represent a compromise: According to a literal interpretation of Article 9, the Elements must be considered to be of a "declarative and systemizing character" (*Ambos* 2001, 65) and hence do not have the same legally binding force as the provisions of the Statute that the United States had called for in their initial proposal.

Article 9 (3) underscores the formally subordinated role of the Elements of Crimes requiring them to be "consistent" with the Statute. However, since the lengthy document which contains 92 provisions was passed with a two-thirds majority by the Assembly of States Parties, it will be hard for the judges of the Criminal Court to ignore it. During the codification process, the United States emphasized on several occasions the purpose of the Elements as necessary clarifications of the core crimes preventing ambiguity of the Statute and hence arbitrary application of its provisions. On the other hand, critics have not only pointed to the complicated language of the Elements (*Politi* 2002, 451), but have also denounced the inclusion of the Elements as a fundamental mistrust against the judges of the Criminal Court and as an obstacle for the development of international criminal law by jurisprudence (see *Cassese* 1999, 163ff.; *Hunt* 2004, 56ff.). As the Elements of Crimes form a novelty to international criminal law, it will be interesting to see how great their actual impact on the jurisprudence of the Criminal Court will be in future trials.

7. Proceedings

The Prosecution headed by the Prosecutor and being an independent institution of the Criminal Court, plays a central role. All cases referred to the Prosecution by a contracting party or by the Security Council (see *infra* 8) must be dealt with. In addition, the Prosecutor is able to initiate investigations, i.e. he holds an *ex officio* authority and may initiate investigations *proprio motu* (Art. 15 (1)). He may rely upon information from states and UN organs, but also from intergovernmental and non-governmental organizations (NGOs), as well as "other reliable sources". In all cases, the Prosecutor is subject to the Criminal Court's control, which means that the actual preliminary investigation must be approved by the Pre-Trial Chamber which is responsible for the judicial aspects of proceedings. If the latter, upon examination of the request and the supporting material, considers that there is a reasonable basis to proceed with an investigation and that the case falls within the jurisdiction of the Criminal Court, it will authorize the start of the investigation (Art. 15 (4)). The Pre-Trial Chamber may issue a warrant of arrest or a summons to appear and hold a hearing to confirm the charges that will eventually be the basis of the later trial.

The case may then be assigned to a Trial Chamber, consisting of three judges. The accused has the right to defense against the charges of the Prosecutor. As of 24 October 2007, 221 persons have been admitted to the List of Counsel who can be called upon at any time to provide legal assistance (www.icc-cpi.int/library/defence/Defense_Counsel_List_English.pdf).

A Code of Professional Conduct for Counsel had already been adopted by the Assembly of States Parties at its fourth session on 2 December 2005 (ICC-ASP/4/Res.1). Moreover, a List of Professional Investigators has been developed which includes the names of persons who can be called upon at any time by the defense counsel, the victims, or their legal representatives in order to assist the proceedings before the Criminal Court.

For the first time in the history of international criminal justice, victims may participate personally or through their legal representatives and represent their views, e.g. file submissions (also before the Pre-Trial Chamber). The Victim's Participation and Reparation Section helps victims to organize their legal representation, if they wish. Upon conclusion of its proceedings, the Trial Chamber issues its decision, which either acquits or convicts the accused person. In the latter case, the Trial Chamber also issues a sentence specifying the penalty. All appeals are decided by the Appeals Chamber which consists of five judges.

The efficiency of the legal prosecution may be limited by the interim regulation for war crimes (Art. 124): Member states may declare, on becoming a party of the Statute, that for a period of seven years after the Statute's entry into force, they are not obliged to accept the jurisdiction of the Criminal Court with respect to a war crime allegedly committed during this time by its nationals or on its territory. This rule, resulting from a French proposal, was criticized as a temporary "partial withdrawal from the Statute" (*Kaul* 1998, 128). As of November 2007, declarations pursuant to Article 124 have been submitted by Co-

lombia and France. Another limitation of the legal prosecution concerns the deferral of investigation or prosecution upon the initiative of the Security Council (Art. 16; see *infra* 8).

In contrast to the Statute of the International Military Tribunal of Nuremberg, which permitted proceedings to be conducted in the absence of the accused, the accused must be present during a trial before the International Criminal Court (Art. 63 (1)). Furthermore, everyone shall be presumed innocent until proven guilty; it is the task of the Prosecutor to prove the guilt of the accused. High priority is placed on the rights of the accused, e.g. he/she has to have adequate time and facilities for the preparation of his/her defense, this means, he/she has the right to be tried without undue delay, to examine the witnesses against him/her, to have the necessary translations, etc.

Other important provisions concern the protection of victims and witnesses. In taking appropriate measures to protect victims and witnesses, the International Criminal Court shall have special consideration for victims of sexual or gender related violence and violence against children, among others. For example, hearings do not have to take place in public. The Victims and Witnesses Unit, established under Article 43 (6), shall provide, in consultation with the Office of the Prosecutor, counseling and assistance for witnesses and victims who appear before the Criminal Court as well as others who are at risk because they are testifying. The Victims and Witnesses Unit may also advise the Prosecutor and the Criminal Court on appropriate protective measures and security arrangements for witnesses (Art. 68 (4)). The detailed functions and responsibilities of the Unit are specified in the Rules of Procedure and Evidence (ICC-ASP/1/3, Rules 16-19) and include, in particular, the protection and security of all witnesses and victims who appear before the Criminal Court through appropriate measures and the establishment of short- and long-term plans for their protection. The Unit shall also provide assistance for victims and witnesses receiving medical and psychological care. Furthermore, it shall, in consultation with the Office of the Prosecutor, elaborate a code of conduct emphasizing the vital importance of security and professional secrecy for all persons and organizations acting for or on behalf of the International Criminal Court (Rule 17). The Unit is also responsible for providing training for its staff regarding the security, integrity, and dignity of victims and witnesses (Rule 18).

The working languages of the Criminal Court are English and French. The deliberations of the judges shall remain undisclosed; in this way, their impartiality is guaranteed. The Criminal Court, which is required to base its decision "only on evidence submitted and discussed before it at the trial" (Art. 74 (2)), may initially apply the Statute, the Elements of Crimes, and the Rules of Procedure and Evidence. Subsequently and where appropriate, it may consult applicable treaties and the principles and rules of international law, and as a last resort also general principles of law derived from national laws. The final decision shall be in writing and shall contain a full and reasoned statement of findings, evidence and conclusions. When there is no unanimity, the Trial Chamber's decision shall contain the views of the majority and the minority. In the event of a conviction, the Trial Chamber shall consider the appropriate sentence to be imposed. The sentence shall be pronounced publicly (Art. 76).

An appeal against the Criminal Court's decision may be made by the Prosecutor or by the convicted person in case of a procedural error or error of fact or law. In addition to these grounds, a convicted person also has the possibility to bring forward "any other ground that affects the fairness or reliability of the proceedings or decision" (Art. 81 (1)). As far as the sentence itself is concerned, an appeal is possible on the grounds of "disproportion between the crime and the sentence" (Art. 81 (2)).

The imposition of the death penalty is excluded and the maximum penalty that may be imposed is a term of life imprisonment (Art. 77 (1) (b)). A sentence of imprisonment shall be served in a state designated by the Criminal Court from a *list of states* which have indicated to the Criminal Court their willingness to accept sentenced persons (Art. 103). As of 2008, only Austria has concluded a so-called "Enforcement of Sentences Agreement" with the Criminal Court; several other states are in the process of negotiating such agreements (cf. Report of the International Criminal Court to the United Nations for 2006-2007, UN Doc. A/62/314 of 31 August 2007, www. iccnow.org/documents/ICC_Report_to_ UN_2006_2007_English.pdf)

As far as reparations to victims are concerned, the Criminal Court, for the first time in history, has the possibility to order the payment of reparation, from one individual to another or collectively, including restitution, compensation, and rehabilitation (Art. 75 (1)). To apply for reparation, victims are required to file a written application with the Registry and are assisted by the Victim's Participation and Reparation Section. Where appropriate, the Criminal Court may order that the award for reparations be made through the *Trust Fund*, which was set up by decision of the Assembly of States Parties for the benefits of victims of crimes and for the families of such victims in September 2002. The Trust Fund conducts its work according to the criteria specified in the Regulations of the Trust Fund for Victims, adopted by the Assembly of States Parties pursuant to Article 79 (3) in December 2005 (ICC-ASP/4/Res.3). Funding is generated through voluntary contributions from governments, international organizations, individuals, and other entities, as well as through money or property arising from fines or forfeiture transferred to the Trust by the Criminal Court pursuant to Article 79 (2). The Secretariat of the Trust Fund is funded by the states parties through their regular contributions to the Criminal Court (about 1 % of the regular budget).

In 2006, the Trust Fund received voluntary contributions of about 1.14 million euros (contributing states were Belgium, France, Germany, Ireland, Liechtenstein, Netherlands, Poland, Slovenia, Spain, Sweden, and the United Kingdom); together with contributions from earlier years, the total balance of the Trust Fund was, as of 30 June 2007, about 2.5 million euros.

8. Relationship between the Security Council and the Criminal Court

The UN Security Council may transfer so-called "country situations" to the Criminal Court in which one or more fundamental crimes, i.e. the crimes listed in Article 5-8, appear to have been committed. In such individual cases, it does not matter whether the state concerned is a party to the Rome Statute or not. The referral of the situation in Darfur to the Criminal Court by Resolution 1593 of 31 March 2005, was the first time that the Security Council made use of this power (see *infra* 13).

The Criminal Court's independence from the Security Council, the latter having the main responsibility to maintain world peace and international security, was a matter of conflict during the process of codification of the Rome Statute. Of particular concern was the question whether a single permanent member of the Security Council can use its veto power to obstruct a Council's decision to refer a situation in which crimes appear to have been committed to the Criminal Court. At present, the Security Council is able to defer an investigation or prosecution for a period of twelve months to be renewed under the same conditions through a joint decision if this is considered necessary to securing international peace and security through Chapter VII of the UN Charter (Art. 16 Rome Statute). The Security Council referred to this power when passing Resolution 1422 in 2002 and Resolutions 1487 and 1497 in 2003 in order to prevent the Criminal Court's jurisdiction over members of peacekeeping forces. Especially with regard to Resolution 1422 and its renewal by

Resolution 1487, the legal validity of the Security Council's actions has been questioned (see *Zimmermann* 2003). Resolution 1422 was passed unanimously by the Security Council as a consequence of extensive pressure of the United States threatening to veto the renewal of the Council's mission in Bosnia and Herzegovina if there was no general exemption of peacekeepers from the Criminal Court's jurisdiction (see *Jain* 2005, 239ff.).

The criticism voiced on Resolutions 1422 and 1487 mainly targeted the Security Council's references to its special competences for international peace and security while there was no evidence of immediate threat. In Resolution 1497, the Security Council did refer to a concrete situation guaranteeing exclusive jurisdiction of states participating in the Council's peacekeeping mission in Lebanon over their nationals. Critics nonetheless consider all three resolutions inconsistent with the Rome Statute pointing to the wording of Article 16 which seems to require case by case decisions rather than general exemptions with automatic renewals (*Jain* 2005, 247; *Zimmermann* 2004, 31f.). Due to rising opposition within the international community, the United States withdrew a proposal to renew the general exemption of peacekeepers in 2004. However, the delicate question of the Criminal Court's jurisdiction over peacekeepers is likely to remain a matter of dispute in the Security Council, especially when US nationals are involved.

9. Relationship between the Criminal Court and the United States of America

In the mid-1990s, US President Bill Clinton supported the establishment of an International Criminal Court and the United States participated actively and with the largest national delegation in the preparatory meetings to the drafting of the statute. The United States proposed the establishment of a permanent International Criminal Court as standing tribunal to the Security Council which would have had the final decision in any case on referrals to the court. However, as negotiations developed in the direction of a more independent court, the United States' opposition grew. When Clinton signed the Statute on his very last day of office, he urged his successor to abstain from ratifying the treaty unless major changes were made in the legal provisions. In May 2002, Clinton's successor, President George W. Bush Jr., notified the UN that the United States would not ratify the treaty: "This is to inform you, in connection with the Rome Statute of the International Criminal Court adopted on July 17, 1998, that the United States does not intend to become a party to the treaty..." (Rome Statute of the International Criminal Court, UNTS 2187, No. 38544, Note 7, 6 May 2002). Since then a hostile US policy towards the Criminal Court has been implemented (see *Cerone* 2007, 277ff.; *Scheffer* 1999, 13ff.).

It has remained an integral interest of the US government to prevent American nationals, particularly members of the armed services, from being subjected to trial before the International Criminal Court without US consent. Since Article 12 of the Rome Statute includes the possibility that the Criminal Court may exercise jurisdiction if the state on whose territory the crime was committed is a state party or has accepted the jurisdiction of the Criminal Court, the USA tries to argue that the Rome Statute violates fundamental principles of international law, e.g. the *pacta tertii nec nocent nec prosunt* rule meaning that a third state which has not ratified a treaty cannot be bound by that treaty without its consent (*Kaul* 2002, 614). Additionally, the United States continues to criticize the power of the Prosecutor to initiate investigations personally, arguing that such initiatives favor politically motivated trials, and undermine the supremacy of the UN Security Council in questions of international peace and security as guaranteed by the UN Charter. The United States has also objected strongly to the inclusion of aggression as a prospective crime in the

Statute (*Scheffer* 1999, 12ff.; *Zimmermann* 2004, 33ff.).

The Bush administration's fundamental opposition to the Criminal Court became most apparent when, in May 2002, the American Servicemembers' Protection Act (ASPA) was passed (H.R. 4775, Title II of Public Law 107-206) forbidding US agencies from any form of cooperation with the Criminal Court and restricting financial military aid to member states of the latter. The ASPA was meant to protect US citizens from the jurisdiction of the Criminal Court ruling that the US may only participate in international peacekeeping missions mandated by the Security Council if the mandate explicitly exempts US soldiers from the Criminal Court's jurisdiction. The Act even contains a clause that enables the American President to intervene with military force in order to enforce the release of US citizens arrested following an arrest warrant. Critics therefore have referred to the Act as "The Hague Invasion Act". Since 2002, the US has furthermore concluded bilateral non-surrender agreements with approximately 100 states containing reciprocal guarantees not to hand over any national of the contracting parties to the Criminal Court (*Cerone* 2007, 296; *Leigh* 2001, 130f.). In some cases, the United States suspended assistance programmes to states that refused to sign or ratify a bilateral non-surrender agreement.

Although fundamental US criticism has not diminished over the past years, the US administration and its agencies currently tend to take on a more pragmatic attitude towards the Criminal Court emphasizing the United States' commitment to fight impunity worldwide. As indications of a more moderate US position towards the Criminal Court, the United States abstained in the 2005 vote on Security Council Resolution 1593 authorizing referral of the Situation in Darfur to the Criminal Court and in 2006 called for the Charles Taylor case of the Special Court for Sierra Leone (SCSL) to be held in The Hague using the facilities of the International Criminal Court (see *Cerone* 2007, 277ff.).

10. International Cooperation and Judicial Assistance

Lacking its own police force or executive power, the Criminal Court depends on effective and speedy international cooperation with member states. For that reason, implementation of Part 9 of the Rome Statute on international cooperation and judicial assistance is especially important. States parties shall cooperate "fully" with the Criminal Court in its investigation and prosecution of crimes (Art. 86). The Criminal Court has the right to transmit requests to states parties for cooperation, either through diplomatic channels, the International Criminal Police Organization, or other appropriate channels. States are not allowed to refuse such cooperation with the Criminal Court. If they fail to comply with a request to cooperate contrary to the Statute's provision, the Criminal Court may make a finding on the issue and refer the matter to the Assembly of States Parties.

The Criminal Court may also transmit a request for the arrest and surrender of a person to any state on the territory of which the person has been found (Art. 89). Since the nationality of a person is not a valid reason for rejecting a request of arrest and surrender by the Criminal Court, a collision with national law may occur in some cases (for example with regard to Germany, Art. 16 (2), German Basic Law (Constitution), see *Schlunck* 1999, 28ff.). Where such a case occurs, the requested state shall immediately consult with the Criminal Court.

Moreover, a state party shall authorize, in accordance with its national procedural law, the transportation of a person being surrendered to the Criminal Court by another state through its territory (Art. 89 (3)). In urgent cases, the Criminal Court may request the provisional arrest of a person sought (Art. 92). Other forms of cooperation concern, *inter alia*, the examination of places and sites, the execution of searches and seizures, the questioning of any person being investigated or prosecuted, and the provision of records and documents.

As was mentioned above (para. 9), numerous bilateral non-surrender agreements have been signed upon pressure of the United States. This amounts not only to a hidden subsequent modification of the Criminal Court ratification bill in the countries concerned, but is also a harsh setback in the fight against impunity.

11. Financing

As experience has shown, the funding of institutions charged with the protection of human rights within the UN system is often difficult. Therefore, the drafters of the Criminal Court's Statute aimed at a wide funding base (*Jurasch* 1999, 17f.).

The financial support for the International Criminal Court is to be made available through assessed contributions by states parties and through funds provided by the United Nations, subject to approval by the General Assembly. This approval is of particular importance in relation to the expenses incurred due to referrals by the Security Council. Furthermore, voluntary contributions from governments, international organizations, individuals, corporations, and other entities are possible in accordance with relevant criteria adopted by the Assembly of States Parties. In 2002, the Assembly of States Parties called for a Committee on Budget and Finance which has served since then as an external expert panel to all Criminal Court budgetary questions. In order to guarantee the Criminal Court's flexibility in case of unforeseen situations, the Committee recommended a yearly Contingency Fund of 15 million euros; however, in 2004, the Assembly of States Party only provided for a yearly 10 million euro fund (*O'Donohue* 2006, 591ff.) until the terms are reviewed again in 2008 (ICC-ASP/3/Res. 4, B).

It is worth mentioning that, with regard to the budgetary performance of the Criminal Court in 2006, only 64.1 million euros of the approved budget of 80.4 million euros were spent. This is due primarily to the fact that, except for the Lubanga trial (see *infra* 13), no trials were initiated although the Assembly of States Parties had provided for more than one trial in the approved budget.

However, the Registrar has proposed a budget for 2008 of 97.57 million euros, which – if accepted by the states parties – would mean an increase of 8.70 million euros or 9.8% from 2007. As the Criminal Court has been transformed in the meantime to a complete functioning court, it has become apparent that, in the future, financial problems will be difficult to avoid through the existing financial regulations. With four current situations, only one case pending before the court, but possibly more to come in the future if arrest warrants are implemented, the budgetary demands of the different organs of the Criminal Court will increase significantly. Already, critics have pointed to the fact that not enough resources have been provided for the outreach programs and victim protection in Uganda and the DRC (*O'Donohue* 2006, 597ff.). It is therefore particularly problematic that the Security Council has referred the situation in Darfur to the Criminal Court, but has rejected to participate in the high costs of the investigations there (*Crook* 2005, 691ff.).

12. Staff Development

As of March 2007, the Criminal Court has recruited a permanent staff of 464 employees, of which approximately 46% are female and 54% are male. Out of the entire staff, 17.59% come from the African Group of States (target: 13.09%), 5.53% from the Asian Group of States (target: 7.69%), 8.04% from the Group of Eastern Europe (target: 7.32%), 11.06% from the Latin American and Caribbean Group of States (target: 14.15%) and 57.79% from the Western European and other Groups of States (target: 57.74%). With regard to weighted geographical representation, the Criminal Court has thus largely fulfilled its objectives (see *ICC*, Ninth Diplomatic Briefing of the International Criminal Court, 29 March 2007).

Major steps towards a fully operational institution were already taken in 2003 when the 18 judges (7 female and 11 male), Chief Prosecutor Luis Moreno Ocampo from Argentina and Registrar Bruno Cathala from France were inaugurated. The judges then elected the Presidency of the Criminal Court, consisting of the President and two Vice-Presidents (Report on the activities of the court, ICC-ASP/2/5). In March 2006, the judges of the Criminal Court re-elected the Presidency of the Criminal Court which is at present composed of President Phillippe Kirsch from Canada, First Vice-President Akua Kuenyahia from Ghana, and Second Vice-President René Blattmann from Bolivia (Report on the activities of the Court, 17 October 2006, ICC-ASP/5/15; see also *Elberling* 2007, 529ff.; *Geiß* 2006, 473ff.).

13. The First Cases before the International Criminal Court

The Prosecutor of the Criminal Court has up to now officially opened investigations in four cases; these arising from the situations in the Democratic Republic of Congo (DRC), in Uganda, in Darfur and in West-Africa.

Except for the situation in Darfur, which was referred to the Criminal Court by Security Resolution 1583 in 2005, all situations were referred to the Office of the Prosecutor (OTP) by means of so-called "self-referrals", i.e. states voluntarily surrendered to the Criminal Court's jurisdiction. The practice of self-referrals has been criticized for releasing governments from resolving persisting domestic problems and from maintaining an effective national judicial system themselves (see *Arsanjani/Reisman* 2005, 392; *Gaeta* 2004, 949ff.). Others, however, have welcomed the self-referrals as clear indications for a growing acceptance of the Criminal Court and hope for greater governmental cooperation, as governments have voluntarily surrendered to the Criminal Court's jurisdiction (*Höpfel/Schweiger* 2006, 222).

In March 2004, the government of the Democratic Republic of Congo turned to the Prosecutor whose investigations so far have mainly focused on crimes committed in the northern region of Ituri since July 2002. As of 2007, the situation in the DRC must be considered the most advanced case of the Criminal Court. Following a February 2006 Criminal Court's arrest warrant, the government of the DRC handed over Thomas Lubanga Dyilo, former President of the "Union des Patriotes Congolais" to The Hague. Lubanga Dyilo has been charged for conscripting and enlisting child soldiers and using them to participate actively in hostilities. In January 2007, Pre-Trial Chamber I of the Criminal Court confirmed reasonable grounds to proceed with a full trial expected to start in September 2007 (see *Elberling* 2007, 532ff.).

The situation in Uganda was referred to the Prosecutor as early as December 2003 with the Ugandan government referring exclusively the investigations of crimes committed by the Lord's Resistance Army (LRA). When, however, the Prosecutor officially opened investigations in June 2004, he made clear that his office would investigate both the responsibility of the LRA as well as the responsibility of the Ugandan government. Pre-Trial Chamber II of the Criminal Court has confirmed four arrest warrants thus far: LRA leader Joseph Kony, his deputy Vincent Otti, and the high-ranking LRA-commanders Okot Odhiambo and Dominic Ongwen. All of them are allegedly responsible for war crimes and crimes against humanity committed in Northern Uganda since mid 2002. They are still at large, and persisting public discussions about a general amnesty for members of the LRA who voluntarily surrender form a challenge to the goal of the Criminal Court to prosecute the criminally responsible in Uganda (see *Arsanjani/ Reisman* 2005, 392; *Akhavan* 2005, 403ff.).

The third situation, regarding the Northern-Sudanese region Darfur, is not only the first one referred to the Criminal Court by the Security Council, but is also expected to be the situation of greatest dimension. It is associated with high costs and, most importantly, with serious political obstacles. With regard to the ongoing conflict and the persistent refusal of the Sudanese government to accept jurisdiction of the Criminal Court in Darfur, it is very difficult for the Prosecutor to implement efficient investigations (see *Kaul* 2005, 380f.). In June 2005, the Prosecutor of the Criminal Court officially opened his Darfur investigations and has since then collected a great number of evidence and testimony; however, investigations have mostly been carried out in refugee camps outside of Sudan. Two arrest warrants were issued by Pre-Trial Chamber III in February 2007: Ahmand Mohmammed Harun, former prominent member of the Sudanese government, and Ali Kushayb, high-ranking leader of the Janjaweed militia in Darfur. Both suspects are charged with crimes against humanity as they are alleged to be involved in a series of attacks against the civilian population in West Darfur between August 2003 and March 2004. The Sudanese government, although obliged to cooperate under Security Council Resolution 1593, has refused to hand over any suspect to the Criminal Court (see *Chicon/ Bibas* 2007a, 42ff.).

In May 2007, the Office of the Prosecutor opened its fourth investigation in the Central African Republic, again following a self-referral of the government in December 2004. While up to this point little information on the progress of the Prosecutor's preliminary analysis of the situation had been given out to public, the Prosecutor has recently revealed that investigation in the Central African Republic will especially focus on the large-scale sexual crimes committed in the conflict between 2002 and 2003 (see *Chicon/Bibas* 2007b, 45ff.).

As four years of investigations have already gone by with few arrest warrants being issued and little progress being visible to the public, Luis Moreno Ocampo has been criticized for being too reluctant in his investigations and for being overly diplomatic in the fulfillment of his tasks (*Cassese* 2006, 434ff.). NGOs and concerned states have also criticized Ocampo for less than fully informing the public about progress made in the investigations of the OTP. Shortly after his appointment as Chief Prosecutor, Luis Moreno Ocampo publicly announced that his priorities were the strict recognition of the principle of complementarity as well as the support of national justice systems, declaring that a number of cases before the Criminal Court could very well be considered a success (see *ICC, OTP*, Policy Paper of September 2003; *Kaul* 2005, 374). He has also pointed out the need for careful and sequential investigations (see *Petit* 2007, 32ff., *Mattioli* 2007, 12ff.).

14. Perspectives

The establishment of the International Criminal Court in The Hague is a turning point in the history of lawmaking which is marked by centuries of combating impunity and lawlessness. With the adoption of the Rome Statute, which itself is an important source of international criminal law, the member states of the UN have made a significant step in the struggle for worldwide respect of human rights, international humanitarian law and the rule of law. A majority of the states has made clear that they are no longer willing to accept large-scale human rights violations and mass atrocities and wish to punish the perpetrators of these grave crimes. They have the duty to fully cooperate with the Criminal Court and implement legislation aiming at bringing perpetrators of international crimes to justice. It is also important to note that according to experts, states which are not yet parties to the Rome Statute also have a duty to prosecute or extradite suspected perpetrators of international crimes (*Bassiouni/Wise* 1995, 20ff.; Human Rights Watch Policy Paper, June 2005, 9).

Doubtlessly, the Criminal Court strengthens the worldwide capacity for the implementation of human rights and the prevention of international crimes.

Still, important steps remain to be taken. As long as the skeptical attitude towards the International Criminal Court of great powers like China, India, and the United States continues, it will struggle to become an efficient universal body of criminal justice. Only wide acceptance, a sound financial basis, including the allocation of adequate resources for the benefit of victims of crimes through budgetary appropriations in the Trust Fund for Victims, and the will of governments to cooperate effectively and comprehensively with this new institution of international law, will ensure its success. Concerning the bilateral non-surrender agreements signed and ratified, parliamentarians, NGOs, and other parts of civil society should make it very clear that impunity for political reasons is will not be tolerated, and that the agreements in question must be revised as a matter of priority.

Sabine von Schorlemer

Lit.: *Abass, A.:* The Competence of the Security Council to Terminate the Jurisdiction of the International Criminal Court, in: TILJ 40 (2005), 263-297; *Akhavan, P.:* The International Criminal Tribunal for Rwanda: The Politics and Pragmatics of Punishment, in: AJIL 90 (1996), 501-550; *Akhavan, P.:* The Lord's Resistance Army Case: Uganda's Submission of The First State Referral to the International Criminal Court, in: AJIL 99 (2005), 403ff; *Ambos, K.:* Establishing an International Criminal Court and International Criminal Code. Observations from an International Criminal Law Viewpoint, in: EJIL 7 (1996), 519-544; *Ambos, K.:* Internationales Strafrecht – Strafanwendungsrecht, Völkerstrafrecht, Europäisches Strafrecht, Munich 2006; *Ambos, K.:* „Verbrechenselemente" sowie Verfahrens- und Beweisregeln des IStGH, in: NJW 54 (2001), 404ff.; *Arsanjani, M.H./Reisman, M.W.:* The Law-in-Action of the International Criminal Court, in: AJIL 99 (2005), 385-403; *Association Internationale de droit pénal:* La justice pénale internationale. Perspectives, Historiques et Contemporaines, in: RIDP 67 (1996), 21-64; *Austin, K./Nell, S.:* Courting Justice in Rome. International Criminal Court Treaty Signed, in: Tribune des droits humains 5, No. 4 (September 1998), 6-9; *Bassiouni, C.M./ Wise, E.M.:* Aut Dedere Aut Judicare: The

Duty to Extradite or Prosecute in International Law, Dordrecht 1995; *Berg, B.:* The 1994 I.L.C. Draft Statute for an International Criminal Court: A Principled Appraisal of Jurisdictional Structure, in: Case Western Reserve Journal of International Law 28 (1996), 221-264; *Cassese, A.:* Is the ICC still facing teething problems?, in: JICJ 4 (2006), 434-441; *Cassese, A.:* The Statute of the International Criminal Court: Some Preliminary Reflections, in: EJIL 10 (1999), 144-171; *Cerone, J.P.:* Dynamic Equilibrium: The Evolution of US Attitudes toward International Criminal Courts and Tribunals, in: EJIL 18 (2007), 277-315; *Chicon, E./Bibas, B.:* ICC at Darfur's doorstep, in: ICC in 2006: Year one, International Justice Tribune, Paris 2007, 42-47 (quoted as: Chicon/Bibas 2007a); *Chicon, E./Bibas, B.:* ICC Makes no Move on the Côte d'Ivoire case, in: Year one, International Justice Tribune, Paris 2007, 52-57 (quoted as: Chicon/Bibas 2007b); *Crook, J.R. (ed.):* Contemporary Practises of the United States Relating to International Law: United States Abstains on Security Council Resolution Authorizing Referral of Darfur Atrocities to International Criminal Court, in: AJIL 99 (2005), 691-693; *Dörmann, K.:* with contributions by Louise Doswald-Beck; Robert Kolb: Elements of War Crimes under the Rome Statute of the International Criminal Court, Cambridge 2002); *Elberling, B.:* The Work of the International Criminal Court in 2006, in: GYIL 49 (2007), 529-548; *Ferencz, B.:* An International Criminal Court, 2 Vols., New York 1980; *Fife, R.E.:* The International Criminal Court, in: NJIL 69 (2000), 63-85; *Fischer, H./Kress C./Lüder, S.R. (eds.):* International and National Prosecution of Crimes under International Law. Current Developments, Berlin 2001; *Gaeta, P.:* The Defence of Superior Orders: The Statute of the International Criminal Court versus Customary International Law, in: EJIL 10 (1999), 172-191; *Gaeta, P.:* Is the Practise of "Self-Referrals" a Sound Start for the ICC?, in: JICJ 2 (2004), 949-952; *Geiß, R.:* The Work of the International Criminal Court in 2005, in: GYIL 48 (2006), 473-487; *German Red Cross/Human Rights Watch/United Nations Association of Germany/Amnesty International:* The International Criminal Court at Work: Challenges and Successes in the Fight against Impunity, Conference Report, Berlin, 21-22 September 2007, www.icc-berlin 2007.de/Conference_Report_31.10.07.pdf; *Graefrath, B.:* Universal Criminal Jurisdiction and an International Criminal Court, in: EJIL 1 (1990), 67-88; *Haase, J./Müller, E./ Schneider, P. (eds.):*

Humanitäres Völkerrecht – Politische, rechtliche und strafgerichtliche Dimensionen, Baden-Baden 2001; *Hall, C.K.:* The Powers and Role of the Prosecutor of the International Criminal Court in the Global Fight Against Impunity, in: LJIL 17 (2004), 121-139; *Höpfel, F./Schweiger, R.:* Der Internationale Strafgerichtshof: erste Schritte, in: Jahrbuch Menschenrechte – Freiheit in Gefahr, Strategien für die Menschenrechte (2006), 218-226; *Human Rights Watch:* Policy Paper: The Meaning of 'the Interest of Justice' in Article 53 of the Rome Statute, June 2005; *Hunt, D.:* The ICC – high hopes, "creative ambiguity" and an unfortunate mistrust in international judges, in: JICJ 2 (2004), 56-70; *International Criminal Court ICC - Office of the Prosecutor:* Paper on Some Policy Issues Before the Office of the Prosecutor, The Hague September 2003, www.icc-cpi.int/library/organs/otp/030905_Policy_Paper.pdf; *International Criminal Court ICC:* Ninth Diplomatic Briefing of the International Criminal Court. Information Package, The Hague, 29 March 2007, www.icc-cpi.int/library/about/ICC_DB9_IP_En.pdf; *International Law Commission:* Question of International Criminal Jurisdiction. Summary, 30 June 2005, http://untreaty.org/ilc/summaries/7_2.htm; *Irmscher, T.H.:* Das Römische Statut für einen Internationalen Strafgerichtshof, in: Kritische Justiz 31 (1998), 472-485; *Jain, N.:* A Separate Law for Peacekeepers: The Clash between Security Council and the International Criminal Court, in: EJIL 16 (2005), 239-354; *Jarasch, F.:* Einrichtung, Organisation und Finanzierung des Internationalen Strafgerichtshofes und die Schlußbestimmungen des Statuts, in: HuV-I 12 (1999), 10-22; *Kaul, H.-P.:* Durchbruch in Rom, Der Vertrag über den Internationalen Strafgerichtshof, in: VN 46 (1998), 125-130; *Kaul, H.-P.:* Der Aufbau des Internationalen Strafgerichtshofes. Schwierigkeiten und Fortschritte; in: VN 49 (2001), 215-222; *Kaul, H.-P.:* Preconditions to the Exercise of Jurisdiction, in: Cassese, A./Gaeta, P./Jones, J. RWD (eds.): The Rome Statute of the International Criminal Court. A Commentary, Oxford 2002, 583-616; *Kaul, H.-P.:* Construction Site for More Justice: The International Criminal Court after two years, in: AJIL 99 (2005), 370-384; *Lee, R.S. (ed.):* The International Criminal Court. The Making of the Rome Statute – Issues, Negotiations, Results, The Hague et. al. 1999; *Lee, R.S. (ed.):* The International Criminal Court. Elements of Crimes and Rules of Procedure and Evidence, New York 2001; *Leigh, M.:* The United States and the

Statute of Rome, in: AJIL 95 (2001), 124-131; *Mattioli, G.:* ICC Prosecutor's First Darfur Case: Some Tough Challenges Ahead, in: The Monitor 34 (2007), 12-14; *Murphy, S.D. (ed.):* Contemporary Practises of the United States Relating to International: Efforts to Obtain Immunity from ICC for U.S. Peacekeepers, in: AJIL 96 (2002), 725-729; *Murphy, S.D. (ed.):* Contemporary Practices of the United States Relating to International Law: U.S. Bilateral Agreements Relating to the ICC, in: AJIL 97 (2003), 200-203; *Murphy, S.D. (ed.):* Contemporary Practises of the United States Relating to International Law: U.S. Efforts to Secure Immunity from ICC for U.S. Nationals, in: AJIL 97 (2003), 710-711; *Murphy, S.D. (ed.):* Contemporary Practices of the United States Relating to International Law: United States Stresses Importance of Accountability, Seeks Lessened Confrontation over the International Criminal Court, in: AJIL 100 (2006), 477-478; *Nanda, V.P.:* The Establishment of a Permanent International Criminal Court: Challenges Ahead, in: HRQ 20 (1998), 413-428; *O'Donhue, J.:* Towards a Fully Functional International Criminal Court: The Adoption of the 2004 Budget of the International Criminal Court, in: LJIL 17 (2005), 579-597; *O'Donohue, J.:* The 2005 Budget of the International Criminal Court: Contingency, Insufficient Funding in Key Areas and the Recurring Question of the Independence of the Prosecutor, in: LJIL 18 (2006), 591-603; *O'Donovan, M.:* Criminalizing War: Toward a Justifiable Crime of Aggression, in: Boston College International & Comparative Law Review 30 (2007), 507-530; *Ooyen, R.C. van :* Auf dem Weg zu einer wirksamen internationalen Strafgerichtsbarkeit: eine Zwischenbilanz, in: IPG 3 (1998), 333-338; *Petit, F.:* Minimalist Investigation in Lubanga's case, in: ICC in 2006: Year one, International Justice Tribune, Paris 2007, 32-36; *Politi, M.:* Elements of Crime, in: Casssese, A./Gaeta, P.et al. (eds.): The Rome Statute of the International Criminal Court. A Commentary, Oxford/New York 2002, 443-473; *Rao, R.S.:* Financing of the Court, Assembly of States Parties and the Preparatory Commission, in: The International Criminal Court. The Making of the Rome Statute – Issues, Negotiations, Results, The Hague et. al. 1999, 399-420; *Reichart, M.:* Die Bemühungen der Vereinten Nationen zur Schaffung eines „Weltstrafgesetzbuches", in: ZRP 29 (1996), 134-137; *Reisman, M.:* The Definition of Aggression and the ICC, in: ASIL Proceedings 2002, 181-192; *Roggemann, H.:* Auf dem Weg zum Ständi-

gen Internationalen Strafgerichtshof, in: ZRP 29 (1996), 388-394; *Rudolf, B.:* Völkerrechtskommission: 48. Tagung – Kodex der Verbrechen gegen die Menschlichkeit abgeschlossen, in: VN 44 (1996), 225-227; *Scheffer, D.J.:* The United States and the International Criminal Court, in: AJIL 93 (1999), 12-22; *Schlunck, A.:* Die Umsetzung des Statuts des Internationalen Strafgerichtshofes in das deutsche Recht unter Berücksichtigung der Rechtshilfe, in: HuV-I 12 (1999), 27-32; *Schweiger, R.:* Der Beitrag des Internationalen Strafgerichtshofes zur Stärkung nationaler Institutionen – Überlegungen anhand der ersten Ermittlungen in Afrika, in: Wiener Zeitschrift für kritische Afrikastudien 9 (2005), 67-87; *Schorlemer, S. von:* Internationales Strafrecht: Theorie und Praxis des humanitären Völkerrechts, in: Ballestrem, K. Graf (ed.): Internationale Gerechtigkeit, Opladen 2001, 193-215; *Shraga, D./Zacklin. R.:* The International Criminal Tribunal for Rwanda, in: EJIL 7 (1996), 501-518; *Sluiter, G.:* Appendix II: An International Criminal Court is Hereby Established, in: Neth. QHR 16 (1998), 413-420; *Stein, T.:* Die Bilaterale Immunity Agreements der USA und Art. 98 des Rom-Statuts, in: Bröhmer, J./Bieber, R./Calliess, C. et al. (eds.): FS Georg Ress, Köln 2005, 155-171; *Szasz, P.C./Ingadottir, T.:* The UN and the ICC: The Immunity of the UN and its Officials, in: LJIL 14 (2001), 867-885; *Theissen, G./ Nagler, M. (eds.):* Der Internationale Strafgerichtshof. Fünf Jahre nach Rom, 27.-28. Juni 2003, Tagungsdokumentation, Berlin, Deutsches Institut für Menschenrechte 2004; *Tomuschat, C.:* Das Statut von Rom für den Internationalen Strafgerichtshof, in: FW 73 (1998), 335-347; *Tomuschat, C.:* Ein Internationaler Strafgerichtshof als Element einer Weltfriedensordnung, in: EA 48 (1994), 61-70; *Tomuschat, C.:* A System of International Criminal Prosecution is Taking Shape, in: International Commission of Jurists. The Review, No. 50 (1993), 56-70; *Wedgwood, R.:* The International Criminal Court: An American View, in: EJIL 10 (1999), 93-107; *Zimmermann, A.:* Die Schaffung eines Ständigen Internationalen Strafgerichtshofes, in: ZaöRV 58 (1998), 47-108; *Zimmermann, A.:* „Acting under Chapter VII (...)" – Resolution 1442 and possible limits of the powers of the Security Council, in: Frowein, J. A. et al (eds.): Verhandeln für den Frieden/ Negotiating for Peace – Liber Amicorum Tono Eitel, Berlin 2003, 253ff.; *Zimmermann, A.:* Der internationale Strafgerichtshof und die Vereinigten Staaten, in: Theissen, G./Nagler, M. (eds.): Der Internationale Strafgerichtshof –

Fünf Jahre nach Rom, 27.-28. Juni 2003, Berlin, Tagungsdokumentation, Deutsches Institut für Menschenrechte, Berlin (2004), 32-37; *Zimmermann, A./Scheel, H.:* Zwischen Konfrontation und Kooperation. Die Vereinigten Staaten und der Internationale Strafgerichtshof, in: VN 50 (2002), 137-144.

Internet: Homepage of the ICC: www.icc-cpi.int.

ICJ – International Court of Justice

I. Introduction

The *International Court of Justice (ICJ)* is one of the few permanent international courts and certainly the most important one. It is the successor of the first permanent international court on a universal level, namely the *Permanent Court of International Justice (PCIJ)* which had been instituted 1920 in the context, but not as an organ, of the → League of Nations.

The PCIJ constituted the first realization of the idea of a World Court, which was conceived to exercise jurisdiction in all kinds of legal disputes between all states. The Council of the League of Nations had been charged in Article 14 of the Covenant of the League of Nations to elaborate proposals for the establishment of such a court. The project was based on the concept that the jurisdiction of the court should be dependent upon the voluntary submission of the states in conflict, after the effort to reach an obligatory jurisdiction had failed. The Protocol of Signature, to which the Statute of the Court was annexed, was opened for ratification and signature on 16 December 1920 and entered into force on 2 September 1921.

The Court thereby established was not an organ of the Organization of the League of Nations, it was, however, in several respects linked to its organs, i.e. with regard to the election of the judges and the expenses of the Court. Although the obligatory jurisdiction could not be realized, the PCIJ constituted nevertheless significant progress as compared to the heretofore existing jurisdiction, which was arbitration, in that it was for the first time provided that the states could submit, before a dispute had arisen, to the jurisdiction for any future dispute (Art. 36 (2) ICJ Statute). Thereby a kind of optional obligation could be established which could come close to a true obligatory jurisdiction if largely accepted by the states. This expectation was however, to be disappointed.

The innovation realized with the establishment of the PCIJ was the fact that the court was a permanent institution with a proper statute and pre-established rules of procedure, not open to changes by the parties to a case; that it provided for public hearings and a pre-established bench of judges representing the principal legal systems of the world; furthermore, that the court was open to all states and that the applicable law was defined in the ICJ Statute; a Registry was instituted in order to assure the communication with the governments and the parties to a case. From its inauguration in 1922 until the termination of its activities in 1940, the PCIJ dealt with 29 contentious cases and rendered 27 advisory opinions.

Already in 1942 and since, projects for the re-establishment or, the creation anew of an international court of justice had been proposed. Contrary to the structure of 1920, the court to be established now was conceived as one of the principal organs of the new world organization. The *Statute of the International Court of Justice* (Text: UNCIO Vol. XV, 355) was finally adopted together with the United Nations Charter during the Conference of San Francisco on 26 June 1945 (→ History of the Foundation of the UN) and the Court was established as the principal judicial organ of the United Nations.

The Charter of the UN underlines explicitly that the PCIJ is to be regarded as the predecessor of the ICJ (Art. 92 UN Charter), even if legally there does exist discontinuity between the two courts. Nevertheless, factual continuity of the two World Courts with regard to its functions and jurisdiction is ensured on the one hand by the nearly unchanged taking over of the Statute of the PCIJ for the ICJ, and on the other hand by the fact that the jurisdiction of the PCIJ under treaties still in force between parties to the new Statute are now referred to the ICJ (Art. 37 ICJ Statute). The same holds true for declarations made under the optional clause of the PCIJ Statute which remain in force for the ICJ (Art. 35 (5) ICJ Statute). The continuous validity of declarations of submission to the jurisdiction of the PCIJ played an important role with regard to the question of the jurisdiction of the ICJ in the significant case brought by Nicaragua against the United States of America (ICJ Reports 1984, 392ff.), which was concerned with the question whether military or paramilitary actions of the United States in the form of assistance given to the underground movement of the contras in order to reach the overthrow of the Sandinista Government and the re-establishment of a democratic regime were legal under international law.

The legal bases for the activity of the ICJ are laid down in the Charter of the UN (Art. 7, Arts. 92 to 96), in the Statute of the ICJ and in the Rules of Procedure. The ICJ is one of the six principal organs (→ Principal Organs, Subsidiary Organs, Treaty Bodies) of the United Nations. Its seat is at The Hague, The Netherlands. As an independent court of justice the ICJ has a special position as compared to the other organs of the UN, in that it is not integrated into the hierarchical structure of the other five principal organs of the UN. The Statute of the ICJ forms an integral part of the UN Charter with the consequence that all member states of the UN are automatically also parties to the ICJ Statute. Under special conditions, a state that is not a member of the UN may appear before the Court and become a party to the ICJ Statute. In fact, only one state, Switzerland, is a party to the Statute without being a member of the UN (→ Membership and Representation of States).

The ICJ has a twofold function: on the one hand the settlement of disputes between states on the basis of international law, and on the other, the delivery of advisory opinions on legal questions at the request of specifically authorized international organs, in particular the → General Assembly and the → Security Council of the UN (Art. 96 UN Charter).

II. Organization

The ICJ consists of 15 judges, five of which are elected every three years for a term of 9 years. The judges may be re-elected. To simplify the matter somewhat, the rather complicated electoral system (Arts. 3-15 ICJ Statute) requires essentially, that the candidates obtain the absolute majority of votes in the Security Council and in the General Assembly, who vote in separate meetings. If, after the third ballot, seats remain vacant, a special procedure involving a "joint conference" consisting of six members, three appointed by the General Assembly and three by the Security Council, may be applied at the request of either the General Assembly or the Security Council. If this procedure also proves unsuccessful, the judges already elected select the judges to fill the vacant seats from among the candidates who obtained votes in the previous ballots (Art. 12 ICJ Statute). No two of the judges may be nationals of the same state (Art. 3 (1) ICJ Statute) and collectively the bench is to represent "the main forms of civilization and of the principal legal systems of the world" (Art. 9 ICJ Statute). In order to comply with this provision the bench included during the last years in general four judges from Western European states, one from the United States of America, two from Latin America, two from Eastern European states and six from Africa and Asia. The five permanent members of the Security Council are always represented in the ICJ by a judge of their nationality. Judges of the ICJ must not only be of a high moral character but must also possess the qualifications required in their respective countries for the appointment to the highest judicial offices, or be jurisconsults of recognized competence in international law (Art. 2 ICJ Statute). In the exercise of their office, the judges are independent of their governments.

In the case of a state which is a party to a contentious procedure before the ICJ and does not have a judge of its nationality on the bench, it may appoint a judge *ad hoc* to sit in the case (Art. 31 ICJ Statute). The institution of the *ad hoc* judge is a relic of the composition of arbitral tribunals and is aimed at reassuring the states that their position will be explained to the court. Nevertheless, it may be asked whether the institution of the *ad hoc* judge should be retained before an independent international court of justice.

As a rule, the Court's functions are exercised by the full court; a quorum of nine judges being required for taking a decision. However, there are some exceptions to this rule. The Court may also sit in chambers. The Statute provides for three kinds of chambers (Arts. 26 to 29 of the ICJ Statute), namely a chamber for summary procedure and chambers for particular categories of cases, as i.e. the chamber for Environmental Matters established in 1993. Furthermore, the parties to a case may form an *ad hoc* chamber (Art. 26 (2) ICJ Statute), determining themselves the number of judges to sit in the chamber. While the first two categories of chambers have never been utilized, *ad hoc* chambers have met positive acceptance by the states in particular for the reason that the involvement of the parties in the formation of such chambers has not been restricted to the determination of the number of the judges composing the chamber, but has, in fact, included the concrete composition of the chamber. This practice raises not only concern with regard to the terms of Article 26 (2) of the Statute, but also with regard to the fact that decisions of a chamber are regarded as decisions of the court (Art. 27 ICJ Statute). Due to the determination of the members of a chamber by the parties it is, however, possible that the judges of the ICJ form the minority in a chamber, as was the case with the intervention of Nicaragua in the Land, Island and Maritime Frontier Dispute between El Sal-

vador and Honduras (ICJ Reports 1990, 92ff.). In this case, the chamber was composed of five judges, two *ad hoc* judges, that is no permanent judges of the ICJ, and three judges from the bench of the ICJ. Moreover the official term of one of the three judges had meanwhile expired. Thus, only two judges actually in office in the ICJ were involved in the decision of the chamber which, according to the principle of majority decision, could theoretically be overruled, so that "a decision of the Court" in the sense of Article 27 of the Statute could have been taken without the support of any acting judge of the ICJ. In the case at hand this fortunately did not happen. Therefore, while there are some problems with regard to *ad hoc* chambers, it must be emphasized that the cooperation of the parties in the composition of the chambers has enhanced the confidence of states in the settlement of disputes (→ Peaceful Settlement of Disputes) through the ICJ, and has become a preferred means for the settlement of disputes.

III. Competence of the Court in Contentious Cases

Only states may be parties in contentious cases before the Court (Art. 34 ICJ Statute). This provision is criticized today as numerous fields of public international law concern individuals, organizations, groups and other legal entities than states, which have to bring their disputes thus either before national courts *or other international courts or tribunals*.

The ICJ is only competent to settle *legal disputes* as defined in Article 36 (2) of the ICJ Statute. In order to prevent the settlement of a concrete case through the ICJ states, therefore, have often objected that the character of the concrete dispute was not a *legal* one, but a political one, as i.e. in the Tehran Hostages Case (ICJ Reports 1980, 3ff.), in the Nicaragua Case (ICJ Reports 1986, 14ff.), in the Nuclear Test Cases between Australia and France and New Zealand and France (ICJ Reports 1974, 253ff. and 457ff.), in the Aegean Sea

Continental Shelf Case (ICJ Reports 1978, 3ff.). However, the jurisdiction of the ICJ in this respect is consistent in holding that an overall political dispute also contains legal elements which may be decided upon by the ICJ. The same holds true if the Security Council, the political organ of the UN, and the ICJ deal simultaneously with a dispute: in such situations the ICJ is not prevented from deciding the case because it is only concerned with the legal aspects of the matter.

The competence of the Court to settle a dispute depends on the consent of the states. The fact that all member states to the UN Charter are automatically also parties to the Statute does not as such constitute a basis for the competence of the ICJ. Although the participants of the San Francisco Conference in 1945 would have preferred to bestow the judicial organ of the UN with obligatory jurisdiction, this idea could not be realized. Therefore no state can become a party in proceedings before the ICJ without its explicit consent; this is the so-called *principle of consent*. Therefore, the question whether the ICJ is competent to hear a concrete case or not, constitutes the central and most often controversial question in proceedings before the Court.

The consent can be expressed in different ways: it may be given in advance, that is to say independently of the existence of a concrete dispute, or *ad hoc*, when a dispute already exists. There are two alternative methods to submit in advance to the jurisdiction of the Court:

a) According to Article 36 (1) ICJ Statute, "the jurisdiction of the Court comprises ... all matters specially provided for in the Charter of the United Nations or in treaties or conventions in force". The latter terms refer to clauses in general dispute settlement treaties or in bi- or multilateral treaties containing a clause according to which disputes arising out of the interpretation or application of the treaty may be brought before the ICJ. There are approximately 300 treaties containing such a provision; they are listed in the *Yearbook of the*

ICJ. The first alternative in Article 36 (1) ICJ Statute referring to matters specially provided for in the UN Charter is, however, not very clear. According to Article 36 (3) of the UN Charter the Security Council should, in making recommendations for the settlement of disputes, also take into consideration, "that legal disputes should as a general rule be referred by the parties to the International Court of Justice". The question of what is the effect of a recommendation of the Security Council to submit a dispute to the ICJ, was at issue in the Corfu Channel Case (ICJ Reports 1947/48, 15ff.), but has not been answered in that case. It seems, however, that such a decision of the Security Council is not mandatory because Article 36 (3) of the Charter uses the term "recommendation". The explanation is to be found in the fact that the formulation in Article 36 (1) ICJ Statute goes back to a proposal dating from a time when the jurisdiction of the Court was still supposed to be obligatory: since this aim could not be realized these terms are of no significance today.

b) The second possibility to submit in advance to the jurisdiction of the Court, is provided for in Article 36 (2) ICJ Statute, and is known as the *optional clause*. According to this provision, the "States Parties to the present Statute may at any time declare that they recognize as compulsory *ipso facto* and without special agreement, in relation to any other State accepting the same obligation, the jurisdiction of the Court in all legal disputes concerning: a) the interpretation of a treaty; b) any question of international law; c) the existence of any fact which, if established, would constitute a breach of an international obligation; d) the nature or extent of the reparation to be made for the breach of an international obligation". Paragraph 3 of the same article provides: "The declaration referred to above may be made unconditionally or on condition of reciprocity on the part of several or certain States, or for a certain time". This clause is what remained from the originally intended obligatory jurisdiction, and the hope once prevailed that all states would make a declaration under this clause. However, the reality proved to be different: only one third of the member states of the UN have made a declaration under the optional clause (63 states as of 15 February 2002) and, out of these states, not even a dozen have made their declaration unconditionally.

The submission to the jurisdiction is compulsory only in relation to states accepting the same obligation: this constitutes the *principle of reciprocity*. If for example State A has made a declaration under Article 36 (2) ICJ Statute and State B has not, the ICJ is not competent to decide an application instituted by State A against State B. A further consequence of the principle of reciprocity resides in the fact that reservations made by one party to a case may also be invoked by the other party. If, accordingly, State A has made a declaration on condition and State B has made a declaration unconditionally, State B may oppose the reservations made by State A to the jurisdiction of the Court because the jurisdiction only covers the extent of the obligation as accepted by both parties. Therefore, the *reservations* are of considerable importance, especially because they are not restricted to the alternatives spelled out in Article 36 (3) of the Statute, but may extend to nearly all matters, since, to further the peaceful settlement of disputes, declarations under Article 36 (2) ICJ Statute made on condition are preferable to not making a declaration of submission at all. The reservations most frequently concern such matters as time limits, the existence of an agreement concerning other means of peaceful settlement of disputes, disputes arising from certain hostilities, disputes with regard to particular countries, i.e. the members of the Commonwealth of Nations, or states to which the submitting state has no diplomatic relations or disputes concerning particular subject-matters such as national defence, regional conflicts, → law of the sea and the like. A reservation which is particularly favored excludes the jurisdiction of the Court for matters

concerning the domestic jurisdiction as well as the one providing that the declaration may be terminated at any time with immediate effect. This latter reservation is, however, without relevance when a case is already pending before the Court. All these kinds of reservations are acceptable as long as it is the Court which can decide whether they are relevant in a particular case or not. However, there exist also reservations which leave it to the state concerned to decide whether they are of relevance in a particular case or not; such reservations are called "automatic reservations" or "escape clauses". The most famous example is the *"Connally Reservation"* first used by the United States of America, and according to which the United States excluded from the compulsory jurisdiction of the ICJ "disputes with regard to matters which are essentially within the domestic jurisdiction of the United States of America as determined by the United States of America" (US Declaration of 14 August 1946, 61 Stat. 1218 (1947), reprinted in: US Department of State Bulletin, Vol. 15, 1 September 1946, 452-453). Whether such an automatic reservation is admissible or whether it is null and whether the nullity of the reservation then extents to the whole declaration has not been clarified to date, but was addressed in several cases (*Norwegian Loans Case*, ICJ Reports 1957, 9ff., 43-66, *Interhandel Case*, ICJ Reports 1957, 105ff., *Fisheries Jurisdiction Case* (Canada v. Spain, ICJ Reports 1998, 432ff.) It is, however, evident that such a reservation is in contradiction to Article 36 (6) ICJ Statute according to which it is the Court which decides in the event of a dispute as to whether it has jurisdiction, the so-called competence-competence.

Besides the possibility to submit in advance to the jurisdiction of the ICJ, which clearly is most favorable to the peaceful settlement of disputes, states may also submit to the jurisdiction when a dispute has already arisen. If in these circumstances states are able to agree at all to submit the dispute to the ICJ, then this means of submission is the most likely to lead to the effective settlement of the dispute through the implementation of the judgment by the state concerned.

There are two possibilities to submit to the jurisdiction of the ICJ *ad hoc*:

a) The states concerned may conclude an agreement, the so-called *compromis*, in order to submit a particular dispute which has already arisen, to the ICJ (Art. 36 (1) ICJ Statute). The jurisdiction of the ICJ is thereby established exclusively for the settlement of the concrete dispute. This means of submission is increasingly used: for example all cases concerning matters of maritime delimitation have been brought before the Court in this way.

b) The jurisdiction of the Court can be accepted by means of *forum prorogatum*. In this alternative, a case is instituted before the Court against a state which has not made any prior act of submission, a fact known also to the applicant party. By instituting proceedings the defendant party has the possibility to give its consent to the jurisdiction by taking the necessary procedural steps. This kind of submission to the ICJ is not provided for in the Statute, but has been accepted by the PCIJ and the ICJ and is laid down in Article 38 (5) of the Rules of Court.

The indispensable condition of the consent to the jurisdiction of those states whose rights or obligations are at stake in a case before the Court, has in practice been the cause for one more problem. There were cases in which the decision on the dispute brought before the Court was not possible without deciding first on the rights or obligations of a third state not party to the case, as for example in the Monetary Gold Case of 1954, which had been brought before the Court by Italy against the Allied Powers. This case was concerned with the Albanian gold that had been removed by the German Armed Forces in 1943 from Rome to Berlin. Italy claimed property over the gold as compensation for the seizure of Italian assets in Albania, although an arbitral tribunal had decided that it belonged to Albania.

The question, however, whether the gold belonged to Italy or not, i.e. whether Albania had committed an internationally wrongful act by seizing Italian assets for which it owed compensation to Italy, could not be decided by the Court without the consent of Albania, because the legal questions at stake concerned acts committed by Albania which the Court was not authorized to deal with in the absence of the consent of Albania. Albania thus was an *indispensable party* to the settlement of the dispute; without its consent the Court had no jurisdiction to decide the case and therefore had to dismiss it. The same situation of an indispensable party led to the dismissal of the application of Portugal against Australia in the *East Timor Case* (ICJ Reports 1995, 90ff.). Portugal claimed in its application the unlawfulness under international public law of a treaty concluded in 1989 between Indonesia and Australia concerning the exploration and use of the continental shelf off the coasts of East Timor. East Timor was at that time still under Portuguese administration ($\rightarrow$ Trusteeship Council), although it had, after having been illegally invaded in 1975 by Indonesia, been annexed to the Indonesian state. Even though the legal recognition of this annexation was controversial, the ICJ found that it could not decide that question without the participation of Indonesia in the proceedings. This situation was not affected by the fact that the subject-matter of the case concerned the undisputed right of the people of East Timor to self-determination ($\rightarrow$ Self-Determination, Right of): the principle of consent to the Court's jurisdiction remains unaffected even if obligations *erga omnes* are at stake such as the right to self-determination. The question of the indispensable party will probably also play a central role in the case instituted before the Court by Liechtenstein against Germany on 1 June 2001.

IV. Proceedings before the Court

The proceedings before the Court are laid down in the ICJ Statute and the

Rules of Court as amended in 1978 (a further amendment being under consideration of the Court). The proceedings consist of a written and an oral part. The written proceedings consist of "the communication to the Court and to the parties of memorials, counter-memorials, and if necessary replies", together with papers and documents in support (Art. 43 (2) ICJ Statute). The oral proceedings, which are conducted in public, consist of the hearing by the Court of witnesses, experts, and advocates. They may include questions addressed by the judges to the parties. The official languages (→ Languages, Official) of the Court are French and English; each document and each communication is translated from one official language into the other. After the oral proceedings the Court deliberates in private and delivers its judgment in a public sitting. The judgment is final and without appeal (Art. 60 of the ICJ Statute) and has no binding force except between the parties to the case and in respect of that particular case (Art. 59 ICJ Statute).

In general, however, the defendant in a case will seek to impede the continuation of the proceedings. Thus, nearly in all cases that have not been instituted on the basis of an *ad hoc compromis,* preliminary objections are raised to the jurisdiction of the Court or to the admissibility of the application. Such *preliminary objections* have to be examined prior to the merits of the case, because in the event of the lack of the competence of the Court or the admissibility of the application the Court is not empowered to decide on the merits. However, in many instances it may be difficult to examine the preliminary objections without examining at the same time already the merits of the case. Therefore, an amendment of the Rules of Court of 1972 has provided for the possibility to join a preliminary objection to the merits if it does not possess an exclusively preliminary character. The reason for this amendment to the Rules of Court were the problems connected with the Southwest Africa/Namibia case brought before the ICJ, where the Court deliv-

ered, in all, two judgments and four advisory opinions (ICJ Reports 1950, 128ff.; 1955, 67ff.; 1956, 23ff.; 1962, 319ff.; 1966, 6ff.; 1971, 16ff.). In the context of preliminary objections it is interesting to note that here, in this case, the Court, by a judgment on the merits of 1966, repealed its judgment of 1962 in which it had dismissed all preliminary objections and had declared the application admissible. The preliminary objections concerned the application of Ethiopia and Liberia against South Africa for the breach of its obligations under the mandate over Southwest Africa/Namibia. In 1966, the Court decided by equality of votes with the casting vote of the President that the applicants had no standing, a question of a preliminary character which had already been examined in the 1962 judgment. This decision of the ICJ provoked a deep crisis of confidence in the Court from which the Court only slowly recovered.

Preliminary objections are regularly raised in cases instituted by unilateral application. The most recent important examples of these have been the following cases: Bosnia and Herzegovina against Yugoslavia, concerning the violation of the Convention on the Prevention and Punishment of the Crime of Genocide (ICJ Reports 1996, 595ff.); Nicaragua against the United States of America concerning military and paramilitary activities (ICJ Reports 1984, 392ff.); the Lockerbie Case (ICJ Reports 1998, 9ff. and 115ff.); the case brought by Iran against the United States of America concerning the aerial incident of July 3, 1988, (ICJ Reports 1996, 803ff.) as well as the case Nauru against Australia concerning certain phosphate lands in Nauru (ICJ Reports 1992, 240ff.). However, all of these, with only one exception, proved unsuccessful. In the latter two cases the findings of the Court in favor of its jurisdiction led to an amicable settlement of the case by the parties concerned. Only the preliminary objections raised in the case Spain against Canada concerning the seizure of the Spanish fishing vessel *Estai* by Canada because of the violation of a

Canadian law on the interdiction of fishing in a certain area was upheld by the Court. Since Canada's declaration under Article 36(2) ICJ Statute contained a reservation concerning all measures of Canada with regard to fishing in the Northwest Atlantic, the ICJ decided in its judgment of 4 December 1998, that with a view to this reservation it had no jurisdiction to decide the case (ICJ Reports 1998, 432ff.).

In order to impede the continuation of the proceedings states have repeatedly decided not to participate in the proceedings and/or not to appear before the Court. According to Article 53 ICJ Statute the *non-appearance* of one of the parties does not lead to the admission of the claims of the applicant. Also in this situation the ICJ has first of all to examine whether it has jurisdiction and whether the claim is well founded in fact and law, insofar as this is possible without the co-operation of one of the parties. As to the case Nicaragua against the United States of America the opinion is prevailing that the proceedings would have had a different result if the United States had participated. Thus, the non-appearing state bears the risk of a judgment delivered on the basis of incomplete evidence, which is an acceptable form of sanction for the failure to appear before the Court. The parties may, however, at any moment change their attitude and participate in the proceedings.

V. Incidental Proceedings

As in national proceedings, there are also in international jurisdiction a series of *incidental proceedings*, the most important of which are *provisional measures* for interim protection and the *intervention*.

1) Interim Protection

Provisional measures for interim protection may be indicated, according to Article 41 of the ICJ Statute, if the circumstances so require in order to preserve the respective rights of either party necessary for the effectiveness of the final judgment. In international ju-

risdiction the decision on provisional measures meets two significant problems. First of all is the question as to what degree the competence of the Court has to be examined, an examination which has to be made speedily with a view to the urgency of the circumstances. The case law of the Court is constant in that it requires merely that there is a provision which, *prima facie*, affords a basis for the Court's jurisdiction. Thus, it is sufficient, for example, that both parties have made a declaration under Article 36 (2) ICJ Statute; reservations which might be relevant need not be examined in this phase of the proceedings.

The second problem concerns the question of the *binding force of provisional measures*. The wording of Article 41 is rather imprecise, as it uses the term "indicate" (*indiquer* in French): "The Court shall have the power to indicate, if it considers that circumstances so require, any provisional measures which ought to be taken to preserve the respective rights of either party" (Art. 41 (1) ICJ Statute).

The differences of opinion concerning the question whether the aim of provisional measures, namely the preservation of the subject-matter of the final – and binding – judgment does require logically also the binding character of provisional measures, remained unsettled until the judgment of 27 June 2001 in the LaGrand case (Germany v. United States of America). This case concerned a violation of the 1963 Convention on Consular Relations in that two German citizens, the brothers Karl and Walter LaGrand, had not been granted the assistance of the German consul before American courts. The brothers LaGrand had been condemned to the death penalty and, after the execution of Karl LaGrand Germany sought to suspend the execution of Walter LaGrand until the decision on the merits by requesting interim protection. Although the Court adopted the measures requested, Walter LaGrand was executed as scheduled, because the United States were of the opinion that interim measures of protection are not binding. In its application Germany had asked the Court, *inter alia*, to decide upon the binding force of interim measures. In its decision the Court reached the conclusion that interim measures have binding effect (cf. ICJ Press Release 2001/16 of 27 June 2001). By this decision the Court terminated the more than 80 years old discussion on the effect of interim measures in a way consistent with the effectiveness of the exercise of its functions.

2) Intervention

The *intervention* in proceedings pending before the ICJ is always admissible in cases concerning the construction of an international convention; all parties to the convention concerned have a right to participate in the proceedings with the consequence that the interpretation given by the Court is equally binding upon them (Art. 63 of the ICJ Statute).

There is, however, another form of *intervention* which serves the preservation of legal interests of a third state which could be affected by the decision in the case (Art. 62 ICJ Statute). In the context of this category of intervention it has long been disputed whether a jurisdictional link between the intervenor and the parties to the case was required, or whether otherwise the parties to the case had to consent to the intervention. This question had not been addressed explicitly by the ICJ in the first two cases of intervention (Tunisia/Libya Continental Shelf Case, Reports 1981, 1ff. and Libya/Malta Continental Shelf Case, Reports 1984, 3ff.), although it seemed to be the true reason for the dismissal of the application which was, however, based on other reasons. It was, finally, an *ad hoc* chamber of the ICJ that, in 1990, took the decision that the existence of a jurisdictional link was not required for the granting of an application to intervene, because the Court would not give a decision on any claims of the intervenor. In order to preserve the legal interests of a third state, that state need not become a party to the proceedings, because no decision will be taken concerning those interests and only the decision on legal interests of the third state would require the consent of the intervenor to the jurisdiction of the Court as well as a jurisdictional link with the parties to the case. This jurisdiction was confirmed by the full Court in the Case Concerning the Land and Maritime Boundary between Cameroon and Nigeria with regard to the application by Equatorial Guinea for permission to intervene (ICJ Order of October 21, 1999).

VI. Judgments

According to Article 59 ICJ Statute the judgment of the Court has binding force only between the parties and is final and without appeal. It is, however, possible for any party to request the interpretation of the judgment by the Court in the event of questions concerning the meaning or scope of the judgment (Art. 60 of the ICJ Statute), or to bring an application for revision of the judgment if some fact of a decisive nature which was not known when the judgment was given is discovered (Art. 61 ICJ Statute). Judgments are taken by a majority of the judges present; in the event of equality of votes, the President has a casting vote. All judges may deliver a declaration or a separate or dissenting vote in order to give additional reasons in the case that they vote with the majority or to give the reasons for their dissent (Art. 57 ICJ Statute, Art. 95 (2) ICJ Rules of Court). The possibility to deliver separate votes is extensively used and often is of great value in order to fully understand the legal reasoning of the Court. Sometimes, however, it is misused for too extensive, not always case-related argumentation.

The enforcement of the judgment is in principle left to the state concerned. However, according to Article 94 (2) of the UN Charter the Security Council may be seized with the enforcement of a judgment if "any party to a case fails to perform the obligations incumbent upon it under the judgment rendered by the Court". The Security Council "may make recommendations or decide upon measures to be taken to give effect to the judgment". Binding measures under

Chapter VII of the UN Charter may, however, only be taken when the conditions for the application of Chapter VII are given. The problematic character of this means of enforcement became evident in the first case in which the Security Council was seized on the basis of Article 94 (2) UN Charter: the recourse of Nicaragua for enforcement of the judgment obtained against the United States of America (ICJ Reports 1986, 14ff.) failed because of the veto of the United States (→ Veto, Right of Veto). Nevertheless, in all the balance concerning the implementation of judgments is positive, even if the implementation is sometimes not an immediate one and only made in an "indirect" manner, as for example in the Nicaragua-USA case, where the United States finally implemented *de facto* the judgment through a programme of economic assistance in favor of Nicaragua, although the USA had declared explicitly that it did not recognize the judgment.

Since its creation the ICJ has considered 96 contentious cases and delivered 74 judgments (until 15 February 2002). At the time of writing (March 2002) 22 cases are on the list of the Court.

VII. Sources of Applicable Law

The ICJ must render its decisions in accordance with international law. The sources of international law are provided in Article 38 of the ICJ Statute, i.e. international conventions, international custom and general principles of law. As subsidiary means for the determination of the rule of law the Court may use "judicial decisions and the teachings of the most highly qualified publicists of the various nations".

The application of international conventions is the least problematic as these are written rules of law. With regard to the other two categories of international law, questions concerning the existence and the precise contents of the rule may arise which the Court has to resolve; a dismissal for the reason of non-existence of law is not admissible (*iura novit curia*). If the parties have so agreed, the ICJ may also decide *ex aequo et bono*, i.e., on the basis of equity. This has, however, never occurred so far in the history of the Court.

VIII. Advisory Opinions

Advisory opinions may not be requested by states, but only by the organs determined in Article 96 of the UN Charter, in particular the General Assembly and the Security Council as well as other organs and → specialized agencies of the UN which have been so authorized by the General Assembly; that is the case for 5 UN organs and 16 specialized agencies. The organs and special agencies so empowered may only request advisory opinions on legal questions arising within the scope of their activities, while the Security Council and the General Assembly may request advisory opinions on any legal question. In contrast to contentious cases it is left to the discretion of the Court whether it will entertain a request for an advisory opinion which, as such, fulfils the requirements of admissibility. Until now, however, the Court has not made use of this discretion. The procedure follows the one in contentious cases, with the difference that international organizations and states may present written or oral statements concerning the question submitted to the Court. Advisory opinions are not invested with legally binding force; agreements may, however, provide for the binding force of the opinion. A considerable number of questions submitted for advisory opinions have had significant influence on the development of international law, such as i.e. the question concerning the admission of a state to membership in the UN (ICJ Reports 1948, 57ff.); reparations for injuries suffered in service of the UN (ICJ Reports 1949, 174ff.); the territorial status of Namibia (ICJ Reports 1971, 16ff.); Western Sahara (ICJ Reports 1975, 12ff.) as well as recently the important advisory opinions concerning the use of nuclear weapons (ICJ Reports 1996, 66ff., request of the WHO; 1996, 226ff., request of the General Assembly).

As of June, 2001, the ICJ has delivered 24 advisory opinions. At time of writing, no requests are pending.

IX. Germany and the ICJ

The Federal Republic of Germany was admitted to the UN in 1973 and thereby became a party to the ICJ Statute. At that time, it had already on five occasions made use of the possibility to recognize the conditions laid down by the Security Council in order to grant access to the Court for non-members of the UN without being a party to the Statute (Art. 35 (2) of the ICJ Statute). Until now, the Federal Republic has been a party in five cases: in 1969 in the dispute with Denmark and the Netherlands concerning the delimitation of the North Sea continental shelf, 1974 in the fisheries jurisdiction cases against Iceland and 2001 in the LaGrand case between Germany and the United States of America concerning the Convention on Consular Relations. Two cases to which Germany is a party, are actually pending before the Court, namely the case brought before the Court by Liechtenstein against Germany concerning questions of expropriation and the case concerning the "Legality of Use of Force" brought by Yugoslavia against ten NATO states one of which is Germany. To date the Court has had two German judges on its bench: from 1975 to 1984 Hermann Mosler, and since 1994 until 2003 Carl August Fleischhauer.

X. Evaluation of the ICJ

The activity of the ICJ shows a positive development after the low mark caused by the Southwest Africa decisions in the sixties and seventies. In particular, states of the so-called "Third World", especially African states, which after the Southwest Africa cases were rather reluctant to approach the Court, now make increasing use of the Court. Since the states of the former Soviet bloc have also now changed their reservation vis-à-vis the Court, since the beginning of the nineties a significant increase of cases pending before the Court could be observed. As of 2001 (June), 24 cases

were on the docket, none of which was a request for an advisory opinion. With a view to revising the time-consuming procedures, the current workload has caused discussion on a simplification of the procedures. These have until now had only partial results, and are continuing.

An evaluation – which is necessarily subjective – of the activity of the Court indicates however, that the ICJ enjoys increasing acceptance, and that in particular the formerly clearly evident "Western" dominated character of the bench and of the parties is diminishing. Furthermore, it has become evident that to go to the ICJ represents, in particular for weaker states, a promising possibility to enforce their rights against powerful states, as is demonstrated , for example, by the case Nicaragua against the United States of America, as well as in the cases brought by Iran against the United States. Although the states parties to a case do not bear the costs of the procedure – the salary of the judges is paid by the UN budget (→ Budget) – they have nevertheless to bear the expenses for their council, which are generally not negligible for poorer states. In order to empower also financially weaker states to approach the Court, the UN → Secretary-General has instituted in 1989 a "Trust Fund" to support those countries. As the contributions to the Fund are voluntary it may be doubted whether the Fund will really provide meaningful assistance, especially in view of the reluctant attitude concerning the payment of the annual assessed contributions of certain member states.

It is, however, not only the number of pending cases which is relevant to appreciate the activity of the Court, because the Court is not the only organ or means for the peaceful settlement of disputes and particular disputes may even preferably be settled by other means. Furthermore, the Court's scope of activity is determined, on the basis of the principle of consent, by the legal questions as formulated in the disputes referred to it; the ICJ is not empowered to raise and resolve legal questions *ex officio*. In the context of the Lockerbie case a highly contentious question arose, namely whether the ICJ has the power to examine the legality of resolutions of the Security Council (→ Resolution, Declaration, Decision) and thus to act like a constitutional court in respect of the rules of the Charter. Even though the ICJ was not instituted as an organ to review the respect of the Charter provisions by other organs, and even though any organ of the UN has the power to interpret the functions accorded to it by the Charter on its own, the Court is undoubtedly not impeded from a review of a resolution of the Security Council which may be incidental to a case, if this is deemed necessary to decide the dispute. Due to the very large discretion accorded to the Security Council the Court could, however, only in the – nearly unimaginable – situation in which the Security Council had neglected norms of *ius cogens,* find in favor of the illegality of a resolution. A finding in this respect would, however, only have binding force between the parties to the case; the ICJ could not declare the resolution null, but any state would be thereby enabled to object such finding of the ICJ to obligations resulting from that resolution.

The role of the ICJ in the context of the maintenance of peace is not easy to evaluate, because it may only be speculated as to whether an existing declaration of submission or the existing jurisprudence of the Court, may have an influence on the attitude of states in controversies. Nevertheless, there are cases in which the prospect that the dispute would be settled by the Court induced the parties to an amicable settlement of their dispute, for example in the dispute between Finland and Denmark concerning the Passage through the Great Belt (ICJ Reports 1991, 12) where it became obvious through the Court's decision on provisional measures, that the legal situation of Denmark was not as promising as had been anticipated. Following the decision in favor of the jurisdiction of the Court, Nauru and Australia also agreed on an amicable settlement concerning their dispute on certain phosphate lands (ICJ Reports 1992, 240ff.); finally, Iran and the United States reached an amicable settlement of the dispute originating from the shooting down of an Iranian Airbus with 290 people on board during the first Gulf War.

In these cases the certainty that the Court would decide the case had a positive effect, in the sense that the states concerned reached by themselves a peaceful settlement of their dispute. It must, however, be noted that these disputes were not among those highly sensitive disputes threatening the international peace. In such cases submission to the jurisdiction of the Court seems rather unrealistic; moreover other organs, in particular the Security Council, are here often more competent to act. With regard to such disputes the ICJ may at most play a role as one link in a chain of several activities aiming at the maintenance of peace if the states concerned have accepted the jurisdiction of the Court. Due to the lack of comprehensive obligatory competence, the ICJ constitutes only one element in the co-operation of several organs serving the maintenance or restoration of peace, however one whose significance is increasing by the far-reaching acceptance of its jurisdiction and its jurisprudence.

To what degree the Court may play a role in the *prevention of conflicts* is even more difficult to evaluate, because here we are confronted with activities taken even before a dispute has arisen, so that the mere possibility of a subsequent engagement of the Court would have to be regarded as influencing the attitude of the parties to the conflict. On the other hand, it may be stated with good reasons that the failure to invest the ICJ with obligatory jurisdiction is of little importance for the function of dispute settlement, because the delivery of a judgment on a dispute does not guarantee the settlement of the dispute. As a mechanism for effectively enforcing judgments does not exist in international law, the implementation of a judgment is, to a rather large extent, left to the states which are the more prepared to implement a judgment, if they indeed desired that the dispute be settled judicially. This is, however, not necessarily the case under an obligatory jurisdiction or under a declaration of submission according to the optional clause, but is more promising in cases of *ad hoc* submission.

Therefore, it is in the first place necessary to convince states to accept judicial settlement of disputes. That there is a close relationship between the already existing experiences, i.e. with the Court's jurisprudence, and the readiness to use the Court for future disputes, is evident. The experience with the activity of the ICJ since the eighties marks a promising step forward; acceptance of the Court has never been as widespread as today.

Karin Oellers-Frahm

Lit.: *1. Publications of the ICJ* (all in English and French): Reports of Judgments, Advisory Opinions and Orders; Pleadings, Oral Arguments, Documents; Yearbook (General information concerning the Court, docket, overview over the jurisprudence, list of declarations made under Art. 36 (2) of the ICJ Statute and of treaties providing for the jurisdiction of the Court); Bibliography; *ICJ (ed.):* The International Court of Justice, (booklet prepared by the ICJ, 172 p., available in several languages);
2. Secondary Literature: Bala, C.: International Court of Justice; its functioning and settlement of international disputes, New Delhi 1997; *Bowett, D.W.:* The International Court of Justice: process, practice and procedure, London 1997; *Damrosch, L.F. (ed.):* The International Court at a Crossroads, New York 1987; *Elias, T.O.:* United Nations Charter and the World Court, Lagos 1989; *Eyffinger, A.:* The International Court of Justice 1946-1996, The Hague et al. 1997; *Guyomar, G.:* Commentaire du règlement de la Cour internationale de Justice, Paris 1983; *Mosler, H.:* Chapter XIV, The International Court of Justice, in: Simma, B. (ed.): The Charter of the United Nations. A Commentary, Munich/Oxford 1994; *Muller, A.S. (ed.):* The International Court of Justice, The Hague et al. 1997; *Rosenne, S.:* The World Court: What it is and how it works, 5th rev. edn., Dordrecht 1995; *Rosenne, S.:* The Law and Practice of the International Court, 1920-1996, The Hague et al. 1997, 4 vols.; *Schlochauer, H.-J./Oellers-Frahm, K.:* The

International Court of Justice, in: Bernhardt, R. (ed.): EPIL., Vol. II, Amsterdam 1995, 1084-1107, with detailed bibliographical indications and a list of cases;
3. Repertories concerning the jurisdiction of the ICJ (and the PCIJ): Hambro, E.: The Case law of the International Court of Justice, 8 vols., comprising the case law from 1923 to 1974, Leiden; *Max-Planck-Institute for Comparative Public Law and International Law:* World Court Digest, Vol. I, 1986-1990; Vol. 2, 1991-1995, Berlin/Heidelberg et al. 1993 and 1997; *Max-Planck-Institute for Comparative Public Law and International Law:* Fontes Iuris Gentium, Series A, Section I, Berlin/Heidelberg/New York, Vol. 5, 1947-1958 (1961), Vol. 6, 1959-1975 (1978), Vol. 7, 1976-1985 (1990); *Oduntan, G.:* The law and practice of the International Court of Justice (1945-1996) Enugu/Nigeria 1999; *Stern B.:* 20 ans de jurisprudence de la Cour internationale de Justice, 1975-1995, The Hague et al. 1998; *Ziccardi-Capaldo, G.:* Repertory of the Decisions of the International Court of Justice, 1947-1992, Dordrecht et. al. 1995.

Addendum

Any updating concerning the International Court of Justice (ICJ) since the beginning of the new century will necessarily relate primarily to its activity which mirrors its acceptance in the international community. This is due to the fact that the Court's jurisdiction is based on consent. Developments or changes in its organization are somewhat unrealistic because the Statute of the ICJ is an integral part of the UN Charter and thus faces the same rather insurmountable hurdles as a revision of the Charter (→ Charter of the UN). Therefore, this addendum will concentrate on developments with regard to the acceptance of the ICJ's jurisdiction *ratione personae*, aspects of procedure because amendments of the Rules and working methods of the Court are admissible as long as they keep within the framework of the Statute, as well as the most relevant aspects of its case law.

Before doing so, it should be mentioned briefly that for the third time a German judge is sitting on the bench: in 2003 Bruno Simma was elected to fill the seat of Carl August Fleischhauer. His term of office ends in February 2012.

1. Jurisdiction

In the context of jurisdiction under Article 36 (1) and (2) of the Statute, developments with regard to declarations accepting the Court's jurisdiction under the optional clause (Art. 36 (2) of the Statute) are of primary importance. This clause was conceived of as a way to introduce (optional) compulsory jurisdiction on the international level (supra III b), so that any increase or decrease of declarations reflects the acceptability of international jurisdiction in the state community. In this regard no remarkable development has taken place. Out of the 192 member states of the UN 65 have made a declaration under Article 36 (2), most of them providing for reservations. However, the number of states accepting the compulsory jurisdiction without reservations is at least slightly increasing. At the beginning of 2008 nineteen states had made a declaration under Article 36 (2) of the Statute without substantial reservations (homepage of the ICJ: www.icj-cij.org), that marks clearly a development in the right direction.

One of the most remarkable developments concerns the decision of the German Government to finally make a declaration under Article 36 (2) ICJ Statute, a declaration that at the time of accession to the UN in 1973 did not seem advisable for several reasons, in particular the special situation of Germany as a divided state. On the basis of a proposal elaborated by a study group of the "Deutsche Gesellschaft für Völkerrecht (German Society of International Law)" in 2007 the text of which is published in "Zeitschrift für ausländisches öffentliches Recht und Völkerrecht" 67 (2007), 825-842, the Government declared on 30 April 2008 its acceptance of the jurisdiction of the ICJ under Article 36 (2) of the Statute. However, Germany does not belong to those few states that accept the Court's jurisdiction without any reservation (text of the German declaration available at UN Treaty Collection (http://treaties.un.org), link: "Status of Treaties", link: "Chapter I", link: "4.").

Germany's declaration contains three temporal reservations concerning: (a) the possibility of withdrawal of the declaration with effect from the moment of notification to the UN Secretary-General making the usual limitation of the declaration for five or ten years redundant; (b) Germany accepts the jurisdiction of the ICJ only with regard to "situations or facts subsequent to" the date of the declaration that excludes disputes concerning the Second World War; (c) the declaration relates only to disputes with states having accepted the Court's jurisdiction at least twelve months prior to the bringing of a dispute before the Court. This reservation is aimed at excluding "surprise" applications by states submitting to the ICJ in order to bring a particular claim, as, for example, was the case for Yugoslavia with regard to its applications in the Kosovo context. A second reservation concerns disputes for "which the Parties thereto have agreed or shall agree to have recourse to some other method of peaceful settlement or which is subject to another method of peaceful settlement chosen by the Parties". This reservation also includes, according to its terms, means of dispute settlement not leading to a judicial – binding – decision, which might be regrettable. At the same time, this kind of reservation serves to avoid a possible collision between dispute settlement mechanisms which raises increasing problems in international law. The most important and controversial reservation, however, concerns the so-called "double armed forces reservation" which excludes from the Court's jurisdiction any dispute which: (a) "relates to, arises from or is connected with the deployment of armed forces abroad, involvement in such deployments or decisions thereon", and (b) "relates to, arises from or is connected with the use for military purposes of the territory of the Federal Republic of Germany, including its airspace, as well as maritime areas subject to German sovereign rights and jurisdiction". According to these reservations disputes concerning the use of German airspace, airports or marine ports by *foreign* states would be excluded from the Court's jurisdiction as well as any dispute relating, in other words, to the involvement of German armed forces in Afghanistan, Iraq or elsewhere. These reservations were somewhat controversial because questions of the use of force, according to one opinion, would best be settled by the ICJ, as a series of recent cases demonstrates. The majority – political – view, on the contrary, referred to the ongoing development of international law on this issue and therefore considered it inappropriate to submit such disputes to the ICJ. Germany is the nineteenth member state of the EU that has made a declaration under Article 36 (2) ICJ Statute which, it is to be hoped, will serve as an example for other states to follow.

2. Procedure

The increase in the case load of the Court beginning with the 1980s led the Court to take measures to improve its working methods and to accelerate proceedings. In 2001, the Court adopted for the first time *"Practice Directions"* which contain instructions to the parties aiming at improving the work of the Court. Meanwhile the Court has adopted more than a dozen of such directions which concern the exchange and content of written pleadings, the production of new documents, time limits with regard to preliminary objections, temporal restrictions on the involvement of the same person as judge *ad hoc* in one case and agent or counsel in another pending case, as well as the involvement in cases before the Court of persons who until recently were part of the Bench or higher officials of the Court. These *Practice Directions* which are reviewed at regular intervals allow the Court to streamline the proceedings through making timely answers to new challenges.

3. Case Law

The number of cases pending before the Court has remained high. Contentious cases come from all over the world reflecting the Court's world-wide acceptance. The litigating states comprise increasingly also parties from the Balkans, the Middle East, Africa, the Far East, Latin America, Asia and the Indian Sub-Continent thus reflecting the role of the Court as "a world court" (cf. list of cases www.icj-cij.org). Most recently, a case has been brought against Russia, which, as its predecessor, the Soviet Union, has never before been a party before the ICJ (cf. *Application of the International Convention on the Elimination of all Forms of Racial Discrimination* (Georgia v. Russian Federation), application of 12 August 2008.) Also the subject matters of the cases are extremely varied. While the attraction of the Court to settle disputes concerning land and maritime boundaries has been maintained, and also other "classic" disputes such as the treatment of nationals by other states continued to reach the Court [cases in this context involve Arabian and African states (Qatar v. Bahrain; Cameroon v. Nigeria; Benin/Niger, Republic of Guinea v. Democratic Republic of Congo) and Latin American states (Nicaragua v. Honduras; Nicaragua v. Colombia; Peru v. Chile; Costa Rica v. Nicaragua; Argentina v. Uruguay), but also Eastern states (Romania v. Ukraine) and Asian states (Indonesia/Malaysia; Malaysia/ Singapore), a first case concerning exclusively environmental questions has been brought by Ecuador against Colombia (*Case concerning Aerial Herbicide Spraying*). More and more significant cases concerning true "cutting-edge" issues were increasingly brought before the Court. Thus, the Court had the opportunity to express again its view on questions of the use of force and self-defence, Article 51 of the UN Charter, some 20 years after the *Nicaragua* case.

These questions came before the Court at the same time in several contentious cases, namely *Armed Activities*

389

on the Territory of the Congo (Democratic Republic of the Congo v. Uganda), *Armed Activities on the Territory of the Congo* (Democratic Republic of the Congo v. Rwanda), *Case Concerning Oil Platforms* (Islamic Republic of Iran v. United States of America) and *Legality of Use of Force* (Serbia and Montenegro v. Belgium and seven other NATO States) and one advisory opinion *(Legal Consequences of the Construction of a Wall in the Occupied Palestinian Territory)*. These conflicts had also been addressed by Security Council resolutions under Chapter VII. One of the main issues in these cases concerned the question whether the right of self-defence under Article 51 UN Charter can also be invoked against armed attacks from non-state actors or only in the case of an attack of one state against another. While the Security Council had interpreted Article 51 UN Charter after September 11, 2001 in the sense that also non-state attacks can trigger the right to self-defence, the ICJ firmly held its view first expressed in the *Nicaragua* case, that the right of self-defence can only be exercised against armed attacks of one state against another.

For the first time the ICJ had to decide on allegations of massive human rights violations, including genocide. In the *Case Concerning Application of the Convention on the Prevention and Punishment of the Crime of Genocide* (Bosnia and Herzegovina v. Serbia and Montenegro) which had its origin in the armed conflict in the Former Yugoslavia, the Court, in its judgment of February 2007 (International Court of Justice, 26 February 2007, General List No. 91, www.icj-cij.org/docket/files/91/13685. pdf), clarified first that genocide can also be committed by a state, not only by individuals, and second elaborated on the special intent required for the crime of genocide. It finally found that genocide had occurred in 1995 in the town of Srebrenica, but that there was no convincing evidence that the acts committed by the army of the Republika Srpska could be attributed to Serbia and Montenegro under the rules of international state responsibility. However, the Court found that Serbia and Montenegro had violated its obligation to prevent the genocide.

In this case, the Court was furthermore called to make a statement for the first time in detail on questions of revision of a judgment under Article 61 of its Statute. The application involved highly complicated questions concerning the membership of Yugoslavia, Serbia and Montenegro in the UN after the dissolution of the Former Yugoslavia. According to Article 61 the existence of a new fact unknown to the Court and the party claiming revision at the time when the judgment was given can open the way for revision if this fact were decisive for the decision. The new fact invoked by Yugoslavia was its accession to the UN in 2000. As, however, the "new fact" must have already existed when the judgment was given, in this case the judgment on jurisdiction of 1996, the Court dismissed the application for revision as inadmissible.

Two further cases have also briefly to be mentioned, namely *Certain Criminal Proceedings in France* (Republic of the Congo v. France) which is still pending and which relates to questions of universal jurisdiction, a topic that has gained currency in the context of the armed conflicts that occurred not only on the European continent at the end of the last century, but also and on an even greater scale in Africa. This case like those concerning use of force and self-defence offer the Court the opportunity to contribute to the clarification of current issues of general relevance. The second case, *Certain Questions of Mutual Assistance in Criminal Matters* (Djibouti v. France) was decided on June 4, 2008. It is particularly interesting because for the first time a Respondent, France, accepted the Court's jurisdiction under the rules of *forum prorogatum*, which means after the application has been brought for the particular case (supra III.b.). This led the Court to explain in greater detail the extent and implications of *forum prorogatum*. As the case concerned a number of judicial proceedings in France and in Djibouti the Court interpreted the Conventions in force between the two parties governing mutual assistance in criminal matters.

Two other recently brought cases are also worth mentioning, namely the case Georgia v. Russian Federation, which for the first time makes Russia a party before the ICJ. The case concerns grave violations of human rights occurring since the dissolution of the Soviet Union and relating in particular to the situation in South Ossetia and Abkhazia, and the Russian military invasion of Georgia in this context on 8 August 2008. As basis of jurisdiction Georgia refers to Article 22 of the Convention on the Elimination of all Forms of Racial Discrimination. The urgent request for the indication of provisional measures brought a week after the application had already been pleaded orally. The main questions to be decided by the Court in its order on the request concern the question whether *prima facie* Article 22 of the Convention offers a basis of jurisdiction and whether the dispute falls at all under the Convention. The other case concerns the request for interpretation of the Avena judgment of 2004 by which the ICJ obliged the United States "to review and reconsider convictions and sentences against Mexican nationals delivered without informing them of their right to consular assistance under the 1963 Vienna Convention on Consular Relations." By its request Mexico seeks clarification of whether the judgment imposed on the United States an obligation of result, namely review or reconsideration of the cases, which was denied by state courts due to their conviction that the single states of the United States, as opposed to the Federation, are not bound by ICJ judgments.

Finally, it has to be reported that the two cases to which Germany was a party have been decided meanwhile. The case brought by Serbia and Montenegro against eight NATO states including Germany has been dismissed for lack of jurisdiction. The other case, Liechtenstein v. Germany, concerning questions of expropriation during World War II was also dismissed according to Germany's argument that the basis of jurisdiction invoked did not cover this dispute *ratione temporis*.

In conclusion, it can be stated that the ICJ, the principal judicial organ of the UN, continues to play a very significant role in international dispute settlement. The fact that, meanwhile, also cases of a highly sensitive character such as the use of force and massive human rights violations are brought before the Court underlines its acceptance in the state community. Under this aspect it remains regrettable that only one of the permanent members of the Security Council, namely the United Kingdom, has made a declaration, although with some reservations, under the optional clause. In this context the acceptance of the Court's jurisdiction by Germany may constitute an example to be followed by others.

Karin Oellers-Frahm

Lit.: *Amr, M.S.M.:* The Role of the International Court of Justice as the Principal Judicial Organ of the United Nations, The Hague 2003; *Ajaghoub, M.M.:* The advisory function of the International Court of Justice 1946-2005, Berlin 2006; *Apostolidis, C. (ed.):* Les arrêts de la Cour Internationale de Justice, Dijon, 2005; *Azar, A.:* L'exécution des decisions de la Cour Internationale de Justice, Bruxelles 2003; *Bedi, S.R.S.:* The development of human rights law by the judges of the International Court of Justice, Oxford 2007; *Eisemann, P.M./Pazartzis,P (eds.):* La jurisprudence de la Cour internationale de Justice, Paris, 2008; *Guillaume, G.:* La Cour Internationale de Justice à l'aube du XXIème siècle, Paris 2003; *Kaufmann, I.:* Wiederaufnahme von Verfahren vor dem Internationalen Gerichtshof, Baden-Baden 2005; *Manouvel, M.:* Les opinions séparées à la Cour Internationale de Justice, Paris 2005; *Papa, M. I.:* I rapporti tra la Corte Internazionale di Giustizia e il Consiglio di Sicurezza, Padova, 2006; *Rosenne, S.:* Provisional Measures in International Law. The International Court of Justice and the International Tribunal for the Law of the Sea, Oxford 2005; *Rosenne, S.:* The Law and Practice of the International Court of Justice, 1920-2005, vols. I-IV, Leiden 2006; *Rosenne, S.:* Interpretation, Revision and

Other Recourse from International Judgments and Awards, Leiden 2007; *Scherer, S.:* Das Konsensprinzip in der internationalen Gerichtsbarkeit, Frankfurt (Main) 2003; *Schulte, C.:* Compliance with Decisions of the International Court of Justice, Oxford 2004; *Simma, B. (ed.):* The Charter of the United Nations. A Commentary, 2 vols., 2nd edn., Oxford 2002; *Spiermann, O.:* International Legal Argument in the Permanent Court of International Justice, Cambridge 2005; *Zimmermann, A./Tomuschat, C./Oellers-Frahm, K. (eds.):* The Statute of the International Court of Justice. A Commentary, Oxford 2006.

Internet: Homepage of the ICJ: www.icj-cij.org.

ILC – International Law Commission

Art. 13 (1) (a) of the UN Charter (→ Charter of the UN) authorizes the → General Assembly to initiate studies and make recommendations for the purpose, *inter alia*, of "encouraging the progressive development of international law and its codification". The General Assembly was thus assigned the role of a motor for the development of international law (→ International Law and the UN) (*Tomuschat* 1991). In fulfilment of this obligation, the General Assembly established with Resolution A/RES/174 (II) of 21 November 1947 a subsidiary organ, the International Law Commission (ILC), whose statute – in its original version – is included in the annex of the founding resolution. The ILC convened for its first session in 1948.

The above-mentioned mandate of the General Assembly for the development of international law has thus been taken over by the ILC in its Statute (UN Doc. A/CN.4/4/Rev.2 (1982)). It is further defined in Art. 15 of the Statute: while *"codification"* is understood as a "more precise formulation and systematization of rules of international law" in fields where there already has been extensive and consolidated state practice, jurisprudence and academic teaching, the term *"progressive development"* implies the "preparation of draft conventions on subjects, which have not yet been regulated by international law or in regard to which the law has not yet been sufficiently developed in the practice of States." (Art. 15 ILC Statute) The ILC Statute attaches to this distinction certain procedural consequences, which, however, remain irrelevant in practice, since the Commission recognized at a very early stage, that a "mechanical" codification of hitherto existing international customary law and of general principles of law through written formulation, is not practicable. Indeed the process of identification of such unwritten law requires creative complementing of legal norms. However, the work of the ILC is not limited to this "restatement" function of codification. It also aims at the consolidation of hitherto unwritten international law by adapting its content to the changing needs of today's increasingly universalized community of states, i.e. the progressive development of international law. Therefore, the ILC generally avoids in its reports statements as to which of the two above mentioned methods it has used in particular, although most of its areas of work and the corresponding results can be attributed – at least in their tendency – to the one or the other function, codification or progressive development of international law.

Originally the ILC consisted of 15 members. This number was increased in several steps to currently 34 – above all in order to assure an adequate representation of Third World countries. This is in accordance with the rules of the ILC Statute, according to which the Commission as a whole should guarantee the representation of the "main forms of civilization and of the principal legal systems of the world" (Art. 8). The current geographical key for the distribution of seats (cf. GA resolution A/RES/36/39 of 18 November 1981) attributes to the → regional groups in the UN the following number of representatives: Western Europe and others: 8; Africa: 8 or 9: Asia: 7 or 8; Latin America 6 or 7; Eastern Europe: 3 or 4. Candidacies of *members* of the ILC are proposed to the General Assembly by the member states. They are elected by the Assembly for a five-year term and are eligible for re-election. They should be generally acknowledged experts of international law. Although the statute remains silent on the status of the members, the members of the Commission do not exercise their duties within the ILC as representatives of their countries of origin but as independent experts, i.e. they are not subject to instructions from their governments. Neither do they work as UN employees.

The Commission meets every year in Geneva for a period of around three months, more recently divided into two sessions.

The subjects which are discussed at the ILC are mostly chosen in agreement between the ILC and the General Assembly (Sixth Committee). Once the initial choice has been made, a working group normally takes over the issue and sets guidelines for the further proceedings. Thereafter, the ILC appoints one of its members as a *Special Rapporteur* who is assigned the most important task, which is to *report* to the plenary (as a rule every year) on his analysis of the topic. At a certain stage of "maturity", these reports will contain *draft articles*. These are discussed in the plenary, to be subsequently handed over to a *drafting committee*. This body is to frame the proposals of the rapporteur in the light of the opinions expressed in the plenary debate and then to present a revised text. This revised text will then again be discussed in the plenary. Finally, the *draft* is voted on in the ILC at first reading.

After every session, the results of the ILC's work are reported to the Sixth Committee of the General Assembly (→ Committees, System of) for examination and UN member states are asked to comment on the draft. In this way, since the Commission documents its work in detail in its annual reports, the member states are given already at an early stage the opportunity to observe the development of the drafts, and to accompany them with critical comments. Unfortunately they generally make insufficient use of this opportunity, which is regret-

table, for only intensive feedback from the governments can ensure that the Commission's drafts will later gain acceptance by a representative group of states. Taking the comments received into consideration, the ILC further deliberates upon the drafts before finally voting on them in a second reading and forwarding it again to the General Assembly.

The decision on the further fate of the Commission's products then lies in the hands of the General Assembly. It can organize a diplomatic conference which will then elaborate a convention on the basis of the ILC draft and which – in case it is successful – might adopt the final text of a convention and open it for signature. Alternatively, the General Assembly can adopt a draft convention by its own decision. Another possibility would be its adoption as a "soft law" text. In exceptional cases, ILC drafts have only been taken note of by the General Assembly.

The procedure thus described is very complicated and extremely tedious. Normally it takes years, and sometimes even decades, from the choice of a subject and the appointment of a special rapporteur until the adoption of draft articles. This is due to factors such as changes of special rapporteurs, the concentration of the ILC work on other issues and the hesitant reaction of states during the intermediate phases of a project. However, whenever the Commission has been requested by the General Assembly to accelerate its procedure, it has always fulfilled this demand and has presented a draft within a short timeframe, as for example its draft of the Statute of an International Criminal Court (→ ICC). Furthermore, the work of the ILC often influences the practice of states and international jurisprudence (particularly that of the International Court of Justice, → ICJ) already before its formal conclusion. Thus it continuously contributes to the development of customary international law.

In 1998 the ILC celebrated its 50th anniversary. In retrospect, the Commission has undoubtedly been more successful in the first half of its existence than it has been in the second. Successful projects of that first period include the drafts of four Geneva Conventions on the Law of the Sea in 1958 (→ Law of the Sea), as well as the Vienna Conventions on Diplomatic and Consular Relations (1961 resp. 1963). The former law of the sea conventions were later replaced by the UN Convention on the Law of the Sea of 1982 (UN Doc. A/CONF.62/122 and Corr.), in the elaboration of which the ILC has not taken part, while the Vienna Conventions on Diplomatic and Consular Relations have gained universal acceptance. In 1966 the Commission adopted draft articles on the law of treaties, which led up to the *Vienna Convention on the Law of Treaties* of 1969 (UNTS Vol. 1155, No. 18232, 331). Despite the fact that this convention has only half of the UN member states as contracting parties, it can be considered as a generally accepted statement of international law on the subject (→ Treaties, Law of). In 1986, the Convention was complemented by the *Vienna Convention on the Law of Treaties between States and International Organizations or between International Organizations* (UN Doc. A/CONF.129/15), which is not yet in force.

Other drafts of the Commission have also been adopted in the form of conventions, but they have either found only a small number of contracting states or they have not yet entered into force. To this group of conventions belong the *Convention on Special Missions* of 1969 (UNTS Vol. 1400, No. 23431, 231), the *Convention on the Representation of States in their Relations with International Organizations of a Universal Character* of 1975 (UN Doc. A/CONF.67/16), the *Convention on the Succession of States in Respect of Treaties* (1978) (UNTS Vol. 1946, No. 33356, 3), the *Convention on Succession of States in Respect of State Property, Archives* and *Debts* (1983) (UN Doc. A/CONF.117/14), the *Convention of the Non-navigational Uses of International Watercourses* (1997), and, most recently, the *UN Convention on Jurisdictional Immunities of States and their Property* (2004).

In other instances, as already mentioned above, the General Assembly gave the work of the ILC the form of a (General Assembly) declaration, as, for instance, on questions of nationality in relation to the succession of states (2000), on prevention of transboundary harm (2001), and the compensation of damages arising therefrom (2006).

Concerning the Commission's draft articles on State responsibility (on which *infra*), the General Assembly took note of them in resolution A/RES/56/83 of 12 December 2001 and commended them to the attention of states "without prejudice to the question of their future adoption or other appropriate action".

A very special case is the impressive Report of a Study Group of the Commission on the topic of "Fragmentation of International Law: Difficulties Arising from the Diversification and Expansion of International Law" finalized in 2006, which constitutes a sort of juridical tool-box for coping with these challenges (UN Doc. A/CN.4/L.682).

One explanation for successes or failures of the Commission's work may lie in the fact that with regard to the subject matters treated in the first group, there already existed to a large extent a consolidated, politically accepted, "cooled-off", body of customary law, which corresponded to a mutuality of interests of the states. It was precisely this element – consideration for the interests of all groups of states concerned – which was lacking in the case of the three last-mentioned conventions of the second group. Moreover, in respect of some issues, the ILC had to face difficulties or was even excluded from the codification process, because in these cases the existing international law was or is going through a phase of significant transformation. This applies particularly to the law of the sea in its development since the 1960s, whose reformulation was from the very beginning entrusted to a diplomatic conference. More recently, this was also the case for the issue of state immunity (before national courts), for which the Commission presented a draft in 1991, and which has been on hold in the Sixth Committee ever since.

The current *working program* of the ILC includes the following topics:
- responsibility of international organizations,
- reservations to treaties,
- shared natural resources (oil and gas),
- effects of armed conflict on treaties,
- expulsion of aliens,
- obligation to extradite or prosecute,
- immunity of State officials from foreign criminal jurisdiction, and
- protection of persons in the event of disasters.

For several important areas of international law (e.g. protection of human rights ($\rightarrow$ Human Rights, Protection of), international environmental law ($\rightarrow$ Environmental Law, International), international economic law ($\rightarrow$ Trade, International Law of), special, separate institutions are assigned with the formulation of rules, that is, in areas in which certain political as well as "technical" obstacles are considered to stand in the way of treatment by the ILC, the Commission somehow being a body composed of "generalists". Many observers see in the increasing specialization of international law and in its growing $\rightarrow$ regionalization, both promoting the development of international law regimes considering themselves as more or less autonomous, a challenge for the continued existence of universal international law. Hence, in addition to dealing with topical issues of the day, the ILC will have to pay more and more attention to the preservation and consolidation of the general international legal basis of international relations.

Bruno Simma

Lit.: 1. The most important documentary source of the work of the ILC is the Year-book of the International Law Commission, which comprises two volumes, the second of which is divided into two parts. Volume I contains the Summary Records of the ILC sessions; volume II/part I contains the documents relevant for the respective sessions,

particularly the reports of the Special Rapporteurs, while part II contains the Annual Report of the ILC to the General Assembly (which is already published in advance as Supplement No. 10 to the General Assembly Official Records in time for the discussion of the ILC work in the Sixth Committee of the General Assembly); *2. Further UN-Publications: United Nations:* The Work of the International Law Commission, 7th edn., New York 2009; *United Nations:* International Law on the Eve of the Twenty-first Century: Views from the International Law Commission, New York 1997; *United Nations:* Analytical Guide to the Work of the International Law Commission 1949-1997, New York 1998; *United Nations:* Making Better International Law: The International Law Commission at 50, New York 1998; *3. Secondary Literature: Sinclair, J.:* The International Law Commission, Cambridge 1987; *Tomuschat, C.:* Die Völkerrechtskommission der Vereinten Nationen, in: VN 36 (1988), 180-186; *Tomuschat, C.:* ILC – International Law Commission, in: Wolfrum, R: (ed.): United Nations: Law, Policies and Practice, Vol. 1, Munich/Dordrecht 1995, 705-713; *Fleischhauer, C.A.:* Commentary to Art. 13, in: Simma, B. (ed.): The Charter of the United Nations. A Commentary, 2nd edn., Vol. I, Oxford 2002, 298-317; *Vallat, F.:* International Law Commission, in: Bernhardt, R. (ed.): EPIL Vol. II (1995), 1208-1216; *Watts, A.:* The International Law Commission 1949-1998, 3 vols., Oxford 1999.

Internet: Homepage of the ILC: www.un.org/law/ilc/index.htm (information on membership, sessions, programme of work, ILC statute, conventions and draft conventions, commission reports and other documentation).

ILO – International Labour Organization

The International Labour Organization (ILO) was founded in 1919 together with the $\rightarrow$ League of Nations in the framework of the post-World War I peace negotiations. After the end of the Second World War and the dissolution of the League of Nations, ILO concluded an agreement with the United Nations in accordance with Article 57 and Article 63 of the UN Charter ($\rightarrow$ Charter of the UN) and thus became the first specialized agency of the United Nations (→ Specialized Agencies) in 1946.

Purposes and Activities

ILO was designed as a means to safeguard fair international competition and to prevent "social dumping" by maintaining minimum labor standards in the workplace on an international legal basis. It is to facilitate social achievements and improvements of working conditions, by introducing them on the basis of reciprocity. It is built upon the conviction, expressed in the ILO Constitution, that "universal and lasting peace can be established only if it is based upon social justice". The 26th General Conference of ILO, convened in Philadelphia to adjust ILO to the post-World War II era, expanded the Organization's goals and included among them the respect for → human rights, the fight against unemployment, distributive justice and social security. According to its mission statement, "the ILO is dedicated to bringing decent work and livelihoods, job-related security and better living standards to the people of both poor and rich countries. It helps to attain those goals by promoting rights at work, encouraging opportunities for decent employment, enhancing social protection and strengthening dialogue on work-related issues".

Throughout its history, ILO's main activity has been regulatory (→ International Law and the UN): conventions and recommendations should, according to the ideas of its founding fathers, form an International Labour Code. While recommendations offer a non-binding framework for national legislation, conventions are legally binding on all member states which have ratified them. The states parties have to report annually on the implementation of the treaty obligations within the framework of an ILO monitoring procedure. In addition to these reports, procedures of representation (by any workers' or employers' organization) and complaint (by governments or International Labour Conference delegates), as set forth in the

ILO Constitution, are meant to guarantee compliance with ILO conventions. However, these procedures do not provide for sanctions in case of continued non-compliance. Their central effect – as often in human rights mechanisms under international law – is thought to be the negative publicity involved in the proceedings of ad hoc committees (to examine representations) and commissions of inquiry (established to investigate complaints), creating pressure to force the reluctant state to abide by its obligations under international law.

ILO has adopted a number of important conventions concerning issues such as the prohibition of forced labour (1930), freedom of association (1948), equal payment (1951), non-discrimination (1958), and prohibition of the worst forms of child labor (1999). Originally, the primary objective of ILO's legislation was to guarantee safe working conditions. More general questions of social security were soon added to the spectrum of the Organization's fields of concern: ILO adopted, for example, conventions on social security – the Social Security (Minimum Standards) Convention 1959 (ILO Convention No. 102) – and on the rights of indigenous peoples – the Indigenous and Tribal Peoples Convention 1989 (ILO Convention No. 169).

To date, a total of 189 conventions have been adopted, while some have been revoked. A number of the ILO conventions can be considered international customary law, and have thus gained universal applicability.

In the course of → decolonization during the 50s and 60s of the 20th century, an operative accent complemented the older normative focus. *Technical cooperation* with developing countries became an important activity of the ILO, in which it cooperates with other subdivisions of the → UN system, most particularly the United Nations Development Programme → UNDP in carrying out projects of development aid, aiming for example at the setting up of occupational health and safety departments, social security systems or worker education programmes.

Since its foundation, ILO has dealt with women worker's rights, among others by adopting a number of conventions and recommendations with regard to women's rights and their protection, pursuing two objectives: the first is the protection of the role and maternal function of women, and the second the promotion of equality of opportunity and treatment for women, in accordance with changing needs of industrial societies (cf. *Gaudier* 1996). To co-ordinate its activities with regard to *gender equality*, ILO works out specific action plans, the most recent being the "ILO Action Plan for Gender Equality 2008/2009" (*ILO* 2008a). A Bureau for Gender Equality supports staff members in ILO headquarters and in the field on matters concerned with gender equality in the world of work and manages a knowledge base on gender issues (cf. www.ilo.org/gender/index.htm). In the understanding of ILO, gender equality refers to equal rights, responsibilities and opportunities that all persons should enjoy, regardless of whether they are men or women.

Research, information and documentation form another major task of the Organization, performed mostly by the *International Labour Office* and by two largely independent educational institutes which originated from ILO: the *International Institute for Labour Studies* (based in Geneva, Switzerland), and the *International Training Centre* (located in Turin, Italy).

Structures

The preeminent and unique feature of ILO's structure is "tripartism". Member state delegations do not consist of government representatives only, but include delegates of employee and employer associations. A 2:1:1 ratio, however, ensures that government representatives cannot be outvoted.

The *International Labour Conference (ILC)*, also called *General Conference*, is the Organization's supreme body. Delegations from all member states (at present 182) discuss and approve *International Labour Standards*, as well as changes in the ILO Constitution, adopt working programmes and elect the members of the Governing Body.

In its structural position, the *Governing Body* is as unique as the principle of tripartism. Its responsibilities include control over the *International Labour Office* and election of its Director-General, adoption of the agenda of the International Labour Conference, and discussion of representations and complaints. The Governing Body is composed of 56 members: 28 government, 14 trade union and 14 employer representatives. The ten member states of major economic importance appoint 10 of the 28 government representatives, i.e. these countries have non-elective, permanent seats in the Governing Body.

The *International Labour Office* is the Organization's secretariat and performs the classical tasks of administration and informational services. Additionally, it engages in research and documentation efforts. The International Labour Office is headed by a Director-General (since 1999: Juan Somavía, Chile).

Member state contributions are the basis of the ILO *budget*. Their respective share is determined according to the United Nations scales of assessment ($\rightarrow$ Budget). The biennial budget for 2008/20009 is 641.7 million US dollars. Most of the operative expenses, particularly for projects of technical assistance, however, are financed by other institutions and organizations of the $\rightarrow$ UN system.

Resources

Conventions and ratifications are accessible on the ILO website. The text of conventions and lists of countries ratifying them are available on the website through the ILOLEX database: www.ilo.org/ilolex/english/convdisp1.htm.

The text of ILO Recommendations is also available at: www.ilo.org/ilolex/english/recdisp1.htm. In print, conventions and recommendations appear in the Record of Proceedings of the Session of the International Labour Conference at which they were adopted and in Series A of the Official Bulletin for the year of their adoption. Every year ILO publishes an annual list of the ratifications of ILO Conventions of the current year.

ILO publishes in regular intervals the "World Employment Report" and the "Global Employment Trends" (cf. *ILO* 2004 and *ILO* 2008b).

Assessment

ILO is unique among the specialized agencies of the UN system. Involving the social partners, the principle of tripartism embodies an institutionalized dialogue among governments, trade unions and employers' organizations on an international level. However, the roles of employers' and employees' organizations are widely divergent among member states. For example, in many states, free trade unions do not exist, so that tripartism, in these cases, is not much more than a sham. Nonetheless, the principle has basically had a positive effect on international regulation and codification efforts in the realm of international labor standards.

ILO can be considered the "social conscience" of the UN system. However, it only has a minor role to play when compared to the much more important (and influential) economic components of the wider system of international institutions, i.e. the Bretton Woods institutions World Bank (→ World Bank, World Bank Group) and International Monetary Fund (→ IMF). Despite that fact, ILO has been pivotal in the development of international human rights standards (→ Human Rights; → Human Rights, Protection of), for example in implementation and control mechanisms. These have originally been developed under the auspices of ILO and have then been adopted by other UN agencies. In appreciation of its merits, ILO was awarded the Nobel Peace Prize in 1969.

Christian Jetzlsperger

Lit.: *Alcock, A.:* History of the International Labour Organization, New York 1971; *Blan-* *chard, F.:* L'Organisation Internationale du Travail: de la guerre froide à un nouvel ordre mondial, Paris 2004; *Gaudier, M.:* The development of the women's question at the ILO, 1919-1994 (ILO Discussion Paper), Geneva 2006; *Ghebali, V.:* The International Labour Organization: A Case Study on the Evolution of UN Specialized Agencies, Dordrecht et al. 1989; *Hüfner, K.:* Die Vereinten Nationen und ihre Sonderorganisationen. Strukturen, Aufgaben, Dokumente. Teil 2: Die Sonderorganisationen, 3rd edn., Bonn 1992; *International Labour Office.* The ILO: what it is, what it does, Geneva 2003; *International Labour Office:* World Employment Report 2004-2005, Geneva 2004 (quoted as: ILO 2004); *International Labour Office:* Rules of the Game: A brief introduction to international labour standards, Geneva 2005; *International Labour Office:* ILO Action Plan for Gender Equality 2008-09, Geneva 2008 (quoted as: ILO 2008a); *International Labour Office:* Global Employment Trends 2008, Geneva 2008 (quoted as: ILO 2008b); *Servais, J.-M.:* International Labour Law, The Hague 2005; *Köhler, P.A.:* ILO – International Labour Organization, in: Wofrum, R. (ed.): United Nations: Law, Policies and Practice, 2 vols., Munich/Dordrecht 1995, Vol. 1, 714-723.

Internet: *Homepage of ILO:* www.ilo.org; *access to ILO Conventions and Recommendations:* www.ilo.org/ilolex/english/index. htm; *access to literature on ILO and labour issues in general:* http://labordoc.ilo.org/; *list of the ratifications of ILO conventions in the current year:* http://webfusion.ilo.org/public/db/standards/normes/appl/index.cfm?lang=EN.

IMF – International Monetary Fund

1. Origins

In July 1944 the United Nations convened an International Monetary and Financial Conference at Bretton Woods (New Hampshire, USA), in which all 44 participating states agreed on a new order for the world monetary and financial system in the post-war era. The backdrop to the gathering was dominated by still vivid memories of inconvertibility and foreign exchange shortages, hyperinflation and deflation, and default on external debt of the preceding decades; thus the motivation to reach an agreement was strong. It was hoped to establish a system which could prevent a recurrence of the disastrous competitive exchange rate depreciations and the breakdown in international economic relations these countries had experienced in the inter-war period.

The agreements they signed there provided for the establishment of the international monetary and trading system known as the "Bretton Woods System". Although the Havana Charter (→ WTO, GATT) was not ratified by the US Congress, leading to the indefinite postponement of the International Trade Organization (ITO), the Conference did prove the birthplace of two major institutions: the *International Bank for Reconstruction and Development (IBRD)* (→ World Bank, World Bank Group) and the *International Monetary Fund (IMF)*. The IMF was established by the "Articles of Agreement of the International Monetary Fund" (UNTS Vol. 2, No. 20 (a)), which entered into force on 27 December 1945 after ratification by 22 states. It began its operations in 1947.

The IMF has its headquarters in Washington, D.C. in conformity to Article XIII, Section I of the Articles of Agreement, which stipulates that the IMF shall have its seat on the territory of the member with the largest capital stock quota. The largest member is the United States of America with a quota of 17.09 per cent (equivalent to SDR 37 billion) and related voting rights of 16.77 per cent (April 2008). If the 15 countries of the euro area were considered a single entity as some observers call for, it would replace the USA as the largest member.

II. Aims

According to the Articles of Agreement the IMF is dedicated to five main purposes: (a) to promote multilateral monetary co-operation; (b) to facilitate international trade and high levels of employment in member countries; (c) to promote exchange stability, maintain orderly exchange arrangements and avoid competitive exchange depreciation; (d) to correct disequilibrium in balances of payments and thus avoid extreme external surplus or deficit on the part of individual countries; (e) to establish a financial support system for countries to correct maladjustments in their balance of payments (cf. Articles of Agreement, Art. I).

III. Status in the UN System, Membership and Organs

In 1947 the IMF received the status of a specialized agency (→ Specialized Agencies) in the → UN system and, was thus endowed with full juridical personality and entitled to conclude internationally binding agreements. Furthermore, the Fund is endowed with all the rights of an autonomous governmental organization, including the right to establish its own budget, recruit its own personnel and to admit new member countries. Thus membership of the UN (→ Membership and Representation of States) is not a prerequisite of membership of the IMF. A total of 185 countries are members (as of 31 December 2008). In principle any country can become a member of the IMF if it accepts the "Articles of Agreement" as the basis for its monetary and financial policies, and pays the appropriate subscription to the authorized IMF depository. The allocated quota determines the voting power with which the country can participate in the internal decision-making processes of the Fund. Countries with the highest quotas therefore have the greatest voting power and influence on IMF policy.

The three key executive organs of the IMF are the *Board of Governors*, the *Executive Board* and the *Managing Director*. The Board of Governors is the highest executive organ of the IMF and meets once a year during the general meeting of the IMF and World Bank. All IMF member countries are represented on the Board of Governors, with voting power weighted according to quotas. The Board of Governors has exclusive powers to decide on the admission or suspension of members (Art. II, Art. XXVI), determining or changing quotas (Art. III) and amendments to the

Articles of Agreement (Art. XXVIII). In the case of violation of the Articles of Agreement, the Board of Governors is not only authorized to exclude a member from access to the general resources of the Fund, but, after the coming into force of the Third Amendment to the Articles of Agreement in November 1992, may also move to suspend that member's voting rights. Furthermore, the Board of Governors is also responsible for the regulation of general business policy and credit lines, in so far as such competence has not already been delegated to the Executive Board (Art. XII, Section 2a). Since 1999, the Board of Governors has been advised by the *International Monetary and Financial Committee (IMFC)* on matters relating to the supervision of the international monetary system.

In practice, however, the bulk of decision-making involved in adopting policies to changed framework conditions has passed to the Executive Board which is responsible for the ordinary conduct of business, including the surveillance of exchange rate policies, the provision of credit lines and consultations with member countries. The Executive Board consists of 24 members, with 5 permanent representatives from the countries with the highest quotas (USA, Germany, Japan, France, and the United Kingdom) and the other 19 directors elected from member countries on a rotational basis. The Executive Board is chaired by the Managing Director, who is elected from its ranks, albeit major members agreed upon until recently that he or she will always be a European. This office is now held by Dominique Strauss-Kahn from France succeeding a short period of the Spanish Rodriguez de Rato and a very short and not particularly successful period of the German Horst Köhler.

IV. Funding: Sources and Uses

Each member is allocated a quota which reflects its share in IMF capital stock. The quota is expressed in *Special Drawing Rights (SDRs);* it is assessed in terms of the country's economic power,

using factors such as gross domestic product (GDP), share of world trade, variability and official foreign exchange reserves. Each country is assigned a basic vote of 750 (before April 2008: 250) plus one vote per SDR 100,000 of its quota; thus, the quota determines a country's maximum financial commitment to the IMF, its maximum amount of borrowing and its voting power. At the time of writing (April 2008) the total amount of quotas is SDR 217.3 billion. The SDR asset is a weighted currency basket consisting of the US dollar, the euro (before 1.1.1999 the German mark and the French franc), the yen and the pound sterling. The value of the SDR is fixed on a daily basis according to the latest value of its constituent denominations on the currency market, and thus is subject to the same exchange rate fluctuations as affect the basket currencies. Some consider the SDR an international reserve asset; created in 1969, the SDR is used in transactions of members among one another, with the IMF and with few authorized "other proprietors" (such as development banks in the → UN System). However, the current relevance of the SDR as a reserve asset is negligible: a mere 2% of members' reserves (not counting gold) are held in SDRs. Of a member's allocated quota, 25% must be paid either in SDRs or in a convertible currency specified by the IMF (this used to be gold) whilst the other 75% can be paid in the member's own currency. Quotas paid in to the IMF General Resources Account are subject to periodic reviews, once every 5 years at the most, and if deemed necessary may be increased (Art. III). Although the Tenth General Review of Quotas in 1994 had opted against an increase of quotas, in January 1998 the Eleventh General Review of Quotas, in acknowledgement of the extraordinarily high levels of finance needed to support the exchange rates of the South-East Asian economies, recommended increasing the quota by 45%, which became effective one year later. Since then, however, there has been no quota increase.

In November 1998 the *New Arrangements to Borrow (NAB)* also came into force. These are intended to supplement the older *General Arrangements to Borrow (GAB)* dating back to 1962, and now cover 26 countries including all the original 11 parties to the GAB. The provisions of both the GAB and NAB allow the IMF to resort to credit lines from governments and central banks in cases where the financial requirements of support measures outstrip its lending capacity. Although the GAB can provide funding to the tune of SDR 17 billion and the NAB SDR 34 billion, the cumulative credit horizon for simultaneous funding from both GAB and NAB is limited to SDR 44 billion. Furthermore, the IMF is empowered to raise money from governments, central banks and on the international capital market – an option to which the IMF has not yet resorted.

When faced with balance of payments difficulties, a member may first call in the amount of its reserve tranche exceeding its quota of IMF stock in domestic currency in the General Resources Account. The reserve tranche allows countries to buy foreign exchange with domestic currency without IMF-imposed conditions or fees. As such it stands in marked contrast to the provision of credit tranches by the regular facilities, *Stand-by Arrangements (SBAs)* and the *Extended Fund Facility (EFF)*, or the special facilities, all of which are subject to conditions and fees by the IMF. The *Special Lending Facilities* comprise the *Compensatory Financing Facility (CFF*, 2000, formerly (1963) as CCFF established), the *Supplemental Reserve Facility (SRF*, 1997) and the *Contingent Credit Lines (CCLs*, 1999-2003). The latter two were established after the currency crisis in emerging markets. At the height of the East Asian crisis the IMF Board of Governors approved the establishment of the SRFs in December 1997; the SRFs were provided for countries which experience exceptional balance of payments difficulties resulting from a sudden and disruptive loss of market confidence and accompanied by a melt-down of foreign exchange reserves; the SRF has a maturity of up to 18 months and is considered additional to the reserve tranche and other lending facilities. CCLs had been considered a precautionary line of defense for solvent members with liquidity problems due to contagion, comparable to a lender-of-last-resort-facility of a central bank, albeit providing international reserves instead of domestic money. However, as no country had ever fallen back on CCLs, the Board let this facility expire at its sunset date in December 2003. The low attractiveness of this lending facility had been due to concerns of countries that private international investors would take the use of CCLs as a signal for imminent default and thereby enforce capital flight. As a reaction to the Mexico crisis, the IMF already adopted a set of procedures called the Emergency Financing Mechanism in September 1995, which should have enabled the IMF Board to approve quick IMF financial support to crisis-afflicted countries.

The ceilings for borrowing arrangements and special facilities vary from 55 % of the quota for the Compensatory Financing Facility up to 300 % of quota cumulative for credit tranches and the Extended Fund Facility. All credits are disbursed to members in a number of instalments and, prior to the payment of each instalment, the IMF reviews economic and monetary policy to ascertain that the beneficiary country is making every effort to overcome its balance of payments problems, and that the agreement on policy adjustments concluded between it and the IMF is being adhered to. Should the IMF find this not to be the case, outstanding installments can be (and at several occasions were indeed) suspended.

Apart from regular IMF facilities such as Stand-By Arrangements and the Extended Fund Facility or the special facilities, the IMF also disposes of a number of concessional instruments. One of these is the *Poverty Reduction and Growth Facility (PRGF)*, which was originally set up in 1987 as the Enhanced Structural Adjustment Facility (ESAF), and became the PRGF in 1999. As a programme with the ordained aim of sustained improvement of the balance of payments position and the promotion of growth in eligible countries, the ESAF was originally scheduled to end in 1994. However, both economic growth and an enduring improvement in the balance of payments position are more long-term processes than mid-term goals, a fact the IMF recognized when it extended the programme's life. Increasingly vocal criticism of the deterrent social impact of IMF policies in the 1990s prompted the change of name to PRGF. Around 50% of IMF members (78 member countries as of August 2007) qualify for eligibility within the terms of the programme which formally consists in the cut-off point of eligibility for the World Bank concessional lending; however, the payment of credits in the form of a three-year agreement is generally dependent on the submission of a so-called Poverty Reduction and Growth Strategy Paper by the candidate country, and on the observance of a number of conditions. Credits can run for a maximum term of 10 years, have a grace period of 5.5 years and a nominal interest rate of 0.5 per cent.

Another concessional instrument is the debt relief granted under the *Heavily Indebted Poor Countries (HIPC) Initiative* which the IMF and IBRD had launched already in 1996. The HIPC Initiative was designed to reduce the foreign debt of those developing countries classified as over-indebted; previous IMF and World Bank measures and programmes had not restored the solvency of candidate countries or provided sufficient growth perspectives. The HIPC Initiative embodies the view that, without the removal of the debt burden, economic development is difficult or even impossible. The circle of countries eligible for this initiative comes from those eligible for PRGF credits. Within the provisions of the HIPC Initiative, remission of debt generally involves a three-year preliminary period during which candidate countries have to prove

that they are able to fulfill conditions required by the PRGF and IDA programmes before debt relief. A debt sustainability analysis in terms of foreign currency, and using generally valid economic indicators, serves as the basis for the debt relief. The original definition of debt sustainability was adjusted in 1999, when the economic indicators were revised downwards (in the so-called HIPC II or Enhanced HIPC Initiative) in order to broaden eligibility for debt remission among the 41 countries of the HIPC group and fix actual debt relief. Although the PRGF Trust and the PRGF-HIPC Trust are both administered by the IMF, financing for these concessional loans does not come from regular members' contributions. Around 50% of the debt relief cost is directly financed by bilateral public creditors and the rest from multilateral lenders, e.g. the African Development Bank, the second largest donor after the World Bank Group, and the Inter-American Development Bank, the fourth largest donor after the IMF. On initiative of the G-8 Gleneagles Summit under the UK Presidency in 2005, the HIPC initiative was complemented by the *Multilateral Debt Relief Initiative (MDRI);* MDRI provides for hundred per cent debt relief to free financial resources within low-income countries to advance *Millennium Development Goals (MDGs).* Participating institutions are the African Development Fund (AfDF), the International Development Association (IDA, → World Bank, World Bank Group) and the IMF, which individually decide upon debt relief; from 2007 on the Inter-American Development Bank decided to also grant debt relief to eligible member countries according to MDRI terms. International donors provide the major part of the MDRI costs. At the time of writing debt relief equivalent to SDR 2 billion under the MDRI has been granted by the IMF.

In total, the IMF had outstanding loans of SDR 16.1 billion of which SDR 6.5 billion classified for concessional loans to 56 countries (as of March 31,

2008); lending under the regular and special facilities was at an all-time low.

V. Activities

The history of the IMF, which commenced its financial operations in March 1947, falls into four substantive phases:

(I) 1947-1973: the creation and maintenance of monetary stability was to be ensured by fixed, albeit adjustable exchange rates with maximum authorized fluctuation of ±1 per cent on IMF-agreed parity. National central banks were obligated to buy foreign currency at the prescribed rates. Changes in parity were only effected during fundamental disequilibria of the balance of payments. In contrast, temporary disturbances or cyclical downturns in the balance of payments were bridged by withdrawals from the reserve tranche, or the provision of credits by the IMF, and if considered necessary they were combined with restrictive monetary policy by affected member states. When the IMF was established, it was intended to make the Fund the central coordinating and surveillance agency for the monetary policies of its members. In practice, however, its functions were mainly limited to implementing the annual Article IV consultations, fixing new parities for fundamental balance of payments deficits and providing information. During this period the tasks of co-ordination, meeting agreements as well as the main burden of providing lines of credit fell to the USA. The unilateral decision of the USA to stop its free trading in gold for international transactions in 1971 and the general transition to flexible exchange rates in 1973 not only entailed the collapse of the Bretton Woods system but also meant a partial eclipse for the IMF itself as its key instrument – fixed exchange rates – had suddenly become obsolete.

(II) 1974-1978: this period is marked by the search for new agendas and organizational forms to deal with the changed conditions of the world economy, and to fill the vacuum left by the collapse of the Bretton Woods system.

The 20-member Committee of the Board of Governors on Reform on the International Monetary System and Related Issues was set up only in 1972 and brought to an end already in 1974. Thus, a speedy return to the order of fixed exchange rates as a major step in the IMF reform was precluded. Finally, in 1976 the IMF undertook the Second Amendment to Article IV, in which floating exchange rates were recognized as permissible if not exactly desirable. This established the right of members to adopt exchange rate arrangements of their choice. At the same time the exchange rate problems of developing countries were increasingly taking centre stage. This was also expressed in the establishment in 1974 of the Development Committee, co-sponsored with the IBRD.

(III) 1979-2005: the search for a new raison d'être came to an end in 1979, even though it was Mexico's 1982 defaulting on its foreign debt, signalling the onset of the debt crisis that first marked the IMF's entry onto the international stage as a major actor. The Guidelines of Conditionality, the register of conditions attached by the IMF to the granting of a loan to an applicant country, underwent three substantial modifications in 1979: a) loans should now be disbursed in several instalments; b) payment of an instalment was dependent on the extent to which a country had implemented the structural adjustment measures attendant on the loan; c) in the case of long-term loans, criteria for reviewing the implementation of prior conditions should now be determined on an annual basis. At the outset "conditionality" was restricted to pure economic criteria, laid down in a "Letter of Intent". This put the prime focus on the flexibility of key prices (such as interest rates or exchange rates but also including basic food stuffs), market liberalization (e.g. commodity and capital markets) and general government deregulation through cut-backs in government intervention and the privatization of public sector companies. However, since the early 1990s a political dimension has been added to the

403

economic aspect, including further conditions such as anti-corruption measures and an emphasis on strengthening democratic tendencies in the borrower country.

Since the introduction of Structural Adjustment Programmes there has been growing criticism of the approach of the IMF both in debtor countries, and from → NGOs in creditor countries. At first, discussions centred mainly on the draconian economic and social consequences such programmes entailed, in particular the destruction of domestic production capacity, the loss of jobs, and the deepening disparities in income distribution. Furthermore, the – in some cases – drastic impact of IMF-financed programmes and projects on the environment was another cause for serious concern. And finally the lack of adequate democratic structures in the institutions and their lack of open and transparent control mechanisms gave rise to a number of restructuring proposals for the Bretton Woods twins themselves.

The IMF's handling of the Asian crisis 1997/1998 and the succeeding currency crises in other emerging market economies fanned once more the flames of controversy and increased the pressure for change. The financial support of the Fund for the crisis-afflicted countries was criticized as too low, too late and too lopsided. Over the years the emergency finance provided by the Fund within its rescue packages continuously increased and exceeded several times the accepted quota limit of cumulative 300 per cent. Between 1995 and 2003 IMF financial support for nine emerging market economies (Argentina, Brazil, Mexico, Indonesia, Republic of Korea, Russian Federation, Thailand, Turkey and Uruguay) reached an amount on average equivalent to 637 per cent of quotas (*Akyüz* 2005, 18). However, considering that the almost bottomless deterioration of their exchange rates could not have been prevented, exceptional emergency finance of the IMF was characterized as being inadequate and provided only after international reserves of the crisis-afflicted countries had al-

ready reached critical levels. In addition, IMF conditionality was only attached to deficit countries which therefore had to carry the whole burden of adjustment; however, misalignments and strong variations of exchange rates among the G-3 currencies constituted a major source of disturbance for countries and had played an important role in almost all major emerging market crises.

In the face of mounting criticism an external evaluation of IMF surveillance was instigated in 1998. Two years later its Executive Board delivered a resolution recommending the establishment of an independent office of evaluation as a further arm to the IMF internal audit. In 1998 the IMF and World Bank also reached an agreement about the form of their collaborative work: in future all joint efforts would be governed by the three principles of clarity about responsibility, early and effective consultation, and separate accountability. Within this period these were the only steps towards a reform of the Bretton Woods twins, although commissions were appointed to investigate far-reaching reform steps and several reports submitted, e.g. the Quota-Formula Review Group, which focused on the revision of quota formula and thereof derived quotas, or the International Financial Institution Advisory Commission appointed by the US Congress, which analyzed the role of the International Financial Institutions and their division of labor (*Williamson* 2000).

In sum, the IMF had moved a very long way from its original design at the time of establishment. The focus of IMF core activities had shifted from temporary or cyclically-induced maladjustments of the balance of payments, to overcoming "structural balance of payments crises" through adjustment programmes. Such programmes were no longer composed purely of monetary and currency policy measures, but included elements of fiscal, trade, industry and social policies, and were a clear indication that the IMF had greatly extended its area of jurisdiction since 1979. The new directions in goals and tasks definition were also reflected in the institutionalization of new credit facilities, with terms of maturity including repayment of up to 10 years. Since the onset of the debt crisis the IMF had not evolved into the key actor in international crisis management, because of the sheer volume of credits it had disbursed, which was somewhat limited in comparison to other public and private capital flows. During its most powerful period the IMF fulfilled the function of the prime informant for public and private creditors alike and, as the guarantor for reform in countries of the South stricken by debt and currency crises. Signing an adjustment programme with the IMF was akin to receiving a seal of quality that would grant a country access to the international capital market. Thus the IMF had not only undergone substantial changes in terms of its original purposes, tasks and repertoire of instruments, but had also achieved a qualitative enhancement of its competence and power in the international economic and monetary order. However, with the outbreak of the Asian crisis the Fund's powerful position faded away.

(IV) 2006 to present: The IMF experiences a deep institutional crisis for which at least three factors may require authorship. First, emerging market economies and oil exporters have accumulated high foreign exchange reserves which serve as war chests in case of a currency or debt crisis; in addition, the regional establishment of foreign exchange swaps and emergency finance facilities is enforced through monetary co-operation by developing countries and emerging market countries themselves; thus, for these countries, the Fund no longer has the role to play in the typical balance of payments crisis it used to manage. Second, early debt repayment by all major emerging market and developing countries let the outstanding non-concessional loans dwindle from an all-time-high of over SDR 70 billion (2003) to an all-time low of under SDR 10 billion (2007); the IMF's main source of income to finance gross expenditures of around 1 billion US dol-

lars (fiscal year 2008) consists in the interest which is charged on the loans; at the time of writing (April 2008) the spending-income gap amounts to 400 million US dollars on an annual basis. Thus, the traditional financial basis of IMF operations is no more sustainable.

Third, the IMF failed to identify the woes of the subprime crisis in time, leaving it to central bankers, finance ministers and private financial actors to deal with the crisis and its implications; only in April 2008 did the IMF provide the first comprehensive analysis (*IMF* 2008a). The IMF's misjudgment of the subprime debacle which turned out to be the worst threat to financial stability in post-war period is explained by the IMF's traditional macroeconomic approach with its preference for balanced budgets, low inflation, good governance and property rights; together with the persuasion that markets would allocate resources in an optimal way. The surveillance of financial markets had not figured as prominent in the IMF analysis as would have been necessary to detect risks for financial stability in time. Thus the IMF increasingly displays a loss of intellectual leadership.

In a sensational speech Mervyn King, Governor of the Bank of England, drew attention to the virtues which John Maynard Keynes ascribed to the IMF and World Bank at their first meeting decades ago and stated: "In recent years the critics have charged that all three of the virtues of universalism, energy and wisdom have been lacking in the IMF. And if not in a deep slumber, then the Fund has appeared to be drowsy. It is an institution, it is said, that has lost its way" (*King* 2006, 2-3).

Mervyn King called for a reform of the IMF with regard to focus, independence and ownership.

A sharper focus would imply limiting IMF analysis to a restricted number of macroeconomic core areas, including the development of the financial sector and capital accounts of respective countries, together with spill-over effects and vulnerability analyses as opposed to non-financial structural areas or typical development aid issues. As a result of refocusing the IMF's field of operation, the mingling of tasks and functions of the Fund and the World Bank could end and the original division of labor could be restored. With regard to independence, the former director of the fiscal affairs department at the IMF who served the IMF for three decades was not very optimistic: "As to the political independence of the Board, it must be noticed that especially the G7 countries tend to send to the Board of the IMF individuals who are relatively low in the political totem pole of their countries. They are for the most part medium level civil servants. These people have no political independence and, on important issues, they simply read the instructions that they receive from their principals in their capitals. ... Major changes would be needed to make the Board, as an institution, more politically independent." (*Tanzi* 2006, 20). Attached to the issue of political independence is the question of ownership and the governance structure of the Fund; for years emerging market countries and developing countries criticized their marginal influence within the Board. In September 2006, the Board of Governors finally accepted an ad-hoc quota increase for the four most under-represented countries China, Mexico, the Republic of Korea and Turkey of total 1.8 per cent of quota volume as a first step to increase voice and vote of emerging markets countries and developing countries. In April 2008 the Board of Governors adopted a quota reform as the follow-up of the Singapore decisions; it comprises a revised quota formula, the tripling of basic votes which favors in particular low income countries, two additional Alternate Executive Directors for African member countries and a shift in both quota shares and votes to developing countries (*IMF* 2008c). However, the aggregate shift in quota shares and votes amounts to 4.9 percent points and 5.4 percentage points respectively only (*IMF* 2008b); even lower is the shift in quota share in favor of emerging market countries and developing countries

which amounts to 2.7 percentage points. Thus, with this cosmetic reallocation of quotas, a shift of power to developing countries within the Fund cannot be expected. Several think tanks and → NGOs even wrote an open letter to the Executive Directors of member countries asking them not to vote against the reform: "We write to express our concern that the proposed reforms fall far short in addressing the challenges facing the IMF in its evolution toward a truly global institution with more balanced and inclusive representation and voting power." (Open Letter 2008). In April 2008, the Executive Board also agreed to change the income model of the IMF towards one that generates more revenues; the IMF's investment policy were to be improved and additional funds, fed by profits from gold sales up to an amount of 400 tons, invested. The then still prevailing income-spending gap should be closed by spending cuts, including the reduction of staff members.

Whether with the above mentioned decisions "the IMF is back" as Dominique Strauss Kahn pompously proclaimed at the press conference before the Spring Meeting in April 2008 (*IMF* 2008d) remains still to be seen.

Commonwealth countries, representing one third of world population, are skeptical that "incremental and ad hoc approaches to reforms" of international financial institutions are sufficiently far-reaching to respond to current crises (*Commonwealth Heads of Government* 2008, 1). They announced that they will pursue the process of redefining both the purpose and governance of the Bretton Woods institutions by organizing "wider international support for an international conference to achieve these goals" (ibid., 3).

Martina Metzger

Lit.: *Akyüz, Y.:* Reforming the IMF – Back to the Drawing Board, Paper presented at the G24 Technical Meeting, Washington, D.C., September 16, 2005, www.g24.org/Akyu 0905. pdf; *Boorman, J.:* An Agenda for the Reform of the International Monetary Fund. Emerging Markets Forum, November 2007, www.

emergingmarketsforum.org/about/pdf/2007%20EMF%20Boorman.pdf; *Bretton Woods Commission (ed):* Bretton Woods: Looking to the Future. Commission Report, Staff Review, Background Papers, Washington, D.C. 1994; *Committee of Eminent Persons to Study Sustainable Long-Term Financing of IMF Running Costs:* Final Report, January 2007 (so-called Crockett Report), www.imf.org/external/np/oth/2007/013107.pdf; *Commonwealth Heads of Government:* Meeting on Reform on International Institutions: Malborough House Statement on Reform of International Institutions, London, 9-10 June 2008, www.thecommon wealth.org/Templates/internal.asp?NodeID=178967/); *Commonwealth Secretariat:* A Commonwealth Initiative to support reform of the IMF and the World Bank, London, May 2008, www.thecommonwealth.org/Templates/internal.asp?NodeID=178967/); *King, M.:* Reform of the International Monetary Fund. Speech held at the Indian Council for International Economic Research, February 20, 2006, www.icrier.org/pdf/icrierspeech_mervynking.pdf; *New Rules for Global Finance (Coalition):* IMF Quota Reform: letter regarding vote on Friday, March 28 2008 (quoted as Open Letter 2008), www.new-rules.org/event/2008Letter_IMF_Quota_Reform050208.htm; *International Monetary Fund:* IMF – Annual Report 2007, www.imf.org/external/pubs/ft/ar/2007/eng/pdf/ar07_eng.pdf; *International Monetary Fund:* Global Stability Report – Containing Systemic Risks and Restoring Financial Soundness, Washington, D.C., April 2008 (quoted as IMF 2008a), www.imf.org/external/pubs/ft/gfsr/2008/01/pdf/text.pdf; *International Monetary Fund:* Executive Board Recommends Reforms to Overhaul Quota and Voice, Press Release No. 08/64, March 28, 2008 (quoted as IMF 2008b), www.imf.org/external/np/sec/pr/2008/pr0864.htm; *International Monetary Fund:* IMF Board of Governors Adopts Quota and Voice Reforms by Large Margin, Press Release No. 08/93, April 29, 2008 (quoted as IMF 2008c), www.imf.org/external/np/sec/pr/2008/pr0893.htm; *International Monetary Fund:* Transcript of a Press Briefing by IMF's Managing Director Dominique Strauss-Kahn, First Deputy Managing Director John Lipsky, and Director of External Relations Masood Ahmed, Washington, D.C., April 10, 2008 (quoted as IMF 2008d), www.imf.org/external/np/tr/2008/tr080410.htm; *Tanzi V.:* Global Imbalances and Fund Surveillance. Paper presented at the G24 Technical Meeting, Geneva, March 16, 2006, available at: www.g24.org/tanz0306.pdf; *Toussaint, E./Drucker, P. (eds.):* IMF/Worldbank/WTO: The Free Market Fiasco (Notebooks for Study and Research No. 24/25, International Institute for Research and Education), Amsterdam 1995; *Williamson, J.:* The Failure of World Monetary Reform 1971-74, Sunbury-on-Thames 1977; *Williamson, J.:* The role of the IMF: A Guide to the Reports (Policy Brief No. 5, Peterson Institute for International Economics 2000), www.petersoninstitute.org/publications/pb/pb.cfm?ResearchID=66.

Internet: Homepage of the IMF: www.imf.org; Homepage of The Bretton Woods Project – Critical Voices on the World Bank and IMF: www.brettonwoods project.org/index.shtml.

IMO – International Maritime Organization

The International Maritime Organization (IMO) was established by the Convention on the Inter-Governmental Maritime Consultative Organization (IMCO), adopted by the United Nations Maritime Conference in Geneva on 6 March 1948 (UNTS Vol. 324, No. 553), which entered into force on 17 March 1959. By decision of the 9th Assembly of IMCO on 14 November 1975 (Resolution A. 358 (IX)), which entered into force on 22 May 1982, the original name *Inter-Governmental Maritime Consultative Organization (IMCO)* was changed to *International Maritime Organization (IMO)*.

The IMO is one of the sixteen → specialized agencies of the United Nations. Its seat is in London.

In accordance with Articles 4-6 of the IMO Convention all UN member states (→ Membership and Representation of States) and all participating states of the Geneva Maritime Conference in 1948, which founded the IMCO, are entitled to become IMO members. All other states can accede to the Convention, if two thirds of the IMO member states agree. Switzerland, which is not a member of the United Nations, entered the IMO in this manner in 1955. 167 states are members of the IMO (as of 31 December 2008).

Purposes

In accordance with the Convention, the IMO promotes cooperation among governments in all technical matters of international ocean shipping. The aim is in particular the international enforcement of the highest possible standards in the fields of maritime safety, efficiency of navigation and prevention and control of marine pollution from ships.

In order to achieve these objectives the IMO is authorized to make recommendations in the form of resolutions of its Assembly. It provides also drafts of international conventions to be submitted for adoption, to conferences convened for this purpose by the IMO. Finally, it interprets these international conventions in daily practice.

Originally, a group of members within the IMO was of the opinion that the IMO should deal with the economic aspects of international shipping, as well. However this met with opposition from important member states, so that the IMO confined itself to technical cooperation. The IMO adopted more than 40 conventions and protocols in several fields of its competence, most of which have entered into force. Among the most important ones are conventions on the shipping routes in international shipping, on technical safety of ships, on maritime search and rescue, on establishing an international maritime satellite net, on prevention of marine pollution by oil or by dumping of hazardous substances and on salvage of ships in distress at sea. In addition to conventions and other formal treaty instruments, the IMO has adopted several hundred *recommendations* dealing with a wide range of subjects. They constitute codes, guidelines or recommended practices on important matters not considered suitable for regulation by formal treaty instruments. Although the IMO recommendations are not binding on member states' governments, they provide guidance in framing national legislation or regulations – an important function of UN specialized agencies in general.

Structure

The main organs of the IMO are the *Assembly*, the *Council*, five *committees* (Maritime Safety Committee, Legal Committee, Marine Environment Protection Committee, Technical Cooperation Committee and Facilitation Committee (for international maritime traffic)) and the *Secretariat*. The Assembly of all IMO member states is the highest main organ and holds its sessions every two years at IMO's headquarters in London. Essential functions of the Assembly, consisting of all member states, are the adoption of technical resolutions, of the budget and of the programme of work, as well as the election of the council members and the approval of the election of the IMO Secretary-General by the Council.

The Council, composed of 40 elected members for a two-year term, meets in session two times a year. It is the principal organ of the IMO between the sessions of the Assembly and coordinates the activities of all other organs.

Most of the IMO's work is carried out in the above-mentioned IMO committees: they prepare draft resolutions for the Assembly and draft conventions in their respective fields of work. The Maritime Safety Committee deliberates on all questions concerning technical safety, assisted by numerous subcommittees, e.g. on navigation, marine radio, containers, rescue operations etc. The Legal Committee concerns itself with conventions, for instance on liability and salvage, the Marine Environment Protection Committee with newly emerging problems and risks of pollution of the marine environment from ships, the Technical Cooperation Committee in collaboration with → UNDP with the promotion of shipping in developing countries, the Facilitation Committee with reducing the formalities and simplifying documentation required of ships when entering or leaving ports.

The IMO Secretariat, directed by the Secretary-General, coordinates administratively the work of all other IMO organs and acts as an information and documentation center.

Recent Challenges

In addition to the "classical" tasks of the IMO in the last decades, new problems have evolved: the increasing problems caused by terrorist attacks on ships, the re-emergence of piracy on a rather large scale, and the intricate legal problems connected with rescuing people attempting to flee from their country of origin by crossing the sea, in particular the Mediterranean. In all three problem areas it becomes obvious that the IMO – like any specialized agency of the UN – is not able to solve the problem on its own, but only in cooperation with other UN bodies.

With regard to terrorist attacks the IMO adopted in 1988 the Convention for the Suppression of Unlawful Acts Against the Safety of Maritime Navigation (UNTS Vol. 1678, No. 29004) which entered into force in 1992, complementing the UN codex of conventions against terrorist attacks.

After the extent of piracy and armed robbery at sea had reached in the late 1980s and early 1990s a considerable level, the IMO established in 1998 a long-term anti-piracy project, consisting of assessment missions in the respective regions, regional seminars and workshops attended by the government representatives from countries with piracy problems and the fostering of regional agreements on implementation of counter-piracy measures. The Regional Cooperation Agreement on Combating Piracy and Armed Robbery against ships in Asia (RECAAP), which was concluded in November 2004 by 16 Asian countries, has in the meantime proved to be a good example of effective regional cooperation in the fight against piracy. In other regions, for example the Red Sea and the Gulf of Aden, the situation is more complicated. Here IMO measures alone do not make sense, a combined programme, consisting of the presence of multilateral military forces, supplemented by UN development cooperation measures and IMO training programmes, is needed and is, in fact, in the phase of implementation.

As regards the asylum-seeking boat people, the IMO has joined forces with the UNHCR to improve the existing treaties governing the rescue regime, in an attempt to strengthen the legal obligation of the coastal states to disembark the refugees and asylum seekers, irrespective of whether they eventually may bring legitimate claims as to their status, lifting thus the burden of the ship masters rescuing the refugees at high sea. For this purpose the Convention for the Safety of Life at Sea (SOLAS) of 1974, in force since 1980 (UNTS Vol. 1184, No. 18961), was amended by IMO Doc. Res. MSC 153 (78), Annex 3, adopted on May 20, 2004, and entered into force on 1 July 2006. It is more than likely that the IMO will also in future have to deal with this problem, having to reconcile the interests of the vessel masters, of the refugees and of the coastal states (cf. *Syring* 2008).

Perspectives

Up to now the IMO has dealt successfully with a great amount of work in establishing international standards and rules in the endeavor to keep pace with growing shipping, above all merchant shipping, and its problems and risks, especially ecological hazards. The IMO has proved its competence and thoroughness. However, from the point of view of the environmentalists, the IMO works very slowly (→ Environmental Protection; → Environmental Law, International). The standards set by the IMO are beyond doubt high and have proved beneficial in many areas: oil pollution of the sea, for example, is less a threat now than it was twenty years ago, the number of collisions between ships has been greatly reduced in areas where IMO-approved traffic separation schemes have been introduced, and the safety of passenger ships has been considerably improved.

But in recent times the effective implementation of IMO standards has posed problems: the IMO has been confronted with increasing problems recently in the fields of maritime safety and navigation, mostly due to economic factors: the average age of the world's ships has risen – old ships are more likely to have accidents ; the fleets of traditional maritime countries, which tend to have good safety records, have declined, while many of the flags that are growing rapidly have relatively poor records. Many shipping companies of industrialized countries have "flagged out" their ships, i.e. they have registered their ships in states that are less uncompromising in the implementation of IMO standards.

The IMO therefore is presently concentrating not only on the effective implementation of the technical norms, but also on improving the education and advanced training of the staff of the national maritime institutions.

Helmut Volger

Lit.: *Boisson, P.:* Safety at Sea. Policies, Regulations and International Law, Paris 1999; *Seidel, P.:* IMO – International Maritime Organization, in: Wolfrum, R. (ed.), United Nations: Law, Policies and Practice, Vol. 1, Munich/ Dordrecht 1995, 734-742; *Syring, T.:* The International Maritime Organization (Reports on International Organizations of the American Society of International Law), www.asil.org/rio/imo.html.

Internet: Homepage of IMO: www.imo.org.

Independent Commissions, Reports of

At the end of the 1970s so-called "Independent Commissions" first appeared on the international agenda, which were established in connection with or on the initiative of different bodies of the United Nations. Some attracted much public attention. In particular, the Independent Commissions headed by Willy Brandt and Gro Harlem Brundtland influenced considerably the international debate on development and environmental policy. Moreover reports of Independent Commissions on security policy, global governance and the reform of the UN system were submitted ($\rightarrow$ Reform of the UN; $\rightarrow$ UN System).

The initiative to establish the Independent Commissions has come from various sources and their working methods and report structures have varied widely. However, all Independent Commissions have had in common that a group of experienced, independent personalities have prepared proposals for the solutions of global problems. They have tried to fill a particular deficit of existing national and international processes, which is a lack of long-term concepts.

The concept of interdependence forms the basis of all reports of the commissions. They begin with an analysis of global problems that cross national boundaries, define common interests and develop solutions derived from the latter ($\rightarrow$ Globalization). The commissions' recommendations aim to give new impulse for important areas of activity. Members of the Independent Commissions are prominent representatives from all regions, with the exception of the South Commission, which consisted only of representatives of the developing countries. The members of the Independent Commissions act as private persons and are independent of any instructions of their home countries. Several governments and foundations have financed the work of the Independent Commissions with financial grants.

The Pearson Commission

In 1969 the *Pearson Commission*, which is a direct precursor of the Independent Commissions of the late 70s, 80s and 90s, presented its report "Partners in Development". Pearson, the then president of the World Bank, had initiated this Independent Commission to strike the balance of 20 years of development policy and to work out strategies for the future. The Brandt Commission took up later on the tradition of analyzing the development policy of the Pearson Report and of other Third World development reports.

The Brandt Commission

In 1977 Robert S. McNamara, the then president of the World Bank, proposed the establishment of an *Independent Commission on International Development Issues* (known as Brandt or North-South Commission). The commission consisted of 18 members, and was headed by Willy Brandt, the former German chancellor. An important aspect of the composition of the Commission was a majority of members (10 of 18) from developing countries. The Commission took up the task of analyzing existing development problems and looking for solutions to overcome poverty. In their report they addressed the political decision makers as well as the public. The Brandt Commission stressed its independence and non-interference with the activities of states and organizations. As the first Independent Commission it was concerned to refute any apprehensions of this new international organ. At the conclusion of its working phase with eight sessions between 1977 and 1980, the North-South Commission presented its report entitled, "North-South: A Programme for Survival".

The notion of common interests of North and South was the basic idea of the analysis and the recommendations. The need to solve the development problems of the south was for the first time substantiated with the argument of global interdependence on the international level. The Brandt Commission identified a lack of capital transfer to the South, and the existing international economic and monetary system as the major obstacles to the development of the South. Consequently the report called for the establishment of an international tax system to provide new financial means for addressing development issues. These means were to be administered by a new organization which was to be established: the World Development Fund. Concrete steps to implement this were to be taken by a high-level North-South summit.

The North-South Report attained considerable publicity and was discussed broadly. But its recommendations have not been taken up on the political level. In 1981 the North-South Summit which the Commission had proposed took place in Mexico, but it did not produce any concrete results. The members of the North-South Commission were very alarmed by the failure to implement any of their recommendations, and by the worsening of the situation in developing countries at that time. Therefore they presented in 1983 a second report which was intended to function as an emergency programme: "Common Crisis, North-South: Co-operation for World Recovery". This report contained concrete proposals for the expansion of development financing, for better cooperation among development countries and for the establishment of a constructive North-South dialogue. These recommendations were not put into practice, too. Nevertheless, the work of the North-South Commission did make a difference by establishing new basic concepts for the dialogue between North and South, and by introducing the issue for the first time in the public discussion in the industrialized nations.

The Palme Commission

The *Independent Commission on Disarmament and Security Issues* (known as *Palme Commission*) was established in 1980. The Commission intended to treat more deeply questions of security policy which had been only touched marginally in the report of the North-South Commission. The former Swedish Prime Minister Olaf Palme was assigned as the chairperson. A special aspect of the composition of the Palme Commission was the membership of two representatives of the Warsaw Pact states. Further six of the (altogether) 17 members of the commission came from developing countries.

The Palme Commission attempted to formulate a concept of military security complementary to the Brandt Report. It aimed at developing guiding principles for global disarmament and armament control. Central to its concern were nuclear weapons, due to their global risk

411

potential. The commission did not analyze the causes of military confrontation, as this would clearly have endangered the consensus of the members of the commission.

Between 1980 and 1982, 12 meetings were held by the Palme Commission. In 1982 its report, entitled "Common Security: A Blueprint for Survival", was submitted to the UN → Secretary General. The report developed a new key concept of "common security", which was not based on confrontation , as had been the concept of deterrence, although, at the beginning of the 80s a new phase of confrontation between East and West had begun, with the discussion on the deployment of medium-range missiles in Europe. Nevertheless the Palme Commission managed for the first time to create a degree of consensus between the members of the different military alliances within the commission. They jointly called for cooperation in dealing with the collective threats, since the confrontation constituted a danger for the security of mankind (→ Collective Security; → Peace, Peace Concept, Threat to Peace).

Even though the East-West conflict was at the center of the analysis, the report nevertheless dealt in depth, too, with the security problems of developing countries. The Palme Commission also took up another issue upon which the Brandt Report had touched only briefly: the relationship between military expenditures and development. A central recommendation was the establishment of a 300 km zone in Central Europe which was to be free of nuclear weapons. Chemical weapons were also to be banned from Europe. The necessity of regional security systems and of the strengthening of the UN system were emphasized.

During the 80s the recommendations of the Palme Commission received scant attention. Only after the end of the East-West conflict in the 90s, the revised concepts of security – as proposed by the Commission came again into favor. However, the Palme concept of common security had been based on an existing East-West confrontation, and could not be used in precisely that form for the development of new multilateral concepts in the post-Cold War setting.

The Brundtland Commission

In 1983 the UN General Assembly called for the establishment of a World Commission for Environment and Development (known as Brundtland Commission), to elaborate a "Global Agenda for Change". Thereupon the UN Secretary General asked the former Norwegian Prime Minister Gro Harlem Brundtland to become the chairwoman and to establish the Commission. The *Brundtland Commission* consisted of 23 members, 13 from developing countries. As with the Palme Commission, two representatives from Eastern Europe also participated. The growing destruction of the environment and its consequences for the future of mankind were the starting point for the work of the commission. Environmental problems were to be identified, interactions between environment and development to be analyzed and ways for the solutions of the problems to be worked out in order to establish a secure, socially just and economically sound perspective. The commission was also to include in its discussions new international forms of cooperation with regard to environmental and development issues, and the role of non-governmental actors.

The work of the Brundtland Commission was characterized by an intensive exchange with Non-Governmental Organizations (→ NGOs). Public hearings of the commission took place on every continent and enabled a broad participation of non-governmental actors. In April 1987 the report of the Commission "Our Common Future", in brief Brundtland Report, was presented to the public.

The report focuses on the concept of "sustainable development". The Commission defined sustainable development as "development that meets the needs of the present without compromising the ability of future generations to meet their own needs" (*World Com-*

mission on Environment and Development 1987, 9). Environmental problems are not primarily discussed from the perspective of the North, but the report includes environmental destruction caused by poverty in the South. The Brundtland Report still maintains that growth is necessary to overcome poverty. In this connection development and growth are not clearly separated in the concept. Since the publication of the Brundtland Report, which introduced the concept of sustainability in the public discussion beyond the academic circles, the concept has been broadly discussed and is today generally accepted.

For the implementation of sustainable development the commission deems it necessary to integrate environmental and development concepts. This strategy should aim at reducing population growth, increasing the agricultural capacities for subsistence and strengthening the resources for renewable energy.

Of all the commission reports to date, the Brundtland Report has attained the greatest public resonance. For the first time, environment and development were perceived on an international level as interdependent problems. In this context the Brundtland Commission recommended to convene a second conference on environment (after Stockholm 1972), to be devoted also to development issues. This led eventually to the Rio Conference on Environment and Development of the United Nations (UNCED) in 1992.

The South Commission

The initiative of Mahathir Bin Mohamad, the Prime Minister of Malaysia, led to the establishment of the *South Commission*. He announced the planned establishment of the Commission at a conference of non-aligned states in 1986 ($\rightarrow$ Non-Aligned Movement and the UN).The South Commission consisted of 28 members exclusively from developing countries. Julius Nyerere, the former President of Tanzania, was asked to become the chairperson. Starting from the insight that "the South does not know the South" (*Stiftung Entwicklung*

und Frieden 1991, 11), the South Commission commenced its work in 1987. The experiences of and the potential for developing countries to contribute to the solution of the global problems were in the focus of the analysis of the North-South relations as well as developmental and environmental issues.

The South Commission presented its report, "The Challenge to the South", after eight sessions in 1990. The focal point of the report is the South's responsibility for its own development. Most of the demands and recommendations are consequently addressed to the South. The members of the Commission confirmed the importance of $\rightarrow$ human rights, participatory development and the ethical norm of social justice. The fight against poverty should be at the center of political activities in the South; but development should not be oriented on the models of the developed nations.

The essential recommendations of the report cover democratization of developing countries and appropriate political reforms to achieve this objective, the foundation of a South Secretariat with regular, institutionalized meetings of the heads of governments of the South, and – based on the latter –, a stronger South-South cooperation. Consequently the South Commission called for coordinated South action within the international monetary institutions, as well as the establishment of a forum for debtor countries and producer associations.

But the analysis described also development hindrances as results of the economic policy of the North, and demanded above all to put an end to the net capital transfer from South to North, a reduction of protectionism, and democratization of the UN ($\rightarrow$ Democratization and the UN) and of the international monetary system ($\rightarrow$ IMF).

The South Report expressed the growing collective self-confidence and self-criticism in the South. Especially the focus on political deficits in developing countries and their potential for developing own solutions gave the report credibility. The report contained a relentless analysis of the mistakes and of

413

the necessary efforts of the South. Its main goal, to strengthen the cooperation of developing countries to better put through common interests, resulted in a general rejection of the report by the governments of developed countries.

The Commission on Global Governance

An initiative of Willy Brandt in 1990 to search for new possibilities for international cooperation in the face of the changes in world politics after 1989, led to first in 1991 to the formation of the "Stockholm Initiative on Security and Global Governance" and resulted in 1992 in the establishment of the *Commission on Global Governance*. The Commission consisted of 28 members (of the 28 members came 19 from developing countries, four representatives from Eastern Europe, the remaining members from the Western countries). The Commission had two Co-Chairpersons – Ingvar Carlsson, former Prime Minister of Sweden, and Shridath Ramphal of Guyana, former Secretary-General of the British Commonwealth.

Founded in times of rapidly changing political processes the commission saw very favorable conditions to develop new forms of international cooperation. The international system was no longer governed by the concept of bipolarity. This gave room for potentially new structures. But at the same time the commission identified an increasing incidence of problems with trans-boundary implications. Part of the commission's mandate was a search for potential actors and structures for a future system of global governance. Existing international institutions were to be analyzed in respect of their potential to function properly in changing conditions and requirements.

In eleven meetings of the commission the report, "Our Global Neighbourhood", was elaborated. The commission integrated NGOs in its work, and highlighted the increased importance of the latter for the envisaged global governance system. The focus of the report is formed by the concept of "global neighbourhood", which describes global se-

curity as collective security. The report tries to give substance to the new catchword "global governance", defining it as the cooperation of governmental and non-governmental actors on all levels of political processes. The commission stressed the necessity to form an international civil society which would include non-governmental organizations, industrial corporations and scientific institutions.

The topics of the preceding commissions were re-analyzed with a new focus on essential international organizations. Consequently the main recommendations aim at a reform of the United Nations and the development of international core values in the form of international legal norms. The proposals for UN reform include a democratization of the → Security Council, the strengthening of the → General Assembly, and the dissolution of both the Economic and Social Council (→ ECOSOC) and of the UN Conference on Trade and Development (→ UNCTAD). A Council for Economic Security should be established as part of the UN system. The International Monetary Fund should be strengthened to effect supervisory organ over the international monetary system.

With a view to the development of common international legal norms the International Court of Justice (→ ICJ) should be strengthened and its compulsory jurisdiction in international disputes should be recognized by all UN member states – being as member states also states parties of the ICJ statute – by means of formally accepting the Court's competence under Article 36 (2) ICJ Statute. As first step for the restructuring of the international system the commission proposed to convene a world conference on global governance. This proposal has not met much acceptance so far. Most of the developing countries, as well as developed countries, opposed the idea of a stronger international system that would lead to a reduction of national → sovereignty.

414

The Weizsäcker-Qureshi Commission

The *Independent Working Group on the Future of the United Nations* was convened by the Ford Foundation in late 1993 on the initiative of UN Secretary-General Boutros Boutros-Ghali. The working group consisted of 12 members (5 from developing countries, 2 from Eastern Europe, 5 from the Western countries) and was co-chaired by Moeen Qureshi, former Prime Minister of Pakistan, and Richard von Weizsäcker, former Federal President of Germany.

The international system had played a major role in the work of all Independent Commissions so far. The Commission on Global Governance placed the UN at the center of its recommendations. At the same time the UN member states discussed the necessary reform of the UN. The working group had in this context the mandate to develop concrete, detailed recommendations and a programme of action for the future of the UN.

Greater efficiency and a strengthening of the UN are the main objectives of the recommendations of the working group. The group stressed the growing pressure on nations caused by the processes of economic → globalization, and by trans-boundary problems. But security and prosperity can be reached only collectively – in other words with the help of the United Nations. The report contains a critical analysis of the UN system, but it also points to the responsibilities of the UN member states, which have restricted until now the competence and the scope of action of the UN. The proposals aim at a more democratic UN system (especially regarding the Security Council) within the framework of a concept of "human security". The UN should be the one and only institution for the solution of national and intergovernmental conflicts, as well as for the coordination of social and economic processes. The establishment of two new principal organs of the UN (→ Principal Organs, Subsidiary Organs, Treaty Bodies), a UN Social Council and a UN Economic Council,

would reduce the powers of the traditionally dominant Security Council. At the same time this three-council model should be structured more democratically and should be provided with more powers. To implement these proposed reforms the UN needs the support of the member states and above all more money. How new financial means might be obtained is a question which the report leaves unanswered.

Assessment

The reports of the Brandt and Brundtland Commissions brought to the public awareness of the international community in the 80s that there are "common interests of survival." These interests cannot be safeguarded by nation states acting individually. The reports of all Independent Commissions have developed new international core values, and have promulgated the concept of "one world".

The UN system itself has not been able up to now to influence the international discussion in a similar manner. Institutional self-interest and financial dependency of the UN on some member states are key hindrances to such reform impulses. On the other hand, has the influence of the Independent Commissions on the UN system not been very far-reaching: some UN world conferences took up the topics of the Independent Commissions in the 90s and developed new concepts which mostly need still to be implemented.

The implementation of the action plans and recommendations of the different reports of the Independent Commissions would be without doubt an essential contribution to the solution of existing global problems. But the characteristic of all Independent Commissions, namely to be able to give impulses "from the outside", carries consequences for the prospects of implementation: the commissions depend completely upon political actors in the UN member states for the implementation of their recommendations.

Heike Henn

415

Annex:

Reports of the Independent Commissions (in chronological order):

Commission on International Development: Partners in Development; Report (Chairman: Lester B. Pearson), New York 1969.

Independent Commission on International Development Issues: North-South: A Programme for Survival. Report of the Independent Commission on International Development Issues [Brandt Report], Cambridge/USA 1980.

Independent Commission on Disarmament and Security Issues: Common Security: A Blueprint for Survival. Report of the Independent Commission on Disarmament and Security Issues [Palme Report]; prologue by Cyrus Vance, New York 1982.

Independent Commission on International Development Issues: Common Crisis North-South: Cooperation for World Recovery. Memorandum of the Independent Commission on International Development Issues [Brandt Memorandum], London 1983.

World Commission on Environment and Development: Our Common Future [Brundtland Report], Oxford 1987.

South Commission: The Challenge to the South. Report of the South Commission, Oxford/New York 1990.

Commission on Global Governance: Our Global Neighborhood: The Report of the Commission on Global Governance, Oxford/New York 1995.

Independent Working Group on the Future of the United Nations: The United Nations in Its Second Half-Century: A Report of the Independent Working Group on the Future of the United Nations, New York 1995 (also available on the Internet: www.library.yale.edu/un/un1e3co.htm from the United Nations Scholars' Workstation at Yale University).

Lit.: *Commission on Global Governance:* Issues in Global Governance: Papers Written for the Commission on Global Governance, London/Boston 1995; *Commonwealth Secretariat:* Common Index and Glossary to the Brandt, Palme and Brundtland Reports of the Independent Commissions on International Development, Disarmament and Security, and Environment and Development, London 1990; *Langmann, A:* Policy Advice on Rearranging the North-South Relationship: the Fortune of the Pearson, Tinbergen (RIO Project) and Brandt Commissions (1968-80), in: Peters, B.G./Barker, A. (eds.): Advising West European Governments: Inquiries, Expertise and Public Policy, Edinburgh 1993, 98-114; *Meyer, B./Schlotter, P.:* Common Security between East and West. Questions Related to the Palme Report, in: Bulletin of Peace Proposals 14 (1983), 219-225; *Rupesinghe, K.:* The Brandt Commission Report 1983. A blueprint for world recovery?, in: Bulletin of Peace Proposals 14 (1983), 283-288; *Rwegasira, D.G.:* National development and South-South cooperation: moving forward. An analytical commentary on the Report of the South Commission, in: African Development Review 3 (1991), No. 1, 90-101; *Softing, G.B. et al. (eds):* The Brundlandt Commission's Report – 10 years, Oslo et al. 1998; *Stiftung Entwicklung und Frieden (ed):* Gemeinsame Verantwortung in den 90er Jahren. Die Stockholmer Initiative zu globaler Sicherheit und Weltordnung, Bonn 1991; *Tandon, Y.:* Towards a common security – alternative perspectives of the Third World, in: Bulletin of Peace Proposals 21 (1990), 385-393; *Wren, B./Heath, E./Ratner, J. et al.:* The Brandt Report and after, in: New Internationalist, No. 104 (Oct. 1981), 7-31.

Addendum

Recent years have seen the continued use of international commissions by governments and international organizations to generate new knowledge and foster consensus building. Prominent examples of government initiatives are the Commission on Intervention and State Sovereignty (Canada), on Human Security (Japan) and the International Task Force on Global Public Goods (Sweden and France). On the side of international bodies, the International Labour Organization drew attention with its Commission on the Social Dimension of Globalization.

Former UN Secretary-General Kofi Annan gained a reputation for relying heavily on high-level panels as the ones on global threats, civil society relations and coherence of UN operational activities. In certain instances member states reacted negatively to such moves since they felt outmanœuvered on sensitive issues. Compared to previous decades, the commissions appointed since the start of the new millennium did not have an impact comparable with the global reach of the Brandt or Brundlandt Commissions, with the possible exception of the Canadian effort on state sovereignty and Annan's security panel.

International Commission on Intervention and State Sovereignty

The International Commission on Intervention and State Sovereignty (ICISS) was set up in 2000 by Canadian Foreign Minister Lloyd Axworthy as a response to the controversial debate on state sovereignty in light of the tragic events in Rwanda and Kosovo. The expert body rephrased the normative consensus by replacing the language of humanitarian intervention with a new concept, the *responsibility to protect*. Its 2001 report emphasizes that state authorities must foremost be held accountable for safeguarding human security within their borders. Only if and when they fail, will the responsibility to prevent, react and rebuild fall onto the international community. Use of force as the last resort must be authorized by the Security Council. The report has resonated strongly with the United Nations and the world public (cf. *Stahn* 2007).

In 2005, the General Assembly adopted in its concluding resolution of the World Summit the *"responsibility to protect"* in a somewhat watered-down version thereby inserting a human dimension into the state-centric concept of sovereignty: "The international community, through the United Nations, ... has the responsibility to use appropriate diplomatic, humanitarian and other peaceful means, in accordance with Chapters VI and VIII of the Charter, to help to protect populations from genocide, war crimes, ethnic cleansing and crimes against humanity. In this context, we are prepared to take collective action, in a timely and decisive manner, through the Security Council, in accordance with the Charter, ... should peaceful means be inadequate and national authorities are manifestly failing to protect their populations from genocide, war crimes, ethnic cleansing and crimes against humanity (United Nations 2005, UN Doc. A/RES/60/1, 16 September 2005, para. 139).

World Commission on the Social Dimension of Globalization

In 2002, the International Labour Organization launched the Commission) with the aim of providing analytical insight and political advice on how to share the benefits of globalization. Its final report of 2004 articulates a number of recommendations on the governance of globalization which would make the world safer, fair, ethical, inclusive and prosperous for the majority within countries and between countries, such as the reduction of unfair barriers to market access for goods in which developing countries have comparative advantage, the increase of Official Development Assistance (ODA) of the industrialized countries to 0.7 per cent of the gross national product, an increased representation of developing countries in the decision-making bodies of the Bretton Woods Institutions and an effective participation in the negotiations of the World Trade Organization WTO (A Fair Globalization 2004, Synopsis)

While the Commission's work did attract some interest, its policy recommendations were not pointed enough to have a significant impact on the global debate.

High-level Panel on Threats, Challenges and Change

In the aftermath of the bitterly divisive war against Iraq, former Secretary-General Kofi Annan established an expert panel, the High-level Panel on Threats, Challenges and Change,) and entrusted it with defining a new framework for collective global security. Its 2004 report "A more secure world: our shared responsibility" (UN Doc. A/59/565,

417

2 December 2004) has made a substantial contribution to reform efforts at the UN which culminated in the Millennium Review Summit of 2005 (cf. 2005 World Summit Outcome, UN Doc. A/RES/60/1).

The panel's comprehensive understanding of security which includes intrastate violence, poverty, terrorism and organized crime was widely accepted by states and civil society (cf. the statements of the member states in the debates of the General Assembly in April 2005 (UN Doc. A/59/PV.87 and 88 of 7 April 2005, A/59/PV.89 and 90 of 8 April 2005; cf. also *Fassbender* 2005, *Ozgercin/Steinhilber* 2005; *Thakur* 2006).

The response to its practical recommendations, however, was more limited. While the call for the creation of a Peacebuilding Commission led to success – General Assembly and Security Council decided in December 2005 in identical resolutions (UN Doc. A/RES/60/180 and S/RES/1645 of 30 December 2005) to establish the Peacebuilding Commission as an intergovernmental advisory body –, the proposals for Security Council enlargement were not enacted in the reform debates in the General Assembly in the following years.

Thomas Fues

Lit.: *Fassbender, B.:* UN Reform and Collective Security (Heinrich-Boell-Stiftung Global Issue Papers No 17), April 2005, www.boell.de/downloads/global/GIP17_ENG_UN-Reform_Sicherheit.pdf; *International Commission on Intervention and State Sovereignty:* The responsibility to protect, Ottawa 2001, www.iciss.ca/pdf/Commission-Report.pdf; *Ozgercin, K./Steinhilber, J.:* Towards a More Secure World? The Work of the High-Level Panel on Threats, Challenges and Change (FES-Briefing Paper), New York, January 2005, http://library.fes.de/pdf-files/iez/global/5010o.pdf; *Stahn, C.:* Responsibility to protect: political rhetoric or emerging legal norm? In: AJIL 101 (2007), 99-120; *Thakur, R.:* The United Nations, peace and security: from collective security to the responsibility to protect, Cambridge et al. 2006; *Thakur, R./Cooper, A./English, J. (eds.):* International commissions and the power of ideas, Tokyo 2005; *United Nations - General Assembly:* A more secure world: Our shared responsibility. Report of the High-level Panel on Threats, Challenges and Change, New York, 2 December 2004, UN Doc. A/59/565; *United Nations - General Assembly:* 2005 World Summit Outcome, UN Doc. A/RES/ 60/1, 16 September 2005; *World Commission on the Social Dimension of Globalization:* A Fair Globalization: Creating Opportunities for All, International Labour Organization, Geneva 2004, www.ilo.org/public/english/wcsdg/docs/report.pdf.

Internet: Homepage of the Commission on Global Governance: www.cgg.ch/home.htm; Homepage of the South Centre, which was established on the initiative of the South Commission: www.southcentre.org.

INSTRAW – International Research and Training Institute for the Advancement of Women

The establishment of the International Research and Training Institute for the Advancement of Women (INSTRAW) was decided upon by the Economic and Social Council of the UN (→ ECOSOC) in its resolution E/RES/1998 (LX) in 1976, as a response to a request by the World Conference for the International Women's Year in Mexico City in 1975 (→ World Conferences). ECOSOC's decision was endorsed by the → General Assembly with resolution A/RES/ 31/135 (1976).

The government of Iran, which had proposed the foundation of INSTRAW at the World Conference on Women, in 1979 withdrew its initial offer of 1975 to host the Institute. INSTRAW therefore took up its work provisionally in New York in 1980. In 1983 it moved to its permanent seat in Santo Domingo in the Dominican Republic. Its foundation was completed when its Statute was adopted by ECOSOC and by the General Assembly in 1984.

According to its statute, INSTRAW seeks to promote the advancement of women by research, training and information. Its aim is to support their inclusion in development as participants as well as beneficiaries. Its programme planning, is inspired by the guiding principles and key concepts of the world conferences, takes particularly the situation in developing countries into account.

The work of the Institute addresses practitioners of development policy, women's organizations, as well as non-governmental organizations (→ NGOs) whose major field of activity is the issue "women and development". Through policy-oriented research, seminars and training materials it provides support for the planning and implementation of development policies that address the needs of women, and take into consideration their role in the development process.

INSTRAW also seeks actively to build up networks by cooperating with other institutes at the national and the regional level. Finally, INSTRAW promotes the establishment of statistical methods for research on the social position and the status of women, and collects research reports, training material and statistical material in databases that are made available for policy planning within and outside the → UN system.

This latter task of INSTRAW was enhanced in 1999, when the General Assembly endorsed the establishment of the Gender Awareness Information and Networking System (GAINS) as the new working method of INSTRAW making use of the new electronic information technologies in the conduct of research on gender equality, the dissemination of the knowledge and information for policy-making, as well as in the empowerment of women through distance education and on-line training.

Being an autonomous research institute within the UN system, INSTRAW is independent of the UN Secretariat (→ Secretariat). However, its activity is supervised by a *Board of Trustees*, which includes eleven members elected by ECOSOC, the Director of INSTRAW (who is a member ex officio), a representative of the UN Secretary-General (→ Secretary-General), one representa-

tive from each Regional Economic Commission of the UN (→ Economic Commissions, Regional) and one representative from the host country (i.e. the Dominican Republic).

The Institute reports to ECOSOC and to the General Assembly. INSTRAW is financed by voluntary contributions to a trust fund from member states, international organizations, NGOs, foundations and private persons.

To use efficiently its limited budget, INSTRAW cooperates closely with the Regional Economic Commissions, with governmental and non-governmental organizations, and with other research institutions.

Within the UN system (→ UN System) it claims a monopoly on research on women's issues. However, to avoid duplication, coordination with the Division for the Advancement of Women in the Secretariat (DAW), the Commission on the Status of Women (CEDAW) (→ Human Rights Conventions, CEDAW), as well as with the UN Development Fund for Women (→ UNIFEM), is necessary (→ Women and the UN). The coordination is mainly effected by the Liaison Office of INSTRAW in New York.

As measure of reform of the UN system (→ Reform of the UN), Secretary-General Boutros-Ghali proposed a merger of INSTRAW with UNIFEM in 1993, rejecting the demand of some states to dissolve INSTRAW. However, as the Fourth Conference on Women in Beijing in 1995 did not take a position on the proposed merger, the proposal was not pursued further.

In the late 1990s INSTRAW was confronted with serious difficulties due to reduced contributions of member states to its trusteeship funds. In 1990 its budget amounted to 2.3 million US dollars; by 2000 the amount had fallen to only 201,408 US dollars. This called into question not only the implementation of planned programmes, but also the existence of the Institute as such. INSTRAW needs urgently additional funding, if it is to continue its valuable research work.

Andreas Blätte

Lit.: *Kardam, N.:* Bringing Women In. Women's Issues in International Development Programms, London 1991; *Pietilä, H. et al.:* Making Women Matter. The Role of the United Nations, 2nd edn., London et al. 1994; *Shields, M.:* Frauenforschung: Unsichtbares sichtbar machen. Das Programm des Internationalen Forschungs- und Ausbildungsinstituts der Vereinten Nationen zur Förderung der Frau (INSTRAW), in: VN 40 (1992), 188-192; *United Nations:* Development Cooperations with Women. The Experience and Future Development of the Fund, New York 1985; *United Nations:* The United Nations and the Advancement of Women 1945-1996, New York 1996; *Winslow, A. (ed.):* Women, Politics and the United Nations, Westport et al. 1995.

Addendum

In the late 90's INSTRAW suffered severely from the political pressure of industrialized countries such as Germany who urged INSTRAW to merge with the → United Nations Development Fund for Women (UNIFEM). It was argued that the two small organizations for the international advancement of women would be ineffective and inefficient – as the German government stated in the Bundestag in 1999 (Deutscher Bundestag – printed paper 14/772, 15 April 1999).

Thus the member countries reduced voluntary contributions for projects drastically in 1995 and the following years. In 1999 the project budget amounted to 15,000 US dollars. Furthermore, they reduced the so-called core budget for the organization and staff of INSTRAW from the average sum of 1.5 million US dollars in the 1980s and early 1990s, to around 500,000 US dollars, reaching its lowest point in 2004 with 87,638 US dollars.

The combination of political pressure and severe financial problems jeopardized INSTRAW and provoked an impetus for reform within INSTRAW, as

well as political support from the Third World countries in the General Assembly. INSTRAW initiated a process of revitalization and reform in order to focus the Institute's work on certain key areas. In 2004, the *Board of Trustees* was replaced by an *Executive Board* comprising ten delegates from member states elected by ECOSOC for a three-year term. The Director of INSTRAW as well as the Under-Secretary-General for Economic and Social Affairs, a representative of the Dominican Republic as the host country of INSTRAW, and a representative of each of the regional commissions of the ECOSOC are ex-officio members of the Executive Board. The Board meets at least once a year in New York.

During the reform process, in 2004 the new Executive Board of INSTRAW set up its Strategic Plan 2004-2007, formulating its vision as follows: "INSTRAW strives to be a recognized leader in strategic and innovative approaches towards achieving gender equality and making a difference in women's lives". It defines four elements of a new approach, comprising inclusiveness, participatory and team-building approaches, respect for diversity, and transparency and accountability. These elements are combined with four concrete goals, namely (1) that policies are based on results of research, the application of lessons learned, and the replication of best practices, (2) to support governments and civil society when mainstreaming gender into policies and programs, (3) capacity building, and (4) to shape a sound and sustainable institution. After being adopted by the Executive Board of INSTRAW the Strategic Plan was explicitly welcomed by the General Assembly in a resolution on the future operation of INSTRAW in December 2004 (UN Doc. A/RES/59/260, 23 December 2004). In the same resolution the General Assembly urged "Member States to make voluntary contributions, particularly during this critical transitional period". The appeal was successful, and the contributions of the member states were increased in the following years (2005 929,361 US dollars for the trust fund, 648,818 US dollars for the projects, 2006 378,836 US dollars for the trust fund and 961,912 for the projects – figures from "Financial Situation of UN-INSTRAW 2007"). Hence it can be assumed that the explicit political support of the majority of the General Assembly saved INSTRAW from a financial breakdown in 2004 and, has secured its existence as an independent entity in the medium term at least,. This impression was confirmed by a report of the Secretary-General on the future work of INSTRAW delivered in September 2005 to the General Assembly, where he spoke explicitly of the "progress achieved in the revitalization of the International Research and Training Institute for the Advancement of Women (INSTRAW)" (UN Doc. A/60/372, 21 September 2005).

The current research projects of INSTRAW include topics such as "Gender, Migration and Remittances", "Gender, Governance and Political Participation", and "Gender, Peace and Security". Additionally, INSTRAW has set up a Gender Mainstreaming Guide and a gender glossary, as well as a "Gender Training wiki" with information on training opportunities, training material, and more useful information which is available at the website.

Irene Weinz

Lit.: *Deutscher Bundestag:* Antwort der Bundesregierung: Finanzierung des UN-Forschungsinstituts INSTRAW, Bundestags-Drucksache 14/772, 15 April 1999, http://dip.bundestag.de/btd/14/007/140077.pdf; *United Nations - General Assembly:* Future operation of the International Research and Training Institute for the Advancement of Women. Report of the Secretary-General, UN Doc. A/60/372, 21 September 2005; *United Nations INSTRAW:* INSTRAW Strategic Framework 2004-2007, www.un-instraw.org/en/images/stories/INSTRAWDocuments/instrawstrategicframework.pdf; *United Nations - INSTRAW:* Financial Situation of UN-INSTRAW. Report by the Director of the Institute, 25 April 2007, UN Doc. INSTRAW/EB/2007/R.5, www.un-instraw.org/en/images/stories/INSTRAWDocuments/financialsituation-25apr2007-final-website.pdf; *United Nations INSTRAW:* Gender Training Wiki, www.un-instraw.org/wiki/training/index.php/Main-Page; United Nations INSTRAW: Gender Mainstreaming Guide, www.un-instraw.org/en/index.php?option=comwrapper&wrap=Mainstreaming& Itemid =228.

Internet: Homepage of INSTRAW: www.un-instraw.org.

International Economic Relations and New International Economic Order (NIEO)

The 6th Special Session of the UN General Assembly (9 April to 2 May 1974) adopted on 1 May 1974 the "Declaration on the Establishment of a New International Economic Order" (A/RES/3201 (S-VI)) and "Programme of Action on the Establishment of a New International Economic Order" (A/RES/3202 (S-VI)) (→ General Assembly). The declaration was adopted against the votes of the United States and several EC states (Federal Republic of Germany, United Kingdom, Belgium, Luxembourg and Denmark), with 117 positive votes of countries of the Second and Third World, and 10 abstentions out of the Western group of countries. The declaration opened with the words *"We, the members of the United Nations, ... solemnly proclaim our united determination to work urgently for THE ESTABLISHMENT OF A NEW ECONOMIC ORDER based on equity, sovereign equality, interdependence, common interest and the cooperation among all States, irrespective of their economic and social systems which shall correct inequalities and redress existing injustices, make it possible to eliminate the of the widening gap between the developed and the developing countries and ensure steadily accelerating economic and social development and peace and justice for present and future generations..."* For the post-colonial countries, this meant above all that more attention would be drawn to the issues of economic development.

Although the proposals of the "Declaration and the Programme of Action" repeat the general goals of the international development strategy, as well as those goals urgently demanded by the developing countries in the → UNCTAD and other fora, there is a number of new concepts in the declaration: the requirement that the developing countries should have their national resources at their disposal and should form producer cartels, the demand for effective participation in the decision-making process of international financial institutions such as → IMF, for the indexation of commodity prices in relation to the prices of the finished products and finally for the control of transnational corporations.

The programme for the establishment of a *New International Economic Order* (NIEO) considers itself as an attempt to initiate discussion on some of the measures needed for a re-organization of the world's economy. Placed in the historical context in which the debate about the NIEO took place, some common factors may be seen. At the time when the former colonies became independent states, the conviction prevailed everywhere that the problems of the young states had their roots in their former political dependence, and that their economic situation would rapidly improve as they gained their independence and participated fully in international economic relations, with the support of regional and international development programmes. By the end of the 60s these hopes had been shattered.

In spite of a prospering world economy and bilateral and multilateral development programmes, the prosperity gap between the industrialized countries and the most of the developing countries had not only become wider, but the economic situation of the developing countries remained disastrous. The regional and international development programmes and in general the mechanisms of the international economic system had not reached the goals they had seemed to promise. The first *"Development Decade"*, proclaimed by the UN General Assembly in 1961 with great expectations, turned out to be failure just as did the *"Alliance for Progress"* between United States and Latin America, created by the Kennedy administration in 1961. Also the association agreements between the EEC and 17 African Francophone states and Madagascar (Jaunde I 1963, and Jaunde II 1969) had not fulfilled expectations. The *United Nations Trade and Development Conference* (UNCTAD) had a promising start in 1964, but could not make much progress at the second conference in 1968, and thus only increased the frustration of the developing countries.

The developing countries started to realize that political independence would remain an illusion if not supported by a minimal economic independence. The insight gained ground that the international mechanisms and structures connecting the Third World with the industrialized states were incapable of meeting their specific interests. Especially the deteriorating *terms of trade*, i.e. the trade exchange terms between the steadily declining commodity prices and the increasing prices for industrial goods, aroused criticism about the existing international economic system. The new states began to think that this system did not work not *for,* but *against* them, or at least that it placed the economically weaker states at a disadvantage.

As a result the demands for fundamental restructuring measures in favor of the developing countries, within the framework of a *New International Economical Order* (NIEO) to be established, became clearer and more distinct.

The growing self-confidence of the states of the Third World, and the getting through of the declaration for the establishment of a New International Economical Order (NIEO) within the framework of the UN, was preceded by a number of political developments and group formations within the Third World. One of these was the foundation of the *Group of 77,* which became the leading voice for these demands in the following years (→ Group of 77 and the UN).

At the beginning of the 70s their demands were endorsed by Non-Aligned Movement (→ Non-Aligned Movement and the UN), which had developed since its meeting in Bandung in 1955 and its official foundation in Belgrade in 1961, to one of the most influential pressure groups of the Third World.

The most striking manifestation of this change can be found in the "Declaration on Non-Alignment and Economic Progress", adopted at the third summit conference of the heads of states and governments in Lusaka/Zambia in 1970, in the pledge of the member states "to cultivate the spirit of self-reliance and to this end to adopt a firm policy of organising their own socio-economic progress and to raise it to the level of a priority action programme; ... to exercise fully their right and fulfil their duty so as to secure optimal utilization of the natural resources in their territories and in adjacent seas for the development and welfare of their Peoples; ... to broaden and diversify economic relationships with other nations so as to promote true interdependence" and "to foster mutual co-operation among developing countries so as to impart strength to their national endeavour to fortify their independence; ... to intensify and broaden to the maximum extent practicable, the movement for co-operation and integration among developing countries at subregional, and inter-regional levels ..." (quoted from: *Jankowitsch/Sauvant* 1978, 86f.)

The fact that the presentation of a body of conceptually compact and politically massive demands of the Third World states to restructure the world economy had not occurred before 1974, was caused by many political factors. The most important was the energy crisis in 1973/1974. It was a great success for the Organization of Petroleum Ex-

porting Countries (OPEC) to use the commodity "oil" as an instrument to gain economic and political power. Furthermore the shift of emphasis in the UN, away from the issues of the East-West conflict to the North-South issues, contributed much: in the course of → decolonization of large parts of Africa and Asia in the 60s, more and more young states of the Third World became members of the UN (→ Membership and Representation of States). This transformed the UN to an increasing extent into a political forum where, they discussed and negotiated their specific interests and concerns (→ History of the UN). Making use of the basic principle of the UN "one state – one vote", the Third World states were, over the course of time, able to dominate especially the General Assembly. Regardless of the different valuation of these developments it is indisputable that the so-called "oil crisis" determined the moment for the demand for an NIEO, because the Algerian president Boumedienne, at the time president of the Non-Aligned Movement, demanded a special session of the UN General Assembly over commodities and development, as a countermove against the energy conference which had been convened by the United States in February 1974 in Washington. This special session subsequently took place as the sixth special session of the General Assembly, held between 9 April and 2 May 1974, where the "Declaration for a New International Economic Order" was adopted.

The main demands of the declaration (D) and the program of action (P) can be assumed as follows:

"Sovereign equality of States, self-determination of all peoples, inadmissibility of the acquisition of territories by force, territorial integrity and non-interference in internal affairs of other States" (D 4.a);

"The right of every country to adopt the economic and social system that it deems the most appropriate for it own development and not to be subjected to

423

discrimination of any kind as a result" (D 4.d);

"Full permanent sovereignty of every State over its natural resources ... including the right to nationalization or transfer of ownership to its nationals" (D 4.e);

" Regulation and supervision of the activities of transnational corporations by taking measures in the interest of the national economies of the countries where such transnational corporations operate on the basis of the full sovereignty of those countries" (D 4.g; P V.a-e);

"Just and equitable relationship between the prices the prices of raw materials, primary commodities, manufactured and semi-manufactured goods exported by developing countries and the prices of raw materials, primary commodities, manufactures, capital goods and equipment imported by them ..." (D 4.j; P I.1.d);

"Extension of active assistance to developing countries by the whole international community, free of any political and military conditions" (D 4k);

"Preferential and non-reciprocal treatment for developing countries ..." (D 4.n);

"Giving the developing countries access to the achievements of modern science and technology, and promoting the transfer of technology and the creation of indigenous technology ... in forms and accordance with procedures which are suited to their economies" (D 4p; P IV.a-e);

"The strengthening ... of mutual economic, trade, financial and technical co-operation among the developing countries, mainly on a preferential basis" (D 4.s; P VII.1.a-h);

"Facilitating the role which producers' associations may play within the framework of international co-operation ..." (D 4.t; P I.1.c);

"Expeditious formulation of commodity agreements ... in order to regulate as necessary and to stabilize the world markets for raw materials and primary commodities; (P I.3.a iii);

"Preparation of an over-all integrated programme, ... for a comprehensive range of commodities of export interest to developing countries" (P I.3.a.iv);

"The setting up of buffer stocks within the framework of commodity arrangements ... with the aim of favouring the producer developing and consumer developing countries and of contributing to the expansion of world trade as a whole" (P I.3.a.xi);

"Improved access to markets in developed countries through the progressive removal of tariff and non-tariff barriers and of restrictive business practices" (P I.3.a.ii);

Reform of the world food system (P I.2.a-i);

Measures to finance and development of developing countries and to meet the balance-of-payment crises in the developing world (P II.2.a-i);

Promotion of the industrialization of the developing countries (P III. a-d);

"Strengthening the role of the United Nations system in the field of international economic co-operation", especially the work of the conference for trade and development of the United Nations (P IX.1-8);

The Declaration and the Programme of Action contained in a *Special Programme (Part X)* a number of demands with regard to the less developed and most seriously affected countries (LDCs) such as:

"Commodity assistance, including food aid ..." (3.c);

"Long-term suppliers' credits on easy terms" (3.d);

"Establishment of a link between the creation of special drawing rights and developing assistance..." (3.g);

"Debt renegotiation an a case-by-case basis with a view to concluding agreements on debt cancellation, moratorium or rescheduling" (3.i).

The demand for a NIEO was without any doubt an enormous political and economic challenge for the industrialized countries, because it aimed in essence at a change of the traditional North-South-Relations (→ North-South-

Relations and the UN) in favor of the developing countries, and it thereby questioned the traditional privileges of the industrialized states. But, in sober fact, the reaction of the Western industrialized countries was astonishing. They saw the demand for a NIEO as assault on the "free" market economy and feared the establishment of a dirigiste international planned economy. But neither the Declaration nor the Programme of Action aimed at establishing a fundamentally new order, but retained the anachronistic principles of the international division of labor, and were basically trade-oriented. Only the goals concerning the commodity policy contained aspects that were likely to give the commodity producers larger slices of the cake. Even the nightmare of commodity cartels modeled after the OPEC was not realistic from the beginning, because it was questionable whether all existing commodities could produce those positive features which oil possessed in order to be able, as "cartel of commodity producers," to push through their own interests against the industrialized countries.

In spite of positive developments within the North-South-Dialogue since 1974, bringing a change from the era of "petition" to an era of "action", "the material results of the achievements to establish an NIEO have remained so far relatively little, compared with the amount and scope of the catalogue of demands of the developing countries. In comparison to the euphoric atmosphere of departure on the side of the developing countries and the hectic political nervousness on the side of the industrialized countries in 1974, today there are everywhere signs of tiredness and wear to be seen." (*Matthies* 1980, 27)

The reasons for this can be attributed to the following factors and developments:
- the lack of consistency and a failure to set priorities in the catalogue of demands;
- the partly deliberate dissipation of the demands through the distribution, by

the industrialized countries, of the negotiations to different conferences and fora;
- the increasing divergence of interests among the developing countries caused by processes of increasing diversification, resulting in a weakened negotiating position;
- a serious lack of structural balance in the relation between the industrialized countries and the developing countries, which could not be resolved by negotiations.

Against the backdrop of a changed political world situation after the dissolution of the Soviet empire and the end of the East-West-Conflict, both of which the Third World had used as instruments to push through their demands, there was a new thinking in the offing at the beginning of the 90s, with regard to the new structure of the international economic relations. The first evidence for this was provided by the resolution on the "Declaration on International Economic Co-operation", adopted by the 18th Special Session of the General Assembly on international economic co-operation on 1 May 1990 (UN Doc. A/RES/S-18/3), where the responsibility of every single state for its own development was pointed out, as well as the particular modes of influence of the industrialized countries on the world economy and the ensuing consequences and results. The same trend was revealed by the results of the UNCTAD IX Conference in Midrand/South Africa 1996, the "Midrand Declaration and A Partnership for Growth and Development" (UN Doc. TD/377, 24 May 1976), where not only the demand for establishing a NIEO was not mentioned anymore in the final documents, but where also in consensus the neo-liberal aim of a growth-oriented economy in the industrialized countries was confirmed, which was expected to give positive impulses to all developing countries. Moreover the removal of the deficits was declared as a task for which every state is responsible on its own. With this statement the debate to establish a NIEO, which had also suited the expectations and needs of the states of the South, seems to be a thing of the past.

Mir A. Ferdowsi

Lit.: *Bartoszewicz, T.:* Institutional Aspects of International Trade in the Eighties: Opportunities and Barriers, in: Development and Peace 2 (1981), 133-142; *Bhagwati, J. N. (ed.):* The New International Economic Order: The North-South Debate, Cambridge 1977; *Galtung, J.:* The North/South Debate: Technology, Basic Human Needs, and the New International Economic Order, New York 1980; *Galtung, J.:* Überlegungen zu einer neuen Weltwirtschaftsordnung. Die alte, neue und zukünftige Ordnung, in: Ferdowsi, M.A. (ed.): Johan Galtung: Self-Reliance. Beiträge zu einer alternativen Entwicklungsstrategie, Munich 1983, 19-45; *Graham, A.:* Die Neue internationale Wirtschaftsordnung – eine schwindende Vision? in: VN 27 (1979), 162-167; *Heinz, U.:* International Economic Order, in: Wolfrum, R. (ed.): United Nations: Law, Policies and Practice, Vol. 2, Munich/Dordrecht 1995, 749-759; *Jankowitsch, O./Sauvant, K.P. (eds.):* The Third World Without Superpowers. The Collected Documents on the Non-Aligned Countries, Dobbs Ferry/USA 1978; *Khushi, M.K./Matthies, V. (eds.):* Collective Self-Reliance: Programme und Perspektiven der Dritten Welt, Munich et al. 1978; *Matthies, V.:* Neue Weltwirtschaftsordnung. Hintergründe – Positionen – Argumente, Opladen 1980; *Mkandawire, T.:* The New International Economic Order, Basic Needs Strategies and the Future of Africa, in: Africa Development 5 (1980), No. 3, 68-90; *O'Manique, J.:* Canadian Decision Makers and the New International Economic Order, in: Canadian Journal of Development Studies 1 (1980), 382-399; *Petersmann, E.-U.:* International Economic Order, in: Bernhardt, R. (ed.): EPIL 8 (1985), 336-343; *Sauvant, K.P./Hasenpflug, H. (eds.):* The New International Economic Order: Confrontation or Cooperation between North and South? Boulder 1978; *Sauvant, K.P.:* Von der politischen zur wirtschaftlichen Unabhängigkeit? Die Ursprünge des Programms der NWWO, in: VN 27 (1979), 49-52; *Streeten, P.:* Approaches to a New International Economic Order, in: World Development 10 (1982), 1-17; *Streeten, P.:* The New International Economic Order: Development Strategy Options, in:

Development and Peace 1 (1980), No. 2, 5-25; *Tetzlaff, R.:* Perspektiven und Grenzen der Neuen Weltwirtschaftsordnung, in: Nohlen, D./Nuscheler, F. (eds.): Handbuch der Dritten Welt, Vol. 1: Unterentwicklung und Entwicklung: Theorien – Strategien – Indikatoren, Hamburg 1982, 273-291; *United Nations Conference on Trade and Development:* Midrand Declaration and A Partnership for Growth and Development, 24 May 1996 (UN Doc. TD/377); *United Nations - General Assembly:* Declaration on the Establishment of a New International Economic Order, UN Doc. A/RES/3201 (S-VI), 1 May 1974); *United Nations - General Assembly:* Programme of Action on the Establishment of a New International Economic Order, UN Doc. A/RES/3202 (S-VI), 1 May 1974); *Williams, M.:* International Economic Organization and the Third World, New York et al. 1996.

Addendum

While the polarized debate on the NIEO has faded away in recent times, tectonic shifts in the world economy and, concomitantly, in the global political order have been evolving since the start of the 21st century. The centre of gravity is shifting from the West to Asia, with China and India as key drivers of global change. Key nations from other continents, such as Brazil, Mexico and South Africa, are also gaining economic and political clout. If one takes the GDP (gross domestic product) at current exchange rates as measure, China has, in the year 2008, overtaken Germany to assume rank three of the global league, after the U.S. and Japan. That country is expected to move on to second place by 2011. On the basis of purchasing power parity, which better reflects economic achievement levels, China and India have already progressed to second and third position, respectively. In 2003, the acronym "BRICS economies", referring to Brazil, Russia, India and China, received worldwide attention. Analysts from the investment firm Goldman Sachs had predicted that this group of countries would catch up with leading industrialized countries in less than 40 years and would become the principal driving force of global demand growth and spending power.

While the newly-gained material strength of emerging powers is beyond dispute, the global governance system still has to accommodate the new players. Unfortunately, the United Nations, particularly ECOSOC, have not been accepted by industrialized countries as platform of policy coordination for the global economy. Outside of the UN's ambit, the then leading industrial countries USA, United Kingdom, Canada, Japan, France, Germany and Italy instead established for this purpose, in the 1970s, the *Group of Seven (G7)*; after Russia joined the group in 1998, the group is called the *Group of Eight (G8)*. Annual G8 summits have turned into major media events with broad political agendas which increasingly attract worldwide criticism and street protest. The G8 is seen by many as an ineffective, undemocratic institution which protects the interests of the West and undercuts universal structures (cf. *Hajnal* 2007). However, it would be unfair to completely dismiss the "rich nations' club", especially from a development perspective, since it has promoted important initiatives such as debt relief for low-income countries and additional assistance to Africa. Increasingly, the G8 has engaged in outreach efforts to include other relevant countries in its debates.

The most advanced step in this direction is a recent German diplomatic initiative, the so-called "Heiligendamm Process (HP)", which provides for a topic-driven policy dialogue continuing until July 2009 between the G8 and five rising economies from the South: Brazil, China, India, Mexico and South Africa,. After some hesitation, this group has begun to project itself onto the international stage as a collective actor, the G5. The HP works on four global issues of critical importance: development, particularly in Africa; innovation and research, including intellectual property rights; and energy efficiency and cross-border investment.

The HP has to manage widely diverging objectives of participating countries. Some G8 countries, such as the USA and Japan, are ambiguous in their mindset, since they tend to see the HP as a covert attempt of summit enlargement, which they oppose. Others from that group, like Great Britain and France, openly favor the formal inclusion of all or at least some of the G5 members and suspect the HP of stalling the momentum in this direction. The G5 countries see themselves as emerging leaders who deserve a place at the apex of the global hierarchy. The HP, in their eyes, can hardly fulfill this ambition, but is rather understood as an intermediate step. In demanding tangible concessions from the global North on a long shopping list of development concerns, e.g. trade, migration, aid, debt and technology transfer, the emerging powers tie the legitimacy of the process to genuine progress for the developing world. The industrialized countries, in contrast, are focused on process and legitimacy by symbolic inclusion without yielding any real power.

The Japanese hosts of the 2008 summit had mixed feelings on the HP, which are possibly linked to their uneasy relationship with China. It was only through intensive diplomatic manœuvring, especially from the German side, that the G5 were officially invited. In order to balance the privileged position of this group, Japan also invited Australia, Indonesia and South Korea to a "Major Economies Meeting (MEM) on Energy Security and Climate Change", enhancing the credibility of the climate initiative by U.S. president Bush, which, many believe, runs counter to UN-sponsored negotiations for a post-2012 agreement. The Hokkaido summit turned into a global event on a scale not witnessed before. Outreach efforts by Japanese hosts led to a record-breaking participation of developing countries with a total of 14 invited leaders, including seven from Africa (cf. *Jaura* 2008). The summit was also, in certain segments, attended by the UN

427

Secretary-General, the Commission of the African Union, World Bank, International Monetary Fund, Organization for Economic Cooperation and Development and International Energy Agency. Thus, international participation came close to the historic Cancun (Mexico) North-South summit on international cooperation and development in October 1981.

Despite the lack of consensus on many issues at the Hokkaido 2008 summit, the HP still holds considerable promise for advancing the North-South dialogue in the global economy. Its long-term impact will, to a large extent, be determined at the 2009 summit hosted by Italy. Much will depend on how divisions within the two country groups will be managed. The G8 will need to find a common position on how to proceed with the summit architecture. Within the G5, underlying tensions between China and India could put a strain on the group's capacity for collective action. In Latin America, Mexico and Brazil vie for leadership while South Africa's claim to regional leadership remains contested and Mexico still has to define its position vis-à-vis the OECD and developing countries. IBSA, the tripartite alliance of Southern democracies, encompassing India, Brazil and South Africa, might gain in relevance as self-directed project of strategic cooperation while, in comparison, the G5 constitutes "only" a relational response to G8 outreach. On the other hand, the emerging constellation of the BRIC countries (Brazil, Russia, India and China), which have recently met at the level of foreign ministers, may prove to be an attractive alternative to any G8-sponsored dialogue. One should, however, not underestimate legitimacy concerns of the G5 in justifying a privileged relationship with the West towards antagonistic audiences in the developing world, the G77 and the Non-Aligned Movement.

After the conclusion of the HP in 2009, the best option for summit reform would be a formal enlargement of the group, preferably following the MEM formula and then adding an Arab country (e.g. Egypt) and a further country from Sub-Saharan Africa like Nigeria. In the medium term, European Union members should agree to be represented by a single voice, the Council President, which would enhance foreign policy integration and, at the same time, take account of Europe's declining weight in the global economy. The reformed summit should strive for close cooperation with the UN system, especially through ECOSOC and UNCTAD, and other multilateral bodies but also provide institutionalized avenues for dialogue with non-state actors, e.g. from civil society and private business.

It is however, highly unlikely, that the UN system (ECOSOC, UNCTAD etc.) will assume a central role for global economic policies in the near to medium-term future. The broad membership base of ECOSOC and its low status vis-à-vis the Security Council and the General Assembly do not provide an environment conducive for policy coordination of global players. UNCTAD) is mainly perceived as a think tank for developing countries with limited significance for the industrialized world. It can be safely speculated that the future international economic order will be characterized by a multi-polar constellation in which Asia will become a decisive actor (*Mahbubani* 2008). Beyond the new summit architecture, other forms of intergovernmental dialogue among leading nations from North and South will become ever more important for international consensus-building such as the G20 (finance) which acts as an informal forum of global financial governance (*Martinez-Diaz* 2007).

Thomas Fues

Lit.: *Cooper, A.F./Antkiewicz, A. (eds.):* Emerging Powers in Global Governance. Lessons from the Heiligendamm Process (Studies in International Governance Series – The Centre for International Governance Innovation (CIGI)), Waterloo/Canada 2008; *Hajnal, P.:* Summitry from G5 to L20: A

Review of Reform Initiatives (Centre for International Governance Innovation (CIGI) – Working Paper No. 20), March 2007, www. cgionline.org; *Jaura, R.:* Add Another Five – In a Way, in: Development Watch, 13 July 2008, www.php.developmentwatch.net/article.php?/sid=418; *Kaplinsky, R./Messner, D.:* Introduction: The Impact of Asian Drivers on the Developing World, in: World Development 36 (2008) 197–209; *Mahbubani, K.:* The New Asian Hemisphere: The Irresistible Shift of Global Power to the East, New York 2008; *Martinez-Diaz, L:* The G20 After Eight Years: How Effective a Vehicle for Developing-Country Influence? (The Brookings Institution – Global Economy and Development Working Paper No. 12), Washington, D.C. 2007, www.brookings.edu; *Whalley, J.:* China in the World Trading System (Centre for International Governance Innovation (CIGI) – Working Paper No. 2), October 2005, www. cgionline.org; *Wilson, D./Purushothaman, R.:* Dreaming with BRICs: The Path to 2050 (Goldman Sachs Global Economics Paper No. 99), New York 2003, http://www2.goldmansachs.com/ideas/brics/book/99-dreaming.pdf.

International Law and the UN

I. Introduction

At its 44th session the → General Assembly of the UN adopted a resolution about the *United Nations Decade of International Law* for the years 1990-1999 (UN Doc. A/RES/44/23, 17 November 1989). The resolution on the Decade of International Law did not have a particular effect on the pace of creation and development of international law. Nevertheless the activities of the → ILC (International Law Commission), which led to the adoption of a "Draft Code of Crimes against Peace and Security of Mankind" by the ILC in July 1996 (YBILC 1996, Vol. II, Part Two, para. 49) which was approved by the General Assembly in resolution A/RES/51/160 of 16 December 1996 (text of the Draft Code: UN Doc. A/51/10, chapter II, para. 30-50) and to the adoption of the "Rome Statute of the International Criminal Court" (→ ICC) which was adopted in July 1998 (UN Doc. A/CONF.183/9, 17 July 1998) by a diplomatic conference of plenipotentiaries on the establishment of an International Criminal Court , were two outstanding achievements in the development of international law during that period.

The development of international law includes the *creation, formation and confirmation* of international legal norms. *Klein* refers in this context to the determination and creation of law. This process differs from national legislative processes in that it involves the direct participation of the subjects of international law as well as non-state actors, non-governmental organizations (→ NGOs) and transnational corporations (TNCs); and is marked by an absence of central legislative organs and specific executive institutions. In contrast to national constitutions, the UN Charter (→ Charter of the UN) does not regulate the creation of norms of international law or their implementation.

In the UN system, initiatives for the development of international law primarily originate in the General Assembly. Still under the impact of the horrors and sufferings of World War II, UN member states entrusted the General Assembly with establishing an international order based on the rule of law which is able efficiently to maintain international peace and security.

In addition especially the → ECOSOC, the → Security Council, the → Secretariat of the → Secretary General and the → ICJ participate in the development of international law.

ECOSOC can make recommendations for the purpose of promoting respect for, and observance of, human rights and fundamental freedoms (Art. 62 (2)), prepare draft conventions with respect to matters falling within its competence (Art. 62 (3)), and call international conferences on such matters (Art. 62 (4)).

The *Security Council*, which can make binding decisions for the maintenance of international peace and security (Arts. 24 and 25), thereby also influences the development of international law, in particular with regard to the prohibition of the use of force (→

Use of Force, Prohibition of) and the → peaceful settlement of disputes.

The *Secretariat* participates in the development of international law through the preparation of draft conventions at the request of the General Assembly and other organs of the UN (→ UN System). The registration of treaties entered into by any member state of the UN is also carried out by the Secretariat (Art. 102). Finally the International Court of Justice is worth mentioning in this context. Its decisions and advisory opinions are important subsidiary means for the determination of rules of international law (Art. 38 (1) ICJ Statute), contributing to the specification of general principles of law and of international customary law.

II. Development

The earliest significant efforts to codify international law were made at the Vienna Congress of 1814-15 and the Hague Peace Conferences of 1899 and 1907. The states parties to the Paris Agreement of 1814 adopted regulations on navigation in international rivers, and on the abolition of slave trade. Both times, in Vienna and The Hague, specialists in international law, either working on their own or within a framework of scientific associations, formulated the respective norms. Two international associations for the codification of international law, both founded in 1873, the *Institut de Droit International* and the *International Law Association*, submitted draft codifications which later became the basis for governmental codification work.

The *Hague Peace Conference* of 1899 adopted, inter alia, the Hague Regulations respecting the Laws and Customs of War on Land and a convention on the peaceful settlement of international disputes. The second Hague Peace Conference of 1907 agreed upon no less than 13 conventions on the laws of war on land and sea, and on the law of neutrality, most of which, however, did not become effective.

In 1930, the → *League of Nations* convened a codification conference with representatives of member states par-

ticipating. This conference has generally been rated a failure. The proposed rules of international state responsibility concerning the rights of aliens were not passed, and only a few articles of the project concerning the territorial seas were provisionally adopted. In 1931, the League of Nations Assembly adopted a resolution on the procedure of codification, which called for a strengthening of the influence of governments in every phase of the codification process. This aspect was later incorporated in the statute of the ILC, and concretized by the establishment of expert committees for the preparation of codifications.

The UN Charter vests the General Assembly with *a right to initiate the development of international law*. The activities of the General Assembly, and its bodies established by it, mainly resulted in a progressive development of international law. In that development the respective organs are guided by the objectives and purposes which are laid down in the preamble of the UN Charter, namely "to save succeeding generations from the scourge of war", "to reaffirm faith in fundamental rights", and "to establish conditions under which justice and respect for the obligations arising from treaties and other sources of international law can be maintained".

III. Competences for the Development of International Law within the Framework of the UN Charter

The UN participates in the development of international law essentially, through the formation and confirmation of law, the elaboration of codification of international law and the interpretation of general international law.

The development of international law amounts to more than a mere enumeration of norms. The process rather covers the sum of activities of the participating UN organs, as well as the variety of necessary steps in their entirety. There is no other international organization participating so intensively and decisively in the establishment and development of international law – the activity of the UN "motorizes" the development of treaty and customary international law (*Simma* 1975, 85). However, the establishment of a legal duty to comply with newly established norms is reserved to the action of the individual states.

Documents are created and debated which express customary international law, and codification of international law, or they are drafted as recommendations. The UN fulfils the tasks of formation of law, preparation of codifications of international law and interpretation of general international law.

The General Assembly, as the only organ to which the Charter expressly assigns the task of developing international law, is supported by several subsidiary organs: its Legal Committee (Sixth Committee), the Special Political and Decolonization Committee (Fourth Committee) (→ Committees, System of), the ILC and → UNCITRAL, and further by special committees, for instance those for → space law, → decolonization and for the revision of the UN Charter, the Special Committee on the Charter of the UN and on the Strengthening of the Role of the Organization (→ Reform of the UN). In addition, the General Assembly established a number of ad-hoc committees, such as the committee preparing the draft of the "Definition of Aggression" resolution (UN Doc. A/RES/3314 (XXIX), 14 December 1974) (→ Aggression, Definition of), the committee elaborating the Declaration on Principles of International Law concerning Friendly Relations and Cooperation among States in accordance with the Charter of the UN (A/RES/ 2625 (XXV), 24 October 1970), and the UN Disarmament Commission (→ Disarmament).

The regulatory basis for the development of international law by the UN is Article 13 (1) lit. a UN Charter, which assigns to the General Assembly the task of encouraging "the progressive development of international law and its codification". This task is connected with the general mandate of the General Assembly stated in Article 11 (1) to "consider the general principles of cooperation in the maintenance of interna-

tional peace and security, including the principles governing disarmament and the regulation of armaments". For that purpose and in order to contribute to the promotion of "international co-operation in the economic, social, cultural, educational and health fields", and with the aim of "assisting in the realization of human rights and fundamental freedoms for all" (Art. 13 (1) lit. b), the General Assembly may initiate studies and make recommendations. For the fulfillment of the tasks of the General Assembly established in Article 13 (1) lit. b the second paragraph of Article 13 refers to Chapters IX and X of the Charter.

Article 22 authorizes the General Assembly to establish "subsidiary organs as it deems necessary for the performance of its functions", while Article 68 authorizes ECOSOC to "set up commissions in economic and social fields, and for the promotion of human rights" (→ Human Rights, Commission on).

1. The unity of progressive development of international law and codification

Following the formulation in Article 13, the ILC, as the most important of the mentioned subsidiary organs, has specified in Article 15 et seq. of its statute the promotion *of progressive development* of international law and its *codification* as its principal task. The progressive development of international law is meant to include "the preparation of draft conventions on subjects which have not yet been regulated by international law, or in regard to which the law has not yet been sufficiently developed in the practice of States" (Art. 15 ILC Statute).

Codification, on the other hand, is understood as the identification and registration of norms of international law, as well as their more precise formulation and systematization. It is, however, not easy to understand why Article 13 (1) lit. a UN Charter and Article 15 ILC Statute make such a distinction between "progressive development" and "codification". This distinction is also not tenable in terms of the theory of international law; every codification includes, to a different degree, at the same time elements of codification and of progressive development (*Fleischhauer* 1994, 271). The border between the formation of international law in the sense of its new creation and the codification of international law is fluid; new rules arise from already existing codifications, and a codification always includes new rules. This connection between progressive development and codification of international law requires that the two be considered as a unity, or parts of a continuum.

Almost all fields of international law are included in this process of development. In turn, a multitude of members of the international community of states is affected. As typical examples one may point to the law of treaties (→ Treaties, Law of), the → law of the sea, the law of diplomatic and consular relations, and → human rights. In the process of development of international law all UN member states are given an equitable opportunity for participation. This aspect has been especially important for the newly independent states → Decolonization).

2. Conferences of Member States to Develop Codifications of International Law

The *General Assembly* has the competence to convene conferences of member states with the task of discussing, finalizing and adopting conventions for the codification of international law. That is preceded by the preparation of draft conventions by the subsidiary organs of the General Assembly, in particular the ILC. The subjects are partly chosen by the ILC itself, partly they are suggested to it by the General Assembly or by ECOSOC. After their adoption by the respective conference, the conventions can be accepted by individual states by way of signing and ratifying or, later, acceding to them. Of the manifold contributions to the development of international law by the ILC the following codificatory works are particularly worth mentioning: the Conventions on the Law of the Sea of 1958 (Convention

on the Territorial Sea and the Contiguous Zone (UNTS Vol. 516, No. 7477, 205), Convention on the High Seas (UNTS Vol. 450, No. 6465, 11), Convention on Fishing and Conservation of the Living Resources of the High Seas (UNTS Vol. 559, No. 8164, 285) and the Optional Protocol of Signature concerning the Compulsory Settlement of Disputes (UNTS Vol. 450, No. 6466, 169), and the Convention on the Continental Shelf (UNTS Vol. 499, No. 7302, 311)), the Vienna Convention on Diplomatic Relations (1961 in Vienna; UNTS, Vol. 500, 95), the Vienna Convention on Consular Relations (1963 in Vienna; UNTS Vol. 596, No. 8638); the Vienna Convention on the Law of Treaties (1969 in Vienna; UNTS Vol. 1155, No. 18232); the Convention on the Succession of States in Respect of Treaties (1978 in Vienna); the Convention on the Succession of States in Respect of State Property, Archives and Debts (1983 in Vienna), and the Rome Statute for the International Criminal Court (1998 in Rome; UN Doc. A/CONF.183/9).

The UN Commission on International Trade Law (→ UNCITRAL), which was established by the General Assembly as a subsidiary organ in 1966 (UN Doc. A/RES/2205 (XXI)), is to play an active role in promoting "the progressive harmonization and unification of the law of international trade". For that purpose it prepares draft conventions in the field of international trade law and submits them to the UN General Assembly which then convenes conferences for the adoption of the conventions. As first draft convention, the convention regarding the statute of prescription (limitation) in international trade of goods was passed at a session of UNCITRAL in 1974 and it was then adopted as convention (UNTS Vol. 1511, No. 26119) by a UN conference, convened for this purpose in June 1974 by the General Assembly through resolution 3104 (XXVIII) of 12 December 1973. In 1980 an additional protocol to the convention was adopted (UNTS Vol. 1511, No. 26120). In 1978 the "Convention on the International Carriage of Goods by Sea" (UNTS Vol. 1695, No. 29215) was adopted by a conference convened for this purpose by General Assembly resolution 31/100 of 15 December 1976. In 1980 the "UN Convention on Contracts for the International Sale of Goods" (CISG) basing on the draft worked out by UNCITRAL was passed by a diplomatic conference (UNTS Vol. 1489, No. 25567).

3. The Codification Process

The General Assembly also participates *directly* in the development of international law when it adopts by a resolution draft conventions prepared by organs of the UN, and calls upon states to sign and ratify them. Outstanding examples of such treaties are the two human rights covenants prepared by the Commission on Human Rights and adopted by A/RES/2200 A (XXI) on 16 December 1966: the International Covenant on Civil and Political Rights (UNTS Vol. 999, No. 14668; → Human Rights Conventions, CCPR), and the International Covenant on Economic, Social and Cultural Rights (UNTS Vol. 993, No. 14531; → Human Rights Conventions, CESCR).

Highly important is also the Treaty on the Non-Proliferation of Nuclear Weapons (in short Non-Proliferation Treaty), first drafted by the Committee on Disarmament (adopted by A/RES/2373 (XXII) on 12 December 1968).

The Statute of the International Criminal Court was developed under the significant participation of the ILC. As early as 1950 the General Assembly decided with resolution A/RES/489 (V) to establish a Committee on International Criminal Jurisdiction with the task of preparing "one or more preliminary draft conventions relating to the establishment and the statute of an international criminal court". This first draft was influenced by the violations of international law by Germany and Japan as well as the judgments of the international military tribunals of Nuremberg and Tokyo. After discussing the report of the committee at the seventh session of the General Assembly in 1952 ex-haustively the Assembly decided with resolution A/RES/687 (VII) to further study "the problems relating to an international criminal jurisdiction" and established a new committee with the same task as the first. This committee presented its report with a revised draft statute for the international criminal court in 1954 (UN Report of the 1953 Committee on International Jurisdiction, UN Doc. A/2645, Annex). Because of the major differences between the USA and the USSR, the General Assembly decided to postpone the debate on the draft statute (UN Doc. A/RES/898 (IX), 14 December 1954). For a long period the work on a statute for an international criminal court paused.

In 1989, initiated by the General Assembly (A/RES/44/39 of 4 December 1989), the work to develop a statute for an international criminal court was taken up by the ILC and in 1994 a draft statute (UN Doc. A/49/10 (SUPP)) was proposed to the General Assembly. In 1996 the General Assembly established by resolution A/RES/51/207 a Preparatory Committee on the Establishment of an International Criminal Court to submit a draft statute which would yield broad consensus among the member states and convened by resolution A/RES/52/160 of 15 December 1997 a "Conference of Plenipotentiaries on the Establishment of an International Criminal Court".

This met in Rome from 15 to 17 June 1998. This conference adopted on July 17, 1998 the "Rome Statute of the International Criminal Court" (UN Doc. A/CONF.183/9). The Model Law on Cross-Border Insolvency adopted in 1997 by the General Assembly (UN Doc. A/RES/52/158, Annex) is the most recent example for the work of UNCITRAL.

4. The interpretation of general international law

The influence that such General Assembly resolutions have exerted on the development of international law can be illustrated by discussing the Friendly Relations Declaration and the Declara-

433

tion on the Granting of Independence. The latter proclaimed, explicitly referring to the UN Charter, the right of all peoples "to complete freedom, the exercise of their sovereignty and the integrity of their national territory" (preamble). All peoples are said to have "the right to self-determination; by virtue of that right they freely determine their political status and freely pursue their economic, social and cultural development" (para. 2). The right to self-determination includes the right of suppressed peoples to resist racist regimes and to fight against them (para. 4). In the Special Committee on Decolonization the provisions of the declaration served as guidelines for its work.

However, the principles of international law specified and concretized in this declaration, in particular the right to self-determination (→ Self-Determination, Right to), also became an important subject of subsequent resolutions of the General Assembly and of international treaties and were also included in national constitutions. This demonstrates the *interrelationship* between processes of social development and the development of international law; it makes obvious how this *interaction* contributes to the progressive development of international law and law in general.

The Friendly Relations Declaration, in which the main principles of international law as contained in the Charter of the UN have been assembled and specified, has had the most extensive influence on the development of international law. Among all the respective resolutions of the General Assembly, it holds a special position. Like all other resolutions of the General Assembly it is not an original, primary source of international law. Nevertheless the Declaration, which was adopted without vote, can be regarded as an *authoritative interpretation* of the principles of international law proclaimed in the Charter, an interpretation which supports states in the application and the interpretation of the principles of the Charter, and guides the further development of those principles. It is in this sense that the ILC designated

the Friendly Relations Declaration a *commentary* for its future activity in the progressive development of international law (Report of the ILC on the second part of its 17th session, 3-28 January 1966, UN Doc. A/6309/Rev.1, para. 76ff.).

The ICJ has confirmed this high importance of the declaration in its judgment in the Nuclear Tests case (Australia v. France). The ICJ relied on the Friendly Relations Declaration when deciding whether the dispute was of a political or a legal nature. It stated that citing the Friendly Relations Declaration means using normative material (ICJ Reports 1974, 361, 366ff.). The ICJ, which has to take its decisions on the basis of international law according to Article 38 (1) of the ICJ Statute, exerts an influence on the development of international law while determining the applicable elements of international law in the concrete case. Thus the ICJ participates in the specification and progressive development of international law through the *interpretation of the customary international law in force and of the international treaties*.

As it describes these basic principles and objectives of the UN Charter and establishes references between the single elements according to the underlying systematics, the binding character of the principles of the UN Charter is transferred to this document, the Friendly Relations Declaration. Thus the declaration supports the states in the application and the interpretation of the principles of the Charter. Also the voting behavior of the states supports this assessment of the declaration: the resolution was adopted without any votes against or abstentions.

Generally here the question arises what character the cited resolutions do actually have. The question involves both, the problem of the *legal sources* in international law and the *formative power* of these documents. Thus the dynamics of international law becomes evident: resolutions are themselves constituent parts of international law, and are apt to enrich international legal norms, or to contribute to the creation of new norms, as may be the case with the right to development. But it cannot be disregarded that resolutions are not sources of international law *per se*, although they can exert a more or less strong influence on it.

International law is agreement law in the forms of treaty law and customary law; those are the only two existing sources of law. The member states of the UN can put the General Assembly in charge of the development of international law and thus initiate and sustain the process of lawmaking, but they cannot ensure and guarantee it. The agreement is the only basis for the validity of international law.

However, there may be doubts in specific cases, whether it is already an international customary legal norm which has been *strengthened* by a resolution, or whether the resolution helps in *promoting* the creation of such a norm, and this norm is thus on its way to an agreement in international law. The common grounds of reaching agreements in international law and of adopting resolutions is the co-ordination, the conjunction of the will of the states and of their interests. But only where legal conviction and certain legal concepts lead to an agreement, do rights and duties arise for the states and the norm becomes legally binding. A resolution lies thus in the approaches of international law agreements; the resolutions are always recommendations for a certain way of behavior. The phrasing of the International Court of Justice in its Namibia Advisory Opinion, speaking of an *operative design* (ICJ Reports 1971, 50) with respect to resolutions, also can be understood in this manner. Resolutions have this effect only when their content has *been commonly accepted*. However, those resolutions are not just proposals or desiderata, but legal demands and thus they constitute specific contributions to the development of international law.

From the richness and variety of resolutions, there follows also consequently a differentiation with respect to the influence which these norms may have in the creation, implementation, consolidation and further development of international law. When one outlines the content of the resolutions of the General Assembly one finds that they refer to the following complexes of problems: *first* to a practice of international law which is confirmed as international customary law (Human Rights Declaration), *second* to customary legal norms which are interpreted (the Friendly Relations Declaration), *third* to a standard or scale which has been set up for the process of law development (Declaration on the Granting of Independence) and *fourth* to situations that concern international conflicts (Namibia Resolution) or topical problem complexes (environmental protection). It might thus be argued that, for example, the Human Rights Declaration and the Friendly Relations Declaration have exerted a larger influence on the development of international law than some conventions.

Resolutions lie within the *grey area between legal demands and legal norms*. In order to judge their influence on the development of international law the voting behavior (→ Voting Right and Decision-Making Procedures; → Rules of Procedure) with respect to a resolution has to be taken into account, as well as the question whether the resolution aims to strengthen extensive existing international law, or intends to promote the creation of new norms and thus has the effect of an authoritative statement (*Frowein* 1976) and performs a law-making function (*Brownlie* 2003, 663). Resolutions have thus an *indirect law-making effect*. A resolution may thus be said to take the middle position between a demand and a norm, as a supportive instrument and guideline for achieving international law agreements and for the preparation of further resolutions.

Finally, a tendency can be observed in that the lengthy establishment of international customary law is complemented by the phrasing of legal convictions in the form of resolutions. Legal conviction (*opinio iuris*) can thus be seen as a catalyst in the process of establishing customary law. The pace of international cooperation has clearly accelerated, and the international interweaving has increased. Much time is saved by creative reliance on legal convictions which in the past would develop over a long period of time and would draw on many and diverse sources. A faster way of developing legal norms than customary law, a way adjusted to the higher pace of development in the social and political fields, has been found in the adoption of resolutions.

The practice of the UN bodies of mentioning certain resolutions recurrently provides the element of repetition which is of importance to the establishment of international customary law. Thus in a certain way, one can apply an analogy to the creation of customary law with resolutions under the aspect of repetition. This does not imply that a steady repetition of the contents of resolutions or its steady citation automatically creates customary law. It rather implies that customary law is stimulated by this practice. Only if the will to agree with a certain practice has been expressed, and if there is an explicit legally binding acknowledgement, are the conditions of achieving the legal quality of customary law met. This is the case through practice, custom or an explicit consent to a codification of customary law. Resolutions thus have an effect on international law without being legal norms.

Their influence on the development of international law increases. Even if the states' willingness to enter into a commitment is absent when the resolutions are passed, they still have an influence on the process of law-making. They cannot establish legal duties, but they can set them up with respect to the expressed expectations for future behavior. Without having a legal character they are legally relevant.

5. The influence of Security Council Resolutions on the Development of International Law

The resolutions of the Security Council under Chapter VII UN Charter, which refer to the maintenance and restoration of peace and international security, are *legally binding*. These particular resolutions are limited to certain situations and are therefore limited to *individual cases*. However, since the 1990s it can be seen that the Security Council, by adopting resolutions under Chapter VII UN Charter, takes over *legislative functions* and during that process international *legal norms are developing*. This runs contrary to the traditional formation of international law, which usually develops through international agreements.

The *legislative function of the Security Council* became obvious when it adopted the resolutions on the establishment of the International Criminal Tribunal on Rwanda (UN Doc. S/RES/955, 8 November 1994) and on the establishment of the tribunal on the former Yugoslavia (UN Doc. S/RES/872, 25 May 1993, and S/RES/1166, 13 May 1998). This is different to the legal basis of the international courts of Nuremberg and Tokyo, which were created by an agreement under international law. Another example of the Security Council's legislative activity was resolution S/RES/1244 (1999), whereby the United Nations Interim Administration Mission on Kosovo (UNMIK) was created; and that mission was vested with far-reaching executive, legislative, and judicial competences. Furthermore, the Security Council used its legislative power in resolutions related to terrorism. Resolution S/RES/1373 (28 September 2001) which concerns the financing of terrorists and terror organizations legally bound the member states to measures against terrorism. The binding effect of that resolution did not originate from an international agreement and it went one step further than the resolutions on Rwanda, the former Yugoslavia and the Kosovo administration. Without an individual situation or case states are subject to obligations by a resolution with an *abstract* and *general* character. This was repeatedly done through resolution S/RES/1540 (2004) concerning the distribution of weapons of mass destruction (WMDs). That resolution concerns the general situation of distribution of WMDs without referring to a particular threat to international peace and security under Chapter VII of the UN Charter. States are generally obligated to take measures which should prevent WMDs falling into the hands of non-state actors.

The legislative function of the Security Council becomes even clearer in the cases of binding resolutions aimed at *individual* entities. Resolution S/RES/1390 (2002), for example, postulates that persons and institutions that are connected to Al-Qaeda can be put on a list by the Security Council, without any further justification by the Security Council or the Security Councils Sanctions Committee. There is no international legal protection against this measure. There are also no effective national legal protections, since Security Council resolutions are binding to the member states. As long as the Security Council's legislative actions, which certainly have a positive effect on international peace, are not enacted in a legal framework, they are doubtful under international law.

Overall the United Nations provides a substantial contribution to the development of international law. That is evident with regard to the resolutions of the General Assembly which promote the creation of international law and which often serve as the preliminary stage for treaties and conventions of international law. An interesting development can be observed with regard to non-state actors which influence the creation of procedural and material law in and outside the United Nations. This leads to a differentiation in content and further development of the sources of international law.

The work of the Security Council implicates a problematic tendency by passing resolutions with legislative charac-

ter, especially the Security Council's on concerning international terrorism. This development involves problems for the states' compliance with and the structure of international law.

Martina Haedrich

Lit.: *Alston, J. D.:* Die Bekämpfung abstrakter Gefahren für den Weltfrieden durch legislative Maßnahmen des Sicherheitsrats – Resolution 1373 (2001) im Kontext, in: ZaöRV 62 (2002), 257-289; *Brownlie, I.:* Principles of Public International Law, 6th edn., Oxford 2003; *de Wet, E.:* Judicial Review as an Emerging General Principle of Law and its Implications for the International Court of Justice, in: NILR 47 (2000), 181-210; *Döhring, K.:* Gewohnheitsrechtsbildung aus Menschenrechtsverträgen, in: Klein, E. (ed.): Menschenrechtsschutz durch Gewohnheitsrecht, Berlin 2003, 67-83; *Fischer, P./Köck, H.:* Völkerrecht, 6th edn., Vienna 2004; *Fleischhauer, C.-A.:* Art. 13, in: Simma, B. (ed.): The Charter of the United Nations. A Commentary, 2nd edn., Vol I, Oxford 2002, 298-317; *Frowein, J. A.:* Der Beitrag der internationalen Organisationen zur Entwicklung des Völkerrechts, in: ZaöVR 36 (1976), 147-167; *Haedrich, M.:* Die Wirkung von Resolutionen der UN-Vollversammlung auf den völkerrechtlichen Rechtsbildungsprozeß, in: Neue Justiz 40 (1986), 441-444; *Johnstone, I.:* Legislation and Adjudication in the UN Security Council: Bringing down the deliberative deficit, in: AJIL 102 (2008), 275-308; *Klein, E.:* Die Vereinten Nationen und die Entwicklung des Völkerrechts, in: Volger, H. (ed.): Grundlagen und Strukturen der Vereinten Nationen, Munich/Vienna 2007, 21-66; *Pellet, A.:* La formation du droit international dans le cadre des Nations Unies, in: EJIL 6 (1995), 401-425; *Simma, B.:* Methodik und Bedeutung der Arbeit der Vereinten Nationen für die Fortentwicklung des Völkerrechts, in: Kewenig, W.A. (ed.): Die Vereinten Nationen im Wandel, Berlin 1975, 79-101; *Singh, N.:* The United Nations and the Development of International Law, in: Roberts, A./Kingsbury, B. (eds.): United Nations, Divided World, 2nd edn., Oxford 1993, 384-419; *Talmon, S.:* The Security Council as World Legislature, in: AJIL 99 (2005), 175-193; *Wolfrum, R.:* Der Kampf gegen die Verbreitung von Massenvernichtungswaffen: Eine neue Rolle für den Sicherheitsrat, in: Dicke, K. et al. (eds.): Weltinnenrecht. Liber amicorum Jost Delbrück, Berlin 2005, 895-908; *Zimmermann, A./Elberling, B.:* Grenzen

der Legislativbefugnisse des Sicherheitsrates
– Resolution 1540 und abstrakte Bedrohung
des Weltfriedens, in: VN 52 (2004), 71-77.

Internet: Website on international law
within the UN homepage: www.un.org/
en/law/

International Organizations, Theory of

The theory of international organizations, understood as a specific form of
political theory, aims to fulfill three
separate but interrelated tasks:
- the scrutiny of international organizations as manifestations of politics in terms of the basic ideas,
  principles and norms underlying
  their existence;
- the development of a conceptual and
  analytical framework in order to
  better understand and explain the
  emergence, functioning and operations of international organizations; and
- the evaluation of competing explanations and prognoses for the development and transformation of
  international organizations as well
  as their constitutive context in
  world politics.

The subject of the theory of international organizations therefore can be seen in
both conceptual and empirical research
undertaken in a systematic and historically orientated way. Such an approach
necessarily implies interdisciplinary
work, e.g. combining early pacifist writing in the history of ideas, international
legal reasoning on the very notion and
implications of international organizations as well as various studies in political science that deal with the concrete
policies and politics of and in international organizations.

Whereas international organizations
as institutions only emerge in the late
19th century with the advent of international bureaus and administrative unions, the challenge of international organization, i.e. the problem of how to
organize the relationship between nations and states, has been a continuing

feature of historical and philosophical
writing (cf. *Schücking* 1909).

A special form of reasoning can be
discerned in the literature of peace plans
which find their most mature expression
in Kant's essay on "Perpetual Peace" of
1795. Based on an explicit philosophy
of history Kant introduced the notion
that peace can best be achieved by a
strategy of promoting the rule of law in
the domestic, international as well as
cosmopolitan realm. He consequently
argued for political systems based on republican principles within states, a federation of free states to organize the relations between states and a cosmopolitan law that anticipates the modern idea
of human rights beyond borders.

Kant's essay not only inspired the current debate on "democratic peace" or a
global rule of law (*Delbrück* 1998), but
also the principles that were later realized in the League of Nations and the
United Nations (cf. *Fröhlich* 1997).
This line of thought also touches upon a
number of classical legal texts that dealt
with emerging forms of "associations of
states" (cf. *Jellinek* 1882). The topicality
of these texts for current problems of
conceptualizing and understanding new
forms of organizations and networks of
global actors can be attributed to the fact
that they already dealt with fundamental
questions of: (a) what constitutes the legal personality of such organizations,
and (b) what implications they have for
the traditional notion and practice of
state → sovereignty. Finally, these
questions of international law are deeply
linked to reasoning on the legitimation,
purpose and performance of international organizations: theories of global justice, world order or universal norms in
world affairs can thus be seen as yet another branch within the theory of international organizations.

The multitude of different forms of
appearance of international organizations implies the need to categorize their
plurality. Understood in a narrow sense,
international organizations are created
by states through treaties that establish
permanent organs and institutions. In
contrast to these international organiza-

tions, non-governmental organizations (→ NGOs) which have experienced a dramatic proliferation in the latter half of the 20th century do not require state participation but rely on civil society groups acting transnationally. International organizations and non-governmental organizations have, however, engaged in a number of cooperative (and sometimes competitive) patterns of interaction. NGOs thus, having gained → observer status with the Economic and Social Council of the United Nations (→ ECOSOC), engage in world conferences and participate in a number of innovative, trilateral alliances or compacts that bring together states, international organizations and civil society (both in the form of non-profit and profit-orientated actors from the private sector) (*Reinicke et al.* 2000).

The theory and practice of international organizations have thus experienced a close interaction, starting with early studies on the functionalist logic underlying the emergence of both the → UN system and the beginnings of European integration (*Haas* 1964). The empirical nature of these early studies was directly linked with a normative outlook that finds a telling expression in the title of Mitrany's book on "A working peace system". While the origins of the theory of international organizations are also closely linked with liberal thought in international relations (cf. *Claude* 1971), already a brief survey of different strands of reasoning is able to distinguish between several traditions (cf. *Meyers* 2008; *Rittberger* 1995).

Realist authors in the tradition of Hans Morgenthau would argue that the state is the primary and unitary actor in international relations. In an inevitably anarchical environment these states seek to guard and promote their national interest through self-help, alliances or various forms of hegemony. The emergence of international organizations with a peacekeeping function thus is a consequence of the security dilemma (*Jervis* 1997) in the international realm. International organizations can alleviate but not solve tensions in international affairs. In neorealist thought the creation and existence of international organizations is a function of the distribution of power within the international system. International organizations depend upon state action and are used by different states as an instrument of their foreign policy.

Liberal authors in the tradition of Kant would challenge the extraordinary position of states and power-seeking in world affairs. International organizations thus emerge as a genuinely new form of social organization aiming to preserve individual rights and conceived of as a form of extension of or analogy to the social contract thinking that underpinned the rise of the modern state. International organizations are thereby linked also to transnational civil society and its inclination toward global solidarity, commerce and communication. More than mere instruments of nation states, they can be regarded as manifestations of world society, a forum of interaction and even actors in their own right. International organizations thus have the potential to not only manage but also transform world affairs.

In between the spectrum of realist and liberal thinking, a number of concrete variations of international organizations theory has developed that partly mirrors the broader development of international theory in political science: conflict theory studies emphasize the role of tensions and structural forces in global politics that are determined by sharp economic differences and the polarity between "centre" and "periphery". This approach has also found echoes in a number of studies emerging from critical theory and dealing not only with economic exploitation of the so-called Third World but also with the hardships and problems of current globalization.

Drawing from both realist as well as liberal assumptions, the rise of regime theory during the 1980s gave a number of impulses also to the study of international organizations in that it refined the categories of international cooperative action. According to *Krasner* (1983) regimes consist of "principles, norms, rules, and decision-making procedures around which actor expectations converge in a given issue-area". Building also on the sophisticated understanding of interdependence put forward by Keohane and Nye, regime theory focuses on the question why and how cooperation establishes itself in the international realm (*Keohane* 1984) thus associating itself with a new institutionalist understanding of international relations where "institutions" need not define themselves through fixed organizational structures but also represent patterns of behavior or relevant normative structures.

A good illustration of various approaches to the understanding of international organizations and institutions can be found in the controversy that followed John J. Mearsheimer's article on the "False Promise of International Institutions" published in "International Security". Mearsheimer expressed a realist viewpoint that criticized not only the liberal institutionalist school but also the arguments from proponents of → collective security and critical theory that all, in his view, share a sympathy for international organizations and their contribution to international affairs. In contrast to that, Mearsheimer limits the relevance of international institutions to being mere arenas for competitive power struggles among states. Even the explanation for cooperation among states is heavily criticized by Mearsheimer who stresses the difference between absolute and relative gains employed in game theory models that underlie his opponents' viewpoint.

The reactions to Mearsheimer for their part questioned a number of Mearsheimer's assumptions and, *inter alia*, dealt with the fundamental problem between agency and structure in international relations. It is no coincidence that the debate over international institutions thus brought to the fore an explicit statement of so-called "constructivist" theorizing by Ruggie and Wendt who joined the debate on the relevance of international organizations. Constructivist thinking is concerned with the "genera-

tive powers" of international organizations, i.e. "[their] ability to constitute or construct new actors in world politics, create new interests for actors, and define shared international tasks" (*Barnett/Finnemore* in Weiss/Daws 2007)

The theory of international organizations has therefore developed a whole set of analytical tools and conceptual distinctions that transform and adapt themselves with the development of international organizations in practice. The current debate on "global governance", i.e. the debate on how new constellations of international and transnational actors (e.g. NGOs, transnational corporations etc.) deal with new policy challenges (e.g. global health, terrorism, climate change, etc.) and thereby transform the institutional as well as normative structures of global politics (e.g. the notion of sovereignty or the structure of "global alliances/ networks") is thus a continuation of a long tradition of thinking about how to best organize the world.

Klaus Dicke / Manuel Fröhlich

Lit.: *Archer, C.:* International Organizations, 3rd edn., London/New York 2001; *Bennett, A.L.:* International Organizations. Principles and Issues, 7th edn., Englewood Cliffs 2002; *Claude, I.L.:* Swords into Plowshares. The Problems and Progress of International Organization, 4th edn., New York 1971; *Chawaszcza, C./Kersting, W. (eds.):* Politische Philosophie der internationalen Beziehungen, Frankfurt (Main) 1998; *Delbrück, J.:* „Das Völkerrecht soll auf einen Föderalismus freier Staaten gegründet sein" – Kant und die Entwicklung internationaler Organisation, in: Dicke, K./Kodalle, K.M. (eds.): Republik und Weltbürgerrecht, Weimar et al. 1998, 180-213; *Dicke, K.:* Effizienz und Effektivität internationaler Organisationen, Berlin 1994; *Fröhlich, M.:* Mit Kant, gegen ihn und über ihn hinaus: Die Diskussion 200 Jahre nach Erscheinen des Entwurfs „Zum ewigen Frieden", in: ZPol 7 (1997), 483-517; *Fröhlich, M. (ed.):* UN Studies. Umrisse eines Lehr- und Forschungsfeldes, Baden-Baden 2008; *Haas, E.B.:* Beyond the Nation-State. Functionalism and International Organization, Stanford 1964; *Jellinek, G.:* Die Lehre von den Staatenverbindungen, Wien 1882; *Jervis, R.:* Cooperation under the Security Dilemma, in: Lehmkuhl, U. (ed.): Theorien internationaler Politik, 2nd edn., Munich/Vienna 1997, 93-106; *Kant, I.:* Perpetual Peace and Other Essays, Indianapolis/Cambridge 1984; *Karns, M.P./Mingst, K.A.:* International Organizations. The Politics and Processes of Global Governance, Boulder/London 2004; *Keohane, R.:* After Hegemony. Cooperation and Discord in the World Political Economy, Princeton 1984; *Keohane, R.O./Nye, J.S.:* Power and Interdependence, 3rd edn., New York et al. 2001; *Kohler-Koch, B. (ed.):* Regime in den internationalen Beziehungen, Baden-Baden 1989; *Krasner, S.D. (ed.):* International Regimes, Ithaca/New York 1983; *Martin, L.L./Simmons, B.A. (eds.):* International Institutions. An International Organization Reader, Cambridge/London 2001; *Meyers, R:* Theorien internationaler Verflechtung und Integration, in: Woyke, W. (ed.): Handwörterbuch internationale Politik, 11th edn., Opladen 2008, 504-520; *Mitrany, D.:* A Working Peace System, Chicago 1966; *Morgenthau, H.:* Politics Among Nations, 6th edn., New York 1985; *Müller, H.:* Die Chance der Kooperation, Darmstadt 1993; Promises, Promises: Can Institutions Deliver? Special Section in: International Security 20 (1995); *Reinicke, W. et al.:* Critical Choices: The United Nations, Networks, and the Future of Global Governance, Ottawa 2000; *Rittberger, V./ Zangl, B.:* International Organization. Polity, Politics and Policies, Houndmills et al. 2006; *Rittberger, V.:* International Organizations, Theory of, in: Wolfrum, R. (ed.): The United Nations. Law, Policies and Practice, Vol. 2, Munich/Dordrecht 1995, 760-770; *Rittberger, V. (ed.):* Global Governance and the United Nations System, Tokyo 2001; *Ruggie, J.G. (ed.):* Multilateralism Matters. The Theory and Praxis of an International Form, New York 1993; *Schücking, W.:* Die Organisation der Welt, Leipzig 1909; *Weiss, T.G./Daws S. (eds.):* The Oxford Handbook on the United Nations, Oxford/New York 2007.

Internet, Websites of the UN System in the

The United Nations has used the Internet since its inception. In the early years the Internet served merely for the exchange of information within the organization, and with the → permanent missions of the member states. As the technology of the Internet developed at increasing speed, the Internet was step by step used to make more and more UN information accessible to the broad public, reacting to the initiatives within the United Nations and in the public to open the world organization, and to make its work more transparent.

As the reform of the United Nations gained more impetus after the end of the Cold War, the UN Secretaries-General Boutros-Ghali and Annan (→ Secretary-General) made ample and skilful use of the Internet for disseminating information about the UN more efficiently among the world public, with the aim of increasing the acceptance of the work of the United Nations in the member states.

Since the middle of the nineties the Department of Public Information (DPI), being part of the UN → Secretariat, works hard to put the relevant information quickly onto the Internet. The UN Internet websites offer access in all six official languages of the UN: English, French, Russian, Arabic, Chinese, Spanish (→ Languages, Official). They support all the new technological facilities (radio broadcasts, television broadcasts), without neglecting the Internet users with older software (who still depend on text-only versions without graphics and frames). A multitude of texts (UN resolutions and other documents, press releases, fact sheets, etc.) can be downloaded; on the respective website it is indicated since what point of time UN documents are accessible via Internet.

1. Internet Access to the UN

The easiest access to the United Nations via Internet is through the UN Headquarters in New York, with the Internet address www.un.org, and in Europe through the UN Office in Geneva, at www.unog.ch. The New York server serves only the → UN system, while the Geneva server offers also information about other inter-governmental organizations and non-governmental organizations (→ NGOs).

A very useful survey of the whole UN system in the Internet is provided by the website www.unsystem.org. It contains the *Official Web Site Locator of the UN System of Organizations*, which provides information about all Internet addresses and e-Mail addresses of UN organs, bodies and → specialized agencies (cf. → Principal Organs, Subsidiary Organs, Treaty Bodies).

2. Overview and General Information

In order to gain an overview of the information provided on UN websites it is most practical to start with the UN Main Website "www.un.org", provided in all six official languages of the UN. It offers links to a large number of information sources, among others about the principal organs of the UN, UN member states (including links to the websites of their permanent missions to the UN), UN reforms and conferences, press releases, UN documents (www.un.org/en/documents), the different fields of activities of the UN (peace and security, economic and social development, human rights, humanitarian affairs, international law), jobs at the UN (link "employment"), procurement, and recent additions on the website, supplemented by a detailed site index (www.un.org/en/siteindex) and a search engine (www.un.org/en/search/) comprising UN documents, press briefings and press releases.

3. Access to the Documents of the Principal Organs

A well-structured gateway to the texts of the UN principal organs (→ General Asembly, → Security Council, Economic and Social Council → ECOSOC, Secretariat, International Court of Justice → ICJ and → Trusteeship Council) is provided on the website "Documents" www.un.org/en/documents/ (as of 1 May 2009):

- with regard to the General Assembly access is provided through links to session documents and verbatim records (stored in the ODS data bank, further information see below) for the sessions since 2001 (56th session) and to all General Assembly resolutions since the first session in 1946, includ-

ing the special sessions and emergency special sessions of the Assembly; for the resolutions since 1997 the access is provided with further links to the respective meeting records and to a search engine concerning GA press releases;

- with regard to the Security Council beside the access to all resolutions since the first session of the Council in 1946 access is provided among others to the meeting records including action taken (resolution, presidential statement, etc.) from 1996 onwards, to reports of the Secretary-General to the Council from 1994 onwards, to the exchange of letters between Council and Secretary-General from 1997 onwards, to presidential statements since 1994 and presidential notes since 1993; to SC mission reports since 1992, and to a search engine referring to UN news and press releases about Security Council matters;

- with regard to the Economic and Social Council links are provided to resolutions and decisions of ECOSOC since 2001, to ECOSOC reports since 2004, to all subsidiary bodies of the ECOSOC (such as CSD and the Economic Regional Commissions), and to a search engine of all ECOSOC documents and texts;

- with regard to the Secretariat with a link to a number of selected reports of the Secretary-General;

- with regard to the International Court of Justice (ICJ) with a link to its Internet website (www.icj-cij.org);

- with regard to the Trusteeship Council with a link to a fact sheet.

4. Background Information for the Internet Search

Helpful detailed background information for the UN document search is provided on the website "United Nations Documentation: Research Guide" of the UN Dag Hammarskjöld Library (www.un.org/Depts/dhl/resguide/) with regard to the different types of UN texts, the respective document numbering systems, the information about the actions of the UN organs and – under the subtitle "Special Topics" detailed links to the UN bodies, their texts and related reference sources for the topics environment, human rights, international law, peacekeeping and budget.

The information and the links are supplemented by Internet training guides on the topics UN Web search, Security Council documents and the two important databases UNBISNET and ODS (see below).

5. UNBISNET – Bibliographic Catalogue and Online UN Text Access

UNBISNET (http://unbisnet.un.org) is the online catalogue of the UN Dag Hammarskjöld Library. The catalogue includes all UN documents issued since 1979 (older documents are successively added to the catalogue) with direct links to many of them, above all to the resolutions of the General Assembly, the Security Council and the ECOSOC since 1946.

The user can also search in special databases for the voting records for all General Assembly resolutions since its 32nd session (1977/78) and for all Security Council resolutions since the first year (1946) together with links to the full texts of the resolutions and for speeches made in the General Assembly beginning with the 38th session (1983/1984), the Security Council beginning with its 38th year (1983), the ECOSOC beginning in 1983 and the Trusteeship Council beginning with the 15th session (1982). Links to the full texts of the speeches are provided.

Furthermore UNBISNET includes commercial book and journal publications held in the collection of the library as well governmental texts of member states and NGO texts.

Thus UNBISNET is most useful in gaining an overview about the documents and other publications on a particular UN-related topic.

It is also of great use when a UN text other than GA, SC or ECOSOC resolutions (which can be easily found on the UN Documentation website) is to be accessed, but the UN document number is not known.

In this case UNBISNET provides information on the UN document number and with the help of this number it can be accessed in the ODS database.

6. United Nations Official Documents System (ODS)

The *Official Document System of the United Nations (ODS)*, http://documents.un.org), a full-text retrieval system for United Nations documents and official records, offers on the "Advanced Search" website two main search areas: "UN Documents" and "Resolutions".

The *"UN Documents"* area provides access to the formal parliamentary documents of the United Nations (i.e. with masthead indicating the name of the body and the document symbol) beginning in 1993.

Not included are:
- most informally published working papers without masthead (conference room papers, "non-papers", etc.);
- press releases and press briefings, which are posted at the UN News Centre (www.un.org/News/);
- UN treaties and conventions (as far as they have not been adopted as GA resolutions); they can be accessed at the UN Treaty Collection site (http://treaties.un.org; see below).
- UN sales publications;
- public information materials published by the UN Department of Information;

The *"Resolutions"* area of ODS provides access to the resolutions of the major UN organs (General Assembly, Security Council, Economic and Social Council, Trusteeship Council) back to 1946. The search may be based upon the UN body concerned, session number, agenda item number, document symbol, language, date, title, etc.). The system also allows full-text searching in all six languages.

The areas "Daily journal - New York" and "Daily journal - Geneva" offer searching for the respective issue of the "Journal of the United Nations" referring to the programme of meetings and the agenda for the UN Headquarters in

New York (further information see below) and of the "Bulletin of Meetings at the Palais des Nations in Geneva".

7. United Nations Treaty Collection

Under Article 102 of the Charter of the United Nations every bilateral or multilateral treaty and international agreement entered into by UN member states shall be registered with and published by the UN Secretariat.

These registered treaties can be found in the *United Nations Treaty Collection* database (http://treaties.un.org/).

The database provides online access to the text of the treaties and international agreements filed and recorded with the secretariat since 1946 in the original treaty language(s) together with translations into English and French.

The search engine offers the search by the popular name of the treaty, the official title, treaty participants and a full text search. Information is also provided on the status of ratification and the state parties.

Furthermore the UN Treaty Collection offers under the link "MTDSG" (Multilateral Treaties Deposited with the Secretary-General) a systematically structured gateway to all multilateral treaties concluded by the United Nations or specialized agencies of the UN family. In addition to the text and the ratification information also the declaration, reservations and objections of state parties to the respective treaties can be accessed.

The link "Overview" on the website includes definitions of key terms as well as a glossary of terms relating to treaty actions.

In a separate database "League of Nations Treaty Series" the international treaties registered and filed at the League of Nations, the predecessor organization of the United Nations, can be accessed.

8. Journal of the United Nations

A very useful source of information is also the online edition of the "Journal of the United Nations" providing information on the programme of meetings and agenda at UN headquarters for a certain day, comprising all UN bodies as well as formal and informal meetings of other organizations with relation to the UN such as the non-aligned movement or Group of 77.

The agendas contain also links to sessional documents which can be accessed and downloaded. As mentioned above the UN journal for a particular day can be accessed in the "advanced search" modus of the ODS database.

The most recent journal can be also be accessed on the UN documentation website: www.un.org/Docs/journal/En/lateste.pdf.

9. Summing up

The UN websites have developed in recent years to a highly efficient and user-friendly information and research instrument. It is highly recommendable that those interested in information about the UN invest some efforts to "dip" into the UN websites and then "dig" deeper to get an impression on the large variety of information accessible on the websites.

Additional information about UN activities together with links to UN documents can also be found on the websites of a number of NGOs, such as www.globalpolicy.org, www.reformtheun.org, www.securitycouncilreport.org, www.unwire.org.

The entry for the first edition written by *Peter M. Schulze* was revised for the second edition by *Helmut Volger*

Intervention, Prohibition of

The prohibition of intervention in the internal affairs of other states results directly from the → sovereignty of states, which is a fundamental principle in international law: as every state has the right to conduct its internal affairs autonomously and independently, any interference or intervention from outside is strictly forbidden.

Explicitly, the Charter of the UN contains only the prohibition of intervention for the organization itself in relation to its member states (Art. 2 (7) UN Charter), but not for individual states in their relations: "Nothing contained in the present Charter shall authorize the United Nations to intervene in matters which are essentially within the domestic jurisdiction of any state ..." However, the Charter contains a comprehensive prohibition for all states with regard to the use of the means of "classical" intervention, the threat or use of force against the territorial integrity or political independence (Art. 2 (4)): "All members shall refrain in their international relations from the threat or the use of force against the territorial integrity or political independence of any state, or in any other manner inconsistent with the Purposes of the United Nations." (→ Use of Force, Prohibition of)

The principle of non-intervention is too fundamental for the relations among sovereign states to be disputed in principle, so the UN General Assembly which considered the legal situation as unsatisfactory, decided to fill the "gap" in the written international legal norms by adopting resolutions (→ Resolution, Declaration, Decision) dealing with the principle of non-intervention: In its resolutions it developed "applicable principles which partly reflect existing customary international law and partly develop the law further." (*Beyerlin* 1995, 805) (→ International Law and the UN).

On 21 October 1965, the General Assembly adopted the "Declaration of the Inadmissibility of Intervention in the Domestic Affairs of States and the Protection of their Independence and Sovereignty" with only the United Kingdom abstaining (UN Doc. A/RES/2131 (XX)). Moreover, the General Assembly adopted on 24 October 1970 in consensus the "Declaration on the Principles of International Law concerning Friendly Relations and Co-operation among States in accordance with the Charter of the United Nations", the so-called "Friendly Relations Declaration" (UN Doc. A/RES/2625 (XXV)), which took over almost literally the wording of the principle of non-intervention from the former declaration.

The two resolutions formulated a "broad" concept of intervention, which also includes the use of non-military force, i.e. intervention and interference by economic, political and other means. The *actus reus* is given when a state is put under so much pressure by one or more states that it performs an act which it would not have done in free self-determination. Protected from intervention, however, are only those internal and external affairs, which are not subject to any rules of international law, but fall – according to their nature – exclusively under the domestic jurisdiction ("domaine réservé") of the state in question.

On 9 December 1981, the General Assembly adopted a further resolution on the principle on non-intervention, the "Declaration on the Inadmissibility of Intervention and Interference in the Internal Affairs of States" (UN Doc. A/RES/36/103) with 120 votes in favor, 22 votes against and 6 abstentions. In contrast to the 1965 and 1970 resolutions, which both reflected to a large extent customary international law, the 1981 resolution was criticized by many Western governments and also by specialists in international law, as in their opinion the declaration tried to extend the prohibition of intervention by a number of political concerns of developing countries (for example, the right of nations to self-determination, permanent sovereignty over natural resources and the demand for a new world information order), thereby completely blurring the outlines of the principle of non-intervention (*Verdross/Simma* 1984, 498).

Since the beginning of the 1990s, some states and above all human rights activists have repeatedly postulated a "right to humanitarian intervention" allowing interventions with the aim to protect the people of a foreign state suffering from massive persecutions and human rights violations by their own state. Such a *"droit à l'ingérence"*, however, in form of an intervention of a state or a group of single states on its own responsibility, is not permissible because of the prohibition of intervention stated in Article 2 (7) UN Charter and the *lex specialis*, the prohibition of the use of force (Art. 2 (4) UN Charter). An intervention or interference in the internal affairs of a state in order to protect the people from massive human rights violations or to prevent a human catastrophe is only admissible if the → Security Council considers them (or their consequences) to be a threat to the international peace and security and decides upon proportionate measures under Chapter VII of the Charter, which are then undertaken as UN-authorized interventions on behalf of the community of states with the purpose of improving the inhumane situation in the state concerned. The first time that this happened was on 5 April 1991, when the Security Council considered the persecution of the Kurds by Iraq as a threat to the peace in S/RES/688 (1991). (See also S/RES/733 (1992), 23 January 1992, on Somalia, and S/RES/827 (1993), 25 May 1993, on former Yugoslavia).

Although there is some concern that this "right of intervention" of the United Nations in favor of the international protection of human rights in cases of gross and systematic human rights violations might be used selectively and might serve as pretext for the pursuit of own political interests of the permanent members of the Security Council which can decisively influence the respective decisions of the Council on the authorization of such an intervention, the cases where such an intervention was decided on so far have shown that the intervention was urgently required and that the human rights situation of the people was improved. Thus it can be argued with some justification that this interpretation of the principle of non-intervention is in accordance with the principles and purposes of the UN Charter.

Isabelle Reinery

Lit.: *Adelmann, H.:* Humanitarian Intervention: The Case of the Kurds, in: International Journal of Refugee Law 4 (1992), 4-38; *Beyerlin, U.:* Humanitarian Intervention, in: Bernhardt, R. (ed.): EPIL 3 (1982), 211-215;

Beyerlin, U.: Intervention, Prohibition of, in: Wolfrum, R. (ed.): United Nations: Law, Policies and Practice, Vol. 2, Munich/Dordrecht 1995, 805-813; *Delbrück, J.:* Die internationale Gemeinschaft vor neuen Herausforderungen: Zur Neubestimmung der Reichweite des Interventionsverbotes der Charta der Vereinten Nationen, in: Heydrich, W./Krause, J. et al. (eds.): Sicherheitspolitik Deutschlands: Neue Konstellationen, Risiken, Instrumente, Baden-Baden 1992; *Lilich, R.B.:* Humanitarian Intervention through the United Nations: Towards the Development of Criteria, in: ZaöRV 53 (1992), 557-575; *Lock, P.:* Intervention, in: S+F 4 (1986), 66-71; *Scheuner, U.:* Intervention und Interventionsverbot, in: VN 28 (1980), 149-156; *Schröder, M.:* Non-Intervention, Principle of, in: Bernhardt, R. (ed.): EPIL 7 (1984), 358-360; *Simma, B. (ed.):* The Charter of the United Nations. A Commentary, Munich/Oxford 1994; *Verdross, A./Simma, B.:* Universelles Völkerrecht: Theorie und Praxis, Berlin 1984.

Addendum

In the context of the principle of the prohibition of intervention and that of the → sovereignty of states the discussion of the responsibility to protect as an emerging norm in international law is arguably the most important new development and has gained considerable momentum in the recent past.

The concept of humanitarian intervention, upon which the emerging concept of a responsibility to protect builds, originates in its modern form in the 19th century. By the end of that century, a majority of scholars supported the idea of the existence of a right of humanitarian intervention. A state which had abused its sovereignty by brutal and excessively cruel treatment of those within its power, whether its nationals or not, was regarded as having made itself liable to action by any state which was prepared to intervene. The doctrine was vague and its protagonists gave it a variety of forms, such as intervention to free a nation oppressed by another, intervention to put an end to crimes and slaughter, intervention to end "tyranny" etc. The Charter of the United Nations introduced some decisive changes as to the question of the legality of the use of armed force by states. Although the Charter makes no express reference to humanitarian intervention, this concept is in conflict with the prohibition of the threat or use of force in Article 2 (4). The concept of humanitarian intervention is further questionable because of the inherent danger of abusive resort to it. On a number of occasions (Dominican Republic 1965, East Bengal 1971, Vietnam 1978, Cambodia 1979, the Central African Republic 1979, Uganda 1979, Grenada 1983, Panama 1989) where the right of humanitarian intervention was, at least implicitly, advanced by the intervening states, it was perceived by the targeted states as an excuse for interference in their internal affairs and thus in violation of their sovereignty. At the beginning of the 21st century, neither legal doctrine nor state practice provided a sufficient basis to justify the so-called "right" to humanitarian intervention under international law.

Following the 1994 genocide in Rwanda and ethnic cleansing in the Balkans and Kosovo in 1995 and 1999, the international community engaged in a serious debate on how to react to gross and systematic violations of human rights. In September 1999, then Secretary-General Kofi Annan reflected – in his speech on presenting his annual report on the work of the organization to the General Assembly – upon "the prospects for human security and intervention in the next century" and challenged the member states to "find common ground in upholding the principles of the Charter, and acting in defence of common humanity" (UN Doc. A/54/PV.4, 20 September 1999, 1 and 3). In his Millennium Report, Kofi Annan repeated the challenge saying that: "if humanitarian intervention is, indeed, an unacceptable assault on sovereignty, how *should* we respond to a Rwanda, to a Srebrenica – to gross and systematic violation of human rights that offend every precept of our common humanity?" (UN Doc. A/54/2000, 27 March 2000, para. 217)

At the end of 2001, the International Commission on Intervention and State Sovereignty (ICISS) set up by the Canadian Government issued a report, entitled "The Responsibility to Protect". The concept affirmed that state sovereignty implied responsibility, and that the primary responsibility for the protection of its people rested with the state itself. The report also stated that where the state failed to act to avert serious harm to its population, through either lack of capacity or will, that responsibility to protect shifts to the wider international community.

In paragraphs 138 and 139 of resolution A/RES/60/1 of 16 September 2005, the "2005 World Summit Outcome" Document, the General Assembly at the level of heads of state and government reiterated the acceptance of a sovereign responsibility and underlined the essential role of the international community and the United Nations to "encourage and help" states meet this responsibility. More specifically, the General Assembly outlines four main obligations of the international community in the responsibility to protect, namely to:
- encourage and help states exercise this responsibility, including through prevention and building capacity to protect their populations from genocide, war crimes, ethnic cleansing and crimes against humanity;
- support the United Nations in establishing an early warning capability;
- use "appropriate diplomatic, humanitarian and other peaceful means, in accordance with Chapters VI and VIII of the Charter", to help protect populations from the four listed crimes; and
- be prepared "to take collective action, in a timely and decisive manner, through the Security Council", should peaceful means be inadequate and national authorities manifestly fail to protect their populations from the above listed crimes. (UN Doc. A/RES/60/1, 16 September 2005, para. 139)

The adoption of this concept represented one of the major achievements of the 2005 World Summit.

Following the momentum that had been created, the Security Council affirmed the concept of a responsibility to protect in resolution S/RES/1674 of 28 April 2006 on the protection of civilians in armed conflict. In light of the Security Council's primary responsibility for the maintenance of international peace and security this affirmation is of major significance.

While the responsibility to protect is not a new legal obligation as such, it is an important political commitment by states which have obligations under international law to prevent, prosecute and punish genocide, crimes against humanity and war crimes. The scope of these obligations is developing through customary law and the jurisprudence of the system of international criminal justice. States responsible for violating the above obligations must, under international law, cease the violation, offer appropriate assurances and guarantees not to repeat the violation and make full reparation for the injury caused. The conceptual foundation of the responsibility to protect is "sovereignty as responsibility". Therefore, the primary obligation is for states to protect their populations from the above crimes. This is coupled with a commitment by the international community to assist states in meeting those obligations. And finally, member states of the United Nations have accepted their responsibility in a timely and decisive manner.

The change towards the responsibility to protect is not just cosmetic. It focuses attention towards a suffering population. For the future, the international community is facing a number of questions to which answers will have to be found. What is already clear, however, is that the concept of the responsibility to protect is an emerging norm in international law, according to which there is a collective responsibility to protect peoples from genocide, crimes against humanity, war crimes and all forms of these crimes can take, including "ethnic cleansing", which is not a distinctly defined international crime and rather describes the intended result of criminal

448

acts. This responsibility lies, first and foremost, with each individual state. However, if national authorities are unable or unwilling to protect their citizens, it falls to the international community to use peaceful means to protect civilians, and ultimately to the Security Council to take enforcement action if necessary. The various facets of this matter will probably occupy the attention of the international community in the years to come. For the United Nations the challenge will be how it can best operationalize the concept of the responsibility to protect.

Markus Pallek

Lit.: *Evans, G.:* The Responsibility to Protect: Creating and Implementing a New International Norm. Address by Gareth Evans, President International Crisis Group, to Human Rights Law Resource Center, 13 August 2007, www.crisisgroup.org/home/index.cfm?id=5036&l=1; *Evans, G.:* The Limits of State Sovereignty: The Responsibility to Protect in the 21st Century (Eighth Neelam Tiruchelvam Memorial Lecture by Gareth Evans, International Centre for Ethnic Studies (ICES), Colombo, 29 July 2007), www.crisisgroup.org/home/index.cfm?id=4967; *Evans, G.:* Crimes against Humanity: Overcoming Global Indifference (2006 Gandel Oration for B'nai B'rith Anti-Defamation Commission by Gareth Evans, University of New South Wales, Sydney, 30 April 2006), www.crisisgroup.org/home/index.cfm?id=4087&l=1; *Evans, G./Sanhoun, M.:* The Responsibility to Protect, in: Foreign Affairs 81 (2002), 99-110; *Hilpold, P.:* The duty to protect and the reform of the United Nations : a new step in the development of international law? In: Max Planck Yearbook of United Nations Law 10 (2006) 35-69; *International Commission on Intervention and State Sovereignty (ICISS):* The Responsibility to Protect. Report, Ottawa 2001; *Luck, E.C.:* Mixed Messages: American Politics and International Organization 1919-1999, 1999; *Luck, E.C.:* UN Security Council – Practice and Promise: A Primer (Global Institutions Series), London/New York 2006; *Luck, E.C./Doyle, M.W.:* International Law and Organization: Closing the Compliance Gap, Lanham/USA 2004; *MacFarlane, S.N./Thielking, CJ./Weiss, T.G.:* The responsibility to protect: is anyone interested in humanitarian intervention? In: TWQ 25 (2004),

977-992; *Responsibility to Protect Center for International Human Rights:* The Responsibility to Protect and the International Criminal Court: America's New Priorities. Conference Report, March 2008, presented by the Responsibility to Protect Center for International Human Rights, Northwestern University School of Law; *Saxer, M.:* The Politics of Responsibility to Protect (Dialogue on Globalization, FES Briefing Paper 2), Berlin, Friedrich-Ebert-Stiftung, April 2008, http://library.fes.de/pdf-files/iez/global/05313-20080414.pdf; *Stahn, C.:* Responsibility to protect: political rhetoric or emerging legal norm? In: AJIL 101 (2007), 99-120; *Thakur, R.:* The United Nations, peace and security: from collective security to the responsibility to protect, Cambridge et al. 2006; *Thakur, R./Popovski, V.:* The Responsibility to Protect and Prosecute: The Parallel Erosion of Sovereignty and Impunity, in: The Global Community, Yearbook of International Law and Jurisprudence 2007, Vol. I; *United Nations - General Assembly:* We the peoples: the role of the United Nations in the twenty-first century. Report of the Secretary-General, 27 March 2000, UN Doc. A/54/2000; *United Nations - General Assembly:* A more secure world: our shared responsibility. Report of the High-level Panel on Threats, Challenges and Change, 2 December 2004, UN Doc. A/59/565; *United Nations - General Assembly:* 2005 World Summit Outcome, 16 September 2005, UN Doc. A/RES/60/1; *United Nations - Security Council:* Protection of civilians in armed conflict, UN Doc. S/RES/1674 (2006), 28 April 2006; *United Nations - General Assembly:* Report of the Secretary-General on the implementation of the Five-Point Action Plan and the activities of the Special Adviser of the Secretary-General on the Prevention of Genocide, UN Doc. A/HRC/7/37, 18 March 2008, 7; *Weiss, T.G.:* The sunset of humanitarian intervention? The responsibility to protect in a unipolar era, in: Security Dialogue 35 (2004), 135-153; *Welsh, J./Thielking, C.J./MacFarlane, S.N.:* The responsibility to protect: assessing the report of the International Commission on Intervention and State Sovereignty, in: Thakur, R. (ed.): International commissions and the power of ideas, Tokyo et al. 2005, 198-220, also in: IJ 57 (2002), 489-512; *Wills, S.:* The „responsibility to protect" by peace support forces under international human rights law, in: International Peacekeeping 13 (2006), 4, 477-488.

ITLOS – International Tribunal for the Law of the Sea

1. Inauguration, Legal Position and Legal Basis

The *International Tribunal for the Law of the Sea (ITLOS)* was established by the *United Nations Convention on the Law of the Sea of 10 December 1982 (LOSC)* (→ Law of the Sea). It convened for the first time at its seat in the Free and Hanseatic City of Hamburg on 1 October 1996. The ceremonial inauguration of the judges during its first public session on 18 October 1996 brought to an end a development which had begun in 1970 with proposals to create a special procedure for the peaceful settlement of seabed disputes. Since November 2000 it has occupied its permanent headquarters Am Internationalen Seegerichtshof 1, 22609 Hamburg, Germany.

ITLOS is the second permanent international court with universal jurisdiction besides the International Court of Justice (→ ICJ). The jurisdiction of this "Tribunal of the Oceans" covers more than 70 % of the earth's surface and comprises (almost) all conceivable questions concerning the sea such as maritime boundaries, navigation, rights of overflight, the laying of submarine cables, marine scientific research, underwater cultural heritage, environmental protection, conservation and utilization of fish stocks, bio-prospecting, as well as the right to exploration and exploitation of the living and non-living resources of the seabed and its subsoil.

ITLOS was established "under the auspices of the United Nations"; but, unlike the ICJ and the two International Criminal Tribunals for the Former Yugoslavia and for Rwanda (→ ICC – International Criminal Court), it is neither a judicial organ of the United Nations nor a subsidiary organ of the Security Council (→ Principal Organs, Subsidiary Organs, Treaty Bodies; → UN System). It is also not an organ of the International Seabed Authority. ITLOS is rather an autonomous international judicial institution with legal personality which may conclude treaties, acquire movable and immovable property and institute legal proceedings. In addition, ITLOS has → observer status at the → General Assembly (A/RES/51/204). Because of its various relations with the United Nations and especially with their Secretary-General provided for partly in the *LOSC*, partly in the *Agreement on Cooperation and Relationship Between the United Nations and the International Tribunal for the Law of the Sea of 18 December 1997* (A/RES/52/251, Annex) and other legal instruments, ITLOS may be counted, without doubt, as a member of the "UN family". This was further underpinned by an exchange of letters between the UN and ITLOS, dated 26th May 2000 and 12th June 2001 respectively, which extended the competence of the UN Administrative Tribunal to the staff of the Registry of ITLOS (ITLOS Yearbook 2001, 145-148). The Tribunal is not, however, a specialized agency of the United Nations in the formal sense (→ Specialized Agencies).

The basic legal rules governing the operation of ITLOS are laid down in Articles 186-191, 279-299 LOSC and in its Annex VI which contains the Statute of the International Tribunal for the Law of the Sea (ITLOS Statute).

2. *"A New Tribunal for a New Law"*

From the outset ITLOS has been deemed, especially by developing countries, a symbol of a new international law of the sea: "a new tribunal for a new law". Henry Kissinger called this new law of the sea the result of one of the "most important, most complex and most ambitious diplomatic undertakings in history": the *Third United Nations Conference on the Law of the Sea*, or in short *UNCLOS III* (Law of the Sea). The negotiations in which more than 150 states participated and which took some nine years (1973-1982) were characterized by the demand of the developing countries for a new international economic order (→ International Economic Relations and New International

Economic Order (NIEO)), which was to find its expression, *inter alia*, in the just distribution of marine resources between the states and by the attempts of coastal states at seaward extension of their sovereign rights and jurisdiction ("creeping jurisdiction"). The negotiations at UNCLOS III were strongly influenced by two procedural principles: the formulation of "package deals" and the "consensus principle". Only after all efforts at consensus had been exhausted, a formal vote was to be taken. On 30 April 1982, the Conference approved the text of the Convention by a formal vote of 130 in favor (among them almost all developing countries), four against (Israel, Turkey, USA and Venezuela), with seventeen abstentions (mostly industrialized nations, among them the Federal Republic of Germany). Although the LOSC was signed on 12 December 1982 by 119 states it should take another twelve years until it entered into force (twelve months after the deposit of the sixtieth instrument of ratification). The main reason for this was that important industrialized countries were opposed to Part XI of the LOSC on the exploration and exploitation of the resources of the seabed and ocean floor and the subsoil thereof beyond the limits of national jurisdiction (the "Area") with its provisions on production policies, participation in revenue, and the transfer of technology as well as the possibility of binding changes to the regime of the "Area" by a three-fourths majority of the states parties to the LOSC. Only the adoption on 28 July 1994 of the *Agreement Relating to the Implementation of Part XI of the United Nations Convention on the Law of the Sea of 10 December 1982 (IA)* which made substantial "modifications" to Part XI of the LOSC, opened the door for ratification by the industrialized states. According to Article 2 IA, the Implementation Agreement and Part XI of the LOSC are to be interpreted and applied together as "a single instrument". In the event of any inconsistency, the provisions of the Agreement shall prevail. The LOSC with its 320 articles, nine extensive annexes and four resolutions (which, without being part of the LOSC, are inextricably linked to it) entered into force on 16 November 1994 (text: UNTS Vol. 1833, No. 31363, 3), the IA on 28 July 1996 (text: (UNTS Vol. 1836, No. 31364, 41). By the end of October 2008, the LOSC had 157 and the IA 135 parties. As regards states parties, the LOSC prevails over the four *Geneva Conventions on the Law of the Sea of 29 April 1958* (the Convention on the High Seas (UNTS Vol. 450, No. 6465, 11), the Convention on the Territorial Sea and the Contiguous Zone (UNTS Vol. 516, No. 7477, 205), the Convention on Fishing and the Conservation of the Living Resources of the High Seas (UNTS Vol. 559, No. 8164, 285), and the Convention on the Continental Shelf (UNTS Vol. 499, No. 7302, 311), the so-called "old law of the sea".

The LOSC creates a comprehensive legal order for the seas and oceans. However, it does not govern by itself all aspects of the law of the sea, but rather constitutes an "umbrella convention" which needs to be implemented and which provides the framework for further development by regional and specific agreements. In its seventeen "parts" the LOSC covers, *inter alia*, the following matters: "territorial sea and contiguous zone", "straits used for international navigation", "archipelagic States", "exclusive economic zone", "continental shelf", "high seas", "regime of islands", "enclosed or semi-enclosed seas", "right of access of landlocked States to and from the sea and freedom of transit", "the Area", i.e. the economic exploitation of the deep seabed, "protection and preservation of the marine environment", "marine scientific research", "development and transfer of marine technology", and "settlement of disputes". The LOSC adopts some time-tested rules of the Geneva Conventions and develops them further or makes them more precise. At the same time, it also introduces novel legal concepts and institutions: the details of the exclusive economic zone (including the concept of sustainable development of marine resources), the protection of the marine environment, marine scientific research, the transfer of marine technology, and the protection of the underwater cultural heritage have been codified for the first time on the international plane. The most fundamental innovation, however, is the principle according to which the seabed and ocean floor and subsoil thereof beyond the limits of national jurisdiction constitute the → common heritage of mankind, over which no state may claim or exercise sovereignty; in particular, no state may appropriate any part of it or its resources. In technical terms, the LOSC is characterized by a "zoning of the sea", i.e. the legal position as regards fishing, navigation, overflight, protection of the marine environment, marine scientific research, protection of underwater cultural heritage, and seabed mining depends on the zone of the sea (internal waters, archipelagic waters, territorial sea, contiguous zone, exclusive economic zone, high seas, continental shelf, or Area) in which one is. In general, it may be said that the further away a zone is situated from the shore, the fewer rights the coastal state possesses or, in other words, the distance of a zone from the coast is inversely proportional to the scope of the coastal state's rights in it. Apart from these substantive innovations, the LOSC also creates three new international institutions: the *International Seabed Authority*, the *International Tribunal for the Law of the Sea* and the *Commission on the Limits of the Continental Shelf*. The first two are to be classified as "autonomous international organizations", the latter as a "treaty organ" of the United Nations (UN Doc. CLCS/5, 11 March 1998). In addition, the "Meeting of States Parties" (SPLOS) and the Office of Legal Affairs of the United Nations Division for Ocean Affairs and the Law of the Sea (DOALOS), which serves as the secretariat of the Convention, play an important role within the system of the LOSC.

451

3. Composition and Organization

a. Judges

ITLOS is composed of 21 independent members (judges) elected by the states parties to the LOSC for a period of nine years; re-election is possible. The first election was held on 1 August 1996. In order to ensure a certain consistency in the Tribunal's jurisprudence a system of rotation was established at the first elections: the terms of office were staggered, so that every three years the terms of seven judges expired. The term of office starts on 1 October. The judges who may not be nationals of the same state must represent the principal legal systems of the world and be "of recognized competence in the field of the law of the sea". In the Tribunal as a whole "equitable geographical distribution" must be assured, a principle that usually (only) governs the composition of the political organs of the United Nations. According to Article 3 (2) ITLOS Statute each of the five geographical groups as established by the General Assembly of the United Nations (→ Regional Groups in the UN) must be represented by no fewer than three judges. The remaining six seats were also distributed by the states parties among the geographical regions leading in practice to the following ratio of distribution: Africa (5), Asia (5), Latin America and the Caribbean (4), Western Europe and others (4), and Eastern Europe (3). Compared to the ICJ (ratio: 3/2/2/6/2), the representation of developing countries on the ITLOS bench is much stronger. While this may lead to greater acceptance of the Tribunal with the majority of states parties, it has led to a certain reservation towards the Tribunal on the part of industrialized states.

The members of the Tribunal are not (yet) full-time judges. They may therefore continue their present occupation or take up a new one. No member of the Tribunal, however, may exercise any political or administrative function, or associate actively with or be financially interested in any of the operations or enterprises concerned with the commercial use of the sea or the seabed. Furthermore, no member may act as agent, counsel or advocate in any case (Art. 7 ITLOS Statute); if a judge has done so prior to his election, he is precluded from participating in the decision (Art. 8 (1) ITLOS Statute).

Besides the elected judges there may also be judges *ad hoc*. If the Tribunal, when hearing a dispute, does not include upon the bench (elected) members of the nationality of the parties to the dispute, each of those parties may choose a judge (not necessarily of its nationality) who participates in the case on terms of complete equality with the other judges.

The judges, when engaged on the business of the Tribunal, enjoy diplomatic privileges and immunities (Art. 10 ITLOS Statute). The details are laid down in the *Agreement on the Privileges and Immunities of the International Tribunal for the Law of the Sea of 23 May 1997* which entered into force on 30th December 2001(text: UNTS Vol. 2167, No. 37925, 271) and, by the end of October 2008, had 36 parties. In addition, the *Agreement between ITLOS and the Federal Republic of Germany Regarding the Headquarters of the Tribunal of 14 December 2004* (UNTS No. I-44269) contains further provisions on the immunities and privileges of the Tribunal, its headquarters and its assets. Prior to the entry into force of this host state agreement (→ Host State Agreements) on 1 May 2007, the legal status of the judges and of other persons, when engaged on the business of the Tribunal in Germany, was governed by the Ordinance Concerning the Privileges and Immunities of the International Tribunal for the Law of the Sea of 10 October 1996 (BGBl. 1996 II, 2517).

b. Experts

Besides the judges, experts may also sit on the bench. In disputes involving scientific or technical matters the Tribunal or one of its chambers may, at the request of a party or *proprio motu*, select in consultation with the parties no fewer than two experts to take part in the hearings and the deliberation without the right to vote (Art. 289 LOSC). This is a manifestation of the fact that many disputes before ITLOS (e.g. over the delimitation of the continental shelf) raise not only legal but, above all, geological, geophysical and hydrographic problems. Experts in the sense of Article 289 LOSC are not "expert witnesses" whose statements may be questioned or refuted by the parties, but "assessors" in the sense of Article 30 (2) ICJ Statute. Their task is to assist the judges in drafting their judgment and to ensure that the judgment is free from technical inaccuracies and in conformity with the present state of science and technology.

c. The Tribunal and the Chambers

The composition of the Tribunal depends upon the subject matter of the dispute and the will of the parties. Irrespective of its composition in a specific case judges *ad hoc* and experts may sit on the bench.

(1) The Tribunal as a Whole

All disputes and applications submitted to ITLOS shall be heard and determined by the Tribunal as a whole, i.e. by all 21 judges, unless the dispute is to be submitted to the Seabed Disputes Chamber in accordance with Part XI, section 5, of the LOSC, or the parties request that it be submitted to a special chamber (Art. 13 (3) ITLOS Statute). A quorum of eleven elected members is required to constitute the Tribunal. The rule on the quorum may be of some importance in the future, as ITLOS, though being a permanent court, is not a "standing court". Of the judges only the President is required to reside at the seat of the Tribunal (Art. 12 (3) ITLOS Statute).

(2) Seabed Disputes Chamber

Disputes arising out of the exploration and exploitation of the resources of the seabed and ocean floor beyond the limits of national jurisdiction, i.e. the "Area", are to be submitted to the Seabed Disputes Chamber (Art. 14, 35-40 LOSC). It consists of eleven judges selected every three years by the judges of the Tribunal from among themselves in such a manner as to ensure the representation of the principal legal systems of the world and equitable geographical distribution. A quorum of seven members is required to constitute the Chamber which elects its President from among its members. It is sometimes called a "tribunal within the Tribunal". At the request of the parties certain seabed disputes may be submitted by the chamber to an *ad hoc* chamber composed of three of its members (Art. 36 ITLOS Statute) or to a special chamber (Art. 188 (1)(a) LOSC). The Seabed Disputes Chamber was first constituted by ITLOS on 20 February 1997 and reconstituted on 4 October 1999. Its members are elected by the Tribunal every three years at the beginning of October; the last election being held on 2 October 2008. As deep seabed mining will not take place in the foreseeable future, the Seabed Disputes Chamber will, for the time being, at best be occupied with giving advisory opinions to the International Seabed Authority (Art. 191 LOSC).

(3) Special Chambers

The Statute of ITLOS distinguishes between obligatory and optional special chambers. According to Article 15 (3) ITLOS Statute, the Tribunal annually forms a five-member Chamber of Summary Procedure which may hear and determine disputes by summary procedure. In addition, the Chamber can prescribe provisional measures in the exercise of the Tribunal's powers, if the Tribunal is not in session or a sufficient number of Members is not available to constitute a quorum (Art. 25 (2)).The Tribunal may form such further chambers, composed of three or more judges, as it considers necessary for dealing with particular categories of disputes (Art. 15 (1)). On the basis of this provision the Tribunal at a meeting on 14 February 1997 established for the first time two standing special chambers which are composed of seven judges each: the Chamber for Fisheries Disputes and the Chamber for Maritime Environment Disputes (ITLOS/ 13, 20 April 1998, 8ff.). On 13 March 2007, the Tribunal formed a third standing special chamber: the Chamber for Maritime Delimitation Disputes which is composed of eight judges (ITLOS/2007/RES.1, 16 March 2007). The members of all special chambers are now elected by the Tribunal every three years at the beginning of October, the last election being held in October 2008 (ITLOS/2008/RES.1, RES.2 and RES.4, 7 October 2008). Other special chambers, e.g. for marine scientific research or underwater cultural heritage, are conceivable. At the request of the parties to a dispute, the Tribunal may also establish an Ad Hoc Chamber to deal with a particular case. The composition of such a chamber is determined by the Tribunal with the approval of the parties (Art. 15 (2)). The first, and so far only, such special chamber, composed of five judges, was formed by the Tribunal on 20 December 2000 to deal with the case concerning the *Conservation and Sustainable Exploitation of Swordfish Stocks (Chile/European Community)* (ITLOS Reports 2000, 148).

4. Competence

a. The Tribunal within the Dispute Settlement System of the LOSC

The states parties to the LOSC are obliged to submit any dispute between them concerning the interpretation or application of the Convention where no settlement can be reached by peaceful means of their own choosing (Art. 279-285 LOSC) after the exhaustion of local remedies (Art. 295 LOSC) to a judicial settlement procedure that leads to a binding decision – compulsory dispute settlement obligation (Art. 286 LOSC). The obligation on states parties to submit disputes to compulsory settlement constitutes a considerable improvement upon the Geneva Conventions on the Law of the Sea which provided for the compulsory settlement of disputes merely in an Optional Protocol (UNTS Vol. 450, No. 6466, 169) which has attracted only 38 ratifications and has never been applied. States parties are, however, not obliged to submit any dispute to ITLOS. According to Article 287 (1) LOSC, states are free to choose at any time on

or after signature of the Convention, by means of a written declaration to be deposited with the Secretary-General of the United Nations, one or more of the following means for the settlement of disputes: ITLOS, the ICJ, an arbitral tribunal constituted in accordance with Annex VII of the LOSC or a special arbitral tribunal constituted in accordance with Annex VIII of the LOSC (for the categories of dispute specified therein). At the end of October 2008, only 36 out of the 157 parties had deposited a declaration positively choosing one of these means of dispute settlement, of which 24 states, including the Federal Republic of Germany, had chosen ITLOS as one of their preferred options (in matters other than the prompt release of detained vessels and crews). For most states ITLOS is still too much of an "unknown quantity"; they wait for the time being to see how the jurisprudence of the Tribunal develops (see for example the declaration of the United Kingdom on the choice of procedure under Article 287, made on 12 January 1998 (ITLOS Yearbook 1998, 99). If a state has not chosen one of the means for the settlement of disputes available under Article 287 (1) LOSC, or if the parties to a dispute have not selected the same means, the dispute is to be submitted to arbitration in accordance with Annex VII, unless the parties otherwise agree (Art. 287 (3), (4), and (5) LOSC). Annex VII arbitration thus constitutes the "default dispute settlement procedure" of the LOSC. Arbitral Tribunals under Annex VII of the LOSC have so far dealt with five cases (see *Southern Bluefin Tuna (Australia and New Zealand v. Japan)*, Award on Jurisdiction and Admissibility, 4 August 2000; *MOX Plant (Ireland v. UK)*, Order No. 6 of 6 June 2008 on Termination of Proceedings; *Maritime Boundary Delimitation (Barbados/ Trinidad and Tobago)*, Award of 11 April 2006; *Maritime Boundary Delimitation (Guyana/ Suriname)*, Award of 17 September 2007; and *Land Reclamation by Singapore in and around the Straits of Johor (Malaysia v. Singapore)* Award on Agreed Terms of 1 September 2005; all available at www.pca-cpa.org/). But, even if all parties to a dispute have chosen ITLOS this does not mean that it may decide the case. If the states parties have agreed, through an international agreement or otherwise, to submit their disputes to a settlement procedure that entails a binding decision, this procedure prevails over ITLOS, unless the parties to the dispute otherwise agree (Art. 282 LOSC). This is of importance for member states of the European Union to the extent that the LOSC has become part of Community law (see Case C-459/03, *Commission v. Ireland*, Judgment of the European Court of Justice of 30 May 2006, [2006] ECR I-4635) and for states that are parties to dispute settlement treaties such as the European Convention for the Peaceful Settlement of Disputes of 29 April 1957 (UNTS Vol. 320, No. 4646, 243), in which the parties have agreed to submit, as a rule, all international legal disputes arising between them to the judgment of the ICJ. The exception in Article 28 (1) of that Convention does not apply here, as law of the sea disputes must *not* be submitted to ITLOS as is shown by Article 282 LOSC.

According to Article 287 (2) LOSC the choice of settlement procedure does not apply in the case of disputes arising from activities in the Area (LOSC Part XI, section 5) which are to be decided by ITLOS through its Seabed Disputes Chamber. Here, the parties may, depending on the circumstances, only choose whether the dispute shall be decided by the Seabed Disputes Chamber itself, its *ad hoc* chamber or a special chamber. Only in one particular case may such a dispute be submitted, at the request of a party, to binding commercial arbitration (Art. 188 (2) LOSC).

Irrespective of whether ITLOS has been chosen by a state party it functions as an "emergency dispute settlement procedure". Pending the constitution of the chosen or, if the parties to a dispute have not taken their choice, the *ipso jure* competent court or arbitral tribunal, ITLOS may, at the request of a party,

prescribe provisional measures (Art. 290 (5) LOSC). In five out of the fifteen cases so far brought before ITLOS, the Tribunal was asked to prescribe provisional measures pending the constitution of the Arbitral Tribunal under Annex VII of the LOSC (Cases Nos. 2, 3 & 4, 10, and 12). In nine other cases, ITLOS was asked to decide on the prompt release of detained vessels and crews because the parties failed to reach agreement, within 10 days from the time of detention, to submit the question of release from detention to any court or tribunal agreed upon by them (Cases Nos. 1, 5, 6, 8, 9, 11, 13-15; all these decisions may be found at www.itlos.org/).

b. Jurisdiction

If states parties have chosen ITLOS as their dispute settlement procedure, it has, in principle, "jurisdiction over any dispute concerning the interpretation and application" of the LOSC (Art. 288 (1) LOSC). Legal issues which are related to the sea but which are not regulated by the LOSC (such as the acquisition of sovereignty over islands) are thus removed from its jurisdiction. The principle of comprehensive jurisdiction laid down in Article 288 (1) LOSC is, however, subject to far-reaching exceptions, especially in favor of coastal states, whose exact scope is yet to be determined by the Tribunal's case law. In part, the LOSC itself excludes certain disputes concerning the exercise by a coastal state of its sovereign rights, marine scientific research or fisheries in the exclusive economic zone from the Tribunal's jurisdiction (*ipso jure* exceptions – Art. 297 LOSC), in part, it gives states parties the right to make a declaration taking out certain disputes on the delimitation of maritime zones, military activities and enforcement activities in regard to the exercise of sovereign rights of the compulsory settlement process (optional exceptions – Art. 298 LOSC). By the end of October 2008, surprisingly, only twenty-five states had comprehensively invoked the optional exclusions clause. These exceptions to the Tribunal's jurisdiction *ratione mate-*

riae constitute the concession which the supporters of compulsory dispute settlement had to make in order to achieve its inclusion in the LOSC.

ITLOS may derive its jurisdiction not only from the LOSC but also from other international agreements related to the purposes of the Convention (Art. 288 (2) LOSC; Art. 21, 22 ITLOS Statute). Thus, according to Article 30 (1) of the Agreement for the Implementation of the Provisions of the United Nations Convention on the Law of the Sea of 10 December 1982 relating to the Conservation and Management of Straddling Fish Stocks and Highly Migratory Fish Stocks of 4 December 1995 (UNTS Vol. 2167, No. 37924, 3), ITLOS also has jurisdiction over any dispute concerning the interpretation or application of this Agreement, if the states parties have chosen it as a dispute settlement procedure. In addition, there are nine other agreements which confer jurisdiction on the Tribunal (see the list of international agreements at www.itlos. org/ under "Proceedings and Judgments – Competence").

In the event of a dispute as to whether ITLOS has jurisdiction, the matter will be settled first by a decision of the Tribunal (Art. 288 (4) LOSC). Similarly, the Tribunal determines in preliminary proceedings whether an application made in respect of a dispute falling under the *ipso jure* exceptions to its jurisdiction constitutes an abuse of legal process.

c. Access (locus standi)

ITLOS is, in principle, open only to states parties of the LOSC (Art. 291 (1) LOSC, Art. 20 (1) ITLOS Statute). According to the definition in Article 1 (2) (2) LOSC, "States Parties" are, however, not only states in the sense of public international law, but also other entities like international organizations (LOSC Annex IX) which have become Parties to the LOSC. Thus, the Tribunal is also open, for example, to the European Community (EC) which formally confirmed the Convention on 1 April 1998, being so far the only non-state entity doing so (cf. Case No. 7, *Conserva-*

tion and Sustainable Exploitation of Swordfish Stocks (Chile/European Community) (ITLOS Reports 2000, 148)). The LOSC thereby takes into account the fact that EC member states have transferred sovereign rights to the Community in areas covered by the Convention. In disputes before the Seabed Disputes Chamber not only states have legal standing but also the International Seabed Authority, the Enterprise, state enterprises and natural or juridical persons (Art. 291 (2), Art. 187 LOSC). It is, however, going too far to assume that also the Tribunal is open to natural and juridical persons for the settlement of their private (shipping law) disputes (*contra Basedow* 1999, 13). While, according to Article 20 (2) ITLOS Statute, the Tribunal is also open to entities other than states parties "in any case submitted pursuant to any other agreement conferring jurisdiction on the Tribunal which is accepted by all the parties" to the case, the term "agreement" in this context does not mean any kind of private agreement but only international agreements in the sense of Article 288 (2) LOSC.

5. Procedure, Applicable Law, Decisions and Their Enforcement

Proceedings before ITLOS are instituted either by notification of a special agreement between the parties, by written application or by a request to prescribe provisional measures or to order the release of a detained vessel and its crew. They consist of two parts: written and oral.

The details of the Tribunal's procedure are laid down in the LOSC, the Statute of ITLOS (Arts. 24-34) and the "Rules of the Tribunal" adopted by ITLOS on 28 October 1997 and amended on 15 March and 21 September 2001 (consolidated text: ITLOS/8, 27 April 2005). In addition, the "Guidelines Concerning the Preparation and Presentation of Cases before the Tribunal" (ITLOS/9, 14 November 2006) and the "Resolution on Internal Judicial Practice of the Tribunal" (ITLOS/10, 27 April 2005) are to be taken into account.

ITLOS applies the provisions of the LOSC, the IA and other rules of international law not incompatible with the Convention in deciding disputes submitted to it (Art. 293 (1) LOSC, Art. 23 ITLOS Statute). This open wording will allow the Tribunal to apply new sources of international law (not mentioned in Art. 38 (1) ICJ Statute), should such sources gain general recognition in the future (→ International Law and the UN). ITLOS also has the power to decide cases *ex aequo et bono*, if the parties so agree (Art. 293 (2) LOSC). The Seabed Disputes Chamber applies, in addition, the rules, regulations and procedures of the International Seabed Authority and the terms of contracts concerning activities in the Area in matters relating to those contracts (Art. 38 ITLOS Statute).

The Tribunal issues orders and renders judgments. All decisions, whether delivered by the plenary or a chamber, are to be considered "as rendered by the Tribunal" (Art. 15 (5) ITLOS Statute). The decisions have binding force and must be complied with by the parties to the dispute (Art. 296 LOSC, Art. 33 ITLOS Statute). The LOSC, however, does not provide for the enforcement of decisions by international organs or sanctions in case of non-compliance. The enforcement of a decision against a state party in another state party would be contrary to the principle of sovereign equality of states. Article 39 ITLOS Statute makes however an exception for decisions of the Seabed Disputes against a state party which are enforceable in the territories of the other states parties in the same manner as judgments or orders of the highest court of the state party in whose territory the enforcement is sought. This may be explained by the commercial character of activities in the "Area". It is nowadays generally accepted that with respect to commercial activities (*acta jure gestionis*) States do not enjoy immunity from enforcement measures against their property in the forum state that does not serve public purposes. In order to make provision for the enforcement of decisions of the Sea-

bed Disputes Chamber, the German Parliament on 6 June 1995 adopted the Act on the Enforcement of Decisions of International Tribunals in the Field of the Law of the Sea – Seegerichtsvollstreckungsgesetz (BGBl. 1995 I, 786 and 2002 I, 564).

6. Evaluation and Outlook

In the first twelve years of its existence ITLOS was able to enter just fifteen cases upon its docket, of which thirteen came to it under its "emergency jurisdiction" for the prompt release of detained vessels and crews and the prescription of provisional measures. Of the remaining two cases, one (Case No. 7) has been pending since December 2000. The time limits of the proceedings in this case have been extended several times at the request of the parties and it seems unlikely that the case will ever be decided by ITLOS. This leaves the Tribunal with just one substantial judgment on the merits (Case No. 2, *The M/V "SAIGA" (No.2) (Saint Vincent and the Grenadines v. Guinea)*). In over a decade, only three states and the EC have thus "chosen" the Tribunal as a means for the settlement of law of the sea disputes. By comparison, the Permanent Court of International Justice issued forty-four substantive judgments and advisory opinions during the first twelve years of its existence, and for the ICJ the equivalent number is twenty-nine. Since 1996, six new maritime disputes were submitted to the ICJ and five to Arbitral Tribunals under Annex VII of the LOSC. Judging by the number of cases, ITLOS can hardly been regarded as a success story. Despite all its outreach and information activities, the Tribunal so far has not been able to endear itself to states parties of the LOSC as a credible means for the settlement of substantive law of the sea disputes. In particular, the high number of (individual or joint) dissenting and separate opinions and declarations by individual judges in the early years have created the image of an unpredictable group of individualistic judges, each of whom seems to know the LOSC best, rather than that of a unified court. It may well take several years and a new generation of judges, which has not been as intimately involved in the negotiations of the LOSC as the present one, before ITLOS can achieve its full potential as a provider of judicial services.

Stefan Talmon

Lit.: *Basedow, J.:* Perspektiven des Seerechts, in: JZ 1999, 9-15; *Churchill, R.R.:* Some Reflections on the Operations of the Dispute Settlement System of the UN Convention on the Law of the Sea During its First Decade, in: Freestone, D. et al. (eds.): Law of the Sea: Progress and Prospects, Oxford 2006, 388-416; *Eiriksson, G.:* The International Tribunal for the Law of the Sea, The Hague 2000; *Klein, N.:* Dispute Settlement in the UN Convention on the Law of the Sea, Cambridge 2005; *Nordquist, M.H. et al. (eds.):* United Nations Convention on the Law of the Sea 1982. A Commentary, Vol. 5, Dordrecht 1989; Vol. 6, The Hague 2002; *Oda, S.:* Dispute Settlement Prospects in the Law of the Sea, in: ICLQ 44 (1995), 863-872; *Rao, P.C./Khan, R. (eds.):* The International Tribunal for the Law of the Sea, The Hague 2001; *Rao, P.C./Gauthier, P. (eds.):* The Rules of the International Tribunal for the Law of the Sea: A Commentary, Leiden 2006; *Seymour, J.:* The International Tribunal for the Law of the Sea: A Great Mistake? In: Indiana J. Global Legal Stud. 13 (2006), 1-35; *Sohn, L.B.:* A Tribunal for the Sea-Bed or the Ocean, in: ZaöRV 32 (1972), 253-264; *Treves, T.:* A System for the Law of the Sea Dispute Settlement, in: Freestone, D. et al. (eds.): Law of the Sea: Progress and Prospects, Oxford 2006, 417-432; see also the publications of the *International Tribunal for the Law of the Sea*: Pleadings, Minutes of Public Sittings and Documents, Vol. 1 (1997) - present; Reports of Judgments, Advisory Opinions and Orders, Vol. 1 (1997) - present; Yearbook, Vol. 1 (1996-1997) - present.

Internet: General information on ITLOS, documents and publications, the decisions of the Tribunal and its press releases may be found on the Court's website: www.itlos. org.

ITU – International Telecommunication Union

The *International Telecommunication Union (ITU)* was established on 9 December 1932 as a merger of two predecessors, the International Telegraph Union, founded in Paris in 1865, and the International Radiotelegraph Conference, which had been founded in 1906 in Berlin. The merger into the ITU was accomplished by the first International Telecommunication Convention, adopted at a conference in Madrid 1932, and in force since 1 January 1934. In 1947 the ITU was restructured at the ITU conference in Atlantic City, by revising the International Telecommunication Convention of 1934.

On 1 January 1949 the ITU became a specialized agency of the UN ($\rightarrow$ specialized agencies) by an agreement with United Nations (UNTS Vol. 30, No. 175). Its seat is in Geneva since 1948, after having been initially located in Berne. Its *membership* is open to all member states of the United Nations, and to any other state with the approval by two-thirds of the ITU member states. At present the ITU has 191 members (as of 31 December 2008).

I. Purposes and Tasks

The main objective of the ITU is to guarantee international cooperation and economic and social development by setting up and extending efficient telecommunication services, and by planning the structures of telecommunication servicees. Since the ITU reform in 1992, its scope of tasks comprises three sectors:

a) *radio communication:* distribution of radio frequencies for the different radio services (broadcasting, marine radio services, air transport radio, radio amateur services) as well as the registration and coordination of the distribution of frequencies and satellite orbits for radio-communication satellites;

b) *standardization of telecommunication:* establishment of worldwide standards in telecommunication, including Internet connectivity;

c) *development of telecommunication:* serving as catalyst for the extension of telecommunication services in the developing countries, in cooperation with the IBRD (→ World Bank, World Bank Group) and the Regional Economic Commissions of the United Nations (→ Economic Commissions, Regional).

II. Organizational Structure

a) *Plenipotentiary Conference:* The Conference is the supreme organ of the ITU, in which all ITU members are represented, and which is convened normally every five years. It determines the general policies for the ITU and elects the members of the other ITU organs.

b) *Administrative Council:* The council comprises 46 members, elected by the Plenipotentiary Conference, and normally convenes annually. It acts in the intervals between the sessions of the Conference on behalf of the latter, and is responsible for the implementation of the decisions of the Conference and of the tasks assigned by the Convention.

c) World or Regional *Administrative Conferences* may be convened in the interval between the sessions of the ITU Conference, to offer an opportunity to react to new technological developments.

d) The telecommunication sector, the sector of standardization and the sector for the telecommunication development of the ITU dispose of their own *advisory organs,* each headed by a director: the International Frequency Registration Board, the International Radio Consultative Committee, the International Telegraph and Telephone Consultative Committee and the Telecommunications Development Board.

e) The *General Secretariat:* Directed by a Secretary-General, who is elected by the ITU Conference. It is entrusted with the administrative and budgetary planning of the ITU, monitors the compliance with the ITU regulations and documents and publishes the results of the work of the ITU organs.

The ITU cooperates closely with other specialized agencies of the UN, e.g. → ICAO, → IMO, → UPU, → UNESCO, and → WMO, as these are all concerned with telephone and radio services.

III. New Challenges

More than any other specialized agency of the UN, the ITU has been forced to address new technological developments (satellite radio services, telefax services, digital radio and television, the Internet) and has had to deal in this context also with the economic and political aspects of these developments. In this process ITU has succeeded in ensuring the further technological development of the telecommunication systems in a worldwide balancing of interests, so that in the meantime the rapid global communication of news, the global transmission of radio and television programmes and the global transfer of data concerning economic transactions, has become feasible.

The economic, social and cultural problems connected with these developments (→ Globalization) were for many years mainly discussed in other UN organs and organizations.

The ITU, as a clearing and organization center of international telecommunication, seemed for a long time to be overtaxed with these latter roles. That is why the debate about the world information and communication order, as it was initiated by the developing countries, was held under the aegis of UNESCO for some decades. The discussions on the question whether the predominance of the Western industrialized countries in the field of private enterprise in the television and radio sector, in the area of news agencies and in the field of satellite telecommunication etc., might result in endangering the freedom of information and of expression, were predominantly held in UNESCO circles and only to a small extent in ITU bodies.

It was at least a first sign of a new awareness of the complex and urgent sociopolitical aspects of the problems in the ITU, that the ITU Conference launched in its 1998 Conference in Minneapolis an initiative for a World Summit on the Information Society, The

459

UN General Assembly responded to this ITU initiative in resolving, with Resolution 56/183 in December 2001, to hold the suggested meeting in the form of a world summit and assigned the ITU the leading managerial role in preparing the summit. The GA expressed in its resolution the wish that the summit would help to find "the global consensus and commitment required to promote the urgently needed access of all countries to information, knowledge and communication technologies for development ... and to address the whole range of relevant issues related to the information society ..." (ibid.).

The *World Summit on the Information Society (WSIS)* was the first gathering of global leaders to address the issues of the information society and was held in two phases. The first took place in Geneva from 10 to 12 December 2003, bringing together over 11,000 participants from 175 countries, including about 50 heads of states and of governments, respectively. The second phase was held in Tunis from 16 to 18 November 2005, with over 19,000 participants taking part from 174 countries, among them more than 1,200 journalists from over 600 media organizations, a remarkably large circle of participants for such a rather abstract summit topic, which made it clear that nowadays the world public considers structures of the information society, in particular the Internet, a highly important global issue. WSIS resulted in four outcome documents addressing the issues of the information society, including the use of information and communication technology (ICT) for development, Internet governance, infrastructure, capacity building and cultural diversity: the *Geneva Declaration of Principles* (Doc. WSIS-03/GENEVA/DOC/4-E, 12 December 2003) and the *Geneva Plan of Action* (Doc. WSIS-03/GENEVA/DOC/5-E, 12 December 2003) in the first conference phase and the *Tunis Commitment* (Doc. WSIS-05/TUNIS/DOC/7-E, 18 November 2005) and the *Tunis Agenda for the Information Society* (WSIS-05/

TUNIS/DOC/6 (Rev.1)-E, 18 November 2005) in the second phase.

The expressed aim of the General Assembly in convening WSIS was to provide an effective means of support to the ITU in developing a global framework to address the challenges by the global information society:

1) The developing countries needed *increased and cheaper access to communications*, in particular to the Internet, a drop in charges for international calls and more efficient national communications systems, in order to be able to take part more efficiently in world trade. They hoped for a "digital solidarity", i.e. the willingness of the developed states to subsidize the building-up of communication facilities in the developing states through a special fund.

2) The problem of *Internet governance* should be solved at the WSIS summit, i.e. the question who will decide in future on the rules, norms and principles in the use of the Internet. Historically the management of important Internet resources such as IP numbers and domain names has been done by the Internet Corporation for Assigned Names and Numbers (ICANN), a US not-for-profit public-benefit corporation based in California and operating through a Memorandum of Understanding with the US Department of Commerce, giving the latter oversight authority on ICANN's policies, to the detriment of the rest of the governments that only have an advisory role through ICANN's Governmental Advisory Committee (GAC) (http:// gac.icann.org).

3) The ITU had previously managed global communication resources, but found itself increasingly sidelined in the new international telecommunication framework, promoted by WTO and WIPO and backed by the rich-country governments and the Bretton-Woods institutions, in which access prices to communications services are exclusively regulated by market forces. The WSIS thus represented an attempt by the ITU to regain a central role within the world information system.

4) The developed nations saw in the Summit an opportunity to promote expansion of their telecommunications companies in the South, to broaden the path opened by the liberalization of the communications markets achieved through the signing in 1996 of the WTO's Telecommunications Agreement.

As it is often the case at UN conferences, the results of WSIS consist in a compromise which does not satisfy many of the wishes of the developing countries, but brings some progress for them:

a) With regard to the financing of communication facilities in the developing countries, the summit documents did not establish an effective funding mechanism, but at least contained some assertive language in this direction.

b) With regard to the Internet governance, the US government successfully prevented any document language weakening its own control position by agreeing to a skillful compromise: the USA agreed to the principle in the Tunis document that all governments should have an equal role and responsibility for international Internet governance; in exchange, the other conference states agreed to the principle that the US government retains control over ICANN. That the US government has also after the Tunis conference retained indeed the Internet control with regard to ICANN is illustrated by the fact that ICANN and the US Department of Commerce signed in September 2006 a new agreement, called "Joint Project Agreement", affirming the old legal construction in new diplomatic language.

c) The most positive outcome of WSIS is perhaps the establishment of the Internet Governance Forum (IGF), having only an advisory role; it is an expression of the intensive participation of civil society organizations during all conference phases and it will doubtlessly develop into an institution where global information and communication policies will be discussed by governments, private enterprises and NGOs on an equal footing, which might contribute to a gradual democratization of the world communication system.

The disparities with regard to communication facilities between developed and developing states – the so-called "digital divide" – have not been effectively diminished through the WSIS conference, the ITU has not strengthened its position in the world information system in relation to WTO and WIPO, but at least the attention of the world public in general and of the politicians in particular has been drawn to this important area of global activities and the existing norms and rules have been discussed at great length. It is up to the ITU to take care that in the years to come the United Nations continues with the debate about this issue.

Helmut Volger

Lit.: *Accuosto, P.:* WSIS wraps up to mixed emotions, in: Third World Resurgence No. 184 (Dec. 2005), www.twnside.org; *Khor, M.:* UN debate on the digital divide, in: Global Trends No. 46, 7 March 2005, www. twnside.org; *Magiera, S.:* ITU – International Telecommunication Union, in: Wolfrum, R. (ed.): United Nations: Law, Policies and Practice, Vol. 2, Munich/Dordrecht 1995, 821-826; *Schrogl, K.-U.:* Die „neue" ITU. Strukturreform einer internationalen Organisation als Routine, in: VN 42 (1994), 97-101; *Tegge, A.:* Die Internationale Telekommunikationsunion: Organisation und Funktion einer Weltorganisation im Wandel, Baden-Baden 1994; *World Summit on the Information Society (WSIS):* Declaration of Principles, 12 December 2003, Doc. WSIS-03/GENEVA/DOC/4-E; *WSIS:* Plan of Action, 12 December 2003, Doc. WSIS-03/GENEVA/DOC/5-E; *WSIS:* Tunis Commitment, 18 November 2005, Doc. WSIS-05/TUNIS/DOC/7-E; *WSIS:* Tunis Agenda for the Information Society, 18 November 2005, Doc. WSIS-05/TUNIS/DOC/6(Rev.1)-E; *WSIS Civil Society:* Much more could have been achieved. Civil Society Statement on the World Summit on the Information Society, revised version, 23 December 2005, www.wsis-cs.org.

Internet: 1. Homepage of ITU: www.itu.int; 2. information on the World Summit on the Information Society: www.itu.int/wsis.

Languages

There is no general regulation for the use of languages for the United Nations proper, i.e. for the six principal organs and their subsidiary organs (→ Principal Organs, Subsidiary Organs, Treaty Bodies), nor for the United Nations system (→ UN System) with its numerous bodies and institutions.

I. Languages of the Principal Organs

In the Charter of the United Nations (→ Charter of the UN), only Article 39 of the Statute of the International Court of Justice (→ ICJ), which is an integral part of the UN Charter, determines French and English as official languages (→ Languages, Official), taking up the → League of Nations tradition. The parties of a dispute may however agree to use one of these languages only and, at the request of any party, the Court may authorize a language other than French or English to be used by that party.

For the five other principal organs, however, the usual language clause is lacking. This means that language arrangements and their modifications are left to the respective → Rules of Procedure. But as the Charter was signed in the five languages "Chinese, French, Russian, English and Spanish", which were declared to be "equally authentic" (Art. 111 UN Charter), these five languages were considered to be official languages, i.e. languages admitted for oral as well as written statements. However, (oral) interpretations and (written) translations were made at first only into the two working languages French and English (→ Languages, Working) as was the practice in the League of Nations. In the → General Assembly and in the → Security Council, the other three official languages gradually came to be used equally as working languages into which the four other official languages were to be interpreted and translated.

By A/RES/246 (III), adopted by the General Assembly on 7 December 1948, the first language to become an additional working language of the General Assembly (and soon afterwards of the Security Council) was Spanish, which had been given up shortly after its introduction by the League of Nations as a working language because of the additional time needed for consecutive interpretation, that being the only usual translation method at that time. But though simultaneous interpretation (which was first used in the multilingual Soviet Union, and was established in the West by its use during the Nuremberg Trials) had by then been established as a new interpretation technique needing no extra time, it took 20 additional years until, by A/RES/2479 (XXIII), adopted on 21 December 1968, the Russian language reached the status of a working language and five more years until finally, by A/RES/3189, adopted on 18 December 1973, the Chinese language (the most difficult language to interpret simultaneously because of its complex linguistic structure) equally became a working language, first of the General Assembly and then of the Security Council. Since then, all five original official languages have the status of working languages in these two organs, so that usually the distinction is omitted and they are referred to only as "the languages".

In the same year when the first German-speaking member state, Austria, was admitted to the UN in 1955, the Arabic member states, using a clause of the → Rules of Procedure, succeeded in having established a small Arabic Translation Unit, fully financed by the regular budget (→ Budget), for translation of a number of selected documents into the Arabic language. In 1973, when the then two German states were admitted to the UN and, on the same date, Chinese became a working language, the Arabic states successfully asked that Arabic be recognized as an official and a working language of the General Assembly and its Main Committees (→ Committees, System of), and shortly afterwards of the Security Council as well. Subsequently, Arabic was recognized as the sixth language of the United Nations - above all with the help of UN world conferences (→ World Conferences).

At this point, the now three German-speaking member states asked for the establishment of a small → German Translation Section, using the same Rules of Procedure clause the Arabic countries had used, and equally having in mind the final status of an official language. Such a German Translation Section was created by A/RES/3355 (XXIX) on 18 December 1974 with the mandate to officially translate into German, as of 1 July 1975, all resolutions and decisions of the General Assembly and of the Security Council (→ Resolution, Declaration, Decision), as well as the annual reports of the → Secretary-General, of the Security Council and of other bodies to the General Assembly and other important texts, these translations being published in the same form as the other versions in the now six official languages. Unlike the Arabic Service, however, the German Translation Section, though fully integrated into the → Secretariat, is not financed by the regular budget but by a trust fund now fed by the user states Austria and Germany, with additional funding by Liechtenstein and Switzerland. To date, German has remained an "additional language" for the official translation of certain documents, in particular of the General Assembly and of the Security Council. There is no interpretation section or service of the UN for interpretation from and into German.

Leading German-speaking representatives such as heads of state or foreign ministers, however, under another rule of the Rules of Procedure, are able to use their own language in the General Assembly or in the Security Council, if they bring their own interpreters with them, who then translate their statements into one of the six official languages (usually English), from which the Secretariat interpreters can translate them into the other five official languages.

Soon after the extension of the Arabic Translation Unit and after the establishment of the German Translation Section, the Joint Inspection Unit published a report (UN Doc. JIU/REP/77/5) which led to a limitation on the admission of "additional languages," by establishing the so-called "user-principle" (payment by "users") and the principle of selectivity (only "necessary" translations into "necessary" languages). This selectivity principle is however hard to put into practice, as all documents are closely interrelated in content as well as in wording, and by the fact that delegates, in any case, will have to speak or write in one of the official and working languages and therefore tend to prepare their statements and documents in the "foreign" language they are planning to use. This is probably the reason for German so far having remained the only "additional language" into which official translations are made, though the member states using other languages such as Japanese, Italian, Hindi or Swahili have shown some unofficial interest in following similar practice in respect of their languages.

The Economic and Social Council (→ ECOSOC) has so far maintained its three working languages: English, French and Spanish. The → Trusteeship Council has practically put itself "out of business" by its successful policy of → decolonization.

Since A/RES/2 (I) of 1 February 1946, the Secretariat which is housing all languages services (translation and interpretation being organized and working separately) and which serves all other organs as well as the UN world conferences, has maintained its two working languages, English and French, for its own work (such as oral and written communication, printed forms, signboards, telephone directories etc.).

II. Languages of the United Nations System

Language regulations in the United Nations System, including its specialized agencies and the multiple other UN bodies and organizations, are even more variegated than for the main organs, their subsidiary bodies and for UN world conferences. Thus, for instance, the oldest specialized agency (→ Specialized Agencies), the Universal Postal Union (→ UPU), founded during the 19th century at a time when French was the dominant diplomatic language, has maintained French as its only official language, whereas in the Asian Development Bank, English is the only official language. In the International Labor Organization (→ ILO) English, French and Spanish are official languages, while Arabic, Chinese, German and Russian have the status of working languages. All international labor conference reports, some Governing Body documents and a selection of other documents are translated into German. From the inception of the ILO in 1919 up to 1933, when Germany resigned from the ILO (and the League of Nations), German together with French and English were official languages. German was reintroduced as a working language in 1951 together with Russian, followed in the 1980s by Chinese and Arabic.

a) For ILO terminology (English/French/German/Spanish/Russian/Arabic/Chinese) see: www.ilo.org/iloterm/

b) For ILO documents and publications published in German see: www.ilo.org/public/german/region/eurpro/bonn/publ.htm

Contact: German Translation Unit, Official Relations and Documentation Branch, 4, route de Morillons, CH-1211 Geneva 22; phone : +41-22-799 78 23.

The official languages of → UNESCO and the World Health Organization → WHO are Arabic, Chinese, English, French, Russian and Spanish. Moreover, there are internal language services for Hindi, Italian and Portuguese at UNESCO and for Portuguese and German at the WHO, where since 1975, German is additionally a "working language" for the European Region (Regional Office at Copenhagen), as provided by Resolution EUR/RC25/R2 of September 2, 1975. This is why there are German versions of numerous WHO documents, including the constitution. These documents can be retrieved on the Internet under www.euro.who.int; phone: 0045-3917-1233 or 1392.

The World Bank (International Bank for Reconstruction and Development (→ World Bank, World Bank Group) and the International Monetary Fund (→ IMF) have no "official languages". Without any official language rules, they work in fact with English (as well as with international translation teams into and from Arabic, English, French, Russian and Spanish, and "from all major Western languages"). The annual World Bank Report is also published in German. The IMF has a small translation capacity with one translator/reviser and a typist for translations into German.

III. General Remarks

Though the United Nations have already limited their languages to six official languages (out of 5000 to 6000 languages spoken today), with equal legal status for each of the six languages, and though the costs for language services are far below 10% of the regular budget (as against about 35% at the European Commission or even over 50% for the European Parliament), there is in practice considerable pressure towards further language limitation, and even towards a monolingual system with English as a worldwide "lingua franca".

Internal meetings of groups, such as of the EU representatives at the UN or of the "Group of 77" with its now 130 members (→ Group of 77 and the UN), are more and more often held without interpreters in one language – English, even in the French-speaking environment of Geneva. As for the meetings of UN bodies themselves, the desire to save time and costs often induces the delegates not to wait for translations of an English original (90% of all UN documents are English originals) into the other languages, but to start discussions right away as soon as the English version is available. This practice is however strongly disapproved and fought in particular by the numerically strong "Groupe francophone" led by France, supported by others of the group of Romance languages. An initiative of that group supported by several other member states (including Germany) led to the adoption, on 2 November 1995, of General Assembly Resolution 50/11 on "multilingualism", which is intended mainly to preserve equality for French with English. The resolution includes as well regulations about language requirements for UN staff members ($\rightarrow$ Personnel). As a rule, staff members are expected to know at least two official languages. This is however a considerable obstacle for applicants from countries where none of the official languages are spoken, and where regional conditions make it necessary to learn foreign languages other than the official languages of the UN. After recruitment, staff members can however improve their linguistic skills (relevant for salary and promotion, as well) in free language courses for all official languages (which included German before some Secretariat units were moved from New York City to Vienna), given in the target language only.

To be admitted to the written and oral examinations for prospective members of translation and interpretation services of the Secretariat, candidates are required to have a university degree (of any discipline), acquired in the language into which they wish to translate. Apart from English, which is the source language for most of the examination papers for candidates who want to translate into a language other than English (whereas for English translators it is French), candidates have to know at least two other official languages. (For more information, write to your respective Ministry of Foreign Affairs)

Besides the Department of Public Information (DPI) at UN Headquarters, most UN organs and organizations as well as their representations in member countries publish information brochures and other material in non-official languages. These publications are distributed by the UN Information Centres (UNICs) established in certain member states, or by the country representatives of the respective UN organization or specialized agency. (For more information see the list of addresses contained

in the annex to this encyclopedia.) Thus one can for example order free copies of the $\rightarrow$ Charter of the UN, of the Universal Declaration of Human Rights ($\rightarrow$ Human Rights, Universal Declaration of), of the International Covenant on Civil and Political Rights ($\rightarrow$ Human Rights Conventions, CCPR) and the International Covenant on Economic, Social and Cultural Rights ($\rightarrow$ Human Rights Conventions, CESCR).

A special case of language use are United Nations $\rightarrow$ stamps. All stamps display the same graphic design, but have English captions when sold in New York, French captions in Geneva and German captions in Vienna.

Ruprecht Paqué

Lit.: *Paqué; R.:* Sprachen und Sprachendienste der Vereinten Nationen in: VN 28 (1980), 165ff.; *Paqué, R.:* Vielsprachigkeit, Mehrsprachigkeit, Einsprachigkeit – zu den Sprachen der Vereinten Nationen und zur Resolution 50/11 der Generalversammlung über 'Multilingualism', in: VN 45 (1997), 61-68; *Tabor, M.:* Multilingualism in International Law and Institutions, Princeton 1980.

Internet: The websites of the Internet homepage of the United Nations Headquarters (www.un.org) are provided in all six official languages: the Internet user begins with the common homepage www.un.org and chooses the respective language button at the bottom of the homepage to continue with the websites in the language chosen. Homepage of the German Translation Section: www.un.org/Depts/german; list of German translations: www.un.org/depts/german/gts/gts0.pdf..

Languages, Official

The term *"official language"* (Fr. *langue officielle;*G. *Amtssprache*) usually refers to a language admitted (in the statutes or in the rules of procedure of an organization or other body) for oral and written statements. It does however not automatically imply that each official language must be interpreted or translated into all other official languages of the respective organization. As the UN Charter ($\rightarrow$ Charter of the

UN) does not contain any language rules except for the International Court of Justice (→ ICJ), the United Nations began its work with the five languages of the five "equally authentic" versions of the Charter (Art. 111 UN Charter): Chinese, French, Russian, English and Spanish. As distinguished from these official languages, however, the respective rules of procedure of the individual organs (→ Rules of Procedure) chose as "working languages" (→ Languages, Working) those languages into which all statements made in an official language had to be interpreted and translated.

To French and English, the two working languages taken over from the → League of Nations, some principal organs (→ Principal Organs, Subsidiary Organs, Treaty Bodies) gradually added Spanish, Russian and Chinese, until all five original official languages had become working languages, too, in the → General Assembly and the → Security Council, so that they were referred to from then on as "languages" only (→ Languages). In 1973, the same year when the then two German states were admitted to the UN, the General Assembly, soon followed by the Security Council, added Arabic as an additional "official and working language", thus enlarging the Arabic Translation Unit which had already been established in 1955. Subsequently, Arabic grew into a full-fledged sixth official language in the two organs, and in other bodies such as the UN world conferences (→ World Conferences). The only other language represented in the UN Secretariat Services (→ Secretariat) is German, which is neither an official nor a working language, nevertheless translations into that language by the → German Translation Section are official UN documents.

Ruprecht Paqué

Lit.: *Paqué, R.:* Vielsprachigkeit, Mehrsprachigkeit, Einsprachigkeit. Zu den Sprachen der Vereinten Nationen und zur Resolution 50/11 der Generalversammlung über "Multilingualism", in: VN 45 (1997), 61-68.

Internet: The websites of the Internet homepage of the United Nations Headquarters (www.un.org) are provided in all six official languages: the Internet user begins with the common homepage www.un.org and chooses the respective language button at the bottom of the homepage to continue with the websites in the language chosen.

Languages, Working

For the principal organs of the UN (→ Principal Organs, Subsidiary Organs, Treaty Bodies), the term *"working language"* (Fr. *langue de travail*; G *Arbeitssprache*) refers to a language into which all oral and written statements in an admitted official language are to be interpreted or translated. "Working language" implies thus a higher status than "official language" (→ Languages, Official), as interpretation and translation have to take place only into these "working languages" and not into the other official languages. For many other bodies and organizations of the UN system (→ UN System), however, "working language" may imply – similar to the situation at the Council of Europe – a lesser status where the use of a "working language" is limited to certain documents or occasions. In the World Health Organization (→ WHO), based on WHO Resolution EUR/RC 25/R of September 1975, German enjoys, in the European region, equal status with English, French, and Russian for the more important documents (Regional Committee documents, policy documents, action plans, etc.), as well as for conferences, while for the internal workings of the WHO regional office, English is used almost exclusively.

Ruprecht Paqué

Law of the Sea

1. Importance, Terminology and Sources

The seas and oceans cover more than 72 per cent of the surface of the earth. Approximately 4 billion people, almost two-thirds of the world population, live in coastal areas and thus many of them live on and with the sea. Its importance for the world climate, for the supply of humankind with food, energy and raw materials as well as for the communication between continents and states can hardly be overestimated. Furthermore, the sea serves as an object of scientific research, as a waste dumping ground and, too, as a naval battlefield.

The term *"international law of the sea"* covers the rules of public international law governing the legal status and relations of and on the sea, the seabed and subsoil, and the airspace above it. The international law of the sea is thus more than the laws governing navigation and shipping and is not to be confused with admiralty or maritime law. It encompasses all the laws relating to the sea in the fields of fishery, economic activity, transport, protection of the environment, underwater cultural heritage, mining, and armed conflicts; it also regulates the acquisition of → sovereignty and jurisdiction over marine areas, as well as marine scientific research and the development and transfer of marine technology.

As a consequence of this diversity of subjects, the international law of the sea is to be found not only in the great law of the sea codifications adopted within the framework of the United Nations but also in hundreds of bilateral and multilateral (international and regional) treaties which do not deal exclusively with maritime legal issues. Despite the existence of numerous treaties, customary international law (cf. Art. 38 (1) (b) ICJ Statute) still plays an important role. As far as the member states of the European Union are concerned, European Community Law is also applicable. This multitude of sources contributes to the complex picture the international law of the sea presents at the beginning of the 21st century.

2. Development of the Law of the Sea within the Framework of the United Nations

a) The First Conference on the Law of the Sea and the Geneva Conventions of 1958

Since its foundation the United Nations is, in accordance with its function laid down in Article 13 (1) (a) of the Charter (→ Charter of the UN), the central forum for the codification and progressive development of the international law of the sea (→ International Law and the UN). At the request of the → General Assembly resolutions A/RES/374 (IV) of 6 December 1949; A/RES/798 (VIII) of 7 December 1953, and A/RES/899 (IX) of 14 December 1954), the International Law Commission (→ ILC) studied the law of the high seas and the territorial sea and in 1956 submitted a detailed final report (UN Doc. A/3159), in which it recommended the summoning of an international conference of plenipotentiaries "to examine the law of the sea, taking account not only of the legal but also of the technical, biological, economic and political aspects of the problem, and to embody the results of its work in one or more international conventions." After consultations in the Sixth (Legal) Committee (→ Committees, System of), the General Assembly in resolution A/RES/1105 (XI) of 21 February 1957 invited all members of the United Nations and its → specialized agencies to the *First United Nations Conference on the Law of the Sea* (UNCLOS I) which met at Geneva from 24 February to 27 April 1958. Eighty-six states participated, and interested international organizations sent observers. On 29 April 1958, the Conference adopted a Final Act (UN Doc. A/CONF.13/37-43) that, apart from nine resolutions, contained four conventions: the *Convention on the Territorial Sea and the Contiguous Zone – TSC –* (UNTS Vol. 516, No. 7477, 205), the *Convention on the High Seas – HSC –* (UNTS Vol. 450, No. 6465, 11), the *Convention on Fishing and the Conservation of the Living Resources of the High Seas – HSFC –*

(UNTS Vol. 559, No. 8164, 285), the *Convention on the Continental Shelf – CSC* – (UNTS Vol. 499, No. 7302, 311), and an *Optional Protocol of Signature Concerning the Compulsory Settlement of Disputes – OP* – (UNTS Vol. 450, No. 6466, 169). The TSC entered into force on 10 September 1964, the HSC on 30 September 1962, the HSFC on 20 March 1966, the CSC on 10 June 1964, and the OP on 30 September 1962. These conventions are still in force; by the end of October 2008, the TSC had 52 parties, the HSC had 63, the HSFC 38, the CSC 58 and the OP 38. The *four Geneva Conventions on the Law of the Sea* to a large extent codified existing customary international law (cf. the Preamble of the HSC). In some areas, however, they also developed new rules of the law of the sea (cf. the North Sea Continental Shelf Cases, ICJ Reports 1969, 37ff.). Nowadays, their practical relevance is limited to interpreting the 1982 Convention on the Law of the Sea, to filling any remaining gaps, and to providing evidence for the existence of a rule of customary international law.

b) The Failure of the Second Conference on the Law of the Sea, 1960

During the First Conference on the Law of the Sea no agreement could be reached on the breadth of the territorial sea. This problem had already defeated the 1930 Hague Codification Conference. Accordingly, the United Nations General Assembly in resolution A/RES/ 1307 (XIII) of 10 December 1958 convened the *Second United Nations Conference on the Law of the Sea* (UNCLOS II) which met at Geneva from 17 March to 16 April 1960. Again, no agreement could be reached: while most of the newly independent states, supported by the Eastern bloc under the leadership of the Soviet Union, advocated a territorial sea of up to 12 nautical miles (nm), the great seafaring nations (which owned more than 80 per cent of the world tonnage) favored the traditional three-mile rule. A compromise formula providing for a six-mile

territorial sea plus a six-mile exclusive fishery zone, in which historic fishing rights were to continue, did not obtain the required majority. The only text which the conference adopted recommended that the United Nations advance the fisheries of less developed countries (UN Doc. A/CONF.19/4.15).

c) The Developments towards the Third Conference on the Law of the Sea

The Geneva Conferences on the Law of the Sea illustrated two problems: first, the traditional division into a (wide) high seas and a (narrow) territorial sea was no longer considered satisfactory by the majority of states and, second, no legally binding limits existed either for the territorial sea, exclusive fishing rights or the continental shelf. This led many states to extend the seaward limit of their territorial sea further and further and to attempt to secure the exclusive use of fish stocks and seabed resources (oil, gasoline) by proclaiming ever broader "fishery zones", "fishery protection zones" or "exclusive economic zones" and continental shelf areas. For example, the Federal Republic of Germany on 20 January 1964 issued a Proclamation on the Exploration and Exploitation of the German Continental Shelf (BGBl. 1964 II, 104). With technical developments progressing, the question of the exploitation of the mineral resources of the deep seabed (e.g. valuable polymetallic nodules – especially manganese nodules – which are scattered across large areas of the seabed at depths of 3000 to 4000 meters) increased in importance. The developing countries feared that a handful of industrialized states on the basis of the freedom of the high seas might exploit the deep seabed resources, thus depriving them of the mineral wealth of the oceans. Experts warned of a "plundering of the seas" (*Graf Vitzthum* 1981). In a verbal note to the → Secretary-General on 17 August 1967 (UN Doc. A/6695) Malta proposed that the seabed and ocean floor underlying the seas beyond the limits of national jurisdiction should be declared the → common heritage of mankind and that their resources should be used in the interests of mankind – the so-called "Pardo Initiative" (cf. UNYB 1967, 41-49). In Malta's view, the traditional concepts of the freedom of the high seas and of sovereignty were no longer adequate to solve satisfactorily for all concerned the problems resulting from the novel commercial uses of the sea. In its resolution 2340 (XXII) of 18 December 1967 the General Assembly established an *Ad Hoc Committee to Study the Peaceful Uses of the Seabed and the Ocean Floor beyond the Limits of National Jurisdiction*, replaced in 1968 by a larger and "permanent" committee (A/RES/2467 (XXII) of 21 December 1968). Two years later, the General Assembly expanded the mandate of the Committee and entrusted it with the task to prepare a comprehensive list of subjects and issues for a new Conference on the Law of the Sea (UN Doc. A/RES/2750 (XXV) of 17 December 1970). In its resolution A/RES/2749 (XXV) of 17 December 1970 (*Declaration of Principles Governing the Seabed and Ocean Floor, and the Subsoil Thereof, beyond the Limits of National Jurisdiction*) the Assembly already set the tone for the conference when it declared the seabed and its resources to be the → common heritage of mankind, the exploration and exploitation of which should be carried out for the benefit of mankind as a whole, irrespective of the geographical location of states. In the preceding year, the Assembly had already (against the votes of some industrialized states) declared that everybody was bound to refrain from all activities of exploitation of the resources of the seabed pending the establishment of an appropriate international regime (UN Doc. A/RES/2574D (XXIV) of 15 December 1969 – the so-called *Moratorium Resolution*).

d) The Third United Nations Conference on the Law of the Sea, 1973-1982

On 16 November 1973, the General Assembly convoked the *Third United Nations Conference on the Law of the Sea* (UNCLOS III) and entrusted it with the task "to adopt a convention dealing with all the matters relating to the law of the sea", bearing in mind that "the problems of ocean space are closely interrelated and need to be considered as a whole" (A/RES/3067 (XXVIII)). The conference met for the first time at New York from 3 to 15 December 1973 to talk about organizational and procedural questions; on 20 June 1974, it held its first substantive session in Caracas. During the following eight years, the conference held twelve sessions of four to six weeks each in Geneva, Caracas, New York and Montego Bay. More than 150 states as well as the United Nations Council for Namibia (a total of some 700 delegates) participated in the conference as full members. Numerous states and territories enjoying self-government but not yet having attained full independence, liberation movements (PLO, SWAPO), non-governmental organizations (→ NGOs), international and supranational organizations and 14 specialized agencies of the United Nations participated as observers without vote. Henry Kissinger called UNCLOS III one of the "most important, most complex and most ambitious diplomatic undertakings in history". The task UNCLOS III was entrusted with already illustrates that, unlike its predecessors, it was not only to codify the existing customary rules but to progressively develop the international law of the sea. This is also shown by the fact that the conference had no report or draft convention of the International Law Commission (→ ILC) as a "Basis of Discussion" to aid its work. From the outset the conference was seen as a political rather than a legal enterprise – indeed, issues of the conference were assigned to the General Assembly's First (Political and Security) Committee and not the Sixth (Legal) Committee (→ Committees, System of). At the beginning of the negotiations there was not so much an exchange of legal argument but a presentation of the respective political and economic positions which were to be taken into account. The negotiations were characterized by the demand of the developing countries for a new international economic order ($\rightarrow$ International Economic Relations and New International Economic Order (NIEO)), which was to find its expression, *inter alia*, in the just distribution of the marine resources between the states and by the attempts of the coastal states at seaward extension of their sovereign rights and jurisdiction ("creeping jurisdiction"). The negotiations at UNCLOS III were strongly influenced by two procedural principles: the formulation of "package deals" and the "consensus principle". According to a gentlemen's agreement, formal votes were to be avoided and were to take place only after all efforts at consensus had been exhausted. This approach heavily influenced the format of the negotiations: after the general debates the work in plenary meetings almost ceased and the discussion of the substantial issues shifted to the committees, subcommittees and working groups (*Jaenicke* 1978). Although the "Working Papers" and "Informal Composite Negotiating Texts" prepared by the committees did not have any formal status and were merely meant to represent an emerging consensus and serve as a basis for subsequent negotiations, the provisions of these texts in many cases soon found their way into national legislations and proclamations. Indeed, states quickly extended their jurisdiction over large parts of the high seas in order not to miss the boat on the new legal developments which might lead to the "dividing up of the seas". For example, the Federal Republic of Germany on 21 December 1976 and 18 May 1978 proclaimed the establishment of exclusive fishing zones in the North Sea (BGBl. 1976 II 1999) and in the Baltic Sea (BGBl. 1978 II 867). Thus, the negotiating texts already exerted substantial influence upon the development of customary international law rules on, *inter alia*, the exclusive economic zone and the continental shelf (cf. Continental Shelf Case (Tunisia/Libya), ICJ Reports 1982, 38, 47-49, 79).

e) The Need for an Implementation Agreement

After all possibilities of reaching consensus had been exhausted the Conference on 3 0 April 1982 approved the final text of the *Convention on the Law of the Sea* (LOSC)and four resolutions (UN Doc. A/CONF.62/122 and Corr.) by a formal vote of 130 in favor (among them almost all developing countries), four against (Israel, Turkey, USA and Venezuela), with seventeen abstentions (mostly industrialized nations, among them the Federal Republic of Germany). Although the LOSC was signed on 12 December 1982 by 119 states it took another twelve years until it entered into force (twelve months after the deposit of the sixtieth instrument of ratification). The main reason for this was that important industrialized countries (among them the USA, the United Kingdom, and the Federal Republic of Germany) were opposed to Part XI of the LOSC on the exploration and exploitation of the resources of the seabed and ocean floor and the subsoil thereof beyond the limits of national jurisdiction (the "Area") with its provisions on production policies, participation in revenue, and the transfer of technology as well as the possibility of binding changes to the regime of the "Area" by a three-fourths majority of the states parties to the LOSC. This opposition led to two parallel regimes governing the "Area": while the Preparatory Commission for the International Seabed Authority and the International Tribunal for the Law of the Sea (PREPCOM), as predecessor of the *International Seabed Authority* which was to be established after the entry into force of the LOSC, from 1987 onwards registered the first enterprises or corporations sponsored by a state under the regime of the LOSC as "Pioneer Investors", whereby they acquired the right to explore (and the inchoate right to exploit) a specific mine site, the states opposing Part XI of the LOSC enacted laws on deep seabed mining while UNCLOS III was still in progress, which provided for a purely national licensing system for the exploration and exploitation of the seabed. For example, Germany on 16 August 1980 adopted a Law on the Interim Regulation of Deep Seabed Mining (BGBl. 1980 I, 1457, amended by a law of 10 February 1982, BGBl. 1982 I, 136). In order to protect their national licenses the states outside the LOSC regime concluded treaties between each other on the mutual recognition of licensed operations and the procedures to be followed in the case of overlapping licenses (ILM 21 (1982), 950; ILM 23 (1984), 1354; ILM 26 (1987), 1502).

In July 1990 Secretary-General Pérez de Cuéllar took the initiative to convene "informal consultations" aimed at achieving reconciliation between the "LOSC Regime" and the "Reciprocating States Regime" thus rendering the LOSC acceptable to all states. These informal consultations, during which fifteen meetings were convened in which the three main non-contracting parties (USA, United Kingdom and Federal Republic of Germany) actively participated, on 28 July 1994 led to the adoption of the *Agreement Relating to the Implementation of Part XI of the United Nations Convention on the Law of the Sea of 10 December 1982 (IA)*. This Agreement made substantial "modifications" to Part XI of the LOSC, seeking to meet the objections of the industrialized states. According to Article 2 IA, the Implementation Agreement and Part XI of the LOSC are to be interpreted and applied together as "a single instrument". In the event of any inconsistency, the provisions of the Agreement shall prevail. The Agreement allowed, among others, the Federal Republic of Germany on 2 September 1994 to become the 67th party to the LOSC (BGBl. 1994 II, 2538); on 4 October 1994 it also ratified the IA (BGBl. 1994 II, 2565).

f) The United Nations Convention on the Law of the Sea 1982

As provided in its Article 308, the LOSC entered into force on 16 November 1994, twelve months after the date of deposit of the sixtieth instrument of ratification (by Guyana). The LOSC (text: UNTS Vol. 1833, No. 31363, 3), comprising 320 articles, nine extensive annexes and four resolutions (which, without being part of the LOSC, are inextricably linked to it) can, without exaggeration, be called one of the most impressive treaties in the whole history of international law. The IA (text: UNTS Vol. 1836, No. 31364, 41) entered into force on 28 July 1996, it had however been provisionally applied by almost all signatory states since 16 November 1994. At the end of October 2008, the LOSC had 157 states parties and the IA had 135.

As regards states parties, the LOSC prevails over the four Geneva Conventions (Art. 311 (1) LOSC). It creates a comprehensive "legal order for the seas and oceans which will facilitate international communication, and will promote the peaceful uses of the seas and oceans, the equitable and efficient utilization of their resources, the conservation of their living resources, and the study, protection and preservation of the marine environment" (para. 4 of the preamble of the LOSC). However, it does not govern by itself all aspects of the law of the sea, but rather constitutes an "*umbrella convention*" which needs to be implemented and which provides the framework for further development by regional and specific agreements. In its seventeen parts the LOSC covers, *inter alia*, the following matters: territorial sea and contiguous zone, straits used for international navigation, archipelagic states, exclusive economic zone, continental shelf, high seas, regime of islands, enclosed or semi-enclosed seas, right of access of land-locked states to and from the sea and freedom of transit, economic exploitation of the deep seabed ("Area"), protection and preservation of the marine environment, marine scientific research, development and transfer of marine technology, and settlement of disputes.

The LOSC adopts some time-tested rules of the Geneva Conventions and develops them further or makes them more precise. At the same time, it also introduces novel legal concepts and institutions: transit passage through international straits, archipelagic waters, the details of the exclusive economic zone (including the concept of sustainable development of marine resources), the seaward limit of the continental shelf and its exploitation beyond 200 nm, the regime of islands and enclosed or semi-enclosed seas, the right of land-locked states of access to and from the sea and freedom of transit, the protection of the marine environment, the development and transfer of marine technology, marine scientific research, the compulsory dispute settlement mechanism leading to binding decisions, the procedure for the prompt release of vessels and crews, and the protection of the underwater cultural heritage have been codified for the first time on the international plane. The most fundamental innovation, however, is the principle according to which the seabed and ocean floor and subsoil thereof beyond the limits of national jurisdiction constitute the common heritage of mankind, over which no state may claim or exercise sovereignty; in particular, no state may appropriate any part of it or its resources. Apart from these substantive innovations, the LOSC also creates three new international institutions: the *International Seabed Authority*, the *International Tribunal for the Law of the Sea* (→ ITLOS), and the *Commission on the Limits of the Continental Shelf*. In addition, the "Meeting of States Parties" (SPLOS) and the Office of Legal Affairs of the United Nations Division for Ocean Affairs and the Law of the Sea (DOALOS), which serves as the secretariat of the Convention, play an important role within the system of the LOSC.

g) *Recent Developments in the Law of the Sea*

The adoption of the LOSC and the IA did not mark the end of the codification of the law of the sea. The *United Nations Conference on Environment and Development (UNCED)*, which met in Rio de Janeiro from 3 to 14 June 1992

(→ Environmental Protection; → Environmental Law, International; → World Conferences) called in its *Agenda 21* for an intergovernmental conference under United Nations auspices "with a view to promoting the effective implementation of the provisions of the LOSC on straddling fish stocks and highly migratory fish stocks", a call which was endorsed by the General Assembly (A/RES/47/192 of 22 December 1992). Such a conference met six times between April 1993 and August 1995 and on 4 August 1995 adopted the *"Agreement for the Implementation of the Provisions of the United Nations Convention on the Law of the Sea of 10 December 1982 relating to the Conservation and Management of Straddling Fish Stocks and Highly Migratory Fish Stocks"* (text: UNTS Vol. 2167, No. 37924, 3). The *Straddling Stocks Agreement* entered into force on 11 December 2001. At the end of October 2008 it had 71 parties. The United Nations continues to remain concerned with the protection of the marine environment and the conservation and management of fishing resources, in particular with sustainable fisheries, the impact of fishing on vulnerable ecosystems, the large scale pelagic drift net fishing on the high seas, the unauthorized fishing in zones of national jurisdiction, and the fishery by-catch and discards (see the Reports of the Secretary-General: UN Docs. A/63/128, A/61/154 and A/57 459).

On 2 November 2001, the General Conference of the United Nations Educational, Scientific and Cultural Organization (→ UNESCO) adopted the *Convention on the Protection of the Underwater Cultural Heritage* which aims to ensure and strengthen the protection of underwater cultural heritage such as submerged shipwrecks and ruins in accordance with the LOSC (Art. 3). The Convention will enter into force on 2 January 2009.

The high profile sinkings of the oil tankers "Erika" (1999) and "Prestige" (2003) prompted action both at the level of the International Maritime Organization (→ IMO) and at European Union level (ERIKA I, II and III legislative packages), aimed at enhancing maritime safety and the prevention of unintentional oil spills.

The threat of terrorism and the proliferation of weapons of mass destruction at sea led to the adoption by the United States and several other states of the *Interdiction Principles for the Proliferation Security Initiative* (2003) and the conclusion, under the auspices of the IMO, of the *Convention for the Suppression of Unlawful Acts against the Safety of Maritime Navigation* (SUA Convention 2005), which is not yet in force. The upsurge in piracy in the Gulf of Aden triggered several resolutions in which the Security Council, acting under Chapter VII, authorized and called upon states to take action against piracy and armed robbery off the coast of Somalia, including the territorial sea of Somalia (S/RES/1814 (2008), S/RES/1816 (2008) and S/RES/1838 (2008)).

3. The Regimes of Marine Zones under the Convention on the Law of the Sea

The LOSC is characterized by a "zoning of the sea", i.e. the legal position as regards fishing, navigation, overflight, protection of the marine environment, marine scientific research, protection of underwater cultural heritage, and seabed mining is dependent upon the zone of the sea in which one is. In general, it may be said that the further away a zone is situated from the shore, the fewer rights the coastal state possesses or, in other words, the distance of a zone from the coast is inversely proportional to the scope of the coastal state's rights in it. Viewed from the coast, the following zones may be distinguished: internal waters, archipelagic waters, territorial sea, contiguous zone, exclusive economic zone, and the high seas. The seabed and subsoil thereof are divided into the seabed subject to the sovereignty of the coastal state, the continental shelf, and the "Area".

a) The Importance of Baselines for the Delimitation of the Maritime Zones

Starting point for the determination of any maritime zone is the baseline, or – in the case of archipelagic states – the archipelagic baseline. The baseline may also be called the "prime meridian of the law of the sea". The (archipelagic) baseline serves as the line from which the seaward limits of the territorial see and the other maritime zones are measured. The course of these lines determines the breadth of the internal waters (or, in case of archipelagic states, of the archipelagic waters) as well as the seaward extension of the other maritime zones and thus indirectly also affects the extent of the high seas and the "Area". Each seaward shift of baselines automatically reduces the high seas and the "Area" – it is this fact that accounts for their geopolitical significance. Where a coastal state cannot expand its maritime zones at the expense of the high seas or the "Area" because it lies opposite another state, the seaward shifting of baselines will not lead to a quantitative but to a qualitative change of the affected maritime areas. The coastal state may employ various methods for determining baselines to suit the different geographic conditions (Art. 14 LOSC). A distinction must be made between the "normal baseline", i.e. the low-water line along the coast (Art. 5 LOSC) and the "straight baselines" (Art. 7 LOSC). According to the wording of the LOSC, both methods stand in a rule-and-exception relationship, a fact that is deliberately ignored by many states in order to extend their jurisdiction farther seawards ("creeping jurisdiction"). Despite its detailed rules for the determination of (straight) baselines in the case of reefs, islands, deeply indented coastlines, bays, mouths of rivers, ports, and atoll entrances (Art. 6-16 LOSC) and for the drawing of closing lines in the case of archipelagic states (Art. 50 LOSC), the Convention leaves open numerous questions in this regard (*Graf Vitzthum/Talmon* 1998, 77-92).

b) The Maritime Zones

(1) Internal Waters, Archipelagic
Waters and the Territorial Sea

Internal waters, archipelagic waters
and *territorial sea* constitute a state's
maritime territory, the so-called *aquito-*
rium, to which, as a rule, the full sovereignty of the coastal state extends (Art.
2 LOSC). Sovereignty does not only extend to the water column, but also to the
airspace above it. In national (water and
mining) law, internal waters, archipelagic waters (if applicable), and territorial sea are also referred to as coastal or
national waters, their outer limit as the
limit of sovereignty.

Internal waters (Art. 8 LOSC) are
those waters of a state between the end
of the permanently dry land (i.e. for the
North Sea the medium tidal high-water
line and for the Baltic Sea the medium-
water level) and the baseline or, in the
case of archipelagic states, the closing
line, Article 50 LOSC). The fact that
these waters lie on the "internal", i.e. on
the landward side of the baseline or
within the closing line have given them
their name. By drawing straight baselines, states may substantially enlarge
their internal waters. In its internal waters the coastal state has the same complete jurisdiction to prescribe and to enforce as on its land territory. As a rule,
no right of innocent passage exists for
the vessels of other states (cf. Art. 8 (2)
LOSC). In a more recent development,
coastal states have, however, repeatedly
consented to restrictions on their sovereignty over internal waters in the interest of a comprehensive protection of the
marine environment (*Graf Vitzthum/*
Talmon 1998, 128-131).

Archipelagic states (like the Bahamas,
Fiji, Indonesia, or the Philippines) may
draw straight archipelagic baselines up
to a maximum length of 125 nm joining
the outermost points of the outermost
islands or drying reefs of the archipel-
ago provided that within those baselines
are included the main islands and an
area in which the ratio of the area of the
water to the area of the land is between
1 to 1 and 9 to 1 (Art. 47 (1) LOSC).

Waters lying within these baselines are
archipelagic waters, in which (unlike in
internal waters) ships of all states enjoy
the right of innocent passage or – where
appropriate sea lanes and air routes have
been designated – the right of archipelagic sea lanes passage (Art. 52 ff.
LOSC).

The belt of waters adjacent to the internal waters of a state and, in the case
of an archipelagic state, its archipelagic
waters, is described as the *territorial sea*
which, according to Article 3 LOSC,
may not exceed 12 nm (measured from
the baselines). The Federal Republic of
Germany by a proclamation of 19 October 1994 (which entered into force on
1 January 1995) expanded its territorial
sea in the North and Baltic Seas to 12
nm (BGBl. 1994 I, 3428). The coastal
state must respect the right of ships of
all states to innocent passage through its
territorial sea; the same, however, does
not apply to overflight of foreign aircraft. The coastal state's jurisdiction
over ships in innocent passage is limited
(Art. 17-26 LOSC). Where the extension of the territorial sea has the effect
of enclosing straits used for international navigation, ships and aircraft of
all states continue to enjoy the right of
transit passage there (Art. 38 LOSC).

(2) Contiguous Zone

Coastal states may claim a *contiguous*
zone adjacent to the territorial sea which
must not extend beyond 24 nm from the
baselines (Art. 33 LOSC). This zone is
subject neither to the sovereignty nor to
the jurisdiction of the coastal state. The
latter has merely certain powers of enforcement to prevent infringement of its
customs, fiscal, immigration or sanitary
laws within its territory or territorial sea,
but no power to prescribe such laws for
that zone. The contiguous zone may
thus be described as a "zone of functional jurisdiction" in which the coastal
state may (only) exercise certain police
powers. The Federal Republic of Germany so far has seen no need to claim a
contiguous zone.

(3) Exclusive Economic Zone

The *exclusive economic zone* (EEZ) is the area beyond and adjacent to the territorial sea up to a distance of 200 nm seaward of the baselines (Art. 57 LOSC) which must be expressly claimed by states. If the coastal state also claims a contiguous zone the two zones will overlap. On 25 November 1994, the Federal Republic of Germany proclaimed an EEZ in the North Sea and in the Baltic Sea (BGBl. 1994 II, 3769). The EEZ, which does not extend to the airspace above it (but includes the seabed and its subsoil), belongs neither to the coastal state's maritime territory nor is it part of the high seas. In it, the coastal state has the right to *exclusive* economic use (except for navigation, overflight and the laying of submarine cables and pipelines) and jurisdiction with regard to the construction of installations and artificial islands, as well as scientific research and the protection of the marine environment (Arts. 56, 58 LOSC). More than 85 % of fishing takes place within the EEZ and over 90 % of the submarine crude oil deposits are presumed to lie in this zone. The recognition of the concept of an EEZ by the LOSC entailed a substantial reallocation of marine resources in favor of coastal states. Other states have access to the living resources of the EEZ only insofar as the coastal state does not have the capacity to harvest the entire allowable catch. In giving other states access to the surplus of the allowable catch, land-locked and geographically disadvantaged states, and here especially developing countries, enjoy a certain preferential treatment (Art. 69-72 LOSC). The EEZ thus constitutes, above all, a coastal state fishing monopoly zone.

(4) The High Seas

According to the negative definition employed in Article 86 LOSC the *high seas* covers all parts of the sea that are not included in the EEZ, in the territorial sea or in the internal or archipelagic waters of a state. No state may purport to subject any part of the high seas to its sovereignty (Art. 89 LOSC). On the high seas all states enjoy – with due regard for the interests of other states – the freedoms of navigation, overflight, of laying submarine cables and pipelines, fishing, construction of artificial islands and scientific research (Art. 87 LOSC). Ships are, as a rule, subject to the exclusive jurisdiction of the state whose flag they fly (*flag state principle*). The only exception is if there is reasonable ground for suspecting that a merchant ship is engaged in piracy, slave trade, illicit traffic in narcotic drugs or sails under a false flag. Apart from the right of hot pursuit (Art. 111 LOSC) the coastal state has no special rights on the high seas. It may, however, in accordance with Article 218 LOSC, undertake investigations and institute proceedings in respect of any violation of applicable international rules and standards on the high seas (but only if the violating vessel is voluntarily within its ports or at its off-shore terminals).

c) The Zones of the Seabed and its Subsoil

(1) Seabed and Subsoil of a State's Maritime Territory

The seabed and subsoil of the internal waters, the archipelagic waters and the territorial sea are under the full sovereignty of the coastal state (Art. 2 (2) LOSC). The coastal state may thus regulate all questions concerning the exploration, exploitation, conservation and use of the living and non-living natural and other resources (e.g. archaeological and historical objects) of the seabed and its subsoil.

(2) The Continental Shelf

The *continental shelf* which was described by the International Court of Justice (→ ICJ) in the North Sea Continental Shelf Cases as "the natural prolongation or continuation of the land territory or domain" of a state (ICJ Reports 1969, 31), comprises, according to Article 76 (1) LOSC, "the seabed and subsoil of the submarine areas that extend beyond its territorial sea". Depending on the geographical situation, a state's continental shelf may extend beyond 200 nm (and even beyond 350 nm) from the baselines (Art 76 (5) and (6)); if it does, the coastal state shall establish it on the basis of recommendations made by the *Commission on the Limits of the Continental Shelf*. The seabed and subsoil of the EEZ are thus always part of the continental shelf (cf. Art. 56 (3) LOSC). The rights over the continental shelf appertain to the coastal state *ipso jure*, i.e. they do not depend on effective or notional occupation or any express proclamation (Art. 77 (3) LOSC). A continental shelf proclamation of the kind made by the Government of the Federal Republic of Germany on 22 January 1964 (BGBl. 1964, II 104) is thus today no longer required. The coastal state exercises over the continental shelf only limited sovereign rights (not sovereignty) for the purpose of exploring it and exploiting its natural (living and non-living) resources. A difficult problem constitutes the delimitation of the continental shelf between states with opposite or adjacent coasts (Art. 83 LOSC). The demarcation of the German continental shelf in the North Sea is governed by the treaties with Denmark, the Netherlands, and the United Kingdom of 28 January 1971 and 25 November 1971 (BGBl. 1972 II, 881, 889, 897) which were concluded following the decision of the ICJ in the North Sea Continental Shelf Cases (ICJ Reports 1969, 3).

(3) The "Area"

The *"Area"* means "the seabed and ocean floor and subsoil thereof beyond the limits of national jurisdiction" (Art. 1 (1) (1) LOSC), i.e. beyond the continental shelf. According to Article 136 LOSC, "the Area and its resources are the common heritage of mankind" over which "no State shall claim or exercise sovereignty or sovereign rights" and of which no part shall be "appropriated" (Art. 137 (1) LOSC). All rights in the resources of the "Area" are vested in humankind as a whole (paying particular attention to the needs of "developing States") on whose behalf the *International Seabed Authority* in Jamaica acts. The "Area" may thus be described as a "communal zone" under international administration. The administration will, however, not gain any practical significance in the foreseeable future, as deep seabed mining is not a profitable venture at present.

4. Evaluation and Outlook

Present-day international law of the sea is characterized by the *zoning* and ever increasing *territorialization* of the sea: the maritime zones in which coastal states exercise sovereignty, sovereign rights or jurisdiction increase in number, extent and importance – at the expense of the high seas. The *internationalization* of the "Area" and the idea of a *community-oriented use of the sea* by coastal states (of which first traces may be found in the LOSC), on the other hand, can hardly balance this development. In order to meet the monumental challenges ahead (marine environmental protection, the provision of food and energy for future generations), the international law of the sea must develop from a zone-based legal order regulating the exploitation of the resources of the sea to an *order of joint and sustainable management* of those resources. Thus, more importance will have to be attributed to norms regulating the management of the resources of the sea, especially the allocation of, for example, fish stocks and mineral resources between states, regions and generations. This new perspective finds its expression in the legal principle of the common heritage of mankind (which is to be preserved, administered and handed down together). A development from sectoral and zonal to comprehensive and integrated cooperation is needed. *Integrated ocean management* remains the great task for the future international law of the sea.

Stefan Talmon

Lit.: *Brown, E.D.:* The International Law of the Sea, Vol. 1: Introductory Manual, Aldershot 1994; *Churchill, R.R./Lowe, A.V.:* The Law of the Sea, 3rd edn., Manchester 1999;

Dupuy R.-J. (ed.): A Handbook on the New Law of the Sea, 2 vols., Dordrecht 1991; *Freestone, D. et al. (eds.):* The Law of the Sea: Progress and Prospects, Oxford 2006; *Graf Vitzthum, W.:* Die Plünderung der Meere, Frankfurt (Main) 1981; *Graf Vitzthum, W. (ed.):* Handbuch des Seerechts, Munich 2006; *Graf Vitzthum, W./Talmon, S.:* Alles fließt. Kulturgüterschutz und innere Gewässer im Neuen Seerecht, Baden-Baden 1998; *Jaenicke, G.:* Die Dritte Seerechtskonferenz der Vereinten Nationen, in: ZaöRV 38 (1978), 438-511; *Lowe, A.V./Talmon, S. (eds.):* The Legal Order of the Oceans: Basic Documents on the Law of the Sea, Oxford 2009; *Nordquist, M.H. (ed.):* United Nations Convention on the Law of the Sea. A Commentary, 6 vols., Dordrecht 1985-2002; *O'Connell, D.P.:* The International Law of the Sea, 2 vols., Oxford 1982-1984; *Sohn, L.B./Noyes, J.E. (eds.):* Cases and Materials on the Law of the Sea, Ardsley 2004; *Treves, T. (ed.):* The Law of the Sea: The European Union and its Member States, The Hague 1997.

Internet: Recent materials and texts of treaties may also be found on the "Oceans and Law of the Sea Home Page" of the United Nations Division for Ocean Affairs and the Law of the Sea: www.un.org/Depts/los/index.htm.

League of Nations

Already in the time prior to World War I the world had become aware that universal wars among the concert of nations would always entail considerable losses for all those involved; and that all wars or at least some wars might be prevented. However, in the course of the Hague Peace Conferences of 1899 (with 26 mostly European countries participating), and of 1907 (with an almost worldwide circle of participants), apart from the codification of regulations of international law concerning land and maritime warfare, the Hague Regulations on Land Warfare and the Convention for the Adoption to Maritime Warfare of the Principles of the Geneva Convention of 1864, only vague agreements about the jurisdiction of the court of arbitration (the Hague Court of Arbitration), intercession and the commissions of inquiry, were realized.

The dreadful experiences of the First World War had demonstrated the need for a new international order for the future. During the war, peace movements in many states had already spoken for a new approach to international relations. And politicians as well as international lawyers had sketched a kind of future league of nations – especially those in the United States, the United Kingdom, France and in the German Empire.

On 10 January 1920 the League of Nations formally came into existence; it would be dissolved on 19 April 1946 – one year after the founding of the United Nations (→ History of the Foundation of the UN). The Covenant of the League had been already adopted in the first phase of the Paris Peace Conference on 28 April 1919, and was a compromise between the US-American and the British drafts.

Accordingly, the League of Nations was designed to be a voluntary association of the member states, establishing as organs a permanent *Secretariat* with its seat in Geneva, a *League Assembly* of the members and a (smaller) *League Council*, which was composed of permanent representatives of the great powers, and alternating members from among other states.

The League's primary goal was to counter attacks against territorial integrity, and on political independence, by collective means (→ Collective Security). To this end, in addition to arbitration, investigation, and jurisdiction, economic and military sanctions against aggressors might also be imposed.

In fact, the League of Nations could not fulfill these far-reaching claims, first of all because of its lack of → *universality*. Though for US-President Woodrow Wilson the League of Nations formed the core of his peace concept, the United States did not become a member due to the U.S. Senate's refusal to ratify the complete peace settlement of Versailles (Versailles Treaty); and they would not until its final dissolution. The German Empire (among other defeated nations) was initially refused admission. Germany, however, joined, rather late in 1926 and withdrew from the League of Nations under the Hitler regime in October 1933. In the interests of achieving a collective security policy, the Soviet Union was granted admission in 1934. In 1940, however, the USSR was expelled as a consequence of its war of aggression against Finland. Japan left the League in 1933 in the course of its East Asian expansionist policy; Italy gave up its seat in 1937. Initially the League of Nations had counted 45 states among its members, out of which three did not actually accede to it, 21 more were to join in the years to come. However, by 1942 altogether 20 states had left the League of Nations.

It proved to be a disadvantage that the League of Nations originally had emerged from an exclusive agreement of the victorious powers; its Covenant constituted a part of the Paris Peace Treaties, discrediting thus in the eyes of the defeated the claim to universality. Not only was the League of Nations actually dominated by the great powers holding a permanent seat in the Council – but it was dominated by European states in general, especially by France and the United Kingdom. These states like most of the other members were not at all prepared to limit their ability to act as great powers, nor to limit their state sovereignty with respect to an international authority. The Treaties of Locarno (1925), being negotiated outside the League of Nations, turned out to be the most significant example of the weakening of the League by its own protagonists.

In the beginning there were clear initiatives coming from the League of Nations for the → peaceful settlement of disputes between smaller states regarding less significant issues, as well as of the disputes concerning the delineation of borders – in the latter case frequently in connection with committees of victorious powers, such as the Supreme War Council, which was finally relieved of its duties by the Paris Ambassadors Conference.

But when in 1931 on the occasion of the Japanese invasion of China, the League of Nations could only rouse itself to a verbal condemnation despite an on-the-spot investigation, and Japan nevertheless withdrew from the League, the decline finally began. The League of Nations did impose economic sanctions against the Italians for their attack on Abyssinia 1935/1936, but these proved to be ineffective. From this time on the League of Nations virtually eked out a shadowy existence. Confronted with the German policy of expansion during peace time, and then during the war, the League was no longer able to set anything against it.

The issue of disarmament constituted a major center of attention for the League of Nations (→ Disarmament), which had already been declared to be of paramount importance by Article 8 of the Covenant. In 1926 a Preparatory Disarmament Commission was convened, the 1932-1934 follow-up of which – a general Disarmament Conference – failed, however, due not only to Germany's intransigence. None of the great powers – especially France – were ready for a substantial reduction of their own military forces, at least not until "security" had been guaranteed.

The League of Nations did nonetheless gain political influence by establishing a forum for the exchange of views, for informing the official agencies and for maintaining private contacts in Geneva. This was true particularly of the days of Aristide Briand, Austen Chamberlain and Gustav Stresemann (1926-1929), at a time when Geneva was of great political significance for a general and mostly informal exchange on international relations.

In addition to the state policy's focal issues of war and peace, the League of Nations brought forth a number of other initiatives. According to Article 23 of the Covenant, the League was to establish a number of social, cultural and economic institutions that aimed at improving the living conditions in an international context. The problems which were addressed by the League institutions included, *inter alia,* financial and economic issues connected with the founding of new nation states, health and industrial safety regulations, anti-slavery, refugees, minorities, the protection of intellectual work, women's rights, as well as drug traffic. In these fields of activities the League of Nations achieved significant progress through the work in committees, at congresses and in part also through legally binding agreements. On the one hand institutions for multilateral cooperation were established for the first time. On the other hand, the rise in transnational relations since the 19th century found an institutional expression with the emergence of the new organizations within the League framework. As a result also a number of non-governmental international organizations (→ NGOs) established their headquarters in Geneva.

With regard to the administration of territories as consequence of the Paris Peace Treaties, the German city Danzig was put as a "Free City" under the control of a High Commissioner of the League of Nations up to 1939. This was a matter of special concern for the German Empire. The Saarland, too, was until 1935 administered by an international governmental commission, being accountable to the League of Nations. The mandatory system of the League of Nations, as laid down in Article 22 of the Covenant, was intended to prepare for independence the former possessions of the Ottoman Empire, as well the former German colonies. But the influence of the mandatory powers, especially that of the United Kingdom and France, remained, with few exceptions, unchallenged and of determining influence.

In recent years a kind of reassessment of the League of Nations has been underway. Broad studies on international relations have underlined the fact that security and disarmament questions played a dominant role during the 1920s and early 1930s, but were generally unsuccessful.

But the League should not be regarded as a monolithic organization, but as a plurality of different activities which centred around the League itself and its sub-organizations, or were encouraged in transnational organizations by the agenda and aims of the League. The League of Nations Union tried to function as a cooperative system of national organizations, but it was by no means the singular or the most important among such attempts. Seen in the light of later developments of the → UN system, in particular during the last two decades, two levels of the League's activities were especially remarkable: the creation of a new kind of forum for public debate and public diplomacy as well as the emergence of a tendency to look for common, global solutions for common problems of the nations in many fields of life, such as education and school standards or ecological standards ("protection of nature"), which were discussed in Geneva in the framework of the League of Nations.

The League system thus became instrumental in world-wide rationalization and scientific discourse. Humanitarian cooperation played a major role, minority rights, starting with Jewish claims, found a focus of debate and recommendations in the League, and encouraged the citizen movement of a *European Minority Congress* (→ Minorities, Protection of). Attempts to prevent trafficking in women were remarkable (report in 1933 of the Commission of Inquiry into Trafficking in Women and Children), as well as the fight against drug traffic.

The trustee system for former German colonies as well as the International Labor Office (ILO) provided norms for the treatment of indigenous populations in parts of the world that were to become the "Third World" a generation later, thus forming a first step towards → decolonization. The *International Relief Organization (IRO)* tried to establish norms in humanitarian aid and disaster relief. The forerunner of the World Monetary Fund, the *Economic and Financial Organization – EFO*, as well as first steps towards a European economic system centred around the Geneva organization. Of course, all these activities were not full-fledged success stories, but they underline the importance of a growing internationalism in humanitarian, economic and scientific questions in the League of Nations system.

Jost Dülffer

Lit.: *1. General Information: Blessing, R.:* Der mögliche Frieden, Munich 2007; *Fuchs, E./Schulz, M. (eds.):* Globalisierung und transnationale Zivilgesellschaft in der Ära des Völkerbundes, in: Zeitschrift für Geschichtswissenschaft 54 (2006), 837-911; *Gerbet, P./Ghebali, V.-Y./Mouton, M.-R:* Société des Nations et Organisation des Nations Unies, Paris 1973; *Henig, R.B. (ed.):* The League of Nations, Edinburgh 1973; *Northedge, F.S.:* The League of Nations. Its Life and Times 1920-1936, Leicester 1986; *Pfeil, A.:* Der Völkerbund. Literaturbericht und kritische Darstellung seiner Geschichte, Darmstadt 1976; *Steiner, Z.:* The Lights that Failed. European International History 1919-1933, Oxford 2004; *Walters, F.P.:* A History of the League of Nations, 2 Vols., London 1952; The League of Nations in Retrospect. Proceedings of the Symposium Organized by the United Nations Library and the Graduate Institute of International Studies, Geneva, 6 - 9 November 1980, Berlin/New York 1983; *2. Research Reports: Gray, W. G.:* What Did the League do, exactly? In: International History Spotlights 1, 2007, www. h-net.org/~diplo/IHS/PDF/IHS2007-1-Gray. pdf; *3. Specific Topics: Bamberger-Stemmann, S.:* Der Europäische Nationalitätenkongreß 1925 bis 1938. Nationale Minderheiten zwischen Lobbyistentum und Großmachtinteressen, Marburg 2000; *Barros, J.:* Betrayal from within: Joseph Avenol, Secretary-General of the League of Nations 1933-1940, New Haven 1969; *Barros, J.:* Office without Power: Secretary-General Sir Eric Drummond 1919-1933, Oxford 1979; *Birn, D.S.:* The League of Nations Union, 1918-1945, Oxford 1981; *Callahan, M.D.:* A Sacred Trust: The League Of Nations And Africa, 1929-1946 Brighton 2004; *Fink, F.:* Defending the Rights of Others: The Great Powers, the Jews, and International Minority Protection, 1878-1938, Cambridge/New York 2004; *Fuchs, E.:* Die internationale Organisation der edukativen Bewegung. Studien zu Transfer- und Austauschbeziehungen im Aufbruch der Moderne. Stuttgart 2007; *Haas, C.:* Die französische Völkerbundpolitik 1917-1926, Dissertation, Cologne 1994; *Hell, S.:* Diplomatie gegen Opiumhöhlen. Siam und die Bemühungen des Völkerbundes zur internationalen Opiumkontrolle, in: Periplus 10 (2000), 154-175; *Kim-*

mich, C.M.: Germany and the League of Nations, Chicago/London 1976; *Kuss, S.:* Der Völkerbund und China: technische Kooperation und deutsche Berater 1928-34, Münster 2005; *Maul, D.:* Menschenrechte, Sozialpolitik und Dekolonisation. Die Internationale Arbeitsorganisation (IAO) 1940-1970, Essen 2007; *Miller, D.H.:* The Drafting of the Covenant, 2 Vols., New York/London 1928, Reprint New York 1969; *Ostrower, G.B.:* Collective Insecurity. The United States and the League of Nations during the Early Thirties, Lewisburg 1979; *Pauly, L.W.:* The League of Nations and the foreshadowing of the International Monetary Fund, Princeton, NJ 1996; *Plettenberg, I.:* Die Sowjetunion im Völkerbund 1934 bis 1939. Bündnispolitik zwischen Staaten unterschiedlicher Gesellschaftsordnung in der internationalen Organisation für Friedenssicherung. Ziele, Voraussetzungen, Möglichkeiten, Wirkungen, Cologne 1987; *Ramonat, W.:* Der Völkerbund und die Freie Stadt Danzig 1920-1934, Osnabrück 1979; *Scheuermann, M.:* Minderheitenschutz contra Konfliktverhütung? Die Minderheitenpolitik des Völkerbundes in den zwanziger Jahren, Marburg 2000; *Schulz, M.:* Deutschland, der Völkerbund und die Frage der europäischen Wirtschaftsordnung, 1925-1933, *Shara, S.-K.:* Der Völkerbund und die Großmächte. Ein Beitrag zur Geschichte der Völkerbundpolitik Großbritanniens, Frankreichs und Deutschlands 1929-1933, Frankfurt (Main) 1978; *Viefhaus, E.:* Die Minderheitenfrage und die Entstehung der Minderheitenschutzverträge auf der Pariser Friedenskonferenz 1919, (no place of publication indicated) 1960; *Wintzer, J.:* Deutschland und der Völkerbund 1918-1926, Paderborn 2006; *Wöbse, A.K.:* Der Schutz der Natur im Völkerbund – Anfänge einer Weltumweltpolitik, in: Archiv für Sozialgeschichte 43 (2003), 177-190.

Internet: Leage of Nation Treaties (database): http://treaties.un.org/Pages/LON.aspx.

Membership and Representation of States

1. Introduction

High on the list of priorities of every new state is to become a member of the United Nations. Membership is considered to be the most distinct confirmation of statehood and symbolizes the official admission to the international community.

Representation of a member state in the United Nations also often serves governments as proof of their legitimacy; its relevance in the field of domestic politics is sometimes even greater than its importance on the international plane.

While the question of representation may always arise if there are two or more groups claiming to be the government of a member state (e.g. Cambodia, 1979-1991), the question of membership usually comes up nowadays – after → decolonization has largely come to an end – only in the context of the disintegration or dismemberment of existing states (Soviet Union, 1991; Yugoslavia, 1991/92) or in cases of secession (Eritrea, 1993; Montenegro, 2006; Kosovo, 2008). With 192 members, the United Nations has almost achieved → universality. After the admission of the pacific "micro-states" (Kiribati, Nauru, Tonga, and Tuvalu) in 1999 and 2000, of Switzerlandand Timor-Leste in 2002 and of Montenegro in 2006, only the Vatican City as well as the special cases of Palestine, Kosovo, and Taiwan remain outside the United Nations. Taiwan's bid to join the UN as a member is incompatible with the "One China Policy" which has been followed by United Nations since 1971. In 2007, the → General Assembly for the 15th consecutive year rejected the inclusion in its agenda of an item entitled the "question of the representation of Taiwan in the UN" and, in 2008, a more moderate request by 16 of Taiwan's allies to consider how it could "participate meaningfully in the activities of the United Nations specialized agencies" met a similar fate. For Palestine and the Vatican City, → observer status provides a way of participating informally in the work of the Organization.

Non-membership in the United Nations does not exclude membership in its special organs and → specialized agencies. Thus, Niue and the Cook Islands are members of the World Health Organization (→ WHO). Membership of the United Nations, however, facilitates the admission to other international organizations and sometimes even gives a legal entitlement thereto.

The basic rules governing membership and representation in the United Nations are laid down in Article 3-6 of the → Charter of the UN, as well as in the → (Provisional) Rules of Procedure of the General Assembly (rules 27-29, 134-138) and the → Security Council (rules 13-17, 58-60) (→ Rules of Procedure).

2. Acquisition of Membership

The Charter distinguishes between the fifty-one original members (Arts. 3 and 110 (4)) and members subsequently admitted. Membership is open to all peace-loving states which (formally) accept the obligations contained in the Charter and, in the judgment of the Organization, are able and willing to carry out these obligations (Art. 4). According to the advisory opinion of the International Court of Justice (→ ICJ), delivered on 28 May 1948 (ICJ Reports 1948, 57ff.), admission must not be made dependent on conditions other than those expressly provided for in Article 4 UN Charter, such as the simultaneous admission of other states in a so-called "package deal". However, the imprecise wording of these conditions leaves the Organization, respectively its member states, with vast discretion which, in practice, has often led to political considerations playing an important role in admission decisions. Thus, as a consequence of the dispute with Greece over the name of Macedonia, the Republic of Macedonia was admitted only under the name of "Former Yugoslav Republic of Macedonia" ("FYROM"). The admission of a new member is effected by a decision of the General Assembly, requiring a two-thirds majority (Art. 18 (2)), upon the recommendation of the Security Council (Art. 4 (2)). The latter, according to Article 27 (3), requires an affirmative vote of nine members including the concurring votes of all permanent members (→ Veto, Right of Veto). The General Assembly is not com-

481

petent to effect the admission of a new member on its own, even if a recommendation of the Security Council is frustrated by a permanent member abusing its veto power, as the ICJ held in its advisory opinion of 3 March 1950 (ICJ Reports 1950, 4ff.). As long as the Russian Federation opposes Kosovo's unilateral declaration of independence there is thus little prospect of Kosovo becoming a member of the UN.

Acquisition of membership by way of succession is not provided for in the Charter. If a member state disintegrates or is dismembered, the successor states do not automatically acquire its membership rights, rather they have to undergo the formal admission procedure (Czech Republic and Slovakia, 1993). If, on the other hand, one or more parts of a member state break away, only the new state (or states) must formally apply for admission, whereas the original state continues its membership (secession of Montenegro from the Union of Serbia and Montenegro, 2006; and of Eritrea from Ethiopia, 1993). In certain cases it may be controversial whether a dismemberment or a secession has occurred. The decision of this question will often be influenced by political rather than legal considerations. Thus, when the President of the Russian Federation Boris Yeltsin informed the UN Secretary-General in a letter dated 24 December 1991 that the membership of the Union of Soviet Socialist Republics in the UN, including the Security Council and all other organs and organizations of the UN system, was being continued by the Russian Federation with the support of the countries of the Commonwealth of Independent States, the position of the Russian Federation was not challenged and it was allowed to carry on the membership of the former Soviet Union including its permanent seat on the Security Council (cf. UN Doc. A/47/2, 277; see also: Repertoire of the Practice of the Security Council, Supplement 1989-1992, UN Doc. ST/PSCA/1/Add.11, 228). In contrast, the while the Federal Republic of Yugoslavia (Serbia and Montenegro) –

FRY – was not allowed to continue automatically the membership of the former Socialist Federal Republic of Yugoslavia (SFRY) on the ground that that state had ceased to exist (UN Doc. S/RES/777 (1992)). Lack of UN membership from 1992 to 2000 prevented the FRY from participating in the work of the General Assembly, its subsidiary organs, and the conferences and meetings convened by it (UN Doc. A/RES/47/1, 22 September 1992; UN Doc. A/47/485, 30 September 1992). It also meant that the FRY was not *ipso facto* a party to the Statute of the ICJ (Art. 93 (1) UN Charter) and that the Court thus was not open to it under Article 35 (1) of its Statute (ICJ Reports 2004, 1307). However, as the membership of the SFRY was never formally terminated or suspended, the Yugoslav missions at the UN Headquarters and offices (staffed by diplomatic personnel from the FRY) continued to function and received and circulated documents. The → Secretariat continued to fly the old flag of the SFRY at UN Headquarters and Yugoslav delegates participated in the work of organs other than Assembly bodies. This amorphous state of affairs may be described as a kind of *de facto* succession into at least some existing membership rights until either the old member state is formally excluded or the new state is formally (re-)admitted. For the FRY the second course was followed: she was admitted as a new member on 1 November 2000 (UN Doc. A/RES/55/12, 1 November 2000). Such admission does not have the effect of dating back to the time when the old state broke up and disappeared (ICJ Reports 2004, 1307).

The Charter also does not provide for informal re-admission after the (temporary) termination of membership. In practice, however, both Indonesia, which withdrew from the United Nations in 1965, and Syria, which in 1958 had joined Egypt to form the United Arab Republic, were allowed to resume their old membership without undergoing the formal procedure of admission. In both cases, membership was considered *ex post* not terminated but only "suspended".

3. Development of Membership

In consequence of the beginning Cold War, during the period from 1945 to 1954 only nine new states could be admitted to membership: many applications were thwarted by majority decisions in the Security Council or a permanent member exercising its veto power, because the applicants were counted among the respective other bloc whose voting power was not to be increased. Members of the Security Council either disputed the statehood or questioned the "peace-loving" character of undesirable candidates. In 1947, there was a "waiting list" of some twenty states desiring to be admitted. Eventually, as a result of growing pressure exercised by the other states (especially in the General Assembly) and a global climate gradually easing off, the admission policy began to change. In 1955, sixteen new members were admitted at one blow. The following procedure was adopted in order to ensure that the applicant states belonging to the Eastern bloc obtained the required two-thirds majority in the Assembly: after an individual assessment and approval of each application in the Security Council where the USSR refrained from exercising its veto power with regard to Western states the individual recommendations of the Council were combined in one resolution which the Assembly could only take or leave, without the possibility of making any changes or amendments (cf. *UNYB* 1955, 22-30).

This collective admission initiated a development which radically changed the face of the Organization. The states admitted during the following years were mainly former African colonies of Great Britain, France, and Spain which had only recently obtained their independence. Already in 1960 the number of members had nearly doubled, amounting to ninety-nine states. As a result of the admission of numerous developing countries the issues of de-colonization and the new international economic order gained prominence especially in the General Assembly (→ International Economic Relations and New International Economic Order (NIEO); → North-South Relations and the UN). Since 1961 the admission policy has normalized and the refusal of an application is nowadays an exception, as in the case of Kuwait which gained its independence in 1961; the USSR vetoed in the Security Council Kuwait's first application for UN membership in November 1961, in May 1963 Kuwait's renewed application for membership was approved by the Security Council and Kuwait became member of the UN by General Assembly resolution A/RES/1872 (S-IV). The Federal Republic of Germany (→ UN Policy, Germany) which had been a member of all specialized agencies and some special organs since the mid-1950s and had maintained a permanent observer mission at the United Nations in New York since 1952 became a member of the Organization only on 18 September 1973 with UN Doc. A/RES/3050 (XXVIII) – at the same time as the German Democratic Republic (→ UN Policy, German Democratic Republic) – after the conclusion in December 1972 of a Basic Relations Treaty between the two German states. In a similar "package deal" the two Koreas (DPRK and ROK) were admitted to membership in 1991 (UN Doc. A/RES/46/1, 17 September 1991). By September 1980 the number of members, now amounting to 154, had more than tripled. As the process of de-colonization has almost been completed, the latest major increase of the membership resulted from the break-up of the (former) USSR, Yugoslavia and Czechoslovakia in the early 1990s. The last state to be admitted to membership was the Republic of Montenegro on 28 June 2006.

Overview of the development of UN membership, 1945-2008:

1945: 51 original member states

admission of new member states:
1946 - 1954:	9 states
1955 - 1964:	55 states
1965 - 1974:	23 states
1975 - 1984:	21 states
1985 - 1994:	29 states
1995 - 2004:	7 states
2005 - 2008:	1 state

4. Termination of Membership and Suspension of Membership Rights

Although the withdrawal from the United Nations is not expressly mentioned in the Charter, it was not generally to be excluded, as is shown by the negotiations during the San Francisco Conference (→ History of the Foundation of the UN). Thus, Indonesia withdrew from the United Nations in 1965 (only to rejoin in 1966), so far being the only state ever to have done so. A Member which has persistently violated the Principles of the Charter may be expelled by the General Assembly upon the recommendation of the Security Council (Art. 6 UN Charter). So far, no state has ever been expelled, although the expulsion of South Africa (because of its apartheid policy) and of Israel were repeatedly demanded. In practice, membership often terminates as the result of the peaceful dissolution of a member state (Czechoslovakia, 1993), its disintegration (Socialist Federal Republic of Yugoslavia, 1992) or the unification of two members (GDR, 1990).

Besides the expulsion of a member state, the Charter provides – as a further sanction – for the suspension of membership rights. In this context a distinction must be made between the temporary suspension from the exercise of all rights and privileges of membership by the General Assembly (Art. 5) and the automatic loss of the right of a state to vote in the General Assembly as a consequence of the non-payment of its con-

tributions to the Organization (including its contributions to the regular budget, the peacekeeping budget (→ Budget) and the costs of the UN *ad hoc* tribunals for the former Yugoslavia and Rwanda) equaling or exceeding the amount due for the last two full years (Art. 19 UN Charter). Only the latter has gained any practical significance. In 2000, a record number of 52 member states, most of them in Africa, lost their voting rights after failing to pay their dues in time (seven of which were later allowed to keep their voting rights for another six months because of the extenuating financial situation in these countries) (cf. UN Doc. A/54/730, 31 January 2000; see also: Countries lose vote in General Assembly over UN debt, in: The Independent, 1 February 2000). Facing a permanent member of the Security Council that, like the USA, withholds a great portion of its contributions (→ Financial Crises; → UN Policy, USA) in order to press ahead with reforms which it considers necessary, the *ipso jure* suspension of voting rights in the General Assembly remains the only sanction the Organization has at hand.

The total collapse of state structures in a member state ("failed state") and the absence of a government capable of appointing representatives and issuing credentials may result in a situation best described as "non-participating UN membership". As a consequence of Somalia's continual state of anarchy between 1991 and 1999 no credentials were presented for any Somali representative and the country's chargé d'affaires a.i. did not participate in the work of the Organization.

5. Representation and Credentials

The question of membership must be distinguished from the question of who is entitled to represent a member state in the Organization. In the organs of the United Nations every member is represented by accredited representatives who must present credentials issued by their state's government, i.e. by the head of state or government or by the Minister of Foreign Affairs. The examination of the credentials is, as a rule, a merely formal act. However, it may gain huge political significance if the legitimacy of a *de facto* government is in dispute. Thus, the General Assembly did not recognize the credentials of the South African delegates from 1974 to 1994 on the grounds that the Apartheid Government was not representative of the country's population. In 1997-1998, the General Assembly for the first time refused to recognize the credentials issued by a Cambodian Government having seized power in a coup d'état. The non-recognition of the credentials of its representatives amounts in fact to a suspension of the state's membership rights in the General Assembly, although the preconditions for such a measure set out in Article 5 of the Charter are not fulfilled.

The question of the legitimacy of the government issuing the credentials also arises if several rival groups claim to be the government of a member state. The United Nations have not always been led by the principle of effectiveness when deciding about the recognition of the credentials in such cases. Thus, Afghanistan was represented from 1996 to 2001 by the Rabbani Government (and not by the Taliban Government which controlled more than 90 % of Afghan territory), Cambodia was represented from 1979 to 1989 by the Cambodian government in exile, and China was represented by the Chinese nationalist Government on Taiwan from 1945 until 1971 when the General Assembly finally decided to recognize the Government of the People's Republic of China as the sole legitimate representative of China (UN Doc. A/RES/2758 (XXVI), 25 October 1971).

The capacity of a delegate to represent a member state may be in doubt, if the government having issued his or her credentials ceases to exist and the new government has not yet appointed a representative. Neither the Charter nor the (Provisional) Rules of Procedure contain any provisions such a case. In 1994, during the Rwandan civil war, the Security Council made the representative of the non-permanent member Rwanda vacate the country's seat "voluntarily", which led to the Security Council temporarily having only 14 members. Upon learning that Baghdad had fallen to US forces and the Government of Saddam Hussein had collapsed, on 9 April 2003 the Permanent Representative of Iraq to the UN declared that the "game was over" and left the UN Headquarters "of its own accord". Iraq continued to be represented for the time being at chargé d'affaires a.i. level until a new Permanent Representative was appointed by the Iraqi Interim Government in September 2004. A compulsory exclusion would not have been admissible, especially in the light of the imminent danger of abuse.

If the government which issues the credentials is in exile and does not exercise effective control over the member state's territory (because of civil war or foreign military occupation) the question of representation will usually depend on whether the government is recognized by other UN member states (Kuwait 1990; Somalia 2000-2006).

Stefan Talmon

Lit.: *Bailey, S.D./Daws, S.:* The Procedure of the UN Security Council, 2nd edn., Oxford 1998; *Conforti, B.:* The Law and Practice of the United Nations, 3rd edn., Leiden 2005; *Hasani, E.:* The Evolution of the Succession process in the Former Yugoslavia, in: Thomas Jefferson Law Review 29 (2006), 111-150; *Jovanovic, V.:* The Status of the Federal Republic of Yugoslavia in the United Nations, in: Fordham ILJ 21 (1998), 1718-1736; *Lloyd, D.O.:* Succession, Secession, and State Membership in the United Nations, in: NYUJILP 26 (1994), 761-796; *Magliveras, K.D.:* Exclusion from Participation in International Organisations, The Hague 1999; *Reisman, W.M.:* The Case of the Nonpermanent Vacancy, in: AJIL 74 (1980), 907-913; *Simma, B. (ed.):* The Charter of the United Nations. A Commentary, 2nd edn., Oxford 2002; *Scharf, M.P.:* Musical Chairs: The Dissolution of States and Membership in the United Nations, in: Cornell ILJ 28 (1995), 29-69; *Ting-Lun Huang, E.:* Taiwan's Status in a Changing World: United Nations Representation and Membership for Taiwan, Annual Survey of International and Comparative Law 9 (2003), 55-99; *Wood, M.C.*: Participation of Former Yugoslav States in the United Nations and in Multilateral Treaties, in: Max Planck Yearbook of United Nations Law 1 (1997), 231-257.

Internet: List of member states, statistical data about the growth in UN membership 1945-2008, and links to the permanent missions of the UN member states: www.un.org/en/members/index.shtml.

Minorities, Protection of

I. Introduction

In almost every state of the world live people whose ethnic, linguistic, or religious identity is different from the majority population. The formation of states often led to borders arbitrarily separating people, who share a common history, culture, religion or social origin; economic pressure and conflict has caused migration movements that continue to change the demography of states.

Throughout history, differences in the ethnic, racial, religious or national identity of people have been used by governments and other political actors as pretexts for discrimination and violence, including genocide. Since World War II, the vast majority of armed conflicts developed from tension related to minorities and violence against ethnic, racial or linguistic minorities has cost more than 10 million lives. Peaceful relationships between minorities and between the minority and majority populations based on mutual respect make an important contribution to the prevention of conflict and human rights violations, including genocide, which is fundamental to the → Charter of the United Nations. Therefore, the protection of minorities is a central task of the United Nations.

II. Development of the International Protection of Minorities

1. Protection of Minorities prior to the Foundation of the League of Nations

The need for the protection of minorities within the territory of a state derived from the separation of nations and states. At the beginning, the protected groups were identified on the basis of religion. However, the provisions of the bilateral agreements between states concerned, e.g. the peace treaties of Augsburg (1555) or of Münster and Osnabrück (1648), went far beyond the regulation of religious liberties and included property, education, customs and law. After the Congress of Vienna (1805), the agreements identified the protected groups on the basis of nation rather than religion. This tradition of bilateral agreements on the protection of minorities continues until today, e.g. in the treaties on friendly relations concluded between Germany and its Eastern European neighbors in 1991-1992.

2. Protection of Minorities under the League of Nations

The → League of Nations applied a system of protection of minorities in situations, where the principle of "one nation, one state" could or should not apply. The regulations on protection favored certain groups of minorities and were basically contained in provisions of the Paris Peace Treaties and other bilateral treaties between the Allied and Associated Powers and states in Eastern Europe and the Balkans (1919-1920). Furthermore, the adequate protection of minorities was one of the criteria that new member states had to meet to join the organization. In addition to a guarantee of equal treatment, the respective provisions of the treaties contained regulations concerning language, culture, and religion. For their implementation, the League of Nations progressively developed a monitoring mechanism of the League Council and created a petition system.

3. Protection of Minorities under the United Nations

In 1945, the Charter of the United Nations (→ Charter of the UN) declaring the universal realization of the principle of non-discrimination on the basis of protection of individual rights and freedoms one of the aims of the organization, discontinued the system of protection of minorities as a group, as developed by the League of Nations. Not long after the entry into force of the Charter, however, it appeared that additional positive measures would be necessary to protect members of minorities against discrimination and to maintain their identity. To this end, the United Nations progressively developed special rights for minorities and practical measures to complement the principle of non-discrimination.

III. Protection of Minorities within the United Nations

1. Definition of Minority

A generally accepted definition of the term minority and, at the same time, an answer to the question to whom exactly special rights and practical measures should apply, could not be found yet. The situations where certain people could form a minority within a state are too different for a general definition to be applied without the risk of arbitrarily excluding certain individuals. However, the absence of such a generally accepted definition has prevented neither the development of special rights, nor their implementation.

The integration of the criteria of the most frequent situations where people could constitute a minority led to the description of a minority that is considered to be the most widely accepted. Pursuant to this description, a minority is "a group numerically inferior to the rest of the population of a state, in a non-dominant position, whose members – being nationals of the state – possess ethnic, religious, or linguistic characteristics different from those of the rest of the population and show, if only implicitly, a sense of solidarity, directed towards preserving their culture, traditions, religion, or language." (*Capotorti* 1979)

There have been discussions whether indigenous peoples could be considered minorities for the purposes of their special protection. Indigenous people may be defined as "those living descendants of pre-invasion inhabitants of land now dominated by others". (*Anaya* 1992)

Some legal instruments, such as the recently adopted United Nations Declaration on the Rights of Indigenous Peoples (UN Doc. A/RES/61/295, 13 September 2007), the ILO Convention Concerning Indigenous and Tribal Peoples in Independent Countries (ILO Convention No. 169, http://www2.ohchr.org/english/law/indigenous.htm), and the Convention on the Rights of the Child (→ Human Rights Conventions, CRC) consider indigenous peoples to be different from minorities. While many indigenous peoples claim special status under international law, the Human Rights Committee and others consider them minorities (see e.g. *Human Rights Committee*, Communication No. 879/1998, Howard vs. Canada (Views adopted on 26 July 2005, eighty-fourth session), UN Doc. A/60/ 40, Vol. II (2005), Annex V, sect. B, 12-28).

2. Legal Basis for the Protection of Minorities

As mentioned above, the legal provisions regarding the protection of minorities could be divided into the right to non-discrimination and special rights for persons belonging to minorities.

a) The Right to Non-Discrimination

The right to non-discrimination is directed towards the "prevention of any action, which denies to individuals or groups of people equality of treatment, which they may wish". Discrimination is understood to "imply any distinction, exclusion, restriction, or preference, which is based on any ground such as race, colour, ... language, religion, ... national or social origin, ... birth or other status, and which has the purpose or effect of nullifying or impairing the recognition, enjoyment, or exercise by all persons, on an equal footing, of all rights and freedoms". (*Human Rights Committee*, General Comment 18 of 10 November 1989, Non-discrimination, UN Doc. A/45/40, Vol. I, Annex VI, lit B, 173-175).

The prohibition of discrimination is contained in a number of international agreements that cover almost every situation, where members of minorities could be denied equal treatment. In addition, at least severe forms of discrimination, such as offences or threats against the life, physical or mental integrity, severe weakening of the conditions of life and deliberate oppression, are prohibited by a peremptory norm of international law.

Provisions regarding non-discrimination are contained in the Charter of the United Nations (Arts. 1 and 55), the Universal Declaration of Human Rights (Art. 2) (→ Human Rights, Universal Declaration of), the International Covenant on Civil and Political Rights (CCPR) (Arts. 2 and 26), the International Covenant on Economic, Social and Cultural Rights (CESCR) (Art. 2), the Convention on the Rights of the Child (Art. 2), the International Convention on the Elimination of All Forms of Racial Discrimination (CERD) (Art. 2 et seq.) (→ Human Rights Conventions, CCPR and CESCR, CRC, CERD), and the Convention against Discrimination in Education of → UNESCO. Pursuant to these provisions, discrimination on the basis of race, language, religion, national or social origin, and birth is prohibited in the exercise of a number of rights. On the basis of these provisions, individual members of minorities can request equal treatment in law or in fact in any case regulated and protected by public authorities.

b) Special Rights

Special rights have been developed within the United Nations with a view to enable minorities to preserve their identity and traditions. In principle, those rights are not privileges, but granted to members of minorities in different situations to alleviate conditions for them to reach, in the long term, the same factual situation as the majority population (affirmative action).

Special rights for members of national minorities are contained in the International Convention on the Elimination of All Forms of Racial Discrimination (Arts. 2 and 4), the International Covenant on Civil and Political Rights (Art.

27), the International Covenant on Economic, Social and Cultural Rights (Art. 13), and in the Declaration on the Rights of Persons Belonging to National or Ethnic, Religious and Linguistic Minorities (UN Doc. A/RES/47/135, 18 December 1992). Notwithstanding its non-binding legal character, the latter is of particular importance as a means of interpretation of Article 27 CCPR.

Special rights of minorities regulate in particular the use of minority languages, the exercise of their religion and cultural activities, contacts to members of their group residing in other countries, possibilities of self-organization and self-administration, and the participation in the political, economic, and cultural life of the state where the members of the minority reside.

c) Right to Self-Determination

Repeatedly, minorities have demanded independence or political autonomy on the basis of their right to self-determination as nations ("peoples") (→ Self-Determination, Right of).

This right is recognized in the Charter of the United Nations, the International Covenant on Civil and Political Rights and the International Covenant on Economic, Social and Cultural Rights.

The terms of minorities and peoples overlap to a certain extent, and their definitions are, therefore, disputed. The right to self-determination includes the right of peoples to decide on their political status and their social, economic and cultural development without interference, and within the state where the peoples live. However, any attempt to destroy the national unity and territorial integrity of a state partly or as a whole, has been declared incompatible with the principles and aims of the United Nations (Declaration on the Granting of Independence to Colonial Countries and Peoples, UN Doc. A/RES/1514 (XV) of 14 December 1960). Within these limits, the right to self-determination has been recognized as a peremptory norm (*ius cogens*) of international law. At least in democratic states, therefore, the independence or autonomy of peoples does not derive from the right to self-determination (Declaration on Principles of International Law concerning Friendly Relations and Co-operation among States in Accordance with the Charter of the United Nations, UN Doc. A/RES/ 2625 (XXV) of 24 October 1970).

Even after most colonies achieved independence, conflicts related to the right to self-determination continued, e.g. in Kosovo or Chechnya. The General Assembly considers the right to self-determination under a separate item of its agenda – "Rights of peoples to self-determination" – based on annual reports of the Secretary-General (cf. for the 62nd session of the General Assembly: Universal realization of the right of peoples to self-determination. Report of the Secretary-General, UN Doc. A/62/ 184, 2 August 2007). However, discussions moved away from questions related directly to minorities towards the rights of the Palestinian people, threats of foreign and military intervention and occupation, and the use of mercenaries as a means of impeding the exercise of the right to self-determination (cf. the debate in the 62nd session of the General Assembly on the item: UN Doc. A/62/PV.76, 18 December 2007).

3. Mechanisms of Implementation

The implementation of the protection of minorities by the United Nations aims primarily at the development of effective national institutions on the basis of precedent, experience and models.

a) General Measures of Implementation

The implementation of contractual obligations of states regarding non-discrimination and special rights, in particular the adoption of national legislation and legal and administrative practices, is monitored by the treaty bodies, established by the different human rights conventions, within the general procedures for the review of periodic reports and individual communications ($\rightarrow$ Human Rights Conventions and their Measures of Implementation).

The Secretary-General and the High Commissioner for Human Rights submit reports upon request to the General Assembly and the Human Rights Council on measures by member states to implement non-treaty obligations related to the protection of minorities, e.g. the rights of indigenous peoples, elimination of racism and racial discrimination, and the right of peoples to self-determination.

b) Special Measures of Implementation

The General Assembly entrusted the United Nations High Commissioner for Human Rights ($\rightarrow$ Human Rights, United Nations High Commissioner for) *inter alia* with the task of promoting and protecting the rights of people belonging to national minorities (UN Doc. A/RES/48/141 of 20 December 1993). The Office of the High Commissioner for Human Rights (OHCHR) contributes to clarifying human rights obligations related to minorities and supports their implementation through technical cooperation with member states. The Office supports the work of the Special Rapporteur on the rights of indigenous peoples and of the Independent Expert on minority issues.

Furthermore, the $\rightarrow$ General Assembly requested the High Commissioner to promote, through a dialogue with the governments concerned, the principles contained in the Declaration on the Rights of Persons Belonging to National or Ethnic, Religious and Linguistic Minorities (UN Doc A/RES/49/192, 23 December 1994, para. 8).

In Resolution 2005/79 the Commission on Human Rights requested the High Commissioner to appoint an *independent expert on minority issues* with a mandate to complement and enhance the work of other UN bodies and mechanisms that address minority rights and minority issues, including the Working Group on Minorities and the treaty monitoring bodies (UN Doc. E/CN.4/RES/ 2005/79).

On this request, endorsed by the ECOSOC in Decision 2005/25, the UN High Commissioner for Human Rights appointed on 29 July 2005 the first Independent Expert on Minority Issues. Importantly, the Independent Expert could – on the basis of the mandate provided by the Commission on Human Rights in resolution 2005/79 – consult directly with governments regarding minority issues (ibid., para. 6 a), and was also mandated to take into account the views of NGOs (ibid., para. 6 e)., offering a unique opportunity for constructive engagement in country situations. The Commission requested the Independent Expert to submit annual reports to the Commission, "including recommendations for effective strategies for the better implementation of the rights of persons belonging to minorities" (ibid., para. 7).

Following the gathering of heads of state and government in New York in September 2005, the General Assembly established the Human Rights Council (UN Doc. A/RES/61/251, 15 March 2006) recognizing the work undertaken by the Commission on Human Rights and the need to preserve and build on its achievements and to redress its shortcomings. The General Assembly decided that the Council shall assume, review and, where necessary, improve and rationalize all mandates, mechanisms, functions and responsibilities of the Commission on Human Rights.

In 2007, the Human Rights Council decided to replace the *Sub-Commission on the Promotion and Protection of Human Rights* by the *Human Rights Council Advisory Committee* that is mandated to function as a think-tank for the Council and to work at its direction. (UN Doc. A/HRC/RES/5/1, 18 June 2007)

Subsequently, the Council decided to establish a *Forum on Minority Issues* to replace the Working Group on Minorities and "provide a platform for promoting dialogue and cooperation on issues pertaining to persons belonging to national or ethnic, religious and linguistic minorities, which shall provide thematic contributions and expertise to the work of the independent expert on minority issues" (UN Doc. A/HRC/RES/6/15,

28 September 2007, para. 1). The Forum "shall identify and analyze best practices, challenges, opportunities and initiatives for the further implementation of the Declaration on the Rights of Persons Belonging to National or Ethnic, Religious and Linguistic Minorities" (ibid.).

The mandate of the Independent Expert on Minority Issues was extended by the Human Rights Council for three years pursuant to resolution 7/6 of 27 March 2008 (UN Doc. A/HRC/RES/7/6).

c) Early-Warning and Prevention

The 1994 Genocide in Rwanda and its aftermath has indicated yet again the close connection between the protection of minorities, the prevention of genocide and the maintenance of international peace and security. UN bodies, NGOs and academics agree that the application of existing international standards may have protected vulnerable groups and addressed many of the concerns held by both the majority and the minority, in particular with a view to their effective participation in public and economic life. They concluded that an institutional mechanism was required to address the root causes of future violent conflict, i.e. discrimination, policies of exclusion, disregard, humiliation or repression, and bring situations at risk to the attention of the Security Council, before military intervention was the only remaining option. Following discussion of different proposals, in July 2004, the Secretary-General appointed a Special Adviser on the Prevention of Genocide with a view to the lessons learnt from the collective failure of the UN to save the people of Rwanda. (Outline of the mandate: UN Doc. S/2004/567, 13 July 2004, Annex)

With a view to preventing religious or ethnic tensions from escalating into conflicts, the High Commissioner for Human Rights may mediate between parties and governments within the more general competence of "preventing the continuation of human rights violations throughout the world". (UN Doc. A/RES/48/141, 20 December 1993)

The Committee for the Elimination of All Forms of Racial Discrimination (CERD) has developed a mechanism for early warning and urgent action, based on the International Convention on the Elimination of All Forms of Racial Discrimination, to prevent or to react in a timely manner to violations of rights under the Convention. The lack of effective legal mechanisms to prevent racial discrimination, the inadequate implementation of monitoring mechanisms, racial propaganda, or a significant flow of refugees into territory of the respective state party could indicate a need for such measures of early warning. In February 2005, CERD invited states parties, civil society organizations and experts to participate in a thematic discussion on the prevention of genocide from the standpoint of racial discrimination. Following the discussion, CERD developed a special set of indicators and decided to strengthen and refine its early warning, urgent action and follow-up procedures in all situations where these indicators suggest the increase possibility of violent conflict and genocide. (UN Doc. CERD/C/67/1, 14 October 2005)

Within her thematic priorities, Gay McDougall, the Independent Expert on Minority Issues emphasizes in her reports that exclusion, discrimination and racism directed at minority groups may result in social unrest based on inequality (cf. the report of 28 February 2008, UN Doc. A/HRC/7/23, para. 47). There is a need to better understand the causes and prevalence of discrimination against minorities in order to put in place effective policies and practices to address such situations, and avoid them. The Independent Expert pointed out to states the significant benefits of legislative and policy reform which seeks to promote effective strategies of social cohesion, equality and non-discrimination. She also stressed the need for mechanisms, including indicators, which allow deteriorating situations to be identified as early as possible in order to avoid grievances developing into violence, conflict or even genocide.

4. Conclusion

There is growing understanding within the UN of the connection between minority rights, human rights, sustainable development and international peace and security. While standard setting and their implementation by different bodies make an important contribution to the protection of minorities, ultimately, the key to finding durable solutions to the plight of minorities will be found on the country level. Therefore, all parts of the UN system should increase their efforts to include the protection of minorities into their cooperation with member states.

Ekkehard Strauß

Lit.: *1. Documents: Capotorti, F.:* Study on the Rights of Persons Belonging to Ethnic, Religious, and Linguistic Minorities, by Francesco Capotorti, Special Rapporteur of the Subcommission on Prevention and Protection of Minorities, UN Doc. E/CN.4/Sub. 2/384/Rev. 1, United Nations, New York 1979; *United Nations - International Convention on the Elimination of all Forms of Racial Discrimination:* Declaration on the prevention of genocide, UN Doc. CERD/C/66/1 of 17 October 2005; *United Nations - International Convention on the Elimination of all Forms of Racial Discrimination:* Decision on follow-up to the declaration on the prevention of genocide: indicators of patterns of systematic and massive racial discrimination, UN Doc. CERD/C/67/1, 14 October 2005; *2. Secondary Literature: Anaya, S.J.:* Indigenous People and International Law, New York 1996; *Baldwin, C./Chapman, C./Gray, Z.:* Minority Rights: The Key to Conflict Prevention (Minority Rights Group International – Report), London 2007; *Bartsch, S.:* Minderheitenschutz in der internationalen Politik, Opladen 1995; *Capotorti, F.:* Minorities, in: Wolfrum, R. (ed.): United Nations: Law, Policies and Practice, Vol. 2, Munich/Dordrecht 1995, 892-903; *Gurr, T. R.:* Peoples Versus States, Washington D.C. 2000; *Horowitz, D.L.:* Ethnic Groups in Conflict, Berkeley et al. 1985; *Omanga Bokatola, I.:* L'Organisation des Nations Unies et la Protection *des* Minorités; Brussels 1992; *Packer, J./Friberg, E.:* Genocide and Minorities: Preventing the Preventable (Minority Rights Group International – Briefing), London 2004; *Ramcharan B.G.:* People's Rights and Minorities' Rights, in: Nordic JIL 56 (1987), 9-38; *Schabas, W.A.:* Preventing Genocide and Mass Killing: The Challenge for the United Nations (Report – Minority Rights Group International), London 2006, www.minorityrights.org; *Thornberry, P.:* International Law and the Right of Minorities, New York 1992; *Thornberry, P.:* Indigenous Peoples and Human Rights, Huntington 2002; *Tomuschat, C. (ed.):* Modern Law of Self-Determination, Dordrecht et al. 1993; *Volger, H.:* Die Reform des Minderheitenschutzes in den Vereinten Nationen, in: Hüfner, K. (ed.): Die Reform der Vereinten Nationen. Weltorganisation zwischen Krise und Erneuerung, Opladen 1994, 173-204.

Internet: Documents on the Independent Expert on Minority Issues: http://www2. ohchr.org/english/issues/minorities/expert/in dex.htm, including on the current situation of minorities in different countries.

NGOs – Non-Governmental Organizations

I. Introduction

A global organization such as the United Nations will become increasingly important as nation states lose their ability to exert an effective influence on problems of increasingly global dimensions. In this regard, the expectations of the United Nations are relatively high. These expectations might even be realized – at least to some extent – if the basis of the United Nations' work is further expanded and improved.

Although the UN is an organization of states, for states, and will remain so in the future – as former Secretary-General Boutros Boutros-Ghali noted in his "Agenda for Peace" (→ Agenda for Peace) – the UN Charter (→ Charter of the UN) offers a basis for the inclusion of non-state actors.

The preamble of the Charter begins with the words "We the peoples of the United Nations ..." As an integral part of the Charter, the function of the preamble is to outline the reasons for the creation of the organization and its general objectives (→ History of the Foun-

dation of the UN). Therefore, the preamble serves as a guideline for the interpretation of the entire Charter.

Especially in the first years after the foundation of the UN, there were many discussions about the interpretation of these introductory words. These discussions focused on the essential question of *who* is meant by the words of the preamble "We the Peoples": is it "we", the states of this world, or is it "we", the "peoples", i.e. all the people and not only the states and their governments? As UN → Secretary-General Dag Hammarskjöld pointed out, the UN is more than just the sum of the governments of its member states. The now-prevailing understanding of the UN Charter assumes that the beginning of the preamble has to be interpreted as referring to "the populations of the member states". It therefore opens the path towards active participation of citizens, and their associations in the member states, in the work of the United Nations. Non-governmental organizations (NGOs) could establish a broader basis for the work of the United Nations, as well as more understanding and acceptance for it, in their respective member nations. These non-governmental organizations often have gained in decades of work a profound experience in different fields, and thus possess capacity and knowledge which might contribute to finding better solutions for the many problems the UN is dealing with, and might thereby improve the reputation of the UN. Besides technical and political experience, they often enjoy a broader acceptance by the population, as their work is "citizen-oriented" and consistent. NGOs offer a possibility to gain and promote the participation of many citizens, for example in the environmental field, or in development aid, not only within their own country, but also on a global scale.

In addition, NGOs in the so-called "countries in transition" or "Second World" could serve as substitute supporting institutions for missing or incompletely developed political structures. Within their national system they could be initiators of actions in the fields of environment, human rights or development, drawing the attention of the public to the problem not tackled so far by the political actors and motivating the politicians to look for solutions in an answer to the public pressure. Regarding their work in the developing countries, the "Third World", NGOs often enjoy higher acceptance among the population, since they carry out small-scale projects and demonstrate a large social commitment. In comparison to international organizations with large-scale projects, NGOs often have been able to gain broader experience in dealing with the local population.

II. The History of the NGOs

With the increasing democratization and industrialization at the beginning of the 20th century, pressure groups having common interests emerged with the aim of developing or maintaining so-called "rights to prosperity". The internationalization of trade led to the internationalization of all kinds of associations. It is not a matter of pure coincidence that the growth of International Governmental Organizations (IGOs) runs parallel to the growth of NGOs. NGOs generally oriented themselves by the work of IGOs, pushed, supported or criticized them, and NGOs have contributed substantially to the foundation of new IGOs. The activities of the Interparliamentary Union (IPU) contributed to the foundation of the → League of Nations and the Permanent Court of Justice, and the activities of the International Federation of Workers' Unions and the Second Socialist International contributed to the foundation of the International Labour Organization (→ ILO).

Nevertheless, until the foundation of the United Nations, there were no established rules for dealing with NGOs, although many of the international organizations were considerably influenced by the NGOs in their work. In the first proposals for the UN Charter – especially in the ones made at Dumbarton Oaks – there was no reference made to NGOs, but massive lobbying from national and international NGOs finally resulted in the formulation of a compromise, as provided in Article 71 of the Charter (→ History of the Foundation of the UN).

The participation of the NGOs according to the UN Charter remains restricted to the fields of activity of the Economic and Social Council (→ ECOSOC), and special procedures are required for establishing a legal basis for the relationship between NGOs and ECOSOC: "The Economic and Social Council may make suitable arrangements for consultation with non-governmental organizations which are concerned with matters within its competence. Such arrangements may be made with international organizations and, where appropriate, with national organizations after consultation with the Member of the United Nations concerned." (Art. 71 UN Charter).

This Article provides the framework for cooperation between the UN and NGOs. However, this provision merely formalized the practice of the → League of Nations, where NGOs had the right to express their opinions in certain committees, to present reports, to initiate discussions, and to propose resolutions and amendments. Moreover, they could be assigned to certain "subsidiary organs". At the World Conference on Disarmament in 1932, NGOs addressed all participants in the plenary session. Apart from the right to vote, NGOs had the right to participate without restrictions in all activities of the League of Nations.

One could argue that the informal rules at the League of Nations granted NGOs more rights and privileges than they have today apart from some NGOs with special relations to UN → specialized agencies and subsidiary organs (→ Principal Organs, Subsidiary Organs, Treaty Bodies) as well as certain NGOs with a special status, which will be discussed further below.

Summing up, it can be said that NGOs have in the drafting of the Charter achieved recognition and legitimization in a special Article. At the same time, they also had to accept a defeat by seeing their activities being restricted to the social and economic field. In other words, access was denied to UN activities in the fields of international politics and international security. Nevertheless the limits on the activities of the NGOs, their exclusion from political aspects, cannot be defined unambiguously. This is especially true with regard to those fields where NGOs have been extremely successful at the international level, e.g. → human rights and → environmental protection. These fields do not only contain social and economic aspects, but have also political and even security dimensions clearly falling into the competence of the → General Assembly and the → Security Council.

III. On the Significance of NGOs

The participation of NGOs in the work of the United Nations is seen – by critics as well as by supporters of Article 71 – as an important addition to the Charter and to international law. On the other hand, there are still controversial discussions within the UN, and in public opinion in member states, about the actual influence of the NGOs. While some consider the influence of NGOs to be substantial and efficient, others consider it to be of minor importance.

An evaluation of the work of NGOs in the UN in an encyclopedia such as this can only be made in form of some general remarks. The consultative status strongly restricts the rights of NGOs with regard to scope and content, and the time ECOSOC can actually dedicate to NGOs has constantly been diminished due to the increasing number of NGOs (estimates surpass 23,000 registered international NGOs), and the resultant increasing number of NGOs with consultative status in relation to ECOSOC – about 3100 in 2008 (as of 18 September 2008, UN Doc. E/2008/INFF/5). The main part of the work of NGOs, however, is not done at ECOSOC itself, but is achieved on the one hand through informal work (lobbying) and in the specialized subsidiary bodies of ECOSOC, resulting in the fact that NGOs usually focus on the latter.

1. Functions of NGOs

In analyzing the work of NGOs up to now, it becomes evident that NGOs have adopted four essential *roles*:

They act as *representatives* and *advocates* of clearly defined interests of their members in the field of public policy.

They are *advisors* who can provide expertise on the basis of their acknowledged competence in special fields, especially where governments and governmental organizations do not have this competence or where their resources are insufficient.

They form a kind of *executive organs of activities of the United Nations*, particularly of their specialized agencies and subsidiary organs, and have thereby become the second-largest provider of development aid in the world (→ Development Cooperation of the UN System).

They offer support for the → UN system in the field of → *public information*, reaching all levels of society. This is particularly important in cases where the media draw a rather polemical picture of the UN (→ Public Opinion and the UN).

It is undeniable that the intensive work by NGOs in the fields of fact-finding, of lobbying and of active implementation of UN activities, has resulted in a remarkable improvement in early international awareness of global problems.

Other aspects of their work certainly are that today violations of human rights cannot pass unobserved and without comment – on the grounds of facts documented by NGOs the states on whose territory the violations occur will be criticized in the UN human rights organs – and that there is an increased international awareness of ecological problems. Also, numerous activities of UN organizations in the field of development assistance receive decisive support in the form of financial donations from the NGOs, and by their local commitment.

Today's NGOs differ from those of the past not only in the vast range of their activities, but also in the social and professional structure of their membership. NGOs are becoming more and more connected through networking, and they become increasingly complex in their organization structures and more aware of their power.

In addition to their traditional primary fields of work (social welfare, improvement of working and living conditions), old and established NGOs have taken over new functions, such as development aid, protection of the environment, as well as other tasks which have been – until recently – considered as being traditional tasks of governments.

2. Phases of NGO Work

In addition to these developments, there has also been a change in the focus of the work of the NGOs. Since the foundation of the United Nations, when underdevelopment and poverty were at the center of attention, four phases and correspondingly four groups of NGO work can be discerned. Issues of universal human rights and development, as well as the abolition of underdevelopment, were the main foci of the first generation of NGOs after the founding of the United Nations.

The facets of the peace movement which emerged during the Cold War (in the late 1960s, and again in the 80s) formed a second phase in the development of NGOs.

In the 1980s the notion of "peace" came to be defined in a broader sense (→ Peace, Peace Concept, Threat to Peace), and ecological movements became an integral part of the international community of NGOs, thus adding the aspects of sustainable development and human rights in the 1990s to the scope of their work.

The end of the Cold War led to a new quality of the human rights movement. The indivisibility of human rights and the cultural particularities of nations, tightly linked with questions of development and peace, stood at the center of the work of the NGOs.

IV. NGOs in the other parts of the UN System

As far as the specialized agencies are concerned, they generally outline their relationship with NGOs in their respective statutes and rules of procedure. They either follow the three-part system of the ECOSOC, or do not categorize them at all. The general trend is that organizations with a broad field of activities tend to classify NGOs, whereas those with specifically defined tasks do not: → ILO, → UNESCO, → FAO and → UNHCR follow the three-part system, whereas → UNIDO, →IAEA, → WHO, → IMO, → WMO, → ITU, → UPU, → WIPO and → ICAO do not apply any classification. → UNCTAD, → UNEP and → UNDP are considered to be exceptions as they have large fields of activities, but do not classify the NGOs. In his report to the General Assembly in 1998 (UN Doc. A/53/170 of 7 October 1998) the UN Secretary-General has given a detailed and comprehensive survey of the role of NGOs in the UN system.

V. The Struggle for Reform: ECOSOC Resolution 1996/31

1. Definition of NGOs

The term "NGO" is widespread in the international discussion, yet it has not been defined comprehensively up to now, due to the history and the heterogeneity of its applications. In order to proceed with a detailed analysis of NGOs, and to find the right demarcations for their political activities within international organizations, frequent attempts have been made to develop a general definition of NGOs. All those attempts have been more or less successful, ending with the compromise definition of the ECOSOC resolution E/RES/1296 (XLIV) of 1968.

The successes of NGOs in the fields of human rights and environmental protection, and the strong influence NGOs exerted at the UN world conferences at the beginning of the 1990s (→ World Conferences), have intensified the pressure to review the ECOSOC resolution

1296. After three years of intensive work, the ECOSOC amended resolution 1296 by resolution E/RES/1996/31 of 25 July 1996. But despite the expectations of many NGOs, the new resolution kept the old standards and mechanism, due to the resistance of a large number of UN member states. Thus, with respect to the definition of NGOs, the new resolution simply took over the definition standards of resolution 1296 (XLIV).

In this article the term "NGO" is used in accordance with its official usage in the UN: it defines an NGO which is entitled to establish consultative relations with the United Nations in the above-mentioned ECOSOC resolution 1296 (XLIV) as well as in the new ECOSOC resolution E/RES/1996/31 of 25 July 1996 as follows:

"The aims and purposes of the organization shall be in conformity with the spirit, purposes and principles of the Charter of the United Nations..." (E/RES/1996/31, para. 2).

"The organization shall be concerned with matters falling within the competence of the Economic and Social Council and its subsidiary bodies..." (para. 1).

"The organization shall have a representative structure and possess appropriate mechanisms of accountability to its members, who shall exercise effective control over its policies and actions through the exercise of voting rights or other appropriate democratic and transparent decision-making processes..." (para. 12).

In this context "non-governmental organization" means that the organization "is not established by a governmental entity or intergovernmental agreement ..." (para. 12).

Still, even this standard has weak points, as for example the Organization of the International Red Cross, which is a recognized, registered NGO, although it has been established by an intergovernmental agreement.

2. Classification of NGOs according to Resolution 1996/31

In resolution 1996/31 the ECOSOC has determined three different categories of NGOs, each with different privileges concerning their cooperation with the UN. The attributed status is subject to periodical examination by the Committee on Non-Governmental Organizations of ECOSOC, and by the Council itself.

The *general consultative status* (former category I or A) is accorded to those NGOs
- which are concerned with most of the ECOSOC activities and which are capable of making substantive and sustained contributions to the work of the United Nations;
- which are closely involved with the social and economic life of the people of the areas they represent;
- and whose membership is broadly representative of major segments of society in a large number of countries in different regions of the world.

These organizations can actively participate in the debates and sessions of the ECOSOC and of its subcommittees. They can also submit written statements and make proposals for the respective agendas.

The *special consultative status* (former category II or B) is accorded to those NGOs working in selected fields of activity covered by ECOSOC and which are known for making substantial contributions. Very often these are human rights organizations. They have all rights of category I except for the one of making proposals concerning the agenda.

The list, called *Roster* (former category III or C) contains all the other NGOs that do not have general or special consultative status, but that (a) the UN Secretary-General, or (b) ECOSOC consider to be capable of making occasional and useful contributions to the work of the Council or its subsidiary bodies, or other UN bodies within their competence. The list also includes (c) those organizations which are in a consultative status or a similar relationship with a specialized agency or a United Nations body. The fact that an organization is on the Roster is not in itself regarded as a qualification for general or special consultative status.

Those organizations on the Roster do have fewer and more limited rights compared with the former two groups of NGOs: they can only attend those meetings concerned with matters within their field of competence. The attendance arrangements may be supplemented to include other modalities, but are determined on a case-by-case basis. Written statements can only be submitted by organizations in consultative status, limited to 2,000 words for NGOs in general consultative status, and to 500 words for those in special consultative status. If a statement exceeds the prescribed length, summaries will be circulated. NGOs on the Roster can only submit oral or written statements (no longer than 500 words) if they have been invited to do so by the Secretary General, the Committee on NGOs of ECOSOC or the Council itself (para. 30). This provision has been made in order to avoid a waste of material (as there are now 192 UN member states and 54 members of ECOSOC), and in recognizing that the ever increasing amount of information makes it impossible for diplomats to read or even discuss long statements.

The right to attend public meetings (para. 29) and conferences convened by ECOSOC – referring to Article 62 (4) of the UN Charter – seems to be rather arbitrary, as every legal person or entity has the right to attend public meetings in the visitors' gallery. It would therefore be a simple matter to declare a session closed to the public, in order to exclude "unpleasant" participants from discussions.

In general, only organizations in consultative status are entitled to make oral presentations – given the approval of the Committee on NGOs of ECOSOC. Also subject to the Committee's approval is any kind of request for admission to hearings, oral statements, etc. The Committee considers itself as the coordinat-

ing body for NGOs, and can and must thus function in a selective manner.

According to paragraph 57 of the resolution, the consultative status of a NGO can be withdrawn or suspended for up to three years on the recommendation of the Committee on NGOs if,

- an organization clearly abuses its status by acting contrary to the purposes and principles of the UN Charter, including unsubstantiated or politically motivated acts against member states of the United Nations which are considered incompatible with those purposes and principles;
- an organization is involved in internationally recognized criminal activities such as illicit drug trade, money laundering or illegal arms trade;
- within the preceding three years, an organization did not make any positive or effective contribution to the work of the United Nations, in particular, of the Council or its subsidiary organs.

The paragraph referring to secret government funding contained in Resolution 1296 was modified in resolution 1996/31, as the organization now must declare any financial support from a government, and must explain to the satisfaction of the Committee on NGOs the reasons for it, and must be convincing that it nevertheless remains independent. As well, the organization must describe the purposes for which such support is required. (UN Doc. E/RES/1996/31, para. 13).

The exclusion of any politically motivated action against member states (resolution 1996/31 para. 57), which already existed in resolution 1296, is doubtful in the legal, as well as in the political sense, as for many existing NGOs an explicit aim is to oppose those political systems that have proven to be incapable of solving economic, political and/or social problems, or which represent the very reason for those problems. Moreover, NGOs – especially those acting in the field of human rights – also oppose those states that violate or even completely reject existing, yet not universally ratified resolutions and treaties.

497

This provision of the resolution has often been misused by certain states. Referring to the principle of → sovereignty, these states have attempted – and certainly will continue to do so in the future – to restrain actions of human rights groups, and to prevent these organizations from criticizing them within the framework of the United Nations.

3. Critical Assessment of the New ECOSOC Resolution 1996/31

a) No Broader Access to the General Assembly

The NGOs had placed their hopes in the new resolution with regard to a broader access to UN organs and institutions. The NGOs had demanded (limited) access to the General Assembly, but without success: Resolution 1996/31 did not even mention the issue of the access of the NGOs to the General Assembly and the Security Council, although the resolution has the title "Consultative relationship between the United Nations and non-governmental organizations", i.e. the title refers to the United Nations in general with all its principal organs. In resolution 1996/31 ECOSOC could at least have made a recommendation or appeal to the other organs to provide NGOs with some kind of access on a consultative basis.

Yet ECOSOC decided to use a form of political statement with less weight than a resolution; it adopted a decision (UN Doc. E/DEC/1996/297, 25 July 1996) in which it "decided to recommend that the General Assembly examine ... the question of the participation of non-governmental organizations in all areas of the work of the United Nations ...". The General Assembly accepted the call to "examine" the question of NGO participation in subsequent years: at its request (UN Doc. A/DEC/52/453, 19 December 1997) the Secretary-General prepared and submitted in July 1998 a report on the arrangements and practices for the interaction of NGOs in the UN system (UN Doc. A/53/170, 10 July 1998) and again, at the request of the General Assembly (UN Doc. A/DEC/53/452, 17 December 1998), the

Secretary-General asked for the views of the member states, specialized agencies and NGOs on the above-mentioned report and submitted a report with the submissions received in September 1999 (UN Doc. A/54/329, 8 September 1999).

The political message of the member states as summarized in the report was quite clear and outspoken: they did not support any formalized access to other UN principal organs except ECOSOC. This was in fact disappointing for the NGOs, but they continued their fight for better access.

b) Lack of Coordinating Body

The coordinating function of the UN Secretariat was emphasized in resolution 1996/31 (ibid., para. 64), but no mention was made about the organizational form. Thus it is small wonder that in subsequent years there was no reorganization of the Secretariat in favor of the interaction with the NGOs. A central coordinating body – similar to the already existing Committee on NGOs of ECOSOC – would certainly have rendered their work more efficient, and would have taken into account the growing reputation and influence of the NGO community.

c) No Defined Legal Status

Further, no formal statements were made in Resolution 1996/31 as well as in subsequent UN texts with regard to the legal status of representatives of NGOs with official status (concerning transportation arrangements, residence and working permits, access to convertible currencies or fiscal regulations in host countries), although their legal status is quite unclear (cf. *Rebasti/Vierucci* 2005). They do not enjoy up to now any kind of privileges or immunities or any specific legal protection. An advisory opinion of the International Court of Justice (→ ICJ), which General Assembly or Security Council can ask for according to Article 96 (1) UN Charter in order to clarify an issue of international law, could have been very helpful for specifying the legal status of NGOs and their representatives, but such an advisory opinion has not been asked for so far. Currently it is entirely up to each state to decide upon its manner for dealing with NGOs – and at present these decisions are often taken in a very restrictive manner.

Only in cases when NGO representatives take part in UN peacekeeping operations under an agreement with the UN Secretary-General with the respective NGO do they enjoy the legal protection provided by the "Convention of the Safety of United Nations and Associated Personnel", in force since January 1999 (UNTS Vol. 2051, No. 35457).

d) Consultation or Participation

Furthermore, Resolution 1996/31 did not abandon the principle of distinction between, on the one hand *participation without the right to vote* which remains the privilege of governments of states not members of the Council or of specialized agencies, and on the other hand, the *arrangements for consultation for NGOs* (para. 18). Yet, such participation without the right to vote in all ECOSOC activities could have elevated the status of NGOs substantially, as they would have had the right to participate actively in discussions, and to circulate statements.

e) National and Regional NGOs

A new aspect was added by merely writing down what already existed in practice: the international character of an NGO is no longer required as an absolute precondition, so that today national, sub-regional or regional organizations can be admitted as well. Thus not only the top organization, but also its independent branches can gain access to the UN system, as for example the → WFUNA and the American UN Society.

f) Participation in World Conferences

One of the most important innovations contained in the resolution is Part VII, which regulates the participation of NGOs in UN → world conferences. Those NGOs who already have an official status at the United Nations can participate in those conferences without ex-

tra application. All other NGOs are treated according to the normal procedure of admission provided by ECOSOC resolutions 1296 and 1996/31. The secretariat of each conference is responsible for the coordination towards the NGOs.

Year	General	Special	Roster	Total
1948	13	26	1	40
1968	17	78	85	180
1992	18	297	409	724
1993	40	334	410	784
1994	40	334	410	784
1995	65	406	415	886
1996	76	468	497	1041
1997	85	582	517	1184
1998	100	742	663	1505
1999	111	918	909	1938
2000	122	1048	880	2050
2001	124	1132	895	2151
2002	131	1197	906	2234
2003	131	1316	903	2350
2004	134	1474	923	2531
2005	136	1639	944	2719
2006	136	1780	952	2869
2007	136	1956	955	3052
2008	137	2072	976	3187

Table 1: Number of NGOs with consultative status at ECOSOC 1948-2008
Source: Homepage of NGO section/DESA (2008), www.esa.un.org/coordination/ngo

VI. A New Effort: The Report of the Cardoso Panel 2004

During the Millennium Summit of the General Assembly 2000, and the World Summit on Sustainable Development 2002 in Johannesburg the NGOs played an important role, some observers even ascribe them a decisive role in Johannesburg for the fact that in spite of the blockade of the USA and other conference states the conference ended with a partial success.

499

This important function in world conferences as well as their increasing significance in the implementation of → humanitarian assistance and in the formulation and implementation of mandates for UN peacekeeping missions have contributed to the decision of Secretary-General Kofi Annan to undertake a new attempt to broaden the access of the NGOs to the United Nations, to simplify the NGO accreditation and to establish an effective UN Secretariat unit in charge of the contacts with the NGOs.

In order to develop concepts for this endeavor Annan appointed in spring 2003 an expert panel under the chairmanship of the former Brazilian president Cardoso with the mandate to develop proposals for re-structuring relations between the UN and civil society. The panel presented its report in June 2004 under the title "We the peoples: civil society, the United Nations ands global governance" (UN Doc. A/58/817 of 11 June 2004), in short called "Cardoso Report".

In relation to the great expectations of the NGOs the Cardoso Report turned out to be rather disappointing. The report contains some useful proposals on simplifying the accreditation process, suggesting this function be entrusted to a new committee of the General Assembly, on financial support for participation of NGOs from developing countries and on strengthening the informal working relations between NGOs and the Security Council having developed since the mid-1990s. But in one of the central questions, the access to the General Assembly, the report remains vague and hardly moves beyond the status quo of E/RES/1996/31 (cf. *Martens* 2005, 2; *Volger* 2005, 17).

The report does not suggest granting NGOs direct access to the formal meetings of the General Assembly in a way comparable to the NGO access to ECOSOC, since this concept is rejected by a lot of member states, but it suggests "the General Assembly should permit carefully planned participation" of NGOs; in particular "the Assembly

should regularly invite contributions to its committees and special sessions" (Cardoso Report, loc. cit., proposal 6) – a suggestion merely repeating the already used practice.

In reaction to the Cardoso Report, Secretary-General Kofi Annan published a report in September 2004 (UN Doc. A/59/354) in which he made a number of pragmatic suggestions on how to develop UN-NGO relations further, including:

- simplifying the NGO accreditation process by establishing a single accreditation for all NGOs through a committee of the General Assembly (ibid., paras. 26-32);
- holding interactive hearings between member states and NGO representatives prior to major events, as well as prior to the opening of the General Assembly (ibid., paras. 10-11);
- formally granting NGOs access to the General Assembly, starting with a formal accreditation to the GA main committees (ibid., para. 25); and
- formulating a code of conduct for NGOs "as an instrument to ensure that NGOs commit themselves to the aims of the Charter and act in a manner that reflects the intergovernmental character of the Organization." (ibid., para. 34).

Also Annan's report was considered by the NGOs as a rather cautious compromise text, since the only substantial demands were the simplification of the accreditation process and the access to the General Assembly, while the interactive hearings had already been practiced at "major events" such as world conferences and should according to Annan's suggestion just be expanded to the annual opening of the General Assembly. The code of conduct was obviously thought of as compensation towards the reluctant member states for granting access to the General Assembly.

The member states reacted to both reports in a very reserved manner in the General Assembly debate in October 2004: they made clear that they were not ready to grant the NGOs more participation rights within the United Nations.

Thus the President of the General Assembly summarized at the end of the debate the disappointing results laconically, reflecting the lack of support for a reform of the NGO participation: "Regarding relations between the United Nations and civil society contained in the Cardoso report, it was recognized that the contributions of non-governmental organizations (NGOs) are important for the work of the United Nations. However, it is clear from discussions that the modalities for their participation and their contribution to the work of the General Assembly still need to be considered." (UN Doc. A/59/PV.20, 5 October 2004, 17-18).

VII. The UN World Summit 2005

In his reform report of March 2005 (*United Nations* 2005a, UN Doc. A/59/2005 of 21 March 2005) preparing the UN World Summit in September 2005 Kofi Annan tried again to persuade the member states to grant the NGOs more participation rights with the argument that the implementation of UN decisions could only succeed with the help of the NGOs: the General Assembly "should ... engage much more actively with civil society – reflecting the fact that, after a decade of rapidly increasing interaction, civil society is now involved in most United Nations activities. Indeed, the goals of the United Nations can only be achieved if civil society and Governments are fully engaged... The General Assembly should ... establish mechanisms enabling it to engage fully and systematically with civil society." (ibid., para. 162).

The hope that the World Summit would follow Annan's suggestion did not come about: the concluding document of the World Summit, the "2005 World Summit Outcome" (*United Nations* 2005b, UN Doc. A/RES/60/1 of 16 September 2005), contained only a very general and vague formulation, where the positive role of "the private sector and civil society, including non-governmental organizations" was appreciated in the implementation of development and human rights programmes and where the importance of their "continued engagement with governments, the United Nations and other international organizations" in these areas was emphasized (ibid., para. 172).

No mention is made of any expansion of the participation opportunities for NGOs or at least of a request to the Secretary-General to examine this issue further. The document simply confirms the current status of the relations between the UN and the NGOs – in the face of the efforts of the NGOs and of the Secretary-General a severe backlash.

Even the fact that, in the preparatory phase of the World Summit, the General Assembly held a two-day informal interactive hearing with business and NGO representatives (cf. United Nations 2005c) cannot be regarded as proof of the interest of the member states in strengthening the dialogue with the NGOs: The hearings took place relatively late in the preparatory phase of the summit and had no recognizable effect on the summit's outcome document. It seemed to have rather a demonstrative and symbolic effect as if the member states wanted to prove that they were open to listen to the NGOs. A similar symbolic event was the participation of a handful of NGO representatives in the World Summit: they could deliver their speeches not before, but after the adoption of the summit declaration, since the summit agenda was delayed, a highly symbolical expression of the minor role of the NGOs.

All in all, the World Summit constitutes a setback for the participation of the NGOs, since the preceding world conferences in the 1990s as well as the UN world conferences in Johannesburg and Monterrey in 2002 had offered broad participation opportunities for NGOs in the preparation phase and during the conferences proper. In deciding on the format of the UN World Summit 2005 the member states had chosen the form of a "high-level meeting" within the plenary session of the General Assembly and had rejected the format of a UN world conference or of a special session of the Assembly – both offering more participation space through their accreditation rules and rules of procedure. Obviously the majority of UN member states did not value broad participation of NGOs at the World Summit.

VIII. Outlook

Since the World Summit 2005 the relationship between the United Nations and NGOs has not changed substantially. No real progress has been achieved: the only positive signs are the annual informal interactive hearings of the General Assembly with NGOs in the years 2006, 2007 and 2008 and the fact that the Security Council agreed in July 2006 to confirm in writing – in the form of a Presidential Note (UN Doc. S/2006/507, 19 July 2006) – the informal formats for the participation of NGOs in the deliberation process within the Security Council which had gradually developed since the mid-1990s. Apart from this little progress the other problems remain unsolved: a highly complicated accreditation process, a lack of financial resources for NGOs from developing countries and the access to meetings of the General Assembly being restricted to some special sessions or meetings of those main committees granting access to NGOs.

This is rather disappointing and does not serve the best interests of the United Nations. National and international solutions can only be successful in the long run if cooperation with civil society is safeguarded. The states must therefore ensure that this dialogue can take place. They should provide a sufficient legal and financial basis for the work of the NGOs within the UN system, even if the interests of the NGOs are not necessarily in accordance with the perception of the states with regard to their own interests. The effective participation of the NGOs is the only way to make sure that grievances and faulty developments, in particular in the social field, are detected in time and that a common acceptance for the regulating function of the UN system can develop.

NGOs with their structures for articulation offer the citizens the possibility to communicate in the organs of the UN political preferences, which are formed independently from their governments. The NGO can also help in the often difficult implementation process of UN decisions in their home countries. Even though NGOs are not the key to the solution of all global problems, they can help to open some doors that would otherwise perhaps remain closed for governments and governmental organizations. The implementation of programmes originating from NGOs and from governments should not be considered as in mutual opposition, but as complementary strategies in solving the problems.

The governments of the UN member states should – in their best interests – start a substantial dialogue with the NGOs about appropriate and effective ways and means of NGO participation, also in the General Assembly – the example Security Council has proven in recent years that a generous informal participation of NGOs keeps the positional status rights of the organ members intact and increases at the same time transparency and political efficiency of the organ. The General Assembly should learn from this example.

The entry of *Peter M. Schulze* of the first edition was revised by *Helmut Volger*

Lit.: *1. Documents: United Nations - ECOSOC:* Consultative relationship between the United Nations and non-governmental organizations, UN Doc. E/RES/1296 (XLIV) of 23 May 1968; *United Nations - ECOSOC:* Arrangements for consultation with non-governmental organizations, UN Doc. E/RES/1996/31 of 25 June 1996; *United Nations - General Assembly:* Arrangements and practices for the interaction of non-governmental organizations in all activities of the United Nations system. Report of the Secretary-General, 10 July 1998, UN Doc. A/53/170; *United Nations - General Assembly:* Views of Member States, members of specialized agencies, observers, intergovernmental and non-governmental organizations from all regions on the report of the Secretary-General on arrangements and practices for the interaction of non-governmental organizations in all activities of the United Nations system. Report of the Secretary-General, 8 September 1999, UN Doc. A/54/329; *United Nations:* UN System and Civil Society – An Inventory and Analysis of Practices. Background Paper for the Secretary-General's Panel of Eminent Persons on United Nations Relations with Civil Society, May 2003; *United Nations - General Assembly:* We the people: civil society, the United Nations and global governance. Report of the Panel of Eminent Persons on United Nations-Civil Society Relations, UN Doc. A/58/817, 11 June 2004; *United Nations - General Assembly:* Report of the Secretary-General in response to the report of the Panel of Eminent Persons on United Nations-Civil Society Relations, 13 September 2004, UN Doc. A/59/354; *United Nations - General Assembly:* In larger freedom: towards development, security and human rights for all. Report of the Secretary-General, 21 March 2005, UN Doc. A/59/2005 (quoted as: United Nations 2005a); *United Nations - General Assembly:* 2005 World Summit Outcome, 16 September 2005, UN Doc. A/RES/60/1 (quoted as: United Nations 2005b); *United Nations - General Assembly:* Informal interactive hearings of the General Assembly with representatives of non-governmental organizations, civil society organizations and the private sector. Note by the President of the General Assembly, 2 September 2005, UN Doc. A/60/331 (quoted as: United Nations 2005c). *2. Secondary Literature: Alger, C.:* The Emerging Roles of NGOs in the UN System, in: Global Governance 8 (2002), 93-117; *Dupuy, P.M. (ed.):* NGOs in international law: efficiency in flexibility? Cheltenham et al. 2008; *Gordenker, L./Weiss, T.G. (eds.):* NGOs, the UN and Global Governance. A Special Issue of the Third World Quarterly, Vol. 16 (1995), No. 3; *Hüfner, K.:* Non-Governmental Organizations, in: Wolfrum, R. (ed.): United Nations: Law, Policies and Practice, Vol. 2, Munich/Dordrecht 1995, 927-935; *Lindblom, A.-K.:* Non-governmental organisations in international law, Cambridge et al. 2005; *Martens, J.:* The Future of NGO Participation at the United Nations after the 2005 World Summit (Friedrich-Ebert-Stiftung – Dialogue on Globalization Briefing Papers), Berlin 2005; *Pentikäinen, A.:* Creating Global Governance. The Role of Non-Governmental Organizations in the United Nations (ed. by the Finnish UN Association), Helsinki 2000; *Rice, A.E./Ritchie, C.:* Relationships between International and Non-Governmental Organizations and the United Nations, in: Transnational Associations 47 (1995), 254-265; *Rebasti, E./ Vierucci, L.:* A Legal Status for NGOs in Contemporary International Law? Paper for the 2005 Research Forum Geneva of the European Society of International Law, www.esil-sedi.eu; *Volger, H.:* Mehr Partizipation nicht erwünscht. Der Bericht des Cardoso-Panels über die Reform der Beziehungen zwischen den Vereinten Nationen und der Zivilgesellschaft, in: VN 53 (2005), 12-18; *Weiss, T./Gordenker, L. (eds.):* NGOs, the UN, and Global Governance, Bouder/London 1996; *Willetts, P.:* From "Consultative Arrangements" to "Partnership": The Changing Status of NGOs in Diplomacy at the UN, in: Global Governance 6 (2000), 191-212; *Willetts, P.:* The Cardoso Report on the UN and Civil Society: Functionalism, Global Corporatism, or Global Democracy, in: Global Governance 12 (2006), 305-324.

Internet: *1) United Nations: a) Department of Economic and Social Affairs:* www.un.org/en/civilsociety/index.shtml;

b) *NGO-website of the UN Department of Public Information:* http://www.un.org/dpi/ngosection/index.asp;
c) *UN Non-Governmental Liaison Service (NGLS):* www.un-ngls.org/spip.php?page=sommaire;
2) Conference of Non-Governmental Organizations in Consultative Relationship with the United Nations (CONGO): www.ngocongo.org/index.php

Non-Aligned Movement and the UN

I. Goals and Purposes

The Non-Aligned Movement (NAM) represents the interests of states in international relations and in the UN which do not wish to belong to any military alliance and stand for the end of colonialism, the realization of the right of self-determination of peoples (→ Self-Determination, Right of), equal rights of races and peoples, nuclear → disarmament and peaceful international cooperation of all peoples and states.

This Movement plays a central role in focusing the UN more towards development issues and its politicization (→ Development Cooperation of the UN

System). It sees its significance above all in giving important impulses to the Group of 77 (→ Group of 77 and the UN).

Goals and objectives of the Movement are elaborated at Summit Conferences and laid down in conference documents. Summit Conferences are conducted as a rule every third year. Once each year a Coordinating Bureau meets on ministerial level (Ministerial Meeting) or – if required – on the level of the UN Ambassadors of member states in New York (→ Permanent Missions). These conferences are used to preparing Summit Conferences of the Movement as well as to coordinating its foreign policy before the annual sessions of the → General Assembly of the UN.

The Movement has its origin in the Bandung Conference, which took place from 18 to 24 April 1955, and was intended to increase the international political role, as well as to improve the international economic and social situation, of the Third World countries. 1 September 1961 is regarded as the date of foundation of the Movement when the representatives of 25 states met and united in Belgrade. In 2001 the Movement included 114 states, with the membership of Yugoslavia being suspended.

At the Summit Conferences as well as at meetings of the Coordinating Bureau the member states of the Movement discuss initiatives and common positions with regard to basic issues of international policy which are on the agenda of the General Assembly of the UN, of Special Sessions of the General Assembly as well as of meetings of other principal organs of the UN (→ Principal Organs, Subsidiary Organs, Treaty Bodies; → UN-System). With respect to important issues of international relations the members of the Non-Aligned Movement appear within the UN – as a rule – as a group of states (→ Groups and Groupings in the UN) and explain the common initiatives and positions. Usually this is done by the representative of the state which is chairing the

504

Movement at the moment. World economic and especially development issues are introduced in the UN organs and supported by the Movement through the Group of 77.

II. The Role of the Non-Aligned Movement in the UN

Inside and outside the UN, the group of non-aligned states appears to the great powers as a great political challenge. This is as true today as it was during the East-West-Conflict and the Cold War. Especially within the UN the fact alone plays an important role that the group of non-aligned states represents about two thirds of the member states of the Organization, thus it has the possibility to influence essentially the content of resolutions and decisions of the General Assembly (→ Resolution, Declaration, Decision). Non-aligned states were and still are undertaking great efforts to increase their influence and their representation in the various organs and bodies of the UN. In particular they are demanding equal participation of the non-aligned states in the → Security Council, especially concerning the rights and duties of the permanent members of the council. They stand for a reform of the UN-Charter (→ Charter of the UN; → Reform of the UN). They are in favor of strengthening the role and functioning of the General Assembly as the main deliberative and decision-making organ of the UN and call for the restoration of the balance between its role and that of the Security Council.

The collapse of the socialist camp and the USSR had serious repercussions on the NAM as well. One of the most important co-founders of the Movement, Yugoslavia, also disintegrated. After the ending of the confrontation of the two main military blocs some voices within the Movement have been raised expressing doubts about the further relevance of the NAM. In view of the changes in world politics a discussion about determining new main goals and principals on which the NAM should concentrate started at the Summits of the Movement in Belgrade in 1989 and in Jakarta in 1992.

The NAM is of the opinion that the world today is still far from being a peaceful, just and secure place and that the main purposes of the Movement are still relevant. It will focus its activities on the establishment of a new world order based on peace, equality among nations and respect for international law and → human rights, and eliminating the serious inequalities between the poor and the rich. Furthermore it will focus on restructuring the existing international economic order (→ International Economic Relations and New International Economic Order (NIEO)), and on sustainable development, which includes economic growth, social development and protection of the human environment (→ Environmental Protection). The Movement stands for strengthening the UN and its reconstruction and democratization (→ Democratization and the UN).

Assessing the real role of the NAM within the UN, the heterogeneous composition of the Movement has to be considered as well as its small economic and financial potential in comparison to the major actors in today's world economy, such as transnational corporations, the USA, the European Union and Japan. Members of the Movement are large, medium-size and small states. Except for a few rich states, the large majority of members are very poor states, at very different socio-economic stages and having very different political systems. These considerable variations within the Movement, and serious development problems as well as different interests, impede common actions as well as the implementation of the various initiatives and demands made at Summits and Ministerial Meetings of the Movement. This also explains why the positions taken by many NAM states in the UN organs often fall short of the agreed common positions of the Non-Aligned Movement.

Wolfgang Spröte

Lit.: *1. Bibliographies: Fritsche, K.:* Blockfreiheit und Blockfreienbewegung – Eine Bibliographie, Deutsches Übersee-Institut, Hamburg in cooperation with the Dokumentationsstelle Bewegung Blockfreier Staaten e.V., Dortmund/Hamburg 1984; *Tandon, J.C./Batra, S./Muley, R.:* Non-Alignment: A Bibliography, New Delhi 1983;
2. Secondary Literature: Institute of International Politics/Review of International Affairs (eds.): Non-alignment in the Eighties, Belgrade 1982; *Jackson, R.:* The Non-Aligned, the UN and the Superpowers, New York 1983; *Jankowitsch, O./Sauvant, K.P. (eds.):* The Third World Without Superpowers: The Collected Documents of the Non-Aligned Countries, 4 Vols., New York 1978ff.; *Matthies, V.:* Die Blockfreien. Ursprünge, Entwicklung, Konzeptionen, Opladen 1985; *Matthies, V.:* Blockfreienbewegung, in: Woyke, W. (ed.): Handwörterbuch Internationale Politik, 6th edn., Opladen 1995, 46-52; *Morphet, S.:* The Non-Aligned in 'the New World Order': The Jakarta Summit, September 1992, in: International Relations 13 (1993), 359-380; *Sauvant, K.P.:* The Group of 77: Evolution, Structure, Organization, New York 1981; *South Centre (ed.):* Non-Alignment in the 1990s. Contributions to an Economic Agenda, Geneva 1992; *Volger, H.:* Blöcke/Blockbildung/Bewegung der Blockfreien Staaten, in: Albrecht, U./Volger, H. (eds.): Lexikon der Internationalen Politik, Munich/Vienna 1997, 75-79; *Willets, P.:* The Non-Aligned Movement. The Origins of a Third World Alliance, London 1978.

Addendum

As the entry on the non-aligned movement and the UN notes the non-aligned deal with a wide range of international economic and political issues. This often enables them to give advice and ideas to the G77 which concentrates on economic questions. Nearly all the non-aligned which had 118 members in 2007, are members of the 130 strong G77 as are many of the 57 members of the Organization of the Islamic Conference. The most influential of these, however, remains the non-aligned because its members deal with so many global issues besides the UN as well as their own foreign policy interests.

The non-aligned were able to consolidate links with China soon after the end-

505

ing of the Cold War. China made clear in 1991 that it would like to become an Observer within the movement since, in the view of most non-aligned, it is too influential to become a member. But it is able to pursue non-aligned interests as a permanent member of the UN Security Council, as well as to use non-aligned support in the UN. It became an Observer in the movement in 1992 because India, which opposed its application, had lost influence in the non-aligned on account of the break up of the Soviet Union.

The Fourteenth Non-Aligned Summit took place in Havana in September 2006. The documents produced showed that a majority continued to remain part of the moderate mainstream of the movement.

Chapter 1 of the main document, called "Final Document" (see below), dealt with global issues and devoted 26 of 128 paragraphs to UN reform. This should include the strengthening of the General Assembly and ECOSOC as well as reforming the Security Council and other relevant UN bodies while addressing systemic issues at the same time (para. 38ff.). These challenges include bolstering multilateralism and the multilateral decision making process as well as updating the role of the organization. The non-aligned are also asked to promote greater democracy, effectiveness, efficiency, transparency and accountability within the UN System and to mainstream the development dimension within the General Assembly, ECOSOC, and the economic sectors of the UN system. The document included chapters on Regional and Sub-Regional Political Issues and Development, Social and Human Rights Issues: the usual chapter on economic questions was dropped.

The Summit both agreed a declaration on methodology and a Declaration on the Purposes and Principles and Role of the Non-Aligned Movement in the Present International Juncture. The Summit heads of state stated "their firm belief that the absence of two conflicting blocs in no way reduces the need to strengthen NAM as a mechanism for the political coordination of developing countries. Now more than ever it is essential that our nations remain united and steadfast and are increasingly active in order to successfully confront unilateralism and interventionism." (Summit Declaration, see below)

The Group of 77 which only started having Summits every five years in 2000 will need time to make their Summits work as well as those of the non-aligned.

Sally Morphet

Lit.: *Non-Aligned Movement:* Final Document of the 14th Summit Conference of Heads of State or Government of the Non-Aligned Movement, Havana, Cuba 11th to 16th of September 2006, Doc. NAM 2006/Doc.1/Rev.3; *Non-Aligned Movement:* Declaration on the Purposes and Principles and Role of the Non-Aligned Movement in the Present International Situation, 14th Summit Conference of Heads of State or Government of the Non-Aligned Movement, Havana, Cuba 11th to 16th of September 2006, Doc. NAM 2006/Doc.3.

Internet: Websites of the Non-Aligned-Movement: a) http://www.nam.gov.za; b) http://canada.cubanoal.cu/ingles/index.html

North-South Relations and the UN

I. Development Prior to the Onset of the First Oil Crisis

Initially the United Nations played no role at all in the reform of North-South relations. These relations may be defined as a conflict between country groups or blocs (in this case, North and South) over form, structure, content and distribution impact of frameworks for economic, financial and cultural transfers between them.

While the UN involvement in these issues later increased, since the end of the 1970s the UN has again experienced a decreasing influence in this field. The fact that the United Nations did not play a major role shortly after World War II is explained by the small number of independent developing countries at that time, and the preoccupation of de-colonizing states (especially in the late 1950s and early 1960s) with their own political consolidation. The United Nations was relevant for those countries, as for those territories yet dependent, mainly as vehicle for the removal of all remaining residues of colonialism, a task to which the UN contributed remarkably effectively (→ Decolonization). In addition, the newly independent countries did not possess at first an instrument for the expression of their collective interests, which later took shape in the Movement of the Non-Aligned Countries (first summit 1961) and the → Group of 77 within the United Nations Conference on Trade and Development (→ UNCTAD, 1964). The Movement of the Non-Aligned Countries (→ Non-Aligned Movement and the UN) confined itself during its first decade to questions of political, not of economic independence. Moreover the growing "bloc" of developing countries within the UN System lacked the political or economic power to pressure others for assistance in their development. Their demands intended foremost to increase official development assistance (→ Development Cooperation of the UN System) and to reorient the programmes of the → specialized agencies of the UN to the needs of developing countries. They demanded also to give the developing countries a more pronounced influence on established multilateral agencies or – alternatively – to create new institutions, more responsive to their needs and interests and organized in a more democratic way (according to the formula „one country, one vote") than were the World Bank (→ World Bank, World Bank Group), → IMF and GATT (→ WTO/GATT).

Developing countries succeeded in winning quite a few concessions in these early years: The World Bank Group was complemented by a new agency for encouraging private investments (the International Finance Corporation, IFC), and – more important – by a soft loan-window (for loans with very favorable rates and long repayment pe-

riods), the International Development Agency (IDA) and new Regional Development Banks were established and finally, at the request of developing countries, the first United Nations Conference on Trade and Development (→ UNCTAD) was convened in 1964, and → UNIDO was founded in 1966. The main achievement of UNCTAD in the following years was that of gaining acceptance for the idea of trade preferences for developing countries. Developing countries, however, did not succeed in pushing through the desired development fund of the United Nations as an alternative to the World Bank, or to achieve any reform in the organizational structures of the Bretton Woods Institutions or GATT.

II. The Programme of a New International Economic Order

From the early 1970s, the traditional international economic order came under strong and rising attack during several UN conferences. Representatives of developing countries held this order responsible for the increasing economic and social gap between North and South, for declining commodity prices, mounting balance of payments deficits and debt burdens of Third World countries. They portrayed their countries as being manipulated by transnational corporations and international institutions dominated by Western countries. This perception was thought to justify the demand for a complete restructuring of the international economic relations, a demand which gained momentum through the oil crisis and the seemingly increasing commodity power of the South. The programme of the New International Economic Order (NIEO) (→ International Economic Relations and New International Economic Order (NIEO)), as presented in the course of several UN conferences up to the end of the 1970s, included:

- easier access for products and services of developing countries to the markets of the North (by lowering duty rates, expansion of trade preferences, lower-

ing of subsidies for structurally weak industries in the North);
- full sovereignty of developing countries over their natural resources, including the right to form commodity cartels; implementation of an Integrated Programme for Commodities for the financing of buffer stocks and other measures; indexing of commodity prices;
- an increase in official development assistance from industrial countries (to 0.7% of their GNP), debt forgiveness for the poorest developing countries, for the others organization of an international debt conference;
- return to fixed currency parities, allocation of new Special Drawing Rights for the financing of development, liberalization of IMF conditionalities;
- increase of the share of developing countries in worldwide industrial production by successive transfer of labor intensive industrial sectors to the South;
- expansion of the technological infrastructure in developing countries, by *inter alia* better and cheaper access of these countries to modern technologies;
- regulation and surveillance of transnational corporations through a code of conduct, prohibiting restrictive business practices;
- establishment of a New International Information Order (NIIO), meaning a less dominating role of Western media in the global flow of information;
- an increase in voting power of developing countries in international organizations dominated so far by the North, and/or strengthening the influence of organizations sympathetic to the interests of developing countries.

1. Negotiation Results

In the negotiation of this agenda within the UN system, very small achievements came about: Apart from the agreement on an *Integrated Programme for Commodities* (UNCTAD Resolution TD/RES/93 (IV) of 30 May 1976, published in: UN Doc. TD/218(Vol.I), 6-9) – later more or less devoid of real func-

tions –, the establishment of some smaller financing funds, in the management of which developing countries had considerable influence and limited concessions in debt relief agreements of the industrialized countries with the developing countries, nothing else of the catalogue of demands of the NIEO was agreed upon. But the developed countries made, however, some concessions in fora outside the UN system in the strict sense and in other international organizations (new financing facilities of the IMF, Lomé Agreement of the European Union).

The main reasons for the poor outcome of the negotiations for the South were weaknesses of the negotiation system inside the UN, rigid block behavior and block voting of developing countries (made necessary by internal cleavages), but most prominently the diminishing commodity power of developing countries and their increasing debt crisis. The latter forced them to postpone demands for structural reform in favor of short-term crisis assistance. This new situation was exacerbated by the crumbling of the socialist block at the end of the 80s, an occurrence which rendered impractical the former strategy of some countries to profit financially by threatening to change sides. The end of the Cold War also facilitated a kind of "roll-back-strategy", engineered by the United States (to a lesser degree by the United Kingdom and Germany), and aimed at those UN organizations which were most sympathetic to radical demands for a New International Economic Order. The withdrawal of the United States and Great Britain from → UNESCO forced this organization to streamline its programme and gradually to abandon the programme of a New International Information Order. Stagnant or shrinking budgets also forced other specialized agencies of the UN (UNIDO, → FAO, UNCTAD) to dismiss staff and to rationalize programme activities. For UNCTAD and UNIDO, the two central institutions assisting the South in formulating the programme of the New International Economic Order, survival was at stake for quite some time. Even the Commission on Global Governance (→ Independent Commissions, Reports) pleaded for a fusion of these organizations with the Economic and Social Council (→ ECOSOC) of the United Nations, as their functions had become obsolete with the end of the Uruguay round of GATT, or were looked after by World Bank, IMF and WTO. This however did not happen, due to some residual resistance of the Group of 77; but the mandates of UNCTAD and UNIDO were reduced and focused on sectors – such as support for the private sector in developing countries, sustainable development, good governance, special assistance for the poorest countries – which were compatible with the interests of industrialized countries and now reflected a more market-friendly position of these institutions. The mandate of UNCTAD was restricted to the analysis of trade policy only; its secretariat was streamlined after UNCTAD IX (1996).

III. The North-South-Dialogue in the 90s and After

In the 90s, the agenda of North-South negotiations within the → UN system switched even more to universal or Western issues, whereas demands for structural reforms of the world economy receded to the back stage. The prominent issue now was now the promotion of → human rights, dominating the UN Conference on Human Rights in Vienna (1993) and the 4th World Conference on Women in Beijing (1995) (→ World Conferences). Both conferences emphasized the universal character of human rights, against considerable resistance of several delegations from developing countries.

In a more limited sense, this change of perspective applies also to the ecological issue, which was dealt with at the first UN Conference on Environment and Development in 1972 (→ Environmental Protection), and was at that time regarded by representatives of some developing countries almost as a conspiracy of the North to obstruct industrial progress in the South. Twenty years later, at the UN Conference for Environment and Development (UNCED) in Rio de Janeiro in 1992, developing countries did still not accept commitments on their part for safeguarding sustainable development. But the common front of the South did experience, however, some erosion (in the question of joint implementation), and the concerns relating to global warming and the depletion of the ozone layer have become universal today.

Some remnants of the New International Economic Order were however revitalized by The World Summit for Social Development in Copenhagen (1995) which resulted for the first time in a common commitment by developing and industrialized countries for the financing of basic social programmes in the South (the so-called 20:20 initiative). This conference furthered endeavors of aid agencies in OECD to concentrate assistance on a couple of measurable aims (foremost on poverty reduction) within a defined time frame. This initiative was taken up by the Millennium Summit of the United Nations in 2000, where in the "Millennium Declaration" of the General Assembly (UN Doc. A/RES/55/2, 8 September 2000) eight development goals and precise indicators for there measurement were identified to be attained in a common effort of industrialized and developing countries (ibid., para. 19f.) by 2015. Structural reforms of the international financing and trade system were envisaged, as OECD countries promised to scale up development assistance, open their markets for products of developing countries and work for a comprehensive settlement of their official debts. A solution of the debt problem of poorer countries was indeed engineered before and after the summit by G7 with the decision to continue and enlarge the HIPC-initiative, cancelling debt of least developed countries with a track record of sound economic policies (= PRSP-process under the aegis of the IMF and the World Bank).

These issues were later taken up by the International Conference on Financing of Development in 2002 (Monterrey/Mexico), where Northern and Southern countries discussed a wide spectrum of economic issues, not too dissimilar to those of the defunct New International Economic Order, but in a far more cooperative spirit and on a more or less common understanding of a road map for international development (cf. *Hofmann/Drescher* 2002). The conference concluded in its final document, the "Monterrey Consensus" (*United Nations* 2002) with pledges for a substantial increase and quality improvement of official development assistance, which where followed for the first time by sincere implementation efforts. Structural reforms, as the introduction of new financing mechanisms for development (Tobin tax etc.) or encroachments of the United Nations on the mandate of WTO, IMF and the World Bank, were sternly opposed by Western countries (cf. *Martens* 2003).

In the end, efforts to change the international division of labor by conference diplomacy under the umbrella of the United Nations have not born fruit, but – at the danger of total economic exclusion of least developed countries and the total neglect of the ecological and social sustainability of globalization – the change has been prevented.

Joachim Betz

Lit.: *Beigbeder, Y.:* Reforming the Economic and Social Sectors of the United Nations: An Incomplete Process, in: Hüfner, K. (ed.): Agenda for Change. New Tasks for the United Nations, Opladen 1995, 239-256; *Betz, J.:* International Relations, North--South, in: Wolfrum, R. (ed.): United Nations: Law, Policies and Practice, Vol. 2, Munich/Dordrecht 1995, 778-788; *Brock, L.:* Nord-Süd-Beziehungen, in: Nohlen, D. (ed.): Lexikon der Politik, Vol. 6, Munich 1994, 330-341; *Dadzie, K.:* The UN and the Problem of Economic Development, in: Roberts, A./Kingsbury, B. (eds.): United Nations, Divided World. The UN's Roles in International Relations, 2nd rev. and expanded edn., Oxford et al. 1993, 297-326; *Diehl P.F. (ed.):* The Politics of Global Governance: International Organizations in an Interdependent World, 2nd edn., Boulder 2001; *van Dijk, P.:* Developing countries and the Doha development agenda of the WTO, London 2006; *Drescher, R.:* In the shadow of the WTO: UNCTAD XI, in: Development and Cooperation 31 (2004), 334-335; *Fues, T./Hamm, B.I. (eds.):* Die Weltkonferenzen der 90er Jahre: Baustellen für Global Governance, Bonn 2001; *Hofmann, M./Drescher, R.:* The Monterrey Consensus. A New Development Partnership, in: Development and Cooperation 29 (2002), 4-5 and 28; *Kaul, I. et al. (eds.):* Global Public Goods. International Cooperation in the 21st Century, New York/Oxford 1999; *Martens, J.:* The future of multilateralism after Monterrey and Johannesburg (Dialogue on Globalization, 10), Bonn 2003; *Sauvant, K.P. (ed.):* Changing Priorities on the International Agenda. The New International Economic Order, Oxford 1982; *Rittberger, V. et al.:* Vereinte Nationen und Weltordnung. Zivilisierung der Internationalen Politik? Opladen 1997; *South Centre (ed.):* What UN for the 21st century. A new North-South divide. Issued by the South Centre on the occasion of the Second South Summit, Doha 2005; *Strotmann, F.N.:* Third World Group Formation in the United Nations, Amsterdam 1977; *Taylor, I./Smith, K.:* United Nations Conference on Trade and Development (UNCTAD), London 2007; *United Nations:* Report of the International Conference on Financing for Development, Monterrey, Mexico, 18-22 March 2002, UN Doc. A/CONF. 198/11, Annex: Monterrey Consensus of the International Conference on Financing for Development (quoted as: United Nations 2002); *Volger, H.:* Die Vereinten Nationen, Munich/Vienna 1994; *Williams, M.:* Third World Cooperation. The Group of 77 in UNCTAD, London/New York 1991.

Internet: a) Homepage of the Group of 77: www.g77.org; Homepages of the Non-Aligned-Movement: www.nam.gov.za and www.cuba noal.cu/; Homepage of UNCTAD: www.unc tad.org.

Observers

When speaking of "blue helmets" one usually thinks of the UN → peacekeeping forces. However, UN observers are also an important element of → peacekeeping operations (→ Peacekeeping). There are three types of observers which can be deployed together or separately:
- UN military observers (UNMOs),

- police observers or monitors, and
- civilian and political observers.

Military observers are usually officers between the ranks of captain and lieutenant-colonel. The first UN military observers were deployed in 1948 in Greece, Indonesia, Palestine, and Kashmir. In September 2008, there were 2,569 military observers deployed worldwide: 751 in the two missions in Sudan, 670 in the Democratic Republic of the Congo, about 200 each in Liberia, Côte d'Ivoire and in Western Sahara, 152 in the Middle East, 126 in Georgia, 44 in Kashmir, 40 in Chad and in the Central African Republic, and 33 in Timor Leste. Additional military, police and civilian observers are deployed by organizations such as the OSCE. Their tasks include supervising armistice and similar agreements, keeping constant liaison with the parties to the conflict, especially with military forces and armed groups. Observers normally operate in teams consisting of two to four officers of different nationality, and report observations (such as troop strengths, changes in positions or armaments along cease-fire lines, etc.). However, their main function lies in their presence: as international observers, they represent an element of outside presence, which ensures objective control, thus contributing – ideally – to the establishment of confidence between the parties to the conflict. Military observers normally wear the uniforms of their home country, with UN badges and the characteristic blue caps or berets. They are normally unarmed.

Police observers usually observe and assist local police forces in (or after) internal conflicts (→ UNCIVPOL).

In addition to the military and police observers, civilian observers and experts are increasingly deployed, to assist peace-building and confidence-restoration missions, or to prepare and supervise elections. Apart from the UN, organizations like the OSCE, EU, OAU/ AU, Commonwealth, OAS, etc. are active in these missions. An example of a purely civilian mission was the UN Observer Mission in South Africa

(UNOMSA, 1991-94) which supported the peace process in that country and during the April 1994 elections numbered 2,120 men and women.

By August 2008, there were 12 political and peace-building missions (six in Africa, and six in Asia), of which three (in Afghanistan, Burundi and Sierra Leone) were directed by the Department of Peacekeeping Operations, and nine by the Department of Political Affairs (DPA).

The DPA is also responsible for → electoral assistance, which evolved over time. Between 1989 and 2005, electoral assistance (including organizational and technical support as well as election observers) was provided to 96 countries.

Like the military observers, civilian observers write reports, but their main function lies in their – often long-term – presence on the spot, thus assisting the parties to the conflict and the local population to gain trust and confidence. The percentage of women in these missions is higher than with the military or police elements, and is actually very beneficial, as women and women's organizations often play vital roles in civil society, including churches and social organizations.

Erwin A. Schmidl

Observer Status

The *observer status* grants to states and entities of international law which are not regular members of the United Nations the right to participate in the meetings of the → General Assembly and other bodies of the UN (→ UN System; → Principal Organs, Subsidiary Organs, Treaty Bodies), as participants without the right to vote (→ Voting Right and Decision-Making Procedures). In the UN Charter (→ Charter of the UN) the matter is not laid down explicitly, however, as the application of observer status is anchored in international customary law. Article 2 (6) of the UN Charter provides that the organization is to ensure that even non-member states act in accordance with the principles of the Charter, insofar as far as this may be necessary to maintain international peace and international security. To do justice to this claim to → universality, the UN integrates regional organizations, non-member states and national liberation organizations as *observers* in the work of the organization.

The legal status of observers in their relation with international organizations is regulated in the *Vienna Convention on the Representation of States in their Relations with International Organizations of a Universal Character* (UN Doc. A/CONF.67/16, 14 March 1975). This Convention has however not yet entered into force, and therefore does not at present provide a general basis for the observer status in international law (→ Treaties, Law of).

Article 7 of the Vienna Convention grants observers the following rights:
- to represent and protect the interests of the sending state in relation to the organization, and to maintain a permanent liaison with it;
- to observe the activities of the organization and to report thereon to the sending state;
- to promote cooperation with the organization, and to negotiate with it.

As the Vienna Convention has not yet entered into force, there remains considerable space in customary international law for the specific delineation of the observer status in the different UN bodies.

In practice, the rights of participation are regulated in the → rules of procedure of the bodies. According to Article 11(2), in conjunction with Article 35(2) of the UN Charter, non-member states have the right to draw the attention of the → Security Council or the → General Assembly to matters relating to international peace and security.

How passive or active the observer status in the respective UN bodies may be, can be deduced from the extent of the rights given to an observer: does (s)he have authorized admission to the respective forum, is (s)he authorized to submit motions concerning the agenda and the voting on decisions or draft texts, respectively, is (s)he authorized to distribute and receive documents via the committee, and does (s)he even have the right to reply?

In this connection the permanent observers who have the right to participate in all sessions, must be distinguished from observers who are only allowed to take part in a single meeting, or in meetings dealing with a certain topic.

It can be the case that the observer in a UN organ is representing a country, which is a member of the UN, but not of the respective body, for example the Security Council. Moreover, → specialized agencies send observers to the UN organs. The role of the observers has changed since the foundation of the UN from a passive to an active one, from a simple "being present" to an active "participation" (*Bartram/López* 1995, 941).

In the history of the UN the observer status was for many states one step on the way to become a full member of the organization (→ Membership and Representation of States). Today there is only one non-member state among the observers: the Holy See. For a long time – from 1946 till 2002 – Switzerland also had remained observer at the UN, as its foreign policy and, in particular its concept of neutrality, had prevented it from applying for full membership (cf. *Bartram/López* 1995, 938). But a change in the attitude of the Swiss population in the late nineties and a referendum held on 3 March 2002 altered the situation completely: a majority of the Swiss population (54.6%) as well as a majority of the Swiss cantons accepted a popular initiative on Swiss membership of the UN. In September 2002 Switzerland became a full member of the United Nations. Observer status has been granted by the General Assembly – according to the interpretation of the UN Charter – as a rule to entities with a sufficient degree of sovereignty, states, enjoying full sovereignty, supra-national organizations which have been entrusted by treaty with a certain amount of sovereignty towards third states (for example the European Union, and the African

Union), and other intergovernmental organizations (e.g. the International Organization for Migration) which have been given measured decision-making powers and which therefore represent, to a certain extent and in certain matters, the common interests of their member states (cf. *Sybesma-Knol* 1998, 373). With the development of liberation movements in the phase of → decolonization the General Assembly granted a number of them observer status, for instance the PLO (Palestine Liberation Movement) in November 1974.

Only hesitatingly and as an explicit exception to the rule the General Assembly granted observer status to the non-governmental organization the International Committee of the Red Cross in 1990 (A/RES/45/6, 16 October 1990). In the debate before the adoption of the resolution, the representatives of the UN member states emphasized that this granting of the observer status was only due to the great merits of the ICRC for the international community and should not constitute a precedent allowing other NGOs to apply for this status (cf. UN Doc. A/45/PV.31, 73ff.).

The majority of non-governmental organizations (→ NGOs) has been so far only granted a minor kind of observer status within the UN with less status and fewer rights than the state and non-state participants with observer status. Their status is called "consultative" status and is granted after being approved on application by the Economic and Social Council (→ ECOSOC). There are three different categories of the NGO-observer status. These differences reflect their respective rights to participation, and are granted to the respective NGOs according to their relevance for the work of the UN, their competence and their supra-regional importance (UN Doc. E/RES/288 (X) of 27 February 1950, E/RES/1296 (XLIV) of 23 May 1968, and E/RES/1996/31 of 25 July 1996). Their participation as observers in the work of the UN is of very high importance for the protection of → human rights (→ Human Rights, Protection of) and the preparation of UN world con-

ferences for the solution of global problems (→ World Conferences), because of the information they gather in the member states and of their high level of expertise.

The hope of many NGOs that the increasing relevance of the NGOs at the UN world conferences in the early 90s (Rio de Janeiro 1992, Vienna 1993, etc.) would result in a greater readiness of the member status to grant them observer status, was not fulfilled. In December 1994 the General Assembly reacted to such an initiative to grant observer status to NGOs flatly: "The General Assembly ... decides that the granting of observer status in the General Assembly should in the future be confined to States and to those intergovernmental organizations whose activities cover matters of interest to the Assembly." (UN Doc. A/DEC/49/426)

The way to more formal recognition and more rights for the NGOs in the United Nations through attaining observer status seems not very promising – neither the so-called "Cardoso Report" on the reform of the relations between United Nations and civil society organizations 2004 (*United Nations* 2004) nor the Outcome Document of the UN World Summit 2005 in September 2005 (*United Nations* 2005) supported this endeavor of the NGOs. Obviously for most UN member states granting observer status implies too much legal and political recognition which they do not want the NGOs to have.

For the NGOs the most promising way of getting more information from and influence on the debates and decisions in the General Assembly will be most likely to continue to be through making use of the informal means of participation – interactive hearings with General Assembly members in the foreground of important meetings such as the World Summit 2005 and participation in special sessions of the Assembly and in the subordinate organs of the General Assembly where the hurdles for participation are lower.

Anne-Kathrin Dippel

Lit.: *Bartram, B./López, D.P.:* Observer Status, in: Wolfrum, R. (ed.): United Nations: Law, Policies and Practice, Vol. 2, Munich/ Dordrecht. 1995, 936-946; *Ginther, K.:* Article 4, in: Simma, B. (ed.): The Charter of the United Nations. A Commentary, 2nd edn., Vol. I, Oxford 2002, 177-194; *Mower, A.G.:* Observer Countries: Quasi-Members of the United Nations, in: IO 20 (1966), 266-283; *Suy, E.:* The Status of Observers in International Organizations, in: RdC 160 (1978-II), 75-179; *Sybesma-Knol, N.:* The Continuing Relevance of the Participation of Observers in the Work of the United Nations, in: Wellens, K. (ed.): International Law: Theory and Practice, The Hague 1998, 371-394; *Sybesma-Knol, N.:* Non-State Actors in International Organizations: An Attempt of Classification, in: Netherlands Institute of Human Rights (ed.): The Legitimacy of the United Nations. Towards an Enhanced Legal Status of Non-State Actors, Utrecht 2004; *United Nations - General Assembly:* We the peoples: civil society, the United Nations and global governance. Report of the Panel of Eminent Persons on United Nations-Civil Society Relations, 11 June 2004, UN Doc. A/58/817 (quoted as: United Nations 2004); *United Nations - General Assembly:* 2005 World Summit Outcome, Resolution adopted by the General Assembly, 16 September 2005, UN Doc. A/RES/60/1 (quoted as: United Nations 2005). /.

Internet: *Information about the list of permanent observers to the UN:*
1) non-member states: www.un.org/ en/members/nonmembers.shtml;
2) intergovernmental organizations: www.un.org/en/members/intergovorg.shtml.

Peace, Peace Concept, Threat to Peace

Peace as Political Category

Peace is the state of social relations on all levels, which allows human beings to develop in dignity, mutual respect and without any prejudice through direct or indirect violence. Peace can be defined as a "process-oriented pattern of the international system, which is marked by decreasing violence and increasing distributive justice" (*Czempiel* 1984).

The purpose of all politics is peace (*Plato*).This concept is still today valid: "The object and the purpose of politics is peace. We have to understand the realm of politics as the area of efforts to make, to keep, to guarantee, to protect and of course to defend peace. Or to say it in other words: Peace is the political category as such" (*Sternberger* 1960). Faced with the existence weapons of mass destruction, we may state for our times without any exaggeration that peace is the condition of survival, the "vital requirement of the technological era" (*C.F. von Weizsäcker* 1963).

Relationship between War and Peace

War times and peace periods alternated again and again during the course of history. But all civilizations accepted the notion of peace as the highest ethical obligation which is expressed in the so-called "golden rule", which already *Kung Fu Tse* (*Confucius*) proclaimed ("What you do not want for yourself, do not do it to other people"), in the *Gospel* ("All what you want that people should do towards you, do it to them equally"), and finally formulated by *Immanuel Kant* in modern judicial language and accepted generally as the Categorical Imperative ("Act in a way that the maxim of your will can become the principle of a general legislation"). The *obligation to peace* that one can find in this notion is normally restricted by the equally old right to self-defense, which as "just war" (*bellum iustum*) already gained admission to the literature of the Roman Empire (*Cicero*). In the forth century *Augustinus* tied the Just War to three decisive conditions: a *just cause* (*causa iusta*) must exist, an *ethically good intention* (*recta intentio*) should be given, and the decision to go to war must be taken by a *legitimate authority* (*legitima potestas*), which was, in the time of *Augustinus,* the Roman Emperor. If war could not be removed from the world, because final peace would be established only after the arrival of God's Kingdom, then peace should at least – thanks to these conditions – be fenced, or domesticated. In the High Middle Ages *Thomas of Aquinas* complemented these three conditions by a fourth: that a war, if justly fought, has to observe the *adequacy of the means* (*debitus modi*). As at this time the authority of the Emperor seemed insufficient for maintaining peace, Thomas extended the notion of *legitimate power* (*legitima potestas*) to the *public authority of the territorial princes or sovereigns* (*auctoritas principis*), so that at the end of the Middle Ages the *just war* (*bellum iustum*) was followed by the *right of war* (*ius ad bellum*). *Niccoló Machiavelli* proclaimed in his essay "The Prince" (Il Principe), published 1532, that the *raison d'être* alone of the territorial prince should command his decisions about war and peace, without any regard to moral scruples. *Thomas Hobbes* formulated about one hundred years later (1651) the philosophical argument to this claim. He presented the state as an artificial entity, as the *Leviathan* (hence the title of his book, originating from the Hebraic word for monster), which is necessary to tame man who distinguishes himself as being his own wolf (*homo homini lupus*). The state personified by the prince enforces pacification inside the territory and represents the interests of the state towards the outside: "The sovereign power ... of whose acts a great multitude, by mutual covenants one with another, have made themselves everyone the author, to the end he may use the strength and means of them all as he shall think expedient for their peace and common defence." (*Thomas Hobbes*, "Leviathan" (1651), chapter 17) The state monopoly of power as the guarantor of peace was established from this point.

Peace as a Norm of International Law

This understanding of war and peace was confirmed by the Westphalian Peace Treaties, and accepted as norm of international law until the First World War. Extremely cruel excesses of warfare, injuring the civilian population, were to be avoided or at least tempered by lawful international agreements and conventions – the so-called Law of War (*ius in bello*).

Only with the founding of the → League of Nations, and finally with the → Charter of the United Nations, the ban of war and the obligation to maintain the peace were declared as the foundation of international relations. The Charter of the UN in Article 1 proclaims as one of its purposes "to maintain international peace and security, and to that end: to take effective collective measures for the prevention and removal of threats to the peace, and for the suppression of acts of aggression or other breaches of the peace, and to bring about by peaceful means, and in conformity with the principles of justice and international law, adjustment or settlement of international disputes or situations which might lead to a breach of the peace". In Article 51 the members of the UN are expressively given "the inherent right of individual or collective self-defence".

Threats to Peace

As threats to peace we understand primarily all assaults aiming at the modification of existing borders with the purpose of pushing through power interests by force, as with the Iraqi attack on Kuwait, which unleashed the Second Gulf War. Grave violations of → human rights, too, are counted among threats to peace, and can become object of an UN intervention (→ Humanitarian Law, International; → Peacekeeping; → Peacekeeping Operations; → Peacekeeping Forces). Closely related to the notion of peace is the notion of *security* as an essential prerequisite of *peacekeeping*. Any security policy that is aimed at a lasting peace ought to respect the interests of all parties in a conflict (→ Collective Security; → Security Council; → Agenda for Peace).

Peace and Conflict Research

Peace and its follow-up problems are the object of *peace and conflict research* (*peace studies*). These analyze the conditions which can safeguard the co-existence of peoples without recurring to violence. Since peace is often disturbed by collective violence – in the past in particular by inter-state wars, recently more and more by social and/or ethno-national outbursts of violence –,

515

the analysis of the causes of war and violence belongs to the most important subjects of peace and conflict research. Further steps include studies about how the use of military force can be limited, if not avoided, through international agreements in the framework of the United Nations or regional alliances of states, e.g. Organization for Security and Co-operation in Europe (OSCE). Studies on military armament and → disarmament, especially nuclear weapons and other means of mass destruction play a decisive role. Of special interest in this context are the concepts of "confidence-building measures", "graduated reciprocation" and "common security", which have been developed during the seventies and eighties in peace research institutes and accepted – though insufficiently – in the realm of international relations. This aspect of peace science can be defined as *research on the causes of war*, aiming at a so-called *"negative peace" (absence of war)* as one of the decisive prerequisites for abolishing international violence.

In the sixties peace and conflict research gained a new quality by introducing the concept of *structural violence (Johan Galtung)*. There is now, after a lengthy and continuing debate on this concept, a high degree of agreement that political suppression, economic exploitation, social pauperization, an absence of development as well as increasing destruction of the environment, are the breeding ground for terrorists and criminal violence, which finally leads to violent conflicts such as the Gulf War, the Yugoslavian wars, the wars in the Caucasus, in the Horn of Africa and in Central Africa and in many other places. Peace research therefore analyses more and more the causes of such violence, and develops models to show how such conflicts may be prevented (→ Preventive Diplomacy), and after an outbreak, might be mediated. Concepts of non-military conflict resolution are at the center of such studies and are developed together with members of different groups which perform on-the-spot practical peace, development or environment as-

sistance (→ NGOs). Through such studies peace research formulates increasingly critical views about basic social structures which are marked by patriarchal traditions and militarization, even in classic democracies. Through such approaches peace research searches for new explanations for peaceless, social situations and offers perspectives to overcome them by strengthening civil societies. These approaches have led recently to the research concept of *the research on the causes of peace* which places the shaping of positive peace at the center of its work.

Peace Utopias and Peace Memoranda

The decisive feature of *positive peace* is, in addition to respect for human rights and the equality of all men and women before the law, the guarantee of the establishment of *justice*, especially in the social area. The notion of *justice* has been stressed in early peace concepts of all civilizations. It was again *Augustinus* who formulated this connection between peace and justice as a principle: *peace is the result of justice (pax iustitiae opus)*. This principle has been persistently defended by the utopians. The word *utopia* (Gr. *u topia* = no land) has been created by the English scholar and statesman *Thomas More* in the form of a description of a journey (1516), and was meant as the projection of an ideal constitution of a state and society. If today many diverse concepts are called "utopias", the original utopias were always associated with a pacified and just society, especially the three classic utopias at the beginning of modern times: *Utopia (Thomas More)*, *Citta del Sole (Tommaso Campanella*, 1602), and *Nova Atlantis (Francis Bacon*, 1624). *More* and *Campanella* expected social peace first of all through restructuring of possessive interests and renewing social ethics, *Bacon* through technical progress. *William Penn* expressed the idea of justice as the prerequisite of peace most clearly in his "Essay Towards the Present and Future Peace of Europe": "As *Justice* is a Preserver, so it is a better Procurer of Peace then [sic!] War. ... *Justice is the means of Peace*; betwixt [sic!] the Government and the People, and one Man and Company and another. It prevents strife and at last ends it. ... Thus *Peace* is maintained by Justice..." (*Penn* 1693, 6ff.)

The last of the great peace memoranda before the French Revolution was written by *Immanuel Kant*, who developed in his tractate "Eternal Peace" (1795) the clear vision of enduring peace under two conditions: independent jurisdiction and republican constitution following the principle of separation of powers as defined by *Charles de Montesquieu* fifty years earlier. *Kant* rejects resolutely the right to war and is astonished "that the word right has not yet fully and pedantically been banned from war politics."

Peace Societies and Pacifism

The peace utopias and peace memoranda did not find much public resonance until the beginning of the 19th century. Only then first "peace societies" were founded following the example of the *Peace Society* founded in London in 1816. They can be considered as the precursors of the modern peace movement. In 1817 the *Massachusetts Peace Society* became active; in 1848 the *Société de la Paix* was founded in Belgium. At the end of the 19th century the notion of "pacifism" became popular. The *Carnegie Endowment for International Peace* was founded in 1910 in New York; one year later followed the *World Peace Foundation* in Boston. A decisive initiative came from *Bertha von Suttner*, an Austrian writer, who published 1889 the novel "*Die Waffen nieder*" (Down the Arms), which inspired *Alfred Nobel*, the Swedish industrialist, to establish the Donation of the Nobel Peace Prize. Von Suttner founded together with *Alfred H. Fried* in 1891 the Österreichische Friedensgesellschaft (Austrian Peace Society), and one year later the Deutsche Friedensgesellschaft (German Peace Society). The first issue of the "Friedenswarte" (Peace Observer), the most important journal of the pacifist movement, was published in 1899. When the Nazis came to power in Ger-

many, the editorial office moved to Switzerland. Today this journal is still sporadically published, once again in Germany. Renowned historians like *Ludwig Quidde,* and professors of law like *Walther Schücking,* dominated the pacifism debate during the twenties, thirties and forties.

In the period between the two World Wars disarmament, international law and the fight against the fascist regimes in Italy, Germany and Spain stood at the center of the pacifist movement. In 1919 the *War Resisters International* (WRI) was founded in London and the *International Peace Bureau* (IPB) was established in Berne, Switzerland. The "International Law Pacifists", as they were called, placed all their hope in the → League of Nations – but in vain. The movement split over the question of "just defense". While French and British pacifists rejected unconditionally war and military service, German pacifists were split in this question. The so-called "Friedenskartell" (Peace Cartel) of the German pacifist groups dissolved on account of these quarrels. Symptomatic of this dilemma was *Albert Einstein*, on the one hand the most prominent and consequent pacifist, who on the other demanded very early military interventions of the democratic states against Hitler and Mussolini, although he continued in his own words to "detest the military". He would have preferred an international police intervention, but because there was no such police force he was in favor of military action.

Peace Movement

The *peace movement* after 1945 gained its most important momentum from its criticism of nuclear armament, whose first spokesmen were *Albert Einstein* and *Bertrand Russell*. The movement started first in Great Britain with the so-called "Easter Marches" and "sit-down blockades" in front of nuclear arms bases, and became well known through the *Campaign for Nuclear Disarmament*. In the United States the peace movement became popular at the end of the sixties through its protest against the

Vietnam War. The American withdrawal from Vietnam was predominantly the consequence of the domestic climate of refusal to do military service and of the political opposition against the involvement in Vietnam. The American anti-racism campaign (*Martin Luther King*) gave an equally strong momentum to the peace movement. Further impulses came from the struggle of India against the British colonial rule, where *Mohandas Karamchand Gandhi* used with success the means of non-violent action.

In the Federal Republic of Germany the peace movement started relatively late. The "Ohne mich" (*count me out*) and "Kampf dem Atomtod" (*fight against atomic death*) campaigns of the fifties found at the beginning little resonance. The Easter Marches had been (wrongly) suspected for a long time to be steered and infiltrated by communists. As a matter of fact they were initiated by Christian non-violent groups (Quaker, Mennonites, Fellowship of Reconciliation and others). Furthermore the increasing conscious objection against war service played an important role. The peace movement reached its peak – as in nearly all other West European states – at the end of the seventies with the support of the "Helsinki Act", which defused the East West Conflict, and still more with the campaign against the so-called "Nachrüstungsbeschluß" (protest against the stationing of American intermediate range rockets). The peace groups received support from the Anti-Nuclear-Power Movement, numerous church groups and the ecology movement. Opinion polls showed that temporarily 70% of the West German population supported the peace movement, which has been, not wrongly, named "nuclear pacifism".

UN and Peace Movement

The United Nations and its organizations (→ UN System; → Principal Organs, Subsidiary Organs, Treaty Bodies) played surprisingly no important role in the peace movement and vice versa, with the exception of → UNESCO, which repeatedly consults peace-oriented organizations, and initiated and still supports the campaign for the "Culture of Peace". The peace movement considers the UN as the right approach to overcome international anarchy, and to contribute thereby to peace-building, and has adopted the "Agenda for Peace" of the then Secretary General Boutros Boutros-Ghali (→ Agenda for Peace) as its own. However, it has lost confidence in the efficiency of the organization, especially since the influence of powerful states, principally the USA, has increased recently.

With the beginning of nuclear disarmament and later, especially with the end of the "Cold War" and the reunification of Germany, the peace movement lost much of its impetus. Neither the Gulf War nor the eruptions of violence in the former Yugoslavia, nor the reduced but still ongoing nuclear armament could re-activate it. It is at present reduced to a core group of traditional pacifists, and concentrates its actions on protests against militarism, right-wing extremism and xenophobia, and on humanitarian assistance and mediation in war-ravaged regions. Today the peace movement opposes the concept of governments to end war by *military intervention* with its own concept of *civilian intervention (Civil Peace Service),* aiming at containing violence at all levels of society. The basic idea is a reversal of the Roman saying *Si vis pacem, para bellum* (if you want peace, prepare war) to *Si vis pacem, para pacem* (if you want peace, prepare peace).

UN Report: A More Secure World

While the UN Charter primarily focuses on peacekeeping and peacemaking in the classical terms of international law by banning war, especially through Chapter VI (Pacific settlement of disputes), and Chapter VII (action with respect to threats to the peace, breaches of the peace, and acts of aggression – particularly through Article 51 "Right to self-defence"), in 2003, the then Secretary-General Kofi Annan convened a *High-level Panel on Threats, Challeng-*

es and Change in order to redefine the threats to peace fifty years after the foundation of the United Nations. He invited the former Prime Minister of Thailand, Anand Panyarachun, to chair the panel, which included other 15 high-ranking members from different states all over the world, among them the five standing members of the Security Council (UN Doc. A/58/612, 28 November 2003).

The Report entitled "A more secure world: our shared responsibility" (UN Doc. A/59/565, 2 December 2004) which the panel handed over to Kofi Annan on 1 December 2004, certainly does not have the authority of the UN Charter, but generates, as the Executive Summary written for the UNDPI brochure version of the Panel Report outlines, "new ideas about the kinds of policies and institutions required for the UN to be effective in the 21st century. In its report, the High-level Panel sets out a bold, new vision of collective security for the 21st century. We live in a world of new and evolving threats, threats that could not have been anticipated when the UN was founded in 1945 – threats like nuclear terrorism, and state collapse from the long-term effects of poverty, disease and civil war. In today's world, a threat to one is a threat to all. Globalization means that a major terrorist attack anywhere in the industrial world would have devastating consequences for the well-being of millions in the developing world. Any one of 700 million international airline passengers every year can be an unwitting carrier of a deadly infectious disease. And the erosion of state capacity anywhere in the world weakens the protection of every State against transnational threats such as terrorism and organized crime. Every State requires international cooperation to make it secure." (A more secure world, Executive Summary, *United Nations* 2004, 1)

Six clusters of threats are named in the Report with which the world must come to terms now and in the decades ahead:
- war between states;

- violence within states, including civil wars, large-scale human rights abuses and genocide;
- poverty, infectious disease and environmental degradation;
- nuclear, radiological, chemical and biological weapons;
- terrorism; and
- transnational organized crime.

The Executive Summary of the Report points to the fact, "that the United Nations and our collective security institutions have shown that they *can* work. More civil wars ended through negotiation in the past 15 years than the previous 200. In the 1960s, many believed that by now 15-25 States would possess nuclear weapons; the Nuclear Non-Proliferation Treaty has helped prevent this" (ibid., 2).

On the other hand we observe that meanwhile India and Pakistan dispose of nuclear weapons, North Korea tried to develop such weapons, but appeared more recently to have refrained under high international pressure from following this policy any further, while Iran is continuing its dangerous nuclear build-up.

Policies for Prevention, But Implementation Lags

The Executive Summary of the Report continues: "Meeting the challenge of today's threats means getting serious about prevention; the consequences of allowing latent threats to become manifest, or of allowing existing threats to spread, are simply too severe. Development has to be the first line of defense for a collective security system that takes prevention seriously. Combating poverty will not only save millions of lives but also strengthen States' capacity to combat terrorism, organized crime and proliferation. Development makes everyone more secure. There is an agreed international framework for how to achieve these goals, set out in the Millennium Declaration and the Monterrey Consensus, but implementation lags. Biological security must be at the forefront of prevention. International response to HIV/AIDS was shockingly

519

late and shamefully ill-resourced. It is urgent that we halt and roll back this pandemic. But we will have to do more." (ibid., 2)

Further on the Report describes the different threats: preventing the spread and use of nuclear, biological and chemical weapons is essential for safeguarding a more secure world. The Report urges negotiations for a new arrangement which would enable the International Atomic Energy Agency to act as a guarantor for the supply of fissile material to civilian nuclear users at market rates.

Terrorism is a threat to all states, and to the UN as a whole. New aspects of the threat – including the rise of a global terrorist network, and the potential for terrorist use of nuclear, biological or chemical weapons – require new responses. The Report urges the United Nations to forge a strategy of counter-terrorism that is respectful of human rights and the rule of law. The spread of transnational organized crime finally increases the risk of all other threats. Combating organized crime is essential for helping states build the capacity to exercise their sovereign responsibilities.

"Of course", the Executive Summary of the Report emphasizes, "prevention sometimes fails. At times, threats will have to be met by military means. The UN Charter provides a clear framework for the use of force. States have an inherent right to self-defense, enshrined in Article 51. Long-established customary international law makes it clear that States can take military action as long as the threatened attack is imminent, no other means would deflect it, and the action is proportionate. The Security Council has the authority to act preventively, but has rarely done so ... Deploying military capacities – for peacekeeping as well as peace enforcement – has proved to be a valuable tool in ending wars and helping to secure States in their aftermath. But the total global supply of available peacekeepers is running dangerously low. Just to do an adequate job of keeping the peace in existing conflicts would require almost doubling the

number of peacekeepers around the world. The developed States have particular responsibilities to do more to transform their armies into units suitable for deployment to peace operations". (ibid., 4f.)

Moreover, the Executive Summary of the Report points out that, once wars have ended, post-conflict peacebuilding is vital: "The UN has often devoted too little attention and too few resources to this critical challenge. Successful peacebuilding requires the deployment of peacekeepers with the right mandates and sufficient capacity to deter would-be spoilers; funds for demobilization and disarmament, built into peacekeeping budgets; a new trust fund to fill critical gaps in rehabilitation and reintegration of combatants, as well as other early reconstruction tasks; and a focus on building State institutions and capacity, especially in the rule of law sector. Doing this job successfully should be a core function of the United Nations." (ibid., 5)

The Executive Summary of the Report ends with the remark that it is "the report is the start, not the end, of a process. The year 2005 will be a crucial opportunity for Member States to discuss and build on the recommendations in the report, some of which will be considered by a summit of heads of State. But building a more secure world takes much more than a report or a summit. It will take resources commensurate with the scale of the challenges ahead; commitments that are long-term and sustained; and, most of all, it will take leadership – from within States, and between them." (ibid., 6)

The Report was followed by a number of other reform reports and programmatic reform declarations such as the Secretary-General's report to the General Assembly 2005 "In larger freedom: towards development, security and human rights for all" (UN Doc. A/59/2005, 21 March 2005) and the "World Summit Outcome Document" (UN Doc. A/RES/60/1, 16 September 2005), adopted by the member states at the end of the UN World Summit in

September 2005. Again – despite the fact that all member states agree with the described scenarios and the proposed measures to reform the present system of collective security, the United Nations themselves and world society is still awaiting that words are followed by actions providing the world with more security and peace.

Karlheinz Koppe

Lit.: *Alger, C.F.:* 1999: The Quest for Peace: What are we learning, in International Journal of Peace Studies, Vol. 4 (1999), Formosa College, Tamkang University, Taiwan, 21-46; *Boulding, E.:* Cultures of Peace. The Hidden Side of History, Syracuse/New York 2000; *Burton, J.W.:* 1962: Peace Theory. Preconditions of Disarmament, New York 1962; *Call, C.T./Wyeth, V.H.:* Building States to Build Peace, Boulder 2007; *Ceadel, M.:* Thinking about Peace and War, Oxford and New York 1987; *Cousens, E.M./ Kumar, C. (eds.):* Peacebuilding as Politics: Cultivating Peace in Fragile Societies, Boulder 2001; *Falk, R./Mendlovitz, S. (eds.):* The Strategy of World Order, 6 vols., New York 1996; *Galtung, J.:* Nonviolence and Deep Cultures: Some Hidden Obstacles, in: Peace Research, Vol. 27, Oslo 1995; *Glad, B. (ed.):* Psychological Dimensions of War, London 1990. *Jeong, H.:* Peace and Conflict Studies. An Introduction, Ashgate/Aldershot 2000; *Kaldor, M.:* New & Old Wars. Organized Violence in a Global Era, London 1999; *Kriesberg, L.:* International Conflict Resolution. The US-USSR and Middle East Crisis, New Haven/London 1992; *Kühne, W. (ed.):* Winning the Peace: Concepts and Lessons Learned of Post-Conflict Peacebuilding, Ebenhausen 1996; *Paris, R.:* At War's End: Building Peace after Civil Conflict, Cambridge 2004; *Penn, W.:* An Essay Towards the Present and Future Peace of Europe by the Establishment of an European Dyet, Parliament or Estates. Reprint of the First Edition London 1693, United Nations Library, Geneva, Series F, Sources on the History of International Organization, No. 1, Hildesheim et al. 1983; *Pugh, M. (ed.):* The UN, peace, and force, London 1997; *Thomas, D. C./Klare, M. T. (eds.):* Peace and World Order Studies, Boulder 1989; *United Nations - Department of Public Information:* A more secure world. Our shared responsibility. Report of the High-level Panel on Threats, Challenges and Change. Executive Summary, New York 2004; *United Nations Association of the United Kingdom:* An Agenda for Peace Ten Years on, London 2002; *Väyrynen, R. (ed.):* The Quest for Peace. Transcending Collective Violence and War among Societies, Cultures and States, London 1989; *Wiberg, H.:* The Peace Research Movement, in: Wiener Beiträge zur Geschichte der Neuzeit, Vol. 11, Vienna 1994, 165-185; *Young, N.:* Peace Movements in History, in: Mendlovitz/Walker (eds.): Towards a Just World Peace, London/Boston 1987.

Peaceful Settlement of Disputes

I. Peaceful Settlement of Disputes in the UN Charter

Chapter VI of the UN Charter, "Pacific Settlement of Disputes", and Chapter VII, "Action with Respect to Threats to the Peace, Breaches of the Peace, and Acts of Aggression" (→ Charter of the UN; → Peace, Peace Concept, Threat to Peace; → Peacekeeping), number amongst the key substantive chapters setting out the ways in which the organization's core aim, "to maintain international peace and security", is to be translated into reality.

In the public perception, of course, Chapter VI of the Charter has mostly been overshadowed by the fixation with the possibilities offered by Chapter VII, or with "peacekeeping measures" (→ Peacekeeping Operations), located somewhere between the two. Routine UN practice, however, has been different: in it, the attempt to realize the precept set out in Article 2 (3) UN Charter that "[a]ll Members shall settle their international disputes by peaceful means" has played a very prominent role. Whether the provisions of the Charter equip the organization with an adequate set of instruments to do this, and whether the → Security Council (the body mainly entrusted to fulfill this task) has done enough to develop these instruments successfully, is, however, questionable.

The key provisions of Chapter VI of the Charter give the Security Council three powers:

- to investigate conflicts to determine whether they are "likely to endanger the maintenance of international peace and security" (Art. 34 UN Charter);
- to recommend "appropriate procedures or methods" to settle disputes peacefully (Art. 36(1) UN Charter);
- to draft its own recommendations for settling conflicts (Art. 37 (2) UN Charter).

II. The Role of the Security Council

In practice, the Security Council has devoted copious attention to disputes referred to it by member states. In most cases, however – particularly at the time of East-West blockade-politics – its responses were confined to appeals to avert or contain violence, and to general recommendations about the joint regulation of disputes. The potential for active peaceful intervention offered by Article 37 (2) UN Charter was only utilized in exceptional cases. The reasons for this lay not only in the differing interests – especially of the veto powers, i.e. the permanent members of the Security Council (→ Veto, Right of Veto) – in the particular cases in question, but probably also, to a much greater extent, in the common interest of these powers in not seeing their room for maneuvers, in their domestic as well as in their foreign policies, curtailed by an effective "regime for the peaceful settlement of disputes". Any substantial advances in realizing the UN precept of peaceful dispute-settlement therefore depend on there being a redefinition of the principles of → sovereignty and non-interference in the internal affairs of states (→ Intervention, Prohibition of) – a move which, in the context of increased global interdependence, is, in any case, overdue.

The end of the old East-West conflict did at least remove some of the earlier obstacles to a more active dispute settlement policy on the part of the Security Council – as demonstrated, above all, by the agreement achieved on a number of Central American conflicts, and by the understanding arrived at on a post-war settlement for Cambodia. This new departure did not, however, lead to a lasting process of systematic reinforcement of peaceful dispute-settlement by the Security Council. Instead, under the pressure of new conflicts in the 1990s, there was a gradual blurring of the dividing-line between peaceful dispute-settlement as set out in Chapter VI of the UN Charter and peace-enforcement as detailed in Chapter VII. In addition, after the rather sobering record on increased peace-keeping operations, the big powers – first and foremost the USA (→ UN Policy, USA) – increasingly turned away from multilateralism and had only selective recourse to the UN's precepts on peacekeeping.

III. The Role of the Secretary-General

The modest record of the Security Council on Chapter VI of the Charter naturally only represents one aspect of UN efforts in the area of peaceful dispute-settlement. In practice, the "gap" left by the Security Council in this area has meant that the → Secretary-General and the latter's representatives (Personal Representatives, Special Envoys) have assumed a key role at the operational level. To begin with, there was still disagreement as to whether the Secretary-General could only do this under express instruction from the Security Council. However, since the publication of the → "Agenda for Peace" in 1992 (UN Doc. A/47/277-S/24111, 17 June 1992) it has been recognized that when it comes to prevention, the UN needs to be involved long before the Security Council concerns itself with an issue, and that the → Secretariat must assume greater responsibility here.

The "Group of Friends of the Secretary-General" was created as an additional instrument, located quasi between the Security Council and the Secretary-General. This is a small group of states comprising several veto-powers and various other key actors, including regional ones, who are willing to assume special responsibility for dispute settlement in particular conflict-fields. Its members monitor the various efforts made to achieve mutually agreed settlement; they maintain contact with all those involved; they develop solutions; and they consult with one another and with the Secretary-General on a regular basis (→ Groups and Groupings in the UN).

The increased operational involvement of the Secretary-General and his representatives, and of the "Groups of Friends", renders the dilemma about (im)partiality more acute: On the one hand, the UN is required, in every conflict, to take a clear stand in relation to its principles and norms, particularly with regard to respect for → human rights; on the other hand, all third-party interventions require a minimum of neutrality, just to be able to build bridges between the parties to the conflict. This dilemma was reflected, for example, in the conflict over Bosnia-Herzegovina, where measures on the Serbian side were openly criticized in the Security Council's statements, whereas the Secretary-General's envoys on the spot took care to refrain from such judgments in their negotiations with the Serbian side.

IV. Means Used in Peaceful Dispute Settlement

If the means listed in Chapter VI of the UN Charter to be used in peaceful dispute-settlement are considered systematically in relation to the degree of third-party involvement, six categories emerge:

The most direct form of peaceful dispute settlement, with no involvement by third parties, is *negotiation* between disputants. This is one of the core elements of classical diplomacy, and, where it has been used effectively, it has undoubtedly prevented countless disputes from escalating into destructive modes of conflict resolution. The possibilities developed by the "Alternative Dispute Resolution" Movement for optimizing negotiations have, however, not yet been fully exploited in the diplomatic framework. Such possibilities include procedures enabling the parties to move on from their more superficial and, in most cases, short-term 'positions' to

their more deeply rooted, "enlightened self-interests", thus increasing the chances for jointly agreed "inclusive solutions".

The weakest form of third-party involvement, albeit often a vital one, is that of *good offices*, in which outside parties try to get disputants to negotiate, or facilitate such negotiations by providing communication facilities and transport, arranging venues, etc., but not themselves acting as mediators. This task is performed by the Secretary-General and his representatives on a regular basis and in a variety of ways (even though this means of dispute settlement is not expressly mentioned in Article 33 UN Charter). They are also increasingly trying to improve coordination between the various bilateral and multilateral negotiating forums that are of relevance to whatever conflict is being dealt with.

A more formalized procedure is the *investigation* of a conflict by an inquiry commission of impartial experts. In terms of international law, this instrument draws heavily on arbitration regulations as already laid down in the Hague Convention on the Peaceful Settlement of International Disputes of 1907 (text: Martens NRG, 3rd Series, Vol. 3, 360). But there is also the "fact-finding mission", less regulated in terms of use and evaluation, which can be used as one element in combination with other forms of dispute settlement. Overall, this instrument now plays a prominent role in international politics, particularly where observance of human rights and the prevention of crisis and violence are concerned. However, in terms of establishing which party is responsible for which causal factors, the importance of investigation and fact-finding in achieving mutually agreed dispute settlements is limited. Instead, it has proved more effective to use this method for monitoring adherence to agreements.

When conflicts appear virtually insoluble, or have become highly escalated, peaceful dispute settlement is dependent upon a stronger form of involvement, in the form of *mediation*. Here, the third

523

party generally assumes responsibility for directing proceedings and makes suggestions as to how the talks with the parties in conflict are to be organized in terms of themes. As regards all the other aspects of the interaction with the parties, there is a whole range of permutations. These extend from "shuttle diplomacy", in which the mediators negotiate separately with each party, through "transformative mediation", in which the mediators confine themselves strictly to steering the process, to "problem-solving mediation", in which mediators can also make suggestions on substantive points.

Informal conciliation and arbitration procedures aim to clarify the facts of the matter at issue, and to work on them from the outset on the understanding that the disputants will ultimately have a solution proposed to them by the third party. Such procedures are not, however, binding on the parties. This distinguishes them from *formal arbitration and judicial rulings*. These are at least binding in international law, provided that the parties concerned are willing to submit to the ruling in question ($\rightarrow$ ICJ).

In practice, there are all sorts of combinations of these means of dispute settlement. Thus, in the 1995 Dayton Accords on Bosnia-Herzegovina, virtually every instrument was employed. All in all, however, the use of legal procedures tends to be the exception. The reasons for this lie, firstly, in the inadequate legal criteria for settling what is now the most prevalent form of dispute – the intra-state conflict, and, secondly, in the tendency of governments to prefer political processes, in which they can play part, over legal procedures, the outcome of which they are less able to predict. Up to now, these factors have also blocked the establishment of effective legal procedures for peaceful settlement of disputes within regional organizations such as the OSCE.

V. Effectiveness of Dispute Settlement Procedures

Empirical research focuses on the effectiveness of "power mediation", in which influential third parties act on the basis of their own interests and are in a position to exert pressure or supply the resources needed to enact particular solutions (*Bercovitch* 1997). How far the claim of effectiveness holds good for the long-term settlement of intra-state conflicts, particularly those of an ethnopolitical kind, is, however, hotly disputed. If nothing else, the discussion about "power mediation" does, however, make it clear that the effectiveness of conflict resolution does not depend only – and probably not even primarily – on the skilled use of diplomatic means in negotiations with the leading figures in parties to a dispute. There are very strong reasons for believing that the diplomatic tools of peaceful dispute settlement have to be viewed in combination with a series of other *measures for promoting peace*.

One of the most important of these is assurance of the *structural stability* of the country or region in question. Social change in developing and transforming societies can only be organized without violence if there is progress in economic development, social justice, democratization ($\rightarrow$ Democratization and the UN), the rule of law, good governance, and the development of a civil society capable of ensuring a fair balance of interests. Development cooperation ($\rightarrow$ Development Cooperation of the UN System), which serves these goals, is therefore an important precondition for peaceful dispute settlement.

A key role is here played by concepts that strengthen the capacity of the political system in question to *resolve conflict in a way that promotes democracy* (e.g. through integrative power-sharing between hostile groups, through the institutionalization of human rights observance, and through the creation of bodies to work through the violent past). Integrating these concepts proactively into mediating efforts opens up opportunities to learn from comparable instances of conflict resolution that have led to lasting settlements (*Harris/Reilly* 1998).

Moreover, experience of lastingly successful peace-agreements shows that the *role of third parties* in these cases was not confined to the diplomatic brokerage of the relevant documents. An important factor was the willingness of the third parties to make a longer-term commitment, in order to assist practically in the implementation of the agreements (*Hampson* 1996).

In the case of protracted and deeply rooted conflicts, dispute settlement at the highest level of leadership is often not enough. It has to be accompanied – and in some cases driven forward – by similar activities at the grass roots level and at the middle levels of leadership. This involves both the enlistment of external non-governmental organizations (→ NGOs) for third-party functions ("track-2 diplomacy") and the broad-based mobilization of semi-partial and impartial *civil society actors* in the country concerned for the purposes of peaceful dispute settlement and the creation of "peace constituencies".

VI. Further Development of Procedures for Peaceful Dispute Settlement

The discussion about the → reform of the UN) has recently focused more intensively on peaceful dispute settlement. Besides the aspects already mentioned, the main points highlighted have been the following:

Since the 'Agenda for Peace' and the 1992 Security Council summit, the topic of conflict resolution has been extended to include *prevention* (misleadingly dubbed → preventive diplomacy in UN terminology). This move was overdue, given that the chances of peaceful dispute settlement are much greater in the early phases of the development of a conflict than when hostilities have broken out. So far, the attempts at implementing this new imperative have not, it must be said, been particularly impressive.

The United Nations is present in almost all zones of crisis and conflict in the world, via a range of special organs and → specialized agencies (→ Principal Organs, Subsidiary Organs, Treaty Bodies), most notably those that are responsible for development cooperation and → humanitarian assistance. Very often, coordination of all the aid in a humanitarian disaster lies in the hands of one of these organizations, e.g. → UNHCR. In conflicts of long duration, these UN organizations, whether they like it or not, have an influence on the political developments on the spot. These mostly unintended effects have led to increased discussion about *codes of conduct* in crises and conflicts and have raised the question of whether the special organs and specialized agencies concerned should not assume a more active role in peaceful dispute settlement at the lower and middle leadership-levels.

In order to prevent the United Nations being overburdened with peacemaking activities, Article 33 (1) UN Charter also allows for parties to a dispute to "resort to regional agencies or arrangements". A number of important contributions to the further development of the instruments of peaceful dispute settlement have been made by the OSCE, particularly through its Permanent Council, its Chairman-in-Office and the latter's representatives, its long-term missions, and its High Commissioner on National Minorities. These developments have led, on the one hand, to a discussion about the establishment of similar instruments within the UN, and, on the other, to suggestions for the creation of "Regional UN Centres for Sustainable Peace" (*Peck* 1998).

The critical discussion about the effectiveness of non-military modes of enforcement (→ Sanctions) and about their sometimes devastating "side-effects" for the civilian population concerned raises the question of whether more thought should not be given to the use of "positive sanctions", of incentives and rewards, for peacemaking. This hitherto neglected means of peaceful dispute settlement does indeed merit closer consideration (*Amley* 1998).

525

The further development of the instruments used by the UN for peaceful dispute settlement should not, however, be viewed in isolation from the reform of other areas of policy relevant to peace. This includes, most importantly: winning back and strengthening the UN's monopoly on the legitimization of force; extending the rule of law at the global level, through the International Criminal Court (→ ICC); and fostering a type of development policy that is geared to peaceful change.

Norbert Ropers

Lit.: *Amley, E.A., Jr.:* Peace by Other Means: Using Rewards in UN Efforts to End Conflicts, in: Den.J.Int'l.L.&Pol. 26 (1998), 235-297; *Bercovitch, J.:* Mediation in International Conflict: An Overview of Theory, A Review of Practice, in: Zartman, I.W./ Rasmussen, J.L. (eds.): Peacemaking in International Conflict. Methods and Techniques, Washington 1997, 125-154; *Czempiel, E.O.:* Die Reform der UNO. Möglichkeiten und Mißverständnisse, Munich 1994; *Debiel, T.:* Handlungsfähige Weltautorität oder Legitimationsbeschaffer à la carte? Friedenspolitische Perspektive für die UNO, in: FW 73 (1998), 443-464; *Franck, T./Nolte, G.:* The Good Offices Function of the UN Secretary-General, in: Roberts, A./Kingsbury, B. (eds.): United Nations, Divided World. The UN's Roles in International Relations, 2nd rev. and expanded edn., Oxford et al. 1993, 143-182; *Hampson, F.O.:* Nurturing Peace: Why Peace Settlements Succeed or Fail? Washington 1996; *Harris, P./Reilly, B. (eds.):* Democracy and Deep-Rooted Conflict: Options for Negotiators, Stockholm 1998; *Kühne, W.* 1993. Blauhelme in einer turbulenten Welt. Baden-Baden 1993; *Matthies, V. (ed.):* Der gelungene Frieden. Beispiele und Bedingungen erfolgreicher friedlicher Konfliktbearbeitung, Bonn 1997; *Peck, C.:* Sustainable Peace. The Role of the UN and Regional Organizations in Preventing Conflict, Oxford 1998; *Skjelsbaek, K.:* The UN Secretary-General and the Mediation of International Disputes, in: JPR 28 (1991), 99-115; *Wolfrum, R.:* Peaceful Settlement of Disputes, in: Wolfrum, R. (ed.): United Nations: Law, Policies and Practice, Vol. 2, Munich/Dordrecht 1995, 982-993.

Addendum

As outlined in recent reports (*High-level Panel on Threats, Challenges and Change* 2004, *Annan* 2006) the UN has broadened its understanding of threats to international security and peace in the last years. Not only inter-state conflicts or internal conflicts are seen as global risks, but also such issues as economic and social threats, genocide, nuclear, radiological chemical and biological weapons, terrorism and transnational organized crime are now so regarded.

Due to these developments UN peace operations shifted from linear-sequenced strategies to a multi-dimensional approach, where civil and military strategies are strongly intertwined and where the UN is often involved in peacemaking, peacekeeping and peacebuilding simultaneously (see *Darby/ McGinty* 2000).

As a consequence, the dividing line between the peaceful settlement of violent conflicts as outlined in Chapter VI of the UN Charter and peacekeeping or peace enforcement operations as set out in Chapter VII has been further blurred. As has been shown for example in the Sudan, UN interventions are no longer mandated with only supporting the implementation of a peace agreement. The United Nations Mission in Sudan (UNMIS) has also the authority under Chapter VII to take necessary actions involving the use of force and it is charged with a range of peacebuilding responsibilities (cf. *Mingst/Karns* 2007). The peaceful settlement of disputes is strongly connected to peacekeeping efforts and peace enforcement operations. Besides this robust peacekeeping operations can be considered as the dominant intervention form of the UN in the last years ("Brahimi Report" 2000, UN Doc. A/55/3005-S/2000/809).

Even if the Human Security Report 2005 (*Human Security Center* 2005) outlined that mediation, negotiation, facilitation and good offices are considered as useful in preventing latent conflicts from becoming violent, and although it highlighted a large demand for

UN peacemaking activities, several shortcomings in this area must be noted. According to the Report of the High-level Panel on Threats, Challenges and Change (UN Doc. A/59/565, 2 December 2004) and the decisions taken at the UN World Summit in 2005 (see concluding resolution: UN Doc. A/RES/60/1 of 16 September 2005), the Secretary-General should place greater emphasis on appointing highly qualified, experienced and regionally expert envoys. In addition to this, their training should be enhanced. Since the Department of Political Affairs (DPA) is considered as a resource on mediation for the UN system as a whole (*DPA* 2007), it necessitates more funding in order to provide more consistent support to its peacemaking envoys.

As recommended by the High-level Panel, it has been decided to establish within DPA the Mediation Support Unit (MSU) in late 2005 (cf. *Gambari* 2006), which serves as a central repository of lessons learned on peacemaking. It should act as a clearing house for best practices and coordinate training for mediators (*DPA* 2007). However, the UN lacks experienced mediators, who are able to master polarized situations (cf. *Crocker* 2007).

Nevertheless, the UN still interacts primarily with governments and other state-based institutions, and is less experienced in cooperating with civil society organizations. For this reason an important point for the reform of UN peacemaking activities can be seen in forging closer ties with other actors working in the peacemaking field, such as regional organizations, NGOs and think tanks (*Gambari* 2006). One possibility for this would be to further extend the special mandate of the UN in the field of peacebuilding. The organization could take a leading role in linking mediation approaches of official and unofficial actors (cf. *Griffiths* 2005).

Daniela Körppen

Lit.: *Crocker, C.:* Peacemaking and Mediation: Dynamics of a Changing Field, New York 2007; *Darby, J./McGinty, R. (eds.):* The Management of Peace Processes, London 2000; *Department of Political Affairs (DPA) in United Nations Secretariat:* Website on conflict prevention, www.un.org/depts/dpa/conflict.html, 22 November 2007 (quoted as: DPA 2007); *Gambari, I.A.:* Making Good Offices Better: Enhancing the UN Peacemaking Capabilities; Center for Strategic and International Studies, Washington DC, 27 February 2006, www.un.org/Depts/dpa/speeches/CSIS%20remarks2.pdf; *Griffiths, M.:* Talking Peace in a Time of Terror: United Nations Mediation and Collective Security, Geneva 2005; *Human Security Center (Liu Institute for Global Issues, University of British Columbia):* Human Security Report 2005. War and Peace in the 21st Century, New York/Oxford 2005, www.humansecurityreport.info; *Mingst, K.A./Karns, M.P.:* The United Nations and Conflict Management: Relevant or Irrelevant?, in: Crocker, C.A. et al. (eds.): Leashing the Dogs of War. Conflict Management in a Divided World, Washington 2007, 497-521; *United Nations - General Assembly/Security Council:* Report of the Panel on United Nations Peace Operations ("Brahimi Report"), UN Doc. A/55/305-S/2000/809, 21 August 2000 (quoted as: Brahimi Report 2000); *United Nations - General Assembly:* A more secure world: our shared responsibility. Report of the High-level Panel on Threats, Challenges and Change, UN Doc. A/59/565, 2 December 2004 (quoted as: High-level Panel on Threats, Challenges and Change 2004); *United Nations - General Assembly:* 2005 World Summit Outcome, UN Doc. A/RES/60/1, 16 September 2005 (quoted as: World Summit Outcome 2005), www.un.org/ga/59/hl60_plenarymeeting.html; *United Nations - General Assembly:* Progress report on the prevention of armed conflict. Report of the Secretary-General, 18 July 2006, UN Doc. A/60/891 (quoted as: Annan 2006).

Peacekeeping

This form of conflict control is not mentioned, let alone described, in the United Nations Charter (→ Charter of the UN). During the Cold War period this technique evolved as a measure to contain armed regional conflicts. At times the power vacuum created by the impact of the → decolonization process could thus be filled, and some regional conflicts could be kept out of the East-West Cold

War orbit; e.g. in Palestine, on Cyprus and in the Congo. Peacekeeping involves the use of military personnel, civilian police and other experts supplied by member states to monitor and supervise cease-fire and truce agreements and to provide not only a pretext and incentive for the parties to a conflict not to renew hostilities, but also to create stability as a prerequisite for lasting peace.

Until the end of the Cold War, Peacekeeping operations (→ Peacekeeping Operations) were usually governed by Chapter VI of the United Nations Charter "Pacific Settlement of Disputes" (→ Peaceful Settlement of Disputes). Such operations require impartiality and neutrality on the part of the UN peacekeepers (→ Peacekeeping Forces), as well as the consent of all parties to the conflict. Additionally the soldiers and/or police officers of a Chapter VI-Peacekeeping Operation may use physical force only as a last resort in self-defense or to resist efforts to disrupt their mission. Peacekeepers are deployed in an area of conflict, often along lines of separation to serve as a buffer between former enemies. Since the second → Secretary-General of the United Nations, Dag Hammarskjöld, decided on their outfit, they are recognized by their light-blue headgear, either berets, caps or helmets, as "Blue Helmets".

Peacekeeping operations are usually established by the → Security Council, which holds primary responsibility under the Charter for the maintenance of international peace and security. The Council provides the political mandate for such operations, whereas the → General Assembly provides the necessary → budget.

In the beginning, the military commanders of peacekeeping operations acted as Heads of Mission. Meanwhile, the Special Representative of the Secretary General (SRSG) is the political leader and head of a mission, while the Force Commander or the Chief Military Observer report through the SRSG to the Secretary-General and through him to the Security Council. This leadership is designated by the Secretary-General

with consent of the Council. The formed units within a peacekeeping force as well as the military observers (→ Observers), who come as individuals, are made available voluntarily by governments of member states. The expenses of troop-contributing countries will in principle be reimbursed by the UN. For this purpose peacekeeping operations are financed from a special "Peacekeeping Support Account", financed by a special assessment of all members of the United Nations.

The earliest activities, which have later been referred to as "peacekeeping operations" were missions of unarmed military observers to monitor cease-fires in Palestine in 1948 and Kashmir in 1949. Both of these missions are still in existence: UNTSO (United Nations Truce Supervision Organization in Palestine) and UNMOGIP (United Nations Military Observer Group in India and Pakistan). In 1956 the Suez crisis, involving the invasion of Egypt by the forces of France and the United Kingdom and simultaneously by Israel, demanded a more substantial arrangement than a group of military observers, who are always unarmed. On the suggestion of Canada UNEF I (United Nations Emergency Force) was authorized by the General Assembly to which the question had been transferred by the Security Council (cf. → Uniting for Peace Resolution; → History of the UN). This peacekeeping force monitored the withdrawal from Egypt of the three invading armies and established a buffer zone between the forces of Israel and Egypt, which existed until 1967, when Egypt's demand for its withdrawal gave rise to the Arab-Israeli War of 1967.

Subsequent peacekeeping operations on the model of UNEF I were established in Cyprus, in the Congo, on Syrian territory, in southern Lebanon and elsewhere (list below). Of these the largest before the end of the Cold War was ONUC (United Nations Operation in the Congo) 1960-64. Though the UN Charter deals with the maintenance of peace only in the context of international security, i.e. between sovereign states (→

Sovereignty), ONUC operated within the boundaries of a single state and therefore also had a large civil affairs component. Such a change of focus of the UN from international to intra-national intervention set the scene for the majority of the UN peacekeeping operations in the 1990s after the end of the Cold War.

These newly initiated peacekeeping missions are of a very different nature from the earlier operations, operating mostly within a single state to contain violence and restore order. These missions have a broad range of functions, including humanitarian assistance and refugee work, all kinds of civil affairs functions, monitoring → human rights, disarming and cantonment of military personnel, civil police work, and preparing, monitoring, and even conducting elections (→ Electoral Assistance).

The majority of peacekeeping operations in the 1990s were quite successful, though their positive results often went unnoticed; e.g. the missions in Namibia, El Salvador or Mozambique. By contrast, those missions, where the mandate was either unclear altogether or based upon faulty assumptions or where the resources did not match the objectives, were widely perceived as failures, in spite of the undoubted fact that the situation in that specific area of conflict would have been infinitely worse without a UN intervention.

In the case of Somalia, the United Nations was drawn into the conflict on the initiative of the United States. There was no cease-fire, let alone peace to be kept, but factional violence was raging. The mandates given to the UNOSOM (UN Operation in Somalia) missions I and II foresaw military protection for the provision of humanitarian aid to the population, who suffered from famine. This part of the mission was successfully completed, and millions of surviving Somalis bear witness to this extraordinary result. But the second part of the UN objective, to transform a failed state into a stable democratically organized society was out of reach of any foreign intervention. If this needed any kind of

confirmation, it can be seen in the desperate present situation of that country (November 2008).

During UNOSOM II when, apart of 130 Blue Helmets from other nations, 18 American soldiers had been killed in the course of an operation entirely, as it happened, US-lead in Mogadishu. The echo of this event within the US media triggered widespread opposition in Washington to agree to any new peacekeeping operations under the flag of the United Nations. Consequently the Security Council became increasingly reluctant to take the necessary actions, even in humanitarian emergencies. This lack of political will proved disastrous when the Council refused to react in any practical way to the onset of genocide in Rwanda in the spring of 1994.

In the former Yugoslavia, mainly on the territories of Croatia, Bosnia-Herzegovina and Macedonia, the United Nations were called upon to intervene, when European institutions had proven unsuccessful. The Security Council provided numerous resolutions, mostly under Chapter VI of the Charter, but the resources made available did not suffice for the demanding operations, especially when "safe areas" were established by the Council and had to be protected. A definition of what a "safe area" actually means for the civilian population therein and the opposing parties to a conflict is still lacking. The attempt to escalate the peacekeeping operation in midstream from a Chapter VI mandate to a Chapter VII operation proved impossible. NATO (North Atlantic Treaty Organization) had first been requested to provide support in the form of air space control, later a humanitarian air-lift was added as well as naval embargo supervision. Finally, in December 1995, when a peace agreement had been signed at Dayton, Ohio, the United Nations had to hand over the responsibility for the complete military operation in Bosnia-Herzegovina to a 60,000 strong NATO-lead "Implementation Force" (IFOR).

While the number of "Blue Helmets" dwindled from nearly 80,000 in 1993 to about 38,000 in 2001 it has since risen to reach 107,000 at the present time (November 2008).

Many Security Council Resolutions establishing peacekeeping operations nowadays refer to Chapter VII of the Charter providing more freedom of action to create the necessary conditions for the proper implementation of the mandates.

Simultaneously more attention has been given to "regional arrangements" as referred to within Chapter VIII of the Charter. Some "regional arrangements" are developing capabilities to act in cooperation with or even on behalf of the United Nations in conducting peacekeeping operations.

The African Union (AU), the European Union (EU), the Economic Community of West African States (ECOWAS), the North Atlantic Treaty Organization (NATO), the Organization of American States (OAS) and the Organization for Security and Cooperation in Europe (OSCE) have successfully cooperated with the United Nations in a number of peacekeeping operations. In some cases, e.g. Bosnia-Herzegovina, responsibility was even passed from the UN to a "regional arrangement", i.e. the EU. It can be assumed, that the trend of such cooperation will continue with the establishment of enhanced operational capabilities within those regional organizations, who have already started working with the Security Council and DPKO. It can be expected, that more "regional arrangements" will be following the same pattern.

Brian Urquhart / Manfred Eisele

The following is a *chronological listing of United Nations peacekeeping operations* (The numbers in brackets refer to the number of fatalities during the missions, as of November 2008:

UNTSO (UN Truce Supervision Organization; Palestine/Israel; 1948-present; (49)

UNMOGIP (UN Military Observer Group in India and Pakistan); 1949-present; (11)

UNEF I (1st UN Emergency Force); Egypt/Israel; 1956-1967; (106)

UNOGIL (UN Observation Group in Lebanon); 1958-1958;

ONUC (UN Operation in the Congo); 1960-1964; (250)

UNSF (UN Security Force in West New Guinea [West Irian]); 1962-1963;

UNYOM (UN Yemen Observation Mission); 1963-1964;

UNFICYP (UN Peacekeeping Force in Cyprus); 1964-present; (179)

DOMREP (Mission of the Representative of the SG in the Dominican Republic); 1965-1966;

UNIPOM (UN India-Pakistan Observation Mission); 1965-1966;

UNEF II (2nd UN Emergency Force); Egypt/Israel; 1973-1979; (55)

UNDOF (UN Disengagement Observer Force); Syria/Israel; 1974-present; (43)

UNIFIL (UN Interim Force in Lebanon); 1978-present; (279)

UNGOMAP (UN Good Offices Mission in Afghanistan and Pakistan); 1988-1990;

UNIIMOG (UN Iran-Iraq Military Observer Group); 1988-1991; (1)

UNAVEM I (UN Angola Verification Mission I); 1989-1991;

UNTAG (UN Transition Assistance Group); Namibia; 1989-1990; (19)

ONUCA (UN Observer Group in Central America); 1989-1992; (250)

UNIKOM (UN Iraq-Kuwait Observation Mission); 1991-2003; (18)

UNAVEM II (UN Angola Verification Mission II); 1991-1995; (5)

ONUSAL (UN Observer Mission in El Salvador); 1991-1995; (5)

MINURSO (UN Mission for the Referendum in the Western Sahara); 1991-present; (15)

UNAMIC (UN Advance Mission in Cambodia); 1991-1992;

UNPROFOR (UN Protection Force) Croatia/Bosnia/Macedonia; 1992-1995; (212)

UNTAC (UN Transnational Authority in Cambodia); 1992-1993; (84)

UNOSOM I (UN Operation in Somalia II); 1992-1993; (8)

ONUMOZ (UN Operation in Mozambique); 1992-1994; (24)

UNOSOM II (UN Operation in Somalia II); 1993-1995; (148)

UNOMUR (UN Observer Mission in Uganda-Rwanda); 1993-1994;

UNOMIG (UN Observer Mission in Georgia); 1993-present; (3)

UNOMIL (UN Observer Mission in Liberia); 1993-1997; (0)

UNMIH (UN Mission in Haiti); 1993-1996; (8)

UNAMIR (UN Assistance Mission in Rwanda); 1993-1996; (26)

UNASOG (UN Aouzou Strip Observer Group) Chad/Libya; 1994-1994;

UNMOT (UN Mission of Observers in Tajikistan); 1994-2000; (7)

UNAVEM III (UN Angola Verification Mission III // MONUA – United Nations Observer Mission in Angola; 1995-1999; (41//22)

UNCRO (UN Confidence Restoration Operation in Croatia); 1995-1996; (17)

UNPREDEP (UN Preventive Deployment Force) Macedonia; 1995-1999; (4)

UNMIBH (UN Mission in Bosnia and Herzegovina); 1995-2003; (12)

UNTAES (UN Transitional Administration for Eastern Slavonia, Baranja and Western Syrmium); 1996-1998; (11)

UNMOP (UN Mission of Observers in Prevlaka) Croatia; 1996-2003; (0)

UNSMIH/UNTMIH/MIPONUH (United Nations Mission in Haiti); 1996-2000; (8)

MINUGUA (UN Verification Mission in Guatemala); 1997-1997; (4)

UNPSG (UN Civilian Police Support Group); Croatia (Follow-on to UNTAES); 1998; (1)

MINURCA (UN Mission in the Central African Republic); 1998-2000; (2)

UNOMSIL (UN Observer Mission in Sierra Leone); 1998-1999; (0)

UNAMSIL (UN Mission in Sierra Leone); 1999-2005; (192)

UNMIK (UN Mission in Kosovo), Kosovo; 1999-present; (54)

UNAMET (UN Assistance Mission in East Timor), East Timor (Indonesia); 1999; (3)

UNTAET (UN Transitional Administration in East Timor); 1999-2002; (21)

MONUC (United Nations Organization Mission in the Democratic Republic of the Congo); Congo; 1999-present; (131)

UNMEE (United Nations Mission in Ethiopia and Eritrea), 2000-present; (20)

ONUB (United Nations Operation in Burundi); 2000-present; (24)

UNAMA (United Nations Assistance Mission in Afghanistan); 2002-present; (11)

UNMIL (United Nations Mission in Liberia); 2003-present; (119)

UNOCI (United Nations Operation in Côte d'Ivoire); 2004-present; (53)

MINUSTAH (United Nations Stabilization Mission in Haiti); 2005-present; (38)

UNMIS (United Nations Mission in Sudan); 2005-present; (40)

UNMIT (United Nations Integrated Mission in Timor Leste; 2006-present; (4)

UNAMID (African Union/United Nations Hybrid Operation in Darfur); 2006-present; (21)

MINURCAT (United Nations Mission in the Central African Republic and Chad); 2007-present.

Lit.: *James, A.:* Peacekeeping in International Politics, London 1990; *Paris, R.:* United Nations Peacekeeping after the Cold War, London 1991; *Rikhye, I.J./Skjaelsbaek, K. (eds.):* The United Nations Peacekeeping: Results, Limitations and Prospects, London 1990.

Internet: Homepage of the Department of Peacekeeping Operations of the UN Secretariat (with maps and detailed information about the ongoing missions: www.un.org/Depts/dpko/dpko).

Peacekeeping Forces

I. Definition/Mission

The Charter of the United Nations ($\rightarrow$ Charter of the UN) does not contain the term "peacekeeping forces", nor any similar term. Such forces have been developed from practical experience in the context of missions to maintain or restore peace. "UN peacekeeping forces" are mainly military formations or formed civilian police units or individuals (military and/or civilian police) serving under a mandate of the United Nations (UN), mostly in the framework of UN → peacekeeping operations.

In recent years a discussion has begun among scientists whether one should replace the term "peacekeeping forces" by "peace forces" to cover the political development from "classical" peacekeeping missions/operations mainly under Chapter VII of the UN Charter, with emphasis on the enforcement element of such undertakings.

Usually peacekeeping forces are made available by their nations, either individually as "military observers" (→ Observers) and/or "UN Police Officers", or in military formations – sometimes also in formed civil police units – as national contingents. In the area of operations these contingents or military observers operate jointly with similar elements from other countries as a multinational "peace-force", or "peacekeeping force". In addition to the military civilian police officers are deployed, in some areas even exclusively. (→ UNCIVPOL/ UNPOL)

Due to the light blue color of their headgear (helmets, berets, caps; always marked with the UN emblem) "UN peacekeeping forces" are often referred to as "Blue Helmets". On 10 December 1988 the "UN Blue Helmets" were collectively awarded the Nobel Peace Prize for their selfless dedication to world peace.

In 1945, when the UN Charter was signed (→ History of the Foundation of the UN), most of the 51 signatory states were still at war with one or more of the "enemy states" (cf. Arts. 53 and 107 UN Charter; → Enemy State Clauses) and still fielded considerable armed forces abroad. Such active duty military forces were meant to be made available for the central task of the new organization, the maintenance of international peace and security (Art. 1 UN Charter).

The Permanent Members of the → Security Council claimed for themselves the "strategic direction of any armed forces placed at the disposal of the Security Council. Questions relating to the command of such forces" were to "be worked out subsequently" (Art. 47 (3) UN Charter). However, such questions were not addressed, thus the issue of command and control of UN peacekeeping forces remains to be settled. The problem was addressed in detail in a report commissioned by UN Secretary-General Kofi Annan and submitted to the Security Council and the General Assembly on 20 October 2000. This comprehensive review by a panel of experts under Lakhdar Brahimi (Algeria) covers most aspects of peacekeeping operations (Report of the Panel on United Nations Peace Operations, 21 August 2000, UN Doc. A/55/305-S/2000/809; known as the "Brahimi Report").

The confrontational East-West conflict during the Cold War prevented the UN from implementing other objectives of the Charter concerning the deployment and eventual use of military force, e.g. the holding of "immediately available national air-force contingents for combined international enforcement action" (Art. 45 UN Charter).

Even the obligations of the member states (Art. 2 (2) and 2 (5) UN Charter) under Article 43 (1) UN Charter "to make available to the Security Council, on its call and in accordance with a special agreement or agreements, armed forces, assistance, and facilities ..." have not been made concrete and practical in form of agreements: the "special agreements" foreseen under Article 43 still wait to be concluded.

The Security Council therefore decided to delegate to "Regional Arrangements" or "Agencies," or to "Coalitions of the Willing" (Chapter VIII UN Charter), the authority to "take action by air, sea, or land forces as may be necessary to maintain and restore international peace and security. Such action may include demonstrations, blockade, and other operations by air, sea, or land forces of Members of the United Nations."(Art. 42 UN Charter)

Consequently UN Secretary-General Boutros Boutros-Ghali recommended to the Security Council in the second edition of his → "Agenda for Peace" (1995) that rapid reaction forces be made available on call within member states, to deter through their very existence any threat to the peace or aggression. In this area he also saw a role for the "Military Staff Committee", which has been generally unemployed since its creation in 1945 (Arts. 46 and 47 UN Charter; *Boutros-Ghali* 1995, 55f.).

In view of the widely accepted necessity to reform the Security Council (→ Reform of the UN) according to the fundamental changes which have affected the political situation in the world, of which the dramatic increase in the number of member states is the most visible (→ Membership and Representation of States), any attempt to give additional competence to the Permanent Members of the Security Council would meet with wide opposition. As the Military Staff Committee symbolizes the privileged position of the Permanent Members of the Council, it can hardly be activated in any form.

Secretary-General Kofi Annan therefore suggested in his reform report "In larger freedom" of March 2005 that all reference to this element be eliminated from the charter (*United Nations* 2005a, para. 219), a demand which was not followed by the member states at the world summit in September 2005; they requested in the "2005 World Summit Outcome" ambiguously "the Security Council to consider the composition, mandate and working methods of the Military Staff Committee (United Nations 2005b, para. 178).

II. Development of Peacekeeping Missions

Based upon Security Council Resolution 48 (1948) of 23 April 1948, establishing a truce commission for Palestine, the first nine military officers were deployed as unarmed "Military Observers" to Israel/Palestine in June 1948. This "UN Truce Supervision Organisation – UNTSO" has been considered the first

"UN Peacekeeping Operation". It has remained continuously in existence since its inception, though its structure and size have undergone changes. At present it consists of 142 Military Observers; its annual budget amounts to ca. 66 million US dollars. UNTSO has suffered 49 casualties. French Commandant René de Labarrière was the first military peacekeeper to be killed in action, while serving the UN in July 1948 in Jerusalem. Meanwhile more than 2,534 "Blue Helmets" lost their lives under the flag of the UN (as of November 2008).

In 1998 the "Dag Hammarskjöld Medal", newly created by the Security Council to mark the occasion of the 50th anniversary of UNTSO's inauguration, was presented to the Labarrière family. (A peculiar aspect of that medal is that it will only be given posthumously to the families of uniformed peacekeepers who were killed in action.)

The second peacekeeping operation, mandated in January 1949, was the "UN Military Observer Group in India and Pakistan – UNMOGIP". With its headquarters alternating every six months between Islamabad and Srinagar, this mission of 44 Military Observers has an annual budget of ca. 17 million US dollars, it has suffered 11 fatalities. It is still in existence, and still tasked to observe the volatile situation in Kashmir.

Of the more recent UN peacekeeping operations, one of the largest was the "UN Assistance Mission in Sierra Leone – UNAMSIL," established in 1998. Its authorized strength grew in various steps to 17,000 "Blue Helmets". Following its predecessor observer mission, UNOMSIL, which had only 90 military observers, civilian police and medical personnel, UNAMSIL had become the point of main effort for the UN in Africa. It was mainly the determined presence of UNAMSIL, which created the conditions under which this most outrageous civil war in Africa could be ended, allowing Sierra Leone to return to a state of peaceful stability. UNAMSIL was officially terminated in 2005 and had suffered 192 fatalities. Af-

533

ter less successful missions in Somalia (UNOSOM II), Rwanda (UNAMIR) and Angola (UNAVEM III) and successful deployments to Namibia (UNTAG), Mozambique (ONUMOZ) and Liberia (UNOMIL; 1993/1997), other peace-keeping operations in Africa are still in a questionable state, e.g. MINURSO (Western Sahara), ONUB (Burundi), UNMIL (Liberia; 2003-present), UNOCI (Côte d'Ivoire) and both missions in Sudan UNMIS and UNAMID.

After a hesitant start with an authori-zation of only 5.537 "Blue Helmets", MONUC (UN Mission in the Democ-ratic Republic of the Congo) has grown into the largest and most complex mis-sion in Africa. MONUC, with its pre-sent strength of more than 18,000 and a mandate, which allows for unusual ro-bustness, has been essential for the sta-bilization of the DRC after years of out-rageous civil war and armed interven-tion of many African states. Through MONUC's contribution not only the country-wide registration of voters suc-ceeded, but also the ensuing parliamen-tary and presidential elections were able to be conducted in an orderly fashion. Whether a promising degree of stability will be developing remains to be seen. But the presence of UN peacekeepers will certainly remain necessary for some time to come. The critical situation es-pecially within the DRC's eastern prov-inces will require the continued, robust international intervention.

Altogether the Security Council has so far mandated 63 peacekeeping opera-tions, in which almost one million "Blue Helmets" have been deployed (as of No-vember 2008). As there have been more than 200 armed conflicts globally, rang-ing in intensity from civil strife to all-out war, it becomes apparent that the Council is hesitant when it comes to the question of international intervention. The tendency of quite a number of member states to avoid precedent-setting interventions on the grounds of human rights violations (→ Human Rights, Protection of), adds to the re-stricted behavior of the Security Coun-cil.

The overall costs of more than sixty years of UN peacekeeping are estimated to amount to about 54 billion US dollars (as of November 2008). In comparison to the money spent annually by member states on defense, this is a modest amount; the US defense budget for the fiscal year 2008 amounts to far more than 500 billion US dollars.

III. Contribution of Peacekeeping Forces

As the UN does not possess any military forces of its own which are or can be made readily available for peacekeeping operations, the Organization depends entirely upon the willingness of member states to provide the necessary military means when the latter are required im-plementing a mandate of the Security Council.

Because of the most complex and time-consuming political decision-mak-ing processes, both within the Security Council and within the → General As-sembly, the Secretaries-General have repeatedly asked for the provision of a "Rapid Reaction Force" to prevent cri-ses from escalating into wars, and to contain armed conflicts before they spread across national boundaries (cf. *Boutros-Ghali* 1995, 18). The political will of member states necessary for the implementation of such an idea has only accepted the establishment of an ex-tremely small "headquarters" for a "Rapid Reaction Force," without pro-viding, however, more than symbolic budgetary resources for it.

The fact that the General Assembly considers and approves the → budget of the United Nations (Art. 17 UN Charter) has an immediate bearing upon the po-litical decisions of the Security Council concerning the establishment of peace-keeping operations and their eventual extension beyond the originally planned end-date. Even if the General Assembly follows the decisions of the Security Council, its participation inevitably leads to delays, if it does not in fact jeopardize the timely start-up of an op-eration and its proper implementation.

The UN Department of Peacekeeping Operations – DPKO has developed a concept for "Stand-by Forces", which meets both the conditions of "Special Agreements" as foreseen by Article 43 UN Charter and the general idea of "Rapid Reaction Forces". This "Stand-by Forces Concept" was therefore explicitly endorsed by the General Assembly on 10 December 1993 (cf. *Boutros-Ghali* 1995, 100f.) Following this concept member states inform the Secretary-General (DPKO) of such military formations, civil police or individuals, which they are willing to provide for UN peacekeeping operations. Details as to type, strength, structure of units, equipment and capabilities, levels of self-sustainment, requirements for air- and sea-lift, necessary warning time, professional and other specific topics to be considered, are to be stored in a "DPKO Stand-by Forces Database".

In bi-lateral negotiations between DPKO and the troop-contributing nations modalities of availability and claims for re-imbursement for contingent-owned equipment are being resolved. Finally, a "Stand-by Forces Agreement" will be signed as a document under international law.

It is generally understood that these agreements are "Letters of Intent". Most of the more than 80 member states (figures as of April 2005), as signatories to such agreements, reserve the right to decide on an actual deployment of their promised contribution only after having assessed the actual political conditions of a given conflict situation as well as the domestic legal situation.

Nevertheless, the "Stand-by Forces Database" considerably accelerates the planning process within DPKO for any future operation. It enabled for example DPKO to react very quickly to the request by the Security Council (SC Resolution 1159 (1998) of 27 March 1998), to deploy an authorized force of 1,350 into the Central African Republic. After only 19 days, UN Secretary-General Kofi Annan reported, that the "UN Mission in the Central African Republic – MINURCA", 1,200 persons strong, was ready for action in the capital of Bangui. The reaction required by General Staffs of the great powers could not have been faster. They expressed their respect for such a performance through the comparably very small DPKO.

Nevertheless the UN has been forced to realize, that considerable shortfalls in contingent-owned equipment and sustainability faced by some troop-contributing countries eventually endanger the proper performance of some missions. Therefore the General Assembly recommended that DPKO facilitate various arrangements to overcome such challenges (UN Doc. A/61/19 (Part II) of 5 June 2007).

A Stand-by High Readiness Brigade (SHIRBRIG) with its multinational planning staff in Denmark was formed as an instrument to overcome the complete lack of forces for ready deployment on the part of the UN. This multinational brigade, consisting of voluntary contributions from a number of member states (ca. 15 of which 12 are European) which have trained and exercised together to the same standards, using the same operating procedures and interoperable equipment. SHIRBRIG maintains a level of readiness for deployment in a UN peacekeeping operation with 15 to 30 days' notice. It can operate for six months and will hand over to follow-on UN forces.

SHIRBRIG first proved its readiness in November 2000 as the advance party for six months for the newly formed UNMEE. In 2003 SHIRBRIG provided the headquarters staff support to the establishment of UNMIL and assisted ECOWAS in the set-up of their UN-authorized operation in Côte d'Ivoire.

This concept appears most promising also for other regions, e.g. Africa (further information cf. *United Nations* 2007).

IV. Command and Control of UN Peacekeeping Operations

As the Security Council holds "primary responsibility for the maintenance of international peace and security" (Art. 24 (1) UN Charter), it also decides on the political direction of any peacekeeping operation, while the General Assembly approves the budget submitted to it by the Secretary-General, who is tasked with the translation of the Council's political guidance into active missions. For the direct command and control of all peacekeeping operations the Secretary-General until recently relied on his Department of Peacekeeping Operations – DPKO. Logistic, technical, and administrative support has consequently been the task of DPKO's "Office of Mission Support" (OMS).

Despite warnings from peacekeeping experts and from the "Special Committee on Peacekeeping Operations and its Working Group on the 2007 substantive sessions" the General Assembly (GA) followed the Secretary General's suggestion and in its resolution A/RES/61/279 of 26 June 2007 stated: [*The General Assembly...*] *"Decides* to establish the Department of Field Support; ..." (ibid., para. 10)

As this new department will have to shoulder the majority of those tasks, which were before covered by the OMS, the General Assembly's warning becomes very understandable, that it is important to preserve "... unity of command in missions at all levels as well as coherence in policy and strategy and clear command structures in the field and up to and including at Headquarters; ..." (ibid., para. 14).

The General Assembly further *"Requests* the Secretary General to ensure a clear chain of command, accountability, coordination and maintenance of an adequate system of checks and balances; ..." (ibid., para. 17) Additionally the General Assembly "... notes that the organizational structure of the Department of Peacekeeping Operations and the Department of Field Support may present some major management challenges; ..." (ibid., para. 22)

Therefore the General Assembly also *"Notes* the unique nature of the reporting line from the head of the Department of Field Support to the Under-Secretary-General for Peacekeeping Operations, and decides that having one

head of department (Department of Field Support) report to and take direction from another head of department (Department of Peacekeeping Operations) shall not set a precedence in the Secretariat; ..." (ibid., para. 26)

The consequences in the field with such lack of clarity related to accountability and reporting remain to be seen.

In the area of a peacekeeping operation either a politician or a diplomat will be entrusted with overall command authority and responsibility as "Special Representative of the Secretary General – SRSG". In some cases a military officer will be appointed as "Head of Mission", either as the "Force Commander – FC" or as "Chief Military Observer – CMO" (cf. *Boutros-Ghali* 1995, 16).

The authority of the Head of Mission may often be limited by restrictions which troop contributing nations – TCNs – may place upon the use of their contingents. Such reservations by TCNs can hamper the mission's freedom of action and endanger the proper implementation of the mandate. Thus the UN hardly ever has complete control over the forces placed at its disposal. Especially contingents from the "North" reserve the right to act only after approval of a specific UN mission is received from national authorities. If such national checks tend to lead to negative results, the burden within a peacekeeping operation may shift to contingents, which are less directly controlled from their capitals. In one case a national contingent had to be relieved from a certain task due to legal reservations concerning the use of military force, brought to bear directly by the government. Another contingent from another continent then took over from the first one, as the implementation of the task was essential for the mandate.

Such problems also stem from the lack of a universally agreed definition of command relations and leadership authority.

By contrast, it is globally understood, that disciplinary matters will remain a national prerogative. Despite the general responsibility of the UN for the activities of their peacekeeping forces vis-à-vis the parties to the conflict and indigenous authorities in the crisis area, the only measure open to the Head of Mission (SRSG or FC/CMO) through DPKO is the repatriation of individuals or whole units at the expense of their own governments.

V. Changes in the Mandates of Peace-keeping Missions

It has become common in the scientific and political debate to categorize peace missions as either "classic" or "complex/multi-functional".

"Classic" peace missions are based on the assumption of consent of both or all parties to a conflict to the mandate of a UN peacekeeping force. Such mandates require the "Blue Helmets" to follow the principles of "impartiality" and "limited use of force", which allow such use only in case of "self-defense". Traditionally UN peacekeeping forces have only been lightly armed as their missions have always been quite similar to that of civilian police. The mandates of "classic" peacekeeping operations have mostly followed the principles of "Pacific Settlement of Disputes" (Chapter VI UN Charter; → Peaceful Settlement of Disputes). Until 1988 almost all deployments of UN peacekeeping forces fell into this category.

The aggressive behavior of some parties to conflicts vis-à-vis UN peacekeeping forces, especially in internal, civil war-like crises have resulted in some fundamental changes. Mandates by the Security Council have since more often been oriented to the principles of enforcement actions as defined in Chapter VII UN Charter. Simultaneously the missions given to UN peacekeeping forces have become increasingly complex. They have been required to monitor armistices, and to organize and control disarmament, demilitarization and demobilization of former combatants, to protect → humanitarian assistance measures, to set up and implement mine-clearing actions, to organize and monitor democratic elections (→ Electoral Assistance), to provide support for the reconstruction of war-destroyed infrastructure and to train cadres for the restructuring or even the reconstruction of armed forces and/or civilian police.

Supporting the establishment of indigenous civilian police, based on the principles of the "Universal Declaration of Human Rights" (→ Human Rights, Universal Declaration of), is of increasing importance in war-torn societies. From 1996 to 2003 the "International Police Task Force – IPTF" in Bosnia-Herzegovina, with 2,027 civilian police officers from more than 50 nations, broke new ground. The IPTF mandate was to monitor, advise and train local and regional police of the institutionally separate Bosnian-Serb and Croat-Bosnian entities, and to support their efforts to restructure into a professional, politically neutral and ethnically unbiased law-enforcement system. As IPTF had no executive authority it was unarmed. The protection of IPTF in emergency situations was guaranteed by the military, at first through NATO's "Implementation Force – IFOR" and later its successor "Stabilization Force – SFOR".

As under-equipped UN peacekeeping forces, trained only for "classic" missions, met with hostilities in the course of their deployment, particularly in the former Yugoslavia (Srebrenica), Somalia and other African missions, some nations decided to better equip their contingents and thus not only provide them with better force protection, but also to prepare them better for the implementation of their complex multi-dimensional tasks. Firstly these missions require a "robust" mandate, usually under the provisions of Chapter VII UN Charter, thus authorizing the "use of all necessary means to implement the mandate". Thus the mission leadership should have more freedom of action, including the possible use of force. UN peacekeeping forces must be adequately trained and equipped for these robust missions.

From 1996 to 1998 the "UN Transitional Administration for Eastern Slavonia, Baranja, and Western Sirmium – UNTAES" set the scene for this new kind of peacekeeping operations: comprising several mechanized infantry battalions, each reinforced by a company of main battle tanks, additional tanks, artillery, mortars, combat helicopters and engineers, this 5,100 person strong formation had the "war fighting" capability to conduct "peacekeeping by deterrence". When it became clear that the situation in the UNTAES area of responsibility allowed for the careful de-escalation of its military capability a complete tank battalion was withdrawn and replaced by dismounted infantry and special police.

Whenever UN peacekeeping forces are capable of responding to worst-case scenarios, they can de-escalate visibly if the situation permits. The opposite case, reinforcing units in the course of an ongoing mission and thus escalating from the requirements and structures of a force which had been established based on the assumption of a benign environment to the capability of the unit to react adequately to conditions of hostility, is not possible. Thus in political terms, UN peacekeeping forces prepared for a Chapter VII mandate can readily be "downgraded" to a mandate under Chapter VI. By contrast, a force only trained and equipped for the peaceful settlement of a crisis cannot be "upgraded" for a mission escalating into an enforcement mission under Chapter VII UN Charter. This lesson was learned the hard way from the bitter experience the UN made in Somalia and the former Yugoslavia (Mogadishu; Srebreniça) (cf. *United Nations* 1999a and 1999b).

VII. Multinationality

Multinationality is a determining feature of international organizations. While regional organizations are confined by ethnic, religious, or geographical factors, multinationality under UN conditions is universal. If the UN is called upon for support, it is the whole world which comes to help, not just interested neighbors. UN peacekeeping forces are always multinationally composed. Therefore even small missions will consist of Blue Helmets from a dozen or so coun-

tries, though some of them may only send very few Military Observers or UN Police officers. In political terms, multi-nationality symbolizes strength, namely the combined political will of all troop-contributing nations to contain or to solve a conflict. In operational terms however, multinationality is a weakness.

Differing from an alliance, which may be based on identity of interests and often also on common values, and enjoying the advantages of an integrated command structure, multinational UN peacekeeping forces are often ill-prepared for co-operation with formations from foreign countries. Interoperability between quite heterogeneous contingents meets with many difficulties.

Though the UN will determine one of the six official UN languages as the command language of a mission, usually English, proficiency in that language can hardly be expected except from a few officers or junior ranks. In one peace mission three West African contingents serving in adjacent areas communicated in Mandingo, spoken by two of the three commanders, of whom one translated into English for the third.

Additional problems arise from the local language in the mission area. Despite the employment of numerous interpreters and translators manifold misunderstandings may cause a multitude of problems. If an interpreter in Bosnia was recognized as Croat or Muslim, he/she could hardly work within the Republica Srpska.

Multinationally composed UN Police can often only convey their findings towards the local police or the civilian population through local translators.

It happens that within a team of four military observers on post in the most remote of places not one speaks the language of another. This renders human communication as one of the great challenges of multinationality.

In July 2000 Secretary-General Kofi Annan requested that before deployment all UN peacekeeping forces must be educated in the principles of the "Universal Declaration of Human Rights":

This will include the necessary respect for the rights of women (→ Women and the UN; → Human Rights Conventions, CEDAW). Problems with armed children belong in the same context. Some parties in civil war scenarios have armed children of ages 10 to 14, introduced them to drugs and cruelly abused them. Due to their immaturity those children cannot be convinced to lay down their weapons and to come to reason, which is why it is so difficult to disarm them. The UN has therefore decreed that no soldiers under the age of 18 will be employed with UN peacekeeping forces (→ Human Rights Conventions, CRC). The minimum age for Military Observers, who do not serve in formed units but as individuals and are always unarmed, as for UN Police Officers, is 25.

Religious rules can have a considerable bearing upon the contingents from societies where religious adherence is strong. Apart from general respect, such religious rules may require special consideration in a number of areas e.g. food supply, provision of blood reserves for medical services, or daily duty routine with fixed times for prayer. Often military chaplains demand the right to inspect food before it may be cooked. Some contingents refuse food supplies from a country of another religion. Medical support, as difficult as it may already be under the linguistic constraints of a multinational mission, can be further exacerbated, if religious rules forbid using blood reserves from an unknown donor, who may not be of the "proper" faith.

Similarities of military rank structures and even of uniforms for both civilian police and the military may lead to the misperception that training standards and professionalism are also comparable. The assumption, that a "Captain" is a "Captain" requires some testing before a determined degree of responsibility can be given to a certain "Blue Helmet."

National principles for leadership, inclusive of the treatment of junior ranks by their superiors, may differ widely. Delegation of authority to lower ranks is rarely known among armed forces which base their system of functionality solely upon rigid obedience. Initiatives taken or suggested by junior ranks can under such circumstances easily be misunderstood as lack of discipline, and thus cause disciplinary problems. Any form of co-operation with civilians is unknown to many military, and vice versa.

While interoperability between different sets of technical appliances can be facilitated through the use of adapters or "black boxes", compatibility among human beings is often difficult.

The underlying cause for many such difficulties is differing sets of values, out of which develop different codes of conduct and varying disciplinary standards.

Despite the unifying effect of the common objective in a UN peacekeeping operation under a mandate from the Security Council, "Blue Helmets" show particular pride for their national heritage. Many contingents come from young nations, who have only relatively recently gained independence and therefore tend to stress their uniqueness, instead of focusing on the unifying commonalties in a UN peacekeeping force.

Contingents who were seen off to the mission personally by their head of state will usually be highly motivated throughout the term of their deployment. Such factors have to be considered if problems with the attitude of some contingents arise during the mandate, especially when the views of the UN leadership and those of national contingent commanders may differ.

A very high degree of mutual tolerance is the indispensable prerequisite for successful multinationality. Without it, internal frictions within the UN peacekeeping force can lead to failure and even result in fatalities, as has happened in Somalia.

Social problems, often marked by great differences in incomes, between the UN peacekeeping force on the one hand, and the local population on the other, as well as among contingents from rich and poor countries, require fine-tuning on the part of the UN peace-keeping force. Though all troop-contributing nations are reimbursed an amount of ca. 1,000 US dollars per "Blue Helmet" per month from the "Peacekeeping Support Account", some will pay their military only a small portion of that, while the payment of other contingents may even exceed that sum. Of course the personal risks for the "Blue Helmets" are equal, irrespective of their income.

In spite of such differences the UN must ensure that their peacekeeping forces follow the same principles. Apart from the "Code of Conduct" for "Blue Helmets", which each of them receives as a pocket card (hopefully in his or her native language, otherwise in the command language of the mission), UN peacekeeping forces ore obliged to obey the Rules of Engagement – ROE. These ROE will be decided upon by the Secretary-General through DPKO after consultation with the SRSG and FC/CMO; they will take into account most specific conditions anticipated for the mission. Generally the ROE grant a considerable amount of freedom of action to the leadership of a mission, i.e. the SRSG/FC/CMO. In no instance have these UN authorities been accused of excessive use of their liberties.

As most military officers serving under the UN flag are accustomed to be kept on a tight rein by their national authorities, they find it difficult to make up their own minds independently within the framework of a UN mission. The loyalty of UN peacekeeping forces remains a latent problem. Situations can develop where obligations towards the own nation, and the challenges under the UN flag may be controversial. The situation of "Blue Helmets" in Rwanda in 1994 may illustrate such a situation, when some contingents could not believe that the Security Council or their national government had actually ordered their withdrawal, forcing them to abandon those who urgently needed protection for their very survival.

UN peacekeeping forces do not fight wars; they know no "enemies". "Blue Helmets" are to keep the peace, or – if need be – enforce it, but they are no "warriors". They do not fight shoulder-to-shoulder, but they work together as friends on a mission. Such conditions facilitate their task. Differences between UN peacekeeping force contingents, which might perhaps even lead to losses in a war, can be handled more easily in a spirit of friendship and mutual support. As the relatively small number of "Blue Helmets" will be thinly spread over often vast territories, such as Angola, Congo, Somalia or Sudan, units enjoy contacts with neighboring formations, rather than encountering problems arising from congestion.

The common objective, to maintain or restore peace in their area of responsibility leads to a feeling of togetherness that will overcome all divisive differences. Thus many "Blue Helmets" return to their home countries with the conviction that they served a just cause. Many of them remain convinced that the principles of → human rights and the fundamental rule of law and democracy, which they supported abroad as peacekeepers, are also worth additional efforts at home.

Manfred Eisele

Lit.: *1. UN Documents: Boutros-Ghali, B.:* An Agenda for Peace. Second Edition, New York 1995; *United Nations:* Report of the Independent Inquiry into the Actions of the United Nations During the 1994 Genocide in Rwanda, UN Doc. S/1999/1257, 15 December 1999 (quoted as United Nations 1999a); *United Nations:* Report of the Secretary-General pursuant to General Assembly Resolution 53/35, The Fall of Srebrenica, UN Doc. A/54/549, 15 November 1999 (quoted as United Nations 1999b); *United Nations:* Report of the Panel on United Nations Peace Operations, UN Doc. A/55/305-S/2000/809, 21 August 2000; *United Nations:* Handbook on United Nations Multidimensional Peacekeeping Operations, Peacekeeping Best Practices Section, Department of Peacekeeping Operations; December 2003; *United Nations:* In larger freedom: towards development, security and human rights for all. Report of the Secretary-General, 21 March 2005, UN Doc. A/59/2005 (quoted as United Nations 2005a); *United Nations:* 2005

World Summit Outcome. Resolution adopted by the General Assembly, 16 September 2005, UN Doc. A/RES/60/1 (quoted as United Nations 2005b); *United Nations:* United Nations Peace Operations: Year in Review 2006, New York 2007 (quoted as United Nations 2007. *2. Secondary Literature: Biermann, W./Vadset, M.:* UN Peacekeeping in Trouble: Lesson Learned from the Former Yugoslavia, Abingdon 1998; *Covey, J. et al. (eds.):* The Quest for Viable Peace. International Intervention and Strategies for Conflict Transformation, Washington 2005; *Eisele, M.:* Die Vereinten Nationen und das internationale Krisenmanagement, Frankfurt (Main) 2000; *Eisele, M.:* Friedenssicherung, in: Volger, H. (ed.): Grundlagen und Strukturen der Vereinten Nationen, Munich/Vienna 2007, 131-161; *Goulding, M.:* The evolution of United Nations peacekeeping, in: International Affairs 69 (1993), 451-464; *Hüfner, K.:* Die Vereinten Nationen und ihre Sonderorganisationen. Teil 3 A: Vereinte Nationen – Friedensoperationen – Spezialorgane, Bonn 1997; *James, A.:* Peacekeeping in the post-Cold War era, in: I J, Vol. L (1995), 241-265; *Jett, D.C.:* Why Peacekeeping Fails, Houndmills/London 2000; *Lehmann, I.:* Peacekeeping and Public Information, London 1999; *Ratner, S.:* The New UN Peacekeeping, New York 1995; *Rudolph, K.:* Peace-Keeping Forces, in: Wolfrum, R. (ed.): United Nations: Law, Policies and Practice, Vol. 2, Munich/Dordrecht 1995, 957-969; *Unser, G.:* Die UNO. Aufgaben und Strukturen der Vereinten Nationen, 6th rev. and expanded edn., Munich 1997; *Volger, H.:* Geschichte der Vereinten Nationen, 2nd rev. and enlarged edn., Munich 2008.

Internet: Homepage of the Department of Peacekeeping Operations (DPKO) of the UN Secretariat (with maps and information on the completed and ongoing peacekeeping missions): www.un.org/Depts/dpko/dpko.

Peacekeeping Operations

I. Purposes of Peacekeeping Operations

Peacekeeping operations (PKO), also called peace operations or peace support operations (PSO), are among the best-known and most important activities of the United Nations. From their characteristic blue headgear they are also known as "blue helmets" or "blue berets" type operations. These include

- the deployment of lightly armed → peacekeeping forces and/or military observers (→ observers) to supervise armistice agreements and de-militarized "buffer zones," in conflicts between states or consolidated entities ("traditional peacekeeping"), and
- the deployment of military forces, military observers, and/or police (→ UNCIVPOL) and other civilian observers and experts to supervise and carry out elections, to administer a territory (e.g. of a former colony on its way to independence), to assist in the resettlement of refugees, to establish a stable administration and a democratic police force, especially in or after such internal conflicts as civil wars, ethnic conflicts, etc. ("wider peacekeeping").
- A third category ("robust operations" or "peace-enforcement") goes beyond peacekeeping, but is usually still counted among the three forms of peace (support) operations.

These three groups are sometimes referred to as "three generations" of peacekeeping. This is incorrect, however, as all three types evolved parallel, and are still important.

In the past decade, additional terms like "Crisis Response Operations" (CRO) or "Peace and Stability Operations" were often used. These usually include peacekeeping missions, but also humanitarian and combat operations which clearly go beyond peacekeeping (cf. *Durch* 2007, 19).

The same applies to the term "Petersberg Missions" (referring to the WEU's ministers' council on the Petersberg near Bonn, on 19 June 1992), which include peacekeeping among the various tasks listed. The "Petersberg missions" were included in the EU's Amsterdam Treaty of 1997.

Peacekeeping operations are often seen as an invention of the UN. This is untrue, however: multinational peace missions gradually developed in the 19th and early 20th century, and to this day a number of important peace operations are undertaken outside the → UN

541

system (with or without a mandate of the UN Security Council).

II. Recent Developments in Peacekeeping Operations

Until 1989 the majority of UN missions dealt with conflicts between states, especially in the Middle East. While these missions (and the crises which led to their deployment in the first place) still continue, after the end of the Cold War a number of internal conflicts erupted which led to a new type of UN peacekeeping operations. Immediately after 1989, the hope for a new and extended role for the UN system to preserve the peace (→ Agenda for Peace of UN Secretary-General Boutros-Ghali 1992) led to a drastic increase in the number of missions, and of personnel deployed: from some 10,000 "blue helmets" before 1989 to 80,000 in 1993-94 with new missions in Cambodia, Somalia, and the former Yugoslavia. This presented the UN with new financial and logistic problems.

These quantitative problems were exacerbated by accompanying qualitative aspects of multi-dimensional peacekeeping operations in internal conflicts, which are more complex and more difficult to administer than the traditional, military-only missions. Also, police and civilian personnel are available in limited numbers only. Communication problems between the different components make unified command more difficult to achieve, especially as often hundreds of → NGOs are involved as well. After the mid-1990s, the number of UN personnel in peacekeeping operations was reduced to 12,000 in 1999, and has since grown again to over 45,000 in late 2001 and to almost 108,000 in 2008. By August 2008, there were 16 UN peacekeeping operations worldwide, totaling 107,876 personnel, of whom 82,230 were military and police, coming from 119 countries. The approved budget for these missions for the period from 1 July 2008 to 30 June 2009 amounts to about 7.3 billion US dollars (figures as of 1 May 2009: note by the Secretary-General on the financing of the peacekeeping operations, UN Doc. A/C.5/63/23).

There have been 66 UN peacekeeping operations since 1948, of which 16 are operational at the time of writing (autumn 2008).

Larger UN operations in 2008 included MONUC (since 1999, in the Democratic Republic of the Congo) with 18,389 uniformed personnel, UNMIL (in Liberia, since 2003) with 12,736 uniformed personnel, and UNIFIL (in Lebanon since 1978, but enlarged in 2006) with 12,295 military troops and observers. The missions in Sudan's Darfur province, in southern Sudan, in Côte d'Ivoire and in Haiti each number around 10,000 peacekeepers.

III. Legal and Political Basis of Peacekeeping Operations

The term "peacekeeping" is not contained in the → Charter of the UN (while the French term "maintien de la paix" is), but the authority for the UN to become involved is obvious from the UN's responsibility for the "maintenance of international peace and security" in general (Preamble, Articles 1 (1), 24, and 26 of the UN Charter). Peacekeeping operations were interpreted as falling between the Charter's Chapters VI (Pacific Settlement of Disputes) and VII (Action with Respect to Threats to the Peace, Breaches of the Peace, and Acts of Aggression), and were therefore often referred to as "Chapter VI ½" activities. In recent years, many operations have been established on the basis of Chapter VII, however.

Generally, peacekeeping operations are mandated by the → Security Council (in some cases by the → General Assembly, → Uniting for Peace Resolution), and are led by the → Secretary General. Troop-contributing countries as well as the host countries are also consulted. Each mission is different, but commonly the use of force only in self-defense and the consent of the host country to the operation are interpreted as necessary conditions for peacekeeping operations. Because "blue helmets" have police-like tasks and are highly "visible" like police, the term "police operations" was occasionally used as well.

The success of a peacekeeping operation depends on the conditions in the theatre, and on the political will of all involved, including the parties to the conflict as well as the troop-contributors and the hegemonic powers. The mandate of the mission, its interpretation by the head of mission (usually the Special Representative of the Secretary-General) and/or the Force Commander, and the – often exaggerated – expectations of the public (both in the field and at home) play an important role. The attempt to copy a successful mission – like the UN Disengagement Observer Force on the Golan Heights (UNDOF), between Syria and Israel, since 1974 – under different circumstances – as in the case of the UN Interim Force in Southern Lebanon (UNIFIL) since 1978 – is usually an invitation for failure.

So far, so-called "robust" peace operations undertaken by the UN, i.e. missions authorized under Chapter VII of the UN Charter to use armed force to achieve their goals, in the terminology of Boutros-Ghali's → "Agenda for Peace" called "peace enforcement", occasionally also known as "Chapter VI ¾" or (more recently) as "Chapter VII" activities, have been less than successful. As a complex organization, the UN lacks the necessary command-and-control mechanisms to direct complex more military operations and combat missions. Missions like the early Congo operation (ONUC, 1960-64) or the later ones in Somalia (UNOSOM I and II, 1991-95) were usually seen as failures which – even though not completely true – damaged the world organization's reputation. More robust operations are therefore usually organized – albeit with UN authorization – by state coalitions acting independently, as in the cases of the allied forces fighting in Korea (1950-53), against Iraq (1991), against the terrorist threat (2001) and in the case of the International Security Assistance Force in Afghanistan (since 2002).

IV. Reform Proposals

In a attempt to learn from the difficulties the peacekeeping operations encountered in the 1990s with regard to the often imprecise content of the mandate, complex command structures, technically unreliable communication between New York and the mission place, inadequate financing, and rather long time needed for deployment, a panel of experts under the Algerian diplomat Lakhdar Brahimi, commissioned by UN Secretary-General Kofi Annan, elaborated a report on peacekeeping operations which was submitted to the Security Council and the General Assembly on 21 August 2000 (UN Doc. A/55/305-S/2000/809). The Security Council as well as the General Assembly have expressed their appreciation for the reform proposals of the "Brahimi Report" as it is called, and some recommendations have been implemented: for example, the deployment time has been reduced, the command structures have been clarified, the financing has been improved, and DPKO has been granted additional posts (cf. *Durch et al.* 2003, 101-108).

Moreover, as recommended by the Brahimi Report, DPKO began using integrated mission task teams to plan peacekeeping operations, the teams consisting of military and police planners from DPKO and representatives of all UN humanitarian and development agencies involved.

The difficult coordination problems of the increasing number of multi-dimensional peace operations motivated the involved departments in the UN secretariat to search in recent years for a far-reaching reform of the joint mission planning. In January 2004, the DPKO Heads of Mission Conference issued a paper on "Integrated Mission Planning Process" (UN Doc. DPKO/HMC/2004/12, 23 January 2004), attempting to clarify the role of DPKO and its relationship with the other departments and stakeholders in the planning process. In May 2005, an expert group, commissioned by the Expanded Core Group of the UN Executive Committee on Humanitarian Affairs (ECHA), presented its "Report on Integrated Missions: Practical Perspectives and Recommendations" (*Eide et al.* 2005). On the basis of this preparatory work the UN Secretary-General approved in June 2006 guidelines for the "Integrated Missions Planning Process (IMPP)" (*United Nations* 2006).

While the guidelines brought more clarity with regard to the lines of command, duties and responsibilities of the different actors in a mission, critics still complained of a lack of system-wide "strategic culture", and of a shared vision among all UN actors as to the strategic objective of the UN missions (*Gowan* 2008a, 453). In an effort to fill this strategic gap, the UN Department of Peacekeeping Operations and the recently established Department of Field Support issued in March 2008 a basic document for this purpose, the "United Nations Peacekeeping Operations – Principles and Guidelines" (*United Nations* 2008). As the two UN departments stipulate in the introduction, this document "sits at the highest level of the current doctrine framework for United Nations peacekeeping. Any subordinate directives, guidelines ... should confirm to the principles and concepts referred to in this guidance document." (ibid., 9) Referring to this overarching, top position among the UN peacekeeping doctrines the 2008 guidelines have also been called the "capstone doctrine", for example in the discussions of a seminar with the title "UN Peacekeeping Operations Capstone Doctrine" in May 2008 in Oslo on the practical implications of the 2008 guidelines (*Coning et al.* 2008), a seminar organized by DPKO and peacekeeping researchers, or in the report of the Norwegian government on "Implementing United Nations Multidimensional and Integrated Peace Operations" (*Norwegian Ministry of Foreign Affairs* 2008).

The 2008 guidelines attempt to bring some orientation into the conceptual debate underlying the debates on peacekeeping operations by offering a common understanding of UN peacekeeping

(cf. *Coning* 2008, 6). To what extent it will be helpful to serve as guidance for peacekeeping missions remains to be seen.

Erwin A. Schmidl

Lit.: *Annan, K.A.:* Peace Operations and the United Nations: Preparing for the Next Century, New York 1996; *Bellamy, C.:* Knights in White Armour; London 1996; *Chopra, J. (ed.):* The Politics of Peace-Maintenance, Boulder et al. 1998; *Collins, C./Weiss, T.G.:* An Overview and Assessment of 1989-1996 Peace Operations Publications (Occasional Papers No. 28), Providence 1996; *Coning, C. de/Detzel, J./Hojem, P.:* UN Peacekeeping Operations Capstone Doctrine. Report of the TfP Oslo Doctrine Seminar, 14-15 May 2008 (Norwegian Institute of International Affairs – Report), Oslo 2008; *Durch, W.J. (ed.):* The Evolution of UN Peacekeeping, New York 1993; *Durch, W.J./Holt, V.K. et al.:* The Brahimi Report and the Future of UN Peace Operations, Washington 2003; *Durch, W.J. (ed.):* Twenty-First-Century Peace Operations, Washington 2006; *Eide, E.B. et al.:* Report on Integrated Missions: Practical Perspectives and Recommendations. Independent Study for the Expanded UN ECHA Core Group, May 2005, New York 2005, http://ochaonline.un.org; *Gowan, R.:* The Strategic Context: Peacekeeping in Crisis, 2006-08, in: International Peacekeeping 15 (2008), 453-469 (quoted as: Gowan 2008a); *Gowan, R.:* UN Peace Operations: Operational Expansion and Political Fragmentation? In: Fischer, M./Rittberger, V. (eds.): Strategies for Peace: Contributions of International Organizations, States and Non-State Actors, Opladen 2008, 109-130; *Kühne, W. (ed.):* Winning the Peace: Concept and Lessons Learned of Post-Conflict Peacebuilding, Ebenhausen 1996; *Norwegian Ministry of Foreign Affairs:* Implementing United Nations Multidimensional and Integrated Peace Operations. A report on findings and recommendations, Oslo May 2008; *Ramsbotham, O./ Woodhouse, T.:* Encyclopedia of International Peacekeeping Operations, Santa Barbara 1999; *Schmidl, E.A./Wimmer, J.:* Friedenserhaltende Operationen, Wien 1998; *Thakur, R./Schnabel, A. (eds.):* United Nations Peacekeeping Operations: Ad Hoc Missions, Permanent Engagement, Washington 2002; *United Nations - Department of Peacekeeping Operations:* Multidisciplinary Peacekeeping: Lessons From Recent Experience, New York 1999; *United Nations:* Report of the Panel on

United Nations Peace Operations, UN Doc. A/55/305-S/2000/809, 21 August 2000; *United Nations - Department of Peacekeeping Operations - 2004 Heads of Mission Conference:* Integrated Mission Planning Process, 23 January 2004, UN Doc. DPKO/ HMC/2004/12; *United Nations:* Integrated Missions Planning Process (IMPP). Guidelines Endorsed by the Secretary-General on 13 June 2006, www.undg.org/docs/8481/ IMPP.pdf; *United Nations - Department of Peacekeeping Operations:* United Nations Peacekeeping Operations: Principles and Guidelines, New York 2008, www.un.org/ Depts/dpko/dpko/selectedPSDG/ index.html; *Williams, P.D./Bellamy, A.J.:* Contemporary Peace Operations: Four Challenges for the Brahimi Paradigm, in: Langholtz, H. et al. (eds.): International Peacekeeping. The Yearbook of International Peace Operations, Vol. 11 (2006), Leiden/Boston 2007, 1-28.

Internet: Homepage of United Nations Headquarters, Department of Peacekeeping Operations: www.un.org/Depts/dpko/dpko.

Permanent Missions

The history of diplomatic representations of states at international organizations dates back to the → League of Nations. At the League, as well as in the early days of the UN, states were represented by diplomatic delegations sent on an ad hoc basis (→ Membership and Representation of States). But the demand for permanent missions increased because of the necessity to participate continuously in the political process and the decision-making of the UN. The → Security Council required the permanent presence not only of the five permanent members, but also of the ten non-permanent members and their staff for the duration of their term, i.e. two years (Art. 23 (2) UN Charter). Also, in times of crisis, it has proved to be useful for member states to have permanent representatives at the UN who could immediately inform their governments of the latest developments and decision-processes. So the General Assembly affirmed explicitly in its resolution A/RES/ 257 A (III) of 3 December 1948 "the practice ... of establishing, at the seat of the Organization, permanent missions of

Member States" and established certain rules for their appointment and accreditation.

Today, the majority of member states have permanent missions in New York, Geneva, and Vienna, though smaller states often tend to appoint the ambassadors of their foreign representations simultaneously as permanent representatives to the UN.

Twice a year the UN Secretariat publishes in printed form and in the Internet a list of all permanent missions to the United Nations at its headquarters in New York in the UN Document Series ST/SG/SER.A. The permanent missions are listed with their addresses, telephone and telefax numbers, e-mail addresses, language of correspondence as well as the names, diplomatic ranks, etc. of all members of their diplomatic personnel. The publication can be accessed in the Internet under: http://missions.un.int/ protocol/bluebook.html.

I. Organizational Structure

The head of a permanent mission is the "Permanent Representative of the Mission to the UN". The staff of the permanent mission is composed of foreign service and administration personnel (the USA additionally have a section for → peacekeeping). The size of the permanent missions varies greatly: while the US mission has a staff of 36 (*Finger* 1992, 13), smaller states sometimes have to make do with less than half of that number (for example, Ukraine has 13 staff members, Antigua and Barbuda has 7). Generally speaking, one can observe an increase in the number of employees of many states' permanent missions due to the increasing number of conferences and committees (→ Committees, System of) dedicated to the subjects of economic development and → decolonization. During the session periods of the → General Assembly and other principal organs (→ Principal Organs, Subsidiary Organs, Treaty Bodies), the permanent missions are reinforced by special delegations. The delegations for the General Assembly are formed by the members of the permanent mission, together with the special delegations and other members of the foreign service of the member state.

II. Legal Status

The permanent missions enjoy an independent status. However, their rights have not, until the present day, been formally established in the UN Charter and UN treaties. The UN Charter (→ Charter of the UN) contains only very few legal statements regarding the representation of the member states: Article 28 (1) states that "The Security Council shall be so organized as to be able to function continuously. Each member of the Security Council shall for this purpose be represented at all times at the seat of the Organization." Regarding the status of the members of the permanent missions, Article 105 (2) provides that: "Representatives of the Members of the United Nations … shall … enjoy such privileges and immunities as are necessary for the independent exercise of their functions in connection with the Organization."

Further basic principles are contained in the *Convention on Privileges and Immunities of the United Nations – CPIUN* – of 13 February 1946 (UNTS Vol. 1, No. 4, 15), to which most UN member states are party. This includes the UN host states United States, Austria and Germany, but not the UN host state Switzerland, which is not a party to the Convention. Instead, Switzerland grants privileges and immunities in accordance with the *Interim Agreement on Privileges and Immunities of the United Nations concluded between the Secretary-General of the United Nations and the Swiss Federal Council* of 11 June-1 July 1946 (UNTS Vol. 1, No. 8). Nonetheless, the almost universal validity of CPIUN adds credibility to the view among international law experts that the Convention is binding even to non-states parties such as Switzerland. However, the Convention only enumerates regulations for the states delegations, not for the permanent missions (*Dembinski* 1988, 49), so that in the end, it is the host state agreements which form the legal bases

for the status of the permanent missions. As a consequence, the privileges of the member states' representatives vary according to the rights granted by the respective host state (→ Host State Agreements). The host state can limit the privileges and immunities strictly along the lines of functional criteria, such as granting diplomats freedom of movement only for the exercise of their official tasks, and regularizing private journeys. In the case of the host state USA, restrictions like these have repeatedly led to tensions with the permanent missions of the East European states during the Cold War (cf. for example the Report of the Committee on Relations with the Host Country, 20 November 1986, UN Doc. A/41/26 (SUPP), 5-7).

There are efforts made in international law to codify the immunities and privileges of the permanent missions, and to grant the representations rights coming near to diplomatic privileges and immunities (*Schütz* 1991, 778). One such attempt is the *Vienna Convention on the Representation of States in their Relations with International Organizations of a Universal Character* of 1975 (UN Doc. A/CONF.67/16, 14 March 1975; reprinted in: *AJIL* 69 (1975), 730-759). Above all, the convention contains the rights of freedom of communication, diplomatic immunity, and freedom of movement for the permanent missions. However, as of 30 December 2008, only 34 states have acceded to the Vienna Convention, among them none of the host states.

III. Functions of the Permanent Missions

1. Collection and Transmission of Information

One focus of the activity of a diplomat working at a permanent mission is the cultivation of contacts and the gathering of information. Permanent representatives have the opportunity to acquire information in the fastest of possible ways, be it through formal channels (meetings, publications, the internet, etc.) or informally, in conversations with ambassadors, representatives of governments, staff members of the → Secretariat etc. Between the sessions of the General Assembly, the permanent representatives maintain continuous contacts with the representatives of other states. Secretary-General Hammarskjöld saw a great value in these mutual contacts of the ambassadors: "Over the years the diplomatic representatives accredited to the United Nations have developed a co-operation and built mutual contacts ... which in reality makes them members of a kind of continuous diplomatic conference, in which they are informally following and able to discuss, on a personal basis, all political questions that are important for the work of the Organization." (*Hammarskjöld*, 2 May 1959, UN Press Release SG/812, quoted after: *Bailey/ Daws* 1998, 167). The exchange of information helps the permanent representatives to receive information from other missions about their respective policies, to test reactions to the policy of their own government, but also to gain important information about UN activities and tendencies through the contact with the → Secretary-General and the Secretariat (*Lindemann* 1973, 244). Many permanent representatives therefore maintain close relations with the Secretary-General and his most important collaborators. Contrary to the provisions of Article 100 of the Charter, which states that the UN staff "shall not seek or receive instructions" from the governments of member states, many staff members of the Secretariat regularly brief their national representation about Secretariat affairs. This close cooperation of Secretariat members with the permanent missions exerts a political influence on the work of the Secretariat, the result being that reports, for example, often tend to acquire a political flavor consistent with the states' interests (*Lindemann* 1973, 266).

For the Secretary-General of the UN, the permanent missions are one of the most important sources of information regarding the position of the countries on individual political issues and poten-

tial crises. The information received allows him to plan the respective actions of the Secretariat, by talking to the representatives about his plans before concrete measures are elaborated. The Secretary-General's close cooperation with those permanent representatives which have a special interest in a particular project, such as mediation in a political conflict, often results in the formation, on an informal level, of a group of diplomats who call themselves "Friends of the Secretary-General for ...," and support him in the execution of his plan, e.g. by introducing it in the General Assembly or the Security Council and by influencing the decision-making process (→ Groups and Groupings in the UN).

2. Implementation of Government Policies in Multilateral Negotiations

Permanent representatives have a political function which they practice in a multitude of ways. Principally, the members of permanent missions have the task of advising their governments in establishing their national UN policies, and in making recommendations. To what extent the opinions of the permanent mission are taken into consideration by the government in its political decisions depends on their respective influence, and their position in relation to the government representatives. The influence of a permanent mission on its national government is strongest in periods in which a certain subject is being negotiated within the context of the UN. During the negotiation phase, the permanent representatives have the most in-depth knowledge of the available data and the different standpoints of the others involved. Even before the governments reach a decision on a certain matter, a permanent representative can make recommendations as to how the decisions could be modified in order to better accomplish the intended objectives (*Finger* 1992, 23; *Pedersen* 1961, 258f.). Usually, the permanent representatives' freedom of action is limited, as they are bound by instructions. Most governments supply their permanent representatives with guidelines for their conduct in order to prevent the representatives from making decisions on their own authority. This obligation to follow instructions can be a disadvantage in circumstances when a decision on a certain situation has to be reached quickly and a government reacts too late (e.g. when communication fails or is delayed for technical reasons). The problem of being subject to instructions lies in the fact that politics and decision-making between state representatives in the UN is a dynamic process, while a government's initial directives cannot take into account the changes of a situation that might occur during the negotiations in a given organ: "In sum, the formulation of policy cannot be considered as at an end when the delegation is instructed and sent to the conference or meeting. There are inevitable changes and readjustments that occur during all the stages of implementation." (*Hyde* 1956, 28). There have been many occasions where initiatives were not implemented or votes were lost due to the fact that a permanent representative was unable to obtain his government's opinion regarding a changed situation in a UN organ (*Lindemann* 1973, 242). In spite of the fact that permanent representatives are often subject to strict instructions from their government, the diplomats nonetheless have sufficient room to manœuvre in the negotiations about standpoints in the UN. In the work in the meetings and assemblies, good tactical cooperation within the group of permanent representatives is necessary, especially within the → regional groups. Success depends upon the personal commitment of the individual representatives and their ability to build majorities. At the same time, they play an important role in UN personnel decisions (→ Personnel), as they are involved in the composition of organs through elections in the General Assembly, the → Economic and Social Council, etc.

3. Influencing the Programme and Personnel Policies of the UN

Having access to the UN Secretariat and the UN Development Programme (→ UNDP) is of great interest to many governments. Many countries, through their permanent missions, seek technical or financial aid from the organization or take advantage of programmes of UN organs, especially in development-related affairs (→ Development Cooperation of the UN System). At the same time, the permanent representatives exert influence on the formulation and implementation of UN programmes, actions and decisions.

The member states are represented in various bodies, such as the General Assembly, the Security Council, the Economic and Social Council (→ ECOSOC), and other UN organs and committees. The larger permanent missions are able to send to the bodies diplomats who have the relevant expert knowledge, while smaller countries tend to have a smaller staff, which consequently has to negotiate questions from the most differing subject areas, sometimes without having the relevant in-depth expert knowledge.

In order to help the new members of permanent missions to gain a better understanding of the services performed by the UN Secretariat and of the negotiation processes and techniques within the UN context, the UN Institute for Training and Research (→ UNITAR) offers orientation courses in New York and Geneva for members of permanent missions.

4. The Permanent Representatives as Quasi-Parliamentarians

Within the → UN system, the permanent representatives practice the functions of a "parliamentary diplomacy", as it is they who negotiate political decisions in the organs and bodies of the UN. The permanent representatives move in a framework of "quasi-parliamentary" processes: discussions, negotiations and voting procedures (→ Voting Right and Decision-Making Procedures). They know each other personally and are often able to come to agreements about the posture they will assume, before the voting takes place in the bodies. It is very common, for example, for the permanent representatives to come to an agreement, prior to a vote, about how their own standpoints – and thus, those of the respective governments – need to be modified in order to reach consensus with the other permanent representatives. The permanent collaboration in thousands of sessions every year (in the UN offices in Geneva alone, more than 8,400 meetings take place each year (*UNITAR* 1998)), as well as the structure of UN decision-making processes, make it necessary to resort to various tactics which are employed in parliamentary diplomacy, such as consensus- and group building. Appropriate timing is also an important tactical instrument. The correct point in time can be a decisive factor in whether a draft resolution passes or not. Conversely, votes can be delayed or stopped entirely by bringing in procedural motions (*Lindemann* 1073, 243).

In this area, diplomats have a certain margin for tactical manœuvring when carrying out their respective government's guidelines and instructions.

5. Opinion Building by the Permanent Representatives of States

Permanent representatives at the UN also have an opinion-building and an image-building function, which they can exercise toward the UN staff as well as toward the representatives of other states and the world public. Richard Petersen, a member of the United States Permanent Mission to the UN for more than 15 years, used to recommend to his colleagues to always dedicate a significant portion of their daily planning to the question of how the UN could most effectively be utilized to convince the world of the policies of one's government (*Finger* 1992, 21). In the public sessions of the General Assembly, the permanent representatives have the opportunity to canvass for their governments' interests and to try to convince the presidents, foreign secretaries, and other state representatives who are present at the opening of the general debate in September of every year. These assemblies also offer the possibility to use the media to gain sympathy for the states, or to clarify one's position regarding the debate on certain subjects in the UN. But in order to be sure of the media's attention, the permanent representatives need to act according to tactical considerations. For example, in order to guarantee the presence of a large number of media representatives, it is of advantage to hold a speech in the General Assembly or the Security Council shortly before noon.

IV. Résumé

Permanent missions play an important role in the formation of the national UN policies, and make possible the functioning of the UN system in practice. It is the permanent missions which connect the organization with its now 192 member states; it is through them that information is transmitted, interests are introduced, and contacts are established, and all this in a multilateral manner. The permanent missions are most important at the time of articulating, launching, and pushing through interests, and to report important developments on the international and the UN level to their respective governments, so that the latter are able to react quickly. Thereby, they offer states the chance to use the UN as an instrument of global multilateral diplomacy for the purpose of coming to an understanding on common solutions to problems – instead of merely pursuing their national interest.

Andrea Roth

Lit.: *1. Documents: UNITAR:* Report on the UNITAR Fellowship Programme in International Affairs Management, Geneva 1998; *United Nations:* Convention on the Privileges and Immunities of the United Nations (CPIU) of 13 December 1946, in: UNTS Vol. 1, No. 4, 15; *United Nations:* The Practice of the United Nations, the Specialized Agencies and the International Atomic Energy Agency concerning their status, privileges and immunities. Study prepared by the Secretariat (UN Doc. A/CN.4/L.118 and Add.1+2), in: ILCYB 1967, Vol. II, 154-324; *United Nations:* United Nations Conference on the Representation of States in their Relations with International Organizations, Vienna, 4 February-14 March 1975, Official Records, 2 vols. (UN Doc. A/ CONF.67/18 and Add.1); *United Nations:* Vienna Convention on the Representation of States in Their Relations with International Organizations of a Universal Character (CRSIO) (UN Doc. A/CONF.67/16, in: AJIL 69 (1975), 730-759; *2. Secondary Literature: Aggrey-Orleans, A.Y.:* The Role, Organization and Work of a Permanent Mission in Geneva, in: Boisard, M.A./Chosssudovsky, E.M. (eds.): Multilateral Diplomacy/La Diplomatie Multi-latérale: The United Nations System at Geneva/Le Système des Nations Unies à Genève; A Working Guide/ Guide de Travail, The Hague et al. 1998, 47-50; *Appathurai, E.:* Permanent Missions to the United Nations, in: International Journal 25, No. 2 (Spring 1970), 287-301; *Bailey, S.D./ Daws, S.:* The Procedure of the UN Security Council, 3rd edn., Oxford 1998, 166ff.; *Dembinski, L.:* The Modern Law of Diplomacy; External missions of states and international organisations, Dordrecht et al. 1988; *Finger, S.M.:* American Ambassadors at the UN: People, Politics, and Bureaucracy in Making Foreign Policy, UNITAR, Geneva 1992; *Gerster, M.:* Art. 105, in: Simma, B. (ed.): The Charter of the United Nations. A Commentary, 2nd edn., Vol. II, Oxford 2002, 1314-1325; *Hammarskjöld, D.:* Do We Need the United Nations? Address Before the Students' Association, Copenhagen, May 2, 1959, www.un.org/depts/dhl/dag/docs/needun.pdf; *Hyde, J.N.:* U.S. Participation in the U.N., in: IO 10 (1956), 22-34; *Lindemann, B.:* Die Organisationsstruktur der Vereinten Nationen und die Mitarbeit der BRD, in: Scheuner, U./Lindemann, B. (eds.): Die Vereinten Nationen und die Mitarbeit der Bundesrepublik Deutschland, Munich/Vienna 1973, 217-306; *Pedersen, R.F.:* National Representation in the United Nations, in: IO 15 (1961), 256-266; *Schütz, H.-J.:* Host State Agreements, in: Wolfrum, R. (ed.): United Nations: Law, Policies and Practice, Vol. 1, Munich/Dordrecht 1995, 581-591.

Internet: (1) Overview of all New York and Geneva missions which have a web site: www.un.int/index-en/index.html;
(2) Overview of the permanent missions in New York with addresses and web sites: www.un.org/Overview/missions.htm;
(3) a) Search for the individual missions: www.un.int/index-en/webs.html;
b) search on the websites of all permanent missions for texts: www.un.int/index-en/search-en.html
(4) Overview of and links to the permanent

representations in Geneva: www.itu.int/TIES/services/missionweb.html.

Personnel

The → General Assembly as well as all Secretary-Generals of the UN (→ Secretary-General) have repeatedly emphasized that they consider the personnel of the United Nations its most important asset. For Dag Hammarskjöld, financial resources were only of value when employed by trained, experienced and devoted men and women: "Such people can work miracles even with small resources and draw wealth out of a barren land." (quoted from *United Nations Department of Economic and Social Affairs* 1998, 1)

Kofi Annan expressed a similar sentiment in a Secretary-General's Bulletin: "Our greatest strength – and the key to success – is the quality of our people, both staff and managers." (*United Nations* 1998, 1)

This esteem finds its expression in the regular budgets (→ Budget) where over 70% of all expenditure relates to staff cost. Numerically though, the size of the work force appears to be quite modest. It is, however, difficult to obtain precise staffing figures since the statistics published by the various entities often show variations which result from the different definitions that are being used. The number of participants in the UN Joint Staff Pension Fund seems to be the most indicative figure as it includes all employees holding a contract of at least six months. According to this measure, the → UN system employed in 1999 over 68,000 persons (excluding the staff of the World Bank Group (→ World Bank, World Bank Group), → peacekeeping forces, short-term employed technical cooperation experts, locally recruited → UNWRA staff, UN volunteers (→ UNV), experts, consultants and other collaborators holding special or contractual service agreements, daily temporary staff and independent outside contractors. Some organizations participate in the Pension Fund, though, who do not belong to the UN system. With about 300 staff members altogether they are a negligible quantity which has been subtracted from the above figure.) To counter the accusation of being a bloated bureaucracy comparisons are being made which, for instance, show that the US State of Wyoming or the City of Stockholm employ more staff than the UN system with its world-wide operations (*Childers/Urquhart* 1994, 28-29). The main proportion of the UN staff (66%) relates to the United Nations proper including the associated relief agencies, programmes and funds (→ Principal Organs, Subsidiary Organs, Treaty Bodies). Another 23,600 persons work in the specialized and other independent organizations (→ Specialized Agencies) (e.g. → IAEA). Almost all organizations have reduced their staff in the past – sometimes considerably (e.g. → UNIDO). In previous statistics of the Pension Fund the staff reductions amounted to a mere 1.75% since cuts were mainly effected by canceling unencumbered posts, and additional temporary staff had often to be hired afterwards.

I. Staffing Concept of the UN Charter

The staffing concept establishes an independent international civil service whose members perform their functions free from any national influence and solely in the interest of the organization, and hence of the world community. This concept, which has its origin in the → League of Nations, has legally been embedded in Article 100 of the Charter (→ Charter of the UN): "In the performance of their duties the Secretary-General and the staff shall not seek or receive instructions from any government or from any other authority external to the Organization"; and "They shall refrain from any action which might reflect on their position as international officials responsible to the Organization." (Art. 100 (1) UN Charter) Each member state, in turn, "undertakes to respect the exclusively international character of the responsibilities of the Secretary-General and the staff and not to seek to influence

them in the discharge of their responsibilities." (Art. 100 (2) UN Charter) This concept has been elaborated on in the Staff Regulations and Rules, the Standards of Conduct in the International Civil Service, the Conventions on the Privileges and Immunities of the United Nations and of the specialized agencies, and the bilateral → host state agreements.

Critics claim that this concept, which Secretary-General Trygve Lie praised as "one of the most important and promising developments of the twentieth century" (*Lie* 1954, 41), has been watered down from its inception by pragmatic compromises. The US enforced between 1951 and 1953 the termination of more than 40 UN officials who had been accused of "anti-American activities". In order to be employed by the United Nations, US citizens – between 1953 and 1956 – required a loyalty clearance from their national security authorities. For the Soviet Union there was no question, as Nikita Khrushchev explained 1961 in an interview, "that there can be no such thing as an impartial civil servant in this deeply divided world, and that the kind of political celibacy which the British theory of the civil service calls for is in international affairs a fiction." (quoted by *Lippmann* 1961). The former East Bloc countries, accordingly, did not only decide who was to be seconded for service to the United Nations, but also expected from their citizens strict partisanship when working in the UN Secretariat and, if need be, even espionage activities. In addition, they closely controlled their private life and confiscated most of their UN income.

Each Secretary-General has so far publicly complained about improper attempts to influence personnel decision. Pérez de Cuéllar stated in his annual report for 1983: "… for while all [States] profess their dedication to the principles of independence and objective international administration, few refrain from trying to bring pressure to bear in favour of their own particular interests." (UN Doc. A/38/1, 5). Securing as many → Secretariat post as possible for their own citizens is not only a matter of national prestige, but is also seen as an opportunity to safeguard oneself against undesirable activities, to influence the work and resource allocation, to give more weight to national positions, or to place protégés. UN staff members are, thus, encouraged to seek the support of their governments in order to gain advantages for themselves or their area of work.

II. UN Personnel Increasingly at Risk

The expectation that the end of the Cold War would offer an opportunity for reviving the international civil service has only partly been met. Not only have attempts to influence personnel decisions not decreased, but since the early nineties staff at many duty stations have been exposed to considerable personal risk, including physical assault, armed robbery, abuse, bodily injury and rape. 198 civilian staff members were killed between 1992 and February 2001. For the first time in 1998 the number of unarmed civilian staff who died a violent death exceeded the death toll of soldiers of the → peace keeping troops. Between 1994 and February 2001 there were 64 cases of hostage taking/kidnapping involving 242 UN personnel. The responsibility for the safety and security of UN staff rests with the host countries. However, states are often not in a position, or are unwilling, to fulfill this responsibility since many duty stations are in areas in which there is no functioning state authority. Only three of the 177 cases involving the violent death of UN personnel have been brought to justice. Locally recruited staff are especially at risk since, as a rule, they will not be evacuated in case of acute danger (148 of the 198 killed were local staff).

The General Assembly, after protracted negotiations, adopted on 9 December 1994 the "Convention on the Safety of United Nations and Associated Personnel" (Annex to A/RES/49/59; UNTS Vol. 2051, No. 35457). State parties to the Convention agree in case of attacks against UN and associated personnel to adopt appropriate measures in order to bring the perpetrators to justice. This includes exchange of information, prosecution of alleged offenders and, if need be, their extradition. The Convention covers military and civilian personnel of the United Nations, the specialized agencies and the IAEA, as well as personnel assigned by a government or deployed by a humanitarian non-governmental organization (→ NGOs), provided that the operation has been authorized by the Security Council or the General Assembly for the purpose of maintaining or restoring peace and security, and that the participating personnel are exposed to an exceptional risk. This excludes, for instance, personnel who happen to be in a crisis area for the performance of their regular functions. Only 87 states had ratified the Convention by 31 December 2008 – the majority of those were countries which would not pose any extraordinary risk to UN staff.

The General Assembly regularly condemns the attacks upon UN personnel and requests member states to fulfill their obligations. These resolutions (→ Resolution, Declaration, Decision) do not seem to have any significance except for their declamatory character. A UN Security Coordinator informs organizations about the situation in crisis areas and introduces, if necessary, security measures such as travel restrictions or evacuations. The *Administrative Committee on Coordination ACC* (→ Coordination in the UN System) has issued procedural guidelines for responding to arrest of, or danger to UN staff. As a matter of principle, no ransom will be paid in the event of abduction or hostage taking. Through a trust fund, to be established out of voluntary contributions of member states, means are being sought for financing additional security measures.

III. Recruitment of UN Personnel

The concept of an independent international civil service presumes competitive recruitment at an early age based on qualifications, lifelong employment, promotion on the basis of merit, and protection and welfare by the organization.

Especially, lifelong employment has come under attack as being too inflexible and not fostering a culture of excellence. Increasing use is being made of fixed-term appointments which, by linking a series of time-limited contracts, offer little security. In addition to the traditional short-term appointments and special and contractual service agreements, new employment arrangements have been introduced, such as appointments of limited duration, hiring of independent contractors and outsourcing of work to service providers. Staff representatives see in such arrangements unfair labor practices which serve the sole purpose of reducing costs and undermining the protection accorded to staff against unjustified termination. Responding to general resource constraints, organizations are also using gratis personnel provided by individual member states. However, under pressure from developing countries, which see in it a means for circumventing recruitment and geographical distribution procedures, the General Assembly has considerably restricted the use of such personnel.

The staff is vertically subdivided into three categories: The General Service Category, comprising support functions ranging from messengers and drivers to secretaries, clerks, technicians, laboratory workers etc.; the Professional Category, which requires as a rule a university degree and which performs the substantive work of the organization; and the Higher Category for directors and assistant and deputy directors/secretaries-general, which differs from one organization to the other. While the upper two categories are almost treated like a single category (Professional and Higher Categories), the movement from the General Service into the Professional Category is not easily effected. For logistical and administrative support of → peacekeeping operations a Field Service Category has been established, which reaches vertically into the Professional Category. There is no horizontal break down into "career paths". However, a common directory of occupa-

tional groups contains over 200 different fields of work, which shows the high degree of specialization of UN staff.

The recruitment of staff is to be guided by the need – in accordance with Articles 8 and 101 of the Charter and the relevant provisions of the Staff Regulations – to secure employees of the highest standards of efficiency, competence and integrity, to prohibit any form of discrimination and to take into account the "geographical principle". The latter means that staff are to be selected on as broad a geographical basis as possible. The General Assembly offered a plausible substantiation for this principle in resolution A/RES/153 (II) adopted in 1947: "… in view of the international character and in order to avoid undue predominance of national practices, the policies and administrative methods of the Secretariat should reflect, and profit to the highest degree from, assets of the various cultures and the technical competence of all Member nations."

The application of the "geographical principle", which according to Article 101 (3) of the Charter is clearly subordinate to the "highest standards of efficiency, competence and integrity", became a controversial subject in the sixties when during the process of → decolonization the joining member states (→ Membership and Representation of States) demanded their share among the staff. A system of "quotas" or "desirable ranges", which had initially been introduced in the United Nations and the larger specialized agencies, foresaw a distribution of posts in the Professional and higher categories (exclusive of linguistic staff) mainly on the basis of the assessed financial contributions. Developing countries objected to this system since it was in their view unfair, and the establishment of a "just" or "balanced" geographical distribution became the predominant personnel policy issue until far into the eighties. Under pressure from developing countries, the weight of the contribution factor has gradually been reduced to 55 %. The weight of the so-called "membership factor", which accords each member state the same

553

share of posts, has been increased to 40%, and additionally a "population factor" with a weight of 5% has been introduced, from which states with a large population benefit.

"Quotas" and "desirable ranges" play an important role in recruiting staff in the Professional and higher categories, and it has to be assumed that, in reality and notwithstanding the ranking given in the Charter, the "highest standards of efficiency, competence and integrity" and the "geographical principle" are attributed equal weight. The General Assembly has promulgated a number of additional recruitment directives, which *inter alia* call for a significant increase in the share of women (who are generally underrepresented in the Professional and higher categories), for a better balance in the linguistic composition of the staff and for more recruitment of young professionals through national competitive examinations, and which restrict the employment of retirees. While the staff of the Professional and higher categories are usually recruited through world-wide vacancy announcement, the personnel of the General Service category, as a rule, are hired from the local labor market.

IV. Conditions of Employment

The inter-agency cooperation in the personnel field, within the framework of the so-called Common System, has been closer than in any other area. The General Assembly has established the International Civil Service Commission (ICSC) as an independent expert body for the co-ordination and regulation of conditions of employment. However, staff representatives have accused the Commission of politicization and of lacking independence and expertise. Staff representatives, who are organized in two large system-wide unions (CCISUA and FICSA), have, therefore, boycotted the work of the Commission for years and demand a comprehensive reform which would give them the right to negotiate their conditions of employment. Member states, however, have left no doubt that they will hold on

to the Commission for reasons of uniformity, equal treatment and cost control in the UN system.

The conditions of employment of the Professional and Higher Categories are subject to the so-called *Noblemaire Principle*, which derives its name from the chairman of a committee in the → League of Nations which formulated it first in 1920. It states that the remuneration of the international staff must also be attractive to candidates from the country with the best paid national civil service. Since the inception of the United Nations the Federal Civil Service of the USA has been considered to be the best paid national civil service in the world. However, since it has been considerably lagging behind salaries in the private sector for many years and since other international organizations, such as the World Bank Group, the OECD and the EU, provide in some cases significantly better conditions of employment, UN organizations and staff representatives have repeatedly asked for a revision. Surveys carried out by the ICSC since 1995 have shown that the German civil service has replaced the US civil service at its top position as the best paid one world-wide. Nevertheless, the General Assembly, mainly for cost reasons, but also because of methodological objections made by Germany, has been unable to reach a decision and to replace the US civil service as comparator for the UN remuneration.

Especially the specialized agencies have been complaining for years about a deterioration of their competitive position particularly when recruiting highly qualified personnel from countries with high salary levels. However, even young professionals are increasingly difficult to retain. The Secretary-General emphasized regretfully that voluntary resignations had exceeded retirements for the first time in 1998. Member states, in spite of these trends, stick strictly to their policy of zero real growth, also for salaries, and are at most prepared to talk about special pay rates for specific occupational groups, or to cost-neutral systems of pay for performance.

Staff of the General Service Category are subject to the *Flemming Principle* (named after the chairman of a UN committee that formulated it in 1949). According to this principle, the conditions of employment of locally recruited staff should be determined on the basis of the best prevailing local conditions of employment. Here, the UN organizations are usually in a strong competitive position since its salaries are keeping pace with the developments in the local labor market and often reach a level corresponding to that of middle positions in the Professional Category. However, through changes in the methodology for determining salaries, the ICSC has reduced General Service pay despite the strong objections of staff representatives.

The United Nations operate their own Pension Fund which is financed from contributions shared between the staff and the organizations. The Fund, which comprises more than 68,000 active participants and 46,000 beneficiaries, owned in 1999 assets in the amount of 15 billion US dollars with a market value of over 25 billion US dollars covering all current and future liabilities. The accumulated assets have repeatedly aroused envy on the part of some member states, who have wished to see them utilized for development purposes. The Pension Fund has always rejected such demands with the argument that it is not a development bank, and that the money of the insured persons must be invested in accordance with the established criteria of security, profitability, convertibility and liquidity.

V. Reform of the UN Human Resources Management

There is general agreement that, as the development of staff potential and motivation leaves presently much to be desired, the management reform process launched by the Secretary-General ($\rightarrow$ Reform of the UN) is bound to fail without a comprehensive reform of human resources management. The objective of the Secretary-General's reform proposals (cf. Renewing the United Nations: A Programme for Reform, UN Doc. A/51/950, 14 July 1997) is the creation of a management culture which strengthens performance and accountability, and improves the efficiency and quality of the staff. The proposals, which mirror the experience in the private sector, do not find support everywhere. Staff representatives see in them in the first instance a synonym for cost reductions and staff cuts. Management warns that developments in the private sector cannot unreservedly be adopted since the international civil service operates within a much more complex framework and has the most heterogeneous staff composition in the world. Many member states, in turn, fear that their ability to influence the staff would be restricted.

VI. UN Personnel in the New Millennium – Challenges and Reforms

Even though the impressive growth of human resources by over thirty per cent since the beginning of the millennium seems to indicate a renewed support by governments of the UN system, the challenges which the international civil service is facing have not subsided. The concept of a truly independent international civil service continues to be called into question in its practical application. One glaring example is the top-most American international civil servant in the Secretariat, whose responsibility ironically included human resources management and who, shortly after his appointment, stated that he had come to the UN at the request of the White House and that his primary loyalty was to the United States of America. Other new appointees also saw their role as partisan and a possibility to promote the political agenda of US-President Bush "in an organization that has clashed bitterly with Republican policymakers over such issues as the impact of global warming and the justification for the war in Iraq" (*Lynch* 2005).

The security of UN staff working in conflict zones has remained precarious.

Between 1 July 2006 and 30 June 2007 over 3,800 security incidents involving United Nations staff members were reported, including 23 murders, 520 attacks, 542 robberies and 127 hijackings (*United Nations* 2007b, Annex III). A number of countries impede the import, deployment and use of essential communications and security equipment for UN operations, which adversely affects the safety and security of personnel. The UN tries to counter such threats to the security and safety of its civilian personnel by promoting internally a culture of security consciousness, including mandatory security training, threat and risk assessment, minimum operating security standards, and critical incident stress management. It also reminds member states of their collective responsibility, according to international law, to ensure the safety and security of UN personnel and to end impunity for crimes committed against them. In December 2005 the General Assembly adopted by resolution A/RES/60/42 the Optional Protocol to the 1994 Convention on the Safety of United Nations and Associated Personnel, which expands the scope of protection (*United Nations* 2005a, Annex).

The transformation of the UN work force from a 'civil service model' designed to master complicated procedures and rules to an 'enterprise model' geared to achieving results has continued. Building on his comprehensive reform programme of 1997, ambitiously named "Renewing the United Nations" (UN Doc. A/51/950, 14 July 1997, *United Nations* 1997), Kofi Annan launched in his last year in office – 2006 – another ambitious management reform entitled "Investing in People" (UN Doc. A/61/255, 9 August 2006, *United Nations* 2006b). It contained, *inter alia*, proposals for streamlining of contractual arrangements and harmonization of conditions of service for field staff. These reforms were considered particularly important in view of the fact that more than 62 % of the staff is now deployed in the field. A cornerstone was the recommendation of one UN contract for all staff members regardless of whether or not they are working at Headquarters or in the field, and replacing traditional civil service-like permanent contracts by more enterprise-like temporary, fixed-term or continuing contracts. The management reform also foresaw more delegation of authority to the Secretary-General and programme managers, who would be held accountable within a result-based management framework. The system of internal justice, which – according to an outside panel of experts – was outmoded, dysfunctional, ineffective and lacking independence (panel report: UN Doc. A/61/205, 28 July 2006, *United Nations* 2005a), has also been fundamentally redesigned.

All these reforms have in common that they are costly (streamlining contracts will cost 23 million US dollars and redesigning the internal system of justice another 23.5 million US dollars) and that they meet resistance from affected staff and member states alike. The management reform, as any other issue, is seen through the North-South divide, and many developing countries consider it "an attempt by rich white countries to gain even more influence over a secretariat already dominated by the North" (*The Economist,* 4 January 2007, 19). Furthermore, any single reform proposal will be thoroughly tested as to whether it might affect the system of geographical distribution and hence the employment opportunities for candidates from member states.

To combat mismanagement, fraud, inefficiency and abuse, the UN has, over the years, introduced a number of oversight processes. Even though the inquiry following the Oil-for-Food scandal had found that "the administrative-control structure [of the UN secretariat, D.G.] had worked to prevent corruption on those elements that fell under its control" (*Mathiason* 2007, 245) and that as far as the UN was concerned there was evidently only one case of corruption (cf. the report of the so-called Volcker Commission, www.iic-offp.org/; see also: *Williams* 2007), the Secretary-General responded to public concerns by establishing a new Ethics Office, rewriting the whistleblower protection policy and devising stronger financial disclosure requirements for his senior staff (cf. UN Doc. ST/SGB/2005/22 of 30 December 2005 and ST/SGB/2006/6 of 1 May 2006 and the websites www.un.org/reform/ethics/index and www.un.org/sg/PublicDisclosure).

The new Secretary-General, Ban Ki-moon, has continued the management reform agenda which had begun during the period of office of his predecessor. However, in a press conference shortly after his appointment, he stated as his goal "to build a staff which is truly mobile and multi-functional, through greater emphasis on career development, training, accountability, and recognition of work performed at all levels" (*United Nations* 2007a). Mobility and multi-functionality of all staff, thus, seems to be his priority, as well as ensuring accountability and performance of senior staff. To the latter end he has engaged himself in a process of dialogue with each of the senior managers and in concluding with them performance compacts for 2007 and 2008.

Dieter Göthel

Lit.: *Ali, A.:* The International Civil Service: The Idea and the Reality, in: Cooker, C. de (ed.): International Administration, The Hague 1990; *Beigbeder, Y.:* The Internal Management of the United Nations Organizations. The Long Quest for Reform, Houndmills/London 1997; *Busch, J.-D.:* Dienstrecht der Vereinten Nationen, Cologne 1981; *Childers, E./Urquhart, B.:* Renewing the United Nations System, Uppsala 1994; *Göthel, D.:* Die Vereinten Nationen: Eine Innenansicht, Bonn 1995; *Göthel, D.:* Im Auftrag der Weltorganisation: Das Personal der Vereinten Nationen im Wandel, in: VN 43 (1995), 99-105; *Lemoine, J.:* The International Civil Service: An Endangered Species, The Hague 1995; *Lindemann, B./Hesse-Kreindler, D.:* Secretariat, in: Wolfrum, R. (ed.): United Nations: Law, Policies and Practice, Vol. 2, Munich/Dordrecht 1995, 1129-1135; *Lynch, C.:* At the U.N., a Growing Republican Presence, in: Washington Post, 21 July 2005; *Mathiason, J.:* Invisible Governance. International Secretariats in Global Politics, Bloomfield 2007; *Pellet, A./*

Ruzié, D.: Les Fonctionnaires Internationaux, Paris 1993; *United Nations:* Convention on the Safety of United Nations and Associated Personnel (Annex to GA Res. 49/59 of 9 December 1994); *United Nations:* Renewing the United Nations: A Programme for Reform. Report of the Secretary-General, UN Doc. A/51/950, 14 July 1997; *United Nations:* Secretary General's Bulletin: Building the Future (UN Doc. ST/SGB/1998/6), Geneva Reproduction 98/23, 31 March 1998, 1; *United Nations Department of Economic and Social Affairs:* Changing Perspectives on Human Resources Development, UN Publication ST/TCD/SER.E/25), New York 1998; *United Nations - General Assembly:* Renewing the United Nations: A Programme for Reform. Report of the Secretary-General, 14 July 1997, UN Doc. A/51/950 (quoted as United Nations 1997); *United Nations - General Assembly:* Optional Protocol to the Convention on the Safety of United Nations and Associated Personnel, UN Doc. A/RES/60/42, 8 December 2005, Annex (quoted as United Nations 2005); *United Nations - General Assembly:* Report of the Redesign Panel on the United Nations system of administration of justice, 28 July 2006, UN Doc. A/61/205 (quoted as United Nations 2006a); *United Nations - General Assembly:* Investing in people. Report of the Secretary-General, 9 August 2006, UN Doc. A/61/255 (quoted as United Nations 2006b); *United Nations - Press Release:* Transcript of Press Conference by Secretary-General Ban Ki-moon at United Nations Headquarters, 11 January 2007, SG/SM/10839 (quoted as United Nations 2007a); *United Nations - General Assembly:* Safety and security of humanitarian personnel and protection of United Nations personnel. Report of the Secretary-General, 7 September 2007, UN Doc. A/62/324 (quoted as United Nations 2007b); *United Nations - Secretariat:* Ethics Office – establishment and terms of reference. Secretary-General's bulletin, 30 December 2005, UN Doc. ST/SGB/2005/22; *United Nations - Secretariat:* Financial disclosure and declaration of interest statements. Secretary-General's bulletin, 10 April 2006, UN Doc. ST/SGB/2006/6; *Williams, I.:* «Öl für Lebensmittel» Das Programm, der 'Skandal' und die Geschichte dahinter, in: VN 55 (2007), 10-15

Internet: Homepage of the Office of Human Resources Management of the UN Secretariat (information on employment opportunities, recruitment through competitive examinations, salaries and internship programmes: www.un.org/Depts/OHRM/index.html.

Preventive Diplomacy

I. The New Concept of Preventive Diplomacy

Since the publication of the 1992 "Agenda for Peace" of then UN → Secretary-General Boutros-Ghali (→ Agenda for Peace), the term *"preventive diplomacy"* has been viewed as an important addition to the spectrum of the UN's peace-promoting activities, beside → "peaceful settlement of disputes" (according to Chapter VI UN Charter), → "peacekeeping operations", and → "peacekeeping" (according to Chapter VII UN Charter) (→ Charter of the UN). The term was coined in 1960 by the then Secretary-General of the UN, Dag Hammarskjöld, who used it to describe UN attempts to contain regional conflicts in which there was a danger of confrontation between the superpowers. In the "Agenda", Secretary-General Boutros-Ghali defined preventive diplomacy more broadly, namely as all "action to prevent disputes from arising between parties, to prevent existing disputes from escalating into conflicts and to limit the spread of the latter when they occur" (*Boutros-Ghali* 1992, 11, para. 20).

More specifically, the "Agenda" cites the following as instruments of preventive diplomacy: early warning, fact-finding missions, confidence-building measures, demilitarized zones, and the preventive deployment of → peacekeeping forces (loc. cit., 13, para 23). In Boutros-Ghali's view, these instruments should be usable both in international and in intra-state conflicts. Furthermore, as envisaged by the "Agenda", preventive diplomacy encompasses all phases of conflict intervention, from crisis management to the termination of wars.

On the one hand, the broad-based approach of 1992 was welcomed as an overdue addition to the UN's spectrum of options for the peaceful settlement of disputes. This was, in the first place, be-

cause the chances of civilized settlement are much more favorable in the early phase of the development of a conflict than in the phases of political confrontation, or indeed at the stage when it is being played out by force; and in the second place because, following the end of the East-West conflict, the possibilities of a joint approach by the permanent members of the → Security Council appeared to be greatly improved.

On the other hand, certain reservations were expressed, particularly by governments from the South, who feared a dilution of the principles of → sovereignty and non-interference (→ Intervention, Prohibition of) and thought that the UN's already scarce resources would be better used combating the "real" causes of conflict in the development domain (→ Development Cooperation of the UN System).

In addition to all this, there were a number of conceptual criticisms. The Agenda idea that "preventive" intervention could encompass the whole course of a conflict was viewed as misleading, and the incorporation of the work on the causes of conflict, including those of a structural kind, was deemed too ambitious. There was also criticism of the fact that the instruments cited, which were extremely diverse in character, were presented as subcategories of "diplomatic" efforts. It would be better, critics said, if the instruments of peaceful dispute settlement were activated as early as possible as "diplomatic" procedures in the narrower sense, and other measures such as the preventive deployment of peacekeeping troops were classified as "preventive actions" (*Lund* 1996; *Peck* 1998).

The broader-based terms *"conflict prevention"* and *"crisis prevention"*, respectively, are now preferred, both in politics and journalism. The problem with the term "conflict prevention", however, is that "conflict" is tacitly equated with "violent conflict", whereas social change necessarily entails conflicts, and the point is therefore not to prevent conflicts in general, but to deal with them in a civilized way. In academic circles, the term *"prevention of violence"* is therefore regarded as more accurate, and a distinction is made between structural and process-based efforts to ensure the peaceful transformation of social upheavals. In this context, *"preventive diplomacy"* is viewed primarily as a process-based activity, encompassing all measures at the macro-political level that promote the early resolution of political disputes.

II. Preventive Diplomacy in Practice

As far as UN practice is concerned, the *Security Council* has so far played only a modest "preventive" role. In general, the Council is already overburdened with managing violent conflicts. Besides this, the very fact that the Council turns its attention to a conflict in its early phase can unintentionally help to escalate that conflict, because it then becomes "internationalized", and the "face-saving" aspect acquires enhanced importance for all those involved. Finally – and this is probably the most important argument – the Council's way of working tends more towards "position-taking" than "problem-solving".

For the same reason, and also because its competence is confined to international disputes, also the → ICJ is also of limited use when it comes to preventive measures. That said, the parties to a conflict may very well bring individual points of contention to the court for a ruling and integrate these into some kind of arrangement negotiated at the political/diplomatic level (instrument of the so-called "compromis" according to Article 36 (1) ICJ Statute).

The more appropriate actors to work with when it comes to preventive diplomacy are therefore: the *Secretary-General*; the persons commissioned by the latter for such purposes; and the "Group of Friends of the Secretary-General" (→ Groups and Groupings in the UN). After several failed attempts at organizational reform (→ Reform of the UN), the "Department of Political Affairs" (DPA), together with a series of sub-departments, was set up within the → Secretariat, as an attempt of improv-

ing the UN's operational base. But resources and staffing in the department (→ Personnel) are so meager that there have so far only been a handful of cases in which the UN has managed to play a preventive part in a regional crisis.

Another key set of UN instruments relating to preventive diplomacy is that comprising the diverse institutions and mechanisms of *human-rights protection* (→ Human Rights, Protection of). The effectiveness of these tools in preventing crises and violence rests partly on a gradual differentiation and "constitutionalization" of principles, norms, rules, and procedures ensuring respect for individual human rights (→ Human Rights; → Human Rights Conventions and their Measures of Implementation). In addition, the monitoring and publicizing of human rights violations, as well as the imposition of reporting requirements on states, have greatly helped to improve early warning of looming crises and conflicts. One area that is greatly in need of further improvement, however – precisely as regards its preventive functions – is the protection of minorities (→ Minorities, Protection of).

All in all, the record of preventive diplomacy within the UN framework has so far been an extremely modest one. The reasons for this, however, do not lie only in the peculiar features of the UN delineated above. Preventive politics in general is confronted with a whole series of obstacles in today's world of states. These include: non-interference in the internal affairs of other states, as required by international law; the unwillingness to intervene in a preventive role unless there is wide public concern; the attention of decision-makers being drawn away from potential conflicts to acute problems; and, last but not least, a lack of the capacities, mandates, and coordination mechanisms needed for effectively targeted preventive measures.

III. Effectiveness of Preventive Diplomacy

Michael S. Lund (1996, 85 ff.) has distilled five "lessons learned" from previous experiences with preventive diplomacy:

(1) For preventive diplomacy to be successful, there need to be long-term incentives for, or ongoing pressure on, the actors in the conflict to come to a peaceful settlement, and this should ideally happen before either side has mobilized its supporters or threatened the other side with coercive measures.

(2) The effectiveness of preventive measures is crucially dependent on the ability to mesh together many different third parties in a coherent strategic approach, using a broadly based bundle of measures.

(3) Effectiveness is also dependent on big powers, regional powers, and the affected neighboring states either at least tolerating the attempts at prevention, or, better still, actively supporting them and refraining from undermining them (either overtly or covertly) by lending support to the one or the other party.

(4) The more moderate the leaders of the disputed groups appear, the greater are the chances of an early, mutually agreed settlement.

(5) The more detached a state's political institutions are from the parties in dispute, the greater the likelihood of finding a peaceful settlement that takes account of the interests of all those involved.

IV. Reforming Preventive Diplomacy

In the debate about ways of strengthening *the instruments of preventive diplomacy*, it is widely agreed that the success of such diplomacy depends on developing and implementing a broad spectrum of reform measures amounting ultimately to a comprehensive *"culture of prevention"* (or "prevention regime", *Lund* 1996). Important contributions to this debate about reform were made in the individual studies and overall report produced by the *"Carnegie Commission on Preventing Deadly Conflict"* (1997) (hereinafter "Carnegie Commission").

The most important aspects of the debate about reform can be summed in under six points:

(1) A key question at one stage was whether attempts to strengthen prevention should center on extending either the UN or regional organizations in an appropriate way, or on linking together non-governmental organizations (→ NGOs) working in relevant domains (*Evans* 1993). An answer to this question has since emerged, in the form, essentially, of a division of labor between all three of these areas, coupled with single-state measures of the kind that have already taken shape in other fields such as crisis management and → humanitarian assistance (*Weiss* 1998). There is unanimous agreement that regional capacities for preventive action should be strengthened, e.g. through jointly run "regional UN centres for sustainable peace" (*Peck* 1998, 225 ff.).

(2) The debate about the enlargement of the Security Council also impinges upon its capacity for preventive diplomacy. Central to this debate is the notion that a "more representative" composition of the permanent membership of this body would enhance the readiness to become involved early on in crisis regions that lie outside the spheres of interest of the big powers (*Carnegie Commission* 1997, xiii).

(3) At the conceptual level, there is the problem of how the tension between the principles of national → sovereignty and non-intervention on the one hand and the effective international protection of human rights on the other can be translated into concrete options for action. The concepts of "human security" and "good governance" are being discussed as possible goals for preventive diplomacy here.

(4) There is broad agreement that effective prevention means, first and foremost, supporting developing and transforming societies in their efforts to manage the necessary social, economic, cultural, and political processes of change in a non-violent way. Power-oriented strategies based on the exertion of political influence should therefore be replaced mainly with incentives, support, and advice, in an effort to strengthen these societies' capacities for dealing

constructively with conflict and plurality.

(5) To attain this goal of increased capacity to deal constructively with conflict in crisis regions, many different institutions and mechanisms need to be created or to combine their efforts, and large numbers of people need to be trained. All this requires considerable resources, as well as a readiness to learn from innovative models. The experiences of the OSCE with its "High Commissioner for National Minorities" and its long-term missions (*OSCE* 1999) are regarded as particularly helpful here, as are the methods of "multi-track" diplomacy developed by various NGOs (European Platform for Conflict Prevention and Transformation 1998). The UN has a key role to play here as a coordinator, but its present resources are utterly inadequate for this (→ Financial Crises; → Budget).

(6) In this connection, some reform proposals point not only to the underfinancing of the UN Secretariat – e.g. for the DPA – , but also to a fundamental structural defect in the form of any social or parliamentary representation within the United Nations still missing (*Czempiel* 1994, 156ff.). For the foreseeable future, the tasks of coordinating and linking preventive measures between the world of states and the societal world will therefore have to be carried out via a number of different channels such as regional organizations, UN → specialized agencies, and coalitions of NGOs. An important bridging function is achieved here by preventive measures that are undertaken jointly in "public-private partnerships" by multilateral or single-state bodies, NGOs, and businesses.

The list of improvements that need to be made to preventive diplomacy would naturally not be complete without some reference to the need for structural measures such as: → disarmament; arms control; action to strengthen "good governance" and the rule of law; and socially sustainable development policy.

Norbert Ropers

Lit.: *Boutros-Ghali, B.:* An Agenda for Peace. Preventive Diplomacy, Peace-Making and Peace-keeping. Report of the Secretary-General pursuant to the statement adopted by the Summit Meeting of the Security Council on 31 January 1992, United Nations (DPI/1247), New York 1992; *Carnegie Commission on Preventing Deadly Conflict:* Preventing Deadly Conflict. Final Report, Washington 1997; *Czempiel, E.O.:* Die Reform der UNO. Möglichkeiten und Mißverständnisse. Munich 1994; *European Platform for Conflict Transformation (ed.):* Prevention and Management of Violent Conflicts. An International Directory, Utrecht 1998; *Evans, G.:* Cooperating for Peace. The Global Agenda for the 1990s and Beyond, St. Leonards 1993; *Lund, M.S.:* Preventing Violent Conflicts, A Strategy for Preventive Diplomacy, Washington 1996; *OSCE (ed.):* OSCE Handbook, Vienna 1999; *Peck, C.:* Sustainable Peace. The Role of the UN and Regional Organizations in Preventing Conflict, Oxford 1998; *Weiss, T.G.:* Beyond UN subcontracting. Task-sharing with regional security arrangements and service-providing NGOs, London/New York 1998.

Addendum

Part A: Broadening of the Concept

When the "Agenda for Peace" was published in 1992 the concept of preventive diplomacy came to encompass all phases of conflict intervention. Over the last years though, the term *preventive action* has been used more regularly than *preventive diplomacy*. This terminological shift refers to the enlargement of the scope and of the methods of crisis prevention (cf. *United Nations Secretariat - Department of Political Affairs* 2007). Today it can be considered less a single technique or method of intervention but as a pro-active orientation and a potential policy that cuts across a wide range of major policy sectors and organizations. These do not only include diplomacy, conflict management and → human rights, but also economic development, democracy building, environment, education, health agriculture and commercial activities, e.g. international trade and natural resource development, play a crucial role in the prevention of violent conflicts (*Lund* 2003).

On the one hand, as outlined in the so-called "Brahimi Report" (UN Doc. A/55/305-S/2000/809, 21 August 2000), the report of an expert group on the reform of UN peacekeeping, the focus has been more on *structural prevention* within the preventive practice of the UN. On the other hand – as Secretary-General Kofi Annan outlined in his report "Prevention of armed conflict" – this structural prevention is characterized by interlinking development, peacebuilding and security strategies. It is assumed that a coordinated and at times integrated approach to peace, development and security interventions is likely to mitigate some of the basic challenges in the area of crisis prevention. Sustainable development and crisis prevention are considered as synergistic goals and the importance of mainstreaming crisis prevention into development policies is stressed. (*Annan* 2001, UN Doc. A/55/985-S/2001/574, 7 June 2001)

Another shift in the agenda for the prevention of armed conflicts grew out of the recognized failure of the international community in the post-cold war period to adequately prevent humanitarian tragedies such as the Rwandan genocide (cf. Report of the Independent Inquiry, UN Doc. S/1999/1257, 16 December 1999). Instead of reacting "too little and too late" to humanitarian crises, the need to enhance the effectiveness of the UN in addressing conflict at all stages was expressed. Having considered its role in the prevention of armed conflict in a debate in November 1999 and again in July 2000, the Security Council met again on this subject on in June 2001 with the above-mentioned report of the Secretary-General as its basis. In a resolution on prevention of armed conflict the Council emphasized: that "early warning, preventive diplomacy, preventive deployment, practical disarmament measures and post-conflict peace-building are interdependent and complementary components of a comprehensive prevention strategy." (UN Doc. S/RES/1366/2001, 30 August 2001). Thus the Council demonstrated a higher political priority for prevention strategies.

Reinterpreting the understanding of state sovereignty has been one basic aspect of this debate. As it was highlighted by the "International Commission on Intervention and State Sovereignty" (ICISS) in 2001, sovereignty is no longer seen as a right but also as a duty of every state to protect its people. It is interpreted now as a dual responsibility: externally, to respect the sovereignty of other states, and internally, to respect the basic rights and dignity of all people within the state. (*ICISS* 2001). If a single state is not able or is unwilling to do so, the international community has the so-called "right of humanitarian intervention" and the "responsibility to protect" civilians – if necessary with coercive and in particular military actions (*ICISS* 2001). Since human rights violations are no longer seen as internal affairs of particular states but as a threat to international peace and security, it is considered as the responsibility of the Security Council, under Article 24 of the UN Charter, to "respond to situations of compelling human need with appropriate measures" (*ICISS* 2001).

One argument brought forward in criticism against this reinterpretation of sovereignty was that it could legitimize also the use of force if a security threat for the whole international community is perceived. Apart from this, some reservations were expressed, especially by governments from the South, to linking the legitimacy of a state and the political authority of a government to the human rights situation within a particular country. It is argued by those governments in the South that the human rights concept of the UN could be considered less as a neutral, universal system of values, but as an established political practice based on certain cultural values.

After the attacks of September 11, 2001, the importance of collective security strategies has been stressed within the UN discourse. In its report "A more secure world: Our shared responsibility" (UN Doc. A/59/565, 2 December 2004) the "High-level Panel on Threats, Challenges and Change" identified a broad range of collective threats which need to be addressed within a framework of preventive actions: economic and social threats, inter-state conflicts, internal conflicts including civil war, genocide, nuclear, radiological chemical and biological weapons, terrorism and transnational organized crime. Once more it is argued that development plays a vital role in addressing and preventing these collective threats, because it helps states to prevent or reverse the erosion of state capacity and it is part of a long-term strategy for preventing civil war. In addition to this it helps combat poverty, infectious disease and environmental degradation (*High-level Panel* 2004).

The use of force for preventive action is also legitimized in the same report with reference to Article 51 and the right to self-defense by arguing that long established customary law makes it clear that "states can take military action as long as the threatened attack is imminent, no other means would deflect it and the action is proportionate." (ibid., Part 3, IX, 1).

Whereas the crisis prevention agenda of the United Nations had been composed of structural and operational initiatives since the "Agenda for Peace", Kofi Annan introduced in his study "Progress Report on the Prevention of Armed Conflict" of 2006 another sphere of action, namely "systemic prevention" (*Annan* 2006, 5, para. 8). This term refers to measures to address global risk of conflict that transcend the borders of particular states, such as efforts to regulate trade in natural resources that fuel conflict, to offer support to private-sector initiatives on conflict sensitive business practices, to develop practical mechanisms to reduce illicit flows of small arms and light weapons, to fight the spread of HIV/AIDS and to pay more attention to the nexus of prevention and migration.

Furthermore the report contains a review of the United Nations capacity in preventing violent conflicts where several shortcomings are identified. It is underlined that until now no significant

progress has been made in the area of strengthening the capacity of the Organization in early warning and the collection of information and analysis. The UN is still lacking the capacity to analyze and integrate data from different parts of the system into comprehensive early warning reports and strategies on crisis prevention (*Annan* 2006, 27, para. 94).

The review also found that the UN's capacity to cooperate with other actors in the field of conflict prevention is very low. Unlike other mandates given to the Organization, the area of crisis prevention lacks a permanent forum for regular discussions with the intergovernmental system and expert groups at the policy level. There is a need, so states the review, to create a platform where a regular dialogue among member states, and between them and the UN system can be undertaken (ibid., para. 95).

Having said this it becomes clear that "crisis prevention" today is a concept with varied meanings and understandings. It can be considered as a loose conceptual framework which includes a broad range of activities and actors. Besides this, it raises the issue of the use and justification of coercive power including military intervention. Since 2001 there is a growing legitimization of the use of military means for maintaining international peace and security. As is shown in the United States National Security Strategy of 2002 preventive action can also be interpreted as an entry point for military pre-emption (*Väyrynen* 2006).

Part B: Institutional Developments

The afore-mentioned conceptual and strategic shifts have been accompanied by new or refined institutional developments, tools and mechanisms. The *Department of Political Affairs (DPA)* in the UN Secretariat is still considered as the focal point of crisis prevention on behalf of the whole UN system.

Even though the General Assembly approved a start-up mediation support capacity within the DPA, the Department remains significantly under-resourced (*Annan* 2006, 26). The Mediation Support Unit works in tandem with the strengthened DPA regional divisions and the Department of Peacekeeping Operations, amongst others. The aim of this Support Unit is to provide mediators and their teams with advice, operational tools and guidance on the key issues they face. Its services are available to all UN partners, governments, NGOs and private individuals (*Annan* 2006).

In addition to this, two further UN entities have been established to play a crucial role in crisis prevention: the *Peacebuilding Commission (PBC)* and the *Human Rights Council (HRC)*.

The PBC was a concrete outcome of the September 2005 World Summit, where the UN's capacity to respond effectively to conflicts through linking peace and security was to be reviewed. The PBC was established to bridge the gap between the signing of a peace accord and post-conflict reconstruction as well as to provide recommendations on the prevention of the recurrence of conflict. It is to interact with the Security Council and the UN Economic and Social Council, and improve the participation of the international financial institutions. Given that the Commission lacks a proactive prevention mandate, it might seem that prevention still has no real home within the UN (*GPAC* 2006, 16).

The HRC was established as subsidiary organ of the General Assembly in 2006 by resolution 60/251 and replaced the UN Commission on Human Rights. One of its main tasks should be to address situations of violations of human rights within countries and make recommendations thereon. Hence, it depends strongly on the cooperation of the particular state. In current discussions it is seen as more difficult for the HRC to take on human rights abuses within 'powerful' countries, while it may be less difficult to do so in countries with less influence. Given that powerful countries such as the USA did not approve the implementation of the HRC, its area of influence is seen as limited (*Human Rights Watch* 2008).

As highlighted in some of the mentioned documents, acting in concert is an important component for safeguarding success in the UN crisis prevention efforts. Therefore organizations such as the World Bank have created a "Conflict Prevention and Reconstruction Unit" in 2001 and have integrated conflict prevention strategies into their funding initiatives.

In order to enhance the cooperation between the UN and civil society organizations and to strengthen the role of NGOs in the prevention of armed conflicts the *"Global Partnership for the Prevention of Armed Conflict"* (GPAC) was created in 2003 (www.gppac.net). Its goal is to develop a comprehensive and coherent global action agenda on crisis prevention and peacebuilding that guarantees a vital role for civil society. On the basis of 15 separate regional action agendas, *People Building Peace: A Global Agenda on the Prevention of Violent Conflict* was adopted by more than 500 organizations in 2005 (*GPAC* 2007, 3).

Part C: Effectiveness of the UN's Crisis Prevention Agenda

Despite these developments several amendments are still needed to upgrade the UN's capacities in preventing violent conflicts. A lot of work has to be done to intensify dialogue and cooperation within the UN system as well as between the UN and civil society to develop a strategic vision of what the organization as whole can accomplish in the area of prevention.

As it is argued in documents of the High Level Panel, in Annan's Report of 2006, and in the decisions of the September 2005 UN World summit, the UN has been less successful in civil – than inter-state-crisis prevention. Besides this, it is emphasized that the Secretary-General must place greater emphasis on the appointment of highly qualified, regional expert envoys and should enhance their training and briefing. Also, in order to provide more consistent support to its peacemaking envoys the DPA needs greater financial support (*Crocker*

2007, 9). More resources are also required for the Secretary-General's capacity for mediation and 'good offices' (*World Summit Outcome* 2005). Finally, a more creative and constructive use of sanctions as a tool for conflict prevention has been requested (*Annan* 2006).

Daniela Körppen

Lit.: *Annan, K.:* The Prevention of armed conflicts, Report of the Secretary-General, United Nations, New York 2001, published by UNDPI as UN sales publication (DPI/2256), also published as UN Document: UN Doc. A/55/985-S/2001/574, 7 June 2001; *Annan, K.:* Progress Report on the Prevention of Armed Conflict. Report of the Secretary-General, United Nations, New York 2006; *Crocker, C.A.:* Peacemaking and Mediation: Dynamics of a Changing Field, New York, IPA, March 2007; *Global Partnership for the Prevention of Armed Conflict (GPAC):* People Building Peace: A Global Action Agenda for the Prevention of Violent Conflict, The Hague 2007 (quoted as: GPAC 2007); *Human Rights Watch:* More business as usual: The work which awaits the Human Rights Council. Report on the Website, www.hrw.org/english/docs/2007/03/12/sudan 15471.htm, 9/2008; *International Commission on Intervention and State Sovereignty (ICISS):* The Responsibility to Protect, Ottawa 2001, in the Internet: www.iciss.ca/report-en.asp; *Lund, M.:* What kind of Peace is being built? A discussion paper prepared on the occasion of the tenth anniversary of Agenda for Peace for the IDRC, Ottawa 2003; *United Nations - General Assembly/Security Council:* Report of the Panel on United Nations Peace Operations, ("Brahimi Report"), UN Doc. A/55/305-S/2000/809, 21 August 2000; *United Nations - General Assembly:* Prevention of armed conflict. Report of the Secretary-General, 7 June 2001, UN Doc. A/55/985-S/2001/574 (quoted as: Annan 2001); *United Nations - General Assembly:* A more secure world: our shared responsibility. Report of the High-level Panel on Threats, Challenges and Change, UN Doc. A/59/565, 2 December 2004 (quoted as: High-level Panel 2004); *United Nations - General Assembly:* 2005 World Summit Outcome, UN Doc. A/RES/60/1, 16 September 2005 (quoted as: World Summit Outcome 2005), further information: www.un.org/ga/59/hl60_plenarymeeting.html; *United Nations - General Assembly:* Progress report

on the prevention of armed conflict. Report of the Secretary-General, 18 July 2006, UN Doc. A/60/891 (quoted as: Annan 2006); *United Nations Secretariat - Department of Political Affairs (DPA):* Website on conflict prevention, www.un.org/depts/dpa/conflict. html, 26 September 2007; *United Nations - Security Council:* Resolution 1366, 30 August 2001 (UN Doc. S/RES/1366 (2001); *Väyrynen, R.:* 2006: Preventive action by military means: A contested approach, in: Global Society 20 (January 2006), 69-86.

Principal Organs, Subsidiary Organs, Treaty Bodies

There is such a variety and multitude of different organs and institutions within the UN system (→ UN System), that it seems to make sense to attempt at least a rough classification of the UN organs, even if one realizes very quickly during this classification procedure that the experts in many cases do not agree with each other, use different names for the same institutions, or make different divisions and groupings.

So a practicable classification should be oriented at the provisions of the UN Charter (→ Charter of the UN), the decisions of the UN organs and the prevailing administrative practices in the UN system.

A. The Different Types of UN Organs

I. Principal Organs

Article 7 UN Charter distinguishes two groups of UN organs: "principal organs" (Art. 7 (1)) and "subsidiary organs" (Art. 7 (2)).

The *principal organs* enumerated in Article 7, → General Assembly, → Security Council, Economic and Social Council (→ ECOSOC), → Trusteeship Council, International Court of Justice (→ ICJ), and → Secretariat, have their bases directly in the Charter, and their functions and powers are laid down in the respective articles of the Charter, whereas *subsidiary organs* are established by a specific organizational decision of a principal organ within the scope of its competence assigned by the Charter

565

of the UN. The Military Staff Committee, which is established to assist the Security Council in questions concerning the military requirements for the maintenance of international peace and security (Art. 47 (1) UN Charter), is the only subsidiary organ whose establishment originates directly from the Charter.

As the UN Charter enumerates all principal organs, this means that new principal organs can only be established by an amendment to the Charter. The same is true for the abolition of principal organs. This is valid, for example, for the → Trusteeship Council, which lost its original function when Palau gained its independence in 1994, since there are no UN trust territories left to administer. Even changes in the composition, the functions and powers can only be achieved through amendments to the Charter. This has been the case when the number of members of the Security Council and of ECOSOC increased through Charter amendments entering in force in 1965 and 1973, respectively.

The enumeration in Article 7 UN Charter places all principal organs, with their specific functions and powers, on the same level of importance; there is no ranking order of the organs. As far as the Charter does not state otherwise, no principal organ is subject to the instructions of other principal organs, but is independent in its respective scope of competence, and can become active on its own initiative.

This is especially true for the relationship between General Assembly and Security Council. The Charter does not give either of the two organs the competence to give instructions to the other, and no relationship of subordination of one to the other can be concluded from any Charter provision.

There is quite a different relationship between General Assembly on the one hand, and ECOSOC and the Trusteeship Council on the other. These two principal organs are independent in their respective scope of competence, but in the discharge of their functions they are "under the authority of the General Assembly" (Arts. 60 and 87 UN Charter, respectively). This means that their activities can be initiated and monitored by the General Assembly.

More complicated is the position of the → Secretary-General as the head of the principal organ the Secretariat, in relation to the other principal organs. Within the framework of his own organizational tasks he disposes of his own field of competence, and can moreover start diplomatic activities, on his own initiative, on the basis of Article 99 UN Charter, in order to prevent the escalation of international conflicts which might constitute a threat to international peace.

On the other hand, he is obliged to organize administratively the work of the other principal organs, to manage the implementation of their decisions, and to assume other tasks with which the other principal organs might entrust him (Art. 98 Charter).

With a certain justification one could speak of a prominent position of the General Assembly as it has the budget power over all activities of the United Nations (→ Budget), and as all other organs have to report to the General Assembly. But the obligation to report does not entail an authority to issue instructions.

With the same justification one could speak of a prominent position of the Security Council because of its important powers in peacekeeping (Chapter VI and VII of the Charter); this all the more as the General Assembly is not allowed (according to Art. 12 Charter) to address any conflict as long as the Security Council deals with the matter, unless the Security Council requests the General Assembly to do so.

A special position is taken by the International Court of Justice (→ ICJ) as the "principal judicial organ of the United Nations" (Art. 92 Charter). Through its judicial independence the ICJ stands outside the relationship system of the other principal organs.

II. Subsidiary Organs

The Charter contains no provisions concerning the composition, competence and scope of duties of "subsidiary organs". No uniform, binding interpretation with regard to this matter can be deduced from the decisions of the principal organs nor from the general administrative practice of the United Nations. As for the subsidiary organs, there is such a large variety of differences with respect to their competence, their extent of autonomy, their limiting as to time etc., that one can develop many different classification schemes, depending on the criteria of division.

With regard to definitions, it is clear at least, that all those UN organs are *subsidiary organs* which have been established according to Article 7 (2) Charter, either by a decision of a principal organ, or by a competent organ on the grounds of an explicit authorization of a principal organ. In the same way the subsidiary organs can be abolished again by decisions of the respective organs.

III. Treaty Bodies

Beside the principal and the subsidiary organs there are also treaty bodies in the UN system, i.e. organs (committees, commissions) established by international conventions and responsible for the implementation and monitoring of the compliance with the respective conventions, which have been adopted by the member states, with the aim of fulfilling the goals and purposes of the United Nations. These organs have developed independently from the United Nations in terms of international law, but are functionally and organizationally linked with the United Nations so closely by these treaties that they are referred to as "treaty bodies" or "treaty organs" of the United Nations. Their reports are to be submitted according to the provisions of the conventions to the competent principal organ of the United Nations, their expenses are completely or at least partly paid from the regular budget of the UN, and their secretarial work is done by the UN Secretariat. In many cases the competent principal organ of the UN is also responsible for the appointment of the members of the treaty body.

Among these treaty bodies are counted: the International Narcotics Control Board (INCB), the Conference on Disarmament, as well as the commissions and committees established by the different human right conventions (→ Human Rights Conventions and their Measures of Implementation) which shall monitor the compliance with the conventions in the contracting states: CERD, CEDAW, CAT, CRC and the → Human Rights Committee.

These treaty bodies are doubtless not subsidiary organs of the United Nations because they have not been established by a principal organ of the UN, nor are they subject to its authority in the sense that the principal organ could change the mandate of the organ, or could give it instructions. On the other hand, the treaty organs are dependent *de facto* in the exercise of their duties upon the services of the UN Secretariat and upon the financial resources of the UN. This implies that their position is in some respect similar to subsidiary organs of the UN, but in other regard the treaty organs possess more autonomy.

IV. Specialized Agencies

Another important group in the UN system are the → specialized agencies, i.e. intergovernmental organizations which are autonomous in terms of international law, such as → WHO, which act on their own, are subjects of international law, and conclude their own international treaties. Specialized agencies are not subsidiary organs of the United Nations, they do not belong to the United Nations in the strict sense of the word as defined by the Charter of the UN, but they can be brought "into relationship with the United Nations" and become part of the more comprehensive UN system (→ UN System) by concluding agreements according to Articles 57 and 63 UN Charter with ECOSOC which are "subject to approval by the General Assembly".

At present there are 17 specialized agencies of the United Nations: → FAO, → ILO, → UNESCO, → UNIDO, → WHO, → ICAO, → IMO, → ITU, → UPU, → WIPO, → WMO, → IMF, → World Bank (IBRD), → IFAD, → UNWTO (UN World Tourism Organization), → IAEA and → WTO/GATT. The latter two (IAEA and WTO/GATT) are commonly counted among the specialized agencies, although they have not concluded relationship agreements with the United Nations according to Article 57 and 63 of the UN Charter, but are in very close cooperation with the UN.

B. The Different Types of Subsidiary Organs

I. Special Organs

Among the subsidiary organs of the United Nations the most important group is formed by the so-called "special organs" (G. Spezialorgane, *Hüfner* 1991, 966). These are organs which were established by the General Assembly to fulfill mostly operative, functionally demarcated tasks. To this group belong *inter alia* → UNICEF, → UNRWA, → UNHCR, → UNHCHR, → UNIFEM, the World Trade Conference → UNCTAD, → UNDP, UNEP, the World Population Fund → UNFPA, and the World Food Programme → WFP.

In establishing these special organs the United Nations reacted to increasing problems in the economic, social and humanitarian fields which could not have been foreseen by the founders of the United Nations, but which fall into the competence of the world organization according to Article 1 (3) and Article 55 of the Charter. Some special organs serve exclusively research and educational purposes in the United Nations, with the aim to increase the efficiency of the UN system (→ UNU, → UNITAR, → UNRISD, → UNIDIR, → INSTRAW, → UNV).

Some authors emphasize the relative autonomy of the special organs, which they display in the exercise of their duties within their scope of competence, in their manner of financing, *inter alia*

through voluntary contributions of the member states, in their organizational structure and personnel policy (cf. *Verdross/Simma* 1984, 97ff.; critically: *Dijkzeul* 1997, 209ff.). But in contrast to the specialized agencies, the special organs do not possess their own legal and political basis in form of an international agreement, nor do they possess their own legal personality.

II. Committees and Commissions

Other subsidiary organs are established by the General Assembly, ECOSOC and the Security Council for the exercise of their tasks. To this group belong the standing and *ad hoc* committees and commissions of the General Assembly (→ Committees, System of), and the commissions of ECOSOC.

In December 2005 General Assembly and Security Council established with concurrent resolutions a subsidiary organ of a new category, a *common subsidiary organ*: the *Peacebuilding Commission* (UN Doc. A/RES/60/180 and UN Doc. S/RES/1645 (2005) of 20 December 2005) as an intergovernmental advisory body for peacebuilding efforts.

III. Legal Commissions

An important role among the subsidiary organs is played by those subsidiary organs working in the legal field: the International Law Commission (→ ILC) promoting the progressive development of international law through its work and the → Human Rights Council.

IV. Organizational, Coordinating and Reform Organs

Another group of subsidiary organs addresses administrative and budgetary matters of the world organization, including the coordination problem (→ Coordination in the UN System) and the reform of the UN system (→ Reform of the UN).

C. Summing Up

This brief survey of the different categories of organs within the UN system has perhaps illustrated the complexity of the organizational structure. This complexity often causes great problems with regard to the concise designation of the different groups of organs, but even more problems, when it comes to informing the world public about the work of these organs.

But, after all, the complex system is the expression of the continuous effort of the world organization to adapt its structures to the changing conditions of the international system as well as to new purposes and goals as they are determined by its member states.

Helmut Volger

Lit.: *Beigbeder, Y.:* The Internal Management of United Nations Organizations. The Long Quest for Reform, Houndmills/London 1997; *Dijkzeul, D.:* The Management of Multilateral Organizations, The Hague et al. 1997; *Hüfner, K.:* UN-System, in: Wolfrum, R. (ed.): United Nations: Law, Policies and Practice, Vol. 2, Munich/Dordrecht 1995, 1361-1368; *Jaenicke, G.:* Article 7, in: Simma, B. (ed.), The Charter of the United Nations. A Commentary, 2nd edn., Oxford 2002, Vol. I, 217-229; *Verdross, A./ Simma, B.:* Universelles Völkerrecht, 3rd edn., Berlin 1984.

Internet: 1. Official Web Site Locator for the UN System: comprehensive and easy-to-use access to all UN sites (including alphabetical and thematic indexes and a system chart): www.unsystem.org; 2. Web Site of the Global Policy Forum on the UN system (links to UN headquarters, UN information services, diverse UN databases etc.): www.globalpolicy.org/links-and-resources-ql/united-nations-system-ql.html.

Public Information of the UN

United Nations Public Information Activities Require Re-orientation

Efforts initiated in 1997 by UN Secretary-General (→ Secretary-General) Kofi Annan at reforming the United Nations (→ Reform of the UN) also included a speedy re-orientation of the Organization's public information activities. "We must ensure that the tale of the activities of the United Nations is told with more vigor and purpose and to greater effect", Mr. Annan wrote on 17 March 1997 in a letter addressed to the President of the → General Assembly on the strengthening of the → UN system (UN Doc. A/51/829). To that end, a sweeping revamping of the United Nations public information capacity was an urgent requirement. Revamping these services would be in line with intergovernmental recommendations, but action to implement these recommendations had not kept pace with the urgent nature of the problem, the Secretary-General stated.

The Secretary-General formulated three principal effects for the reorientation of public information. First, United Nations information activities should in future be geared to providing communications and outreach services to the media, non-governmental organizations (→ NGOs) and other re-disseminators, utilizing the latest media technologies and techniques. Second, the information capability of the → Secretariat should be more intimately linked with and directly supportive of the activities of the substantive departments. And third, resources should be decentralized and refocused on the country and regional levels and greater use should be made of local resources.

Just one month later, he mandated a high-level task force (see Annex 1), chaired by former World Bank Vice President Mark Malloch Brown, with the preparation of a report on the reorientation of United Nations public information activities. The report was presented on 27 June 1997 under the title "Global Vision – Local Voice, A strategic communications programme for the United Nations" (UN Doc. A/AC.198/1997/CRP.1, *United Nations* 1997).

Respected But Not Enough Supported

The Report underlines that the United Nations remains well respected. Even in the United States, thought to be home to the Organization's most persistent critics, more than 60 % of Americans, when polled, routinely express support for the Organization (→ Public Opinion and the UN). But this attitude is only occasionally translated into strong public backing. In such an environment, it is no surprise when determined minorities suspicious of the UN agenda can have a disproportionate influence on US policy towards the UN (→ UN Policy, USA).

Of course, political setbacks as in Bosnia, Somalia and Rwanda have taken their toll, but even more lasting damage has been inflicted worldwide by the perception of the Organization as a "distant, global bureaucracy with little direct relevance to the lives of ordinary people", stereotypes often used by UN critics.

This needs not be so, the Report argues. Poll after poll, in both industrialized and developing countries, had shown that people's concerns revolve around issues which are at the core UN agenda: fighting crime, drugs and disease, securing employment, education and social services, promoting development, protecting the environment (→ Environmental Protection) and human rights (→ Human Rights, Protection of). All of them important UN issues, but only rarely is UN ownership and relevance to them recognized or known.

By its internationalism, its worldwide presence and its agenda, the UN, according to international experts, has the potential to make people everywhere recognize the Organization as an indispensable global institution. But while some of the problems surrounding the less flattering perceptions of the UN could be addressed by better communications and advocacy work, any significant improvement in global support would only take place if this is accompanied by reforms in the way the UN conducts its business. The reform programme initiated by the Secretary-General was therefore a minimum threshold requirement for restoring universal public confidence in the Organization. Good communications would reinforce the reform process internally and externally, the Report maintains.

While the conclusions and proposals arrived at by the experts were not entirely uncontroversial in all their parts, a substantial number of the Report's recommendations were eventually included in a new concept of strategic objectives and operational priorities for future pub-

lic information activities of the world organization.

The Original Mandate

The United Nations public information mandate originates from one of the very first resolutions adopted by the General Assembly (→ Resolution, Declaration, Decision) in 1946 on the organization of the UN Secretariat. In that resolution (A/RES/13 (I) of 13 February 1946), the Assembly declared that "the United Nations cannot achieve its purposes unless the peoples of the world are fully informed of its aims and activities". In the same resolution, the Assembly approved the recommendations of the Technical Advisory Committee on Information, contained in an annex to the resolution and spelling out in detail the policies, functions and organization of the UN Department of Public Information (DPI).

According to these recommendations, the Department was to be so organized and directed as "to promote to the greatest possible extent an informed understanding of the work and purposes of the United Nations among the peoples of the world". To this end, the Department was primarily to assist and rely upon the cooperation of the established governmental and non-governmental agencies of information to provide the public with information about the United Nations. By no means was the Department to engage in "propaganda", but it should, on its own initiative, engage in positive informational activities that would supplement the services of existing agencies of information to the extent that these might be insufficient.

As a general guidance, the Department was requested to give the press "the fullest possible direct access to the activities and official documentation of the Organization". When negotiating agreements with → specialized agencies, the coordination of information services and the need for a common information policy was to be taken into consideration. In order to ensure that peoples in all parts of the world receive the fullest possible information about the United

Nations, the Department was to establish branch offices at the earliest practical date.

Finally, the recommendations of the Technical Advisory Committee of 1946 also included the establishment by the United Nations of its own radio broadcasting station, cooperation with educational institutions and non-governmental organizations, the operation of reference libraries, regular analysis of opinion trends, especially the extent to which an informed understanding of the work of the United Nations is being secured.

Except for a brief reform approach at the end of the 1980s, the structure of the Department for Public Information – called Department or Office at times – remained largely unchanged until the 1990s.

The Committee on Information

While a special Advisory Committee had early been foreseen to serve as the principal policy-making body on public information matters, the General Assembly's Special Political Committee (→ Committees, System of) filled this role for many years, assisted by a Consultative Committee for Press and Public Information. In 1978, the General Assembly established a Committee to Review United Nations Public Information Policies and Activities (UN Doc. A/RES/33/115C, 18 December 1978), later to be known as the "Committee on Information". Originally composed of 41 member states, the Committee has been gradually enlarged over the years to reach 96 members in 2001. The fact that today almost half of the UN membership is represented in that Committee indicates the increased relevance member states attach to the Organization's information policy, as well as to their ability to influence this policy.

For more than 20 years the Committee's mandate has remained unchanged. Three central tasks were assigned to the Committee. It was requested by the General Assembly (UN Doc. A/RES/34/182, 18 December 1979):

- to continue to examine United Nations public information policies and activities, in the light of the evolution of international relations … and of the imperatives of the establishment of the new international economic order and of a new world information and communication order;
- to evaluate and follow-up the efforts made and the progress achieved by the United Nations system in the field of information and communications; and
- to promote the establishment of a new, more just and more effective world information and communication order intended to strengthen peace and international understanding and based on the free circulation and wider and better balanced dissemination of information and to make recommendations thereon to the General Assembly.

The obviously political orientation of this mandate resulted during the following years in numerous polarizations between the "Group of 77" developing countries (→ Group of 77 and the UN) and the Western industrialized states. Only recently has the work in the Committee proceeded largely by consensus.

The Reorientation of Public Information

In the early 1990s, a completely changed international landscape confronted the United Nations with the need to adjust its focus to these changes. New tasks also arose for the United Nations public information activities. Hand-in-hand with the political developments in the post-Cold War era, dramatic technological progress brought basic new requirements which were only to be met by a profound revamping and reorientation of the Organization's public information activities. Within a few years, the Department not only had to cope with the quantum leaps in learning to use new information technologies efficiently, but had also to redefine its most important strategic objectives and functional priorities.

Based on the expert report "Global Vision – Local Voice", as well as comments on and reactions thereto, the Secretary-General presented, in his 1998 report to the General Assembly on questions relating to information (*United Nations* 1998), a general framework for the new public information concept. The broad objectives of the new orientation for United Nations public information activities were defined in that report as follows:

- to place the communications and information functions at the heart of the strategic management of the Organization, given the central role in building public and political support for the United Nations;
- to help develop a culture of communications throughout the Organization, in order to communicate, in cooperation with the programmes, funds and specialized agencies, the direct relevance of every aspect of its work to the daily lives and concerns of people everywhere;
- to project the Organization as an open, transparent and public institution that has the capacity to meet the principal peace, development and human rights objectives enshrined in the Charter of the United Nations ($\rightarrow$ Charter of the UN);
- to strengthen the Organization's ability to communicate at the country and regional levels – the levels at which public opinion is created – and to ensure that the global messages of the United Nations both reflect and are tailored to national orientations;
- to continue to strengthen the Organization's capacity to use the latest information technologies to reach audiences around the globe;
- to follow closely the strategic guidance and direction of the General Assembly on the implementation of mandates, while accepting much greater responsibility for formulation of specific programmes designed to meet mandated goals;
- to develop and strengthen the capacity to deploy given resources flexibly to meet exigent challenges, while maintaining the commitment to mandated priorities; and

- to strengthen further the Department's capacity to work together with other parts of the Organization to design and implement communication and information strategies for their substantive and thematic objectives.

New Challenges

Further steps to implement the new conceptual framework for a re-orientation of the United Nations public information activities were summarized in April 1999 in another report of the Secretary-General (UN Doc. A/AC.198/1999/2, 10 April 1999), addressing new trends and challenges. While maintaining and expanding the Department's capacity to use the "traditional" media – print media, radio and television – for dissemination of information, the use of the Internet became the spearhead of the information revolution in the United Nations. Meanwhile available in all its six official languages ($\rightarrow$ Languages, Official), the UN website (www.un.org) has become the Organization's most important and efficient dissemination tool ($\rightarrow$ Internet, Websites of the UN System in the). During the first four months of 1999 no less than 45.8 million hits were counted, as compared to 25 million hits during the same period in 1998. The UN website was accessed by users from 150 countries. While the majority of users are still based in developed countries, developing countries are increasingly catching up. The information offer is being further expanded by local websites maintained by United Nations Information Centres in local languages including German (the list of the local websites in local languages: http://unic.un.org/around/world/unics/en/whatWeDo/)

Step-by-step the manifold multimedia opportunities offered by the Internet are being fully utilized, and used for the transmission of radio and video programmes as well as for photographs. The daily press briefings by the Spokesman for the Secretary-General were among the first live Internet broadcasts from New York. Already in December 1997, the Third Conference of the Parties to the United Nations Framework Convention on Climate Change, meeting in Kyoto, Japan, was broadcast live on the Internet. Thus, millions of people around the globe were able to follow in real time the making of important decisions on the reduction of greenhouse gases and global warming, and to participate in interactive chat sessions. Meanwhile, webcasts from UN conferences on the Internet have become a standard information feature.

Fundamental changes have also been initiated in the area of the "traditional media". A more effective news gathering and delivery system transmits available information via electronic mail and computerized facsimile distribution directly to the news desks of key media organizations. Personal op-ed articles by the Secretary-General and other senior UN officials are being placed in major daily newspapers through the network of UN Information Centers worldwide. More effective delivery systems using short wave, satellite, digital audio, telephone feeds, electronic audio-file transfers and other Internet-based mechanisms are being established to ensure better use of UN radio programmes. The Department is also following technical innovations available on the Internet that could enhance the use of television and video clips on the United Nations website. Brief video programmes, such as "UN in Action" continue to be seen by millions of viewers through cooperative arrangements with CNN International and national broadcasters. The change to digital television technology presents considerable technical and financial challenges to the Organization but is planned to be fully implemented in the first decade of the new millennium. The role of the Department of Public Information in developing information and communication strategies for the thematic priorities in the area of economic and social development, the promotion of human rights or of peace and security remain a continuing challenge to the Department.

A newly important area of activity relates to the establishment and mobilization of new partnerships in civil society. In order to foster a stronger relationship with the business community, an area of particular interest to the Secretary-General (see Annex 3), the Department launched a new website (www.un.org/partner) in January 1999 to serve as a new virtual enterprise liaison service, helping corporations to locate the UN services they require. Additional efforts are aiming at an even further integration of non-governmental organizations (already today some 1,600 NGOs are associated with the Department) and at the extension of contacts to educational institutions, from primary schools to universities, and from adult education to research institutes.

In the area of publications and library services numerous technical as well as substantive innovations have taken place. Just one of many examples is the continuing move of the Dag Hammarskjöld Library in the direction of a "virtual library", offering full texts of all United Nations documents in all official languages on the Internet ($\rightarrow$ Documentation System; $\rightarrow$ Publications), and servicing a network of well over 350 depository libraries ($\rightarrow$ Depository Libraries).

Implementation of the new public information concept also required some structural changes. A Director of Communications was appointed in the Office of the Secretary-General to assist in developing an overall communications strategy for the Organization and to coordinate efforts to ensure coherence and clarity in the delivery of United Nations messages. To this end, he convenes weekly meetings of the Communications Group composed of representatives of the various parts of the Secretariat engaged in communications functions. The Department of Public Information now also has its own strategic communications planning group. A Media Response Group reacts more quickly to misinformation or criticism of the United Nations in the media. A Central Writers' Group, capable of responding

573

quickly to the need for clear, coherent information material on breaking stories generates customized scripts which can be used for live radio broadcasts or for direct posting on the Internet.

Finally, communications efforts at the field level require greater attention, if the message from the "Global Vision – Local Voice" report is to be understood in a meaningful way. UN Information Centers, the networking of various UN organizations, funds and programmes working in the field, already clustered together in a local "United Nations House" in many cases, will play an important role in this endeavor, as will a review of the experience made with the integration of UNICs in United Nations Development Programme field offices (→ UNDP). With their established contacts over many years with Government officials and media, Parliamentarians and non-governmental organizations, schools and universities, their know-how of the local information networks and their access to sources of information and re-disseminators, the United Nations Information Centers will remain the essential link of the Organization to an effective local implementation of the new information policy.

The organizational switches for a re-orientation of the United Nations public information activities have been put in place, the concepts have been defined, the frameworks established, the instruments tuned. How harmoniously this new instrument will perform will however depend on the substantive successes the Organization will be able to achieve, and on the extend to which it will receive from its member states the human resources and the political and financial support required for implementing mandated tasks. There certainly will be no lack of enthusiasm on the part of the Organization's staff to achieve these aims.

Axel Wüstenhagen

Annex 1:

The Task Force on the Reorientation of United Nations Public Information Ac-

tivities, established by the Secretary-General, was chaired by former World Bank Vice President Mark Malloch Brown and comprised the following members: Peter Arnett, Foreign Correspondent, CNN; Joan Ganz Cooney, Chairman of the Executive Committee of the Children's Television Workshop; Raghida Dergham, Senior Diplomatic Correspondent, Al-Hayat, and President of the UN Correspondents Association; Djibril Diallo, Director of Public Affairs, UN Development Programme; Lelei Lelaulu, Office of the Executive Coordinator for United Nations Reform and Editor of Secretariat News (Secretary of the Task Force); M. Salim Lone, Chief, Publications, UN Department of Public Information (Rapporteur); Hironobu Shibuya, President of Pacific Basin Partners, Inc.; Ambassador Juan Somavia, Permanent Representative of Chile to the United Nations.

Annex 2:

In an address to the World Economic Forum on 31 January 1999, Secretary-General Kofi Annan proposed a Global Compact for the promotion of a set of common values. The Compact encompasses nine principles, drawn from the Universal Declaration of Human Rights, the ILO's Fundamental Principles on Rights at Work and the Rio Principles on Environment and Development and it asks companies to act on these principles in their own corporate domains. Thus, the Compact promotes good practices by corporations; it does not endorse companies. It is not a regulatory instrument or code of conduct, but a value-based platform designed to promote institutional learning. World business leaders are being challenged to help build the social and environmental pillars required to sustain the new global economy and make globalization work for all the world's people. The Global Compact concept is based on the idea that as markets have gone global, so, too, must the idea of corporate citizenship and the practice of corporate social responsibility.

(For further information see www. unglobalcompact.org.)

Lit.: *United Nations:* Global Vision, Local Voice, A strategic communications programme for the United Nations. Report of the Task Force on the Reorientation of United Nations Public Information Activities, June 1997; *United Nations:* Informationsfragen, Bericht des Generalsekretärs, 16 October 1998, UN Doc. A/53/509.

Addendum

In the new millennium the UN Department of Public Information (DPI) continued to follow up on the recommendations made by the Task Force on the Reorientation of United Nations Public Information Activities in its report "Global Vision, Local Voice – A strategic communications programme for the United Nations" (UN Doc. A/AC.198/ 1997/CRP.1) by submitting further reports of the Secretary-General on DPI reform (in 2000 UN Doc. A/AC.198/ 2000/2, in 2001 UN Doc. A/AC.198/ 2001/2 and in 2002 UN Doc. A/AC.198/ 2002/2).

In particular, the 2002 report contained an explicit criticism of the performance of the DPI together with a new mission statement and a set of suggested goals for the work of DPI.

The Need for Further Reform

The 2002 report explicitly stated with regard to the Department of Public Information "a number of critical deficiencies, which adversely affect its ability to deliver its work programme effectively and with the greatest impact." (A/AC.198/2002/2, para. 11) The report saw the fundamental problem of the DPI in the "prevailing ambiguity surrounding its mission" as well as in the "lack of definition in the target audiences for the Department's various activities." (ibid., para. 12).

It related the lack of clarity with regard to its mission to the manifold mandates (more than hundred) given by the General Assembly to the DPI. The proliferation of mandates "has not only created a heavy workload for the Depart-

ment, but has contributed to the fragmentation of its activities ..." (ibid., para. 12).

Concerning the target audiences the report detected manifold target groups: UN member states and their delegations, researchers, a well-informed segment of the public with an interest in the UN and, last but not least, the public at large. To some extent the DPI relied in its work on intermediaries (mass media, NGOs and educational institutions), another part of its work was addressed directly to the public.

Moreover the DPI had failed to evaluate the impact of its activities adequately, being of the opinion that the DPI activities "must be performed because they are mandated rather than because they are demonstrably effective." (ibid., para.15).

In addition to these structural problems within the department, the DPI was increasingly confronted with criticism in the sessions of the Commission on Information: the developing countries criticized the insufficient number of UN information centres in developing countries and demanded a transfer of resources from UN information centres in developed countries to developing countries for the setting-up of new information centres. Member states with official languages other than English and French criticized the small number of DPI information material in the other official languages of the UN and other states complained about the lack of information material in languages other than the UN official languages. The big "payers" in the UN criticized the lack of efficiency of the DPI and urged rationalization measures in order to save money. The other Secretariat Departments complained of an insufficient degree of communication and coordination achieved by the DPI.

New Mission Statement: Coordinator of UN Communications Content

In contrast to the former DPI goal of developing its own information content and of conveying it to diverse target audiences the report proposed a reduction in and concentration of the tasks of the DPI:

"The Department of Public Information's)mission is to manage and coordinate United Nations communications content – generated by the activities of the Organization and its component parts – and strategically to convey this content, especially through appropriate intermediaries, to achieve the greatest public impact." (ibid., para. 19)

Thereby it should focus in particular on key intermediaries, such as the media, NGOs and educational institutions, rather than attempting to reach the public at large. This multiplier approach promised more efficiency and lower costs than the direct outreach. In other words, the DPI should concentrate more on applying its communication expertise in crafting and conveying the information content obtained from other UN offices and Departments rather than creating the bulk of its communications content on its own. That meant first of all establishing better working relations with the other UN entities in order to obtain firsthand information from them.

The Concept of Regional Information Centres

While this part of the 2002 reform report contained a pragmatic concept for an adequate reformulation of the DPI's goals in general, the report contained in the part dealing with the UN Information Centres – in disguised diplomatic language – concrete proposals for restructuring the network of Information Centers. Referring to the necessity to "maximize the limited resources available to Information Centres", the report recommended taking up the suggestion made already in the above-mentioned Report of the Task Force of the year 1997, namely to establish a number of regional information centres – "hubs" – to replace the large number of information centers in the respective region, "especially in areas where linguistic commonalities facilitate regionalization." (ibid., para. 53)

The report made it clear that it considered above all the developed countries as the area, where such regional "hubs" should be established: the question "is whether the Organization needs to maintain United Nations Information Centres in high-cost developed countries, whose populations have relatively greater access to a wide range of sources of information than their counterparts in the developing world." (ibid., para. 54)

Here the report reveals the massive pressure from developing countries to obtain more UN Information Centres, financed in their opinion by the resources saved through the establishment of regional hubs in developed countries, and the demand to get from DPI more information material in languages other than the six official UN languages (cf. ibid., para. 54).

Putting the New Concept into Practice

The Commission on Information endorsed the new concept submitted in the 2002 SG report in its session in April 2003 (cf. UN Press Releases PI/1475 of 29 April 2003 and PI/1477 of 30 April 2003).

In June 2003 Secretary-General Annan announced that nine information centers in Western Europe, among others the UNICs in Paris, Bonn, London and Copenhagen, would be closed by the end of the year and "be replaced by a regional hub in Brussels" (UN Press Briefing of 12 June 2003) and in December 2003 the General Assembly adopted with resolution A/RES/58/101B the new concept for the work of the DPI.

In paragraph 40 the General Assembly explicitly affirmed the plan of the Secretary-General to establish a Western European hub.

In 2004 and the following years the DPI began to put the new concept into practice, with mixed results: with regard to its information policy some remarkable improvements could be observed – more and detailed information on the DPI Internet website, an online edition of the UN Chronicle, and later on free access to a number of important databanks, such as UNBISNET, containing the bibliographic information on all UN documents, other UN texts and secondary literature available at the Dag Hammarskjöld Library at UN Headquarters in New York, and the Official Document System of the United Nations (ODS), comprising direct access to the texts of all UN documents issued since 1993 and to all GA and SC resolutions since 1945.

The Regional Hub in Brussels

On the other hand the DPI, the Secretary-General and the General Assembly contributed to a severe damage inflicted on the network of UN information centres by the decision to close nine UN Information Centres (UNICs) in Western Europe and to replace them by the Regional UN Information Centre in Brussels. This decision was taken rather quickly, neither NGOs nor journalists, diplomats and politicians of the respective member states had been given adequate opportunities to participate in the debate or to develop alternative suggestions. After the General Assembly had agreed on the closure in December 2003, the nine UNICs were closed in a few weeks, the move of staff, equipment, books, etc. took place at high speed and on 30 January 2004 the Brussels "hub" was opened in the presence of Secretary-General Kofi Annan (cf. UN Press Release SG/SM/9136/Rev.1 of 30 January 2004) – indeed a hasty measure, which later on proved to be a mistake in many regards: the closure of the UNICS, the move to Brussels and the maintenance of the Regional Centre proved to be more costly than estimated (cf. the statement of the Tunisian representative in the session of the Committee on Information on 19 April 2005, UN Press Release PI/1645; see also the SG report on the rationalization of the UNICS 2005, *United Nations* 2005, para. 6).

Moreover valuable contacts with the mass media, NGOs representatives and academic experts were severely impeded through the move to Brussels, as an evaluation of the UN public information situation in Western Europe, under-

taken in late 2005 with the expert assistance of a communication consultant, and published in 2006 as report of the Secretary-General (UN Doc. A/AC.198/2006/1) revealed: "... in 2005 the Centre [the Regional United Nations Information Centre Brussels, H.V.] had not yet fully adjusted to this new regional approach. It was still grappling with the challenges of a dramatic change in the established patterns of doing business and of serving the media and civil society in a large and distant geographical area from a centralized location. The physical distance from their key local partners was seen by some staff at the Centre as a major obstacle in maintaining the necessary rapport with the media and civil society, in taking part in important media events and in developing new partnerships. Though new methods of functioning, in particular by electronic and telephonic means, had been envisaged, this physical distance from their target audiences had led in some cases to a decline in contacts and activities and had reduced the visibility of the United Nations in the countries concerned. As a result, the Centre has yet to achieve the visibility and standing that had been hoped for in the countries it serves. This problem was exacerbated by the lack of adequate travel funds, which made frequent visits impossible. ... Some desk officers have been able to mobilize travel funds from Governments or the organizers of the events they have been invited to support, such as non-governmental organizations and educational institutions. ... Efforts to energize the regional United Nations Associations in European countries to serve as civil society partners of the Centre have also made uneven progress, despite the cooperation of the World Federation of United Nations Associations." (Report of the Secretary-General on the continued rationalization of the network of United Nations information-centres, *United Nations* 2006, para. 29). Even the then Director of RUNIC Brussels Fodha had to admit in a speech held before the Working Group on the UN of European Council Members in May

2004: "It must be clear that the nine country officers [in RUNIC Brussels, H.V.] can not offer the same intensity and complexity of service as those former UNICs." (RUNIC Press Release 19 May 2004).

The criticism inside the UN and in the member states about the closure of the nine UNICs was so massive and outspoken that the UN Secretariat changed in subsequent years its policy and gave up in early 2005 its original intention to establish further regional information hubs – a "lesson learned" from Brussels (cf. report of the Secretary-General on the further rationalization of the network of UN information centres, 22 February 2005, UN Doc. A/AC.198/2005/3, para. 52).

Prospects for the Work of the DPI

Striking a balance between the work of the DPI and the situation of the UN public information in general, there are successes and failures on the balance sheet:

- The information of the public worldwide has been improved considerably; the more than sixty UN information centres provide more than fifty local UNIC websites, many of them also in languages other than the six official UN languages.
- The Internet information sources provided by the different UN institutions are nowadays excellent, search engines and data banks grant access to a large variety of UN documents, background papers, session records and multilateral treaties deposited and registered at the UN Secretariat.
- In contrast to this abundance of primary texts such as UN documents it is much more difficult to obtain UN texts giving critical evaluations of the processes and events in the United Nations; the information brochures and books published by the DPI, for example "The United Nations Today" (New York 2008), are mostly written from an idealistic point of view, sound often rather naive and do not contain much criticism. This makes the DPI material in general not very attractive.

- There is no systematic and fruitful cooperation between DPI staff and UN-interested journalists, which could have the long-term effect of encouraging journalists to write in-depth reports on UN events, thus broadening the understanding of the UN in the world public; it is very telling that Hollywood movies playing in the UN buildings such as "The Interpreter" have a stronger public information impact than a lot of DPI actions.
- Contrary to the mission statement of 2002 which gave the cooperation between the DPI and other UN Departments and Offices a high priority, there is still an obvious lack of effective day-to-day cooperation, for example between the DPKO and the DPI. Particularly in the peacekeeping area closer cooperation would be very helpful in the effort to prevent DPKO and the peacekeeping missions from being unfairly criticized (cf. *Lehmann* 1999).
- The DPI has not been very successful in assisting Secretary-General Kofi Annan in defending himself during the Oil-for-Food investigations and the ensuing public debate against polemical allegations; the UN Association of the USA did in this respect a better job than the DPI.
- The DPI still has a staff problem. As Barbara Crossette commented critically in an Internet article in July 2003 (*Crossette* 2003), the DPI is extremely overstaffed in comparison to other UN Departments, and moreover its staff follows more often bureaucratic rules instead of journalistic concepts and is more interested in keeping their jobs than in explaining the UN to the public. There is a lack of journalists inside the DPI, since many member states have considered the DPI just as another UN unit, where they could place their people to provide them with good jobs. Since much of the DPI budget is spent on the staff expenses there is not enough money left for keeping pace with technological innovations; the DPI equipment is often outdated, while it would be impor-

tant to offer interesting material on the Internet, in particular to young people; the UN CyberSchoolBus (www.un.org/Pubs/CyberSchoolBus/) as Internet platform for school children is a very modest achievement in this respect.

- Instead of taking the structural problems of the DPI enough into account, the Commission on Information and the General Assembly repeat the same phrases about public information policy every year, with the General Assembly underlining for example still in its routine resolution 2008 on "Questions relating to information" (A/RES/100 A-B of 5 December 2008) "the importance of rationalizing the network of United Nations information centres, and in this regard, requests the Secretary-General to continue to make proposals in this direction, including the redeployment of resources where necessary" (ibid., para. 29), as if the move to Brussels had not been a complete failure; this lesson has obviously not been learned so far by a lot of UN member states.

What is Needed

The DPI needs no further reorientation and rationalization papers, but an intensive structural reform of its staff, which might prove difficult, but which would increase its efficiency considerably: the size of the staff of the Department should be reduced; vacancies should be filled with journalists instead of UN diplomats.

The DPI should also change its style of work. It should introduce weekly cabinet-style meetings with staff people from all UN Departments, UN programmes, funds and specialized agencies where they should discuss priorities of UN public information policy, decide on who is going to publish what publication and plan and implement "joint ventures", i.e. common publications, something rare in the UN landscape with all its separate "kingdoms". At least USG Kiyo Akasaki, head of the DPI, informed the Commission on Information in April 2008, that he had

held "a series of consultations with the heads of departments and offices to identify specific areas of cooperation" and that he "sought to be more proactive in ensuring coordination across the United Nations system on selected priorities" (UN Press Release PI/1827 of 28 April 2008) – a first step on the way to an improved UN public information policy.

In particular the contacts with UN journalists should be given more attention; they should be encouraged to realize more media projects (movie and tv films, radio features, etc.) about the UN. The DPI should take over in this respect the role of the helpful impresario in the background, enabling the journalists to do their journalistic work freely – quite an adventure in the still rather bureaucratic UN offices, but such media projects would stir up the UN melancholy to the better.

What the UN does is interesting and mostly valuable. It needs to be told more interestingly and more professionally to the public. The UN should invest more ideas in its public information policy, it is worth the trouble.

Helmut Volger

Annex 1:

In 2008, the *Committee on Information* (www.un.org/ga/coi) comprised the following 110 UN members states: Algeria, Angola, Argentina, Armenia, Austria, Bangladesh, Belarus, Belgium, Belize, Benin, Brazil, Bulgaria, Burkina Faso, Burundi, Cape Verde, Chile, China, Colombia, Congo, Costa Rica, Côte d'Ivoire, Croatia, Cuba, Cyprus, Czech Republic, Democratic People's Republic of Korea, Democratic Republic of the Congo, Denmark, Dominican Republic, Ecuador, Egypt, El Salvador, Ethiopia, Finland, France, Gabon, Georgia, Germany, Ghana, Greece, Guatemala, Guinea, Guyana, Hungary, Iceland, India, Indonesia, Iran, Ireland, Israel, Italy, Jamaica, Japan, Jordan, Kazakhstan, Kenya, Lebanon, Liberia, Libya, Luxembourg, Madagascar, Malta, Mexico, Monaco, Mongolia, Morocco, Mozambique, Nepal, Netherlands, Niger, Nigeria, Pakistan, Peru, Philippines, Poland, Portugal, Qatar, Republic of Korea, Republic of Moldova, Romania, Russian Federation, Saint Vincent and the Grenadines, Saudi Arabia, Senegal, Singapore, Slovakia, Solomon Islands, Somalia, South Africa, Spain, Sri Lanka, Sudan, Suriname, Switzerland, Syria, Thailand, Togo, Trinidad and Tobago, Tunisia, Turkey, Ukraine, United Kingdom, United Republic of Tanzania, United States, Uruguay, Venezuela, Viet Nam, Yemen, Zimbabwe.

Lit.: *Crossette, B.:* Ahead Of Information Summit, U.N. Should Examine Itself, in: U.N. Wire, 28 July 2003 (www.unwire.org); *Lehmann, I.:* Peacekeeping and Public Information. Caught in the Crossfire, London et al. 1999; *United Nations - General Assembly:* Global Vision, Local Voice – A strategic communications programme for the United Nations. Report of the Task Force on the Reorientation of United Nations Public Information Activities, 14 August 1997, UN Doc. A/AC.198/1997/CRP.1; *United Nations - General Assembly:* Reorientation of United Nations activities in the field of public information and communications. Report of the Secretary-General, 25 March 2002, UN Doc. A/AC.198/2002/2; *United Nations - General Assembly:* Further rationalization of the network of United Nations information centres. Report of the Secretary-General, 22 February 2005, UN Doc. A/AC.198/2005/3 (quoted as: United Nations 2005) *United Nations - General Assembly:* Continued rationalization of the network of United Nations information centres. Report of the Secretary-General, 14 February 2006, UN Doc. A/AC.198/2006/1 (quoted as: United Nations 2006).

Internet: Homepage of the United Nations: http://www.un.org; link to UN Information Centres: www.un.org/aroundworld/unics.

Public Opinion and the UN

The United Nations is often referred to as a "world public" in common metaphorical language: *forum* (of the world as a market and as a place of negotiations and bargaining), *arena* (of arguments or struggle for power), *platform/*

speaker's stand, (world's) *stage,* as well as *theatre, drama.* Other typical metaphors for the UN are: *town/city hall of the world, world parliament* and often even *world government* or, negatively, *debating society/club.* Furthermore: *bridge (between the worlds ...); world police, fire brigade* (for "blue helmet" operations and the like); the *tool* or *instrument* United Nations is also called *seismograph* (of international relations conceived as natural catastrophes) or (their) *mirror* and *magnifying glass.* These, commonly used metaphors and concepts are mostly wrong in substance, but they show what most people expect, implicitly, and often despite better knowledge, of the United Nations. The UN has to recognize, clarify and solve any problems one can think of, be it political, social or cultural. Of course, these high expectations cause subsequently disappointment and criticism in form of sweeping generalizations. Often the same people, who have such high expectations, blame explicitly, despite better knowledge, "the UN" for inactivity, incompetence and inefficiency. The → UN system is indeed an essential part of the global political public, but at the same time in terms of political coverage and public opinion it is an object of publicity itself, and of the mechanisms to establish and to influence the public perception.

I. The Role of the Mass Media in International Politics

The nature and extent of the influence of the mass media on decision-making in politics, especially in foreign policy, are controversial. However, the thesis is plausible that the (media) public has a specific importance which is growing parallel to the growth of the media system. The media "presentation" – or even "production" – of "the UN" has developed typical patterns of presenting and of perception: Generally, conflicts and dissention are (over)emphasized by superficial "war reporting". The travelling diplomacy of the → Secretary-General and other UN heads, as well as certain phases of formal debating – often only the voting, are in the focus of the media; reports are regularly made about the → Security Council. The other UN bodies (→ Principal Organs, Subsidiary Organs, Treaty Bodies) are almost ignored. In most media, the reports on the so-called "world conferences" (→ World Conferences) are also restricted to the "highlights" such as the opening ceremony featuring the heads of state and government. Because of their immediate visual appeal and tendency to focus on topicality, television reports tend to reduce the image of the UN above all to pictures of scenes of conflict, often regardless of the question for what reason and in how far the UN is involved in the conflict. The problem in reporting on activities of or within the UN is that there people often speak in a highly formal manner of affairs and of situations that have already been amply discussed, debated or written about ; such static discussion situations, particularly in diplomatic negotiation committees, are difficult to visualize, whereas seemingly "effective" acting, i.e. actions of all kinds such as white vehicles driving around or helpful "blue helmets", are easy to visualize and thus are "transmittable" in terms of television reporting.

During the second Gulf War of 1991/1992 a new problem emerged with regard to television reports. More important than the prohibition by the USA, presumably derived from their Vietnam war experience, on the publication of any pictures other than photos approved or even "selected" by censuring US military authorities was the politically active function of the media reports themselves. CNN, the American private television programme, which was the first to broadcast the start of the actual fighting in this war, became well-known even to the last newspaper reader, and became a topic itself: In the debate about the UN operation some years later in Somalia the *bon mot* was coined that virtually the Security Council has a "16th member", a "sixth" permanent member with veto right - the television programme CNN. The intervention in Somalia was made rather difficult to

implement and became more and more problematic to a large extent because of the changing mood of the US public, being strongly influenced by television reports of CNN (cf. *Goodman* 1992), and because of the American "stop-and-go" policy being decisively influenced by these changes in the US public opinion (→ UN Policy, USA). Since the end of the East-West confrontation, public perceptions and discussions, influenced by television programmes such as CNN, have gained their own political relevance in international affairs, having been formerly conducted secretly and well isolated from every-day political affairs. This is significant in particular for the superpower USA, where usually the citizens are sparsely concerned with external matters. But nowadays the viewers in all member states of the UN are strongly influenced by the pictures they see on television.

Media reports focus the perception of the public, and thus influence decision-making processes (cf. *Iyengar/Simon* 1993; *Domke et al.* 1998). The pressure to change procedures of communication and decision-making comes from the quantitative and structural expansion of the media system and from the resulting changes in political public opinion. These changes restrict the traditional autonomy of the ministers of foreign affairs (cf. *Miller* 2007). Meanwhile decision-making processes in managing crises and conflicts have changed considerably due to the potentially unlimited "real time" live television reports, creating time pressures, as well as strong political effects caused by sudden changes in the political "mood" of the public in reaction to television coverage (cf. *Jordan/Page* 1992). Thus politicians are tempted to react without taking enough time for discussion and reflection and to present themselves on the public stage created by the electronic media as resolutely acting protagonists in accordance with the – and often abruptly changing – expectations of the public as they appear in the printed and electronic media. Similar changes are also to be found in the once relatively discreet and secret realm of classical diplomacy between states. When international organizations emerged in the second half of the 19th century, the "classical" impenetrable bilateral diplomacy had been supplemented by "semi-transparent" multilateral consensus-oriented negotiation diplomacy. Now new forms of actually or seemingly transparent "public diplomacy" are developing beside the two existing forms of diplomacy: representatives of states communicate and negotiate in and through the media. Thus negotiations are no longer restricted to representatives of the state, but civil society actors are also gaining weight in the negotiations.

II. The Changing Public Image of the UN

Interests and motives of the actors on the "stage of the world", and the inherent laws of the media shape the presentations of issues and activities of "the UN". Against the dynamics of the national public in the member states, the public relations work of the UN has slim chances. The UN → Secretariat makes some efforts, however, to tie in with the traditional image of the UN as peacekeeper and pioneer for social and humanitarian progress, and to maintain this image in the world public through a trustworthy public information policy in the face of fundamental criticism, often one-sided and polemic (→ Public Information of the UN). Public opinion polls with regard to the UN are rare, disparate and suffer often from the vague framing of the questions. Generally, UNICEF and UNESCO are the best known and best appreciated UN organizations, although it is obvious that the opinions of the public are not rooted in any profound degree of knowledge about the work and structure of the world organization.

The blockades of the Security Council in the times of Cold War, caused by the confrontation of the superpowers, had dampened the early hopes of fruitful activity of the world organization. Later the behavior of many governments of the "young nations" of the "South",

forming since the 1960s the majority in the UN General Assembly provoked large parts of the public in the "North-West" of the world, i.e. the Western industrialized countries, and frustrated particularly the American public. Apparently, after the end of the confrontation of the blocs, the times seemed to have changed in favor of the UN: the UN seemed now to be more capable of acting in the interest of the "new world order".

After a low mark in the public opinion during the mid-eighties, for example in the countries of the European Community, a high enthusiasm was noted in opinion polls on the UN at the end of the 80s: in the Federal Republic of Germany, where usually the numbers of positive statements were lower in comparison to the other western countries, the positive estimation of the UN was doubled in these few years, amounting now to nearly 50 percent of the interviewed, whereas the number of explicitly negative-minded voices fell to under a tenth. However, the second Gulf War demonstrated the rather weak position of the United Nations in relation to the foreign policy of a hegemonic coalition of powers, which led to some disillusionment among those who had hoped for a central role of the United Nations since the superpowers had ended their blockade of the Security Council. When the Somalia operation was declared by influential governments and large parts of the media – in contrast to the facts, but as a consequence of the disappointed high expectations and the media coverage – as a failure of "the UN", the public appreciation of that operation was changed into a negative, and polemical criticisms of its ineffectiveness became a favorite topic of many media. The conflict in former Yugoslavia was considered, in the opinion of a rather critical, but frequently poorly informed western public, as a crucial test for the UN, even though the UN initially was not directly engaged. However, the slow political progress in the Balkans offered just routine pictures of negotiations, ceasefires, patrolling peacekeeping forces, with no glorious events of success which could be covered on television.

The "war against terror" is a serious challenge for the UN and at the same time a menace to the world's opinion of the world organization. As the US disregarded the UN at the beginning of the US intervention in Iraq the organization seemed to prove to be both brave and weak. In the long run, it is to be hoped that the third Gulf war will strengthen the position of multilateralism, even in US opinion.

Since the early years of the UN, US foreign and public information policies have had a special significance for the image of the UN. Whether idealistic approval of the UN – expressed by leading politicians and the media after the foundation of the UN in the second half of the 1940s – or the negative conspiracy theories brought forward against the UN in the time of McCarthyism in the early 50s and again during the Reagan administration in the 1980s, changes in public opinion in the USA always reflected a precarious relationship of the superpower to the world organization (cf. *Scott/Withey* 1958; *Hero* 1977; *Millard* 1993): a relationship that is on the level of political decision-making determined by the dynamics of US foreign policy doctrines (isolationism vs. hegemonic interventionism, connected with burden-sharing in multilateral cooperation), but is also more and more influenced – cognitively as well as emotionally – by the electronic media. In fact, unilateralism offers a hegemonic power, in the opinion of many politicians, many more advantages than multilateralism. Therefore it is hard to imagine that the US political decision-makers will accept to be politically influenced by the UN.

In the opinion of the vociferous neo-conservative and fundamentalist right wing movements in US politics the UN is considered even as the enemy of American interests, because those people are convinced that the UN has transformed the countries of the Third World into a coalition of anti-Western nations. The criticism of the alleged inefficiency

and waste of money was often advanced with populist verve by members of the US Congress, whereas the American public makes more distinctions in its views with regard to the UN. From its beginnings the UN always has been comparatively popular among the US citizens, sometimes it was even more valued than the US government. In the late 1990s, up to three quarters of Americans had a positive opinion of the UN and widely appreciated the UN membership of the USA (cf. *Wirthlin Worldwide* 1998). Amidst the dangers and challenges of the first decade of the new century, most Americans believe the UN should be stronger in playing its necessary role in the world, but they have specific reservations about UN performance (comprehensive analysis of polls of the American public over the past decade, *International Policy Attitudes/WPO*). Like the rest of the world, Americans favor a considerable increase in UN power: large majorities think the UN should be able to go into countries to investigate human rights abuses, command a standing UN peacekeeping force, regulate international arms sales, and much more; most Americans support adding new permanent members to the UN Security Council even to the disadvantage of the USA (see *The Chicago Council on Global Affairs* and *Program on International Policy Attitudes/WPO* 2006/2007).

Most of the reservations about the UN are connected with its alleged inefficiency, and with the fear that the world organization could restrict American sovereignty. Variations in the approval of the UN depended above all on the assessment of the success or failure of peacekeeping operations, whereby this evaluation of the UN peacekeeping is strongly influenced by the media. It is indeed interesting that American public has obviously a more positive opinion of the UN than the politicians assume (cf. *Kull et al.* 1997). Thus, it is still a structural problem of the UN in respect to the US public opinion, that this approval of the majority of the US public cannot be used to balance the political influence of the very active interest groups in the US Congress which are either indifferent to the UN or strongly criticize it.

Beyond the USA, all over the world a clear desire for increased UN power is to be found, combined with a universal support for dramatic reforms of the UN (cf. *GlobeScan* and *Program on International Policy Attitudes* 2005).

It is not clear what image the UN does actually have in general in the countries of the "South". At least we know from opinion polls that Latin Americans trust the UN more than their own institutions.

In practice the political and economic elites in the Third World regard and use the UN system as a negotiating mechanism, service organization and source of financial resources.

All in all, the UN image in the Third World states should be quite good, if only because of its usefulness. In poorer countries or those that suffer from conflicts, probably, for many the blue flag of the UN is likely to have a more positive significance than the power insignia of the own state (cf. Diven 2008).

III. The Symbolic Function of the United Nations

The United Nations or, strictly speaking, the global problems of mankind addressed by it such as peace, fight against poverty, the protection of the biosphere, etc. have either no or insufficiently organized lobbies in the USA as well as in Europe and the other countries of the West. Most UN topics suffer from abstraction and cognitive distance from the daily political world of the national public. The national public in the industrialized countries is normally cognitively as well as emotionally far away from the peoples in the South afflicted more directly and more strongly by "global" problems; the interests of both groups of peoples diverge strongly while communication between them hardly takes place.

That is why the symbolic function of the United Nations is of such great importance (cf. *Hurd* 2002). Even though the UN has no material means itself and

no power, it can nevertheless "heal" – in the sense of the above mentioned metaphoric images – global problems which are seemingly intractable or not solvable in the near future, "simply" by acting and speaking symbolically in the world "forum", in an appeal to the "conscience" of the community of states, a symbolic "prayer of mankind addressed at itself", as Conor Cruise O'Brien, staff member of UN Secretary-General Dag Hammarskjöld, has put it. The symbolic action at least keeps the situation open and allows further communication.

In this sense, the staging of "world conferences" has had considerable significance for the public perception of the UN, which should not be underestimateed. For example, the Rio Earth Summit of 1992 connected "state theatre" with high-ranking "actors", with a supreme topic that affects all. The summit certainly has raised public awareness of the problem of global environmental problems, even though it has not succeed so far in making the states draw the necessary conclusions in form of effective implementation measures. But it has made the world aware of the problem and presented suggestions for its solution. This is quite an achievement for a powerless and symbolic world forum.

Reinhard Wesel

Lit.: *Brewer, P.R. et al.:* International Trust and Public Opinion About World Affairs, in: American Journal of Political Science 48 (2004), 93-109; *Crossette, B.:* Media, in: Weiss, T.G./Daws, S. (eds.): The Oxford Handbook on the United Nations, 275-284; *Diven, P.J.:* The Determinants of International Support for the United Nations. Unpublished manuscript of a paper presented at the Annual Conference of the International Studies Association at San Francisco in March 2008; *Domke, D. et al.:* Media Priming Effects: Accessibility, Association and Activation, in: International Journal of Public Opinion Research 10 (1998), 51-74; *Goodman, W.:* How Much Did TV Shape Policy, in: New York Times, 8 December 1992; *Gowing, N.:* Media Coverage: Help or Hindrance for Conflict Prevention? Diagnostic Paper, Carnegie Commission on Preventing Deadly Conflict, New York 1996; *Hurd,*

L: Legitimacy, Power, and the Symbolic Life of the UN Security Council, in: Global Governance 8 (2002), 35-51; *Hero, A.O.:* The United States Public and the United Nations, in: Proceedings of the Academy of Political Sciences 32 (1977), 17-29; *Iyengar, S./Simon, A.:* News Coverage of the Gulf Crisis and Public Opinion. A Study of Agenda-Setting, Priming and Framing, in: Communication Research 20 (1993), 365-383; *Jervis, R.:* Perception and Misperception in International Politics, Princeton 1976; *Kertzer, D.I.:* Ritual, Politics, and Power, New Haven 1988; *Lehmann, I.:* Peacekeeping and Public Information: Caught in the Crossfire, London 1999; *Kull, S. et al.:* The Foreign Policy Gap: How Policymakers Misread the Public. A Report of a Study by the Center for International and Security Studies of the University of Maryland and its Program on International Policy Studies, College Park/ MD 1997; *Millard, W.J.:* International Public Opinion of the United Nations: A Comparative Analysis, in: International Journal of Public Opinion Research 5 (1993), 92-99; *Miller, D.B.:* Media Pressure on Foreign Policy: The Evolving Theoretical Framework, New York 2007; *Neumann, J.:* Lights, Camera, War – Is Media Technology Driving International Politics? New York 1996; *Rotberg, R./Weiss, T.G. (eds.):* From Massacres to Genocide – The Media, Public Policy, and the Humanitarian Crises, Harrisonburg 1996; *Ramey, Carl R.:* Mass Media Unleashed: How Washington Policymakers Shortchanged the American Public, Lanham 2007; *The Pew Research Center for the People and the Press:* Views of a Changing World, June 2003, http:// people-press.org/reports/pdf/185.pdf; *Scott, W.A./Withey, S. B.:* The United States and the United Nations: The Public View 1945-1955, New York 1958; *Sills, J.B. (ed.):* Public Attitudes toward the U.N. Hearing before the Subcommittee on International Operations of the Committee on Foreign Relations, United States Senate, 59th Congress, 1st session, 27 July 1977, Washington 1977; *Torgler, B.:* Trust in International Organizations: an empirical investigation focusing on the United Nations, in: Review of International Organizations 3 (2008), 65-93; *United Nations Department of Public Information:* What Do Americans Really Think of the UN, UN Doc. DPI/1963/Rev.1, New York 1998; *United Nations Department of Public Information:* United Nations Worldwide Public Opinion Polling Programme (1989-1992) – Cross-Country Analysis of Key Findings, New York 1992; *Volger, H.:* Das Bild der Vereinten Nationen in der öffentlichen Meinung, in: Volger, H. (ed.): Grundlagen und Strukturen der Vereinten Nationen, Munich 2007, 363-389; *Wesel, R.:* Die symbolischen Vereinten Nationen, in: Schorlemer, S. v. (ed.): Praxis-Handbuch UNO, Berlin et al. 2003, 591-613.

Internet: Homepages of the United Nations Association of the USA (www.unausa.org) and of the Global Policy Forum (www. globalpolicy.org), using the text searching function (search word: public opinion); periodic news and reviews of polls on the public opinion of the UN provides WordPublicOpinion (WPO), a project managed by the Program on International Policy Attitudes at the University of Maryland): www.worldpublicopinion.org; cf. www.americans-world. org.

Publications

The United Nations produce not only an enormous number of official documents (→ Documentation system) that are used as working papers for the meetings of numerous UN organs and bodies, it is also active as a publisher and releases approximately 900 new titles in multiple languages per year. Among these are introductions to the work of the UN, studies and monographs in specific subject areas, such as international relations, economics, environment, sociology, international law, → human rights and demography, compilations of laws and documents, conference reports, teaching materials and posters, as well as statistics and databases. In total, more than 4,000 titles are currently in print: approximately 2,100 titles in English and the remaining titles in the other five official languages (→ Languages, Official) of the UN, Arabic, Chinese, French, Russian and Spanish. International statistics are normally published in multilingual editions. Slightly over 10 % of the 2,100 English-language titles fall into the category United Nations/ reference works/ general, about 10 % cover political sciences (predominantly studies on disarmament issues), slightly over 20 % belong to the domain of social sciences (women, narcotic drugs, health, nutrition, social development), about 10 % cover international law (trade law (→ Trade, International Law of), international environmental law (→ Environmental Law, International), human rights, international criminal law, → law of the sea), just under 20 % fall into the category → environmental protection/sustainable development, 30 % belong to the domain of economics (international trade, economic development, development aid, transnational corporations, energy, industrial development, agriculture, transfer of technology, transport, and technological development), and just under 7 % cover the areas demography and human settlements.

United Nations publications are primarily directed at experts and practitioners in the fields and professional domains mentioned above. However, a number of UN publications are widely popular or are of particular importance because topics are covered with a worldwide scope or because they supply global situation reports and data. Among others, the following titles fall into this category:
- The United Nations today,
- Yearbook of the United Nations,
- International instruments of the United Nations,
- Statistical yearbook,
- Demographic yearbook,
- United Nations disarmament yearbook,
- United Nations blue books series,
- The blue helmets,
- World statistics pocketbook,
- Report on the world social situation,
- The world's women: trends and statistics,
- State of the world's children,
- The progress of nations,
- World population prospects,
- The state of world population,
- Human rights: a compilation of international instruments,
- The work of the International Law Commission,
- United Nations treaty series,
- World economic and social survey,
- Trade and development report,
- The least developed countries report,
- World investment report.

With respect to journals published by the UN, the *United Nations chronicle,* the *Law of the sea bulletin, CEPAL review* and the *Monthly bulletin of statistics* are among the more popular titles.

A complete catalogue can either be requested from the UN publications offices and sales agents listed below or it can be consulted on the UN homepage at http://unp.un.org/catalog.aspx.

An increasing number of key UN publications are published on behalf of the United Nations by major commercial publishers, including the *Human development report* of the United Nations Development Programme (→ UNDP), the *Global environment outlook* of the United Nations Environment Programme (→ UNEP), *The state of the world's refugees* of the High Commissioner for Refugees (→ UNHCR) or the *World drug report* of the United Nations Drug Control Programme.

Whereas the majority of UN publications are issued in print and CD-ROM formats, an increasing number of titles (currently approximately 700) are also made available as electronic books for online purchase and immediate download. Many key publications can be freely consulted, sometimes in their entirety, sometimes in excerpts, on the publications web pages of the issuing UN agency. The content of a large number of UN publications can also be searched using Google Book Search.

The United Nations Publications Board has overall responsibility for the execution of the publications programme, including coordination, production, costing, and setting organization-wide policies and standards governing the sale and marketing of published materials, external publishing, as well as copyright (cf. UN Doc. ST/SGB/2005/ 15 of 24 May 2005).

Overall revenue earned from the sale of UN publications or the sale of license fees to access online resources, such as the *United Nations Commodity Trade Database* or the electronic version of the *Monthly bulletin of statistics,* has been declining due to free online availability of many publications. It makes up only a minute portion (approximately 0.066%) of the income of the United Nations (not considering budget contributions by UN member states).

United Nations publications can be consulted in → Depository libraries, the UN Libraries in Geneva and New York, as well as in UN Information Centres (see listing in annex), or they can be purchased from the UN sales offices in Geneva and New York:

> United Nations Sales Office and
> Bookshop
> Palais des Nations
> CH-1211 Geneva 10
> Switzerland
> Phone: +41 (22) 917-2613/14
> Fax: +41 (22) 917-0027
> E-mail: unpubli@unog.ch

> United Nations Publications
> 2 United Nations Plaza
> New York, NY 10017
> USA
> Phone: +1 212-963-8302
> Fax: +1 212-963-3489
> E-mail: publications@un.org

> United Nations Bookshop
> Visitors Lobby GA-32
> 1st Avenue and 46th Street
> New York, NY 10017
> USA
> Phone: +1-800-553-3210 (Toll-free
> for USA and Canada)
> +1-212-963-7680
> Fax: +1-212-963-4910
> E-Mail: bookshop@un.org
> Internet: http://bookshop.un.org

The → specialized agencies, such as the World Bank (→ World Bank/World Bank Group), the World Health Organization (→ WHO) or → UNESCO run their publication programmes and associated sales offices or book shops independently from the United Nations. A complete list of sales agents worldwide can be found at http://unp.un.org/distributors.aspx.

Ramona Kohrs

Lit.: *United Nations Secretariat:* Publications Board. Secretary-General's bulletin, 24 May 2005, UN Doc. ST/SGB/2005/15.

Internet: United Nations publications homepage: http://unp.un.org.

Reform of the UN

The capacity for reform is an essential requirement for the survival of political institutions. Institutional reforms usually aim at two results: (a) to preserve an institutional setting as a whole for the sake of the political programs, purposes, norms and values embodied in a given structure and (b) to constantly adapt institutional structure to ever-changing contexts and circumstances. Inevitable as this process may seem, the political obstacles for institutional reform are formidable: most organizations tie reform efforts to high standards of political consensus as every change in the institutional setting is not only perceived as an adequate answer to future challenges but also as a disturbance of the status quo which in itself captures a balance of power and diverse interests. In addition, the imperfect solutions of the political realm typically fall short of a number of rather technocratic proposals from outside the institution. Reform efforts thus combine questions of power, legitimacy and efficiency.

The reform history of international organizations dates back to the founding period of the → League of Nations. Article 24 of the Covenant of the League laid the basis for an ultimately failed attempt to consolidate all technical international organizations and administrative unions under the common roof of the League. Already this first effort highlights a central challenge to reform in international organizations: coordination. Vested political interests, turf wars and the resilience of already established structures and processes hinder attempts to create a consistent, concerted and rational division of labor. As a consequence, a number of rather obvious reform plans need a considerable amount of time from their first conceptualization to implementation. The 1939 "Bruce-Report" on the development of international cooperation in economic affairs is a case in point. Although it was not realized in the League of Nations period it nonetheless paved the way for the constitutive inclusion of economic affairs in what later on came to be chapter IX of the United Nations Charter (→ Charter of the UN).

The United Nations underwent several phases of reform efforts. While the first two decades were dominated by the formation of its specific institutional structures and practices, the 1960s and 1970s saw increasing demands from developing countries to better represent their problems and influence in the → UN system. The 1980s were shaped by budgetary and management reforms which were strongly advocated by the US government that even withheld part of its contributions in order to promote its agenda (→ Budget; → Financial Crises). The discrepancy between the big donor countries and the majority in the → General Assembly of the UN already became quite obvious.

The 1990s clearly started with a new boost in UN support and activities. But the expanding role of the UN especially in the → peacekeeping sector (cf. Boutros-Ghali's → "Agenda for Peace", UN Doc. A/47/277-S/24111, 17 June 1992) also came with a number of fundamental failures. Again, reform initiatives from member states, civil society and, not least, from the UN → Secretariat itself proliferated. → Secretary-General Kofi Annan prepared two complementary plans for reform in his "Renewing the United Nations: A Programme for Reform" (UN Doc. A/51/950) and "Strengthening of the United Nations: an agenda for further change" (UN Doc. A/57/387), submitted in 1997 and 2002, respectively. These initiatives (although implemented only in part by member states) did indeed result in a number of changes in the structure and practice of the world organization (cf. a chronology of reform measures of the principal organs of the UN from 1996 to 2006 on the UN website: www.un.org/reform/chronology.html). In the wake of the Iraq conflict in 2003, Kofi Annan discerned yet another "fork in the road"

(UN Press Release SG/SM/8891 of 23 September 2003) for the UN system: The concurrent stress on fundamental institutional structures (e.g. the → Security Council) and conceptual ideas (e.g. → collective security) had once again created a critical mass of reform pressure that went beyond a simple "stocktaking" on the occasion of the world organization's 60th birthday in 2005.

The need to simultaneously adapt to changing circumstances, reconcile shifts in the power structure among member states, avoid failures from the past, yield to financial and budgetary restrictions while at the same time defending, upholding and renewing the basic consensus and standards of the UN Charter (→ Charter of the UN) led to recurring and time-consuming reform initiatives and not least to a considerable amount of improvisation and makeshift policies. This already hints at a number of quite diverse instruments and ways of reform in the → UN system, of which only the strongest is an amendment or revision of the charter. This option is tied to high standards of consensus among member states. Article 108 spells out the double requirement of (a) a two-thirds majority of member states in the General Assembly supporting any change of the Charter as well as (b) the subsequent ratification of amendments by two-thirds of the UN's member states – including ratification by all permanent members of the UN Security Council. Tied to similar standards of consensus, a revision of the Charter according to Article 109 was initiated in 1955 but did not materialize into concrete reform debates. So far there are only three amendments of the Charter that have been realized: In 1965 the membership of the Security Council was increased from 11 to 15 (Arts. 23 and 27) and the membership of → ECOSOC from 18 to 27 (Art. 61). Three years later the concurrent adaption of Article 109 came into force and in 1973 ECOSOC membership was once again increased from 27 to 54 members.

Below the threshold of "constitutional" amendments, the Charter as well as the organization's internal rules vest a broad variety of reform powers in the main organs (→ Principal Organs, Subsidiary Organs, Treaty Bodies). The Security Council, the General Assembly as well as ECOSOC all have the power to change and adopt their respective rules of procedure as well as create and establish new or subsidiary organs.

In addition to that the format of → world conferences also has led to the establishment of institutions through multilateral treaties – *inter alia* the Commission on Sustainable Development, the Secretariat of the UN Convention to Combat Desertification or the Office of the UN High Commissioner for Human Rights (→ Human Rights, United Nations High Commissioner for).

Additionally, the Security Council established topical committees on sanctions or terrorism as well as tribunals e.g. on the former Yugoslavia and on Rwanda thus applying its power to establish subsidiary organs and/or to take measures under Chapter VII of the Charter. By enlarging the scope of its mandate under Article 39 in order to react to the predominantly intra- and transnational security threats after the Cold War, the Council has employed yet another way of "reforming" the UN.

Last but not least, the Secretariat and even more specifically the → Secretary-General can play an important part in the reform process by either (a) making use of the leeway he has as chief administrative officer of the UN in shaping the management structure of the Secretariat (also through the appointment of → personnel) and by (b) making use of the established role as formulator of ideas and innovator of conceptual reforms through his speeches, reports or the creation of commissions of experts, etc. These options are, however, balanced by the power of the General Assembly to ultimately approve the UN's budget. Regarding personnel, finance, management and coordination, the ACABQ, a subsidiary committee of the General Assembly's fifth main committee (→ Committees, System of) with recommendatory functions in finance and management questions and the Committee for Programme and Coordination (CPC), which functions as the main subsidiary organ of ECOSOC and the General Assembly for planning, reviewing, programming and coordination, play a substantial role together with a broad variety of further ad hoc committees, etc.

Reform measures, therefore, are typically developed in the interaction of various UN organs and not by single-handed action of just one main organ or part of the UN system. The opportunities for delay, obstruction and blockade are as numerous as the number of autonomous actors involved. Of particular importance is the lack of any close relationship between the UN proper and the → specialized agencies. The General Assembly has no power to take decisions which are binding for any specialized agency. Accordingly, reform measures aimed at the UN system as a whole are dependent upon the specialized agencies' cooperation.

And yet, the UN has proved its ability to react to new challenges by establishing new institutions throughout its history. An outstanding case in point is the establishment of → peacekeeping forces by Secretary-General Dag Hammarskjöld. By inventing the "Blue Helmets", he ensured the capacity of the UN to act for the maintenance of international peace and security even under Cold War conditions. At the same time he introduced an innovative element of peacekeeping and conflict prevention into UN practices. A second example is the establishment of programs of technical assistance for developing countries (→ Development Cooperation in the UN) which was progressively accompanied by processes of institution building. It eventually led to the establishment of → UNDP, which in turn underwent political, structural and administrative reforms in several steps starting in the 1990s. In the field of environment and technology the UN established → UNEP and the Committee for Science and Technology for Development which in 1992 was transformed into a commission of ECOSOC.

This institution-building stimulated some member states to establish domestic administrative branches in the fields of environmental and technological policy. On the other hand such institution-building processes (exemplified also by the creation of → UNCTAD) revealed some kind of political ambivalence in so far as the two thirds majority of the Group of 77 (→ Group of 77 and the UN) used the establishment of new bodies to institutionalize programs under the so-called New International Economic Order (→ International Economic Relations and New International Economic Order (NIEO)). Irrespective of the controversy surrounding these innovations one has to realize an overall tendency of a proliferation of new institutions while at the same time only few established organs were abolished. And this again leads to increased demand for coordination among those entities.

Institution-building is just one way of trying to keep track of the organizational growth and the expanding of the scope of the UN's activities. Both in the area of social and economic cooperation (cf. the 1969 "Jackson Report") but also in the conduct of peace missions the demand for coordination and the implementation of lessons learned in order to avoid failure has become a standard tool for the UN (cf. the 2000 "Brahimi Report", UN Doc. A/55/305-S/2000/809).

The topicality of recommendations from the "Bertrand Report" (UN Doc. A/40/988; JIU/REP/85/9) of 1985, the 1994 report of the "Independent Working Group on the Future of the United Nations" or the study by *Childers and Urquhart* (1994) all underline the fact that the problem does not so much lie with a lack of information or insight but rather with a lack of political will.

Against this background, the tenure of Secretary-General Kofi Annan can be described as a particularly reform-loaded time encompassing: (a) reforms of the UN's administrative structure; (b) institutional reforms within the UN system; and (c) conceptual reforms regarding the operative principles of the world organization in a time of globalization and new threats to state and human security.

Starting with a plan for renewing the UN system in 1997 (UN Doc. A/51/950), Annan paid close attention to the introduction of a new management style throughout the UN system (cf. *GAO* 2006). Although he was successful in reorganizing and focusing the UN's bureaucracy (*inter alia*, by introducing a new Chief Executives Board for Coordination), which found the remarkable appreciation of even the General Accounting Office of the USA (*GAO* 2004), the problems surrounding the management of the Oil-for-Food program and peace missions led him to issue an urgent plea for still more reforms in the UN's administrative structure. Annan's 2006 report on "Investing in the United Nations" (UN Doc. A/60/692) defines goals that still serve as a measure for Secretary-General Ban Ki-moon who followed up Annan's efforts.

With regard to institutional reforms Annan made use of the employment of a high-level panel whose 2004 recommendations on "A more secure world: our shared responsibility" (UN Doc. A/59/565 of 2 December 2004) he transformed into an outline for action for the 2005 world summit in his reform report of March 2005 "In Larger Freedom" (UN Doc. A/59/2005 of 21 March 2005).

The "2005 World Summit Outcome" (UN Doc. A/RES/60/1, 16 September 2005) brought the establishment of a new Peacebuilding Commission as well as the substitution of the Commission on Human Rights (→ Human Rights, Commission on) by a new human rights body, the → Human Rights Council, but it failed to take action on the contested issue of Security Council reform, although Annan had pressed with urgency for a resolution of that issue which has been on the agenda of the UN for decades. In contrast to that, reform of the → General Assembly and the → ECOSOC did not receive that amount of attention although the recent financial

590

crisis may open up new venues for revitalizing the latter.

While it may not be regarded as institutional in its character, the opening up of the → UN system to the participation of civil society actors both in the form of non-governmental organizations (→ NGOs) and the profit-oriented private sector (cf. the 2004 "Cardoso Report" on the relations between UN and civil society, UN Doc. A/58/817, 11 June 2004) also marks a reform of how the UN is operating. New institutions like the Global Compact, the Global Fund or Kimberley Process (partly working outside but in close consultation with the UN system) established networks of global governance that complement the UN's institutional setting.

Last but not least, Annan took leadership in trying to spell out the consequences of an ever more globalized world and the new threats it poses to states and peoples in the 21st century. In part he could build upon the remarkable conceptual work that his predecessor Boutros-Ghali had done in a series of reports (1992 → "Agenda for Peace" (UN Doc. A/47/277-S/24111), 1994 → "Agenda for Development" (UN Doc. A/48/935), and 1996 "Agenda for Democratization" (UN Doc. A/51/761)).

Annan's Millennium report "We the peoples: the role of the United Nations in the twenty-first century" (UN Doc. A/54/2000, 27 March 2000) and a series of speeches on the relationship between security, development and human rights helped to define new standards of conduct in world affairs. Human security and the still nascent idea of the "responsibility to protect", as formulated in the 2005 outcome document can be seen as substantial reforms of an organization consisting of member states that jealously guard the tradition of their sovereign rights.

Looking at the balance sheet of reform in the UN system made up of a multitude of – successful and unsuccessful – reform measures with conceptual, operational or institutional characteristics one can conclude that reform is no exception to the rule. It seems fair to judge that constant reform is the UN's modus operandi – hindered by a number of factors and actors who all have their part in the success and failure of the world organization and the efforts to reform itself.

Klaus Dicke / Manuel Fröhlich

Lit.: *Archibugi, D.:* The Reform of the UN and Cosmopolitan Democracy, in: JPR 30 (1993), 301-331; *Bertrand, M.:* Some reflections on the Reform of the United Nations, UN Doc. JIU/REP/85/9-A/40/988 of 6 December 1985; *Bertrand, M.:* The Historical Development of Efforts to Reform the UN, in: Roberts, A./Kingsbury, B. (eds.), United Nations, Divided World. The UN's Roles in International Relations, 2nd edn., Oxford 1993, 420-436; *Childers, E./Urquhart, B.:* Renewing the United Nations System, in: Development Dialogue, 1994, No. 1, 1-213; *Commission on Global Governance:* Our Global Neighbourhood, Oxford 1995; *Czempiel, E.-O.:* Die Reform der UNO. Möglichkeiten und Mißverständnisse, Munich 1994; *Dicke, K.:* Reforming the United Nations. The 1990s and Beyond, in: Japanese-German Center Berlin (ed.): The Role of the United Nations in the 1990s, Symposium 27-31 August 1990, Berlin 1991, 79-86; *Dicke, K.:* Effizienz und Effektivität internationaler Organisationen, Berlin 1994; *Dicke, K.:* Reform of the UN, in: Wolfrum, R (ed.): United Nations: Law, Policies and Practice, Vol. 2, Munich/Dordrecht 1995, 1012-1024; *Fassbender, B.:* UN Security Council Reform and the Right of Veto. A Constitutional Perspective, The Hague 1998; *Fröhlich, M.:* Leitbild Global Governance. Zur Reform der Vereinten Nationen, in: Vorländer, H. (ed.): Politische Reform in der Demokratie, Baden-Baden 2005, 135-157; *Fröhlich, M.:* The Ironies of UN Secretariat Reform, in: GG 13 (2007), 151-159; *Hüfner, K. (ed.):* Die Reform der Vereinten Nationen. Die Weltorganisation zwischen Krise und Erneuerung, Opladen 1994; *Hüfner, K. (ed.):* Agenda for Change. New Tasks for the United Nations, Opladen 1995; *Hüfner, K./ Martens, J.:* UNO-Reform zwischen Utopie und Realität. Vorschläge zum Wirtschafts- und Sozialbereich der Vereinten Nationen, Frankfurt (Main) et al. 2000; *Independent Working Group on the Future of the United Nations:* The United Nations in its Second Half-Century, New York 1994, reprinted in: Hüfner, K. (ed.), Agenda for Change, Opladen 1995, 271-312; *Jackson, R.:* Capacity of the United Nations Development System, 2 vols., Geneva 1969; *Kaspersen, A.T./Leira, H.:* A fork in the road or a roundabout? A narrative of the UN reform process 2003 – 2005 (Norwegian Institute of International Affairs), Oslo 2006; *Luck, E.C.:* Reforming the United Nations. Lessons from a History in Progress, New Haven 2007; *Luck, E.:* Principal Organs, in: Weiss, T.G./Daws, S. (eds.): The Oxford Handbook on the United Nations, Oxford 2007, 653-674; *Malloch Brown, M.:* Can the UN be Reformed? Holmes Lecture 2007, in: Global Governance 14 (2008), 1-12; *Malone, D:* Ingredients of success or failure in UN reform efforts (accessible at www.un-globalsecurity. org); *Müller, J. (ed.):* Reforming the United Nations: The Struggle for Legitimacy and Effectiveness, Leiden et al. 2006; *South Centre:* Enhancing the Role of the United Nations, Geneva 1992; *South Centre:* For a Strong and Democratic United Nations. A South Perspective on UN Reform, Geneva 1996; *South Centre:* The United Nations crisis and its reform, in: South Bulletin 97/98, 28 February 2005, 59-63; *Taylor, P. (ed.):* Documents on Reform of the United Nations, Aldershot et al. 1997; *United Nations - General Assembly:* Renewing the United Nations: A Programme for Reform, Report of the Secretary-General, 14 July 1997, UN Doc. A/51/950; *United Nations - General Assembly:* We the peoples: the role of the United Nations in the twenty-first century. Report of the Secretary-General, 27 March 2000, UN Doc A/54/2000; *United Nations - General Assembly/Security Council:* Report of the Panel on United Nations Peace Operations, 21 August 2000, UN Doc. A/55/305-S/ 2000/809; *United Nations - General Assembly:* Strengthening of the United Nations: an agenda for further change. Report of the Secretary-General, 9 September 2002, UN Doc. 57/387; *United Nations - General Assembly:* We the peoples: civil society, the United Nations and global governance. Report of the Panel of Eminent Persons and United Nations – Civil Society Relations, 11 June 2004, UN Doc. A/58/817; *United Nations - General Assembly:* A more secure world: our shared responsibility. Report of the High-level Panel on Threats, Challenges and Change, 2 December 2004, UN Doc. A/59/565; *United Nations - General Assembly:* 2005 World Summit Outcome, 16 September 2005, UN Doc A/RES/60/1; *United States General Accounting Office:* United Nations: Reforms Progressing, but Comprehensive Assessments Needed to Measure Impact, February 2004, GAO-04-

339, quoted as: GAO 2004; *United States Government Accountability Office:* United Nations: Management Reforms Progressing Slowly with Many Awaiting General Assembly Review, October 2006, GAO-07-14 (quoted as: GAO 2006); *Volger, H.:* UN-Reform ohne Charta-Revision? Der Stand der Reformbemühungen nach dem Millenniums-Gipfel, in: Schorlemer, S. von (ed.): Praxis-Handbuch UNO, Berlin et al. 2003, 733-753; *Volger, H.:* Mehr Partizipation nicht erwünscht. Der Bericht des Cardoso-Panels über die Reform der Beziehungen zwischen den Vereinten Nationen und der Zivilgesellschaft, in: VN 53 (2005), 12-18; *Volger, H.:* Die Reform der Vereinten Nationen, in: Volger, H. (ed.): Grundlagen und Strukturen der Vereinten Nationen, Munich/Vienna 2007, 487-571; *Weiss, T. et al.:* UN Voices. The Struggle for Development and Social Justice, Bloomington/Indianapolis 2005; *Weiss, T.G./Crossette, B.:* The United Nations: The Post-Summit-Outlook, in: Foreign Policy Association (ed.): Great Decisions – 2006 Edition, New York 2006, 9-20; *Weiss, T.G./ Daws S. (eds.):* The Oxford Handbook on the United Nations, Oxford/New York 2007; *Yale Center for the Study of Globalization (ed.):* Reforming the United Nations for Peace and Security, New Haven 2005.

Internet: Homepages on UN reform that also contain the reports and documents cited above: www.un.org/reform; www.reformtheun.org; www.globalpolicy.org.

Regional Groups in the UN

I. General

Regional groups exist within the United Nations system ($\rightarrow$ UN System) only as unofficial groupings ($\rightarrow$ Groups and Groupings in the UN). They reflect in part shared ideologies from the early days of the UN, although today the focus is on regional solidarity. The UN Charter ($\rightarrow$ Charter of the UN) does not mention regional groups, although they have become a fixed feature of the UN system. The regional groups principally act as electoral bodies, which take the preliminary decisions on the composition of nearly all important UN organs ($\rightarrow$ Principal Organs, Subsidiary Organs, Treaty Bodies). The composition and structure of the regional groups have constantly changed during the Organization's existence. Since 1995 at the latest, commentators have been considering how the groups could be adapted to the changes wrought by the close of the East-West conflict in the late 1980s.

II. Origins

The origins of today's regional groups can be traced back to a gentlemen's agreement concluded by the United States and the then Soviet Union in 1946, regarding the distribution of the six non-permanent seats on the → Security Council between the 51 (46) founding members of the organization (→ History of the UN). The "main groups" recognized were Latin America (2 seats), Middle East (1), Eastern Europe (1), Western Europe (1) and the British Commonwealth (1). While the Soviet Union was of the opinion that decisions by the regional groups were to be endorsed by the → General Assembly, the United States viewed the division as a one-off without binding consequences. States such as India subsequently voiced their dissatisfaction with the division (*Bailey* 1988). Its basis was however not to be understood as representative, but rather as distributive (in the following years for example, Greece, Turkey and Yugoslavia occupied the "Eastern Europe" seat).

III. Gradual Entrenching of the Group System

The regional group system has since become firmly established. In the course of enlarging the Security Council in 1963 from 11 to 15 members, a reallocation of the seats was undertaken and recorded in General Assembly decisions (UN Doc. A/RES/1990 (XVIII) and A/RES/1991A (XVIII) of 17 December 1963). This geographical distribution was later also applied to the Economic and Social Council (→ ECOSOC) (A/RES/2847 (XXVI) of 20 December 1971) and was ultimately stipulated for "principal organs" of the UN (A/RES/33/138 of 19 December 1978). From July 1978 the monthly regional group chairs have been published in the official UN journal. The five groups as redrawn in 1963 are still in existence today.

IV. Geographical Distribution

The five regional groups in existence since 1963 are the Group of African States (GAFS), the Group of Asian States (GASS), the Group of Latin American and Caribbean States (GRULAC), the Group of Eastern European States (EEC) and the Group of Western European and Other States (WEOG). The composition of the last group, which also includes the most important western states outside of Europe, shows the extent to which the distribution of 1963 was built on the East-West confrontation, which at that time divided the UN. The members of the individual groups are listed below:

GAFS (53): Algeria, Angola, Benin, Botswana, Burkina Faso, Burundi, Cameroon, Cape Verde, the Central African Republic, Chad, the Comoros, Congo-Brazzaville, Congo-Kinshasa, Côte d'Ivoire, Djibouti, Egypt, Equatorial Guinea, Eritrea, Ethiopia, Gabon, Gambia, Ghana, Guinea, Guinea-Bissau, Kenya, Lesotho, Liberia, Libyan Arab Jamahiriya, Madagascar, Malawi, Mali, Mauritania, Mauritius, Morocco, Mozambique, Namibia, Niger, Nigeria, Rwanda, São Tomé and Principe, Senegal, Seychelles, Sierra Leone, Somalia, South Africa, the Sudan, Swaziland, United Republic of Tanzania, Togo, Tunisia, Uganda, Zambia, Zimbabwe;

GASS (53): Afghanistan, Bahrain, Bangladesh, Bhutan, Brunei Darussalam, Cambodia, China, Cyprus, Democratic People's Republic of Korea, Fiji, India, Indonesia, Iran, Iraq, Japan, Jordan, Kazakhstan, Kuwait, Kyrgyzstan, Lao People's Democratic Republic, Lebanon, Malaysia, Maldives, Marshall Islands, Micronesia, Mongolia, Myanmar, Nauru, Nepal, Oman, Pakistan, Palau, Papua New Guinea, Philippines, Qatar, Republic of Korea, Samoa, Saudi Arabia, Singapore, Solomon Islands, Sri Lanka,

Syrian Arab Republic, Tajikistan, Thailand, Timor-Leste, Tonga, Turkmenistan, Tuvalu, United Arab Emirates, Uzbekistan, Vanuatu, Viet Nam, Yemen;

GRULAC (33): Antigua and Barbuda, Argentina, Bahamas, Barbados, Belize, Bolivia, Brazil, Chile, Colombia, Costa Rica, Cuba, Dominica, Dominican Republic, Ecuador, El Salvador, Grenada, Guatemala, Guyana, Haiti, Honduras, Jamaica, Mexico, Nicaragua, Panama, Paraguay, Peru, Saint Kitts and Nevis, Saint Lucia, Saint Vincent and the Grenadines, Suriname, Trinidad and Tobago, Uruguay, Venezuela;

WEOG (28): Andorra, Australia, Austria, Belgium, Canada, Denmark, Finland, France, Germany, Greece, Iceland, Ireland, Israel, Italy, Liechtenstein, Luxembourg, Malta, Monaco, Netherlands, New Zealand, Norway, Portugal, San Marino, Spain, Sweden, Switzerland, Turkey, United Kingdom;

EEC (21): Albania, Armenia, Azerbaijan, Belarus, Bosnia and Herzegovina, Bulgaria, Croatia, Czech Republic, Estonia, Georgia, Hungary, Latvia, Lithuania, The Former Yugoslav Republic of Macedonia, Montenegro, Republic of Moldova, Poland, Romania, the Russian Federation, Serbia, Slovakia, Slovenia, Ukraine.

V. Non-Aligned States

As of 31 May 2008, Kiribati belonged to no group (cf. *New Zealand Ministry of Foreign Affairs and Trade* 2008: United Nations Handbook 2008/09, 16). Joining a regional group is often difficult for tactical and political reasons, not least because it requires consensus in the prospective group. Existing, long-term voting arrangements within individual groups, such as in WEOG for ECOSOC, mean that groups are reluctant to accept new additional members. These were the main hurdles at which Israel's previous attempts to join either GASS or WEOG had failed.

VI. Special Cases

Turkey is a member of WEOG and GASS. For electoral matters it is however a member of WEOG only. The United States counts as a member of WEOG for electoral purposes, but is otherwise a mere observer, not a full member of the group. Israel has been a "temporary" member of the WEOG since May 2000, but only in New York and under proviso as regards putting up candidates. Observer in WEOG as a non-UN member state is the Holy See.

VII. Functions

The main significance of the regional groups lies in their work as electoral committees for appointments to seats, and to ensure the geographical distribution of the various offices (*Schorlemer* 1995, 75). They implement the principle that "the composition of the various organs of the United Nations should be so constituted as to ensure their representative character" (A/RES/33/138, 19 December 1978). This principle applies to the elections to the non-permanent seats on the Security Council, to the Economic and Social Council (ECOSOC) and to all other important UN bodies. Exceptions are the Committees of Experts, which are formed on the basis of expertise regardless of region. The regional group principle customarily also plays a role for the office of the → Secretary-General and the President of the General Assembly (see No. 3 above and Rule 31 of the → Rules of Procedure of the General Assembly, which expressly stipulates the principle in abbreviated form for the election of the vice-president). While the office of the President of the General Assembly is filled according to a strict rotation of the regions, a comparable model has only recently emerged for the election of the Secretary-General and is not viewed so strictly (most recent Secretary-Generals are U Thant/GASS, Waldheim/WEOG, de Cuellar/GRULAC, Boutros-Ghali/Annan/GAFS and Ban Ki-moon/GASS). EEC has not presented a candidate so far. The re-election of Annan in 2001 represented *de facto* a third consecutive

GAFS term which had not been objected to at the time.

The regional groups work according to the consensus principle. Candidates who are endorsed by them are as a rule elected by the General Assembly in the subsequent election. The endorsement of a regional group is not binding on others; it is legally permissible for groups to field competing candidates. As a rule, candidates endorsed by a group are elected. There have been sporadic attempts by regional groups to take over substantive issues (e.g. the motion by Arab states in 1998 to discuss the reform of the Security Council within the GASS). Such attempts have so far tended to meet a cool reception. Most UN member states are of the opinion that the jurisdiction of the groups should not be extended beyond electoral arrangements (exception: GAFS with its sub-groups, based on OAU principles, for Eastern, Western, Central, Southern and Northern Africa; similar developments also in the GRULAC sub-group of CARICOM). The practice according to which the Chairpersons of the five groups make statements at ceremonial occasions in the name of their groups (e.g. on the occasion of the election of the Secretary-General, the election of the President of the General Assembly) is within the scope of this restrictive framework. The Chairpersons of the regional groups are frequently asked to pass on communications and information about current events to their members. This they normally do with no added comment.

VIII. Procedure

The regional groups meet at irregular intervals (every four to six weeks, more frequently if necessary), usually on UN premises. The member states are represented at UN Ambassador or expert level. The Chair of each group rotates monthly and the new appointee is announced in the official UN journal. The Chairs of the regional groups meet on a monthly basis with the President of the General Assembly for informal briefings.

IX. Deficits and Need for Reform

The great variation in size (from 53 to 21) between the regional groups is far from ideal. Moreover, it is increasingly the case that individual states are carefully distancing themselves politically from their groups. EEC members Bulgaria, the Czech Republic, Estonia, Hungary, Latvia, Lithuania, Poland, Slovakia and Slovenia have since 1999/2004 become members of NATO and of the European Union (EU). Most of them are increasingly aligning themselves with WEOG. At the same time, within WEOG intensified coordination between the 15 EU partners ($\rightarrow$ European Union, Common Foreign and Security Policy at the UN) means that other WEOG members such as Australia, the United States, Canada and New Zealand feel themselves to be excluded from decision-making processes and disadvantaged in general. Australia also seems to be seeking greater involvement with its neighbors in the South Pacific (*Downer* 1997). The 21 Arab states are divided between GAFS (10) and GASS (11). In the long run, Israel will not remain satisfied with the present interim solutions. There are thus compelling grounds for reorganizing the groups in the near future. A new classification would, not least, do justice to the altered circumstances, brought about by the end of the East-West confrontation, under which groups within the UN now work.

X. Proposals for Reform

As part of the work on the reform of the Security Council ($\rightarrow$ Reform of the UN), in September 1995 Australia (*Australian Government* 1995) proposed a new distribution for the regional groups, based on a division into seven groups: Western Europe (24 members), Central and Eastern Europe (22), Middle East and the Maghreb (19), Africa (43), Central Asia and the Indian Ocean (17), East Asia and Oceania (25) and America (35). This proposal would remove the "other" states from the WEOG, and would also create a homogenous Middle-Eastern group. The creation of the Oceania group would respond to the demands of other states from the South Pacific. Nevertheless, a great disparity as regards the size of the groups would remain (43 to 17).

A Canadian study in 1997 (*O'Brien* 1997) proposed the creation of nine new groups: Eurasia (21 members), Asia/Pacific (25), the Mediterranean/Gulf (19), Northern Europe (20), Southern Europe (19), North Africa (23), South Africa (23), America (19), the Caribbean (16). At first glance this proposal would seem to overcome many of the current system's weaknesses. However it remains to be seen whether regions and alliances such as the EU, Africa (with its subordinate AU structures) or the Caribbean (with its close ties to Central America), which have so far been united in their groups, would accept such a division.

The inclusion of states which are not fully integrated into any group would be achieved in the course of implementing either of these models, or indeed any other more comprehensive one. Any reorganization will have to take into careful consideration the effect that it would have on an enlarged Security Council with more than five permanent and ten non-permanent seats.

Ingo Winkelmann

Lit.: *Australian Government:* Possible Models for Enlarging the Security Council, UN Document A/49/965 of 15 September 1995, 65-67; *Bailey, S. D/Daws, S.:* The procedure of the UN Security Council, 3nd edn., Oxford 1998; *Downer, A.:* Revamp to reflect the world, in: International Herald Tribune of 3 October 1997; *New Zealand Ministry of Foreign Affairs and Trade:* United Nations Handbook 2008/09, Wellington 2008, 14-16; *O'Brien, T.:* The United Nations: Legacy and Reform, Wellington 1997 (CSS Working Paper 6/97); *Peterson, M.J.:* „Freunde des Präsidenten" und andere Helfer – Informelle Verhandlungspraktiken in der Generalversammlung der Vereinten Nationen, in: VN 37 (1989), 121-125; *Schorlemer, S. von:* Blocs and Groups of States, in: Wolfrum, R. (ed.): United Nations: Law, Policies and Practice, Vol. 1, Munich/Dordrecht 1995, 69-77; *Schorlemer, S. von:* "Gemeinsam stärker"?: Regionalgruppen in der UNO, in: Dicke, K./Fröhlich, M. (eds.): Wege multilateraler Diplomatie, Baden-Baden 2005; *Talmon, S.:* Participation of UN Member States in the Work of the Organization: A Multicultural Alternative to Present-Day Regionalism? In: Yee, S./Morin, J.-Y. (eds.): Multiculturalism and International Law, Leiden 2009, 239-275; *Whitfield, T.:* Friends indeed? The United Nations, Groups of Friends, and the Resolution of Conflict, Washington, D.C. 2007..

Regionalization

Regionalization generally refers to the formation of regionally organized economic and political integration areas, as well to as a growing orientation of the political actors towards regions. This development stands in direct contrast to the multilateral or universalist orientation (→ Universality), as it is advanced by the United Nations and other global organizations. In this context the term *region* is not only understood in geographical terms, but it includes also other aspects, such as political affiliation or economic development. Tendencies in direction towards regionalization can be observed in security policy and in the military field, in the protection and promotion of → human rights as well as in the area of economic development and integration. The following analysis will emphasize the latter aspect and its implications for the world trade system.

I. Regionalization within and outside the UN System

Based on universalist principles, the Charter of the United Nations does not "...[preclude] the existence of regional arrangements or agencies for dealing with such matters relating to the maintenance of international peace and security as are appropriate for regional action ..." (→ Charter of the United Nations, Chapter VIII, Art. 52 (1)). The maintenance of the international → peace (→ Peace, Peace Concept, Threat to Peace) and security (→ Peacekeeping) is the only domain for which the UN Charter has explicitly provided *regional arrangements*. The settling of regionally limited conflicts should primarily occur within the framework of regional arrangements, before they are referred to the → Security Council (UN Charter Art. 52 (2); see also Art. 33 (1)). Nevertheless, the Security Council must be informed of the measures taken on the basis of regional arrangements (Art. 54). Furthermore, regional arrangements and institutions must comply with the purposes and principles of the United Nations (Art. 52 (1)). Apart from that, the UN Charter does neither define any further the nature of regional arrangements nor regions as such. Prominent examples for regional security arrangements are the "Organization for Security and Co-operation in Europe" (OSCE), the "Organization of American States" (OAS) and the "Organization of African Unity" (OAU). The tendency towards regionalism in the field of peace and security, however, is most developed in exclusively military alliances, such as NATO, the "Western European Union" (WEU) and the former Warsaw Pact.

Regionalist tendencies in this domain are not only tolerated by the → General Assembly, but they are actively supported. In recent years, the call for a stronger cooperation between UN organs and regional organizations has gained urgency particularly in the field of conflict prevention (→ Preventive Diplomacy). Regional organizations seem to be especially suited for this task, since a successful prevention has also to take into consideration the economic, social and ethnic roots of conflicts. This concession to regional organizations does not constitute a renunciation of the universal peace concept, on the contrary, it makes allowances for the fact that maintaining and making peace in different states at different times requires different measures and concepts (→ Peaceful Settlement of Disputes).

However, despite the fact that the concept of regionalization is limited in the UN-Charter to the maintenance of peace and security (in a strictly military sense), a growing tendency towards regionalization can be observed within as well as outside the UN system and in other areas.

As regional organs within the UN system in the field of development assistance, five regional economic commissions (→ Economic Commissions, Regional) have been established by the Economic and Social Council (→ ECOSOC). The commissions for Africa (ECA), Latin America and the Caribbean (ECLA), Western Asia (ESCWA) and Asia and the Pacific (ESCAP) are responsible for the development policies of the respective regions. Their goal is to promote economic development through consulting and exchanging information, and they also elaborate concrete development plans and projects. The economic commission for Europe (ECE), whose members are identical with those of the OSCE, was in the past the only trans-bloc platform for the economic East-West relations. After the political change in the former Communist states, the ECE supports the Eastern European states, and the successor states of the former Soviet Union, in their transition to market economies. The economic commissions are subordinate to the Economic and Social Council (ECOSOC), to whom they are obliged to report on their work annually or bi-annually.

Recently, a discussion about the position and dependence of the economic commissions has begun, with the former UN Secretary General (→ Secretary General) Boutros Boutros-Ghali speaking in favor of their strengthening and greater independence. But there are also voices arguing against increasing their autonomy, and the issue is not yet resolved. The regional economic commissions cooperate closely with other regional organizations located outside the UN system. In the case of the African and Asian Development Bank, the commissions have even actively supported the foundation of these bank institutions.

The tendency towards regionalization is furthermore evident in the decision-making processes of the United Nations. On the universal level of the General Assembly or the United Nations Conference on Trade and Development (→

UNCTAD), the formation of blocs (→ Groups and Groupings in the UN) has taken place aimed at agreeing on a common voting behavior. The largest and most important blocs are the Group of 77 (→ Group of 77 and the UN) and the Western industrial countries, with the members of the European Union as their most influential sub-group (→ European Union, Common Foreign and Security Policy at the UN). Further, elections and nominations often follow geographical patterns. Therefore, a balanced geographical distribution (→ Regional Groups) is always taken into consideration at the election of the non-permanent members of the → Security Council, the composition of the Economic and Social Council, the appointment of the President of the General Assembly as well as at the hiring of the Secretariat personnel (→ Secretariat; → Personnel).

Outside the UN system, there is increasing overlap of tasks of the UN organizations with those of regional organizations looking after tasks that fall under the competence of the UN. The protection and implementation of human rights (→ Human Rights, Protection of; → Human Rights Conventions and their Measures of Implementation) is an example: The regional efforts for the protection of human rights are explicitly welcomed by the General Assembly, since they represent specific regional values and preferences. For instance, the "African Charter on Human and Peoples' Rights" of 1981 ("Banjul-Charter") and the "European Convention for the Protection of Human Rights and Fundamental Freedoms", which entered into force in 1953, belong to such regional conventions. In the domain of economic co-operation there is overlap among the activities of the regional development banks and the Bretton Woods Institutions → IMF and the World Bank (→ World Bank, World Bank Group), which are → specialized agencies of the UN.

II. Growing Regionalization in the World Trade System

Special attention was paid to the growing regionalization in the world trade system (→ International Economic Relations and New International Economic Order (NIEO)). In this context, regionalization is an expression of the intensifying regional economic relations, and could be understood as the result of historical processes of regional economics. For example, 85 per cent of the world trade is handled between the European Union, the USA and Japan, without formal trade agreement.

In contrast to these regionalizing processes stands *regionalism,* which is a deliberate policy aiming at the promotion of such regional concentrations, and thereby the deliberate establishment of discriminating trade agreements, for example in form of regional trade blocs. More important – in terms of trade policy – are those trade agreements negotiated on the state level, since they lead to a growing regionalism within the world trade system. While the UN organs specialized on economic questions focus their activities mainly on development problems (→ Development Cooperation of the UN System), these regional trade agreements concentrate rather on the economic integration within the respective region. Therefore we speak of specialization, rather than of competition, in this field. Depending on the extent of integration, one can distinguish between preferences zones, free trade zones, tariff unions, common markets and economic unions. The latter may lead to monetary unions; a common currency, however, is not an indispensable prerequisite for the functioning of an economic union. To establish the conditions for a zone of preferences, an accommodation of technical standards is required first, for example in the field of customs controls and means of transportation. These services are provided, for example by, the Economic Commission for Europe. In these processes, a rising level of integration is always connected with a loss of sovereignty of the member states, (→ Sovereignty) in foreign as well as in domestic trade.

Since World War II there have been two *major waves of regionalization movements*, leading to 179 regional trade agreements registered at GATT/WTO (→ WTO, GATT); 103 of which are still in force today. The *first phase of regionalism* took place during the 1950s and 1960s and was characterized by the foundation of the European Economic Community in 1957 and the European Free Trade Association (EFTA) in 1959, as well as of numerous other regional trade agreements in developing countries (e.g. the Latin American Free Trade Association (LAFTA), the Andean Pact, the OAU, and the Organization of South-East Asian Nations (ASEAN). For the decolonized developing countries (→ Decolonization), regional integration with like-minded nations was an opportunity to escape from dependence on the former colonial powers and on the few available export markets of the industrialized countries. In addition, the then-prevailing development theory of import substitution called for cutting off the national economies from the world market in order to promote the building-up of indigenous industries. But since the isolated industrialization of every single country would lead to an inefficient allocation of resources, due to insufficient market size, cooperation on a regional level seemed more promising. The major part of integration efforts among developing countries failed, however, or did not lead to the expected success. The main reason for this development was competitive and non-complementary economic structures, i.e. the participating countries exported the same or similar products. Their major trade partners were mostly located outside the integration area, so that – in spite of the preferential access for suppliers from the region – the intra-regional trade stagnated. As a result of this, of the agreements resulting from the first phase of regionalization, only the Western European integration achieved significant progress. Although the Western

European states, too, had rather competitive economic structures, here there was an opportunity for trade with differentiated products, i.e. similar, but not identical products. This option does not exist for developing countries, which as a rule export mining and agricultural products.

The 1980s witnessed a revitalization of regionalism on the European level with the decision to establish the internal market of the European Community (EC) and the European Economic and Monetary Union. But also the developing countries in the different regions signed more trade agreements, again, as the foundation of the Southern Common Market (MERCOSUR) in 1994 and the Asian Free Trade Area among the ASEAN states of 1992 demonstrate.

The *creation of North-South alliances* was particularly remarkable within this *second wave of regional agreements*, by which are meant those integration efforts between industrialized and developing countries. Examples are the entry of Mexico into the North American Free Trade Agreement (NAFTA) in 1994, and the foundation of the Asian-Pacific Economic Co-operation (APEC) in 1989. These North-South alliances correspond to the existing trade relations of the involved partners, and they offer therefore more perspectives for interregional trade than did their predecessors of the 1960s. The heterogeneity of the participating countries concerning their size, economic performance, as well as their cultural and political background, seems to remain nevertheless problematic. These differences often lead to delays in negotiations on further integration steps, and North-South alliances which go beyond tariff unions are surely doomed to fail, if compensating transfer payments of the richer to the poorer countries do not take place.

How do those regional integration tendencies affect global trade? Although regional trade agreements contradict the principles of the most-favored nation treatment and of non-discrimination, as laid down in the GATT Agreement, the globally orientated WTO, which is responsible for this domain, assumes a rather positive effect. Article 24 of the GATT Agreement allows explicitly free-trade zones and tariff unions, under the condition, that the resulting level of protection is not higher than the level of the single countries before the conclusion of the regional agreement, and that the reduction of trade barriers among the participating countries includes all significant areas of trade. The effects of those regional integration efforts can be divided into "trade-creating" and "trade-transforming" effects. Depending on whether the trade volume increases through the preference of regional providers, or whether it decreases through the disadvantaging of non-regional providers, regional agreements can affect the liberalization of world trade positively or negatively. This static analysis, developed in the 1950s by Jacob Viner, refers primarily to the creation of tariff unions and leaves aside the dynamic effects, which become effective particularly when entering a common market.

The larger sales market created by the regional agreement offers the providers the chance to realize economies of scale. Furthermore, the consumers within the region as well as outside benefit from the price reduction made possible by the decrease of fixed costs. Moreover, the competitive pressure within the region increases through the growing number of providers, which offers also the possibility for declining prices. By these effects, the real income increases and thereby increases as well the import tendency within the integration zone, also with regard to imports from other countries. This means that, even if the static effect of trade re-channeling exceeds the trade-creating one, the regional trade agreements can – due to the previously described dynamic effects – nevertheless positively affect other states, too.

Finally, the participants of regional integration efforts expect faster and easier access to technologies and advantages in their search for foreign direct investment.

III. Reasons for the Tendencies towards Regionalization

An explanation for the growing trend towards regionalization with regard to the UN as well as to the world trade system has to take into account – according to the different features of regional concepts – several different aspects:

The expectations articulated in multilateral organs have often not been met. For example, the tariff reductions of the eight negotiation rounds of GATT have lead to an increased use of non-tariff trade barriers, and have not contributed to a liberal free-trade system to such an extent as the reduced tariffs might have led one to expect. Also the claim for universal peace as pursued by the United Nations can be realized – in the face of the large number of regional conflicts – only with the help of specific regional approaches for conflict resolution.

Political and economic developments are often the reason why the intended universalism cannot be implemented. Regionalization in the field of security policy – with the creation of NATO and the Warsaw Pact – was an inevitable result of the Cold War. Regional organizations have to be seen as a reaction to changes in political and economic circumstances.

National interests can be better pursued in smaller organizations. The large institutions with universal claims, such as the IMF or the World Bank Group, are dominated by the capital-giving group of Western industrialized countries. Regional organizations such as the regional economic commissions offer the developing countries the only chance to promote or even put through their own interests. In addition to that, as is known from the theory of collective action, the costs for coordination rise disproportionately to the number of members of an organization. Large organizations also offer opportunities for jumping on the bandwagon, where members of the organization benefit from its existence without being willing to contribute to its provision and maintenance. In contrast to that, a smaller group offers more transparency, and thereby the opportunity for sanctioning such egoistic behavior of member states.

The setting-up of multilateral organizations often requires taking into account the desires of certain groups of states. Chapter VIII of the UN Charter, for example, is not the expression of a theoretical concept of deliberate deviation from the universalist concept of the Charter. Rather the explicit recognition of regional organizations for the maintenance of international peace and security was the result of a compromise due to pressure from Latin-American states and countries of the Arab League (→ History of the Foundation of the UN).

Regionalization within the universal organization of the UN system offers the possibility to gather and bundle the interests and votes of one region. In this way, concrete concerns are more likely to be realized than if the (small) states concerned come out in favor of them individually. Finally, this concentration of power increases the potential for threats in the case of an unsuccessful representation of interests.

IV. Regionalization versus Multilateralism

Within the UN system as well as at the level of world trade, the question arises whether growing trends towards regionalization promote or hinder the desired multilateralism. But there is no clear and simple answer that would be valid for the whole range of formal and informal regional agreements. The effectiveness of regional organizations in the global system depends largely on the features of the respective regional agreement. Depending on how open the regional community is for new members, and how strongly it demarcates from other states, the evaluation will differ from case to case. The growing regionalization in the field of politics and economy is definitely not linked to a fundamental renunciation of the universal principle, but can also be understood as a path towards that goal: the regional approach can prevent overstretching the

global system by representing the national interests of the individual member states and by assuring their support for the universal order. This applies particularly to those international organizations whose growing number of members makes them less and less similar to the small, homogeneous groups they were at their foundation in the post-war era. The increasing structural and development differences of the member states make regional sub-groups appear as necessary mediators between nation states and global organizations. The goal of every global order should not be simply "multilateralism at all costs", but the increase of the welfare of all participants. If regional organizations turn out to be more effective in that sense, their resources should be used.

On the other hand, it would be wrong to neglect completely the risks of regional tendencies for the global system. Those dangers always exist, since the members of regional organizations consider the latter as advantageous, while they leave aside the question what consequences this choice might entail for the rest of the world. Therefore, one must find institutional mechanisms to reduce possible negative effects of the regional approach. An important instrument in this direction is the strengthening of multilateral institutions. It is their task to coordinate regional organizations, to prevent the abuse of power of single large regions as well as to prepare and install trans-regional structures with regard to institutions. In this aspect, too, universalism and regionalism rather complement than exclude each other.

Birgit Reichenstein

Lit.: *Beyerlin, U.:* Regional Arrangements, in: Wolfrum, R. (ed.): United Nations: Law, Policies and Practice, Vol. 2, Munich/Dordrecht 1995, 1040-1051; *Kimminich, O.:* Peace-keeping on a Universal or Regional Level, in: Wolfrum, R. (ed.): Strengthening the World Order: Universalism versus Regionalism, Berlin 1990, 37-47; *OECD:* Regional Integration and the Multilateral Trading System, Paris 1995; *Schreuer, C.:* Promotion of Economic Development by International Law at the Universal and/or the Regional Level, in: Wolfrum, R. (ed.): Strengthening the World Order: Universalism versus Regionalism, Berlin 1990, 71-91; *Schreuer, C.:* Regionalization, in: Wolfrum, R.(ed.): United Nations: Law, Policies and Practice, Vol. 2, Munich/Dordrecht 1995, 1059-1067; *Speyer, B.:* Regionale Integration. Eine eigenständige Liberalisierungsstrategie für die Weltwirtschaft, Wiesbaden 1997; *Vierucci, L.:* WEU: A Regional Partner of the United Nations? Paris 1993; *WTO:* Regionalism and the World Trading System, Geneva 1995.

Addendum

Today, one important aspect of regionalization within the UN system is the commitment of regional organizations, for example the African Union (AU) or NATO, or supranational organizations such as the European Union (EU) in the field of peace and security (cf. *Graham* 2006).

In recent years, the role of regional organizations has changed significantly, and contributions by those organizations are not only welcomed, but explicitly asked for. The reasons brought forward in the political debates are that regional organizations are closer to regional crises or conflicts, that they are more likely to be accepted by regional actors or groups involved in the conflicts, and that they have a vital interest in the solution of regional conflicts (*Graham* 2005; *Felício* 2006).

In 1991, the Special Committee on the Charter of the United Nations and on the Strengthening of the Role of the Organization was asked by the General Assembly to consider the role of regional organizations with regard to the maintenance of international peace and security (UN Doc. A/RES/46/58, 9 December 1991, para. 4 (a)). In 1994, the General Assembly adopted the "Declaration on the Enhancement of Cooperation between the United Nations and Regional Arrangements or Agencies in the Maintenance of International Peace and Security" (UN Doc. A/RES/49/57, 9 December 1994), in which it called for the solution of local conflicts through regional arrangements and un-

derlined their potential in solving such disputes.

In 2004, the "High-level Panel on Threats, Challenges and Change" called in its report "A more secure world: Our shared responsibility" (UN Doc. A/59/565, 2 December 2004) for "fuller and more productive use of the Chapter VIII provisions" (para. 270), stressing the contributions by regional organizations to peace and security issues. The Panel members argued that regional organizations could be a vital part of the multilateral system. With regard to regional peace operations, they emphasized the need for authorization by the Security Council according to Chapter VIII of the Charter of the United Nations (ibid., para. 272).

In his report "In larger freedom: towards development, security and human rights for all" (UN Doc. A/59/2005, 21 March 2005,), Secretary-General Kofi Annan asked for the improvement of coordination between the United Nations and regional organizations (ibid., paras. 213-215).

The Security Council took up the issue of cooperation with regional organizations in peacekeeping with greater intensity in April 2003, when it held a public meeting with regional organizations on the topic of the "The Security Council and regional organizations: Facing New Challenges to International Peace and Security" (see Press Release SC/7724, 11 April 2003) and dealt again with the issue in a public meeting with regional organizations in July 2004. In a presidential statement (UN Doc. S/PRST/2004/27, 20 July 2004) the President of the Security Council emphasized in this context the "important role" of the regional organizations "in the prevention, resolution and management of conflicts, including ... addressing their root-causes". In 2005, the Security Council even used the highly official form of a resolution to call for the development of a stronger and closer cooperation between regional organizations and the United Nations and to invite such organizations to support the efforts of the United Nations in the field of peace and security (UN Doc. S/RES/ 1631 (2005)). It mentioned their effective potential in conflict prevention and crisis management, in post-conflict stabilization, and in addressing the illicit trade in small arms and light weapons.

Also in 2006 and 2007 the Security Council dealt with the issue and underlined the importance of regional organizations in maintaining peace and security in presidential statements of the council (UN Doc. S/PRST/2006/39, 20 September 2006; S/PRST/2007/7, 28 March 2007).

Since 1994, high-level meetings between the UN and regional as well as other intergovernmental organizations are organized by the Department of Political Affairs of the UN → Secretariat in order to strengthen cooperation in peacekeeping (cf. the report of the high-level meeting in 2005: UN Doc. A/60/ 341-S/2005/567, 8 September 2005).

These meetings are complemented in Europe since 1993 by tripartite annual meetings between United Nations, the Council of Europe, the Organization for Security and Co-operation in Europe (OSCE) and other international organizations (cf. Joint Communiqué of the Meeting on 14 February 2007, UN Doc. SEC.GAL/28/07).

In the field of peacekeeping, for example, several missions are led by regional organizations: AMIS, the African Union mission in the Sudan, monitors and observes compliance with the Humanitarian Ceasefire Agreement of 2004. On 21 February 2007, AMISOM, the African Union mission in Somalia, was authorized by the Security Council to assist with the implementation of the National Security and Stabilization Plan and to contribute to humanitarian assistance (see resolution UN Doc. S/RES/ 1744). By resolution S/RES/1671 of 25 April 2006, the Security Council mandated the deployment of the European Union mission EUFOR RD Congo in the Democratic Republic of the Congo to observe the presidential and parliamentary elections. In 1999, the KFOR mission, led by NATO, was established in order to build a transitional

administration and support the development of democratic institutions and structures within Kosovo (see resolution UN Doc. S/RES/1244).

The fight against international terrorism is another field in which regionalization and the commitment of regional organizations is increasingly asked for. In the Global Counter Terrorism Strategy, adopted by the General Assembly in September 2006 (UN Doc. A/RES/ 60/288), not only states, but international, regional and sub-regional organizations are explicitly encouraged to support the implementation of this plan of action, for example by creating counter-terrorism mechanisms or centers. In this regard, for example the European Union has become an important partner to the United Nations. In order to support states in implementing Security Council resolution S/RES/ 1373 (2001), asking all member states to prevent the support of terrorist acts by listing different measures such as the suppression of financing of terrorism or the exchange of information, the European Union has provided technical assistance to states in need.

To create a scientific potential for analysing the trend towards regionalization, the United Nations University (UNU) established in 2001 a unit for Comparative Regional Integration Studies (UNU-CRIS) in Bruges (Belgium), which has published a wealth of studies on the different aspects of regionalization. The studies prove that regionalization remains an important aspect within the UN System, having grown even more important in the field of peace and security within recent years, and that regional organizations continue to play an important role in world politics.

Irene Weinz

Lit.: *Felício, T.:* Conflict Prevention and Peace-Building in the Regional Context. UNU-CRIS/DPA Seminar Report (UNU-CRIS Occasional Papers 0-2006-20), Bruges 2006; *Graham, K.:* Regionalisation and Responses to Armed Conflict, with Special Focus on Conflict Prevention and Peacekeeping (UNU-CRIS Occasional Papers 0-2005-

21), Bruges 2005; *Graham, K.:* UN-EU Cooperation on Security: In Search of Effective Multilateralism and a Balanced Division of Tasks, in: Wouters, J. (ed.): The UN and the EU: An Ever Stronger Partnership, Leuven 2006; *United Nations:* The Partnership between the UN and the EU. The United Nations and the European Commission working together in Development and Humanitarian Cooperation, Brussels 2006, http://ec. europa.eu/europeaid/reports/un_ec_report_ final_march_2007_en.pdf; *United Nations - General Assembly:* A more secure world: Our shared responsibility. Report of the High-level Panel on Threats, Challenges and Change, 2 December 2004, UN Doc. A/59/565; *United Nations - General Assembly:* In larger freedom: towards development, security and human rights for all. Report of the Secretary-General, 21 March 2005, UN Doc. A/59/2005.

Internet: Homepage of AMIS: www.amis-sudan.org; Homepage of EUPOL RD Congo: www.consilium.europa.eu/cms3_fo/showPage.asp?id=1303&lang=en; Homepage of KFOR: www.nato.int/kfor/; Homepage of United Nations University – Comparative Regional Integration Studies: www. cris.unu.edu.

Research about the UN

International organizations with political objectives are an achievement of the 20th century. The first practical attempt to institutionalize the maintenance of peace was the foundation of the → League of Nations after World War I. Despite the fact that this turned out to be a failure, the political leaders in the forties did again look for "peace through an international, global organization". This was to be the cornerstone of the new world order after World War II. In 1945 the United Nations took the place of the League of Nations which was dissolved in 1946 (→ History of the Foundation of the UN).

Both organizations are based on theoretical approaches and conceptions that were developed in Western Europe since the beginning of the 17th century (→ International Organizations, Theory of). The political realization of both organizations was achieved by two US Presidents. Therefore it is evident that

especially in the USA scientists and journalists looked intensively and in detail into both the activities and the chances of success of these new international organizations. This is especially valid for studies on the foundation and the early development of the United Nations. Even today the UN literature, which has in the meantime filled up whole shelves, is still dominated by English-speaking publications.

I. The Beginning of German UN Research (1948 – 1972)

After the total defeat of Germany in World War II it took more than a decade until the United Nations was taken up as a topic in both German states, which came into existence in 1949. In the initial phase of German research, in both the FRG and GDR there was a concentration on the respective domestic political development, and on the ideological safeguarding of one's own political system. This thematic concentration of the respective academic disciplines and of the institutions of political education was caused by external political influences from the respective political systems. So on the one hand the researchers in the FRG focused on "the Science of Democracy", while the researchers in the GDR on the other hand paid special attention to the "Building up of Socialism".

In 1968 the first West German anthology on new UN literature was published. Volker Rittberger complained in a book review that there was a "lack of competent German literature about the United Nations" (PVS 1968). In the preface to a UN bibliography that was published in the same year, Gilbert Ziebura struck a similar critical balance: one must regret that "the United Nations is not given the place it deserves – despite or even because of its imperfection –, neither in the public opinion nor in scientific research" (*Hüfner/Naumann* 1968). An important reason for the obvious lack of interest by German researchers was the fact that the participation of West Germany in the United Nations' activities was initially very limited (→ UN Policy, Germany).

Although the FRG had gained access to the system of the United Nations in 1950 already with its admission to the → FAO, and although it joined other → specialized agencies of the UN and participated in the work of numerous subsidiary organs of the UN, programmes and funds (→ Principal Organs, Subsidiary Organs, Treaty Bodies) – for instance the FRG was a member of the Economic Commission for Europe (ECE) since 1956 (→ Economic Commissions, Regional) – the first German UN monographs did not appear before the mid-sixties. These publications were for the most part descriptive overviews of the entire → UN system (*Siegler* 1966) and of the peacekeeping activities (→ Peacekeeping) of the UN (*Schlüter* 1966). These were supplemented by a first comprehensive study on the participation of the FRG in the system of the United Nations, presented by the Research Institute of the Deutsche Gesellschaft für Auswärtige Politik (German Society for Foreign Politics) (*Dröge et al.* 1966). In 1967 the translation of an essay based on personal experience, written by a British journalist (*Boyd* 1967), became the first paperback on the United Nations in German.

In the FRG very few scientific journals dealt with the world organization in the fifties and sixties. In this context the bimonthly magazine "Vereinte Nationen" (United Nations) had specific status as a specialist journal on the UN. It was first published in 1952 by the German United Nations Association (Deutsche Gesellschaft für die Vereinten Nationen – DGVN) in Heidelberg, which was founded following the example of United Nations Associations that already existed in other countries.

The West German scientific UN literature, which lay far behind the Anglo-Saxon in quantity as well as in quality, focused in this phase on general UN problems, with the UN Charter (→ Charter of the UN) as a special point of interest – and this mainly from the point of view of international law. Specific

problems, however, such as peacekeeping, economic and social development (→ Development Cooperation of the UN System), human rights protection (→ Human Rights, Protection of) or financing the organization (→ Budget; → Finance Crises) were to a large extent ignored.

In the beginning there was also little willingness to understand and to locate the world organization as a political phenomenon in the academic education at West German universities. Only experts in international law dealt with the UN topic in their teachings (*Czempiel* 1971). Working still in the shadow of university professors of international law like Georg Dahm, Wilhelm Grewe (who published the Charter of the United Nations with a translation in German and an introduction in 1948) and Karl Josef Partsch or Ignaz Seidl-Hohenveldern, who all worked during the post-war era, their young co-workers in particular developed a growing readiness to obtain knowledge about international organizations and also about the United Nations, and to convey it to the students. Today many of those former youngsters have become experts on the United Nations in the field of international law.

The persistent lack of interest shown by social scientists is also reflected in the number of doctoral theses in Germany since 1945 dealing with the UN. Generally, their number per year did not increase from the end of World War II to the mid-seventies, with a clear predominance of theses from the field of international law. Between 1948 and 1953 only 9% of the theses were written in economics, political science and social sciences. In the sixties, this proportion increased to 20%, with this trend continuing in the seventies. Nevertheless, there continued to be a predominance of theses in international law. Only in the eighties there occurred a marked change. The interest of the scientific community involved in the UN increased in general (50 theses in this phase against 37 in the seventies) as well as the proportion of those written in the fields of economics, political and social sciences; 32% of the theses on the UN belonged to the latter group, while 34% were written in international law.

This trend continued in the nineties. Among the 53 theses on UN issues written between 1990 and 1998, 15 (i.e. 28%) were written in the disciplines of economics, political science and social sciences and the remainder in international law. (These figures were compiled by Helmut Volger.)

This continuing lack of interest in issues surrounding the UN was mirrored by the failure to establish academic chairs and curricula at German universities for these subjects. Only hesitatingly and with a clear distance in time, political science took the UN topic as a field of research. Not before the early sixties, when the first academic chairs for international politics were established in the FRG, did the United Nations find entrance as a research topic in political science. Now the political scientist and journalist Klaus Mehnert succeeded – in the framework of "open lectures" – to get students interested in the UN topic even at a Technical University, such as the RWTH in Aachen.

In the GDR, which had in vain tried to become part of the UN system since the fifties (→ UN Policy, German Democratic Republic), the UN research focused up to 1973 mainly on finding a scientific basis for the demand of the GDR to become a "member with equal rights" in the world organization (*Bruns* 1978). Nevertheless, in comparison to the FRG, more scientific articles with reference to the United Nations were written and published in the GDR. Moreover the "Liga für die Vereinten Nationen (League for the United Nations)", founded in 1954, edited a series of periodical publications, one of them being a yearly balance sheet of the UN system called "UNO-Bilanz".

II. New Impetus for UN Research (1973 – 1989)

On 18 September 1973 the two German states became members of the United Nations. This led to a considerable increase of interest in the jurisprudence and political science in the UN system, and in the past and future roles of the two "newcomers".

In order to satisfy the increasing need for information in the West German public, a number of introductory study books concerning the structures, functions and history of the world organization were published (e.g. *Unser* 1973; *Hüfner/Naumann* 1974). Also the federal and regional centers for political education, which up to then were mainly focused on domestic political problems, edited more publications on the United Nations than before. Thus in 1970, on the occasion of the 25th anniversary of the United Nations, a synoptic survey was published (*Hüfner/Naumann* 1970).

Important impulses for the activation of UN research in the two German states came also from the two UN associations, the Deutsche Gesellschaft für die Vereinten Nationen – DGVN (German Society for the United Nations) in the FRG and the Liga für die Vereinten Nationen (League for the United Nations) in the GDR. They encouraged projects aiming at more intensive scientific UN research and initiated the publication of sophisticated standard works. Thus the "Handbuch der Vereinten Nationen" (Handbook of the United Nations) was published in 1977 under the editorial guidance of the research council of the DGVN. In 111 entries this handbook mirrored the fact that the level of UN research had obviously been consolidated by that time (*Wolfrum et al.* 1977).

In the former GDR two of the most prominent UN researchers started already in 1974 an ambitious publication project. They were both leading staff members of the Institute for International Relations at the Academy for Political Science and Jurisprudence in Potsdam-Babelsberg, which was a kind of a leading institution for the foreign policy research in the GDR. The state publishing house of the GDR annually published two volumes of a collection of documents, originally planned for a total of 17 volumes, later expanded to 20 volumes. In all volumes an introduction preceded UN texts (mainly statutes and resolutions) in the official UN languages English and French (→ Languages, Official), as well as in German (*Sprötel Wünsche* 1974 ff.). In 1974 the first volume was published and up to 1985, 13 more volumes appeared. In 1989, just before the unification of Germany, the last two volumes came out. This series was edited with great competence, and found broad recognition as reference book also in the West.

To a large extent UN reports and analyses that continuously accompanied the political developments were – if one takes the scientific journals in the FRG into consideration – to be found predominantly in the above-mentioned journal "Vereinte Nationen (United Nations)", with periodical journals like "Archiv des Völkerrechts" (Archive of International Law) and "Europa-Archiv" (European Archive) (today "Internationale Politik" (International Politics), increasingly dealing with UN issues.

In the GDR at least two topical UN issues were covered in each issue of the monthly journal "Deutsche Aussenpolitik" (German Foreign Policy), which was edited by the UN League and the above-mentioned Potsdam Institute. Other periodicals, such as "Staat und Recht" (State and Law), also dealt with UN subjects.

In contrast to the heterogeneous West German UN publications, which tackled a broad spectrum of questions and a multiplicity of competing observations and evaluations, there was only one view upon the UN in research in the GDR. This perspective culminated in the attempt to prove that the GDR and its socialist brother countries played an active and constructive role on the side of the developing countries in building up the United Nations as a "peace instrument" – against the resistance of the "imperialistic" states (cf. *Bruns* 1978).

III. German UN Research Catches Up with the International Level of Research since the early 1990s

With regard to its subjects and questions, political science is very strongly oriented towards current affairs. Therefore it is not astonishing that historic upheavals always lead to a boom in research and publications. This holds particularly true for the now all-German UN research in the eventful nineties.

A comprehensive survey (*Knapp* 1997) containing comments of high expertise provides information on the wide range of literature that has been published on the United Nations since 1993.

The increased interest in the United Nations was also reflected in a number of specialized periodicals, in single contributions as well as in UN-focused issues (e.g. on the occasion of the 50th anniversary of the world organization), in journals such as "Vereinte Nationen" (United Nations) and "Die Friedens-Warte (Journal of International Peace and Organization).

With the rapprochement of the two superpowers USA and USSR in the second half of the eighties, a process of change in world politics began. This was reflected first in a most obvious way in the United Nations as the microcosm of international politics. The consequences of the changed climate were reflected particularly in that UN organ, which had been blocked over decades to a large extent in its capacity to act, the → Security Council (see also: → History of the UN).

Numerous regional conflicts that had appeared to be insoluble until then, could now either be settled through missions of UN peacekeeping forces (→ Peacekeeping Forces), or could at least be brought nearer to resolution. Even coercive military measures (→ Sanctions) against an aggressor, in this case in the Second Gulf War (1990/1991), mandated on the basis of Chapter VII of the UN Charter, were decided upon in consensus by the Security Council and implemented. One spoke of a "renaissance of the United Nations," and the developing countries were promised a "peace dividend" for the future. It did not seem to be a sheer dream anymore to realize a "New World Order", with the United Nations as its main actor. But soon disillusionment followed the rash euphoria, and also the United Nations suffered from serious setbacks, especially in the area of peacekeeping. On the occasion of the 50th anniversary of the United Nations not only the media spoke of an "overburdened birthday boy" (German newspaper "Die Welt") and of a "Organization celebrating its jubilee which is in need of reform" (German newspaper "Frankfurter Allgemeine Zeitung") – altogether the media saw "little reason to celebrate" (German newspaper "Die Tageszeitung").

In the German UN research after the unification of the two states, both the "hausse" and the following "baisse" of the world organization were strikingly reflected in the same way as the focus of the UN research orients itself towards the concrete UN activities and problems. At the beginning of the 90s two important, almost simultaneous publications reflected the increased public interest and vigorously demonstrated the efficiency and capability of German UN research, and have taken their place as standard reference literature (cf. *DGVN* 1996). After lengthy preparatory work Bruno Simma, an expert in international law, edited the first German commentary on the United Nations Charter, comprising more than 1200 pages. About 60 scientists, diplomats and UN officials contributed to it (*Simma* 1991). In 1994 it was followed by a revised English edition (*Simma* 1994). Also in 1991 Rüdiger Wolfrum, specialist in international law, published a completely revised edition of the "Handbuch der Vereinten Nationen" (Handbook of the United Nations) that now comprised 158 entries and offered a comprehensive and critically evaluating look on the entire spectrum of the United Nations. More than 90 experts, predominantly specialists in international law, but also political scientists and UN practitioners, participated in the work. In 1995 this

reference work was published in a revised English edition in two volumes under the title "United Nations: Law, Policies and Practice" (*Wolfrum* 1995). The two books were supplemented by the publication of a bilingual collection (English and German) of UN documents in three volumes in 1995 and 1996 with the title "The System of the United Nations and its Predecessors" (*Knipping et al.* 1995/96). In 2002 Bruno Simma published a second revised English edition of his commentary on the UN Charter "The Charter of the United Nations. A Commentary" (*Simma* 2002).

These reference works were supplemented in 2000 by a concise encyclopedia on the UN in one volume, edited by Helmut Volger, with the title "Lexikon der Vereinten Nationen" (*Volger* 2000), offering a comprehensive survey of the structures and problems, but also of more recent developments in the United Nations. To the contributing authors belonged specialists in international law, political scientists, journalists, active and former UN officials and diplomats as well as members of NGOs. In 2002 followed the English edition of this German encyclopedia, "A Concise Encyclopedia of the United Nations" (*Volger* 2002). As had been the case with the English editions of the books of Wolfrum and Simma, the English-speaking reviewers appreciated the book as providing the rare opportunity to get to know European UN research. As Ruth Wedgwood wrote in her book review: "One great virtue of the volume is to open up to English readers the work of European scholars whose research is less familiar in the confines of the American academy." (*Wedgwood*, book review, in: AJIL 99 (January 2005), 284-287, 286).

The works mentioned here form – for the German-speaking research landscape – a solid scientific foundation, and an important integrating resource for the multiplicity of the investigations on specific questions.

These books are complemented in UN historiography by an important pioneer work of Helmut Volger, who published the first "History of the United Nations" in German (*Volger* 1995), particularly acclaimed by the German historiography (cf. *Dülffer* 1995).

The "Rediscovery of the United Nations", being also the title of an anthology of UN texts and research contributions of Günther Doeker and Helmut Volger (*Doeker/Volger* 1990), in Germany in the 1990s led to a marked increase of the German UN publications.

Among the up to 15 new publications each year, there were fundamental study books (for instance *Volger* 1994 or *Rittberger/Mogler/Zangl* 1997) and groundbreaking analyses of specific fields of duties and problem areas (e.g. *Kühne* 1993), but also – especially on the paperback market – books that were often written by self-proclaimed UN experts for publishing houses seeking quick profits.

But the majority of research literature contained thorough and thoughtful analyses of the UN activities, dealing with an increasing number of issues in reaction to the expanding scope of activities of the UN in the 1990s: in view of the increase in peacekeeping operations (→ Peacekeeping Operations) and the changing forms of the peacekeeping missions at the end of the eighties and the beginning of the nineties, this topic was taken up and analyzed intensively in comparative case studies (cf. for instance *Knapp* 1997, *Eisele* 2000). While the "classical" missions were given a positive evaluation in the specialized literature, the peacekeeping operations of the "second generation" and "third generation" caused controversies (cf. *Hufnagel* 1996), as well as the completely different form of authorization by the Security Council used now for military missions, above all in the Second Gulf War. The question of the legitimacy of humanitarian interventions (→ Humanitarian Law, International) in case of serious violations of human rights developed into a controversy among researchers, particularly among specialists in international law (cf. e.g. *Debiel/Nuscheler* 1996; *Pape* 1997; *Hasse/Müller/ Schneider* 2001).

Apart from discussing the different aspects of humanitarian intervention, an increasing number of books dealt with the significance of the United Nations with regard to the further development of international law: Christian Tomuschat's anthology on the occasion of the 50th anniversary of the foundation of the UN, for example, presented (in English) German contributions together with contributions from international researchers from Europe and overseas dealing with the different legal aspects of United Nations work (*Tomuschat* 1995), while Bardo Fassbender rendered in his (English) monograph a in-depth analysis of the legal aspects of the Security Council reform (*Fassbender* 1998).

On the occasion of the 50th anniversary of the 1948 Universal Declaration of Human Rights (→ Human Rights, Universal Declaration of) many projects, symposia and publications dealt with the protection of human rights (e.g. *Baum/ Riedel/Schaefer* 1998; *Tomuschat* 2000; *Hasse/Müller/Schneider* 2002; *Opitz* 2002).

In contrast to these efforts the research concerning UN development assistance (→ Development Cooperation in the UN System) remained at least quantitatively of lesser importance. In 1994 for instance the "Agenda for Development" by the UN Secretary-General at that time received hardly any attention in German academic circles. This policy field in the UN framework was only analyzed in detail in German UN research when the key word of "sustainable development" found acceptance in an almost inflationary way in the entire development policy.

But still up to the present, there is no comprehensive monograph in the German language on development co-operation within the UN system. The study of Stephan Klingebiel (*Klingebiel* 1998) on the efficiency and the reform of the UN Development Programme → UNDP, however, provides an important contribution to this systematic analysis, as well as Rainer Tetzlaff's monograph on the World Bank and the IMF (*Tetzlaff* 1996), later supplemented by the excellent systematic contributions on development cooperation and development research of Inge Kaul in the first edition of this encyclopedia (*Kaul* 2002a and 2002b).

One aspect of this important policy field of the United Nations however did turn out to be a relevant, long-lasting topic for scientific research: the uncontrolled growth of aid programmes and funds, the overlapping and insufficient co-ordination between the UN bodies – a field that is open to further proposals for reform, recently analyzed in a briefing paper by Martina Vatterodt (*Vatterodt* 2007).

IV. Dominant Topic Since the mid-90s: UN Reforms

Since the mid-90s the extensive issue of UN reform (→ Reform of the UN) assumes an outstanding rank in research. Hardly any publication on the world organization does not take a position concerning this subject. While the necessity for reform is basically undisputed, less agreement exists when it comes to the scope and depth of such a reform, and to concepts and strategies.

In the UN literature one can differentiate among three reform categories, which are connected to one another, regarding the objectives and the scope of the reform:

a) reforms, with the priority goal of greater efficiency and effectiveness in the central scope of the duties of the UN: The capacity to act as well as the ability to implement one's objectives is to be increased by clearer objectives, modifications to the instruments and a more effective co-ordination. Included here are demands for administrative improvements, as well as reforms in the area of finances and → budget.

b) reform concepts aiming at the structural-institutional reorganization of the United Nations: To this group belongs the reform of the Security Council as well as reforms concerning the amalgamation and the dissolution, respectively, of existing UN organs or the foundation of new ones.

c) reforms which are directed towards a basic modification of the principles and the character of the world organization: All concepts that belong to this category have in common that they want a far-reaching root-and-branch reform, in the long run they want a "new" UN. Often the suggestions come down to a transformation of the intergovernmental organization into a global supranational institution with competences in its own right. This concept which was developed some hundred years ago, thereby still exercises a certain utopian fascination.

For all three reform categories the German researchers, supplemented by independent working groups and non-governmental organizations (→ NGOs) have supplied – in conjunction with international discussion – problem analyses, partly with a prognostic pretention, sophisticated concepts or detail proposals. Here should be mentioned the comprehensive structural analysis by Klaus Dicke (*Dicke* 1990), the considerations concerning the reform of UN peacekeeping by Ernst-Otto Czempiel (*Czempiel* 1994) and the two anthologies edited by Klaus Hüfner (*Hüfner* 1994 and 1995). The first of the two, with the title "Die Reform der Vereinten Nationen" (Reform of the United Nations) summarizes the discussion results of a "Berlin Working Group" of twelve UN researchers from the FRG and from the former GDR on UN reforms. The second book, "Agenda for Change" (1995) represents (in English) a new and positive trend in German UN research: the linking-up to the UN research in Anglo-Saxon and French languages. This book is a collection of the results of an international workshop organized from the International Institute for Peace in Vienna in 1993. In the year 2000 Klaus Hüfner and Jens Martens have complemented the general surveys on UN reform by the first comprehensive survey and critical analysis of all reform proposals for the economic and social field of the United Nations (*Hüfner/Martens* 2000), a valuable addition to the reform literature.

Rather new as topic of UN research is the role of the UN in the processes of globalization: two books written within the framework of the "Stiftung Entwicklung und Frieden" (Foundation Development and Peace), founded 1986 on the initiative of Willy Brandt, attempt to give the reader some basic orientation about "globalization", "global governance" and the chances and challenges for the UN (*Brühl et al.* 2001; *Fues/ Hamm* 2001). Their publications have been increasingly complemented in recent years by working and policy papers of the Deutsche Institut für Entwicklungspolitik (German Development Institute) and of the Friedrich Ebert Stiftung on globalization and global governance as well as on UN reforms in general (cf. *Fues/Loewe* 2005; *Messner/ Wolff* 2005; *Martens* 2005a and 2005b; *Ozgercin/Steinhilber* 2005; *Ozgercin* 2005).

As the debate in the United Nations as well as among the academics of its member states about the role of the UN in the new millennium intensified after the year 2000 with its large UN gathering, the millennium assembly adopting the Millennium Declaration with its Millennium Development goals, this debate was also reflected in German UN research by an increasing number of publications.

This debate intensified once again, as the 60th anniversary of the United Nations in the year 2005 approached. Both attempts for a top-to-bottom reform of the United Nations initiated by Kofi Annan – the "High-level Panel on Threats, Challenges and Change", which presented in December 2004 its report "A more secure world: our shared responsibility" (UN Doc. A/59/565) and his own reform report "In larger freedom" of March 2005 (UN Doc. A/59/ 2005) as well as the reform package passed by the Millenium+5 Summit – the "2005 World Summit Outcome Document" (UN Doc. A/RES/60/1 of

16 September 2005 – provided a strong impetus for German UN research to deal in detail with these proposals and their relevance.

Numerous publications appeared which on the one hand analyzed the broad spectrum of reforms (for instance *Varwick/Zimmermann* 2006; *Leininger* 2005; *Volger* 2003 and *Volger* 2005) and on the other hand questioned reform approaches for sections such as the UN environmental policy (*Subkus* 2004). As in Germany, politics and media very soon reduced the discussion about comprehensive UN reform only to the debate about the reform of the Security Council and the aspiration of the German Government for a permanent seat within the Council, German UN research often focused on this aspect with quite controversial appraisals. Indeed, while concerning this question just a few autonomous investigations were published (*Andrae* 2002; *Fröhlich/Märker/Hüfner* 2005; *Hellmann/Roos* 2007), a multiplicity of entries in relevant scientific journals paid special attention to this aspect. The best orientation in this complex field is still provided by Ingo Winkelmann's overview article from the year 1997 (*Winkelmann* 1997).

Furthermore, in recent years the United Nations and its main fields of activities has been the subject of numerous symposia and publications in Germany. Among these publications were, for instance, two comprehensive anthologies, which for one thing analyzed with a highly pragmatic orientation the broad fields of activities of the UN in the light of global challenges (*Schorlemer 2003*) and for another convey a very well-founded insight into the current discussion about the principles and structures of the United Nations (*Volger* 2007). Furthermore, completely revised editions of introductory study books (*Unser* 2004; *Gareis/Varwick* 2006) and updates concerning the historical development of the world organization (*Volger* 2008) were published. Compared to the nineties, the number of publications concerning UN peacekeeping is apparently declining: the topics of discussions were, among other things, UN peace missions in Africa (*Debiel* 2003), the problem of sanction regimes (*Werthes* 2003; *Horn* 2003) and the problems of the UN governing conflict areas. The same applies to UN development cooperation with only one publication striking a critical balance of this aspect of the Millennium+5 summit (*Fues/Loewe* 2005). Also the academic debate about the global compact and global public goods has been taken up in German book publications rather seldom, with the exception of the books of Inge Kaul, one of the "parents" of the concept of global public goods (*Kaul* 1999 and *Kaul* 2006).

It is remarkable that numerous publications have recently been dealing with the role and the personality of individual UN Secretaries-General – Dag Hammarskjöld (*Fröhlich* 2002), Boutros Boutros-Ghali (*Paepcke* 2004), Kofi Annan (*Fröhlich* 2004; *Bauer* 2005). Two comprehensive works focus on the International Criminal Court (ICC), which was established by a diplomatic conference in Rome in 1998 through the Rome Statute and began its work in 2002 – on the one hand, it is the effectiveness of the ICC that is asked for (*Heilmann* 2006) and on the other, the contribution of the ICC to safeguarding permanent peace (*Nietsche* 2007) that is evaluated. The current topic of women's rights within the UN was taken up by two anthologies, which reflect the discussion about the gender problem from the point of view of international law (*Schorlemer* 2007; *Rudolf* 2007).

As the relation between the European Union (EU) and the United Nations became increasingly politically important from the mid-nineties, German UN research began to concentrate – but hesitatingly – on this topic. In particular the support of the EU within the scope of the European Security and Defence Policy (ESDP) as a UN partner to safeguard peace is the main topic taken up in symposia, reports, papers and entries in both anthologies (cf. *Wouters/Hoffmeister/Ruys* 2006) and scientific journals.

Increasing attention has been paid in recent years to a hitherto neglected research field, the group processes and processes of decision-making in the UN system: an anthology edited by Klaus Dicke and Manuel Fröhlich (*Dicke/ Fröhlich* 2003) deals in detail with the mechanism of multilateral diplomacy, while the monograph of Jochen Prantl focuses on the role of informal groups of states in the decision-making of the UN security council (*Prantl* 2006). This field of reseach is likely to gain even more importance in the future.

Unfortunately, German UN research still pays little attention to UN-Subsidiary Organs and Treaty Bodies although they play an important role within the UN system. Only on the occasion of its 50th anniversary was an encyclopedically composed monograph (*Schriefer/ Sandtner/Rudischhauser* 2007) about the International Atomic Energy Agency (IAEA) published. In contrast with former times, German UN policy plays currently no essential part in German UN research. It is only sporadically taken up as topic in anthologies and scientific journals concerning the German foreign policy and mostly in connection with the German ambition for a permanent seat within the Security Council. The most recently published monographs about Germany and the United Nations also deal with this question (*Freuding* 2000; *Andreae* 2002).

V. The Situation of the German UN Research At Present

As heretofore, German UN research is still concentrated in a limited number of universities (Kiel, Munich, Tübingen, Berlin, Hamburg and recently in Duisburg, Bochum, Potsdam, Jena, Dresden and Erfurt) and in a few renowned research centres, which are either financially supported by the government or by private sponsors.

Heretofore these institutions work largely autonomously, which means that German research is splintered both institutionally and contextually and thus it consists still more or less of uncoordinated single research activities, often with the high idealistic input of the researchers and with creative research approaches, but without sufficient cooperation with other research projects and without an efficient platform for the publication of the research findings.

Being concerned about this heterogeneity within German UN research, the Research Council of the German UN Association invited scientists and UN practitioners working in the ministries for foreign affairs and for development cooperation to join them in a symposium titled "UN Research in Germany". The aim of this conference, which took place in Berlin in December 2005, was to locate and evaluate German UN research.

These obvious deficits within United Nations research had already been the chief motive for the foundation of the "Forschungskreis Vereinte Nationen" (Research Group United Nations) in Potsdam/Germany in 1999 (www. forschungskreis-vereinte-nationen.de).

This research network was founded through the personal incentive of a few scientists and practitioners. There is no formal membership and the circle considers itself as an informal association of those who are interested in a better cooperation within German UN research and in an improved dialogue between scholars and practitioners. The members describe their research group as an information service and a network of German UN research.

Since 2000 they annually host the interdisciplinary organized "Potsdamer UNO-Konferenz" (Potsdam UN Conference). These conferences are organized together with the Human Rights Centre of the University of Potsdam and supervised by its coordinator – since its foundation this office has been administered by Helmut Volger – who works together with a concept group composed of members of the Forschungskreis. The papers presented at the Potsdam UN conferences are published in conference brochures (cf. *Klein/Volger* 2000, 2001, 2002, 2003, 2004, 2005, 2006, and 2008, www.forschungskreis-vereinte-nationen.de/text/brosch.html).

The above-mentioned Berlin conference in 2005 on UN research showed that concerning the development of this research topic there is a considerable need for discussion in the academic community and between academics and politicians. To meet this need, the organizers not only published relevant reports presented at the conference in a brochure (*Deutsche Gesellschaft für die Vereinten Nationen* 2006), but also decided to hold a further symposium on the topic the following year. In December 2006 the Research Council of the German UN Association hosted a further symposium with the title "UN Studies". Based on the growing awareness that UN-relevant research reports cannot be assigned to just one scientific field, the aim was to analyze how to cooperate and use synergies more efficiently. In comparing the own situation with that of "European Studies", which have been recently becoming more and more important in academic teaching and research in Germany, the question was discussed at the 2006 symposium whether to establish methodologically comparable "UN Studies". "UN Studies" – so one of its protagonists – "describes the intensive dealing with the principles, the institutions and functions of the world organization understood as a broad term and problem" (*Fröhlich* 2008). Based on the preliminary work of the conference in 2006, the anthology "UN Studies" (*Fröhlich* 2008) was published in 2008, which outlines and constitutes the concept of a new academic teaching and research field.

In the first part of the book, scientists of UN-relevant disciplines present information about connecting factors and options of UN Studies. In the second, concrete experiences with such scientific programmes, teaching fields and cooperation as well as its required relevancy to practice are discussed. For the further development of German UN research the establishment of a "Centre for UN Research" is one of the proposed objectives (*Volger* 2008a, 261).

As a first step towards establishing UN Studies as a research field and

613

teaching discipline Helmut Volger has recently suggested in a contribution for the journal of German scientific libraries that the academic libraries should establish a comprehensive and systematic bibliography of monographs and contributions to anthologies and learned journals referring to the United Nations, its structures, functions and activities (*Volger* 2008b).

While the project of establishing "UN studies" in Germany as field of research and of academic teaching is still in an early stage, since the nineties the supply of university lectures and courses on the topic United Nations has been considerably improved and is still improving. A survey of the newer curricula shows that topical UN issues (with the focus on UN functions and structures, peacekeeping, human rights and reform) are more and more offered as courses at the universities, in particular in the framework of political science and international law.

VI. Summing Up

Drawing the conclusions from the results of the German UN research one has to state that it has attained a remarkable level. Political counseling and political education profit from the findings, even if the transfer possibilities have not yet been fully exhausted, since parliament and government make only occasional use of the scientific resources when preparing their decisions. Parliamentary hearings on UN topics and mandates of the government for expert groups to do research on UN issues are still the exception and not the rule.

In order to gain more attention and acknowledgement in the international scientific community – especially in the Anglo-Saxon area – the German research results should be increasingly accessible in the English language, as Ruth Wedgwood has wished it in the above mentioned book review of the first edition of this encyclopedia.

Therefore it is to be hoped that this second English edition of the "Lexikon der Vereinten Nationen", of which this contribution is a part, might further im-

prove this international knowledge of the German UN research.

Günther Unser

Lit.: *I. Bibliographies and Bibliographic Commentaries:*
Deutsche Gesellschaft für die Vereinten Nationen (ed.): Die Vereinten Nationen in der Literatur. Blaue Reihe Nr. 63, Bonn 1996; *Hüfner, K./Naumann, J.:* Zwanzig Jahre Vereinte Nationen. Internationale Bibliographie, Berlin 1968; *Knapp, M.:* 50 Jahre Vereinte Nationen: Rückblick und Ausblick im Spiegel der Jubiläumsliteratur, in: Zeitschrift für Politikwissenschaft, 7 (1997) 423 – 481.
II. Collections of UN Documents:
Knipping, F./ Mangoldt, H. von/Rittberger, V. (eds.): Das System der Vereinten Nationen und seine Vorläufer, 3 vols., Munich 1995/96; *Spröte, W./Wünsche, H. (eds.):* Die Vereinten Nationen und ihre Spezialorganisationen. Dokumente, 16 vols., Berlin (East) 1974 – 1988.
III. Handbooks and Commentaries:
Simma, B. (ed.): Charta der Vereinten Nationen. Kommentar, Munich 1991; *Simma, B. (ed.):* The Charter of the United Nations. A Commentary, Munich/Oxford 1994; *Simma, B. (ed.):* The Charter of the United Nations. A Commentary, 2nd edn., Oxford 2002; *Unser, G.:* Die UNO – Aufgaben, Strukturen, Politik, 7th edn., Munich 2004; *Volger, H. (ed.):* Lexikon der Vereinten Nationen, Munich/Vienna 2000; *Wolfrum, R. (ed.):* Handbuch Vereinte Nationen, Munich 1977; *Wolfrum, R. (ed.):* Handbuch Vereinte Nationen, 2nd edn., Munich 1991; *Wolfrum, R. (ed.):* United Nations: Law, Policies and Practice, 2 vols., Munich/Dordrecht 1995.
IV. Readers, Monographs and Articles in Journals:
Albrecht, U. (ed.): Die Vereinten Nationen am Scheideweg. Von der Staatenorganisation zur internationalen Gemeinschaftswelt, Hamburg 1998; *Andreae, L.:* Reform in der Warteschleife. Ein deutscher Sitz im Sicherheitsrat?, Munich and Vienna 2002; *Bauer, F.:* Kofi Annan. Ein Leben, Frankfurt(Main) 2005; *Baum, G./Riedel, E./Schaefer, M. (eds.):* Menschenrechtsschutz in der Praxis der Vereinten Nationen, Baden-Baden 1998; *Beise, M.:* Die Welthandelsorganisation (WTO), Baden-Baden 2001; *Beyerlin, U.:* Umweltvölkerrecht, Munich 2000; *Biermann, R./Simonis, U.E.:* Eine Weltorganisation für Umwelt und Entwicklung. Funktion, Chancen, Probleme (Policy Paper 9 – Stiftung Entwicklung und Frieden), Bonn 1998; *Biermann, R./Simonis, U.E.:* Institutionelle

Reform der Weltumweltpolitik? Zur politischen Debatte um die Gründung einer Weltumweltorganisation, in: Zeitschrift für Internationale Beziehungen 1 (2000), 163-183; *Bothe, M./Dörschel, T.(eds.):* UN Peacekeeping: A Documentary Introduction, The Hague 1999; *Brock, L./Brühl, T.:* Nach dem UN Reformgipfel. Vorschläge zur Stärkung der kollektiven Friedenssicherung (Policy Paper 24 – Stiftung Entwicklung und Frieden), Bonn 2006; *Bruns, W.:* Die UNO-Politik der DDR, Stuttgart 1978; *Bruns, W.:* Die Uneinigen in den Vereinten Nationen: Bundesrepublik Deutschland und DDR in der UNO, Cologne 1980; *Cede, F./Sucharipa-Behrmann, L. (eds.):* Die Vereinten Nationen – Recht und Praxis, Vienna/Munich 1999; *Czempiel, E.-O.:* Macht und Kompromiß. Die Beziehungen der BRD zu den Vereinten Nationen 1956 – 1970, Düsseldorf 1971; *Czempiel, E.-O.:* Die Reform der UNO. Möglichkeiten und Mißverständnisse, Munich 1994; *Debiel, T./Nuscheler, F. (eds.):* Der neue Interventionismus. Humanitäre Einmischung zwischen Anspruch und Wirklichkeit, Bonn 1996; *Debiel, T.:* UN-Friedensoperationen in Afrika. Weltinnenpolitik und die Realität von Bürgerkriegen, Bonn 2003; *Delbrück, J.:* Die Effektivität des UN-Gewaltverbots, in: FW 74 (1999), 139-158; *Deutsche Gesellschaft für die Vereinten Nationen (ed.):* UNO-Forschung in Deutschland (Blaue Reihe No. 15), Berlin 2006; *Dicke, K.:* Effizienz und Effektivität internationaler Organisationen. Darstellung und kritische Analyse eines Topos im Reformprozeß der Vereinten Nationen, Berlin 1994; *Dicke, K./Fröhlich, M.(eds.):* Wege multilateraler Diplomatie. Politik, Handlungsmöglichkeiten und Entscheidungsstrukturen im UN-System, Baden-Baden 2005; *Doeker, G. (ed):* Die Vereinten Nationen – Rolle und Funktion in der internationalen Politik, Munich 1976; *Doeker, G./Volger, H. (eds.):* Die Wiederentdeckung der Vereinten Nationen, Opladen 1990; *Droege, H. et al.:* Die Bundesrepublik Deutschland und die Vereinten Nationen, Munich 1966; *Ehrhart, H.-G./ Klingenburg, K.:* UN-Friedenssicherung 1985-1995. Analyse und Bibliographie, Baden-Baden 1996; *Eisele, M.:* Die Vereinten Nationen und das internationale Krisenmanagement. Ein Insider-Bericht, Frankfurt (Main) 2000; *Fahl, G.:* Der UNO-Sicherheitsrat. Analyse und Dokumentation nach dreißigjährigem Bestehen, Berlin 1978; *Fassbender, B.:* Reforming the United Nations, in: FW 73 (1998), 427-442; *Fassbender, B.:* UN Security Council Reform and the Right of Veto. A Constitutional Perspective, The Hague et al. 1998; *Fenner, C.:* Der globale Pakt der Vereinten Nationen, Freiburg 2004; *Ferdowsi, M./Opitz, P.J. (eds.):* Macht und Ohnmacht der Vereinten Nationen. Zur Rolle der Weltorganisation in Drittwelt-Konflikten, Munich et al. 1987; *Fink, U.:* Kollektive Friedenssicherung: Kapitel VII UN Charta in der Praxis des Sicherheitsrates der Vereinten Nationen, 2 vols., Frankfurt (Main) 1999; *Fleischhauer, C.-A.:* Der Internationale Gerichtshof und die Staatengemeinschaft am Ende des Jahrhunderts, in: Die Friedens-Warte 74 (1999), 113-125; *Frei, D.:* Die Organisation der Vereinten Nationen (UNO). Eine Einführung in 15 Vorlesungen, ed. by D. Ruolff, Grüsch/Switzerland 1990; *Freuding, C.:* Deutschland in der Weltpolitik: Die Bundesrepublik Deutschland als nichtständiges Mitglied im Sicherheitsrat der Vereinten Nationen in den Jahren 1997/78 und 1987/88 und 1995/96, Baden-Baden 2000; *Fröhlich, M.:* Dag Hammarskjöld und die Vereinten Nationen. Die politische Ethik des UNO-Generalsekretärs, Paderborn 2002; *Fröhlich, M. (ed.):* Die Vereinten Nationen im 21. Jahrhundert. Reden und Beiträge 1997-2003 von Kofi Annan, Wiesbaden 2004; *Fröhlich, M. (ed.):* UN Studies: Umrisse eines Lehr- und Forschungsfeldes, Baden-Baden 2008; *Fröhlich, M./Hüfner, K./Märker, A,:* Reform des Sicherheitsrats. Modelle, Kriterien und Kennziffern, Berlin 2005; *Fues, Th./Loewe, M.:* Between Frustration and Optimism: The Development Outcome of the Millennium+5 Summit (Deutsches Institut für Entwicklungspolitik (DIE) Briefing Paper 7), Bonn 2005; *Gareis, S.B.:* Der Wandel der Friedenssicherung durch die Vereinten Nationen, in:APZ, No. 27-28(2002), 19-25; *Gareis, S.B./Varwick, J.:* Die Vereinten Nationen. Aufgaben, Instrumente, Reformen, 4th edn., Opladen/Farmington Hills 2006; Opladen 2002; *Griep, E.:* Neue Maßstäbe für die UN-Friedensmissionen. Der Brahimi-Report und seine Folgen, in: VN 50 (2002), 61-66; *Hasse, J./Müller, E./Schneider, P. (eds.):* Humanitäres Völkerrecht – Politische, rechtliche und strafgerichtliche Dimensionen, Baden-Baden 2001; *Hasse, J./Müller, E./ Schneider, P. (eds.):* Menschenrechte – Bilanz und Perspektiven, Baden-Baden 2002; *Heilmann, D.:* Die Effektivität des Internationalen Strafgerichtshofs, Baden-Baden 2006; *Hellmann, G./Roos, U.:* Das deutsche Streben nach einem ständigen Sitz im UN-Sicherheitsrat (INEF-Report 92/2007), Duisburg 2007; *Horn ,A.:* Multilaterale ökonomische Sanktionsregime der Vereinten Nationen. Konzepte, Probleme, Resultate, Frank-

furt (Main) 2003; *Horn, A.:* Vereinte Natio-
nen – Akteure und Entscheidungsprozesse,
Berlin 2007; *Hufnagel, F.-E.:* UN Friedens-
missionen der zweiten Generation. Vom Puf-
fer zur Treuhand, Berlin 1996; *Hüfner, K.
(ed.):* Die Reform der Vereinten Nationen,
Opladen 1994; *Hüfner, K. (ed.):* Agenda for
Change. New Tasks for the United Nations,
Opladen 1995; *Hüfner, K./Martens, J.:*
UNO-Reform zwischen Utopie und Realität.
Vorschläge zum Wirtschafts- und Sozial-
bereich der Vereinten Nationen, Frankfurt
(Main) 2000; *Hüfner, K./Naumann, J.:* 25
Jahre Vereinte Nationen. Bundeszentrale für
politische Bildung, Bonn 1970; *Hüfner,
K./Naumann, J.:* Das System der Vereinten
Nationen, Düsseldorf 1974; *Jarasch, F.:* Er-
richtung, Organisation und Finanzierung des
Internationalen Strafgerichtshofs und die
Schlußbestimmungen des Statuts, in: Huma-
nitäres Völkerrecht (1999), 1, 10-22; *Kaul,
H.-P.:* Arbeitsweise und informelle Verfah-
ren des Sicherheitsrats. Beobachtungen eines
Unterhändlers, in: VN 46 (1998), 6-13;
Kaul, H.-P.: Durchbruch in Rom. Der Ver-
trag über den Internationalen Strafgerichts-
hof, in: VN 46 (1998) 125-130; *Kaul, H.-P.:*
Der Aufbau des Internationalen Strafge-
richtshofs. Schwierigkeiten und Fortschritte,
in: VN 49 (2001) 215-222; *Kaul, I./Grun-
berg, I./Stern, M.A. (eds.):* Global Public
Goods. International Cooperation in the 21st
Century, New York 1999; *Kaul, I./Concei-
cao, P. (eds.):* The New Public Finance.
Responding to Global Challenges, New Y-
ork/ Oxford 2006; *Keil, I./Volger, H.:* Die
Umweltpolitik der Vereinten Nationen, in:
Hüfner, K. (ed.): Die Reform der Vereinten
Nationen. Die Weltorganisation zwischen
Krise und Erneuerung, Opladen 1994, 81-98;
Keil, I./Lobner, S.: UNO – Weltpolizei auf
dem Prüfstand. 38 Jahre Friedensmissionen
vom Suez bis Kambodscha, Müns-
ter/Hamburg 1994; *Klein, E. (ed.):* The Mo-
nitoring System of Human Rights Treaty
Obligations, Berlin 1998; *Klein, E./Volger,
H. (eds.):* Bilanz ein Jahr nach dem Millen-
nium – Reformkonzepte und deren Imple-
mentierung. 3. Potsdamer UNO-Konferenz
vom 29. bis 30. Juni 2001, Potsdam 2001;
Klein, E./ Volger, H.(eds.): Die Vereinten
Nationen und Regionalorganisationen vor
aktuellen Herausforderungen. 4. Potsdamer
UNO-Konferenz vom 28. bis 29. Juni 2002,
Potsdam 2002; *Klein, E./Volger, H. (eds.):*
Die deutsche UN-Politik 1973-2003.
5. Potsdamer UNO-Konferenz vom 27. bis
28. Juni 2003, Potsdam 2004; *Klein,
E./Volger, H. (eds.):* Integrative Konzepte
bei der Reform der Vereinten Nationen.

6. Potsdamer UNO-Konferenz vom 25. bis
26. Juni 2004, Potsdam 2004; *Klein,
E./Volger, H. (eds.):* Chancen für eine Reform der Vereinten Nationen? 7. Potsdamer
UNO-Konferenz vom 24. bis 25. Juni 2005,
Potsdam 2006; *Klein, E./ Volger, H. (eds.):*
Ein Jahr nach dem UN-Weltgipfel 2005. Eine Bilanz der Reformbemühungen. 8. Potsdamer UNO-Konferenz vom 23. bis 24. Juni
2006, Potsdam 2006; *Klein, E./Volger, H.
(eds.):* Die Vereinten Nationen in den internationalen Beziehungen. 9. Potsdamer UNO-
Konferenz, 28. Juni 2008, Potsdam 2009;
Klingebiel, S.: Leistungsfähigkeit und Reform des Entwicklungsprogramms der Vereinten Nationen, Cologne 1998; *Koll, T.:* Die
Weltbank. Struktur, Aufgaben und Bedeutung, Berlin 1988; *Köllner. L.:* Militäraus-
gaben und Finanzielle Abrüstung. Ein sicherheitspolitisches Programm der Vereinten
Nationen, Munich 1981; *Köster, K.:* Bundesrepublik Deutschland und Vereinte Nationen
1949-1963, Frankfurt (Main) 2000; *Kühne,
W.:* Blauhelme in einer turbulenten Welt,
Baden-Baden 1993; *Kühne, W.:* Zukunft der
UN Friedenseinsätze. Lehren aus dem Brahimi-Report, in: Blätter für deutsche und internationale Politik 45 (2000), 1355-1364;
Kühne, W./Baumann, K.: Reform des Sicherheitsrates zum 50jährigen Jubiläum. Aus-
wertung und Analyse der Stellungnahmen
der Mitgliedstaaten im Überblick, Ebenhausen 1995; *Lehmann, I.:* Peacekeeping and
Public Information. Caught in the Crossfire,
London 1999; *Leininger,J.:* Die Reform der
Vereinten Nationen – Chancen auf eine Erneuerung zivilgesellschaftlicher Beteiligung?, Berlin 2005; *Liese, A.:* Menschenrechtsschutz durch Nichtregierungsorganisationen, in: APZ, No.. 46-47 (1998), 36-42;
Löwe, V.: Peacekeeping-Operationen der UN
– Aspekte einer Beteiligung der Bundesrepublik Deutschland, Münster/ Hamburg
1994; *Lüder, S.R.:* Völkerrechtliche Verantwortlichkeit bei Teilnahme an „Peace-
Keeping"-Missionen der Vereinten Nationen, Berlin 2004; *Martens, J.:* "In larger
freedom": the report of the UN Secretary-
General for the Millennium+5 Summit 2005,
Friedrich Ebert Stiftung (Dialogue on globalization: Briefing papers- FES Berlin), Electronic ed., Bonn 2005 (quoted as Martens
2005a); *Martens, J.:* The development agenda after the 2005 millennium+5 summit: a
checklist of uncompleted tasks, Friedrich
Ebert Stiftung (Dialogue on globalization:
Briefing papers- FES Berlin), Electronic ed.,
Bonn 2005 (quoted as Martens 2005b); *Martens, K.:* NGO's and the United Nations: Institutionalization, Professionalization and

Adaptation, New York et al. 2005 (quoted as Martens 2005c); *Messner, D./Nuscheler, F. (eds.):* Weltkonferenzen und Weltberichte, Bonn 1996; *Messner, D./Wolff, P.:* The Millennium Development Goals – Thinking beyond the Sachs Report, Deutsches Institut für Entwicklungspolitik (DIE), Briefing Paper 5, Bonn 2005; *Metzger, M./Reichenstein, B. (eds.):* Challenges for International Organizations in the Twenty-First Century. Essays in Honor of Klaus Hüfner, Basingstoke et al. 2000; *Münzing, E.:* Die UNO – Instrument amerikanischer Außenpolitik? Die UNO-Politik der Bush-Administration 1988-1992, Münster/Hamburg 1995; *Nitsche, D.:* Der Internationale Strafgerichtshof ICC und der Frieden, Baden-Baden 2007; *Oberthür, S.:* Umweltschutz durch internationale Regime. Interessen, Verhandlungsprozesse, Wirkungen, Opladen 1997; *Oberthür, S./Ott, H. E.:* Das Kyoto-Protokoll. Internationale Klimapolitik für das 21. Jahrhundert, Opladen 2000; *Opitz, P.J./Rittberger, V. (eds.):* Forum der Welt – 40 Jahre Vereinte Nationen, Munich 1986; *Opitz, P.J.:* Menschenrechte und Internationaler Menschenrechtsschutz im 20. Jahrhundert, München 2002; *Ozgercin, K.:* Collective security and the United Nations: the work of the high-level panel on threats, challenges and change, New York 2005, (Dialogue on globalization: Briefing papers – FES New York), Bonn 2005; *Ozgercin, K./Steinhilber, J.:* Toward a more secure world? The report of the high-level panel on threats, challenges and change, New York 2005, (Dialogue on globalization: Briefing papers – FES New York), Bonn 2005; *Paepcke, H.:* Die friedens- und sicherheitspolitische Rolle des UN-Generalsekretärs im Wandel. Das kritische Verhältnis zwischen Boutros Boutros-Ghali und den USA, Baden-Baden 2004; *Pape, M.:* Humanitäre Intervention. Zur Bedeutung der Menschenrechte in den Vereinten Nationen, Baden-Baden 1997; *Partsch, K.J.:* Human Rights, in: Wolfrum, R. (ed.): United Nations: Law, Policies and Practice, Vol. 1, München/Dordrecht 1995, 603-611; *Paschke, K.T.:* Innenrevision in den Vereinten Nationen – Eine neue Erfahrung, in: VN 46 (1998), 41-45; *Prantl, J.:* The UN Security Council and Informal Groups of States: Complementing or Competing for Governance? Oxford 2006; *Prittwitz, V. .v (ed.):* Institutionelle Arrangements der Umweltpolitik, Opladen 2000; *Rittberger, V./Mogler, M./Zangl, B.:* Vereinte Nationen und Weltordnung, Opladen 1997; *Rittberger, V. (ed.):* Anpassung oder Austritt: Industriestaaten in der UNESCO-Krise. Ein Beitrag zur vergleichenden Aussenpolitikforschung, Berlin 1995; *Roggemann, H.:* Die internationalen Strafgerichtshöfe. Einführung, Rechtsgrundlage, Dokumente, 2nd edn., Berlin 1998; *Rudolf, B.:* Frauen und Völkerrecht. Zur Einwirkung von Frauenrechten und Fraueninteressen auf das Völkerrecht, Baden-Baden 2007; *Rupprecht, J.:* Frieden durch Menschenrechtsschutz: Strategien der Vereinten Nationen zur Verwirklichung der Menschenrechte weltweit (Demokratie, Sicherheit, Frieden, Vol. 153), Baden-Baden 2003; *Scheuner, U./Lindemann, B. (eds.):* Die Vereinten Nationen und die Mitarbeit der Bundesrepublik Deutschland, Munich/Vienna 1973; *Schlüter, H.W.:* Diplomatie der Versöhnung. Die Vereinten Nationen und die Wahrung des Weltfriedens, Stuttgart 1966; *Schlüter, H.W.:* Der Sicherheitsrat der Vereinten Nationen, Bonn 1977; *Schorlemer, S. v.:* Menschenrechte und „Humanitäre Interventionen", in: IP 55 (2000), 41-48; *Schorlemer, S. v. (ed.):* Praxishandbuch UNO. Die Vereinten Nationen im Lichte globaler Herausforderungen, Heidelberg 2003; *Schorlemer, S. v. (ed.):* Globale Probleme und Zukunftsaufgaben der Vereinten Nationen (Sonderband 1 der Zeitschrift für Politik), Baden-Baden 2006; *Schorlemer, S. v. (ed.):* Die Vereinten Nationen und neuere Entwicklung der Frauenrechte, Frankfurt (Main) 2007; *Schriefer, D./Sandt-ner, W./ Rudischhauser, W.:* 50 Jahre Internationale Atomenergie-Organisation IAEO, Baden-Baden 2007; *Siegler, H. v.:* Die Vereinten Nationen – Eine Bilanz nach 20 Jahren, Bonn et al. 1966; *Simonis, U.E.:* Weltumweltpolitik. Grundrisse und Bausteine eines neuen Politikfeldes, 2nd edn., Berlin 1998; *Stoecker, F.W.:* NGOs und die UNO: die Einbindung von Nichtregierungsorganisationen (NGOs) in die Strukturen der Vereinten Nationen, Frankfurt (Main) 2000; *Strauss, E.:* Prävention von Menschenrechtsverletzungen als Aufgabe internationaler Organisationen. Rechtsgrundlagen und inhaltliche Ansätze (Schriften des Menschenrechtszentrums der Universität Potsdam, Vol. 11), Potsdam 2001; *Subkus, R.:* Reform der Vereinten Nationen im Umweltbereich, Berlin 2004; *Suchsland-Maser, U.:* Menschenrechte und die Politik multilateraler Finanzinstitutionen – Eine Untersuchung unter völkerrechtlichen Gesichtspunkten an den Beispielen der Weltbank, des Währungsfonds und regionaler Entwicklungsbanken (Studien zum Öffentlichen Recht, Völker- und Europarecht, Vol. 1), Potsdam 1999; *Tetzlaff, R.:* Weltbank und Währungsfonds: Gestalter der Bretton-Woods-Ära, Opladen 1996; *Tomuschat, C.*

(ed.): The United Nations at Age Fifty. A Legal Perspective, The Hague 1995; *Tomuschat, C.:* Die Lage der Menschenrechte 50 Jahre nach der Allgemeinen Erklärung, in: Jahrbuch Internationale Politik 1997-1998, Munich 2000; *Tomuschat, C.:* Völkerrecht ist kein Zweiklassenrecht. Der Irak-Krieg und seine Folgen, in: VN 51 (2003), 41-46; *Varwick, J.:* Weltorganisation zwischen Anspruch und Wirklichkeit. Zu den Reformperspektiven der Vereinten Nationen nach ihrem 50. Geburtstag, in: Gegenwartskunde 45 (1996), 555-589; *Varwick, J.:* Die Vereinten Nationen im Ausgang des Jahrhunderts. Zur Reformdebatte der Weltorganisation, in: Politische Bildung 1999, 29-43; *Varwick, J./ Zimmermann, A.:* Die Reform der Vereinten Nationen – Bilanz und Perspektiven, Berlin 2006; *Vatterodt, M.:* Reform of the United Nations Development Cooperation: Despite Progress, still a Long Way to go to Achieve more Coherence (DIE Briefing paper 10/2007), Bonn 2007; *Volger, H.:* Der Wandel der Perzeption von Abrüstung, Entwicklung und Konversion in der UNO, Frankfurt (Main) 1987; *Volger, H.:* Die Vereinten Nationen, Munich/Vienna 1994; *Volger, H.:* Geschichte der Vereinten Nationen, Munich/ Vienna 1995 (2nd edn. Munich/Vienna 2008); *Volger, H.:* Neue Strukturen für die Vereinten Nationen, in: IP 56 (2001), 9-15; *Volger, H.:* UN-Reform ohne Charta-Revision? Der Stand der Reformbemühungen nach dem Milleniums-Gipfel, in: Schorlemer, S. v. (ed.): Praxishandbuch UNO. Die Vereinten Nationen im Lichte globaler Herausforderungen, Berlin et al. 2003, 733-753; *Volger, H.:* Machtpoker um den Weltsicherheitsrat, in: Blätter für deutsche und internationale Politik 49 (2004), 1375-1381; *Volger, H.:* Mehr Partizipation nicht erwünscht. Der Bericht des Cardoso-Panels über die Reform der Beziehungen zwischen den Vereinten Nationen und der Zivilgesellschaft, in: VN 53 (2005), 12-18; *Volger, H.:* Vereinte Nationen: Große Reform klein gemacht, in: Blätter für deutsche und internationale Politik 50 (2005), 1290-1294; *Volger, H.:* Grundlagen und Strukturen der Vereinten Nationen, Munich/ Vienna 2007; *Volger, H.:* Bausteine für eine Reform der UNO-Forschung und -Lehre in Deutschland: Praktische Erfahrungen eines UNO-Forschungsnetzwerks, in: Fröhlich, M. (ed.): UN-Studies. Umrisse eines Lehr- und Forschungsfeldes, Baden-Baden 2008, 247-261 (quoted as Volger 2008a); *Volger, H.:* Die Vereinten Nationen als Arbeitsgebiet für wissenschaftliche Bibliotheken in Deutschland: Plädoyer für den Aufbau einer zentra-len Dokumentations- und Bibliographiestelle für die UN-Forschung, in: Zeitschrift für Bibliothekswesen und Bibliographie 55 (2008), 272-277 (quoted as Volger 2008b); *Werthes, S.:* Probleme und Perspektiven von Sanktionen als politisches Instrument der Vereinten Nationen, Münster 2003; *Winkelmann, I.:* Bringing the Security Council into a New Era: Recent Developments in the Discussion on the Reform of the Security Council, in: Max Planck Yearbook of United Nations Law, Vol. 1 (1997), 35-90; *Wollenberg, S.:* Die Regierung von Konfliktgebieten durch die Vereinten Nationen, Baden-Baden 2007; *Wouters, J./Hoffmeister, F./Ruys, T. (eds.):* The United Nations and the European Union: An Ever Stronger Partnership, The Hague 2006; *Wündisch, M.:* Die United Nations Joint Inspection Unit als Instrument zur Einführung organisatorischer Rationalität in internationalen Organisationen, Frankfurt (Main) et al. 1998; *Zitka, F.:* Wandel und Kontinuität. Amerikanische UNO-Politik 1977-1993, Frankfurt (Main) 1996.

V. Journals:
Archiv des Völkerrechts, Tübingen; Blätter für deutsche und internationale Politik, Bonn; Die Friedens-Warte, Berlin; Humanitäres Völkerrecht – Informationsschriften, Bonn; S+F. Vierteljahresschrift für Sicherheit und Frieden, Baden-Baden; Vereinte Nationen, Baden-Baden; Zeitschrift für ausländisches öffentliches Recht und Völkerrecht, Stuttgart.

Internet: Bibliographies of German UN research publications:
a) website of the UN Information Centre Bonn on UN literature:
www.uno.de/bibliothek/tipps.htm;
b) website of the Forschungskreis Vereinte Nationen (Research Group United Nations) on UN literature: www.forschungskreis-vereinte-nationen.de/text/literatur.html;
c) website of the Deutsche Gesellschaft für die Vereinten Nationen (UN Association of Germany) with information on brochures, research papers, leaflets : www.dgvn.de.

Resolution, Declaration, Decision

The Charter of the United Nations (→ Charter of the UN)does not specify in which form the principal organs (→ Principal Organs, Subsidiary Organs, Treaty Bodies) of the UN shall express their views. According to Chapter IV, for instance, the → General Assembly may discuss questions and make recommendations (Art. 10), consider certain issues (Art. 11 (1)), initiate studies (Art. 13 (1)), or approve the → budget (Art. 17 (1)), but it is not said how the respective resolutions shall be called, nor what legal effect they may have. Article 18, 25 and 27 speak of "decisions" of the General Assembly and the → Security Council, respectively.

In practice, the General Assembly distinguishes between *"resolutions"*, *"declarations"* and *"decisions"*. A *"resolution"* is the most general form for making observations and recommendations. The term comes from the constitutional law of the United States of America where it describes an official expression of opinion of a parliamentary assembly, in particular one of either house of the Congress, which does not, or does not yet, have the character of a statute. A typical resolution of the General Assembly begins with the words "The General Assembly", to be followed by a *preamble* (which refers to earlier relevant resolutions, outlines the history of the origins of the resolution, and states in a number of so-called considerations the main reasons for its adoption), and an *operative part* consisting of the actual declaration or recommendation.

A *"declaration"* is also adopted as a resolution. However, the solemn name is reserved for statements which the General Assembly considers to be of outstanding importance. In particular, principles of a political or legal nature have been "solemnly proclaimed" in the form of a declaration. Major examples of such documents are the Universal Declaration of Human Rights of 12 December 1948 (A/RES/217 (III)) (→ Human Rights, Universal Declaration of), the Declaration on the Granting of Independence to Colonial Countries and Peoples of 14 December 1960 (A/RES/1514 (V)) (→ Decolonization), and the Declaration on Principles of International Law concerning Friendly Relations and Co-operation among States in accordance with the Charter of the United Nations of 24 October 1970 (Annex to A/RES/2625 (XXV), "Friendly Rela-

tions Declaration"). In the case of the → Charter of Economic Rights and Duties of States of 12 December 1974 (A/RES/3281 (XXIX)) the General Assembly, seeking to enhance the importance of the declaration, even chose a name which in the United Nations is usually reserved for the founding instrument of the Organization.

Up to the thirtieth regular session (1975), the resolutions of the General Assembly (A/RES) were numbered consecutively, with bracketed Roman numbers indicating the session in which a resolution had been adopted. If the Roman number was preceded by the letter "S" or "ES", the resolution had been passed in a "special session" or "emergency special session" of the General Assembly, respectively. Beginning with the thirty-first session (1976), this system was changed. Since then, an Arabic number first indicates the session; it follows, separated by an oblique stroke (/), another Arabic number designating the respective resolution (→ Documentation System).

In a narrower sense than that implied by Article 18, the General Assembly uses the name *"decision"* for internal organizational acts, like elections and appointments of members of its subsidiary organs and of other UN principal organs, determinations of dates of sessions and of the agenda, or rulings on budgetary questions.

From the *designation* of a statement made by the General Assembly one cannot conclusively infer its *legal effect*. Apart from exceptions in the internal sphere of the Organization, like decisions on the admission of new members (→ Membership and Representation of States) or the approval of the budget, the General Assembly has only the power to make *recommendations*. Even the designation of a resolution as a "declaration" or a "Charter" does not give its contents a legally binding character. The Assembly is not a "world legislator". This, however, does not mean that its resolutions are legally meaningless. First, all member states are obliged to take note of, and seriously to consider,

619

an Assembly resolution. Second, resolutions can contribute to the development of new customary international law or general principles of international law (→ International Law and the UN) (see, for instance, the Universal Declaration of Human Rights or the Declaration on the Inadmissibility of Intervention in the Domestic Affairs of States and the Protection of their Independence and Sovereignty of 21 December 1965 (A/RES/2131 (XX)). They can also give expression to, or interpret, existing norms of international law (see, for instance, the "Friendly Relations Declaration"). Frequently, the substantive content of a resolution has later been included in an international treaty and thus become binding on the parties to the treaty (see, for instance, the Declaration on the Elimination of all Forms of Racial Discrimination of 20 November 1963 (A/RES/1904 (XVIII)). In summary, one can say that "although lacking the requisite qualities of a world legislator, the United Nations has become a powerful motor for norm-setting by taking the lead in initiating reform and organizing the relevant drafting processes" (*Tomuschat* 1999, 306).

Expressing the views of the organs mainly responsible for the application of the UN Charter, resolutions of the General Assembly and the Security Council are of importance to the interpretation of the Charter. Within the limits of the objective meaning of the rules of the Charter, they can also progressively develop those rules through their practice. Beyond that, amendments of the law of the Charter must be brought about in the formal procedures of Article 108 and 109 of the UN Charter.

The UN Charter refers to all resolutions of the *Security Council* as "decisions" (see Arts. 25 and 27). According to Article 25, members of the UN are obliged "to accept and carry out the decisions of the Security Council in accordance with the present Charter". Decisions taken by the Council may have different effects (cf. *Delbrück* 2002, 454-455). The Council can, for instance, make recommendations with respect to

a pacific settlement of disputes (see Art. 36). By contrast, decisions of the Council under Chapter VII of the Charter, adopted in the form of a resolution, are legally binding on all states and members of the international community. They are usually characterized by the opening formulation "The Security Council ..., Acting under Chapter VII ..., Decides (demands, insists)". They require a determination of the existence of a threat to the peace, breach of the peace, or act of aggression in accordance with Article 39 of the Charter. It is, however, not necessary that the Council expressly refers to that article. With a terminology developed in the context of the European Community, the binding resolutions of the Council can be counted among the "secondary law" of the United Nations (in contradistinction to the "primary law", *i.e.*, the UN Charter).

Following the terrorist attacks of September 11, 2001, the Council began to adopt, under Chapter VII of the Charter, resolutions characterized by the general and abstract character of the obligations imposed (see, for instance, S/RES/1373 (2001) of 28 September 2001 on the prevention and suppression of the financing of terrorist acts). The obligations are phrased in neutral language, apply to an indefinite number of cases, and are not usually limited in time. In the legal literature, these resolutions are seen as the beginning of an "international legislation" (cf. *Talmon* 2005).

The practice of the Security Council distinguishes between *"resolutions"* and *"decisions"*. The latter term is generally used for determinations of procedural and organizational questions. All other statements (recommendations as well as binding decisions, in particular those adopted under Chapter VII of the Charter) are styled "resolutions". Council resolutions (S/RES) are consecutively numbered; in brackets, the year is added in which a resolution was adopted. This manner of numbering emphasizes that the Council is not only a permanent, but also a continuously functioning organ of the UN (see Art. 28 (1) of the UN Charter). Today, new resolutions of the Council are immediately posted on the UN website (→ Internet, Websites of the UN System in the). All resolutions of the Council and the General Assembly are also published in the Yearbook of the United Nations, together with notes on the drafting history and subsequent developments.

Under the heading of "decisions" the official records of the Security Council also publish *verbal statements and letters of the President of the Security Council*. These express views on political questions which might have been made the subject of a resolution as well. Presidential statements require a consensus of all fifteen members of the Council. Often, such statements are meant to give, on a level less formal than that of a resolution, expression to the Council's concern about a situation threatening international peace and security. In other statements, certain states are urged to comply with their obligations arising from the UN Charter (see, for instance, the statement of the President of the Security Council regarding the situation in Angola of 19 May 1999 (UN Doc. S/PRST/1999/14)) or from earlier resolutions (see, for instance, the statement of 16 June 2008 (UN Doc. S/PRST/2008/21), urging the Government of Sudan and all other parties to the conflict in Darfur to cooperate fully with the International Criminal Court, consistent with resolution 1593 (2005), in order to put an end to impunity for the crimes committed in Darfur). Since 1994, such "Presidential Statements" are designated with the symbol "S/PRST", which is followed by the year in which a statement was made, and a consecutive number.

Bardo Fassbender

Lit.: *Bailey, S.D./Daws, S.:* The Procedure of the UN Security Council, 3rd edn., Oxford 1998; *Delbrück, J.:* Article 25 of the Charter, in: Simma, B. (ed.): The Charter of the United Nations: A Commentary, 2nd edn., Oxford 2002, 452-464; *Peterson, M.J.:* The General Assembly in World Politics, Boston 1986; *Sloan, B.:* United Nations General Assembly Resolutions in Our Changing World, Ardsley-on-Hudson/NY 1991; *Talmon, S.:* The Security Council as World Legislature, in: AJIL 99 (2005), 175-193; *Tomuschat, C.:* International Law: Ensuring the Survival of Mankind on the Eve of a New Century. Collected Courses of the Hague Academy of International Law, Vol. 281 (1999), 1-438.

Internet: UN Documentation Research Guide - General Assembly Resolutions/Decisions: www.un.org/Depts/dhl/resguide/gares.htm; UN Documentation Research Guide - Security Council Resolutions: www.un.org/Depts/dhl/ resguide/scres.htm.

Rules of Procedure (General Assembly, Security Council)

Articles 21 and 30 of the → Charter of the UN empower the → General Assembly and the → Security Council, respectively, to adopt their own *rules of procedure*. In this respect the Charter follows the example of modern state constitutions which, as a rule, regulate the organization and procedure of collective constitutional organs (in particular parliaments) in general terms only, leaving it to the bodies themselves to decide on the details. Articles 21 and 30 of the Charter can also be traced back to Article 5 (2) of the Covenant of the → League of Nations which provided that "all matters of procedure at meetings of the Assembly or of the Council ... shall be regulated by the Assembly or by the Council".

The rules of procedure of the General Assembly and the Security Council are legal norms. Hierarchically, they are subject to the rules of the UN Charter. Since the rules of procedure have a great impact on the course and, to some extent, also the outcome of the discussions of the two principal political organs of the UN, they are of considerable political importance and have often been very controversial.

The *General Assembly* adopted its rules of procedure in the second session on 17 November 1947. They became effective on 1 January 1948 and have since then been amended several times. The 163 rules are concerned with the procedure of the Assembly itself and that of its committees (→ Committees, System of), in particular the summoning of the Assembly, its agenda, the official and working languages (→ Languages, Official; → Languages, Working), the examination of credentials of member states' representatives, the election of the President and Vice-Presidents of the Assembly, the conduct of business, voting (→ Voting Right and Decision-Making Procedures), the admission of new members of the UN (→ Membership and Representation of States), and the election of members of other organs (Security Council, Economic and Social Council (→ ECOSOC), → Trusteeship Council, International Court of Justice (→ ICJ)) by the Assembly.

According to Rule 163, the rules of procedure can be amended by a decision of the Assembly, taken by a majority of the members present and voting. A number of rules repeat articles of the UN Charter verbatim.

The procedure of the *Security Council* is still guided by the provisional rules of procedure of 24 June 1946. The adoption of these rules was preceded by considerable differences of opinion between member states, especially about the voting procedures and the modes of exercise of the right of veto (→ Veto, Right of Veto) of the permanent members.

A number of states favored the "case-by-case approach" of the Council of the → League of Nations which adopted rules of procedure only in 1933. According to Article 27 (2) of the Charter, decisions of the Security Council on procedural matters shall be made by an affirmative vote of nine members; the right of veto does not apply. Insisting on the "provisional character" of the rules of procedure, the members of the Council wish to retain the possibility of changing the rules in a given case, and also informally. In the practice of the Council, some rules have indeed often been ignored or breached without compromising, in the view of the Council, the validity of its decisions.

The provisional rules of procedure of the Security Council deal, in particular, with the calling of meetings, the agenda, the functions of the presidency of the Council (which is held in turn, for one calendar month, by the states members of the Council in the English alphabetical order of their names), and the conduct of business. As regards voting, Rule 40 simply refers to the UN Charter.

The rules do not mention the so-called "informal consultations" of Council members, which since the early 1990s have become highly important. They are held in advance of official Council meetings between all members (as "consultations of the whole"), or the permanent members, or members being especially interested in a certain matter. It is in the course of these meetings that decisions are actually made which subsequently are only formally adopted or announced in the official meetings. As a rule, consultations take place behind closed doors and cannot be attended by non-invited states. No official records are kept. For those reasons, today the background and causes of a Council decision, and the motives of the members having initiated and supported it, often remain obscure (for critical analysis, see, e.g., *Reisman* 1993).

The Council has recognized that the lack of transparency of its decision-making process, and the ensuing negative impact on the legitimacy of Council decisions, are problematic, but the steps it has taken so far to improve the situation (like the introduction of "open briefings" in 1998) have not silenced the critical voices.

Since 1994, the issue of an improvement of the working methods of the Council has been discussed in the "Open-ended Working Group on the Question of Equitable Representation on and Increase in the Membership of the Security Council and Other Matters related to the Security Council", established by General Assembly resolution A/RES/48/26 of 3 December 1993 (for the latest report of the Working Group, see UN Doc. A/62/47 of 9 October 2008).

Bardo Fassbender

Lit.: *1. Texts: a) United Nations - General Assembly:* Rules of Procedure of the General Assembly (embodying amendments and additions adopted by the General Assembly up to September 2007, UN Doc. A/520/Rev.17, New York 2007; reprinted in: *Simma, B. (ed):* The Charter of the United Nations. A Commentary, 2nd edn., Oxford 2002, Vol. II, 1385-1405; *b)Security Council:* Provisional Rules of Procedure of the Security Council, UN Doc. S/96/Rev. 7, adopted by the Security Council at its 1st meeting and amended at its 31st, 41st, 42nd, 44th and 48th meetings, on 9 April, 16 and 17 May, 6 and 24 June 1946; 138th and 222nd meetings, on 4 June and 9 December 1947; 468th meeting, on 28 February 1950, 1463rd meeting, on 24 January 1969; 1761st meeting, on 17 January 1974; and 2410th meeting, on 21 December 1982, New York 1983; reprinted in: *Bailey, S.D./Daws, S.:* The Procedure of the UN Security Council, 3rd edn., Oxford 1998, 441-454;
2. Secondary literature: Bailey,S.D./Daws, S.: The Procedure of the UN Security Council, 3rd edn., Oxford 1998; *Reisman, W.M.:* The Constitutional Crisis in the United Nations, in: AJIL 87 (1993), 83-100; *Fitschen, T.:* Art. 21, in: Simma, B. (ed.), loc.cit., Vol. I, 399-420; *Wasum-Rainer, S./Jahn-Koch, I.:* Art. 30, in: Simma, B. (ed.), loc. cit., Vol. I, 563-572.

Internet: a) Rules of Procedure of the General Assembly: www.un.org/ga/ropga.shtml; Provisional Rules of Procedure of the Security Council: www.un.org/Docs/sc/scrules.htm.

Sanctions

I. Sanctions in the UN Charter

UN sanctions belong to the area of maintaining international peace and security. Therefore, they are dealt with in Chapter VII of the UN Charter ($\rightarrow$ Charter of the UN). If the $\rightarrow$ Security Council determines – according to Article 39 UN Charter – that a threat to the peace or breach of the peace exists, it can impose sanctions against the peace-disturbing party according Article 41:

"The Security Council may decide what measures not involving the use of armed force are to be employed to give effect to its decisions, and it may call upon the Members of the United Nations to apply such measures. These may include complete or partial interruption of economic relations and of rail, sea, air, postal, telegraphic, radio, and other means of communication, and the severance of diplomatic relations" (Art. 41 UN Charter).

In general, sanctions are considered as the last measure before military action. According to the Charter the Security Council can decide on the use of armed force in cases of threats to the peace or breaches of the peace, when it considers "that measures provided for in Article 41 would be inadequate or have proved to be inadequate ..." (Art. 42 UN Charter)

If the Security Council decides on sanctions, they are binding on all member states according to Articles 25 and 48. Sanctions are not punishments; they are international measures designed to bend wills. They are meant to demonstrate to the respective state the disapproval of the international community and to change, through their coercive pressure, its peace-endangering behavior. At the same time, there is a preventive effect: the target state – as well as others – is to be deterred from further incriminating acts.

In order to achieve the desired change in the behavior of the target country, sanctions must be efficient, effective, and successful. Efficiency here means the translation into legal and administrative provisions of the member states. Trade partners, friends and neighbors of the target country must cooperate. Sanctions may be judged to be effective if they actually result in the intended negative impact on the reputation and/or the economy of the targeted country or organization. In the cases of comprehensive sanctions or of arms embargoes, this will require effective control systems, such as those applied at considerable effort and expense against Iraq and Yugoslavia. However, sanctions can only reach full success where they actually influence the policies of the state at which they are directed, i.e. where this state fulfils the conditions stipulated in the sanctions resolutions ($\to$ Resolution, Declaration, Decision) and no longer engages in the behavior classified as constituting a threat to the peace.

The Charter had intended to provide the Security Council with an instrument of obvious attractiveness: a means which, in case of conflict, can have a stronger impact than attempts of diplomatic mediation while still remaining below the threshold of military intervention. If sanctions are imposed, statesmen finding themselves exposed to pressure of public opinion in their own country in a specific case can always point out that something is done in any case to confront the threat to the peace. And the use of armed force is not excluded, should the sanctions turn out to be inadequate (Art. 42 UN Charter).

II. Sanctions as Practiced in the UN

During the first forty-five years of the existence of the United Nations the sanctions instrument was hardly utilized. This was due to the deadlock in the Security Council during the Cold War ($\to$ History of the UN) when, as a rule, such proposals had to expect the veto of the opponent ($\to$ Veto, Right of Veto). During that period, sanctions resolutions were passed only twice: firstly against Rhodesia in the form of diplomatic, financial, and comprehensive economic sanctions (1968-1979) and secondly as an arms embargo against South Africa (1977-1994).

Since 1990, however, the sanctions resolutions of the Security Council have been numerous. Special attention has been drawn to the comprehensive economic sanction regimes imposed against Iraq and the Federal Republic of Yugoslavia (Serbia and Montenegro,) and the package of measures imposed against Libya in 1992, including diplomatic and financial sanctions, and have included also the disruption of air traffic and a partial embargo. Other sanctions regimes have been put into force against

Afghanistan, Ethiopia and Eritrea, Haiti, Liberia, Rwanda, Sierra Leone, Somalia, Sudan, a military government in Sierra Leone, and the UNITA in Angola. In the case of the Federal Republic of Yugoslavia the Security Council decided unanimously on the grounds of the political changes which had taken place – above all the establishment of a democratic government – to lift the sanctions and to end the work of the respective sanctions committee (UN Doc. S/RES/1367 (2001) of 10 September 2001). In the case of Libya the Security Council adopted on 8 April 1999 a Presidential Statement (UN Doc. S/PRST/1999/10), in which it noted that the conditions for suspending the aerial, arms and diplomatic sanctions against Libya had been fulfilled, i.e. the sanctions were suspended (details about the sanctions under Chapter VII of the Charter of the UN: www.un.org/News/ossg/sanction.htm).

III. Problem Areas

In the meantime, we can thus draw on some experience from the application of sanctions. In the $\to$ General Assembly, in the Security Council, and in scholarly circles they have become subjects of intensive discussion, which has led to a number of proposals for reform. Such proposals were also submitted by UN $\to$ Secretary-General Boutros Boutros-Ghali in January 1995 in his "Supplement to An Agenda for Peace" (UN Doc. A/50/60-S/1) ($\to$ Agenda for Peace). In order to sharpen the (in his view) "blunt" instrument, he recommended to create a "mechanism" which would allow a more reliable assessment of the impact of sanctions, to secure the availability of $\to$ humanitarian assistance, and to render support to affected third countries.

Even critics maintain that sanctions are justified where and as far as they prevent a disruption of peace without recourse to war. In UN practice during this decade, however, problems have appeared which indicate a need for reform. Such weak points are found in the spheres of politics, law, and ethics.

Therefore, the selection of sanctions and the practice of their imposition have to be carefully examined.

As clearly shown in the case of Iraq, the execution of the sanctions regime was seriously flawed and the political calculations on which the system of sanctions is based cannot be considered as being reliable. Similarly, the so-called "Wagenburg" (barricade of wagons) effect could already be observed in the case of the sanctions imposed against Rhodesia: In times of international pressure, the people rally around the flag and put internal political disagreement aside. In Iraq, the sanctions were actually used to justify increased repression by the rulers. In South Africa, on the contrary, one could count on a strong internal opposition ready to accept the evil of sanctions as a means to achieve democracy and → human rights.

Obviously, Security Council resolutions are political decisions and not those of a court of justice. Equal cases are without hesitation decided differently, especially if the interests of permanent members of the Security Council are involved. Thus, sanctions were imposed against Haiti by the Security Council (UN Doc. S/RES/841 (1993), 16 June 1993) and recently in a rather doubtful case against Iran with Resolution 1737 (2006) of 23 December 2006, but not against Nigeria or Burma, and of course not against the Russian Federation in the Chechnya war. One of the results of this unevenness is an unfortunate North-South divide.

The sanctions taken against Libya on the grounds of Security Council Resolution 748 (1992), just to mention another example, were indirectly a case of dispute in international law, because Libya filed in March 1992 at the International Court of Justice (→ ICJ) two separate applications instituting proceedings against the USA and the United Kingdom (ICJ Communiqué No. 92/1, 3 March 1992) with the aim to obtaining a judicial decision on the lawfulness of the sanctions imposed by the Security Council. The ICJ, however, did not decide on the legal actions of Libya, as in 2003 the ICJ closed the files at the request of the concerned parties, Libya, the USA and the United Kingdom (ICJ Reports 2003, p. 152ff., and ICJ Reports 2003, p. 149ff.).

Some member states, without taking any part in the disturbance of peace, are disproportionately affected by sanctions. To find a solution for the special economic problems of these so-called "third states", consultations with the Security Councils are recommended in Article 50 UN Charter. In practical terms, this provision of the Charter has so far proved ineffective; and the claim for "denial damage" of third states (e.g. the states bordering the Danube in the case of the sanctions against the Federal Republic of Yugoslavia) has not met any recognition in the community of states. According to the Coalition Treaty of 1998, the then German Federal Government intended to advocate the creation of sanctions funds and supported this idea within the United Nations, but without success; up to now the UN has not established such funds.

The ethical problem connected with sanctions arises basically from the fact that civilian populations suffer more from economic sanctions than political elites, and can even end up as "political hostages" in the dispute, as in Iraq. If sanctions result, as witnessed there, in catastrophic humanitarian consequences, the ethical questions can reach the dimension of legal relevance. Human rights belong to the core of goals and principles of the United Nations which the Security Council has also to follow in the execution of its mandate according to Article 24 (2) of the Charter. Hence, the peremptory rights of the people affected by sanctions – particularly the right to life, health, food, water, housing, and clothing – must be taken into account. Starvation is not allowed in any case. The line of the tolerable is clearly overstepped if sanctions contribute to bring about a situation where a large part of the population falls below subsistence level.

In such cases it is also not sufficient to guarantee access of humanitarian aid (→ Humanitarian Assistance). What can the people of an internationally proscribed country expect to receive from the limited assistance resources available, especially if the suffering people live far away from the countries of the wealthy North? Even the "oil for food" programme, created because of such considerations, has so far not proven to be an effective success in terms of relieving the misery of the people.

IV. Proposals for Reform

The problems indicated here point to the need to review and to reform the practice of sanctions. Thus an intensive discussion has begun in the Security Council, particularly in its Working Group on General Issues on Sanctions established in 2000, but also in the Commission on Human Rights (→ Human Rights, Commission on), whose Subcommission on the Promotion and Protection of Human Rights commissioned Marc Bossuyt to prepare a working paper on "The Adverse Consequences of Economic Sanctions on the Enjoyment of Human Rights, which he submitted in June 2000 (UN Doc. E/CN.4/Sub.2/2000/33, 21 June 2000). The debate within the organs of the UN is accompanied by a vivid discussion in → NGOs, in scholarly circles and research institutions: so the Bonn International Center for Conversion organized at the request of the German Foreign Office and in cooperation with the UN → Secretariat since 1999 two major conferences and a number of working group meetings – to collect and elaborate suggestions for improvements in arms embargoes and travel sanctions in particular, the debating process is called "Bonn-Berlin Process" (*Brzoska* 2001). Similar conferences were organized in London by the Humanitarian Policy Group and the Relief and Rehabilitation Network (*Brabant* 1999b) and in Interlaken by the Swiss Federal Office for Foreign Economic Affairs together with the United Nations Secretariat (details in *Brabant* 1999a (bibliography) and on the website of the UN Working Group on General Issues on Sanctions www.un.org/sc/com mittees/sanctions/initiatives.htm).

The prevailing tendency in recent years in applying sanctions tends to use the instrument of sanction, as far as possible, as a scalpel instead of a cudgel. In other words, one talks about targeting or "smart" sanctions. As areas of sanctions application, Article 41 UN Charter mentions economic relations, traffic, communications and diplomatic relations. It is generally accepted that these examples are not all-inclusive, and that the Security Council is free in the choice of sanctions.

It is doubtful whether the establishment of international tribunals should be considered as a sanction. One could argue that this would be the easiest way to justify legally such a decision of the Security Council. In any case, this question will become less relevant since the International Criminal Court (→ ICC) has now been established in The Hague after the Statute of Rome had reached its sixtieth ratification in 2002.

So far, the most important fields of sanctions have been

- culture and sports (suspension of exchanges, exclusion from international events);
- diplomacy (reduction or closure of diplomatic missions, exclusion from international organizations, ban on entry of officials);
- transport and communications (ban on air and sea traffic, suspension of rail and road transport and of post and telecommunication links);
- security (arms embargo, termination of military and intelligence co-operation);
- finance (freezing of foreign assets, ban on financial transfers);
- trade (partial or total boycotts and embargoes); and
- criminal justice (international tribunals).

As in medicine, there are means with different degrees of effects and dosages available in this "kit" of sanctions. Therefore, a careful assessment of the desirable and achievable result and of the unavoidable damage is necessary. The principle of proportionality of means should also apply in politics. Comprehensive economic sanctions should only be used as means of last resort in case of urgency. A targeting strategy should always try to hit and influence first and foremost the political elites and decision makers. Clearly, the expenditure involved is also a factor to be considered. The damage caused by arms embargoes may be limited. However, it is difficult and rather expensive to enforce them effectively. In many cases, as experience has shown, they merely contribute to drive arms trade underground and to push arms prices upward.

In total, the reform proposals can be summarized as follows:

- The aims of the sanctions and the conditions for their removal should be unequivocally stated in advance.
- Sanctions should be imposed for a limited period of time in order to require a new resolution for their renewal or prolongation.
- It should be clearly confirmed that the United Nations is bound by human rights and humanitarian international law (→ Humanitarian Law, International) in the implementation of sanctions.
- The choice of sanctions instruments has to be based on a thorough analysis of the impact to be expected. For this assessment and for the continuing observation of the sanction regimes, a precise procedure has to be developed. Decisive criteria should be the proportionality of means, target group orientation, and the chances of political success.
- Arms embargoes should only be imposed if there is a good chance for their implementation. Expressions of disapproval should have preference over economic pressure, partial boycott and limited embargo over comprehensive economic sanctions. A higher measure of creativity is recommended, not the least in view of modern developments in technology and communications.

- Third countries suffering substantial damages from obeying sanctions should receive adequate compensation. For this purpose, a sanctions hardship fund should be established.
- The United Nations should exercise "exclusive power" in the area of peace-related sanctions.
- This should be incorporated into an international convention which should also define aims, principles and procedures of sanctions law.
- The implementation of sanctions should be entrusted to a UN Sanctions Council.

Manfred Kulessa

Lit.: *1. (Commented) Bibliography: Brabant, K. van (ed.):* Sanctions: The Current Debate: A Summary of Selected Readings (Overseas Development Institute) London 1999 (brochure; Internet: www.oneworld. org/odi) (quoted as: Brabant 1999a); *2. Secondary Literature: Bessler, M./Garfield, R./McHugh, G.:* Sanctions Assessment Handbook: Assessing the Humanitarian Implications of Sanctions, United Nations Office for the Coordination of Humanitarian Affairs, New York 2004; *Boudreau, D.:* Creating a United Nations Sanctions Agency, in: International Peacekeeping 4 (1997), 115-137; *Brabant, K. van:* Can Sanctions Be Smarter?: The Current Debate: Report of a Conference Held in London, 16-17 December 1998, London 1999 (quoted as: Brabant 1999b); *Brzoska, M. (ed.):* Smart Sanctions: The Next Steps. The Debate on Arms Embargoes and Travel Sanctions within the 'Bonn-Berlin Process', Baden-Baden 2001; *Cortright, D./Lopez, G.A.:* The Sanctions Decade: Assessing UN Strategies in the 1990s, Boulder 2000; *Cortright, D./Lopez, G.A./Gerber-Stellingwerf, L.:* Sanctions, in: Weiss, T./Daws, D. (eds.): The Oxford Handbook on the United Nations, Oxford 2007, 349-369; *Doxey, M.P.:* United Nations Sanctions: Current Policy Issues, Halifax 1997; *Fisler Damrosch, L.:* Enforcing Restraint – Collective Intervention in International Crimes, New York 1993; *Horn, A.:* Multilaterale ökonomische Sanktionsregime der Vereinten Nationen, Frankfurt (Main) 2003; *Hufbauer, G.C./Schott, J./Elliott, K.A.:* Economic Sanctions Reconsidered: History and Current Policy, Washington 1990; *Kulessa, M.:* Von Märchen und Mechanismen – Gefahren und Chancen der

Sanktionen des Sicherheitsrats, in: VN 44 (1996), 89-96; *Kulessa, M./Starck, D.:* Peace through Sanctions? Recommendations for German UN Policy (SEF-Policy Paper 7), Bonn 1997; *Starck, D.:* Die Rechtmässigkeit von UNO-Wirtschaftssanktionen in Anbetracht ihrer Auswirkungen auf die Zivilbevölkerung, Berlin 2000; *United Nations - Security Council:* Enhancing the Implementation of United Nations Security Council Sanctions. A Symposium, 30 April 2007, United Nations, New York. Annex to the letter dated 12 September 2007 from the Permanent Representative of Greece to the United Nations addressed to the President of the Security Council, UN Doc. S/2007/734, 13 December 2007; *Wallensteen, P./Staibano, C. (eds.):* International Sanctions: Between Words and Wars in the Global System, New York 2005; *Weiss, T.G./Cortright, D./Lopez, G.A./Minear, L.:* Political Gain and Civilian Pain – Humanitarian Impacts of Economic Sanctions, Lanham/Oxford 1997.

Internet: 1. Information on sanctions and sanction committees: www.un.org/sc/committees/; 2. Information on UN documents and press releases, sanction policy studies, bibliographies and additional links: www.globalpolicy.org/security-council/sanctions.html.

Secretariat

I. Introduction

In order to give to the world organization which they were creating, a stable organizational structure, the founding states of the UN in San Francisco devised an international Secretariat which – under the direction of the → Secretary-General – would support the other principal organs in their work with regard to organization (→ Principal Organs, Subsidiary Organs, Treaty Bodies), would record their decisions and monitor their implementation, and would conduct communications with the member states. This concept of a single (unitary) secretariat for all bodies of the UN had prevailed after initial debates about whether distinct secretariats for each of the four principal organs → General Assembly, → Security Council, → Economic and Social Council (ECOSOC) and → Trusteeship Council

would be better. But since the founding states concentrated more on the competences of the Secretary-General and on the procedure of his appointment, the provisions of the → Charter of the UN in Chapter XV, regulating the composition of the Secretariat (Articles 97-101), remained imprecise. This made it easy for the member states to interfere time and again in the personnel policy (→ Personnel) and the daily work of the Secretariat, but also to express vehement, often unjustified criticism about alleged confusion of competences, bureaucratic proliferation and wastefulness.

When discussing the structures, the working methods and the achievements of the Secretariat one has to take into account first the regulations of the Charter, and second the organizational demands made by the → UN system on the Secretariat as its organizational service center. In addition, there are the political functions of Secretariat as being responsible for the (legal) representation of the UN, and for presenting the UN image to the outside, which includes the implementation of the decisions of the Security Council, the General Assembly and ECOSOC.

II. Secretariat and Secretary-General

The fact that the Secretariat is enumerated as a principal organ in Article 7 of the Charter makes it evident that the founding states wanted to upgrade the Secretariat in comparison to the Secretariat of the → League of Nations, as the Secretariat was to assume important political functions, beside the administrative-organizational tasks. Nevertheless, the functions of the Secretariat cannot be considered as separate from those tasks and competences which the Charter explicitly ascribes to the Secretary-General in Article 98 and 99, especially as the Charter does not ascribe any explicit specific functions to the Secretariat. The Charter merely states in Article 97: "The Secretariat shall comprise a Secretary-General and such staff as the Organization may require. The Secretary-General shall be appointed by the General Assembly upon the recommendation of the Security Council. He shall be the chief administrative officer of the Organization." This means that the tasks of the Secretariat result from the tasks and competences of the Secretary-General mentioned explicitly in the Charter in relation to the Security Council, the General Assembly, the ECOSOC, and the Trusteeship Council, as well as from those other functions entrusted to him additionally by those four principal organs. The Secretariat plays the role of the "instrument", with the help of which the Secretary-General fulfills his tasks; though he has also tasks which go beyond the bounds of the Secretariat, e.g. as the chief administrative officer of the United Nations, thus he is more than merely the administrative head of the Secretariat.

III. Tasks

The Secretariat supports the work of the other principal organs as well as the work of subsidiary organs of the General Assembly, such as → UNCTAD, → UNDP, → UNEP and → WFC. Other subsidiary organs such as → UNICEF. → UNRWA, → UNITAR and → UNFPA had been given at their establishment direct responsibility in administrative and personal matters.

From the general task to support the work of the UN organs results a large number of tasks which can be roughly divided into the following areas: organization, collecting and processing of information, editing of texts, preparation of decisions, implementation of decisions, communication, consultation and public relations work.

The Secretariat prepares the sessions of the UN bodies in terms of organization. It collects social and economic data and information about political conflicts and violations of human rights, and edits them in a large number of reports and studies upon which the decisions of the UN bodies are to be based. The Secretariat staff prepares draft texts, such as draft resolutions for the Security Council or the General Assembly, in close co-operation with the respective bodies. The staff also assists in preparing the

decisions during the private meetings of the numerous informal groups taking place before the sessions proper (→ Groups and Groupings in the UN).

When decisions have been made in the UN bodies, the Secretariat organizes their implementation. For example, with regard to peacekeeping missions (→ Peacekeeping, → Peacekeeping Forces, → Peacekeeping Operations), the staff of the Department of Peacekeeping Operations conducts negotiations with those states which have stated their readiness to supply contingents for peacekeeping troops, negotiations concerning specific troop levels, equipment scales, transport routes – a gigantic task, especially considering that more than 15 states may contribute contingents to a single peacekeeping mission.

The Secretariat documents the work of the United Nations in registering the texts in all the different stages, placing them in the archives and in editing the minutes of all meetings (for further information: see UN Documentation: Research Guide, www.un.org/Depts/dhl/resguide/index.html). Furthermore, its departments edit summarizing surveys on the work in their respective field of work, such as disarmament or human rights.

The Secretariat receives all communications from individual persons, non-governmental organizations (→ NGOs) or governments of the member states, forwards them to the competent UN organs and informs the state governments about the decisions of the UN organs.

It gives advice to politicians and experts from the member states concerning economic and social problems, provided this does not belong to the competence of special UN organs. It informs the public via the mass media about the activities of the UN (→ Public Information of the UN) and – since the middle of the nineties – it uses to an increasing extent the Internet to inform the public directly (→ Internet, Websites of the UN System in the). It conducts surveys about the reports and comments on the work of the UN published in the mass media (→ Public Opinion and the UN).

IV. Structure

As provided in the Charter, the Secretariat is structured in a predominantly hierarchical manner: all officials derive their competences directly or indirectly from the Secretary-General, the departments and offices being headed by Under-Secretaries-General or Assistant Secretaries-General who are appointed by the Secretary-General. The departments and offices are further subdivided into smaller units. The concrete structure of the Secretariat depends to a large degree on the range and quality of problems with which the United Nations may be faced at any given moment. The Secretary-General can thus react to the emergence or diminishing of task areas by adding small units, offices or even departments, or by closing them. This has often been the case throughout the → history of the UN. In each successive decade the Secretaries-General have implemented far-reaching structural changes in the Secretariat.

But the competence of the Secretary-General in terms of personnel policy, which should enable him to implement those structural changes, is in practice restricted in its effect by several factors. In his personnel policy the Secretary-General has to abide by regulations established by the General Assembly (Art. 100 (1) UN Charter). These regulations deal with the ratio of women among the UN officials (→ Women and the UN), the age structure, the distribution with regard to the official languages (→ Languages, Official) and the balanced geographic distribution. The latter principle has repeatedly resulted in conflicts. According to Article 101 (3) of the Charter, the Secretary-General has to pay due regard "to the importance of recruiting the staff on as wide a geographical basis as possible". The General Assembly has tried to define this principle for practical purposes by establishing "desirable ranges", i.e. national minimum and maximum quotas for the number of UN officials from one state on the basis of the state's assessed contribution to the UN budget (→

Budget), a system which was amended several times in favor of the member states from the Third World with rather small contributions to the budget.

On the one hand, such a broad, truly international composition of the Secretariat is desirable, but on the other, this quantification of demands leads to problems concerning the professional qualification of many UN officials. A member state will hardly be ready to refrain from "its" share of the posts in the Secretariat, even if it may have no qualified applicants for the positions at that moment.

In the case of the more powerful states the influence on the personnel policy reaches far beyond the quantitative dimension. Since the foundation of the UN in 1945 the five permanent members of the Security Council (P5) have succeeded in securing the highest-ranking posts under the Secretary-General, as a rule the position of the head of a department, by exerting massive pressure on the Secretary-General. In the meantime this "principle" has taken on nearly the quality of customary law. This massive interference of the P5 clearly violates the duty of all member states – laid down in Article 100 UN Charter – "to respect the exclusively international character of the responsibilities of the Secretary-General and the staff and not to seek to influence them in the discharge of their responsibilities." Notwithstanding, the P5 have for decades sought constantly to "influence" the Secretary-General in his personnel policy.

As well, via the distribution of the financial resources at the planning of the budget, the member states can exert an indirect influence on the personnel policy of the Secretary-General, as they can enforce staff reductions. This all the more, since the USA has put through a change in the established budgeting procedure, through its frequent delaying in the payment of its assessed contributions to the UN regular budget (→ Financial Crises). This has resulted in a *de facto* revision of the respective provisions of the UN Charter by General Assembly Resolution A/RES/41/213 of 12 December 1986, which makes it virtually impossible that the main payers can be outvoted on the budget. The USA has beyond doubt forced – through its continuing refusal to pay its contributions – Secretary-Generals Boutros-Ghali and Annan to a policy of massive job cuts, a policy which has inflicted damage on the UN by a massive loss of expert knowledge, since the UN has no facilities preserving its institutional experience, no "institutional memory".

V. Structural Reforms under Boutros-Ghali and Annan

Nevertheless Boutros-Ghali and Annan, as experienced experts on UN administrative matters, have tried to make a virtue of necessity: With more consistency and courage and in spite of the resistance of influential member states, they have reduced the number of highly paid "chieftains", i.e. of the Under-Secretaries-General and of the Assistant Secretaries-General, and have reduced the large number of departments and offices by mergers.

V.1. Annan's Reform Concept 1997

In addition to this, Annan has been the first Secretary-General to undertake a profound reform of the leadership structure of the Secretariat, laid down in his conceptual reform programme of 1997: "Renewing the United Nations: A Programme for Reform" (UN Doc. A/51/950 of 14 July 1997). Annan replaced the strictly hierarchical structure which had caused high losses in efficiency through the strict principle of personal responsibility of all heads of department towards the Secretary-General, who was not able to coordinate more than 10 departments efficiently, with a completely new structure. He clustered the departments of the Secretariat into four Executive Committees which are responsible for the different fields of work of the Secretariat: (1) Peace and Security, (2) Economic and Social Affairs, (3) Humanitarian Affairs, (4) Development. Human Rights, as the fifth main task shall be dealt with in all four commit-

tees as a cross-cutting issue. The four Executive Committees hold at least one meeting per month to co-ordinate their work. These comprise the respective departments of the Secretariat as well as the heads of the subsidiary organs of the UN working in the same field. Thus the Executive Committee for Peace and Security comprises the Department for Political Affairs (DPA), the Department for Peacekeeping Operations (DPKO), the Office for the Coordination of Humanitarian Affairs (OCHA), the UN Development Programme (UNDP), the Office of Legal Affairs (OLA), the Office of the UN Security Coordinator as well as representatives of the Executive Office of the Secretary-General.

Furthermore, in September 1997, Secretary General Annan introduced in the management of the Secretariat a "cabinet style": a *Senior Management Group* or "Cabinet" made up of all Under-Secretaries-General meeting weekly under the chairmanship of the Secretary General, and making video conferences with the heads of the UN subsidiary organs, to coordinate the work and to determine the focus of their activities.

Since spring 1998 the UN Secretary-General is supported by a *Deputy Secretary-General*. This post was established by the General Assembly with resolution 52/12B of 19 December 1997 as part of the reform package proposed by Annan (→ Reform of the UN). The Deputy Secretary-General is to assist the Secretary-General in coordinating the UN system and in the implementation of the reform proposals. A further focus of his work is the → development cooperation of the UN.

With this package of reform measures Secretary-General Annan had initiated the most ambitious structural reform project within the UN so far and – to the astonishment of many UN experts knowledgeable about the systemic resistance within the UN against reforms – with remarkable success. Even the rather critical US General Accounting Office (GAO) stated in a report of the year 2000 with regard to the UN reforms: "The United Nations has substantially implemented initiatives to build more cohesive leadership structure and has partly integrated the activities of U.N. agencies in the field." (*GAO* 2000, 8)

V.2. Reform of the UN Peacekeeping

Shortly after Annan had started his first reform initiative in 1997 and almost at the same time when he prepared with the Secretariat staff the Millennium Summit 2000 he began another reform in an area he was particularly familiar with as former Head of Department: UN peacekeeping. He convened in March 2000 a high-level panel under the chairmanship of Lakhdar Brahimi with the mandate to develop concrete and practical recommendations for the reform of UN peacekeeping. The panel presented in record speed in August 2000 a concise and pragmatic report (UN Doc. A/55/305-S/ 2000/809 of 21 August 2000) with a number of recommendations concerning among others the increase in staff of the Department of Peacekeeping Operations, the financing of UN peacekeeping, the formulation of mandates, and the improvement of logistics. Annan succeeded in getting many of the recommendations implemented rather quickly if measured in UN terms – most probably because the panel was chaired by an expert with a high UN reputation and because the recommendations did not contain ideologically sensitive issues and did not touch superpower interests, but involved simply practical measures.

V.3. Annan's Reform Package 2002

To supplement his first reform package of 1997 Kofi Annan submitted in 2002 a second package to the General Assembly in his report "Strengthening the United Nations: an agenda for further change" (UN Doc. A/57/387 of 9 September 2002) with some reform initiatives expanding on those introduced in 1997 and others reflecting new priorities. The reform programme included a reorganization of the budget and planning system to make it less complex and more transparent for the evaluation of results; a thorough review of the UN

programme of work in order to identify mandates and activities no longer relevant; improving UN human rights protection activities, in particular at the country level and by reforming the reporting procedures of the human rights treaty bodies (→ Human Rights Conventions and their Measures of Implementation) and by strengthening the Office of the High Commissioner for Human Rights; establishing a high-level panel to examine the relationship between the United Nations and civil society (→ NGOs) and enhancing UN → public information, in particular the UN information services.

Evidently Annan was able to stir up a reform mood also in the General Assembly. It endorsed the whole reform package with some slight, rather symbolic admonitions: "*The General Assembly ... Requests* the Secretary, while implementing the provisions of the present resolution, to continue to take into account the views and comments expressed by Member States and to respect fully the Charter of the United Nations and the relevant decisions and resolutions of the General Assembly ..." (UN Doc. A/ RES/57/300 of 20 December 2002).

Again Annan succeeded in implementing to a surprising extent his reform initiative. In another report of the year 2004, the US General Accounting Office stated that Annan had implemented his 1997 reforms already to 60 % and his 2002 reform concepts already to 38 % (*GAO* 2004, 2). He succeeded in fact in reorganizing and strengthening the UN human rights protection, to start a review process for outdated General Assembly mandates and to reform to some extent the planning and budgeting process.

Not so successful was Annan in the long run with regard to the reform of the UN public information activities: besides some progress, in particular related to the improved Internet websites of the UN and the large-scale access to UN documents and bibliographic information via Internet, there were some setbacks: the premature regionalization of UN information centres in Western Europe as a model for further regionalization measures proved to be a total flop, the quality of UNDPI publications did not essentially improve, and the Department remained rather over-staffed and bureaucratic (cf. *Crossette* 2003).

Also the attempt to start a reform of UN-NGO relations through a high-level panel (named "Cardoso Panel" after its chairman) proved to be not really successful: The panel presented in June 2004 a rather cautious and uninspired reform report (UN Doc. A/58/817 of 11 June 2004) moving not far beyond the *status quo*. Annan reacted with his own reform report (UN Doc. A/59/354 of 13 September 2004), urging the General Assembly to grant formal access to NGOs, to expand the Secretariat unit dealing with NGOs and to subsidize the work of NGOs from developing countries, but the Assembly turned down all recommendations. Thus the conditions in the Secretariat for servicing NGOs were not improved.

V.4. Annan's Reform Package 2006

The next reform initiative which Annan started in 2006 took place in difficult conditions. Annoyed by Annan's outspoken criticism of the US Iraq policy, in particular of the US military intervention in Iraq in spring 2003, the US administration, the US congress and the media began an increasing polemical attack against Annan and the work of the Secretariat, having its peak in allegations of fraud and embezzlement in connection with the Oil-for-Food Programme, a programme to provide Iraq with food and medical drugs and the like in spite of the UN sanctions against it in exchange for oil on the grounds of Security Council resolutions and under the control of a Council sanctions committee, but in practice organized by Secretariat staff.

An independent inquiry commission, appointed by Kofi Annan, explicitly endorsed by Security Council resolution S/RES/1548 (2004) and chaired by Paul Volcker, former Chairman of the United States Federal Reserve, indeed found in its concluding report issued in autumn 2005 (cf. *Independent Inquiry Committee* 2005, Vol. I) legally incorrect behavior by some Secretariat officials, but no personal responsibility of the Secretary-General for these criminal acts. On the other hand, the report stated a "dilution of individual and institutional responsibility" of the Security Council (ibid., 60) and a lack of effective controls in the Secretariat which was in the opinion of the Committee "ill-equipped in terms of experience and capacity" (ibid., 61). The Committee consequently recommended in its report to create the position of a Chief Operating Officer with authority over all aspects of administration, to be appointed by the General Assembly on recommendation of the Security Council and directly subordinate to the Secretary-General. Moreover an independent oversight board should be established, the management performance review improved and the financial disclosure requirements within the UN expanded (ibid., 63-65).

The UN World Summit of the heads of state and government of the member states in September 2005 agreed to the proposals made in the report of the Independent Inquiry Commission as well as in the pre-summit reform report of Kofi Annan "In larger freedom" (UN Doc. A/59/2005 of 21 March 2005) in order to improve the working of the Secretariat: (1) establishment of an Ethics Office and development of a system-wide code of ethics for UN personnel; (2) greater whistle-blower protection (for people informing UN authorities about illegal acts within the UN system); (3) strengthening oversight capacity; and (4) full financial disclosure by UN staff (cf. concluding resolution of the summit: "2005 World Summit Outcome", 16 September 2005, UN Doc. A/RES/60/1, para. 161).

In the subsequent months of 2005 and 2006 the summit decisions were implemented and have improved the situation with regard to oversight, financial transparency and ethical standards considerably (cf. report of the *US Government Accountability Office* 2008, 2).

All in all Annan achieved – despite some setbacks an the end of his second term of office – a far-reaching restructuring and re-focusing of the UN Secretariat, as far as such reforms are achievable in such a complex multi-cultural bureaucracy with a multitude of tasks and scarce resources.

VI. No Further Reforms? The Secretariat under Ban Ki-moon

When Secretary-General Ban Ki-moon entered office in January 2007 he made clear in his public statements that did he did not intend to develop further reform initiatives, but wanted to consolidate the existing structures. Consequently he introduced only two changes within the Secretariat: he divided the large Department of Peacekeeping Operations into two departments by establishing the new Department of Field Support, with responsibility for the support and logistic service to all UN field operations. Originally Ban Ki-moon had wanted to create two independent departments in this area, but the majority of the member states in the General Assembly forced him to change his plans in so far that the head of the new Department of Field Support was made to report to the head of DPKO who retains the overall authority for UN peacekeeping.

The second reform matter was the downgrading of the Department of Disarmament Affairs to an Office for Disarmament Affairs. Here again the General Assembly forced him to keep the rank of the head of the office on the level of an Under-Secretary-General. Critical observers of the downgrading assumed that the Secretary-General followed in this case a tacit agreement with the USA which does not like a strong UN institution for disarmament.

VII. The Present Structure of the Secretariat

At present the Secretariat has the following structure: the top organizational level is formed by the Secretary-General and his small Executive Office of the Secretary-General (EOSG). The second level is formed by ten departments and offices respectively, being headed by Under Secretary General:
- Department of Political Affairs (DPA)
- Office of Disarmament Affairs (ODA)
- Department of Peacekeeping Operations (DPKO)
- Department of Field Support (DFS)
- Department for the Coordination of Humanitarian Affairs (OCHA)
- Department of Economic and Social Affairs (DESA)
- Department for General Assembly Affairs and Conference Management (DGACM)
- Department of Management (DM)
- Department of Public Information (DPI)
- Office of Legal Affairs (OLA)
- Office of Internal Oversight Services (OIOS)

The latter office was established in 1994 under particular pressure from the USA. Unlike the heads of the other departments its head is appointed by the General Assembly, to which that USG is responsible. Equipped with special competences, the USG is supposed to examine the activities of all UN bodies with regard to efficiency, to uncover waste of money and corruption and to make recommendations for improvement. (→ Control Mechanisms of the UN, Internal and External) In the years since its establishment OIOS has resulted in uncovering many cases of mismanagement, the resolution of which has led to considerable reductions of costs.

Beside the said departments and offices the SG has also under his direction:
- the UN Office at Geneva (UNOG) (→ UN Office Geneva)
- the UN Office at Vienna (UNOV) (→ UN Office Vienna)
- the UN Office at Nairobi (UNON) (→ UN Office Nairobi)
- the five regional economic commissions of the UN (→ Economic Commissions, Regional).

A number of subsidiary organs are linked via their own secretariats in organizational terms with the Secretariat, but have a large degree of autonomy: → UNHCR, → OHCHR, → UNCTAD, → UNEP, → UN-Habitat, → UNRWA, and the Office for Drug control and Crime prevention (ODCCP). The following subsidiary organs do not report over the SG to the principal organs, but directly: UNHCR to ECOSOC, UNRWA to General Assembly.

V. Summing Up

If one tries to draw a conclusion, after this survey on the tasks and structures, about the reform measures, and about the weaknesses and strengths of the Secretariat, the strengths of the Secretariat outweigh the weaknesses by far. The Secretariat has admittedly shown time and again a strong tendency to develop into an organizational "jungle", to put a large number of less qualified people in important positions and to incur high costs. But these cases of mismanagement have been and are still rendered transparent by public criticisms, and to an increasing extent by the internal inspection of OIOS. Abuses are generally promptly dealt with, and are to some degree prevented by reform measures.

It is quite evident that in such a complex international secretariat, with 192 members of the General Assembly functioning as a "supervisory board", and the Secretary-General as the "Chief Executive Officer", cases of mismanagement are to some extent unavoidable.

The strengths of the Secretariat, which it has amply demonstrated in its history, lie in its ability to adapt rather quickly to changing tasks by means of improvisation, to establish an effective international cooperation beyond the borders of languages of cultures and to develop a sustainable sense of responsibility.

In many conflict situations the Secretariat has rendered extraordinary services. For example, at the establishment of the first UN peacekeeping force UNEF I, an organizational concept was developed and carried into effect in just a few hours; truly a masterpiece.

The reform measures of Boutros-Ghali and Annan – if one can evaluate them at such an early stage – seem to be not only adequate measures for the reduction of cost and the increase of efficiency, but Annan's cabinet style of management – if kept by his successors – might prove helpful to uncover coordination problems and lack of clarity concerning the respective tasks, and to search effectively for appropriate solutions.

Further job cuts or reduction of funds would damage the Secretariat considerably in its efficiency – this is at least the perception of the Secretariat staff, and which seems largely born out by available statistical data. The world community cannot afford to damage the functioning of the Secretariat: it renders important services for the world organization and thus in the end for the people in the member states.

Helmut Volger

Lit.: *I. UN documents: United Nations – Secretariat:* Organization of the Secretariat of the United Nations (Secretary-General's Bulletin), UN Doc. ST/SGB/1997/5, 12 September 1997; *United Nations - Secretariat:* Status, basic rights and duties of United Nations staff members (Secretary-General's Bulletin), UN Doc. ST/SGB/2002/13, 1 November 2002; *United Nations - Secretariat:* Protection against retaliation for reporting misconduct and for cooperating with duly authorized audits or investigations (Secretary-General's Bulletin), UN Doc. ST/SGB/2005/21, 19 December 2005; *United Nations - Secretariat:* Ethic's Office – establishment and terms of reference (Secretary-General's Bulletin), UN Doc. ST/SGB/2005/22, 30 December 2005; *United Nations – Secretariat:* Financial disclosure and declaration of interest statements (Secretary-General's Bulletin), UN Doc. ST/SGB/2006/6, 10 April 2006;

II. Reports from other sources: Independent Inquiry Committee into the United Nations Oil-for-Food Programme: The Management of the United Nations Oil-for-Food Programme; Vol. I: The Report of the Committee, September 7, 2005, www.iic-offp.org; *US General Accounting Office:* United Nations: Reform Initiatives Have Strengthened Operations, but Overall Objectives Have Not Been Met, 10 May 2000 (quoted as: GAO 2000); *US General Accounting Office:* United Nations: Reforms Progressing, but Comprehensive Assessment Needed to Measure

Impact, February 2004, GAO-04-339 (quoted as: GAO 2004); *US Government Accountability Office:* United Nations: Progress on Management Reform Has Varied, November 2007, GAO-08-84; *US Government Accountability Office:* United Nations: Management Reforms and Operational Issues, 24 January 2008, GAO-08-246T (quoted as: GAO 2008);

III. Secondary Literature: Bailey, S.D.: The Secretariat of the United Nations. United Nations Study No. 11, edited by the Carnegie Endowment 1962 (w/o place of publication); *Crossette, B.:* Ahead Of Information Summit, U.N. Should Examine Itself, in: U.N. Wire, 28 July 2003 (www.unwire.org); *Dicke, K.:* Reformen des Sekretariats und die veränderte Rolle des Generalsekretärs, in: Hüfner, K. (ed.): Die Reform der Vereinten Nationen. Die Weltorganisation zwischen Krise und Erneuerung, Opladen 1994, 225-239; *Fiedler, W.:* Commentary to Art. 97, in: Simma, B. (ed.): The Charter of the United Nations. A Commentary, 2nd edn., Vol. II, Oxford 2002, 1191-1205; *Jonah. J.:* Secretariat: Independence and Reform, in: Weiss, T.G./Daws, S. (eds.): The Oxford Handbook on the United Nations, Oxford et al. 2007, 160-174; *Lindemann, B./Hesse-Kreindler, D.:* Secretariat, in: Wolfrum, R. (ed.): United Nations: Law, Policies and Practice, Vol. 2, Munich/Dordrecht 1995, 1129-1135; *Meron, T.:* The UN Secretariat: The Rules and the Practice, Lexington 1977; *Meron, T.:* Charter Powers of the UN Secretary-General with regard to the Secretariat and the Role of General Assembly Resolutions, in: ZaöRV 42 (1982), 731-779; *Pitt, D./Weiss, T.:* The Nature of United Nations Bureaucracies, London 1986; *Winchmore, C.:* The Secretariat: Retrospect and Prospect, in: IO 19 (1965), 622-639.

Internet: *1. Documents of the Secretariat:* www.un.org/documents/secretariat.htm; *2. Information about Secretariat activities:* www.un.org/News/ossg/sg/index.html

Secretary-General

I. Introduction

The most prominent figure, almost the symbolic expression of the world organization as a whole, is the Secretary-General of the United Nations. He represents the UN in the world's public opinion, the UN is identified with him, as he travels restlessly as mediator to the world's conflict zones, exhorting and admonishing the member states not to forget the poor in the world, the hungry, the refugees and the victims of the massive violations of → human rights all over the world.

And all this in spite of the rather powerless and administrative position which the UN → Charter of the UN provides for the Secretary-General, compared with the competences of the → General Assembly and the → Security Council. But all the holders of this office since the foundation of the UN have managed skillfully and convincingly to widen, step by step, the competences of this office in daily practice, interpreting the Charter in crisis situations to legitimize this additional competence of the Secretary-General, since the other institutions (General Assembly, Security Council) were not able to act according to the Charter goals for the protection of international peace and security. This expansion of competences was either tacitly or expressively tolerated by the General Assembly and the Security Council, sometimes accompanied by an initial massive resistance from among the permanent members of the latter.

These introductory remarks may illustrate why a text dealing with the Secretary-General has to consider two aspects of this office simultaneously: the Charter provisions as well as the political practice of the incumbents, who worked hard to attain new rights and competences for this office, reaching beyond the provisions of the Charter to rights and competences which are nowadays considered to be in accordance with the Charter, on the grounds of customary international law.

The incumbents of this office have interpreted its functions and competences quite differently, and have changed the role of the Secretary-General in the UN system considerably within the limits drawn by other principal organs of the UN. The former holders of the office of the Secretary-General since the foundation of the UN were: Trygve Lie (Norway) from 1 February 1946 to 10 April 1953; Dag Hammarskjöld (Sweden) from 10 April 1953 to 18 September 1961; Sithu U Thant (Burma) from 3 November 1961 to 31 December 1971; Kurt Waldheim (Austria) from 1 January 1972 to 31 December 1981; Javier Pérez de Cuéllar (Peru) from 1 January 1982 to 31 December 1991; Boutros Boutros-Ghali (Egypt) from 1 January 1992 to 31 December 1996; Kofi Annan (Ghana) from 1 January 1997 to 31 December 2006. The present incumbent (since 1 January 2007) is Ban Ki-moon (Republic of Korea).

II. Secretary-General and Secretariat

Most surprisingly the UN Charter does not count the Secretary-General, but the → Secretariat as among the principal organs in the enumeration in Article 7. But the Charter provisions for the Secretariat in Chapter XV (Arts. 97-101) point to the fact that the two – Secretariat and Secretary-General – shall cooperate as a functional unit on the one hand, but that the range of functions is different in spite of overlapping areas: The Secretariat is the organizational center of the → UN System which is to prepare the work of the other principal organs, to manage the implementation of their decisions, and to keep in permanent touch with the member states. The Secretariat consists of the Secretary-General and the staff which works under his authority and for whom he is responsible (Art. 97).

In addition to this the Secretary-General is the "chief administrative officer" of the United Nations as a whole (Art. 97). Furthermore Articles 98 and 99 entrust the Secretary-General with important tasks and functions in the fields of → preventive diplomacy and → peacekeeping. Thus the Secretary-General and Secretariat are not identical institutions.

III. Position of the Secretary-General

The Secretary-General is appointed by the General Assembly upon the recommendation of the Security Council (Art. 97). In the Security Council a qualified two-thirds majority is required and thus a veto (→ Veto, Right of Veto) of one

the permanent members can block the appointment of a Secretary-General candidate by the General Assembly, since the General Assembly cannot appoint a candidate without the recommendation of the Security Council. The Charter does not contain any provisions concerning the term of office and the possibility of reappointment. Thus the first General Assembly had to make a decision on this matter. Pursuant to the conditions of appointment fixed by UN Doc. A/RES/11(I) of 24 January 1946 on the election of the first Secretary-General, the term of office is for five years, with a possibility of reappointment for another full term. Only once has the UN deviated from this rule: when the Security Council could not find a consensus for a recommendation to the General Assembly at the end of Trygve Lie's first term of office, the General Assembly extended on 1 November 1950 the term of office by three more years without recommendation of the Security Council (UN Doc. A/RES /492(V) of 1 November 1950; voting record: 48 yes, 5 no, 8 abstentions). This bypassing of the UN Charter proved to be a Pyrrhic victory in the end, as the East European states, which had tried to prevent Lie's reappointment by means of the veto of the USSR in the Security Council, refused any form of cooperation in the ensuing months, so that Lie had finally to give in and, in a formal statement before the General Assembly, resigned his office on 10 November 1952 (UN Doc. A/2253 of 10 November 1962, cf. UNYB 1952, 90-91).

As the example clearly illustrates, the mode of the Secretary-General's appointment secures the permanent members of the Security Council a far-reaching influence on the election. But this makes sense as both – Security Council and Secretary-General – have to cooperate closely in protecting international peace and in fulfilling the other tasks of the UN: a policy of the UN in direct conflict with the superpowers would not have any chance of success.

In the legal terms of the Charter provisions the Secretary-General is independent from any influence from the member states in his administration of office: according to Article 100 (1) he is not allowed "to receive or seek instructions from any government or from any other authority external to the Organization." According to Article 100 (2) the member states undertake "not to seek to influence" the Secretary-General and the staff "in the discharge of their responsibilities."

Unfortunately the governments of the member states often ignored and still ignore this legal obligation and this is to the detriment of the Secretary-General's reputation and standing. They have exerted and they still exert considerable influence on the personnel policy of the Secretary-General, and they try to install their candidates in key positions in the Secretariat. Already the first Secretary-General, Trygve Lie, had to accept a "Gentlemen's Agreement" with the five permanent members (P5) of the Security Council: they claimed for their respective countries one of the most high-ranking positions under the Secretary-General, i.e. of the heads of the departments of the Secretariat, and this tradition has been maintained to this day.

Not only the P5, but also many other influential states demand "traditional positions". This struggle for power and influence of the member states makes the work of the Secretary-General extremely difficult as he is often prevented from filling vacancies with the best qualified → personnel.

The Secretary-General is well advised, on the other hand, to search for a continuous and close coordination with the governments of the member states by means of their UN ambassadors at the → permanent missions of the states in New York, as he has necessarily to rely on the support of many states in all the different UN bodies and institutions, in the early phases of debating and planning, if he wants to get majorities for his initiatives, and even more so when it comes to the implementation of decisions. The better the Secretary-General cultivates these essential contacts, the more he can get accepted in

the bodies of the United Nations. A typical instrument for this canvassing and log-rolling of the Secretary-General for his initiatives are the so-called "friends of the Secretary-General", i.e. informal groups of UN ambassadors from the different regional groups of the UN, constituting themselves as a support group for the Secretary-General for a certain project (→ Groups and Groupings in the UN).

IV. Administrative Tasks

The Secretary-General is the "chief administrative officer" of the UN (Art. 97 UN Charter). In this capacity he appoints the staff of the Organization, i.e. all UN officials. In fulfilling this duty he has to be concerned for the efficiency of the Secretariat as well as for the professional competence of the staff, their personal integrity and an adequate geographical distribution (Art. 101 (3)) – often an extremely difficult balancing act.

The Secretary-General is required to submit an annual report to the General Assembly on the work of the Organization, and he takes part in all meetings of the General Assembly, of the Security Council, of ECOSOC and of the → Trusteeship Council (Art. 98). He has the right to intervene in the deliberations in the organs according to the → rules of procedure of the organs, which also entrust him with the important function of preparing the provisional agendas of the General Assembly, Security Council, ECOSOC and Trusteeship Council. He has the right to request the inclusion of supplementary items which he considers to be of importance in the agenda of the General Assembly. The final decision about the agendas lies with the organs themselves.

The Secretary-General convenes Special Sessions of the General Assembly at the request of the Security Council or of a majority of the members of the UN (Art. 20 UN Charter).

He prepares the budget plan for the Organization and is responsible for the implementation of the → budget. He coordinates the collection of information data in the Secretariat concerning the different fields of activity of the UN, and organizes the submission of studies and reports to the different UN organs.

Particularly the annual report to the General Assembly provides him with the significant opportunity to give a summarized overview of the work of the Organization in its different areas of responsibility, but also to criticize the flow of work within the Organization as well as the attitude of the member states, to make suggestions for improving the efficiency of the Organization and to point to new challenges in politics and social life which the UN will have to face in the future. The annual report is thus the clearest expression of the political responsibility of the Secretary-General, of the eminent political tasks he has to fulfill beside his administrative tasks.

IV.1. Coordinator of the UN System

The Secretary-General also plays a key role in coordinating the work of the entire UN system, in particular in the coordination between the UN and the → specialized agencies, which latter tend to emphasize their autonomy (→ Coordination in the UN System). The Secretary-General is also the chairman of the board charged with the coordination among the UN organs, the United Nations System Chief Executives Board for Coordination (CEB), replacing since 2002 its predecessor as coordination body, the Administrative Committee on Coordination (ACC), but the UN Secretary-General acts here only as "primus inter pares" in the group of the heads of the specialized agencies and programmes. In the face of the strong "quasi-autonomous" position of the specialized agencies, on the grounds of their own legal treaty basis, the Secretary-General can only convince and persuade, but cannot coordinate effectively.

IV.2. Architect of Reforms

The efforts of the Secretary-General to increase the efficiency of the UN and to lower its expenses are also part of his responsibility as chief administrative officer.

This zest for reform of the Secretary-General (→ Reform of the UN) has been intensified since the late seventies by the polemical criticism from the USA, as well as by parts of the mass media all over the world, but even more by the repeated → financial crises of the UN, which have been caused by a long-lasting withholding of assessed budgetary contributions by the USA (→ UN Policy, USA) and the arrears of many other member states. That is why the Secretaries-General since Pérez de Cuéllar's term of office have intensified the attempts to reform the UN. They have submitted reports on this topic, have encouraged independent commissions to work out reform studies (→ Independent Commissions, Reports of) and have presented their own reform concepts.

In particular Boutros-Ghali and Annan have presented detailed reform concepts, and have begun to implement structural reform measures in the Secretariat: they reorganized the department structure in reducing their number, decreased the number of jobs, etc. While Boutros-Ghali set first examples of restructuring and of reducing bureaucratic "undergrowth", Annan made use of his two terms of office to develop and implement far-reaching reform measures within the Secretariat: he grouped the Secretariat units into thematic executive committees, established regular meetings of these committees, comprising also the respective heads of UN programmes and funds, and introduced "cabinet"-like weekly meetings of his Executive Office and the heads of the Secretariat Departments. He modernized the budget planning and the procurement procedures as well as the mission planning and logistics in UN peacekeeping and introduced a staff performance review and an efficient human resources management. Even if some of his reform concepts were cut back or prevented by fears of the member states of losing influence in the Secretariat and/or the resistance of the staff members feeling put under pressure to produce substantial results in their work after decades of "work-to-rule", Annan succeeded in increasing the capacity of the Secretariat for learning, communication, and performance evaluation. This difficult task succeeded since Annan with his charismatic attitude evoked for quite some time a sense of pride and identification with the UN in the staff.

With regard to the reform of the other UN organs and UN bodies, there has been so far an evident lack of political will to implement the reform proposals which Boutros-Ghali and Annan had carefully developed in reform "agendas" (Boutros-Ghali) and in comprehensive reform reports (Annan), based on the work of high-level panels. In particular the most carefully prepared UN World Summit 2005 showed that convincing concepts of reform based on the idea of the common responsibility for global peace and security and human well-being do not suffice if the member states see more their national interests and only to a lesser degree the common interest. Neither the Security Council nor the Economic and Social Council (ECOSOC) were actually reformed at the reform summit, but as a small-scale reform the General Assembly agreed on the establishment of a new organ, the Peacebuilding Commission as a common advisory organ of the Security Council and General Assembly in peacebuilding matters and on replacing the Commission on Human Rights, subsidiary organ of ECOSOC, by a new human rights organ, the → Human Rights Council as a subsidiary organ of the General Assembly.

Annan's example illustrates that the UN Secretary-General can only devise reform concepts with the help of experts and high-level panels and provide the political foundation for reforms by negotiations with key UN ambassadors, but the concrete implementation of his concepts depends on the political climate within the United Nations, on the interests and fears of the smaller member states as well as on the interests of the "big payers", in particular the USA. It all depends on the question whether they all are interested in reform and in what kind of reform.

IV.3. The Role of the Secretary-General in International Law

In terms of international law the Secretary-General represents the Organization as a whole: the diplomatic representatives of the member states are accredited to him, he checks the accreditations of the representatives of states and organizations taking parts in meetings of UN organs or in UN conferences (with the exception of the General Assembly and → ECOSOC where their own credentials committees check the accreditations). The Secretary-General represents the UN in the negotiation and signing of agreements with states and other institutions on the demand of other principal organs of the UN. He is responsible for implementing and keeping to the → Host State Agreements and represents the Organization in any kind of legal action or lawsuit. A great number of multilateral international treaties provide for the Secretary-General as depositary, which means the treaties as well as the ratification documents are deposited with him, and are registered and published by him. According to Article 102 UN Charter, this is also valid for all the international treaties of UN member states which they have concluded since the UN Charter came into effect: these are also registered and are published in the United Nations Treaties Series → UNTS (http://treaties.un.org).

The Secretary-General receives all communications for the UN organs and is responsible for forwarding UN documents to the member states and to other international organizations.

Furthermore he is in charge of the entire public information work of the UN (→ Public Information of the UN).

V. Tasks Entrusted to the Secretary-General

Besides his administrative tasks, the Secretary-General fulfills tasks which are entrusted to him by the other principal organs in accordance to Article 98 of the Charter. This is particularly the case in the field of → peaceful settlement of disputes and of → peacekeeping.

At the request of the Security Council the Secretary-General offers his "good offices" to the conflicting parties, i.e. he offers his mediation services to the parties, tries to bring the parties to a common conference table by means of "shuttle diplomacy" and presents proposals for a conflict management to them. Furthermore he undertakes "fact-finding missions" on demand of the Security Council in order to explore the situation in conflict zones and to provide the Council with information as a basis for its own initiatives with regard to a particular conflict.

The Security Council – and in exceptional cases the General Assembly (→ Uniting for Peace Resolution) – mandate the implementation of peacekeeping missions and/or the command over the → peacekeeping forces of the UN (→ Peacekeeping Operations) to the Secretary-General. These peacekeeping mandates can be more or less precise, depending on the degree of consensus reached in the Security Council. In case the mandate is rather imprecise the Secretary-General, supported by his Secretariat's Department of Peacekeeping Operations, has the difficult task of taking the necessary concrete decisions on the precise operational mandate of the peacekeeping contingent, its composition, etc. on his own.

During the Cold War those imprecise mandates were often the case due to the lack of effective cooperation between the USA and the USSR in the Security Council. This led repeatedly to severe controversies about the decisions of the Secretary-General in the Security Council and in the General Assembly, as was the case with Hammarskjöld's decisions on the peacekeeping force in the Congo.

Since the superpowers have begun to cooperate better in the Security Council at the end of the eighties, the mandates for peacekeeping missions have become much more concrete and detailed. But now the problem for the Secretary-General lies with the complexity of the mandates: he has to implement complex mandates providing for the observance of truces, the reconstruction of administrative structures, the organization of general elections and a host of other matters. At the same time he has to safeguard the financing of the peacekeeping missions by budgetary measures, not an easy task in the face of the many peacekeeping missions being carried out simultaneously, especially with the background of payment arrears and delays of the member states.

There are also important tasks in the social and economic field which are entrusted to the Secretary-General, in particular in the field of the protection of human rights (→ Human Rights; → Human Rights, Protection of). In this area the General Assembly very often instructs the Secretary-General to assist in the re-establishment of the human rights in a member state. In this context the Secretary-General can offer his "good offices" or can send a board of inquiry to the respective country, but this can only be with the consent of the host government in question.

VI. Political Competences according to Article 99 UN Charter

When the UN Charter was created in 1945, the founding members of the UN wanted to establish a certain counterweight to the Security Council which bears the main responsibility for the maintenance of international peace, in particular for those cases when the Security Council is not in a position to act due to a lack of agreement. Therefore the Secretary-General was given the option with Article 99 UN Charter "to bring to the attention of the Security Council any matter which in his opinion may threaten the maintenance of international peace and security".

In the history of the UN so far this Article 99 has proved to be a very important and substantial legal basis for the political activities of the Secretaries-General. And this not in a direct way, as the Secretaries-General have seldom referred formally to Article 99, when they invoked the Security Council in an international crisis, but they referred to it very often in an indirect way. When they practiced their "quiet diplomacy" of fact-finding and mediation in international conflicts, they tacitly referred to their implicit powers according to Article 99, reasoning that the Secretary-General's responsibility for international peace and security according to Article 99 as "guardian" of peace would imply of necessity the competence to determine the causes of conflicts and to explore conflict resolutions measures before the Security Council becomes involved in the conflict management.

The direct referral to Article 99 has proved to be neither necessary nor even to be recommended. First, every member state has, according to Article 35 (1) UN Charter, the competence to bring any threats to international peace to the attention of the Security Council. Second, a formal invocation of the Security Council by the Secretary-General might be not very useful in an international crisis: this formal act could increase the political tension in the conflict area and, furthermore, the Secretary-General would risk to lose his role as impartial mediator, who stands outside the sphere of the "political" principal organs Security Council and General Assembly, if he invokes the Security Council.

As the history of the UN shows, the Secretary-General has more success if he can act without publicity and public discussions, relying alone on the political and moral authority and reputation of his office, and of his person. The "quiet diplomacy" of the Secretary-General enables the conflicting parties to surrender positions derived from the conflict without loss of face when the Secretary-General provides them with a realistic and reliable evaluation of the situation, supplementing this evaluation with well-balanced proposals for compromise, which offer good prospects of being accepted by the majority of UN member states.

In relying on their implicit competences due to Article 99 the Secretaries-General have deliberately taken the risk that the General Assembly and/or Security Council might criticize their behav-

ior afterwards, or might approve it by their respective resolutions or – as it was often the case – tolerate it without comment.

The thesis that both organs – General Assembly and Security Council – accept tacitly this important fact-finding and mediation work of the Secretary-General is demonstrated by the fact that both organs have adopted no decisions or resolutions recommending that the Secretary-General might end his mediation work. But that does not mean that the member states, in particular the superpowers, would not often express behind closed doors their irritation or annoyance about some mediation activities of the Secretary-General, or would even express their criticism publicly in the meetings of the two organs. Nevertheless all Secretary-Generals have defended and maintained the mediating role of the Secretary-General in spite of criticism and have thus contributed to the political prestige of the office. They began this preventive work with mediating activities and later extended it to fact-finding missions in conflict areas, and in cases of massive and systematic violations of human rights. The latter proved to be very helpful in cases where the human rights bodies, being genuinely competent for the protection of the human rights, could not reach consensus about an official inquiry mission by the respective treaty body.

What makes this "independent" work of the Secretary-General even more remarkable is the fact that the legal basis for this type of activity is neither clear nor reliable. The Secretaries-General have extended their competence simply on their own initiative. While this activity is not contested on legal grounds, as far as the mediating role is concerned, as the Charter provides the Secretary-General (in Article 99 UN Charter) with the competence to assist the Security Council in the search for pacific settlements of disputes, there had been for a long time a considerable controversy about his competence to establish fact-finding missions. But in the meantime a consensus has been reached with the member states that the opportunity to collect timely and sufficient information about international conflict zones constitutes an essential precondition for the use of Article 99 to invoke the Security Council in an international crisis.

VII. The Relationship between Secretary-General and the Superpowers

The answer to the decisive question as to what concrete competences beyond the provisions of the Charter, and on what source of political influence the Secretary-General would rest, has depended and still depends on the relationships among the superpowers, and between the superpowers on the one hand and the Secretary-General on the other. The more the relationship between the superpowers deteriorated in the Cold War, the smaller became the chances for the Security Council to agree on measures for conflict resolution. In some cases, the General Assembly tried to fill this gap: on the grounds of the controversial "Uniting for Peace Resolution" it claimed the right to discuss the situation in conflict areas and to make recommendations for the conflict resolution. But more often, and with more success and support, the Secretary-General tried to fill the gap created by the inactivity of the Security Council in peacekeeping.

This was particularly the case with Dag Hammarskjöld. He filled this gap with his self-confident and charismatic personality and with his visionary ideas, and claimed to develop the Charter in a creative way. He said repeatedly in controversies about his competences in meetings of the Security Council that he believed "that it is in keeping with the philosophy of the Charter that the Secretary-General ... should be expected to act without any guidance from the Assembly or the Security Council should this appear to him necessary towards helping to fill any vacuum that may appear in the systems which the Charter and traditional diplomacy provide for the safeguarding of peace and security." (SC 837th meeting, 22 July 1958, cf. UN Doc. S/PV.837, para. 12)

Thus his courage in undertaking to "fill the vacuum" was the basis for the establishment of the first UN peacekeeping force UNEF I in the Suez Conflict 1956, when – resting on an idea of the Canadian UN delegate Lester B. Pearson – Hammarskjöld worked out the concept for peacekeeping forces. He managed to gain the support of the majority of the states in the General Assembly and to reach the consent of the troop-contributing countries as well as of the conflict parties. And he did all this without any clear legal basis in the Charter, he just interpreted the *ratio legis* of Chapter VII of the Charter in a very extensive manner, and succeeded in obtaining the consent of the majority of states.

At that point in time the office of the Secretary-General might be reckoned to have had reached *de facto* the height of its power. This growth in power of the Secretary-General during the Congo conflict provoked the hostile opposition of the USSR against the Secretary-General. On behalf of the USSR, Krushchev demanded from the General Assembly the replacement of the post of the Secretary-General by a three-person committee, consisting of one representative of the Western states, one representative of the Socialist countries and one representative of the non-aligned states (cf. GAOR, 869th meeting, para. 142-153, 23 September 1960).

But he failed: the majority of states saw in this proposal the danger that the conflict structures of the Security Council might be transferred to the leadership level of the Secretariat, and the USSR proposal was rejected. They preferred an active Secretary-General who might make mistakes and might transgress the limits of his competences, to a safe committee in a permanent stalemate, incapable of acting (cf. GAOR, 883rd meeting, para. 4-12, 3 October 1960; also UN Press Release SG/966 of 3 October 1960).

Despite the fact that the blockage of the Security Council caused by the Cold War continued, the Secretaries-General succeeding Hammarskjöld were not able to continue the active leadership role in the style of Hammarskjöld, much less were they able to develop the role further. First, they did not have that kind of charismatic personality, which had enabled Hammarskjöld to win the support of the world's public opinion; second, the power structure in the General Assembly changed profoundly when the UN admitted from the early sixties a large number of new members, those states which had gained their independence in the → decolonization process. Thus it became more difficult to mobilize reliable majorities in the General Assembly in support of the Secretary-General. The new members were naturally more interested in the economic and social problems of their groups of states (→ Group of 77 and the UN; → Non-Aligned Movement and the UN), thus the Secretaries-General shifted the focus of their work to this area (→ International Economic Relations and the New International Economic Order (NIEO)).

The role of the Secretary-General in peacekeeping was also restricted by the fact that the superpowers refused in several international conflicts where they were direct parties to the conflict to accept the involvement of the UN. That is why U Thant's diplomatic initiatives for mediation in the Vietnam War failed in the end, for instance: the USA rejected any mediating role by U Thant (cf. *Finger* 1988, 124ff.). On the other hand, U Thant had been able just a few years earlier to stop the escalation of the conflict between the USA and the USSR in the Cuban missile crisis through his mediating role as both sides (Kennedy and Krushchev) were dependent on a third party offering them a face-saving compromise and thus accepted U Thant as mediator (cf. *Finger* 1988, 120-124; *Luard* 1989, 392ff.; list of relevant UN, US and USSR documents in: *Volger* 2008, 121ff.).

As the historical examples illustrate, the active role of the Secretary-General is based on three preconditions: the stalemate of the superpowers in the Security Council, the strong personality of

the office holder and – as is often overlooked – the readiness of the Permanent Five to tolerate an active policy by the Secretary-General.

The rapprochement between the superpowers and between them and the UN in the course of the CSCE process and other bloc-bridging development dynamics, gave the Security Council again a larger capacity to act in the field of peacekeeping. Now the Secretary-General in his role as the creative "fill-in" peacekeeper was less in demand, and his real political weight as an active element in the UN system decreased.

The greatest problem confronting the United Nations since the end of the Cold War is the tendency towards hegemonic policy and unilateralism, which can be observed to an increasing extent in the foreign policy of the USA in the eighties (cf. *Zitka* 1997, 288ff.). The USA reduces severely the Secretary-General's capacity to act by its long-lasting partial budgetary payment withholdings, and this effect is even enhanced by its selective attitude towards peacekeeping matters and human rights affairs, oriented on its trade interests.

This indifference of the USA towards the UN and polemical criticism – often tinged with hostile undertones – towards the Secretary-General as a symbol of multilateralism was clearly expressed in the polemical media campaign in the USA directed against Boutros-Ghali, which increased in intensity in 1996, when Boutros-Ghali's reappointment was on the agenda. There was a large number of discriminatory and disrespectful statements of US politicians made in Congress and in the media. This was paralleled by the stubborn veto policy of the USA in the Security Council in the straw polls concerning the reappointment of Boutros-Ghali. Several times the outcome was fourteen yes-votes and one no-vote (of the USA), until the other Council members finally gave in and presented other candidates for the Secretary-General.

His successor Annan was able to benefit in his first term of office from the fact that the US administration considered him as their "choice" and as an administratively experienced UN reformer, treated him in a friendly manner and accompanied his reforms with appreciative comments and supported his re-election in 2001.

But when Annan criticized frankly the intervention of the US-led coalition troops in spring 2003 in Iraq as "illegal" and lacking the necessary authorization through the UN Security Council (BBC Interview with Annan, 16 September 2004), the US administration and the US media showed a large measure of hostility towards Annan in the same way as they had before towards Boutros-Ghali. The apparent lack of support of the US administration for Annan's reform concept in 2005 was a decisive cause for the failure of the reform attempt, which was clearly demonstrated by the arrogant behavior of US ambassador John Bolton in the informal General Assembly negotiations in summer 2005, when he virtually demanded the re-negotiation of the whole reform package (cf. David Usborne, The US vs The UN. American ambassador seeks to scupper UN's global strategy with 750 amendments after just three weeks in the job, in: The Independent, 26 August 2005).

But the role of the superpower should also not be over-estimated. In many cases the political support of the large majority of small, medium and large member states of the UN and the political attitude of the world public in general towards the UN has proved to be important enough to counter-balance the US influence. The adoption of the Rome Statute for an International Criminal Court in 1998 against the outspoken and massive opposition of the USA as well as the encouraging results of the Johannesburg World Summit on Sustainable Development 2002 – again in a political fight against US opposition – illustrate that a courageous Secretary-General can become the speaker and "centre forward" of the "team" of the majority of UN member states. It is in phases of hegemonic dominance that the United Nations needs a strong Secretary-General and it is appreciated by most member states, when the incumbent shows strength and courage. Opinion polls proved that the public in the member states was impressed by Annan's quiet, self-confident and dignified attitude as Secretary-General in negotiations, by the clarity of his political analysis and by the strength of his moral appeals in his public speeches. It was in recognition of his clear moral stance and visionary force that the Nobel Peace Prize Committee awarded him together with the Organization of the United Nations the Nobel Peace Prize of the year 2001.

His successor Ban Ki-moon is still in the phase of developing his own standpoint towards the super-power USA, preferring so far a low profile with regard to criticisms of the UN policy of the USA, but at least in the Climate Conference in Bali 2007 he demonstrated that he is able to forcefully criticize obstructive US behavior at a UN conference and has contributed considerably to the change in the US position at the Bali conference (cf. CBS News: U.S. Bends To Critics, OKs Climate Roadmap, 15 December 2007). To be respected by the majority of member states the UN Secretary-General needs to win a certain independence of and distance from US political positions.

VIII. The Political Role of the Secretary-General in the International System

Within the highly complex, ever-changing network of multilateral diplomacy of the United Nations the dilemma of the Secretary-General constitutes at the same time his chance: he has to define in his person the standpoint of multilateral diplomacy, a kind of diplomacy which has always to stand its ground against the states' tendency towards bilateral diplomacy, and which often lacks coherence, consistence and orientation on global problems.

All the UN Secretaries-General so far have – after having learned enough in their first years in office about the conditions for and chances of their work as Secretary-General – succeeded in defining such a personal and convincing standpoint – with different emphasis on the various aspects of his role according to his personality, his understanding of the office and the political circumstances during his term of office, some laying the emphasis more on the negotiating function and good offices, others accentuating more the reform necessities and the common goals to be achieved, some underlining the moral stance.

Regardless of his personal interpretation of his office, each Secretary-General is expected to take a clearly marked standpoint to the situation of the United Nations with regard to its structures, finances and working conditions as well as to the role of the United Nations in international conflicts and in the face of the global problems. His standpoint shall – in an almost symbolical way – give global orientation for the other UN organs or – to be more precise – for the governments of the states represented in these organs. He represents the global concepts for the solution of global problems which they have to take into consideration if they really want to make progress in solving the problems. He represents a kind of "categoric imperative" of world politics. According to the changing constellations and conditions of international politics his standpoint is sometimes more appreciated and his initiatives are taken up in the UN system, in particular in the General Assembly and the Security Council, sometimes his standpoint is not appreciated and is criticized as unrealistic and idealistic and his initiatives are not taken up. Notwithstanding the success of his efforts the main significance of his role lies in the clarity and strength of his standpoint taken up towards the politicians of the member states and the world public. His role is a political and a public role, marking concrete political challenges for the politicians to meet and setting desirable medium-term and long-term goals for the world public to strive towards in order to make their politicians put these issues eventually on the political agenda.

The difficult task of the Secretary-General, namely to fulfill an integrating role within the world organization, to offer a set of political goals for the actors of world politics, and to motivate the member states to decide on and implement adequate decisions, seems to be nearly impossible to execute, since states are reluctant to give higher priority to common goals over national interests and even more reluctant to surrender even portions of their sovereignty to the world organization. But – as the history of the UN illustrates – the Secretary-General is often helped by the astonishing fact that – despite all the setbacks and difficulties in that organization's history – the people in the member states invest, time and again, their hope in the Secretary-General of the UN, as the bearer of possibilities for the pacific resolution of conflicts, and as the "lawyer" for the weak and the people without rights. They accept him as the "world conscience", as the "educator of the world", and as someone who cannot influence effectively daily politics, but who repeatedly *can* articulate the aspirations and goals of long-term developments and *can* encourage mankind to develop new initiatives for the solution of global problems.

Helmut Volger

Lit.: *1. Public Papers and Other Texts of UN Secretaries-General:*
Annan, K.: The Secretary-General and the UN Budget, in: Rivlin, B./Gordenker, L. (eds.): The Challenging Role of the UN Secretary-General. Making "The Most Impossible Job in the World" Possible, Westport/London 1993, 98-107.
Annan, K.: Report of the Secretary-General: Renewing the United Nations: A Programme for Reform (UN Doc. A/51/950 of 14 July 1997).
Annan, K.: Making Globalization Work for the Poor, in: The Independent, 12 December 2000.
Boutros-Ghali, B.: Empowering the United Nations, in: Foreign Affairs, (Winter 1992/93), 89-102.
Boutros-Ghali, B.: Friedenserhaltung durch die Vereinten Nationen: Eine neue Chance

für den Weltfrieden, in: EA 48 (1993), No. 5, 123-131.

Boutros-Ghali, B.: Globalisierung und Erwachen der Nationen. Der UN-Generalsekretär vor der Deutschen Gesellschaft für die Vereinten Nationen, in: VN 41 (1993), 1-10.

Boutros-Ghali, B.: An Agenda for Peace. Preventive Diplomacy, Peacemaking and Peace-keeping. Report of the Secretary-General pursuant to the statement adopted by the Summit Meeting of the Security Council on 31 January 1992, New York 1992 (United Nations Doc. DPI/1247).

Boutros-Ghali, B.: New Dimensions of Arms Regulation and Disarmament in the Post-Cold War Era. Report of the Secretary-General, 27 October 1992, UN Doc. A/C.1/47/7.

Boutros-Ghali, B.: Improving the Capacity of the United Nations for Peace-Keeping, Report of the Secretary-General, 14 March 1994, UN Doc. A/48/403-S/26450.

Boutros-Ghali, B.: Agenda for Development. Report of the Secretary-General, 6 May 1994, UN Doc. A/48/935.

Boutros-Ghali, B.: New Departure on Development, in: Foreign Policy, No. 98 (Spring 1995), 44-49.

Boutros-Ghali, B.: Unvanquished, New York 1999.

Hammarskjöld, D.: The Servant of Peace. A Selection of the Speeches and Statements of Dag Hammarskjöld (ed. by W. Foote), London 1962.

Lie, T.: In the Cause of Peace: Seven Years with the United Nations, New York 1954.

Pérez de Cuéllar, J.: The UN Simply Must Be Made To Succeed, in: New York Times Week in Review, October 20 (1985), 21E.

Pérez de Cuéllar, J.: The Role of the UN Secretary-General, in: Roberts, A./Kingsbury, B. (eds.): United Nations – Divided World, 2nd edn., Oxford 1993, 125-142.

Pérez de Cuéllar, J.: Anarchy or Order. Annual Reports 1982-1991, New York 1991.

Pérez de Cuéllar, J.: Pilgrimage to Peace: A Secretary-General's Memoir, New York 1997.

Public Papers of the Secretaries-General of the United Nations, Vol. I: Trygve Lie 1946-1953, selected and edited with a commentary by A.W. Cordier and W. Foote, New York/London 1969.

Public Papers of the Secretaries-General of the United Nations, Vol. II: Dag Hammarskjöld 1953-1956, selected and edited with a commentary by A.W. Cordier and W.Foote, New York/London 1972.

Public Papers of the Secretaries-General of the United Nations, Vol. III: Dag Hammarskjöld 1956-1957, selected and edited with a commentary by A.W. Cordier and W. Foote, New York/London 1973.

Public Papers of the Secretaries-General of the United Nations, Vol. IV: Dag Hammarskjöld 1958-1960, selected and edited with a commentary by A.W. Cordier and W. Foote, New York/London 1974.

Public Papers of the Secretaries-General of the United Nations, Vol. V: Dag Hammarskjöld 1960-1961, selected and edited with a commentary by A.W. Cordier and W. Foote, New York/London 1975.

Public Papers of the Secretaries-General of the United Nations, Vol. VI: U Thant 1961-1964, selected and edited with a commentary by A.W. Cordier and M. Harrelson, New York/London 1976.

Public Papers of the Secretaries-General of the United Nations, Vol. VII: U Thant 1965-1967, selected and edited with a commentary by A.W. Cordier and M. Harrelson, New York/London 1976.

Public Papers of the Secretaries-General of the United Nations, Vol. VIII: U Thant 1968-1971, selected and edited with a commentary by A.W. Cordier and M. Harrelson, New York/London 1977.

U Thant, S.: Toward World Peace. Addresses and Public Statements, 1957-1963, New York 1964.

U Thant, S.: Portfolio for Peace. Excerpts from the Writings and Speeches of U Thant, 1961-1968, 2nd edn., New York 1970.

U Thant, S.: View from the UN, Newton Abbott 1978.

Waldheim, K.: Der schwierigste Job der Welt, Vienna et al. 1978.

Waldheim, K.: Building the Future Order, New York 1980.

Waldheim, K.: The Challenge of Peace, London 1980.

Waldheim, K.: In the Eye of the Storm: The Memoirs of Kurt Waldheim, London 1985.

2. Secondary Literature: Boudreau, T.E.: Sheathing the Sword: The UN Secretary-General and the Prevention of International Conflict, New York 1991; *Bourloyannis, M.-C.:* Fact-finding by the Secretary-General of the United Nations, in_ New York Journal of International Law and Politics 23 (1990), 641-669; *Cordovez, D.:* Strengthening United Nations Diplomacy for Peace: The Role of the Secretary-General, in: UNITAR (ed.): The United Nations and the Maintenance of International Peace and Security, Dordrecht et al. 1987, 161-175; *Dicke, K.:* Reformen des Sekretariats und die veränderte Rolle des Generalsekretärs, in: Hüfner, K. (ed.): Die

Reform der Vereinten Nationen. Die Weltorganisation zwischen Krise und Erneuerung, Opladen 1994, 225-239; *Fiedler, W.:* Commentary to Art. 97, in: Simma, B. (ed.): The Charter of the United Nations. A Commentary, Munich/Oxford 1994, 1019-1032; *Fiedler, W.:* Commentary to Art. 97, 98, 99, in: Simma, B. (ed.): The Charter of the United Nations. A Commentary, Vol. II, 2nd edn., Munich/Oxford 2002, 1191-1230; *Finger, S.M.:* American Ambassadors at the UN. People, Politics, and Bureaucracy in Making Foreign Policy, New York/London 1988; *Forsythe, D.P.:* The UN Secretary-General and Human Rights, in: Rivlin, B./ Gordenker, L. (eds.): The Challenging Role of the UN Secretary-General: making "the most impossible job in the world" possible, Westport/USA 1993, 211-232; *Franck, T. M.:* The Secretary's Role in Conflict Resolution: Past, Present and Pure Conjecture, in: EJIL 6 (1995), 360-387; *Franck, T.M./Nolte, G.:* The Good Offices Function of the Secretary-General, in: Roberts, A./Kingsbury, B. (eds.): United Nations, Divided World. The UN's Roles in International Relations, 2nd edn., Oxford 1993, 143-182; *Fröhlich, M.:* Dag Hammarskjöld und die Vereinten Nationen. Die politische Ethik des UN-Generalsekretärs, Paderborn/Munich et al. 2000; *Gordenker, L.:* The UN Secretary-General and the Maintenance of Peace, New York/London 1967; *Goulding, M.:* The UN Secretary-General, in: Malone, D.M. (ed.): The UN Security Council. From the Cold War to the 21st Century, Boulder/London 2004, 267-279; *Holcombe, A.N. (ed.):* The UN Secretary-General: His Role in World Politics, New York 1962; *Jackson, W.D.:* The Political Role of the Secretary-General under U Thant and Kurt Waldheim: Development or Decline? in: World Affairs 140 (1978), 230-244; *James, A.:* U Thant and His Critics, in: The Yearbook of World Affairs 20 (1972), 43-64; *James, A.:* The Secretary-General: A Comparative Analysis, in: Berridge, G.R./ Jennings, A. (eds.): Diplomacy at the UN, Basingstoke 1985, 31-47; *James, A.:* The Secretary-General as an Independent Political Actor, in: Rivlin, B./Gordenker, L. (eds.): The Challenging Role of the UN Secretary-General ..., loc. cit., 22-39; *Kanninen, T.:* Leadership and Reform: The Secretary-General and the UN Financial Crisis of the late 1980s, The Hague et al. 1995; *Lash, J.:* Dag Hammarskjöld's conception of his office, in: IO 16 (1962), 542-566; *Lentner, H.H.:* The Diplomacy of the United Nations Secretary-General, in: The Western Political Quarterly 18 (1965), 531-550; *Lippmann, W.:* Dag

Hammarskjöld – United Nations Pioneer, in: IO 15 (1961), 547-548; *Luard, E.:* A History of the United Nations, Vol. 2: The Age of Decolonization, 1955-1965, London 1989; *Meisler, S.:* United Nations: The First Fifty Years, New York 1995 (the chapters on Trygve Lie (21-35), Dag Hammarskjöld (75-134), Sithu U Thant (135-184), Kurt Waldheim (185-222), Javier Pérez de Cuéllar (239-277) and Boutros Boutros-Ghali (278-329); *Meisler, S.:* Kofi Annan: A Man of Peace in a World of War, New York 2007; *Morr, H. v.:* Secretary-General, in: Wolfrum, R. (ed.): United Nations: Law, Policies and Practice, Vol. 2, Munich/Dordrecht 1995, 1136-1146; *Nayar, M.G.:* Dag Hammarskjöld and U Thant: The Evolution of Their Office, in: Case Western Reserve Journal of International Law 36 (1974), 36-83; *Newman, E.:* The UN Secretary-General from the Cold War to the New Era – A Global peace and Security Mandate? Houndmills/ Basingstoke/ London 1998; *Newman, E.:* Secretary-General, in: Weiss, T.G./Daws, S. (eds.): The Oxford Handbook on the United Nations, Oxford et al. 2007, 175-192; *Paepcke, H.:* Die friedens- und sicherheitspolitische Rolle des UN-Generalsekretärs im Wandel: Das kritische Verhältnis zwischen Boutros-Ghali und den USA, Baden-Baden 2004; *Ramcharan, B.G.:* The Good Offices of the United Nations Secretary-General in the Field of Human Rights, in: AJIL 76 (1982), 130-141; *Ramcharan, B.G.:* The history, role and organization of the "cabinet" of the United Nations Secretary-General, in: Nordic JIL 59 (1990), No. 2/3, 103-116; *Rivlin, B./Gordenker, L. (eds.):* The Challenging Role of the UN Secretary-General ..., loc. cit., 1993; *Rivlin, B.:* The UN Secretary-Generalship at Fifty, in: Bourantonis, D./ Wiener, J. (eds.): The United Nations in the New World Order: the World Organization at Fifty, Houndmills/London 1995, 81-104; *Rovine, A.W.:* The First Fifty Years: The Secretary-General in World Politics 1920-1970, Leyden 1970; *Schwebel, S.M.:* The Origins and Development of Article 99 of the Charter, in: BYIL 28 (1951), 371-382; *Schwebel, S.M.:* UN Secretary-General, in: EPIL 5, Amsterdam 1983, 341-345; *Skjelsbaek, K.:* The UN Secretary-General and the mediation of international disputes, in: Journal of Peace Research 28 (1991), 99-115; *Szasz, T.:* The Role of the Secretary-General. Some Legal Aspects, in: NYUJ of Int'l L& Pol 24 (1991), 161-198; *Traub, J.:* The Best Intentions: Kofi Annan and the UN in the Era of American Power, London 2006; *Urquhart, B.:* Hammarskjöld, New York 1972;

Urquhart, B.: Selecting the world's CEO: remembering the Secretaries-General, in: Foreign Affairs 74 (1995), 21-26; *Urquhart, B.:* The Role of the Secretary-General, in: Maynes, C.W./Williamson, R.S. (eds.): U.S. Foreign Policy and the United Nations System, New York/London 1996, 212-228; *Volger, H.:* Geschichte der Vereinten Nationen, 2nd rev. edn., Munich/Vienna 2008; *Zitka, F.:* Wandel und Kontinuität. Amerikanische UNO-Politik 1977-1993, Frankfurt (Main) 1997.

Internet: 1. UN websites: a) website "UN Secretaries-General": www.un.org/Overview/ Secretary-General/index.html (contains statements and other texts of the present office holder as well as UN documents and information sheets about the former Secretary-Generals and a bibliography); b) for resolutions of the General Assembly: www.un. org/documents/resga.htm; c) for press releases: www.un.org/documents/pressga.htm; 2. Website of the Global Policy Forum on UN Secretaries-General: www.globalpolicy. org/secgen/index.ht

Security Council

1. General

The Security Council is the second principal organ of the United Nations (→ Principal Organs, Subsidiary Organs, Treaty Bodies) named in Article 7 (1) of the UN Charter (→ Charter of the UN): → General Assembly, Security Council, Economic and Social Council (→ ECOSOC), → Trusteeship Council, International Court of Justice (→ ICJ), and → Secretariat. "Primary responsibility for the maintenance of international peace and security" is conferred upon it (Art. 24 (1) UN Charter). This, combined with the fact that only it has the power to create law binding on all member states, is responsible for its elevated position, that has in turn led some to speak of a "Board of Directors" (*Geiger* 1991). The composition and powers of the Security Council were based on the international political situation at the end of World War II, and have been adapted in line with developing UN practice and pursuant to the first revision of the Charter of 1965. It is not just since the beginning of the 1990s that the working methods and the composition of the Security Council have been considered urgently in need of reform in order to maintain the functionality of → the UN system.

2. Concept

The idea of a new order of world peace which emerged in the course of World War II, with the goal of replacing the order propagated by the unsuccessful → League of Nations, originated primarily with the United States (*Schäfer* 1981; *Rivlin* 1966) (→ History of the Foundation of the UN). Following the *Declaration by United Nations* on 1 January 1942, in which 26 states participated, it was made clear by the Moscow Declaration (30 October 1943) and the Conferences in Teheran (1 December 1944), Dumbarton Oaks (late summer 1944) and Yalta (February 1945), that the major victorious powers, the United States, the United Kingdom, the Soviet Union, as well as France and China, intended to play a leading role in this new order (*Eitel* 1994). Small and medium-sized states objected vociferously at first, but at the San Francisco Conference (spring 1945) ultimately supported the concept. The transfer of special responsibility to the Security Council and thus to the five "Great Powers", the future permanent members, was part of a central compromise (*Geiger* 1994) at the San Francisco Conference.

3. Composition

Pursuant to Article 23 of the UN Charter, the Security Council comprises the five permanent members – the Republic of China (in 1971 replaced by the People's Republic of China), France, the Union of Socialist Soviet Republics (since 1991 the Russian Federation has taken over the UN membership and the seat in the Security Council), the United Kingdom and the United States – as well as ten non-permanent members. The ten non-permanent members are selected on a regional basis from countries from Africa, Asia, Latin America and the Caribbean, Eastern Europe, and "Western Europe and other states" (→

Regional Groups), and are elected by the → General Assembly for a term of two years. Five are replaced every year. The main criterion for selection is a country's "contribution ... to the maintenance of international peace and security and to the other purposes of the Organization" (Art. 23 (1) UN Charter). The criterion is general enough not to exclude any UN member from standing for election. In cases of doubt, the political climate has been sufficient to prevent individual countries standing. No member state has yet failed at the formal hurdle. Nor are candidates examined to see if they contribute to the functioning of the Security Council (ensuring quick and effective action, see below). Functional considerations are as a rule outweighed by those of foreign policy prestige and profile. States which have most frequently held non-permanent seats on the Security Council (as of June 2007) include Japan (9 times), India (6) and Pakistan (6) for Asia; Brazil (9), Argentina (8) and Colombia (6) for Latin America and the Caribbean; Egypt (5) for Africa; Canada (6) and Italy (6) for Western Europe and others and Poland (5) for Eastern Europe. 80 states have, for various reasons, not yet served on the Security Council.

4. Dominance of the Permanent Members

The five permanent members of the Security Council (P5) exercise considerable influence over the machinery and decisions of the Security Council (cf. *Delon* 1991). The influence is generally based on experience and years of cooperation with those offices in the → Secretariat which serve and administrate the Security Council. The resulting specialist knowledge and almost untouchable informational advantage is heightened by a certain solidarity between the P5 (→ Groups and Groupings in the UN). Furthermore, the permanent seats are equipped with a right of veto (→ Veto, Right of Veto). Using a veto prevents the UN from intervening in a particular situation (*Eitel* 1994). Bearing in mind this potential for dominance, it is

perhaps unexpected that of the permanent members mentioned in Article 23 (1) one is no longer a UN member (Republic of China), and one no longer even exists (Union of Socialist Soviet Republics). This anachronism confirms the need for a comprehensive reform of the Security Council (see below). (→ Reform of the UN).

5. Competence

Primary responsibility for the maintenance of international peace and security has been conferred by the UN member states on the Security Council, to ensure prompt and effective action by the United Nations (Art. 24 (1) UN Charter). The responsibility of the General Assembly, based on Article 10 *et seq.* of the UN Charter, takes second place – not least due to the unstable nature of the General Assembly, as caused by its large membership. The Security Council has exclusive competence for adopting effective, binding measures, in particular mandatory measures (*Delbrück* 1994). Whether a threat to the peace or breach of the peace justifying such measures exists (cf. Art. 39 UN Charter), is a matter for the Security Council to determine; in this it is granted considerable scope for discretion in order to maintain its functionality (*Herdegen* 1995). The jurisdiction of the International Court of Justice remains unaffected by the Security Council considering the same dispute. The Security Council has specific powers laid down in Chapter VI (Peaceful Settlement of Disputes), Chapter VII (Action with Respect to Threats to the Peace, Breaches of the Peace, and Acts of Aggression), and Chapter VIII (Regional Arrangements) of the Charter, to enable it to fulfill its mandate.

In addition to procedural issues and questions of organizational law, resolutions on peace-keeping make up about three quarters of the work of the Security Council (*Eitel* 1994).

Peacekeeping resolutions deal with international tensions and hotspots, as well as attacks, interventions and acts of aggression perpetrated by one state against another. In situations where there is merely a threat to the peace, the Security Council often limits itself to expressing its regret and calling for restraint or negotiations. These less operative measures normally remain within the framework of Chapter VI of the Charter.

In the more threatening situations with which Chapter VII is concerned, peacekeeping measures may be taken and economic or arms embargoes imposed.

Embargoes (→ Sanctions) have in the past been imposed on Afghanistan, Al-Qaida and the Taliban, Côte d'Ivoire, the Democratic Republic of Congo, the Democratic People's Republic of Korea, Eritrea/Ethopia, Iran, Iraq/Kuwait, Serbia-Montenegro, Libya, Haiti, Angola (UNITA), the states of the former Yugoslavia, Liberia, Rwanda, Sierra Leone, Somalia and Sudan (for further information on the sanctions cf. in the Internet: www.un. org/sc/committees).

Typical peacekeeping measures include the deployment of troops ("blue helmets") and the authorization of so-called "coalitions of the willing" or other organizations (e.g. Iraq/Kuwait, Albania, Bosnia and Hercegovina, Kosovo). The European Union, too, is gaining profile with UN-authorized peace missions. Since the founding of the UN, a total of 63 peacekeeping missions ("blue helmets") have taken place (PKMs) (→ peacekeeping; → peacekeeping forces; → peacekeeping operations), of which 17 were still in place in 2008 (as of 30 April 2008). Successful examples from the past include the peacekeeping operations in Namibia, Mozambique, El Salvador, Georgia, Haiti, East Slavonia and Central Africa. Set-backs in Somalia, Rwanda and Bosnia and Herzegovina however have led to widespread calls for the Security Council to be quicker in issuing clearer and more flexible mandates for peacekeeping missions. The withdrawal of "blue helmets" should be better cushioned by relief organizations, observers and police forces (*Voorhoeve* 1998). Since the mandate issued by the Security Council is often the result of tough political wrangling, and so tends to represent a formal compromise, intentionally open to interpretation, it will not be easy for the Security Council to take heed of these reasonable demands in practice.

6. Meetings

The frequency of Security Council consultations has constantly increased. At present *"informal consultations"* between the 15 Council members, which are closed to non-members, take place almost every morning. As soon as a matter is ready for decision, the Security Council convenes a *"formal meeting"*, which is public but usually only of a ceremonial nature. The distinction between the two forms of session is of considerable practical and political significance. "Consultations" have developed from the chats over coffee to which the President of the Security Council invited his colleagues to swap opinions in an informal framework. In the course of the 1970s these consultations became a standard form of meeting for the Security Council, for which a special consultation room with all standard equipment was made available. In this room, resolutions are prepared, sponsored and discussed. The non-members only have access to the consultations once their format changes to that of an official session. Then, in the official meeting room, all UN members can be privy to the formal decisions and statements of the individual Security Council members. The permanent members of the Security Council in particular have wished to ensure in the past that those UN members whose interests are specially affected or who are the parties to the dispute (Articles 31 and 32 UN Charter) may only participate in the consultations once they have reached this stage. A formal argument for this is that at the previous stage the Security Council does not meet collectively, but as individual member states (*Aust* 1995). Within the framework of the discussions on reform of the Security Council (see below), many UN mem-

651

bers have backed a Czech proposal, which would allow affected member states to participate earlier, at the stage of informal consultations, since these have now become the main type of meeting for the Security Council, and the provisional Rules of Procedure of the Council (→ Rules of Procedure) state that public meetings are the norm (Rule 48).

In the late 1990s, the Security Council increasingly called public meetings at which current topics were discussed by all those with a special interest (banning anti-personnel mines, measures of so-called practical disarmament (→ Disarmament), deployment of police forces in peacekeeping operations, rule of law etc.). In addition to the option of inviting "other persons" to consultations and information-sessions (Rule 39 of the Rules of Procedure), the Council has in recent times made increased use of the *"Arria" formula*. This formula meets the needs of the practice whereby member states may participate in briefings from and exchanges of opinion with outsiders, without calling formal Security Council meetings. "Arria" meetings, to which invitations are issued by one member of the Security Council in agreement with the President of the Council, thus take place outside the Council's premises (cf. *Volger* 2007, 544-558).

7. Presidency, Agenda

The Presidency of the Security Council rotates monthly. Every non-permanent member holds the Presidency at least once during its two-year membership of the Council. Details are set out in the Council's provisional Rules of Procedure (Rules 18-20; for more information see *Jahn/Wasum* 1994). These also state that the provisional agenda for each meeting of the Security Council shall be drawn up by the Secretary-General and approved by the President of the Security Council (Rule 7). The agenda of formal Council meetings is published in the daily UN Journal. The Secretariat and each Presidency draw up a monthly overview of the topics which require ac-

tion by the Security Council. These overviews are distributed informally.

The role of the President of the Security Council is an important one. It is up to the President to decide, after consulting the other members, whether to include items on the agenda or to permit their discussion under the heading "any other business". Informal consultations for this purpose take place at the start of every month and continue as necessary. The President is further responsible for subsequently informing the press and member states about the agenda and results of informal meetings. He has a not inconsiderable discretion in the performance of this duty.

There is a tendency in the Security Council, particularly among the permanent members, to avoid formalizing working methods as Rules of Procedure, and to follow fixed rules as little as possible. The dominant interest is in interpreting the existing fragmentary "provisional" rules as pragmatically as possible. This often stands in contrast to the wishes of the non-members who would prefer the Security Council to be bound by clear, fixed rules, thus making its actions more predictable.

8. Decision-Making and Voting Methods

The Security Council makes its opinion known through decisions and recommendations. "Softer" forms of action are formal Presidential Statements and informal press briefings by the President. In the latter case, the members of the Security Council often content themselves with giving the President broad guidelines to which he is to speak. The text for formal Statements is on the other hand negotiated in detail and adopted by consensus.

Security Council decisions on procedural matters are made by an affirmative vote of nine members (Art. 27 (2) UN Charter). All other matters require the concurring votes of the five permanent members (Art 27 (3) first sentence). This rule in effect gives the permanent members a right of veto. They also have a right of veto as regards the often tricky question of whether a matter is a procedural matter or "other" matter (so-called "double veto"). Criteria to differentiate the two are contained in GA resolution A/RES/267 (III) of 14 April 1949 (see also *Simma/Brunner* 1994). The voluntary abstention by a permanent member is not deemed to be veto (*Unser* 1997). A veto is often avoided by taking the position of the permanent members into account in advance ("hidden veto").

Even if the right of veto has seldom been used since the end of the East-West conflict (*Klein* 1997), and the Security Council has in the 1990s increasingly acted by consensus, clarifying the requirements for exercising the veto and its extension to potential new permanent members is a focus of the debate on reforming the Security Council (*Fassbender* 1998).

9. Subsidiary Organs

The Security Council has exercised its right to establish subsidiary organs (Art. 29 UN Charter). These include the Military Staff Committee (cf. Art. 47 UN Charter), the Committee on Admission of New Members and the Committee on Council Meetings away from Headquarters (→ Committees, System of). The Committee of Experts on Rules of Procedure meets fairly regularly to discuss current procedural matters. In practice, the Sanctions Committees, established for each sanctions regime, are the most significant subsidiary organs. The Chairpersons and Vice-Chairpersons of these committees are selected from the non-permanent members of the Council. Committee members too are drawn solely from Security Council member states. The ad-hoc tribunals for Rwanda and the former Yugoslavia are likewise classified as subsidiary organs (see *Oellers-Frahm* 1995). This is not true of the International Criminal Court, whose Statute was adopted at the Rome Conference in 1998 (→ ICC) (UN Doc. A/CONF.183/9 of 17 July 1998), which has an independent basis in international law (Art. 126 of the Statute of the Court). Nonetheless, the Court's Statute grants the Security Council a range of powers: it may refer a Chapter VII situation to the Prosecutor (Art. 13 (b) Statute of the Court); it may, in a resolution adopted under Chapter VII, request the Court to refrain from investigating or prosecuting a case for a period of 12 months, and it may renew such a request (Art. 16); it has a right to be informed in certain cases if states fail to cooperate with the Court (Art. 87 (5) and (7)). During the Rome Conference, the permanent members of the Security Council (especially the US and China) tried to obtain wider powers for the Security Council, but failed.

10. The Need for Reform

It is beyond question that the Security Council needs reform. On 24 October 1995 the UN member states expressly stated in their declaration on the occasion of the 50th anniversary of the United Nations that the Security Council must be enlarged and its working methods reviewed (No. 14). Most statements by UN member states in the major General Debates and debates of substance at the General Assemblies since 1992 are in line with this demand. In 1992/1993, 79 states communicated their opinions on reform of the Security Council to the Secretary-General (UN Doc. A/RES/47/62 of 11 December 1992; response in UN Doc. 48/264 of 29 July 1993 with addenda). Numerous states of their own accord named Germany and Japan as possible new permanent members. The General Assembly thereafter established a Working Group on the matter (A/RES/48/26 of 3 December 1993), which began its work in January 1994.

Material reasons for reforming the Security Council include: (1) the fact that important countries from the developing world have a legitimate claim to be permanently represented on the Security Council; (2) the growing influence exercised by leading economies such as Japan and the reunified Germany on the international stage; (3) the fact that the UN has 192 members; (4) the fact that the circle of permanent members is now charmingly anachronistic (see above) and no longer representative; (5) the lack of transparency of the Security Council's working methods; (6) the potential loss of credibility and authority of the Security Council due to the above deficits.

11. Previous Attempts at Reform

The Security Council has already been reformed once, in 1965, at the behest of a group of developing countries. At that time the increased membership of the UN (from 51 to 113) led the Council to be enlarged from eleven to the current fifteen members by the addition of four non-permanent seats (A/RES/1991A (XVIII) of 17 December 1963). Although only one permanent member voted in favor of the reform (China), all remaining (permanent) members subsequently ratified the amendments to the Charter. Apart from the enlargement of the Economic and Social Council, the reform of the Security Council marks the only successful use of Article 108 to revise the Charter. Attempts to enlarge the Council to 21 members, made ever since the 1970s by a smaller group of states led by India, remained without success until 1993, when the Working Group on reform was established (*Koroula/Kanninen* 1995; *Winkelmann* 1997).

12. The Debate on Reform

The Working Group on reform of the Security Council has met frequently since 1993 and has since published annual reports, each of which has been taken note of by the General Assembly. Extensive consultations have been held on thematic "clusters" – enlargement (cluster I) and working methods (cluster II). Numerous opinions on both these topics have been submitted by individual member states and both Chairpersons of the group. The spring of 1997 saw the submission of the first comprehensive proposal for the reform of the Security Council, the so-called "Razali Plan" (named after Razali Ismail, at the time the Malaysian President of the General Assembly), which led to a crystallization of the group's work. The plan

(*United Nations* 1997) foresaw enlarging the Security Council by five permanent seats (three for the developing countries from the three major regions, two for industrialized states) and up to four non-permanent members, thus creating a future total of 24 members. This goal, which takes into account the interests of both larger and smaller states in better representation, would be part of a framework plan to be adopted by the General Assembly. As a second step, the candidates for a permanent seat would present their case to the General Assembly. And as a third step, the resulting substantive Charter amendments would be adopted on the basis of Article 108 of the UN Charter. The original five permanent members would agree to use their right of veto only if clearly defined conditions were met, and to give reasons for each exercise of their veto. The new permanent members would have the same veto rights, or at least a collective veto right (to be exercised by two of the new members together) limited to Chapter VII for a transitional period. All reform steps would be reviewed by the General Assembly after 10-15 years (so-called periodic review).

Supporters of the "Razali-Plan" have tried to improve on its details. States which reject the proposal have used procedural means to block it (e.g. Italian draft resolution UN Doc. A/52/L.7 of 22 October 1997; opposing this, the German proposals in UN Doc. A/52/L.47 of 1 December 1997; the discussions resulted in Resolution A/RES/53/30 of 1 December 1998, which provides for a legally dubious vote by two-thirds of the members of the UN beyond the scope of Article 108 of the UN Charter).

The fact that the intensive reform debate has so far failed to produce results is not due to a shortage of legitimate candidates willing to become permanent members of the Security Council. Brazil, Egypt, Germany, India, Indonesia, Japan, Nigeria and South Africa have all directly or indirectly let their ambitions be known. The reason that progress is so slow lies rather in the regional animosities among countries in the South (Argentina and Mexico vs. Brazil, Pakistan vs. India, Egyptian mistrust of Nigeria and South Africa) as well as in sensitivities in the North (China vis-à-vis Japan, Italy vis-à-vis Germany). Tactical considerations provide an additional brake (e.g. Egypt's and Indonesia's interest in winning more time).

13. Models for Reform

Beside the "Razali-Plan" (see para. 12 above), more than a dozen proposals for enlarging the Security Council have been submitted in the course of the discussions. Consultations between the Finnish and Thai Chairpersons and 165 member states in the spring of 1997 showed that a very large majority favored increasing the number of both permanent and non-permanent seats. New permanent members (five) should, in their opinion, be selected from the developing and industrialized countries. Total figures ranging from 26 to the "low twenties" were mentioned (UN Doc. A/51/147 (Supplement No. 47) of 8 August 1997, Annex VII).

There is agreement that in the course of implementing the possible options, the working methods of the Council may also be altered and anchored in its Rules of Procedure. Such changes would for example concern the participation of non-members in discussions (Articles 31 and 32 of the UN Charter), discussions with non-members who provide troops, improved and accelerated communication of the substance of informal consultations, cushioning the effect of sanctions regimes on third states, working methods in the Sanctions Committees (cluster II topics, see above; cf. *Alvarez* 1995).

14. New Initiatives 2003

In 2003, the then Secretary-General *Annan* urged member states in his famous "fork in the road" speech (cf. the record of the speech in: UN Doc. A/58/PV.7, 23 September 2003, 2-4) to tackle the topic of the composition of the Council with more urgency, in order to strengthen the legitimacy of the decisions of the

Council. The *High-level Panel on Threats, Challenges and Change* elaborated two enlargement options in its 2004 report "A more secure world" (UN Doc. A/59/565 of 12 December 2004). In 2005, *Annan* took these options up in his report "In Larger freedom" (UN Doc. A/59/2005 of 21 March 2005). "Model A" provided for a total of 24 council seats, among them six new permanent (with no veto) and three new non-permanent seats. "Model B" provided for 24 seats as well, creating 9 new non-permanent seats of which 8 would be renewable every four years Both models represented in essence main streams that had developed during discussions in the past within the relevant Working Group (see para. 12 above).

15. Comprehensive Draft-Resolutions

Following a thorough debate of the two models, three draft-resolutions were introduced into the General Assembly, marking thus an important new development of the debate. Together with 24 co-sponsors, Brazil, Germany, India and Japan presented in July 2005 a draft-solution based on "Model A" and the "Razali-Plan", with 25 seats and two new permanent seats for Africa (UN Doc. A/59/L.64). A week later, 43 member states of the African Union presented a draft resolution proposing a Council of 26 seats, including two permanent and five non-permanent seats for Africa (UN Doc. A/59/L.67). A third group, 12 UN member states led by Italy, followed shortly later with yet another draft-resolution that proposed 5 permanent and 20 non-permanent members, the latter being re-eligible, with the consent of the respective $\rightarrow$ regional groups (UN Doc. A/59/L.68). The debate of the draft resolutions did not result in a vote however, mainly due to Chinese and US resistance and a lack of resolve of the African Union and its members to go ahead and vote. The World Summit Outcome in autumn 2005 limited itself to supporting an early reform of the Security Council

(UN Doc. A/RES/60/1, 16 September 2005, *United Nations* 2005, para. 153).

The President of the General-Assembly nominated in 2007 five "facilitators" to conduct consultations with the membership on how to move the process forward. In reports of May and of June 2007 (see UN Doc. A/61/47, annexes), the facilitators made an attempt to outline an intermediary approach, entailing inter alia the creation of a category of Council membership not currently provided for in the Charter.

16. European Action

The idea of a European seat on the Security Council has been repeatedly put forward by Italy. Given the current stage reached by the Common Foreign and Security Policy (CFSP) (→ European Union, Common Foreign and Security Policy at the UN), plans for a European seat must be considered as not yet adequately thought through and presently unrealistic (*Winkelmann* 1998 and 2003). Bearing in mind the detailed regime set out in Article 19 TEU, no state of the European Union (EU) – with the exception of Italy – has therefore spoken out in favor of such a seat. A European seat would only be attainable if France and the United Kingdom were to combine the two seats they have at present. And if there were a permanent EU seat, none of the 27 EU partners, who together provide almost 40% of the UN budget, could stand for election to a non-permanent seat of their own. In the General Assembly too, the 27 EU votes would have to be reduced to only one. The presence of Europe would thus be diminished rather than enhanced. Any future development of the CFSP will have to create ways to overcome these contradictions.

17. The Way Ahead

The UN remains an indispensable forum for crisis management and discussion. The Security Council is its central decision-making body and "location of transnational agreement" (*von Simson* 1993). Without having its structures thoroughly overhauled and adapted to economic and political realities, the Council will not be able to fulfil its role in the long term (*Kühne/Baumann* 1995). The Iraq crisis 2003 showed that the authority of the Council, upon which its decisions are founded, is suffering. Only by amending Article 23 *et seq.* of the Charter comprehensively can this trend be averted. Today, the General Assembly has available substantial draft resolutions to vote for reform of the Council. If interim approaches are helpful in supporting this process, they should be used. Both – interim approaches and final reform – depend on the political will of the (two-thirds) majority of the UN membership.

Ingo Winkelmann

Lit.: *Alvarez, J.:* The Once and Future Security Council, in: WQ, Spring 1995, 5-20; *Aust, A.:* The procedure and the practice of the Security Council today, in: Dupuy, R.-J. (ed.): Le développement du rôle du conseil de sécurité, The Hague 1995, 365-374; *Bailey, S.D.:* The UN Security Council and Human Rights, New York 1994; *Bailey, S.D./Daws, S.:* The procedure of the UN Security Council, 3rd edn., Oxford 1998; *Bedjaoui, M.:* The New World Order and the Security Council, Dordrecht 1994; *Blum, Y.:* Proposals for UN Security Council Reform, in: AJIL 99 (2005), 632-649; *Bourantis, D.:* The History and Politics of UN Security Council Reform, London 2005; *Bruha, T.:* Security Council, in: Wolfrum, R. (ed.): United Nations: Law, Policies and Practice, Vol. 2, Munich/Dordrecht 1995, 1147-1161; *Delbrück, J.:* Arts. 24 and 25, in: Simma, B. (ed.): The Charter of the United Nations. A Commentary, Vol. I, 2nd edn., Oxford 2002, 442-464; *Delon, F.:* Le rôle joué par les membres permanents dans l'action du conseil de sécurité, in: Dupuy, R.-J. (ed.): Le développement du rôle du conseil de sécurité, The Hague 1995, 349-364; *Delpech, T.:* Dreierdiplomatie der Zukunft, in: IP 54 (5/1999), 33-66, *Dupuy, R.-J. (ed.):* Le développement du rôle du conseil de sécurité, The Hague 1995; *Eitel, T.:* Auswirkungen von Erklärungen des Sicherheitsrats auf das nationale Recht, Sitzungsbericht Q zum 60. Deutschen Juristentag, 1994; *Eitel, T.:* Bewährungsproben für den Sicherheitsrat der Vereinten Nationen, in: FW 74 (1999), 1-2, 126 ff.; *Fassbender, B.:* UN Security Council Reform and the Right of Veto, The Hague 1998; *Fassbender, B.:* All illusions shattered? In: Max Planck Yearbook of United Nations Law 7 (2003), 183-218; *Franck, T.,* Collective Security and UN reform, in: Chicago Journal of International Law 6 (2000), 597-611; *Geiger, R.:* Art. 23: in: Simma, B. (ed.): The Charter of the United Nations. A Commentary, Vol. I, 2nd edn., Munich/ Oxford 2002, 437-442; *Herdegen, M.:* Der Sicherheitsrat und die autoritative Konkretisierung des VII. Kapitels der UN-Charta, in: FS R. Bernhardt, Berlin 1995, 103-119; *Hoffmann, W.:* United Nations Security Council Reform and Restructuring, Livingston/USA 1994; *Hofstötter, B.:* Einige Anmerkungen zur Reform des Sicherheitsrats der Vereinten Nationen, in: ZaöRV 66 (2006), 143-165; *Jahn-Koch, I./Wasum-Rainer, S.:* Art. 30, in: Simma, B. (ed.): The Charter of the United Nations. A Commentary, Vol. I, 2nd edn., Munich/Oxford 2002, 563-572; *Klein, E.:* Die Internationalen und Supranationalen Organisationen als Völkerrechtssubjekte, in: Graf Vitzthum, W. (ed.): Völkerrecht, 3rd edn., Berlin 2004, 295-356; *Koroula E./ Kanninen, T.:* Reforming the Security Council: The international negotiating process with the context of calls to amend the UN Charter in the new realities of the Post-Cold War era, in: Leiden Journal of International Law 8 (1995), 337-346; *Kühne, W./Baumann, B.:* Reform des VN-Sicherheitsrats zum 50jährigen Jubiläum, Ebenhausen 1995; *Müller, J. (ed.):* Reforming the United Nations, Leiden 2006; *Oellers-Frahm, K.:* Die Einsetzung des „Internationalen Tribunals über Kriegsverbrechen im ehemaligen Jugoslawien" durch den Sicherheitsrat, in: FS R. Bernhardt, Berlin 1995, 733-751; *Permanent Mission of the Federal Republic of Germany:* Reform of the Security Council. The German Position, Vol. I/Vol. II, New York 1996/1997; *Rivlin, B.:* UN Reform from the standpoint of the United States, Tokyo 1996; *Schäfer, M.:* Die Funktionsfähigkeit des Sicherheitsmechanismus der Vereinten Nationen, Berlin 1981; *Simma, B./Brunner, S./ Kaul, H-P.:* Art. 27, in: Simma, B. (ed.): The Charter of the United Nations. A Commentary, Vol. I, 2nd edn., Oxford 2002, 476-523; *Simson, W. von:* Der Staat als Teil und als Ganzes, Baden-Baden 1993; *United Nations - General Assembly:* Open-Ended Working Group on the Question of Equitable Representation on and Increase in the Membership of the Security Council and Other Matters Related to the Security Council. Conference Room Paper by the Bureau, 29 May 1997, UN Doc. A/AC.247/1997/CRP.8 (quoted as United Nations 1997), retrievable in the Internet under: www.globalpolicy.org/security/docs/crp8.htm; *United Nations - General Assembly:* 2005 World Summit Outcome, 16 September 2005, UN Doc. A/RES/60/1 (quoted as United Nations 2005); *Unser, G.:* Die UNO - Aufgaben und Strukturen der Vereinten Nationen, 6th edn., Munich 1997, 85-112; *Varwick, J./Zimmermann, A. (eds.):* Die Reform der Vereinten Nationen – Bilanz und Perspektiven, Berlin 2006; *Volger, H.:* Die Reform der Vereinten Nationen, in: Volger, H. (ed.): Grundlagen und Strukturen der Vereinten Nationen, Munich/Vienna 2007; 487-571; *Volger, H.:* Geschichte der Vereinten Nationen, 2nd edn., Munich/ Vienna 2008; *Voorhoeve, J.:* Lehren für die Zukunft – UN-Friedenssicherung im Wandel, in: IP 53 (1998), 41-48; *Willens, K. C.:* Resolutions and Statements of the UN Security Council (1946-1992): a thematic guide, Dordrecht 1993; *Winkelmann, I.:* Bringing the Security Council into a New Era, in: Max Planck Yearbook of United Nations Law 1 (1997), 35-90; *Winkelmann, I.:* Germany's Role in the Security Council of the United Nations – Past and Present Engagement, Future Participation and European Accentuation, in: GYIL 46 (2003) 30-63.

Internet: a) Website with background information on the Security Council, members, functions and powers, sanctions: www.un. org/Docs/scinfo.htm; b) link to SC resolutions: www.un.org/documents/scres.htm; link to other SC documents: www.un.org/Docs/ sc.htm.

Self-Determination, Right of

I. History

Self-determination has become of relevance for international law, partially arising from the so-called "Fourteen Points" of US President Wilson as presented to the drafters of the Paris Peace Treaties following World War I. This document combines the philosophical idea of self-determination with the concept of nation state. This combination of concepts allowed peoples to establish their own state, or at least to develop their autonomy within the framework of a multi-ethnic state. In the activities of the → League of Nations the principle of self-determination played a role in connection with the protection of minorities (→ Minorities, Protection of)

657

and with the mandated territories. During World War II the principle of self-determination influenced the Anti-Hitler Coalition. This is reflected in the so-called *Atlantic Charter*, a declaration of principles concerning the concept of the post-war world order formulated by US President Roosevelt and the British Prime Minister Churchill in 1941 during a meeting on board of a ship on the Atlantic (→ History of the Foundation of the UN). In this charter they declared the respect of the right of all peoples to choose the form of government under which they will live. During the codification of the UN Charter (→ Charter of the UN) the Soviet Union proposed to include in the document an obligation to respect the equality and self-determination of all peoples. This obligation is explicitly mentioned in Article 1 (2) and 55 of the UN Charter. The wording of those articles makes it clear that self-determination is a principle and not a legally binding norm. Its realization is one of the aims of the world organization. It was the state practice which developed the legal quality of the right of self-determination as customary international law (analysis see *Thürer* 1985). Of utmost importance for the development of the right of self-determination was the process of → decolonization. The struggle for independence by the peoples under colonial rule has been supported mainly by A/RES/1514 (XV), adopted by the General Assembly on 14 December 1960, the Declaration on the Granting of Independence to Colonial Countries and Peoples, which explicitly speaks of the right of all peoples to self-determination. GA Resolution A/RES/1803 (XVII) of 14 December 1962 (Permanent Sovereignty over Natural Resources) contains also a list of rights of peoples which are in that case limited to the economic aspect of self-determination. The International Covenant on Civil and Political Rights (→ Human Rights Conventions, CCPR) and the International Covenant on Economic, Social and Cultural Rights (→ Human Rights Conventions, CESCR) of 16 December 1966, represent the codification

of the subjective right of all peoples to self-determination. The so-called "Friendly Relations Declaration" of the General Assembly (Declaration on Principles of International Law concerning Friendly Relations and Co-operation among States in accordance with the Charter of the UN, UN Doc. A/RES/2625 (XXV) of 24 October 1970) confirms this right. The economic aspect of that norm has been underlined by resolution A/RES/3281 (XXIX) of 12 December 1974 (Charter of Economic Rights and Duties). Today self-determination is the "guiding principle of legitimacy underlying the international law order" (*Thürer* 1995), which regulates the relationship between states and peoples: according to this understanding of self-determination state sovereignty (→ Sovereignty) is not an end in itself, but is to protect the rights of the people and the human rights, as sovereignty is only justified as long as it serves these fundamental purposes.

II. Normative Content

In modern international law there is no doubt about the existence of the legally binding norm of self-determination (*Tomuschat* 1983; *Tomuschat* 1993). Already in 1975 in the Western Sahara Advisory Opinion (ICJ Reports 1971, 31 and ICJ Reports 1975, 31ff.) the International Court of Justice (→ ICJ) spoke of a "right to self-determination". In the Nicaragua Case the ICJ underlined explicitly the customary law character of that norm (ICJ Reports 1986, 14ff.). The inclusion of the right to self-determination in the two UN Human Rights Covenants supplemented the international customary law character by treaty law. The numerous cases of decolonization in the sixties and seventies have confirmed the opinion in international law that the right to self-determination in this context has acquired a quality of *ius cogens* (*Kadelbach* 1992). Thus, the ILC found that the right to self-determination was – after the norm of the prohibition of aggression by the state – was the second most mentioned norm of international law which was quoted by the states as example for a *ius cogens* norm (YBILC 1976 II/2, 121).

III. Contents of the Right of Self-Determination

The most authoritative and comprehensive formulation has been given by the UN General Assembly in the "Friendly Relations Declaration" of 1970. According to this document, "all peoples have the right freely to determine without external interference their political status and to pursue their economic, social and cultural development", and "every state has the duty to respect this right in accordance with the provisions of the Charter". This declaration (→ Resolution, Declaration, Decision) does not differentiate between the external and internal aspect of self-determination, however state practice and the literature often do.

External self-determination means a change in the legal status of a territory, and is therefore "the core aspect of the right to self-determination" (*Murswiek* 1994). According to the Friendly Relations Declaration there are three possible "modes of implementing" that right: "[t]he establishment of a sovereign and independent State, the free association or integration with an independent State or the emergence into any other political status freely determined by a people". As yet the state practice does not provide clear rules in connection with external self-determination (ICJ Reports 1975, 110). It is obvious that there is tension between the norm of external self-determination and equally important norm of sovereign equality of states, which includes respect for the territorial integrity and the internal affairs of states. Under these circumstances, the acceptance of the norm of self-determination by the states results from the insight that every state which does not represent the will of its people is not really a stable one. Immediately after the decline of suppression such a state will break down (*Oeter* 1992). The right of a people to establish its own state is *ipso jure*: there is no need to fulfill any precondition. Even the annexa-

tion by another state – as in East Timor until 1999 – does not abrogate the right of a people to self-determination. There is no doubt that international law connects the right to self-determination directly with the right to establish an independent and sovereign a state. This became evident when the ILO Convention 169 (Convention Concerning Indigenous and Tribal Peoples in Independent Countries) was drafted in 1989 (→ ILO). When the signatory states of this convention accepted that the indigenous form "peoples" and not only "populations", it was specified in Article 1 (3) of the Convention that the "use of the term 'peoples' in this Convention shall not be construed as having any implications as regards the rights which may attach to the term under international law". However, the establishment of an independent and sovereign state is not necessarily the consequence of the implementation of the right to self-determination. This was made clear by the ICJ in an Advisory Opinion on Western Sahara (ICJ Reports 1975, 12). There are also other possible forms of political status which can be freely determined by a people as a mode of implementing the right of self-determination, and the possibility of the free association or integration with another state. The right to self-determination does not exist independently; the international community has been involved in guiding and accompanying peoples striving for self-determination continuously, in the phase of decolonization as well as later on. The implementation of the right to self-determination concerns issues affecting the foundations of the international system and the world order, respectively, and therefore is no longer an internal affair of one people, if the competent organs of the UN so decide (*Tomuschat* 1995). In the case of former Yugoslavia, the community of states has practiced its right of co-determination to a large extent. In 1991, during the beginning of the crisis, most states rejected the demand for secession of Slovenia and Croatia, but changed their position after the use of force by the Yugoslavian People's Army, and after the failure of mediation attempts. The community of states accepted step by step the demand for independence by the different peoples of the Yugoslav republics (*Weller* 1992).

The implementation of the right to self-determination in the present world is surrounded by controversy. Doubtless it has been one of great successes of the UN to establish procedures for the implementation of the right to self-determination of colonial peoples which led in the long run to the end of the European colonial empires. However, even this process has not been free of contradictions. One of these contradictions, which had far-reaching consequences, is that newly independent states were obliged to respect their own borders, even if these had been drawn arbitrarily by the former colonial power, dividing the traditional territories of ethnic groups (*uti possidetis* principle). The ICJ has underlined in the Border Dispute between Burkina Faso and Mali the legal importance of the *uti possidetis* principle and has called it a general principle which is logically attached to independence, because it protects the stability of newly independent states (ICJ Reports 1986, 554). In close relationship with external self-determination, there is the controversial problem of secession. Secession is the separation of part of territory of a state carried out by the resident population with the aim of creating a new and independent state. The predecessor states continue to exist within new borders, but remain – from a legal point of view – identical as subjects of international law. Secession violates the territorial integrity of the existing state. Therefore some authors insist that secession is a violation of international law. Also the UN has in the past rejected demands of secession. This position was underlined by the former UN Secretary-General U Thant concerning Biafra: "[T]he United Nations has never accepted and does not accept and I do not believe it will ever accept the principle of secession of a part of its Member State" (UN Chronicle, No. 2/1970,

660

10). Therefore the Biafra case was never debated in the UN. The Friendly Relations Declaration can be interpreted as an endorsement of the right to secession in cases in which the government does not represent the whole people without discrimination. In cases where severe acts of discriminations against a people occur, the right of self-determination provides the people with a kind of right of self-defense, which can be enforced even by the use of force: the secession would be a kind of defense of fundamental human rights. In general, international lawyers do not reject legality of secession completely, but underline its exceptional character. However, there is no international law instrument prohibiting or allowing secession. To avoid problems of secession, many authors recommend that autonomy regulations allow the implementation of the right to self-determination (*Suksi* 1998, *Tomuschat* 1993).

The issue of internal self-determination deals with the relationship between peoples and their governments because it empowers peoples to determine the internal order of a state. The term internal self-determination was first used by Indonesia in 1949 when the UN demanded that the population of a territory be allowed to determine by a democratic procedure the status of their territory.

Due to the fact that this is in principle an internal affair of every state, most states have attempted – for reasons connected with their sovereignty – to emphasize the external aspect of the right to self-determination. This is reflected by resolutions passed every year by the UN General Assembly on the topic of the agenda "Universal Realization of the Right of Peoples to Self-Determination" (for example A/RES/51/84 of 28 February 1997). These resolutions deal only with external self-determination. However the impressive number of resolutions condemning the apartheid policy of South Africa tends to support the conclusion that internal developments within a country may also be regarded as violations of the right to self-determination. This does not mean that international law prescribes specific forms of government, for example the democratic form, and prohibits other forms. If a people chooses another kind of state organization, then the international community has no right to interfere in that decision.

The international community does not evaluate different political systems; the UN Charter only demands of the states in its preamble "to practice tolerance and live together in peace with one another as good neighbors". In the Nicaragua Case the ICJ reaffirmed that ideological questions are not part of international law regulations (ICJ Reports 1986, 263). The proposal to lay down in the UN Charter that all UN member states should be constituted democratically came up already during the codification of the UN Charter in San Francisco in 1945, but was rejected as interference in internal affairs of member states (*Ginther* 1994). The only exception of the indifference of international law towards different political systems are Nazi and fascist regimes. Those ideologies have, for example, been condemned expressly by the General Assembly in resolution A/RES/36/162 of 16 December 1981. Yet, after the Cold War many authors underline the democratic component of the right to self-determination. They argue that self-determination means that peoples have the right to play an active role in the determination of their affairs in freedom and equality. Exactly that is the main feature and normative content, respectively, of democracy (*Heintze* 1998). Another connection between self-determination and democracy is their common origin, and the fact that free self-determination is a precondition for any comprehensive implementation of human rights.

Self-determination involves also an economic aspect. It results from the formulation of Article 1. (1), second sentence of both Human Rights Covenants, from Article 47 of the International Covenant on Civil and Political Rights and Article 25 of the International Covenant on Economic, Social and Cultural Rights. According to those articles all peoples freely determine their economic development and freely dispose of their natural wealth and resources, without prejudice to any obligation arising out of international economic cooperation. Self-determination means therefore a permanent sovereignty of peoples in that field.

V. The Holders of the Right to Self-Determination

The holders of the right of self-determination are the peoples. States do not need any recourse to that right because are sovereign. According to Article 1 of the Human Rights Covenants, all peoples are holders of the right to self-determination. This right is not limited to peoples under colonial oppression. In the past, however, some states have tried to limit this concept to colonially oppressed peoples. For example, there has been the reservation of India on Article 1 of the Covenant on Civil and Political Rights, saying that the scope of that treaty is limited to "peoples under foreign domination and that these words do not apply to sovereign independent States or to a section of a people or nation – which is the essence of national integrity."

France, Germany and the Netherlands rejected that reservation rightly and underlined that all peoples have the right to self-determination. Nevertheless, the question whether certain groups form a people or not is basically a question of ethnology. Therefore there is no binding definition of the term "people" in international law.

"Peoples" as holders of rights constitute a non-determined legal term which requires in each single case a specific determination, a determination which implies as well a decision about values. However, the state practice allows some general conclusions which groups of persons are being considered as peoples. Basics elements are, according to that state practice, a common feeling of identity and the political will to be a people. A fundamental precondition for demanding self-determination is the po-

661

litical organization of the people, and the establishment of bodies which represent the people (*Ermacora* 1983).

This organizing of a people is also the precondition for partial subjectivity of peoples under international law, because the peoples can bear – within a certain framework – legal rights and duties in international law.

Connected with that subjectivity is the question of the international recognition of representative bodies of peoples. Such a recognition is commonly understood as the acceptance of the demand of that people for self-determination by other states. The literature increasingly states that the act of recognition can have beside the declaratory effects also a constitutional one (*Hilpold* 1993).

One cannot exclude such a consequence in the case of the recognition of representative bodies of peoples. However, even non-recognition does mean automatically that a people has no right to self-determination.

According to state practice, the recognition of a people which is in the process of implementing its right to self-determination, is legal (*Dugard* 1987). The UN General Assembly recognized liberation movements as authorized representatives of peoples under colonial oppression in the 1970s, basing its decisions on recognition on decisions of the relevant regional organizations, which meant, in the case of southern Africa, the OAU, and in the case of Palestine the League of Arab Countries. The recognition by the UN was also the precondition for the establishment of an → observer status at the UN for national liberation movements. However the non-recognition by the UN does not automatically mean that the people concerned has no right to self-determination (*Tanca* 1993).

There is a strong tendency among the community of states to reduce the content of the norm of self-determination in its internal aspect.

The UN General Assembly Declaration on the Rights of Indigenous Peoples of 13 September 2007 (UN Doc. A/RES/61/295) is continuing this trend

that has been observed for quite some time. It appears that today's meaning of self-determination is found precisely in its internal aspect.

Article 3 of this Declaration repeats the content of Article 1 of the UN Human Rights Covenants – Article 4, however, limits this right by arguing that indigenous peoples "have the right to autonomy or self-government in matters relating to their internal and local affairs". Moreover Article 46 of the Declaration states explicitly that nothing in the Declaration "may be interpreted as implying for any … people … any right to engage in any activity or to perform any act contrary to the Charter of the United Nations or construed as authorizing or encouraging any action which would dismember or impair, totally or in part, the territorial integrity or political unity of sovereign and independent States."

Even this very weak understanding of self-determination was rejected by four leading states (the USA, Canada, Australia and New Zealand) with large indigenous peoples within their borders. Australia declared its dissatisfaction with the reference to self-determination in the Declaration and underlined its understanding that self-determination applied only to situations of decolonization and the break-up of states into smaller states with clearly defined population groups. These groups were denied political or civil rights.

This interpretation is not in accordance with the wording of the norm. However, this approach is quite common and therefore the states avoid applying the norm. Even in the case of Kosovo the international community did not mention the right to self-determination. Instead they prefer to argue, that the Kosovars were violated in their basic human rights and therefore it had not been any longer possible for them to live under Serbian rule.

It remains to be seen if the emerging new interpretation of sovereignty in the concept of the responsibility to protect since the 2005 world summit will also have an impact of the attitude of the multi-ethnic states with regard to the self-determination of the peoples living on their territory.

Hans-Joachim Heintze

Lit.: *Bayefsky, A.:* Self-determination in international law: Quebec and Lessons Learned, The Hague 2000; *Bowen, S. (ed.):* Human Rights, Self-determination and Political Change in the Occupied Palestinian Territories, The Hague 1997; *Brölmann, C. (ed.):* Peoples and Minorities in International Law, Dordrecht 1993; *Cassese, A.:* Self-Determination of Peoples – A Legal Reappraisal, Cambridge 1995; *Dugard, J.:* Recognition and the United Nations, Cambridge 1987; *Ermacora, F.:* The Protection of Minorities before the United Nations, The Hague 1983; *Fotrell, D. (ed.):* Minority and Group Rights in the New Millennium, The Hague 1999; *Ginther, K.:* Art. 4, in: Simma; B. (ed.): The Charter of the United Nations. A Commentary, 2nd edn., Oxford 2002, 177-194; *Heintze, H.-J.:* Selbstbestimmungsrecht und Minderheitenrechte im Völkerrecht, Baden-Baden 1994; *Heintze, H.-J. (ed.):* Selbstbestimmungsrecht der Völker – Herausforderung der Staatenwelt, Bonn 1997; *Heintze, H.-J.:* Selbstbestimmungsrecht und Demokratisierung, in: Reiter, E. (ed.): Jahrbuch für internationale Sicherheitspolitik 1999, Hamburg 1998; *Hilpold, P.:* Die Anerkennung der Neustaaten auf dem Balkan, in: AVR 31 (1993), 387-408; *Kadelbach, S.:* Zwingendes Völkerrecht, Berlin 1992; *Musgrave, Th. D.:* Self-determination and National Minorities, Oxford 1997, *Murswiek, D.:* Die Problematik eines Rechts auf Sezession – neu betrachtet, in: AVR 31 (1993), 307-332; *Nowak, M.:* CCPR-Commentary, Kehl 1993; *Oeter, S.:* Selbstbestimmungsrecht im Wandel, Überlegungen zur Debatte um Selbstbestimmung, Sezessionsrecht und "vorzeitige" Anerkennung, in: ZaöRV 52 (1992), 741-780; *Skurbaty, Z.A. (ed.):* Beyond the One-Dimensional State: An Emerging Right to Self-Determination, Leiden 2005; *Suksi, M. (ed.):* Autonomy: Applications and Implications, The Hague 1998; *Tanca, G. J.:* Foreign Armed Intervention in Internal Conflict, Dordrecht 1993; *Thürer, D.:* Self-Determination, in: Bernhardt, R. (ed): EPIL 8, Amsterdam 1985, 470-476; *Thürer, D.:* Der Wegfall effektiver Staatsgewalt: „The Failed State", in: Berichte der Deutschen Gesellschaft für Völkerrecht, Vol. 34, Heidelberg 1995, 9-45; *Tomuschat, C.:* The protection of minorities under Art. 27 of the International Covenant on Civil and Political Rights, in: Bernhardt, R. et al. (eds.): FS Hermann Mosler, Berlin 1983, 615-634; *Tomuschat, C. (ed.):* Modern Law of Self-determination, Dordrecht 1993; *Tomuschat, C.:* Die internationale Gemeinschaft, in: AVR 33 (1995), 1-20; *Weller, M.:* The International Response to the Dissolution of the Socialist Federal Republic of Yugoslavia, in: AJIL 86 (1992), 569-607; *Weller, M.:* The Self-Determination Trap, in: Ethnopolitics 4 (2005), 3-20; *Wenzel, N.:* Das Spannungsverhältnis zwischen Gruppenschutz und Individualschutz im Völkerrecht, Berlin 2008.

Sovereignty

According to a widely shared view, *sovereignty* has two complementary and mutually dependent dimensions: within a state, a sovereign power makes law with the assertion that this law is supreme and ultimate, *i.e.* that its validity does not depend on the will of any other, or "higher", authority. Externally, a sovereign power obeys no other authority. At the beginning of the modern state, the *internal dimension* of sovereignty addressed the problem of "intermediate" powers in a certain territory (such as a princedom or a city), independent in a legal or actual sense, which an emerging "central power" sought to subjugate. The *external claim* to sovereignty was directed against powers outside that territory. This latter dimension is today also referred to as "sovereignty in international law" or "independence".

The notion of sovereignty, which is closely related to the idea of the modern state, has an almost mythical quality. Although (or perhaps just because) its contours are so blurred, it has played a prominent role in modern constitutional and international legal theory, as well as in politics. Since the French jurist and philosopher Jean Bodin introduced the notion into the theory of state in the sixteenth century, it has been resorted to as an argument in a concrete political fight – as a description of what was desired or aspired to rather than of what really existed. At the beginning of the modern European system of states, the notion was used to establish and defend the independence of the French King from the Pope and the Emperor of the Holy Roman Empire, and the supremacy of the King's orders over those of particularistic powers in what became France. Today sovereignty of states is often used as an argument against a more intense political and economic integration on a regional as well as a universal level. (For the history of the idea of sovereignty, see *Hinsley* 1986, *Quaritsch* 1970 and 1986, and *Hofmann* 1967; for the etymology *Klippel/Boldt* 1990)

I. Historical Development

In its long history since the sixteenth century, the idea of sovereignty has proved highly adaptable. So far, it has survived many precipitous funeral speeches, and also the charges that it is standing in the way of a system of international governance adequate to ensure the future existence of mankind. The idea accompanied and fostered the rise of the modern rational state as an entity possessing comprehensive jurisdiction over a defined territory and the people living therein. However, it was only in the nineteenth century (at a time of decline of the doctrine of natural law according to which even a sovereign prince had been regarded as bound by certain fundamental rules of religious or moral origin) that a claim to an unrestrained power over the law was derived from the concept. The ideas of *sovereignty* and of the *nation state* joined, reinforcing each other and leading to what later was called the "anarchy of sovereignty" of the nineteenth and twentieth century (*Kimminich* 1997). Now the emphasis of the notion shifted from building and perfecting an effective state authority to competing with other nations. "Sovereign nation states", constructed and understood as closed, self-contained entities facing one another, fought over political, economic and military power. Understandably, in retrospect the idea of sovereignty was seen as having supported political developments that led to the two world wars.

Accordingly, the notion entered a state of crisis in the twenties of the last century and in particular after 1945. In Western Europe, it was countered with the new guiding idea of *supranationality*, which was meant to reconcile the autonomy of states with their intensified cooperation. In international law, the notion of *solidarity* of all member states of the *international community* was advanced. The transformation was described as a change from a *"law of co-existence"* to a *"law of cooperation"* – or a "move of international society from an essentially negative code of rules of abstention to positive rules of cooperation" (*Friedmann* 1964). On the other hand, the new states emerging from → decolonization strongly emphasized their sovereignty in order to consolidate their independence from the former colonial powers.

II. Sovereignty after 1945

Since the UN was established in 1945 (→ History of the Foundation of the UN), the traditional notion of sovereignty has experienced profound *modification and limitation*. In 1934, *Heller* still referred to sovereignty as a "highest, exclusive, irresistible and independent power" of a state. Today, such a power no longer exists, neither actually nor in a legal sense. Step-by-step, and following the experience of a steadily increasing interdependence of states, the "sovereign state" of the past, seen as essentially not bound by law, turned into a territorial organization with a large number of international legal obligations (arising with, without, and even against its will) – an organization which in the complex structure of the universal legal order is endowed with the highest degree of autonomy.

The → *Charter of the UN* does not speak of "sovereignty" as such but proclaims the "principle of the sovereign equality" of all members of the UN (Article 2 (1)), and the → General Assembly stated in its so-called "Friendly Relations Declaration" of 1970 ("Declaration on Principles of International Law concerning Friendly Relations and Cooperation among States in accordance with the Charter of the United Nations",

664

Annex to A/RES/2625 (XXV)), adopted by consensus: "All States enjoy sovereign equality. They have equal rights and duties and are equal members of the international community, notwithstanding differences of an economic, social, political or other nature." (for a commentary on Art. 2 (1), see *Fassbender/Bleckmann* 2002). This combination of *sovereignty* (which the Charter relegated to the position of an attributive adjective modifying the noun "equality") and *membership in the international community* makes it clear that, in the age of the UN, a state's right to independence is conditioned by its obligation to protect and promote community values and aims. In the UN system this obligation is put in concrete form by the binding decisions of the → Security Council (for the role and function of the Council in the international legal order, see *Fassbender* 1998b). In particular, no state can evade its obligation to respect and protect the fundamental → *human rights* of the persons under its jurisdiction. More recently, this idea has been expressed and strengthened by the concept of the "Responsibility to Protect". In the words of the 2005 World Summit Outcome, "[e]ach individual State has the responsibility to protect its populations from genocide, war crimes, ethnic cleansing and crimes against humanity. This responsibility entails the prevention of such crimes, including their incitement, through appropriate and necessary means" (UN Doc. A/RES/60/1 of 16 September 2005, para. 138). If necessary, the international community, through the Security Council, will take appropriate collective action to ensure that states exercise that responsibility. Increasingly, states are also held to be bound to observe basic principles of democratic government.

The *legal independence* of a state from other subjects of international law is a precondition for its sovereignty. "A state is sovereign if it is subject only to international law, *i.e.* if it is a direct and immediate subject of international law without any intervening authority" (*Verdross/Simma* 1984). At the same time,

sovereignty entails the right to political independence and territorial integrity. The General Assembly and the Security Council today usually refer to sovereignty as a part of this triangle of rights.

A sovereign state enjoys a principally unlimited international legal personality and capacity to perform international legal acts. This distinguishes it from other subjects of international law, in particular intergovernmental organizations, which have a limited legal personality defined by the respective founding treaty. One used to say that sovereign states are the only "natural" or "born" persons of international law, whereas all others are "made" in the sense that they are brought into existence by an act of international law. Because of their sovereignty, all states are juridically equal, the smallest just as much as the most powerful, and have, in principle, the same position in international conferences and organizations ("one state, one vote"). Sovereignty involves a right of participation in the international community. A sovereign state is protected by the prohibition of the threat or use of force (Art. 2 (4) UN Charter) (→ Use of Force, Prohibition of) and the duty of states not to intervene in matters within the domestic jurisdiction of any other state (→ Intervention, Prohibition of). In accordance with international law, a sovereign state is entitled freely to determine its constitution and its political, social, economic and cultural order, which the other members of the international community must respect. If a state has a democratic constitution, its sovereignty protects a space of democratic self-determination (→ Self-Determination, Right of). A sovereign state possesses jurisdiction over its citizens as well as over foreigners and stateless persons present in its territory (albeit limited by the obligation to safeguard their fundamental human rights and freedoms), and within its territory an exclusive power to use physical force to enforce its law. Further, a sovereign state has the right to determine its future legal status. It can, for instance, decide to form a union with, or to become an

665

integral part of, another state. Only sovereign states can become a member of the UN and most of the other intergovernmental organizations (→ Membership and Representation of States). In the age of the UN, the most important limitation of the rights formerly entailed in sovereignty is the abolition of the *jus ad bellum* (the right the wage war against another state) by the UN Charter. This instrument has put the international use of force under the exclusive control of the Security Council, the only exception being a state's temporary right to self-defense according to Article 51 (→ Collective Security).

Up to the present, the sovereign state is the "standard member" of the international community. It is regarded as an "indispensable element of the international legal order": "States have a special public interest task to fulfill ... [T]he complex structure of today's legal order is based on fully operational units of governance which assume the legal responsibilities enshrined in treaties and other sources [of international law] for their territorial areas of competence" (*Tomuschat* 1999). International law endeavors to maintain a uniform global system of sovereign states, and therefore sometimes generously attributes sovereignty to states whose independence is doubtful not only in actual but also in legal terms. The legal concept of a "non-sovereign state" today mainly serves the purpose of explaining the status of constituent parts of federal states (such as the United States of America, Germany or Switzerland) which for political and historical reasons are accorded a limited statehood by the respective federal constitution.

III. Constitutionalization of International Law

A more recent school of thought in international law understands the legal development of the international community since the foundation of the → League of Nations as a process of constitutionalization (see *Fassbender* 1998a; *Macdonald/Johnston* 2005). The adoption of the Covenant of the League in 1919 and, subsequently, the UN Charter is seen as a gradual effort to give the international community a constitution expressing systematically and in writing its fundamental values and the rules which shall protect them and ensure a peaceful coexistence and cooperation of all nations of the world. The international community is not just perceived as a sum, or addition, of the interests of the individual states but as an entity committed to humankind as a whole, having its own legal personality and purposes which it can set against the opinion and action of a recalcitrant state. This *constitutional approach to international law* seeks to reestablish a category of priority norms existing independently of the will of the individual states, in this formal quality similar to those norms which were accepted as natural law until the early nineteenth century. The approach recognizes a *hierarchy of rules* of international law in which the constitutional rules of the international community enjoy the highest rank and the greatest firmness. At the same time, the notion of constitution takes up elements of organization and institutionalization characteristic of modern state constitutions. It is this constitutional view of the present international legal order which leads to a *definition* of sovereignty that reflects the strongly increased orientation of the individual state towards community values and goals: *sovereignty is the legal authority and autonomy of a state as defined and guaranteed by the constitution of the international community* (cf. *Kelsen* 1944; *Fassbender* 2003). It denotes the entitlement of a state to autonomous development and self-responsibility within the limits set by international law. Accordingly, sovereignty is neither static nor "natural". In a process that has placed ever more constraints on the freedom of action of states, its substance has changed, and will further change in the future.

Bardo Fassbender

Lit.: *Fassbender, B.:* The U.N. Charter as Constitution of the International Community, in: ColJTransL 36 (1998), 529-619; *Fassbender, B.:* UN Security Council Reform and the Right of Veto: A Constitutional Perspective, The Hague et al. 1998; *Fassbender, B.:* Sovereignty and Constitutionalism in International Law, in: Walker, N. (ed.): Sovereignty in Transition, Oxford 2003, 115-143; *Fassbender, B./Bleckmann, A.:* Article 2 (1), in: Simma, B. et al. (eds.): The Charter of the United Nations: A Commentary, 2nd edn., Vol. I, Oxford 2002, 68-91; *Heller, H.:* Staatslehre, 1st edn. Leiden 1934, 6th edn., Tübingen 1983; *Hinsley, F.H.:* Sovereignty, 2nd edn., Cambridge 1986; *Kelsen, H.:* The Principle of Sovereign Equality of States as a Basis for International Organization, in: Yale Law Journal 53 (1944), 207-220; *Kimminich, O.:* Einführung in das Völkerrecht, 6th edn., Tübingen 1997; *Klippel, D./Boldt, H.:* Souveränität, in: Brunner, O. et al. (eds.): Geschichtliche Grundbegriffe, Vol. 6, Stuttgart 1990, 98-154; *Macdonald, R.St.J./Johnston, D.M. (eds.):* Towards World Constitutionalism: Issues in the Legal Ordering of the World Community, Leiden et al. 2005; *Quaritsch, H.:* Staat und Souveränität, Frankfurt (Main) 1970; *Quaritsch, H.:* Souveränität: Entstehung und Entwicklung des Begriffs in Frankreich und Deutschland vom 13. Jahrhundert bis 1806, Berlin 1986; *Tomuschat, C.:* International Law: Ensuring the Survival of Mankind on the Eve of a New Century. Collected Courses of the Hague Academy of International Law, Vol. 281 (1999), 1-438; *United Nations - General Assembly:* 2005 World Summit Outcome, 16 September 2005, UN Doc. A/RES/60/1; *Verdross, A./Simma, B.:* Universelles Völkerrecht, 3rd edn., Berlin 1984; *Volger, H.:* Geschichte der Vereinten Nationen, 2nd edn., Munich/Vienna 2008.

Space Law

Space law is made up of a series of international instruments that regulate the activity of states and private persons in the universe in which no → sovereignty exists. Space law was created in the framework of the United Nations when, in 1959, the → General Assembly founded for this purpose the *Committee on Peaceful Uses of Outer Space*

(COPUOS) with A/RES/1472 (XIV) of 12 December 1959.

The Vienna-based *United Nations Office for Outer Space Affairs* serves as secretariat for the Committee (www.oosa.unvienna.org). The Office disseminates space-related information to member states through its International Space Information System.

The *Treaty on Principles Governing the Activities of States, in the Exploration and Use of Outer Space, including the Moon and Other Celestial Bodies* of 27 January 1967 (UNTS No. 8843) has fundamental significance. It is commonly referred to as the *Outer Space Treaty*. It provides that exploration and utilization of outer space are to serve for the benefit of all states and all mankind (→ Common Heritage of Mankind). Outer Space is not subject to national appropriation, and should only be used for peaceful purposes. A contracting state is as much responsible for its activities as it is for private legal persons under its authority. Hence it is also liable for damages. The state will therefore demand from private persons acting in outer space a corresponding insurance coverage (*Reijnen* 1992). The *Convention on International Liability for Damage Caused by Space Objects* ("Liability Convention") of 29 March 1972 stipulates for the first time an unlimited international absolute liability. According to this, the launching state is liable for damages that were caused on the surface of the earth or to aircraft in flight. In the event of damage in outer space, however, liability for intentional and negligent acts is applicable, although this has been frequently criticized as impracticable. The *Agreement Governing the Activities of States on the Moon and Other Celestial Bodies* ("Moon Agreement"), adopted by the General Assembly with A/RES/34/68 on 5 December 1979 (UNTS Vol. 1363, No. 23002), provides that the moon and its natural resources are the common heritage of mankind and consequently should only be explored on the basis of an international order, when this becomes technically possible. Thus the

Moon Agreement corresponds to the concept of a New International Economic Order (→ International Economic Relations and New International Economic Order (NIEO)), and that is why it has also not been ratified by the leading outer space powers. The *Convention on Registration of Objects Launched into Outer Space* ("Registration Convention"), adopted by the General Assembly with A/RES/3235 (XXIX) on 12 November 1974 (UNTS Vol. 1023, No. 15020), obliges all contracting states to establish a system of registration of these objects, and to provide the UN with registration number, date and location of the launch, basic orbital parameters and the basic function, which seems to be practicable with regard to eventual questions of liability. In practice, however, the outer space powers do not so far comply adequately with these obligations. The *Agreement on the Rescue of Astronauts, the Return of Astronauts, and the Return of Objects Launched into Outer Space* ("Rescue Agreement"), adopted in 1967 by the General Assembly with A/RES/2345 (XXII), aims at providing international assistance in event of emergency.

Beside these treaties, a number of resolutions of the UN General Assembly belong to the codex of space law. Of these resolutions, of paramount importance is A/RES/37/92 of 1 December 1982, containing the *Principles Governing the Use by States of Artificial Earth Satellites for International Direct Television Broadcasting*. This instrument stipulates that broadcasting above a foreign state is subject to prior consent. Western states consider this provision as a limitation of the freedom of information, and therefore voted against this resolution. On the other hand the *Principles Relating to Remote Sensing of the Earth from Space* (A/RES/41/65 of 2 December 1986) were adopted by consensus. According to this resolution, such sensing requires the prior consent of the observed state. However, this list of principles is characterized by a number of deficits which limit its significance. For example, it is only applicable to civil remote sensing. Military satellites are thereby excluded, as is the increasing dual use (the simultaneous civil and military utilization) of celestial bodies. Moreover, commercialization was not taken into account (*von Kries* 1996). Finally, adherence to the principles cannot be controlled. By A/RES/47/68 of 14 December 1992 *Principles Relevant to the Use of Nuclear Power Sources in Outer Space* were adopted. They represent an important step towards a limitation of nuclear power sources to the absolutely necessary, and are supposed to prepare the ground for legally binding rules (*Benkö et. al.* 1997). Up to now the latter have not yet been agreed upon.

The *Declaration on International Cooperation in the Exploration and Use of Outer Space for the Benefit and in the Interest of All States, Taking into Particular Account the Needs of Developing Countries* (A/RES/51/122 of 13 December 1996) is the outcome of North-South dialogue which has been continuing since 1988 and had been confrontational for quite some time before consensus was reached. This declaration gives the obligations for cooperation as provided in the Outer Space Treaty a concrete shape, by calling upon the outer space powers to cooperate in the use of the universe for the mutual benefit of all.

This effective decrease of confrontation is symptomatic for modern space law (*Heintze* 1994). Likewise, the Third UN Conference on the Exploration and Peaceful Uses of Outer Space (UNISPACE III) in Vienna in 1999 has underlined in its basic documents (the "Vienna Declaration on Space and Human Development" and the "UNISPACE III Action Plan") the goal of a common and mutually beneficial use of outer space research (cf. press release UNISPACE III SPACE/V/9, 30 July 1999). Further current problems of space law are the regulations concerning outer space debris (space rubbish) and the protection of life on earth against space dangers (*Benkö/Schrögl* 1997).

Yet the exact scope of application of space law is still not agreed upon in detail: the precise delimitation between outer space without jurisdiction, and air space belonging to state territory, has not up to now not been codified , thus states still consider as valid in international law a customary delimitation at 100-110 km above the surface of the earth.

Scholars regret a decline of the normative power of space law. The Outer Space Treaty of 1967, as an example, has been ratified by 98 states and signed by further 27 states (as of 1 January 2008). However, the Moon Treaty of 1979 counts only thirteen ratifications and 4 signatures (as of 1 January 2008). Increasingly, it is up to the General Assembly to interpret obligations of the community of states concerning the outer space (see *United Nations* 2007a and 2007b). These activities are important but cannot replace the establishment of legally binding agreements.

Other recent challenges of space law constitute the increasing space tourism and the enactment of national space laws by many states. The national laws are important instruments to guarantee the responsibilities of states for the activities of non-state actors in outer space.

The US President authorized in August 31, 2006 a new national space policy (National Security Presidential Directive 49, text: www.fas.org/irp/offdocs/nspd/indec.html) which plays an important role against the background of the planned space based defense shield. During the negotiations it was argued that the existing space law does not prohibit the placing or using of weapons, with exception of weapons of mass destruction, in and through space.

Scholars consider this approach troubling because legitimate concerns about national security cannot sweep aside the existing treaty and customary law. Especially there are some concerns that the activities of the USA might lead to the militarization of outer space which is not in accordance with the agreed use of this space in the interest of whole mankind and only for peaceful purposes.

Hans-Joachim Heintze

Lit.: *Abeyratne, P.:* The Use of Nuclear Power Sources in Outer Space and its Effect on Environmental Protection, in: JSL 25 (1997), 17-28; *Benkö, M./Schrogl, K.:* The UN Committee on the Peaceful Uses of Outer Space: Adoption of a Declaration on 'Space Benefits' and Other Recent Developments, in: ZLW 46 (1997), 228-248; *Dallmeyer, D.G./Tsipis, K. (eds.):* Heaven and Earth: Civilian Uses of Near-Earth Space, The Hague 1996; *Diederiks-Verschoor, I.H./Kopal, V.:* An Introduction to Space Law, 3rd edn., Gif-sur-Yvette 2008; *Goedhart, R.:* The Never-Ending Dispute: Delimitation of Air Space and Outer Space, Gif-sur-Yvette 1996; *Gorove, S.:* Cases on Space Law: Texts, Comments and References, Mississippi 1996; *Heintze, H.-J.:* Entwicklungstendenzen des Weltraumrechts, in: ZLW 43 (1994), 293-306; *Hettling J.K.:* Satellite imagery for verification and enforcement of public international law, Cologne 2008; *Jasani, B. (ed.):* Peaceful and Non-Peaceful Uses of Space, New York 1991; *Kries, W. v.:* The UN Remote Sensing Principles of 1986 in Light of Subsequent Developments, in: ZLW 45 (1996), 166-179; *Malanczuk, P.:* Review of the Regulatory Regime Governing the Space Environment: The Problem of Space Debris, in: ZLW 45 (1996), 37-62; *Meredith, P.L./Robinson, G.S.:* Space Law: A Case Study for the Practitioner, Dordrecht 1992; *Mosteshar, S. (ed.):* Research and Invention in Outer Space: Liability and Intellectual Property Rights, Dordrecht 1995; *Reijnen, B.:* The United Nations Space Treaties Analysed, Gif-sur-Yvette 1992; *Robinson, G.S.:* The U.S. National Space Policy: Pushing the Limits of Space Treaties?, in: ZLW 56 (2007), 45-57; *United Nations – General Assembly - Committee on the Peaceful Uses of Outer Space:* Space debris mitigation guidelines of the Scientific and Technical Subcommittee of the Committee on the Peaceful Uses of Outer Space, 6 March 2007, UN Doc. A/AC.105/890, Annex IV; *United Nations - General Assembly:* Recommendations on Enhancing the Practices of States and International Intergovernmental Organizations in registering Space Objects, UN Doc. A/RES/62/101 of 17 December 2007 (quoted as United Nations 2007a); *United Nations - General Assembly:* International cooperation in the peaceful uses of outer space, UN Doc. A/RES/62/217 of 22 December 2007 (quoted as United Nations 2007b); *United States of America:* U.S. National Space Policy. National Security Presidential Directive (NSPD) 46, www.fas.org/irp/offdocs/nspd/index.html; *Viikari, L.:*

The Environmental Element in Space Law, 2008; *Wertz, J.R. (ed.):* Reducing Space Mission Cost, Dordrecht 1996.

Internet: Information on space law on the homepage of the UN Office for Outer Space Affairs, website for space law: www.oosa. unvienna.org/SpaceLaw/; information on the UNISPACE III Conference in Vienna: www. un.org/events/unispace3/

Specialized Agencies

I. Introduction

According to the → Charter of the United Nations specialized agencies are intergovernmental organizations which are brought into relationship with the United Nations in accordance with the provisions of Article 57 and 63 of the Charter, in order to promote the goals of the United Nations as postulated in Article 55 of the Charter:

"(a) higher standards of living, full employment, and conditions of economic and social progress and development;

(b) solutions of international economic, social, health, and related problems; and international cultural and educational co-operation; and

(c) universal respect for, and observance of, human rights and fundamental freedoms for all without distinctions as to race, sex, language, or religion."

With the foundation of the United Nations the pre-conditions for a broad range of specialized agencies were created which have "wide international responsibilities, as defined in their basic instruments, in economic, social, cultural, educational, health and related fields" (Art. 57 of the Charter). Together with the UN and its Funds and Programmes they form the → UN system.

Organizations such as the → Universal Postal Union (UPU) and the → International Telecommunication Union (ITU), that had been in existence long before the → League of Nations and had no legal relationship with it, received the status of specialized agencies of the UN, as did the → International Labour Organization (ILO) which had been created jointly with the League of Nations.

Other international organizations maintaining ties with the League of Nations were either merged to specialized agencies or replaced by newly created specialized agencies. The Charter (cf. Art. 57) specifically mentioned such fields as culture, education and health, for the foundation of new specialized agencies.

During the period 1945 - 1986 several other specialized agencies were founded (cf. Table 1, p. 675). Today, the → UN system includes 17 specialized agencies. The → International Atomic Energy Agency (IAEA) and the → World Trade Organization (WTO) are often included in the organizational charts, although these are not specialized agencies according to Article 57 of the Charter.

The decisive basic idea consisted in the assumption that through increased co-operation in the fields mentioned above existing conflicts and sources of potential wars could gradually be reduced. In this context, the elimination of poverty and social injustice was understood as a concrete contribution to implement the peace mandate of the United Nations. This "functional approach" demanded, therefore, a stronger engagement of the member states in solving concrete-practical problems. Article 56 of the Charter explicitly states that "all Members pledge themselves to take joint and separate action in co-operation with the Organization for the achievement of the purposes set forth in Article 55".

II. Purposes and Tasks

The purposes and tasks of the specialized agencies, which in their respective fields serve the overall purpose of the UN, namely the maintenance of international peace and security, are broadly spread. In practice, there is no activity of a state which does not fall into the field of competence of one of the specialized agencies of the United Nations. Indeed, the broad range of specialized agencies of the UN reflects the activities to be found, for example, in a large number of Federal Ministries in Germany.

As expressed already by the term "specialized agencies", those organizations are equipped by special professional competencies which they are to exercise in a global context. The purposes and principles of the specialized agencies are basically not of a political nature which, however, does not imply that they act non-politically, although the general political mandate lies explicitly with the → General Assembly of the UN. Since we deal with intergovernmental organizations, it may happen, even in the case of the so-called "technical organizations" that decisions are affected by general political considerations.

III. Relationship Agreements

As mentioned above, specialized agencies are brought into relationship with the United Nations through agreements which are concluded by the → Economic and Social Council (ECOSOC) according to Article 63 of the Charter. Those agreements must be approved by the General Assembly. The first agreement was concluded in 1946 with → ILO (UN Doc. A/RES/50 (I), 14 December 1946). This set the example for many of the relationship agreements concluded afterwards.

Later on, for example in the cases of → WIPO (UN Doc. A/RES/3346 (XXIX), 17 December 1974), → IFAD (UN Doc. A/RES/ 32/107, 15 December 1977), → UNIDO (UN Doc. A/RES/ 40/180, 17 December 1985), great importance was attached to the obligation of cooperation.

The ECOSOC may co-ordinate the activities of the specialized agencies through consultations with and recommendations to them, the General Assembly and to the members of the UN (Art. 63, para. 2).

In order to co-ordinate the activities of the specialized agencies among themselves and with the UN, the ECOSOC established in 1946 the *Administrative Committee on Co-ordination (ACC)*, originally composed of the UN Secretary-General and the executive heads of the specialized agencies and IAEA (→

Coordination in the UN System) . Its successor body, the *UN System Chief Executives Board (CEB)*, set up in 2000, is also chaired by the Secretary-General, but is larger in its composition. It comprises the heads of the Specialized Agencies, including the → World Bank and the → IMF as well as the → WTO, and the heads of the UN programmes and funds.

Based upon Article 63 of the Charter the conditions for the co-ordination of activities of the specialized agencies towards the UN and among each other are laid down in almost standardized relationship agreements.

They contain, *inter alia*, the right of the UN to have a say in matters of admission of non-members of the UN to the specialized agencies, furthermore the mutual right to propose issues to be put on the (partner's) agenda, and the obligation of the specialized agencies to forward recommendations of the UN to the organs of the specialized agencies competent for the passing of resolutions, and to support all other organs of the UN in pursuing their tasks. The specialized agencies have the right to ask the → International Court of Justice for advisory opinions on legal matters. The relationship agreements provide both parties with the mutual claim to the exchange of materials and documents and contain provisions concerning the co-ordination of administrative and technical services as well as the exchange of statistical materials in order to avoid duplication of work within the member states and between the specialized agencies and the UN. It is also envisaged harmonizing the different staff regulations in order to facilitate a greater flexibility and mobility of staff within the UN system.

Furthermore, representatives of the United Nations have the right to attend the sessions of all the bodies of the specialized agencies and to participate in the deliberations (without the right to vote). Vice versa the representatives of the specialized agencies have the right to participate and to take the floor at the sessions of the → Economic and Social

Council and of the Main Committees and other organs of the General Assembly; this participation being restricted however to "items of the agenda relating to … matters within the scope of activities of the Organization and other matters of mutual interest" (cf. for example the relationship agreement between the United Nations and the → UN Industrial Development Organization of 17 December 1985, UNTS 1412, 937, Art. 3). Since their representatives are seated behind the representatives of the member states, the participation rate has sunk dramatically over the years and has not led to the desired communication and cooperation.

IV. Charter Provisions

In addition to Article 63 of the Charter mentioned above, there are ten further articles in the Charter related directly or indirectly to the specialized agencies.

In Article 17 (3) it is said that the General Assembly "shall consider and approve any financial and budgetary agreements with specialized agencies referred to in Article 57 …" Furthermore, the General Assembly "shall examine the administrative budgets of such specialized agencies with a view to making recommendations to the agencies concerned". These recommendations are related to the co-ordination function of the → General Assembly; they do not imply a central function vis-à-vis the specialized agencies, for which the General Assembly has no competencies.

Article 58 of the Charter contains an extremely soft formulation which says that the United Nations "shall make recommendations for the co-ordination of the policies and activities of the specialized agencies".

Article 60 of the Charter draws the attention to the fact that the → General Assembly and, under its authority, the → Economic and Social Council are responsible for the discharge of "the functions of the Organization".

In Article 62 of the Charter, the Economic and Social Council is provided with the authority to make recommen-

dations to the specialized agencies concerned with respect to international economic, social, cultural, educational, health, and related matters.

Furthermore, Article 59 of the Charter draws the attention to the possibility of creating new specialized agencies, if required for the accomplishment of the purposes set forth in Article 55 of the Charter.

Article 64 of the Charter authorizes the Economic and Social Council to "take appropriate steps to obtain regular reports from the specialized agencies". Article 66 of the Charter empowers the Economic and Social Council "to perform services, with the approval of the General Assembly, at the request of Members of the United Nations or at the request of specialized agencies".

Article 70 of the Charter provides that representatives of the specialized agencies may participate, without vote, in the deliberations of the Economic and Social Council and in those of the commissions established by it, and that the representatives of the ECOSOC may participate in the deliberations of the specialized agencies.

V. Membership

Membership in one or more specialized agencies does not necessarily require a membership within the UN, although, vice versa, a membership within the UN almost automatically allows a membership in some of the specialized agencies (e.g. WHO, UNESCO). The → Federal Republic of Germany, for example, has been, since long before its admission to the UN, a member of all specialized agencies. Switzerland, although a member in all specialized agencies, continued not to be a member of the United Nations proper until 2002, when it applied for membership and was admitted on 10 September 2002.

The principle of universal membership is a goal aimed at for the UN as well as for all specialized agencies, although some of them have reached it only recently. This has been the case, *inter alia*, for the monetary-financial organizations, such as the → International

Monetary Fund (IMF) and the → World Bank Group (IBRD, IFC, IDA), where many former socialist states and developing countries for long did not apply for membership, due to the fact that voting power is weighted in these organizations according to the economic position of the respective member. But nowadays, all specialized agencies are close to realizing the principle of universal membership.

A special form of "coordinated membership" exists in the Bretton Woods Institutions: members of the → IBRD must be members of the → IMF, and only members of the IBRD may become members of the → IFC and the → IDA.

Notwithstanding the fact that specialized agencies are to be considered as intergovernmental institutions based upon governmental treaties, not only states as such are eligible for membership. Some agencies, such as → FAO, → ITU, → UPU, → UNESCO and → WHO, in fact also admit as associated members territories which do not (yet) possess the basic features of statehood. A unique feature of → ILO is the principle of tripartite (2+1+1) participation in its Constitution: each member state is represented in the plenary organ by two government delegates plus two delegates representing the national workers' and employers' organizations, respectively. This 2+1+1 structure is also maintained in other ILO decision-making organs. Relatively new is the option introduced by FAO: since November, 1991, the Organization also admits "member organizations"; up to now, only the European Union (EU) fulfills the admission criteria as a "regional economic integration organization", whereby – depending upon the item on the agenda – either the EU with 27 votes en bloc or the single EU members as member states of FAO are allowed to vote (the → WTO Constitution contains a similar provision since 1995).

VI. Organizational Structures

The following three basic categories of specialized agencies can be distinguished:

(1) *specialized agencies within a broadly defined scope of tasks* concerning social, cultural and humanitarian affairs (FAO, ILO, UNESCO, UNIDO, WHO);

(2) *technical specialized agencies* (ICAO, IMO, ITU, UNWTO, UPU, WIPO, WMO); and

(3) *monetary-financial specialized agencies* (IMF, World Bank Group, IFAD).

Although all the specialized agencies are based on different constitutions which depend in their content on their specific goals and tasks, some common features can be identified:

(a) In all specialized agencies there exists a *plenary organ* in which all member states are represented. The majority of specialized agencies grants to each member state one vote in the plenary organ ("one state – one vote" principle). Exceptions are the monetary-financial organizations (IMF, World Bank Group and IFAD) where voting power depends upon the financial contributions of each member state.

(b) *Meetings* are held annually (IMF, ILO, World Bank Group, WHO) or every two years (FAO, UNESCO), or at even longer intervals (ICAO, ITU, UPU).

(c) All specialized agencies have an *executive body* (Council, Board) which is responsible for the supervision of the implementation of policies between the plenary meetings.

(d) All specialized agencies are run by a *Secretariat* with a Secretary-General or Director-General or President at the top, who is elected for a minimum of three and a maximum of six years, respectively, and may be re-elected several times (except, e.g., ITU, UNESCO, UPU).

VII. Financing

The financial resources of the specialized agencies come mainly from three sources:

(1) The *regular budget* consists on the income–side primarily of obligatory contributions of the member states, determined by an assessment scale based

673

upon their economic capacity to pay. The maximum (ceiling) is 22.00%; the minimum (floor) in most cases is 0.001% (except IMF, World Bank Group, IFAD).

(2) The member states pay voluntary contributions to the special funds and programmes of the UN (e.g., UNDP, UNFPA, UNICEF) which finance the implementation of programmes and projects of the specialized agencies, especially within the framework of Multilateral Technical Cooperation ($\rightarrow$ Development Cooperation of the UN System). These flows, which have decreased dramatically since the early 1990s, are listed in the extraordinary budgets of the specialized agencies.

(3) Finally, there are voluntary, mostly project-related financial contributions by member states to the specialized agencies which are also listed in their extraordinary budgets ("multi-bi arrangements"). In addition, private financial flows, although still at a moderate level, have increased in recent years ("private-public partnership").

In most specialized agencies the financing is based upon obligatory membership contributions. The members must contribute annually – according to the scale of assessments – to the budget of the specialized agencies. This scale differs from organization to organization depending upon the total membership. Many specialized agencies (ILO, FAO, WHO, UNESCO, UNIDO) apply the scale of assessments of the UN. Some technical specialized agencies (ITU, UPU, WIPO) have established a system of different classes of contributions for their members; the class is determined by the member state itself. Other technical specialized agencies (ICAO, IMO, WMO) apply a "mixed system" where the contributions of the members are partly based upon the UN scale of assessments and partly upon the object of their activities (e.g., tons/kilometres capacity in the case of ICAO, registered shipping tonnage in the case of IMO) or upon an "own" scale of assessments (WMO). The payment record, mostly motivated by political considerations and highly influenced by the major contributors, differs considerably; the technical specialized agencies ITU, UPU and WIPO have the best records, whereby the latter has considerable own income from fees for certain administrative services.

The monetary-financial specialized agencies do not charge obligatory contributions for membership; administrative costs are financed through their returns.

VIII. Outlook

Despite the close legal and real relationship between the UN and the specialized agencies, many problems of co-ordination exist. *Inter alia*, this is due to the fact that the governmental representatives in the specialized agencies usually are not sent by the respective Foreign Ministries, but by the respective Ministries in charge of the matter in question. As long as co-ordination at the national level of the individual members cannot be achieved, those member states may decide quite differently in different fora due to the diverging interests of the respective ministries. Since the specialized agencies developed meanwhile a strong life of their own, the desired co-ordination fails due to the resistance of these specialized agencies as well as that of the respective ministries of the individual member states.

Most recently – in November 2006 – a high-level expert group mandated by the UN Secretary-General to work out recommendations for the improvement of system-wide coherence in the areas of development, humanitarian assistance, and the environment, recommended in its panel report "Delivering as One" the establishment of "One United Nations for development - at the country level" with "one leader, one programme, one budget and, where appropriate, one office" (*United Nations* 2006, 11). For the time being, this model is going to be implemented in a small number of selected countries – however, without the inclusion of the Bretton Woods Institutions.

Klaus Hüfner

Table 1: Specialized Agencies of the United Nations, 1946-2000

Year	Organization
1946	ILO (International Labour Organization), Geneva FAO (Food and Agricultural Organization), Rome UNESCO (UN Educational, Scientific and Cultural Organization), Paris
1947	IMF (International Monetary Fund), Washington, DC IBRD (International Bank for Reconstruction and Development), Washington, DC
1947	ICAO (International Civil Aviation Organization), Montreal GATT (General Agreement on Tariffs and Trade), Geneva[1]
1948	UPU (Universal Postal Union), Berne WHO (World Health Organization), Geneva
1949	ITU (International Telecommunication Union), Geneva
1951	WMO (World Meteorological Organization), Geneva
1957	IAEA (International Atomic Energy Agency), Vienna[1] IFC (International Finance Corporation), Washington, DC[2]
1959	IMO (International Maritime Organization), London[3]
1961	IDA (International Development Organization), Washington, DC[2]
1974	WIPO (World Intellectual Property Organization), Geneva
1977	IFAD (International Fund for Agricultural Development), Rome
1986	UNIDO (UN Industrial Development Organization), Vienna
1995	WTO (World Trade Organization), Geneva[1]

[1] No specialized agency according to Article 57 of the Charter.
Since 1 January 1995 GATT – as a treaty as well as an institution – is in the still ongoing process of being embedded in the World Trade Organization.
[2] Affiliates of the IBRD.
[3] Former IMCO (Inter-Governmental Consultative Organization).

Lit.: *Beigbeder, Y.:* The Internal Management of United Nations Organizations. The Long Quest for Reform, Houndmills/London 1996; *Hüfner, K.:* Die Vereinten Nationen und ihre Sonderorganisationen: Strukturen, Aufgaben, Dokumente. Teil 2: Die Sonderorganisationen (DGVN-Texte 41), Bonn 1992; *Hüfner, K.:* Die Vereinten Nationen und ihre Sonderorganisationen. Teil 3: Finanzierung des Systems der Vereinten Nationen 1971-1995. Teil 3B: Sonderorganisationen – Gesamtdarstellungen – Alternative Finanzierungsmöglichkeiten (DGVN-Texte 46), Bonn 1997; *Klein, E.:* United Nations, Specialized Agencies, in: Bernhardt, R. (ed.): EPIL 5, Amsterdam 1983, 349-369; *Meng, W.:* Arts. 57-60, in: Simma, B. (ed.): The Charter of the United Nations. A Commentary, Munich/Oxford 1994, 796-825; *Pitt, D./Weiss, T.G. (eds.):* The Nature of United Nations Bureaucracies, London/ Sydney 1986; *Seidl-Hohenveldern, I.:* 125. Specialized Agencies, in: Wolfrum, R. (ed.): United Nations: Law, Policies and Practice, Volume 2, Munich 1995, 1202-1208; *United Nations - General Assembly*: Delivering as one. Report of the High-Level Panel on United Nations System-wide Coherence in the areas of development, humanitarian assistance and the environment, 20 November 2006, UN Doc. A/61/583; *Williams, D.:* The Specialized Agencies and the United Nations – The System in Crisis, London/New York 1987.

Internet: 1. Links to the websites of the different specialized agencies on the Website of the UN Official Website Locator (in alphabetical order as well as in thematic groups: www.unsystem.org; 2. Information on the financial situation of the specialized agencies on the Homepage of the Global Policy Forum: www.globalpolicy.org/finance/ tables/index2.htm; 3. Information on the UN System Chief Executives Board for Coordination: www.unsystemceb.org.

Stamps

The United Nations is the only international organization which is entitled to publish and use its own stamps, this right being based on agreements with the governments of Austria, Switzerland and the United States. These stamps are available to all stamp collectors worldwide, but can be used only for mailings from the UNPA Post offices at UN Headquarters in New York, at the United Nations Office in Geneva (UNOG) in the "Palais des Nations" and at the United Nations Office at Vienna (UNOV).

The UN stamps are designed by artists selected from 500 designers in 40 countries by an international competition for each individual issue. The chosen designs are printed at the best security printing offices in various parts of the world. Each of the three UNPA Post Offices offers the same stamps and services, the stamps being distinguished only by the three languages English, French and German and the respective currency (US dollar, Swiss franc and Austrian schilling which has been replaced on new issues as of 1 January 2002 by the common European currency Euro).

Orders for stamps or postcards and envelopes with printed postage stamps in mint condition may be addressed to the United Nations Postal Administration (UNPA) in New York, Geneva and Vienna or may be made online at the UNPA homepage.

The New York office is responsible for all stamp orders originating from countries outside Europe, the UNPA offices in Vienna is in charge of European orders.

The New York address is "United Nations Postal Administration, P.O. Box 5900, Grand Central Station, New York, N.Y. 10163-5900, USA, e-mail: unpanyiquiries@un.org.

The Vienna address is "United Nations Postal Administration (UNPA) at Vienna", International Center Vienna, A-1400 Vienna, United Nations, P.O. Box 900 – Austria; e-mail: UNPA-Europe@unvienna.org).

Ruprecht Paqué

Lit.: *United Nations Postal Administration (UNPA) (ed.):* The United Nations Stamps – an Introduction.

Internet: 1. Homepage of UNPA, New York: http://unstamps.un.org; 2. Homepage of UNPA in Vienna: www.unvienna.org/unov/en/unpa.html.

Terminology

In response to diverse and wide-ranging demands of United Nations language staff for terminology and nomenclature, a terminological database has been compiled. UNTERM is a multilingual terminology database which provides United Nations nomenclature and special terms in all six official UN languages - English, French, Spanish, Russian, Chinese and Arabic. The database is mainly intended for use by the language and editorial staff of the United Nations to ensure consistent translation of common terms and phrases used within the Organization. It was eventually put on the Internet to facilitate the efforts of people around the world who participate in the work of the United Nations but do not have access to the Secretariat's intranet. The database can be accessed at http://unterm.un.org/

UNTERM contains around 70,000 entries in 6 official languages and is updated daily. The database is maintained by the terminology team of the Terminology and Reference Section, Documentation Division, DGACM. Terminological queries may be directed to the section via the "Feedback" function on the UNTERM website.

Furthermore, the Translation Services of the six official languages (Arabic, Chinese, English, French, Russian and Spanish) have compiled numerous terminology lists for internal use for various specific subject matters, available for consultation at the Dag Hammarskjöld Library of the → Secretariat.

There is also a terminology database maintained by the German Translation Section, called DETERM, which is equally accessible to the public on the Internet. This database (in English, German, French, and Spanish) contains organizational names, acronyms, conventions, declarations and other terms frequently used in the United Nations system. The records contained in DETERM are primarily based on the German Translation Section's current translation work, which covers only a limited area of UN activities, i.e. essentially resolutions and decisions of the General Assembly and the Security Council, annual reports of the Secretary-General and of the Security Council, and similar documents.

Wrongly Used Terms

Depending on the context, the abbreviation UN for the United Nations can mean either the community of all member states, *or* the "Organization of the United Nations" functioning as the "executive organ" of the former or may refer to both. The United Nations normally refers to itself in its own documents and publications as "the organization" ("l'organisation") only. In French, the acronym is (l')ONU (in tables without article) for "Organization des Nations Unies". In German, the community of UN member states as well as the organization is often referred to as "UNO" though this acronym for "United Nations Organization" is not used in English. The official German acronym in UN documents and governmental documents is "VN" for "Vereinte Nationen", not UN (e.g. VN-Politik, VN-Organe).

Another important distinction is to be made between the United Nations proper (i.e. the said community of member states or the six main organs of the organization) on the one hand and the so-called "United Nations System"(Fr. système – also organisme – des Nations Unies) or "family" on the other hand (→ UN System), with its numerous other bodies and their various organizational affiliations (→ Principal Organs, Subsidiary Organs, Treaty Bodies), in particular the so-called → "specialized agencies" ("institutions spécialisées"; in German "Sonderorganisationen", in Austria and the former GDR "Spezialorganisationen"), because of their legal special status according to Article 57 UN Charter, for special fields such as health (→ WHO), food and agriculture (→ FAO) or education, science and culture (→ UNESCO).

A distinction often overlooked is the one between *Committee* (Fr. Comité; G. Ausschuss) and *Commission* (Fr. Commission; G. Kommission). Thus, for instance, the "Human Rights *Committee*" (Comité des droits de l'homme; Menschenrechtsausschuss) of the International Covenant on Civil and Political Rights, adopted on 19 December 1966, is by no means identical with the "*Commission* on Human Rights" (Fr. Commission des droits de l'homme; G. Menschenrechtskommission), a subsidiary body of the Economic and Social Council (→ ECOSOC) already created in 1946, with which it is easily confused.

Likewise the title "resolution" (résolution; Resolution) is sometimes confused with a "decision" (Fr. décision; G. Beschluss, not "Entscheidung"). Though, indeed, a resolution is a special form of a decision (therefore volume titles such as "Resolutions and other decisions of the General Assembly" etc.), a resolution is distinguished from a "simple" decision by its formality, especially by its separate preamble (Fr. préambule; G. Präambel) and operative part (Fr. dispositif; G. Beschlussteil), and by their strictly standardized beginnings of paragraphs (in French "paragraphe" for the preambular part, but "alinéa" for the operative part; in German "Absatz" for the non-numbered preambular paragraphs and "Ziffer" for the numbered paragraphs of the operative part, not "Paragraph").(cf. also → Resolution, Declaration, Decision)

Rule for the Use of Acronyms

Acronyms, i.e. "neologisms" composed of the capitalized first letters of mostly very long institutional names like UN for "United Nations", UNESCO for "United Nations Educational, Scientific and Cultural Organization" or UNITAR for "United Nations Institute for Training and Research" etc. are to be distinguished from *abbreviations* like Ph.D., Mr., Mme etc. Acronyms are words, formed of the initial letters of a title, and are pronounceable, as in NATO, whereas O.S.C.E. cannot be pronounced, and forms no word; it is an abbreviation.

As opposed to German, where in most cases the English acronyms have been adopted without change (but should be used with the article for the grammatical gender of the German form), French acronyms of the UN bodies and institutions are mostly based on their French names (such as l'ONU for UN, FMI for IMF or ONUDI for UNIDO etc.) which creates a difficulty for simultaneous interpretation but is a considerable help for the general public in "deciphering" and thus recognizing the meaning of an acronym by dissolving it into its components.

For historical reasons, the spelling of the English UN texts (which make up about 90% of the originals for translations) does not follow the American, but the British spelling (thus e.g. programme, not program).

Ruprecht Paqué

Internet: UNTERM terminology database: http://unterm.un.org/. DETERM terminology database: http://unhq-appspub-01.un.org/dgaacs/gts_term.nsf

Trade, International Law of

I. Introduction

There is no unanimously recognized definition of "International Law of Trade". It might be defined as the totality of multilateral provisions in international treaty and common law that apply to cross-border trade, whereby "trade" refers not only to the exchange of goods but also to that in services. The term "International Law of Trade" (or International Law of Commerce) is more accurate than "International Trade Law", which does not explicitly exclude the trade-related items of (national) Private International Law. In line with this definition, questions of commercial customs *(lex mercatoria)* are, among other matters, attached to Private International Law, rather than the International Law of Trade. Nonetheless, Private Interna-

tional Law is linked to the International Law of Trade whenever international treaties harmonize provisions on the conflict of laws between participating countries (e.g. EEC Convention on the Law Applicable to Contractual Obligations; UN Convention on Contracts for the International Sale of Goods). International Organizations (→ WTO, → ITU, → ICAO, etc.) that deal with world trade must be distinguished from non-governmental organizations (→ NGOs), such as the International Chamber of Commerce (ICC). International Law of Trade – by itself a subset of the International Law of Economics – is not a clearly delineated domain in Public International Law. Rather, it is a multiform amalgamation of somehow trade-related rules.

International Law of Trade is characterized by a low degree of institutionalization and the predominance of treaty law (→ Treaties, Law of). The UN and its → specialized agencies exerted considerable influence on its structure. Although several multilateral trade agreements had been concluded during the 19th century, the year 1947 marked the true birth of modern International Law of Trade, when the *General Agreement on Tariffs and Trade (GATT)* was signed. In 1994, the Agreement Establishing the World Trade Organization (WTO) successfully brought into being, for the first time, a common international framework for the conduct of trade relations. The convention comprises a set of annexes, encompassing "GATT 1994" and further trade-related agreements (→ WTO, GATT) and instruments. While GATT had sometimes been referred to as a "magna carta of world trade" even before 1994 (*Hailbronner/Bierwagen* 1988), the elaborate WTO system, together with accession of most of the former socialist countries and many developing states to it, has at least taken on some features of a "constitution of global economy" (for details see *Oeter* in: Hilf/Oeter 2005, § 1 Index No. 39ff.). Most provisions of International Law of Trade are purpose-oriented, focussing on the liberalization of world trade and the dismantling of trade barriers. This is particularly true of *GATT, GATS (General Agreement on Trade in Services)* and *TRIPs (Agreement on Trade-Related Aspects of International Property Rights)*. However, economic development and → environmental protection may call for restrictions to free trade. These conflicting aims are typical of the International Law of Trade. Even regional trade organizations (customs unions and free trade areas), which frequently liberalize domestic trade and simultaneously erect trade barriers at their edge, are somewhat opposed to the objective of *universal* liberalization of trade. The WTO/GATT system tries to balance those opposing interests, notably by establishing general and specific exceptions to the trade rules.

II. WTO/GATT: "Magna Carta" of World Trade

A brief outline of the key features of the WTO/GATT '94 system is given here, because most trade-related instruments either refer directly to the system's trade rules or need to be brought into line with them.

The WTO/GATT .rules came in force 1 January 1995. Negotiations had started in 1986 with the so-called Uruguay Round. The WTO "complex" encompasses 16 "multilateral" agreements, binding to all parties to the WTO – in particular GATT 1994 (containing the unchanged wording of GATT 1947), GATS and TRIPs. Furthermore, there is an agreement on (expanded) dispute settlement (Understanding on Rules and Procedures Governing the Settlement of Disputes), the Marrakesh Protocol to the GATT and a series of "understandings" on GATT obligations. "Plurilateral" agreements (originally four, only two of them still being in force) are binding only on those WTO members that have accepted them. The WTO Agreement connects all these legal instruments. The WTO was established as a permanent institutionalized platform for negotiation and arbitration on issues of world trade. As early as 1948, the Havana Charter had envisaged an international trade organization (ITO). Because of that Charter's failure, however, the organization never materialized (*Senti/ Conlan* 1998, 12f.; *Hauser* 1995). While ITO was conceived as a specialize agency within the "UN Family" (Art. 57, 63 UN Charter), WTO is not. Encompassing 153 member states (as of 23 July 2008) it is on the verge of → universality. Still, this undoubted success has not facilitated decision-making within WTO, and the near-failure of the present "Doha ["Development"] Round" (since 2001) has given evidence that agreement on the liberalization of world trade as a common goal could not altogether cover up old conflicts (→ International Economic Relations) between industrial and developing states (concerning, *inter alia*, topics like agricultural products, notably farming subsidies, or intellectual property).

The WTO/GATT system rests upon a set of principles of international trade, among these the principles of the mostfavored nation, national treatment (both of these principles granting non-discrimination) and reciprocity. Notably GATT provides for general or merchandise-related exceptions and contains a number of protective clauses. (For details, see → WTO/GATT).

Most regional trade-related agreements, especially those establishing customs unions and free-trade areas, seek to fit within this pattern, insofar as basic freedoms of trade and non-discrimination are granted and interference with competition declared unlawful. Yet, at the same time, customs unions and freetrade areas, in spite of being permitted for by WTO rules (Art. XXIV (4), (5), (8) GATT), appear to be exceptions to a global approach towards free trade. What justifies their admittance is the expectation that many steps toward trade liberalization will initially be taken within homogeneous economic blocs and later catalyze progress on a global level (cf. *Weiler* 2000). Most of world trade is still done within and between those blocs. Customs unions (which abolish internal duties, but establish common external tariffs, Article XXIV (8) lit. a GATT) must be distinguished from free trade areas (which minimize internal barriers to trade and have no common foreign tariff, but preserve, at least potentially, internal duties, Article XXIV (8) lit. b GATT; e.g.: EFTA, NAFTA). The highest level of integration is attained by common markets, where the customs union concurs with legal harmonization, liberalization and integration of all economic sectors (e.g. EU/EC) (*Herdegen* 2007, § 11; *Dolzer* 2007, Index No. 93ff.). The political reality of world trade is marked by the juxtaposition and combination of these regional legal instruments.

III. Sectorial Treaty-Based Regimes

Although the WTO/GATT complex covers almost all forms of trade in goods and services, some traded items are submitted to specific regimes (most of which have been in operation for decades). Some agreements lay the foundations for international organizations; others contain material provisions regulating infrastructure and technology. Most conventions pertain to network goods and services.

The *Universal Postal Union* (→ UPU), created in 1874, is now a specialized UN agency that ensures the working of international postal transport, as laid down in a multitude of agreements (Universal Postal Convention, Postal Parcel Service Agreement, Postal Payment Services Agreement, etc.).

Cross-border *telecommunications infrastructure* is the domain of the *International Telecommunication Union* (→ ITU), founded as early as 1865 under the name of the International Telegraph Union. As a specialized agency of the UN, ITU (that states – 191 by the end of 2008 – as well as private organizations of many kinds ["sector members"] have the right to join) provides a forum for co-operation and co-ordination. Hence, it controls rather than liberalizes trade in services. In the scope of WTO, the GATS annex on telecommunications (enacted on 15 February 1997) was an important step towards dismantling lo-

cal monopolies. Therefore, the ITU lost some of its importance vis-à-vis the WTO complex (cf. *Grewlich* 1997, 165ff.).

International transport (as the carrying out of trade) is regulated by a multitude of agreements that apply – with the exception of the UN Convention on the Multimodal International Transport of Goods of May 25, 1980 (UN Doc. TD/MT/CONF/16; ILM 1980, 938) – to certain means and items of transport. Some of them focus upon the transport networks (roads, railways, waterways, airspace), others upon transport-specific trade rules. The 1944 Chicago Convention on International Civil Aviation (UNTS Vol. 15, No. 102, 295) is an important codification. Together with a framework of secondary law, the convention provides for free international air transport of passengers and goods (freedoms of air transport). The Chicago Convention is part of the statute of the International Civil Aviation Organization (ICAO), which is the specialized agency of the UN dealing with matters related to air safety and profitability of air transport.

Sea freight law is dominated by the International Convention for the Unification of Certain Rules of Law Relating to Bills of Lading (LNTS No. 2764) of August 25, 1924 (known as the "Hague Rules"), as amended in 1968, giving rise to what is now referred to as "Hague-Visby Rules" (UNTS Vol. 1412, 121). These rules promote trade by standardizing norms and behavior. The UN Convention on the Carriage of Goods by the Sea (the "Hamburg Rules") of 30 March 1978 (ILM 1978, 608) establishes further-reaching, uniform rules for sea transports, notably in the interest of developing countries.

International agreements on harmonization of Private International Law or national trade law also foster world trade. As a subsidiary organ (Art. 22 UN Charter) of the UN → General Assembly, the UN Commission on International Trade Law (→ UNCITRAL), founded in 1966, renders valuable service by elaborating conventions (e.g. the

"Hamburg Rules"), guidelines and model regulations (like the "Model Law on Electronic Commerce" of 1996). UNCITRAL was the driving force behind the UN Convention on Contracts for the International Sale of Goods (CISG) adopted in Vienna on 11 April 1980 (UNTS Vol. 1489, No. 25567, 3; ILM 19 (1980)), 671) (*Herdegen* 2007, § 10, Index No. 11ff.; *Schlechtriem* 2005; → UN Office Vienna). The agreement, which codifies *Private* International Law, is at the same time a document of *Public* International Law. According to its Article 1, the Convention applies to contracts of sale of goods between parties whose places of business are in different states under the condition that the states are contracting states or that the rules of private international law lead to the application of the law of one of its 70 contracting states (as of December 2006). On 3 July 2008, UNCITRAL approved a draft Convention on Contracts for the International Carriage of Goods Wholly or Partly by Sea (UN Doc. A/CN.9/WG.III/WP.101 and A/CN.9/658). UNCITRAL has also engaged in codification of rules on electronic commerce and composed a United Nations Convention on the Use of Electronic Communications in International Contracts, adopted by the → General Assembly on 23 November 2005 and signed (as of 31 December 2007) by 18 countries (source: www. uncitral.org).

IV. World Trade and Aid to Development

Foreign aid helps developing countries improve their chances on the world market and thus makes an indirect contribution to the promotion of international trade. Likewise, comprehensive integration of developing countries in the world trade system may have this effect ("aid by trade"), provided that developing states are partially exempted from strict application of the rules governing world trade for a transitional period in order to facilitate their integration into the mechanisms of world trade. *The UN Conference on Trade and De-velopment* (→ *UNCTAD*), which was created in 1964, is a subsidiary organ of the General Assembly but virtually acts like an independent international organization. In 1967, it pushed through the exemption from the principle of reciprocity for less developed countries. Moreover, these countries were released from the duty to respect the most-favored nation principle (Art. XXXVI (8) GATT). Many commodity agreements, some of which are listed below, owe their existence to UNCTAD lobbying. In the 1970s, the debate on the developing countries' (somewhat obscure) claim for a "right to development" pervaded the work of the Conference (→ International Economic Relations and New International Economic Order (NIEO); cf. *Dupuy* 1981), which subsequently focussed on restrictions of world trade in the interest of poorer countries. Discussions with industrial countries were consequently heavy with ideology and remained without tangible result (*Bryde/Kunig/Oppermann* 1986).

International Commodity Agreements do not intend to restrict trade. Rather, they aim at channeling it in the interest of developing countries that export raw materials. By counteracting price deterioration, these agreements sustain producer states' economies. Commodity agreements, in the narrow sense, are negotiated among producer and purchaser states. These must be differentiated from commodity cartels, which unite producer states that have a common interest in keeping product prices high.

The Organization of the Petroleum Exporting Countries (OPEC), the best known of all these cartels, is an international organization founded in 1960 by petrol-exporting countries and comprising 13 members (as of 31 December 2007). Generally, commodity cartels (*Ipsen-Gloria* 2004, § 46, Index No. 37, 39) do not promote development, on the contrary: while most of them lack the power to harm developed states, the economic catch-up of less developed countries that do not have raw materials at their disposal may be impaired by commodity cartels.

The extension of the worldwide net of *commodity agreements* is among the most significant achievements of the UN policy of trade and development. Although some agreements were already concluded after World War II (for wheat, sugar, tin, coffee, olive oil), a catalyzing effect on further agreements was not felt until 1964, when the UN Conference for Trade and Development assembled for the first time. In 1976, UNCTAD adopted by consensus Resolution 93 (IV) providing for the Integrated Programme for Commodities. However, the practical relevance of this programme remained modest (*Tomuschat* 1992b, 687).

Some of the commodity agreements initiated by UNCTAD can be categorized as international organizations, yet none belong to the "UN family" in legal terms. The agreements follow a variety of approaches. Some merely stipulate mutual notification and consultation, while others aim to optimize market structures. Agreements that include rules for intervention may be categorized as either buffer stock or quota systems (*Pelikahn* 1990, 174ff., 264ff.; *Tomuschat* 1992a; *Herdegen* 2007, § 10).

The *buffer stock* mechanism, an elaborate system of intervention, requires the commodity organization to act like an enterprise. To stabilize prices, available market stocks for specific goods are monitored. Whenever a surplus accumulates, the organization buys goods and resells them once the commodity has become scarce on the global market. On the basis of the Integrated Programme for Commodities, the Common Fund, an international financial organization, was established in 1980. Although it was ambitiously conceived, the fund lacks sufficient financial backing and has had modest impact so far (*Pelikahn* 1990, 606ff.; *Tomuschat* 1992a).

The frequently employed *quota systems* refrain from direct market participation. Instead, the commodity organization sets targets ("quotas") – for production, sales, imports, but mostly export – that are binding on its member states. Quota systems lack their own logistic facilities. Hence, their capacity to respond flexibly to the market situation is restricted. Unlike the buffer stock system, which keeps market mechanisms working, the merits of price stability through quotas are mitigated by the restrictions imposed on market freedoms.

Commodity funds lessen the impact of price fluctuations on developing countries and thus enable these nations to act as reliable partners within the global trade system. However, funds are not immune to economic risks. This is shown by the failure of the International Tin Council, which was the first International Organization to declare itself insolvent in 1985 (*Pelikahn* 1990, 222ff.; *Herdegen* 2007, § 10, Index No. 2). The future of commodity agreements is uncertain, not only because most of them failed to meet the expectations, but also because alignment with the WTO/GATT system is mandatory pursuant to Article XX (h) GATT. Not only is the interest in their adoption fading, but also gradually shifting from developing towards commodity-dependent industrial states, as the rising demand for some raw materials worldwide (and also growing domestic requirements in some industrializing states) have caused shortages in some raw materials and the subsequent price increases as well as difficulties of allocation threaten to destabilize their economies.

V. Trade Embargoes: Interference with World Trade

Trade embargo law *(Ress* 2000), which regulates a specific form of economic discrimination, is also part of the International Law of Trade. A trade embargo restricts or stops imports and/or exports of goods, services, know-how or capital from or to a state and aims to generate sufficient (political) pressure in order to reach a not trade-related, foreign affairs objective. The embargo is imposed on the state itself, its nationals or enterprises under its jurisdiction; while a boycott is organized by individuals, an embargo is decided upon and enforced by states

(*Gornig* 1990, 114f.; *Ress* 2000, 6ff.). Sometimes a distinction is made between import and export embargoes, as well as between capital and transport embargoes. The embargo is a traditional instrument of foreign politics. Its serves predominantly political and strategic purposes (the "COCOM list", for example, was a list of strategic goods subject to an embargo that 14 Western states imposed on socialist countries), but they may also be punitive (e.g. the wheat embargo that the USA imposed on the Soviet Union after her invasion of Afghanistan) (*Kausch* 1985/1995, 60).

Embargoes must not violate international treaty or customary law. In general, countries are not required to trade with other states or even to maintain existing trade relations. A trade embargo is just an unfriendly act, except to the extent that provisions of a treaty prohibit restrictions on trade. It is just a contentious issue whether non-compliance with WTO/GATT rules may in the case of embargoes be justified as a reprisal (*Hahn* 1996) under the condition that the other state has violated rules of public international law and that the measure is proportional to the preceding infringement – or whether the "non-compliance procedures" provided by the WTO system supersede this right, possibly to the extent of making it a "self-contained régime" (cf. *Dahm/Delbrück/Wolfrum* 2002, 987f.). Under rare and extreme circumstances embargoes imposed by states can be seen as illicit, if, for example, the measures taken amount to use of force (→ Use of Force, Prohibition of) or intervention (→ Intervention, Prohibition of) (Art. 2 (4), (7) UN Charter) (cf. *Gornig* 1990, 115ff.), such as a trade blockade threatening the basic supply of the whole population. It is also controversial whether embargoes may be imposed on third states that refuse to ostracize a state for violating fundamental → human rights or promoting terrorism (e.g. the United States' "Helms-Burton Act" and "D'Amato Act", 1996), or whether such third-party sanctions should rather

be regarded as illicit interference in other states' affairs (*Meng* 1997, 275ff.).

Trade embargoes ("complete or partial interruption of economic relations") can also be imposed by the UN → Security Council as measures taken under Chapter VII of the Charter pursuant to its Article 41 (→ Sanctions) , to be implemented by UN member states. Although this kind of embargo is a response to a threat to the peace, breach of the peace or act of aggression (Art. 39 UN Charter), the Council is not endowed with a monopoly in imposing trade restrictions, as Article 41 UN Charter involves neither use of force nor intervention (see *Frowein/Kirsch*, in: Simma 2002, Art. 41, Index No. 11; *Schröder* 2007, Index No. 117). Since 1990, this right has been used more frequently not only against states (trade sanctions against Iraq, Yugoslavia, Libya, Somalia, Iran, etc.) (*Langenfeld* 1995, 64ff.; *Ress* 2000, 53ff.; *Stephanides* 1998; *Cortwright/Lopez* 2000), but also "smart" or "targeted" sanctions against individuals charged with terrorism, whose bank accounts had to be frozen. In some events, it was the General Assembly that in (non-binding) resolutions (→ Resolution, Declaration, Decision) called upon the UN member states to impose an embargo (e.g. on South Africa at the time of apartheid).

Jörn Axel Kämmerer

Lit.: Bryde, B.-O./Kunig, P./Oppermann, T. *(eds.):* Neuordnung der Weltwirtschaft?, Baden-Baden 1986; *Cortwright, D./Lopez, G. A.:* The Sanctions Decade: Assessing UN Strategies in the 1990s, Boulder 2000; *Dahm, G./Delbrück, J./Wolfrum, R.:* Völkerrecht, 2nd edn, Berlin 1989 (Vol. I/1) and 2002 (Vols. I/2, I/3); *Dolzer, R.:* Wirtschaft und Kultur im Völkerrecht, in: Graf Vitzthum, W. (ed.): Völkerrecht, 4th edn., Berlin et al. 2007, 491-576; *Gornig, G.:* Die völkerrechtliche Zulässigkeit eines Handelsembargos, in: Juristenzeitung 45 (1990), 113-123; *Grewlich, K.W.:* Konflikt und Ordnung in der globalen Kommunikation. Wettstreit der Staaten und Wettstreit der Unternehmen, Baden-Baden 1997; *Hahn, M.J.:* Die einseitige Aussetzung von GATT-Verpflichtungen als Repressalie, Berlin et al.

1996; *Hailbronner, K./Bierwagen, R.M.:* Das GATT – Die Magna Charta des Welthandels, in: Juristische Ausbildung 20 (1988), 318-329; *Hauser, H.:* Das neue GATT: Die Welthandelsordnung nach Abschluß der Uruguay-Runde, Munich 1995; *Herdegen, M.:* Internationales Wirtschaftsrecht, 6th edn., Munich 2007; *Hilf, M./Oeter, S.:* WTO-Recht, Baden-Baden 2005; *Ipsen, K.:* Völkerrecht, 5th edn., Munich 2004; *Kausch, H.G.:* Embargo, in: Bernhardt, R. (ed.): EPIL, Vol. II (1995), 58-63 (quoted as: Kausch 1985/1995); *Langenfeld, C.:* Embargo (Addendum 1995), in: Bernhardt, R. (ed.): EPIL II (1995), 63-67; *Meng, W.:* Wirtschaftssanktionen und staatliche Jurisdiktion - Grauzonen im Völkerrecht, in: ZaöRV 57 (1997), 269-327 *Pelikahn, H.-M.:* Internationale Rohstoffabkommen, Hamburg 1990; *Petersmann, U. (ed.):* International Trade Law and the GATT/WTO Dispute Settlement System, London et al. 1997; *Ress, H.-K.:* Das Handelsembargo. Völker-, europa- und außenwirtschaftsrechtliche Rahmenbedingungen, Praxis und Entschädigung, Berlin et al. 2000; *Schlechtriem, P.:* Commentary on the UN Convention on the International Sale of Goods (CISG), 2nd edn., Oxford et al. 2005; *Schröder, M.:* Verantwortlichkeit, Völkerstrafrecht, Streitbeilegung und Sanktionen, in: Graf Vitzthum, W. (ed.): Völkerrecht, 4th edn., Berlin et al. 2007, 577-636; *Seidl-Hohenveldern, I.:* International Economic Law, 2nd edn., Dordrecht et al. 1992; *Senti, R./Conlan, P.:* WTO. Regulation of World Trade after the Uruguay Round, Zürich 1998; *Simma, B. (ed.):* The Charter of the United Nations. A Commentary, Munich 2002; *Stephanides, J.:* A Brief Overview of United Nations Applied Sanctions. Background paper prepared by the UN Sanctions Secretariat for the Seminar on Targeting UN Sanctions, Interlaken, March 1998; *Tomuschat, C.:* Commodities, Common Fund, in: Bernhardt, R. (ed.): EPIL, Vol. I (1992), 683-686 (quoted as: Tomuschat 1992a); *Tomuschat, C.:* Commodities, International Regulation of Production and Trade, in: Bernhardt, R. (ed.): EPIL, Vol. I (1992), 686-692 (quoted as: Tomuschat 1992b); *Weiler, J.J.H. (ed.):* The EU, the WTO and the NAFTA: towards a common law of international trade? Oxford 2000; *Weiss, F.:* The WTO and the Progressive Development of International Trade Law, in: NYIL 29 (1998), 71-115.

Internet: *Information about international trade law:* a) at the Homepage of WTO: www.wto.org; access to important WTO agreements and other documents: www. docsonline.wto.org; b) about multilateral treaties concerning international trade: at the Homepage of the United Nations Treaties Series (UNTS): http://untreaty. un.org; c) about UPU: www.upu.int; d) about ITU: www.itu.int; e) about UNCITRAL: www. uncitral.org; f) about UNCTAD: www. unctad.org; g) about OPEC: www.opec.org.

Treaties, Law of

I. Introduction

International treaties are the primary source of international law. Consequently they are the prevalent and most important instrument for the development of international law (→ International Law and the UN). Correspondingly, Article 13 (1) lit. a of the UN Charter (→ Charter of the UN) states that the → General Assembly shall initiate studies and make recommendations to encourage the "progressive development of international law and its codification". A *"treaty"* under international law is *any agreement governed by international law and concluded in written form between one or more states and one or more international organizations or between international organizations*. The particular designation of this agreement is of no relevance: in the practice of the states very different designations are used, for example *agreement, convention, pact, charter, protocol*. Whether a document in question is a treaty is to be determined by the interpretation of the content. According to the number of parties to the treaty a distinction is made beween *bilateral* and *multilateral treaties*: A bilateral treaty refers to two subjects of international law; a multilateral treaty to more than two subjects.

The law of treaties, which regulates the conclusion, the validity and the termination of agreements, was for long only applicable as customary law, and was not codified by the International Law Commission (→ ILC) until the sixties. This was effected in two independent agreements, whose development lasted 17 and 11 years (respectively).

The first of these, the *"Vienna Convention on the Law of the Treaties"* of 23 May 1969 (UNTS Vol. 1155, No. 18232, 331), in short VCLT, regulates exclusively treaties concluded between states, and entered into force in 1980. The second, the *"Vienna Convention on the Law of the Treaties between States and International Organizations or between International Organizations"* of 21 March 1986 (UN Doc. A/CONF.129/15; reprinted in ILM 25 (1986), 543ff.) has not yet entered into force as the number of ratifications required for entry into force has not been reached. As of 20 March 2002 26 states have ratified the Convention; necessary for the entry into force are 35 ratifications. This is indicative of states' reluctance to concede to international organizations a comprehensively equal status, even as they can no longer neglect the increasing significance of these subjects of international law. There exists an international need for regulation, particularly regarding → host state agreements and technical assistance through international organizations. Both Vienna Conventions relating to the Law of Treaties contain to a large extent parallel provisions preventing a fragmentation of the Law of Treaties. With that has come a substantially equal treatment of states and international organizations. Only a few articles differ in their contents, to take into consideration the special qualities of international organizations. The conventions are complemented by the "Vienna Convention on the Succession of States" of 23 August 1978 (UN Doc. A/CONF.80/16/Add.2). This contains rules which are explicitly excluded by the two other Vienna Conventions. Being controversially discussed for a long time, the convention on state succession entered nevertheless into force 6 November 1996, as the newly independent states of East and Southeast Europe declared their succession or accession to the convention. Nevertheless the practical importance of the Convention on the Succession of States is trifling.

II. Conclusion and Entry into Force

Subjects of international law, states as well as international organizations can use their treaty-making power only by their organs. Subjects of international law appoint their organs and determine their competence to conclude treaties. Sometimes there do not exist clear rules on the authorized organs. This refers also to the United Nations. For example, Article 63 (1) UN Charter does not state clearly whether the competence to conclude treaties on the relation of the UN to the → specialized agencies belongs to the → General Assembly, or the Economic and Social Council (→ ECOSOC). The organs have to prove their competence to act bindingly under international law by submission of a power of attorney (Art. 7 (1) lit. a VCLT). Also persons are considered as representing a state – i.e. without submission of a power of attorney – to have the right to conclude a treaty, if from the practice of the represented state or other circumstances it appears consistent that the person is to be considered as representative of the state (Art. 7 (1) VCLT). Further, heads of states, heads of government and ministers of foreign affairs are considered as representing their states without having to produce appropriate full powers, as well as heads of diplomatic missions and representatives accredited by states to an international conference or to an international organization, for that particular purpose, i.e. to adopt the text of a treaty (Art. 7 (2) VCLT).

According to the conclusion of treaties, a distinction is to be made between the single and the composed procedure. The negotiation of the draft of a treaty often takes place by bodies of international organizations or in diplomatic conferences. The provisional result will be confirmed by initialing the text if the negotiator and the signatory are different persons.

In the single procedure the subsequent signature constitutes the binding force of the treaty. However, in most cases the composed procedure takes place.

That means the signatory only records the acceptance of a draft to be authentic. Thereafter the treaty has to be ratified, i.e. first the internal procedure of consent, the participation of the constitutional organs of the states (for example Article 59 (2) Basic Law (Constitution of the Federal Republic of Germany), and then the ratification under international law, i.e. on the international level the treaty-concluding party declares its will to be bound (deposit or exchange of the instruments of ratification).

A treaty enters into force at the date fixed by the states (Art. 24 (1) VCLT), or, if such a agreement is lacking, as soon as consent to be bound has been established for all negotiating states (Art. 24 (2) VCLT). After entry into force a treaty becomes binding for an accessing state, if a state declares its consent to be bound by the treaty (Art. 24 (3) VCLT). In practice most of the multilateral treaties include a rule according to which the treaty enters into force after a certain number of states have ratified. According to the Vienna Convention on the Law of Treaties the instruments and declarations of intent are to be deposited and are to be kept in custody (Arts. 76-77 VCLT). Additionally, according to Article 102 (1) UN Charter, the treaty shall be registered with the UN Secretariat (→ Secretariat) and published by it. This rule has the aim of rendering international relations transparent and to prevent secret diplomacy. The neglect of the rule to register each treaty does not cause invalidity of a treaty, but the parties cannot subsequently invoke the provisions of the treaty before the UN organs (Art. 102 (2) UN Charter), in particular before the International Court of Justice (→ ICJ).

III. Scope of Treaties

With the entry into force of a treaty, the question will arise as to the extent to which the treaty is binding upon the parties. In principle the treaty is binding upon each party in respect of its entire territory (Art. 29 VCLT), and in the dimension of time *ex nunc,* i.e. since the date of the entry into force (Art. 28 VCLT), if the parties do not conclude otherwise. If the parties to the treaty conclude a succeeding treaty relating to the same subject, the new treaty is binding (Art. 30 (2) VCLT). If in the case of a multilateral treaty not all parties are also parties to the new treaty, the former treaty remains in force between the former parties (Art. 30 (4) lit. b VCLT). In the event of a conflict between the obligations of the UN member states under the UN Charter and their obligations under any other international treaty, according to Article 103 UN Charter, their obligations under the Charter prevail. Most multilateral treaties admit reservations. By a reservation a contracting party declares before entry into force that specific provisions of the treaty are not valid for it, or are valid only in a modified form. The reservation is to be distinguished from a declaration of interpretation; declarations of interpretation have importance only with regard to the interpretation of a treaty.

In principle reservations are allowed, unless the treaty explicitly prohibits reservations, or the treaty provides that only specific reservations, which do not include the reservation in question, may be made or the reservation in question is considered to be incompatible with the object and purpose of the treaty (Art. 19 lit c. VCLT). Reservations allow the states to protect their interests and, at the same time, be party to a great number of multilateral treaties. If a reservation remains without objection, the rule is applicable between the state which has made the reservation and the other states only in the modified form of the reservation. If a state makes an objection to a reservation, the rule in question is not valid between the state parties. The rest of the treaty enters into force, unless a contrary intention is expressed by the objecting state (Art. 21 VCLT).

If objections are made against the treaty of foundation of an international organization, in principle the competent organ of the organization has to accept the reservation to become valid. With regard to the United Nations, the General Assembly has this competence since it decides on the admission of new members based on a recommendation of the Security Council (→ Membership and Representation of States). Nevertheless the UN Charter contains no rules on reservations.

IV. Interpretation of International Treaties

With the Vienna Conventions the rules of interpretation existing in customary international law became codified. Article 31 (1) of the two Vienna Conventions states: "A treaty shall be interpreted in good faith in accordance with the ordinary meaning to be given to the terms of the treaty in their context and in the light of its object and purpose". In accordance with the "objective theory" the Vienna Convention on the Law of Treaties follows the principle that the will of the parties is expressed primarily in the text of the treaty. Additional enclosures, protocols, together with subsequent agreements and "subsequent practice in the application of the treaty which establishes the agreement of the parties regarding its interpretation", and with "any relevant rules of international law applicable in the relations between the parties" (Art. 31 (2) and (3) VCLT) are to be taken into account. The "travaux préparatoires" have only subsidiary importance as complementary means of interpretation (Art. 32 VCLT). Beside these general rules of interpretation for the interpretation of foundation treaties of international organizations, the principle of the *effet utile* has to be observed. That means a treaty has to be interpreted in such a way that the aim of the treaty and its regulation purpose are reached to the best possible extent, so that the *intended benefit effect*, the *effet utile*, is reached. Finally the *implied powers doctrine* is also valid with regard to the UN Charter, i.e. in interpreting the Charter one is entitled to draw conclusions from explicitly prescribed duties in the Charter which may lead to other, not explicitly mentioned rights, which are necessary to the fulfillment of the prescribed duties.

V. Termination of Treaties

The termination of a treaty may take place in conformity with the provisions of the treaty, especially when a time limit has expired. Further, a treaty can terminate by consent of all parties to the treaty (Art. 54 lit. b VCLT), or be suspended (Arts. 57 and 58 VCLT). Foundation treaties to international organizations often include a procedure to modify the statutes relating to the changing circumstances, for example Article 109 of the UN Charter. A treaty can also be terminated through the declaration of the will of a party. Withdrawal or denunciation are possible according to the rules of Article 54 of the Vienna Convention on the Law of Treaties, if the treaty in question contains provisions for denunciation of withdrawal (Art. 54 lit. a VCLT) or "it is established that the parties intended to admit the possibility of denunciation or withdrawal" or "a right of denunciation or withdrawal may be implied by the nature of the treaty." (Art. 56 (1) lit. a and b VCLT). Finally termination can take place by reasons of later fundamental change of the circumstances existing at the time when the treaty was concluded (Art. 62 VCLT). This can be the case if a new peremptory norm of general international law (*ius cogens*) emerges. In this case each treaty which is in conflict with this norm becomes void and terminates (Art. 64 VCLT). Also in some cases the change of essential circumstances constituting the inherent basis of the contract can allow according to Article 62 (1) VCLT) termination or withdrawal under certain conditions (*clausula rebus sic stantibus*).

VI. Effects of Armed Conflicts on Treaties

In 2004 the ILC decided to include the topic "Effects of armed conflicts on treaties" in its programme of work. In 2005 the UN Secretariat submitted a study on this topic to the ILC (UN Doc. A/CN.4/550 of 1 February 2005).

In 2008 the ILC adopted on first reading a set of 18 draft articles and transmitted them to governments for comments until 2010 (cf. ILC Report 2008, UN Doc. A/63/10, Chapter V, C). The draft articles are an important amendment to the VCLT. They follow the idea, that the outbreak of an armed conflict does not necessarily terminate or suspend the operation of treaties.

However, whether a treaty is susceptible to termination resort shall be had to the nature, extent and the effects of the armed conflict and the subject matter and the numbers of parties of the treaty. A party to the conflict has to notify its intention to terminate or to withdraw from a treaty. The notification takes effect upon receipt by the other state party(ies). However, this shall not affect the right of a party to object to the notification. A state exercising its right to self-defense is entitled to suspend the operation of a treaty incompatible with the exercise of that right. On the other hand, an aggressor state shall not be entitled to such a right if the effect would be the benefit of that state. All the regulations do not apply on a list of treaties mentioned in an Annex to the Draft Articles, among them treaties relating to international humanitarian law, human rights, the protection of the environment and multilateral law-making treaties.

VII. Reservations to Treaties

In 1993 the ILC included the topic "Reservations to treaties" in its programme of work. In the following years the ILC prepared draft guidelines and – starting in 2000 – each year provisionally adopted some draft guidelines – in 2000 five, in 2001 twelve, in 2002 eleven, in 2003 eleven, in 2004 five, in 2005 two, in 2006 seven, in 2007 nine and in 2008 eight draft guidelines (cf. ILC Reports UN Docs. A/55/10, 2000; A/56/10, 2001; A/57/10, 2002; A/58/10, 2003; A/59/10, 2004; A/60/10, 2005; A/61/10, 2006; A62/10, 2007; A/63/10, 2008).

To expand its knowledge of the practical problems connected with reservations to treaties, the ILC held in July 2007 a meeting with representatives of UN human rights bodies and regional human rights bodies to exchange views on the issue of reservations to treaties

(UN Doc. ILC(LIX)/RT/CRP.1, 26 July 2007).

The slowness of the working methods of the ILC in this case is due to the very nature of the instrument which is to be elaborated. The ILC works out a "Guide to Practice" and not a draft treaty. Although the ILC still has a large number of guidelines to discuss and adopt, it is reasonable to suppose that the second part of the "Guide to Practice" might be concluded in 2009.

Brigitte Reschke

Lit.: *Aryal, R.S.:* Interpretation of Treaties, 2003; *Aust, A.:* Modern Treaty Law and Practice, 2nd edn., Cambridge 2007; *Bowman, M.J.:* The Multilateral Treaty Amendment Process – A Case Study, in: ICLQ 44 (1995), 540-559; *Fitzmaurice, M./Elias, O.:* Contemporary Issues in the Law of Treaties, Utrecht 2005; *Gardiner, R:* Treaties and Treaty Materials: Role, Relevance and Accessibility, in: ICLQ 46 (1997), 643-662; *Gardiner, R.:* Treaty Interpretation, Oxford 2008; *Gomaa, M.:* Suspension or Termination of Treaties on Grounds of Breach, The Hague 1996; *Goodman, R.:* Human Rights Treaties, Invalid Rservations. and State Consent, in: AJIL 96 (2002), 531-560; *Heintschel von Heinegg, W.:* Die völkerrechtlichen Verträge als Hauptrechtsquelle des Völkerrechts, in: Ipsen, K.(ed.): Völkerrecht, 5th edn., Munich 2004; *Hilpold, P.:* Das Vorbehaltsregime der Wiener Vertragsrechtskonvention, in: AVR 34 (1996), 376-425; *Kirgis, F.L.:* Reservations to Treaties and United States Practice, in: ASIL Insights, May 2003, www.asil.org; *Klabbers, J.:* The Concept of Treaty in International Law, The Hague et al. 1996; *Klein, E./Pechstein, M.:* Das Vertragsrecht internationaler Organisationen, Der Konventionsentwurf über Verträge zwischen Staaten und Internationalen Organisationen im Vergleich zur Wiener Vertragsrechtskonvention von 1969, Berlin 1985; *Köck, H.F.:* Zur Interpretation völkerrechtlicher Verträge, in: ZÖR 53 (1998), 217-237; *Lim, C./Elias, O.:* The Role of Treaties in the Contemporary International Legal Order, in: Nordic JIL 66 (1997), 1-21; *Linderfalk, U.:* On the Interpretation of Treaties: The Modern International Law as Expressed in the 1969 Vienna Convention on the Law of Treaties, Dordrecht 2007; *Seibert-Fohr, A.:* The Potentials of the Vienna Convention on the Law of Treaties with Respect to Reservations to Human Rights Treaties, in: Ziemele, E. (ed.): Reservations to Human Rights Treaties and the Vienna Convention Regime, Leiden 2004, 183-211; *Szasz, P. C.:* General Law-Making Process, in: Joyner, C. (ed.): The United Nations and International Law, Cambridge 1998, 27-64; *Torres-Bernárdez, S.:* Interpretation of Treaties by the International Court of Justice following the Adoption of the 1969 Vienna Convention on the Law of Treaties, in: Hafner, G. et al. (eds.): Liber Amicorum – Professor Ignaz Seidl-Hohenveldern in honour of his 80th birthday, The Hague et al. 1998; *United Nations - International Law Commission:* Second Report on Reservations to Treaties, by Alain Pellet, Special Rapporteur, Annex 1: Bibliography concerning Reservations to Treaties, 8 April 1999, UN Doc. A/CN.4/478/Rev.1); *Wolfrum, R./Röben, V. (eds.):* Developments of International Law in Treaty Making, Berlin/Heidelberg 2005.

Internet: *1. Documents:* The Vienna Convention on the Law of Treaties: www.un.org/law/ilc/texts/treaties.htm; *2. Information* on the international treaties, their status of ratification, as well as additional information on the legal procedures and terms ("Treaty Handbook") on the Homepage of UN Treaty Collection: www.untreaty.un.org/English/; *3. Information* on diverse datatbases with regard to international treaties: www.asil.org/treaty1.cfm.

Trusteeship Council

During the discussions about the structure of the United Nations at the preparatory conference of Dumbarton Oaks, and the foundation conference of San Francisco in the first half of 1945 (→ History of the Foundation of the UN), it became necessary to decide the future of the mandated territories of the → League of Nations, i.e. the former German and Turkish colonies of the First World War that had been entrusted, in the framework of the peace treaties, to mandate powers for administration under control of the League of Nations.

It was agreed to continue the system of mandated territories in a modified form as trusteeship system. In that system were to be included as well the overseas colonies of Japan in the Pacific Ocean, and the colonies of Italy in Africa, that had been brought under control of the Allied powers towards the end of the Second World War.

The USA intended to include also the colonies of all other colonial powers and to connect the establishment of the trusteeship system with an explicit declaration for the right to self-determination (→ Self-Determination, Right of), and the promise to grant independence in the near future to all dependent territories with a view to safeguarding the rapid → decolonization of all colonies under the control of the United Nations. This project failed because of opposition from the United Kingdom and France.

In Article 77 (1) lit. c of the Charter of the United Nations (→ Charter of the UN), it was left to the discretion of the colonial powers to place voluntarily their colonial territories under UN control. This possibility was not used by any colonial power.

Likewise an explicit codification of the right to self-determination was not reached, nor a binding promise in the UN Charter to grant the independence to the colonies, but only – as provided in Article 73 of the UN-Charter – an obligation for all member states that "have or assume responsibilities for the administration of territories whose peoples have not yet attained a full measure of self-government ... to ensure, with due respect for the culture of the peoples concerned, their political, economic, social, and educational advancement" and "to develop self-government, to take due account of the political aspirations of the peoples, and to assist them in the progressive development of their free political institutions," provided in the general clause "according to the particular circumstances of each territory and its peoples and their varying stages of advancement".

In this context "self-government" – in contrast to "independence" – was understood only as internal autonomy, while maintaining the present status under international law of limited → sovereignty. That means that the UN founding states did not lay down any binding guaranties relating to the granting of independence, but only vague promises

689

with regard to internal autonomy as far as "the particular circumstances" and "their varying stages of advancement" would permit. Thus the intention of the USA to safeguard a regulated course of decolonization, under the control of the UN and in the framework of the trusteeship system, had failed.

During the next decades, on the one hand colonial states continued to resist the inclusion of their colonies into the trusteeship system, with the argument that the administration of their colonies was a matter falling exclusively within their domestic jurisdiction, and interference by other states would constitute a violation of the prohibition of intervention ($\rightarrow$ Intervention, Prohibition of) as laid down in Article 2 (7) of the UN Charter. On the other hand, non-colonial states among the UN member states tried to secure the United Nations a surveying right over the colonies. In application of Article 73 UN Charter, the $\rightarrow$ General Assembly had already, with Resolution A/RES/66 (I) of 14 December 1946, defined seventy-four colonies as "territories without self-government" in the sense of Article 73. With the "Declaration on the Granting of Independence to Colonial Countries and Peoples" (UN Doc. A/RES/1514 (XV)), adopted on 14 December 1960, the General Assembly confirmed the following principles: all peoples have the right to self-determination; submission under foreign rule is contrary to international law; and the granting of independence is to be initiated as soon as possible.

During the whole period of decolonization the General Assembly dealt with the development in the dependent territories through reports and resolutions. There are still – in the year 2001 – about twenty territories without self-government, that are taken care of by the United Nations. Thus Article 73 UN Charter has formed an important basis in international law for the activities of the United Nations concerning colonial territories – beyond the context of the trusteeship system.

The trusteeship system as such was limited to the few mandate territories of the League of Nations and the above-mentioned former Japanese and Italian possessions. Trusteeship administration meant an administration of the colonies by an administrating power under the control of the United Nations; the UN had the authority to determine an administering authority (a member state, a group of states or the UN itself). The administering authority and the United Nations were to conclude a trusteeship agreement regulating the details of the trusteeship.

Within the trusteeship system provided in the UN Charter the General Assembly, the $\rightarrow$ Security Council and the Trusteeship Council – according to the enumeration in Article 7 of the UN Charter also a principal organ – control, in cooperation, the administration of the trust territories. The Trusteeship Council was – until its cessation of active work in 1994 – composed of all trust states, all permanent members of the Security Council as well as that number of non-trust states elected by the General Assembly necessary to reach a parity with the trust states in the Trusteeship Council.

There are three different types of the development of the trusteeship in trust territories to be distinguished in UN history:

(1) For the former mandate territory of the League of Nations Palestine, the General Assembly decided with Resolution A/RES/181 (II) on 29 November 1947, which included the scheme for Palestine's partition that the mandate should end no later than 8 August 1948. This resolution came into existence after the United Kingdom had practically handed over its mandate to the United Nations. The mandate ended in fact with the declaration of the state of Israel on 14 May 1948.

(2) The majority of colonial territories gained their independence comparatively quickly during the 50s and early 60s; some stragglers were left as trust territories until the 90s. Palau – the last trust territory – was granted its independence in 1994.

(3) There was a long-lasting international conflict about the South African League of Nations' mandate territory German South-West Africa, later named "Namibia". South Africa refused to put its territory under the trusteeship system with the argumentation that since the dissolution of the League of Nations South Africa would no longer be subject to mandate obligations, but would derive its rights from military conquest. Neither an advisory opinion of the International Court of Justice (→ ICJ) that said South Africa had still obligations under international law as former mandate power, nor numerous resolutions of the General Assembly that declared the presence of South Africa in Namibia as contrary to international law and requested it to give up the administration of Namibia, brought a change of South Africa's conduct. Not before the end of the 80s and after long negotiations, the United Nations succeeded in convincing South Africa to grant Namibia's independence. In 1990 Namibia became independent after holding free elections under UN electoral observation.

With the independence of Palau, the last remaining trust territory, on 1 October 1994 and the termination of the respective Trusteeship Agreement by Security Council Resolution 956 (of 10 November 1994) and Palau's admission as member of the United Nations on 15 December 1994 the Trusteeship Council completed the task entrusted to it under the Charter with respect to the territories that had been placed under the Trusteeship System of the United Nations (cf. UN Press Release ORG/1211/Rev.1 of 2 January 1996). The amendment to the rules of procedure of the Trusteeship Council contained in Trusteeship Council Resolution T/RES/2200 (LXI) of 25 May 1994, was now applied: in this amendment the Council dropped the obligation to meet annually and agreed to meet as occasion required – by its decision or the decision of its President, or at the request of a majority of its members or the General Assembly or the Security Council. As there are no longer UN member states "administer-

ing trust territories", the Council is – in accordance to Article 86 UN Charter the Council – now only composed of the permanent members of the Security Council.

There are proposals to give the Trusteeship Council a new function, e.g. as Environmental Council (→ Environmental Protection) of the United Nations. UN → Secretary-General Kofi Annan, for example, proposed in his reform programme "Renewing the United Nations: A Programme for Reform" of 14 July 1997 (UN Doc. A/51/950) to reconstitute the Trusteeship Council "as the Forum through which Member States exercise their collective trusteeship for the integrity of the global environment and common areas such as the oceans, atmosphere, and outer space." ("Renewing the United Nations", para. 85) It should serve to link the United Nations and civil society in addressing these areas of global concern. (→ Environmental Protection; → NGOs)

But such a new dedication that would imply a change of the Council's composition requires as well an amendment to the Charter, as would the dissolution of the Trusteeship Council. Such an amendment requires a two-thirds majority of the members of the General Assembly as well as the ratification by two-thirds of the members of the United Nations, including all the permanent members of the Security Council.

In the course of the reform debate in the year 2005 Secretary-General Kofi Annan made in his reform report "In larger freedom" (UN Doc. A/59/2005 of 21 March 2005) the suggestion to replace the obsolete Trusteeship Council by a Human Rights Council (ibid., paras. 166 and 181-183.).

The General Assembly followed at the World Summit 2005 Annan's recommendation only partly and did not make a connection between the two councils, the Trusteeship Council and the suggested Human Rights Council. In paragraphs 157-160 of its resolution A/RES/60/1 "2005 World Summit Outcome" the General Assembly "resolved to create a Human Rights Council", a decision which was put into practice – after further negotiations among the UN member states – in March 2006 with A/RES/60/251.

With regard to the Trusteeship Council the GA simply stated, that the Assembly "should delete" the respective Chapter of the UN Charter on the Trusteeship Council and the references to the Council in the Chapter on the Trusteeship System (UN Doc. A/RES/60/1, para. 176). But so far this recommendation has not been put into practice.

Annan's suggestion to give the Trusteeship Council a new task as Human Rights Council was obviously not followed because the majority of states did not want to establish a human rights organ as principal organ of the United Nations (→ Principal Organs, Subsidiary Organs, Treaty Bodies), but decided to give it a lesser status as subsidiary organ of the General Assembly.

Some optimists still hope that the General Assembly might decide to restructure the Trusteeship Council as UN Environmental Council – as was suggested in Annan's 1997 reform concept – with the council retaining the rank of a principal organ. This would perhaps provide the UN environmental policy with more impact, but the example of the rather clumsy and ineffective ECOSOC illustrates that UN principal organs are not always effective and powerful. Anyway, decisions on the Trusteeship Council might be slow in coming. As long as the General Assembly finds no sufficient consensus about the structural reform of the other principal organs – General Assembly, Security Council and ECOSOC – it will most probably make no decision about the Trusteeship Council.

Helmut Volger

Lit.: *Ermacora, F.:* Trusteeship System/ Trusteeship Council, in: Wolfrum, R. (ed.): United Nations: Law, Policies and Practice, Vol. 2, Munich/Dordrecht 1995, 1259-1266; *United Nations - General Assembly:* Renewing the United Nations: A Programme for Reform. Report of the Secretary-General, 14 July 1997, UN Doc. A/51/950; *United Na-*

tions - General Assembly: In larger freedom: towards development, security and human rights for all. Report of the Secretary-General, 21 March 2005, UN Doc. A/59/2005; *United Nations - General Assembly:* 2005 World Summit Outcome, 16 September 2005, UN Doc. A/RES/60/1.

Internet: Information on the Trusteeship Council: www.un.org//tc.htm.

UNCITRAL – United Nations Commission on International Trade Law

Within the → UN system, UNCITRAL can be located in two different ways: On one hand it belongs to the group of institutions dealing with the economic, social or legal aspects of worldwide trade. This group includes for instance such organizations as → UNCTAD, → UNIDO, → WTO/GATT, as well as the less- known UN Economic Commission for European Trade Facilitation. On the other hand UNCITRAL, together the International Law Commission (→ ILC) and the Sixth Committee of the → General Assembly (→ Committees, System of), constitute the "Principal Legal Bodies of the United Nations": the three columns of international law within the United Nations (*ITL* 1998).

I. History

In the early 1920s the "International Institute for the Unification of Private Law" (UNIDROIT) was created as an international organization with the primary goal to harmonize the different national trade laws, and can thus be seen as a forerunner of the UNCITRAL (*UNCITRAL* 1992). But it took several decades until, in 1962, during a conference of the "International Association of Legal Science", the overall necessity was recognized that "*an international agency of the highest order, possibly at the level of the United Nations, should be charged with the task of coordination* [*of international trade law; the author*]" (*UNCITRAL* 1992). The next attempt to harmonize national trade laws (i.e. the sale of tangible products) through an international conference in the Netherlands in 1964 failed, however. Due to that failure Hungary entered a motion during the nineteenth regular session of the UN General Assembly that the UN should concern itself with possible measures for harmonizing international trade law. Following a recommendation of the Sixth Committee of the General Assembly the → Secretary-General was asked to prepare a report *"that would review the work in the field of harmonization or unification of the law of international trade ... and consider the future role of the United Nations and other agencies in the field."* (*UNCITRAL* 1992). As result of the report submitted to the twenty-first regular session of the General Assembly, this principal organ of the UN adopted Resolution 2205 (XXI) on 17 December 1966, including the decision to create the *UNCITRAL "which shall have for its object the promotion of the progressive harmonization and unification of the law of international trade"*. (UN Doc. A/RES/ 2205 (XXI), I)

II. Organizational Structure

UNCITRAL, which is located at the → UN Office Vienna, is assigned as an organ for international trade law (→ Trade, International Law of) to the UN Office of Legal Affairs. It runs a bureau with currently 10 legal specialists for international law (including the Secretary of UNCITRAL) and 7 office staff members, forming the secretariat of UNCITRAL. Additionally there is a varying number of unpaid interns in the secretariat. The secretariat has a biennial budget of currently 3,440,000 US dollars, and the Commission itself has a biennial budget of 337,040 US dollars (cf. UN Doc. A/54/6/Rev.1).

UNCITRAL consists since 1973 of 36 members (originally 29) representing the different geographically defined groups of UN member states: 9 from African states, 7 from Asian states, 5 from Eastern European States, 6 from Latin American and Caribbean states, and another 9 from the group of West European and Other States (→ Regional Groups in the UN). The members of

UNCITRAL are elected by the General Assembly for a term of six years, with the terms of half of the members expiring every three years.

Since January 2001 the commission has been considering an increase of the total number of members to 50-60 member states because *"the large number of States that had participated as observers* [43 during the 34th session;] *and had made valuable contributions indicated that there existed a considerable interest beyond the thirty-six States that were currently members."* (UN Doc. A/CN.9/500). The Commission has currently four permanent working groups (I: Privately Financed Infrastructure Projects; II: International Arbitration and Conciliation; IV: Electronic Commerce and V: Insolvency). This number will be increased in 2002 by two more such working groups (III: Transport Law and VI: Security Interests) (*UNCITRAL* 1998/1 and *UNCITRAL* 2001/1). The Commission meets usually only once a year, the working groups meet usually twice a year for a two-week session each, alternating between New York and Vienna. Due to the increase of working groups (from three to four, then to six in 2002), working groups will in the future only meet twice a year for a one-week session each, because UNCITRAL is entitled by the General Assembly to six, two-week working group sessions per year only. The meetings of the Commission and its working groups are open for all other members of the UN as well as for specially invited non-governmental organizations (→ NGOs). Among the latter are UNIDROIT, the "Hague Conference on Private International Law" and the "International Chamber of Commerce", with whom UNCITRAL is in permanent and intensive exchange about the latest developments in trade law. (*UNCITRAL* 1992; *UNCITRAL* 1998/2)

III. Tasks of UNCITRAL

The main task of the Commission is *the coordination of all organizations and institutions concerned with international trade law.* Furthermore the

693

Commission has been assigned the task to find solutions for problems raised by the ongoing → globalization of trade by further developing or harmonizing conventions, model laws and rules for practically all sectors of trade among persons and/or enterprises as well as among states. The commission has the important right to deal with any given subject, *"taking any other action it may deem useful to fulfil its functions"* (A/RES/2205 (XXI) of 17 December 1966), i.e. UNCITRAL does not need an assignment by the General Assembly in order to concern itself with a certain topic (*UNCITRAL* 1998/2).

This lenient guideline becomes all the more understandable when we consider the broad spectrum of possible issues: from the signing of a contract for sale, to the transportation and delivery of tangible goods, to the different ways of payment (for instance via letter of credit), and settlement of disputes between manufacturer, merchant and customer – the Commission has to cover all problems and issues of international trade. And there is a long list of other topics the Commission has dealt with or is currently dealing with, such as procurement by governments and their subsidiaries (for instance for the construction of power plants or hydro-electric dams), the duration and coverage of warranties or, in recent times, the problems arising from electronic commerce via the internet (*UNCITRAL* 1998/1). It seems evident from this enumeration above of possible topics that there is a great demand for harmoniztion of the different national rules and laws in order to facilitate or even to enable international trade. UNCITRAL works out recommendations for the Sixth Committee of the General Assembly, and also draft resolutions or conventions for the General Assembly, and develops model laws for the incorporation of universal rules into national legislation.

Some of the major achievements of UNCITRAL are for instance the so-called "Hamburg Rules" (1978), regulating the transport of tangible goods by ship. Or the "United Nations Convention on Contracts for the International Sale of Goods"(1980) as well as the "UNCITRAL Model Law on International Commercial Arbitration" (1985), or the "UNCITRAL Model Law on Electronic Commerce" (1996) – to name just a few. (*ITL* 1998)

Another focus of UNCITRAL lies on the training and information of lawyers and legal specialists in developing nations and countries in transition. For this task a number of conferences are organized in these countries by UNCITRAL, and the Commission hosts a number of interns every year from such countries (*UNCITRAL* 1998/1).

IV. Evaluation of UNCITRAL and Criticism

In his speech at the 25th anniversary conference of UNCITRAL the former UN Secretary-General Boutros-Ghali underlined the importance of the work of the commission for the international economic and political development: "the standardization of international trade law promises to be one of the most important means of facilitating international exchanges and thereby foster economic development. ... Difference in law can ... create an impenetrable thicket of norms in which only the most powerful can find their way – and all this to the detriment of those who are comparatively weak." (*UNCITRAL* 1992, 1f.)

Has UNCITRAL really been able to fulfill its important task after all? The above mentioned conventions and laws created or phrased by the commission and implemented by a large number of UN member states seem to confirm the positive statement of Boutros-Ghali. And even if some of the important conventions have been ratified by only a small number of nations so far ("Hamburg Rules" by only 28 states, "Convention on Contracts for the International Sale of Goods" by 61 states, as of 15 March 2002), the influence of such conventions is considerable, particularly if the nations with the highest shares of global trade are among the signatories and/or ratifying member-states. Whoever has studied the long and tedious process of the creation of GATT or WTO will not be astonished by the equally long and tedious process of establishing universal legal rules for international trade accepted and implemented by the majority of UN-member states. In this regard UNCITRAL has certainly more than fulfilled its expectations.

This positive evaluation however can not be extended to the primary task of coordinating international trade law. "There is a multiplicity of intergovernmental and non-governmental organizations active in the field of international trade law. A report of the UNCITRAL Secretariat in 1988 listed 40 such … organizations. … Unfortunately, the General Assembly did not give the Commission institutional resources to carry out the coordination role it had been assigned." (*UNCITRAL* 1992, 18) The obvious lack of adequate funding as shown above (compare also → Financial Crises) can be regarded as a major cause for the ongoing multi- level definition and formulation of – parallel at best and contradictory at worst – rules and models by UNCITRAL, and a large number of other institutions and organizations. Even though pluralism is an important ingredient for an international democratic order, a pluralism of law is certainly a detriment to international trade, as it creates incalculable risks for the trading parties and hinders the exchange of goods, tangible and intangible. However, this problem can be found in many other parts and sectors of the wide network of the United Nation system, and can only be adequately dealt with within the overall → reform of the UN.

Another result of the meager funding of such an important commission can be found in "the relatively low incidence of expert representation from developing countries as sessions of the Commission and particularly of its working groups during recent years, owing in part to inadequate resources to finance travel of such experts." (Report of the Sixth Committee, UN Doc. A/49/739 of 1 December 1994, 4)

As a remedy UNCITRAL created a trust fund, i.e. voluntary contributions of the wealthier nations, for the financing of travel expenses (cf. UN Doc. A/CN.9/500 of 9 May 2001, para. 10). But this can only help to ease the financial burden for the developing nations, without treating the source of the problem. It is therefore inevitable that any decision to increase the number of members of the commission has to go hand in hand with a significant or at least proportionate increase of the budget of UNCITRAL.

Patrick Oliver Ott

Lit.: *Internet Homepage of the University of Tromsö,* Norway, Law Faculty (quoted as *ITL* 1998); *Joyner, C.:* The United Nations and International Law, Cambridge 1997; *Käde, A.:* UNCITRAL - United Nations Commission on International Trade Law, in: Wolfrum, R. (ed.): United Nations: Law, Policies and Practice, Vol. 1, Munich/Dordrecht 1995, 1267-1273; *Schachter, O. et al.:* United Nations Legal Order, Cambridge 1995; *UNCITRAL:* UNCITRAL - The United Nations Commission on Trade Law, New York 1986; *UNCITRAL:* Uniform Commercial Law in the twenty-first century, Congress of the UNCITRAL 18-22 Mai 1992, New York 1992; *UNCITRAL*: UNCITRAL Yearbook, Vol. XXVII, 1996, New York 1997; *UNCITRAL: Internet Homepage of UNCITRAL* (quoted as UNCITRAL 1998/1); *UNCITRAL:* Information of Jeanette Tramhel, Legal Officer, UNCITRAL, given to the author on 10 December 1998 (quoted as UNCITRAL 1998/2).

Addendum

UNCITRAL – due to the increased demand for uniform trade law standards in a globalized world – has faced a growing workload in this first decade of the new millennium. To meet this challenge, it has considerably increased the number of its permanent working groups since 2002. The Commission currently has six permanent working groups (I: Procurement (since 2004); II: International arbitration and conciliation; III: Transport law (since 2002); IV: electronic commerce; V: Insolvency law; VI: Security interests (since 2002)).

The growing interest of the UN member states in its work made it necessary for UNCITRAL to ask the General Assembly to expand the membership of UNCITRAL in order to enhance its working capacity and to improve its representativeness. Through Resolution A/RES/57/20 of 19 November 2002, the Assembly further increased the Commission membership from 36 to 60 states.

The opposition of the budgetary and oversight institutions of the United Nations to the necessary increase in personnel in the International Trade Law Branch of the UN Office of Legal Affairs (OLA), which is in charge of servicing UNCITRAL, therefore often referred to as the UNCITRAL Secretariat, caused delays and created obstacles. In spite of a growing workload the staff resources had remained roughly the same since the late 60s.

Hence, the UN Legal Counsel Hans Corell, in his opening speech at UNCITRAL's 35th session in June 2002, warned the UN member states that if the staff working for UNCITRAL were not significantly strengthened, UNCITRAL would have to reduce its work programme (*Corell* 2002, 9).

Unfortunately, according to Hans Corell, the Advisory Committee on Administrative und Budgetary Questions (ACABQ), the key institution in the budgetary process (→ Budget), was not convinced that the proposal to upgrade the International Trade Law Branch in the UN Secretariat to a Division by raising the staffing size, would meet the criterion set by the General Assembly, namely that it be within the limits of the resources available (quoted from: *UNIS Vienna* 2003). For Corell, the statement of the ACABQ about the increase in staff seemed to be a result of a critical report of the Office of Internal Oversight Services on the in-depth evaluation of the OLA submitted in April 2002 (UN Doc. E/AC.51/2002/5 of 9 April 2002, para. 66). OIOS recommended considering other options, in particular the benefit of new working methods, before increasing staff re-

sources. The General Assembly followed in its 2002 resolution on the work of UNCITRAL and on the strengthening of its secretariat the line of argumentation of OIOS (UN Doc. A/RES/57/19 of 19 November 2002). The critical attitude of OIOS is difficult to understand in view of the fact that the budget proposal for 2002-2003 was achieved by streamlining and increasing efficiencies within the OLA. This made it possible for those resources to be redeployed from other parts of the Legal Office to the UNCITRAL Secretariat.

In the Secretary-General's bulletin of 1 August 2008 (ST/SGB/2008/13) establishing the organizational structure of the OLA the International Trade Law Branch is now mentioned as International Trade Law Division (ITLD). It currently has 14 legal experts and seven office staff members.

UNCITRAL itself has now (October 2008) a biennial budget of 486,500 US Dollars and the ITLD a budget of 6,128,300 US Dollars (UN Doc. A/62/6 (Sect. 8)).

There are three important projects completed by UNCITRAL since 2002:

(1) adopted on 7 July 2003, the "Model Legislative Provisions on Privately Financed Infrastructure Projects" are intended to assist domestic legislative bodies in the establishment of a legislative framework favorable to privately financed infrastructure projects;

(2) adopted on 25 June 2004, the "UNCITRAL Legislative Guide on Insolvency Law" is to assist the establishment of an efficient and effective legal framework to address financial difficulties of debtors. It is intended to be used as a reference by national authorities and legislative bodies when preparing new legislation and regulations or reviewing the adequacy of existing laws and regulations;

(3) on 23 November 2005, the General Assembly adopted the "United Nations Convention on the Use of Electronic Communications in International Contracts", which had been adopted by the Commission and

which aims to enhance legal certainty and commercial predictability where electronic communication is used in relation to international contracts.

In the last years the significance of the projects mentioned earlier concerning transport law, the trade of goods and arbitration has increased, which can be deduced from a steadily growing number of ratifications.

Thus, the "United Nations Convention on the Carriage of Goods by Sea" (Hamburg Rules) has now been ratified by 33 states, the "Convention on Contracts for the International Sale of Goods" by 70 states, and the "UNCITRAL Model Law on International Commercial Arbitration" has been incorporated into the legislation of more than 50 states (figures as of 30 May 2008, UN Doc. A/CN.9/651). The provisions of these projects, used in the great majority of private contracts concerning transboundary traffic of goods, play a considerable role in the practice of international economic law.

The future will show if the latest reform projects of UNCITRAL will have a similar success. On 3 July 2008, UNCITRAL approved the "Draft Convention on Contracts for the International Carriage of Goods Wholly or Partly by Sea" (Report of UNCITRAL, forty-first session, 16 June - 3 July 2008, UN Doc. A/63/17, Annex I). The draft convention was submitted by UNCITRAL to the General Assembly with a view of adopting it as UN Convention (UNCITRAL decision, 3 July 2008, UN Doc. A/63/17, para. 298). With respect to the number of Commission member states, a considerable number of ratifications can certainly be expected.

Felix Boor

Lit: *Corell, H.:* Opening Speech at UNCITRAL's 35th session by Mr. Hans Corell, Under-Secretary-General for Legal Affairs (The Legal Counsel), New York, 17 June 2002, www.un.org/law/counsel/english/uncitral2002.htm; *United Nations - Economic and Social Council - Committee for Programme and Coordination:* Report of the Office of Internal Oversight Services on the in-depth evaluation of legal affairs. Note by the Secretary-General, UN Doc. E/AC.51/2002/5, 9 April 2002; *United Nations - General Assembly:* United Nations Commission on International Trade Law. Status of conventions and model laws. Note by the Secretariat, 30 May 2008, UN Doc. A/CN.9/651; *United Nations Information Service (UNIS Vienna):* Legal Committee Told of Initiatives on Global Trade Rules, UN Press Release GA/L/3230, 7 October 2003 (quoted as UNIS Vienna 2003)

Internet: a) Homepage of UNCITRAL: www.uncitral.org; b) Website of the University of Tromsö, serving with commission of the UN as "International Trade Law Monitor": http://itl.irv.uit.no/trade_law/papers/UNCITRAL.html, with links to other institutions of international law and trade; c) "UN Workstation" of Yale University; keyword: „International Trade": www.library.yale.edu/un/unhome.htm; d) for legal searches: the data bank CLOUT of UNCITRAL with collection of cases in all languages of the UN: www.un.or.at./uncitral/clout.

UNCIVPOL – United Nations Civilian Police

"Civilian Police" (CIVPOL or UNCIVPOL) is the UN term for uniformed international police in → peacekeeping operations (→ Peacekeeping). The term has been chosen to distinguish it from the military police (provost) units normally included in military forces.

The term "civilian police" was coined when in 1964 the new UN Peacekeeping Force in Cyprus (UNFICYP) included a police component: 30 police officers per district were attached to the UN force to supervise and monitor the Cypriot police in cases involving inter-community relations, thereby reassuring the population. Initially, 173 police officers from Australia, Austria, Denmark, New Zealand, and Sweden were deployed.

Recently, the term "CIVPOL" has been replaced in official UN documents by the term "UN Police" – in part, because "civilian police" was sometimes misinterpreted to signify plain-clothes men.

Police are of less importance in (traditional) peacekeeping missions in inter-state conflicts, when an international military presence supervises, for example, a cease-fire line (→ Peacekeeping Forces). However, in internal conflicts, often involving inter-ethnic tensions, police play an important stabilizing role.

Starting with the 1989-90 Namibia mission (UNTAG), most UN operations after the Cold War included strong police components. Normally, UN police are not to replace local police or to enforce the law themselves, but rather to supervise, assist and train existing or newly established indigenous police forces. This might include joint training programmes and even joint patrols. The aim is to help the new or reformed local police to (re-)gain the confidence of the local population.

Police play an increasingly important role in peacebuilding processes (→ Agenda for Peace).

Usually, CIVPOL personnel (like military → observers) are not armed. They wear their national police uniforms with additional blue berets or caps, and UN insignia.

Certain problems have resurfaced in many operations. These include insufficient personnel selection and pre-mission training, lack of Basic English and driving skills, lack of mission-specific preparation such as cultural awareness training, and often less-than-democratic police traditions in their home countries. Consequently, the UN was often criticized for insufficient CIVPOL activities. Since 1995, however, the UN Secretariat (→ Secretariat) and its Department of Peacekeeping Operations have increasingly been involved in the selection processes in certain countries, resulting in some improvements.

One problem remains: few (Western) countries are able to spare significant numbers of police officers for lengthy periods of time. The maintenance of adequate personnel remains difficult, however, over longer periods.

At the time of writing (autumn 2008), seven peacekeeping operations included more than 1,000 police personnel. These were the missions in Haiti (MINUSTAH) 1,916 police; Darfur (UNAMID) 1,845; Timor Leste (UNMIT) 1,534, Kosovo (UNMIK) 1,499; Côte d'Ivoire (UNOCI) 1,127; Liberia (UNMIL) 1,094 and Democratic Republic of the Congo (MONUC) 1,051. The total number of UN police personnel was about 9,500.

From 2003, the EU became increasingly engaged in police missions as well, especially by taking over the UN police in Bosnia-Herzegovina in 2003.

Erwin A. Schmidl

Lit.: *Lewis, W./Marks, E.:* Police Power in Peace Operations. Civilian Police and Multinational Peacekeeping: A Workshop Series of the Center for Strategic and International Studies, Washington D.C. 1999; *Oakley, B. et al. (eds.):* Policing the New World Disorder, Washington D.C. 1998; *Schmidl, E.A.:* Police in Peace Operations, Vienna 1998; *United Nations - Department of Public Information:* UN Police Magazine: Building Institutional Police Capacity in Post-Conflict Environments, New York 2006, www.un.org/Depts/dpko/UNPolice_mag.pdf.

Internet: Information on UN Civilian Police: www.un.org/Depts/dpko/dpko/intro/police.htm and www.un.org/Depts/dpko/dpko/civpol/civpol1.html.

UNCTAD – United Nations Conference on Trade and Development

In 1964, the United Nations Conference on Trade and Development (UNCTAD) was established as a special organ of the UN General Assembly (→ General Assembly) to advocate a basic restructuring on behalf of the developing countries. UNCTAD's foundation is generally considered to be a milestone on the way to institutionalizing the North-South-Dialogue (→ North-South-Relations and the UN), as well as being the complement to the system of international economic organizations which was established in Bretton Woods (→ World Bank, World Bank Group; → IMF).

The establishment of UNCTAD was the consequence of a process. Since the beginning of the early 60s, the problems of the developing countries had appeared in three fields, together with the limited ability of so-far existing UN bodies to support them in these problems having become obvious. These were the questions of a) favorable loans and investments, b) (terms of) trade and c) access to technological know-how.

The developing countries maintained that the time had come both to call for action for the foundation of → specialized agencies as well as for commissions within the → UN system: having founded the International Development Association (IDA) on 5 December 1959 with the consent of the industrialized countries, the General Assembly had already established a suitable frame for providing funds to cover the most important development needs of the developing countries. These funds were more elastic and a lesser financial burden on the balance of payments of the receiving countries than loans under customary conditions. However, the fulfillment of the demands in the area of trade had a long time in coming, though the world market share of the developing countries' exports decreased between 1953 and 1961 from 27% to some 21%. On the one hand, reasons for this were the technological innovations in agriculture, which in turn led to considerable increase in the worldwide supply of agricultural products, and, on the other hand, the substitution of raw materials through synthetic materials. Due to the low price elasticity in the demand of these goods, the slump in prices of primary goods could not be compensated by an increase in demand. With prices for industrial products increasing at the same time, Terms of Trade for the developing countries noticeably deteriorated. The result was an accumulated trade deficit on the part of the Third World, which could not be balanced even by increased transfer payments through economic aid.

Capital needed for the industrialization process was not sufficiently available, and the slogan "trade instead of aid" became the major demand of third-world countries. From the view of the economically weak countries, no inter-national organizations, which might have contributed to their better integration into the world economy, existed at the beginning of the sixties. The passing of a resolution concerning "World trade as a main instrument for economic development" (UN Doc. A/RES/1707 (XVI) on 19 December 1961, at the 16th regular session of the General Assembly, meant a significant step towards improving the conditions of world trade for developing countries, which, in the meantime, had attained a strong position within the UN system. The resolution recommended a conference on world trade, but and determined the topics and the structure.

In 1962, 36 developing countries convened in Cairo to discuss "aspects of economic development". This conference is seen as another decisive step towards the establishment of a world trade conference. It concluded with the "Cairo Declaration", in which the developing countries expressed their will to pursue their own concerns in the future. The breakthrough was attained when, on 3 August 1962, the Economic and Social Council (→ ECOSOC) decided to summon a conference on trade and development (UN Doc. E/RES/917 (XXXIV), which had been initiated by the developing countries. On 8 December 1962, this decision was approved explicitly by the 17th session of the General Assembly (UN Doc. A/RES/1785 (XVII).

The convening of the conference was, however, preceded by lengthy disputes: the industrialized countries were only willing to establish the conference as a subsidiary body to the ECOSOC (→ Principal Organs, Subsidiary Organs, Treaty Bodies). Finally, agreement on the foundation as a "special organ" of the GA was reached with a compromise: the developing countries gave up their plan to establish an organization exclusively concerned with aspects of development, and they agreed to limit UNCTAD's responsibility to the trade between countries on different developmental levels and to the trade between developing countries and countries with different economic and social systems. Additional objectives and responsibilities were laid down in the founding resolution which was approved on 30 December 1964, during the 19th session of the General Assembly (UN Doc. A/RES/1995 (XIX):

- to promote international trade, especially between countries with different levels of development, aiming at accelerating economic growth in developing countries;
- to formulate and implement principles and guidelines for international trade and linked problems of economic development;
- to coordinate activities of other UN institutions dealing with international trade and linked problems of economic development and to cooperate with General Assembly and ECOSOC in this field;
- to take measures to achieve negotiations and multilateral agreements in the field of international trade, as well as
- to assume a central role in harmonizing trade and development policies of states and regional economic organizations.

The crucial impulses to formulate these demands were given by Raoúl Prebisch, a renowned economist and Executive Director of the UN Economic Commission for Latin-America and the Caribbean – ECLAC (→ Economic Commissions, Regional). In the run-up to the first UNCTAD conference in Geneva in 1964, Prebisch also took the lead in working out a common position for the Latin-American countries. Based on the assumption of a "trade gap" in the trade between developing and industrialized countries (*Prebisch* 1968) to the detriment of the former, Prebisch took the view that a totally free trade and the international economic order of the postwar-period had resulted in the exploitation of the developing countries. The ensuing continually rising deficits in the balance of payments barred the developing countries from any industrializing process. For Prebisch there was no doubt that the international community was legally obliged to establish a new international economic order to the benefit of the developing countries (→ International Economic Relations and NIEO).

Already in the preparation phase of the conference, Prebisch, who was elected Secretary-General of UNCTAD at the conference, succeeded in forging the different interests of the developing countries into common denominators, and to translate this into a package of demands that was supported by all developing countries:

- unconditional reduction and finally abolishment of all trade barriers that existed to the disadvantage of the developing countries;
- increase in the export of primary goods to the industrialized countries at stable prices;
- opening of the markets for finished and semi-finished products from developing countries;
- granting of further trade preferences in the area of invisible trade, especially easing the burden of freight and insurance costs.

At the first UNCTAD conference in 1964, a group of developing countries formed the "Group of 77" (→ Group of 77 and the UN) and became the voice for their claims. In the following years, this group successfully contributed to increasing the acceptance of UNCTAD and its aims.

The first UN Conference on Trade and Development took place in the League of Nations Palace in Geneva from 23 March to 16 June 1964. In the number of participating countries it reached a new level: about 2000 delegates from 119 countries negotiated for improving the integration of developing countries into the world economy.

According to the 1964 founding resolution, every member state of the UN or a member of any of its specialized agencies is also automatically a member of UNCTAD. UNCTAD is structured as follows. The *Conference*, convening every four years, functions as a permanent subsidiary body of the General Assembly. The *Trade and Development Board,* also created by the founding resolution, is the permanent executive organ of UNCTAD which convenes regularly between the conferences, at least twice a year. The Trade and Development Board created main committees on a) commodities, b) manufactures, c) services and financing relating to trade, d) shipping, e) transfer of technology, and f) economic cooperation among developing countries.

The administrative authority lies with the General Secretariat, which is headed by a Secretary-General. Till the mid-90s, it was subdivided into eight departments: conference and foreign relations; research; trade policy; commodities; finished products; services; financial aspects of trade; trade with socialist countries. The annual UNCTAD budget is drawn from the UN regular budget ($\rightarrow$ Budget). In 1995, it amounted to about 57.5 million US dollars.

Negotiations within the UNCTAD are based on internal groupings. Group A (Afro-Asian states) and Group C (Latin-American states) have united to the "Group of 77". Group B comprises the industrialized countries of Western Europe as well as Australia, Canada, New Zealand, the United States and the Holy See. Till the decline of the Soviet Union, Group D consisted of the Eastern industrialized countries. Votes are taken by the "one-state, one-vote" principle ($\rightarrow$ Voting Right, Decision-Making Procedures).

Though it was originally intended to hold conferences every two or three years, a four-year-rhythm to convene was practiced right from the beginning. In 1972, it was codified by an agreement to hold conferences every four years. So far, on only one occasion was there a three-year interval: between UNCTAD IV (1976) and UNCTAD V (1979).

Conferences until the year 2000 have been:
UNCTAD I (1964 in Geneva);
UNCTAD II (1968 in New Delhi);
UNCTAD III (1972 in Santiago de Chile); UNCTAD IV (1976 in Nairobi); UNCTAD V (1979 in Manila);
UNCTAD VI (1983 in Belgrade);
UNCTAD VII (1987 in Geneva);
UNCTAD VIII (1992 in Cartagena de Indias, Columbia);
UNCTAD IX (1996 in Midrand, South Africa) and
UNCTAD X (2000 in Bangkok).
Beside Raúl Prebisch (1964-1969), three of his successors have decisively influenced the structure of the organization and its political weight: Gamani Corea (1974-1984) from Sri Lanka, Kenneth K. S. Dadzie (1984-1994) from Ghana and the former Brazilian finance minister Rubens Ricupero (since 1995).

The greatest success of UNCTAD is commonly considered to have been the establishment of the "Common Fund for Commodities", which was adopted at UNCTAD IV in Nairobi in 1976. This fund was aimed at
- improving the Terms of Trade for the benefit of the developing countries,
- establishing stable price ratios in commodity trading,
- avoiding excessive price fluctuations,
- securing a price level that is profitable, but also fair for consumers,
- promoting a balance between supply and demand in a growing worldwide commodity trade.
But even though this reform project was put into effect in 1989 and is seen as UNCTAD's greatest success so far, the industrialized countries at the same time put up some obstacles. They prevented the "Integrated Programme for Commodities" which would have been a prerequisite for the functioning of the funds, and replaced all theretofore existing commodity agreements with buffer stocks, whose financing the common fund was to guarantee (*Melchers* 1996, 147).

This development is even more remarkable when the paramount importance of this topic for the developing countries with regard to their excessively high dependence on commodities is taken into account. For even as late as 1995, the export of raw materials of 35 American, 45 African, 11 West-Asian, 7 South- and Southeast-Asian developing countries and 8 in the Oceanic region made up 50 % or more of their overall exports (*UNCTAD* 1995, 80).

The fact that UNCTAD was ultimately denied success in many fields and could therefore not fulfill the hopes and expectations of the developing countries can largely be attributed to UNCTAD's founding concepts. Once having accepted the proviso clause, as demanded by the industrialized countries, that UNCTAD should neither transgress nor overlap responsibilities of other existing international organizations, especially GATT, the developing countries allowed for existing structures to be cemented: GATT has remained the powerful "club" of the rich industrialized world (→ WTO, GATT), while UNCTAD has just been granted a political role as the key forum of the poor.

The role of UNCTAD was even more seriously affected when economic policy in the USA changed to a neo-liberal course. The United States not only challenged the whole multilateral economic system, but also criticized the alleged politicization, the content of its orientation and the efficiency of UNCTAD (→ UN Policy, USA).

In addition, the debts crisis and the fall of the commodity prices in the 1980s as well as the dissolution of the Eastern Bloc at the beginning of the 1990s, severely weakened the negotiating power of the Group of 77. Thus, UNCTAD's acceptance as a platform for negotiating aspects of trade and development from that point increasingly declined.

Trying to adjust UNCTAD to this development, its members accepted major elements of neo-liberalism at UNCTAD VIII in Cartagena (1992), recognizing the positive effects of → globalization and of a liberalization of the world economy on developing countries as well (*Jessen* 1992).

But the pressure to go ahead with reforms has increased since the mid-90s. With the final establishment of the World Trade Organization (WTO) in January 1995, those developing countries which had joined the WTO started to turn to the new organization, hoping to make their problems heard there. This in turn led to questions of UNCTAD's

future role and its right to exist. On the other hand, a number of independent commissions (→ Independent Commissions, Reports of) had been set up on the occasion of the 50th anniversary of the UN to work out reform potentials of the world organization (→ Reform of the UN). In order to revive the economic and the social sectors, these commissions recommended creating a "Security Council for World Economy", a "UN Economic Council" or a "Council for Economic Security", that should either coordinate the work of the existing specialized agencies or should integrate in or merge the great number of existing institutions, such as UNCTAD, → UNIDO, → UNDP, in the new institution.

Especially the "Commission on Global Governance" considered UNCTAD's goal of strengthening the negotiation power of the developing countries to be outdated. The commission recommended dissolving UNCTAD as well as UNIDO and ECOSOC, and replacing them by a "Council for Economic Security". Negotiations on trade, including preliminary hearings, were to come under the responsibility of WTO, and those on other aspects of development were to be handled by IMF and World Bank (*Commission on Global Governance* 1995, 304-313).

In November 1995, the Group of 77 and the Movement of Non-Aligned States (→ Non-Aligned Movement and the UN) published a position paper titled "Why UNCTAD?" (published in: epd-entwicklungspolitik 21 (1995), p-v) in which they expressed their will to preserve UNCTAD in its present form. Nevertheless, they could not prevent the adoption of important reforms at UNCTAD IX in Midrand, South Africa, in 1996. By making "promoting growth and sustainable development in a globalizing and liberalizing world economy" the conference's main economic topic, they took up the most crucial economic issue after the end of the Cold War while at the same time stressing UNCTAD's right to exist and underlining the necessity of such an organization as a counterpart to the Bretton Woods institutions

and the WTO. Three major challenges of globalization were pointed out for most developing countries:
- loss of national autonomy in political decision-making: imitating the development course of the East-Asian "dragon states" is not possible because they achieved their export successes through government funds and a strategy of selective integration into the world market;
- financial risks: the liberalization of international financial markets not only enabled capital transactions for the benefit of the developing countries, but was also followed by a heightened instability because of sudden changes in the expectations of foreign investors;
- marginalization through globalization: Because of weak points on the supply side (low technological capacities, lack of know-how and education, insufficient infrastructure, financial bottlenecks of small-level producers), especially the least developed countries (LDCs) are of little interest for foreign investors (*Melchers* 1996, 150).

Though the continued existence of UNCTAD as an important forum for opinion and consensus building in the North-South-Dialogue is basically guaranteed since the Midrand conference, the "old UNCTAD" no longer exists. Apart from being assigned new working fields, UNCTAD was as well considerably tightened up in its institutions. Now the UNCTAD Secretariat is intended mainly to fulfill the function of an opinion-leader, with primarily analytic research work along the lines of an "OECD of the South" (*Hüfner* 1997, 156).

In the foreground stands thereby its function as mediator between the industrialized countries and the developing countries in solving questions of common interest. In this context UNCTAD is to put special emphasis on articulating the interests of the LDCs, and to support their integration into the world market and the WTO. Furthermore, UNCTAD is to concentrate on the aspect of development when dealing with the issues

presented. Based on the concentration on the needs of the LDCs, it was agreed that aspects concerning LDCs should not be dealt with in the framework of a separate field of work, but should be dealt with as a cross-sectional topic in all activities and departments of UNCTAD.

Additionally, UNCTAD's working field was adapted to that of the WTO and its position towards the WTO was made clear. Agreement was reached that the following topics should be handled as cross-sectional topics by UNCTAD in the future: sustainable development, fight against poverty, empowerment of women, LDCs and South-South cooperation (*Melchers* 1996, 152).

With these decisions, UNCTAD's reorientation became obvious. The demand for a New International Economic Order, for North-South negotiations on fair trade and similar far-reaching conceptions have been abandoned. Moreover, more clearly than ever UNCTAD has placed the poor countries' own responsibility for their economic development and growth in the focus, and has assigned the aid of donor countries only an accompanying and complementary role.

The institutional reorganization concentrated on reducing the number of commissions subordinated to the UNCTAD Council. Their number was reduced from seven to three, with the following tasks: (1) trade with goods, services and commodities, (2) investments, technology and linked financial aspects, (3) measures of concrete technical cooperation.

These commissions are to convene once a year for five days at the most and, if required, to summon three-day-long expert rounds on specific topics, with a maximum of ten per year. By taking those measures, it is intended to decrease the annual days of meetings from 130 to 70.

Doubtless the UNCTAD will continue to exist as the platform for the North-South dialogue concerning aspects of trade and development within the UN-system. But its main task in future will

703

be to look after and support the marginalized countries and losers of the globalization process. With that, UNCTAD claims to be "the conscience" of the poor countries, as Secretary-General Boutros Boutros-Ghali formulated in his opening address (*Boutros-Ghali* 1996, 3). Nevertheless, this development of UNCTAD can be considered to be a "victory of reason over ideology".

In the founding period of UNCTAD the idea of an ethic-oriented global spirit was prevalent, but turned out to be of no influence on the processes of world economy. It has meanwhile been replaced by a new responsibility- and result-oriented ethics (*Lammert* 1996, 58). It is not surprising that the G-7 states welcomed the agreed reforms at their economic summit in Lyon in June 1996: "UNCTAD IX was a major milestone in the renewal of UNCTAD. In close partnership with the other member States, we succeeded in reforming UNCTAD's intergovernmental machinery and in refocusing its work on a small number of priorities to promote development through trade and investment with the aim of facilitating the integration of developing countries in the international trade system. We are committed to the implementation of these reforms. The LLDCs [sic!; i.e. least developed countries, the author] will be the major beneficiaries of this action. We also welcome the initiative of WTO and the renewed UNCTAD to enhance mutual cooperation with each other, with due regard to their respective mandates." (*Lyon G7 Summit 1996:* Economic Communiqué, para. 44).

Mir A. Ferdowsi

Lit.: *Bauerochse, L.:* UNCTAD VII: Und es bewegt sich nichts, in: Der Überblick 23 (1987), 62-65; *Borman, A.:* Die Entwicklungsländer im Polarisierungsprozeß des Welthandels, in: Fischer, B. (ed.): Die dritte Welt im Wandel der Weltwirtschaft, Hamburg 1992, 33-60; *Boutros-Ghali, B.:* Address by Dr. Boutros-Ghali, Secretary-General of the United Nations, at the Inaugural Ceremony of the Ninth Session of the UNCTAD, Midrand/South Africa, 27 April - 11 May 1996, 1-4; *Dams, T.:* UNCTAD IV: Noch kein Ausweg aus der Krise, in: VN 31 (1983), 118-124; *Fabius, W.:* Fünfundsiebzig suchen einen Weg zur Entwicklung. Erträglicher Ausgang der Welthandelskonferenz in Genf, in: VN 12 (1964), 133-137; *Habermayer, W.:* Internationale Rohstoffabkommen als Beispiel des Nord-Süd-Dialoges, Frankfurt (Main) 1985; *Höffkes, P.W.:* UNCTAD VII – Eine Hoffnung für mehr Vernunft im Nord-Süd-Dialog, in: Politische Studien 39 (1988), No. 289, 154-159; *Hüfner, K.:* Die Vereinten Nationen und ihre Sonderorganisationen. Teil 3: Finanzierung des Systems der Vereinten Nationen 1971-1995. Teil A: Vereinte Nationen – Friedensoperationen – Spezialorgane, DGVN-Texte 45, Bonn 1997; *Jessen, Ch.:* UNCTAD VIII in Cartagena – ein Neubeginn? in: NORD-SÜD aktuell 6 (1992), 116-121; *Kommission für Weltordnungspolitik:* Nachbarn in einer Welt, edited by Stiftung Entwicklung und Frieden, Bonn 1995; *Lammert, N.:* Sieg der Vernunft über die Ideologie. Ergebnisse von UNCTAD IX, in: IP 55 (1996), No. 8, 55-58; *Lyon G7 Summit 1996:* Economic Communiqué: Making a success of globalization for the benefit of all, Lyon 28 June 1996, edited by the Canadian Department of Foreign Affairs and International Trade 1996; *Melchers, K.:* Totgesagte leben länger. Nach UNCTAD IX: eine gestraffte Organisation mit Zukunft, in: VN 44 (1996), 147-153; *Prebisch, R.:* Towards a New Trade Policy for Development, United Nations, New York 1964; *Prebisch, R.:* Für eine bessere Zukunft der Entwicklungsländer, edited by Schmidt, J.L./Domdey, K.H., Berlin 1968; *Raghavan, Ch.:* UNCTAD VII and the Promise of Geneva, in: Development and Peace, Vol. 9 (1988), 30-38; *Rothstein, R. L.:* Global Bargaining. UNCTAD and the Quest for a New International Economic Order, Princeton 1979; *Steuernagel, A.:* Zur politischen Ökonomie multilateraler Wirtschaftsorganisationen. Ein Beitrag zur Reformdebatte der Vereinten Nationen, Münster 1997; *Talpin, G.:* Neubelebung der UNCTAD, in: Finanzierung & Entwicklung 29 (1992), No. 2, 36-37; *UNCTAD:* Commodity Yearbook 1995, Geneva 1995; *UNCTAD:* The history of UNCTAD 1964-1984, New York 1985; *UNCTAD:* UNCTAD Statistical Pocket Book, New York et al. 1994; *Wolfrum, R.:* Commodity Agreements/Common Fund, in: Wolfrum, R. (ed.): United Nations: Law, Policies and Practice, Vol. 1, Munich/Dordrecht 1995, 138-148.

Addendum

During recent years, UNCTAD has been able to consolidate its (peripheral) position in the international system, although this has not been free from controversy. In a recent report, UNCTAD's Panel of Eminent Persons (*United Nations* 2006a, 1) called for decisive action: "UNCTAD is at a crossroads, defined by a growing conflict between the reality of its success and the perception of its redundancy."

So far, demands for the dissolution of the organization have led nowhere. It is obvious that the G77/China will not let go of an innovative think tank which is geared towards their agenda. Though they may dislike the overall framework of its analytical work, Western countries have accommodated to UNCTAD since it refrains from intergovernmental negotiations and decision-making. A further factor for UNCTAD's recognition is the appointment of a respected international civil servant as Secretary-General. Supachai Panitchpakdi, a former Director-General of WTO, began his four-year term in September 2005, following his appointment by the UN General Assembly.

UNCTAD XI (2004 in São Paulo) has enriched the North-South debate by insisting on the need for "policy space" in national decision-making (cf. the key text "São Paulo Consensus", UN Doc. TD/410, 25 June 2004). This notion is often used by developing countries in questioning the neoliberal orthodoxy propagated by the dominant institutions of global economic governance. UNCTAD XII in Accra/Ghana (2008) will address the opportunities and challenges of globalization for development. The conference will also examine how the growth in South-South trade, investment and aid is transforming the world economic landscape (cf. Report of the Secretary-General of UNCTAD to UNCTAD XII "Globalization for development: Opportunities and Challenges", UN Doc. TD/413, 4 July 2007).

UNCTAD's reputation as a reliable source of analysis and policy advice is undisputed. It produces an impressive array of periodical publications such as the reports on world investment, trade and development and on LDCs which are well received in policy circles and academia. The organization's special focus on the poorest countries and on Africa has gained in relevance since the unequal distribution of benefits from globalization is increasingly recognized as a paramount challenge for the international community. UNCTAD statistics, e.g. its "World Investment Directory Online" database, as well as its analytical work on financial markets and foreign debt have become oft-cited reference documents.

Increasingly, UNCTAD engages in operational activities in support of developing countries, a move seen critically by those who plead for system-wide coherence (cf. *United Nations* 2006b). One highly praised example is the Blue Book programme, which assists African governments in strengthening their investment environment.

The South Centre, an intergovernmental think tank of developing countries, has proposed that UNCTAD should play a more prominent role in global economic governance (*South Centre* 2007). A further proposal – of G77/China – refers to the creation of a new UNCTAD Commission on Globalization and Development Strategies which would support the reinvigoration of UNCTAD's role as the primary think tank in the UN system in this field.

In 2006, a Panel of Eminent Persons established by the Secretary-General of UNCTAD presented reform proposals to better position UNCTAD strategically through strengthening its core areas of work (*United Nations* 2006a). The Panel also recommended to replace the high-level segment of the Trade and Development Board either by a multi-stakeholder dialogue (i.e. including representatives of civil society and the business sector) or by a biennial Global Forum for Trade, Investment and Development. It remains open if member states from North and South will agree on expanding UNCTAD's mandate and

705

resources or if the organization will remain locked into a niche of the global governance system.

Thomas Fues

Lit: *South Centre:* Getting UNCTAD XII right: Recommendation on Theme and Sub-Themes. Analytical Note, SC/GGDP/AN/GPG/3, Geneva 2007, www.southcentre. org/index.php?option=com_docman&task= doc_download&gid=203&Itemid=69; *United Nations:* Enhancing the Development Role and Impact of UNCTAD. Report of the Panel of Eminent Persons, New York and Geneva, June 2006, UN Doc. UNCTAD/OSG/2006/1 (quoted as: United Nations 2006a), www.unctad.org/sections/edm_dir/docs/osg20061_en.pdf; *United Nations - General Assembly:* Delivering as one. Report of the High-level Panel on United Nations System-wide Coherence in the areas of development, humanitarian assistance and the environment, UN-Doc. A/61/583, 20 November 2006 (quoted as: United Nations 2006b).

Internet: Homepage of UNCTAD: www. unctad.org.

UNDP – United Nations Development Programme

I. Origins

The *United Nations Development Programme* (UNDP) was established in 1965 by the → General Assembly (UN Doc. A/RES/2029 (XX) of 22 November 1965) and began work in 1966. UNDP was the result of the merging of two existing UN bodies: the *Expanded Programme of Technical Assistance* (EPTA) and the *Special Fund* (SF). EPTA, which had been set up in 1949, operated in the area of technical cooperation, mainly through the assignment of experts. The *Special Fund*, established in 1958, had the task of preparing major development projects. These two bodies were merged to reduce duplication and concentrate financial resources.

In 1970 the General Assembly adopted the "Consensus Resolution" (UN Doc. A/RES/2688 (XXV) of 11 December 1970), which was based on the recommendations of a study of the efficiency of the UN's development cooperation carried out under the guidance of Sir Robert Jackson: "A Study of the Capacity of the United Nations Development System", also known as the *"Capacity Study"* (UN Doc. UN/DP/5).

The *"Capacity Study"* analyzed various structural, organizational and financial problems associated with the UN's development cooperation, which are frequently encountered in the same or a similar form even today. The main warning issued by the study has also remained valid: unless UN development cooperation has a central "brain", it may well suffer the same fate as the dinosaurs.

The "Consensus Resolution" assigns fundamental and overarching responsibilities for the → UN system's technical cooperation to UNDP. From the outset this met with opposition from other bodies in the UN system (such as the → specialized agencies and, in the 1990s, → UNICEF) which would rather act as autonomously as possible. Even today many of the statements and recommendations made in the *"Capacity Study"* remain valid, even though in recent years the reform agenda has brought a clearer allocation of rights and duties to the UNDP.

II. Tasks and Objectives

UNDP is the world's largest technical cooperation agency operating on the basis of non-repayable contributions (*grants*). Its funding consists of the governments' annual voluntary contributions.

UNDP plays a *key role* in the United Nations' development cooperation (→ Development Cooperation of the UN System). At the time of its establishment it was assigned overarching functions relating to the *UN's operational development tasks* (as distinct from its non-operational activities, i.e. advisory, standard-setting and normative tasks).

In principle, UNDP's task is to act as the *sole, central guiding, financing and coordinating body for the technical cooperation of the UN system as a whole. Financial cooperation* (i.e. credits and investments) does not fall within the terms of reference of UNDP or the other UN funds and programmes; these tasks are performed primarily by the World Bank (→ World Bank/World Bank group) and the regional development banks.

Until the end of the 1990s and unlike other operational UN bodies active in the field of development cooperation, UNDP has not been subject to any specific substantive or sectoral restrictions (e.g. "children" in UNICEF's case and "population" in the case of → UNFPA). In 1994 and 1996 the Executive Board defined UNDP's substantive objectives through a *core mission* and a *mission statement*, which placed the emphasis on *"sustainable human development"*.

UNDP seeks to contribute to the achievement of this objective by offering to help develop *institutional and structural capacities* (*"capacity-building"*) so that development programmes, especially in the area of poverty reduction, may be planned and implemented. In conjunction with large reforms of the UNDP this roughly delineated agenda was replaced by five central areas of activity (see chapter 4 of this article).

III. Members, Organization and Staff

Any of the UN's member states, its specialized agencies and the → IAEA (*International Atomic Energy Agency*) are free to participate in UNDP. There is no UNDP membership in any narrower sense of the term.

UNDP is what is known as a *subsidiary body* of the General Assembly (→ Principal Organs, Subsidiary Organs, Treaty Bodies). It is administered under the authority of the General Assembly and the → Economic and Social Council (ECOSOC).

UNDP itself is composed of an *Executive Board, the Secretariat of the Executive Board*, an *Administrator* and his staff. The *Executive Board* (known as the *Governing Council* until 1994) is the body that oversees and guides UNDP's policy. It meets in three annual sessions each year. One of its important tasks is to discuss and approve the *Country Co-operation Frameworks*. UNDP's Executive Board is also responsible for UNFPA. It has 36 members in accordance with the following regional breakdown: 8 from African countries, 7 from Asian countries, 4 from eastern European countries, 5 from Latin America and the Caribbean and 12 from western European and other countries. This results in a distribution of votes which, in theory, gives the group of developing countries a majority. In practice, however, the principle of consensus dominates. The UNDP Executive Board, whose members are elected by ECOSOC, is made up of representatives from 36 countries around the world. These serve on a rotating basis for a term of 3 years, only a third of the members being replaced each year so that a degree of continuity may be maintained. Despite a reduction in size in 1994, the Executive Board is regarded as being, on the whole, rather cumbersome and not very professional.

The *Executive Board Secretariat* facilitates the work of the Board by reviewing and editing all documentation for submission to the Board. It is responsible for logistical efficiency and provides information to Board members.

The *Administrator* conducts UNDP's business. He is nominated by the UN's Secretary-General (→ Secretary-General) after consultations with the Executive Board and confirmed in office by the General Assembly. Till 1999 only US nationals have been appointed Administrator, a practice that has been heavily criticized in the 1990s. In 1999 this practice was given up when UN Secretary-General appointed Mark Malloch Brown (United Kingdom) as UNDP Administrator and the appointment was confirmed subsequently by the General Assembly. Since August 2005 UNDP's new Administrator is Kemal Dervis. He is particularly interested in the connection between democracy and economic growth.

UNDP has about 6,900 staff members. Most of them work in regional and national offices and not in New York where UNDP's headquarters are located.

In the 1990s Germany attempted unsuccessfully to have UNDP's head office transferred to Bonn (→ UN in Bonn).

UNDP administers various other funds and programmes of the UN system that receive separate contributions. They are the following:
- United Nations Volunteers (→ UNV),
- United Nations Capital Development Fund (UNCDF),
- United Nations Development Fund for Women (UNIFEM).

UNDP is also involved in the administration of the *Global Environmental Facility* (GEF) together with the World Bank and → UNEP (→ Environmental Protection).

An important feature of UNDP is its large network of *country offices*, which it maintains in a total of 166 countries (as of February 2007). Its local representatives are known as *Resident Representatives*. As a rule, they also serve as *Resident Coordinators*, as which they are appointed by the UN Secretary-General. This means that they perform a wide range of tasks for the UN. Regional offices were established in Bangkok, Johannesburg, Bratislava and Colombo.

IV. Use of Resources and Focal Areas of Activity

UNDP cooperates with over 170 countries. Some 5,000 measures are currently being implemented at country level. Besides belt-tightening, a major part of the reforms of the nineties was UNDP's formulation of key domains. They are the following:
(i) Democratic Governance
(ii) Poverty Reduction
(iii) Crises Prevention and Recovery
(iv) Energy and Environment
(v) HIV / AIDS

In each of these five fields UNDP fights for the guarantee of human rights and the empowerment of women. Thus there has been the change recommended by most experts: UNDP has sharpened the focus and reduced its activities.

In 2005 most expenditures have been made in the domain of democratic governance, accounting for 47% of our operational activities, followed by poverty reduction (25%), crisis prevention and recovery (12%), energy and environment (11%). This highlights UNDP's clear commitment to democratic governance as a base of sustainable economic development and peace, and its focussing on human security as a broad concept which includes political, social and economic aspects of security.

In regional terms the planned distribution of core resources (see chapter 5 of this article) in 2004 focused on Africa (39%) and Asia and the Pacific (27%).

V. Working and Operating Methods

In principle, UNDP does not as a rule play a direct role as a *financing and co-ordinating body* during the actual implementation of projects and programmes. The rule is rather that, wherever possible, the developing country should take responsibility during *implementation (national execution)*. The proportion of projects and programmes implemented in this way rose sharply in the 1990s (1990-1991: 14%, 1996-1997: 79%). In 2004 *national execution* amounted to 60% of total expenditures. Where these tasks cannot be performed by programme countries themselves, they are entrusted to other implementing agencies. Traditionally, the UN's specialized agencies have occupied a strong position in this context (this being especially true of the *"big five"*: → FAO, → ILO, → UNESCO, → UNIDO and → WHO). In the *Office for Project Services (OPS)*, now no longer part of UNDP, the latter long had major implementing capacities of its own. Non-governmental organizations (→ NGOs) may also be entrusted with project implementation. The governments of developing countries that would like to see UNDP as their partner have particular reservations about the increased involvement of the NGOs.

Through its country offices UNDP provides direct *advisory services* for the governments of the various programme countries, besides managing projects and programmes. These services extend in particular to the formulation and elaboration of objectives and concepts relevant to development policy and to the *coordination* of the various bi- and multilateral donor contributions. In the context of donor coordination UNDP organizes *round tables* primarily for the poorer developing countries (the World Bank has a similar instrument for most other countries in its *consultative group meetings*).

UNDP's main area of activity consists of *country-related programmes*, although it also has *regional, interregional* and *global programmes*. A special instrument (TCDC – *Technical Cooperation among Developing Countries*) is meant to help foster South-South cooperation.

Until the end of 1996 country programming pivoted on the *Indicative Planning Figure (IPF)*. The IPF was used to calculate the financial volume for a planning cycle of five years, which proved to be too long a planning period. The criteria for the IPF calculation were population, gross national product per capita and a number of other development indicators. At the beginning of 1997 the programming system was replaced with a new method, based on a "rolling" three-year planning procedure and so allowing greater flexibility. The criteria for the calculation of the aid volume are guided by the indicators used at an earlier stage. The most important change introduced by the new programming procedure is the possibility of offering development incentives. In contrast to the "entitlement quota" that used to be set, the scale of resources may now be varied for development reasons (increased or decreased).

VI. Financing and Its Impacts

UNDP's financial resources consist of *voluntary contributions*. Some are used to finance its main programme activities (*core contributions*). Most of these resources are provided by the industrialized countries, with a relatively strong commitment from the *like-minded countries* (i.e., in particular, Denmark, Finland, the Netherlands, Norway, Sweden and – with reservations – Canada). Many developing countries (including India, China, Cuba, Thailand and Sri Lanka) also participate in the financing of the main programme; in other words, they contribute to the financing of all UNDP activities and are at the same time recipients and thus direct beneficiaries. Many developing countries therefore identify particularly closely with UNDP. Germany's contributions to the main programme decreased in the period from 1997 to 2005. In 1997 Germany's share of the main programme amounted to 9.1%; in 2005 it constituted only 3.5%. Besides the main programme, other of UNDP's financing mechanisms, known as *non-core resources*, are gaining in importance. They comprise *third party co-financing* and *local resources channelled through UNDP by programme country*. Since the mid-1990s these *non-core resources* have exceeded the resources provided UNDP's actual main programme. In 2005 the budget of the UNDP was 4.5 billion US dollars. Whereas the un-earmarked *core-budget* increased little in the last few years and the *local resources channelled through UNDP by programme country* were more or less stable, it was the earmarked *third party co-financing* that experienced high growth with the result that the UNDP's budget nearly doubled in the period from 2001 to 2005.

The principal problem with these resources is that, as UNDP and its Executive Board have limited access to them, they are not really subject to UNDP's development standards.

*Table 1: Gross Income Received
in 2005 (preliminary)*
(in million US dollars)

*(Ranked by top contributors
to core resources)**

Donors	Core Resources	Co-financing
The Netherlands	111.88	79,41
Norway	108.91	85.82
United States	105.00	140.76
Sweden	99.40	75.85
Japan	82.43	131.35
United Kingdom	80.74	173.63
Denmark	62.38	24.62
Canada	46.69	77.83
Switzerland	40.31	14.48
Germany	32.05	75.78
France	28.01	12.91
Italy	19.40	41.12
Finland	19.15	14.36
Belgium	18.32	22.37
Ireland	18.30	10.82
Spain	8.15	4.27
Australia	5.30	22.10
Austria	5.14	5.29
New Zealand	4.79	11.42
India	4.42	—
China	3.25	18.00
Cuba	2.71	—
Saudi Arabia	2.00	6.16
Mexico	2.00	2.35
Portugal	1.80	4.37
Luxembourg	1.55	6.45
Republic of Korea	1,00	2.57

*All donors to core resources contributing
1 million US dollars or more.

*Source: United Nations Development Programme
– Annual Report 2006.*

Additionally UNDP is supported by non-bilateral funding sources. In 2005 the European Commission provided over 400 million US dollars to non-core-resources, the World Bank around 80 millions; a further 80 millions were allocated by the multilateral fund of the Montreal Protocol.

Little can be done to bring influence to bear on focal areas of activity and countries assisted. This may have an adverse effect on principles of impartial and multilateral operation.

Particularly where the trust funds are concerned, there are also many opportunities for the various donor countries to pursue project-related "micro-management", which is administration-intensive for UNDP. The trust funds are very much a reflection of tendencies to bilateralize UNDP, in that donor countries do not really relinquish their hold on their financial resources. However, the tendency of "bilateralization" reveals states' skepticism of some of the UNDP's concepts and concrete programmes, on the one hand, while on the other hand, it indicates states' belief in the strengths of the UNDP: its credibility and its network.

In 2005 the resources allocated to the main programme amounted to 921 million US dollars (compared to 761 million US dollars and 1,022 million US dollars in 1991) and *non-core resources* jumped to 2,500 million US dollars (compared to 1,250 million US dollars in 1997 and only 268 million US dollars in 1991). For 2007 the Executive Board set the target for main programme resources at 1,100 million US dollars.

VII. Reform Policy and Assessment

In the past UNDP has failed to perform its tasks appropriately. It has in fact been regarded as a weak development institution, owing partly to its small financial endowment of well below US$ 1billion (2006). The major donor countries in particular stress that UNDP is not efficient or effective enough. Governments of developing countries, on the other hand, appreciate the fact that UNDP allocates resources with few strings attached and – compared to other development institutions – provides considerable opportunities for involvement in decision-making. They are critical, however, of its inadequate financial endowment, which makes its mandate impracticable in many respects.

In 1999 UN reacted to the criticism of donor states by launching the Multi-Year Funding Framework (MYFF), a concept that combines long-term strategies with the evaluation of on-going projects. In this vein UNDP allows donors to link their financial contributions to results, programme performance and aid effectiveness. UNDP's own 2005 MYFF report ascertains that more can still be done to further results-based culture at country-level by strengthening measurement and monitoring.

In many ways UNDP suffers directly from the weaknesses that afflict all the UN's operational activities. It was a serious structural mistake to assign so many tasks and overall responsibility to UNDP without equipping it with appropriate implementing instruments or giving it sufficient political support in the performance of these tasks.

Its weaknesses notwithstanding, however, UNDP's strengths are often overlooked. On the conceptual and practical side UNDP has much to offer in terms of important approaches, experience and potential (the coordinating mechanism of the *round tables* at country level, limited outside control of measures, enabling programme countries to identify more closely with UNDP's activities than with other donors', etc.). Furthermore, as Craig Murphy (*Murphy* 2006) argues, UNDP has demonstrated its learning aptitude, pragmatism, openness and flexibility. These strengths should receive far more attention in the development debate.

In the international development debate UNDP has succeeded in attracting attention primarily through the *Human Development Report* (HDR), which has appeared annually since 1990 (→ Human Development Reports). In the first half of the 1990s at least, the concept of "sustainable human development" jointly developed and propagated by the HDR and UNDP was often seen as a criticism of the World Bank and its development paradigms. The Human Development Report should not, however, be equated with UNDP and its policy. The political disputes within UNDP in the early 1990s reflected the absence of a majority in favour of a UNDP that en-

dorses the *Human Development Report* conceptually and in practice.

In the 1990s UNDP has undertaken a number of *reforms* itself (i.e. reforms initiated by the Administrator or the Executive Board). Major efforts have been made, for example, to focus UNDP's activities, to set concrete areas of activity, to overhaul the programming system completely and to involve the programme countries far more closely in implementation (*national execution*). The Administrator has made numerous attempts in the latter half of the 1990s to reorganize UNDP internally and to save costs. These efforts have led, for example, to a 19 % cut in administrative costs (1992-1997), to a 31 % reduction in regular headquarters staff and to new accountability mechanisms, but they have also resulted in "reform fatigue" among the staff.

In addition, the Secretary-General has endeavoured to reform the whole of the UN's development cooperation, which has had a particular impact on UNDP in many respects (→ Reform of the UN). UNDP has, for example, been assigned the chairmanship of the Executive Committee of the newly established *United Nations Development Group (UNDG)*, which is meant to help improve coordination and to attain the MDGs. Wide-ranging efforts are also being made to approximate the administrative and budgetary procedures of the major UN funds and programmes. UNDP also plays an important role in the attempts to achieve more targeted cooperation and greater coherence among the various funds and programmes through the establishment of a single programme framework (*United Nations Development Assistance Framework* (UNDAF).

On the whole, the efforts made in the last 15 years to reform UNDP and to incorporate it more firmly into the UN should be rated positively. In many respects today's UNDP bears little similarity to the UNDP of the late 1980s, because it has very largely succeeded in changing into a more efficient and competitive actor on the development stage.

Although the reforms are rated positively by the majority of the member states, they are not sufficiently appreciated and rewarded. Thus, despite the changes for the better, the financial commitment is waning, significantly in some cases.

Both the programme countries and the main contributing countries need to become more aware of the development "costs" that will arise if UNDP, rather than being strengthened, is weakened further (especially because of the lack of financial resources and of willingness to accept reforms). Many member states generally have no clear idea of how and with what instruments UNDP should operate in the future. Equally, questions concerning the division of labor between UNDP on the one hand and the World Bank and other donors on the other are becoming increasingly significant. The question of the profile that a future UNDP should have is therefore of prime importance and continuing relevance.

Stephan Klingebiel

The update of the article was assisted by
Marius Hildebrand

Lit.: *Centre for Development Research, Assessment of UNDP:* Developing Capacity for Sustainable Human Development, Report Prepared for the Governments of Denmark, India, Sweden, and the United Kingdom, Copenhagen 1996; *Department for International Development:* Working in Partnership with the United Nations Development Programme (UNDP), London 2005, www.dfid. gov.uk/pubs/files/undpis04-07.pdf; *Dervis, K:* Governance and Development, in: Journal of Democracy 17, (2006), 153-159; *Executive Board of the United Nations Development Programme and the United Nations Population Fund:* Second multi-year funding framework, 2004-2007, 13 August 2003, UN Doc. DP/2003/32, www.undp.org/execbrd/ pdf/dp03-32e.pdf; *Executive Board of the United Nations Development Programme and the United Nations Population Fund:* Annual review of the financial situation, 2004. Report of the Administrator, 2 August 2005, UN Doc. DP/2005/33, www.undp.org/ execbrd/pdf/dp05-33e.pdf; *Gwin, C./Morrison, K.M.:* The United Nations and Development, in: United Nations Association of the United States of America (ed.): A Global Agenda: Issues Before the 53rd General Assembly of the United Nations, New York 1998, 89-102; *Klingebiel, S.:* Effectiveness and Reform of the United Nations Development Programme (UNDP), London/Portland 1999; *Murphy, C.:* "Ploughing the sea"? UNDP and the future of global governance, in: Murphy, C. (ed.): United Nations Development Programme, Cambridge 2006, 331-357; *Sahlmann, H./Blank, B.:* UNDP – United Nations Development Programme, in: Wolfrum, R. (ed.): United Nations: Law, Policies and Practice, Vol. 2, Munich et al. 1995, 1284-1290; *United Nations Development Programme:* Annual Report 2006: Global Partnership for Development, New York 2006; *United Nations Development Programme:* Annual Report 2007: Making Globalization Work for All, New York 2007; *United Nations Development Programme:* Annual Report 2008: Capacity Development: Empowering People and Institutions, New York 2008.

Internet: Homepage UNDP: www.undp.org.

UNEP – United Nations Environment Programme

1. Status and Structures

UNEP was established in 1972 as a result of the first UN environment conference in Stockholm. As a "programme" its status is on lower level than that of an independent specialized organization, like the → UNDP. UNEP is the only UN institution headquartered in a developing country, in Nairobi, Kenya. UNEP took a sharp rise in visibility and political presence during the eight years when Klaus Töpfer was its Executive Director (1998-2006). Töpfer, former German environment minister, energetically regained ground for UNEP in the international institutional setup. He was succeeded by another German, Achim Steiner, previously Director of IUCN, heading UNEP since 2006.

UNEP's supreme decision-making body is the *Governing Council* (GC), with 58 states as members, elected by the UN General Assembly for 4 years. The regional distribution is: 16 African states, 13 Asian states, 6 Eastern European states, 13 states from the group of Western Europe and Others, 10 states from Latin America and the Caribbean. Its budget is rather modest, approximately 140 million US dollars biennially. Apart from its headquarters in Nairobi, UNEP has some regional offices: New York (North America), Geneva (Europe), Bangkok (Asia-Pacific), Mexico City (Latin America/Caribbean), Bahrain (West Asia), and Nairobi (Africa). These regional offices operate with minimal staff and budgetary resources, and some depend heavily on external funds and support from "national focal points" (partly → NGOs, partly semi-governmental institutions).

2. UNEP's Objectives

UNEP's activities are focused to a large degree on putting environmental issues on the agenda of international politics, and on initiating co-operation with other global, regional and increasingly also national institutions. UNEP also plays an important role in compiling information and making it available to decision-makers with the authority of a United Nations institution, often jointly with other UN organizations. Particularly important is the "Global Environmental Outlook – State of the Environment" (GEO), UNEP's flagship publication, together with the *Global Resource Information Database* (*GRID*, www.grid.unep.ch/) and the *Global Environment Monitoring System* (*GEMS*, www.gems-water. org/). UNEP further plays important roles in the protection of the seas as secretariat for the "Global Programme of Action for the Protection of the Marine Environment from Land-Based Activities" (www.gpa.unep.org), agreed in 1995, and increasingly the regulation of hazardous waste and harmful substances have moved to center stage in UNEP's activities.

UNEP has increasingly initiated new forms of cooperation, not only with governments but also with the private sector, in particular the financial sector. In Paris UNEP maintains an *Industry and Environment Unit* (www.uneptie. org) coordinating UNEP's Sustainable Production and Consumption Programme which focuses on such cooperative operations. UNEP also acts as secretariat for a number of international environmental agreements, such as the Basel Convention on the Control of Transboundary Movements of Hazardous Wastes and their Disposal, Stockholm Convention on Persistent Organic Pollutants (POPs), the Convention on International Trade in Endangered Species of Wild Flora and Fauna (CITES) and the Convention on Migratory Species (CMS) (→ Environmental Law, International). UNEP plays a catalytic role in intergovernmental negotiations for new conventions like the Stockholm Convention which was negotiated in 2001 and entered into force in 2004.

3. UNEP's Role in the UN System and the UN Reform Process

It is a widely heard opinion that UNEP, ironically, was one of the losers in the 1992 Rio Convention on Environment and Development (UNCED) and the Rio follow-up process. UNEP was not assigned a clear role in this Rio process, and instead the Commission on Sustainable Development (→ CSD) was established and given the task of co-ordinating the Rio follow-up. However, 16 years after Rio it is clear that the CSD cannot properly fulfill this task and the need for a strengthened UNEP is gradually recognized across the international community. As early as 1997 and 1998, attempts were made to define a new role for UNEP in the post-Rio world. The landmark 19th session of UNEP's Governing Council in 1997 passed the "Nairobi Declaration" (Annex I to Decision 19/1 of the Governing Council of UNEP of 7 February 1997, reprinted in: UN Doc. UNEP/GC.19/34, 17 June 1997) which tackled some of the key weaknesses in UNEP's operations. In 1998, Secretary General Kofi Annan established the *"Task Force on Environment and Human Settlements"*chaired by Klaus Töpfer to make proposals for the future of both Nairobi-based UN institutions. Its report "Environment and human settlements" (UN Doc. A/53/463), deliver-

713

ed to the Secretary-General in June 1998 and presented to the General Assembly in October 1998, supported the reform process initiated by the GC and made a number of proposals for strengthening UNEP. A key outcome was the establishment of the *Global Ministerial Environment Forum*, a forum of environment ministers meeting biannually which has become quite productive and is increasingly becoming a competitor for the CSD.

At the 10th Special Session of the GC in 2008 in Monaco, Achim Steiner presented the Draft UNEP Medium-Term Strategy for 2010-2013 (UN Doc. UNEP/GCSS.X/8) a year ahead of schedule. This paper called for a stronger focus of UNEP on six key activities – climate change, disasters and conflicts, ecosystem management, environmental governance, harmful substances and hazardous waste, resource efficiency – and some financial and organizational changes. The GC decision *"welcomes"* the MTS and *"authorizes"* the Executive Director to use the Strategy in formulating the programmes of work and budgets in the coming years (UN Doc. UNEP/GCSS.X/10, 14).

There are also important discussions in the wider UN reform process affecting environmental governance and UNEP's role. At the 2005 Millennium Development Goals Review Summit, the Secretary-General was requested to present a strategy for the reform of the environment, development and humanitarian aid sector.

The President of the General Assembly then in January 2006 decided to ask Ambassadors Maurer of Switzerland and Heller of Mexico to conduct informal consultations about how member states think about such a reform (comprehensive documentation of this process at www.reformtheun.org/index.php/united_nations/c495?theme=alt2). They first presented an options paper in 2007 and in 2008 subsequently two updated versions (all available at www.un.org/ga/president/63/issues/environmentalgovernance.shtml) and have acted rather courageously in favour of a strengthened UNEP. This process is likely to last for some time. Whether the governments that traditionally oppose a stronger role for UNEP like the US or India are going to soften their stance, remains to be seen.

The proposal to upgrade or transform UNEP into a fully-fledged UN Environment Organization (UNEO), on equal footing with specialized agencies such as the → WHO or → FAO, has been championed for a number of years mainly by a number European governments such as Germany or France. Chancellor Kohl proposed it at the summit review five years after Rio, and President Chirac was pushing for it, thus support for this idea has gradually increased, but it is still far from reaching consensus. In the consultations carried out by Ambassadors Maurer and Heller, the EU has called for an *ad hoc* open-ended working group to work out what the financial and legal consequences of such an upgrading would be. So far it is somewhat unlikely that such a highly symbolic move will take place in the near future. As questionable as the motives of the opponents are, it is however also doubtful whether in reality it would result in there being such a big difference between a strengthened UNEP and UNEO. A stronger UNEP, in whatever form it takes, is very likely as a result of the current UN reform procedures, for even the most stubborn opponents are slowly conceding that the status of environmental problems are no longer on the fringes but have long taken center stage in global politics.

Jürgen Maier

Lit.: *Esty, D. et al (eds.):* Global Environmental Institutions – Perspectives on Reform, London 2002; *Holtrup, P.:* Eindämmung der Umweltzerstörung: Aufgabe für eine globale Umweltorganisation? In: Wagner, W. et al. (eds.): Jahrbuch Internationale Politik 1999-2000, Munich 2001, 13-23; *Rechkemmer, A.:* Towards an International Environmental Organization, Baden-Baden 2005; *UNEP:* Annual Report of the Executive Director; *UNEP:* The State of World Environment (annually); *UNEP:* Industry and Environment (quarterly); *UNEP:* UNEP

News (bi-monthly); *United Nations Task Force on Environment and Human Settlements:* Report to the Secretary-General, 15 June 1998, New York 1998.

Internet: *Homepage of UNEP:* www. unep.org; *UNEP Industry and Environment Unit:* www.unepie.org/; *International Institute for Sustainable Development, Earth Negotiations Bulletin (reports on the sessions of the Governing Council of UNEP and on other important UNEP meetings):* www.iisd. ca; further: www.ecologic-events.de/ieg-conference/en/index.htm; www.reformtheun.org/index.php/united_nations/c495?theme=alt 2.

UNESCO – United Nations Educational, Scientific and Cultural Organization

I. Introduction

UNESCO (United Nations Educational, Scientific and Cultural Organization) was founded on the initiative of the Conference of Allied Ministers of Education, set up during World War II. Also the → Charter of the UN contains provisions which designate the founding of an international organization for education and culture (cf. Arts. 13, 55 and 62 UN Charter).

On 16 November 1945 representatives of 37 states meeting in London signed UNESCO's Constitution and *Preamble* in which the signatories – still under the shock of crimes against humanity committed by Fascism – declared "that since wars began in the minds of men, it is in the minds of men that the defences of peace must be constructed". This idealistic idea (reduction of enemy images, positive concept of peace) expresses the hope that education towards an ideal human being will lay the foundations for securing world peace (→ Peace, Peace Concept, Threat to Peace).

The founding members of UNESCO could refer to a number of models. In 1922, the Council of the → League of Nations set up an *International Committee of Intellectual Co-operation*, composed of 12, later 15 prominent scientists, which served as an advisory body of the Assembly and the Council of the League of Nations without an adminis-

trative apparatus of its own. (The Committee worked as advisory organ from 1922 until 1946 when its role was taken over by UNESCO.)

In 1925, France, responding to a request by the Assembly of the → League of Nations, after the latter had been unable to secure funding to maintain a significant office in Geneva, created the *International Institute for Intellectual Co-operation*, a legally independent institution with a secretariat of its own, financed by the French government. The International Committee of Intellectual Co-operation continued to exist as the Institute's Board of Trustees.

From the beginning, conflicts surrounded the creation of UNESCO: Should it be a governmental or a non-governmental organization? (→ NGOs) Should the Organization be concerned solely with education and culture ("UNECO") or should it encompass further areas, such as science and communication? Should UNESCO work on the basis of a global scientific humanism, or should it be strictly functional and limited to practical activities accepted by the majority of its members?

II. Purposes and Functions

UNESCO's Constitution (UNTS Vol. 4, No. 52) entered into force on 4 November 1946; on 14 December 1946, an agreement of 4 June 1946 between UNESCO and the → Economic and Social Council confirming its status as a → specialized agency of the UN (UN Doc. A/77 of 30 October 1946) was approved by the → General Assembly in resolution 50 (I) in accordance with Articles 57 and 63 of the → Charter of the UN.

UNESCO's *purpose* is "to contribute to peace and security by promoting collaboration among the nations through education, science and culture in order to further universal respect for justice, for the law and for the human rights and fundamental freedoms which are affirmed for the peoples of the world, without distinction of race, sex, language or religion by the Charter of the United Nations".

715

To realize this purpose, UNESCO has the following functions, as laid down in its Constitution (Art. 1):
- to advance the "mutual knowledge and understanding of peoples through all means of mass communication, and to that end to recommend such international agreements as may be necessary to promote the free flow of ideas by word and image";
- to "give fresh impulse to popular education and to the spread of culture";
- to "maintain, increase and diffuse knowledge" by recommending international conventions to conserve and protect the world's inheritance of books, works of art and monuments of history and science, "by encouraging international co-operation in all branches of intellectual activity", and by "initiating methods of co-operation calculated to give the people of all countries access to the printed and published material produced by any of them".

The concrete steps to achieve these objectives are laid down in *medium–term strategies* covering a period of six years (C/4 documents which are conceived as a rolling strategy, allowing for a revision every two years). The 34th General Conference held in October 2007 in Paris adopted the sixth medium-term strategy for 2008-2013 (UNESCO Doc. 34 C/4) and the two-year programme 2008-2009 (UNESCO Doc. 34 C/5) which were discussed by the Executive Board after being drafted by the Secretariat. The Midterm Strategy 34C/4 is structured around five programme-driven objectives for the entire organization which are designed to respond to specific global challenges and represent the core competencies of UNESCO within the → UN system. Those five overarching objectives are divided into 14 strategic programme objectives (cf. section V.). In his introduction, the Director-General claims: "UNESCO's comparative advantage within the United Nations system is its ability to respond to complex contemporary problems in a comprehensive and relevant manner through intersectoral and inter-

disciplinary action". (UNESCO Doc. 34 C/4, 5)

III. Membership

According to UNESCO's Constitution, membership of the UN (→ Membership and Representation of States) carries with the right to *membership* of UNESCO. States which are not members of the UN may be admitted to membership upon recommendation of the Executive Board by a two–thirds majority vote of the General Conference. The Federal Republic of Germany is member of UNESCO since 11 July 1951.

Between 1946 and 1956, UNESCO's membership rose from 28 to 80 and reached 161 in 1984. At the beginning of the 1990s, UNESCO's membership further increased due to the political changes in Central and Eastern Europe and the collapse of the former USSR. As of October 2008, UNESCO has 193 member states and 6 associate members.

During the middle of the 1980s, the United States and United Kingdom left the Organization accusing UNESCO of over-politicizing its work and of poor internal management. Whereas the United Kingdom returned to the Organization in 1997, the United States continued to refuse to re-enter UNESCO until October 2003 (→ UN Policy, USA; → UN Policy, United Kingdom).

IV. Organizational Structure

The organs of UNESCO are: the General Conference, the Executive Board and the Secretariat headed by a Director-General.

The *General Conference* as UNESCO's supreme decision-making and supervisory body meets (since 1954) in ordinary session every two years. Voting follows the principle „one state - one vote", but since 1976 the practice has been to take decisions by consensus. The General Conference also elects the members of the *Executive Board*, which (since 1995) has 58 members and meets at least twice a year. It functions as a link between the General Conference and the Secretariat. The members are elected according to a system of electoral groupings by which each region is allocated a specific number of Board seats: Group I (Western Europe and North America): nine seats; Group II (Eastern Europe): seven seats; Group III (Latin America and the Caribbean): 10 seats; Group IV (Asia and the Pacific): 12 seats; Group V (Africa and Arab States): 20 seats.

During the course of the last 60 years an increasing "governmentalization" of the *Executive Board* could be observed, leading, on the one hand, to a stronger political-administrative control of the Director-General, and on the other hand – very much to the disadvantage of UNESCO – to a clear decline of the intellectual level of the debates. Up until 1954, the members were elected as independent individuals, as "representatives of the intellect", who should act on behalf of the General Conference. Since then – in response to the Cold War a compromise solution – the members have no longer been independent representatives of the General Conference, but politicians representing their countries; immediate re-election after four years was not possible any longer. Since 1993, member states are elected "in order to increase UNESCO's efficiency" (Japan); they are eligible for immediate re-election.

The *Secretariat* with a staff of about 2000 (two thirds at UNESCO Headquarters in Paris, one third in the field) is headed by a Director-General (1999-2009: Koichiro Matsuura, Japan), elected by the General Conference upon the recommendation of the Executive Board. A new Director-General will be elected by the 35th General Conference in October 2009 for a term of four years (one re-election is possible). The Secretariat has a number of sectors which cover different areas of work. In the light of the manifold tasks of UNESCO the competitive thinking and acting in sectors leads to tremendous problems of co-ordination. In his reform programme, the present Director-General tries to realize the demands towards a better concentration of activities and a secured multi-disciplinary orientation.

In UNESCO's Constitution, a feature unique among the UN's → specialized agencies is the recommendation to set up *National Commissions for UNESCO* which fulfill in a bridging function two tasks in the member states: on the one hand, advising the government and informing the public, and on the other serving as a UNESCO liaison office in order to keep up the manifold contacts with the numerous national → non-governmental organizations and thereby also to function as a co-ordination unit for the implementation of UNESCO's programme. Those functions can be best performed in pluralistic-democratic societies which allow such a differentiation.

V. Programme Priorities

In the sector of *education* the major emphasis is on improving *literacy* and *basic education* ("Attaining quality education for all and lifelong learning") and more recently, due to a German initiative, on vocational and technical education, which could be best implemented as an inter-agency activity together with the International Labour Organization (→ ILO). UNESCO intends to strengthen its global lead and coordination role for *"Education for All"*; furthermore, policies and tools for quality education and lifelong learning will be developed, taking into due account the promotion of education for sustainable development. In 1995, the report of the International Commission for Education in the 21st Century, chaired by Jacques Delors, was presented which gave new impulses for the work in the sector of education ("learning to live together – learning to know – learning to do – learning to be"). Worldwide, some 7,900 UNESCO Associated Schools undertake concrete work within the area of international peace education in 176 member states; in Germany, over 150 schools joined this programme.

In the sectors of *natural and social sciences*, UNESCO supports, in particular in the developing countries, the *de-*

velopment and improvement of academic research and training facilities ("Mobilizing science knowledge and policy for sustainable development", 34 C/4, 19) and promotes international networks for academic and technical basic research, *inter alia*, in environment research and the management of social transformation ("Addressing emerging social and ethical challenges", UNESCO Doc. 34 C/4, 22).

In the sector of *culture* the most famous focus is the *"List of the World Cultural Heritage"*. This list today (as of 10 July 2008) contains a total 878 cultural and natural monuments in 145 countries, including 33 in Germany, which are protected by the 1972 UNESCO Convention concerning the Protection of the World Cultural and Natural Heritage (→ Common Heritage of Mankind). The overarching objective is: "Fostering cultural diversity, intercultural dialogue and a culture of peace" (UNESCO Doc. 34 C/4, 25). It contains, *inter alia*, the strengthening of the contribution of culture to sustainable development and stresses the importance of the dialogue among cultures.

In the sector of *communication, information and informatics* UNESCO works world-wide toward the right of information and the freedom of the press ("Building inclusive knowledge societies through information and communication", UNESCO Doc. 34 C/4, 29). This includes the *International Programme for the Development of Communication (IPDC)* for the training of journalists as well as the establishment of regional news agencies and communication infrastructures in developing countries.

The new Medium-Term Strategy for 2008-2013 mentions Africa and gender equality as priorities to be translated into action in all of UNESCO's fields of competence (34 C/4, p. 8, 9 and 10). Moreover, specific interventions are foreseen for youth in rural areas and marginalized groups, the least developed countries and the small island developing states. A human rights-based approach to programming is envisaged (UNESCO Doc. 34 C/4, 8).

VI. Financing

The General Conference approves the budget, which is prepared by the Director-General, along with the two-year programme of work, and recommended by the Executive Board, and determines the scale of assessments, based on the scale of assessments of the UN.

In 2008, the United States had to pay 22%, Japan 16.626, Germany 8.578, United Kingdom 6.643, France 6.302, and Italy 5.080% of the UNESCO budget. In 2008, the regular budget had a total of 315.5 million US dollars; this corresponds to about 50% of a university budget in Germany. Germany's contribution to the 2008 regular budget amounted to about 27 million US dollars.

As of 30 June 2008, only 95 member states have paid their 2008 contributions in full. Among them were Japan, Germany, United Kingdom and France. The United States did not pay their contributions assessed for 2008 (= 69.4 million US dollars) nor contributions due for previous years (= 19.1 million US dollars). Also, Italy had a 100% contribution due for 2008 of 16.0 and China of 8.4 million US dollars. 27 member states have paid only part of their 2008 contributions and 71 member states have made no payment at all for 2008.

VII. Outlook

UNESCO's field of work is extremely broad; its tasks became more and more complex and are supposed to cover the major problems world-wide on the basis of an extremely small budget, ranging from the articulation of the global dependencies and through solution proposals to abolish them, to the strengthening of international solidarity to secure the survival of human-kind.

Therefore, UNESCO can perform only modest functions – the Organization can offer an "intellectual forum" for a worldwide exchange of ideas, views and experiences on current issues in the fields of education, science, culture and communication. UNESCO can – in its function as a "think tank" – make proposals, develop concepts, design projects and finance pilot programmes ("multiplier function"). UNESCO also performs a "service function" as a clearing house by constantly processing information in all its fields of work. Finally, through its conventions, agreements and protocols it can promote international co-operation.

Klaus Hüfner

Lit.: *Bernecker, R. (ed.):* Kultur und Entwicklung. Zur Umsetzung des Stockholmer Aktionsplans. Bonn 1998; *Delors, J. et al.:* Learning: The Treasure Within. Report to UNESCO of the International Commission for the Twenty-first Century (Delors Report), Paris 1996, http://unesdoc.unesco.org/images/0010/001095/109590eo.pdf; *Deutsche UNESCO-Kommission (ed.):* Kultur des Friedens. Ein neues UNESCO-Project zur Erhaltung des Weltfriedens, Bonn 1998; *Hüfner, K.:* UNESCO und Menschenrechte, Berlin 2008; *Hüfner, K./Reuther, W. (eds.):* UNESCO-Handbuch. Bonn 2005; *UNESCO:* Medium-Term Strategy 2008-2013 (UNESCO Doc. 34C/4), Paris 2008; *UNESCO:* Approved Programme and Budget 2008-2009 (UNESCO Doc. 34 C/5), Paris 2008.

Internet: Homepage of UNESCO: www.unesco.org.

UNFPA – United Nations Population Fund

The *United Nations Population Fund* was originally founded in 1967 as a UN Trust Fund, following General Assembly resolution A/RES/2211 (XXI) of December 1966 which recommended the support of programmes of population policy. In three decades of practical work, UNFPA became the centre of world-wide support to population policy and reproductive health. Institutionally, UNFPA is a sister organization of → UNDP and is supervised by the same Executive Council which is elected by → ECOSOC. Otherwise, UNFPA is a UN programme of its own that has been, in recent years, increasingly involved in the efforts of UN reform (→ Reform of the UN) and systems of coordination (→ Secretariat). Within the United Na-

tions Development Group (UNDG), UNFPA closely cooperates with UNDP, → UNICEF, and → WFP. UNFPA is supported in its work by a functional commission of ECOSOC, the Commission on Population and Development (CPD).

In the industrialized countries, UNFPA is mainly known through the annual publication of the *world population report* "State of World Population" and its leading role in the *UN Population Conferences* (Romania 1974, Mexico 1984), culminating 1994 in the *United Nations International Conference on Population and Development (ICPD)* in Cairo (→ World Conferences). The "Programme of Action" as agreed there in its concluding resolution (UN Doc. A/CONF. 171/13 of 18 October 1994) contains a far-reaching catalogue of goals and measures in policy fields of population, migration, women, family, and health. At the same time, industrial and developing countries have pledged their support to population programmes on national and international levels. Thus, a concrete framework for global population policy has been carved out, including quantitative targets for primary education, maternal mortality, access to family planning services, etc., but also for the funding of related programmes. One third of the total expenditure is to be financed by the donor countries of the North.

The implementation of the ICPD Programme of Action, as agreed there, was since then evaluated in February 1999 at an international expert meeting in The Hague/Netherlands, called "The Hague Forum" (cf. *UNFPA* 1999), held on 8 to 12 February 1999 and organized by UNFPA, and in a special session of the UN General Assembly from 30 June to 2 July 1999, which adopted in a resolution a set of "Key Actions" for the further implementation of the ICPD Programme of Action (UN Doc. A/S-21/2 of 2 July 1999), including a new set of benchmarks in four areas: education and literacy; reproduction and health care and unmet need for contraception; maternal mortality reduction and HIV/AIDS.

In 2004, progress was evaluated again at the 37th session of the United Nations Commission on Population and Development in New York (*UNFPA* 2004).

In the developing countries, UNFPA is mainly known because of its country programmes agreed upon with the respective government. Following the conditions of the country, these programmes can be centered on demography (e.g. assistance in conducting a census or research), on family planning, on areas of health such as "mother and child" and "reproductive health", in sexual education, in fighting HIV/AIDS, or in the promotion of women. In these programmes, UNFPA co-operates closely with the → specialized agencies of the UN system and other international organizations (e.g. International Planned Parenthood Federation – IPPF). UNFPA is active in 150 countries and maintains offices of representatives in most of them. Technical advice is rendered through UNFPA regional centres.

UNFPA itself is funded from voluntary contributions of governments and (to a limited extent) from donations of private persons and foundations. In total, UNFPA receives financial support from more than one hundred governments. Most OECD donor governments prefer to support population activities through multilateral channels because of its often politically and culturally sensitive character. Thus, UNFPA has achieved, as the largest internationally financed programme, a definite priority in this field of → development co-operation.

Regrettably, UNFPA's relationship to the host nation of its New York headquarters is obscured by unfortunate irritations. UNFPA owes its existence to a large extent to the initiative and early support of the USA. But Washington has repeatedly refused to contribute to UNFPA during the last two decades. While its government had signaled its substantive and financial support at the Cairo ICPD and since, the US Congress linked for example its vote on the aid bill for the fiscal year of 1999 with a veto against funding of UNFPA (→ UN

Policy, USA). The reason given for such decisions, as in earlier years, was the erroneous allegation of UNPA's support of human rights abuses in China's population policies. UNFPA has been able to compensate most of the loss of income through increased contributions from other countries. The Bush administration used this policy of payment reductions towards UNFPA again in the years 2002 and thereafter using the same false allegation concerning UNFPA's policy towards China as pretext; in the years 2006 and 2007 the Bush administration replaced the wrong accusation with the demand for a comprehensive administrative reform of UNFPA as a precondition for its willingness to pay in full.

In contrast to the polemical criticism brought forward by conservative politicians in the USA and by several US administrations, the facts in the UNFPA reports show that UNFPA has been successful in four decades of its work:
- in developing a strong concept for a global population policy and basing it on a broad consensus within the international community;
- in organizing the co-ordination and division of labor in the area of international support for population activities, and;
- in establishing, in co-operation with the governments of developing countries, solid and recognized programmes of advice and support in this field.

UNFPA is therefore rightly considered as a successful United Nations undertaking.

Manfred Kulessa

Lit.: *Brown, L.R./Gardner, G./Halwell, B.:* Beyond Malthus: Sixteen Dimensions of the Population Problem (Worldwatch Paper 143), Washington 1998; *Engelman, R. et al.:* Rethinking Population, Improving Lives, in: Worldwatch Institute (ed.): State of the World 2002, New York/London 2002, 127-148; *Freudenschuß-Reichl, I.:* Population Issues at the United Nations, in: Cede, F./ Sucharipa-Behrmann, L. (eds.): The United Nations: Law and Practice, The Hague et al. 2001, 245-255; *UNFPA:* Report of the International Forum for the Operational Review and Appraisal of the Implementation of the Programme of Action of the ICPD, The Hague, 8-12 February 1999 (www.unfpa. org/icpd/icpd5/meetings/hague_forum/reports /forumrept.htm) (quoted as UNFPA 1999); *UNFPA:* Investing in People. National Progress in Implementing the ICPD Programme of Action 1994-2004; *UNFPA:* ICPD at Ten. The World Reaffirms Cairo. Official Outcomes of the ICPD at Ten Review, New York 2005; *UNFPA:*State of World Population, annual publication (Internet: www. unfpa.org/swp); *Wittrin, H.E..*: UNFPA – United Nations Population Fund, in: Wolfrum, R. (ed.): United Nations: Law, Policies and Practice, Vol. 2, Munich/Dordrecht 1995, 1314-1321.

Internet: Homepage of UNFPA: www. unfpa.org; Homepage UN Department of Economic and Social Affairs – Population Division: www.un.org/esa/population/unpop. htm; Homepage of the Commission on Population and Development (CPD): www.un. org/esa/population/cpd/aboutcom.htm.

UN Guards

The blue-uniformed "UN Guards", also called "UN Security Guards", are a familiar sight to any visitor to the UN offices in New York, Geneva, Vienna, or Nairobi, as well as in smaller UN offices (→ UN Office Geneva; → UN Office New York; → UN Office Nairobi; → UN Office Vienna,; → UN in Bonn). Their task is above all the guard and security service at the entrances and on the UN premises.

When the United Nations failed after 1945 to establish standing UN forces, UN → Secretary-General Trygve Lie proposed in 1948 the establishment of a "UN Guard Force" of 800 men to support UN missions in the field (cf. *UNYB* 1947/48, 419-425; *Luard* 1982, 345f.). This plan was thwarted by the Soviet Union and its allies who did not want to give the UN a (para-)military capacity of its own. Therefore, Lie's plan was modified and eventually led with resolution A/RES/297 (IV) of 22 November 1949 to the establishment of the non-uniformed UN Field Service for the administrative and logistic support of UN

→ peacekeeping forces and → peacekeeping operations.

In 1991, a special "UN Guards Contingent in Iraq" (UNGCI) was established to protect the humanitarian activities of → UNHCR for Kurdish refugees after the Gulf War (→ Humanitarian Assistance). This mission numbered 500 personnel and was drawn from various UN offices, augmented by personnel from a number of UN member states. All members of UNCGI were withdrawn at the time of the evacuation of UN international staff in Iraq in March 2003.

All members of UNGCI wore blue UN uniforms in place of their national uniforms, and thus can be regarded as the first truly "international force", even though the experiment was less than successful otherwise, and the UN Guards proved not suited to operate as a police mission in the field (→ UNCIVPOL).

Erwin A. Schmidl

Lit.: *Luard, E.:* A History of the United Nations. Vol. 1: The Years of Western Domination, 1945-1955, London/Basingstoke 1982; *Schmidl, E.A.:* Police in Peace Operations, Vienna 1998.

UN-HABITAT

formerly **UNCHS – United Nations Centre for Human Settlements (Habitat)**

I. The United Nations Centre for Human Settlements (UNCHS) 1977-2001

The United Nations Centre for Human Settlements (UNCHS), usually referred to as *"Habitat"*, a subsidiary organ of the → General Assembly (→ Principal Organs, Subsidiary Organs, Treaty Bodies) was founded in 1977 by the General Assembly (UN Doc. A/RES/32/162 of 19 December 1977) as the hub of the United Nations activities related to human settlement and their development. It served as the secretariat for the *United Nations Commission on Human Settlements (UNCHS),* seated in Nairobi, (→ UN Office Nairobi).

The task of the *Commission on Human Settlement*, also established pursuant to General Assembly resolution A/RES/32/162 of 19 December 1977, was to develop goals, priorities and guidelines for a human settlement policy of the United Nations.

II. Habitat I Conference 1976 in Vancouver

In the early seventies an international discussion began about urban living environments, how they should be utilized, and related problems. The developing nations increasingly felt the pressure of their fast growing populations and a decreasing availability of living space that led to growing slums, especially in their capitals and population centers. The industrialized nations encountered increasing problems with the unforeseen and rapid process of urbanization. In this context, questions about human settlements and housing were first discussed in the framework of the United Nations at the United Nations Conference on the Human Environment 1972 in Stockholm. Later the same year the General Assembly agreed to a recommendation of the United Nations Environment Programme (→ UNEP) to hold a conference of all UN member states, to discuss guidelines and the foundation for a policy concerned with human settlement.

The conference was organized by UNEP and held in Vancouver, Canada from 31 May to 11 June 1976. It came to be known as Habitat I. As the final document the *"Vancouver-Declaration On Human Settlements"* (UN Doc. A/CONF.70/15 of 11 June 1976) was adopted. This declaration of principles included 64 recommendations that were regarded as necessary to ensure the bare essentials for human habitation (e.g. shelter, clean water, sanitary installations).

III. Habitat II 1996 in Istanbul

The second conference within the framework of UNCHS was held in Istanbul from 3 June to 15 June 1996.

Habitat II was the last conference of the series of global meetings of the 90s (→ World Conferences) It focused on the growing phenomenon of urbanization and its related problems. Especially developing nations were struggling with the rapid growth of their urban agglomerations.

With this rapid growth of cities in the poorer nations, the problems of shortage of housing and ecological destruction were becoming more and more serious. Also, human rights issues and questions concerning family planning were discussed at the so-called "Urban Summit" in Istanbul.

About 20,000 people participated in the conference, as well as 130 representatives of states and about 5,000 members of non-governmental organizations (→ NGOs). At the end of the negotiations in which the NGOs played an important role, the "Istanbul Declaration" on Human Settlements" and "The Habitat Agenda" (UN Doc. A/CONF.165/14 of 7 August 1996, Annex I and II).for the future activities of the secretariat were adopted. The right to shelter as a human right was confirmed again in the declaration, but just as a non-committing goal, so that no citizen can deduct a legal claim towards his government. The greatest success of Istanbul was the shift of focus in the attitude of the member states, away from the mere state measures to implement the often only vague formulated goals which made it necessary to integrate the → NGOs more substantially in the work of the conference. Even though the conference did not produce any tangible results and did not formulate a strategy to deal with the problem of increasing urbanization, the public attention and heightened awareness of the topic was the most important result of the conference.

IV. Istanbul+5 Follow-up 2001

Like most of the UN world conferences of the 1990s, Habitat II was followed by a review conference five years later, here in the form of a special session of the General Assembly in 2001, with the task to review and evaluate the implementation of the *Habitat Agenda* of the Istanbul Conference 1996. The General Assembly confirmed in its concluding resolution "Declaration on Cities and Other Human Settlements in the New Millennium" (UN Doc. A/RES/S-25/2 of 9 June 2001) explicitly the basic principles of the Habitat Agenda and called for greater efforts of the states to provide adequate housing.

V. New Structures – New Chances?

Some months after the special session on the Habitat Agenda the General Assembly decided to strengthen "the mandate and status of the Commission on Human Settlements and the status, role and functions of the United Nations Centre for Human Settlements (Habitat)", as the title of the respective resolution (UN Doc. A/RES/56/206 of 21 December 2001) indicated it: the Commission and its Centre were transformed with effect from 1 January 2002 into "the United Nations Human Settlement Programme, to be known as UN-Habitat" (ibid., I). Thus UN-Habitat has changed from a commission to a genuine UN programme as subsidiary organ of the General Assembly, the Commission being transformed into the Governing Council of the Programme, the Centre being transformed into the secretariat of the Programme. The Governing Council meets biennially – the Commission had held annual meetings, while the composition of the Governing Council, its size and the key for the seats for the different regional groups of the UN remained the same compared to the Commission.

Whether this obvious upgrading in terms of organizational status is followed by concrete measures of the decisive UN bodies with a view of improving the housing situation of many people remains to be seen; at least the issue is taken seriously as an important item on the UN agenda.

Helmut Volger

Lit.: *Bauer, F.:* Aus dem Bereich der Vereinten Nationen – Wirtschaft und Entwick-

lung, in: VN 44 (1996), 218-220; *Schiavone, G.:* International Organisations. A Dictionary, 2nd edn., London/Basingstoke 1995; *Smith-Bizzarro, D./Nagle, A.G.:* Habitat – Commission on Human Settlements, in: Wolfrum, R. (ed.), United Nations: Law, Policies and Practice, Vol. 1, Munich/Dordrecht 1995, 567-571; *United Nations - General Assembly:* Strengthening the mandate and status of the Commission on Human Settlements and the status, role and functions of the United Nations Centre for Human Settlements (Habitat). Resolution adopted by the General Assembly, 21 December 2001, UN Doc. A/RES/56/206; *United Nations Non-Governmental Liaison Service (NGLS):* Istanbul+5: UN General Assembly Review of the Habitat Agenda, in: NGLS Roundup 79 (August 2001), www.un-ngls.org).

Internet: Homepage of UN-Habitat: www.unhabitat.org;

UNHCR – United Nations High Commissioner for Refugees

On 3 December 1949, the → General Assembly of the United Nations adopted a resolution that recognized the responsibility of the UN for the international protection of refugees (UN Doc. A/RES/319 (IV)). To fulfill the task, it was at the same time decided to establish the Office of the *United Nations High Commissioner for Refugees (UNHCR)* as per 1 January 1951. The High Commissioner is elected by the General Assembly on the nomination of the UN → Secretary-General. There have been 10 High Commissioners since UNHCR was founded. UNHCR's mandate was originally established for just three years. This was subsequently extended to periods of five years until in 2003 the UN General Assembly removed the time limitation on the Office's mandate altogether (UN Doc. A/RES/58/153).

According to its *Statute* (UN Doc. A/RES/428(V) of 14 December 1950) UNHCR is a humanitarian organization. Core function: Providing "international protection". Since establishing the office, the statute has not been changed.

Refugee definition: a person who is outside the country of his/her nationality owing to a well founded fear of persecution for reasons of race, religion, nationality, membership of a particular social group or political opinion (Statute, II, para. 6).

International protection of refugees is the "raison d'être" of the Office. The most important international agreement is the 1951 *Convention Relating to the Status of Refugees* (UNTS Vol. 189, No. 2545), also called *The Geneva Refugee Convention.*) The 1951 Convention includes a time and geographical limitation "as a result of events occurring in Europe before 1951". This was lifted in 1967 through an additional protocol, the *Protocol Relating to the Status of Refugees* (UNTS Vol. 606, No. 8791). 144 states are currently *parties* to the Convention and 144 to the Protocol (as of 1 October 2008).

The 1951 Convention regulates the rights and duties of a recognized refugee in his country of asylum and offers an internationally binding definition of the term "refugee" (Convention, Art. 1) using substantially the same definition as in the UNHCR Statute. A main element of the 1951 Convention is the so-called principle of *non-refoulement*, which prohibits expulsion and return of a refugee to territories where "his life or freedom would be threatened on account of his race, religion, nationality, membership of a particular social group or political opinion" (Convention, Art. 33). The aim of the 1951 Convention is to provide (recognized) refugees with a range of rights based on four different standards of treatment, depending on the right in question. UNHCR, according to the preamble to the Convention, has the task to "ensure implementation of international agreements to protect refugees".

Other important references for UNHCR's work are the *regional refugee conventions* such as *the Convention of the Organization of African Unity (OAU)* of 1969 and *the Cartagena Declaration on Refugees* of 1984. Both documents expand the definition of refugees to include individuals displaced over international borders owing, among other things, to events seriously disturbing public order.

International refugee law forms the basis for the activities of UNHCR though over the course of decades, these have been considerably expanded. Apart from providing international protection for refugees, UNHCR is tasked with finding permanent or "durable" solutions for refugees. There are three such solutions: Voluntary repatriation to the country of origin, integration in the country of asylum, or resettlement to a third country.

In most cases and when conditions allow, voluntary repatriation is the preferred solution. UNHCR assists refugees not only to return but to reintegrate in their country of origin. Since its creation, UNHCR has assisted approximately 50 million people to renew their lives in their home countries.

Originally UNHCR was not given a role in the delivery of material assistance. This changed when in the course of → decolonization and nation-building UNHCR's sphere of action was extended beyond Europe to other continents, including many countries that were not able to provide refugees with assistance themselves.

In the course of time, assistance to refugees and host countries through the funding, co-ordinating and implementing of aid programmes gained in importance for the work of UNHCR.

The mandate of the Office also covers stateless people and efforts to reduce statelessness. Statelessness occurs in different situations, including discrimination against minority groups in nationality legislation, failure to include all residents in the body of citizens when a state becomes independent, and in situations of conflicts between the laws of states. Traditionally, UNHCR has focused on providing legal advice to states but has also extended its services to provide operational support and ensure inter-agency collaboration.

Over the decades, succeeding UN Secretaries-General also asked UNHCR to assist internally displaced persons. Especially after the end of the Cold War a number of ethnic and intra-state conflicts broke out, leaving millions of people internally displaced. UNHCR was frequently asked to give humanitarian aid (→ Humanitarian Assistance) within extensive UN operations in areas of conflict.

To address gaps in the humanitarian response to situations of internal displacement, in 2005 the → UN system agreed on a more predictable approach, designating lead agencies in critical sectors. UNHCR was given responsibility for the protection, emergency shelter and camp coordination and management areas. UNHCR operations on several continents have since grown to cover the protection and assistance needs of *internally displaced persons (IDPs)*, who significantly outnumber refugees.

The development of UNHCR from a Europe-based and Europe-oriented office with mainly legal tasks to a worldwide and operational humanitarian organization is reflected in the statistical data: At the beginning of the 1970s UNHCR had responsibility for approximately 2.5 million refugees. Ten years later, the number of refugees exceeded 8.2 million. At the beginning of 2008, there were more than 31 million persons of concern to UNHCR, including over 11 million refugees.

While in 1970 UNHCR's budget amounted to approximately 8.3 million US dollars, ten years later it had grown to approximately 500 million US dollars. With the conflict in the former Yugoslavia and the exodus from Rwanda, UNHCR's budget in the 1990's rose to more than one billion US dollars. In 2008, the organization had total financial requirements of more than 1.8 billion US dollars and more than 6,300 staff members working in 110 countries.

The nature of UNHCR's funding has hardly changed since its foundation. The Office is almost exclusively financed by voluntary contributions from governments and the European Commission. There is also a very limited subsidy – about 2 % of the UNHCR budget – from the regular → budget of the United Nations.

The UNHCR programme and budget are approved by the *UNHCR Executive Committee*. This body of 76 governments meets once a year in plenary sessions in Geneva to examine UNHCR's programmes and budget. In addition the Committee adopts each year resolutions concerning all aspects of international protection of refugees, contributing to the further development of international refugee law.

UNHCR co-operates with a number of other UN organizations, especially the World Food Programme (→ WFP), the UN Children's Fund (→ UNICEF), the World Health Organization (→ WHO), the UN Development Programme (→ UNDP) and the Office for the Coordination of Humanitarian Affairs (OCHA) as well as the International Committee of the Red Cross, the Federation of Red Cross and Red Crescent Societies, the International Organization for Migration (IOM) and more than 600 non-governmental organizations (→ NGOs).

Operations in conflict and civil war areas have intensified cooperation with the UN High Commissioner for Human Rights (→ Human Rights, United Nations High Commissioner for) and UN and regional → peacekeeping forces (cf. also → peacekeeping; → peacekeeping operations).

Cooperation with a variety of actors, including the World Bank (→ World Bank, World Bank Group), is pursued to help bridge the gap between relief and development. UNHCR participates actively in the "Early Recovery" clusters for internal displacement led by UNDP as well as with the UN Peacebuilding Commission and in the "Delivering as One" initiative.

Along with traditional challenges such as ensuring the sustainability of solutions for refugees, UNHCR faces new tests related to the increasingly mixed nature of many present-day population flows. The ability to detect people in need of international protection amid broader migratory movements is a pressing concern. At the same time, climate change is complicating and exacerbating forced displacement. With ever greater reliance on partnership, UNHCR is responding to the larger numbers of ever more complex displacement in the 21st century.

Athar Sultan-Khan

Lit.: *United Nations High Commissioner for Refugees:* Convention and Protocol Relating to the Status of Refugees, Geneva, available at www.unhcr.org/protect/Protect/3b66c2aa 10.pdf; *United Nations High Commissioner for Refugees:* The State of the World's Refugees 2006, Geneva 2006, www.unhcr.org/static/publ/sowr2006/toceng.htm.

Internet: 1) Homepage of UNHCR: www.unhcr.org; 2) Homepage of Refworld, UNHCR-organized information system containing a vast number of reports on refugees, policy documents and documents relating to international and national legal frameworks compiled from UNHC's global network, governments, non-governmental organizations, academic institutions and judicial bodies: www.refworld.org.

UNICEF – United Nations Children's Fund

With the aim of supporting the children in Europe, who were affected by the consequences of World War II, with food, medicine and clothes, the UN General Assembly (→ General Assembly) established with Resolution 57 (I) of 11 December 1946 the *"United Nations International Children's Emergency Fund" (UNICEF)*. In 1953 the General Assembly decided to continue the fund indefinitely (UN Doc. A/RES/802 (VIII) of 6 October 1953). Its name was changed to the *United Nations Children's Fund,* but the acronym UNICEF retained.

Today UNICEF helps children in the poorest and least developed countries on the earth. Its scope of duties is manifold. The principal focus of its activities is on long-term programmes for improving health, food and water supply of children, as well as the education of children and the social infrastructure in developing countries. UNICEF also takes part in the emergency and reconstruc-

tion aid of the → UN system (→ Humanitarian Assistance).

In December 1989 the *Convention on the Rights of the Child (CRC)* was adopted by the General Assembly (UN Doc. A/RES/44/25 of 20 November 1989, Annex, in: GAOR 44th Session, Resolutions, 166; UNTS Vol. 1577, No. 27531) (→ Human Rights Conventions, CRC). In this convention UNICEF is assigned the task of supporting the newly created Committee on the Rights of the Child (cf. Art. 45 of the CRC). With the exception of one state – the USA, which has signed the convention in 1995 but not yet ratified it – all UN member states (→ Membership and Representation of States) have become members of the Convention, so that this convention is the human rights convention with the broadest support (→ Human Rights, Protection of; → Human Rights Conventions and their Measures of Implementation).

I. Structures

As a special organ of the United Nations (→ Principal Organs, Subsidiary Organs, Treaty Bodies) with a semi-autonomous status and its headquarters in New York, UNICEF reports to the General Assembly through the Economic and Social Council (→ ECOSOC).

The *Executive Board* of UNICEF is made up of the delegates of 36 UN member states elected for a three-year term by ECOSOC according to the system of equitable regional representation. The Board meets in one annual and up to three regular sessions per year and reviews the work of UNICEF, decides on measures, applications and projects and commits funds for programmes and administrative costs. The *Executive Director* of UNICEF is appointed by the UN Secretary-General (→ Secretary-General), in consultation with the Executive Board. The Executive Director is responsible for the implementation of the programmes and policies, and for the appointment and direction of UNICEF staff.

A large part of the activities of UNICEF takes place in the eight *region-*

al offices. These offices are supplemented by 125 country offices (source: *UNICEF*: Annual Report 2001). Central offices in Copenhagen, Florence, Geneva, Brussels and Tokyo, disseminate information, maintain relations with nongovernmental organizations (→ NGOs) and support the *national committees*. The 37 *national committees*, most of which have their seat in industrialized countries, help to generate a better understanding of the work of UNICEF.

UNICEF works in close cooperation with national governments, NGOs and → specialized agencies of the UN such as → ILO, → FAO, → UNESCO, → WHO, → UNDP, → UNFPA, IBRD (→ World Bank, World Bank Group) and IFAD. Furthermore there are working relations with → UNEP, OCHA (emergency relief programmes) and → UNHCR (United Nations High Commissioner for Refugees).

II. Financing

UNICEF is financed almost exclusively by voluntary contributions from the UN member states and from private donors. In 2000 UNICEF had altogether 1.111 billion US dollars at its disposal (source: *UNICEF:* Annual Report 2001). Two-thirds of the resources income were made up of the voluntary contributions from governments. Main donor states were the USA, Norway and Sweden. Much of the remaining third of the income came from the net profits of privately organized fund raising, such as the sale of greeting cards. In this context the national committees are of high importance in appealing to the governments and the public in the industrialized countries to mobilize the necessary funds for the UNICEF programmes.

III. Perspectives

UNICEF is at present the only organization worldwide which addresses exclusively the needs and interests of children. In the more than 50 fifty years of UNICEF's existence a large variety of internationally renowned personalities such as Danny Kaye, Audrey Hepburn, Sir Peter Ustinov and many others have engaged themselves as ambassadors of good will and special envoys for the interests of children, and have thereby increased the degree of publicity of UNICEF all over the world. UNICEF has indeed developed into one of the draw cards of the United Nations. Moreover the awarding of the Nobel Peace Prize in the year 1956 has contributed to its positive reputation. Also in the future UNICEF will be faced with increasing challenges to a larger extent than ever before. Additionally the setting-up and implementation of programmes in East Europe offers UNICEF a new field of activity.

Jana Mittermaier

Lit.: *Eibach, G.:* UNICEF – United Nations Children's Fund, in: Wolfrum, R. (ed.): United Nations: Law, Policies and Practice, Vol. 2, Munich/Dordrecht 1995, 1323-1328; *Hüfner, K.:* Die Vereinten Nationen und ihre Sonderorganisationen, Strukturen, Aufgaben, Dokumente. Teil 2: Die Sonderorganisationen, Bonn 1995; *UNICEF:* Facts about UNICEF (annually); *UNICEF:* The State of the World's Children Report (annually); *UNICEF:* Annual Report 2001, New York 2001 (Internet: www.unicef.org/ar01).

Addendum

The sixth decade of the work of UNICEF was marked by some important achievements with regard to the human rights status of children as well as to the public awareness of the problems to be solved: UNICEF played an active role in drafting and promoting two Optional Protocols to the Convention on the Rights of the Child which were adopted by the UN General Assembly in 2000 and entered into force in 2002. These were the Optional Protocol to the Convention on the Rights of the Child on the Sale of Children, Child Prostitution and Child Pornography (UNTS Vol. 2171, No. 27531) and the Optional Protocol to the Convention on the Rights of the Child on the Involvement of Children in Armed Conflict (UNTS Vol. 21713, No. 27531). Both have been ratified as of December 2008 by more than 120 states. They are important milestones in the legal protection of children.

UNICEF played also an important role in the convening of the Security Council for a meeting in the form of an open debate on children and armed conflict in January 2003 (cf. the record of the meeting in UN Doc. S/PV.4684 and S/PV.4684 (Resumption I) of 14 January 2003 and UN Press Release SC/7631). This debate increased considerably the political pressure on those states violating human rights with regard to children in armed conflicts. UNICEF also played a key role in securing the release of children from armed forces and other combatant groups in several Asian and African states (cf. *UNICEF* 2006, 29).

UNICEF has expanded – under the pressure of the circumstances – its classical role in promoting the nutrition, health and education of children through the dimension of participating actively in the legal and political fight for the freedom, safety and basic human rights of children endangered in many innerstate conflicts and civil wars.

To mobilize more political support for the fight against malnutrition, diseases and poor education facilities facing children in many parts of the world, UNICEF formed in 2001 together with five other organizations working with children the "Global Movement for Children" and worked out a ten-point agenda to "change the world with children" (*UNICEF* 2006, 30).

This initiative led eventually to a special session of the General Assembly on children in May 2002, another "World Summit for Children" about twelve years after the "World Summit for Children" in New York in September 1990 (cf. *United Nations* 1990). At the special session, world leaders agreed on an outcome document titled "A World Fit for Children" (UN Doc. A/RES/S-27/2 of 10 May 2002) which committed the UN member states to completing the unfinished agenda of the 1990 World Summit for Children and included 21 specific goals for the next decade, for example

to increase net primary school enrolment to at least 90 per cent by 2010.

The special session was also unique among UN meetings in another respect: it encouraged the participation of children. Over 400 children from more than 150 countries took part in the UN Children's Forum in May 2002 in New York, which came up with a common statement that was eventually read to the UN General Assembly by two of them (cf. *UNICEF* 2002).

As more and more children were affected in recent years by natural disasters, conflicts, or other forms of crises, UNICEF realized that it had to clarify its role in such emergencies: it revised and expanded its "Core Commitments for Children in Emergencies", defining the most important tasks for UNICEF on short-, medium-, and long-term scales (cf. *UNICEF* 2005).

In the sixth decade of its work as a UN organization UNICEF has greatly expanded its field of work – in response to the increasing need for the worldwide protection of children as well as in response to a greater willingness to invest political power and financial resources in the improvement of the living conditions for the world's children – and has included human rights protection, disaster relief and political advocacy in its scope of activities. In fact it has evolved from being an emergency fund for children, then a UN programme fighting for better health conditions and better education facilities for children to a complete development agency, working together with other UN organizations and NGOs for more rights, better chances and living conditions for those in need, with the special emphasis on the children.

Helmut Volger

Lit.: *UNICEF:* Core Commitments for Children in Emergencies, New York 2005; *UNICEF:* 1946-2006: Sixty Years for Children, New York 2006; *UNICEF:* Children's Forum report. Report on the Meeting of the Under-18 delegates to the UN Special Session on Children, New York 2002; *UNICEF:* Annual Report 2007, New York 2007;

United Nations - General Assembly: World Declaration on the Survival, Protection and Development of Children, UN Doc. A/45/625, 18 October 1990, Annex (quoted as: United Nations 1990); *United Nations – General Assembly:* A World Fit For Children (UN Doc. A/RES/S-27/2 of 10 May 2002).

Internet: Homepage of UNICEF: www.unicef.org; of particular interest is the annual report "State of the World's Children", containing information texts on a specific issue of UNICEF work (e.g. nutrition, education etc.) together with a lot of statistical figures and graphic illustrations; for example the report for 2008 can be accessed at www.unicef.org/sowc08/docs/sowc08.pdf.

UNIDIR – United Nations Institute for Disarmament Research

I. Purpose

The *United Nations Institute for Disarmament Research (UNIDIR)* is an autonomous research institute within the framework of the United Nations. The Institute was established by the → General Assembly in its Resolution A/RES/34/83M of 11 December 1979. It was first proposed by President Valery Giscard d'Estaing of France in a speech before the First UN Special Session on Disarmament in 1978 (→ Disarmament).

It is the purpose of UNIDIR to conduct applied *research* on questions relating to disarmament and international security. The research programme is geared to the needs of the United Nations and its member states. In discharging its duties, the Institute draws on the expertise, insight and experience of a variety of professions. The field is interdisciplinary, and it is not limited to the academic domain. In hiring its staff, recruiting its consultants and planning its projects, the Institute is seeking a fair geographical distribution of resources. Contacts are maintained with nongovernmental organizations (→ NGOs) active in the field.

Being located in the Palais des Nations in Geneva, UNIDIR attends to the agenda of the *Conference on Disarmament (CD)*, which is working in the same building. While maintaining its independence also in relation to the CD, the Institute may contribute to the clarification of issues being discussed at the CD, or coming up for negotiation in this forum. However, once the CD has agreed on a negotiating mandate, the role of UNIDIR is modest. Then, the politics of the matter under negotiation, and the negotiating intricacies and details, are firmly within the domain of diplomats and their governments.

II. Mode of Work

The Institute has a small core staff in Geneva. For the implementation of its research programme, it relies largely on project-related, short-term contracts. It hires the services of, or develops cooperation with, individual experts and research organizations, while ensuring that multi-disciplinary approaches are applied. The Institute has a fellowship programme which enables scholars from developing countries to come to Geneva to undertake research on disarmament and security issues at UNIDIR, and which helps ensure the participation of researchers on an equitable political and geographical basis.

UNIDIR cooperates closely with the Office for Disarmament Affairs (until 2007, the Department for Disarmament Affairs) in New York and with its branch in Geneva (→ Secretariat) to ensure complementarity and coordination. Full use is being made of United Nations services for purposes of coordination, economy and cost-effectiveness.

UNIDIR benefits greatly from close contacts with the UN and its member governments. These contacts are part and parcel of the rationale of the Institute, and are a significant determinant and asset for the direction and quality of UNIDIR's research. The statutory formula of autonomy within the framework of the UN, therefore, represents an optimal combination. In this way, UNIDIR enjoys independence as well as proximity to the actors it is asked to serve. This is a unique and fruitful platform for the conduct of applied research, especially when in the 1990s the role of the United

Nations in security affairs was significantly enlarged.

UNIDIR receives a small subvention from the regular → budget of the United Nations (of the order of 220,000 US dollars per year). In addition, it seeks voluntary contributions from member states and grants from public and private foundations. These grants are usually earmarked for specific projects. The mixed nature of the funding of the Institute is also a means of guaranteeing its autonomous character: the impact of UNIDIR's publications is predicated on the independence with which the Institute is seen to conduct its research. However, with such a modest contribution from the United Nations, it is a demanding task to raise the necessary financial support for Institute. This requires much work and ingenuity on the part of the leadership of the Institute.

The first Director of the Institute was Mr Liviu Botha, Rumania. He was followed by Mr Jayantha Dhanapala, Sri Lanka (1987-1992), Mr Sverre Lodgaard, Norway (1992-1996), Ms Patricia Lewis, United Kingdom (1997-2008) and Ms Theresa Hitchens (since 2009).

III. Research Programme

Through the last decade, UNIDIR's research programme has been structured into three main headings:

(1) *Global security and disarmament:* UNIDIR activities in the area of global security and disarmament address the contentious issues surrounding international arms control regimes and the links between disarmament, conflict and security. Through its research projects, meetings and publications, the Institute supports the Conference on Disarmament, the General Assembly and other forums by contributing in-depth, forward-looking thinking to security dialogues. UNIDIR remains committed to strengthening arms control regimes after their entry into force through its research on treaty implementation, verification and compliance.

(2) *Regional Security and disarmament:* UNIDIR activities on regional security and disarmament cast the spotlight on specific regions of the world, which are subject to tension, violent conflict and where the availability of various categories of armaments generate region-specific or trans-regional security issues. Recently, the Institute has been focusing on West Africa, South Asia and the Middle East. In addition, UNIDIR's expert group meetings and annual fellowship programme bring together professionals who would not normally have the opportunity to work collaboratively. While recognizing that one-size-fits-all solutions are not appropriate, learning about other regions' initiatives can inspire and encourage more open thinking, and thus lead to further successes.

(3) *Human security and disarmament:* UNIDIR activities on human security and disarmament include cross-cutting research on small arms collection, weapons as a public health issue, and security-building measures – such as peace-building, humanitarian action and the impact of landmines. The Institute actively seeks to involve civil society groups and NGOs in disarmament and security debates. Inclusive methodologies and approaches, such as participatory evaluation and monitoring techniques, are used to ensure that the voices and reflections of those most affected by violence, conflict and weapons proliferation are heard.

The Institute has always had to strike a difficult balance between, on the one hand, a variety of requests for studies of a broad range of diverse issues and, on the other, the limitation and concentration of efforts necessitated by its limited resource base.

The main lines of research are determined by the Board of Trustees of the Institute (see "The Secretary-General's Advisory Board on Disarmament Matters", below).

IV. Cooperation with and among Research Institutes

Four recurrent activities come under this heading:

(1) maintenance and development of UNIDIR's computerized *information*

and documentation system, DATARIS, on who is doing what in the field of security and disarmament research;

(2) publication of *Disarmament Forum,* the journal succeeding UNIDIR Newsletter;

(3) convening of *regional conferences,* held with the dual purpose of examining region-specific issues of security, arms control and disarmament and of fostering cooperation with and among research institutes in the areas concerned;

(4) convening of *conferences* and other smaller group activities in support of initiatives aimed at improving *communication* and *access to data.*

(5) The *Geneva Forum:* Together with the Centre on Conflict, Development and Peacebuilding (CCPD) of the Graduate Institute of International and Development Studies and the Quaker United Nations Office, UNIDIR organizes an ongoing discussion series known as the Geneva Forum. The Geneva Forum is an intellectual space in which expertise on a broad range of disarmament issues is shared among government delegates, United Nations personnel, NGOs, international media and academics.

V. Publications

"Disarmament Forum" is the quarterly journal of UNIDIR, and its flagship publication with global distribution. It is bilingual (English and French), and each issue is available on-line in its entirety.

The other main branch of UNIDIR's publications is its series of Books and Reports. These aim primarily at informing the diplomatic, academic and NGO communities concerned with arms control and disarmament about policy-relevant themes, options and analysis. Reference materials on disarmament-related topics are available in the Lexicon for Arms Control, Disarmament and Confidence-building, published in Arabic, English, Korean and Spanish.

The UNIDIR website comprises the full range of its publications as well as of its past and current activities.

VI. The Secretary-General's Advisory Board on Disarmament Matters

The First UN Special Session on Disarmament also resolved to set up an *Advisory Board on Disarmament Studies.* While the Cold War blocked agreement on important issues, studies of controversial subjects could still be undertaken. The Board was asked to advise the → Secretary-General on various aspects of studies and research carried out under the auspices of the United Nations. It was also asked to serve as the Board of Trustees for UNIDIR; to give advise on the implementation of the UN Disarmament Information Programme (from 1982 to 1989 named the World Disarmament Campaign); and, at the specific invitation of the Secretary-General, to provide him with advice on matters within the area of disarmament and arms limitation.

Conducted by governmental experts, the studies were usually rich on official lines of reasoning and short on agreed recommendations. When the Cold War ended and cooperation between the major powers was much expanded, governmental studies became of lesser relevance. This part of the Board's mandate therefore shrunk accordingly. Much the same can be said for the Disarmament Information Programme.

Currently composed of some 20 members from all major regions of the world – a mix of senior diplomats and senior members of the academic community – the Board has two main functions: to advise the Secretary-General on disarmament matters, and to be the Board of Trustees for UNIDIR. It usually meets twice a year, once in New York and once in Geneva, in the presence of the Secretary-General and/or the High Representative (until 2007, Undersecretary General) for Disarmament Affairs.

Over the years, UNIDIR has become an essential element in the United Nations system (→ UN System) in the field of disarmament. Due to its autonomy and expertise and its comprehensive contacts with member states as well as NGOs, it is in a position to offer high-quality contributions to disarmament affairs.

UNIDIR's mode of work – its flexibility in planning, fund-raising and cooperation with others – sets an example of how a UN institution with small resources at its disposal can, nevertheless, make a significant contribution towards meeting the needs of member states.

Sverre Lodgaard

Lit.: *1) UNIDIR reports: a) annual reports: United Nations - General Assembly:* Report of the Director of the United Nations Institute for Disarmament Research 2006, 25 July 2006, UN Doc. A/61/180; *United Nations - General Assembly:* Report of the Director of the United Nations Institute for Disarmament Research 2007, 26 July 2007, UN Doc. A/62/152; *United Nations - General Assembly:* Report of the Director of the United Nations Institute for Disarmament Research 2008, 28 July 2008, UN Doc. A/63/177; *b) Other UNIDIR reports: UNIDIR in cooperation with the UN Department of Disarmament Affairs (DDA):* Disarmament as Humanitarian Action – A discussion on the occasion of the 20th anniversary of the United Nations Institute for Disarmament Research (UNIDIR), Geneva 2001; *UNIDIR:* Implementing the United Nations Programme of Action on Small Arms and Light Weapons. Analysis of the National Reports Submitted by States from 2002 to 2008, authors: S. Cattaneo and Sarah Parker, Geneva 2008; *2) Other UNIDIR publications: Borrie, J./ Thornton, A.:* The Value of Diversity in Multilateral Disarmament Work, UNIDIR, Geneva 2008; *Dhanapala, J. with Rydell, R.:* Multilateral Diplomacy and the NPT: An Insider's Account, UNIDIR, Geneva 2005; *Miller, D./Rudnick, L.:* The Security Needs Assessment Protocol: Improving Operational Effectiveness through Community Security, UNIDIR, Geneva 2008; *Tulliu, S./Schmalberger, T.:* Coming to Terms with Security. A Lexicon for Arms Control, Disarmament and Confidence Building, UNIDIR, Geneva 2004, bilingual edition English/Spanish; also available in English/Arabic and English/Korean (both UNIDIR, Geneva 2004); also available an edition in French (UNIDIR, Geneva 2007); *UNIDIR (ed.):* Security in Space: The Next Generation. Conference Report 31 March - 1 April 2008, Geneva 2008; *Wolter, D.:* Common Security in Outer Space, UNIDIR, Geneva 2006; *3) periodicals: Disarmament Forum* (quarterly, bilingual (English-French) journal, edited by UNIDIR.

Internet: Homepage of UNIDIR: www.unidir.org.

UNIDO – United Nations Industrial Development Organization

The *United Nations Industrial Development Organization (UNIDO)* was formed in 1966 by changing the *UN Centre for Industrial Development* as part of the → Secretariat of the United Nations into an autonomous organization of the United Nations by a resolution of the UN General Assembly (UN Doc. A/RES/2152 (XXI) of 17 November 1966). At that time the developing countries could not push through their demands for a parity of UNIDO with other UN → specialized agencies. After lengthy negotiations in the second half of the 70s the Statute for UNIDO as a specialized agency was adopted on 8 April 1979 and at the end of 1985 all preconditions for the statute coming into force were fulfilled. Accordingly the relationship agreement between UNIDO and the UN could be concluded in compliance with Art. 57 UN Charter (UN Doc. A/RES/40/180 of 17 December 1985) by which UNIDO became the 16th specialized agency of the UN.

UNIDO's *General Conference* of 172 member states (as of 3 December 2007) meets every second year, elects the *Director-General* and the *Industrial Development Board* of 53 member countries and approves the budget and the work programme. The seat of UNIDO is Vienna.

To the broader public UNIDO became known by its *"Lima Declaration"* of 1974, formulating the goal of raising the industrial production of developing countries to a quarter of the global level of production by the year 2000.

Its *mandate* is to support the *industrial competence and capacity* of *developing countries*, and in recent years also of the reform countries of the former Eastern bloc. At the same time, UNIDO advocates *international cooperation* in the field of *industrial development*, e.g. by supporting partnerships, the codification of treaties, the elaboration of standards and the collection of statistics. In addition, UNIDO offers technical cooperation services. Finally, UNIDO has established a facility in support of private investment which is increasingly used for South-South cooperation. UNIDO created a network of six international technology centers to support the exchange of new and advanced technologies on a global scale.

UNIDO has been active in practically all fields of industry, often through programmes of exchange and training. In technical cooperation, major areas of emphasis are agro-based industries, chemical industry, and mechanical engineering. Priority is given to programmes of global economic integration, environment and energy, support of small scale industries, investment and technology, and rural industries.

The debate about UN reforms (→ Reform of the UN) brought UNIDO into a major crisis. The discussion was not limited to the question of UNIDO's work efficiency, but touched, as an issue of principle, on the question whether its area of work should better be left to the private sector. The United States withdrew in 1996, and similar moves were discussed in government circles of the United Kingdom and Germany in 1997, though both countries did not declare their withdrawal. UNIDO reacted with a reform package, including substantial streamlining of organization, action programme, and budget. These measures came into force in 1998.

In 2004 UNIDO started a second round of programme reforms which further focused its activities and technical services responding to development priorities. These reforms enabled UNIDO to retain its capacity to act in the key areas of its work.

New emphasis is laid in the work of UNIDO on trade-related capacity building and on the work related to the "Montreal Protocol on Substances that deplete the Ozone Layer" (→ Environmental Law, International).

With regard to its finances, total contributions amounted in 2005 to 138 million US dollars (80 million US dollars from governments, 45 million US dollars from the Montreal Protocol Multilateral Funds, and 13 million US dollars from other sources). Technical assistance expenditure was reported at the level of 112 million US dollars.

Manfred Kulessa

Lit.: *Hobohm, S.:* UNIDO, in: Altmann, J./ Kulessa, M. (eds.): Internationale Wirtschaftsorganisationen, Stuttgart 1998, 239-47; *Rau-Mentzen, B.L./Koppenfels, G.v.:* UNIDO – United Nations Industrial Development Organization, in: Wolfrum, R. (ed.): United Nations: Law, Policies and Practice, Vol. 2, Munich/Dordrecht 1995, 1329-1334; *Scholtes, P.R.:* Formulating industrial strategies and policies in the context of restructuring economies; some preliminary thoughts, in: Industry and Development 33 (1993), 43-51; *UNIDO:* Wege in die Zukunft, Vienna 1996; *UNIDO:* The globalization of industry: Implications for developing countries beyond 2000, Vienna 1996; *UNIDO:* Annual Report, Vienna; *UNIDO:* Industrial Development Report 2005: Capacity building for catching-up. Historical, empirical and policy dimensions, Vienna 2005.

Internet: Homepage of UNIDO: www.unido.org.

UNIFEM – United Nations Development Fund for Women

UNIFEM (United Nations Development Fund for Women) emerged from the *Voluntary Fund for the United Nations Decade for Women (VFDW)* in 1985 by a decision of the → General Assembly of the UN (A/RES/39/125). The VFDW had been founded in 1976 at the recommendation of the World Conference on the International Women's Year in Mexico City in 1975 (→ World Conferences), to help to realize the aims of the International Decade for Women (→ Women and the UN); it took up its work in 1978. The seat of UNIFEM is in New York. Though associated with the → UNDP, it is legally independent from it.

UNIFEM offers direct technical and financial aid to support women's initiatives in developing countries. Projects for poor women in LDCs are of particular concern. UNIFEM also promotes the inclusion of women in development by means of their active participation when planning, carrying through and evaluating programmes and projects. A matter of controversy is the support for projects in Eastern Europe from 1994 onwards. When planning and carrying through projects, UNIFEM requires the support of the UNDP, the Regional Economic Commissions (→ Economic Commissions, Regional) and of → specialized agencies of the UN.

The activities of UNIFEM are closely connected with those of → INSTRAW (*International Research and Training Institute for the Advancement of Women*). Therefore → Secretary-General Boutros Boutros-Ghali proposed a merger of INSTRAW and UNIFEM in 1993 as a matter of the reform of the UN (→ Reform of the UN). However, as the issue was not taken up by the Fourth World Conference on Women in Beijing in 1995, it has not been pursued further.

The most important source of income of UNIFEM are voluntary contributions from the member states of the UN. Today, the Nordic states are the most important donors. Further means are obtained from women's organizations, foundations, corporations and private persons. After the World Conference on Women in 1980 in Copenhagen, UNIFEM had to deal with a serious financial crisis – the conference's explicit support for the PLO sparked off the loss of support of the American Women's movement and thus of the US as the most important donor. However, the results of the World Conference on Women in Nairobi in 1985, in particular the association of UNIFEM with the UNDP brought about a consolidation of the financial situation. In 2000 UNIFEM had a budget of 26.7 million US dollars UNIFEM supports various projects and activities in about 100 developing countries.

UNIFEM is persistently confronted with serious budget constraints, and is only able to support half of the projects considered deserving of its support. Being a small programme of development aid (→ Development Cooperation of the UN System), UNIFEM cannot on its own guarantee the adequate involvement of women in the process of development. Therefore it is important that other organs giving development aid, such as the UNDP and the World Bank (→ World Bank, World Bank Group) include women's concerns in the programmes.

Andreas Blätte

Lit.: *Kardam, N.:* Bringing Women In. Women's Issues in International Development Programms, London 1991; *Pietilä, H. et al.:* Making Women Matter. The Role of the United Nations, 2nd edn., London et al. 1994; *Snyder, M.:* Women, Poverty and Politics. A UN Fund for Women, London 1995; *United Nations:* Development Cooperations with Women. The Experience and Future Development of the Fund, New York 1985; *United Nations:* The United Nations and the Advancement of Women 1945-1996, New York 1996; *Winslow, A. (ed.):* Women, Politics and the United Nations, Westport et al. 1995.

Addendum

The role of the *United Nations Development Fund for Women UNIFEM* has expanded since the year 2000 through successive General Assembly resolutions and decisions of the UNDP/ UNFPA Executive Board, which is the board in charge of decisions with regard to UNIFEM. The United Nations reform process, the Millennium Development Goals (MDGs) and the Security Council resolution 1325 (2000) – calling for a stronger participation of women in conflict prevention, peacekeeping and peacebuilding – have strengthened UNIFEM's role as a bridge and convener, bringing together the UN system, governments and non-governmental organizations (NGOs) and have brought UNIFEM together with other development cooperation entities increasingly into the arena of policy dialogue and guidance (cf. *UNIFEM* 2004a, 10ff.): UNIFEM focuses its current work on four areas: Ending violence against women, reversing the spread of HIV/AIDS among women and girls, achieving gender equality in democratic governance in times of peace as well as war and strengthening women's economic security and rights. UNIFEM also stands up for the abolition of the female genital mutilation in Africa.

UNIFEM has played an active political role in recent years in achieving its goals by urging UN institutions and conferences to review the actual progress made in these areas and to establish new goals with regard to gender equality: In June 2000 the UN General Assembly held a special assembly – "Beijing+5" – to review progress in the implementation of the Bejing Declaration and the Bejing Platform for Action, adopted at the Fourth UN World Conference on Women in 1995, in particular with regard to gender equality. The General Assembly adopted on 10 June 2000 a political declaration and a resolution on "further actions and initiatives to implement the Beijing Declaration and Platform for Action" (UN Doc. A/RES/S-23 /2 and A/RES/S-23/3).

In the same year the General Assembly adopted in September the "Millennium Declaration" (UN Doc. A/RES/ 55/2 of 8 September 2000) establishing the "Millennium Development Goals" (MDGs) to be achieved until 2015. One aim of the MDGs is to bring gender equality forward and to strengthen the role of women.

Also in 2000 UNIFEM organized together with the Nyerere Foundation the All-Party Burundian Women's Peace Conference in Arusha, the first women and peace conference in Africa, in an effort to give Burundian women a greater voice in the peace process in their country (www.afrol.com/News/bur001_wom ens-conference.htm).

Furthermore the UN Security Council summoned in October 2000 a council meeting about women, peace and safety and passed resolution S/RES/1325, the first resolution establishing a political framework in which the protection of women and their role in creating peace can be discussed at greater length. UNIFEM welcomed this action of the Security Council as a landmark resolution addressing for the first time ever the impact of conflict on women, recognizing women's role in preventing and solving conflict and calling for the equal participation and full involvement of women in efforts to maintain and promote peace and security. The resolution has been translated so far into 70 languages, gender advisors in peacekeeping operations have now become a standard feature (cf. *UNIFEM* 2005a).

In 2001 UNIFEM increased its efforts in the struggle against HIV/Aids. In the following years UNIFEM supported the reconstruction of the legislative and the reconstruction of Afghanistan in general and the role of women in it (cf. *UNIFEM* 2004b). The important role women have to play in mobilizing the peoples for security and justice in the 21st century is illustrated magnificently in the Dag Hammarskjöld Lecture 2004 given by Noeleen Hoyzer, the Executive Director of UNIFEM, a lecture which examines the consequences of armed conflicts for women and their role in peace-building work (*UNIFEM* 2004c). The direct cooperation with women in peacekeeping missions is an essential part to achieve peace. Unfortunately the international society is not a good role model for the cooperation with women in peacekeeping missions in post-conflict regions. The UN did not keep their promise to involve more women in such missions. At the time of writing only 2-5 % of women work as peacekeepers.

In the deliberations and concluding document of the UN world summit 2005 which took place in New York the leading heads of states and of governments affirmed an increased international interest to bring women's rights forward.

During this world summit UNIFEM published its new report "Progress of the World's Women 2005: Women, Work and Poverty" (*UNIFEM* 2005b). The important message of this report is, to minimize poverty you need to consider the work of women in the informal sector. UNIFEM therefore supports women especially in South Asia who work in the informal sector.

As a small organization within the UN, UNIFEM can solve problems only partially. The support of other important development organizations within the UN is therefore a key element for achieving more progress for women in the future.

Sabrina Neutz

Lit: *United Nations – General Assembly/ Economic and Social Council:* Organizational Assessment: UNIFEM – Past, Present and Future, Report submitted to the UNIFEM Consultative Committee by the Advisory Panel, 1 December 2004, UN Doc. A/60/62-E/2005/10, Annex (quoted as: UNIFEM 2004a); *UNIFEM:* Supporting Women's Leadership and Participation in the Reconstruction of Afghanistan. Fact sheet, March 2004 (quoted as: UNIFEM 2004b), www.unifem. org/about/fact_sheets.php?StoryID=92; *UNIFEM:* Women, War and Peace: Mobilising for Security and Justice in the Twenty-first Century. Speech by N. Hoyzer, Executive Director UNIFEM, 22 September 2004 (quoted as: UNIFEM 2004c), www.unifem. org/news_events/story_detail.php?StoryID= 173; *UNIFEM:* Security Council Resolution 1325 turns 5. Feature, 31 October 2005 (quoted as: UNIFEM 2005a); *UNIFEM:* Progress of the World's Women 2005: Women, Work & Poverty, New York 2005 (quoted as: UNIFEM 2005b).

Internet: www.unifem.undp.org, www.unifem.org, www.unifem.de.

UN in Bonn

Bonn became rather late a UN site compared to the others in Europe: Geneva (→ UN Office Geneva), Vienna (→ UN Office Vienna), Rome (seat of the → FAO) and Paris (seat of the → UNESCO). Bonn's career as UN site began with the Convention on the Conservation of Migratory Species of Wild Animals (CMS) administered by the UN Environment Programme → UNEP setting up its secretariat in Bonn in 1984.

But the genuine development into a UN site began with the decision of the German Federal Parliament in the Berlin-Bonn Act of 1994 which also contained, among other regulations concerning the move of the German Federal Government and the Federal Parliament from Bonn to Berlin, the declared intention to develop Bonn as a compensation measure into a centre for international and supranational organizations.

Looking for the big ones

Since then, the German Federal Government made several attempts to invite large UN organizations to take their seat in Bonn. The first two invited UN organizations, → UNDP and → UNICEF, declined the invitation, most probably because their organizational heads were Americans and because their host state was the USA. The USA, as host state, defended – as Dieter Göthel analyzes in his book on the United Nations in Germany – its "possessions" as host state, since UN organizations not only provide political status, but also economic advantages in the form of jobs for host state citizens, the purchasing power of the international personnel, and the demand for hotel beds and airline tickets connected with conferences held by the respective UN organization (*Göthel* 2002, 279). Also the third attempt, to invite the GATT delegations preparing in 1994 the foundation of the World Trade Organization WTO (→ WTO/ GATT) in the WTO Preparatory Committee to decide for Bonn as seat of the WTO was not successful. Germany competed with Switzerland which invited the WTO to be located in Geneva (cf. WTO Document GW/01 of 22 June 1994). Germany took a group of GATT delegation heads even from the WTO conference seat Marrakesh on a visit to Bonn, where – according to informed circles – the delegates found however the conference room facilities would be inadequate.

The decision taken in the respective Subcommittee of the WTO Preparatory Committee in favor of Geneva reveals in its reasoning that a UN site like Geneva already the seat of a number of UN organizations has a considerable advantage over Bonn, since Geneva is "already host to some international organizations with which WTO is expected to establish a close working relationship" (WTO document PC/BFA/W/1 of 22 July 1994). As its predecessor organization GATT already had its seat in Geneva, there was also the logical argument in favor of Geneva since "the transition from GATT to the WTO" would be in this way "as smooth and secure as possible" (ibid.). In other words, it is difficult for a new UN site such as Bonn to win the seat of a large UN organization.

Building on the Little Ones

After these disappointing attempts Germany focused its efforts more on smaller UN organizations, with more success: in 1996 Bonn became seat of the United Nations Volunteers Programme (→ UNV). To prepare the legal basis for this headquarters of an UN organization Germany concluded in 1995 a host state agreement (→ Host State Agreements) with the United Nations (UNTS Vol. 1895, No. 32310). In 1996 the United Nations Framework Convention on Climate Change (UNFCCC) accepted the German offer to take its seat in Bonn. On this occasion the Federal Government officially handed over certain premises in Bonn to the United Nations in a ceremony with the then → UN Secretary-General Boutros Boutros-Ghali to the United Nations. The above-mentioned host state agreement of 1995 was expanded and supplemented in 1996 by a second agreement concerning the UN premises in Bonn (UNTS Vol. 1911, No. 32554).

In the same year the United Nations Information Centre Bonn opened as one of the more than seventy branch offices of the UN Department of Public Information, providing information about UN activities to the public, academic scholars and journalists and organizing press conferences on current events related to the UN.

Slow But Steady Growth

In subsequent years slowly but steadily Bonn became the seat of a number of small UN units, subdivisions of larger UN organizations in the field of environmental protection, education, health and UN research.

In response to the growing needs for sufficient working space for the group of UN organizations, the German Federal Government decided in 2003 to place the large part of the former German Federal Parliament area completely at the disposal of the UN. In 2006 this "UN Campus" was inaugurated by the then Secretary-General Kofi Annan and the German Federal Chancellor Angela Merkel.

At present there are sixteen UN organizations having its seat in Bonn, comprising a personnel of about 650 people (cf. Annex below).

Learning the Role as Host State

While Germany has been apparently eager to become host state to a large number of UN organizations, it has had on the other hand time and again problems in implementing its host state role in practice to the satisfaction of the UN organizations. The main problem in this context was office accommodation. Thus, for example, UNFCCC Executive Secretary Zammit Cutajar during a conference in Bonn in June 2000 complained that the office facilities for the UNFCCC secretariat would be far from being satisfactory. He criticized above all the lack of an overarching decision-making process of the German authorities and the delayed planning and budget decisions concerning the accommodation facilities. He also criticized that diplomats from foreign countries were running into difficulties in obtaining visas before departure from their home country to enter Germany to attend UN meetings in Bonn (*UNFCCC – Secretariat* 2000).

Although the Federal Government of Germany started in 2003 with the above-mentioned project of converting the existing facilities of the former plenary hall and other buildings of the

German Federal Parliament in Bonn for UN purposes, there have been significant delays in completing the construction work. This causes problems in particular for the UNFCCC Secretariat which has to cope with an increasing secretariat staff due to the rapid expansion of the "Clean Development Mechanism" (CDM) after the Kyoto Protocol had entered into force in February 2005. UNFCCC Executive Secretary de Boer complained in an interview with a German newsmagazine in January 2009 that the UNFCCC still could not move into the buildings where Germany's Federal Parliament once was located, so that the working conditions for the UNFCCC secretariat had become very unsatisfactory (*Schwägerl* 2009).

Apparently the German authorities still have room for improvement in providing the services of a host state. If Germany wants to invite further UN organizations to take their seat in Bonn it should provide the UN organizations in Bonn in time with sufficient accommodation and solve the visa problems in the same manner as Switzerland and Austria.

In order to avoid such problems in future, the host state Germany should organize its host state services towards the UN organizations more efficiently. So far the UN organizations can approach the Mayor of Bonn and a Special Representative of the German Federal Foreign Office for the UN organizations in Bonn. Perhaps Germany should follow the Swiss example: it has established a Diplomatic Committee for consultation and discussion, where representatives of the host country meet regularly representatives of the UN organizations and where questions of privileges, immunities, housing, transport and security of the personnel can be discussed with a view to expressing opinions and proposing solutions to the host country.

It were advisable that Germany would follow the example of Austria and Switzerland also in another aspect, the aspect of diplomatic status. Both countries have accredited Permanent Mission to the UN not only in New York, but also in the host cities. Austria has established a Permanent Mission to the UN in Vienna, Switzerland a Permanent Mission to the United Nations Office and other international organizations in Geneva. By establishing a Permanent Mission to the UN organizations in Bonn Germany would demonstrate a higher appreciation of the UN organizations located in Bonn. Of course this would entail negotiations with the United Nations Secretariat about the status of the UN site in Bonn with the aim of establishing in Bonn as in Geneva, Vienna and Nairobi a full-fledged UN Office with a Director-General as head of the office. In this way the large number of smaller and medium-sized UN organizations in Bonn would obtain an administrative structure, and an office coordinating common services such as conference, procurement, safety and information services. Thus Bonn would without doubt improve its reputation as a UN site.

Helmut Volger

Lit.: *Göthel, D.:* Die Vereinten Nationen: Eine Innenansicht, Berlin 2002; *Preparatory Committee for the World Trade Organization - Subcommittee on Budget, Finance and Administration:* Seat of the WTO – Candidates and Selection Procedures, 22 June 1994, WTO Doc. GW/01; *Preparatory Committee for the World Trade Organization:* Seat of the World Trade Organization, WTO Doc. PC/BFA/W/1, 22 July 1994; *Schwägerl, C.:* UN Climate Secretariat Complains about German Office, in: Spiegel Online, 15 January 2009, www.spiegel.de/international/germany/; *UNFCCC - Secretariat:* UN official appeals to German Government for better support in Bonn, 13 June 2000, Press Release.

Annex:

UN Organizations in Bonn

1. UN Organizations with Seat in Bonn:

- *Secretariat of the Convention on the Conservation of Migratory Species of Wild Animals (CMS):* set up in 1984 in Bonn;
- *United Nations Volunteers programme (UNV):* since 1996 seat in Bonn;

- *United Nations Framework Convention on Climate Change Secretariat (UNFCCC):* since 1996 seat in Bonn;
- *Secretariat of the Agreement on the Conservation of Population of European Bats (UNEP/EUROBATS):* opened in Bonn 1996;
- *Secretariat of the United Nations Convention to Combat Desertification (UNCCD):* set up in 1999 in Bonn;
- *Secretariat of the Agreement on the Conservation of African-Eurasian Migratory Waterbirds (UNEP/ AEWA):* set up in 2000 in Bonn;
- *World Health Organization – European Centre for Environment and Health (WHO-ECEH):* set up in Bonn in 2001;
- *UNESCO International Centre for Technical and Vocational Education and Training (UNESCO-UNEVOC):* established in Bonn in 2002;
- *United Nations University – Institute for Environment and Human Security (UNU-EHS):* set up in Bonn in 2003;
- *World Tourism Organization Consulting Unit on Biodiversity and Tourism for Tsunami Affected Countries (UNWTO):* set up in Bonn in 2006;
- *United Nations Secretariat for the International Strategy for Disaster Reduction – Platform for the Promotion of Early Warning (UN/ISDR-PPEW):* established in Bonn in 2007;
- *United Nations University – Vice-Rectorate in Europe (UNU/ViE):* set up in Bonn in 2007;
- *United Nations University – International Human Dimensions Programme on Global Environmental Change (UNU-IHDP):* set up in Bonn in 2007;
- *UN-Water Decade Programme on Capacity Development (UNW-DPC):* set up in Bonn in 2007
- *Space-Based Information For Disaster Management and Emergency Response (UN-SPIDER):* set up in Bonn in 2007;
- *Secretariat of the Agreement on the Conservation of Small Cetaceans of the Baltic and North Seas (UNEP/ ASCOBANS):* opened in Bonn in 2007.

2. UN System Liaison Offices in Bonn

United Nations Information Centre (UNIC): 1996 - 2004

The UN Information Centre in Bonn, one of the 70 branches of the New York Department of Public Information, established in 1996, earned a good reputation among scholars and journalists, but was regrettably dissolved together with eight other West-European UN information centres in 2004 in favor of a European Regional Information Centre (UNRIC) in Brussels, leaving in Bonn only a small liaison office with UNRIC Brussels.

3. UN Organizations and Liaison Offices in Germany outside Bonn

- *International Labour Organization (→ ILO) – Office in Germany:* Berlin
- *International Tribunal for the Law of the Sea (→ ITLOS - Seat:* Hamburg
- *UNESCO Institute for Education (→ UNESCO):* Hamburg
- *United Nations High Commissioner for Refugees (→ UNHCR) - Regional Representation for Austria, the Czech Republic and Germany:* Berlin
- *World Food Programme (→ WFP) – Liaison Office:* Berlin
- *World Bank – Liaison Office:* Berlin

UNITAR – United Nations Institute for Training and Research

I. Background and History

The idea of a UN Training and Research Institute was mentioned for the first time in a 1962 resolution of the → General Assembly (UN Doc. A/RES/1827 (XVII) of 18 December 1962). The General Assembly requested the → Secretary-General "to study the desirability and feasibility of establishing a United Nations institute or training programme ... ; the frame of reference might include such fields as: (a) Training of personnel, particularly from the developing member states, for administrative and operational assignments with the United Nations and the specialized agencies, both at Headquarters and field operations and for national service; (b) Advanced training for persons now serving in such posts; (c) Research and seminars on operations of the United Nations and the specialized agencies."

In May of the following year the Secretary-General proposed the establishment of the United Nations Institute for Training and Research (UNITAR) in a report to the Economic and Social Council (→ ECOSOC) (UN Doc. E/3780 of 28 May 1963).

The founding of UNITAR followed the recommendation of the Economic and Social Council to the General Assembly, which commissioned the Secretary-General in 1963 with the establishment of a United Nations training and research institute recalling the above mentioned resolution 1827 (UN Doc. A/RES/1934 (XVIII) of 11 December 1963) (*Narasimhan* 1990, 7).

Two years later, in 1965, UNITAR became operational in New York "… for the purpose of enhancing the effectiveness of the United Nations in achieving the major objectives of the Organization ... in particular the maintenance of peace and security and the promotion of economic and social development …" in UN member states (Statute of UNITAR, Article 1).

In 1987 the General Assembly requested that the Institute be restructured, focusing more on training activities (UN Doc. A/RES/42/197 of 11 December 1987). As a result of a continued financial crisis of UNITAR in the late eighties, a process of structural change was initiated in the early nineties. This resulted in far-reaching cuts to both the Institute's activities and the number of personnel. Following a resolution of the General Assembly, the headquarters of the Institute were moved from New York to Geneva and merged with the Institute's European Office (UN Doc. A/RES/47/227 of 4 May 1993).

After a period of institutional and financial consolidation, UNITAR reopened an office in New York in October 1996.

As of 2001, the Institute opened in Hiroshima a liaison office for Asia and Pacific. Its objective is to fulfill the mandate of UNITAR through training activities based on the priorities and needs of the countries in the region

II. Set-Up and Financial Structure

UNITAR is an autonomous body within the → UN system. Nominated by the UN Secretary-General, the Executive Director heads the Institute as its principal policy-maker with the over-all responsibility for its organization, direction and administration.

The *UNITAR Board of Trustees* is responsible for providing policy guidance to the *Executive Director* and for reviewing the budget. It is composed of at least eleven high-level members, including former UN staff, government officials, diplomats or prominent representatives from academia or the private sector. The UN Secretary-General, the Presidents of the UN General Assembly and the Economic and Social Council, as well as the Executive Director of UNITAR serve as ex-officio members of the Board of Trustees.

UNITAR's budget amounts to 36 million US dollars for the biennium 2008-2009. Funding for the Institute derives entirely from voluntary contributions, grants and earmarked project funds from various UN member states or other partner organizations. In contrast to other research entities of the UN system, UNITAR receives no funding from the regular UN → budget.

At the end of 2007 the General Assembly decided to streamline the reporting arrangements of UNITAR through the consolidation of the reports of the Secretary-General and the Executive Director of the Institute. The new consolidated report of the Secretary-General is to be submitted every two years to the Economic and Social Council rather than to the General Assembly (UN Doc. A/RES/62/210 of 19 December 2007).

III. Structure and Activities

Following a restructuring process started in 2007, UNITAR consists of the *Office of the Executive Director* as well as of three departments, namely: Support Services, Research and Training.

The *Support Services Department* regroups UNITAR common services to support the core activities of UNITAR world-wide. The Institute's New York and Hiroshima offices are included in this department.

The *Research Department* develops research activities on knowledge systems and knowledge management conducive to delivering better training. It also performs monitoring and evaluation functions useful to the Training Department and affiliates. UNITAR has identified knowledge systems as a differentiating advantage that can enhance its capacity to offer high-quality and innovative training for the development of the capacities of adult learners. Knowledge systems are the combination of methodologies, tools and skills required to build, strengthen, use and retain capacity. This is an area in which no other UN entity is specialized, allowing UNITAR to build synergies and complementarities within the UN system.

The *Training Department* is in charge of developing training contents, functional capacity and training methodologies as well as of organizing and delivering training activities. It also manages the coordination with affiliates, such as the CIFAL Centres (International Training Centres for Local Authorities) and accredited networks of training providers. The Training Department is responsible for the bulk of the Institute's operational activities, which are organized around thematic clusters in three units: Environment, Governance and Peace, Security and Diplomacy.

The Institute's *Environment Unit* comprises training and capacity development activities in the areas of Climate Change, Biodiversity, Chemicals and Waste Management and Environmental Governance.

The *Governance Unit* offers Programmes on Public Finance & Trade, E-governance and Local Development.

The *Peace, Security and Diplomacy Unit* conducts Programmes on International Law, Multilateral Diplomacy, Peacemaking & Conflict Prevention as well as Peacekeeping.

The Institute develops training activities in close collaboration with organizations inside and outside of the UN system, incorporating the work of regional partners as well as national development strategies.

IV. Target Groups and Methodology

UNITAR's training programmes are designed for UN member states. Training initiatives are primarily developed for diplomatic personnel, representatives from ministries and other government entities, academia as well as non-governmental organizations (→ NGOs).

Every year the Institute provides training to 80,000 professionals through different forms of training and capacity development activities. These can take place in the form of: face-to-face seminars, briefings, lecture series, workshops, fellowship programmes, tailormade training courses and study tours as well as through distance and e-learning opportunities.

Additional training tools are systematically developed and published in form of handbooks, training packages and CD-ROMs.

The training approach of UNITAR follows the principle of continuous evaluation of its training activities and equally comprises assessments of specific national, regional or sub-regional capacity development needs.

One of the most successful concepts, the *national profile concept*, which is now used by several UNITAR training programmes, was originally created in 1994 by the Chemicals and Waste Management Programme. Based on a multistakeholder approach, the National Profile provides a comprehensive overview and assessment of the existing national legal, institutional, administrative, and technical infrastructure. In this respect, it offers a useful basis for identifying national chemicals management priorities and for initiating targeted and coordinated action. In 2007, over 100 countries, including several OECD member states, have prepared or are preparing a

741

National Profile following the UNITAR National Profile Guidance Document.

V. Perspectives

Over the past decades UNITAR has acquired a unique expertise, accumulating experience, knowledge and capacities to design and implement a variety of training activities. The small size of the Institute and its independence within the United Nations system enable it to respond with a high degree of flexibility to new challenges in the area of training and research.

The pragmatic and practice-oriented approach to training has proved to be the right path for the Institute. UNITAR has increased the number of its training programmes continuously and has successfully established strong institutional cooperation, two trends that will mark the work of the Institute in the future.

In its 2007-2009 Strategic Reform Plan, UNITAR established the goal of becoming a centre of excellence, measured by international standards, recognized within and outside the United Nations system for its standard-setting methodologies, high-quality training and research capacity on knowledge systems (*UNITAR* 2007).

Marina Walter / Daniela Bottigelli

Lit.: *Narasimhan, C.V.*: How and why UNITAR was established, in: UNITAR (ed.): 25 years of training and research for the United Nations, New York 1990, 7-11; *UNITAR*: 2007-2009 Strategic Reform Plan, July 2007; *UNITAR*: Statute of UNITAR, as promulgated by the Secretary-General in November 1965 and amended in March 1967, June 1973, June 1979, May 1983, April 1988, December 1989 and December 1999; *United Nations - General Assembly*: A/RES/1827 (XVII) of 18 December 1862; A/RES/1934 (XVIII) of 11 December 1963; A/RES/42/197 of 11 December 1987; A/RES/47/227 of 4 May 1993; A/RES/62/210 of 19 December 2007; *United Nations - General Assembly*: Report of the Executive Director of the United Nations Institute for Training and Research, UN Doc. A/53/14, Supplement No 14, New York 1998; *United Nations*: Report of the Secretary-General to the Economic and Social Council (ECOSOC), UN Doc. E/3780 of 28 May 1963.

Internet: www.unitar.org.

Uniting for Peace Resolution

To some extent the Uniting for Peace Resolution, passed as A/RES/377 (V) by the → General Assembly (GA) on 3 November 1950, with 52 votes in favor, 5 against and 2 abstentions, put the carefully balanced system of → collective security, of the United Nations under a tough test and challenged it severely, especially the respective competences of the → Security Council and of the General Assembly. Since the world organization had been set up predominantly according to the concepts and goals of the great powers USA, USSR and the United Kingdom, these powers had taken care that, in the UN Charter, the main responsibility for the maintenance of international peace and security had been given to the Security Council, with the Charter assigning the functions and powers as follows:

a) The General Assembly has only an advisory and subsidiary function with regard to peace and security: it "may consider the general principles of cooperation in the maintenance of international peace and security ... and may make recommendations ... to the Members or the Security Council or to both." (Art. 11 UN Charter) According to the Charter it may not take any decisions in these matters.

b) In the framework of the Charter, the role of the GA is only passive. When the Security Council is active, the GA has to step aside in a conflict; while the Security Council "is exercising its functions assigned to it" in a dispute, "the General Assembly shall not make any recommendations with regard to that dispute ... unless the Security Council so requires." (Art. 12 (1))

c) The Security Council on the other hand, is entitled by the Charter in cases of threats to the peace or breach of the peace to make not only recommendations, but to "decide what measures shall be taken ... to maintain or restore international peace and security" (Art.

39) and the UN member states are bound "to accept and carry out the decisions of the Security Council" (Art. 25).

In other words, the UN Charter postulated a clear division of labor with regard to the maintenance of peace, the primary, acting role being given to the Security Council, the secondary, only advisory role given to the General Assembly. This division of labor makes sense as long as the permanent members of the Security Council act according to their tasks depicted in the UN Charter, but it creates a kind of power vacuum when the Security Council does not act because it is blocked by disagreements and by veto threats of one or more of the P5.

This happened rather dramatically during the Korean conflict. At the time when the conflict erupted in June 1950, the Soviet Union boycotted all meetings of the Security Council because the permanent members USA, the United Kingdom and France refused to abide by the Soviet request and pass China's permanent seat on the Council, which had been given through the UN Charter to the Republic of China (Taiwan) (Art. 23 UN Charter), to the People's Republic of China, which had gained control over the Chinese mainland and established itself as state in 1949 (→ UN Policy, China). In the roughly six months' absence of the USSR since January 1950, the Security Council was able to act quickly and decisively with regard to the Korean War. When the Soviet Union returned to the Council in August 1950, it blocked all further resolutions on Korea with its veto (→ Veto, Right of Veto). Thus the Security Council was unable to take any further decisions on this matter. The United States, however, had in this phase of the Cold War a particular interest in maintaining the UN's capacity for action in matters of security policy (*Nolte* 1995, 1341; FRUS 1950 II, 303ff.). Therefore, it asked to place an item entitled "United Action for Peace" on the General Assembly's agenda, which after some debates subsequently led to the adoption of the *Uniting for Peace Resolution* which po-

litically and legally provides the General Assembly, when the Security Council is in a political conflict unable to act because of the lack of unanimity of the permanent members, with the power to take decisions in the form of recommendations to the member states to take measures, including the use of force – according to the Charter only the Security Council is entitled to take such a step.

In the "Uniting for Peace Resolution" the General Assembly reaffirms the purpose of the UN stated by the → Charter of the UN "to maintain international peace and security" and the primary responsibility of the Security Council in this area. It emphasizes – and this passage contains an explicit criticism of the practice of the Security Council – with regard to this task "the duty of the permanent members to seek unanimity and to exercise restraint in the use of the veto".

But, and this is a challenge to the position of the Security Council, the resolution states further that "failure of the Security Council to discharge its responsibilities on behalf of all the Member States ... does not relieve Member States of their obligations or the United Nations of its responsibility ... to maintain international peace and security".

In other words, in such a situation all the member states, in whose interests the Security Council is bound to act and who are present in the General Assembly, are entitled to take over the decision-making. Thus the General Assembly "resolves that if the Security Council, because of lack of unanimity of the permanent members, fails to exercise its primary responsibility for the maintenance of international peace and security in any case where there appears to be a threat to the peace, breach of the peace, or act of aggression, the General Assembly shall consider the matter immediately with a view to making appropriate recommendations to Members for collective measures, including in the case of a breach of the peace or act of aggression the use of armed force when necessary to maintain international peace and security."

Since the General Assembly is only for certain periods in session, the resolution provides for this situation a special kind of session: "If not in session at the time, the General Assembly may meet in emergency special session ..."

If the General Assembly had applied the Uniting for Peace Resolution to the full extent in the way it had been conceived, it would have challenged in fact the political prerogative of the Security Council and would have caused a power fight between the two principal organs. But this did not happen. The General Assembly did not recommend the use of force as envisaged under the Uniting for Peace procedure (cf. *Schrijver* 2006, 14). Up to now, it has never recommended the use of force under this resolution. One explanation for this self-restraint could be that the Assembly has been well aware of the great importance of the norm of the prohibition of force in the Charter, including the risk of eroding this norm by a use of the Uniting for Peace procedure authorizing the use of force through the General Assembly. Another reason could be the wish of the General Assembly not to risk conflicts with the permanent members of the Security Council by recommending the use of military force (cf. *Schrijver* 2006, 15).

In a form of wise self-restraint the resolution has been used by the General Assembly in subsequent years only to establish a new form of UN peace-maintaining activity and moreover to give the General Assembly the opportunity to convene quickly to discuss an acute political conflict. Employing the Uniting for Peace procedure, the Assembly established in 1956 a peacekeeping operation in the Middle East (UNEF I), in fact the first UN peacekeeping force (→ Peacekeeping; → Peacekeeping Forces; Peacekeeping Operations). In the course of the years the Uniting for Peace procedure has become a part of the institutional structures of the UN, used quite often for the convening of Emergency Special Sessions of the General Assem-

bly in political conflicts when the Security Council is reluctant to deal with the matter.

So far, ten Emergency Special Sessions of the General Assembly have been called:

1	Middle East	1-10 November 1956
2	Hungary	4-10 November 1956
3	Middle East	8-21 August 1958
4	Congo question	17-19 September 1960
5	Middle East	17 June – 18 September 1967
6	Afghanistan	10-14 January 1980
7	Palestine	22-29 July 1980 20-28 April 1982 25-26 June 1982 16-19 August 1982 24 September 1982
8	Namibia	3-14 September 1981
9	Occupied Arab territories	29 January – 5 February 1982
10	Occupied East Jerusalem and the rest of the Occupied Palestinian Territory	24-25 April 1997 15 July 1997 13 November 1997 17 March 1998 5, 8 and 9 February 1999 18 and 20 October 2000 20 December 2001 7 May 2002 5 August 2002 19 September 2003 8 December 2003 16-20 July 2004 17 November 2006 15 December 2006 15-16 January 2009

Table 1: Emergency Special Sessions

The legitimacy and lawfulness of the Uniting for Peace Resolution and the authority attributed to the General Assembly by the resolution were disputed from the outset, within the UN and among international lawyers and legal scholars (cf. *Woolsey* 1951; *Vallat* 1952). The question was decided mostly in favor of the General Assembly in an Advisory Opinion issued by the International Court of Justice (→ ICJ) in 1962 (Certain Expenses of the United Nations. Advisory Opinion, ICJ Reports 1962, 150-180).

The General Assembly did not, all in all, use the Uniting for Peace Resolution as a means of shifting the power balance, to reach decision-making functions in the maintenance of peace. This function stayed alone with the Security Council.

But the General Assembly has used the resolution repeatedly to demonstrate its political opposition to political and military actions of one or more of the P5, for example in the Suez Crisis 1956, in expressing its criticism against France and the United Kingdom, and in the case of the revolt in Hungary, to show its fierce opposition against the USSR.

The significance of the resolution, however, has decreased since the early 1990s as the Security Council's capacity for action increased with the end of the Cold War (→ History of the UN; *Nolte* 1995, 1347).

In general terms, the General Assembly has established with the use of the Uniting for Peace procedure the accepted interpretation of the UN Charter with regard to its functions and powers that the Assembly can also assume responsibility for matters relating to peace and security beside the Security Council.

Helmut Volger

Lit.: *Andrassy, J.:* Uniting for Peace, in: AJIL 50 (1956), 563-582; *Nolte, B.:* Uniting for Peace, in: Wolfrum, R. (ed.): United Nations: Law, Policies and Practice, Vol. 2, Munich/Dordrecht 1995, 1341-1348; *Schrijver, N.J.:* The Future of the Charter of the United Nations, in: Max Planck Yearbook of United Nations Law 10 (2006), 1-34; *Stein, E./Morrissey, R.C.:* Uniting for Peace Resolution, in: Bernhardt, R. (ed.): EPIL 5 (1983), 379-382; *United States Government, Department of State:* Foreign Relations of the United States, 1950 (quoted as: FRUS), Vol. II: The United Nations; The Western Hemisphere, Washington 1976; *Vallat, F.A.:* The General Assembly and the Security Council of the United Nations, in: BYIL 29 (1952), 63-104; *Woolsey, L.H.:* The Uniting for Peace Resolution of the United Nations, in: AJIL 45 (1951), 129-137;

Internet: Information about UN Emergency Special Sessions: http://www.un.org/ga/sessions/emergency.shtml

Universality

Universality of the United Nations means its aim to have as members, as far as possible, all states of the world. This was already proclaimed in the Moscow Declaration of 1943 (→ History of the Foundation of the UN), which announced the Allied Powers' plan to establish "a general international organization, based on the principle of the sovereign equality of all peace-loving states, and open to membership by all such states, large and small, for the maintenance of international peace and security" (*Goodrich/Hambro* 1949, 571-572). Today, that aim is almost achieved. Switzerland, which for reasons of its neutrality had not joined the Organization, became a member in 2002 after the Swiss people had agreed to this step in a referendum. By its own free choice, the State of the Vatican City still remains outside the Organization (the Holy See participates as an observer (→ Observer Status) in the work of the → General Assembly). However, the cases of the Republic of China (Taiwan), the membership of which is rejected by the People's Republic of China because of its "One-China-Policy", and of the Republic of Kosovo, which declared its independence in 2008 but has not been universally recognized, demonstrate that political controversies between states can still run contrary to the universality of the UN.

By comparison with the UN, the → League of Nations, the first organization intended to unite all states of the world in a global "community of peaceful cooperation" (*Schücking/Wehberg* 1931, 56), lacked universality right from the start because of the non-participation of the United States. Other countries belonged to the League only for a limited period of time, e.g. the Soviet Union (1934-1939), Japan (1919-1933) and Germany (1926-1933).

The *principle of universality* is implied in the constitutional structure established by the → Charter of the UN. The goals of the UN stated in the preamble and Article 1, in particular the maintenance of international peace and security, can only be achieved with a membership as universal as possible. Universality is a pre-condition of the effectiveness of the UN as an embodiment of the organized international community. Accordingly, Article 4 (1) of the Charter opens the Organization to all "peace-loving states which accept the obligations contained in the present Charter and ... are able and willing to carry out these obligations". Procedurally, the admission of a state requires first a recommendation of the → Security Council and subsequently a decision of the General Assembly (see Article 4 (2) of the Charter) (→ Membership and Representation of States). The recommendation is subject to the right of veto of the permanent members of the Security Council (→ Veto, Right of Veto).

Contrary to the principle of universality, the East-West conflict led to a mutual blockade of applications for membership between 1946 and 1955. None of the two sides was prepared to allow the admission of a state regarded as belonging to the opposing camp, and a corresponding increase of "enemy" influence. That policy was pursued despite an advisory opinion of the International Court of Justice (→ ICJ) of 28 May 1948, (ICJ Reports 1948, 57ff.) which had answered in the negative the question of the General Assembly whether a member state could make its consent to an admission dependent on a fulfillment of conditions other than those set out in Article 4 of the Charter. In that period, only nine out of 31 applicants were admitted to membership. However, a "package deal" of December 1955 ended the long controversy and led to the recommendation of the

Security Council to admit simultaneously sixteen states (→ History of the UN). In the following two decades the process of → decolonization resulted in a great increase in the number of UN members. In 1945, the Organization had 51 original members. Twenty years later, the number had more than doubled (to 117). By 1975, after most European overseas colonies had gained independence, it had further increased to 144. Thus, the UN succeeded in integrating the new states established after 1945, which generally regarded the Organization as a guarantor of their often precarious statehood. In the early 1990s, it was especially the dissolution of the Soviet Union and the former Socialist Federal Republic of Yugoslavia which led to another increase in membership. In 1990, the unification of Germany and of Yemen, respectively, ended the membership of the German Democratic Republic and of the People's Democratic Republic of Yemen. Today (in March 2009), the UN has 192 members (→ Annex, Member States of the UN).

Apart from Indonesia (1965-1966), no member state ever tried to leave the UN. The Charter is intentionally silent on the question of withdrawal, but at the UN founding conference of San Francisco (→ History of the Foundation of the UN) it was recognized that under certain conditions a member is free to leave the Organization.

In the course of decolonization, the principle of universality became so strong that in practice the Article 4 (1) condition was dropped (according to which a state applying for membership must actually be able to carry out the obligations contained in the Charter and, in particular, to contribute meaningfully to the system of → collective security provided for in Chapter VII). A number of "micro-states", like the island states of the Caribbean and the Pacific, were admitted to the UN although they did not meet that condition. When in the 1990s the small West European states Liechtenstein, San Marino, Andorra and Monaco, and the Pacific islands formerly administered by the United States as a trust territory ($\rightarrow$ Trusteeship Council), applied for membership, even certain formal limitations of their independence were generously overlooked in favor of the "universal vocation" of the UN (*Ginther* 2002, 178).

For an organization striving for universality, the divided states of Germany, Korea and Vietnam constituted a particularly difficult problem. Here, in the time of the East-West conflict the antagonistic political beliefs and goals of the two blocs, and the legal claims serving them, clashed with particular ferocity. The two German states could only become members of the UN (in 1973) after they had regulated, with the approval of the United States, the USSR, the United Kingdom and France, their relations in the "Basic Treaty" of 1972. An earlier application for the admission of East Germany (of 1966), which had expressly referred to the principle of universality, had not been successful ($\rightarrow$ UN Policy, Germany; $\rightarrow$ UN Policy, German Democratic Republic).

In accordance with the principle of universality, non-member states have been accorded $\rightarrow$ observer status by the UN. The same applies to liberation movements representing peoples who have a right to self-determination ($\rightarrow$ Self-Determination, Right to) and are on the way towards establishing their own statehood. The observer status permits the respective states and peoples to participate in certain ways in the work of the United Nations, and gives, vice versa, the UN a possibility to influence them with a view to advancing its goals and purposes. Further, a number of intergovernmental organizations, among them the African Union, the League of Arab States and the European Community ($\rightarrow$ European Union, Common Foreign and Security Policy at the UN), have received a standing invitation to participate as observers in the work of the General Assembly, and maintain permanent offices at UN Headquarters.

Universality of the UN, understood as an invitation of all states to join the Organization, is one of the reasons supporting the UN's assertion of a right to establish standards of conduct for all members of the international community. According to Article 2(6) of the Charter, the UN shall ensure that states which are not members of the Organization act in accordance with the principles of the Charter "so far as may be necessary for the maintenance of international peace and security". Since 1977, the Security Council has addressed its binding resolutions under Chapter VII to "all States", including non-member states.

If it is true that today all states, as members of the international community, are equally obliged to heed the rules of the UN Charter as the constitution of that community (*Fassbender* 2009), then all states are also equally entitled to membership and participation in the community's organs ($\rightarrow$ Principal Organs, Subsidiary Organs, Treaty Bodies). According to such a constitutional view, UN member states cannot grant or deny membership to states not yet belonging to the Organization just as they like. Article 4 (1) of the Charter must therefore be read as entitling every sovereign and "peace-loving" state to membership in the United Nations. The latter requirement is met if a state credibly accepts the fundamental constitutional principles of the international community as enshrined in the Charter and other instruments based upon it. This means that every UN member state is obliged to vote in favor of a particular application for membership if those conditions are met. It is that right to membership in the UN through which the principle of universality is realized.

The possibility of expelling a state from the Organization (Article 6 of the Charter) is not in accord with the principle of universality. In fact, in the history of the UN it has never been used. To prevent a state permanently from participating in the work of the community organs is incompatible with the very idea of an international community living under a constitution. A (temporary) suspension of a state which has seriously violated the rules of the Charter "from the exercise of the rights and privileges of [UN] membership" (Art. 5) is a sufficient – and constitutionally acceptable – means of sanctioning a state in case of such violations.

Bardo Fassbender

Lit.: *Czerwinski, G.:* Das Universalitätsprinzip und die Mitgliedschaft in internationalen universalen Verträgen und Organisationen, Berlin 1974; *Fassbender, B.:* The United Nations Charter as the Constitution of the International Community, Leiden/Boston 2009; *Ginther, K.:* Art. 4, in: Simma, B. (ed.): The Charter of the United Nations. A Commentary, 2nd edn., Vol. I, Oxford 2002, 177-194; *Grant, T.D.:* Admission to the United Nations Charter, Leiden/Boston 2009; *International Court of Justice:* Conditions of Admission of a State to Membership in the United Nations (Article 4 of the Charter). Advisory Opinion of May 28th, 1948, in: ICJ Reports 1948, 57ff.; *Schücking, W./Wehberg, H.:* Die Satzung des Völkerbundes, 3rd edn., Vol. I, Berlin 1931.

UN Office Geneva

On 18 April 1946 the → League of Nations, which had been virtually inactive since the beginning of World War II, was formally dissolved by decision of the League Assembly and its assets were turned over to the United Nations, the successor of the League (A/RES/79 (I), 1 August 1946; cf. also *UNYB* 1946/47, 111-112). On the same date, the Host Country Agreement between the UN and Switzerland (UNTS Vol. 1, 163) was signed (→ Host State Agreements). The → General Assembly had adopted in its first regular session resolution A/RES/24 (I), endorsing the recommendations of the League of Nations Committee (a body created to administer the transition period) thus inheriting much of the estate of the League, together with the administration of several League of Nations Conventions and Programmes (cf. *Luard* 1982, 71f.; → History of the Foundation of the UN).

Thus, the League's Headquarters in Geneva, the Palais des Nations, which had been built between 1929 and 1938, became the seat of the UN "European Office". In 1966 it was renamed to "United Nations Office at Geneva (UNOG)".

From the very beginning, the UN Office in Geneva was a centre for multilateral diplomacy, serving as the venue of a number of important international efforts in solving regional conflicts, from the conference on Korea and the Four Power Summit on Germany in the fifties, the conferences on Indochina, the Middle East peace conference and the negotiations to solve the Iran – Iraq conflict to the International Conference on Former Yugoslavia in the nineties and the negotiations on Afghanistan. Other important developments were marked by Geneva conferences on commodities, the → Law of the Sea and the international combat of HIV/AIDS.

The establishment, in Geneva, of the UN Economic Commission for Europe (ECE) in 1947, as the first of eventually five Regional Economic Commissions; the establishment of the Office of the UN High Commissioner for Refugees (UNHCR) (→ UNHCR) in 1951; the creation of the UN Conference on Trade and Development (→ UNCTAD) in 1964; the transformation of the Geneva based Centre for Human Rights into the Office of the UN High Commissioner for Human Rights (OHCHR) (→ Human Rights, United Nations High Commissioner for) in the nineties have further strengthened the importance of Geneva as a UN Office. The UN presence in Geneva therefore goes far beyond UNOG itself and encompasses many entities with global or regional responsibilities.

Today, Geneva is the second largest UN hub and more than 160 out of the 192 UN member states (→ Permanent Missions) and two observer missions (→ Observer Status) are accredited with UNOG.

Most UN specialized agencies and UN funds and programmes headquartered elsewhere have established liaison or regional offices in Geneva, many of them situated on UNOG premises.

The presence of important parts of the United Nations, of five → specialized agencies of the UN System ($\rightarrow$ ILO, $\rightarrow$ WHO, $\rightarrow$ ITU, $\rightarrow$ WMO and $\rightarrow$ WIPO), and of other International Organizations, such as the World Trade Organization ($\rightarrow$ WTO), and the International Organization for Migration (IOM) and of the organizations of the International Red Cross and Red Crescent Movement (International Committee of the Red Cross – ICRC – and International Federation of Red Cross and Red Crescent Societies – IFRC) have influenced the move of many other institutions to Geneva, especially those focussing on $\rightarrow$ human rights and humanitarian affairs ($\rightarrow$ Humanitarian Assistance).

These frequently consult on operative activities with the respective UN bodies. Currently, some 350 non-governmental organizations ($\rightarrow$ NGOs) are accredited with UNOG, who promotes the development of their partnership with the UN and facilitates contacts between NGOs and other organizations of the UN system.

Whereas most of the substantive responsibilities are vested in other UN entities, UNOG's role is mainly that of managing policies and providing a wide range of services, including conference facilities, buildings management, security services, information technology, human resources management, financial management and other support services.

UNOG is directed by a Director-General at the rank of Under-Secretary-General, who represents the Secretary-General in Geneva. As such, s/he is responsible for the UN's host country relations. The Director-General is also the Designated Security Official for Switzerland, coordinating security issues among the UN, funds, programmes and specialized agencies in Switzerland. S/he also assumes leadership for efforts to enhance common services (such as procurement) among these UN entities.

In his personal capacity, the Director-General of UNOG serves also as the Secretary-General of the Conference on Disarmament (CD) ($\rightarrow$ Disarmament), and is the Personal Representative of the Secretary-General of the UN to the Conference. Regrettably, for almost a decade, the Conference has not been very active due to its failure to reach an agreement on its programme of work.

UNOG is the custodian and manager of the Palais des Nations, a historical complex, which was extended in 1973 with the addition of a new office and conference building – funded by the Swiss Government –, and of a number of other premises, including the Palais Wilson and the International Environment House (IEH). In that capacity, UNOG provides office space (some 2,800 offices) and related buildings management services to UNCTAD; the Secretariat of ECE; the Geneva Office of the UN Office for the Coordination of Humanitarian Affairs (OCHA) ($\rightarrow$ Humanitarian Assistance); the Regional Office for Europe of the UN Environment Programme (UNEP) and many other entities, for example the UN Institute for Disarmament Research ($\rightarrow$ UNIDIR); the UN Institute for Training and Research ($\rightarrow$ UNITAR); the UN Research Institute for Social Development (UNRISD); the Inter-agency Secretariat of the International Strategy for Disaster Reduction (ISDR); the Joint Inspection Unit of the UN system (JIU); the Geneva Office of the Office of Internal Oversight Services (OIOS); the Secretariat of the Conference on Disarmament; the UN Compensation Commission (UNCC).

Given its extensive conference facilities, UNOG is the most important UN conference center worldwide. Up to 10,000 meetings annually are held or serviced by UNOG, about a quarter of which with interpretation. In addition to conference facilities and interpretation, UNOG provides translation and publication services. UNOG's conference facilities are used by entities of the UN, but also by specialized agencies, governments, NGOs or other International Organizations, e.g.,
- the Human Rights Council, its Committees and various human rights treaty bodies;
- the Economic and Social Council ($\rightarrow$ ECOSOC), alternating with New York;

- the Trade and Development Board of UNCTAD;
- the Economic Commission for Europe (ECE) and its various technical bodies;
- the Executive Committee of UNHCR;
- the World Health Assembly of the WHO;
- the International Labour Conference of the ILO;
- the International Law Commission (→ ILC).

UNOG also provides advisory and other services for UN conferences hosted by governments in other locations.

As a common services provider UNOG provides services in procurement, travel, transportation and other areas to more than 60 UN system entities in Geneva and other duty stations. UNOG's human resources services cover more than 3,500 staff members in more than 30 client offices in Geneva, but also in Bonn, Germany (UN Framework Convention on Climate Change – UNFCC; UN Convention to Combat Desertification – UNCCD) and Turin, Italy (UN System Staff College – UNSSC). More than 4,000 staff members are payrolled by UNOG. UNOG also administers the health insurance for close to 20,000 staff members and retirees.

The UN Information Service (UNIS) in Geneva (→ Public Information of the UN) reaches out to more than 200 journalists permanently accredited by UNOG, and to a large number of other media. As a result of the closure of UN Information Centers in most Western European countries, the role of UNIS Geneva has become even more important.

The UNOG Library, which had been founded in 1919 as the League of Nations Library and moved to its current building in 1936, holds more than 1 million books, 9,000 periodicals and over 4 million documents. It is one of the most complete collections in Europe of works on international, constitutional and administrative law. The Library is the custodian of the archives of the League of Nations and in charge of the records

management at UNOG. The Library is also managing the UNOG Cultural Activities Programme, a programme designed to promote cultural dialogue and understanding with the partnership of member states and international organizations.

Written by *Hans J. Lassen* in 2001, revised by *Egbert C. Kaltenbach* in 2007

Lit.: *Centre for Research on International Institutions (ed.)*: International Geneva Yearbook. Vol. 1, Lausanne 1985; *Club Diplomatique de Genève (ed.):* La vocation internationale de Genève, no place and year of publication indicated (Geneva 1998); *Hay, A. (ed.):* Encyclopédie de Genève, Tome 8: Genève, ville internationale, Geneva 1990; *Luard, E.:* A History of the United Nations. Vol. 1: The Years of Western Domination, 1945-1955, London/Basingstoke 1982; *Ordzhonikidze, S.:* The United Nations at 60: Advancing its Objectives in the New Millennium (UNOG Annual Report 2005), United Nations, Geneva 2006; *Ordzhonikidze, S.:* Translating commitments into action (UNOG Annual Report 2006), United Nations, Geneva 2007; *Pallas, J.-C.:* Histoire et Architecture du Palais des Nations, Nations Unies, Genève 2001; *Spinelli, P.P.:* Genève et la vie internationale, no place and year of publication indicated (Geneva 1963); *Taveau, V.:* Au coeur du Palais des Nations, Geneva 2006; United Nations: The Library of the United Nations Office at Geneva, Geneva 2003; *United States Mission to the United Nations in Geneva (Publ.):* The Briefing Book on International Organizations in Geneva, Geneva 2004.

Internet: Homepage of the United Nations Office at Geneva: www.unog.ch; Homepage of the Library of the United Nations Office at Geneva: www.unog.ch/library..

UN Office Nairobi

The decision to establish in Nairobi a further main office of the United Nations, in addition to the headquarters in New York and the European offices in Geneva and Vienna, was made rather late, in the year 1996. The → General Assembly decided to integrate the two UN organizations already located in Nairobi – the United Nations Environment Programme (→ UNEP) and the United Nations Centre for Human Settlements (Habitat) (→ UN-HABITAT) in a United Nations Office, the *United Nations Office at Nairobi (UNON)*. UNON provides both UN organizations with administrative and support services, including information technology and conference services.

UNEP was established in Nairobi in 1972, Habitat in 1977. At the time of its foundation UNEP was the first UN organization to take its seat in a developing country, and it is still the only major UN institution with a seat in a developing country. Beside UNEP, only the seats of the Regional Economic Commissions of the UN (→ Economic Commissions, Regional) and the Regional Secretariats of the Convention to Combat Desertification are located in developing countries.

So the history of the UN Office Nairobi can also be regarded as the history of the struggle for the representation of the United Nations in the Third World. It speaks for the dominant position of the major financial contributors in the United Nations, the UN special organs and the → specialized agencies (→ UN System), that so far no other important UN organization has taken its seat in the Third World. Only UNRWA has moved it headquarters through a decision of the UN Secretary-General in 1996 from Vienna to Gaza, a move which had been highly advisable because of the regional focus of its work in the Near East.

At the beginnings of the 90s there were even diplomatic efforts by the industrialized countries of the West to move the seat of UNEP from Nairobi to Geneva. Only the steadfast opposition of the African member states and of other Third World states prevented this move.

When this attempt failed, the Western countries tried at least to merge UNEP and Habitat in order to save costs. As first measure in this direction, which considerably weakened the position of Nairobi in the UN system, → Secretary-General Boutros-Ghali abolished the post of the Executive Director of Habi-

tat, which had the rank of Under-Secretary-General. Boutros-Ghali decided that UNEP and Habitat should be directed jointly by the Executive Director of UNEP.

Secretary-General Kofi Annan, however, decided to upgrade the position of Nairobi by establishing a further main UN Office in addition to New York, Geneva and Vienna.

But Nairobi still is an office with restricted resources: compared with the offices in Geneva and Vienna it has a small staff, few financial resources and has also been discriminated against so far in budgetary procedures. The diplomats of the Group of 77 (→ Group of 77 and the UN) had to exert considerable pressure so that the office in Nairobi would not be financed any longer predominantly from the budgetary resources of UNEP and Habitat, but – like Geneva and Vienna – mainly from the regular → budget. As result of their diplomatic attempts the General Assembly requested the Secretary-General in Resolution 55/220 of 22 December 1997 to bring the financial arrangements for Nairobi into line with those of similar UN offices, i.e. Geneva and Vienna. Nevertheless, the Third World countries did not succeed in achieving a quick improvement of the situation. The Secretary-General made, for the period 1998 to 2001, only a commitment "to increase gradually the regular budget component of the budget of the United Nations Office at Nairobi" (cf. United Nations General Assembly, Proposed programme budget for the biennium 2000-2001, UN Doc. A/54/6 (Sect. 27G) of 23 March 1999), which meant in practice an increase of 15 per cent for the regular budget component.

The debate about the move of both institutions or at least the massive decrease of their financial resources initiated by the Western industrialized countries was not finished with this first budgetary decision. A UN Task Force consisting of ministers, ambassadors, UN officials and NGO representatives (→ NGOs) chaired by UNEP Executive Director Klaus Töpfer, which had been commissioned by the Secretary-General Kofi Annan to examine the potential for reform in the field of environmental protection within the UN system, saw itself (in its report submitted to the 53rd General Assembly 1998) in a position to reject the proposal to merge UNEP and Habitat.

The report recommended instead providing UNON with organizational and financial resources appropriate to its status as a major UN office: "The UN Office at Nairobi (UNON) should have arrangements in keeping with its status." They recommended the establishment of better communication capabilities and "adequate access to the Regular Budget of the United Nations". The Task Force even asked the other UN organizations to establish activities at Nairobi "so as to transform the UN compound into a fully active UN Office." (*United Nations Task Force on Environment and Human Settlements* 1998, para. 32ff.)

The same position was taken by Töpfer when he presented the report to the public at a press conference in July 1998 in New York. He rejected plans for a removal of the two organizations from Nairobi and their merger: "The recommendation was not to merge these two institutions". He emphasized that Nairobi was the only UN headquarters in the Third World. (quoted from: Journal of the Group of 77, No. 2-1998; cf. also UN Press Briefing 2 July 1998)

What seems remarkable in this context is the timing of the debate about Nairobi: the UN Office in Nairobi was established on 1 January 1996. One-and-a-half years later the Third World states and Klaus Töpfer had to protest in public against the Western plans to "dry out" UNON, and to demand equal treatment with the other UN offices. This manner in which the Western states treat the developing countries in the United Nation is indeed questionable: who pays the money can determine where the institutions are located. That they might sacrifice much of their credibility with regard to the principle of equality in the United Nations is obviously not foremost in the minds of Western politicians.

The majority of developing states also supported in the following years the fight for adequate financial means for Nairobi and the demand for financing the UN office increasingly from the regular budget and to a lesser extent from the programme budgets of UNEP and Habitat. Thus the General Assembly welcomed in resolution A/RES/54/249 of 23 December 1999 "the commitment of the Secretary-General to increase gradually the regular budget component of the United Nations Office in Nairobi, with a view to easing the administrative costs levied on the substantive programmes of the United Nations Environment Programme and the United Nations Centre for Human Settlements (Habitat)" (ibid., para. 175). The resolution reaffirmed the above- mentioned resolution A/RES/52/220, in which it requested the Secretary-General to bring the financial arrangements of the UN Office in Nairobi in line with those of similar United Nations administrative office [Geneva and Vienna, H.V.]. (ibid., para. 181)

As an important step to strengthen the use of UNON for UN conferences the General Assembly decided in the same resolution "to establish a permanent interpretation service at the United Nations Office at Nairobi) (ibid., para. 180).

In other words, from its foundation in January 1996 until autumn 2000 the UN Office Nairobi worked as a "third-class" office, working in meetings and conferences with interpretation staff borrowed from New York, Geneva and Vienna.

The next step of progress for the UN Office Nairobi was achieved in January 2002 with the change of Habitat through General Assembly resolution A/RES/56/206 of 21 December 2001 into "the United Nations Human Settlement Programme, to be known as UN-Habitat", a genuine UN programme as subsidiary organ of the General Assembly, headed by an Executive Director with the rank of an Undersecretary-General. As a result, Nairobi comprised two UN programmes, UNEP and UN-HABITAT, which strengthened its status.

As was hoped for, the establishment of a permanent interpretation service as well as the increasing political weight of UNEP attracted more major conference events, using the facilities at Nairobi (cf. G77-Statement in the 57th session of the General Assembly, 24 October 2002, www.g77.org/Speeches/102402.htm), a fact, which was also welcomed by the General Assembly members in resolution A/RES/56/242 of 24 December 2001 (ibid. para. 10), which also noted "with satisfaction that the conference-servicing facility at the United Nations Office at Nairobi is becoming organizationally, functionally and in terms of the budget an integral part of the Department of General Assembly Affairs and Conference Services" (ibid. para. 7).

Due to the efforts of the then UNON Director Klaus Töpfer and the support of Secretary-General Kofi Annan the General Assembly approved with regard to the budget an expansion of the UN Office in Nairobi through new buildings.

The work began in 2003 and was scheduled to be completed in 2005, providing additional space for UN-HABITAT needing more space after having been transformed to a full-fledged programme – again a small, but important step on the difficult way for UNON to become a sustainable UN Office. Almost symbolically, the construction of the new facilities experienced repeatedly significant delays, as an UN official in charge of the building measures reported in November 2008 to the Fifth Committee of the General Assembly (cf. UN Press Release GA/AB/3881, 26 November 2008).

The fight for the improvement of the organizational, budgetary and political status of the UN Office in Nairobi remained also on the agenda in the following years. Thus a representative of the G77 criticized in a statement in the Fifth Committee of the General Assembly in October 2006 the still existing inequality in the status of the UN offices with Nairobi being the only office "that has to rely on extrabudgetary resources for nearly half of its funding of conference services" and which has to fund central planning and coordination functions exclusively from extrabudgetary resources (*Group of 77* 2006). And still in December 2007 the UN member states repeated in a General Assembly resolution its already often repeated request to the Secretary-General "to continue to bring the financial arrangements of the United Nations Office in Nairobi in line with those of similar United Nations administrative offices (UN Doc. A/RES/62/236, 22 December 2007, para. 125).

The UN Office in Nairobi is still at a disadvantage in relation to New York, Geneva and Vienna, a shameful fact for an organization committed to the equality of all people in all continents, regardless of color, race and social status.

The United Nations should respect and implement their own decisions and strengthen the UN Office Nairobi, even if against the opposition of the Western member states with the big purses.

The UN Office Nairobi is without doubt an indicator of the seriousness of the dialogue between North and South (→ North-South Relations and the UN). It is highly desirable that the governments of the industrialized countries of the North stop their attempts to bring about the abolition of the only UN office in the Third World by using their budgetary powers, but should recognize the advantages of developing Nairobi as a UN conference center. In supporting the further development of the UN Office Nairobi to becoming an essential conference centre and hub for regional offices of UN programmes and specialized agencies, the developed states could prove that they appreciate the North-South dialogue and the role of the developing states in the UN.

Helmut Volger

Lit.: *Deen, T.:* Environment: Task Force Rejects Merger Of Two U.N. Bodies, in: World News – InterPressService (IPS), 5 July 1998 (Internet: www.oneworld.org/ips2/jul98/05_13-007.htm); *Group of 77:* Statement by the Representative of Venezuela, on behalf of the Group of 77 and China, on agenda item 116 (pattern of conferences), before the Fifth Committee of the 57th session of the United Nations General Assembly, New York 24 October 2002, www.g77.org/Speeches/102402.htm; *Group of 77:* Statement on behalf of the Group of 77 and China by Ms. Karen Lock, Permanent Mission of South Africa to the United Nations, on agenda item 121 (pattern of conferences), before the Fifth Committee of the United Nations General Assembly, New York 17 October 2006, www.g77.org/Speeches/101706b.htm; *United Nations Task Force on Environment and Human Settlements:* Report to the Secretary-General, 15 June 1998, New York 1998; *United Nations:* Proposed programme budget for the biennium 2000-2001, Part VIII Common Support Services, Section 27G – Administration Nairobi, (UN Doc. A/54/6 (Section 27G) of 23 March 1999); *U.N.* task force proposes new environment management group, in: Journal of the Group of 77, No. 2/1998 (Internet: www.g77.org/Journal/2-98/6.htm); *United Nations - General Assembly:* Questions relating to the proposed programme budget for the biennium 2000-2001, UN Doc. A/RES/54/249 of 24 December 1999; *United Nations - General Assembly:* Pattern of conferences, 24 December 2001, UN Doc. A/RES/56/242.; *United Nations - General Assembly:* Questions relating to the proposed programme budget for the biennium 2008-2009, UN Doc. A/RES/62/236 of 22 December 2007; *United Nations – General Assembly:* Construction of New Facilities at Nairobi Office Has Experienced Significant Delays, UN Press Release GA/AB/ 3881 of 28 November 2008; *United Nations:* Press Briefing by Executive Director of UN Environment Programme, 2 July 1998.

Internet: Homepage of UNON: www.unon.org.

UN Office New York

The seat of the United Nations is New York City; the organization's permanent headquarters is located here with five of its six principal organs: → Security Council, → General Assembly, Economic and Social Council (→ ECOSOC), → Trusteeship Council and → Secretariat.

The sixth principal organ, the International Court of Justice → ICJ has its seat in The Hague (Netherlands).

Beside these five principal organs, most of the subsidiary organs (→ Principal Organs, Subsidiary Organs, Treaty Bodies) also meet regularly in New York: the permanent and temporary committees (→ Committees, System of) hold the major part of their sessions here. Many UN programmes and funds (→ UN System) have their seat in New York as well (see Annex). The → specialized agencies of the UN maintain liaison offices at the UN Headquarters in New York.

All 192 member states of the UN (→ Membership and Representation of States) maintain → permanent missions in New York.

Decision on the Seat of the UN

The → Charter of the UN contains no regulation with regard to the seat of the UN. So the General Assembly had to decide on the issue. In its first session, held in London, the General Assembly decided on 14 February 1946 in resolution A/RES/25 (I) that the United Nations should take its permanent headquarters in the USA "in Westchester (New York) and/or Fairfield (Connecticut) counties, i.e. near to New York City" and in a further resolution the General Assembly decided on 14 December 1946 (UN Doc. A/RES/100 (I)) that the headquarters be established in New York City, "in the area bounded by the First Avenue, East 48th Street, the East River and East 42nd Street ..."

On the same day the Secretary-General was authorized by another resolution (UN Doc. A/RES/99 (I)) to start negotiations with the appropriate authorities of the USA about a headquarters agreement as legal basis for the UN headquarters, providing the privileges, immunities and facilities needed for such a seat.

On 26 June 1947 the respective agreement between the United Nations and the United States was signed (UNTS

Vol. 11, No. 147) and came into force on 21 November 1947 through a mutual exchange of notes.

The agreement confirms that the "headquarters district shall be under the control and authority of the United Nations" (cf. → Host State Agreements). The UN headquarters district has thus a status similar to national embassy premises.

Furthermore the legal basis for the UN staff working in the UN headquarters and for the diplomats visiting the UN seat is constituted by the Convention on the Privileges and Immunities of the United Nations of 1946 (UNTS Vol. 1, No. 4).

Being accommodated for the first years rather provisionally in several New York sites, the United Nations could in 1952 move into the new-built headquarters building complex at the East River.

In subsequent years the original complex of buildings was expanded by several further buildings.

Since in the following decades the buildings were not rebuilt, the headquarters buildings have come recently to need extensive renovation. It took many years of difficult negotiations until in December 2007 the General Assembly decided to appropriate financial resources (UN Doc. A/RES/62/87, 10 December 2007) for the renovation programme which will take about five years.

Relations with the Host Country

With the increasing political tensions of the Cold War in the late 1950s and 1960s members of the permanent missions in New York felt restrained and discriminated against by measures of New York City authorities as well as by US federal authorities with regard to the freedom to move within the USA, the staff size of their permanent missions and to the access to entry visas for delegations from their home countries attending meetings of UN organizations in New York. These grievances led to the request by the General Assembly in December 1969 to the Secretary-General in Resolution A/RES/2618

(XXIV) to "undertake an examination of those conditions which adversely affect the delegations and staff of the United Nations in New York and to consider taking all necessary measures to alleviate the effect of such conditions" (para. 6), to examine even the "possibility and desirability of relocating all or part of certain units of the United Nations" (para. 4).

Eventually the problems led to the establishment of the Committee on Relations with the Host Country by a General Assembly resolution in December 1971 (UN Doc. A/RES/2819 (XXVI); to its 14 members belongs of course the USA. The committee attempts since then to alleviate the tensions caused by the differing views on the freedom to move, the denial of visas and the parking habits of mission members between the US authorities on the one side and the UN staff and members of the permanent missions on the other (cf. → UN Policy, USA).

In particular, during the administration of President Ronald Reagan (1981-1989), UN staff and representatives of member states criticized that the work of the UN was impeded by restricting the travelling possibilities of East European diplomats in the USA, and by refusing visas to international diplomats for different reasons (cf. for example the respective committee report of 1986, UN Doc. A/41/26, para. 18). A rather conspicuous example for these problems was the denial of an entry visa to PLO Chairman Yasser Arafat who wanted to take part in the 43rd session of the General Assembly in 1988. This led eventually to the decision of the General Assembly to move with its sessions temporarily – from 13 to 15 December 1988 – to Geneva so that Arafat was able to participate (cf. *Reisman* 1989).

Together with General Assembly resolutions criticizing the policy of Israel in the Near East and others demanding radical reforms of the international economic order, these problems with the host state USA were replied to in the US mass media and by a number of US congress politicians and State Department officials by suggesting the United Nations should leave the USA (cf. *Franck* 1985, 202; *Parsons* 1993).

Since the rapprochement of the USA under President Bush Senior to the UN in reaction to the offer for cooperation by the Soviet leader Gorbachev this criticism and unfriendliness on the side of the host state towards the UN has become less, though the differing political views on the role of the UN remain, as well as the grievances brought forward by the member states in the Committee on Relations with the Host Country (cf. for example the committee report of 2008, UN Doc. A/63/26 of 3 November 2008).

Without doubt the host country USA benefits from the UN headquarters in New York, which fosters the US economy through the demand for goods and services, hotel beds and airline tickets for UN staff and member state delegations. And the United Nations benefits from the central geographical location, the quality of the communication services and the great number of journalists and TV programmes available in New York. As it is important for the UN to attract attention to its debates and decisions, New York is all in all a suitable place for its seat.

Helmut Volger

Lit.: *Franck, T.M.:* Nation against Nation. What Happened to the UN Dream and What the US Can Do about It, New York 1985; *Luard, E.:* A History of the United Nations, 2 vols., London et al. 1982/1989; *Parsons, A.:* The UN and the National Interest of States, in: Roberts, A./Kingsbury, B. (eds.): United Nations, Divided World. The UN's Roles in International Relations, 2nd rev. and exp. edn., Oxford 1993, 104-124; *Reisman, M.:* The Arafat Visa Affair: Exceeding the Bounds of Host State Discretion, in: AJIL 83 (1989), 519-527.

Internet: www.un.org

Annex:

I. Programmes and Funds of the UN located in New York:

- United Nations Children's Fund (→ UNICEF);
- United Nations Development Programme (→ UNDP);
- United Nations Office for Project Services (UNOPS);
- United Nations Development Fund for Women (→ UNIFEM);
- United Nations Fund for International Partnerships (UNFIP);
- United Nations Population Fund (→ UNFPA).

II. Commissions and other Subsidiary Organs of the UN, meeting in New York:
- Ad Hoc Interagency Meeting on Women;
- Advisory Committee on Administrative and Budgetary Questions (ACABQ);
- United Nations Chief Executives Board for Coordination (CEB) and its subcommittees;
- Interagency Meeting on Language Arrangements, Documentation and Publications (IAMLADP);
- Interagency Network on Women and Gender Equality (IANWGE);
- Inter-Agency Working Group on Evaluation (IAWG);
- International Civil Service Commission (ICSC);
- Panel of External Auditors of the United Nations;
- United Nations Board of Auditors;
- United Nations Communications Group;
- United Nations Development Group (UNDG);
- United Nations Geographic Information Working Group (UNGIWG);
- United Nations Information and Communication Technologies Task Force (UNICTTF);
- United Nations Joint Staff Pension Fund (UNJSPF);
- United Nations High Representative for the Least Developed Countries, Landlocked Developing Countries and Small Island Developing States (OHRLLS);
- United Nations Resident Coordinators Network (RCNet).

UN Office Vienna

Along with New York, Geneva and Nairobi, Vienna is one of the four headquarters of the United Nations. The *Vienna International Centre (VIC)*, commonly known as "UNO City", was designed by the Austrian architect Johann Staber. Opened on 23 August 1979, it has been rented to the United Nations for 99 years at a symbolic rate of 1 Austrian schilling (7 cents) annually.

More than 4,000 employees from over a 100 countries work for the Vienna-based organizations. Numerous international conferences and meetings are held annually at the Vienna International Centre. Events of a much larger dimension are held in the adjacent Austria Center.

Located at the Centre are the United Nations Office at Vienna (UNOV), the United Nations Office on Drugs and Crime (UNODC), the United Nations Industrial Development Organization (→ UNIDO), the International Atomic Energy Agency (→ IAEA), the Preparatory Commission for the Comprehensive Nuclear-Test-Ban Treaty Organization (CTBTO PrepCom), the United Nations Commission for International Trade Law (→ UNCITRAL) and the United Nations Register of Damage Caused by the Construction of the Wall in the Occupied Palestinian Territory (UNRoD).

Other United Nations organizations and entities with offices in Vienna are: the United Nations Postal Administration (UNPA), the United Nations High Commissioner for Refugees (→ UNHCR), the United Nations Scientific Committee on the Effects of Atomic Radiation (UNSCEAR), the United Nations Environment Programme (→ UNEP), the United Nations Office for Project Services (UNOPS) and the Joint United Nations Programme on HIV/AIDS (UN AIDS).

United Nations Office at Vienna (UNOV)

The United Nations Office at Vienna (UNOV) provides administrative support to VIC-based programmes in conference planning, language interpretation and building security. The Director-General of UNOV represents the Secretary-General in dealings with the host country and diplomatic missions in Vienna.

United Nations Information Service (UNIS) Vienna

The network of United Nations information centres (UNICs), services and offices links the Headquarters with people around the world. Located in 57 countries, these field offices of the Department of Public Information (DPI) help local communities obtain up-to-date information on the Organization and its activities. Each of these centres and services provides information support for the affiliated countries.

The United Nations Information Service (UNIS) Vienna is responsible for the public relations work of the United Nations offices and for the Visitors Service. At the same time, it functions as the United Nations Information Centre for Austria, Hungary, Slovakia and Slovenia. (→ Public Information of the UN)

United Nations Commission on International Trade Law (UNCITRAL)

The *United Nations Commission on International Trade Law (→ UNCITRAL)* is the core legal body of the United Nations system in the field of international trade law.

Its mandate is to remove legal obstacles to international trade by progressively modernizing and harmonizing trade law. It prepares legal texts in a number of key areas such as international commercial dispute settlement, electronic commerce, insolvency, international payments, sale of goods, transport law, procurement and infrastructure development. UNCITRAL also provides technical assistance to law reform activities, including assisting member states to review and assess their law reform needs and to draft the legislation required to implement UNCITRAL texts.

The UNCITRAL Secretariat is located in Vienna and maintains a website at www.uncitral.org.

The United Nations Industrial Development Organization (UNIDO)

The United Nations Industrial Development Organization (→ UNIDO) is the specialized UN agency that promotes sustainable, environmentally friendly industrial development, with the goals of promoting employment and reducing poverty. It provides tailor-made solutions to today's industrial problems by offering a package of integrated services addressing three key concerns at policy, institutional and enterprise levels: ensuring a sound environment, creating productive employment and building a competitive economy. Further information: www.unido.org.

International Atomic Energy Agency (IAEA)

The *International Atomic Energy Agency (IAEA)*, the first UN organization in Vienna (established in 1957), serves as the world's central inter-governmental forum on scientific and technical cooperation in the nuclear field. The basic task of the IAEA is to support countries in the peaceful use of nuclear energy, e.g. in agriculture, health care, energy production and other fields in compliance with IAEA safeguards. It also verifies that nuclear materials and nuclear installations supplied by its programmes, or by request of its member states, are not used for military purposes (Further information at: www.iaea.org).

Office for Outer Space Affairs (OOSA)

The *United Nations Office for Outer Space Affairs (OOSA)* is the office responsible for promoting international cooperation in the peaceful uses of outer space (→ Space Law). The Office implements the decisions of the General Assembly and of the Committee on the Peaceful Uses of Outer Space. It has the dual objective of supporting the intergovernmental discussions in the Committee and its Scientific and Technical (S&T) and Legal Subcommittees, and assisting developing countries in using

space technology for development. In addition, it follows legal, scientific and technical developments relating to space activities, in order to provide technical information and advice to member states, international organizations and other United Nations offices. Further information at: www.oosa.unvienna.org.

United Nations Office on Drugs and Crime (UNODC)

The *United Nations Office on Drugs and Crime (UNODC)* is a global leader in the fight against drugs, crime and terrorism, which remain three of the greatest threats to the peace, security and well-being of humanity. UNODC operates in all regions of the world through an extensive network of field offices and relies on voluntary contributions, mainly from governments, for some 90 per cent of its budget.

The three pillars of the UNODC work programme are:

1) an operational response made possible by the political ownership of the states concerned, technical assistance from UNODC headquarters and the involvement of the Office's worldwide network of field offices;

2) research and analytical work to increase knowledge and understanding of drugs and crime issues an ensure that policy is evidence-based; and

3) a strong legal framework that helps states fight drugs, crime and terrorism according to the rule of law. Further information: www.unodc.org.

International Narcotics Control Board (INCB)

The *International Narcotics Control Board (INCB)* is the independent and quasi-judicial monitoring body for the implementation of the United Nations international drug control conventions. It was established in 1968 pursuant to the Single Convention on Narcotic Drugs, 1961, and had predecessor bodies under earlier drug control treaties going back as far as the time of the → League of Nations. The mandate of INCB is to monitor and promote Government compliance with the provisions of the international drug control conventions. These conventions recognize that drugs often have legitimate scientific and medicinal uses that must be protected but that the abuse of drugs gives rise to public health, social and economic problems. About 250 substances are controlled under the conventions. Further information at: www. incb.org

Preparatory Commission for the Comprehensive Nuclear-Test-Ban Treaty Organization (CTBTO)

The 1996 *Comprehensive Nuclear-Test-Ban Treaty (CTBT)* bans all nuclear explosions on Earth. The main tasks of the Preparatory Commission for the Comprehensive Nuclear-Test-Ban Treaty Organization) (CTBTO) are to promote Treaty signatures and ratifications and to establish a global verification regime capable of detecting nuclear explosions underground, underwater and in the atmosphere. When complete, the regime will consist of 337 monitoring facilities worldwide, supported by an International Data Centre in Vienna, and on-site inspections. As of November 2008, 180 countries had signed and 145 countries had ratified the CTBT. Nine additional, specific countries need to ratify the Treaty for it to enter into force. Further information at: www.ctbto.org.

Helmut Volger,
on the basis of information texts from the UN institutions depicted in the entry

Internet: Homepage of UN Office Vienna: www.unvienna.org/unov/index.html; Information about UN entities in Vienna: www.un vienna.org/unov/en/unsecretariat.html.

UN Policy, China

In parallel with the varied and eventful internal developments during the first six decades of its history, the People's Republic of China has made several changes in its policy towards the United Nations. In retrospect three phases can be distinguished, which might be characterized as *disapproval, revolution* and *growing stability.*

I. First Phase: Rejection of the United Nations

The first phase began in October 1950 when, acting upon a request of the People's Republic of China, the UN → Security Council decided that it could send a representative to a session of the Council discussing the Korean War. There the People's Republic - together with → North Korea – was branded as the "aggressor" in the Korean War. From that time Beijing rejected the United Nations as an "instrument of US imperialism". China even pursued for some time - hand in hand with the Indonesia of Sukarno, which had left the UN in 1965 - a plan to found a kind of counter-organization, with its seat in Djakarta.

II. Second Phase: China aspires to a Leading Role in the Third World

The second phase began on 25 October 1971. On this day the → General Assembly of the UN – in a spontaneous reaction to the announced visit of US president Nixon in China – decided upon the admission of the People's Republic of China), and the simultaneous exclusion of the Republic of China (Taiwan) from the United Nations.

Beijing made use of this chance to pursue, from this time on, three goals:
- to work for the isolation of Taiwan, which until then – under the name "Republic of China" - had pushed the competitor People's Republic of China almost to the wall in diplomatic affairs;
- to denounce its main adversary at that time, the "hegemonic" Soviet Union, as often as possible; and
- to become a kind of spokesman for the Third World.

The "Province Taiwan" was indeed – step by step – pushed out not only of the UN and the → specialized agencies (→ ILO, → UNESCO, → WHO, → WMO etc), but also out of the four financial institutions of the → UN system, namely the → IMF, the World Bank, the IFC and the IDA (→ World Bank, World Bank Group). Concurrently, many countries severed their diplomatic relations to Taiwan. As a result Taiwan

759

– until today – has only diplomatic representations with a small number of states (23 in 2008, and mostly in Africa and Central America).

In the same way the People's Republic of China did all in its power to "isolate maximally" the "hegemonic" Soviet Union, which had become its main opponent since 1968 (Prague, Ussuri incidents). To reach this goal, China made an effort to win over as many Third World countries as possible. Already in December 1971 China inflicted on the Soviet Union a crushing voting defeat in connection with the war between India and Pakistan. Additionally, Beijing used the UN committees (→ Committees, System of) as instruments for its own purposes, for example in the Seabed Council (→ Law of Sea), China attacked Moscow's alleged striding sea-lane strategy. In the Committee on Decolonization (→ Decolonization), where China would shortly thereafter assume the presidency, it denounced the Soviet invasion of Prague, as well as Moscow's policy in Outer Mongolia.

Furthermore China denounced the Soviet Union, in the United Nations Conference on Trade and Development → UNCTAD and in the Special Political Committee of the General Assembly as being partly responsible for the increasing poverty in the world, and for increasing environmental damages (as consequences of ABC weapons).

To strengthen its fight against Moscow, China moreover began to politicize the term "aggression" (→ Aggression, Definition of) which is central to the UN Charter (→ Charter of the UN). While the European representatives demanded a brief and abstract definition, the Soviet Union an enumerative one, and the representatives of the Anglo-American conception of law demanded a case-law interpretation, the representatives of the People's Republic of China did not aim at a "judicial concept", but a "political concept" of this term: in their understanding "aggression" should be what 95 % "of all peoples" perceive as an aggression, in a specific situation. This decision-focused procedural approach, to decide political questions individually, case by case, which was at that time frequently used in Chinese domestic policy, was now to be transferred by China to its UN policy wherever the "maximal isolation" of the main enemy of the Third World and China, the "Soviet hegemonism", was at issue.

The isolation of Moscow could only be successful if China reached a "maximal solidarity" with the Third World countries. Accordingly China oriented its policy on this guiding principle, and it never failed to refer to itself as a developing country and therefore an authentic member of the Third World. This common feature was emphasized in 1974 in the proclamation of the "Third World Theory" by Deng Xiaoping.

III. Third Phase: Chinese Growing Cooperation in the United Nations

In December 1978 - two years after the death of Mao and the fall of the so called "gang of four", the third phase of the Chinese foreign policy began: The reformists under the leadership of Deng Xiaoping reorganized the foreign policy from "class struggle to modernization", which meant a turn of 180 degrees, and brought the new course into line with the slogan "peace and development". In particular it became reconciled – during the 1990s – with its former main enemies, the Soviet Union/Russia and Vietnam.

In concrete terms this change occurred in three directions: *First*, Beijing tried to transfer its "theory of relations" - practiced for many centuries - to the new interdependence relationships in the international system. Thus China advocates multilateralism and democratization of international relations ("broadest consensus among member states through consultation") and the realization of a "harmonious" world. A new world order in the 21st century is considered necessary, setting forth a common stand on major international issues, such as UN reforms, globalization, North-South-cooperation and world trade. This means, according to Beijing, that a concept is to be advocated where not the nation is in the foreground, as in the "realistic school" of Morgenthau, rather one where the relationships among the nations are central. Where this is successful, the "security" of the nations is not the main issue, rather peace ("harmony") among the participants of the international system is crucial. Conflicts are then not regarded as unavoidable ("national interests are inviolable!"), but have to be "argued away" ("xie" is the most commonly used term, meaning consultation and balance). Thus there is no "zero sum game", but a positive "sum game". Thus where interdependence is successfully practiced, the single nation will not win at the expense of the others, but every participant can profit through "mutual" coordination ($\rightarrow$ International Organizations, Theory of).

For the implementation of this network-thinking China considers the United Nations to be the world's most comprehensive, representative and authoritative forum. It is irreplaceable in this function and should be strengthened in its role. An UN-led global system should be set up to deal with new threats and challenges on the basis of the UN-Charter and international law.

Accordingly China is not a "Njet"-member in the UN, but has used the veto right ($\rightarrow$ Veto, Right of Veto) only six times up to now (as of 15 July 2008): in 1972 to prevent Bangladesh from being admitted to the UNO, in 1973 to stop a resolution on the ceasefire in the Yom Kippur War, in 1977 to keep back ceasefire observers from Guatemala, in 1999 to prevent the extension of the mandate for the UN preventive deployment force UNPREDEP in the Republic of Macedonia (which – as in the case of Guatemala – had recognized Taiwan), in 2007 to save Myanmar from becoming criticized on its human rights record, and in 2008 to stop a resolution criticizing and sanctioning the undemocratic Mugabe regime in Zimbabwe.

In contrast to its theory of interdependence, however, China in certain aspects is behaving in a very nationalistic manner, particularly with regard to the issues of Taiwan and Tibet – or in its new Africa-policy, where it tries to cooperate closely with some oil-producing countries as Sudan or Nigeria and to neglect, in an unobtrusive way, the "rest" of the continent.

Contrary to the expectation of many third world countries, that China should become an active proponent of the Non-Aligned Movement, the PRC played a rather passive role in this respect and became really active only when its national interests were at stake, as in the cases of Macedonia (1999) and Guatemala (1997) when it vetoed peacekeeping missions, because these nations had taken up diplomatic relations with Taiwan.

Second, China dissociated itself very quickly from its former function as a revolutionary troublemaker (which had been emphasized so much under the leadership of Mao Zedong), and returned to its traditional role of maintaining order and stability. No less a man than Deng Xiaoping used the term "wending" (stability) as his favorite phrase, while knowing that stability depends on economic welfare. Consequently in the 1990s the economy moved into the political "centre" of the whole policy of the Communist Party of China. The PRC maintains that the Millennium Declaration of the General Assembly of the United Nations adopted in September 2000 (UN Doc. A/RES/55/2 of 8 September 2000) should be carried out to the letter, that countries should strengthen economic and technological exchanges and cooperation so as to gradually change the economic world order which is, according to China, "unfair and unreasonable". In this way the goals of coexistence and mutual benefits for the economic globalization should be achieved.

According to the new course, China developed more interest for other, so far neglected UN organs, in particular for $\rightarrow$ UNDP and for $\rightarrow$ UNIDO, which in turn reacted positively and assigned to China numerous development programmes, ranging from fresh-water fish cultures to the development of the use of biogas, silkworm raising, to acupuncture, fundamental health protection, small hydro-power stations and "comprehensive development in villages". Moreover UNDP described the Chinese HDI- and GEM-policy (→ Human Development Reports; → Development Cooperation of the UN System) as exemplary.

In the 1990s the People's Republic of China signed numerous security agreements, for example the Non-Proliferation Treaty and the Comprehensive Test Ban Treaty (→ Disarmament) and organized several UN conferences, among others a UN conference on population and the Fourth World Conference on Women (→ World Conferences).

After the "September 11 incident", China moreover strengthened its cooperation with the UN on the issue of anti-terrorism. In November 2001 it acceded to the Convention for the Suppression of Terrorist Bombing and signed the international Convention for the Suppression of Financing Terrorism.

Beijing furthermore changed its position in peacekeeping operations (PKOs). For more than 20 years it had opposed them and refused to contribute money to any operation. In 1988, however, it joined the special committee on PKOs and sent its first military observers the following year and the first company of engineers to Cambodia in April 1992. Since then, China's participation in UN PKOs has spectacularly increased by type and numbers of personal and location of missions. Until 2007 the PRC has sent more than 3,000 military personnel to 13 PKOs, among others to Mozambique, Western Sahara, Liberia, Afghanistan, Congo, East Timor, Bosnia and Herzegovina, Kosovo, and Haiti.

The reasons for this change of outlook may have been: (1) boosting influence; (2) promoting the reputation for the ill-famed PLA (People's Liberation Army) and the PAP (People's Armed Police);

(3) discouraging Taiwan from seeking recognition by granting aid (in the case of Haiti this policy failed: Haiti continued to recognize Taiwan in spite of the PRC's PKO-support).

Third, the People's Republic of China demanded that the "Five Principles of Peaceful Coexistence" (→ sovereignty, non-aggression, non-interference, equality and peaceful coexistence), which it originally had initiated with others in 1954, should become a leitmotif for a new international policy: a goal which did not prevent the People's Republic from becoming one of the five permanent members of the → Security Council with a hierarchical preponderance.

Within the "Five Principles" Beijing laid the main emphasis on "non-interference", particularly as far as the issues of human rights and of Taiwan were concerned, not however with regard to the participation in PKOs.

Regarding the issue of → human rights, China continued advocating its understanding that the western interpretation is not "universal". It takes the view that different cultures have rather developed their own conceptions (for example in China social rights have more importance than individual rights) and that the "human rights issue" is misused by "certain superpowers" as a pretext for interfering in domestic affairs (→ Human Rights, Protection of).

Some allies of Taiwan argue that the exclusion of the successful and democratically ruled island-republic deviates from the spirit of the Universal Declaration of Human Rights, ignoring the fundamental human rights of 23 million people. They assert that Taiwan is tragically caught between the PRC's claim that the island is just a province of China and the right of the people of Taiwan to self-determination. Arguments of this kind failed however to convince the PRC to relinquish its claim to be the government of the whole of China. Indeed it has vetoed all of the petitions which Taiwan has filed since 1991 to rejoin the United Nations, from which Taiwan was excluded on October 25, 1971.

With regard to the intensive debate on the reform of the Security Council before, during and after the UN World Summit in September 2005, China argued that only a concept getting the broadest possible majority in the General Assembly should be voted on and that the General Assembly should take the necessary time for reform (cf. UN Doc. A/59/PV.111, 11 July 2005, 13-14, and UN Doc. A/60/PV.48, 10 November 2005, 3). In other words, it rejected in diplomatic disguise all reform models presented to the General Assembly and all proposals for increasing the number of permanent members of the Security Council with veto right. Here again, the PRC did not fulfill the expectations of the Third World countries that it would fight for their interest to be more strongly represented in the Security Council, but fought for the preservation of its own privileged position as permanent member of the Council.

Oskar Weggel

Lit.: *Boardman, R.:* Post-socialist World Orders. Russia, China and the UN System, New York 1994; *Choedon, Y.:* China and the United Nations, Colorado Springs 2001; *Feinerman, J.V.:* Chinese Participation in the International Legal Order. Rogue Elephant or Team Player?, in: The China Quarterly, No. 141, March 1995, 186-210; *Fravel, M.T.:* China's Attitude Toward U.N. Peacekeeping Operations since 1989, in: Asian Survey, No. 36, November 1996, 1102-1121; *Gill, B.:* Rising star: China's new security diplomacy, Washington/D.C. 2007; *Davis, M. (ed.):* Chinese Values and Human Rights: legal, philosophical and political perspectives, New York 1995; *Hu, R./Chan, G./Zha, D.:* China's International Relations in the 21st Century: Dynamics of Paradigm Shifts, Lanham 2001; *Tsang, S. (ed.):* If China attacks Taiwan: military strategy, politics and economics (Asian security studies), New York 2006; *Ikenberry, J.:* The Rise of China and the Future of the West, in: Foreign Affairs 87, No. 1 (Jan./Feb. 2008); *Kent, A.:* China, the United Nations and Human Rights: The Limits of Compliance (Pennsylvania Studies in Human Rights), Philadelphia 1999; *Kim, S.S.:* China, the United Nations, and World Order, Princeton/N.J. 1979; *Kornberg, J.F./Faust, J.R..:* China in world politics: policies, processes, prospects, 2nd ed., Vancouver 2005; *Kulessa, M.:* China in den Vereinten Nationen, die Vereinten Nationen in China, in: VN 37 (1989), 12-16; *Kurlantzick, J.:* Charm offensive: how China's soft power is transforming the world. New Haven 2007; *Ogden, S.:* China's Position on U.N. Charter Review, in: Pacific Affairs, 52 (1979), 210-240; *Pfeifenberger, W.:* Die UNO-Politik der Volksrepublik China, Erlenbach/Zürich 1978; *Permanent Mission of the People's Republic of China to the United Nations:* Position Paper of the People's Republic of China on the United Nations Reform, 7 June 2005 (quoted as: PRC 2005); *Qian, Q.:* Rede vor der UNO-Vollversammlung, in: Beijing Rundschau, Nr.34, 21.10.1997, 8-11; *Shirk, S.L.:* China: fragile superpower, New York 2007; *Vatikiotis, M.:* Asia: Towards Security Cooperation (International Peace Academy – Working Papers), New York 2007; *Zhao, Q.:* Interpreting Chinese foreign policy, New York 1996.

Internet: Homepage of the Permanent Mission of China at the United Nations in New York: www.china-un.org.

UN Policy, France

Together with the USA, the United Kingdom, Russia, and China, the French Republic is the → Security Council's fifth permanent member with veto power (→ Veto, Right of Veto). As an important former colonial power and victorious ally in World War II, France became a founding member of the United Nations (→ History of Foundation of the UN). Due to → decolonization and nuclear armament France's relationship with the UN was difficult and distanced for the first years. About 1965, the situation changed. France became the 'spokes country' of the developing world. But from different international activities – like interventions in Africa – there arose questions of France's credibility. The end of the Cold War has opened up new possibilities. France actively participates in the work of the no-longer blocked Security Council, and participates intensely in peacekeeping (→ Peacekeeping, → Peacekeeping Operations). Contributing 68.37 million US

Dollars to the UN budget in 1998, France is the fourth largest financial contributor to the UN. (→ Budget)

I. Principles of French UN Policy

The United Nations are not the highest priority for the French foreign policy. The fundamental principles of independence and of preserving France's rank in the world determine the French foreign policy. The United Nations is in this context of minor significance. At the same time, the United Nations functions as a foreign policy instrument, an important source of information and a barometer of international diplomacy. French people's interest in and knowledge of the UN is low as – correspondingly – is public pressure on the French government and its policy towards the United Nations (→ Public Opinion and the UN).

II. France and the Foundation of the United Nations

During the time of the UN foundation, the political influence of France was low. Though France received a permanent seat with veto power in the Security Council, this decision was not taken before June 1944 with the "Tentative Proposals for a General Organization" which were the basis for the first draft of the UN Charter. The provisional French government of General de Gaulle was not invited to the following, important conferences of Dumbarton Oaks and Yalta. France could not influence substantial topics before the UN-founding conference of San Francisco (25 April to 26 June 1945), where important aims were achieved. French became an official language (→ Languages, Official) and one of the working languages (→ Languages, Working) of the United Nations. Plans for international trusteeships and mandates on French colonial areas were prevented (→ Trusteeship Council). In San Francisco, France signed the UN Charter (→ Charter of the UN) and became a founding member of the United Nations.

III. France and Decolonization

Decolonization affected France's relationship to the United Nations very much, as the United Nations put strong pressure on the former colonial power France. One example is the "Declaration on the Granting of Independence to the Colonial Countries and Peoples", General Assembly resolution A/RES/1514 (XV) of 14 December 1960. It was not only former colonies putting pressure on France, but also the USA and the USSR. The French government regarded any pressure as intervention in internal affairs (→ Intervention, Prohibition of; → Sovereignty). From the French point of view, colonies were an integral part of French national territory and the peoples' right on self-determination (→ Self-Determination, Right of) was guaranteed within the French empire as well. Several colonial wars showed France's uncompromising attitude and provoked massive international criticism. The result was a far-reaching isolation of France within the United Nations.

In 1954, the Indochina war ended after eight years and in 1956, France recognized the independence of Morocco and Tunisia. In the same year, the Suez crisis finally showed the limits of colonial powers Great Britain and France, and peaceful decolonization of Black Africa started. With the end of the Algerian war (1954-1962), decolonization was mainly finished for France. The French government was relieved of international pressure, and their relationship with the United Nations normalized.

Due to the community of Francophone states, numerous bilateral treaties and the Franc Zone (Communauté Financière Africaine), former African colonies stayed under French influence and remained a central field of interest to France. Due to its special position in Africa, France defined itself as 'spokesman' of the developing world and therefore France's position in the Security Council was legitimized in its opinion. For Africa, France interpreted this role as a power of order, resulting in numerous interventions of France in African states in the late seventies. France thus often faced accusations of neo-colonialism.

IV. France in the Security Council

Permanent membership in the Security Council was central for French UN policy. The veto power was perceived as adequate recognition of France's rank in the world. French possibilities to pursue and implement its interests on its own as a medium-sized power were and still are limited. Therefore, the Security Council's ability to act has been crucial for France ever since. During the East-West-Conflict, France criticized both the USA and the USSR for paralyzing the Security Council as it hindered the implementation of French political goals. France blamed the United States and the Soviet Union for neglecting their responsibility for international peace and security (→ Peace, Peace Concept, Threat to Peace). Though deeply rooted in the west, France did not always follow the United States, as the Middle East Conflict clearly showed. In 1967, France supported the condemnation of Israel's aggression. Since then, its attitude towards the PLO has been rather positive.

Since 1945, France has not used the veto power more than 18 times (compared to a total of 237 vetoes), and the last use was before the end of the Cold War. In 1956, France vetoed most spectacularly in the Suez crisis, together with the United Kingdom. Both states blocked the Security Council in order to follow their own colonial interests. Individually, France used the veto twice: 1947 on a minor dispute between the Netherlands and Indonesia, and 1976 on the question of the Comoros' self-determination, a former French colony. Ten vetoes concerned South Africa. Together with the USA and the United Kingdom, France prevented resolutions against the apartheid regime from 1974 to 1977. As a consequence, France lost significantly in terms of credibility with Africa and the developing world. In 1977, the situation improved when France supported a weapons' embargo against South Africa (→ Sanctions).

V. Nuclear Power France

In 1960, France became an atomic power, building up its own nuclear force. Ever since, the so-called "force de frappe" has been an integral part of French policy, guaranteeing independence and world power attributes. French strategy follows the principle of minimal deterrence: credibility and political decisiveness are more important than the number of nuclear weapons.

Most UN members condemned French nuclear testing. France evaluated this as propaganda of the existing nuclear powers USA, USSR, and the United Kingdom, denying France the status of a nuclear power. France declined any UN efforts on → disarmament, considering them as measures to maintain American and Soviet superiority. From the French point of view, a precondition for further negotiations was that all other nuclear powers would disarm to the lower level of the French force. French proposals not taken into account appropriately resulted in a French boycott of the Disarmament Commission from 1962 on. France started exporting nuclear plants all over the world, e.g. to Israel and Iraq.

With the end of the Cold War, nuclear weapons lost some importance, and in 1992, France joined the Non-Proliferation Treaty of Nuclear Weapons. Three years later, the French government carried out nuclear tests on the Mururoa atoll. At the same time, it promised to join the Comprehensive Test Ban Treaty. These demonstrations of the French policy of independence caused international protests of UN member states.

VI. French Contributions in the Field of Security since the End of the East-West-Conflict

After the end of the East-West-Conflict, France participated actively in the crisis management of emerging conflicts by contributing to UN → peacekeeping operations. With the Security Council able to act again, France, as a medium-sized power, used its position to play a more prominent role in the settlement of conflicts. But in playing this role, France had to accept the central position of the United States of America and the limits of its own influence. Though only having limited power, France as a permanent member bears a large part of responsibility for success or failure of UN operations, and can lose in this task considerable influence with regard to its role as traditional 'spokesman' for the developing world. For French governments the Security Council's mandate is a precondition for any military intervention. → Preventive Diplomacy should be used more to prevent conflicts (→ Peaceful Settlement of Disputes). France supports the integration of regional security organizations (→ Regionalization) and considers peace conferences an appropriate measure for negotiations, for example also in the Middle East conflict.

Since the end of the Cold War, French contributions to UN peacekeeping operations have been very high in terms of finance and participation. France's support increased to approximately 8% of all peacekeeping operations in 1997 (corresponding to 80.6 million US dollars). France is one of the main contributors to UN → Peacekeeping Forces. With a share of more than a sixth of the UN peacekeeping forces in the middle of the nineties, France at times has had doubled the US contribution. French activities concentrated on its own sphere of interest, mainly former colonies.

In 1978, France participated for the first time in a "Blue Helmet" operation (→ Peacekeeping). France was strongly committed to its former colony Cambodia, in mediating between civil war parties until a peace treaty was signed in 1993 in Paris. During UN administration (UNTAC), in 1993, France sent 14,000 men to Cambodia. In the second Gulf war, France contributed 12,000 men as an ally in the coalition against Iraq. Since the end of the war, France has not actively supported military actions as a response to the reoccurring

Iraq crisis (especially in terms of UN sanctions), but remains reserved.

In the subsequent UN operations in Somalia, Rwanda, and the Balkans, France showed a strong presence. Likewise "Operation Turquoise" – a unilateral humanitarian operation in Rwanda – which took place from 22 June to 22 August 1994 – was executed under French command. A humanitarian safety zone was established, and a regional refugee catastrophe prevented.

Since then, France has actively participated in Kosovo as member of the contact group seeking political solutions to the conflict. Also in the Balkans, France took part in UNPROFOR, and the NATO-led Implementation Force (IFOR) and its successor, the Stabilization Force (SFOR), in Bosnia Herzegovina.

VII. France and the Reform of the Security Council

France does not disapprove of a reform the Security Council (→ Reform of the UN), but French privileges – especially the veto power – have to be guaranteed. A further precondition for enlargement is to ensure the Security Council's ability to act. Therefore, France prefers an enlargement by five more permanent members without veto power. Two seats should go to Germany and Japan, the remaining three to states of the South. Also the number of non-permanent members should be augmented, without French preference for a specific number.

France declines the idea of a shared European seat with veto power that would replace both the French and the British seat. Due to the Maastricht Treaty (1992) France is obliged not only to inform but also to consult on its Security Council decisions with the other European member states. Latest developments show that a common European position is not in fact standard (→ European Union, Common Foreign and Security Policy). For example, France's position to the Iraq conflict differed significantly from the United Kingdom's point of view. Regarding principles of French foreign policy it is unlikely that

France will ever decide against its own interests in the Security Council.

VIII. France and Development Issues

French development policy concentrates on Africa. It started after the difficult time of decolonization. France tried not to connect development assistance with pushing its own specific society model, as other industrial states did. This eased cooperation with many countries and strengthened France's position in the United Nations, although France's role as mediator in the North-South-Dialogue (→ North-South-Relations and the UN) became more and more difficult. Even in recognizing the right of self-determination (→ Self-Determination, Right of) for the Southern states, France did not implement this concept in practice, as this would have resulted in a loss of power for France.

In 1998, France was the second-ranked donor country of official development assistance. Generally speaking, it is mainly African states that profit from French development funds. These funds are primarily distributed as bilateral aid, or via the European Union. Therefore, French development policy is not focused on the United Nations. Within the United Nations (→ Development Cooperation of the UN System), France mainly supported the following institutions and programmes by contributing voluntary funds in 1998: → UNDP (13.3 million US dollars), → UNHCR (8.3 million US dollars), → UNICEF (8 million US dollars), and the World Food Programme → WFP (3.3 million US dollars). In the 1990s, French UN policy basically centered on security topics and did not focus on development.

IX: France and the Protection of Human Rights

Traditionally, the protection of human rights (→ Human Rights, Protection of) is an important topic for France. France not only supports the UN High Commissioner for Human Rights (→ UNHCHR), but strongly encouraged the founding of the International Criminal Court (→

ICC) at the UN conference in Rome in 1998. Upon French initiative, humanitarian interventions under UN mandates were established. These are considered crucial to protecting human rights. Another focus is on → UNESCO, according to France's sense of mission in terms of French culture. This fundamental idea of a cultural mission reaches back to 1925, when France initiated the founding of the International Institute for Intellectual Co-operation, a model for UNESCO.

X. Summing Up

In spite of some difficulties in the first years, France has always been an important member state of the United Nations. In particular France has contributed much in the field of security, with significant contributions during the last decade. Although France's influence in the so-called Third World has decreased, France has been and still is a spokesman for these states. Traditionally, France emphasizes the importance of human rights and their protection and the work of the United Nations in the cultural field.

Ursula Stiel

Lit.: *Dulphy, A.:* La politique extérieure de la France depuis 1945, Paris 1994; *Grand, C.:* Kleine Geschichte der Force de frappe, in: Blätter für deutsche und internationale Politik 41 (1996), 474-485; *Lewin, A.:* France and the United Nations (1945-1995), Paris 1995; *Pons, F.:* Les Casques bleus francais - 50 ans au service de la paix dans le monde, Paris 1995; *Smouts, M.-C.:* France and the United Nations system, in: Alger, C.F. et al. (eds.): The United Nations system: The policies of member states, New York et al. 1995; *Woyke, W.:* Frankreichs Außenpolitik von de Gaulle bis Mitterand, Opladen 1987; *Zorgbibe, C.:* La France, l'ONU et le maintien de la paix, Paris 1996.

Addendum

The United Nations continues to be a key diplomatic instrument for French foreign policy. France's unqualified attachment to the Organization flows from a recognition that both share the same principles and purposes but also from pragmatic expediency. Paul Wolfowitz, when United States Deputy Secretary of Defence, encapsulated this reality with irony and characteristic exaggeration commenting that the only place where France would still be a great power was at the Security Council (*Sur* 2004, 145). It is in France's national interest to work towards a strong world organization fit to meet the challenges of the twenty first century.

1. France, a proactive supporter of the United Nations

As a matter of principle, France stands right behind the Secretary-General, as the most emblematic embodiment of the United Nations. During the oil for food scandal, especially in 2004, the *annus horribilis* of Kofi Annan – as Annan called it in a press conference in December 2004 (cf. *United Nations* 2004) –, France demonstrated more than once its unflinching support for the embattled Secretary-General. In 2006, when it became clear that the United States and China were backing Ban Ki-moon for the post of Secretary-General, France, that had always argued that candidates had to be fluent in the two working languages of the → Secretariat (→ Languages, Working), English and French, hastily delivered a French fluency diploma to Mr. Ban who is still enrolled in a beginner course! In a break with United Nations traditions, in 2008, President Nicolas Sarkozy invited Mr. Ban to be the guest of honor of the national day parade on 14 July to mark the sixtieth anniversary of the Blue Helmets (→ Peacekeeping Forces).

In return, France expected to be given strategic functions at the Secretariat. Since 1997, a French senior official fills the post of Under-Secretary-General for peacekeeping operations. In August 2008, the new incumbent, Ambassador Alain Le Roy took the helm of a department that oversees the operations of about 90 000 peacekeepers in 16 missions.

2. France as a Mover and Shaker in the Security Council

The permanent membership in the Security Council enables France to stand for policies that are its own and may be at variance with the positions of other members of the European Union (→ European Union, Common Foreign and Security Policy at the UN). The Iraqi crisis in 2003 was a case in point. It will be part of the legacy of President Jacques Chirac of France to threaten a French veto (→ Veto, Right of Veto) in the early months of 2003 against a second resolution by the Security Council – after resolution 1441 of 8 November 2002 – authorizing an intervention of the coalition forces led by the USA and Great Britain in Iraq. France's policy contributed to bolstering the determination of the developing countries that were non-permanent members of the Security Council, who were at the time under heavy-handed pressure from the Unites States to vote in favor or at least abstain in the event of the formal consideration of such a text by the Council. France will be remembered for making it impossible for the United Nations to give its blessing to the United States-United Kingdom military intervention in Iraq and for demonstrating that in certain instances the Security Council may adopt stands different from those of the superpower. The event dealt a blow to the appreciation of the United Nations in the United States but improved its image in most of the rest of the world.

With regard to Africa, France has skilfully used its membership in the Security Council to protect its interests while obtaining for its operations the legitimacy that comes with Security Council resolutions. This was the case in 2004 with the Operation Licorne in Côte d'Ivoire (Security Council resolution S/RES/1528 (2004), 27 February 2004, establishing the UN Operation in Côte d'Ivoire (UNOCI) and authorizing the French forces to use all necessary means to support UNOCI) and in 2007 with the deployment of EUFOR Tchad/RCA in Tchad (Security Council resolution S/RES/1778 (2007), 25 September 2007, approving the establishment in Chad of a multidimensional presence, including a European Union operation).

In 2006, at the time of the war in Lebanon, France played an important part in the negotiations at the Security Council that resulted in a significant strengthening of the United Nations Interim Force in Lebanon (UNIFIL) (Security Council resolution S/RES/1701 (2006), 11 August 2006, authorizing an increase in the force strength to a maximum of 15,000 troops). In a departure from a policy that followed the fiascos in former Yugoslavia and Rwanda, to no longer participate massively in United Nations peacekeeping operations, France sent 1900 soldiers to Southern Lebanon as part of UNIFIL. France continues to be a major financial contributor to peacekeeping covering 7 % of its costs.

3. France's Support for the Enlargement of the Security Council

In 2008, President Nicolas Sarkozy stated that he would promote the enlargement of the Security Council by five more permanent members without veto power, Germany, Japan, India, Brazil and a "great African power". The French President is using official visits to pursue this objective, pledging recently for instance French support to the candidacies of India and South Africa. This public diplomacy is a token of France's keen interest in seeing the Council reformed as soon as possible. According to an Indian United Nations expert, Shashi Tharoor, there is another reason for this attitude: "If reform is delayed by another decade, ... the clamour for replacing" the seats of London and Paris "with one permanent European Union seat would mount and could prove irresistible (*Tharoor*, The Times of India, 18 May 2008, "It's essential for Security Council to reform").

4. France and Development Issues

French development programmes continued to be implemented mainly through bilateral or European channels. As a re-

sult, France is playing a junior league role in the United Nations development system (→ Development Cooperation of the UN System), with few nationals represented in the bureau of intergovernmental committees of programmes and funds as well as in their senior staff.

In terms of development orientations, France's policy as articulated at the → General Assembly and at the → Economic and Social Council is aligned with the European Union position. However, during his 12 years presidency, Jacques Chirac launched a few original initiatives that highlighted French enthusiastic commitment to multilateralism as the best tool to advance world solidarity. In 2004, as part of international efforts to find supplementary financing for development, the President started discussion on a solidarity tax on airline tickets to buy drugs for pandemics like AIDS and malaria. The United Nations "took note with interest" of the initiative at the 2005 World Summit (*United Nations* 2005, para. 23d) and UNITAID, the International Drug Purchase Facility, was inaugurated at UN Headquarters in 2006 (see www.unitaid.eu).

The second initiative of the French President, an exploratory discussion on the creation of a UN organization for the environment, was short-lived in face of conflicting national interests and in the absence of political will to agree on common policies (see www.onue.org).

As for international efforts to address climate change, France intends to participate actively in the negotiations of the instrument to succeed the Kyoto Protocol to be concluded in 2009. However, for such international negotiations on trade, development and environment, the major actor remains the European Union with member states' national visibility on the wane.

5. France and the Promotion and Protection of Human Rights

In 2006, France voted in favor of the General Assembly resolution establishing the new Council on Human Rights and confirming Geneva as the human rights hub (UN Doc. A/RES/60/251, 15 March 2006). The same year France was elected on the new 47 members Human Rights Council. While France speaks loudly of the universality of human rights and rejects attempts to give undue weight to national and regional particularities, its voice at the Council is muted by that of the European Union. Members of the Union, whether sitting or not on the Council, consult ahead of debates and adopt a common position advocated later on by their members on the Council. As a result, while criticizing the South for its "bloc logic", the European Union is also perceived by many as a monolithic group.

As part of France's sense of mission in terms of French culture, the country played a key role along with Canada in the adoption by the → UNESCO General Conference on 20 October 2005 of a new Convention on the protection and promotion of the diversity of cultural expressions.

France is an active proponent of the new responsibility to protect civilians, adopted by the 2005 World Summit. In 2008, after the cyclone Nargis devastated Myanmar, it attempted unsuccessfully to have the Security Council invoke this principle to force the junta to open up the country to → humanitarian assistance.

6. Summing up

With Nicolas Sarkozy's presidency, France has abandoned a policy of overreliance on the power of international organizations, and is back to the view that the real power lies with governments. Nevertheless, France is well aware that it entertains with the United Nations a mutually reinforcing relationship. As stated by Foreign Minister Bernard Kouchner on 11 March 2008, French new diplomacy is more practical, multifaceted and realistic (*Kouchner* 2008). In this context, France will continue to insist on the relevance of the United Nations in world affairs and work toward effective multilateralism.

Thérèse Gastaut

Lit.: *Dejammet, A.:* Supplément au voyage en Onusie, Paris 2003; *Kouchner, B.:* Keeping the Peace, in: Le Monde, 11 March 2008, www.ambafrance-uk.org; *Sur, S.:* Le Conseil de sécurité dans l'après 11 septembre, Paris 2004; *United Nations:* Transcript of Press Conference by Secretary-General Kofi Annan at United Nations Headquarters, 21 December 2004, UN Press Release SG/SM/9655, 21/12/2004; *United Nations - General Assembly:* 2005 World Summit Outcome, UN Doc. A/RES/60/1, 16 September 2005; *Védrine, H.:* Rapport pour le Président de la République sur la France et la mondialisation (2007), www.diplomatie.gouv.fr/fr/IMG/pdf/france_mondialisation-3.pdf.

Internet: a) Homepage of the Permanent Mission of France to the United Nations: www.undp.org/missions/france; b) Homepage of the French Foreign Ministry (website on French UN policy): www. france. diplomatie.fr/frmonde/nuoi/index.htm.

UN Policy, German Democratic Republic

The German Democratic Republic (GDR) was a member of the United Nations from 18 September 1973 to 2 October 1990 (→ Membership and Representation of States).

The GDR was admitted by the → General Assembly on the recommendation of the → Security Council under Chapter II, Article 4 of the Charter of the United Nations (→ Charter of the UN), without restrictions being placed on its newly gained membership.

When the United Nations General Assembly at the opening of its 28th session in September 1973, acting on the Security Council's unanimous recommendation and a joint resolution (A/RES/3050 (XXVIII) of 18 September 1973), admitted the two German states, the German Democratic Republic and the Federal Republic of Germany (FRG), by acclamation as members no. 133 and 134, the event was welcomed internationally, and especially in Europe, as a success of progressing politics of détente, and as a significant development in of international cooperation.

United States Ambassador Scali noted on this occasion that the entry of the two

German States was a culmination of diplomacy inside and outside the United Nations, in which process all the sides had come to recognize the realities of today's world (cf. GAOR, 28th session, 2111 7th plenary meeting).

The representative of the Soviet Union, Y. Malik, stated that the event was one of truly historic importance in the evolution of post-war international relations in Europe and the world at large, and in the history of the United Nations (cf. GAOR, loc. cit.). GDR Foreign Minister Otto Winzer pledged the GDR's unreserved support for the purposes of the United Nations, and assured the Assembly of his government's willingness to engage in constructive co-operation (cf. GAOR, loc. cit.).

For the international community of states, the membership of both German states appeared to have settled "the German question". Today, the GDR's past membership can only be reviewed against the background of how international relations had been developing, especially in the years since 1949. After World War II and subsequently, hegemonic global politics had produced a dual German statehood in an antagonistic East-West bloc setting. It was therefore logical that the two German states would become members of the United Nations with the marks of the same East-West divide. With contrasting contents and objectives and firmly anchored in the antagonistic blocs with their ideological confrontation, these two memberships formed part of the balance of interests and of the interaction of forces on the international stage at that time. It is noteworthy that the two German states were the only ones of the nations divided after World War II, who could join the United Nations during the era of the East-West confrontation. Situated right in the center of Europe, both were considered to be an important, and indeed dependable factor for either side's international strength, political and military doctrines and current interests in the 1960s and 1970s, so that their membership in this most important international organization came to be accept-

able. UN membership placed both states on an equal footing. For the GDR, it completed the world-wide recognition it had long been seeking. Bilaterally, co-operation at the UN opened up avenues and areas for a constructive relationship between the two states in the Organization, certainly with the understanding that each other's partnerships or bloc affiliation would be duly observed.

As to how the UN figured in their mutual relationship, it is enlightening to note what Foreign Minister Genscher (FRG) said in an interview on 30 September 1988: that the two German states shared an identity of positions on a number of issues on the UN's agenda. And they were agreed, he added, that problems which the Federal Republic of Germany would have to argue and resolve with the German Democratic Republic should better be handled under their Treaty on Basic Relations than on the stage of the UN, because "at the UN there would be a great deal of prestige involved ... whereas we are interested in a businesslike approach to resolving the problems." (quotes translated from *Bruns* 1988)

I. Policy Objectives and Fields of Action

The policy concept of the GDR, similar to the then-current Soviet approach, saw the UN both as an international tribune and as a door to wide-ranging opportunities for scientific, technological and cultural exchanges which the multilateral Organization would offer. At the time when the two Germanys were being admitted to the UN, the shapes of cooperation at diverse levels and on a diversity of matters were beginning to emerge in Europe. These subsequently took full shape in the CSCE process, and brought forth an awareness that international and regional cooperation meant not just struggle between the systems, but also trade, scientific and cultural exchange, and participation in discussions on problems in public health, communications, environmental protection, radio frequency assignment, technology transfer, standardization, codification of international law, all of which

771

were of common interest to all the countries, regardless of their political system.

Basic to the conduct of the GDR at the UN was its philosophy to use foreign policy potentials for the governance and maintenance of its own purposes, and to influence the changing international environment in keeping with its own interests – an aim which in fact all nations of the world pursue in international relations. Its dominant focus in this context was on working towards an international environment of peace for its own existence and development.

Naturally, there were specific factors weighing on the policy of the GDR. Firstly, there was its subordination to the Soviet policy in Europe with its hegemonic claims. There was also of course the interaction between the two German states as a main stage of the East-West confrontation over more than forty years. Although being adversaries, the two states were bound up with each other and constantly interacting, for better or for worse.

What needs further to be taken into account is the fact that the international significance of their existence and of their mutual relationship constituted the international component of the German question, as it involved the interests of the other European nations, as well as those of the USA and the USSR. What appeared feasible or unfeasible in the relationship between the Federal Republic of Germany and the German Democratic Republic was always an indicator of either positive or negative developments in world politics. And, finally, there were contradictions between the GDR's domestic and its external policies, which restricted the scope for independent action in the conduct of its foreign relations.

The GDR acquired a status of considerable acceptance at the UN. Quite rightly, Wilhelm Bruns in 1988 noted in the journal *Vereinte Nationen* published in Bonn: "A continuous recording and analysis of their voting behavior makes us realize that the GDR needs much less seldom to deviate from the majority than the Federal Republic of Germany."

His summary: "All in all, East Berlin's policy at the UN can sooner be judged as conforming with the majority than Bonn's policy." (translated by the author from: *Bruns* 1988) Throughout the 17 years of its membership, the GDR was an engaged actor in the UN's various major activities in the political field. It spoke up for observing and strengthening the 1969 Treaty on the Non-proliferation of Nuclear Weapons (NPT), and supported or sponsored resolutions on nuclear → disarmament. It submitted draft resolutions on the non-use of nuclear weapons, the cessation of the nuclear arms race, nuclear disarmament, and the prohibition of neutron nuclear weapons, which were adopted by the General Assembly.

The GDR called for negotiations to ban nuclear weapon tests and to start nuclear disarmament, and this stance met with approval from the non-aligned and neutral countries. And when the two superpowers resumed their talks on disarmament in the 1980s, the GDR approved of this development explicitly. That was the time when the Warsaw Pact changed its position on the verification of compliance issue, and subsequently the GDR supported efforts, co-sponsored by the Federal Republic of Germany, to have agreed guidelines for confidence-building and transparency. The breakthrough on the verification issue had the greatest effect on the ongoing negotiations on banning chemical weapons – a matter which the GDR considered to be of high priority.

In that period the GDR and the Federal Republic, together with Czechoslovakia, launched an initiative for a chemical-weapon-free zone in Europe as a forerunner for a world-wide ban. Although a resolution to this end at the UN was not directly supported by the Federal Republic, the move was of consequence in so far as representatives of the three countries since 1984 held periodic consultations on the chemical weapons problem. Negotiations on the conclusion of a convention banning chemical weapons are known to have led to success in 1992, under the chairmanship of a German diplomat.

As far as UN activities on economic matters are concerned, the GDR played a major part in the drafting of the final documents at the 1974 General Assembly's Special Session on the establishment of a New International Economic Order (→ International Economic Relations and the New International Economic Order (NIEO). The GDR also participated, from the beginning, in the special committee charged with preparing a code of conduct for transnational corporations, and held the committee's chairmanship for a number of years. In the UN Economic Commission for Europe (→ Economic Commissions, Regional) it co-sponsored resolutions on eliminating obstacles to trade, establishing a system of European inland waterways, modernizing traffic rules, and creating guidelines to avoid and control environmental pollution.

The GDR was prominently engaged in efforts related to colonialism (→ Decolonization). Every year it sponsored draft resolutions, mostly together with African representatives, and thus had a considerable standing with countries of the so-called Third World. It took a dedicated stance as a member of the Committee against Apartheid. The GDR earned international credit for its engagement in the implementation of the UN Plan for Namibia, which was co-authored by the Federal Republic of Germany. In 1989, Namibia was the first country to receive contingents from both German states in UNTAG, the UN peacekeeping mission (→ Peacekeeping; → Peacekeeping Forces; → History of the UN).

The GDR provided modest contributions to the UN voluntary development aid programmes (→ Development Cooperation of the UN System). Like all the Eastern European countries, it preferred bilateral channels for the bulk of its assistance for Asian, African and Latin American states. Therefore, the GDR's share in 1988 in the UN voluntary aid programmes with an equivalent of 2.6 million US dollars in national currency was just 0.1% of the total sum of those programmes.

On several occasions the GDR had the issue of neo-fascism placed on the UN agenda. It is noteworthy that the General Assembly, taking up a GDR proposal, declared 8 and 9 May 1985 as days of commemorating the victory over nazism and fascism in World War II, and of fighting neo-fascist phenomena.

The GDR was periodically represented on UN organs (→ Principal Organs, Subsidiary Organs, Treaty Bodies) under the rule of rotation. The Federal Republic of Germany and the GDR agreed not to obstruct the election of representatives one or the other of them would nominate. Each supported the election of the other into the Security Council, and of each of the other's nominee for the General Assembly presidency. In 1980/81 the GDR served as a non-permanent member on the Security Council, and GDR Deputy Foreign Minister Peter Florin was elected president of the 42nd General Assembly session in 1987.

The GDR considered that the UN Conferences on the Law of the Sea, held consecutively from 1974 to 1983 (→ Law of the Sea), were very important. As a member of the group of "land locked and geographically disadvantaged states", and having quite a few interests in common with other such members, which were frequently dissimilar to those of the big coastal states (including the USSR), it tried to look after its own interests as much as it could. It supported the Federal Republic of Germany's request to have the International Tribunal for the Law of the Sea (→ ITLOS) seated in Hamburg.

Concerning → human rights, the GDR one-sidedly emphasized the economic and social ones. Its draft resolutions on the indivisibility and interdependence of economic, social, cultural, civil and political rights were endorsed by the General Assembly. Existing deficits in the GDR's human rights practice were hinted at every now and then, but were not seen as a ground for condemnation or for instituting any kind of fact-finding procedures.

In the final phase of the GDR's existence, the de Maizière Government continued to pursue an active policy vis-à-vis the UN. In the foreign policy chapter of his inaugural speech Prime Minister Lothar de Maizière explicitly pledged a continued international policy in accordance with the UN Charter. (cf. *Maizière* 1990, 210 ff.)

II. End of the UN Membership of the GDR

The GDR Government decided to discontinue the country's membership of the UN and the related intergovernmental agencies as from 3 October 1990. In a letter dated 27 September 1990 and handed over to UN Secretary-General Pérez de Cuéllar, the GDR Government declared that due to accession to the territory of the Basic Law of the Federal Republic of Germany under its Article 23, the prerequisites under international law for a continuation of the GDR's memberships had ceased to exist. Lothar de Maizière underlined his confidence that the united Germany, as the single German member of the UN, would remain dedicated to the provisions of the Charter in the spirit of the formal declarations of both German states of 12 June 1973 (cf. *Maizière* 1990, 157).

Foreign Minister Hans-Dietrich Genscher assured the UN Secretary-General in a letter dated 3 October 1990 that by the German Democratic Republic's accession to the Federal Republic of Germany on 3 October 1990 both German states formed a single sovereign state which, as a member of the United Nations, remained committed to the provisions of the Charter in the same way as stated in the formal declaration of 12 June 1973.

Since then, the Federal Republic of Germany has chosen the shorter version "Germany" as the country's name at the UN (→ UN Policy, Germany). Addressing the General Assembly at its 45th session, Foreign Minister Genscher stated that the united Germany having a bigger weight, it would not aspire to gain "more power", but be mindful of its "greater responsibility". (translated from the German original version in: *Auswärtiges Amt* 1995, 207ff.).

III. Four Phases of GDR Policy vis-à-vis the UN

The GDR's policy vis-à-vis the UN can be divided into four chronological phases: The first (1949-1955) may be described as one of "forced standoffishness". The second extended from 1955 to 1966 and saw some participatory activities practiced, particularly in subsidiary organs like the Economic Commission for Europe, in spite of the impact of the Hallstein Doctrine. The third phase was marked by the first request for admission in 1966 and reached up to 1972/73. The fourth phase began with the GDR's admission to membership and lasted until 1990.

Concerning the phases of the GDR's policy towards the UN, Wilhelm Bruns (*Bruns* 1988) asked the question when they began. At what moment was it appropriate to speak of a GDR policy vis-à-vis the UN? As early as the founding of the GDR (1949); with the Soviet Union's declaration vesting sovereignty in the GDR (1955); when majority relations changed in the UN General Assembly (1960), with the GDR's first application for membership (1966), or later, when the GDR became a member of UNESCO (1972)? Bruns gives four reasons for seeing the year 1960 as the initial moment: (1) Since that year the GDR had continually presented statements, stressing its legitimate right to membership. (2) The programme and the statutes of the Socialist Unity Party (SED) of 1963 formulated, for the first time, a claim to UN membership. (3) The early 1960s saw signs of the GDR's will to seek and face a decision on its international status, which led to its first application for membership in 1966. (4) In the GDR itself, the year 1960 was seen to have ushered in an all-embracing policy towards the UN (cf. *Steininger* 1964).

In the first phase of its UN policy, the GDR was seeking to obtain the membership of UN → specialized agencies. In 1952, the Soviet Control Commission for Germany supported the GDR's effort to achieve membership of the Universal Postal Union (→ UPU), somewhat later of the International Telecommunication Union (→ ITU) and, in 1953, of the World Meteorological Organization (→ WMO) (cf. *Dokumente zur Aussenpolitik der DDR,* Vol.1, 1966, 360 ff.). Starting in 1947, experts from the four zones of occupation in Germany took part in the Universal Postal Congresses as experts under the aegis of the Occupying Powers. The same happened at the Congress in Brussels in 1952 (cf. *Sasse* 1959, 13). Since 1947 the four zones of occupation, later the Federal Republic and the GDR, paid to the UPU portions of the membership contribution incumbent on Germany, 70 per cent and 30 per cent respectively. Pursuant to Article XIX of the Final Act of the Universal Postal Convention, an easier procedure of admission was established with respect to Germany's membership of the UPU. Accession was to be notified to the Belgian Government, which would then inform the other UPU members. The GDR Government, with backing from the Soviet Control Commission for Germany, transmitted to Belgium as the depositary state its declaration of accession to the UPU on 11 February 1955. The Belgian Government accepted the declaration, but did not circulate it. When, however, the Federal Republic of Germany declared its accession on 21 March 1955, Belgium notified this accession to all the other UPU members.

In the second phase of its policy towards the UN, the GDR attempted to achieve membership in → UNESCO → ILO and the ITU, and was anxious to become involved in the discussion of specific European economic and related matters in the Economic Commission for Europe.

The third phase was essentially characterized by the GDR Government's first application for admission to the UN in 1966. This application by the GDR came as a surprise to some quarters (cf.

Frankfurter Allgemeine Zeitung, 3 March 1966): "East Berlin's move has caused surprise in New York." However, the timing of the application should have been viewed as a logical consequence of the claims to UN membership which the GDR had been voicing over the years (cf. Statement by the Ministry of Foreign Affairs in: *Foreign Affairs Bulletin* (FAB) 38/60: "Claim to cooperation within the UN justified"; Statement of the Foreign Affairs Committee of the People's Chamber, 26 November 1962, in: *FAB* 46/62; article in *Neues Deutschland* (28 July 1962) on Khrushchev's visit to Berlin; "GDR Foreign Minister Lothar Bolz pleads for admission of both German states to the UN at the 9th People's Chamber session on 19 November 1964" in: *Neues Deutschland,* 20 November 1964).

In the memorandum substantiating its request for admission, the GDR derived the legitimacy of its right to membership (cf. *Dokumente zur Aussenpolitik der DDR,* Vol. 1, 1966, 650-652) from the United Nations principle of → universality and from the requirements stipulated in Article 4 of the UN Charter.

The United States, the United Kingdom and France intervened and prevented the request from being placed on the agenda of the Security Council. It was clear that the request would anyway have foundered on the veto of the Western permanent members (→ Veto, Right of Veto). Since the President of the Security Council refused to disseminate the application document because of the contested state quality of the GDR, Secretary-General U Thant had it forwarded informally to the members of the Security Council, and the three Western permanent members then declared in a letter that the "Soviet Zone" was not a free state and, therefore, had no legal right to UN membership (translated by the author from: *Czempiel* 1985, 185 ff.).

Following this application, discussions about UN membership for Germany intensified, preparing the ground for the admission of both German states later. Characteristic of this phase was what Walter Gehlhoff, the Federal Republic of Germany's Permanent Representative (→ Permanent Missions) from 1971 to 1974, said: "My predecessors always had to watch most closely that the GDR was not possibly recognized by the United Nations. This task still mattered during my term of assignment. But it was ... a fighting retreat." (translated from *Gehlhoff* 1991, 21).

Bernhard Neugebauer

Lit.: *Auswärtiges Amt (ed.):* Deutschland in den Vereinten Nationen, 2nd edn., Bonn 1995; *Brecht, E. et al.:* Kaum miteinander, selten gegeneinander, meist nebeneinander, in: VN 41 (1993), 1251-32; *Bruns, W.:* Die UNO-Politik der DDR, 2nd edn., Stuttgart 1980; *Bruns, W.:* Die Uneinigen in den Vereinten Nationen. Bundesrepublik Deutschland und die DDR in der UNO, 2nd edn., Cologne 1981; *Bruns, W.:* Vom Nebeneinander zum Miteinander? Bundesrepublik Deutschland und Deutsche Demokratische Republik 15 Jahre nach dem UN-Beitritt, in: VN 36 (1988), 141-146; *Czempiel, E.-O.:* Deutschland und die Vereinten Nationen, in: VN 33 (1985), 185-190; *Gehlhoff, W.:* Der Weg der Bundesrepublik Deutschland in die Vereinten Nationen, in: Deutsche Gesellschaft für die Vereinten Nationen (ed.): Die Vereinten Nationen und deutsche Politik – aus persönlicher Sicht. Deutsche UN-Botschafter berichten, Bonn 1991, 18-39; *Maizière, L. de:* Regierungserklärung des Ministerpräsidenten der DDR vor der Volkskammer. Protokoll der Volkskammer der DDR, April 1990, 210-212 (quoted as: *Maizière* 1990a); *Maizière, L. de:* Schreiben des Ministerpräsidenten der DDR an den Generalsekretär der Vereinten Nationen, reprinted in: VN 38 (1990), 157 (quoted as: *Maizière* 1990b); *Ministerium für Auswärtige Angelegenheiten der DDR (ed.):* Dokumente zur Außenpolitik der DDR, Vol. 1, Berlin 1966; *Rittberger, V.:* Die beiden deutschen Staaten in den Vereinten Nationen, in: Deutsche Gesellschaft für die Vereinten Nationen (ed.): Die beiden deutschen Staaten in den Vereinten Nationen, Bonn 1990, 5-20; *Sasse, H.:* Der Weltpostverein, Frankfurt (Main) 1959; *Steininger, P.A.:* UNO-Bilanz 1964, Dresden 1964.

Addendum

Lit: *Bock, S. et al. (eds):* Alternative deutsche Außenpolitik? DDR-Außenpolitik im Rückspiegel (II), Münster/Hamburg 2006; *Deutsche Gesellschaft für die Vereinten Nationen (ed.):* „Kaum Miteinander, selten gegeneinander, meist nebeneinander." Zur Politik der beiden deutschen Staaten in den Vereinten Nationen. Workshop der DGVN und des Verbands für Internationale Politik und Völkerrecht VIP am 17. Oktober 2006 in Berlin (DGVN Blaue Reihe, No. 102), Berlin 2007; *Göthel, D.:* Die Vereinten Nationen. Eine Innenansicht, 2nd rev. edn., Berlin 2002; *Knapp, W.:* Eine erfolgreiche Emanzipation. Drei Jahrzehnte deutsche Mitgliedschaft in den Vereinten Nationen, in: VN 51 (2003), 207-214; *Neugebauer, B.:* Zur Mitgliedschaft der beiden deutschen Staaten in der UNO (Schriften zur Internationalen Politik, H. 8 (2006), ed. Verband für Internationale Politik und Völkerrecht e.V., Berlin 2006.

UN Policy, Germany

Germany and later Japan were the reason for the foundation of the United Nations. It was founded on grounds of the experiences of World War II, provoked by Germany, and founded by those 50 states that had declared war on Germany. This origin found its expression in the → enemy state clauses of the UN Charter (Articles 53 and 107) (→ Charter of the UN). These had become obsolete for Germany since 1973 at the latest, when the Federal Republic of Germany and the GDR (→ UN Policy, German Democratic Republic) were admitted to the United Nations as "peace-loving states which accept the obligations contained in the present Charter and, in the judgment of the Organization, are able and willing to carry out these obligations". (Art. 4 UN Charter)

I. The Relationship between Germany and the UN

The relationship between Germany and the United Nations developed in three phases to its present state:

1. Period I: 1945-1949

In the few first years between the end of World War II in 1945, and the foundation of both the Federal Republic of Germany and the German Democratic Republic (GDR) in 1949, the defeated and occupied Germany was partly an object of the United Nations. The UN Relief and Rehabilitation Administration (UNRRA), already founded during the emergence of the UN in 1943, for the purpose of repatriating people deported by Germany, together with other similar UN organizations in charge of this group of people (→ UNHCR) and the organization for the protection of children (→ UNICEF), were already at work on the territory of Germany governed by the occupation powers.

The division of Germany being a concomitant of the Cold War became a topic of the United Nations twice. In 1948/1949, the → Security Council dealt with the Berlin Blockade by the Soviet Union, but did not reach any decision because of a veto by the latter. The Berlin Blockade was ended by direct negotiations between the USA and the Soviet Union (→ History of the UN).

Two years later, during the Cold War that was now leaving its mark on European politics already in a specific way, the Federal Republic and the three Western occupation powers asked the → General Assembly to examine the holding of free elections for a German National Assembly in all four occupation zones. The undertaking ended in 1952 when the examining board established by the General Assembly was refused entry into the GDR. From then on, the division of Germany was no longer a topic for the UN. Moreover, the Federal Republic and its allies developed the common policy of not letting the German division become a UN topic because of the imponderabilities connected with it.

2. Period II: 1949-1973

In the second period, lasting from the foundation of the Federal Republic and the GDR (1949) to the accession of both German states to the United Nations (1973), German relations with the UN were matter of concern for the Federal Republic only.

Directly after its foundation, the Federal Republic put its interest in a speedy admission to international organizations. Furthermore, its foundation was part of the integration of West Germany into Western Europe and the North Atlantic Treaty Organization (NATO). Article 24 of the Basic (Constitutional) Law, the German Constitution, which declares that the Federal Republic is allowed to "join a system of mutual and collective security" under the condition of restricting its rights of sovereignty by transferring "rights of sovereignty to intergovernmental institutions", was placed in the constitution with the United Nations forming the background as the then only existing system of that kind (→ Collective Security), and against the background of the newly forming military alliance of the NATO. In the Deutschlandvertrag (German Contract) of 1954 which ended the regime of the occupation powers and prepared the accession of the Federal Republic to NATO, the Federal Republic obliged itself "to conduct its politics in accordance with the principles of the United Nations".

In the first years of the Federal Republic, when the major objective of its foreign policy was to re-enter the international community of peoples, the United Nations was generally seen as a kind of a higher institution and court of appeal. In important declarations relating to international affairs in the Bundestag (Lower House of the German Federal Parliament) and on other occasions one referred explicitly to the "purposes and principles of the United Nations".

Even before its accession to the European Council (1951), which was important for its European policy, the Federal Republic had already been admitted in 1950 to one of the large → specialized agencies: the Food and Agricultural Organization (→ FAO). Thanks to the support of its allies, the Federal Republic was in 1952 able to establish an observer mission (→ Observer Status) at the United Nations (like Switzerland and the Holy See), which was then dominated by the Western countries until the emergence of the Third World in the 1960s. In 1954 a further observer mission was established at the second UN office in Geneva (→ UN Office Geneva).

In 1955, six years after its foundation and at the time when it obtained its – restricted – sovereignty and joined NATO, the Federal Republic of Germany had become a member of all specialized agencies, such as the cultural organization → UNESCO, the health organization → WHO and the labour organization → ILO. Moreover, it was a member of those special organs directly related to the General Assembly, such as the children's organization → UNICEF and the organization for refugees → UNHCR, which was less important to the Federal Republic with regard to the topics dealt there, but more so with regard to UN policy in general. The UN membership of the Federal Republic at that time (→ Membership and Representation of States) differed from a full membership only in that it was neither a member of the General Assembly nor of the Security Council.

The Federal Republic used its UN membership somewhat with restraint until German reunification in 1990. Its UN policy was not an unimportant, but a subordinate component of its foreign policy. In contrast to the former European colonial powers (→ Decolonization), there did not exist any historically conditioned guidelines to world politics for the Federal Republic. Furthermore, during Cold War integration in the Western bloc had taken priority for the UN policy of the Federal Republic, as it had for all its other political considerations. German UN policy, too, was not predominantly national in view of the international position of the Federal Republic at this time, but was integrated into the policy of the Western European Union (EU) and that of the Western European-American alliance.

Within this framework, the Federal Republic conducted a UN policy that was often and accurately called the policy of an "active non-membership", until its full UN membership in 1973.

Within this policy framework the Federal Republic gained in a certain way reputation and political weight, just because it did not represent any specific national demands or interests (as the former European colonial powers did), and did not develop any ambitions in world and power politics since, although it was member of all UN organizations, it was not a member of the two organs being primarily concerned with power politics, the General Assembly and the Security Council.

The only, in the classical sense of the word, "national" goal of the then foreign policy and thus of the UN policy of the Federal Republic was the assertion of the "claim for the right of exclusive representation", i.e. the claim to be the only legitimate German state. To do justice to this goal, the Federal Republic had to prevent states other than communist states from recognizing the GDR under international law. The means for this end was the "Hallstein Doctrine", named after the then secretary of state of German Federal Foreign Office. This doctrine stated that the Federal Republic would immediately break off diplomatic relations with any state that recognized the GDR under international law. The doctrine constituted the core element of the foreign policy of the old Federal Republic. Accordingly, it established diplomatic relations even with the smallest and most distant states founded in the period of decolonization, and was – in contrast to many other states – present with embassies in those states.

The objective of this policy within the UN was to prevent the GDR from entering UN organizations. The prevention of a majority in favor of an admission of the GDR turned out to be more complicated than the prevention of the diplomatic recognition of the GDR by single states. Nevertheless, the undertaking was successful until shortly before the admission of both German states as full members of the United Nations (1973). The foundation for the implementation of the Hallstein Doctrine was the rigid confrontation between the Eastern and the Western bloc, the limited opportunities of the GDR and of the other Eastern bloc countries outside their bloc, and the economic possibilities of the Federal Republic.

3. Period III: 1973-1990

The third phase, lasting to the present, was formed by the 17 years of UN membership of the two German states (1973-90). It was a result and consequence, respectively, of the Ostpolitik and the policy of the détente introduced by the CDU-CSU-SPD government (1966-69) and carried out by the SPD-FDP government (1969-82).

The double German UN membership was preceded by the revision of the Hallstein Doctrine and by the Treaty on the Basis of Relations between the two German states (1972). Already in 1967, the Federal Republic had entered diplomatic relations with communist Romania. In 1968, it re-established the diplomatic relations with Yugoslavia, which had been broken off in accordance with the Hallstein Doctrine in 1957 when Yugoslavia had established relations with the GDR. The intensity of this break in the foreign policy of the Federal Republic was still evident, when the Treaty on the Basis of Relations was ratified and the admission of the GDR to the UNESCO was to come: the Federal Republic fought at that point in time vehemently and successfully against the admission of the GDR to the World Health Organization (WHO).

All in all, the claim for sole representation of the Federal Republic had limited the room for manoeuvre within the UN. It had led to a certain "self-tying" in foreign politics, and had even left the Federal Republic open to blackmail. Furthermore, there had been frequently been high political and economic cost to be paid to its Western allies, and sometimes to Third World countries, for the maintenance of this policy.

The 17-year-long German double role, with two equal German member states at the UN (1973-90), was neutral regarding German policy. Neither of the two German states attempted to force the world organization to deal with what was considered still as the "German Question" after the conclusion of the German-German Treaty on the Basis of Relations (1972). The international community of states regarded this question as settled after the admission of the two German states to the United Nations. Neither of the two German states differed in any respect from other UN members. For instance, they took over rotationally the chairmanship in the General Assembly (the Federal Republic in 1980, the GDR in 1987) and in all other bodies, as did all UN member states.

The phase of East-West détente in the first half of the 1970s, which had made possible the consensus of the Eastern and Western states on the admission of both German states to the UN, facilitated also a German-German co-existence within the UN. Of course, the positions of the two German states remained conditioned by their affiliation to the Eastern and the Western blocs, respectively, in accordance with the then-prevailing bloc situation. The position of the Federal Republic was conditioned in this way to a lesser extent, that of the GDR to a larger extent.

The Federal Republic as a full member with improved status, continued indeed with the whole spectrum of UN activities, just as it had already done as an "active non-member". The GDR took part in the UN in a rather selective manner. It avoided some organizations, such as the World Bank Group (→ World Bank, World Bank Group), for ideological reasons; it avoided others, like development organizations, because of its lack of foreign exchange.

The different positions of both German states were clearly shown in their voting behavior, especially in the General Assembly. The voting of the Federal Republic was permanently characterized by a doubled consideration: first, by the consideration for the Western bloc and the transatlantic alliance, and second, by the consideration for the

East-political connections resulting from its position at the interface between East and West. This frequently led to abstentions (which occasionally were called the typical "German vote" in a friendly and mocking tone, by some of their allies).

On the other hand, the GDR, tied to the strict East bloc discipline, found itself with its voting behavior within the mainstream of opinion-forming in the General Assembly, which was marked by the prevalence of the East bloc states and – as mentioned before – by majorities of the Third World states in the 1970s and the first half of the 1980s.

The relations between both German representations in the organizations of the UN were correct but insubstantial, as they were between the two embassies in third countries. It says something about this relationship that only the initiative of the Federal Republic, the GDR and Austria for the establishment of a German Translation Bureau (→ German Translation Section) in the → Secretariat can be quoted as example of the then German-German common interest.

With its full UN membership, with its attitude of taking the German question out of international politics and with its initiatives related to its East-policy, the Federal Republic had enlarged its room for manoeuvre in foreign policy in general and specifically in UN matters. This was both despite of *and* because of its unchanged continuing integration into the European Community (EC) and NATO. It made use of this situation in combining the continuing lack of its own national power with the power factors of NATO and the EC. The Federal Republic compensated its power deficits by the fact that, as a member of EC and NATO, it had "something behind it".

With this policy it went along with the line of foreign policy of the smaller member states of the EC and NATO, however, its legitimization was more convincing due to the higher potentials it contributed to the EC and NATO. In accordance with this line of policy the Federal Republic made intensive use in the United Nations of the opportunities

of the European Political Co-operation (EPC) of the EC member states, today called Common Foreign and Security Policy (CFSP) (→ European Union, Common Foreign and Security Policy at the UN). The CFSP had been established in 1970, simultaneously with the German-German Treaty on the Basis of Relations (Grundlagenvertrag), the activation of the German Ostpolitik, and the admission of both German states to the UN.

II. The UN Policy after the German Reunification in 1990

The UN policy of the unified Germany in its entirety stands in the continuity of the foreign policy of the former Federal Republic. A new component of power politics, however, has been added since the reunification. According to the principle that a larger Germany is willing to assume greater international responsibilities, the unified Germany strove for a permanent seat on the UN Security Council and started to make use of its military power to serve political purposes. Both new components are interrelated, and both have been very controversial in Germany.

The demand for a permanent German seat on the Security Council was expressed in the forty-second session of the General Assembly in September 1992, within the framework of the beginning of discussions about the → reform of the UN in the run-up to the 50th anniversary of the UN (1995). The demand was justified by the argument that Germany is the third-largest payer of contributions to the UN (→ Budget) and a "natural candidate" for a permanent seat on the Security Council, comparable to Japan striving also for a permanent seat on the Council (→ UN-Policy, Japan).

Accordingly, the German participation in the reform debate served more to pursue this demand, than to promote the reform. This however met little response in the European Union. As to the UN reform, this German policy was rather more obstructive than beneficial. At the beginning of 1998, the discussion about the historically first technical amendment of the UN Charter regarding the establishment of two permanent seats for Germany and Japan in the Security Council, almost slowed down to zero. The unified Germany gradually participated to an increasing extent in military missions in the framework of the UN, in particular in Somalia and in the former Yugoslavia (1993).

In 1994, the Bundesverfassungsgericht (Federal Constitutional Court) decided that such military missions serving not the self-defense of the state, but political purposes, are constitutional according to Article 24 of the Grundgesetz (German Federal Constitution), provided that they are based on a mandate of the Security Council and on a decision of the Bundestag (German Federal Parliament)(→ Peacekeeping; → Peacekeeping Operations; → Peacekeeping Forces).

In parallel, Germany supported as a NATO member the new NATO policy which it had pursued under the leadership of the USA since the Gulf War (1990/91). This new NATO strategy (1991) expressed a political will to act more independently, and finally even without any mandate of the UN Security Council. The Kosovo War was fought by the 19 NATO states right from the beginning outside the framework of the United Nations, and in particular without a mandate of the Security Council. As UN members, the coalition members violated the international law of the UN Charter; moreover, Germany violated its own constitutional law.

The coalition government of SPD and Bündnis90/Die Grünen, in office since 1998, seems unwilling to pursue any longer the demand for a permanent seat in the UN Security Council. It participated in the NATO war against Serbia, but it was the first government of the NATO member states with an initiative to lead crisis management back into the framework of the United Nations.

Hans Arnold

Lit.: *Albrecht, U.:* Deutschland und die Vereinten Nationen, in: Hüfner, K. (ed.): Die Reform der Vereinten Nationen, Opladen 1994, 253-271; *Arnold, H.:* Deutschlands Größe – Deutsche Außenpolitik zwischen Macht und Mangel, Munich 1995; *Auswärtiges Amt:* 25 Jahre Mitgliedschaft Deutschlands in den Vereinten Nationen, Bonn 1998; *Brecht, E./Florin, P./Weyel, V.:* Kaum miteinander, selten gegeneinander, meist nebeneinander. Ein Gespräch über die Zeit der deutschen Zweistaatlichkeit in den Vereinten Nationen, in: VN 41 (1993), 125-132; *Bruns, W.:* Vom Nebeneinander zum Miteinander? Bundesrepublik Deutschland und Deutsche Demokratische Republik 15 Jahre nach dem UN-Beitritt, in: VN 36 (1988), 141-146; *Könitzer, B./Martens, J. (eds.):* UN-williges Deutschland – der WEED-Report zur deutschen UNO-Politik, Bonn 1997; *Tomuschat, C.:* Deutschland und die Vereinten Nationen, in: Kaiser, K./Krause, J. (eds.): Deutschlands neue Außenpolitik, Vol. 3, Munich 1996, 97-106; *Unser, G.:* Die UNO Aufgaben und Strukturen der Vereinten Nationen (Chapter 8: Deutschland und die Vereinten Nationen), 6th edn., Munich 1997; *Volger, H.:* Geschichte der Vereinten Nationen, Munich/Vienna 1995; *van Well, G.:* Germany and the United Nations, in: Wolfrum, R. (ed.): United Nations: Law, Policies and Practice, Vol. 1, Munich/Dordrecht 1995, 558-566.

Addendum

I. UN Policy during the Schröder/ Fischer Government (1998-2005)

Hans Arnold has rightly stated in the preceding entry that the German Schröder/Fischer coalition government had not been in the first years after taking office in 1998 very much interested in pursuing with greater diplomatic efforts the demand for a permanent seat on the Security Council in the context of a widely demanded reform of this principal organ: Thus in their coalition agreement of 1998 the SPD and the Alliance 90/The Greens had formulated rather reservedly: "Germany will make use of the possibility of becoming a permanent member of the Security Council of the United Nations when the reform with regard to greater regional balance has been finished and if before then the principally preferred European seat in the Security Council cannot be attained" [translation of the author] Only reluctantly the Government showed more interest in a candidacy for a permanent seat. On the occasion of his first speech at the UN General Assembly in September 1999 Foreign Minister Fischer slightly increased the political weight of his demand, while still avoiding the direct claim for a permanent seat: "Reform [of the Security Council, H.V.] must involve enlargement to include both more permanent and non-permanent members ... As the Assembly knows, Germany has for some time now expressed its willingness to assume more and lasting responsibility. We stand by this unreservedly." (UN Doc. A/54/PV.8, 12)

In 2000, the German government changed its position more clearly in its statements at the United Nations: Chancellor Schröder affirmed in his speech at the UN Millennium Summit in early September 2000 explicitly the German interest in a permanent seat, but still avoided the appearance of a claim, emphasizing instead the willingness to take over the responsibility: "The Council must become both more efficient and more representative. Should the numbers of permanent members be increased, Germany would be prepared to shoulder this responsibility." (UN Doc. A/55/PV.3, 6 September 2000, 35)

Foreign Minister Fischer repeated in his speech during the General Debate of the General Assembly on 14 September 2000 the claim only indirectly in quoting his chancellor: "Last week Chancellor Schroeder reaffirmed Germany's willingness to take on more responsibility in this connection." (UN Doc. A/55/PV.14, 17). This does not sound a very self-confident claim, but more like a modest one.

To give the German hitherto rather low profile in its UN policy more contours, Chancellor Schroeder and Minister Fischer supported in their speeches explicitly the implementation of Secretary-General Annan's concept of a "Global Compact (UN Doc. A/55/PV.3, 35 and PV.14, 15, respectively) as well as the implementation of the Millen-

nium Development Goals (UN Doc. A/55/PV.3, 35 and PV.14, 14, respectively) to improve by 2015 the living conditions for the majority of people in a large number of states in the Third World, contained in the Millennium Declaration which was adopted at the end of the Millennium Summit. And both politicians supported – in marked contrast to the fierce opposition of the US administration – the early entry into force of the Statute of the International Criminal Court (→ ICC) (Schröder: UN Doc. A/PV.55/3, 35; Fischer: A/PV.55/ 14, 15). Fischer referred in his speech even indirectly, but clearly discernibly to the diplomatic fight of the US administration against the ICC: "I call upon all States to respect the integrity of the Statute of the International Criminal Court, to sign and to ratify it ...", alluding at the US attempts to keep states from signing the Statute by threatening to curtail their development assistance and/or military aid.

In subsequent years the German government, actively supported by bilateral diplomatic efforts, the further signing of the Statute by UN member states and after the entry into force in 2002 the setting-up of the ICC in The Hague, in providing the new court with staff and financial resources. This engagement in support of the ICC in spite of the US opposition enhanced Germany's political reputation among numerous UN member states.

1) The Attitude towards the Wars in Afghanistan 2001 and in Iraq 2003

The same clear-cut attitude showed the German government with regard to the wars in Afghanistan – to a lesser degree – and in the Iraq with great consequence. The German government considered, like many other western governments, Security Council resolution 1368, which condemned the terrorist attacks of September 11, 2001 as threat to the international peace and security and confirmed the right to individual and collective self-defense, as sufficient legal basis for the military intervention of the US-led coalition in Afghanistan overthrowing the Taliban regime, but Germany did not take part in the military operation itself.

The government agreed however to take part in military engagement after the US-coalition intervention and asked the German Federal Parliament in November 2001 for the necessary agreement as it has been prescribed by the judgment of the Bundesverfassungsgericht (German Federal Constitutional Court) in 1994 for military missions of the Bundeswehr (Armed Forces of the Federal Republic of Germany). Since members of the SPD parliamentary group and members of the parliamentary group of Bündnis 90/Die Grünen (Alliance 90/The Greens) announced their disagreement in advance, Schroeder connected the vote on the Bundeswehr participation in the military operations in Afghanistan and at the Horn of Africa with a vote of confidence (cf. German Bundestag printed papers 14/7396 and 7440 of 7 and 14 November 2001, respectively). Because the CDU/CSU parliamentary group agreed to the Bundeswehr mission, but did not want to support Schröder politically, the Chancellor reached by a margin of just two votes the necessary parliamentary majority (German Bundestag, 16 September 2001, stenographic record 14/202, 19892f).

In order to distinguish its role from the role of the US-British coalition troops in Afghanistan, the German government decided to participate only in military measures securing the peace-building efforts of the international community within the framework of the international force ISAF.

The Schröder/Fischer government saw its role in Afghanistan in supporting the UN-led peace-building and reconstruction efforts. It supported actively the efforts to find a political solution for Afghanistan and hosted in this context an important conference in Bonn, the so-called "Petersberg-Conference" in December 2001, as well as subsequent meetings. This active involvement earned Germany much respect, in particular in the conflict region itself.

While the German government supported to a certain extent the US-British intervention in Afghanistan, it took from the beginning a different attitude with regard to the Iraq. The government emphasized already at an early point of time, for example in the general debate of the GA in September 2002, its opposition to a premature military solution in the Iraq. Foreign Minister Fischer underlined: "Even if it becomes very difficult, we must do everything possible to find a diplomatic solution ... We do not ... want any automatism leading to the use of military force ... we feel deep scepticism with regard to military action." (UN Doc. A/57/PV.6, 17)

When in spring 2003 the USA and Great Britain attempted to reach a Security Council resolution explicitly authorizing their planned military intervention in the Iraq, Germany, at that time non-permanent member of the Council, organized to a great extent the opposition of the non-permanent members against this draft resolution, in this work supported by the permanent members France and Russia (cf. *Dalgaard-Nielsen* 2003). This rather courageous stance of the German UN ambassador Pleuger and Foreign Minister Fischer earned again Germany much respect and sympathy among the other member states.

Germany had thus without doubt developed a higher profile in its UN policy, but had since then lost the support of the US administration for its enterprise to obtain a permanent seat in the Security Council.

2) Security Council Reform Debate in the General Assembly 2005

As Germany had indeed improved since 2000 its political standing within the United Nations its foreign policy actors were quite optimistic about the prospects of success when the German government started in autumn 2004 a common initiative with India, Brazil and Japan, called the "Group of Four", for the reform of the Council in form of a draft resolution, suggesting the expansion of the Council by six new permanent seats (2 for Africa, 2 for Asia, 1 for Latin

America and 1 for the Western European regional group) and four new non-permanent seats. The new permanent members should get the right of veto, but should suspend the use of the veto until a UN Charter review conference 15 years later.

The Group of Four were in early 2005, when the informal debates in the GA began, quite optimistic, but the complete lack of support from the USA for Germany, India and Brazil, combined with an demonstrative support of Japan's candidacy in appreciating its supporting role during the US-British Iraq intervention in 2003, together with the reluctant attitude of the Russian Federation and of China reduced their chances, when the Group of Four eventually tabled its draft resolution in July 2005. Their chances for success were eventually destroyed by the decision of the African states to table in July 2005 their own draft resolution instead of joining the G4 Group in a common compromise reform resolution and by the fact, that a third group of countries gathering round Italy tabled another draft resolution, containing a Council expansion of only non-permanent members, but with longer terms of office.

Germany had to learn in this case that in the UN not always good work is instantly rewarded, since there are highly complex power structures in the UN with rapidly changing political coalitions.

3) German Green UN Profile

Germany played also in another respect a higher profile role than in the decades before: in the area of environmental protection. Since Germany had become host of the Secretariat of the UN Framework Convention on Climate Change (UNFCCC) in 1996 and the German Klaus Töpfer had been appointed as head of the UN Environment Programme → UNEP in 1998, Germany had focused its political efforts in the UN also on this field, which had been somewhat neglected so far by German governments.

In line with the strong environmental orientation of the Social-Democratic-Green government, much political energy had been invested in diverse conferences dealing with environmental protection and its Environment Minister Jürgen Trittin as well as Chancellor Schröder played above all an important role at the World Summit on Sustainable Development in Johannesburg 2002, when the USA and a number of developing countries blocked real progress on a global scale. Chancellor Schröder brought his political authority to bear when he advocated strongly in his speech at the Johannesburg Conference the prompt ratification of the Kyoto Protocol (→ Environmental Protection; → Environmental Law, International) and invited the Johannesburg delegates to an international conference on renewable sources of energy (cf. UN Press Release ENV/DEV/686 of 3 September 2002), which was eventually held in Bonn in June 2004.

Here again Germany was able to successfully demonstrate that its political and economic weight when effectively used could bring progress into multilateral negotiations in the UN system.

4) Not Enough Money for Development?

Not so convincing was in this phase – as it had been also in the decades before – Germany's UN policy in the field of development cooperation. While the German government verbally repeated strong support for the increase in Official Development Assistance (ODA) by all developed states – for example at the Millennium Summit in 2000 and at the Monterrey Conference on Financing for Development in 2002 – it did not sufficiently implement its promises in this regard: instead of increasing its ODA over 0.3 per cent of its GNP and then to even higher percentages, the ODA remained below 0.3 per cent and many voluntary contributions to UN development programmes were reduced over the years (cf. *Hüfner* 2008).

*II. UN Policy of the Great Coalition
Since 2005*

While the preceding phase of German
UN policy of the Schröder/Fischer government from 1998 to autumn 2005 was
characterized by severe conflicts of interest between Germany and the USA
on the one hand and by some remarkable positive achievements of Germany
as an influential UN "player" on the
other, the UN policy of the Great Coalition Government of Chancellor Merkel
has displayed so far an apparent lack of
highlights as well as of conflicts.

While Germany is still hoping to
reach somewhere in the future a permanent seat in the Security Council, the
Council reform debate has virtually
come to a halt, since the three different
groups described above still keep stead-
fastly to their positions.

Germany participates in a number of
UN peacekeeping missions with about
300 troops, military observers and policemen (as of 31 December 2008;
source: UNDPKO) as well as with a
large number of civil experts. Moreover
it participates with about 7.000 soldiers
in UN-mandated peacekeeping operations of NATO and other organizations,
such as KFOR in Kosovo and ISAF in
Afghanistan.

It invests much brain power and many
financial resources in crisis prevention,
in particular in the training of personnel
for peace-building projects. Furthermore
Germany has earned some merits in
starting together with Switzerland and
Sweden an UN initiative on the development of so-called "smart" sanctions,
i.e. sanctions better targeted and doing
less harm to third party states (cf. Report of the Security Council Working
Group on General Issues of Sanctions,
29 December 2005, UN Doc. S/2005/
842, para. 5).

Germany has also invested political
impact in the disarmament area, among
others, with regard to the ban of certain
types of mines and in the implementation of the conventions on the prohibition of biological and chemical weap-

ons. It is also a lead country on the issue
of the UN register of conventional arms.

All in all, Germany offers presently
the image of a motivated and diligent
UN member state, but without remarkable large-scale projects or political initiatives in the UN fields of activities.
One can get the impression that the
United Nations does not have a high priority on the political agenda of the
Merkel government.

This evaluation might seem unfair,
because Germany fulfills quite a number
of tasks as a UN member state to the
satisfaction of the other member states,
but the UN still needs more in the face
of the global challenges: it needs national politicians with courage and concepts who are able to stir up new debates and to bring the United Nations to
new decisions, for example in the field
of environmental protection, where progress is slow.

The biennial reports of the Federal
Government to the Bundestag on the
United Nations as well as the debates in
the Bundestag on UN topics reflect this
soberness of the current German UN
policy. In the reports the German participation in diverse UN projects and
programmes is described, the German
staff members are listed, the budget figures too, but no critical comments are to
be found and no reform concepts or visions are developed in the reports (see
for example the report for the years
2006 and 2007: *Deutscher Bundestag*,
16 July 2008, printed paper 16/10036).
The parliamentary debates refer mainly
to the prolongation of the agreement to
the German contingents' presence in
UN missions, general thematic debates
in the parliament are seldom and thus
the United Nations are rarely the topic
of the mass media, even if they are
nowadays more present in the media
than in the decades before.

German UN policy can now – if it
wants to – make use of a large amount
of detailed and critical UN research. An
increasing number of adequately trained
people with academic background is
available for jobs in the UN system. It is
a positive sign in this context that a few

785

years ago Germany for the first time reached the so-called "desirable range", i.e. the number of positions Germany is entitled to fill in the UN Secretariat according to a distribution key developed by the United Nations, with financial contributions to the budget of the UN and member state population being the main factors in determining the "desirable range" of staff representation at the UN.

In other words Germany is present in the United Nations with dedicated staff members, among them the Undersecretary-General Angela Kane (Head of the Secretariat Department of Management) and Achim Steiner (Head of UNEP); but Germany should be more present in terms of ideas and initiatives. The German UN Association as well as the other UN-related NGOs should motivate the German Federal Government into giving UN policy a higher priority, even if Germany is at present not invited to take over other attractive UN positions and has only a small chance of gaining a permanent seat in the Security Council. If Germany is elected again with some probability in September 2010 as non-permanent member of the Council for 2011 and 2012, it should prove its value to the United Nations by bringing with it a bundle of interesting and challenging projects, propositions and plans.

Helmut Volger

Lit.: *Dalgaard-Nielsen, A.:* Gulf War. The German Resistance, in: Survival 45 (2003), 99-116; *Deutscher Bundestag (ed.):* Bericht der Bunderegierung zur Zusammenarbeit zwischen der Bundesrepublik Deutschland und den Vereinten Nationen ..., No. 16/10036, 16 July 2008; *Dicke, K.:* Was tun? UNO-Politik nach dem Irak-Krieg, in: Die politische Meinung 2003, No. 405, 25-29; *Haber, H.:* Schwerpunkte der deutschen UN-Politik für die Ratsmitgliedschaft 2003-2004, in: Klein, E./Volger, H. (eds.): Die deutsche UN-Politik 1973-2003 (Potsdamer UNO-Konferenzen, Vol. 4), Potsdam 2004, 33-40; *Hüfner, K.:* Die deutsche UNO-Politik, in: Jäger, T. et al. (eds.): Deutsche Aussenpolitik. Sicherheit, Wohlfahrt, Institutionen, Normen, Wiesbaden 2007, 485-501; *Hüfner, K.:* Peanuts für die UNO? Das deut-

sche Finanzengagement seit 1960, Frankfurt (Main) 2008; *Knapp, M.:* Eine erfolgreiche außenpolitische Emanzipation. Drei Jahrzehnte deutsche Mitgliedschaft in den Vereinten Nationen, in: VN 51 (2003), 207-214; *Knapp, M.:* Vereinte Nationen, in: Schmidt, S. et al. (eds.): Handbuch der deutschen Außenpolitik, Wiesbaden 2007, 727-746; *Opitz, P.J.:* Deutschland und die Vereinten Nationen, in: Opitz, P.J. (ed.): Die Vereinten Nationen. Geschichte, Struktur, Perspektiven, 5th rev. edn., Munich 2007, 285-302; *Pleuger, G.:* Deutschland im Sicherheitsrat. Bilanz aus zwei Jahren als gewähltes Mitglied, in: VN 53 (2005), 1-4; *Scheuermann, M.:* Deutschland in den Vereinten Nationen. Auf dem Weg zu mehr weltpolitischer Verantwortung, Neuried 2007; *Volger, H.:* Geschichte der Vereinten Nationen, 2nd edn., Munich/Vienna 2008.

Internet: 1. Homepage of the German Federal Foreign Office, Department for Global Issues, the United Nations, Human Rights and Humanitarian Aid: www.auswaertiges-amt.de/3-auspol/3/index.htm (Information about the UN, UN institutions in Germany and the German UN policy); 2. Homepage of the German Permanent Mission to the United Nations, New York: www.germany-info. org/UN/index.htm; 3. Homepage of the German Permanent Mission to the United Nations, Geneva: www3.itu.int/Missions/Germany.

UN Policy, Japan

Japan's role in international politics after the Second World War has a lot in common with that of Germany, even if one takes into account the major regional and geo-strategic differences between both countries: In the era after the Cold War both states built up a stronghold against communism under the military umbrella of the USA. In that they became junior partners of the USA. At the same time both states – although being the losers of the Second World War – developed into economic superpowers. After the end of the East-West conflict and the collapse of the socialist world, both nations were called upon to take over greater responsibility in the field of world politics. The necessary process of adapting to the new constellations in world politics turned out to be extremely difficult for Japan as well as for Germany. With this background, it is scarcely surprising that both states show a number of parallels in the development of their relationship to the United Nations.

After the foundation of the United Nations Japan, like Germany, remained excluded from UN membership (→ Membership and Representation of States), being a so-called "enemy state" (→ Enemy State Clauses). Japan, however, could become the 80th member of the international organization at the end of 1956. This happened after two previous applications for membership had failed, both times because of the veto (→ Veto, Right of Veto) of the USSR (1952 and 1955).

The inferno of the atom bombs dropped on Hiroshima and Nagasaki in August 1945 and its consequences had led to an unconditional surrender by Japan, felt as a humiliation by the Japanese. Therefore – not only under the pressure of the USA – Japan "forever" renounced war as a means of its foreign policy, as stated in the post-war constitution of 1947, which was shaped by pacifism. At the same time Japan committed itself "to have no land neither sea nor air forces anymore". (Article 9 of the Japanese constitution) Japan's security was to be ensured by a defensive alliance with the USA (*Dore* 1997).

This security anchorage however turned out to be insufficient, when the Cold War broke out, and especially when the military confrontation in Korea began in the early fifties. On the one hand Tokyo was pushed to increase its own defense capability though the creation of so-called "Self-Defense Forces", provided by law in 1954, on the other hand the government searched for an entrance into the system of → collective security of the United Nations as an additional warranty for its national security.

I. The Early Phase of Japan's UN Policy

In December 1956 Japan entered the political stage of the world in New York "with high expectations and enthusiasm" (*Ogata* 1995). In his maiden speech before the UN → General Assembly, the then Minister of Foreign Affairs defined the three basic principles of the future Japanese UN policy: he promised a foreign policy centered around the UN, he announced a cooperation with all democratic states and he insisted on a strong identification with the Asian group within the United Nations (→ Regional Groups in the UN).

Until the end of the sixties, the *first phase* of the Japanese UN policy was characterized by the fact that Japan very soon recognized the limited capacity of the United Nations to act with regard to security issues, and thus also with regard to Japan's own security problems. Therefore the principle of adjusting its own security policy to that of the United Nations took more and more a back seat. Tokyo was only concerned to give the USA strong political support in the UN bodies, for instance in the common rejection of the demand of Bejing to be recognized as legal representative of China. Additionally, special attention was given to the problems in the Asian region, especially to the unsolved Korea conflict. In 1958 and in 1966 Japan was elected as non-permanent member of the → Security Council. This prestigious success confirmed the self-confidence of the meanwhile economically stronger country. Following this achievement, Japan's then Minister of Foreign Affairs expressed at the end of the sixties, in the plenary meeting of the General Assembly, for the first time – indirectly – the desire to become a permanent member of the Security Council. He also demanded to have the enemy-state clauses deleted from the UN Charter (*Ogata* 1995).

II. Japan and the North-South Conflict

The *second period* of Japan's UN-policy was entirely focused on the North-South-conflict, which dominated the United Nations in the seventies. In the arguments over the conflict strategy of the Group of 77 (→ Group of 77 and the UN), which aimed at a new economic system for the world, Japan took part in the defense of the industrial countries that were in favor of free market principles. Still, it also shared the position of development countries in a few important questions – as its voting record in the General Assembly in these years documents (→ North-South Relations and the UN).

For an industrial power, which is to a large extent dependent upon the import of energy and of raw materials as well as dependent on export markets, the creation and maintenance of good relations with the supplier and customer countries are vital parts of its existential interests. Thus, during the crisis in the Middle East that was heated up by the oil boycott of the Arab countries in 1973, Tokyo disassociated itself from its US protection. It openly supported the attitude of the Arabic States, for instance in demanding the implementation of the Security Council Resolutions 242 and 338. In 1974 the government also quintupled its financial contributions to the → UNRWA.

In the middle of the seventies, supported by its grown financial power, Japan took third place in the list of contribution payers of the regular UN → budget. Thanks to an extensive financial support for the project, Japan finally managed to establish the United Nations University (→ UNU), in Tokyo. Since 1977 Japan has been a member of all organizations belonging to the UN system (→ UN system) and in the seventies it again managed to be represented two times in the Security Council (in 1971/72 and in 1975/76). Although Japan did decidedly pursue its own interests in the United Nations during this phase, it did not "show a mature UN policy" yet (*Bauer* 1994).

III. Japan's Growing Involvement in the UN

In a *third period*, during the eighties, the Japanese government established a more coherent UN policy. At that time the world organization was in a critical political and financial state and on top of

that the USA had to a large extent lost its interest in the UN – it even threatened to withdraw from the United Nations (→ UN Policy, USA). Japan committed itself to revitalize the organization and concentrated on three areas: a restructuring of the administrative and financial system of the UN (→ Reform of the UN), a strengthening of the peacekeeping functions of the UN (→ Peacekeeping), and an expansion of the → humanitarian assistance.

On the occasion of the 40th anniversary of the United Nations in 1985 Japan initiated the appointment of a Group of High-Level Intergovernmental Experts – known as the "Group of 18" – that were to examine the "structural and administrative efficiency" of the organization. One year after its establishment the Group of 18 presented in its report a list of 71 quite practical recommendations for reform measures (UN Doc. A/41/49, 15 August 1986). They advised, for example, a new budgetary procedure, which was in fact later on put into practice by a respective resolution of the General Assembly (A/RES/41/213, 19 December 1986; → Financial Crises).

Japan's effort to improve the peacekeeping capacity of the United Nations in the beginning of the eighties had at its basis a conceptual change of the nation's own security doctrine. In this new doctrine the concept of security gets a wider interpretation: "comprehensive security", i.e. multidimensional security, which does not only limit itself to the protection against military threats, but which also includes the defense against political and especially against economic dangers. With this re-orientation in the sense of a strongly economical security policy Japan committed itself to *multilateralism*, which was expressed in the initiative for international cooperation presented by the government in 1988.

Being in 1981/82 and in 1987/88 again in the position of permanent member of the Security Council, Japan developed new initiatives with regard to the further development of the UN in the areas of peacekeeping and international security politics. On the one hand it focussed on → disarmament, particularly in the field of nuclear weapons, and on the other hand it presented numerous suggestions concerning the increase of the efficiency and the extension of the peacekeeping instruments. These initiatives partly encountered little approval of the Western nations (*Ogata* 1995).

In the eighties a very substantial instrument of the Japanese UN policy was the high financial contribution to the UN system; Japan ended up being the second largest contributor to the regular UN budget. (1986: 10,84%). Pretty soon it also became the second most important payer of voluntary contributions behind the US, though Japan concentrated on particular UN institutions. Since Asia at that time dealt with waves of refugees, Japan put a marked emphasis on humanitarian assistance in the context of the UN refugee assistance (→ UNHCR), for which they spent six times as much in the beginning of the eighties as they had done before. Besides this Tokyo contributed the worldwide largest proportion to the Official Development Assistance (ODA), and gained thereby an outstanding position as international sponsor (→ Development Cooperation of the UN System).

IV. Japan's New Role in the UN

However, with the end of the Cold War and the removal of the bipolar power structures, the Japanese foreign policy faced new challenge making it necessary to examine its international status as a civil economic power. In this context one can take the Second Gulf War (1990/91) as a turning point where Japan, according to its pacifist status, took part only indirectly in paying large amounts of money to the war chest of the Allies. However, Tokyo suddenly realized that others accused Japan of a "cheque-book-diplomacy" and it felt pushed into the position of a "fare-dodger" of the USA. In the nineties, when the international community and the United Nations as part of it were confronted with an ever growing number of conflicts, Japan could not insist on its foreign policy of remaining inactive in the field of military force. Accompanied by turbulent internal quarrels Japan re-orientated its foreign policy (*Volger* 1993).

A new period, the *fourth period* of Japan's UN policy began marked by a more active role of Japan. The newly propagated emphasis of Japan's UN policy is in line with the previous programmatic statements, for instance – apart from reforms in order to raise the efficiency and effectiveness of the international organization – the reinforcement of the peace-keeping capacity of the United Nations is a top priority for Japan. But in this particular field – especially with the participation of Japanese troops in → peacekeeping operations – one can witness how the relationship between Tokyo and the United Nations has changed profoundly in practice, and one can see a "new quality" in Japan's international activities (*Bauer* 1994).

For a long time Tokyo had rejected an active participation in UN operations, in that it would always point to its pacifist constitution, with its restrictive clause in Article 9. Meanwhile, since the beginning of the seventies, there had been government-internal considerations of a possible participation of Japanese armed forces. These were only presented to the domestic public at the end of the eighties. These plans however met with the opposition of the population – as it was shown in polls – and influential political parties rejected them because they found them incompatible with the constitution. A long, partly bitter internal controversy took place until on 15 June 1992 the parliament finally adopted the so-called Blue-Helmet Law, after several unsuccessful previous attempts to get it through. The law with the title "Cooperation for the United Nations Peacekeeping Operations and other Operations", composed of 27 articles enabled Japan to take part in "traditional" UN peacekeeping missions up to an upper limit of 2,000 lightly-armed soldiers. A participation in UN peace-enforcement activities is specially forbidden according to this law (*Stein* 1996).

A few months later, in September 1992, a contingent of 600 Japanese Self-Defense Forces was deployed on the UNTAC mission in Cambodia. This turned out to be the most extensive participation by Japan. It was followed by two, at least in terms of figures, more modest military blue helmet operations in Mozambique (ONUMOZ) and – since the beginning of 1996 – at Golan Heights (UNDOF) in the Near East. At the end of 1998 only 44 Japanese soldiers were left in UN services. Thus in recent times the Japanese engagement concerning the delegation of personnel for the UN-peacekeeping operations keeps within reasonable limits. The participation of Japan in the new field of → electoral assistance is also limited to a few cases (for instance in Angola and in El Salvador) with a total of 80 persons. However, in covering the financial costs of the peacekeeping missions, Japan contributed approximately 18 % of the budget in 1998, which was the second highest contribution after the USA.

Another weakness of the Japanese UN policy lies in the fact that Japan is under-represented among the staff in the → Secretariat as well as in the total → UN system. Japanese only rarely find themselves in hierarchically high UN positions (at present Undersecretary-General Kenzo Oshima, the Head of the Office for the Coordination of Humanitarian Affairs (OCHA), and Koichiro Matsuura, the Director-General of → UNESCO, are the rare exceptions to this). Japan contributes about 18 percent of the regular UN budget of 1998 and 1999 as the second largest contributor, pays almost double the sum of the third-ranking Germany and it contributes more than France, Great Britain and China – which all have a permanent seat in the Security Council – pay together. Still, Japan is not represented accordingly in the UN Secretariat. In 1997 Japan was allowed to provide personnel for 200 positions of the higher service (→ Personnel) in accordance with its fi-

nancial performance, yet only 104 positions were taken up by Japanese (*Drifte* 1998).

It becomes clear that Tokyo still sees high financial contributions as one of the main elements of its UN policy and of its foreign policy in general. Japan is not only one of the chief financiers of the United Nations; it remains the world's biggest sponsor of the ODA, even though it is confronted with economic problems since the middle of the nineties and even though absolute contributions have declined in the meantime.

For Japan – particularly when one considers its perspective of security centered around economics – the financial transfer is one of its most important instruments of security within its foreign policy.

Apart from this, Tokyo considers the Security Council to be the second central field of action for Japanese UN policy. Together with Brazil, which became a member of the UN in 1945, Japan is the nation that was most often a non-permanent member of the Security Council. Both have been non-permanent members of the Council no less than eight times (in the nineties Japan had the seat in 1992/93 and 1997/98).

Japan's performance as a non-permanent member, however, bears no proportion to the respective "advertising campaign" for the country's membership in the Security Council in the African and Asian regional groups before the election takes place. It is a general opinion that Japanese activities in the Council in the nineties were limited to "contributions with regard to procedures and to organizing majorities" (*Drifte* 1998).

Although Tokyo's efforts to attain the status of a permanent member of the Security Council show a certain consistency since the late seventies, this demand is presented in the General Debate of the UN General Assembly for the first time in 1992/93 and since then regularly in the Assembly. Hereby Tokyo always – using the same formulation over and over again – reminds the other UN members of its renunciation of the use of force which is prescribed by the Japanese constitution and which makes only a limited participation of Japan in future UN peacekeeping operations possible (cf. also *Akashi* 2001, 76).

In the Working-Group of the General Assembly which has been discussing the Security Council reform since 1993, Tokyo expressed its favor for a model that foresees a "limited" growth of both the permanent and non-permanent members. According to this model the reformed Security Council should however "not contain much more than 20 members" since then its "efficiency" would be endangered.

The reorganization of the structure of the Security Council is only one of the reform subjects that Japan chose to deal with actively during the last few years. Japan's efforts in the direction of a general UN reform, a third element of its UN policy, are concentrated on the area of peacekeeping and the areas of administration and finances. In the area of peacekeeping Japan puts most stress on suggestions for the prevention of conflicts (→ Preventive Diplomacy). In the area of administration and finances it handed in an extensive suggestion for financial reform in the spring of 1996 (*Japan – Ministry of Foreign Affairs* 1998). The suggestions for reform made by UN Secretary-General Kofi Annan – "Renewing the United Nations: A Programme for Reform" (UN Doc. A/51/ 950 of 14 July 1997) – can also count on full support by Japan. Japan articulates its opinion concerning reform in both the General Assembly plenary and the Reform Working Group of the General Assembly. Recently the old demand to remove the enemy state clauses from the UN Charter receded into the background.

For years now the catchword of the UN-centered diplomacy runs through the Japanese foreign policy like a *leitmotif*. This target was officially proclaimed on the occasion of Japan's entry into the UN in 1956, and it is referred to over and over again. Whether this claim was fulfilled or not remains a difficult question to answer, however, it is certain that Japan cannot claim to have shown a continuous intensive UN engagement during those more than forty years. In the course of time the Japanese government has put different accents in its UN politics, due to changing interests in its foreign policy and changing international and regional political conditions.

As a reaction to the end of the East-West-Conflict and the following turmoil in world politics, the Japanese UN policy first of all reacted by taking up a greater global responsibility, also in the area of peacekeeping. In the meantime, however, it becomes clear that Japan is still looking for a specific role within the United Nations. Its wish to have a permanent seat in the Security Council is more or less openly brought into connection with its high financial contributions to the organization, and is seen as a question of prestige. But how Japan is going to use this position remains an open question. This also shows a parallel to the German UN policy.

Günther Unser

Lit.: *Akashi, Y.:* Peace-Building and Peacekeeping Operations – Roles of the Security Council, in: Japanese-German Center Berlin (ed.): The United Nations in the 21st Century: Japanese, German and U.S. Perspectives. Symposium, 21-22 September 2000, Berlin 2001, 70-76 (further information: www.jdzb.de); *Bauer, F.:* Japans Verhältnis zu den Vereinten Nationen, in: Bredow, W./ Jäger, T. (ed.): Japan – Europa – USA, Opladen 1994, 183-208; *Becker, B./Rüland, J. (eds.):* Japan und Deutschland in der internationalen Politik, Hamburg 1997; *Dore, R.:* Japan, Internationalism and the UN, London/ New York 1997; *Drifte, R.:* Wendungen zum Multilateralismus – mit Vorbehalten. Die japanische VN-Politik ..., in: VN 36 (1988), 102-107; *Harrison, S.S./Nishihara, M. (eds.):* UN Peacekeeping. Japanese and American Perspectives, New York 1995; *Japan - Ministry of Foreign Affairs (ed):* United Nations and Japan, Tokyo 1998; *Ogata, S.:* Japan's Policy towards the United Nations, in: Alger, C.F. et al. (eds.): The United Nations System: The Policies of Member States, Tokyo et al. 1995; *Owada, H.:* The Reform of the UN and its Organs, in: Japanese-German Center Berlin (ed.): The United Nations in the 21st Century: Japanese, German and U.S. Perspectives. Symposium, 21-22 September 2000, Berlin 2001, 13-21; *Rhode, M.*: Japan in der UNO, in: Japan aktuell, No. 3/1997, 163-170; *Stein, T.:* Japans Beteiligung an UN-Einsätzen, in: Konrad-Adenauer-Stiftung – Auslandsinformationen 13 (1996), No. 3, 84-95; *Takasu, Y.:* Factors Influencing the Foreign Policy of Japan – Particularly as it Relates to UN Policy, in: Japanese German Center Berlin (ed.): The Role of the United Nations in the 1990s, Symposium, 27-31 August 1990, Berlin 1991, 196-205; *Volger, H.:* Japan – eine Weltmacht sucht ihre Rolle, in: Blätter für deutsche und internationale Politik 38 (1993), 445-456.

Addendum

The year 2006 marked the 50th anniversary of Japan's admission to the United Nations in 1956. On December 18 in 2006, the Ministry of Foreign Affairs held a commemorative ceremony of this anniversary in the presence of Emperor Akihito. The government of Japan took the opportunity to confirm the excellence of its partnership with the UN and to reaffirm its determination to further contribute to the work of the Organization (cf. the address of Prime Minister Shinzo Abe at the commemorative ceremony, www.mofa.go.jp/policy/un/50th/address_pm.html). Even though over the last 50 years commitment and dedication to the UN have become a basic principle of Japanese foreign policy, we cannot say – in contrast to the statement asserted by the Japanese government in 1952, when it submitted its application for UN membership – that Japan has always accepted the obligations contained in the UN charter without reservations and undertaken "to honor them by all means at its disposal" (quote from: Address of the Japanese Foreign Minister Mamoru Shigetsu before the UN General Assembly on the occasion of Japan's admission to the UN on 18 December 1956, www.mofa.go.jp/policy/un/address5612.html). For many years Japan's UN policy had been restricted by the Japanese constitution as

well as by the general attitude of the Japanese people towards foreign policy.

In recent years, however, changes in global and regional politics – for instance the end of the Cold War – and the resultant consequences for the United Nations have led to an expansion of Japan's scope of action in its UN policy. Its activities within the world organization, have been mainly influenced by the transformation of its long time pacifist-minded security- and defense policy (see Article 9 of the "peace constitution") through the more active role of its military – journalists and scientists speak of Japan plotting "a less pacifist role" and even of "remilitarizing Japan" (*Tom Larimer*, Japan Plots a Less Pacifist Role, Time, 20 September 2001; *Gavan McCormack*, Remilitarizing Japan, in: New Left Review 29 (2004), 29-45). In this regard, the September 11 2001 terror attacks upon the USA turned out to be important occurrences with long-term effects. Due to the attacks upon its closest ally, the Koizumi government that had been in office since spring 2001 expanded the ambits of the Japanese foreign and security policy. The vast majority of the Japanese population was initially in favor of the Japanese military joining the US-led anti-terror-alliance (cf. *Larimer* 2001).

In October 2001 both chambers of the Japanese parliament passed an anti-terrorism bill, which allowed the dispatch of Japanese Self-Defence Forces (SDF) to warships and war-torn regions in Afghanistan – but for logistical support only (cf. Diet Passes Antiterrorism Special Measures Law, in: FPCJ Japan Brief, 9 November 2001, http://fpcj.jp/old/e/mres/japanbrief/jb_250.html). In December 2001, the "Law Concerning Cooperation for United Nations Peacekeeping Operations and Other Operations" – the so-called "PKO Bill" – from 1992, already revised in 1998 to enable SDF involvement in international election-monitoring by regional organizations, was once more revised and made thereby possible the expansion of the scope of action of Japanese SDF units in international operations (cf. Japan's Record on International Peace Operation Activities, www.pko.go.jp/ PKO_E/cooperation/progress_e.html).

In the middle of 2003, the Japanese parliament established through the adoption of the "Iraq Reconstruction Assistance Special Measures Law" the legal basis for the dispatch of SDF troops to Iraq, which were deployed to help supply the population with water and medicine (cf. Diet Enacts Iraq Reconstruction Law – Self-Defense Forces to be Dispatched to Provide Assistance, in: FPCJ Japan Brief, 29 July 2003, http://fpcj.jp/old/e/mres/japanbrief/ jb_157.html). At the beginning of 2004, without the authorization of the United Nations Security Council and against the resistance of the people of Japan, approximately 550 members of Japanese air, naval and land forces were assigned by the Japanese Government on a two-year mission in the non-combat zone in the south-east of Iraq, the largest overseas dispatch of SDF hitherto (cf. Government Issues Order to Dispatch SDF, in: FPCJ Japan Brief, http://fpcj.jp/ old/e/mres/japanbrief/jb_133.html).

The Japanese people remained even more skeptical towards the Japanese military involvement in Iraq: opinion polls taken before and after the Japanese deployment showed that only about 30 % of the Japanese supported the deployment of SDF to Iraq; in August 2002 14 % supported the Japanese involvement, 77 % opposed it; in December 2002 26 % were for and 65 % against; in January 2003 20 % for and 69 % against; in March 2003 27 % for and 65 % against; and in April 2003 29 % for and 63 % against (source: opinion polls taken by Asahi Shimbun, quoted in: Paul Midford, Japanese Public Opinion and the War on Terrorism/East-West Center – Policy Studies No. 27).

There was a heated debate in the Japanese parliament on the issue, and even within the ruling Liberal Democratic Party there were politicians who took a cautious attitude towards the mission (cf. Government Issues Order to Dispatch SDF, ibid.).

According to political analysts this military engagement can be interpreted as the continued cautious effort of the Japanese government to establish a normalization of the country's military policy as they would like to consider it (cf. *Oros* 2007). Given the potential threat of China and North Korea in regional politics, the forward-pushing government of Koizumi strove for a transformation of the Self-Defense Forces into a powerful professional army which safeguarded Japanese interests in the world – if need be also with weapons.

Yet the Japanese people reacted to the expansion of the Japanese involvement in Iraq with increasing opposition. A Nikkei poll taken in December 2003 after Prime Minister Koizumi had announced the further deployment mentioned above in a television press conference on 9 December 2003, found a great majority opposed to dispatch (52 % with 33 % in favor (quoted after *Midford* 2006, 35).

But the skepticism of the majority in Japan did not hinder the government from pursuing a more active security policy in the following years.

The ambition for a more active and independent security policy was the essence of the "National Defence Program Outline" (NDPO), adopted by the Japanese government on December 10, 2004 (cf. *Tatsumi* 2004). The new NDPO proposes a policy of building a "multifunctional, flexible, and effective defense force", and states with regard to peacekeeping missions, "the international peace cooperation activities of the Self-Defense Forces will be positioned appropriately." (NDPO 2004, quoted in: Cabinet Approves New National Defense Program Outline, in: FPCJ Japan Brief, 13 December 2004, http://fpcj.jp/ old/e/mres/japanbrief/jb_62.html). Consequently, at the end of 2005 the Koizumi government, which won the elections, took the last and decisive step towards the creation of a new legal basis and produced a draft constitution for Japan on the occasion of the 50th anniversary of the ruling Liberal Democratic Party (LPD). The government made a wide-ranging modification to article 9 of the constitution, allowing Japanese forces to operate at international level to maintain peace and security and to participate in collective defensive actions: "The military forces for self-defense may engage in activities conducted in international co-operation to secure peace and security of the international community" (quoted from LDP proposal for a new Japanese constitution, as published in parts in: BBC News, 28 October 2005, http://news.bbc.co.uk/go/pr/fr/-/2/hi/asia-pacific/4384806.stm)

It must be pointed out that the draft constitution, adopted by the Japanese lower parliament chamber in April 2007 and still subject to a public referendum that could take place at the earliest in 2010 and would need approval from a majority of voters, merely reproduces what has already become reality in Japan's security policy. Since the change of government in autumn 2006, it is in question whether Koizumi's policy of stronger military engagement in UN peacekeeping will be continued. Despite the passing of a law in January 2008 that authorizes further logistical support against terrorism in Afghanistan, his successors are acting with reserve concerning security policy. This is also due to the fact, that public support for such an active Japanese UN policy in peacekeeping still meets great reserve in the Japanese public: in an opinion poll taken in October 2006 shortly after Prime Minister Abe took office, only 25.4% were of the opinion that Japan should participate in peacekeeping operations in the future "more actively than before", while 50.6% said it "should participate at the current level", and 14.6% said it "should participate at a minimal level" (Survey of the Japanese Cabinet Office, 11 December 2006, para. 3).

How did the transformation of Japan's security policy influence the country's active participation in the United Nations, not least implemented at US pressure on Tokyo to contribute more to both its own defense and the regional security of the Asia-Pacific region? In the Diplomatic Bluebook 2007 the Japanese government gives the assurance: "Japan regards international cooperation as one of the main pillars of its diplomatic policy and therefore has been conducting active diplomacy through the UN as well as making contributions to this organization both in terms of finance and personnel." (*Ministry of Foreign Affairs, Japan*, Diplomatic Bluebook 2007, Chapter 3, A (d), 19)

Japan is still the second most important contributor to both the UN budget and the United Nations peacekeeping operations. But in view of the joint African Union/United Nations Hybrid operation (UNAMID) with up to 20,000 military personnel in Darfur authorized by Security Council in July 2007 (cf. www.un.org/Depts/dpko/missions/unamid/), critics in Japan are warning against the skyrocketing costs of UN peacekeeping and the Japanese government attempts to reduce its share of the UN expenses. While Japan paid a share of 19.468 per cent of the regular budget from 2004 to 2006, the country pressed to lower its share to 16.624 per cent in the assessment period from 2007 to 2009 after years of demanding a recalculation of the scale of assessment. (cf: Statement of Japan's Deputy UN Representative Shinyo at the Fifth Committee on 10 October 2006, www.mofa.go.jp/announce/speech/un2006/un0610-3.html).

Furthermore, Japan is one of the major providers of financial contributions to UN development cooperation and humanitarian aid.

Additionally Japan pays voluntary contributions to UN funds and programmes of about one billion US dollars per year. Regarding staff participation to UN-Peacekeeping Operations, Japan's contribution of military troops has – despite the extended political mandate of the Self-Defense Forces – been decreasing in recent years. While in spring 2002, 467 troops of the Self-Defence Forces were deployed in UN peacekeeping operations (as of 31 March 2002), in January 2008 only 38 Japanese were deployed (30 soldiers at UNDOF, 6 Military Observers at UNMIN in Nepal and 2 policemen at UNMIT in Timor-Leste) (www.un.org/Depts/dpko/dpko/contributors).

Compared with the country's assessed share of the UN budget, Japan is chronically under-represented by the number of its officials in the UN Secretariat. A report of the UN Secretary-General of 31 August 2007 still counts Japan among the group of underrepresented countries, i.e. the number of its nationals appointed to posts in the Secretariat subject to geographical distribution is below the "desirable range" of posts, a number of posts each member country is entitled to on grounds of its share of the regular UN budget, its size of population and other factors defined by the General Assembly (United Nations - General Assembly, Composition of the Secretariat. Report of the Secretary-General, 31 August 2007, UN Doc. A/62/315).

Despite the obvious reluctance towards the deployment of personnel in peacekeeping operations, Japan's government continuously expands the country's engagement in security issues within the world organization. Japan not only integrated in its foreign policy the concept of "human security" drafted at the beginning of 2003 by a UN Commission with the Japanese former UN High Commissioner for Refugees Sadako Ogata as Vice-Chairwoman, in its report "Human Security Now" (*Commission on Human Security* 2003) but it also made a substantial financial contribution to the "UN Trust Fund for Human Security" (cf. www.mofa.go.jp/policy/human_secu/index.html).

Like Brazil, Japan has already been elected nine times as a non-permanent member of the Security Council, and as early as 2009 Japan will return to the most powerful organ of the United Nations.

Tokyo is one of the initiators and founding members of the Peacebuilding Commission (PBC) established in December 2005 by resolutions of the General Assembly (UN Doc. A/RES/60/180) and of the Security Council (UN Doc. S/RES/1645 (2005)). The purposes

of this new intergovernmental advisory body are to combine development cooperation and measures to improve the security situation in the states concerned, as the current Chair of PBC, Japan's foreign ministry announced at the symposium "Building Peace – Japan and the UN" numerous diplomatic events for the year 2008 (Symposium "Building Peace – Japan and UN" Summary, January 28, 2008, www.mofa.go.jp/policy/un/pko/symposium0801.html).

Against the background of its painful experience with the use of nuclear weapons (Hiroshima and Nagasaki 1945) and being concerned about the danger nuclear terrorism, Japan has more than any other country worked hard in promoting disarmament and the non-proliferation of nuclear weapons under UN authority, in particular with regard to the nuclear activities of Iran and North Korea (cf. *Ministry of Foreign Affairs of Japan*, Japan's Disarmament and Non-proliferation Policy, 3rd edn., Tokyo March 2006, www.mofa.go.jp/policy/un/disarmament).

Thus the Japanese foreign ministry expressed its disappointment that no concrete recommendations concerning disarmament had been adopted in the Outcome Document of the 2005 World Summit (UN Doc. A/RES/60/1, 16 September 2005). Furthermore Japan strongly supports the realization of the UN Millennium Development Goals by the target date of 2015, especially in such important areas as education, control of epidemics, drinking water supply and waste water disposal. As Japanese representatives stated at the UN General Assembly's High-Level Event on Climate Change in September 2007 in New York, Japan stands ready to adopt profound measures against climate change (cf. www.mofa.go.jp/policy/environment/warm/cop/state07 09.html).

Japan, which ratified the Kyoto Protocol in 2002, proposes to the international community three principles for a comprehensive package on how to proceed beyond Kyoto's first period which is due to expire at the end of 2012: (1): "... all major emitters must participate

...". (2) "... the framework must be flexible and diverse ...". (3) "... it must achieve compatibility between environmental protection and economic growth ..." (ibid.).

In January 2006, the Japanese Ministry of Foreign Affairs published a document entitled "United Nations Reform: Priority Issues for Japan", pointing out its standpoint on United Nations Reform (www.mofa.go.jp/policy/un/reform/priority.html).The program paper is divided into four main sections (Development, Security, Human-Rights, Institutional Reform). Although the Japanese government confirms in the introductory paragraph: "comprehensive reform is necessary to strengthen the UN's function", it leaves no doubt about its political priorities in the next sentence: "In particular, reform of the Security Council is a matter of special urgency for enhancing the credibility and effectiveness of the Organization as a whole."

In other words, Japan's primary goal is to hold a permanent seat in the Security Council. Particularly in view of Japan's significant financial contributions to the UN system, the country feels discriminated against in its present position and has been for a long time requesting a larger role as a permanent member in a reformed Security Council. (cf. *Weiss* 2005; *Shin'yo* 2003).

In September 2004, Japan together with Brazil, Germany and India, presented to the public the G4 draft resolution, which was tabled as draft resolution in the General Assembly in July 2005 (UN Doc. A/59/L.64, 6 July 2005). The draft resolution proposed adding six new permanent members, with no veto power, and four non-permanent members.

Since none of the three competing draft resolutions for Council reform – the "Group of Four" Resolution, the "Uniting for Consensus" Resolution of Italy and its co-sponsors (UN Doc. A/59/L.68, 21 July 2005), and the draft resolution of the African Union (UN Doc. A/59/L.67, 14 July 2005) – could win a sufficient majority of states, none

of the three resolutions were put to the vote into 2005.

In January 2006, as the three co-initiators resubmitted the draft resolution without any specific modification to the original G4 proposal to the Plenary of the General Assembly (UN-Doc. A/60/L. 64), Japan was no longer co-sponsor of the resolution, but presented its own reform concept.

In a press conference in early January 2006, Japanese Cabinet Secretary Shinzo Abe explained to the press, that Japan would attempt to develop a reform proposal which could win a greater support of member states and would discuss this proposal with the USA (Evelyn Leopold, Japan says working on own U.N. reform proposal, Reuters News Agency, 6 January 2006). In February 2006, it was leaked to the press that Japan tried in negotiations with the USA and China to win their support for its council reform proposal: Japan proposed to expand the council membership from 15 to 21. The status of new permanent membership would be given to countries that stand as candidates and win the support of at least two thirds of the UN membership, i.e. 128 countries. They would not be given veto power. Other candidates would become semi-permanent members with terms longer than the two years for current non-permanent members. Japan did not obtain much support for his compromise, in particular from the USA, and thus withdrew its proposal in March 2006 – but not its claim for a permanent seat in the Council. (cf. Japan Unlikely to Submit New Security Council Reform Plan by September, Japan Economic News Wire, 19 March 2006)

Although in 2007 and 2008 in New York there has been some talk of a new momentum for UN Security Council reform, so far there is no solution in sight. The presidents of the 2006, 2007 and 2008 sessions of the General Assembly have attempted – supported by a number of member states – to give the reform debate some fresh impetus by suggesting negotiations about intermediate solutions for ten or fifteen years, in the hope of overcoming the stalemate caused by the lack of willingness of the above-mentioned different reform proponents to find a compromise. Japan supports at present this intermediary approach: "Japan would participate in the intergovernmental negotiations actively and in a flexible manner, with a view to achieving concrete results during the session" (Japanese UN-representative in the reform debate at the 62nd General Assembly on November 12, 2007; www. un.org/News/Press/docs/2007/ga10656. doc.htm). However, so far no progress has been achieved in the Council reform debate, since the groupings are still clinging to their different initial positions of 2005.

It remains to be seen how far the probable result of the reform debate – no permanent seat in the Council for Japan – for the near future at least – will have an impact on Japan's UN policy, whether it will weaken or strengthen the ambition of its government to gain more influence and status in the United Nations.

Günther Unser

Lit: *Brook, M.:* Increasing Japanese military role in the international arena, in: Asian Defence Journal (2004) No. 10, 8-12; *Cabinet Office of Japan:* Public Opinion Survey on Diplomacy, 11 December 2006, published by The Mansfield Asian Opinion Poll Database 2008, (www.mansfieldfdn.org/polls/ poll-06-17.htm); *Coulmas, F.:* Japan's Bid for a Permanent Seat on the UN Security Council, in: Asien – The German Journal on Contemporary Asia, Issue No. 100 (July 2006), 18-22; *Demming, R.M.:* Japan's constitution and defense policy: entering a new era? In: Strategic Forum (2004) No. 213, 8ff.; *Drifte, Reinhard:* Japan's Quest for a Permanent Security Council Seat: A Matter of Pride or Justice? New York 2000; *Fouse, D.:* Japan's FY 2005 National Defense Program Outline: New Concepts, Old Compromises, in: Asia-Pacific Center for Security Studies, Vol. 4, No. 3, March 2005; *Green, M.J.:* Japan's Reluctant Realism: Foreign Policy Challenges in an Era of Uncertain Power, New York 2001; *Green, M.J.:* The Iraq War and Asia: Assessing the Legacy, in: The Washington Quarterly, Spring 2008, 181-200; *Hughes, Ch.W.:* Japan's security

agenda: military, economic, and environmental dimensions, Boulder, Col. 2004; *Hughes, Ch.W.:* Japan's security policy, the US-Japan alliance, and the "war on terror": incrementalism confirmed or radical leap?, in: Australian Journal of International Affairs, 58 (2004) 427-445; *Izumikawa, Y.:* The evolution of Japan's post-conflict contributions: From reluctant player to an honest broker?, in Peace Forum 18 (2004) 30, 30-46; *Kaseda, Y.:* The Iraq war and Japan's military transformation, in Peace Forum 18 (2005) 31, 20-32; *Kitaoka, S.:* Die Vereinten Nationen innerhalb der japanischen Außenpolitik seit Kriegsende, in: Botschaft von Japan, Neues aus Japan, No. 6/2005; *Konishi, W.S.:* Putting the Cart Before the Horse: Does Abe have public support for his „proactive diplomacy"? Commentary C07-2, 12 February 2007, in: The Mansfield Asian Opinion Poll Database, 2007 (www. mansfieldfdn.org/polls/commentary-07-2.htm); *Larimer, T.:* Japan Plots a Less Pacifist Role, in: Time, September 20, 2001, (www.time.come/time/world/article/0,8599,175626,00. html); *Lind, J.M.:* Pacifism or passing the buck? Testing theories of Japanese security policy, in: International Security 29 (2004) 92-121; *Luck, E.:* Tokyo's Quixotic Quest for Acceptance, in: Far Eastern Economic Review, May 2005, 5-10; *Luckner, K.:* Japans Rolle in der UNO. Grundlagen für einen ständigen Sitz im Weltsicherheitsrat?, Baden-Baden 2006; *McCormack, G.:* Remilitarizing Japan, in: New Left Review 29 (2004), 29-45; *Midford, P:* Japanese Public Opinion and the War on Terrorism: Implications for Japan's Security Strategy, (Policy Studies No. 27), East-West Center, Washington 2006; *Ministry of Foreign Affairs of Japan:* United Nations Reform: Priority Issues for Japan, January 2006 (www.mofa.go. jp/policy/un/reform/priority.html); *Ministry of Foreign Affairs of Japan:* Japan in the Security Council – our Viewpoint, Tokyo 2006; *Ministry of Foreign Affairs of Japan:* Japan's Disarmament and Non-Proliferation Policy, 3rd edn., Tokyo March 2006, www. mofa.go.jp/policy/un/disarmament/policy/pa mph0603. html; *Ministry of Foreign Affairs of Japan:* Diplomatic Bluebook 2007, Tokyo, March 2007, www.go.mofa.jp/policy /other/bluebook/2007/html; *Murphy, C.:* Testing Japan's pacifist resolve, in Far Eastern Economic Review 169 (2006) 9, 19-22; *Oros, A.L.:* Listening to the People: Japanese Democracy and the New Security Agenda. Commentary C 07-3, February 20, 2007 in: The Mansfield Asian Opinion Poll Database, 2007 (www.mansfieldfdn.org/polls/ commentary-07-3.htm); *Pyle, K.B.:* Japan's historic change of course, in: Current History 105 (2006) 692, 277-283; *Shin`yo,T.:* Reforming the Security Council, in: Japan Review of International Affairs 17 (2003) No. 3, 185-200; *Soeya, Y.:* Japanese security policy in transition: the rise of international and human security, in: Asia-Pacific Review 12 (2005) 1, 103-116; *Szechenyi, N.:* A turning point for Japan's self-defence forces, in: The Washington Quarterly 29 (2006) 4, 139-150; *Tatsumi, Y.:* National Defense Program Outline: A New Security Policy Guideline or a Mere Wish List? In: Japan Watch, 20 December 2004 (Center for Strategic and International Studies Washington); *Weiss, T.:* Overcoming the Security Council Reform Impasse. The Implausible versus the Plausible (Dialogue on Globalization/Occasional Papers No 14), Friedrich Ebert Stiftung, New York 2005.

Internet: 1. Homepage of the Permanent Mission of Japan to the UN in New York: www.un.int/japan; 2. Website of the Japanese Ministry of Foreign Affairs on Japan's UN policy: www.mofa.go.jp/policy/un/index.html.

UN Policy, Russian Federation

I. The Russian Federation "Continues" the UN Membership of the USSR

On 24 December 1991 Boris Yeltsin, President of the Russian Federation (Russia), wrote a short letter to then UN Secretary-General Javier Pérez de Cuéllar. In this, Yeltsin stated that the past UN membership of the USSR would be "continued" by the Russian Federation (cf. UN Doc. A/47/2, 277).

From that moment Russia took the place of the dissolved Soviet Union in the organs of the world organization, with all the rights and duties involved – thus Russia also took the seat of a permanent member in the → Security Council. (A corresponding amendment to Article 23 of the UN Charter (→ Charter of the UN) was made neither then, nor later on. As before, the article refers to the "USSR" as permanent member.) This procedure was contested to some extent in international law; but it was made expressly with consent of the ten other members of the Common-

wealth of Independent States (CIS), the loose confederation of states which came into existence as a consequence of the collapse of the USSR (*Daley* 1992).

The Russian leadership considered Russia not as an ordinary "successor state" in the sense of international law (→ Membership and Representation of States), but as a special kind of "continuity state". This is why it appreciated the international acceptance of its particular status as a first meaningful success of its foreign policy. Thus Kozyrev, Russian Minister of Foreign Affairs, declared with self-confidence: "To be a 'continuity state' means that the connection to the external world was handed over to Russia. In this way we have inherited the seat of the Soviet Union in the Security Council – that is a demonstration of our role as a superpower." (Rossijskaya Gazeta, 21 January 1992) The continuity in terms of power politics thus determined Russia's thinking with regard to foreign policy. In this important position, equipped with the right of veto (→ Veto, Right of Veto), Russia further belonged to the "global players" at the actual center of power of the United Nations.

II. UN Policy of the USSR under Stalin

A look back at the establishment phase of the world organization shows that without granting the superpowers a privileged position in the Security Council, the UN would never have come into existence after the end of World War II. The Soviet Union as one of the former allied powers and, at the same time, as the only socialist state, attached particular importance to keeping the right of veto as a "locking device" for the protection of its own interests. It demonstrated consistency in the defense and application of this privilege during ensuing decades. Moscow showed much less consistency in its general attitude towards the UN; the Kremlin's appreciation of the UN changed repeatedly and considerably through the years.

Already towards the end of the forties the situation of the UN was marked by a dangerous power-political and ideological dualism. This dualism would later on become the leading image of the whole international scenery, since it split the world into two blocs – the beginning of the era known as the Cold War. In the period until 1952 Moscow and its few socialist allies saw themselves pushed into a minority position and felt themselves politically isolated in the organs of the United Nations, which were dominated by the West ($\rightarrow$ UN System; $\rightarrow$ Principal Organs, Subsidiary Organs, Treaty Bodies). In view of the "capitalist encirclement", the Soviet leadership threatened repeatedly to withdraw from the organization, and showed little readiness to cooperation with others. Finally, the Soviets boycotted the Security Council at the beginning of 1950.

III. UN Policy under Khrushchev

After Stalin's death in 1953 Soviet foreign policy – also towards the United Nations – underwent a re-orientation, which assumed fixed outlines when Khrushchev became Secretary-General of the Communist Party of the Soviet Union in spring of 1955. Following the UN admission of numerous "younger" developing countries and the increasing significance of development problems, the Soviet Union now pursued a more offensive UN strategy. As a "natural" ally in the fight against Western neocolonialism, it looked for political closeness to the Third World states. Thereby it engaged itself – at least rhetorically – in the field of development policy, which became increasingly more important.

Because of these global changes at the beginning of the sixties, the United Nations, for the first time, had moved into the center of Soviet policy. Primarily it was Khrushchev personally who sought to make use of the United Nations as an "advertising forum" and as a stage for Soviet policy, based on national interest. In September 1960 during the 15th General Assembly he spent more than three weeks in New York, and broke all speakers' records by his frequent appearances on the rostrum of the General Assembly. Hereby he submitted spectacular suggestions, such as complete, world-wide disarmament within four years. He also demanded drastic structural UN reforms ($\rightarrow$ Reform of the UN) in the sense of an adjustment of the $\rightarrow$ Charter of the UN to the new "distribution of power in the international arenas", in that he, for instance, wanted to replace the Secretary-General as head of the Secretariat by a collective executive organ consisting of three persons each of whom would present a group of states, i.e. the Western states, the Socialist states and the Third World, a plan which came to be known as the "troika" proposal, since the Secretariat would be made comparable to the three-in-hand Russian horse carriage, the troika (cf. *Luard* 1989, 204f.).

IV. UN Policy under Brezhnev

After the fall of Khrushchev in October 1964, the collective leadership under Brezhnev and Kosygin first acted carefully and reservedly with regard to foreign policy. The Minister of Foreign Affairs, Gromyko, who had outlined the respective Soviet UN policy in the general debates of the General Assembly since 1957, with only a two-year interruption, now gradually showed a shift of emphasis of the Soviet UN policy using the worn-out slogan of "reinforcement of the UN". Instead of tackling extensive structural reforms, the United Nations should be developed into a still more effective instrument of $\rightarrow$ peacekeeping, and this under strict adherence to the provisions of the Charter of the UN. The Soviet Union concentrated its efforts on the field of security policy; one could say that it unfolded veritable "fireworks" of both disarmament and arms control suggestions in the UN organs and committees ($\rightarrow$ Committees, System of) during the seventies. At the beginning of the eighties deep breaks in the already unstable "united front" of Moscow and the Third World became apparent, on the one hand because the USSR did not participate in concrete development UN activities and, on the other because, at the end of 1979, Moscow had intervened in Afghanistan, a non-aligned country.

Year after year an overwhelming majority of states in the → General Assembly condemned the Soviet intervention. The official statements of the Soviet leadership in the UN organs did, of course, not mention at all the weakened Soviet position within the United Nations. Just as little did they deal with the fact that the dramatic financial crisis of the organization in the middle of the eighties (→ Financial Crises) had also been caused by the Soviet refusal to fulfill its obligation towards the payment of its assessed contributions. Thus Moscow's speeches and declarations on the occasion of the 40th anniversary of the United Nations in 1985 were abundant with self-praise; this use of propagandistic and empty formulas, however, would soon belong to the past

V. UN Policy under Gorbachev

Looking back, it is clear that when Michail Gorbachev took office as Secretary-General of the Communist Party in March 1985, an era of profound re-orientation and re-organization of almost all areas of Soviet politics began. In foreign affairs a process started in which this "new thinking" gradually assumed clearer outlines. The fundamental transformation with regard to foreign policy also contained a conceptual re-orientation of the Soviet UN policy. In the years 1987/88 Gorbachev personally designed an outline of which the key part – taking into account global thinking and global responsibility – represented a "comprehensive security system" (*Unser* 1990). Within a complex global security system, i.e. including all relevant areas of peaceful human cohabitation, the UN system with branches all over the world, should be assigned a dominant and exclusive role ("Toward comprehensive security through the enhancement of the role of the United Nations", Aide-mémoire of the USSR submitted to the United Nations, 22 September 1988, UN Doc. A/43/629). The United Nations should become dominant regarding certain func-

tions within the area of security policy. There the world organization should not only provide the framework, the skeleton of the security system, it should also offer the necessary equipment.

The revaluation of the role and the authority of the United Nations aimed at three areas:
- increase of the effectiveness of the principal organs in consideration of the special, prominent position of the Security Council;
- creation of new UN organs (e.g. an environmental organization); and
- financial reorganization of the United Nations.

Gorbachev's new thinking, directed at a world order model with the United Nations at its center, found its counterpart in the new Soviet behavior within the international organization. It was the Soviet Union which in the long run caused a renaissance of the United Nations in the area of peacekeeping. In the middle of the eighties, the Soviet attitude virtually undermined the US policy of dissociation from the world organization under President Reagan (cf. *Weiss/Kessler* 1990, 104f.) (→ UN Policy, USA). Thus the USA finally gave up its hesitant attitude in relation to multilateral conflict regulation in the hands of the Security Council. The Security Council increasingly functioned as a clearing house between the two world powers.

The willingness to cooperate was submitted to a severe test with the outbreak of the Second Gulf War, i.e. with the invasion of Kuwait by Iraqi troops at the beginning of August 1990. Thanks to the reconciliation of interests between the USA and the Soviet Union, the Security Council reacted with unprecedented determination. At the same time, however, under US guidance a "historic precedent" (in the opinion of Voronzov, Soviet UN ambassador at the time) was created by the military anti-Saddam coalition

VI. UN Policy under Yeltsin

At the end of the Second Gulf War in January 1992, during the historic meeting of the Security Council members – for the first time in its history on the level of the heads of state and of government, the Russian president, Boris Yeltsin, took the opportunity to underline that the Russian Federation would continue the active UN policy which had been introduced by Gorbachev in the name of the USSR. At the same time he announced the readiness of his government to take part in future UN operations in the field of peacekeeping.

Russia's basic view of the United Nations over the course of time is embedded in the foreign policy guidelines of Moscow. This view can be described by comparing the respective statements of the Russian government representatives in the general debates at the beginning of the new sessions of the UN General Assembly.

"Russia", according to the credo of Boris Yeltsin when addressing the General Assembly in September 1994, "is undergoing changes and regaining its identity, but in every respect it remains a great power." It is conscious of its responsibility as a permanent member of the Security Council (UN Doc. A/49/PV.5).

Following this line of thought the thesis of winners and losers of the Cold War is being rejected, and a warning against the danger of a unilateral world order – with the USA as the leading power – is posted ("The idea of supremacy is extremely dangerous" – stated Yeltsin in 1994).

Instead of this, Russian politicians fall back on a slogan out of Gorbachev's concept of UN reorganization. They propagate the foundation of a "comprehensive system of security" (based on a far-reaching concept of security), a multilateral world order on the basis of the equality of states and justice. This should be developed under the auspices of the United Nations. Peacekeeping, with the protection of human rights (→ Human Rights, Protection of) and protection of minorities (→ Minorities, Protection of) is granted priority. It is clear that here Russia puts also the main emphasis of its own foreign policy, in

particular in relation to the republics of the former Soviet Union which are united under the roof of the Commonwealth of Independent States (CIS).

It is obvious that Russia persists in giving the United Nations a more important position, and it especially insists on the importance of the Security Council in the field of peacekeeping. Again and again Russia points to the Charter provision concerning the main responsibility of the Security Council for international peace and security, and it demands the adherence to all resolutions made by the Security Council. The Russian representatives postulate the following statement in each meeting of the General Assembly: all use of armed force must be authorized by the Security Council and should be monitored by it. Therefore Moscow also pleads for a reactivation of the Military Staff Committee in accordance with Article 47 of the Charter. In recent years Russian government representatives repeatedly expressed themselves critically regarding the multitude of imposed UN → sanctions and spoke of a questionable "syndrome of sanctions".

The Russian view about a security structure promoting world peace is not based on the pillar of a global UN protection system only, but also includes – in the sense of decentralization – regional security systems. The emergence of the latter should be coordinated by the United Nations and their existence should be ensured by the interaction between Security Council and the regional organizations in accordance with Chapter VIII of the UN Charter. Here again and again the CIS and the Organization for Security and Co-operation in Europe (OSCE) are referred to, and their significance is pointed out.

It is evident that Moscow has a particular interest in the stabilization of these regional organizations, which in the sense of Russian military doctrine enclose the "nearby foreign countries" (*Raevsky/Vorobev* 1994). Thus the Russian efforts in the area of the CIS pursue the object of becoming a regulatory power or "policeman" under a UN mandate (*Zagorski* 1996). In the beginning of 1995 the Russians expressed the desire to obtain an official UN mandate (blue helmet status) for their troops stationed in Georgia, Tajikistan and other neighboring republics. But the soldiers should nevertheless remain under the direct command of Moscow. This demand led to a sharp controversy with then UN Secretary-General Boutros-Ghali, who gave an unmistakable rejection to this demand.

Up to the era of Gorbachev, the Soviet Union traditionally critically judged or even rejected the → peacekeeping operations of the United Nations. Since 1991, however, Russia has not only advocated the development and enhancement of that instrument, moreover, it took part in different UN operations in providing both financial resources and personnel (so among others in MONUA, UNIKOM, MINURSO and UNMIBH) (as of February 2002: 372 soldiers and civilians).

Since the beginning of the nineties, at least, there has been discussion about a UN reform (→ Reform of the UN). In this discussion Russia accentuates the necessity of change and it pleads for a "well-considered" process of reorganization that includes the whole UN system. Moscow is against short-sighted, selective modifications, and therefore radical suggestions are looked upon with great reservation. The line of thought followed throughout by Russia aims at an improvement of the effectiveness and efficiency of the United Nations on the basis of the present UN Charter (*Boardman* 1994). Therefore Russia strongly supports the → "Agenda for Peace", published by former UN Secretary-General Boutros-Ghali in June 1992. This re-organization plan offers – in the opinion of Russia – a concept after which both the peacekeeping and the security "capacity" of the United Nations can be made stronger and more efficient within the context of the Charter and its provisions, i.e. without amendments of the Charter.

The suggestions brought forward by Russian representatives in the General Assembly and in UN committees almost always refer to the area of international peace and security, in particular to disarmament. They also wish to see an improvement in the protection of both minorities and human rights. On the other hand there are hardly any new suggestions concerning development cooperation (→ Development Cooperation of the UN System), and the existing financial and budgetary problems (→ Budget) are also not dealt with, probably because of the Russian arrears. Russia praises the reform steps that have been initiated by Secretary-General Kofi Annan since 1997 (cf. UN Doc. A/51/950 of 14 July 1997) only in very general terms.

Its attitude towards a reform of the Security Council initially showed a strong reservation. Until 1998 there are only passing remarks concerning this topic in the statements in the general debates. The written statements and the contributions in the respective UN Working Group do contain more concrete statements, but they also include warnings against proceeding too quickly.

The necessity to modify the composition of the Security Council in order to obtain a better regional balance has been recognized by Russia in the meantime, although Yeltsin still praised the "current composition of this organ" at the beginning of 1992. But for the Russian leadership the "effectiveness" of the modes of decision and operation of the "central United Nations organ bearing primary responsibility for the maintenance of international peace and security" remains the supreme criterion, as Russia states in its official reply to the request of UN Secretary-General Boutros-Ghali addressed to the member states to submit written comments on a possible review of the membership of the Security Council in 1993 (UN Doc. A/48/264, 20 July 1993). In the UN Working Group on the Reform of the Security Council, Russia did not make a commitment to one particular model of reorganization. It did indicate that it is in favor of a "limited" to "minimal" numerical extension of the Council. New permanent members – Russia mentioned Germany and Japan as possible candidates – should be granted the right of veto, which should not be changed at all: "… Russia continues to firmly oppose any restriction … of the veto, be it through amendment to the Charter or otherwise." (Statement by a Representative of the Russian Federation in the Working Group on Security Council Reform on Veto Issue, 24 March 1999; source: Permanent Mission of Russia to the UN, Internet page)

VII. UN Policy under Putin

Russia's foreign policy is still based on the document "The Foreign Policy Concept of the Russian Federation" which was confirmed by President Vladimir Putin in June 2000 (*Putin* 2000). In his speech on "Russia's role within global politics" at the 43rd Munich Conference on Security Policy, Putin made some pointed statements concerning Moscow's national identity. Regarding "unilateral and frequently illegitimate actions" especially of the USA, he reasserted "that the unipolar model is not only unacceptable but also impossible in today's world" (www.securityconference. de/konferenzen/rede.php?menu_2007=& menu_2008=&menu_konferenzen=& sprache=en&id=179&).

In Putin's era, the commitment to and the demand for multilateral action runs through Russian declarations of foreign policy principles. "There is no alternative to tackling the existing problems through multilateral diplomacy." (Russian Foreign Minister Sergey Lavrov during the General Debate of the 61st Session of the UN General Assembly in September 2006; www.un.int/russia/new/ MainRoot/Statements/ga/GA61.htm).

The world order of the 21st century has to be based on collective mechanisms of solutions, the priority of right and a wide democratization of international relations. For Russia the United Nations has to remain the main regulation centre for international relations. As a matter

of principle, the use of force – as a last resort – can only be considered legitimate if the decision is sanctioned by the Security Council of the United Nations.

Two occurrences at the beginning of the 21st century initially caused a shock and are having a lasting influence on international politics: first, the September 11, 2001 terrorist attacks upon New York and Washington and, second, the beginning of the war in Iraq in March 2003. The world-wide threat through international terrorism and the arbitrary military course of action of the USA and its allies, have confronted the United Nations and its member states with new challenges.

The United Nations immediately reacted to the terror attacks upon the USA ("one of the most dramatic points during my mission in New York" – said retrospectively the former Russian UN-Ambassador Lavrov; (*Lavrov* 2005, 24). The Security Council unanimously categorized the attacks as a threat to world peace (S/RES/1368, para. 1), called for counteractions (para. 3 and 4) and confirmed the right of individual and collective self-defence (preamble). In another unanimously passed resolution (S/RES/1373), for the first time in its history, the Council acted in the manner of an international legislator and committed the member states to large-scale measures against terrorism. With the same resolution, the Council established the Counter-Terrorism Committee (CTC), a special control regime: "A robust antiterrorist coalition was formed." (*Lavrov* 2005, 24) Without doubt, one of the few impressive moments of collective action within the UN in recent times.

In his speech at the Security Council summit in September 2005 in New York President Putin focused on the war against terror: "Our common task is to create a truly solid front in the fight against this evil." (UN Doc. S/PV.5261, 14 September 2005, 4) In this process the UN and especially the Security Council have to be strengthened in their position as "the coordinating centre, the headquarters of the international antiterrorist front." (ibid., 4). Russia would support this course and would be willing to cooperate closely. He referred (ibid., 4) in his speech explicitly to the "International Convention for the Suppression of Acts of Nuclear Terrorism", which was initiated by Russia and passed by the General Assembly in April 2005 (UN Doc. A/RES/59/290, 13 April 2005).

Russia was the first to sign that Convention and the first among nuclear powers to ratify it in October 2006; in July 2007 the Convention became effective (UNTS No. 44004). Russia also forcefully demanded the realization of a common strategic approach to fighting terrorism with a global counter terrorism strategy, which was finally approved by the General Assembly in September 2006 (UN Doc. A/RES/60/288, 8 September 2006).

Already before the 2003 Iraq war, in autumn 2002, the unity of the anti-terrorist coalition within the Security Council concerning the joint action against the Taliban regime in Afghanistan was about to break up. In particular when "under the specious pretext of stopping the proliferation of weapons of mass destruction, the UN Security Council was urged to authorize an intervention against a sovereign state – Iraq." (*Lavrov* 2005, 24) Russia forcefully advocated a political solution, as Lavrov retrospectively described in detail – "we were against the military solution" (so also Russian Foreign Minister Igor *Ivanov* 2003, 35) – and warned against the consequences of military action without the authorization of the Security Council. What, after all, amounted to unilateral action by the United States and its allies was from the viewpoint of Russia's foreign policy "one of the most dramatic manifestations of unilateral approaches to dealing with acute international problems, and a serious challenge to multilateralism" (former Deputy Foreign Minister of Russia, Iurii *Fedotov* 2004). In Russia's judgment the Iraq war raised the awareness that there is no alternative to multilateralism, as embodied in the UN.

In the current conflicts with North Korea and Iran about their nuclear programmes, Russia pleads for a negotiated settlement "solely by politico-diplomatic methods" (the Russian Foreign Ministry in a press release concerning the passing of the resolution 1803 in March 2008, in which the Security Council put considerable pressure on Iran; www. mid.ru/brp_4.nsf). Russia reused this conflict as an opportunity to make a claim for strengthening the non-proliferation regimes on a generally acceptable basis (Address by Sergey *Lavrov*, Minister of Foreign Affairs at the 62nd UN General Assembly in September 2007, UN Doc. A/62/PV.11, 28 September 2007, 15-18). The situation with the non-proliferation regimes is far from being ideal, and serious problems in that area are closely connected with the stagnation of the disarmament process. At the same time, it has to be ensured in the opinion of the Russian government that the benefits of peaceful atomic energy are legitimately accessible to all states. Questions of disarmament and corresponding abuses (for example concerning aerospace) are doubtlessly one of the basic principles of Russia's UN policy.

In one of the most difficult regional conflicts, the by now escalated Kosovo-question, Russia supports the Serbian position on the illegal character of the unilateral proclamation of the province's independence, running counter to Security Council resolution 1244. For Moscow it is certain: "The situation in Kosovo remained under the close control of the UNSC." (Russian Foreign Ministry in a press release from April 1 2008; www.mid.ru/ brp_4.nsf)

To cope effectively with the growing variety of peace-threatening challenges, Russian UN policy is aimed at the strengthening of the organizational and legal framework of UN peacekeeping activities. "It will be in our common interest to use more actively the UN peacekeeping capabilities." (*Lavrov*, Address at the 62nd General Assembly, September 2007, see above) At the end of 2007, Russia contributed 293 peacekeepers, which ranks it as number 43 in the list of states dispatching personnel to UN peacekeeping operations. Russia contributed its major contingent of 143 troops, military observers and police to UNMIS in Sudan. Russian proposals to reform and modernize the UN peacekeeping instruments (cf. *Fedotov* 2004, 12) include the revitalization of the UN Military Staff Committee, the subsidiary body of the UN Security Council. The gist of this proposal is to tap the expertise of professional military experts in analyzing the various aspects of peacekeeping activities.

The upgrading of the Committee consisting of the "Chiefs of Staff of the permanent Members of the Security Council" (UN Charter Art. 47) "would be conducive to intensifying the UN's military component" (*Fedotov* 2004, 12). With regards to the creation of peace-promoting political instruments, Russia was an active proponent of the establishment of the Peacebuilding Commission (PBC) in December 2005 – an important tool of international assistance in stabilizing the situation in countries that have emerged from acute crisis.

One central doctrine of the Russian UN policy reads as follows: "The interest of asserting the principle of multilateralism requires consolidation of the UN's central role not only in matters of peace and security but also in socio-economic, humanitarian, and environment spheres." (*Fedotov* 2004, 13) Accelerated efforts to achieve the Millennium Development Goals (especially in Africa) are demanded, whereby at the same time the need for increased engagement of international development assistance is underlined. Russia is one of the fastest growing economies of the world and is now a very important donor country. By its own account, Russia has written off or undertaken to write off 11.3 billion US dollars of African countries' debt (*Lavrov,* Address to the General Assembly 2006, UN Doc. A/61/PV.15, 21 September 2006, 30). Moscow considers climate protection as another outstanding global issue the UN has to face and Russia made the plea for

an effective approach to climate change that requires agreed and scientifically-based solutions that are realistic, balanced, and do not undercut the countries' rights to development (*Lavrov,* Address to the General Assembly 2007, see above).

The Russian government strongly supports UN human rights protection but stresses that the main responsibility rests with the states themselves, while international institutions and mechanisms play only a supplementary role contributing to the achievements of these goals. Moscow strongly condemns the practice of using human rights issues as a pretext for interference in the internal affairs of states (cf. Position of the Russian Federation at the 62nd Session of the UN General Assembly; www.un.int/russia/new/MainRoot/docs/interview/240807indexen.htm).

Russia was one of the states, which supported the substitution of the criticized UN Commission on Human Rights (→ Human Rights, Commission on) through the UN Human Rights Council (UNHRC), an absolute necessity for a qualitative improvement of UN work in the human rights sphere. In the first election of the 47 members for the Council, Russia represented the Eastern European group and obtained the best results. The government took this as another proof of Russia's high renown – not only within the UN: "This result demonstrates Russia's prestige and role in the system of international relations" (*Lukiyantsev* 2006, 55).

In Russian statements concerning UN issues, claims and proposals for reforms are mentioned more and more often in recent years. At the 60th Session of the General Assembly on September 15, 2005, President Putin outlined Russia's cautious plan for reforms as follows: "Indeed, there is a need to adjust the Organization to new historic realities. But this process should be constructive. It should take into account both the lessons learned and the positive experience gained by the United Nations. And this process must unite, not separate." Only on the basis of wide consent a real strengthening of UN's authority and legitimacy could be achieved (*Putin* 2005, Address to the General Assembly on the occasion of the High-level Plenary Meeting, 15 September 2005, UN Doc. A/60/PV.5, 4).

Moscow supported the work of the High-level Panel on Threats, Challenges and Change, which was also joined by Yevgenii Primakov, former prime minister of Russia (cf. *Fedotov*, 10) and appreciated Kofi Annan's reform report "In larger freedom: towards development, security and human rights for all" (UN Doc. A/59/2005, 21 March 2005) as a result of a the panel process: "The report's principal value is that it aims to strengthen the security system with the UN Security Council at the top, streamline the Organization's structure, and make it more effective in various spheres." (*Zaemsky* 2005, 29)

During the debate about the report at the General Assembly at the beginning of April 2005, the Russian representative asserted that the Security Council adopt a resolution on the principles of the use of force, but its formulations must not impair the Council's ability to take relevant decisions (UN Doc. A/59/ PV.87, 7 April 2005, 6; see also UN Press Release GA/10338).

The Russian position on the three draft resolutions for the reform of the Security Council, presented at the 59th General Assembly (2005) – the Group of Four, the "Uniting for Consensus" group and the African Union – was ambivalent (cf. Ambassador Denisov, UN Doc. A/59/PV.112, 12 July 2005, 7-8; cf. also *Zaemsky*, 7). On the one hand Moscow had supported the candidateship of Brazil, Germany, India and Japans as well as that of some developing countries, but on the other Russia was put off by the consequences of a crucial vote on the draft that does not enjoy the maximum possible support of the member states – hence the Russian plea for continuing the search for an acceptable formula for a controlled, limited enlargement based on a broad consensus in the interests of strengthening the UN (cf. *Denisov* 2005, ibid.).

Concerning the power of veto of new members, the Russian government changed its position in summer 2005. In contrast to former Russian viewpoints – new permanent members should be provided with the power of veto – Russia now took a more reserved stand: "We believe that the right of the veto should not be granted *a priori* before the list of new permanent Security Council members is determined." (Russian UN Ambassador Denisov at the General Assembly Plenary on 12 July 2005, UN Doc. A/59/PV.112, 8; cf. also UN Press Release GA/10368). In other statements concerning the reform of the UN Security Council Russia formulates – beside the call for a broad consensus among member states – the claim for a limited membership (for example "20 plus") and for the expansion of the Security Council without affecting its effectiveness. The position paper the Russian Ministry of Foreign Affairs presented at the 62nd session of the UN General Assembly (2007/08) confirmed this three-part Russia's reform position, connected with the warning: "... it is unacceptable to rush decisions in that regard as that would inevitably antagonize international relations." (Position of the Russian Federation, 24 August 2007, www.un. int/russia/new/MainRoot/docs/interview /240807indexen.htm).

Although Russia considers the expansion of the Security Council as the key component of UN reforms, other fields should also be included in the reform process. Thus among other items the activities of the General Assembly should be streamlined, the task of coordination of the Economic and Social Council ($\rightarrow$ ECOSOC) should be improved and within the scope of the reform of the management system, especially the effectiveness of the Secretariat should be enhanced (cf. the position papers of the Russian Foreign Ministry presented at the 61st and 62nd General Assembly (for the 61st: www.un.int/russia/new/ MainRoot/docs/interview/060831index-en.htm; for the 62nd cf. above).

The Russian Foreign Minister Sergey Lavrov, who represented Russia as one of the most experienced UN ambassadors in New York from 1995–2005, affirmed: "Russian diplomacy will continue its policy aimed at enlarging the UN's role and effectiveness in the today's world." (*Lavrov* 2005, 29) Further on, the political leadership in Russia will support the Russian UN policy –"... today, the UN is as important for Russia as it was 60 years ago" (*Zaemsky* 2005, 12) – which means that Russian cooperation within the UN is also of use for the national interest of the Russian Federation.

During his visit to Moscow in spring 2008, Secretary-General Ban Ki-moon found appreciative words for the position Russia represents at present within the UN: "The Russian principle of a multipolar world is close to the notion of multilateralism – the bedrock of the United Nations." (UN Press Release SG/SM/11507 of 10 April 2008)

Günther Unser

Lit.: *Allison, R.:* Peacekeeping in the Soviet Successor States, Paris 1994; *Belonogov, A.:* We have no other UN, in: International Affairs, Moscow, No. 4, 2003, 64-79; *Boardman, R.:* Post-Socialist World Orders. Russia, China and the UN System, Houndmills et al. 1994; *Daley, T.:* Russia's „Continuation" of the Soviet Security Council Membership and Prospective Russian Policies toward the United Nations, Santa Monica 1992; *Denisov, A.:* Speech of the Russian UN Ambassador Denisov at the 59th session of General Assembly, 12 July 2005; UN Doc. A/59/PV.112, 7-8; *Fedotov, I.:* United Nations. Guarantor of International Peace and Stability, in: International Affairs, Moscow, No 1, 2004, 1-7; *Fedotov, I.:* Challenges to Multilateralism and the UN, in: International Affairs, Moscow, No. 3, 2004, 6-14; *Ivanov, I.:* A New Foreign-Policy Year for Russia and the World, in: International Affairs, Moscow, No. 6, 2003, 33-38; *Lavrov, S.:* My Years on East River: Apropos the 60th Anniversary of the Global Organization, in: International Affairs, Moscow, No. 4, 2005, 22-29; *Lavrov, S.:* Address by the Russian Minister of Foreign Affairs Sergey Lavrov at the 61st Session of the UN General Assembly, UN Doc. A/61/PV.15, 21 September 2006, 27-30; *Lavrov, S.:* Address by the Russian Minister of Foreign Affairs Sergey Lavrov at the 62nd Session of the UN General Assembly, UN Doc. A/62/ PV. 11, 28 September 2007, 15-18, also: www.un.int/russia/new/MainRoot/Statements/ga/GA62/ga_docs/Statement280907en.htm; *Lukasuk, J.J.:* Rußland als Rechtsnachfolger in völkerrechtliche Verträge der UdSSR, in: Osteuropa-Recht, 39 (1993), 235-245; *Lukiyantsev, G.:* Council to Replace Commission: Human Rights Problems in the UN, in: IA, Moscow, No. 5, 2006, 51-56; *MacFarlane, S.N./Schnabel, A.:* Russia's Approach to Peacekeeping, in: International Journal, No. 2/1995, 294-324; *Mandelbaum, M. (ed.):* The New Russian Foreign Policy, New York 1998; *Putin, V.:* The Foreign Policy Concept of the Russian Federation. Press Release of the Permanent Mission of the Russian Federation to the United Nations, New York, 28 June 2000, www.un.int/russia/pressrel/2000/00_07_01.htm#english; *Putin, V.:* Address to the General Assembly on the occasion of the High-level Plenary Meeting, 15 September 2005, UN Doc. A/ 60/PV.5, 3-4; *Raevskij, A./Vorobev, J.N.:* Russian Approaches to Peacekeeping Operations, New York and Geneva 1994; *Treniu, D.:* Russians as Peacemakers, in: Politik und Gesellschaft, (1994) No. 3, 257-266; *Unser, G.:* Die Sowjetunion in den Vereinten Nationen, Cologne 1990 (BIOST-Bericht No. 4/ 1990); *Weiss, T.G./Kessler, M.A.:* Moscow's U.N. Policy, in: Foreign Policy No. 79, Summer 1990, 94-112; *Zaemsky, V.:* UN Summit: The Need for Change, in: IA, Moscow, No. 5, 2005, 1-12; *Zagorski, A.V.:* Machtpolitik oder kooperative Friedenserhaltung? Rußlands militärische Einsätze in der früheren Sowjetunion, in: VN 44 (1996), 56-60.

Internet: Homepage of the Permanent Mission of the Russian Federation to the UN: www.un.int/russia.

UN Policy, United Kingdom

The active policy of the United Kingdom with regard to the United Nations dates from before the foundation of the organization when, in 1941, the British Prime Minister Winston Churchill signed the Atlantic Charter together with US President Franklin D. Roosevelt (→ History of the Foundation of the UN). Since then the UK has employed its strong position in the UN to achieve its foreign policy goals. However, the United

Kingdom has in many cases adhered to the principles and decisions of the UN as guiding its foreign policy.

The focal points of the UN policy of the UK were:
- its permanent membership in the → Security Council with the right of veto (→ Veto, Right of Veto);
- since the end of the Cold War, an increasing participation in peacekeeping missions (→ Peacekeeping; → Peacekeeping Operations; → Peacekeeping Forces);
- an intensive involvement in the process of → decolonization,
- an active role in the → reform of the UN.

Additionally, the UK played as co-sponsoring power a decisive role when the → General Assembly adopted the → Uniting for Peace Resolution in 1951, giving in cases of veto-blockades of the Security Council the General Assembly the right to make recommendations in peacekeeping matters.

It is more or less an ironic turn of the UN history, that the UK had to accept in 1956 during the Suez Crisis, that the USA and the USSR used after the French and British vetoes in the Security Council against a ceasefire resolution the Uniting for Peace Resolution to enable the General Assembly to take over the initiative, including the establishment of the first real peacekeeping mission UNEF I.

I. Britain's Role in the Founding of the United Nations

In the Atlantic Charter, which contains several principles for the maintenance of international peace and security, the President of the United States, Franklin D. Roosevelt, and the Prime Minister of the UK, Winston Churchill, agreed in 1941 on some guiding principles for a post-war world order. At the subsequent conferences in Moscow, Teheran, Dumbarton Oaks and Yalta, Churchill introduced concepts which differed significantly in several points from Roosevelt's views.

The British position at the negotiations has to be considered from two points of view: Firstly, the UK tried to compensate its declining status as a world power with a strong position in the UN. Secondly, it attempted to draw the main attention of the international community to Europe, because both world wars had their origin in Europe and were also mainly fought there.

Thus the British Prime Minister intended to replace the system of → collective security, which had failed already in the → League of Nations, by three regional councils to guarantee international peace and security: In 1943 Churchill suggested regional councils for Europe and Asia, and one for the western hemisphere. The great powers would have been represented in each of the councils. These regional councils would have constituted the basis for a global council for the maintenance of international stability (cf. *Luard* 1982, 19f.). Concerning a possible veto right, the UK tried to restrict the use of the veto to substantive questions touching directly the interests of the great powers.

But in the remaining time till the foundation of the UN in San Francisco President Roosevelt managed to push through in the subsequent negotiations of the four powers almost all of his positions against the opposition of the UK, including the question of the use of the veto. According to Roosevelt's concept, after World War II only the great powers USA, USSR, UK, China and (later) France should be responsible for international stability.

Another Briton who played a prominent part beside Churchill in the founding of the UN was the economist John Maynard Keynes. He took over the chairmanship of the British delegation for the negotiations on the economic institutions within the UN system, and contributed significantly to its present organizational structure. Keynes was very critical of the Treaty of Versailles and saw, after World War II, an opportunity to contribute to world peace by establishing a stable economic and currency system. The suggestions he made at the conference in Dumbarton Oaks were based on three principles: firstly, a demand-orientated economic policy, in whose framework deficit spending was to be an instrument for reaching the supreme goal of full employment; secondly, the establishment of the economic and financial institutions World Bank (→ World Bank, World Bank Group) and International Monetary Fund (→ IMF), as well as an international trade organization; and thirdly, a mechanism of fixed exchange rates. With the formulation of his principles, and his theoretical works of the 1920s and 1930s, Keynes laid the academic foundations of the economic system of the UN, although the concrete design of the economic structures was more oriented on the US proposals. Keynes became the first executive director of the International Monetary Fund in 1947.

Although the UK in the persons of Churchill and Keynes was not able to overcome the prevailing influence of the USA in decisive matters, the UK nevertheless succeeded in maintaining within the United Nations structure something of the prestige and influence which it had traditionally enjoyed in international politics: The UK had played a decisive role in the League of Nations, and was one of the victorious powers of the Second World War. This privileged status found its expression in the fact that the UK acceded to one of the five permanent seats in the Security Council, and filled traditionally many high level posts in the Secretariat since then.

II. The Policy of the UK in the Security Council

The conduct of the UK in the Security Council showed where the priorities of its foreign policy lay in relation to the United Nations, with which states the UK cooperated primarily and where its interests collided with those of the majority of UN member states. The most important indicator for this are the 32 vetoes of the UK, which were all interposed before the end of the Cold War, and which reveal two main features of the British UN policy. First, two thirds of the vetoes were interposed together with vetoes of the USA, which under-

lines the close cooperation between the two countries during the Cold War; second, it indicates the special meaning the decolonization process had for the UK, and that its interests in that regard were often opposed to those of the majority of UN member states.

One of the first elementary decisions with which the UN members changed the legal framework of the UN was the above-mentioned Uniting for Peace Resolution. The conduct of the UK regarding this resolution was influenced by two conflicting aims: on the one hand, the UK was one of the sponsors of the resolution in the → General Assembly, but on the other hand it emphasized that its use could also be directed against British interests by circumventing a potential veto in the Security Council. In the end, however, the UK voted in the General Assembly in favor of the resolution.

III. The Suez Crisis

The UK was one of the main actors in the Suez crisis, in whose settlement the United Nations played a decisive role. In July 1956 the Egyptian president Nasser declared the nationalization of the Suez Canal to counterbalance the withdrawal of promises for financial support for the construction of the Assuan dam given by the UK, the USA and the World Bank. After diplomatic initiatives failed to reach an agreement, the UK and France called on the Security Council. The Security Council demanded in a resolution to respect the → sovereignty of Egypt, but also to enable the free transit through the canal. Further negotiations were interrupted through Israel's military attack against Egypt. The UK supported Israel by demanding – through an ultimatum and the threat of using military force – from both states to withdraw its troops to a point ten miles behind the respective bank of the Suez Canal. But at that point of time the Israeli troops had not even reached this line ten miles east of the Suez Canal.

Before the British ultimatum elapsed, the USA brought in a draft resolution in the Security Council which asked for the complete withdrawal of the Israeli troops. This draft resolution was blocked with the first British veto in the Security Council. The day after the British ultimatum elapsed the UK started to bomb Egypt. Referring to the Uniting for Peace Resolution the Security Council called on the General Assembly to deal with the situation. The UK argued that it would withdraw its troops if UN troops separated Egyptian and Israeli forces. This proposal was taken up after a Security Council resolution had been adopted demanding the withdrawal of the British and French troops. The result was the deployment of a UN peacekeeping force (→ Peacekeeping Forces) to which the UK finally agreed, due to pressures from the USA and the world public.

With the withdrawal from its former position in the conflict the UK had accomplished the re-opening the Suez Canal and thus its main political goal, although the proceeding of the UN in settling the conflict did not correspond with the British desires.

IV. Britain's Role in Peacekeeping Operations

The behavior of the UK in the Suez crisis was of importance for its UN policy in two regards: first, the deployment of the first peacekeeping forces replaced the system of collective security; and second, the conduct of the UK in the crisis was very untypical for its later much more constructive peacekeeping policy in the Security Council and its participation in peacekeeping operations.

The UK worked on improving the quality of the missions by enhancing its effectiveness. This policy found its expression – amongst others – in the demands raised already in the 1960s to broaden the legal basis of the missions' mandates from traditional peacekeeping to peacemaking and to install a stand-by contingent of UN troops for rapid deployment. But the UK was – like the other P5 members – for a long time mostly excluded from direct involve-

ment in peacekeeping missions, as the peacekeeping "philosophy" of the UN said that it was not recommendable for the role of the "impartial observers and peacekeepers" to consist of military units of the great powers, as the countries in the conflict region might fear own interests of the great powers in their presence in the region. The only exception in this period was Cyprus, where the UK has been involved as contributor to the peacekeeping mission UNFICYP from the beginning in March 1964. After the end of the Cold War this situation changed considerably and the P5 were asked to contribute to peacekeeping missions, particularly in complex missions with a "robust" mandate.

Consequently the UK presented its concepts of a comprehensive and effective peacekeeping several times in the 1990s and joined – in accordance with the 1992 "Agenda for Peace" (→ Agenda for Peace) – the demands for broadening the use of → preventive diplomacy and post-conflict peace-building.

V. The Process of Decolonization

After the Second World War the UK had to deal with the issue of decolonization which became a reason for tensions with the UN several times, because the UK did not see any need to solve this problem within the framework of the UN system. Its readiness to let the UN participate in the decolonization process of its colonial territories became even less when in the 1960s former colonies became members of the UN (→ Membership and Representation of States) and started complaining in the General Assembly about the lengthy and conflict-prone decolonization process. The UK did not want to accept the restriction of its own capacity to act caused by its being a member of the → Trusteeship Council and the Committee on Decolonization. Together with the fact that the UK had different kinds of legal and political relationships with its former colonies, this fact caused the problem that during the whole decolonization process no coherent pattern of proceeding developed which could have been applied to all former non-independent regions. In some cases the transfer of sovereignty to the area formerly administered by the UK happened in a peaceful manner through the resolution of trusteeship agreements and holding of plebiscites. In other cases the handing-over of the mandates was followed – sooner or later – by violent conflicts, as the examples South Rhodesia, Palestine, India and Cyprus made clear.

Palestine and India are the most important examples of the first of four decades of decolonization. Due to the decline of British power in particular in the Middle East the UK found itself compelled to give the mandate over Palestine back to the UN. The results were the proclamation of the state of Israel, the ensuing first war between Israel and the Arab countries and a conflict which remains unsolved to the present. The division of the Indian subcontinent into one part, dominated by a Hindu majority, and the Muslim Pakistan was also accompanied by conflicts. The result of granting the independence to the two states were three wars between India and Pakistan and the dispute over Kashmir. Although the UK tried in the first decade to accomplish decolonization in accordance with the principles of Chapter XI of the UN Charter ($\rightarrow$ Charter of the UN), the UN was not involved in the decisive issues of the political developments in both cases.

The most portentous case in the second decade of decolonization was the handing-over of the sovereignty of Cyprus to the Greek and Turkish Cypriots in 1960. The resulting power vacuum caused a conflict lasting until today.

In general the second decade of decolonization was characterized by the granting of independence to thirty former British territories without self-government so far, although the UN did only play a minor role in this process. The conflict over South Rhodesia dominated the third decade of the decolonization process. The fact that another twelve colonial territories became independent remained therefore almost unnoticed. The unsuccessful efforts to achieve a peaceful settlement of the conflict in South Rhodesia within the UN became the main feature of this decade. The most important events of the fourth and last decade were the independence of South Rhodesia as Zimbabwe, the maintenance of British sovereignty over the Falklands in the Falkland crisis and the signing of the agreement dealing with the handing-over of Hong-Kong to the People's Republic of China.

In the Falkland conflict the United Nations was able to act as mediator in the background, although one conflict partner was a permanent member of the Security Council, the UK. Beside the condemnation of the Argentine invasion as breach of peace (UN Doc. S/RES/502 (1982), 3 April 1982) through the Security Council UN Secretary-General Pérez de Cuéllar was commissioned by the Council with Resolution 505 to negotiate a ceasefire agreement between the two powers, a second draft resolution asking both sides for a ceasefire was introduced, this time vetoed by the UK (cf. *Spence* 1985, 67). Later on the General Assembly called for further mediating initiatives of the Secretary-General, which the UK officially rejected, but informally accepted. The settlement of the conflict was lastly found in bilateral negotiations, but without doubt the United Nations had a de-escalating effect on the conflict and the UK as great power has – to some extent – accepted this mediating role.

VI. Other Focal Points

Other focal points of the British UN policy were the support for the non-proliferation regime for nuclear weapons ($\rightarrow$ Disarmament), development issues ($\rightarrow$ Development Cooperation of the UN System) and the respect for $\rightarrow$ human rights. The UK significantly contributed to the Partial Test Ban Treaty and was in the early 1960s one of the first countries to strive for a total ban. In this context the UK took over an important mediating role between the two superpowers USA and USSR.

The support of the UK for the developing countries in the UN was ambivalent and led to a lot of criticism from the majority of UN member states. The main point of criticism was primarily that the UK – like the majority of UN member states – never paid the 0.7 per cent of its gross national product as development aid which the industrialized countries had obliged themselves to pay. Furthermore was the UK one of the six countries to vote in the General Assembly against the → "Charter of Economic Rights and Duties of States" and it left → UNESCO in 1985. On the other side the UK increased several times its voluntary contributions to the → specialized agencies of the UN in the 1990s (→ Development Cooperation of the UN System).

The fact that the UK signed every important human rights convention (→ Human Rights, Protection of; → Human Rights Conventions and their Measures of Implementation) showed its constructive attitude towards the global respect for human rights. Apart from that the UK did not pursue any special interests concerning human rights, but followed the general line of the human rights policy of the Western countries.

VII. The UN Policy after the End of the Cold War

With the end of the Cold War the aims of the British UN policy have changed, too. In the face of the rising expectations towards the UN the UK first of all supports a reform of the organization (→ Reform of the UN) with the aim to improve its efficiency. The UK considers this to be necessary because the problems of the future can only be solved with a cooperation of all UN member states, as the British Foreign Secretary Robin Cook emphasized in his speech to the UN General Assembly on 23 September 1997: "The challenges we face are global challenges ... And so the United Nations should have a bigger role than ever before. If it appears to be less relevant, it is not for want of challenge, but for want of reform." (Source: text as published by the UK Mission to

the UN on its Internet homepage, 1 October 1997)

Therefore an important step – in the opinion of the UK – would be the reform of the Security Council. With regard to the different reform options the UK favors an extended Security Council with Germany and Japan and developing countries as new permanent members and also additional non-permanent members However, the UK has made clear repeatedly that while it supports the reform efforts in general, it does not accept reform proposals to restrict the right of veto of the permanent members.

Before the background of the global economic crises at the end of the 20th century the UK demands appropriate security and control mechanisms in order to enhance the transparency of international capital flows.

Further features of its UN policy in recent years are an intensive cooperation with the USA and an active participation in peacekeeping missions and in its further development.

Gregor Kolk / Alexander Theodoridis

Lit.: *Barker, E.:* The British between the Superpowers, Toronto/Buffalo 1983; *Childs, D.:* Britain since 1939 – Progress and Decline, London 1995; *Douglas, R.:* World Crisis and British Decline 1929 – 56, New York 1986; *HMSO Publication Centre:* Aspects of Britain; Chapter: Britain and the UN, London 1994; *Hugh, T.:* The Suez Affair, London 1966; *Goodwin, L.G.:* Britain and the UN, New York 1957; *Jensen E./ Fisher T.:* The United Kingdom - The United Nations, London 1990; *Luard, E.:* A History of the United Nations, Vol. I: The Years of Western Domination, 1945-1955, London/Basingstoke 1982; *Porter, B.:* Britain, Europe and the World 1850-1986: Delusions of Grandeur, Boston/Sydney 1987; *Sked, A./Cook, C.:* Post-War Britain 1945-1992, 4th edn., London 1993; *Smith, M./ White, B./Smith, S.:* British Foreign Policy; Tradition, Change & Transformation, London 1988; *Smith, S./Clarke, M.:* Foreign Policy Implementation, Boston/Sidney 1985; *Spence, J-E.:* The UN and the Falkland Crisis, in: Berridge, G.R./Jennings, A. (eds.): Diplomacy at the UN, London 1985, 59-72; *Tugendhat C./Wallace, W.:* Options for British Foreign Policy in the 1990's, London

1988; *Young W. J.:* The Foreign Policy of Churchill's Peacetime Administration 1951-1955, Leicester 1988.

Addendum

The United Kingdom's policy towards the United Nations needs to be studied from at least three levels of analysis: firstly, the Europeanization of British foreign policy in general and UN policy in particular; secondly, Britain as a permanent member of the UN Security Council; and thirdly, (special) security relations with the United States.

Europeanization of British UN Policy

EU membership has significantly impacted on British foreign policy, leading to a process of socialization and adaptation defining the parameters of its policies towards the United Nations, especially with regard to the General Assembly. With the Common Foreign and Security Policy of the European Union ($\rightarrow$ European Union, Common Foreign and Security Policy at the UN) evolving, Britain has become entangled into a web of coordination frameworks seeking conversion of EU member states' foreign policies (cf. *Paasivirta/Porter* 2006; *Verbeke* 2006). The voting pattern of EU members in the General Assembly may illustrate that point: Overall, EU voting cohesion has tended to increase over time despite subsequent rounds of enlargement (cf. *Sucharipa* 2002, 24ff.; *Luif* 2003).

At the same time, the Europeanization of British UN policy has not prevented the government from pursuing alternative options outside the European mainstream. Especially on strategic matters that are discussed in the General Assembly's First Main Committee (Disarmament and International Security), Britain (together with France) have displayed a rather distinct voting pattern, given their status as nuclear powers and permanent member of the UN Security Council. This has been particularly evident since the mid-1990s, with both countries' voting pattern rather coincid-

ing with the United States (cf. *Luif* 2003, 35).

The United Kingdom and the Council

Permanent membership on the UN Security Council poses a three-fold challenge to the United Kingdom: first, to meet its obligations under the UN Charter; second, to uphold the common positions of the European Union in accordance with Article 19.1 TEU; and thirdly, to protect UK vital interests.

To formulate a British foreign policy in this framework become particularly difficult, when the British government chooses to give the US-UK relationship priority over the UN and EU aspects:

The dispute over Iraq in 2002/03 exposed this dilemma, when the Blair government tried to accommodate the competing and often conflicting demands of supporting the US administration's policy goal to overthrow the regime in Baghdad, maintaining domestic support, especially within the Labour Party, and trying to limit the damage within the European Union (cf. *Hill* 2006).

Inside the Security Council, the United Kingdom sought to perform the role of bridge-builder between the United States and other members of the Council, which became however increasingly difficult the more Washington pushed for military action. While Prime Minister Tony Blair succeeded in forcing the US administration to engage the Security Council by adopting Resolution 1441 (2002), which decided that Iraq had been in material breach of its obligations, he did not succeed to secure a mandate that would have explicitly authorized the invasion (cf. *Malone* 2006).

While Blair publicly still fought for this authorizing second Council resolution, he had in early 2003 secretly already given in to the political line of the US administration, as is proven by a secret memo of a Bush-Blair meeting on 31 January 2003 in Washington, which later was leaked to the press (*Norton-Taylor* in "The Guardian", 3 February 2006): In this talk Bush made it clear that he would start the Iraq intervention with or without the second Council resolution. According to the memo Blair did not object to this standpoint, indeed a close alignment with the USA in this issue.

(Special) US-UK Security Relations

This close alignment of British and US security policies, being not always to the same extent the basis of the relationship of the two governments in general, became particularly pronounced during Tony Blair's term of office (1997-2007). Yet, the proximity of Anglo-American relations tended to be the result of external factors, e.g. the terrorist attacks of 11 September, 2001, rather than domestic variables.

With the external factors changing, this (special) relationship will be unavoidably affected. The deep divisions in Anglo-American relations during the Suez Crisis of 1956/57 and the Vietnam War of 1965-1975 provide ample evidence to support this view. Although one may expect the continuation of close UK-US relations under Prime Minister Gordon Brown's term of office (since June 2007), one should not ignore the policy areas where their foreign policies diverge, e.g. the commitment to the International Criminal Court ($\rightarrow$ ICC), the engagement with Africa, questions of how to address global inequality and justice, how to support so-called failing states, and how to address climate change effectively. Especially in those policy areas, one may expect a distinct UK profile.

Climate change may serve as one example here ($\rightarrow$ Environmental Protection). On the initiative of the United Kingdom, the Security Council, for the first time, held an open debate in April 2007 to explore the relationship between Energy, Security, and Climate, raising awareness for the security risks flowing out of a changing climate, which may impact on potential drivers of conflict such as access to energy, water, food, population movement, and border disputes. The debate set the tone for the subsequent General Assembly informal thematic debate on "Climate Change as a Global Challenge," mobilizing over half of the UN membership to express their ideas on how to address the problem.

Jochen Prantl

Lit.: *Briscoe, N.:* Britain and UN peacekeeping, 1948-67, Basingstoke 2003; *Foreign and Commonwealth Office:* The United Kingdom and the United Nations, July 2006, available at www.fco.gov.uk/Files/kfile/34 4530%20CM6892_Web.pdf; *Hill, C.:* The European Powers in the Security Council: Differing Interests, Differing Arenas, in: Laatikainen, K.V./Smith, K.E. (eds.): The European Union at the United Nations: Intersecting Multilateralisms, Basingstoke 2006, 49-69; *Luif, P.:* EU cohesion in the UN General Assembly (European Union - Institute for Security Studies - Occasional Paper No. 49), Brussels, December 2003; *Malone, D.M.:* The International Struggle Over Iraq: Politics in the UN Security Council 1980-2005, Oxford 2006; *Norton-Taylor, R.:* Blair-Bush deal before Iraq war revealed in secret memo, in: The Guardian, 3 February 2006, www.guardian.co.uk/frontpage/story/ 0,,1701214,00.html, quoted in: Volger, H.: Geschichte der Vereinten Nationen, 2nd, rev. edn., Munich/Vienna 2008, 388; *Paasivirta, E./Porter, D.:* EU coordination at the UN General Assembly and ECOSOC: a view from Brussels, a view from New York, in: Wouters, J./Hoffmeister, F./Ruys, T. (eds.): The United Nations and the European Union: An Ever Stronger Partnership, The Hague 2006, 35-48; *Sucharipa, E.:* Die Europäische Union in den Vereinten Nationen, in: Klein, E./Volger, H. (eds.): Die Vereinten Nationen und Regionalorganisationen vor aktuellen Herausforderungen (Potsdamer UNO-Konferenzen, Vol. 3), Potsdam 2002, 7-31; *Verbeke, J.:* EU coordination on UN Security Council matters, in: Wouters, J./Hoffmeister, F./Ruys, T. (eds.): The United Nations and the European Union: An Ever Stronger Partnership, The Hague 2006, 49-60.

Internet: Homepage of the Permanent Mission of the UK to the UN: www.ukun.org..

UN Policy, USA

The United States is midwife ($\rightarrow$ History of the Foundation of the UN; $\rightarrow$ History of the UN), host, largest contributor and by far the most powerful and therefore most influential member state of the United Nations. The world organization's development largely depends on policy priorities in Washington. Traditionally the US government considers the UN as an integral tool of its foreign policy apparatus. According to its perceived national interest the government in Washington will either try to instrumentalize, marginalize or even obstruct the United Nations. Their respective course of action will be determined by the tactical options available.

The United States' permanent seat in the UN → Security Council assures almost complete control over its agenda and action in international security and conflict management. The UN decision-making on economic matters, however, cannot be controlled in the same manner, as there is no right of veto in the respective UN institutions. Consequently, Washington turns its attention to the → IMF and the World Bank (→ World Bank, World Bank Group), where Western donor countries command significant voting privileges. In environmental and development policy the UN's agenda-setting power and institutional dynamics limit Washington's influence (→ Environmental Protection; → Development Cooperation of the UN System). In these fields the US government practices therefore either unilateral action and or bilateral cooperation.

American policy towards the United Nations is determined by ideological, domestic, and institutional factors. The ideological factor in governmental decision-making is strongest early in a new administration. Presidential initiatives, programmatic speeches, and the incumbent's perception of the UN system set the tone in US-UN relations. The incoming President defines the position of his administration in the traditional UN-policy spectrum ranging from multilateralist or internationalist views on the one hand, to unilateralist and isolationalist approaches on the other.

The leading role of the President in US foreign policy is even stronger in UN policy. The ideological factor is more than the sum of presidential beliefs, it is a strategic instrument itself. As is true on all foreign policy issues, ideology is an important component of the American political culture. It is used to legitimize foreign policy goals domestically and internationally, and to camouflage decisions based on simple self-interest.

During the further course of a presidency, the influence of the ideological factor diminishes. It is the domestic influences, the media, special interests, and institutional conflicts that determine the US government's decision-making. The drift towards a more pragmatic, case-by-case approach grows stronger. High expectations are reduced, crusades are postponed and the realities of international politics are taken more seriously into account. The specifics in New York, the number and variety of issues debated there, the large number of diplomatic players, the national interests and sensibilities involved, and the various levels of conflict tend to obstruct the central function of ideological systems, which reduces complexity.

The more an administration place the United Nations in the spotlight of its foreign policy rhetoric – positively or negatively – the more the organization comes to the attention of American special interest groups – even more so, if the issue concerned is subject to international negotiations. The United Nations might turn from being a stage of international conflict into becoming a player itself, and in some cases even an adversary of domestic interest groups. This development was illustrated best in the negotiations concerning the → Law of the Sea Convention, or the dispute over the New World Information Order within → UNESCO in the early 80s.

The periodic pragmatization in US policy toward the United Nations corresponds to diminishing influence of US interest groups. The far-reaching US control of the United Nations on security policy, a pragmatic US approach on UN reform and the exclusion of the Organization from disarmament and global economic policy, limits the policy options for American interest groups. An organization which the US government considers and treats as *one* foreign policy instrument *among others* tends to vanish from the American policy agenda, and the activity of special interest groups ceases.

For the American media, there is no general interest in the United Nations. US coverage of the UN focuses on security policy and conflict resolution. Journalists tend to follow a rather superficial foreign policy concept. International developments are reflected in the US media as consequences of traditional power politics (→ Public Opinion and the UN). Surprisingly enough, up to a few years ago the United Nations had no public relations concept for dealing with the host country. While even small and regional powers keep public affairs officers in Washington, the United Nations had left it mostly to the Americans in government and in the media to comment, analyze, and judge events and developments in New York. Misunderstandings and wrong descriptions of the decision-making realities in the UN headquarters are an almost inevitable result, as the events in and coverage of Somalia 1992-1993 show. Under these circumstances it was and still is tempting for the US administration to try to turn the UN into a scapegoat for the indecisiveness of the relevant great powers. UN Secretary-General Kofi Annan has obviously recognized this problem and started several reform initiatives to increase the efficiency of the UN public relations work (→ Public Information of the UN).

With their foreign policy initiatives interest groups, the media, as well as the executive and legislative branches of government, look for the highest possible approval in public opinion. Even though, as the examples of Somalia, Rwanda, and Iraq have shown, the attention span of the American public is limited, public opinion tends to favor a pragmatic approach in US foreign policy over ideologically motivated activism. Nevertheless, the presidential system of government demands both general pragmatism as well as some national guidance, and visionary leadership. These opposing demands force the American presidents to adjust to varying and sometimes even conflicting expectations at home.

The 70s brought a widening gap in UN policy priorities between the executive and legislative branches of the US government. Congress reacted earlier than did the administration to a growing skepticism in the American public towards the United Nations. The traditional rivalry between Congress and the White House in foreign policy supported a trend of many members of Congress to distance themselves from the UN. Especially since Carter's open internationalism was – in the face of the Soviet invasion in Afghanistan and the UN debate on a "New International Economic Order" (→ International Economic Relations and New International Economic Order (NIEO) – a view shared only by a clear minority on Capitol Hill. This growing gap led Congress to use its most powerful policy instrument, the power of the purse, against the United Nations. In holding back ever larger shares of the US contributions to the UN, Congress pursued a policy, totally independent from, and later even opposed to the White House. By the end of the 1980s Congress basically controlled American UN policy through its financial boycott, and tried to influence directly and even to dominate the UN agenda (→ Financial Crises).

Generally, Congress will try to influence foreign and UN policy whenever it expects thereby to gain advantage it its ongoing rivalry with the President. The politically and ideologically motivated financial boycott of the United Nations is an exceptional case of legislative action in US foreign policy. On 7 June 1985, the US Senate passed the so-called Kassebaum Amendment, which reduced the regular US membership contribution to the United Nation unilaterally by 20%. Only if the United Nations would change its voting procedures on all decisions relevant to the → budget and introduce a weighted voting system reflecting member states' contributions, would regular payments be resumed. Even the Reagan administration, otherwise not known for its UN-friendliness, complained about that legislation's inconsistency with international law, and the limitations the Kassebaum Amendment placed on its UN policy options.

The administrative structure of American UN policy differs significantly from the regular US foreign policy apparatus. It derives from the prominent status of the US Permanent Representative to the United Nations. He or she is a ranking cabinet member with direct access to the president. No other ambassador commands his own channels of communication to the White House. This independence has almost always generated rivalry between the State Department and the US Mission to the UN. The permanent representative is hard to limit to the role of messenger within the chains of command and reporting within the State Department bureaucracy. Various UN Permanent Representatives, most effectively Andrew Young (1977-1979) and Jeane J. Kirkpatrick (1981-1984), followed their own foreign policy priorities, independent from the Secretary of State and in direct communication with the President and Congress. The ambassadorial independence sometimes turned into a serious coordination problem in American UN policy (cf. *Finger* 1988). The infighting between the UN ambassador and the Secretary of State during the Falkland War greatly diminished the effectiveness of Washington's diplomacy in that conflict. The smooth cooperation between Secretary Baker and Ambassador Pickering on the other hand was essential for forming the legendary anti-Iraq coalition of 1990/91 and for passing the historic resolutions 678 and 687 in the UN Security Council.

The influence the United Nations itself can exercise on American UN policy depends on a combination of different factors. On security and human rights issues it is important how the United Nations is perceived within the

US government. If for example the US president considers the United Nations to be a significant forum for international debate, the United Nations can try to use that openness to draw the United States into the international decision-making process and thereby influence the administration in Washington. But in instances when the US government sees the United Nations as an arena for ideological conflict between nations, or as a scapegoat, the UN looses its influence in Washington. Finally, if the US President perceives the UN simply as a tool for political coordination between governments, then the United Nations is limited to be exactly that.

The perception of a possible role for the United Nations within the US government shifts with changes in the international framework. After the Cold War the United States was the sole undisputed superpower. Its dominance in the United Nations was unprecedented, as demonstrated during the Second Gulf War and by the comprehensive set of sanctions against Iraq. After the breakdown of the Soviet Union, Washington was able to dominate the United Nations. Before 1988/89 the superpower rivalry alone prevented Washington from completely integrating the UN Security Council into its own foreign policy apparatus.

Since 1992 – after new differences with Russia and China, international annoyance about more than 1 billion dollars of American debt to the UN, and decreasing willingness on the part of developing countries to cooperate with the United States, American dominance has been again challenged. Consequently Washington has distanced itself from the UN. While President Clinton in 1992 publicly asked for a standing UN military task force, only two years later, in 1994, he argued the opposite and was not even willing to place any American soldiers under UN command. In a basic document on its foreign policy, the classified Presidential Decision Directive 25 "U.S. Policy on Reforming Multilateral Peace Operations", of which an executive summary was published (reprinted in: ILM 33 (1994), No. 3, 795-815), the Clinton government in May 1994 even claimed the right to unilateral military intervention to defend US national interests.

After the disasters in Somalia, Rwanda, and in former Yugoslavia, the lost elections in Congress 1994, and in reaction to the growing isolationalist mood in the US public, the Clinton administration turned away from collective peacekeeping altogether (cf. *MacKinnon* 2000, 64ff.).

Through its → specialized agencies and global conferences (→ World Conferences) the United Nations can exert some functional pressure on participating governments to achieve consensus and compromise. Other than in the UN Security Council where the veto powers can prevent decision and action at any time, in UN conferences and multilateral negotiation fora, like the UN Conference on Environment and Development, the UN Conference on the Law of the Sea or the negotiations on the International Criminal Court (→ ICC), its ability to block a negotiation process is limited. In these instances it is the United States government that is under pressure to adjust.

Generally, the United Nations does not command efficient sanction leverage towards its most powerful member state to influence its internal decision-making. US policy decisions towards the United Nations are determined by Washington's perception of international developments, by domestic financial and political necessities, by the rivalry between the legislative and executive branches of government, and by internal administrative conflicts. During the 1970s and 1980s the institutional conflict between Congress and the White House, as well as that between the State Department and the US Mission in New York, played a significant role in UN policy formulation. In the last decade it has been public opinion, the media, and the need for pragmatic international crisis management by the president that has determined American UN policy. The policy toward the

United Nations has become to a large extent a function of US domestic politics. The United Nations has grown more dependent on US decision-making, without a corresponding capacity to influence its outcome.

Frank Zitka

Lit.: *Bennis, P.:* Calling the Shots. How Washington Dominates Today's UN, New York 1996; *Boutros-Ghali, B.:* Unvanquished: A US-UN Saga, New York 1999; *Coate, R. (ed.):* US Policy and the Future of the United Nations, New York 1994; *Finger, S.M.:* American Ambassadors at the UN. People, Politics, and Bureaucracy in Making Foreign Policy, New York/London 1988; *Gregg, R.W.:* About Face? The United States and the United Nations, Boulder/London 1993; *Laurenti, J.:* US Reluctance and UN Revival, in: International Spectator 34 (1999), No. 4, 13-20; *Lehmann, I.:* Peacekeeping and Public Information. Caught in the Cross-Fire, London 1999; *MacKinnon, A.:* The Evolution of US Peacekeeping Policy under Clinton: a Fairweather Friend? London 2000; *Maynes, C.W./Williamson R.S. (eds.):* US Foreign Policy and the United Nations System, New York/London 1996; *Parsons, A.:* The UN and the National Interests of States, in: Roberts, A./Kingsbury, B. (eds.): United Nations, Divided World: The UN's Role in International Relations, 2nd rev. and expand. edn., Oxford 1993, 104-124; *Zitka, F.:* Wandel und Kontinuität. Amerikanische UNO-Politik 1977-1993, Frankfurt (Main) 1997.

Addendum

The terrorist attacks of September 11, 2001, on New York and Washington, killing 2,974 people, mostly civilians – significantly more than the number of US combatants losing their lives in the Japanese aerial attacks on Pearl Harbor in December 1941 – impacted deeply on US foreign policy, including US-UN relations. While terrorism had only been inconsistently dealt with by the General Assembly and the Security Council prior to the direct attacks on US soil, it became a persistent and a systematic focus of the United Nations in the aftermath (cf. *Weiss et al.* 2007).

The policy shift has been testimony of the extent to which the United Nations is influenced essentially in its political decisions by the United States. Resolution 1368, adopted by the Security Council one day after the terrorist attacks, for the first time explicitly acknowledged that using force in response to non-state violence was in accordance with "the inherent right of individual or collective self-defence" under Article 51 of the UN Charter, which, in essence, legitimized subsequent US intervention in Afghanistan. The Council resolution also called on UN member states to strengthen cooperation in preventing and suppressing terrorist acts, including its financing. Council Resolution 1373 of September 28, 2001, further specified this call and requested member states to adopt comprehensive measures, whose implementation would be monitored by a newly established committee for this task, the Counter-Terrorism Committee (CTC).

On the one hand, the George W. Bush Administration sought to invoke multilateral support for the so-called "War on Terrorism" through the United Nations framework; on the other hand, despite talking up the potential role of multilateral instruments in countering terrorist activities, the United States has been far more reluctant to provide the United Nations with substantial means to engage in expanded counter-terrorist activities (cf. *Luck* 2004). The turn to the United Nations in exchange for multilateral assistance was greeted with skepticism by large parts of the UN membership because of the selectivity of US foreign policy choices, which did not spill over into other key areas of global concern such as land mines, the reduction of greenhouse gases (Kyoto Protocol) (→ Environmental Protection), or the International Criminal Court (→ ICC).

US selectivity has also been the predominant policy pattern with regard to UN reform and adaptation. While the US administration strongly supported joint efforts to promote the implementation of the Millennium Development goals, enlarging Security Council membership did not rank very high on the policy agenda. The lukewarm US support for Council reform evaporated in summer 2005, when the Group of Four (Brazil, Germany, India, and Japan), the African Union, and the Italian-led 'Uniting for Consensus' group tabled three competing draft resolutions in the UN General Assembly. This shift reflected US concerns that the strong focus on Security Council adaptation might effectively endanger the implementation of the other parts of the UN reform agenda (*Volger* 2007, 523-533).

Yet, US foreign policy-making has remained remarkably consistent with its long-term pattern to seek the best of two worlds, that is, pursuing policy goals with a maximum degree of flexibility while seeking the greatest possible international support in exercising leadership. Such pattern is rooted in US exceptionalism rather than based on any suggested unilateral or multilateral teleology. While there is a strong convergence on substance across Presidential administrations, the divergences in style, that is, public diplomacy, *are* considerable. The controversial appointments of John Negroponte (2001-2004) and John Bolton (2005-2006) as US permanent representatives to the UN amply illustrated that cultivating multilateral relations with the wider UN membership was not a priority of the Bush Administration and is not until now. While a number of colleagues at UN Headquarters appreciated the wider goals that both ambassadors were trying to achieve, their abrasive style remained a matter of concern among UN members and alienated even US allies.

The US invasion of Iraq, commencing on March 18, 2003, strongly reflected the failure of US public diplomacy to unite the Security Council on a strategy to deal with the Iraqi regime in Baghdad. At the same time, it exposed the inability of the Council as a whole to see Iraq as a problem that could only be addressed collectively (cf. *Malone* 2006). The ambiguous wording of Council Resolution 1441, adopted in November 2002, which decided that Iraq had been in material breach of its obligations under Resolution 687 (1991), in particular through its failure to cooperate with the UN inspection team and the IAEA, temporarily concealed the deep divisions among the larger UN membership, the rift in transatlantic relations, and the diverging views among members of the European Union and the Arab League. The US invasion constituted a complete exit from the multilateral framework of the United Nations, only thinly masked by the engagement of a loose 'coalition of the willing,' (cf. *Moss* 2003; *Johnstone* 2004)

While the extent of US ambivalence towards international institutions fully materialized in the US National Defense Strategy of March 2005, which underlined that "our strength as a nation will continue to be challenged by those who employ a strategy of the weak using international fora, judicial processes, and terrorism" (*United States* 2005, 5), the bi-partisan Congressional Task Force on the United Nations, chaired by former House Speaker, Newt Gingrich, and former Senate Majority Leader, George Mitchell, concluded the same year "that an effective United Nations is in America's interest" (*United States Institute of Peace* 2005, v). US foreign policy will need to re-strike a bargain between hegemonic power and international institutions. Dealing with the legacy of Iraq and defining the role of the UN in this conflict zone as well as in other conflict regions in a constructive dialogue with the other UN member states constitutes one of the prominent challenges the next US Presidential Administration will need to address.

In this task the new President can count on a bi-partisan group in US Congress supporting a constructive US-UN relationship and rejecting the populist phrases of UN-bashing conservatives, as the above mentioned Senator George Mitchell underlined in a Congress hearing in February 2007, where he re-confirmed the statements of the task force report of 2005 and stated: "An effective UN can serve the American people well ... because the UN can serve as a valuable instrument for promoting democratic political development, human rights, economic self-sufficiency and the peaceful settlement of disputes." (*Mitchell* 2007)

But as the history of US-UN relations illustrates this re-approachment might be a long and complicated travel.

Jochen Prantl

Lit.: *Foot, R./MacFarlane, S.N./Mastanduno, M. (eds.):* The United States and Multilateral Organizations, Oxford 2003; *Forman, S./Lyman, P./Patrick, S.:* The United States in a Global Age: The Case for Multilateral Engagement (Center on International Cooperation Working Paper), New York 2002, www.cic.nyu.edu/archive/pdf/US_Global _Age.pdf; *Johnstone, I.:* US-UN Relations after Iraq: The End of the World (Order) As We Know It? In: EJIL 15 (2004), 813-838; *Luck, E.C:* Mixed Messages: American Politics and International Organization 1919-1999, Washington, D.C. 1999; *Luck, E.C.:* The U.S., Counterterrorism, and the Prospects for a Multilateral Alternative, in: Boulden, J./Weiss, T.G. (eds.): Terrorism and the UN: before and after September 11, Bloomington 2004 74-101; *Malone, D./Khong, Y. F. (eds):* International Perspectives on U.S. Unilateralism and Multilateralism, Boulder 2003; *Malone, D.M.:* The International Struggle Over Iraq: Politics in the UN Security Council 1980-2005, Oxford 2006; *Mitchell, G.J.:* Prepared Testimony of Senator George J. Mitchell on the Future of the United Nations before the Committee on Foreign Affairs, U.S. House of Representatives, 13 February 2007, www.internationalrelations.house.gov/110/m it021307.htm; *Moss, K.B.:* Reasserting American Exceptionalism – Confronting the World. The National Security Strategy of the Bush Administration, in: Internationale Politik und Gesellschaft/International Politics and Society, 3/2005, 135-155; *Patrick, S./Forman, S. (eds.):* Multilateralism and U.S. Foreign Policy: Ambivalent Engagement, Boulder 2002; *Scowcroft, B.:* United Nations Reform and the U.S. (Brookings Briefing, Moderator Ivo Daalder), 8 Februrary 2005 (transcript), www.brookings.edu/comm/events/20050208. pdf; *Tharoor, S.:* Why America Still Needs the United Nations, in: Foreign Affairs, Sept./October 2003; *United States of America - Congressional Research Service:* United Nations Reform: U.S. Policy and International Perspectives, 22 January 2007 (CRS

Report for Congress), Washington 2007; *United States of America - Department of Defense:* The National Defense Strategy of The United States of America, Washington, D.C., March 2005; *United States Institute of Peace:* American Interests and UN Reform. Report of the Congressional Task Force on the United Nations, Washington, D.C. 2005; *Walker, M.:* Bush v. Annan: Taming the United Nations, in: World Policy Journal, Spring 2005, 9-18; *Weiss, T.G./Forsythe, D.P. et al.:* The United Nations and Changing World Politics, 5th edn., Boulder 2007.

Internet: Homepage of the US Mission to the UN: www.un.int/usa.

UNRWA – United Nations Relief and Works Agency for Palestine Refugees in the Near East

With over fifty years of service, a staff of approximately 22,000, and an annual budget of more than 310 million US dollar, UNRWA is not only one of the oldest and largest UN agencies, but also one of the least known outside expert circles.

The *United Nations Relief and Works Agency for Palestine Refugees in the Near East (UNRWA)* occupies a unique position within the framework of the United Nations system (→ UN System; → Principal Organs, Subsidiary Organs, Treaty Bodies).

The Agency is a subsidiary body of the United Nations. It is headed by the *Commissioner General* who, while being appointed by the Secretary General in consultation with the *Advisory Commission*, is the only head of a UN Agency who reports directly to the → General Assembly (cf. Annual Reports since 1950).

The Advisory Commission, on which sit representatives from Belgium, Egypt, France, Japan, Jordan, Lebanon, the Syrian Arab Republic, Turkey, the United Kingdom and the United States of America, and since 1994 the Palestine Liberation Organization (PLO) with observer status (→ Observer Status), has, as its name indicates, no decision-making powers.

UNRWA was created following the first Arab-Israeli war of 1948 as a provisional organization, to provide immediate → humanitarian assistance to Palestine refugees within the framework of a limited *mandate*, in combination with short-term employment through public works programmes. It was only on 1 May 1950 that UNRWA finally started operations from its new headquarters in *Beirut* on the basis of General Assembly Resolution 302 (IV) of 8 December 1949.

In 1978 due to the turmoil of the civil war in Lebanon, the Organization was forced to evacuate and move its central administration offices to *Vienna*.

In 1996 following a politically inspired decision of the UN Secretary-General (a symbolic gesture in support of the 1993 Autonomy Agreement), the headquarters were transferred from Vienna to *Gaza* and *Amman*. It remains to be seen if the ultimate aim of greater organizational efficiency has thus been achieved.

As a consequence of the inability of the international community and the immediate parties to the Middle East conflict to find a political solution, and thus to solve the problem of Palestine refugees, the General Assembly has been obliged to extend the original three-year mandate of the Agency repeatedly since its inception, with the current *mandate* ending on 30 June 2002.

Unlike the definition of refugees under the various UN and other international conventions serving as a basis for the → UNHCR, that used by UNRWA is confined to *Palestine Refugees* intended as "persons whose normal place of residence was Palestine between June 1946 and May 1948, who lost their homes and means of livelihood as a result of the 1948 Arab-Israeli conflict, and who took refuge in Jordan, Lebanon, the Syrian Arab Republic, the Jordanian-ruled West Bank or the Egyptian-administered Gaza Strip." Anyone who falls under this definition and is registered with UNRWA is entitled to enjoy the support and services of the

Agency. The UNRWA definition is extended to include the offspring of the original 1948 refugees. Hence, the figure of *registered refugees* of 914,000 in 1950 rose to over 3.8 million by 2001 (Jordan 1,639,718; Syria 391,651; Lebanon 382,973; West Bank 607,770; Gaza Strip 852,626).

With an annual budget of 310.4 million US dollars (2001), UNRWA endeavors to cover the basic needs of the refugees for *Education* (primary and secondary schools as well as vocational training), *Primary Health Care* (prevention and hygiene) and *Social Welfare* (food aid, social assistance and development aid). Since the early 90s, in particular since the *Autonomy Agreement* of 1993, the Agency has been increasingly involved in development projects. In the framework of its *Peace Implementation Programme* and its *Income Generation Programme* (516 projects from 1993-2001 totaling 255,448,432 US dollars) the Agency has implemented projects for infrastructure improvements (sanitation in refugee camps, construction of housing, schools and medical centers, etc.), as well as measures for the *Income Generation Programme*. These programmes are funded from resources outside the regular budget.

With the exception of a small amount from the regular budget of the UN, UNRWA is almost exclusively financed (95%) through *voluntary contributions* from a limited number of major donor countries. Following the European Union (Commission and Member States) 47% are the USA (29%), Japan (10%), the Gulf States (4,5%) and Canada (2,5%).

The Agency spends approximately two-thirds of its annual budget on administrative costs for its staff of 22,644. It is worthy of note, however, that apart from its 120 international civil servants, almost all of the UNRWA personnel are locally recruited Palestinians, the vast majority of whom have refugee status. Thus, UNRWA is not only one of the largest UN organizations operating in the region, but it is also a major em-

ployer in the area. Moreover, most of UNRWA's employees work directly in occupations such as, *inter alia*, teachers, doctors, nurses, social workers, and in sanitation services. The total administrative costs of the Agency are no more than 12% of its overall budget.

With its roots stemming from one of the longest and most volatile conflicts since World War II, in spite of its strictly humanitarian mandate, or perhaps even as a consequence of it, UNRWA became a political factor in regional politics based on its economic and socially stabilizing role in Gaza and the West Bank and to a lesser extent in Lebanon and Jordan. UNRWA's future, ideally its dissolution, is, therefore, inextricably linked to developments in the peace process in the Middle East.

(All calculations and statistical information based on: UNRWA IN FIGURES. Public information Office, UNRWA, Gaza June 2001; UNRWA Homepage, Internet: www.un.org/unrwa)

Hans Peter Kotthaus

Lit.: 1. *Printed Publications: Morris, B.:* The Birth of the Palestinian Refugee Problem, Cambridge 1987; *Morris, B.:* 1948 and After: Israel and the Palestinians, Oxford 1999; *Said, E.:* The Question of Palestine, 2nd expand. edn., New York 1992; *Schönborn, M. (ed.):* Politisches Lexikon Nahost/Nordafrika, Munich 1994; *United Nations:* Report of the Commissioner-General of the United Nations Relief and Works Agency for Palestine Refugees in the Near East. 1 July 1997 – 30 June 1998, New York 1998 (UN Doc. A/53/13, 30 June 1998); *UNRWA Public Information Office:* UNRWA. A Brief History 1950-1982, Vienna 1982; *UNRWA Public Information Office:* Palestine Refugees and UNRWA – 45th Year, Vienna 1995; *Viorst, M.:* Reaching for the Olive Branch: UNRWA and Peace in the Middle East, Washington 1989; 2. *Publications which can be accessed via Internet: Brynen, R.:* Palestinian Refugees and the Middle East Peace Process. Paper originally prepared for the New Hampshire International Seminar/Yale-Maria Lecture in Middle East Studies, University of New Hampshire, 3 April 1998; published in the Internet in the Palestine Refugee ResearchNet

(PRRN), McGill University, Montreal 1998, Internet address: www.arts. mcgill.ca/MEPP /PRRN/papers/UNH.htm; *Pulfer, G./Gassner, J.D.:* UNRWA – Between Refugee Aid and Power Politics. A Memorandum Calling Upon the International Responsibility for the Palestinian Refugee Question. Alternative Information Center (AIC) Project for Palestinian Residency & Refugee Rights, Jerusalem 1997; Internet address: www. badil.org/ Refugee/ref1.htm; *Tamari, S.:* Return, Resettlement, Repatriation: The Future of Palestinian Refugees in the Peace Negotiations (Final Status Strategic Studies of the Institute for Palestine Studies), Beirut/Washington/Jerusalem 1996; published in the Internet in the Palestine Refugee ResearchNet (PRRN), McGill University, Montreal 1998, Internet address: www.arts.mcgill.ca/MEPP/ PRRN/papers/tamari2.htm

Addendum

In the absence of a solution to the Palestine refugee problem, the General Assembly of the UN has repeatedly renewed UNRWA's mandate, recently extending it with Resolution A/RES/59/ 117 of 10 December 2004 until 30 June 2008.

As of 31 December 2007 UNRWA counted in its official statistics 4.56 million registered Palestine refugees (*UNRWA* 2008a), compared with 3.1 million in 2001.

In recent years the living conditions of the Palestine refugees have deteriorated. According to UNRWA sources, the present living conditions are said to be as miserable as in 1967.

In 2007, UNRWA launched an emergency appeal for 246 million US dollars (cf. *UNRWA* 2007b). With the emergency programme (West Bank and Gaza Strip), UNRWA focuses on provision on food aid, cash assistance and temporary job creation. Since 2000 macroeconomic compression (high unemployment rates, restriction on trade) constitutes a socio-economic crisis (cf. *UNRWA* 2007d and *UNRWA* 2008b).

The European Commission (EC) plans to contribute to the General Fund 264 million euros over the years 2007-2010 (cf. *UNRWA* 2007c) and started with 66 million in 2007 which identifies the EC as one of the largest contributors besides the United States, Sweden, Norway, the United Kingdom and Canada. UNRWA signed recently a 4.5 million US dollar contribution by the OPEC Fund for International Development to credit its microfinance programme.

Originally envisaged as a temporary organization, UNRWA has gradually adjusted its programmes to meet the changing needs of the Palestine refugees. Today, UNRWA is the main provider of basic services – education, health, relief and social services – to over 4.8 million registered Palestine refugees in the Middle East.

Denise Junker

Lit.: *I. Sources for the statistical data: 1. Printed Publications, accessible via Internet:*
UNRWA: The United Nations and Palestine Refugees. Public Information Office, UNRWA Headquarters Gaza, January 2007, 4-7 (quoted as: UNRWA 2007a), www.un.org /unrwa/publications/pubs07/UN&PR_en.pdf;
UNRWA: UNRWA Emergency Appeal 2007. Public Information Office, UNRWA Headquarters Gaza, 2007 (quoted as: UNRWA 2007b), www.un.org/unrwa/ publications/pubs 07/EA_en.pdf;
UNRWA: The European Commission and UNRWA: Improving the lives of Palestine refugees. Public Information Office, UNRWA Headquarters Gaza. April 2007 (quoted as: UNRWA 2007c), www.un.org/unrwa/publications/pubs07/ EC&UNRWA_07.pdf;
UNRWA: UNRWA in Figures. Public Information Office, UNRWA, Gaza, February 2008 (figures as of 31 December 2007) (quoted as: UNRWA 2008a), www.un.org/ unrwa/publications/pdf/uif-dec07.pdf;
II. General sources:
UNRWA: Prolonged Crisis in the Occupied Palestinian Territory: Recent socio-economic Impacts on Refugees and Non-Refugees, Public Information Office, UNRWA Headquarters Gaza, November 2006 (quoted as: UNRWA 2007d), www.un.org/ urwa/publications/pubs07/RecentScEcImpacts. pdf;
UNRWA: Prolonged Crisis in the Occupied Palestinian Territory: Socio-economic De-

velopments in 2007, Public Information Office, UNRWA Headquarters, Gaza, July 2008 (quoted as: UNRWA 2008b), www.un.org/unrwa/publications/pubs08/SocioEconomicDevelopments_23July08.pdf.

Internet: 1. *General Information:* Homepage of the UNRWA: www.un.org/unrwa and www.un.org/Depts/dpa/qpal/index-f1.htm;
2. *UNRWA documents and other UN documents on the Palestine conflict:* www.un.org/Depts/dpa/qpal/p_refugs.htm and http:// domino.un.org/UNISPAL/NSF (UN Information System on the Question of Palestine);
3. *Other links (universities etc).:*
a) Homepage of the AIC Project for Palestinian Residency & Refugee Rights: www.badil. org/Refugee/ref1.htm;
b) Homepage of the Palestinian Refugee ResearchNet of McGill University/Canada: www.arts.mcgill.ca/MEPP/PRRN/prmepp.htm.

UN Simulations, Model United Nations

Simulations of political processes, of deliberation bodies and negotiating committees and of their methods and procedures, are an old analytical and didactic instrument, also applicable to town halls, parliaments, courts of justice, and others – especially to the cognitively far-away world of international relations. Designed in most cases as role plays, simulations are used, on the one hand, to evaluate complex scenarios (such as military activities), and on the other, they serve for the training of negotiators and decision-makers (for example in diplomacy) as well as in the education of students at schools, colleges and universities or in the general political education.

I. UN Simulations

The aim of UN simulations as a teaching method is to make the students familiar with the structure and function of the principal organs and committees of the world organization (→ Principal Organs, Subsidiary Organs, Treaty Bodies; → Committees, System of). The idea is to promote an understanding of international relations and their connec-

tions more thoroughly through authentically simulated multinational diplomacy and intergovernmental decision-making processes, rather than just through abstract information and analysis of problems alone. The participants are to resolve situations and conflicts actively and on their own, and to experience realistically the rules and restrictions of international negotiations "in practice". The play elements as well as the emotional and group-dynamic processes should lead to a more intense experience and a more thorough comprehension. Intensive preparation with regard to the role of the country which one is to represent is essential to an effective simulation, just to "play" the role of the country does not suffice. It is necessary to find out a spectrum of facts about the role of this country in the context of the UN, about the problems and difficulties of the topics to be discussed in the simulated negotiations. The aim of the preparation will be to provide the depth and the multiple views on any given issue, and to avoid the typical danger of role-playing, namely to learn just the official points of view, and the positions of the state representatives, which would lead to a superficial and one-sided simulation. The motivation for such a strenuous and extensive preparation is provided by the engagement for and during the game; the first practical experiences in the play (e.g. the work with procedural questions or the informal negotiation of resolution texts between country groups) lead to deeper and diverse insights; the necessary modification of their own, and appreciation of others' perspectives, force the students to consider carefully seemingly "obvious" positions, and to question their previous judgments and prejudices.

The United Nations, more precisely some of its principal organs, subsidiary bodies and manifold committees in the → UN System are simulated all over the world in hundreds of Model UN activities both in small groups such as school classes and in larger conferences of up to thousands of role players. In the USA there are more than hundred major UN simulations with more than 10,000 participants, often organized by the students themselves. Some large and well-known Model UN conferences, mostly organized by universities (e.g. Harvard/ HNMUN, Harvard World Model or American University in Cairo/CIMUN), try to bring national and /or international activities together.

II. National Model United Nations (NMUN) in the USA

The US-American National Model United Nations (NMUN) – www.nmun.org – is the biggest and most professional UN simulation – actually a combination of some bigger and smaller models. Founded in 1947, it continued the simulation of the League of Nations (Model League of Nations, founded in 1923). This Model UN which has since been held annually, takes place in the week before Easter in New York, and is held partially in the official rooms at UN headquarters itself. More than 3,500 students take part, coming from the USA, as well as from universities from all over the world. The National Collegiate Conference Association (NCCA), which is organizes the simulation, is a non-profit, non-governmental organization. Being acknowledged by the UN as an NGO ($\rightarrow$ NGOs), it cooperates closely with the world body. Students who took part in former years are also responsible for the organization of the Model UN.

The structure, major issues and procedures of the NMUN mirror political reality as closely as possible. For one week, from early morning until late evening, every university group represents one UN member state (or NGO), as they were assigned months before, in the different UN committees and organs. Before the sessions of the simulation begin the delegates have the opportunity to meet the representatives of the permanent mission of "their" country. There they can compare the positions they have prepared with the official policies of the country. Sometimes they have also the opportunity to be briefed by diplomats and UN officials for the work in their committees. At the end of the conference the plenary sessions of the principal UN organs, such as the General Assembly or ECOSOC, discuss and vote upon the resolutions that the committees have worked out. The competition with other universities for the prestigious awards is a principal motivator, beyond the fun at the game.

Students from different regions and cultures meet and get to know intensively the respective style of discussion and work of others. The students realize quickly that the most important points are not discussed in the formal but in the informal sessions. There, it is important to become the speaker of a group; for this it is necessary to show negotiating skills and strategic behavior and, at the same time to develop an insight into the logic of other positions. Of course, the "diplomats" have to follow the rules of diplomatic conduct and procedures.

An intense preparation of the subject matters of the role, if possible in English from the very beginning, and a resulting group identity are the precondition to "make it" in New York, and even to win an award. To represent "their" country actively and to bring in their own initiatives the players have to be familiar with the politics of this country and with the UN System itself. All this can only be achieved through well-rehearsed and efficient team work. The NMUN is no "playground" for "would-be diplomats", but a hard training programme that develops analytical and social skills which are adequate to the challenges of modern diplomacy today and that prepares the students for work in international affairs.

III. UN Simulations in Germany

In Germany, UN simulations at school and universities are used as a learning method. An annual German Model UN (GerMUN) and various other nation-wide model conferences (e.g. Ham-MUN) are now, more than 60 years after the foundation of the UN, well established. Networking associations like Deutsche Model United Nations (DMUN) and Junges UNO-Netzwerk

Deutschland (JUNON) have developed from a broad variety of groups and conferences. An increasing number of universities (early adopters having been Free University Berlin, and the universities of Bonn, Greifswald, Hamburg, Magdeburg, Munich, and Tübingen), respectively their departments of political science and international law, hold their own smaller simulations, and participate for example at GerMUN or the classical New York NMUN. Mostly participants from the previous year's MUN group form a team that organizes the subsequent course, and thus provide a form of "social memory" of the learning experience for the new participants.

The costs of a well-organized simulation are high; those for the well-prepared participation at an international Model UN are even higher. To enable talented students to participate without unbearably high costs for themselves, support by public or private sponsors is necessary. Model UN activities are supported by the German Federal Foreign Office, the DAAD (German Academic Exchange Service), and as well by foundations such as the Robert-Bosch-Stiftung. Established UN models have to assure the quality of the participants and the organizers; and they have to keep up with the real developments in the international relations and the UN system. Thus today also civil society elements, such as NGOs, press and other media, are integrated into Model United Nations conferences.

Reinhard Wesel

Lit.: *Blätte, A./Wesel, R.:* Simulation von politischen Prozessen. Einsatz des Planspiels: Model United Nations, in: Polis, 2001, 1, 16-19; *Coplin, W.D. (ed.):* Simulation in the Study of Politics, Chicago 1970; *Greenblat, C.S.:* Designing Games and Simulations. An Illustrated Handbook, Newbury Park 1988; *Flores, F.A. (ed.):* A Guide to Delegate Preparation 1998-1999. Model United Nations, New York 1998; *Guetzkow, K./Alger, C. et al.:* Simulation in International Relations. Developments for Research and Training, Englewood Cliffs/USA 1963; *Herz, D./Jetzlsperger, C.:* Die Beteiligung der Universität München am National Model United Nations 1987-1997, in: Juristische Schulung 6 (1997), 11f; *Hüfner, K.:* UNO-Planspiele. DGVN-Texte 44, Bonn 1995; *McIntosh, D.:* The Uses and Limits of the Model United Nations in an International Relations Classroom, in: International Studies Perspectives, Vol. 2 (2001), 269-280; *Ments, M. van:* The Effective Use of Role-Play. Practical Techniques for Improved Learning, 2nd edn., London 1999; *Muldoon, J.P.:* The Model United Nations Revisited, in: Simulation and Gaming 26 (1995), 27-35; *Scapple, K.:* Model United Nations: Out of the Closet and Into the Classroom, in: International Studies Notes 34 (1999), 3, 8-13; *Schwenker, M./Wesel, R.:* "Handlungsorientierung" für die UNO: Zur Anwendung von Erfahrungen aus akademischen Lehrsimulationen der Arbeit der Vereinten Nationen im Politikunterricht, in: Massing, P./Roy, K.-B. (eds.): Politik – Politische Bildung – Demokratie. FS Gotthard Breit, Schwalbach/Ts. 2005, 207-218; *United Nations Association of the United States of America:* How to plan a Model U. N. Conference, New York 2002.

Internet:
1. *Model UN Web Site on the UN Homepage:* http://cyberschoolbus.un.org/modelun/index.asp;

2. *Web Site of the World Federation of United Nations Association:* www.wfuna.org/site/c.rvIYIcN1JwE/b.3783407/;

3. *Web Links to the US Model UNs:*
   a) UNA-USA: www.unausa.org, link to Model UN;
   b) NMUN/NCCA: www.nmun.org;
   c) Harvard Model UN, Harvard World Model UN: www.hnmun.org, www.worldmun.org;
   d) American University in Cairo/CIMUN www.cimun.com;
   e) American Model United Nations International: www.amun.org;
   f) Berkeley Model United Nations: http://bmun.net;
   g) Model United Nations Network: www.modelunnetwork.org;

4. *Web Links to German Model UNs:* www.spun.de, www.model-un.de/international, www.dmun.de and www.junges-uno-netzwerk.de;

5. *Other European Model UNs:*
   a) Geneva International Model United Nations: www.gimun.org;
   b) The Hague International Model United Nations: www.thimun.org/main.html.

UN System

In the official documents of the United Nations (UN) as well as in the secondary literature the term "UN system" has been fully accepted. First of all, this term implies that the UN is not identical with the UN system which includes, in addition to the UN and its six principal organs (→ General Assembly, → Security Council, → Secretariat, Economic and Social Council (→ ECOSOC), → Trusteeship Council, and International Court of Justice (→ ICJ) and their subsidiary organs (→ Principal Organs, Subsidiary Organs, Treaty Bodies) and the special organs (i.e. special funds and programmes) established by the → General Assembly, also the → specialized agencies as well as the autonomous organizations → WTO and → IAEA (cf. chart 1).

This definition of the UN system, often also called "UN family", has not been undisputed. In earlier times, i.e. before the collapse of the socialist system at the end of the 1980s, the so-called Bretton Woods institutions → IMF and → IBRD and also the later founded "daughters" → IFC and → IDA were not taken into account because of their special institutional-organizational features in terms of membership, financing and internal voting procedures, and also because of their distance from the UN concerning their activities, although they, from the formal, legal point of view, always belonged to the UN system.

Chart 1 provides a first overview of the UN system; it shows only the "tip of the iceberg" which serves as a proxy to the real complexity of the total system. The description of the UN system refers to the history of an increasing number of institutions, some of which existed already before the founding of the UN, as well as to the increasing complexity of relationships which exists between those independent institutions and thus characterizing the structure of the UN system.

Institutional Multiplicity

Within the organizational structure we have to deal with a great number of institutions. In this context, two dimensions are to be differentiated: the horizontal and the vertical. The horizontal dimension refers to the definition of the system and its environment which is easier to be described for the individual institutions than for the system as a whole. The vertical dimension refers to the hierarchy, the "depth" of the system.

Therefore, chart 1 fails to convey the real complexity of the system as it describes only the UN with its six principal organs as defined in Article 7 para. 1 of the Charter (→ Charter of the UN) plus 16 *special organs (funds and programmes)* and refers to only some *subsidiary organs* of the principal organs (→ General Assembly, → Security Council, → Economic and Social Council (ECOSOC) without indicating the respective organs of the autonomous → specialized agencies. Most of the specialized agencies have established three own *"principal organs"* (such as *assembly, council* and *secretariat*) and their *"subsidiary organs"* as well as *"special organs"* (there are about 20 special organs in the cases of → WHO and → FAO and about 10 in the cases of → UNESCO and → ILO) which are functionally equivalents to those of the UN.

At the same time chart 1 does not provide a regional differentiation of the UN and of its specialized organs (the → UNDP has offices in more than 166 countries and → UNICEF in 127) as well as of the specialized agencies with a great number of *regional offices* (in the case of UNESCO there are 52 field offices, → FAO is present in 78 countries and → ILO in 43 countries, → WHO has 145 country offices) – except the regional economic commissions (→ Economic Commissions, Regional) of the ECOSOC, which possesses in addition about 45 subsidiary organs. In sum: the UN system is characterized by a *functional-institutionally* and *regional-specific differentiated structure* not only within the UN but also in the relationships between the UN and its specialized agencies. This structure cannot be reproduced in a single organigram.

Specialized Agencies

The UN system cannot only be differentiated by the legal-organizational types of organs (unlike the UN special organs, the 17 legally independent specialized agencies are brought into relationship with the UN through agreements with the UN (Articles 57 and 63 of the Charter) and have their own rules, membership, organs and budgets) but also by *functional differentiation*, namely:

(a) institutions with more general objectives, e.g. the UN with a large number of special organs and the five "huge" specialized agencies → FAO, → ILO, → UNESCO, → UNIDO and → WHO, which tend to deal with all problems despite of their selective concentration on certain economic-social aspects;

(b) so-called technical organizations with a high number of members from the beginning on and with relatively small budgets, which set up and monitor general rules in the fields of worldwide shared interests (→ UPU, → ITU, → IMO, → WMO, → WIPO and IAEA); and

(c) so-called financial and monetary organizations with their particularities concerning membership, financing and internal decision-making rules (IMF, IBRD, → IDA, → IFC, and also → IFAD).

Non-governmental Actors

Most of the institutions of the UN system are *inter-state organizations* composed of government representatives. However, there are exceptions such as councils of experts, e.g. the Council of → UNU, or the → ILO based on the principle of tripartite membership, consisting of equal representation not only of two government representatives but also of one employees' and employers' representative each per member state. Furthermore, the *"borders" of the UN system* are not clearly to be defined since, e.g., a worldwide network of uni-

versities and scientific institutions is affiliated with the UNU. Also numerous non-governmental-organizations (→ NGOs) are connected with the UN system, e.g. through consultation arrangements with the ECOSOC as provided in Article 71 of the Charter of the UN or through similar arrangements with the specialized agencies (particularly distinct in the case of → UNESCO).

The Co-ordination Problems within the UN System

The relations between the UN and the specialized agencies are to be analyzed by referring to three types of documents: the Charter of the UN, the constitutions of the respective specialized agencies and the relationship agreements. It is important to mention that neither the Charter of the UN nor the relationship agreements foresee concrete rules for co-ordination of the work of the specialized agencies within the context of a common policy of the UN system (→ Co-ordination in the UN System).

The General Assembly can make recommendations to the specialized agencies on budgetary matters (Art. 17 para. 3 UN Charter); the ECOSOC can co-ordinate the activities of the specialized agencies only through recommendations (Art. 62 para. 2 UN Charter).

The, in most cases, similar *relationship agreements* do not represent an effective co-ordination instrument. Moreover, the agreements with the Bretton Woods institutions imply that certain information is confidential even vis-à-vis the UN. Besides the relationship agreements, there are numerous *bilateral agreements* between specialized agencies on the one hand and between individual specialized agencies and UN special organs on the other. Those agreements refer to concrete common fields of activity and are of a different character when compared with the relationship agreements mentioned above.

The UN Charter is based on a centralized UN structure with the General Assembly on the top and the subordinated ECOSOC (Art. 60 UN Charter) and the primary responsibility for the maintenance of international peace and security of the Security Council (Art. 24 UN Charter) on the one hand and on the concept of a *functionally differentiated and regionally decentralized* overall system on the other. This led to the foundation of numerous *co-ordination committees* at various levels of the UN system in the course of the development of the UN, which, however, have not been able to fulfill expectations.

In this matter, one should distinguish between three complementary approaches:

- an *inter-state co-ordination* through the General Assembly and its Advisory Committee on Administrative and Budgetary Questions (ACABQ) on the one hand, and through the Economic and Social Council and its *Committee for Programme and Coordination (CPC)*, founded in 1962 as a subsidiary organ, on the other. Since 1987, CPC reviews the strategic framework in the off-budget years and the programme budget in the budget years (→ Budget) and thus occupies a central position for the co-ordination of the budget and programme planning of the UN. Its decisions must be reached by consensus;

- an *inter-organizational coordination* mainly through the *Administrative Committee on Co-ordination (ACC)* which – following a reform in 2000 – was enlarged and renamed *United Nations Chief Executives Board for Co-ordination (CEB)*, but also through the International Civil Service Commission (ICSC), founded by the General Assembly in 1974, and through the Joint Panel of External Auditors; and finally;

- a *co-ordination of administrative and management methods* through the *Joint Inspection Unit* (JIU), which began to function in 1968 and has acted as an independent controlling system within the UN system since 1978. The Bretton Woods institutions and the IFAD do not participate in the work of the JIU. In 1994, the *Office of Internal Oversight Services* (OIOS) was

been established and is responsible only for the UN and its special organs (→ Control Mechanisms in the UN, External and Internal).

As a result of the autonomy exercised by the specialized agencies, the CEB in which the Secretary-General acts as a "primus inter pares", must be seen as a new attempt towards collective steering with a view to reduce the problems of competence overlapping and competition among them and with the UN programmes and funds. The CEB has expanded into a 28-member body meeting twice a year and being comprised of the specialized agencies (including the Bretton Woods institution and the WTO) and the special organs. The ACABQ discontinued its annual examination of the budgets of the specialized agencies at the beginning of the 1970s, since they barely paid any attention to its reports. Furthermore, there have been a multitude of expert committees since the 1960s dealing – often caused by the so-called → financial crises – with the inspection of the work of individual institutions or parts of the UN system and putting forward reform proposals (→ Reform of the UN) for a reconstruction of the whole system, particularly in the field of development policy (→ Development Cooperation of the UN System).

At present, two key management tools are applied for the purpose of improved co-ordination in this field: the *UN Development Assistance Framework (UNDAF)* and the Common Country Assessment (CCA). UNDAF is seen as a common strategic framework for the operational activities of the UN institutions at the country level and is supposed to provide for a collective, coherent and integrated UN system response to national priorities and needs as expressed in the CCA.

However, no comprehensive success has been reached up to now. On the contrary, the competition, particularly in the field, between the parts of the UN system, i.e., between special organs and specialized agencies as well as among each other is still too strong. The different interests of the member states have not allowed profound reforms, e.g., in the case of ECOSOC with its huge subsidiary structure or with respect to a stronger centralization of the multilateral development policy of the specialized agencies. It is an open question whether the efforts of the present → UN Secretary-General, Ban Ki-moon, carried out under huge financial constraints, will have more success than those of his predecessors.

Summary

The co-ordination problems have grown because of the shifting of tasks and the increase of institutions, particularly in the 1960s and 1970s, despite all efforts to develop appropriate solutions. Here, one can distinguish between *functional, institutional, regional and financial co-ordination problems* at and between individual levels of the UN system. *Inter alia*, the problems result from the fact that the government representatives in the various institutions of the UN system come from different national ministries whose UN policy lacks a co-ordination at the national level. Therefore one can conclude that the UN system with regard to its functions and structures represents an imperfect generalization of the modern nation state at the global level. On the other hand, an improvement of the co-ordination mechanisms can only be reached if the member states are able and willing to eliminate the respective deficits both at the national level and at the level of the UN system.

Therefore, the question can be raised whether the UN system indeed represents a "complex system" which is characterized by a high degree of coordination. On the contrary, one can conclude that the UN system is nowadays a complicated and diffuse structure characterized through loosely linked *networks* and through partly *de jure*, partly *de facto* autonomously acting institutions. The optimum between centralized co-ordination and monitoring of the programmes and their regionally decentralized implementation has not yet been reached. This is true for the work of the UN special organs under the responsibility of the General Assembly and the ECOSOC and for the specialized agencies in their work with each other as well as for the UN system as a whole.

In late 2006, the High Level Panel's Report on UN System-wide-Coherence "Delivering as one" was issued (UN Doc. A/61/583 of 20 November 2006) which recommended the implementation of a "One UN" programme seeking to integrate the leadership, programme management and budget control for UN activities at the country-level and urging the creation of a single Resident Coordinator as a focal point for this integration to reduce overlap and redundancy. The new Secretary-General Ban Ki-Moon welcomed the findings of the panel report initiated by his predecessor Kofi Annan in a report of 3 April 2007 commenting on the panel report (UN Doc. A/61/836) and announced his "broad support for the principle of a stronger, more coherent United Nations and for the recommendations contained in the report." (ibid., para 3). Whether the pilot phase in which eight countries are involved will lead to major progress in the programme implementation of the UN system without undertaking corresponding reforms at the "upper levels" remains to be seen. It may be some sign of hope that the General Assembly took up the topic in a closed session in February 2008 and that in March 2008 at a conference organized by the Stanley Foundation the Permanent Representatives of important UN member states discussed the issue together with high officials of the UN Secretariat (*Stanley Foundation* 2008). Perhaps the member states are moving with some cautious steps forward on the long road to more coherence in the UN system.

Klaus Hüfner

Lit.: *Beigbeder, Y.:* The Internal Management of United Nations Organizations: The Long Quest for Reform, Houndmills/London 1997; *Childers, E./Urquhart, B.:* Renewing the United Nations System. In: Development Dialogue, No. 1/1994, 1-213; *Dijkzeul, D.:* The Management of Multilateral Organizations, The Hague et al. 1997; *Elmandjra, M.:* The United Nations System. An Analysis, London 1973; *Fomerand, J./Dijkzeul, D.:* Coordination, Economic and Social Affairs, in: Weiss, T.G./Daws, S. (eds.): The Oxford Handbook on the United Nations, Oxford 2007, 561-581; *Freiesleben, J.v.:* System-Wide Coherence, in: Center for UN Reform Education (ed.): Managing Change at the United Nations, New York 2008, www.centerforunreform.org; *Fues, T.:* The Prerequisite to UN Leadership in Development: System-wide coherence, in: World Economy & Development in brief, 8 May 2006, www. world-economy-and-development.org; *Hüfner, K.:* UN-System, in: *Wolfrum, R.* (ed): United Nations: Law, Policies and Practices, Vol. 2, Munich 1995, 1361-1368; *Stanley Foundation (ed.):* One UN Pilots: Aligning UN Capabilities in Support of National Development. 39th United Nations Issues Conference, March 14-16, 2008, accessible at: www.stanleyfoundation.org; *Szazs, P.C.:* The Complexification of the United Nations System, in: Max Planck Yearbook of United Nations Law 3 (1999), 1-57; *United Nations - General Assembly:* Delivering as One. Report of the High-level Panel on United Nations System-wide Coherence in the areas of development, humanitarian assistance and the environment, 20 November 2006, UN Doc. A/61/583; *United Nations Non-Governmental Liaison Service (NGLS):* United Nations System. A Guide for NGOs, 10th edn., New York 2003; *United Nations Non-Governmental Liaison Service (NGLS) with Sidhu, G.:* Intergovernmental Negotiations and Decision Making at the United Nations: A Guide, 2nd Updated Edition, New York/ Geneva 2007.

Internet: Homepage of the Official Web Site Locator for the United Nations System of Organizations (with an alphabetical index and a classification according to different categories of organizations): www.unsystem.org.

The UN System

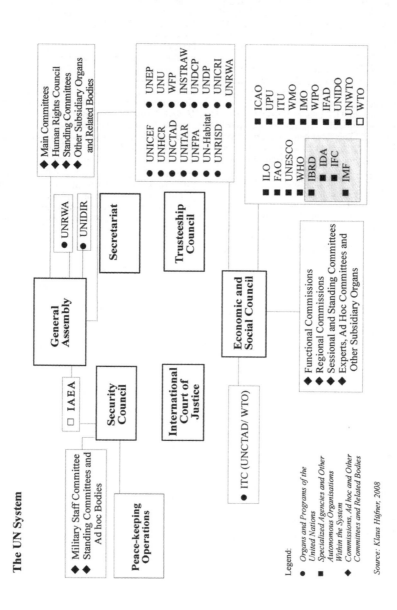

General Assembly

- ● UNRWA
- ● UNIDIR

- ◆ Main Committees
- ◆ Human Rights Council
- ◆ Standing Committees
- ◆ Other Subsidiary Organs and Related Bodies

Secretariat

- ● UNICEF
- ● UNHCR
- ● UNCTAD
- ● UNITAR
- ● UNFPA
- ● UN-Habitat
- ● UNRISD
- ● UNEP
- ● UNU
- ● WFP
- ● INSTRAW
- ● UNDCP
- ● UNDP
- ● UNICRI
- ● UNRWA

Trusteeship Council

- ■ ILO
- ■ FAO
- ■ UNESCO
- ■ WHO
- ■ IBRD
- ■ IDA
- ■ IFC
- ■ IMF
- ■ ICAO
- ■ UPU
- ■ ITU
- ■ WMO
- ■ IMO
- ■ WIPO
- ■ IFAD
- ■ UNIDO
- ■ UNWTO
- □ WTO

□ IAEA

Security Council

- ◆ Military Staff Committee
- ◆ Standing Committees and Ad hoc Bodies

Peace-keeping Operations

International Court of Justice

Economic and Social Council

- ● ITC (UNCTAD/ WTO)

- ◆ Functional Commissions
- ◆ Regional Commissions
- ◆ Sessional and Standing Committees
- ◆ Experts, Ad Hoc Committees and Other Subsidiary Organs

Legend:

- ● *Organs and Programs of the United Nations*
- ■ *Specialized Agencies and Other Autonomous Organisations Within the System*
- ◆ *Commissions, Ad hoc and Other Committees and Related Bodies*

Source: Klaus Hüfner, 2008

832

UNTS – United Nations Treaty Series

Pursuant to Article 102 of the United Nations Charter (→ Charter of the UN), all international agreements entered into by any member state of the United Nations shall be registered with and published by the United Nations Secretariat (→ Secretariat).

Since 1946, these agreements have been published in the single-series *United Nations Treaty Series (UNTS)*, which is the most comprehensive global collection of treaties and contains both bilateral and multilateral treaties. The *UNTS* is an extensive reference source with more than 2400 volumes published containing the references and texts or more than 60,000 registered treaties and related actions (as of 1 August 2008).

The purpose of imposing the obligation on member states to register international agreements was to make international relations more transparent and to prevent secret diplomacy, an intention also provided for by Article 18 of the Covenant of the → League of Nations.

The registration process is regulated by the regulations to give effect to Article 102 of the UN Charter, which were adopted by the General Assembly in Resolution 97 (I) of 14 December 1946 and later modified several times (1946, 1950 and 1978) – the "Regulations to give effect to Article 102 of the Charter of the United Nations" (*UNTS* Vol. 859/860, p. VIII).

Article 102 (1) of the UN Charter does not define the international agreements to be registered. The regulations to give effect to Article 102 provide that all international agreements shall be registered whatever their form and descriptive name. The Treaty Section of the Office of Legal Affairs reviews all international agreements submitted for registration to ensure that they have entered into force, have been concluded by at least two parties possessing treaty-making capacity, e.g. sovereign states or intergovernmental organizations and that such parties intend the agreement to be legally binding at international law.

All subsequent actions to a registered treaty, such as the addition of parties, amendments or withdrawals, must also be registered, according to Article 2 of the implementation regulations. All integral parts of a treaty, including annexes, protocols, maps and the like, must be submitted with the treaty for registration.

The Treaty Section of the Office of Legal Affairs in the Secretariat has the competence to examine summarily whether a submitted treaty is capable of being registered, i.e., whether the treaty meets the requirements of international law, including the *Vienna Convention on the Law of Treaties*, 1969 (→ Treaties, Law of), as well as applicable General Assembly resolutions. After examination by the UN Secretariat, which consults the concerned states or organizations if necessary, it is the task of the Secretariat to publish the treaties. According to Article 12 of the implementation regulations, the publication of treaties in the *UNTS* is in the original language(s) as well as in English and French translation. Over 140 languages have appeared in the *UNTS*.

In addition, Article 10 of the implementation regulations provides that those international agreements not subject to registration under Article 102 of the UN Charter may be "filed and recorded" by the Secretariat and also published in the *UNTS*. This is the case, for instance, with treaties between the United Nations and other intergovernmental organizations or the United Nations and a state not member of the UN, because the Article 102 obligation is directed at member states.

Due to the immense financial and organizational expenditures involved in publishing the large number of treaties submitted for registration, Article 12 of the implementation regulations was modified so that currently a number of categories of treaties are no longer published in full. The limited publication policy extends, for example, to assistance or co-operation agreements of limited scope; agreements for assistance in financial, commercial, administrative or technical matters; agreements relating to the organization of conferences, seminars or meetings; and agreements that are to be published elsewhere by the UN Secretariat or specialized or related agencies. Lengthy lists of products attached to trade agreements are also not published in full and agreements of the European Union are published in the *UNTS* in English and French only. The categories above generally allow for the full texts to be found elsewhere in full, thus fulfilling the spirit of Article 102 of the UN Charter while streamlining the publication load for the Treaty Section.

Article 102 (2) of the UN Charter provides for a penalty for the failure of member states to register a treaty – the parties may not invoke that treaty before any UN organs, the International Court of Justice (ICJ), for example. However, it is not clear whether the ICJ would disallow a legal argument or defense based on the non-registration of a treaty with the UN Secretariat, as the Court has not yet applied the sanction of Article 102 (2) in any of its cases. The *UNTS* may also be accessed on the Treaty Section's website – http:// treaties.un.org. The website contains the database of the *UNTS* and is also the authoritative source of information on the over 520 multilateral treaties deposited with the UN Secretary-General. Varied online research tools, including sorting and filtering options, complex queries and view/print options, enable users to search for and view treaties grouped by subject matter (extradition, for example, or financial assistance) or by party. A full text search capability is functional for all main databases, including the full texts of treaties registered with and published by the UN Secretariat online in the *UNTS*. The *UNTS* online provides an extensive resource to assist governments in the negotiation and drafting of treaties as well as researchers on a particular subject or the evolution of treaty relations between specific parties.

The entry of *Claudia Shirin Weisser* of the first edition was revised by *Sherry Holbrook*

Lit.: *Knapp, U.:* Art. 102, in: Simma, B. (ed.): The Charter of the United Nations. A Commentary, 2nd edn., Oxford 2002, 1277-1292; *Kohona. P.T.B.:* The United Nations Treaty Collection on the Internet – Development and Challenges, in: Environmental Policy and Law 32 (2002), 120-130; *Schröder, M.:* Codification and Progressive Development of International Law within the UN, in: Wolfrum, R. (ed.): United Nations: Law, Policies and Practice, Vol. 1, Munich/Dordrecht 1995, 100-109; *Goodrich, L./Hambro, E./Simmons, A.P.:* A Charter of the UN. Commentary and Documents, New York 1969; *United Nations Treaty Section:* Treaty Handbook (Online Publication: http://untreaty.un.org).

Internet: Homepage of the United Nations Treaty Section: http://treaties.un.org (access to the treaty databases)

UNU – United Nations University

I. Introduction

In 1969, UN Secretary-General U Thant (→ Secretary-General) proposed the creation of a *United Nations University (UNU)* in order to strengthen the international scientific co-operation on the basis of problem-orientated, multi-disciplinary research activities about world problems (among others, population growth and world food, management and use of natural resources, energy problems, the role of science and technology in the development process). At the same time, the expansion of research and training capacities in the developing countries has been envisaged.

II. Establishing as a Network / Position within the UN System

The → General Assembly ratified the establishment of the UNU with Headquarters in Tokyo in resolution A/RES/2951 (XXVII) of 11 December 1972. De facto, the work of the UNU did not commence until autumn 1975. It is a world-wide *network of academic and scientific institutions dealing with global problems*; besides a number of associated institutions, 13 research and training centres/programmes, among them the UNU World Institute for Development Economics Research (UNU/

WIDER) in Helsinki, the UNU Institute for New Technologies (UNU/INTECH) in Maastricht, the UNU International Institute for Software Technologies in Macau, the UNU Institute for National Resources in Africa (UNU/INRA) in Accra, the UNU Institute for Advanced Studies (UNU/IAS) in Tokyo, the UNU Programme for Biotechnology in Latin America and the Caribbean (UNU/BIOLAC) in Caracas, the International Leadership Academy (UNU/ILA) in Amman and the UNU International Network on Water, Environment and Health (UNU/INWEH) in Hamilton, Canada, belong to it.

In January 2007 the UNU set up an International Human Dimensions Programme on Global Environmental Change (UNU-IHDP) in Bonn, Germany. Also, the UNU Vice-Rectorate (UNU-ViE) was established in May 2007 in Bonn to enhance the presence of the UNU and to ensure the visibility of its activities in Europe.

Although the UNU is a special organ of the General Assembly and functions under the joint sponsorship of the UN and → UNESCO, it is not an intergovernmental organization, but an academic institution: according to its Charter the UNU enjoys "the academic freedom required for the achievement of its objectives, with particular reference to the choice of subjects and methods of research and training, the selection of persons and institutions to share in its tasks, and freedom of expression".

III. Organizational Set-up

The UNU consists of: (a) a *Council* which serves as the governing board of the University; (b) a *Rector*; (c) a *University Centre* with a staff responsible to the Rector; and (d) the already above-mentioned *research and training centres and programmes.*

The *Council* is composed of 24 members serving six-year terms in their individual capacity; it meets at least once a year and is the most important decision-making body which, *inter alia*, approves the work programme and adopts the budget.

The *Rector* (since 1 September 2007: Konrad Osterwalder, Switzerland) serves for five years and is eligible for re-appointment for one more term. He is the most senior academic official and administrator and bears the overall responsibility for leading, organizing and administering the *programmes* of the UNU, supported by the *University Centre*.

IV. Financing

The UNU receives no funds from the regular budget of the UN. The main source of funding is the revenue from a permanent *Endowment Fund* to which the member states of the UN make voluntary contributions. This financing mechanism, which is unique within the → UN System, was made possible only by a pledge on the part of Japan to contribute 100 million US dollars within five years (*Hüfner* 2006, 215-217). The 1981 target of 500 million US dollars until 2005 could be reached by only 50%, until 2005 230 million US dollars had been pledged and 224 million US dollars received. In addition, the UNU receives income from states and non-governmental sources (foundations, universities, individuals) for the implementation and support of specific programme activities. The UNU also benefits from counterpart and cost-sharing support as well as from additional contributions for UNU-related academic activities paid directly from cooperating institutions. In 2007, the UNU received about 28 million US dollars: 24 million US dollars were contributed from governments, among them 6.6 million US dollars from Japan, 4.85 million US dollars from Malaysia and 4.17 million US dollars from Germany.

V. UNU's Mission

Under the UNU Charter, the University aims to fulfill its mission by performing five key roles: (a) to be one international community of scholars; (b) to form a bridge between the UN and the international academic community; (c) to serve as a think-tank for the UN system; (d) to contribute to capacity-building, especially in developing countries; and (e) to serve as a platform for dialogue and new, creative ideas.

UNU's present activities are grouped in two *main programme areas*: *peace and governance*, and *environment and sustainable development*. They cover five thematic areas: 1. peace and security; 2. good governance, from local to global; 3. development and poverty reduction; 4. environment and sustainability; and 5. science, technology and society.

Within the framework of the two main programme areas, the UNU has published under the imprint United Nations University Press a large number of anthologies and monographs which exert an important impact on the academic debates in the UN member states about these issues; for instance: the anthology edited by Edward Newman and Ramesh Thakur on multilateralism (*Thakur/Newman* 2006), the anthology on "Global Governance and the United Nations System", edited by Volker Rittberger (*Rittberger* 2002), the study by Andrew Cooper of UN → world conferences (*Cooper* 2004), the anthology by Cooper, English and Thakur on the diplomacy in the era of global governance (*Cooper/English/Thakur* 2002), the anthology by the same editors on the role of international commissions and their reports (*Thakur/Cooper/English* 2005) and the anthology edited by Ginkel and others on "Human Development and Environment" (*Ginkel* 2001).

VI. Outlook

Without doubt, the function of the UNU as a think-tank for the UN system is of utmost importance, but the large number of its often extremely heterogeneous research activities on the one hand and its financial problems on the other has prevented the UNU from fulfilling its intended strategic role in a visible way. The fact that many other research activities exist within other UN institutions must also be taken into account. There is no clear division of labor or cooperation within the UN system; in contrast to the Economic and Social Council (→

ECOSOC) which merely acknowledges receipt of the UNU reports, the General Assembly has drawn already several times the attention to those weaknesses. In future, the UNU intends to strive for a closer content-oriented collaboration with UNESCO, since their constitutional goals are very similar and their partners within the (world) science system are identical.

Beyond the UN system, the UNU will also, as its new rector mentioned in the UNU Annual Report 2007, interact more closely with national governments and civil society. Also, the present asymmetry in the geographical distribution of UNU units will be reduced through twinning arrangements with partners in the South. Furthermore, the UNU intends to introduce own graduate programs in close collaboration with other high-level universities.

Klaus Hüfner

Lit.: I. UN Documents: *United Nations - Joint Inspection Unit:* The United Nations University. Enhancing Its Relevance and Effectiveness, Geneva 1998 (JIU/REP/98/3; UN Doc. A/53/392 of 15 September 1998); II. UNU Publications: *Cooper, A.:* Tests of Global Governance: Canadian Diplomacy and United Nations World Conferences, Tokyo 2004; *Ginkel, H. v. et al. (eds.):* Human Development and the Environment, Tokyo 2001; *Newman, E. at al. (eds.):* Multilateralism under Challenge: Power, International Order, and Structural Change, Tokyo 2006; *Rittberger, V. (ed.):* Global Governance and the United Nations System, Tokyo 2002; *Thakur, R./Cooper, A./English, J. (eds.):* International Commissions and the Power of Ideas, Tokyo 2005; III. Secondary Literature: *Hüfner, K.:* UNU – United Nations University, in: Wolfrum, R. (ed.): United Nations: Law, Policies and Practice, 2 vols., Munich/Dordrecht 1995, Vol. 2, 1369-1376; *Hüfner, K.:* Die Finanzierung des VN-Systems, 1971-2003/2005, Bonn 2006; *Narasimhan, C.V.:* History of the United Nations University – A Personal Perspective, Tokyo 1994; *Simai, M.:* Science and Global Governance: The Story of United Nations University, in: Metzger, M./Reichenstein, B. (eds): Challenges for International Organizations in the 21st Century, London 2000.

Internet: Homepage of the United Nations University: www.unu.edu.

UNV – United Nations Volunteers

On 7 December 1970, the UN → General Assembly passed resolution A/RES/ 2659 (XXV), establishing the United Nations Volunteers (UNV) as a volunteer-based programme and as a subsidiary organ of the General Assembly of the United Nations (→ Principal Organs, Subsidiary Organs, Treaty Bodies). It is an operational programme in the → development cooperation of the UN system. As a volunteer-based programme UNV is both unique within the UN family (→ UN System) and in its scale as an international undertaking, which recruits and supports mid-career women and men in their service in sectoral and community-based development projects, → humanitarian assistance and the promotion of → human rights and democracy. UNV is also the global advocate of the distinctive contributions of volunteerism for development.

From 1971 onwards, UNV has placed about 300,000 professionally qualified and experienced experts into projects of multilateral co-operation. Since the year 2000, UNV has further expanded its scope and field of action.

UNV is one of the programmes administered by → UNDP. In July 1996, UNV accepted the invitation of the Federal Republic of Germany and became the first UN organization to move its headquarters to Bonn (→ UN in Bonn).

At present, around 8,000 volunteers (UNVs) are working in over 140 countries, about half in Africa. Generally, governments and international organizations are UNV's partners in technical co-operation. Traditionally, agriculture, economy, technology, health and education are the main fields of activity. UNV work mostly at the grassroots and often live in villages.

Since the early nineties, UNVs became also increasingly involved in humanitarian aid, human rights work (→ Human Rights, Protection of), democratization (→ Democratization and the UN) and peace-building operations of the UN (→ Peacekeeping Operations; → Peacekeeping), e.g. in Cambodia, East Timor, Mozambique, South Africa, Yugoslavia, Somalia, Rwanda and Angola.

From 1992 until 2007 UNV volunteers have taken part in 44 peacekeeping operations, with over 11,300 volunteers completing more than 16,000 mission assignments during this period. In 2007, over 2,995 UNV volunteers supported 18 UN peacekeeping and special political operations in 18 countries. UNV volunteers serve as civilian peacekeepers in special development situations within the areas of crisis and post-crisis humanitarian assistance, conflict prevention, peace-building and support to post-conflict electoral processes. The tasks include demobilization, disarmament, re-integration, political affairs, civil administration and human rights, as well as medical, administrative, logistical and technical roles (*UN Volunteers:* UNV and peacekeeping, Fact Sheet, May 2008).

The distinctive contribution made by UNV volunteers to peacekeeping operations has been strongly endorsed by the UN Secretary General and highly estimated by DPKO: General Assembly resolution A/RES/59/296 of 22 June 2005 on financing the UN peacekeeping operations, "acknowledges the valuable contribution of the United Nations Volunteers in the United Nations system … and takes note of DPKO's intention to continue its efforts to exploit the potential for increased use of UNV volunteers in peace-keeping operations in those functions or skills which are not normally available in the Secretariat or which are limited." (UN Doc. A/RES/ 59/296, para. XI).

In the meantime, the area of support in crisis situations, reconstruction, rehabilitation and prevention of disasters, has become an area of programme concentration which has led UNVs also to Central America as well as to some of the former republics of the Soviet Union.

The volunteers of UNV are not, as is sometimes assumed, well-meaning youngsters ready to assist, but are well qualified, trained and experienced experts of an average age of forty years (similar to those of the German Volunteer Service and other European volunteer organizations), who generally can draw on about ten years of professional experience. The multinational composition of the volunteer corps is something special: UNVs are of more than 160 different nationalities, mostly (over 75%) from developing countries. They receive no salary, but reimbursement of expenses and a living allowance. As a rule, contracts cover a two-year period. However, UNV retained the necessary flexibility to react to the realistic nature of a request: humanitarian assignments, in particular, can be of shorter duration.

Some short-term expert programmes that were developed in UNDP have in the meantime been integrated in the programmes of UNV: notably TOKTEN (Transfer of knowledge through expatriate nationals) and UNISTAR (UN short term advisory resources). TOKTEN recruits experts who live in a foreign country for a short-term assignment while UNISTAR recruits top managers and engineers for voluntary advisory services in developing countries. With the inclusion of these programmes, UNV became the official focal point for all volunteer service within the UN development system.

UNV became also the focal point for the International Year of Volunteers (2001) in line with its mission of global advocacy of the distinctive contribution of volunteerism for development.

In reaction to General Assembly Resolution A/RES/57/106 of 13 February 2003 dealing with the follow-up of the International Year of Volunteers, UNV established the World Volunteer Web website (www.worldvolunteerweb.org) as a global clearing-house for information and resources linked to volunteerism for use in campaigning, advocacy and networking.

UNV is funded from UNDP programme funds (about 50%), from other UN programme budgets, from its own special fund (UNV Special Voluntary Fund) and earmarked contributions from donor countries such as Belgium, Japan and Germany.

Manfred Kulessa

Lit.: *Baker, B.:* UNV – United Nations Volunteers, in: Wolfrum, R. (ed.): United Nations: Law, Policies and Practice, Vol. 2, Munich/Dordrecht 1995, 1377-1381; *United Nations Volunteers (ed.):* A Globalizing World: Roles for Volunteers? Fourth UNV Intergovernmental Meeting, Bonn, Germany, 30 November – 4 December 1997, Bonn 1997; *United Nations Volunteers (ed.):* Volunteers for Peace, Bonn 1998; *United Nations Volunteers (ed.):* United Nations Volunteers at a glance. The key statistics from 1997, Bonn 1998; *United Nations Volunteers (ed.):* Making Distinctive Contributions, Annual Report 2005/2006, Bonn 2006; *United Nations Volunteers:* Report of the Administrator, UN Doc. DP/2008/34, 4 April 2008.

Internet: United Nations Volunteers: www.unv.org; World Volunteer Web: www.worldvolunteerweb.org.

UNWTO – World Tourism Organization

The World Tourism Organization (UNWTO) is a specialized agency of the United Nations (→ Specialized Agencies) and the leading international organization in the field of tourism. It serves as a global forum for tourism policy issues.

Its seat is in Madrid (Spain). Its membership includes 154 member states as full members, seven territories or group of territories not responsible for their external relations as associate members and, as affiliate members, some 370 intergovernmental and non-governmental organizations (→ NGOs) with special interests in tourism, and commercial and non-commercial bodies and associations with activities related to the aims of UNWTO or falling within its competence (figures as of 1 September 2008).

History

The origins of the UNWTO stem back to 1925 when the International Congress of Official Tourist Traffic Associations was formed at The Hague. In 1934 the Congress became the International Union of Official Tourist Propaganda Organizations (IUOTPO). In 1946, with international travel numbers increasing, the IUOTPO restructured itself into the *International Union of Official Travel Organizations (IOUTO)* as a technical non-governmental organization.

Towards the ends of the 1960s the IUOTO realized that for exercising more influence in its field of activity it had to establish itself as an intergovernmental body: the 20th IOUTO General Assembly in 1967 in Tokyo declared the need of establishing IOUTO as an intergovernmental body in cooperation with the United Nations, but with complete administrative and financial autonomy. In 1970, the IUOTO General Assembly voted in favor of forming the World Tourism Organization (WTO) in adopting the Statutes of the WTO. In January 1975 the WTO Statutes entered into force and the WTO started its work.

In December 1977 the UN General Assembly (→ General Assembly) approved with Resolution 32/156 the Agreement of Cooperation and Relationships between the UN and the World Tourism Organization.

In 2003 the WTO General Council (in WTO resolution 453 (XV)) and the United Nations General Assembly (in UN Doc. A/RES/58/232) agreed to establish WTO as specialized agency of the UN.

Change of Abbreviation to UNWTO

The frequent confusion between the two WTOs in the UN family – World Trade Organization and World Tourism Organization – led in December 2005 to a change of the abbreviation of the World Tourism Organization from WTO to UNWTO by approval of the General Assembly of the World Tourism Organization, after UN Secretary-General Kofi Annan (→ Secretary-General) had given his consent to adding the UN's initials to the abbreviation WTO (cf. UNWTO Press Release 1 December 2005).

Purposes

UNWTO helps its members participate in tourism as one of the world's largest industries. By promoting and developing tourism, it aims to foster economic growth and job creation and to provide incentives for protecting the environment and cultural heritage of tourist sites.

UNWTO's programme of work includes among others: competitiveness and trade in tourism services, development assistance, education and knowledge management, and sustainable development of tourism.

Global Code of Ethics for Tourism

At the request of its General Assembly meeting in 1997 a special committee of the World Tourism Organization worked out a draft document for a Global Code of Ethics. Then the World Tourism Organization asked the Commission for Sustainable Development (→ CSD) as well as its member countries and NGOs for comment. After this consultation process the resulting *Global Code of Ethics for Tourism* was adopted by its General Assembly meeting in 1999.

The United Nations Economic and Social Council (→ ECOSOC) asked in a resolution of July 2001 the UN General Assembly to give recognition to the Code of Ethics; in December 2001 the UN General Assembly declared in Resolution 56/212 that it "takes note with interest of the Global Code of Ethics for Tourism ... which outlines principles to guide tourism development and to serve as a frame of reference for the different stakeholders in the tourism sector, with the object of minimizing the negative impact of tourism on the environment and on cultural heritage while maximizing the benefits of tourism in promoting sustainable development and poverty alleviation as well as understanding among nations." (ibid., para 1).

The UN resolution, recognizing formally the Code of Ethics, gives a concise outline of the purposes of the Code as well as of the complex task of the UNWTO in general, namely to balance the economic interests of the tourism host countries with the protection of the environment and of the cultural heritage.

Structure

The UNWTO *General Assembly*, the supreme body of the organization, meets every two years to approve UNWTO's budget and programme of work. Every four years it elects the UNWTO Secretary-General.

The General Assembly has established six *Regional Commissions* covering Africa, the Americas, Europe, the Middle East, East Asia and the Pacific, and South Asia. These commissions normally meet once a year.

The *Executive Council* is UNWTO's governing body, responsible for ensuring that the UNWTO carries out its work and adheres to the budget. It is elected by the General Assembly, comprising 30 member states and in addition – without voting rights – an associate member and affiliate member, selected by their respective groups. The Executive Council meets at least twice a year.

The Secretariat headed by the UNWTO Secretary-General is responsible for implementing UNWTO's work programme.

UNWTO is an executing agency for the UN Development Programme (→ UNDP) and has cooperation agreements with the UN Environment Programme (→ UNEP), UN Regional Economic Commissions (→ Economic Commissions, Regional) and other specialized agencies (→ FAO, → ICAO, → IMO, → UNESCO, → WMO, and → WHO).

Evaluation

Considering the enormous economic effects of global tourism on the gross national product, in particular of developing countries, it was logical and necessary to establish a specialized agency with the task to bring together on an international level the different stakeholders and to give expanding global tourism a satisfying legal and ethical framework. The Global Code of Ethics for Tourism is an important step on this direction.

UNWTO is confronted currently with considerable challenges for global tourism – piracy and terrorist attacks on tourists, failing states with civil wars, and the effects of the global climate change on nature and tourism infrastructure (cf. *UNWTO* 2008). It will have to look for solutions together with the other organizations of the → UN system.

Helmut Volger

Lit.: *Dicke, K.:* WTO – World Tourism Organization, in: Wolfrum, R. (ed.): United Nations: Law, Policies and Practice, Vol. 2, Munich/Dordrecht 1995, 1501-1504; *UNWTO - General Assembly:* Global Code of Ethics, UNWTO Doc. RES/406 (XIII), Santiago (Chile), September - October 1999, www.world-tourism.org/code_ethics/pdf/RES406-English.pdf; *UNWTO:* UNWTO at the UN General Assembly – Tourism Acting on Climate and Poverty Imperatives, UNWTO Press Release, 14 February 2008; *Vellas, P.:* Tourism (WTO), in: Bernhardt, R. (ed.): EPIL 9, Amsterdam 1986, 376-378.
Internet: www.unwto.org.

UPU – Universal Postal Union

I. History

The *Universal Postal Union (UPU)* was established as the General Postal Union in 1874 by a congress of 22 states in Berne, concluding a Treaty Concerning the Establishment of a General Postal Union, which entered into force on 1 July 1875. It received its present name in 1878 at the second congress in Paris. It is the second oldest international organization after the International Telecommunication Union → ITU. On 1 July 1948 it received by agreement with the United Nations the status of a → specialized agency of the United Nations. Its seat is Berne. 191 states are members of the UPU (as of 31 December 2008).

The UPU's current Constitution dating from the 1964 UPU Vienna Congress and the UPU General Regulations, containing the provisions relating to the operation of the UPU, has been revised and supplemented at a number of further congresses (most recently in Beijing 1999 and Bucharest 2004).

II. Purposes and Functions

The UPU is the primary forum for co-operation between postal services. It is the only international organization representing the interests of the worldwide postal sector in a neutral fashion. It maintains a genuine universal network for the mutual exchange of postal items, establishes the rules for international mail exchanges among its member countries and makes recommendations to modernize products and services and to improve the quality of service for customers.

In 2006 there were approximately 660,000 post offices worldwide with more than five million post employees that delivered 439 billion letter-post items and 6.2 billion parcels.

The original convention on the letter post service has been complemented in the meantime by conventions on further postal services such as parcel service, airmail service, postal giro, post office savings banks and newspaper post service. Notwithstanding their membership in the UPU, states must accede to these conventions explicitly for those conventions to have legally binding force for them.

The UPU aims to achieve worldwide unimpeded fast exchange of postal items through, among other things, the protection of postal traffic, the unification of weight units, payment and accounting principles, and has been rather successful in realizing these goals.

The UPU maintains working relationships with the United Nations programmes such as → UNDP and → UNEP and with specialized agencies such as → ITU, → ICAO, → ILO and WTO (→ WTO, GATT). It also collaborates with the World Bank (→ World Bank, World Bank Group) to promote postal development and reform.

The UPU works as a financial clearing office for the compensation for different financial expenses in postal services. For a hundred years it had been simply assumed, as a rule, that every postal administration kept its received fees undivided and that the compensation for the transport services of the postal administration of the destination country would be achieved by retaining the fees for the sending of postal goods in the opposite direction (principle of non-division and reciprocity). But the precondition for a smooth functioning of this simple and unbureaucratic system is that nearly the same number of letter post items is sent in both directions. After many developing countries became independent during the 1950s and 1960s an imbalance arose. Those who received more letters than they sent incurred service costs which exceeded revenues through postal charges.

Therefore the UPU Congress held in Tokyo in 1964 ruled that all sender post office administrations must make compensation payments to all consignee post office administrations; these compensation payments have been increased several times. In addition, the UPU gives technical support to developing countries in modernizing their postal services, as in developing countries between 14 and 25 % of the population is still without access to postal services (as of December 2008, cf. *UPU* 2008).

III. Organizational Structure

The UPU has the following main organs:

Congress: It consists of representatives of the member states, and acts as the highest organ of the UPU. It meets every five years, reviews and revises the instruments of the Universal Postal Union, determines the work programme and the budget and elects the Executive Council and the Director-General.

Council of Administration: It is made up of 41 elected members, meets annually and acts as an implementation and coordination organ during the time between the UPU congresses.

Postal Operations Council: It consists of 40 experts elected by the Congress. It is to investigate technical, operational and commercial problems of postal service, deliver studies and reports and elaborate standards.

International Bureau: It is directed by a Director-General and serves as the central administrative organ of liaison, information, consultation and coordination organ for the postal administrations of the UPU members.

Consultative Committee: the youngest UPU body established in September 2004 by the 23rd Universal Postal Congress. Comprising 25 members, it consists of external postal stakeholders (delivery service providers, trade unions and → NGOs representing mail customers), giving them a voice in the deliberations of the UPU.

IV. Perspectives

The UPU has proved to be an effective planning and clearing office for global postal services. Its biggest challenge is at present the structural change of postal items, the reduction of letter post items through the increase of e-mail letters with the corresponding decrease of revenues through postage fees, as well as their shifting into the sector of telecommunication. In this technological and economic situation it is the main task for the UPU to develop together with the ITU and other international organizations adequate solutions for the organizational and economic problems linked to these technological changes (cf. *UPU* 2004).

In this context, the UPU has actively participated in the second part of the ITU World Summit on the Information Society (WSIS), held in Tunis (Tunisia) in November 2005, in presenting a seminar on the role of postal services in the information society (www.upu.int/upu_information_society/en/index.shmtl), where the UPU emphasized the important role the postal services are able to play in developing effective global networks for the diverse electronic services. Thus the UPU contributes through its work towards making connections in and between developing countries' communities more effective through the postal sector and towards reducing the

"digital gap", i.e. the backlog of the developing countries with regard to the access to the Internet, which exists in some fields, while in other the developing countries have already made progress: as of 2005 32 % of the industrialized countries and 43 % of the developing countries offer Internet access, 29 % and 26 %, respectively, offer electronic mail services, 82 % and 49 %, respectively, offer online postal services (cf. *UPU* 2005). All in all, this represents quite some success for the UPU, which former UN Secretary-General Kofi Annan underlined: "... [T]he UPU has become one of our most valuable, yet largely unheralded, forums of international cooperation and exchange." (quoted in: *UPU* 2008)

Helmut Volger

Lit.: *Magiera, S.:* UPU – Universal Postal Union, in: Wolfrum, R. (ed.): United Nations: Law, Policies and Practice, Vol. 2, Munich/Dordrecht 1995, 1382-1386; *Universal Postal Union - International Bureau:* Guide to Postal Reform and Development, Berne 2004; *Universal Postal Union:* The postal sector: your partner in delivering the information society. Paper presented at the Postal Symposium during the World Summit on the Information Society (WSIS) - Tunis 2005, UPU, Berne 2005; *Universal Postal Union:* 10 reasons why the world needs the UPU, Berne 2008.

Internet: Homepage of UPU: www.upu.int; UPU Constitution and UPU General Regulations: www.upu.int/acts/en/constitution_general_regulations.shtml

Use of Force, Prohibition of

Article 2 (4) of the UN Charter (→ Charter of the UN) provides a comprehensive prohibition of the use of force. Article 2 (4) states that members shall refrain "in their international relations from the threat or use of force against the territorial integrity or political independence of any state, or in any other manner inconsistent with the Purposes of the United Nations."

The prohibition of the use of force belongs to the fundamental provisions of modern public international law ($\rightarrow$ International Law and the UN). The International Court of Justice ($\rightarrow$ ICJ) considers in its Nicaragua Judgment (Case concerning Military and Paramilitary Activities in and against Nicaragua (Nicaragua vs. US), Judgment of 27 June 1986, ICJ Reports 1986, 14, 98ff.) the prohibition of the use of force to be part of customary international law. Furthermore the majority of writers on international law, as well as the practice of states, accept the prohibition of the use of force as being part of *ius cogens*. Hence the prohibition of the use of force is valid not only between UN member states, but among all states. However, on the domestic level the validity of the prohibition is not accepted, for example in non-international armed conflicts.

In comparison with the League of Nations Covenant ($\rightarrow$ League of Nations) and the Briand-Kellogg Pact, Article 2 (4) of the UN Charter prohibits comprehensively the use of force or the threat of force. Therefore the use of armed force "short of war" as well as even the threat of force are included. But "force" as defined by Article 2 (4) refers – according to the prevailing view – only to military force. Not only the direct use of force is prohibited, i.e. the open incursion of regular military forces into the territory of other states or cross-border shooting into that territory, but also the use of indirect armed force (*Randelzhofer* 1994), for example through the establishment and acceptance of unofficial bands organized in a military manner, such as irregulars, mercenaries, or rebels on its own territory to be used for violent acts against a third state or the support of terrorist acts in foreign countries. In particular developing countries and the socialist states tried to extend the prohibition of the use of force also to economic and political force, e.g. embargoes on imports, blocking of bank accounts, etc. But the majority in the community of states does not accept this concept.

According to the UN Charter exceptions to this absolute prohibition of the use of force are – apart from the now obsolete $\rightarrow$ Enemy State Clauses – only allowed in two cases: individual or collective self-defense (Art. 51 UN Charter), and collective enforcement measures of the United Nations according to Chapter VII of the UN Charter within the system of $\rightarrow$ collective security.

In addition to this the governments of several countries have on various occasions expressed their view that the use of force in order to protect their nationals abroad would be a further exception to the prohibition of the use of force. Examples are the forcible protection action by Belgium for Belgian citizens in the Congo in 1964, Israel's forcible freeing of hostages at Entebbe (1976), similar US attempts in Iran (1980) and Panama (1989), Germany's evacuation by plane of 120 persons from 22 nations (among them 20 Germans) from Tirana (1997) under fire. Beside attempts to qualify a threat to their nationals abroad as an armed attack requiring self-defense (Art. 51 UN Charter), the states argue that the prohibition of the use of force must not restrict their right to protect their nationals, including the use of force if necessary, especially in cases of violation of $\rightarrow$ human rights of their nationals. But this opinion involves the danger that it may be misused for the enforcement of other interests, and may erode the prohibition of the use of force. Accordingly the state practice concerning the evaluation of an intervention for the protection of own nationals differs, so that there is no corresponding rule of customary international law justifying this state behavior as an exception to the prohibition of the use of force.

After the prohibition of the use of force was infringed several times in the era of the East-West Conflict within the framework of the blocs (cf. for example the so-called Brezhnev Doctrine), at the beginning of the nineties the hope arose after the collective action against the Iraqi aggression against Kuwait that the prohibition of the use of force could now become the guiding principle of the community of states ("New World Order" of US-President Bush). Since then international politics have been charac-

843

terized by a large increase of conflicts as well as by the decay of political authority. The conflicts in Former Yugoslavia, Azerbaijan, Georgia and Chechnya, as well as events in Somalia, Rwanda and Haiti, have shown that new threats to international peace and security today (→ Peace, Peace Concept, Threats to Peace) have emerged in the intra-state area (*Donner* 1995). In connection with these trends the legal evaluation of humanitarian intervention (→ Humanitarian Law, International) has achieved increasing importance, with humanitarian intervention being an additional special problem concerning the limits of the prohibition of the use of force (*Heintze* 1997). Finally the enforcement of the prohibition of the use of force as norm *erga omnes* has been discussed recently. This approach refers to the question whether states have the right to enforce rules of common interest, if necessary with armed force. As the law stands at present the right of single states to enforce *erga omnes* rules includes only the right to carry out reprisals, but not the use of armed force. Also in the future the system of collective security of the United Nations will remain the central instrument for the enforcement of the prohibition of the use of force.

After September 11 the question arose whether a right to anticipatory or pre-emptive self-defense exists (cf. *Kirgis* 2002, *Bothe* 2003; a survey of the relevant literature in: *Corten* 2005). According to the traditional understanding of responses to actual armed attacks it does not. However, against the background of modern weaponry the question seems to be justified. Nowadays the attack can be launched with tremendous speed and there is nearly no time to react. In particular, geographically small states have employed pre-emptive strikes in self defense. Israel did in 1967 and this interpretation of self-defense was not condemned by the United Nations. The legal problem involved is that a too early pre-emptive strike might constitute a violation of the prohibition of the use force. If self-defense is allowed where an armed attack is imminent one has to

accept that the burden of proof is on the state which exercises this right. In any case the used means of response have to be proportional (cf. ICJ Reports 1986, p. 94, para. 176; ICJ Reports 1996, p. 245, para. 41).

The USA notified in a letter to the UN Security Council on 7 October 2001 that their exercise of the right to self-defence might require "further actions with regard to other organizations and other states" (UN Doc. S/2001/946), which can be interpreted that they claimed at least an extended and also pre-emptive right to self-defense. In this case the USA argued that the attack of September 11 constituted an armed attack and the NATO and the UN shared that viewpoint.

Another issue connected with the prohibition of the use force is humanitarian intervention. The NATO bombing of Yugoslavia without authorization by the UN Security Council in 1999 was justified by the humanitarian necessity to support the majority of the population of Kosovo being victimized by massive human rights violations. After the conflict, the Security Council adopted Resolution S/RES/1244 (1999) which decided upon the deployment of UN troops in Kosovo. There was no formal condemnation of the NATO action. The increasing acceptance of the "Responsibility to Protect" means that there is a tendency to consider humanitarian interventions without authorization of the Security Council under certain circumstances as an exception to the prohibition of the use of force. Doubtless there is a tension between the categorical prohibition of the use of force and the collective responsibility for the protection of human rights.

The US-led war against Iraq in 2003 was the starting point for a debate on the use of force against dictatorships. The majority of states and legal scholars argued that there is no justification for the invasion of Iraq. Three permanent member states of the Security Council and the non-permanent member states openly denounced in 2003 the invasion and refused any direct assistance (cf. for example the Council meeting of 7 March 2003, UN Doc. S/PV.4714).

In the reform report of Secretary-General Kofi Annan "In larger freedom" of March 2005 (UN Doc. A/59/2005, 21 March 2005) he criticized explicitly the unilateral use of force without the authorization of the Security Council: "The task is not to find alternatives to the Security Council as source of authority but to make it work better." (ibid., 126) He recommended that the Council should adopt a resolution on the principles for the authorization of the use of force (ibid.).

In somewhat weaker and ambiguous wording the UN member states spoke in the "2005 World Summit Outcome Document" with regard to the use of force of "the obligation of all Member States to refrain in their international relations form the threat or use of force in any matter inconsistent with the Charter." (UN Doc. A/RES/60/1, 16 September 2005, para 77) That may be considered as a rather implicit criticism of the states taking part in the military invasion in the Iraq in 2003. In any case it constitutes a confirmation of the conviction of the large majority of states that the use of force shall be authorized explicitly by the Security Council.

Brigitte Reschke

Lit.: *Blokker, N./Schijver N. (eds.):* The Security Council and the Use of Force: Theory and Reality – A Need for Change? Leiden 2005; *Bothe, M.:* Terrorism and the Legality of Pre-emptive Force, in: EJIL 14 (2003), 227-240; *Bruha, Th.:* Use of Force, Prohibition of, in: Wolfrum, R. (ed.): United Nations: Law, Policies and Practice, Vol. 2, Munich/ Dordrecht 1995, 1387-1399; *Byers, M./Nolte G. (eds.):* United States Hegemony and the Foundations of International Law, Cambridge 2003; *Corten, O.:* The Controversies Over the Customary Prohibition of the Use of Force: A Methodological Debate, in: EJIL 16 (2005), 803-822; *Dinstein, Y.:* War, Aggression and Self-Defence, 2nd edn., Cambridge 1994; *Donner, M.:* Die Begrenzung bewaffneter Konflikte durch das moderne jus ad bellum, in: AVR 33 (1995), 168-218; *Heintze, H.-J.:* Interventionsverbot, Interventionsrecht und Interventionspflicht im Völkerrecht, in: Reiter, E. (ed.): Maßnahmen zur internationalen Friedenssicherung, Graz 1997, 163-194; *Herdegen, M./ Rensmann, T.:* Is there a Specific German Approach to the Prohibition of the Use of Force?, German Yearbook of International Law 50 (2007), 349; *International Court of Justice:* Military and Paramilitary Activities in and against Nicaragua (Nicaragua v. United States of America). Merits, Judgment, in: ICJ Reports 1986, 14ff.; *International Court of Justice:* Legality of the Threat or Use of Nuclear Weapons. Advisory Opinion, in: ICJ Reports 1996, 226ff.; *Ipsen, K.:* Gewaltverbot – Interventionsverbot – Nichteinmischung, Elemente der Gemeinsamen Sicherheit, in: Heintze, H.-J. (ed.): Von der Koexistenz zur Kooperation, Völkerrecht in der Periode der Ost-West-Annäherung Ende der 80er Jahre, Bochum 1992, 1-12; *Kirgis, F.:* Pre-emptive Action to Forestall Terrorism, in: ASIL Insights, June 2002, www.asil.org; *Kreß, C.:* Gewaltverbot und Selbstverteidigungsrecht nach der Satzung der Vereinten Nationen bei staatlicher Verwicklung in Gewaltakte Privater, Berlin 1995; *Kreß, C:* Die Rettungsoperation der Bundeswehr in Albanien am 14. März 1997 aus völker- und verfassungsrechtlicher Sicht, in: ZaöRV 57 (1997), 329-358; *König, D. et al. (eds.):* International Law Today: New Challenges and the Need for Reform? Berlin/Heidelberg 2008; *Randelzhofer, A.:* Use of Force, in: Bernhardt, R. (ed.): EPIL 4 (1982), 265-275; *Randelzhofer, A.:* Art. 2 (4), in: Simma, B. (ed.): The Charter of the United Nations. A Commentary, 2nd edn., Oxford 2002, 112-136; *Shaw, M.N.:* International Law, 6th edn., Cambridge 2008; *Wolfrum, R.:* The Attack of September 11, 2001, the Wars Against the Taliban and Iraq: Is There a Need to Reconsider International Law on the Recourse to Force and the Rules in Armed Conflict? In: Max Planck Yearbook of United Nations Law 7 (2003), 1-78.

Veto, Right of Veto

Like few other provisions of the United Nations Charter (→ Charter of the UN), the veto right is reputed to symbolize the world organization's dependence on the will of the permanent members to cooperate in the → Security Council. The prominent position of the permanent members entitled to exercise the veto right has given occasion to repeated criticism. Nevertheless, critics often overlook that the codification of the veto right protecting the national interests of the permanent members of the Security Council was the precondition for the foundation of the United Nations (→ History of the Foundation of the UN).

The legal basis for the *veto right* is provided in Article 27 of the Charter, which regulates the voting procedure (→ Voting Right and Decision-Making Procedures) of the permanent members of the Security Council. This article (the so-called "*Yalta Formula*") was included in the Charter after protracted negotiations among the USA, the United Kingdom and the Soviet Union at the Yalta Conference in February 1945. Under Article 27(1) of the Charter every member of the Security Council has one vote. Articles 27(2) and 27(3) are decisive for the veto right, and distinguish decisions on procedural matters from decisions on non-procedural matters. Article 27(2) determines that nine votes are required for decisions "on procedural matters" (before the Security Council was enlarged in 1965, seven votes had been sufficient). Article 27(3) regulates decisions "on all other matters". In non-procedural decisions of the Council, an "affirmative vote of nine members including the concurring votes of the permanent members" is required. A *veto* is thus a negative vote from any of the five permanent members, even if nine members vote in favor of a draft (→ Resolution, Declaration, Decision). With the principle of unanimity of the permanent members the "Big Five" enjoy a privileged position in the Council, as against the non-permanent members. Each of the five permanent members is able to prevent decisions of the Security Council which do not concern procedural matters in the narrower sense.

In practice, the distinction between procedural and non-procedural matters has turned out to be difficult. The superpower antagonism has fostered a broad interpretation of the political issues and thus of the veto right, except of technical or organizational matters relat-

ing to the tasks of the Security Council. If it is controversial, whether a decision is to be classified as concerning procedural or non-procedural matters, the procedural decision on this question is made according to Article 27(3), allowing the permanent members to use their veto in this procedural question. Therefore, the permanent members de facto have a *double veto right*.

Article 27(3) knows explicitly only two exceptions from the veto right. When decisions are taken under Chapter VI of the Charter (Pacific Settlement of Disputes) and under Article 52(3) of the Charter (pacific settlement of local disputes through regional arrangements or regional agencies), the conflict parties must abstain from voting, if they are permanent or non-permanent members of the Security Council.

The political practice of the Security Council has developed two more exceptions: Contrary to the wording of Article 27(3), which states that a non-procedural decision needs the consent of all permanent members, the abstention from voting or the absence of permanent members are not considered as veto.

This has been of political importance, in particular during the Korea war. The Soviet Union boycotted the meetings of the Security Council from 13 January to 1 August 1950 in order to press for a permanent membership of the People's Republic of China in the Security Council, and to replace the Republic of China (Taiwan) as a permanent member. Then, without running the risk of a negative vote from the USSR, the Security Council was able to decide on the mandate for an international military intervention in Korea.

This unique historical situation pointed to the fact that the Security Council was only able to fulfil its most important duty, the primary responsibility for maintaining international peace and security (→ Peace, Peace Concept, Threat to Peace) when not blocked by a veto. The Charter had left no possibility to the → General Assembly to impose military or other sanctions. So – still in 1950 – the Charter underwent for the first time a de facto amendment with the → *Uniting for Peace Resolution* of the General Assembly, on the initiative of the US Secretary of State, Dean Acheson. The respective Resolution A/RES/377 (V) of 3 November 1950 encountered strong opposition from the Soviet Union, since the extended competence of the General Assembly codified in this resolution circumvented the veto right of the permanent members in the Security Council, and represented in the opinion of the USSR a violation of the principle of unanimity of the great powers. Nevertheless, due to the real power distribution between the superpowers, the "Uniting for Peace Resolution" could be applied only in a few cases (for instance, during the Suez Crisis 1956) and thus did after all not supplant the veto right.

Since the foundation of the United Nations, the veto practice showed considerable discontinuities over the decades with regard to number of vetoes in general and with regard to the respective permanent member using the veto. Until the end of 2000, the five permanent members have used their veto in 247 cases. The 232 vetoes between 1946 and 1989 reflect the then superpower confrontation in the Security Council. During this era, the Soviet Union used 115 vetoes and the United States used it 67 times. France and Great Britain used the veto 18 and 30 times respectively, Taiwan (permanent member until 1971) and the People's Republic of China each have been responsible for only one veto.

The distribution of the vetoes of the permanent members over the years shows that the great powers vetoed decisions more or less frequently during the various phases of the superpower struggle. From 1946 to 1961, the USSR used 99 vetoes, when it was extensively isolated in world politics at the climax of the Cold War. Of these 99 vetoes, 51 vetoes blocked new applications for membership (17 vetoes were used against nine applications in 1955 alone), since the USSR feared to lose political influence in an enlarged world organization containing new members who

would side with the western countries (→ Membership and Representation of States). From 1962 on, the USSR used the veto significantly less frequently (from 1961 to 1989, altogether 16 vetoes). There were two reasons for this remarkable change. Firstly, the USSR used the United Nations more intensively as forum to cooperate with the former colonies (→ Decolonization). Secondly, the relationship of the superpowers improved gradually from confrontation to cooperation.

The USA, who could rely on the dominance of the Western states in the General Assembly during the two decades following World War II, used its veto in the Security Council in 1970 for the first time. Up to 1989, the USA blocked 67 decisions. France and Great Britain also used the most of their vetoes between 1970 and 1989.

Since 1990 only 11 vetoes have been recorded (USA: 1990 2, 1995 1, 1997 2, 2001 2; Russia: 1993 1, 1994 1 (Russia replaced the USSR in the Security Council in 1992), China: 1997 1, 1999 1 (as of 1 January 2002). The new climate in world politics, in particular the increasing endeavor of the USA and Russia to reach consensus solutions (→ History of the UN) has moved the veto as "fighting instrument" into the background.

"Quiet diplomacy", preceding the meetings of the Security Council, has today gained increased importance. Contrary to past practice, drafts are not put to the vote if it turns out in the preliminary stage that they are not likely to gain the majority of votes. Instead, the members negotiate backstage under the pressure of the veto right of the great powers until a consensus, above all among the permanent members, is reached.

Whether the reform of the United Nations (→ Reform of the UN), as it has been discussed for many years, particularly the reform of the Security Council, will lead to a modification of the veto right, remains doubtful. In the view of the five permanent members, the use of the veto right is the last resort for protecting their national interest. Therefore they are not likely to accept any reduction of this right.

Volker Löwe

Lit.: *Bailey, S.D./Daws, S.:* The procedure of the UN Security Council, 3rd edn., Oxford 1998; *Fahl, G.:* Die Vetos im Sicherheitsrat der Vereinten Nationen (1970-1982), in: VN 31 (1983), 84-90; *Fassbender, B.:* UN Security Council Reform and the Right of Veto, The Hague et al. 1998; *Löwe, V.:* Die Vetos im Sicherheitsrat der Vereinten Nationen (1983-1990), in: VN 39 (1991), 11-15; *Patil, A. V.:* The UN veto in world affairs, 1946-1990: a complete record and case history of the Security Council's veto, London 1992; *Schindlmayr, T.:* Obstructing the Security Council: The Use of the Veto in the Twentieth Century, in: Journal of the History of International Law 3 (2001), 218-234; *Sellen, K. L.:* The United Nations Security Council veto in the new world order, in: Military Law Review 138 (1992), 187-262.

Addendum

Between January 2000 and October 2007, the → UN Security Council adopted 496 resolutions, thus further increasing the number of resolutions per year since the end of the Cold War. Despite this increased output, and major controversies affecting the UN's work, permanent members have made use of their veto power only 13 times. This figure is slightly higher than during the 1990s, when the permanent members cast seven vetoes, but remains a far cry from that for the period between 1945 and 1989. Just as during the 1990s, the clear majority of vetoes (ten) has been cast by the United States, with Russia (two) and China (one) following at a considerable distance (cf. for data and subjects of the vetoes: *Global Policy Forum* 2008). The decrease in the actual use of the veto suggests that it is no longer seen as a 'fighting instrument'.

Yet there is no reason for complacency. Instead of casting a veto directly, permanent members have often threatened to veto controversial draft resolutions if these were tabled unchanged. This 'indirect' use of the veto, also called "hidden veto" (cf. *Bailey/Daws* 1998, 249-250), has enabled them to obtain changes to the drafts, and notably to water down proposed sanctions (e.g. in resolutions on the Darfur crisis or Iran's nuclear program). Experience since 2000 suggests that the veto today is mainly used indirectly, and as such remains crucial. As Ambassador Curtis Ward, representing Jamaica, then elected member of the Council, put it in a wrap up discussion on the work of the Security Council in August 2001, "the mere presence of the threat of the veto … determines the way the Council conducts its business." (UN Doc. S/PV. 4363, 31 August 2001, 7)

Both direct and indirect uses of the veto have continued to prompt criticism. The point was made very clearly in the report of the *High-level Panel on Threats, Challenges and Change*, which noted that "the ability of the five permanent members to keep critical issues of peace and security off the Security Council's agenda has further undermined confidence in the body's work" (UN Doc. A/59/565, 2 December 2004, *United Nations* 2004, para. 246). Yet an outright abolition of the veto power is politically not feasible, since it requires the assent of the P5 states; which for the foreseeable future, none of them (including those members of the European Union, a potential successor to their seat) is going to give.

Rather than seeking to abolish the veto, realistic reform initiatives have aimed to curb the P5's discretion in employing it. Two proposals have gained particular support: on a procedural level, permanent members that veto a resolution should be required to explain their decision; as a substantive exception, no veto should be exercised in the event of genocide and other large-scale killing, ethnic cleansing or serious violations of international humanitarian law.

Neither reform initiative has so far borne fruit:

(i) With respect to the substantive exception, this is unsurprising, as it entails an important restriction of the P5's prerogative. Even though the spirit of the reform proposal must be welcomed, it does indeed have serious practical shortcomings, as neither of the proposed exceptions is self-explanatory: the scenarios used to describe situations in which P5 states could no longer veto Security Council resolutions (e.g. the perpetration of "serious violations of international humanitarian law") require an evaluation of a complex situation on the spot. It seems doubtful whether the reality of international conflict management can be captured by hard and fast rules of the type advocated by reformists. Rather one should hope that during future humanitarian crises, public pressure will force P5 states not to cast a veto.

(ii) As regards the procedural requirement that any veto be explained, the P5 have so far resisted outside pressure as well. Yet a reform on this point seems more likely, in particular because it does not place too heavy a burden on the permanent members, especially if 'indirect uses' of the veto need not be justified. Given the broad coverage of major Security Council debates, states' representatives, even without a formal obligation to that effect, tend to make public the reasons for their vote on draft resolutions. It may thus be cautiously hoped that a duty to explain formal vetoes may become accepted as part of the ongoing general reform of the Security Council's working methods.

Finally, the veto has been an important factor in the debates about an enlargement of the Security Council. States seeking permanent representation on the Council have had to make up their mind whether they would also seek a right of veto. Not all contenders have adopted the same position on this point: Initially, states united in the G4 group aimed to be treated like the current permanent members, i.e. claimed a right of veto. After considerable debate and in order to secure support for their reform proposals, they subsequently decided to drop that claim. Para. 5(b) of the tabled framework resolution on Security Council reform (UN Doc. A/59/L.64, 6 July 2005) testifies to the internal struggle

among G4 States; it provides "[t]hat the new permanent members shall not exercise the right of veto" until an eventual review of the reform. Had this proposal been accepted, it would de facto have created a new class of Security Council members, namely permanent members without a veto power. By contrast, the African Union's reform proposal (UN Doc. A/59/L.67, 18 July 2005) insists that the new permanent members should be accorded "the same prerogatives and privileges as those of the current permanent members, *including the right of veto*" [italics added by the author, C.T.].

Interestingly, in order to justify their claim, some of the candidates for new permanent seats relied on the principle of equality, i.e. claimed a right to be treated equally with current permanent members. This claim seems rather curious given that the veto itself is a major obstacle to the equality of states. What is more, a reform that seeks to ameliorate the problem of representation while at the same time expanding the circle of veto powers could hardly claim to increase the legitimacy of the Security Council. In this respect, the High-level Panel rightly noted the "anachronistic character" of the institution of the veto and recommended that "under any reform proposal, there should be no expansion of the veto" (*United Nations* 2004, para. 256).

Since proposals for an enlargement of the Security Council came to a halt after the debates in the General Assembly in 2005, debates about the veto power of new permanent members have subsided for the time being. During the recent attempts at re-starting the reform process, there seems to be a growing consensus that if there will be new permanent members of the Council at all, they will not be accorded a right of veto

Christian J. Tams

Lit.: *Blokker, N.:* Towards a second Enlargement of the Security Council? A Comparative Perspective, in: Blokker, N./ Schrijver, N. (eds.): The Security Council and the use of force. Theory and reality. A need for change? Leiden 2005, 253-260; *Bourantonis, D.:* The History and Politics of UN Security Council Reform (Routledge Advances in International Relations and Global Politics, Vol. 41) (2005); *Fassbender, B.:* On the Boulevard of Broken Dreams: the Project of a Reform of the UN Security Council after the 2005 World Summit, in: International Organizations Law Review 2 (2005), 391-402; *Fassbender, B.:* All illusions shattered? Looking back on a decade of failed attempts to reform the UN Security Council, in: Max Planck Yearbook of United Nations Law 7, 183-218; *Global Policy Forum:* Subjects of UN Security Council Vetoes, New York 2008, www.globalpolicy.org/security/membship/veto/vertosubjj.htm; *Rittberger, V./Baumgärtner, H.:* Die Reform des Weltsicherheitsrats. Stand und Perspektiven, in: Varwick, J./Zimmermann, A. (eds.): Die Reform der Vereinten Nationen. Bilanz und Perspektiven, Berlin 2006, 47-66; *Schindlmayr, T.:* Obstructing the Security Council : the use of the veto in the twentieth century, in: Journal of the History of International Law 3 (2001), 218-234; *United Nations - General Assembly:* A more secure world: our shared responsibility. Report of the High-level Panel on Threats, Challenges, and Change, UN Doc. A/59/565, 2 December 2004, quoted as: United Nations 2004; *Winkelmann, I.:* Deutschlands Position bei der Reform des Sicherheitsrats, in: Varwick, J./Zimmermann, A. (eds.): Die Reform der Vereinten Nationen. Bilanz und Perspektiven Berlin 2006, 67-83; *Wouters, J./Ruys, T.:* Security Council Reform: a New Veto for a New Century?, in: Revue de droit militaire et de droit de la guerre 44 (2005), 139-174.

Internet: Information about the use of the veto (statistical data) and articles about and political statements on the veto: www. globalpolicy.org/security/membship/veto.htm.

Voting Right and Decision-Making Procedures

In the organs of the United Nations ($\rightarrow$ Principal Organs, Subsidiary Organs, Treaty Bodies), the principle of *equal voting power* applies ("one state, one vote"). That principle is a consequence of the sovereign equality of states (Art. 2 (1) of the UN Charter, $\rightarrow$ Sovereignty). Notwithstanding differences of an economic, social, political or other nature, each member state has the same formal voting power (see for the $\rightarrow$ General Assembly Art. 18 (1), for the $\rightarrow$ Security Council Art. 27 (1), for the Economic and Social Council ($\rightarrow$ ECOSOC) Art. 67 (1), and for the $\rightarrow$ Trusteeship Council Art. 89(1) of the UN Charter).

In none of the organs is unanimity of member states required for the adoption of a resolution ($\rightarrow$ Resolution, Declaration, Decision). By making it possible that a state may be outvoted, the $\rightarrow$ Charter of the UN left behind the opinion prevailing in the international law of the nineteenth and early twentieth century that, because of its sovereignty, a state cannot be committed against its expressly declared will. By contrast, the Covenant of the $\rightarrow$ League of Nations still required, as a rule, decisions of the Assembly and the Council to be taken with "the agreement of all the Members of the League represented at the meeting" (Art. 5). The *principle of majority rule of the UN* is based on the belief that there exists an international community with a sufficiently strong community spirit that allows a minority defeated in a vote to accept the majority view (for the concept of the international community, see *Paulus* 2001). That principle is a prerequisite for an effective formulation of will in a system relying on binding decisions and $\rightarrow$ sanctions, which, for its part, is necessary for achieving the goals of the UN, in particular the exclusion of war as a means of national policy (*Schwarz-Liebermann* 1953).

In accordance with the notion of legal equality of states, the UN Charter has retained the principle of *equal voting power* of all member states. It has not introduced a system of weighted voting in which states are accorded different numbers of votes. An initiative of the United States Congress of 1985, seeking to give UN member states in decisions on budgetary questions a voting power equivalent to their contribution to the $\rightarrow$ budget (the so-called Kassebaum Amendment), failed ($\rightarrow$ UN Policy, USA).

Weighted voting, a method which can apply different criteria for the allocation of votes, was first introduced in the nineteenth century in European federal systems. In the legislative assemblies, in which the states members of the federation were represented, votes were allocated to states in proportion to the size of their territory and population (see, for instance, Article 4 of the Founding Act of the German Confederation of 1815, and Article 6 of the German Constitution of 1871). In contrast, the Constitution of the United States of America of 1787 gives each state the same representation by two senators, each of them having one vote (Art. I, sec. 3, clause 1). Since the last third of the nineteenth century, weighted voting was also applied in intergovernmental organizations dealing with "technical" (i.e. "non-political") matters, for instance the International Institute of Agriculture in Rome (later absorbed by the Food and Agriculture Organization, → FAO). After World War II, the method was introduced in international finance institutions like the World Bank (→ World Bank, World Bank Group) and the International Monetary Fund (→ IMF).

The equal voting power of member states in the UN was increasingly criticized, when, in the wake of → decolonization, a great number of territorially very small and/or sparsely populated states were admitted to the UN. How unequal the actual conditions are in which states find themselves is demonstrated by the scale of contributions of member states to the regular → budget of the UN as determined by the General Assembly according to the respective economic strength. At present (2008), 54 of 192 members only contribute the minimum of 0.001 %, and 46 states each contribute 0.01 % or less (see UN General Assembly Res. 61/237 of 22 December 2006, "Scale of assessments for the apportionment of the expenses of the United Nations 2007-2009"). This means that more than half of the membership carries together less than 1 % of the expenses of the Organization, whereas the three largest contributors (the United States of America, Japan and Germany) together bear more than half of the regular budget. However, proposals, advanced in the 1970s, to introduce an "associated membership" for micro-states with limited voting rights were not realized.

A loss of a member state's right to vote in all or only particular organs of the United Nations can result from a suspension "from the exercise of the rights and privileges of membership" (Art. 5 of the UN Charter). According to Article 19, a member state which is in arrears in the payment of its financial contributions to the Organization for two years loses its right to vote in the General Assembly unless the Assembly "is satisfied that the failure to pay is due to conditions beyond the control of the Member". However, it is the practice of the Assembly to allow a member state which is behind in its payments to participate in certain votes, especially on resolutions to be adopted "by consensus" (for explanation of this method, see below). In the Chapter on the Security Council, a provision similar to that of Article 19 is missing. In the view of the founders, the Council should be able to function regardless of possible arrears of its members.

As a rule, for decisions of the *General Assembly* a *simple majority* is sufficient (Art. 18 (3) of the Charter). Only *decisions on "important questions"*, which are listed individually in Article 18 (2), require a *qualified majority of two-thirds of the members present and voting*. A simple majority can determine additional categories of questions to be decided by such a majority (Art. 18 (3)). Accordingly, the → rules of procedure of the General Assembly, which regulate details of the Assembly's decision-making, set forth further decisions for which a two-thirds majority is necessary. Article 18 (2) and (3) are not applied in the committees of the Assembly where for all decisions a simple majority suffices (→ Committees, System of).

"Consensus" is a method of voting which, although it is not mentioned either in the Charter or in the rules of procedure of the General Assembly or the Security Council, has become highly

significant. Resolutions and decisions adopted "by consensus" or "without a vote" are accepted without a formal vote taking place. Instead, the President of the General Assembly or the Council, or the chairman of a committee or subsidiary organ, declares a resolution to have been approved.

In the past, the expression "adopted by consensus" indicated a strong form of general agreement, whereas an adoption "without a vote" suggested a weaker one. Today, this distinction has become less pronounced. Resolutions adopted by consensus are usually preceded by negotiations and consultations in which a compromise is reached that allows a broad majority to accept the text or, at least, not to reject it openly. Without blocking the adoption, a state can express its particular disagreement by "disassociating" itself from the consensus. The consensus procedure was especially favored by Western states, which since → decolonization have been in the minority in the General Assembly, whereas developing countries rather criticized it as a circumvention of the "one state, one vote" rule. On the other hand, those latter states came to realize that resolutions passed against the opposition of the industrialized states are only of relative worth because they are largely ineffective.

Substantive decisions of the *Security Council* require an affirmative vote of nine members (out of fifteen), "including the concurring votes of the permanent members" (Art. 27 (3) of the UN Charter). Accordingly, each of the five permanent members has the possibility and the right to prevent a draft resolution from being adopted by casting a negative vote (for details, see *Fassbender* 1998). This right is called the *"right of veto"* (→ Veto, Right of Veto). It has an effect already before a formal vote is taken, because usually a draft resolution is not put to the vote if the opposition of a permanent member is known. While the text of the Charter requires an express approval of a decision by the permanent members ("concurring votes"), the established practice of the Council

recognizes that decisions can be taken in the absence of a permanent member as well as in the case of its non-participation in the vote or its abstention from voting. In other words, to make use of its veto power a permanent member must cast a negative vote. The right of veto does not apply to decisions on procedural questions (Art. 27 (2) of the Charter).

According to Article 27 (3) of the Charter, permanent as well as non-permanent members of the Council who are "a party to a dispute" that is being discussed by the Council shall abstain from voting – but only if the resolution is about the pacific settlement of disputes (→ Peaceful Settlement of Disputes) as provided for in Chapter VI and Article 52 (3) of the Charter. This means inversely that a party to a dispute retains its right to vote if the vote concerns decisions under Chapter VII. In the practice of the Council, the restriction imposed by Article 27 (3) has often been disregarded.

Although a permanent member of the Security Council numerically has the same voting power as every other member, its right of veto actually enhances this power enormously. A permanent member alone can obstruct a decision, while it needs a negative vote of at least seven non-permanent members to have the same effect. The status of the permanent members, which effectively exempts them from the Charter system of sanctions, constitutes an important exception to the principle of sovereign equality of all UN member states, and has, as such, been criticized heavily since the foundation of the Organization. In the discussions about a reform of the Security Council (cf. *Fassbender* 1998, *Fassbender* 2003; → Reform of the UN), which have been held since the early 1990s, many states, among them those united in the → Non-Aligned Movement and the African Union, have demanded an abolition or considerable restriction of the right of veto.

Article 31 and 32 of the UN Charter provide for the participation of a state not being a member of the Security

Council in the discussions of the Council when its interests are especially affected or if it is a party to a dispute under consideration by the Council. In addition, Article 44 grants a state not represented on the Council, which shall provide armed forces in accordance with Article 43, a right to participate in the decisions of the Council. However, until now this provision has not been applied.

For consultations of the Council with states supporting UN peace-keeping operations with armed forces ("troop-contributing countries)", an own procedure has been developed (→ Peacekeeping, → Peacekeeping Forces, → Peacekeeping Operations). Individual members of the Council meet the representatives of those countries, and the President of the Council informs the other Council members of the results of these conversations (see Presidential Statement of 28 March 1996 (S/PRST/1996/13), reprinted in *Bailey/Daws* 1998, Appendix XII(e)).

In the practice of the Security Council, the adoption of resolutions by *consensus* has become increasingly common. Many procedural motions are now approved without a vote. They relate, for instance, to the agenda, the suspension or adjournment of meetings, invitations to participate, a reference of matters to subsidiary organs, the composition of such organs, requests for information, and decisions that consideration of a particular stage of a matter has been completed (*Bailey/Daws* 1998, 259).

Bardo Fassbender

Lit.: *Bailey, S.D./Daws, S.:* The Procedure of the UN Security Council, 3rd edn., Oxford 1998; *Fassbender, B.:* UN Security Council Reform and the Right of Veto: A Constitutional Perspective, The Hague 1998; *Fassbender, B.:* All Illusions Shattered? Looking Back on a Decade of Failed Attempts to Reform the UN Security Council, in: Max Planck Yearbook of UN Law 7 (2003), 183-218; *Koo, W., Jr.:* Voting Procedures in International Political Organizations, New York 1947; *Paulus, A.L.:* Die internationale Gemeinschaft im Völkerrecht, Munich 2001; *Schwarz-Liebermann von Wahlendorf, H.A.:* Mehrheitsentscheid und Stimmenwägung, Tübingen 1953; *Thiele, C.:* Regeln und Verfahren der Entscheidungsfindung innerhalb von Staaten und Staatenverbindungen, Berlin/Heidelberg 2008; *Wolfrum, R.:* Voting and Decision-Making, in: Wolfrum, R. (ed.): United Nations: Law, Policies and Practice, Vol. 2, Munich/Dordrecht 1995, 1400-1407; *Wolfrum, R.:* Art. 18, in: Simma, B. (ed.): The Charter of the United Nations: A Commentary, 2nd edn., Vol. I, Oxford 2002, 352-362.

WFC – World Food Council

Following a recommendation of the World Food Summit of 1974, the UN → General Assembly established the *World Food Council (WFC)* by Resolution 3348 (XXIX) of 17 December 1974 as one of its special bodies (→ Principal Organs, Subsidiary Organs, Treaty Bodies).

Its task were to direct and coordinate the work of the UN system (→ UN System) concerning world "food" issues, as the actual relief measures were carried out by → specialized agencies of the UN such as the Food and Agricultural Organization (→ FAO), the International Fund for Agricultural Development (IFAD) or the World Food Programme (→ WFP). According to a regional quota system, 36 members participated in annual meetings of the Council.

The main tasks of the WFC were to analyze the world food situation, submit improvement proposals, and maintain the public awareness of the world food problem. Its functions were restricted to advising and initiating. Its "national food strategies" aimed at making food production in developing countries independent from external support. Additionally, in order to create long term global food security, the WFC seeked to improve the mechanisms of food distribution. Financial support of the WFC was provided within the regular UN → budget and amounts to 5 million US dollars for 2 years.

In comparison to other world "food" institutions, the WFC was a late-comer, which led to disputes about responsibilities with the other institutions in this field, and thus made it difficult for the WFC to define its own field of functions within the UN system. Therefore, the Council concentrated mainly on public relations work for the world food problem, an area in which it had great success.

By General Assembly Resolution A/RES/50/227 (1995) FAO and WFP took over the functions of the World Food Council WFC and consequently WFC was discontinued.

Barbara Hofner

Lit.: *Hüfner, K.:* Die Vereinten Nationen und ihre Sonderorganisationen. Strukturen, Aufgaben, Dokumente. Teil 1: Die Haupt- und Spezialorgane, DGVN-Texte 40, 2nd edn., Bonn 1995, 171; *Talbot, R.B.:* Historical dictionary of the international food agencies: FAO, WFP, WFC, IFAD, Metuchen, NJ 1994; *Wolf, K.D.:* WFC – World Food Council, in: Wolfrum, R. (ed.): United Nations: Law, Policies and Practice, Vol. 2, Munich/Dordrecht 1995, 1408-1413; *Wolf, K.D.:* World Food Problems, in: Wolfrum, R. (ed.): United Nations: Law, Policies and Practice, Vol. 2, Munich/Dordrecht 1995, 1460-1465.

Addendum

Lit.: *Overseas Development Institute:* Global Hunger and Food Security after the World Food Summit (ODI Briefing Paper 1/1997, www.odi.org.uk/Publications/ briefing/1-97.html; *Deutsche Stiftung für Internationale Entwicklung (DSE) et al. (eds.):* Welternährungssicherung mit dem UN-System – Änderungen der Prioritäten des Welternährungsrates erforderlich? Konferenz des Entwicklungspolitischen Forums der DSE in Zusammenarbeit mit dem Präsidenten des Welternährungsrates der Vereinten Nationen (UN/WFC) in Berlin am 23.1.1982, Berlin 1982; *Sharp, R.:* Cautious Optimism at the World Food Council, in: Food Policy 8 (1983), 264-267; *Wallerstein, M.B./Austin, J.E.:* The world food council at three years: Global food system manager? in: Food Policy 3 (1978), 191-201.

Friederike Hoffmann

WFP – World Food Programme

In 1961 the United Nations and the Food and Agricultural Organization → FAO established by parallel resolutions of the UN → General Assembly (UN Doc. A/RES/1714 (XVI)) and of the FAO Conference the food aid organization of the UN, the *World Food Programme (WFP)*, with the goal of making the fight against global hunger, poverty and malnutrition more efficient (→ UN System; → Specialized Agencies). In 1966, after a three-year experimental period, it became a permanent organization with its headquarters based in Rome.

WFP's main task is to transfer excess food production from industrialized countries to developing countries. Although the WFP is an autonomous organization, the Director-General of the FAO has to approve any provision of food aid.

In 1994 WFP defined its mission for the coming years along three general lines:

(1) "Food for Life" is food aid for emergency situations particularly for refugees or victims of natural disasters, which adds up to more than 50% of all aid provided through WFP.

(2) "Food for Growth" focuses on development projects for the most vulnerable groups such as children, mothers and the elderly.

(3) "Food for Work" programmes pay work with food to allow communities to devote more funds to essential development projects.

The *decision-making structure* of the WFP was changed in 1996, when the former executive body, the *Committee on Food Aid Policies and Programmes (CFA)* was reconstituted into its current form – the *WFP Executive Board*. The Board consists of 36 members, of which 18 are elected by the Economic and Social Council of the United Nations (→ ECOSOC) and 18 by the Council of the Food and Agricultural Organization (FAO). Each member serves a three-year term and is eligible for re-election. The Board is headed by an Executive

Director, and reports to the FAO. The Board is responsible for approving programmes and budgets.

WFP is funded entirely by voluntary contributions from more than 60 governments and some private corporations. The donations can be made either in cash, food or services. The major donors are the USA (796 million US dollars in 2000), Japan (260 million US dollars in 2000) and the EU (118 million US dollars in 2000). In the year 2000 the total expenditure for emergency operations and development projects in 83 countries amounted to 1.49 billion US dollars and 3.7 million tons of food which helped 83 million people. Altogether during the last 30 years, the WFP has invested 24 billion US dollars and 43 million tons of food aid. About one third of global food aid comes from WFP, whereby more than half of this goes to emergency relief. Most of the emergency relief is provided by the International Emergency Food Reserve (IEFR), which is part of WFP's administration.

Although all these numbers show WFP's success, it has been criticized for its approach. Critics argue that the supply of food works against "self supply" in developing countries. However, WFP is responsible for food distribution problems and is focused on the redistribution of food; it is not a development organization (→ Development Cooperation of the UN System). WFP mainly aims to help individuals and insists that hunger is unacceptable in a world of abundance.

Barbara Hofner

Lit.: *Hüfner, K.:* Die Vereinten Nationen und ihre Sonderorganisationen. Strukturen, Aufgaben, Dokumente. Teil 1: Die Haupt- und Spezialorgane, DGVN-Texte 40, 2nd edn., Bonn 1995, 172-175; *Talbot, R.B.:* Historical dictionary of the international food agencies: FAO, WFP, WFC, IFAD, Metuchen, NJ 1994; *Wolf, K.D.:* WFP – World Food Programme, in: Wolfrum, R. (ed.): United Nations: Law, Policies and Practice, Vol. 2, Munich/Dordrecht 1995, 1414-1418; *Wolf, K.D.:* World Food Problems, in: Wolfrum, R. (ed.): United Nations: Law, Policies and Practice, Vol. 2, Munich/Dordrecht 1995, 1460-1465; *World Food Programme:* World Food Programme News; *World Food Programme:* Tackling hunger in a world full of food: Tasks ahead for food aid, Rome 1996.

Addendum

The World Food Programme (WFP) remains the major actor in the field of emergency hunger relief. Providing 56% of the total food aid delivered in 2006, the organization directs 90% of its resources and finances to emergency relief. With the Tsunami in Asia, the earthquake in Pakistan, and the enduring crisis in Sudan, the overall budget rose significantly to 2.7 billion US dollars in 2006. The WFP's cooperation with the FAO on both the policy and operational level is exceptionally good; a successful example of hand-in-hand cooperation is the Food-for-Work Programme. While the WFP delivers food, the FAO provides technical guidance for agricultural advancement.

In response to the critique that WFP would do damage to the local and regional market by its gratis food import programmes from overseas, the WFP expanded local purchases when possible and continues the distribution without charge, thus keeping the impact on local and regional markets as low as possible. Howver, these efforts depend on the donors' contributions. The USA remains the largest donor with total contributions between 1.4 billion US dollars in 2003 and 1.1 billion US dollars in 2006. However, donations-in-kind remain the majority of U.S. contributions, owing to US national commercial, labor, and shipping interests, thus limiting the WFP's efforts to be more flexible.

Friederike Hoffmann

Lit.: *Buettner, M.:* Streitfall Nahrungsmittelhilfe: Kritische Differenzierung tut Not, in: Weltnachrichten (ed. Austrian Development Agency), No. 1/2007, www.ada.gv.at/view.php3?f_id=9609&LNG=de&version=; *Clay, E.J.:* Responding to Change: WFP and the Global Food Aid System, in: Development Policy Review 21 (2003), 697-709; *Clay, E.J.:* Food aid, tying and trade distortion: a proportionate response (paper for the International Conference "Food Aid: exploring the challenges", Berlin 3-5 May 2007); *Food and Agriculture Organization:* Working Together, Issue 7, December 2005, ftp://ftp.fao.org/docrep/fao/008/a0263e/a0263e00.pdf; *Marchione, T.J.:* Foods Provided through U.S. Government Emergency Food Aid Programs: Policies and Customs Governing Their Formulation, Selection and Distribution, in: The Journal of Nutrition 132 (2002), 2104-2111; *OECD*: The Development Effect of Food Aid. Does Tying Matter? (The Development Dimension), Paris 2005; *World Food Programme:* Statement by Deputy Executive Director of the World Food Programme Mr. John Powell, Food Aid Seminar, World Trade Organization, Geneva, Switzerland, May 17, 2005, http://documents.wfp.org/stellent/groupspublic/documents/newsroom/wfp0706472.pdf; *World Food Programme:* WFP Biennial Management Plan (2006-2007), UN Doc. WFP/EB.2/2005/5-A/1, Rome 2005, http://wfp.org/eb/docs/2005/wfp077004~2. pdf.

Internet: Homepage of WFP: www.wfp.org.

WFUNA – World Federation of United Nations Associations

I. Introduction

The World Federation of United Nations Associations (WFUNA), located in New York and Geneva, was founded on 2 August 1946 in Luxembourg upon the initiative of the British United Nations Association (UNA-UK). The founding of WFUNA was based upon the fundamental concept found in the preamble of the → Charter of the UN ("We, the Peoples of the United Nations"). In this sense WFUNA defines itself as a "peoples' movement for the United Nations", which functions on a voluntary, honorary basis and is the only international nongovernmental organization (→ NGOs) to concentrate exclusively on mobilizing the (world) public (→ Public Opinion and the UN) in favor of the principles and purposes of the UN and its → specialized agencies and supporting their work. WFUNA has Category One Consultative Status at the → ECOSOC and also consultative or liaison links with other UN institutions.

II. Membership

According to the WFUNA Constitution, one national United Nations Association (UNA) per state can become a member if it accepts the general objectives of the Federation. WFUNA distinguishes between members (108 as of September 2008) and associated organizations (5) such as, e.g., the International Academy of Ecological Reconstruction and Sokka Gakkai International.

The figures mentioned above indicate already that WFUNA has never been in the position to increase its membership commensurate with the development of the membership in the UN (→ Membership and Representation of States). Europe's interest in the Federation continues to dominate with 38 UNAs (= 35.2 % of the membership). The highest fluctuation rate is in Africa with presently 25 UNAs, of which about 50 % are unable to pay their dues regularly. Nevertheless, its first goal remains to establish UNAs in all member states of the UN. For this purpose, regional coordination among UNAs in support of regional efforts will be enhanced.

III. WFUNA-Youth

WFUNA-Youth is the official youth section of WFUNA connecting 41 United Nations Youth Associations and UNA Youth Programmes/Sections. It is an integral part of WFUNA but takes its decisions on project and budgetary matters autonomously. WFUNA-Youth aims to strengthen the national activities of its members through different capacity-building measures for its members including Project Management Workshops and handbooks to enable them to successfully carry out projects to inform the young public about the UN. In 2006, the first official WFUNA-Youth Meeting took place in Buenos Aires.

IV. Organizational Set-up

According to the WFUNA Constitution the organs of the Federation are the Plenary Assembly, the Executive Committee and the Secretariat headed by a Secretary-General. But during the 1990s, a far-reaching financial crisis of the Federation led to considerable organizational deficits and a legitimation crisis.

The Plenary Assembly as the principal organ now meets only every three years instead of every two years as it did before. It convened in 2003 in Barcelona and in 2006 in Buenos Aires. The next Plenary Assembly is planned for 2009 to take place in Seoul.

The Executive Committee, which consists of 17 individuals elected for four years and a representative of WFUNA-Youth, meets twice a year; at present; its meetings take place primarily in New York City instead of, as in the past, in Geneva. President of the Federation is Hans Blix (Sweden), former Director-General of the → IAEA. Secretary-General since 2006 is Pera Wells, the first woman to hold this position.

V. Perspectives

Due to the small, geographically unbalanced membership and the modest revenues (2007: about 90,000 US dollars) as well as the dependence on fundraising activities for projects it is difficult to anticipate positive future perspectives. Not only a generation change (cf. section III), but also a new focus of orientation is urgently needed. Whereas until the 1980s the overcoming of the East-West conflict stood at the centre of interest, which offered UNAs of differing "closeness to government" WFUNA as forum for an informal and unofficial exchange of views, a gap suddenly opened up at the beginning of the 1990s for several reasons:

(1) The economically no longer secured UNAs of the former socialist countries were confronted with a complex transformation process which bound the societal forces to solve their internal problems.

(2) The North-South problem has been superimposed by → globalization processes which have also led to a marginalization of the Federation.

(3) Many other NGO actors have appeared on the scene, who are also involved in UN affairs, although primarily interested and specialized in selected issues.

Since active membership of WFUNA continued to decrease and the financial situation became increasingly worse, individual members of the UNA-USA took the lead in the renewal of WFUNA and in shaping future directions; a foundation ("Friends of WFUNA") has been founded that allows US citizens or companies to make tax-deductible contributions to WFUNA. Furthermore an approach of → regionalizationis undertaken in Europe by the UNA/EU Liaison Group, in order to be able to address again actual world problems of the → UN system through inter-regional cooperation mechanisms.

Klaus Hüfner

Lit: *Hüfner, K.*: WFUNA – World Federation of United Nations Associations, in: Wolfrum, R. (ed.): United Nations: Law, Policies and Practice, 2 vols., Dordrecht/ Munich 1995, 1419-1424; *World Federation of the United Nations:* WFUNA submission to the Cardoso panel on UN relations with civil society, New York 2003.

Internet: Homepages of *WFUNA:* www. wfuna.org, and *WFUNA-Youth:* www. wfuna-youth.org.

WHO – World Health Organization

History of WHO

At the beginning of the twentieth century, different international organs were established as forerunners of the World Health Organization. In 1902, the International Sanitary Bureau, which was later changed into the Pan-American Health Organization (PAHO), was established in Washington, D.C. In 1903, the l'Office International d'Hygiène Public (OIHP) was created in Paris and in 1919, parallel to the Paris Office, the Health Organization of the → League of Nations.

It took more than twenty-five years before it was decided to establish a new, independent international health organization. The International Health Conference, which met in New York in 1946, adopted the constitution of the *World Health Organization (WHO)*, which entered into force on 7 April 1948. (UNTS 14, No. 221; www.who.int/governance/eb/who_constitution_en.pdf).

Mandate and Task

The aim of WHO is for all peoples to attain the highest possible status of health according to the definition stipulated in the Preamble to its Constitution: "Health is a state of complete physical, mental and social well-being and not merely the absence of disease or infirmity."

To support this global aim, the Organization has two principal functions:
- To act as the guiding and coordinating body for international health work;
- To provide appropriate technical support in response to governments' requests.

These two main tasks are complementary to each other, and constitute a solid basis for the work of the Organization. WHO also develops proposals for international conventions, regulations, and agreements. Additionally, it issues recommendations for the international nomenclature of diseases, and develops, defines, and promotes international standards, criteria and guidelines for food and biological substances, drugs, as well as chemical and physical agents.

The Structure of WHO

The *World Health Assembly (WHA)* is the highest decision-making organ of the Organization. It is convened each year in May at the WHO Headquarters in Geneva, and is attended by delegations from its member states, who currently number 193 (as of 1 October 2007). As WHO is a specialized agency of the United Nations (→ Specialized Agencies) responsible for health, the delegations at the World Health Assembly consist mainly, but not necessarily, of representatives of the health sector of the member states.

The main functions of the *World Health Assembly* are:
- To determine the policies of WHO; and

- To review and approve proposed biennial programme budgets.

The *Executive Board*, consisting of 34 members who are technically qualified in the field of health, are nominated by their respective member states for three-year terms. They represent the six *regions* of WHO, namely:
- The African Region (7);
- The American Region (6);
- The Eastern Mediterranean Region (5);
- The European Region (8);
- The Southeast Asian Region (3); and
- The Western Pacific Region (5).

Member states who are also members of the → Security Council of the United Nations are represented on the Executive Board continuously, with a break of one year after a three-year period. The Executive Board meets at least twice each year, with the principal meeting normally being held in January, and a second shorter meeting in May immediately after the Assembly.

The main functions of the Executive Board are:
- To give effect to the decisions and policies of the World Health Assembly; and
- To advise the World Health Assembly and facilitate its work.

A special feature of WHO is its *decentralized structure*. The six *regions* (see above) consist of a *Regional Committee* and a *Regional Office*. The Regional Offices are located in:
- Brazzaville – African Region
- Washington D.C., USA – American Region;
- Cairo, Egypt – Eastern Mediterranean Region;
- Copenhagen, Denmark – European Region;
- New Delhi, India – Southeast Asian Region; and
- Manila, Philippines – Western Pacific Region.

Each Regional Office is headed by a Regional Director who is nominated by the respective Regional Committees and appointed for a five-year term (renewable once) by the Executive Board. The Regional Committees are responsible for:

- Formulating regional policies; and
- Monitoring regional activities.

In 147 countries, WHO is represented by a WHO Representative or a Liaison Oficer who is responsible for WHO's activities in their respective countries and for the support of their respective governments in the planning and management of national health programmes. In some countries, WHO has project centres dealing with specific programmatic subjects, for example in Kobe, Japan the WHO Centre for Health Development (WKC) focusing particularly on urban health and health equity (www.who.or.jp); in Lima, Peru the Pan American Center for Sanitary Engineering and Environmental Sciences (CEPIS) (www.cepis.org.pe); and in Rome, Italy the European Centre for Environment and Health (www.euro.who.int/globalchange).

In addition, WHO also has liaison offices responsible for the cooperation with important international institutions and organizations, for example in Brussels the Office at the European Union (WEU) which is mainly responsible for the co-operation with the institutions of the European Union, but also with the Organization for Economic Co-operation and Development (OECD) in Paris, the Council of Europe in Strasburg, and the Organization for Security and Co-operation in Europe (OSCE) in Vienna. Moreover, WHO is represented in New York at the United Nations; in Addis Ababa at the Organization of African Union (OAU).

A special feature of WHO is its *collaborating centers*. These are existing national institutions which are not subject to the authority of, but designated by, the Director General based on strict criteria. WHO can rely on the experience and knowledge of more than 900 of such centers in over 100 countries supporting WHO programmes (www.who.int/collaboratingcentres/en/index.html).

Moreover, WHO has official relations with numerous non-governmental organizations ($\to$ NGOs). The relations between WHO and these NGOs follow specific principles agreed upon by WHO's Governing Bodies.

Secretariat

The work of WHO is managed by the Secretariat. It consists currently of some 8000 health and other experts and support staff on fixed-term appointments, working at headquarters, in the six regional offices, and in countries.

The Secretariat is headed by the Director-General who, after being nominated by the Executive Board, is appointed (renewable once) by the World Health Assembly. The current Director-General is Dr Margaret Chan as of 9 November 2006.

The structure of Headquarters is based on nine broad programme areas organized in clusters that are led by Assistant Directors-General.

These clusters are (as of 1 November 2007):
- Health Security and Environment
- HIV/AIDS, TB, Malaria and Neglected Tropical Diseases
- Information, Evidence and Research
- Noncommunicable Diseases and Mental Health
- Family and Community Health
- Health Technology and Pharmaceuticals
- Health Systems and Services
- Health Action in Crisis
- General Management

The structure of Regional Offices does not need to follow necessarily that of Headquarters.

The Budget of WHO

The budget of WHO consists of assessed contributions of its member states which are oriented on the scale of assessments for the membership contributions of the UN member states ($\to$ Budget) and are based on the size of the population and the economy of the respective countries. The assessed contributions vary from 22 % for the United States to 0.01 % for the majority of the developing countries. The assessed contributions represent the regular budget of WHO.

Additionally, WHO receives voluntary contributions from its member states and other sources, which comprise the so-called extra-budgetary resources. The regular budget approved by the 60th World Health Assembly in May 2007 for the biennium 2008 - 2009 amounts to a total assessment on members of about 958 million US dollars. For the 2008-2009 biennium, WHO's extrabudgetary resources are estimated to be about 3 268 640 000 US dollars, bringing the total effective working budget to about 4.2 billion US dollars for this biennium. The allocation of the regular budget and the voluntary contributions to Headquarters and the six Regional Offices and the source of funding are shown in Table 1.

Table 1: Proposed WHO Budget 2008-2009 by Organizational Level and Source of Funding (in thousand US dollars)

Organizational Level	Assessed Contribution	Voluntary Contributions	Total
Headquarters	325,047	850,883	1,175,930
African Region	213,342	980,598	1,193,940
Region of the Americas	81,501	197,000	278,501
Southeast Asian Region	103,938	387,600	491,538
European Region	63,283	211,480	274,763
Eastern Mediterranean Region	91,570	373,400	464,970
Western Pacific Region	80,159	267,679	347,838
Total	958,840	3,268,640	4,227,480

Source: WHO Document A/MTSP/2008-2013 PB/2008-2009 Original: English

Over the last few years, the voluntary contributions to WHO increased by more than 200% reflecting a significant change by its members and all other donors in the assessment of the importance of protecting and promoting global public health. This change in attitude is to a great extent a result of the increasing threats to global public health from emerging or re-emerging diseases such as the severe acute respiratory syndrome (SARS), the avian flue, HIV/AIDS, malaria and TB and the need to strengthen global health security(see below).

Achievements

Setting the Goal of Health for All

Among the numerous policy initiatives, programmes and projects WHO has launched since its inception in 1948, the movement "Health for All" occupies a prominent place.

In 1977 the World Health Assembly decided that "all governments and WHO establish as the most important social goal for all peoples of the world the achievement of a level of health which would enable them to lead socially and economically productive lives". At the International Conference on Primary Health Care in Alma Ata in 1979, the Alma-Ata Declaration was adopted that emerged as a major milestone of the twentieth century in the field of public health. It identified primary health care as the key to the attainment of the goal of Health for All (www.who.int/hpr/NPH/docs/declaration_almaata.pdf).

Subsequently, in 1981, the World Health Assembly unanimously adopted the global strategy of "Health for All" by the year 2000. The movement "Health for All" was born.

"Health for All" does not mean that all diseases and disabilities will disappear or that health professionals will be able to care for everybody. Rather, it means that all health resources are equitably distributed, and that all human beings have access to basic care. "Health for All" means that health starts at home, at school and at the workplace and that people learn how to prevent diseases and to mitigate unavoidable diseases and disabilities. It also means that people recognize that disease is not inevitable, and that they, therefore, can – to some extent – shape their own lives and the lives of their families in such a way that they are not impaired by avoidable diseases.

2008 marks the 30th anniversary of the Declaration of Alma-Ata and the 60th anniversary of WHO. On this occasion, WHO will dedicate the topic of primary health care to next year's World Health Report underlining WHO's continuous commitment to aspire to the historic goal of "Health for All" set in Alma Ata.

Eradication and Elimination of Diseases

WHO has succeeded in eliminating and mitigating important diseases since its establishment in 1948. The best known example is the eradication of *smallpox*. When, in 1967, WHO started its international effort to eradicate smallpox, an estimated 15 million people suffered from this horrible disease. About 2 million people died, millions where disfigured and, at times, survived only with serious disabilities, such as blindness. In 1980, WHO was able to certify the eradication of this disease.

Significant progress was also made in the fight against *river blindness*, a tropical disease and globally the second biggest cause of the loss of sight. In 1974, WHO, together with three other organizations of the United Nations, established the Onchocerciasis Control Programme (OCP). Today, more than 30 years later, no traces of this disease can be found in about 1.5 million people who had formerly been suffering from it. Currently, more than 300,000 cases of losses of sight have been avoided through the implementation of the OCP.

Dracunculiasis (guinea-worm disease) continues to be a major public health problem among many rural communities in Africa, which depend upon unprotected water sources for drinking. Nevertheless, the Global Programme to Eradicate Dracunculiasis continued to make considerable pro-

gress, reducing the number of endemic countries from 11 in 2004 to 9 in 2005 and the number of reported cases dropped from 892 055 in 1989 to 10674 in 2005 (Weekly Epidemiological Record, No.18, 5 May 2006).

The Global Polio Eradication Initiative is the largest public health initiative the world has ever known (www. who.int/mediacentre/events/2006/ g8summit/polio/en). As a result of this Initiative, by late 2003 *poliomyelitis* had been eliminated from all but six countries and fewer than 1000 children had been paralyzed by the disease during that year. The Initiative spearheaded by the World Health Organization, Rotary International, US Centers for Disease Control and Prevention and UNICEF, is a unique collaboration of governments, international organizations the private sector, civil society and over 20 million volunteers.

Leprosy has been eliminated from 113 out of 122 countries where leprosy was considered a public health problem in 1985. An additional 13 countries achieved the elimination target since 2000 (www. who.int/mediacentre/factsheets/fs101/en). According to the latest available information, intensive efforts are still needed to reach the leprosy elimination target in five countries: Brazil, India, Madagascar, Mozambique, and Nepal.

Through the *expanded programme on immunization* established by WHO in 1974, each year, millions of children were saved. This programme aimed at the immunization against child diseases, which can be prevented through immunization, for example: diphtheria, tetanus, measles, and poliomyelitis. In January 2000, jointly with other agencies, the Global Alliance for Vaccines and Immunization (GAVI) has been launched. GAVI is dedicated to ensuring that all children, however poor, have equal access to immunization. Significant progress has been made by GAVI in achieving this goal. Today, almost 90% of the children are immunized globally.

The Fight against HIV/AIDS, Malaria and Tuberculosis

Much of the work that WHO does and the goals that it seeks to achieve are inextricably bound with the Millennium Development Goals (MDGs), including the fight against HIV/AIDS, malaria and TB (Goal 6). From 1986, WHO lead the responsibilities on AIDS in the UN, aiding countries to develop much-needed national AIDS programmmes. By the mid-1990's HIV/AIDS was spreading so rapidly, no single UN organizations could provide the coordinated level of assistance needed to address the many factors of the epidemic. Therefore, the UN took an innovative approach bringing together six organizations to help form a co-sponsored programme (ECOSOC resolution E/RES/1994/24, July 1994). As a further measure to dramatically increase resources to fight three of the world's most devastating diseases, and to direct those resources to areas of greatest need the Global Fund to Fight AIDS, Tuberculosis and Malaria was created in 2001 (www.the globalfund.org/en/about/how/).

All these initiatives supported by the work of many non-governmental and private organizations have made significant progress in the fight for HIV/AIDS but it is understood by those involved that the road ahead remains long and tough (*Network* 2002: The Durban AIDS Conference & Beyond; Challenge of partnership in the Global Fight Against AIDS).

Malaria has been with man for thousands of years and the fight against the "King of Diseases" is still ongoing (cf. *Litsios* 1996). Malaria kills more than one million people a year – most of them children under five in Africa. In fact, on average a child in Africa dies every 30 seconds from a malaria infection caused by the bite of a mosquito. WHO's target, and that of the Roll Back Malaria Partnership (www.rbm. who. int), is to cut malaria by half by 2010, with the goal of reaching the MDG target by 2015 (*WHO* 2007a).

Tuberculosis is still a major cause of death worldwide, but the global epidemic is on the threshold of decline (*WHO* 2007b). WHO – in collaboration with the Stop TB Partnership (www.stoptb. org) – leads the global drive to expand the use of DOTS (Directly Observed Treatment Short Course Therapy), the internationally recommended strategy to fight TB. DOTS is now being used in 187 countries.

Combating the Spread of the Avian Influenza

In 1996, the first confirmed cases of avian influenza virus H5N1 were located in Guangdong Province, China. One year later, Hong Kong reported the first human infections (*WHO:* H5N1 Avian Influenza: Timeline 8 May 2006). While avian influenza is still being considered an animal disease, up till today (17 October 2007), 331 confirmed human cases and 203 deaths in a total of 12 countries have been reported to WHO (www.who.int/csr/disease/avian_in fluenza/country/cases_table_2007_10_17/ en/index.html). This does not mean, however, that a new pandemic has emerged, as several prerequisites have not been fulfilled, including the transmission between humans. Nevertheless, huge efforts are being spent by WHO coordinating the global response to human cases of H5N1 avian influenza and monitoring the corresponding threat of an influenza pandemic (*WHO:* Director-General's report on avian and pandemic influenza: developments, response and follow-up; Documents A60/7, A60/8 and A60/INF.DOC./1).

Control of the Severe Acute Respiratory Syndrome (SARS)

SARS was recognized at the end of February 2003. WHO coordinated the international investigation with the assistance of the Global Outbreak Alert and Response Network and worked closely with health authorities in the affected countries to provide epidemiological, clinical and logistical support. A total of about 8000 cases were reported to WHO out of which 774 died based on data from 31 December 2003 (www.who.int/csr/sars/country/table2004_04_21/en/index.html).

Global Public Health Treaties

WHO Framework Convention on Tobacco Control (FCTC)

For the fight against non-communicable diseases, in particular, cancer and cardiovascular diseases, WHO developed the WHO Framework Convention on Tobacco Control (FCTC). This Convention was unanimously adopted by WHO's member states in 2003, as the first global public health treaty designed to reduce tobacco-related deaths and the huge tobacco-associated global burden of disease. At present, 151 member states of WHO have become parties to the WHO FCTC, i.e. the provisions of the convention are legally binding in these member states (www.who.int/tobacco/framework/countrylist/en/).

International Health Regulations (IHR)

In June 2007, the world started to implement the International Health Regulations which where adopted by the WHA in 2005. This legally-binding agreement will significantly contribute to international public health security by providing a new framework for the coordination of the management of events that may constitute a public health emergency of international concerns. It will also improve the capacity of all countries to detect, assess, notify and respond to public health threats. It provides for the mandatory notification of four diseases (smallpox, poliomyelitis due to a wild type poliovirus, human influenza caused by a new subtype and severe acute respiratory syndrome (SARS)), and the assessment of events involving diseases with potential serious public health impact and to spread internationally (www.who.int/csr/ihr/prepare/en/).

Strategic Health Operations Centre

Another recent innovation is the WHO Strategic Health Operations Centre. Using the latest technology, the centre is used during disease outbreaks and hu-manitarian emergencies to coordinate information and response between countries, WHO and other partners (www.who.int/csr/en/; www.who.int/hac/en/).

WHO Commissions

The report of WHO's *Commission on Macroeconomics and Health* (WHO Document 55th WHA A55/5: Report of the Director General, 23 April 2002) shows how the → globalization of the economy and other global changes affect human health. In summary, it provides compelling evidence that better health for the world's poor is not only an important goal in its own right, but can act as a major catalyst for economic development and poverty reduction.

The *Commission on Social Determinants of Health (CSDH)* was set up in March 2005 by the late Dr Lee Jong-Wook, then Director-General of WHO in response to the dramatic inequalities that dominate global health today, and with the goal to "marshal scientific evidence as a lever for policy change – aiming toward practical uptake among policymakers and stakeholders in countries". Nine central thematic areas are investigated in "Knowledge Networks" including globalization, women and gender equity, social exclusion, employment conditions, early childhood development, health systems,, urban settings and diseases of public health impact. The ninth thematic area, "Measurement and Evidence", examines the development of methodologies and tools for measuring the causes, pathways and health outcomes of policy interventions. The Commission's report, including recommendations for action will be presented to WHO's Director-General in early 2008 (www.who.int/social_determinants/resources/interim_statement/csdh_interim_statement_intro_07.pdf).

Normative Work

WHO also develops international norms and standards. For example, the *International Classification of Disease (ICD)* and the International Classification of Functioning, Disability and Health (ICF), which are international standards used for clinical and epidemiological purposes. In 1977 the first *Essential Medicines List* appeared, two years after the World Health Assembly introduced the concepts of "essential drugs" and "national drug policy".

156 countries today have a national list of essential medicines.

In the context of the Codex Alimentarius Commission, WHO established more than 200 standards for biological agents. Jointly with FAO, WHO has developed about 240 food safety standards and about 3,350 limiting values for pesticide residues and other food contaminants. In all WHO member states, *WHO's drinking water quality guidelines* are used when dealing with the need for safe drinking water and safe wastewater disposal. Similar guidelines were developed by WHO for air quality.

In the area of chemical safety, more than 230 Environmental Health Criteria (EHC) documents have been developed within the framework of the International Programme for Chemical Safety (IPCS), which is led by WHO. *Environmental Health Criteria documents* are considered the most comprehensive peer reviewed documents concerning risk assessment of important chemicals and other environmental agents. More recently, *Concise International Chemical Assessment Documents (CICADS)* are being published within IPCS. They summarize the information considered critical for risk characterization in sufficient detail to allow independent assessment, but are concise not repeating all the information available on a particular chemical.

These are only some examples of achievements and substantive work accountable to WHO over the last 60 years. Further information, particularly on important programmes related to the prevention and control of noncommunicable diseases and mental health, the protection of the human environment, including the quality of air, water and food; and the health effects and mitigation and adaptation measures related to climate change are available on WHO's extensive web site (www.who.int). A good up-to-date summary of WHO's work is provided by the publication "Working for Health: an Introduction to the World Health Organization" (*WHO* 2007a).

The Future Global Health Agenda

Eleventh General Programme of Work (GPW), 2006–2015

WHO's work over almost 60 years has been based on general programmes of work. In 2006, the 59th WHA adopted the 11th GPW covering a 10-year period from 2006 to 2015, coinciding with the time-frame for achieving the Millennium Development Goals adopted by the heads of state in 2000. The 11th GPW is based on a seven-point global health agenda that charts the broad strategic framework and direction for the work of WHO member states, their partners and the Secretariat. The seven points are (http://whqlibdoc.who.int/publications/2006/GPW_eng.pdf):

1. investing in health to reduce poverty
2. building individual and global health security
3. promoting universal coverage, gender equality and health-related human rights
4. tackling the determinants of health
5. strengthening health systems and equitable access
6. harnessing knowledge, science and technology
7. strengthening governance, leadership and accountability.

As of the biennium 2008-2009, a *six-year medium-term strategic plan* (www.who.int/gb/e/e_amtsp.html), encompassing three biennial budget periods, will form the framework for WHO's results-based management, within which the global health agenda will be addressed. Expected achievements over the period of the medium-term strategic plan reflecting the Director-General's agenda for action, notably health development and security, systems and evidence, partnerships and performance, are described in 13 strategic objectives (WHO Document A/MTSP/2008-2013PB/2008-2009). They provide clear, measurable and budgeted expected results for the

Organization. They also promote collaboration across disease-specific programmes by capturing the multiple links among the determinants of health and health outcomes, policies, systems and technologies.

Wilfried Kreisel

Lit.: *Litsios, S.:* The Tomorrow of Malaria (Ecotrends No. 4) Wellington 1996; *World Health Organization - Regional Office for Europe:* Working for health: an introduction to the World Health Organization, Geneva 2007 (quoted as WHO 2007a); *World Health Organization:* Global tuberculosis control: surveillance, planning, financing, WHO Report 2007, Geneva 2007 (quoted as WHO 2007b).
Internet: Homepage of the WHO: www.who.int.

WIPO – World Intellectual Property Organization

The World Intellectual Property Organization (WIPO) was founded on 14 July 1967 in Stockholm by the Convention Establishing the World Intellectual Property Organization (UNTS Vol. 828, No. 11846). In 1974 it became, with UN General Assembly resolution 3346 (XXIX), a specialized agency of the United Nations (→ Specialized Agencies). Its seat is in Geneva.

It is WIPO's purpose to promote the protection of intellectual property through the collaboration of states worldwide. Intellectual property is defined extensively, comprising all rights that ensue from intellectual activities in commercial, scientific, literary and artistic fields. Industrial property relates to the protection of inventions, trademarks and industrial designs; copyright relates to the protection of literary, musical, artistic, photographic, cinematographic and audiovisual works.

WIPO administers "unions" (unions of states) as international administrative unions and contracts on the protection of several fields of intellectual property. These unions are the Paris Union for the Protection of Industrial Property (established in 1883) and the Berne Union for the Protection of Literary and Artistic Works (established in 1886). Under the "roof" of the Paris Union other unions for partial areas of the protection of industrial property were founded. They were integrated into WIPO at the Stockholm Conference for the establishment of an international organization in this field in 1967.

Tasks

The tasks of WIPO are:
- the conclusion of new international conventions and the modernization of the national legislation in the field of the protection of intellectual property;
- providing technical support to developing countries;
- the collection and publication of information;
- support in the effort to obtain simultaneous protection in several states for inventions, trademarks and industrial designs;
- the promotion of administrative cooperation among the member states.

Membership

Every state that is a member of one of the two unions (Paris or Berne), as well as every other state that is a member of the United Nations or of one of their specialized agencies, or is a contracting party to the Statute of the International Court of Justice (→ ICJ), or is invited by the General Assembly of WIPO, is entitled to become a member of WIPO. As of 31 December 2008, 184 states are members of WIPO.

Structure

Under the direction of WIPO all unions, i.e. the Paris and the Berne union as well as the special unions, continue to exist with their own assemblies of representatives and executive committees, with competence for their budget and their program planning. WIPO itself, as the holding organization, disposes of a General Assembly and a Conference, a Coordination Committee, a Secretariat, and a Director-General. The General Assembly consists of those members who belong to at least one of the unions.

It ensures administrative cooperation between the unions, and is authorized to give instructions to the Secretary-General and to the Coordination Committee.

The Conference is an assembly of all WIPO members, including the ones who are not members of a union. It is concerned with general questions of the protection of intellectual property through cooperation among the states, and holds its sessions simultaneously with the General Assembly and the assemblies of the unions, at the same location, every three years.

The Coordination Committee, composed of the representatives of those states being represented in the Executive Committees of one of the two main unions, discusses the administrative and budgetary matters of the organization. The *"International Bureau for Intellectual Property"* is the most important organ of WIPO and serves as a secretariat for WIPO as a whole, as well as for the single unions. It maintains five international registration services (patents, trademarks, industrial designs, designations of origin, audiovisual works).

As the highest public servant of the WIPO and its unions, the Director-General heads the International Bureau. He is nominated by the General Assembly of WIPO and must be accepted by the assemblies of the Berne and Paris Unions. The Director-General acts as depository of the majority of international conventions which WIPO administers on the protection of intellectual property (IP). WIPO is financed by membership dues and fees for administrative services, such as filing an international application for patent protection.

Recent Developments

WIPO is, as with many other UN organizations, marked by trade conflicts between the Western industrial countries and the Third World (→ North-South-Relations and the UN; → International Economic Relations and New International Economic Order (NIEO)). Since WIPO's foundation the industrialized countries have called for increased protection of their intellectual property

rights (IPRs), whereas developing countries have called for increased transfer of intellectual property, especially in the field of technical inventions, to promote their economic development. The industrialized countries, moved the problem of the IPRs to the Uruguay negotiation round of the General Agreement on Tariffs and Trade GATT (→ WTO/GATT), where political pressure could be organized on a much higher level than at WIPO and where concessions of the developing countries in the field of IPRs could be negotiated in exchange for concessions of the developed countries with regard to improved market access for the developing countries. So the developed countries reached an agreement on Trade-Related Intellectual Property Rights (TRIPS) (UNTS Vol. 1869, No. 31874), which was put in 1994 under the "roof" of the newly founded World Trade Organization, WTO (cf. WTO Agreement, UNTS 1867, No. 31874).

By establishing a new much higher harmonization floor of the national patent systems, enforced through the WTO's trade sanction system, TRIPS imposed developed country patenting standards on the whole developing world, regardless of the different national levels of industrialization.

This far-reaching harmonization was "sold" to the reluctant developing countries by means of the argument that a multilateral agreement on patents would mean an end to bilateral pressure from rich countries to further strengthen their domestic patent systems. In practice quite the opposite has happened: as the minimum standards of TRIPS were considered by the developed countries to be not strong enough in terms of patent rights, they began a series of negotiations to achieve further patent standards in bilateral, subregional and regional agreements (*GRAIN* 2001, 1). "TRIPS-plus" patent protection, i.e. more than the standards of TRIPS, was successfully brought forward from the developed countries as a condition for market access, direct investment or even development assistance (*GRAIN* 2003).

One might assume that WIPO felt in this situation outmanœuvered and superfluous, but on the contrary, WIPO interpreted its role now as junior partner of WTO: in close cooperation with the WTO Secretariat it endeavored to assist in the implementation of TRIPS standards in developing countries.

As many developing countries criticized, WIPO pushed in this situation its own pro-western concept of the patent agenda, namely establishing a world patent system, rather than serving the best interests of its clients, which would have meant finding a suitable consensus between patent protection and development needs.

This WIPO approach found its most obvious expression in a memorandum on the "WIPO Patent Agenda" of the Director-General of WIPO submitted at the 36th Series of Meetings of the Assemblies of the WIPO member states (WIPO Doc. A/36/14 of 6 August 2001). It had the title "Agenda for Development of the International Patent System" and skillfully advocated the establishment of a world patent system.

The establishment of such a system would be of great use to industrialized countries which are interested in a large scope of patentability, including basic research results and even business methods.

For the developing countries it would mean the end of patent policy as a tool for national development strategies, for example by excluding domestic plants from patenting through foreign commercial corporations.

These prospects for the developing countries caused them to organize political resistance against the "Patent Agenda": they rallied round the "Development Agenda", a proposal brought forward by Argentina and Brazil on the occasion of the WIPO General Assembly in August 2004 (WIPO Doc. WO/GA/31/11 of 27 August 2004).

The Development Agenda requires that WIPO should integrate the development dimension in the IP system and WIPO's activities and should facilitate the transfer of technology from the developed states to the developing states, both demands being in the opinion of the sponsor states in accordance with established UN goals and values. The paper argues that WIPO as member of the UN system should be "fully guided by the broad development goals that the UN has set for itself, in particular in the Millennium Development Goals. Development concerns should be fully incorporated into all WIPO activities." (ibid., III).

Almost immediately upon presentation, the proposal gathered another eleven co-sponsors and became the focus for developing country negotiations at WIPO. In this ongoing debate, NGOs are actively involved, supporting the developing countries with well-developed research and statistical data about patents and their economic effects.

The Development Agenda is an expression of widespread criticisms among the developing states that WIPO has failed to establish sufficient links between development and IPRs and has not properly assessed the actual impact on countries of the patent rules it supports and the technical assistance it delivers (cf. *May* 2007, 164).

The WIPO representatives of the developed states do not accept these criticisms. So it remains to be seen whether WIPO will integrate the development issue in a better way than before.

One positive impact of the debate about the Development Agenda can already be stated: WIPO has started to discuss the matter with a number of other UN agencies and with NGOs, the debate gets more media coverage than previous debates and is monitored more closely by NGOs.

This constellation in WIPO illustrates the problems involved in the division of labor in the UN system: the specialized agencies are well equipped to solve intricate global problems, but they tend to favor "technical" solutions, often in the interest of the developed states, and lose sight of the global context, of the value orientation of the UN. Therefore the quality of their work would without doubt benefit from greater public attention and participation of other UN bodies in the debates of the respective specialized agencies.

Helmut Volger

Lit.: *GRAIN:* "TRIPS-plus" through the back door, July 2001, www.grain.org/briefings/?id=6; *GRAIN:* One global patent system? WIPO's Substantive Patent Law Treaty, October 2003, www.grain.org/briefings/?id=159; *May, C.:* The World Intellectual Property Organization and the Development Agenda, in: Global Governance 13 (2007), 161-170; *South Centre:* Agendas on Patents. South Bulletin 48, 15 December 2002, www.southcentre.org; *South Centre:* Establishing A "Development Agenda" for the World Intellectual Property Organization (WIPO): Commentary on Proposal by Argentina and Brazil (South Centre Analytical Note SC/TADP/AN/IP/3), September 2004, www.Southcentre.org; *Stoll, T.:* WIPO – World Intellectual Property Organization, in: Wolfrum, R. (ed.): United Nations: Law, Policies and Practice, Vol. 2, Munich/Dordrecht 1995, 1431-1440; *WIPO - Assemblies of the Member States:* Agenda for Development of the International Patent System, WIPO Doc. A/36/14 of 6 August 2001; *WIPO General Assembly:* Proposal by Argentina and Brazil for the Establishment of a Development Agenda for WIPO, WIPO Doc. WO/GA/31/11 of 27 August 2004.

Internet: Homepage of WIPO: www.wipo.int.

WMO – World Meteorological Organization

The *World Meteorological Organization (WMO)* – successor to the semi-governmental International Meteorological Organization (IMO) founded in 1879 – was established in 1950 by ratification of the 1947 convention on the world organization for meteorology (UNTS Vol. 77, No. 998). The WMO became in 1951 one of the → specialized agencies of the United Nations by approval of a corresponding agreement through the UN → General Assembly. Its seat is Geneva.

It is concerned with worldwide establishment and standardization of mete-orological observation technologies in order to coordinate its use for the welfare of mankind.

Membership

All states with own meteorological services that are members of the United Nations are entitled to membership in the WMO; non-member states of the UN require the consent of two-thirds of the WMO's members. Not only sovereign states are entitled to membership, but also non-sovereign territories may also join (→ Sovereignty). The Dutch Antilles and French Polynesia, for example, are members of the WMO. The WMO has 188 members – 182 member states and 6 member territories – (as of 31 December 2008), and is one of the specialized agencies of the UN with the highest number of members.

Structures

The WMO consists of five main organs, the *World Meteorological Congress*, the *Executive Council*, six regional associations, eight technical commissions and the *Secretariat*. The World Meteorological Congress, as assembly of the delegates of all members of the WMO and supreme body of the organization, meets once every four years, to determine long-term plans for the general policy of the organization as well as the four-year budget.

Furthermore it adopts technical standards for meteorological practice, elects the President of the WMO and the members of the Executive Council and appoints the Secretary-General at the proposal of the President. The Executive Council is composed of 37 members, 27 directors of national meteorological services, the President, the Vice-President and the presidents of the six regional associations. It conducts all activities of the organization in accordance with the decisions of the Congress. The six regional associations (Africa, Asia, Europe, North and Middle America, South America, Western Pacific) coordinate the implementation of the WMO Congress decisions concerning their respective regions, discuss meteorological questions from a regional point of view and present recommendations to the Congress and the Executive Council. The technical commissions are concerned with several fields of meteorology such as instruments and observation systems, atmospheric research, climatology or maritime meteorology and present recommendations to the Congress and the Executive Council. The Secretariat is headed by the Secretary-General. It acts as an administrative, documentation and information center and is responsible for public relations.

Tasks

Since its establishment, the WMO has played an important role in contributing to the safety and welfare of humanity. Within the framework of the WMO programmes national meteorological and hydrological services contribute substantially to protection against natural disasters, to safeguarding the environment and to enhancing the economic and social stability of different sectors of society in such areas as food security, water resources and transport.

The WMO promotes the establishment of networks for making meteorological, climatological, hydrological and geophysical observations, as well as the exchange, processing and standardization of related data. It furthers the application of meteorology to public weather services, agriculture, aviation, shipping, the environment, water issues and the mitigation of the impacts of natural disasters.

The WMO Activities

The most important activities of the WMO are:

The *World Weather Watch Programme*, the most important of all WMO programmes, combines data processing and coordinates observation and communications systems that are operated by members, to put meteorological and connected geophysical information at the disposal of meteorological and hydrological services. The programme includes a warning system for tropical tornadoes for more then fifty states, as well as an observation programme for instruments and methods.

The *World Climate Programme* promotes the understanding of climatic proceedings by internationally coordinated research and observation of climatic changes, to be able to warn against possible impacts on land and people. Its studies on climatic impacts are coordinated with the United Nations Environment Programme (→ UNEP).

Other WMO main programmes concern themselves with world water stocks, the observation of the ozone layer, the practical utilization of meteorological findings for agriculture, aviation and seafaring, with education and technical collaboration.

The WMO and the Environment

The WMO plays a leading role in the international efforts to monitor and protect the environment: in collaboration with other UN agencies and national meteorological services it supports the implementation of a number of environmental conventions (www.wmo.int/pages/about/Environmentalconventions_en.html) (→ Environmental Protection; Environmental Law, International) and provides advice and assessments to governments on related matters.

In 1988 the WMO established together with the UN Environment Programme (UNEP) the *Intergovernmental Panel on Climate Change (IPCC)* tasked to evaluate the risk of climate change caused by human activity. The role of the IPCC as a scientific intergovernmental body (www.ipcc.ch) is to assess on a comprehensive, objective and transparent basis the scientific and socio-economic information relevant to understanding the scientific basis of the risks of human-induced climate change. The IPCC bases its assessments mainly on peer-reviewed and published scientific literature. It publishes its assessments in reports, in particular on topics relevant to the implementation of the UN Framework Convention on Climate Change (UNFCCC). Because of its high quality, IPCC reports are widely appreciated and cited in almost any debate related to climate change. National and international responses to climate change generally regard the IPCC as authoritative. In 2007, the IPCC was awarded the Nobel Peace Prize for its work together with Al Gore.

Evaluation

The WMO is an illustrative example for the potential great political significance of the work of the so-called "technical" specialized agencies. If they work together with other UN bodies and develop instruments such as the IPCC to assess the scientific findings and to make the results known to the broad public, they can play an effective role within the activities of the → UN system.

Helmut Volger

Lit.: *Jarraud, M.:* Challenges and Opportunities Ahead for WMO, in: UN Chronicle 2004, Issue 1; *Koenig, C.:* WMO – World Meteorological Organization, in: Wolfrum, R. (ed.): United Nations: Law, Policies and Practice, Vol. 2, Munich/Dordrecht 1995, 1441-1449.

Internet: Homepage of WMO: www.wmo.int.

Women and the UN

The UN Charter of 1945 (→ Charter of the UN) is the first international document which condemns discrimination based on sex, and which contains sex-equality provisions in a number of its articles. The Charter defines as purposes of the UN: the maintenance of international peace, self-determination of all peoples, international co-operation and the respect for human rights and fundamental freedoms of all people. Guided in particular by the UN norm of equality between men and women, this article examines the UN gender politics and the role of women within the UN institutions (→ UN System) from the beginning of the organization until today.

Laying the Foundation: Creating the Legal Basis for Equality

From the inception of the UN until the mid 1960s, the organization's activities regarding the status of women addressed the question of legal equality in civil and political rights (→ Human Rights Conventions, CCPR). For example, in 1945, only 30 out of the 51 UN founding member states granted women the right to vote and to vie for political posts (*UNDPI* 1996). In addition, women were discriminated against in many areas of civil law in most countries, most notably in family and marriage laws. However, the focus on political and civil rights of the individual was not only a reaction to the world-wide discrimination against women in this area. It also mirrored the numerical predominance of the Western nations in the UN at that time, who, together with the member states from Latin America, favored these so-called "first generation" human rights over economic and social human rights, "the second generation" rights.

The *Commission on the Status of Women* (CSW) has always been and is still the main inter-governmental policy-making body on women's issues within the UN. It is administered by the *Division for the Advancement of Women* (DAW), the UN's institutional center on women's policies located at the UN → Secretariat in New York. CSW was constituted in February 1946 as a subcommission to the Charter-based *Commission on Human Rights* (CHR), the predecessor of today's → *Human Rights Council.* A few months later, it acquired independent status as a Commission under the *Economic and Social Council* (→ ECOSOC) on an equal footing with the CHR. At the outset CSW consisted of 15 rotating member states, with other UN member states as observers. Today, CSW has 45 member states, which in their annual meetings set the standards and guiding principles for the UN's women's politics. The original mandate by ECOSOC enables the Commission to prepare "recommendations and reports to ECOSOC on promoting women's rights in political, economic, social and educational fields. The Commission shall also make recommendations to the Council on urgent problems requiring immediate attention in the field of women's rights" (UN Doc. E/RES/2/11, 21 June 1946). It was expanded in 1988 to include the Commission's responsibility to monitor the implementation of the decisions and conclusions of the women's world conferences (see below) (→ World Conferences).

In 1948, during the negotiations on the *Universal Declaration of Human Rights (UDHR)* (→ Human Rights, Universal Declaration of), CSW and the female members of the government delegations to the CHR were successful in lobbying for the adoption of gender-neutral language in the declaration, and for the inclusion of an article on equality between men and women. With their pressure, the originally intended version "All men are created equal" was changed to "All humans are created equal". The UDHR together with the UN Charter form the normative reference points for CSW's standard setting activities. During the 1950s and 1960s the Commission drafted the following conventions, which were adopted by the UN General Assembly (GA):
- Convention on the Political Rights of Women (1952) (UNTS Vol. 193, 135)
- Convention on the Nationality of Married Women (1957) (UNTS Vol. 309, 65)
- Convention on Consent to Marriage, Minimum Age for Marriage and Registration of Marriages (1962) (UNTS Vol. 521, 231).

While these conventions are binding international treaties, they lack a mechanism to monitor their implementation. Unlike these documents, the most comprehensive and most important of all treaties on women's rights – the *Convention on the Elimination of all Forms of Discrimination* (CEDAW) (→ Human Rights Conventions, CEDAW) from 1979, another product of CSW, – provides for a monitoring procedure: the Committee to CEDAW consists of in-dependent experts who regularly monitor the convention's implementation in all those states who have ratified it.

CSW was also consulted in the drafting of these important anti-discrimination conventions by the → ILO and → UNESCO:
- ILO Convention No. 100 on Equal Remuneration (1953)
- ILO Convention No. 111 on Discrimination (Employment and Occupation) (1960).
- ILO Convention No. 156 on Workers with Family Responsibilities (1981)
- UNESCO Convention against Discrimination in Education (1962).

While CHR's powers on confidential complaints – so-called communications – were gradually expanded, its mandate to review communications by women on the violation of their rights, was limited for over thirty years by the "no power to take any action" doctrine (*Reanda* 1992). After decades of debates on this issue, CSW was granted the authority to appoint a working group to review confidential communications "which appear to reveal a consistent pattern of reliably attested injustice and discriminatory practices against women" (Draft Res. X/E/1980/15, in: *Reanda* 1992) and to prepare a report with recommendations to ECOSOC. In contrast to its sister body CHR, CSW is not allowed to initiate any investigation or action based on such communications. Another problem for the work of CSW is the lower institutional and financial resources compared to those of the CHR/Human Rights Council. While CHR, and now the Council, meets annually for six weeks, CSW's sessions were for two weeks, and only bi-annually until 1986. Since then, the Commission meets every year for two weeks. While the CHR/Human Rights Council has a large number of special rapporteurs and working groups, CSW has only the one standing working group to deal with communications and ad-hoc working groups for the drafting of documents, such as the Optional Protocol to the CEDAW (see below). Until the end of the 1960s, CSW's reports and recommendations on women's issues, for example the early reports on traditional cultural practices or on the under-representation of women in the UN system, were largely ignored within the organization. In summing up, one can conclude that during the first phase of UN women's politics, activities of standard setting dominated. Apart from that, politics to improve the status of women did not have a high priority as such within the UN organization.

The International Decade on Women 1976 – 1985: Women and Development

On December 18, 1972, the UN General Assembly decided to declare 1975 as the *International Year of Women* (IWY) and to hold a world conference for women in Mexico City in the same year. By this announcement, the UN recognized the fight against women's worldwide discrimination as an important political task for the organization. One factor that had led to this recognition was the international search for new approaches in development policies (→ Development Research, Development Theories): the failure of modernization theories and strategies in producing development and the absence of their expected "trickle down effects" became dramatically apparent at the end of the 1960s: poverty, famine and poor health were on the increase in the "developing countries". In addition, for the first time studies showed that women were disproportionately affected by poverty, malnutrition, poor health and poor education. At the beginning of the 1970s, international development organizations realized that their newly developed programmes to combat poverty by satisfying the basic needs of the population, e.g. through the World Bank's *Basic Needs Strategy* (→ World Bank, World Bank Group), needed to include women as key target groups (*Pietilä/Vickers* 1994; *Staudt* 1997). Moreover, prior to the first *World Conference on Population* in Bucharest in 1974, the northern donor countries identified the control of population growth in development countries as a key condition for eco-

nomic development. The relevance of targeting women as carriers of development was well expressed by the then World Bank President Robert McNamara, who stated during the Population Conference that education and economic prosperity reduce women's fertility rates. Consequently, since the founding of the UN Population Fund (→ UNFPA) in 1969, family planning programmes, which exclusively targeted women, had gradually acquired an important role in development policies (→ Development Cooperation of the UN System).

The growing national women's movements world wide were another influential factor in the declaration of the IYW. Women's movements not only put political pressure on their own governments, but they increasingly lobbied on the international level for action on the discrimination against women on the global level. Hence, behind the idea for the IYW were international women's non-governmental organizations (→ NGOs), which were disappointed by the lack of progress in UN women's politics. They had launched the idea with CSW and successfully lobbied its representatives to propose it to ECOSOC. From there the recommendation went to the General Assembly where it was adopted, albeit after long debates and not without resistance by some delegations.

The IYW and the first *World Conference on Women* in Mexico dealt with three themes, which later became the motto for the *UN Women's Decade* (1976-1985) and beyond: equality between men and women (*equality*); integration of women into development (*development*); participation of women in the creation of world peace (*peace*). The 133 states at the Mexico Conference adopted a Plan of Action, which included, *inter alia*: activities for increasing the number of women in decision-making positions; programmes to integrate women into the labor market and into education; programmes for the improvement of women's nutrition, health conditions, housing situations and for family planning. Issues of migration, trafficking in women, and forced prostitution were also already touched upon at the Mexico meeting (*UNDPI* 1996).

The Mexico Conference laid the foundation for the UN agenda on women. Out of the three issue areas for the IYW the agenda initially emphasized development. The Women-in-Development (WID) approach, which aims at integrating women into development by improving women's economic and social status and by securing women's rights, became the leading motto of the international women's decade. It was based on the insight that women had been ignored as subject and target groups of development programming.

At the Mexico summit, states decided to announce the *Women's Decade*, for several reasons: The lack of knowledge about the full extent of discrimination against women and its causes had become apparent, while at the same time the need for action was recognized. However, the political discussions about the approaches and measure for improving women's status was only at its very beginning. Hence, the international community decided to hold two more world conferences to assess the progress in implementing the Mexico Plan of Action in 1975: in Copenhagen in 1980 and in Nairobi in 1985. For the approximately 6,000 women who participated in *the Mexico NGO Forum* which was held parallel to the official conference, the meeting was the beginning of international networking and co-operation among women's groups and women's movements world-wide.

The themes of the second *World Conference on Women* in Copenhagen in 1980 – work, health, education – became the core policy areas of the entire decade. At the third women's world conference, the *United Nations Conference to Review and Appraise the Achievements of the UN Decade for Women* in Nairobi, in 1985, the international community had to realize that the high goals for the improvement of women's status globally were not being met. Only an insignificantly small num-

ber of women had profited from the national and international programmes that had been designed and implemented during the decade. This was clearly demonstrated by the statistics of the new *World Survey on the Role of Women in Development* (*UNDPI* 1995b). Nevertheless, the women's decade also yielded some successes, mostly in terms of new institutions:

The ad-hoc fund for women-specific development programmes which was set up in 1976, was institutionalized as a permanent *UN Development Fund for Women* (→ UNIFEM) in 1985.

In 1980, the *UN Research and Training Institution for the Advancement of Women* (→ INSTRAW) took up its work in New York. Since 1983, INSTRAW operates from its permanent location in Santo Domingo in the Dominican Republic.

Many of the UN institutions and → specialized agencies, such as → UNDP, the World Bank, → ILO, created small administrative units for women's issues, so called Women-in-Development desks.

In 1979 the afore-mentioned → Convention on the Elimination of All Forms of Discrimination Against Women (CEDAW) (→ Human Rights Conventions, CEDAW) was adopted by the General Assembly (UN Doc. A/RES/34/180 of 18 December 1979) and entered into force in 1981 (UNTS Vol. 129, No. 20378).

On the national level, the International Decade gave governments an impetus for legal and policy measures to combat women's discrimination and enhance women's status. Another result of the Decade was a heightened awareness of the systematic oppression of women world wide. UN organizations had produced a number of reports and studies in evidence of this. The international activities of women and women's groups, which were often financially supported by UN organizations, and the networking between organizations expanded substantially during the decade. Hence, 15,000 women participated in the *Non-Governmental World Conference of Women, Forum '85*, in Nairobi, held

873

parallel to the official intergovernmental world summit.

The intergovernmental conference adopted the *Nairobi Forward-looking Strategies for the Advancement of Women (FLS)*. This document includes a catalogue of recommendations and measures for the implementation of the decade's three goals: under the theme *equality* (para. 43-92), it enumerates political, legal and socio-economic measures to abolish *de-facto* discrimination of women and to promote women's participation in social and political decision-making arenas. Under the issue of *development* (para. 93-231), the FLS for the first time acknowledged the subjective and autonomous status of women as actors in development, i.e. as decision makers, administrative planners as well as beneficiaries of development. The decade's third theme, *peace*, which had largely been ignored during the decade, gained more prominence in the Nairobi document (para. 232-276). The FLS called for an increase in women's participation in peace making activities and in peace research, on the national and international levels. Very importantly, the international community acknowledged for the first time that the attainment of peace (→ Peace, Peace Concept, Threat to Peace) implies an end to all forms of violence against women.

In the wake of the Nairobi-conference, the Women-in-Development (WID) approach, which had dominated institutional UN politics during the women's decade, began to be criticized by feminists. They pointed to the fact that WID conceptualizes women as "deficient" beings who need to catch up in terms of education, qualification etc., without analyzing the causes of the unequal distribution of resources and the women's relative chances to access them. The critics argued that this approach ignored the fact that the social, economic, political and legal relationships between men and women were power relationships. They pointed at the dissatisfying institutional set-up in development programmes, where WID often translated into separate women-specific projects, administered by separate institutional WID desks. At the same time, the conceptual frames for institutionalized development policies and programmes remained unchanged. At the end of the 1980s, evaluations of WID field projects predominantly showed that the projects brought additional work burdens for women while producing only minimal surplus income, on an often irregular basis. Consequently, these projects did not significantly enhance women's financial autonomy nor did they contribute to the improvement of women's situation and their social insecurity.

In sum, the women's decade saw the women's legal equality approach, which had been prominent during the first phase of UN women's politics, replaced by the development approach which in turn had grown to become a women and development paradigm.

This had brought along a shift in the strategies to fight discrimination against women: the legal strategies of the first twenty-five years had, despite the adoption of Convention on the Elimination of All Forms of Discrimination (CEDAW) in 1979 and its entering into force in 1981, been by and large replaced by strategies based on social and economic policies.

Although these strategies may have tackled some of the key problems involved for the enhancement of women's status, their implementation by governments is by less binding, less obligatory than legal strategies as they are dependent on the political will and discretion of governments.

Change of Paradigm: Women's Rights are Human Rights

Today, the women's human rights paradigm dominates women's politics and programmes within all UN organizations. While the legal approach of the early UN years aimed at creating separate women's rights instruments, today's goal is broader: it aims at integrating women's human rights into all legal matters and policy areas of the UN system. The paradigmatic shift from the development framework towards the human rights framework is a result of the criticisms of the development approach of the 1980s by the international women's movement.

By the 1990s, many women's organizations entered the international political stage to articulate women's interests on a large scale and in a variety of policy areas beyond traditional women's politics. They had become very professional in their political activities and influential as international pressure and lobbying groups (Chen 1996).

The first UN Conference where women's organizations became visible outside the classical women's conferences was the UN *Conference on Environment and Development* (UNCED) in Rio de Janeiro in 1992 (→ Environmental Protection). The final document, the so-called *"Agenda 21"*, strongly emphasized women's participation, and the support of women in creating sustainable development, and in environmental policies.

However, the breakthrough for a global women's movement was the *World Conference on Human Rights* in Vienna in 1993. During and prior to the conference, women's movements all over the world began to link their demand for women's rights on the national and the international level to the general human rights framework (*Tomasevski* 1993).

This was part of a global campaign under the slogan *women's rights are human rights*, which had taken off two years prior to the Vienna Conference. The campaign made visible and condemned all forms of discrimination against women as human rights violations, in particular all forms of violence against women. Its highlight was a public "tribunal" on women's human rights violations in Vienna parallel to the official conference, where survivors of various forms of violence spoke about their experiences. The campaign, the tribunal and the professional lobbying by representatives of women's NGOs on the human rights of women successfully influenced the final conference

document, to include large passages on women's human rights.

In the *Vienna Declaration and Programme of Action* the international community for the first time acknowledged: "The human rights of women and of the girl-child are an inalienable, integral and indivisible part of universal human rights ... Gender-based violence and all forms of sexual harassment and exploitation, including those resulting from cultural prejudice and international trafficking, are incompatible with the dignity and worth of the human person, and must be eliminated." (UN Doc. A/CONF.157/23; Chapter 1, para. 18) In paragraph 38, the conference "stresses the importance of working towards the elimination of violence against women in public and private life". Hence, the UN for the first time acknowledged *women's protection against human rights violations in the private sphere* as a task for international law and politics.

After this summit, in December 1993, the UN General Assembly adopted the *Declaration on the Elimination of Violence against Women* (UN Doc. A/RES/ 48/104).

Although without a legally binding character (→ Resolution, Declaration, Decision), it represents an international agreement about the definition of violence against women and on the measures to be taken by governments for its elimination. Globally it has been widely used as a reference document for reforms in national laws on violence against women. In the Declaration's definition, violence against women encompasses "physical, sexual, and psychological violence occurring in the family", "within the general community", and "perpetrated or condoned by the State, wherever it occurs" (Art. 2).

In 1994, the Commission on Human Rights appointed a Special Rapporteur on Violence Against Women, Including Its Causes and Consequences (UN Doc. E/CN.4/RES/1994/45), whose mandate was based on the Vienna Declaration. In the annual reports to the Commission on Human Rights and the Human Rights Council, respectively, the Rapporteur has presented detailed analyses of numbers, phenomena, causes and consequences of violence against women. She has also made suggestions for national and international legal and policy measures to combat violence. Every year, the Rapporteur conducts fact-finding missions to selected countries on issues that she deems to be pertinent. These included for instance North- and South Korea on the issue of war crimes (1995), Poland on the issue of trafficking in women (1996), the USA (1998) on the issue of violence against women in prisons as well as Turkey (2006) on suicides of women and Ghana on domestic violence and cultural violence (2007). During her visits, the Rapporteur collects information from governmental as well as non-governmental organizations. Since the inception of the post, the Rapporteur's work has been an important catalyst for debates and resolutions on women's human rights at the Commission on Human Rights, ECOSOC and the General Assembly. Beyond this, the high standard of analysis of legal questions and the research have significantly contributed to the advancement of women's human rights within the other UN organs.

After their success in Vienna, women's organizations applied the human rights framework to many women's issues, which they articulated during the various UN world conferences of the 1990s.

The introduction of the term *reproductive rights* in connection with the *right to reproductive health* caused a new thinking in population politics at the *World Conference on Population* in Cairo in 1994. The conference established the concept of comprehensive sexual and reproductive health and rights (SRHR) for women and men during their life cycle. The respect for and the implementation of women's rights are since then seen to be key for successful population policies. States agreed to provide universal access to services in SRHR that support the realization of those rights. In this context, the improvement of women's social, economic and political status in the context of changing power relationships between men and women became a political goal in population policies.

With the women's human rights paradigm, the WID-policies of the 1970s and 1980s, which had been based on a *basic needs* approach, were replaced by a *basic rights* approach. The *basic rights* – or women's human rights – approach has become the foundation for women's and gender-based policies in the UN until today. It emphasizes the international and national responsibility for the implementation of women's rights. It also entails women's claims to being recognized as autonomous individuals with entitlement to rights and with the right to make their own decisions in all areas of life.

The debates at the *Fourth World Conference on Women* in Beijing in 1995 were dominated by the women's human rights language. This is strongly reflected in the conference's outcome document, the *Beijing Platform for Action (PfA) and the Beijing Declaration* (Report of the Fourth World Conference on Women, Bejing, 4-15 September 1995, UN Doc. A/CONF.177/20, Annex I and II).

Prior to the conference, two UN reports on women were published, which for the first time since the first *World Conference on Women* in 1975, reported some progress. The UNDP *Human Development Report* of 1995 (→ Human Development Reports) *and The World's Women 1995* (*UNDPI* 1995a) found that the gap between men and women in education had been reduced by 50% since 1975. The average life expectancy in development countries had increased faster for women than for men, and the access of women to health care had significantly improved. On the other side, however, this had not automatically led to an increased participation of women in economic and political decision-making, as the UNDP report concludes. Moreover, poverty, with 70% of the poor being women, still has a female face.

The negotiations between the 189 states during the Beijing conference were difficult, because women's claims for their rights in all areas of life were at issue. At the outset of the conference, the draft document entailed more bracketed phrases than any other UN conference document ever before, indicating the controversies between the states.

At the end of the conference, the result was a document which did not go significantly beyond previous existing standards. However, it was also a victory over attempts by some countries to undermine those standards. New in the document is the right of women to "have control over and decide freely and responsibly on matters related to their sexuality ... (para. 96)". This clause had been rejected in Cairo and was also subject to strong controversies again 1995 in Beijing.

The *Beijing Platform for Action (PfA)* identifies twelve central areas of *Strategic Objectives and Actions*, among them not only violence against women and women's human rights, but also women and poverty, women and the economy, women and armed conflict as well as the girl-child. In the area of the girl child, the states were unable to agree on the unequivocal equal right of girls to inheritance.

The NGO-Forum parallel to the official meeting was, with 30.000 participants the largest NGO meeting ever at an UN conference. However, NGO representatives had only little influence on the governmental meeting, because the NGO meeting was located 35 km away from the official meeting, with only insufficient shuttle transport.

Despite these challenges, the PfA is the most comprehensive policy standard for global women's politics at all levels – at the local, the national and the international – until today. It spells out tasks for governments, the UN system as well as NGOs. This document has become the single most important global reference document for women's organizations around the globe. It provides women's movements with the political legitimacy for their various demands for improving women's situations in their respective countries (e.g. for African countries cf. *Wölte* 2002).

The PfA requires governments to develop national implementation strategies. For the first review of the PfA's implementation, the *UN Special Session of the General Assembly to review the implementation of the Beijing Platform for Action: Women 2000: Equality, Development and Peace for the 21st century* (also called "Beijing +5") in June 2000, the UN prepared a document of 135 government reports which offered a mixed picture (*United Nations ECOSOC*: Review and Appraisal of the Implementation of the Beijing Platform for Action, 19 January 2000, UN Doc. E/CN.6/2000/PC/2).

It found an increase in governments' awareness of the promotion of women's status, which translated into a) more high level national machineries for women's/gender issues, b) more gender mainstreaming activities into administrative institutions; c) law reforms, particularly in the area of violence against women, inheritance and land rights; and d) an increase of women's representation in political bodies.

On the other hand, ECOSOC's report and various other reports by UN organizations for the Beijing +5 conference showed that the results of these activities were limited: the average number of women in political and economic decision-making positions world-wide had only risen marginally. While more women were in the formal work sector and the wage gap had narrowed (mostly due to the decrease of male wages) and the number of women living in poverty continued to increase (*UNIFEM* 2000). UNIFEM assessed that despite the fact that 44 countries had improved their laws on violence against women by 2000, there was no improvement in the *de facto* situation of violence against women and girls.

The outcome document of the Beijing+5 meeting (UN Doc. A/S-23/10/Rev.1) emphasized the women's human rights approach. In addition, it explicitly acknowledged female genital mutilation, honor killings and marital rape as human rights violations and dealt with the issue of HIV/Aids within the human rights frame. With reference to further action for implementing the Beijing goals, governments committed to concrete targets and indicators in four areas: a) abolishment of all laws discriminating against women by 2005; b) closure of the gap in primary and secondary education between girls and boys, and free and compulsory universal primary education for both girls and boys by 2015; 50 % improved adult literacy levels, especially for women by 2015; c) universal access to primary health care by 2015; and d) reiteration of the 50/50 gender balance in all posts of the UN secretariat at the professional level.

In March 2005, ten years after the Beijing conference, the UN conducted another review of the PfA implementation. This time, the review took place during a regular CSW session and not in the General Assembly. The meeting was also characterized by the attempts of several countries to water down some of the previously achieved standards, in particular with regard to women's reproductive and sexual rights. This could, however, be prevented by the lobbying of women's groups and by the majority of nations being in favor of women's human rights.

In the end, the meeting endorsed the PfA and the resolutions of the Bejing +5 meeting but did not come forward with new areas of protecting women's human rights. The conference found that political representation of women had continued to increase globally as did the access of girls to primary education. The goal to abolish all discriminatory laws had not been met, and also the 50/50 gender balance in the UN Secretariat had not been reached.

Since progress in many other areas was lacking, the CSW adopted ten resolutions for future actions (UN Doc. E/CN.6/2005/2). Some of them reiterated older issues, such as gender mainstreaming in national programming and the recommendation to create the post of an *UN Special Rapporteur on Dis-*

criminatory Laws. Others picked up new themes, for instance the resolutions on women, the girl child and HIV/Aids; on reducing demand for trafficking women and girls from all forms of exploitation; and on integrating a gender perspective in post-disaster relief with particular reference to the tsunami disaster.

On a regional level, substantial progress in the protection of women's human rights was achieved with the adoption of the *Protocol to the African Charter on Human and Peoples' Rights on the Rights of Women in Africa* by the African Union in July 2003 in Maputo, Mozambique. The Protocol came into force on November 25th following the 15th ratification by Togo. As of October 2007, 24 states had ratified the document.

The Protocol's significance lies in the fact that it is the only regionally generated document specifically on the rights of African women. Also, it entails rights of women that have not been acknowledged in another international or regional document, such as the right to abortion on medical grounds or after rape, and the ban of female genital mutilation. At present, the Protocol only has a very weak monitoring mechanism by the African Commission on Human rights, and it lacks a complaint mechanism.

Mainstreaming Gender: Today's Core Institutional Strategy

The *Fourth World Conference on Women* moved the strategy of *gender mainstreaming* squarely onto the agenda of the UN organizations. The notion of *gender* captures the differently constructed social roles of men and women, which are organized in terms of gendered power relations.

In contrast to the women-specific approach which had informed the WID strategy, the gender concept is based on a broader perspective which includes both women and men and the structural character of gender relationships. Feminist scholars in development policies came up with the concept of *gender and development* (GAD) (e.g. *Moser* 1993) as an answer to the criticism of the WID approach. GAD aims to transform gender relationships in society, politics and institutions towards comprehensive equality between women and men.

It has been translated into the institutional strategy of *mainstreaming gender*, which pursues the systematic integration of the gender perspective into all mainstream policy and programme activities within development organizations.

Today, *gender mainstreaming* has expanded to become the core institutional strategy within all UN organizations to implement equality between men and women.

In July 1997, the Economic and Social Council (→ ECOSOC) passed a comprehensive and important resolution (UN Doc. E/RES/1997/17, in: UN Doc. E/1997/97 (SUPP)), in which it calls upon all organizations of the UN family "to mainstream a gender perspective into all policies and programmes." (para. 3) It clarifies the concept of gender mainstreaming and spells out detailed recommendations as well as requirements for the UN institutions for applying a gender perspective in all areas of UN activities, such as in research, policy development, advocacy/dialogue, legislation, resource allocation, and planning, implementation and monitoring of programmes and projects.

Within the UN, the *Office of the Special Adviser to the Secretary-General on Gender Issues and the Advancement of Women* (OSAGI) monitors the mainstreaming of gender perspectives in the programmatic, normative and operational work of the UN system. The *Special Advisor,* in the rank of an Assistant Secretary-General, is also the chair of the *Inter-Agency Network on Women and Gender Equality* (IANWGE) – a network of gender focal points of currently about 25 international as well as regional UN entities. It has been central in promoting and coordinating *gender mainstreaming* throughout the UN.

To implement *gender mainstreaming*, capacity-building is necessary in UN institutions at the level of the individual as well as at organizational levels. Important instruments are gender trainings for changes in attitudes and values as well as technical support in devising and implementing gender programming with regard to management and policy issues, such as humanitarian aid, health, access to water, etc.

A recent report of the OSAGI (UN Doc. E/2007/64 of 10 May 2007), based on responses to a questionnaire from 40 UN organizations, comes to the conclusion that there is considerable variation in the strengthening of capacity and the implementation of gender mainstreaming among UN organizations.

It also identifies a gap between the conceptual understanding of gender mainstreaming and its implementation in the day-to-day work of staff. Of the 40 organizations 22 had a specific strategy for capacity development and training for *gender mainstreaming*, while the remainder used an ad-hoc approach. Also, training in most institutions is voluntary and up to the interest of staff. Most often, gender and programme officers participated in the trainings. Trainings, however, must be expanded to include all staff. Only UNDP, UNESCO, UNEP as well as some regional commissions have mandatory trainings for all staff.

Other, earlier reports also found that financial allocations and the commitment of top management in an organization to *gender mainstreaming* are often limited.

For example, while UNDP developed a detailed *Gender-in-Development Programme* in 1999, it had at the same time only committed 10 % of its global budget to the improvement of women's status and to gender mainstreaming. The World Food Programme (WFP), under the leadership of a woman, stands out as a positive exception. It commits 60 % of its country resources to the improvement of women's situations in those countries, where selected socio-economic indicators show a lower status of women, in e.g. income, education or health, by at least 25 % compared to men (cf. UN Doc. A/51/322 of 3 September 1996, para. 66-68).

Essential for effective *gender mainstreaming* are a strong organizational commitment, a sufficient budget, a systematic strategy, an action plan and mandatory and regular trainings at all levels. Today, UNDP, UNIFEM, UNFPA, UNHCR and the World Bank are among those with strategy, action plan and budget.

In terms of equal employment for women in higher positions, progress within the UN Secretariat and UN organizations has been slow (see www.un.org/womenwatch/osagi/fpgenderbalancestats.htm, accessed December 2007). The target of 50/50 gender equality by the year 2000 has not been met. In 2006, 37.43 % of all so-called Professional and Higher-level Staff (P-1 to P-5 and D-1 to USG) in the UN Secretariat were women. This number has improved only by 1.3 % since 1999 (cf.: UN Doc. E/CN.6/2000/4 of 27 January 2000).

In general, the number of women still decreases the higher the position is: at the decision-making levels (D1-USG) only 25.3 % were women in the UN Secretariat.

While this is an overall increase since 1999 by eight percent, there has been a slight decrease since 2004, when it had already reached 29 %. Only UNFPA has consistently achieved the 50/50 goal at the Professional and Higher-level Staff since 1999. → UNITAR has also recently reached this goal, and UNICEF as well as UNESCO are close to reaching it. Of all UN Organizations only four are currently headed by women: → UNICEF, → UNIFEM, → UNFPA and → UNWRA.

War and Peace

The international campaign *Women's Rights are Human Rights* raised the issue of war crimes against women. War crimes were traditionally given little attention in international politics. Also, knowledge about the pervasive and globally existing violence against women during and after wars was limited until the beginning of the 1990s. Today,

research shows that crimes against women are an integrated part of most warfare, in particular when civilians are the victims.

As a result of the campaign and of the horrific crimes against women in the wars in Former Yugoslavia and Rwanda in the early 1990s, gender-specific war crimes have been put onto the agenda of international humanitarian and criminal law.

The statutes of the ad-hoc tribunals on war crimes in Yugoslavia and in Rwanda list rape as a crime against humanity (Art. 3). The Rwanda tribunal also includes rape and forced prostitution as a grave breech of the Common Article 3 of the Geneva Conventions on War. As a result of intense lobbying of *The Women's Caucus on Gender Justice*, a network of women's human rights and peace organizations, the statute of the *International Criminal Court* (→ ICC), is even more comprehensive: rape, forced prostitution, sexual slavery, enforced pregnancy and forced sterilization are subsumed under the categories Crimes Against Humanity (Art. 7) and War Crimes (Art. 8) (UN Doc. A/CONF.183/9 of 17 July 1998). In addition, gender-based persecution of a group not only in times of war, but also in the absence of war, falls under the jurisdiction of the court. The statute provides for a witness protection unit, which *inter alia* is to be responsible for the care and protection of survivors of gender-based violence, who are willing to testify before the court.

In 1998, the *International Criminal Tribunal for Rwanda*, ICTR in its verdict against Jean-Paul Akayesu, handed down not only the first genocide conviction by an international court, but the first conviction for rape as an act of genocide. With its decision on "Foca" in 2001, the *International Criminal Tribunal on Former Yugoslawia* also wrote history. It found three Bosnian Serb men guilty of raping Bosnian Muslim women in Foca – some as young as 12 and 15. It was the first time an international court had judged a combination of sexual enslavement and rape to be a crime against humanity.

Before the ICC there are currently four situations at various stages of proceedings: Darfur, Sudan; Democratic Republic of Congo; Northern Uganda; Central African Republic. Investigations only marginally include rape in the first three. However, in May 2007, ICC's prosecutor announced formal investigations into crimes committed in the Central African Republic during 2002 and 2003, with focus on gender-based crimes. At the end of 2007, none of the trials had officially been opened, yet.

So far, women and women's perspectives and concerns still only play a marginal role in conflict resolution and peace politics and policies today. This is despite a variety of UN documents calling for the integration of women in peace politics and activities at national and international levels, some of them dating back to the early 1980s. (UN Doc. A/RES/37/63 of 3 December 1982). The Nairobi FLS (para. 239) and the Beijing PfA (para. 142) reinforced this recommendation. Among other things, the PfA advocates for an increase in the presence of women in Peacekeeping Operations (→ Peacekeeping; → Peacekeeping Operations). In the 1990s, the share of women in civil components was about one third, while they only accounted for 1.7% of all military and police personnel (*UNDAW 1995*) (→ Peacekeeping Forces; → UNCIVPOL). Until December 2007 the number of women in the military operations had only marginally increased to 2,0%. The Department of Peacekeeping Operations (DPKO) is among the UN departments staffed with the lowest number of women in leadership positions.

Missions with civilian mandates tend to have higher representation of women: the election and human rights mission to Guatemala had the highest proportion of women (48.7%) in any UN mission ever, followed by the mission to Haiti (39.2%) (*UNDAW* 1995).

Case studies on UN missions, such as the UNTAG mission in Namibia 1989-1990 and the civil observer mission (→ Observers) to South Africa, UNOMSA, show that missions which have both, a strong mandate for civil and peace-consolidating activities and a high percentage of female staff in all positions, yield the best successes in terms of implementing the mission goals (*UNDAW* 1995; *Olsson* 1999). The presence of women was helpful in building rapport with the local population, and for finding constructive conflict resolutions. Moreover, it reduced the risk of sexual harassment and violence against the female population by peacekeeping soldiers. The contacts with the female staff encouraged local women to articulate their specific needs and interests. Often, local women felt mobilized to organize politically by forming their own organizations and to thus join their voices to the peace process.

In the past, UN peacekeeping troops have become known to be involved in sexual abuse in several missions, e.g. in Bosnia-Herzegovina, Kosovo, Liberia and most recently in the Democratic Republic of Congo. UN Secretary-General Annan reacted with a bulletin titled "Special measures for protection from sexual exploitation and sexual abuse (UN Doc. ST/SGB/2003/13 of 9 October 2003) to which all personnel within the UN is bound. Moreover the Special Committee on Peacekeeping Operations asked in its 2005 report (UN Doc. A/59/19/Rev.1 (SUPP), para. 56) the Secretary-General to prepare "a comprehensive report with recommendations" on the issue, a report, which Annan submitted in March 2005 – "A comprehensive strategy to eliminate future sexual exploitation and abuse in the United Nations peacekeeping operations" (UN Doc. A/59/710 of 24 March 2005). Conduct and discipline units in peacekeeping operations were established in November 2005. Today, about 20 missions have such units which act as advisers to heads of mission and address all forms of misconduct. In 2006, 357 allegations were reported from the peacekeeping missions. The allegations are investigated and when found substantiated, the personnel in question is sent back home where sending countries decide about the legal consequences (cf. the 2007 Report of the Secretary-General on the issue, UN Doc. A/61/957 of 15 June 2007, Annex IV). With regard to the 357 allegations in 2006 82 investigations conducted by the United Nations could be completed, in 65 cases the allegations were determined to be unsubstantial, in 16 cases the allegations were determined to be substantial and the cases were forwarded to the member states or other institutions in charge for further action (UN Doc. A/61/957, Annex V).

In order to move the participation of women in peace processes more on the international agenda, the → Security Council of the UN adopted resolution S/RES/1325 on women, peace and security on 31 October 2000. It marked the first time the Security Council addressed the impact of armed conflict on women and recognized the under-valued and under-utilized contributions women make to conflict prevention and peacemaking. The resolution aims at integrating a gender perspective as well as the participation of women at all aspects of peacekeeping and peace-building. The Council has committed to mainstreaming gender into all of its resolutions. UN member states are encouraged to devise national plans of action to implement the resolution.

Five years later, in 2005, progress in implementing the resolution had been slow. Until 2004 only 39 out of 261 Security Council resolutions included reference to gender perspective or women. Also, women's civil society organizations in war-torn societies had not been adequately supported (*NGO Working Group on Women, Peace and Security*, 2005).

As a result, the UN adopted a system-wide action plan for the implementation of resolution 1325 from 2005-2007 (UN Doc. S/2005/636). It was the first of its kind with indicators for actions, strategies and output for all UN agencies and programmes. In 2007, 11 out of 18 peacekeeping missions have full-time

gender advisors, 7 have gender focal points (UN Doc. S/2007/567). Secretary-General Ban Ki-moon appointed Ellen Margrethe Løj of Denmark to serve as his Special Representative, i.e. head of the mission, for Liberia, one of the largest UN missions. Only two other operations, Angola in 1992/93 and Bosnia-Herzegovina in 1997, were led by women (*Olsson* 1999). In February 2007, the Liberia mission, for the first time ever in UN history, deployed an all-female police contingent from India to Liberia. As a result, the Liberian National Police received three times the usual number of female applicants in the month following the deployment. Despite these singular positive developments, many more efforts are necessary to integrate women in all decision-making processes and institutions regarding issues of conflict and peace at the local, national and international levels as well as in other peacekeeping missions.

(Re-)emerging Issues and Perspectives

A number of other topics have emerged or reemerged in women's politics within the UN since the beginning of 21st century. Very importantly, trafficking of women and girls for sexual exploitation has been moved on the UN agenda by the international women's movement. Not a new phenomenon, the UN already in 1949 adopted the *Convention for the Suppression of the Traffic in Persons and of the Exploitation of the Prostitution of Others* (UN Doc. A/RES/317 (IV), 2 December 1949; UNTS Vol. 96, No. 1342). The convention however focuses on prostitution and does not give an adequate definition for today's situation. The drastic increase of global trafficking and commercial sexual exploitation of women and children in the wake of economic and technological globalization made new interventions necessary.

In 2000, the Protocol to Prevent, Suppress and Punish Trafficking in Persons, especially Women and Children, supplementing the United Nations Convention on Transnational Organized Crime (UN Doc. A/55/383; UNTS No. 39574) was adopted in Palermo, in short: the Palermo Protocol. It entered into force in December 2003 and applies to 130 states parties (as of December 2008). The Palermo Protocol gives a comprehensive definition of trafficking in persons. This international standard has been widely adopted into legislation and policy making by regional organizations as well as states. It has led to numerous national, regional and international legal and political efforts to combat trafficking in women and children.

Women's health, in particular women's reproductive and sexual health and rights, has also become an important policy issue. The risk of women to get infected by the HIV/Aids virus and the high rate of new infections among women world wide has underlined the need to improve women's access to reproductive health services.

The Commission on Women as well as other major organizations, such as the → WHO and → UNFPA have adopted resolutions and started programmes to promote safe access of women to reproductive and sexual health and rights.

The unequal status of women also features in the *Millennium Development Goals* (MDGs) from 2000. As a blueprint agreed to by all the world's countries, the MDGs promote eight goals to improve the situation of the world's poorest, ranging from halving extreme poverty to halting the spread of HIV/AIDS and providing universal primary education, all by the target date of 2015. Goal number three refers to promoting gender equality and women's empowerment, with emphasis on reducing gender disparity in primary and secondary education preferably by 2005, and at all levels by 2015. Goal number five aims at reducing maternal mortality by three quarters by 2015.

The MDGs have galvanized unprecedented efforts by international development organizations, the UN and governments. The ongoing monitoring shows improvements in some sectors, in particular regarding better access of girls to primary education and a reduction of child as well as maternal mortality

world wide (www.un.org/ millennium-goals/index.html).

The MDGs and also the recent *World Bank Gender Action Plan* of 2006 have moved development issues and the situation of women in developing countries back on the UN's agenda on women.

The importance of women's economic activities for society's economic development at large has been rediscovered. Under the heading "smart economics" strategies have been designed by the World Bank and other international donors for women's empowerment in all economic sectors, including the private sector. Some critics argue that this shift and these recent documents tend to ignore the women's human rights perspective, which for example are not emphasized in the MDGs.

30 Years of Women's Politics in the UN: Coming a Long Way

Women and women's politics in the UN have come a long way since the first *World Conference on Women* in Mexico in 1975. Progress has been substantial in some respect: women's and gender issues now feature prominently on the UN's agenda; important international documents spell out, protect and advance the realization of women's rights and gender equality in almost all international policy areas. The women's human rights paradigm and the gender mainstreaming strategy were key elements for this success. The global women's movement was the main political force behind it. Women have entered the UN and been able to influence women's politics from within, albeit not to the extent as to which women would wish to do, as their numbers in the UN are still low.

Yet, after 30 years, some of the problems have not been solved: women are still not adequately represented at all levels of political decision-making. While there has been progress in changing discriminatory laws worldwide, such laws are still to be found in many countries. Also, this progress at the top has often not – or only very slowly – trickled down to make an impact in women's everyday realities, in particular with regard to violence. Hence, a study of the Secretary-General (UN Doc. A/61/122/Add.1, 6 June 2006) shows that violence against women has not decreased and is not adequately punished, a core issue of the women's movement since the 1970s. The Secretary-General in 2007 has pledged new programmes and strategies to combat gender-based violence against women and girl children and the impunity for these crimes.

Today's challenge is therefore to implement all the goals formulated so far and to realize the advancement of women's rights on the grounds, in the countries. For this end, tools and strategies have to be reviewed and refined to integrate more effectively and comprehensively a gender perspective into all policy activities at international, national and local levels.

In addition, the political and legal emphasis on the women's human rights paradigm needs to be upheld in all of these activities in order to prevent its weakening in international and national political decision making and strategizing.

Hence, there has been a recent tendency within in the UN to move away from a rights-based perspective back to a more developmental and economically oriented perspective on gender equality and women's empowerment.

This is not only reflected in the general weakening of the human rights approach in many countries in the aftermath of September 11, 2001, but also in the resistance of many states to expand the human rights agenda of women, specifically.

Women and their movements must continue to be instrumental in keeping up political pressures on UN organizations, decision-makers and delegations to prevent the political and legal weakening of existing standards on women's human rights and concepts of gender equality.

The implementation of women's human rights and gender equality globally, requires a continuous and serious commitment by all states and international organizations to the goals of equality and women's human rights. The United Nations should continue to be at the forefront of this commitment.

Sonja Wölte

Lit.: *Chen, M.:* Engendering World Conferences: The International Women's Movement and the UN, in: Weiss, T.G./Gordenker, L. (eds.): NGOs, the UN, and Global Governance, 139-158, Boulder/London 1996; *Moser, C:* Gender Planning in Development. Theory, Practice and Training, London 1993; *NGO Working Group on Women, Peace and Security:* From Local to Global: Making Peace Work for Women. Security Council Resolution 1325 – Five Years on Report, New York 2005; *Olsson, L.:* Gendering UN Peacekeeping. Mainstreaming a Gender Perspective in Multidimensional Peacekeeping Operations, Report No. 53, Department of Peace and Conflict Research, Uppsala 1999; *Peters, J./Wolper, A. (eds.):* Women's Rights, Human Rights. International Feminist Perspectives, London/New York 1995; *Pietilä, H./Vickers, J.:* Making Women Matter. The Role of the United Nations, London/New Jersey 1994; *Reanda, L.:* The Commission on the Status of Women, in: Alston, P. (ed.): The United Nations and Human Rights: A Critical Appraisal, Oxford 1992, 265-303; *Tomasevski, K.:* Women and Human Rights, London/New York 1993; *UNDAW (United Nations Division for the Advancement of Women):* The Role of Women in United Nations Peace-keeping, in: Women 2000, No. 1/1995, New York December 1995; *UNDPI (United Nations Department for Public Information):* The World's Women 1995: Trends and Statistics, New York 1995 (quoted as: UNDPI 1995a); *UNDPI:* The 1994 World Survey on the Role of Women in Development: Women in a Changing Global Economy, New York 1995 (quoted as: UNDPI 1995b); *UNDPI:* The United Nations and the Advancement of Women 1945-1996, UN Blue Book Series Vol.VI, New York 1996; *UNDPI:* The World's Women 2000: Trends and Statistics, New York 2000; *UNDPI:* The World's Women 2005: Trends and Statistics, New York 2005; *UNIFEM:* Progress of the World's Women 2000, Biennial Report, New York 2000; *Wichterich, C.:* Frauen der Welt. Vom Fortschritt der Ungleichheit, Göttingen 1995; *Wölte, S.:* Claiming Rights and Contesting Spaces: Women's Movements and the International Women's Human Rights Discourse in Africa, in: Braig, M./Wölte, S. (eds.): Common Ground or Mutual Exclusion? Women's Movements and International Relations, London/New York 2002, 171-188.

Internet: Selected Websites on Women/ Gender and UN organizations: Women and the UN: www.un.org/womenwatch; World Bank: www.worldbank.org/gender; UNDP: www.undp.org/gender/homepage.html; UNIFEM: www.unifem.undp.org; Women's Human Rights Net: www.whrnet.org; International Criminal Court: www.iwm.org/wcgj; Women's Initiative for Gender Justice: www.iccwomen.org.

World Bank (IBRD), World Bank Group (IFC/IDA/MIGA/ICSD)

I. Origins

In July 1944 the United Nations convened an International Monetary and Financial Conference at Bretton Woods (New Hampshire, USA), in which all 44 participating states agreed on a new order for the global financial and monetary system in the post-war era. The backdrop to the gathering was dominated by the still-vivid memories of inconvertibility and foreign exchange shortages, hyperinflation and deflation, and default on external debt of the preceding decades; thus the motivation to come to an agreement was strong. It was hoped to establish a system which could prevent a recurrence of the disastrous competitive exchange rate depreciations and the break-down of international economic relations these countries had experienced in the inter war period.

The agreements they signed there provided for the establishment of the international monetary and trading system known as the "Bretton Woods System". Although the Havana Charter (→ WTO/ GATT) was not ratified by the US Congress, leading to the indefinite postponement of the International Trade Organization (ITO) and its replacement by the provisional solution GATT, the Conference proved to be the birthplace of two major institutions: the *International Monetary Fund* (→ IMF) and the *International Bank for Reconstruction and Development (IBRD)*, established

by the "Articles of Agreement of the International Bank for Reconstruction" (UNTS Vol. 2 No. 20 (b)). The IBRD began its operations in 1946.

Apart from the IBRD itself, the World Bank Group consists of the International *Finance Corporation (IFC)*, the *International Development Association (IDA)* and the *Multilateral Investment Guarantee Agency (MIGA)*. The IFC was established in 1956, followed by the IDA in 1960 and the MIGA later in 1988. IBRD and IDA together are known as the "World Bank". The *International Center for the Settlement of Investment Disputes (ICSID)*, founded in 1965, is under the auspices of the World Bank.

The IBRD has its headquarters in Washington D.C. in conformity with Article V, Section 9 of the Articles of Agreement, which stipulates that the IBRD shall have its seat on the territory of the member with the greatest number of shares. The largest member is the United States of America with a share of 16.84% and related voting rights of 16.38% (April 2008). If the 15 countries of the euro area were to be considered as one single entity, as some observers call for, it would replace the USA as the largest member.

II. Purposes

The IBRD is dedicated to the following objectives:
(a) assisting the reconstruction of war-torn economies;
(b) assisting world economic growth;
(c) assisting economic and social progress, particularly in developing countries (cf. Articles of Agreement of the IBRD, Art. I).

The activities of the three World Bank affiliates provide a complement to the stated goals of the IBRD, by focusing on particular aspects of the IBRD agenda, and especially on those concerned with less developed countries (LDCs). The core activities of the other World Bank Group institutions may be summarized as follows:
(a) promotion of private, publicly non-guaranteed investment in developing countries (IFC);

(b) reducing poverty and promoting economic growth in LDCs by means of high-concessionary credits, so-called "soft loans" (IDA);

(c) promoting foreign direct investment for productive purposes, particularly in LDCs by underwriting non-commercial risks (MIGA);

(d) arbitration and conciliation in disputes between foreign investors and recipient countries (ICSID).

III. Status in the UN System, Membership and Organs

In 1947 the IBRD was accorded the status of a specialized agency ($\rightarrow$ Specialized Agencies) in the United Nations System, and was thus endowed with full juridical personality and entitled to conclude internationally-binding agreements. The IFC received special agency status in 1957 and the IDA in 1961. Furthermore, the IBRD is endowed with all the rights of an autonomous governmental organization including the right to establish its own budget, recruit its own staff and to admit new members. In order to join the IBRD a country must first become a member of the IMF (Art. II, Section 1, Articles of Agreement). A member state's quota in the IMF determines the amount of new IBRD members' capital subscription and accordingly the voting power within the Bank. Thus, the governance principle prevailing within the IMF, that countries with the highest quotas have the greatest voting power and influence, also applies to the IBRD. Membership in any of the World Bank's affiliated institutions is dependent on membership in the IBRD and therefore ultimately on IMF membership. There are 185 member states in the IBRD compared to 179 in the IFC, 171 in the MIGA, 166 in the IDA, and 143 in the ICSID (as of May 2008).

The three main executive organs of the IBRD are the *Board of Governors*, the *Executive Directors* and the office of the *President*. The Board of Governors is the highest executive organ of the IBRD and meets once a year during the annual meeting of the IBRD and IMF. All member states are represented on the Board of Governors with voting rights weighted to reflect the value of their shares. The Board of Governors has exclusive powers to decide on the admission or suspension of members, the increase or decrease in capital stock and the distribution of the net income of the Bank (Art. V). Most other activities can be – and in fact usually are – delegated to the Executive Directors who are responsible for the day-to-day running of the Bank and together make up the Board of Directors of the IBRD. There are 24 Executive Directors, five from the countries with the highest shares in the capital stock (USA, Japan, Germany, France and the United Kingdom), and one representative each from China, the Russian Federation and Saudi Arabia, with the remaining 16 board members elected on a rotational basis from the other IBRD member states. The Executive Directors select a President who, subject to its general direction on matters of policy, is responsible for conducting the "ordinary business of the Bank" (Art. V, Section 5 b). The President – currently Robert B. Zoellick – may not be a Governor or Executive Director. Robert B. Zoellick followed former US Deputy Secretary of Defense Paul Wolfowitz who stepped down as IBRD President after only two years following a series of scandals, involving the Riza affair and poor judgement in appointing senior management. Since its foundation, all IBRD Presidents have been US nationals.

The IFC, IDA and MIGA all have a similar organizational structure to that of the IBRD: a Board of Governors, Executive Directors answerable to the Board of Governors, and a President responsible for the conduct of ordinary business. The IFC and IDA are administered by the IBRD; the President, Governors and Executive Directors of the IBRD are ex-officio as are the President, Governors and Executive Directors of both the IFC and IDA, provided they are elected by an IBRD member who is also a member of these two institutions. IBRD and IDA also share the staff and headquarters. The only common office

886

of the World Bank and the MIGA is that of the President. Even so, the World Bank affiliates IFC and MIGA display the same share-weighted voting power as the IBRD and IDA; as might be expected, the group of industrialized nations holds the major part of capital stock in the IBRD, IDA, IFC and MIGA. ICSID has an Administrative Council and a Secretariat for the day-to-day business; in addition, ICSID maintains a Panel of Conciliators and a Panel of Arbitrators for the settlement of disputes.

IV. Funding: Sources and Uses

When a country joins the IBRD, it pays up to a maximum of 20% of its subscribed capital stock of which 2 percentage points must be paid in gold or US dollars and the other 18 percentage points may be in its own currency denomination. The remaining amount of 80% of its subscribed capital stock is subject to calls to meet obligations of the Bank arising from its operations. At the end of fiscal year 2007, total subscribed capital amounted to 190 billion US dollars of which only 11.5 billion US dollars or around 6% were paid in (*World Bank* 2007a). The amount of capital stock in form of shares a member country may hold within the IBRD is dependent on the country's quota within the IMF; thus, the IMF quota determines both a country's commitment to the IBRD and its voting power within the IBRD. Each country is assigned a basic vote of 250 plus one vote per share which has a par value of SDR 100,000. On the basis of their capital shares the industrialized countries have the absolute majority of votes within the IBRD, IDA; IFC and MIGA.

The largest and most important source of finance for the IBRD are private international capital markets, where it trades in debt securities at normal market interest rates. The huge volume of guarantee capital backing the IBRD is a measure of its high reputation and credit worthiness: to date all the bonds it sells have always had an AAA rating, allowing the IBRD to use the leverage of its equity in the international markets very

effectively. A further source of income for the IBRD stems from selling user's debentures (so-called swap transactions), and the repayment of disbursed loans. The IBRD makes non-concessionary loans to member countries at interest rates that reflect its cost of borrowing. In accordance with the Articles of Agreement, an IBRD loan must fulfill five particular conditions: (a) in accordance with the stated objectives of the IBRD, loans may only be granted for reconstruction and development investment. However, there is a lack of clear criteria as to what constitutes such investment; (b) repayment must be underwritten by a governmental guarantee even if the borrower comes from the private sector; (c) the borrower must tender proof that under current market condition no other economically viable finance for the requested investment is available other than the IBRD; (d) no form of contract tie-up may be attached to the loan on the part of the IBRD; and (e) the decision whether a loan be granted or not should be based exclusively on economic considerations and may not be influenced by political aspects although, once again, there is a lack of clear criteria as to what constitutes an "economic" and what a "political" aspect (cf. Articles of Agreement of the IBRD, Art. III).

In general, loans from the IDA are interest-free, set at a term between 20-40 years, with a 10-year grace period. The only additional costs are an administration fee of 0.75%. All IDA borrowers belong to the state sector. Over 80% of an IDA loan comes in the form of a subsidy which puts IDA credit in the category of development assistance, where a subsidy of at least 25% is required. Only the least developed countries, with current annual per capita income of up to 1,065 US dollars are eligible for IDA credits. As its capital assets are steadily depleted through the high-concessionary loans it grants, they need to be regularly refilled in so-called Replenishments. The 15th Replenishment in 2007 provided IDA with financial resources of 41.6 billion US dollars; it was the largest replenishment round in IDA history and included the former IDA borrowers China and Egypt as donors. To date the volume of loan repayments and capital stock from initial membership subscriptions has played only a negligible role in financing IDA credits.

In contrast to the IMF, accumulated IBRD and IDA new loans have steadily increased over the years up to an amount of 24.5 billion US dollars, with law, justice and public administration on the one hand and on the other transportation as the two major sectors to which the loans have been channeled (as of June 2007). However, it is IDA which experiences a major increase in demand for its concessional financing; IBRD outstanding loans have decreased from 116 billion to 98 billion US dollars (2007).

The World Bank Group is also a major participant in debt relief initiatives. Launched by the IMF and IBRD in 1996, the *Heavily Indebted Poor Countries (HIPC)* Initiative was designed to reduce the foreign debt of those developing countries classified as over-indebted; previous IMF and World Bank measures and programmes had not restored the solvency of candidate countries or provided sufficient growth perspectives. The HIPC Initiative embodies the view that, without the removal of the debt burden, economic development is difficult or even impossible. The circle of countries eligible for this initiative comes from those eligible for PRGF credits. Within the provisions of the HIPC Initiative, remission of debt generally involves a three-year preliminary period during which candidate countries have to prove that they are able to fulfil conditions required by the PRGF and IDA programmes before debt relief. A debt sustainability analysis in terms of foreign currency, and using generally valid economic indictors, serves as the basis for the debt relief. The original definition of debt sustainability was adjusted in 1999, when the economic indicators were revised down (in the so-called HIPC II or Enhanced HIPC Initiative) in order to broaden eligibility for

debt remission among the 41 countries of the HIPC group and establish actual debt relief. Although the PRGF Trust and the PRGF-HIPC Trust are both administered by the IMF, the major multilateral financial contributor is the World Bank via IDA. Around 50 % of the debt relief cost is directly financed by bilateral public creditors and the rest comes from multilateral lenders, e.g. the African Development Bank, which is the second largest donor after the World Bank Group, and the Inter-American Development Bank, which is the fourth largest donor after the IMF.

On the initiative of the G-8 Gleneagles Summit under UK Presidency in 2005, the HIPC initiative was complemented by the *Multilateral Debt Relief Initiative (MDRI)*, which provides for hundred percent debt relief for eligible debt to free financial resources within low-income countries to advance *Millennium Development Goals (MDGs)*. Participating institutions are the World Bank Group, the African Development Fund (AfDF), and the IMF, which individually decide upon debt relief; from 2007 on, the Inter-American Development Bank decided to also grant debt relief to eligible member countries according to MDRI terms. While international donors provide the major part of the MDRI costs, two-thirds of this debt relief are being granted by the World Bank via IDA.

In contrast to the practice in the IBRD, capital stock to the IFC must be paid in full and is used as a means of finance. The IFC provides capital for companies in developing countries with the important proviso that IFC investment may only be granted as external finance and not as investment in company equity. Equally, the IFC is prohibited from exercising managerial rights in any enterprise for which it provided finance. With the exception of the governmental guarantee for loan repayment, all the above mentioned IBRD restrictions apply equally to IFC activities (cf. Articles of Agreement of the IFC, Art. III). As all IFC business activities are underpinned by the principle of maintenance of assets, IFC investment must charge real positive rates of interest and take full account of loan default risks.

Authorized contributions paid in by member countries on joining the MIGA – an obligatory 10% mainly in convertible currency and 10% in the form of non-negotiable promissory notes with the remaining 80% on call – constitute the main liable equity capital covering obligations arising from contracted guarantees (MIGA Convention, Art. II). However, the insured party must first furnish substantive proof of loss resulting from a non-commercial risk such as currency transfer, expropriation, breach of contract of the direct investment by the host country, or war or civil disturbance. Yet particularly with reference to the last kind of risk, clear substantive proof is often difficult to furnish, as the hunger revolts following IMF structural adjustment measures in Africa, or the civil unrest in Indonesia and Malaysia during the Asian Crisis, have eloquently shown.

V. Activities of the World Bank

The main activity of the IBRD is to raise money on international capital markets with a view to providing multilateral, mostly long-term finance for specific projects. Since it began operations, the IBRD has followed a number of different strategies which may be ascribed to particular historical phases:

(1) 1946-1967: This phase was dominated by the catching-up strategy with the sole aim of quickening the pace of economic growth. Scarce domestic savings were identified here as the main obstacle to the adjustment of per capita incomes between industrialized and developing countries. It was assumed that the projected investment needed to raise income levels in underdeveloped countries would be far in excess of their savings. Furthermore, a lack of modern know-how was observed in developing countries. In order even to countenance the catching-up process in developing countries, it was considered necessary first to complement their domestic savings with external savings in the form of loans and to provide them with modern technology. Capital provided by the IBRD in conjunction with the increasing technology transfers of its technical assistance was intended to close their capital and technological gaps. The IBRD's main focus was on technical planning, financing and supervision of capital-intensive large-scale projects, in particular in agriculture, power supply and roads. Such was the backdrop to the establishment of the IFC, intended to mobilize private-sector capital, and the IDA with its aim of ensuring that developing countries too poor to gain loans at usual market conditions could also have access to investment to initiate a catching-up process. During the 1960s, however, it became ever more apparent that this strategy was not working in terms of the reduction of poverty, and more equitable income distribution in developing countries. Only a handful of countries had gained the status of so-called emerging markets, and the economic and social conditions of the populations of developing countries had hardly changed at all.

(2): 1968-1979: The coming to office of a new World Bank President, Robert McNamara, also saw a switch of strategy to 'distribution with growth' (distribution *with* and not merely *through* growth). In 1968 McNamara asked the Commission for International Development, chaired by Lester Pearson, to develop a new concept for the Second Development Decade of the 70s. Its eponymous Report was published in 1969. The Report's recommendations prioritized investment to help the most disadvantaged sections of the population – investment in rural integrated development and the social infrastructure in education, health care, water supply and urban development. The Report also laid great emphasis on the need to involve people themselves at community level. Even so, the actual IBRD practice of loan disbursement continued to be dominated by mammoth infrastructure projects, especially in the electricity supply and transport sectors, and this may be attributed to a large extent to the

reservations of receiver governments themselves about the Pearson Report: had the Report's recommendations been consistently carried out, this would have meant a substantial loss of income and assets for the very sections of society from which the government was recruited. However, in spite of the fact that few of its recommendations were ever implemented in practice, the Report itself had a major impact in shaping the program agendas of other organizations in the UN system. Its recommendations were enshrined in the Basic Needs Strategy of the International Labour Organization (→ ILO) and were taken up once more in the 1980s by the United Nations Development Programme (→ UNDP) in its Human Development Index (HDI).

(3) 1980-2005: Against a backdrop of mounting debt and ever decreasing distribution flexibility, the strategy which emphasized social issues has been abandoned in favor of debt management. Debt management focused on re-establishing external solvency to indebted developing countries. To this end in 1980 special instruments such as the Structural Adjustment Loan (SAL) with a term of up to 6 years and the Sectoral Adjustment Loan (SECAL) were introduced. Such loans had substantially shrunk the financial horizon vis-à-vis usual IBRD loans with their average terms of 12-15 years. At the same time there had been a move away from project financing to general programme financing: SECAL credits were not concerned with investment in specific projects but rather with the financing of restructuring programs for entire sectors such as agriculture, industry, foreign trade or finance; in contrast SAL loans were designed as support for structural adjustment measures and to finance current account deficits during the adjustment period, and thus should rather fall under the jurisdiction of the IMF. The conditions attached to the granting of a loan had been sharpened in line with the economic and political prescriptions established by the IMF. At the outset "conditionality" was restricted to pure economic criteria; this put the prime focus on the flexibility of key prices (such as interest rates or exchange rates, but also including basic food stuffs), market liberalization (e.g. commodity and capital markets) and general government deregulation through cut-backs in government intervention and the privatization of public sector companies. However, since the early 1990s a political dimension has been added to the economic one, including further conditions such as anti-corruption measures and an emphasis on strengthening democratic tendencies in the borrower country. These were also clearly delineated in a so-called "Letter for Development" signed between the creditor country and the IBRD.

The increasingly close bonds between the IBRD and the IMF – or rather the ascendancy of the IMF over the IBRD – was also evidenced by the fact that general approval of a SAL or SECAL credit first required a Stand-By Arrangement with the IMF, or at least that the borrowing country could fulfill the conditions to qualify for such an arrangement. The original division of labor between the IBRD and IMF, with long-term development investment on the one hand, and short-term balance of payments assistance on the other, had been gradually superseded during the 1980s by a joint policy of structural adjustment, whose implementation was a key precondition for debt rescheduling and the continued access of developing countries to public and private capital. The second field of activity for the IBRD – the provision of technical assistance – might receive much less public attention but had in fact rapidly expanded during this phase. The IBRD expended an annual budget for technical assistance in excess of 2 billion US dollars for the selection and implementation of loan-related projects and programs. Thus, the IBRD budget for technical assistance had become far larger than that of the United Nations Development Programme, which should have been the actual central coordinating agency for technical assistance in the UN System. Whilst the IBRD had consistently adopted its procedures and policies to follow those of the IMF – a process of emulation into which the Asian crisis introduced the first slight note of verbal discord – the relationship between the IBRD and UNDP was fraught by increasing rivalry.

Since the introduction of structural adjustment lending there has been growing criticism of the procedures of both the World Bank and the IMF in debtor countries, and from → NGOs in creditor countries. At first, discussions were mainly centred on the draconian economic and social consequences such programmes entailed, in particular the destruction of domestic production capacity, the loss of jobs, and the deepening disparities in income distribution. Furthermore, the – in some cases – drastic impact of structural adjustment programmes and projects on the environment was another cause for serious concern. And finally the lack of adequate democratic structures in the institutions and their lack of open and transparent control mechanisms gave rise to a number of restructuring proposals for the Bretton Woods twins themselves.

In 1998 the World Bank and the → IMF reached an agreement about the form of their collaborative work: in future all joint efforts would be governed by the three principles of clarity about responsibility, early and effective consultation, and separate accountability. Within this period these were the only steps towards a reform of the Bretton Woods twins although commissions were appointed to investigate far-reaching reform steps and several reports submitted, e.g. the Quota-Formula Review Group, which focused on the revision of quota formula and thereof derived quotas (*IMF* 2000), or the International Financial Institution Advisory Commission appointed by the US Congress, the report which analyzed the role of the International Financial Institutions and their division of labor and was in short called "Meltzer Commission Report" after the chairman of the Commission (*International Financial Institution*

Advisory Commission 2000; cf. also *Williamson* 2000).

(4) 2006 to present: The main critics focus on the IMF, although they are also applied to the World Bank; the World Bank shares a similar responsibility for the partially devastating impacts of its adjustment policy; its policy has not resulted in either enhancing growth or poverty reduction (*Easterly* 2005); its governance structure is characterized by the same lack of voice and ownership for developing countries and emerging market economies; moreover, the Bretton Woods twins have not "developed as a forum for serious multilateral cooperation" (*Woods* 2008, 2).

One consequence of the World Bank not being the main target of the critics is that in comparison with the IMF it is less severely hit by the institutional, financial and legitimacy crisis. Accordingly, the World Bank has not proposed any governance reforms on its own initiative. Instead, it has waited to see whether and to what extent IMF governance structures will be changed and will most probably take them over thereafter. Structural adjustment lending was abolished in 2004 and development policy lending introduced; however, this is mainly a rhetorical change, as conditionality attached to both development policy lending and investment lending has remained, albeit to a lesser degree than during the 1980s and 1990s; equally the disbursement of development policy loans and investment loans occurs in tranches based on so-called satisfactory performance. Like the IMF the World Bank is confronted with a shrinking operating income due to a decreasing loan volume and less demand by middle-income borrowers; alone between 2003 and 2007 the operating income declined by 50 % from 3 billion to 1.6 billion US dollars (*World Bank* 2007a). The IBRD reacted on the erosion of its financial basis by raising the maximum amount of the loan limit and cutting loan fees several times. In addition, the World Bank has broadened the range of financial products it offers; borrowers may use hedging products, e.g. interest rate swaps, currency swaps and commodity swaps or interest rate caps and collars. In 2004, Tunisia and Colombia were the first member states to use the hedging products; the former only for outstanding World Bank loans and the latter for its entire debt portfolio.

Since 2006 the World Bank has embarked on a process of developing a long-term strategy for itself; the then-chief economist François Bourguignon and his team prepared a review of 2 decades of World Bank policies; in addition, they identified four core areas which should figure more prominently on the World Bank agenda (*World Bank* 2007b). 10 years after the East Asian crisis and in the middle of the subprime loans debacle and exploding fuel and food prices, World Bank President Zoellick presented six strategic themes on which the World Bank should focus; four of these themes refer to country groups (poorest countries, middle-income countries, fragile states and the Arab World); the others comprise knowledge as one of the assumed core competences of the World Bank and enhanced support for the delivery of global public goods, e.g. public health and environment. At the time of writing (June 2008), the World Bank together with major donors and developing countries have finalized the design for the Climate Investment Funds (CIF) which shall be approved by the Board soon and the funds established thereafter; it is still not clear whether these funds will be in the form of loans, grants or a mix of both; moreover, funding for fossil energy projects, e.g. coal is not excluded.

In contrast to observers who stress that further action is not necessary, Commonwealth states, representing one third of world population, have expressed their concern that "incremental and ad hoc approaches to reforms" of international financial institutions are not a sufficient response to current crises (*Commonwealth Heads of Government* 2008, 1). They announced that they will pursue the process of redefin-

ing both the purpose and governance of the Bretton Woods institutions by organizing "wider international support for an international conference to achieve these goals" (ibid., 3).

Martina Metzger

Lit.: *Birdsall, N./Kapur D:* The hardest job in the World: Five crucial tasks for the new president of the World Bank. An agenda for the next president of the World Bank prepared by a Center for Global Development working group, June, 2006. www.cgdev.org/content/publications/detail/2868; *Bretton Woods Commission (ed):* Bretton Woods: Looking to the Future. Commission Report, Staff Review, Background Papers, Washington, D.C. 1994; *Commonwealth Heads of Governments:* Meeting on Reform on International Institutions: Marlborough House Statement on Reform of International Institutions, London, 9-10 June 2008. www.thecommonwealth.org/Templates/internal.asp?NodeID=178967; *Commonwealth Secretariat:* A Commonwealth Initiative to support reform of the IMF and the World Bank, London, May 2008, www.thecommonwealth.org/Templates/internal.asp?NodeID= 178967; *Easterly, W.:* What did structural adjustment adjust? The association of policies and growth with repeated IMF and World Bank adjustment loans, in: Journal of Development Economics 76 (2005), 1-22; *IMF Executive Board:* Report to the Executive Board of the Quota Formula Review Group, April 28, 2000 (quoted as: IMF 2000), www.imf.org/external/np/tre/quota/2000/eng/qfrg/report/index.htm; *International Financial Institution Advisory Commission:* Report (Chairman: Allan H. Meltzer), Washington, March 2000, www. house.gov/jec/imf/meltzer.pdf; *Kapur, D./Lewis, J.P./Webb R. (eds.):* The World Bank: Its first half century, 2 vols., Washington 1997; *Williamson, J.:* What Should the World Bank Think about the Washington Consensus? In: The World Bank Research Observer 15 (2000), 251-264; *Woods, N.:* The Globalizers: the IMF, the World Bank and its borrowers, Ithaca, New York 2006; *World Bank:* Structural and Sectoral Adjustment: World Bank Experience, 1980-92, Washington, D.C. 1995; *World Bank:* Annual Report 2007, Washington, D.C. 2007 (quoted as World Bank 2007a); *World Bank:* Meeting the Challenges of Global Development. A Long-Term Strategic Exercise for the World Bank

Group, Washington, D.C. 2007 (quoted as World Bank 2007b).

Internet: Homepage of the IBRD: www.worldbank.org; Homepage of ICSID: www.worldbank.org/icsid; Homepage of IDA: www.worldbank.org/ida; Homepage of IFC: www.ifc.org; Homepage of MIGA: www.miga.org; Homepage of The Bretton Woods Project – Critical Voices on the World Bank and IMF: www.brettonwoods project.org/index.shtml.

World Conferences

World conferences are commonly called those international conferences which are held under the auspices of the United Nations, involving broad participation of the world's states, and concerned with global problems. As a rule such conferences, based on consensus, adopt *declarations* (→ Resolution, Declaration, Decision) and *programmes of action* that may constitute preliminary stages of conventions and regimes binding under international law (→ International Law and the UN).

If we include here the four climate conventions held in connection with the UNCED *Framework Convention on Climate Change* (Rio de Janeiro 1992) which took place in Berlin (1995), Geneva (1996), Kyoto (1997), and Buenos Aires (1998) (→ Environmental Protection; → Environmental Law, International), we find that, since 1990 the following world conferences were convened in rapid succession, all of which differed in one way or another from the "first generation" of world conferences:

World Conferences since the End of Cold War: Components of Global Governance

In September 1990 the *"World Summit for Children"*, was held in New York and attended by a large number of heads of state and government who, in a spectacular act, signed the Declaration on the Protection and Development of Children. In this prelude to the "Convention on the Rights of the Child" (→ Human Rights Conventions, CRC) → UNICEF recognized a major step forward in the struggle against the exploitation of children.

In June 1992 the *UN Conference on Environment and Development* (UNCED) was held. This so-called *"Earth Summit"* attended by 15,000 delegates from 178 countries, 115 heads of state or government, and 7,000 journalists and representatives of non-governmental organizations (→ NGOs), is seen not only as the largest and most expensive conference ever held, but also as the one that generated the greatest international attention and impact. Beside the *"Agenda 21"* (UN Doc. A/CONF. 151/26/Rev.1 (Vol. I), Annex II), a comprehensive plan of action for sustainable development, and the *"Rio Declaration"* (ibid., Annex I), adopted in the place of a legally binding "Earth Charter" which found no consensus, the conference adopted the *Framework Convention on Climate Change* (UNTS Vol. 1771, No. 30822), the *Convention on Biological Diversity* (UNTS Vol. 1760, No. 30619), a *"Forest Declaration"* (UN Doc. A/CONF.151/26/Rev.1 (Vol. I), Annex III), and suggested in Chapter 12, para. 12.40 of the "Agenda 21" the elaboration of a *convention to combat desertification* through an intergovernmental negotiating committee under the aegis of the General Assembly. The *Convention to Combat Desertification* (UNTS Vol. 1954, No. 33480) was in fact adopted in June 1994 by the respective international negotiating committee and entered into force in December 1996. The Rio conference further suggested setting up a *Commission on Sustainable Development* (→ CSD) as subsidiary organ (→ Principal Organs, Subsidiary Organs, Treaty Bodies) of the United Nations Economic and Social Council (→ ECOSOC), which was to be given the task of monitoring the UNCED follow-up process and the implementation of "Agenda 21".

ECOSOC and the General Assembly followed this suggestion and established the CSD through UN Doc. E/RES/1993/207 and A/RES/47/191, respectively.

In July 1993 the *World Conference on Human Rights* was held in Vienna, which acknowledged the principles of the universality and indivisibility of → Human Rights as well as recognizing, by consensus, the long-controversial "right to development" (cf. the conference results in: Vienna Declaration and Programme of Action, UN Doc. A/CONF.157/23). Women's organizations saw in the recognition of universal women's rights (→ Women and the UN) progress in the development of human rights. Critics, on the other hand, pointing to an inflationary proliferation of postulates, noted a lack of improvement in the protection of human rights (→ Human Rights, Protection of). One concrete result was the establishment of a UN High Commissioner for Human Rights that had long been called for (→ Human Rights, United Nations High Commissioner for).

In April/May 1994 the UN *Global Conference on the Sustainable Development of Small Island Developing States* in Barbados considered, as part of the Rio Conference's follow-up process, the special problem of the rise of sea levels due to the warming of the earth's atmosphere and called for energetic measures aimed at reducing emissions of greenhouse gases.

In September 1994 the UN *International Conference on Population and Development*, convened in Cairo. It was attended by some 3,500 official government representatives, nearly 4,000 representatives of NGOs, and 3,800 journalists. This so-called *"World Population Conference"* adopted a comprehensive plan of action aimed at reducing population growth, promoting women and improving "reproductive health". The conference pointed to the links between living conditions and generative behavior (→ UNFPA).

In March 1995 the *UN Summit for Social Development* was held in Copenhagen. This so-called *"World Social Summit"*, committing itself "to the goal of eradicating poverty in the world", adopted with its "Copenhagen Declaration on Social Development and Pro-

gramme of Action (UN Doc. A/ CONF.166/9, Chapter I, 1) to a strategy against poverty, unemployment, and social marginalization, calling for the primacy of poverty alleviation in international development policy (→ Development Cooperation of the UN System).

In September 1995 the *Fourth World Conference on Women* was held in Beijing, which adopted the *"Bejing Declaration and Platform for Action"* for "equality, development, and peace" (UN Doc. A/CONF.177/20/Rev.1, Chapter I, 1). While it made headlines chiefly thanks to protests of women's organizations, which were kept away from the venue as a means of heading off possible protests, the conference did – like the world conferences on human rights and population – succeed, once again, in focusing attention on the strategic role of women in the development process.

In June 1996 *HABITAT II* (→ UN-HABITAT), the so-called *"Urban Summit"*, met in Istanbul, and considered problems of urbanization, homelessness, and migration. This conference showed clear signs of fatigue.

In June 1996 the *"Plant Summit"* was held in Leipzig on genetic plant resources, which – like the four climate conferences and the Barbados conference – can be seen as a follow-up conference to the Rio summit.

In November 1996 the *World Food Conference* met in Rome, and adopted a plan of action on worldwide food security.

The common thread intertwining these world conferences of the 1990s was *"sustainable development"*.

Conferences in the New Millennium

The first of the world conferences in the new millennium was the *Millennium Summit* in the framework of the General Assembly at the turn of the millennium that focused on the Millennium Development Goals (MDGs) in its concluding *Millennium Declaration* (A/RES/55/2, 8 September 2000).

It was followed in 2001 by the world conference on racism, racial discrimination and xenophobia, with its controversies around the definition of racism (cf. the report of the conference: UN Doc. A/CONF.189/12) and in September 2002 by the Johannesburg Summit on Sustainable Development. In contrast to the Rio summit of 1992, "Rio+10" stressed the importance of social development (water supply and disposal) and energy for sustainable development (cf. Political Declaration and Plan of Implementation, UN Doc. A/CONF.199/20, Chapter I).

Three world conferences with lesser international media attention were the two summits on the information society (WSIS) in Geneva (2003) and Tunis (2005) and the world conference on disaster prevention (2005).

Other conferences organized by the United Nations (such as the 3rd UN Conference on the Least Developed Countries in 2001, or the 2002 Monterrey Conference on Financing for Development) might, due to the large number of participants and the global range of subjects, also be counted among world conferences. Because of the acuteness of the food crisis, the Food Summit in June 2008 gained more media attention than some of the other world conferences that dealt with more specific problems, in which only specialists took more than a general interest.

"PrepCons" for Consultation and Coordination

Each of the main conferences was preceded by preparatory conferences (in UN talk "PrepCons") convened at the national, regional, and global level and concerned with defining positions and exploring possible compromises. The EU presidency, for instance, in each case undertook efforts aimed at formulating a uniform EU negotiating position, albeit not always successfully (→ European Union, Common Foreign and Security Policy at the UN). Coordination between the EU and the United Sates was even more difficult in that the USA was, as a rule, at pains to uphold its hegemonic interests (→ UN Policy, USA). NGOs were also already involved in this preliminary phase of the

consultation process. They too were forced, in an often laborious discussion process, to coordinate their positions with an eye to enlarging their scope of influence and showing themselves up to the task of negotiating with the diplomatic professionals.

Trying to Safeguard Implementation: the Follow-up Conferences

As an important element in its planning of the main conferences of the 90s the United Nations considered the follow-up. The aim was to safeguard the full implementation of the conference decisions and keep the public interested in the global issue. A series of follow-up meetings, mostly held as special sessions of the General Assembly, was organized by the UN Secretariat: in 1997 "Rio + 5" (19th special session of the GA), in 2000 "Beijing + 5" with the title "Women 2000" (23rd special session of the GA) and "Copenhagen + 5" on "Social Development" (24th special session of the GA). But these follow-up meetings failed to generate a political impact comparable to that of the conferences of the 1990s. Yet they organized to some extent and with some success the further implementation of the conference results of the 1990s.

The First and Second Generations of World Conferences

Apart from the "World Children's Summit" and the Copenhagen "World Social Summit", these world conferences on specific issues were convened for the second (UNCED, HABITAT, the World Human Rights Conference, and the World Food Conference), the third (the World Population Conference), or indeed for the fourth time (the World Women's Conference), though in each case the organization, agenda and targets had been adapted to take account of the new conditions in a changed world.

It is mainly for two reasons that a distinction is made between a *first* and a *second generation* of *world conferences*. First, the earlier world conferences were convened under the twofold burden of the Cold War and a confrontational phase of the North-South tensions. The ideological clashes this involved prevented the emergence of viable results concretely geared to solving problems. The West complained of a "tyranny by majorities" on the part of the developing countries, which were backed by opportunistic flanking protection from the East.

Second, the most recent world conferences had grown into mammoth events attended by thousands of participants. The novel element here was, above all, the new role played by increasingly transnationally networked NGOs. True, they remained barred from the negotiations between official government delegations, but they were included in more or less intensive consultation processes with many governments at the preparatory and main conferences, even to the point of being incorporated in the official delegations of some governments. NGOs owed this enhancement of their role for the most part to their function of representing social groups in the process of shaping public opinion, but also to their growing competence in the issues under negotiation.

If the main characteristic of *"global governance"*, as defined by the *Commission on Global Governance*, is cooperation between governmental and nongovernmental actors, then it must be said that a good measure of global governance was already being practiced at these world conferences. Unlike the case of the Vienna Congress, the participating states are no longer able to proceed as they see fit, in diplomatic exclusivity. The world economy and world society is no longer confined to the role of backdrop to the world of states. It now interacts with it. The world conferences have, though, clearly shown that states continue to have the last word in that it is they alone that are capable of positing binding international law. On occasion NGOs tend to overestimate their influence on the negotiations and actions of states.

Costly "Summitry" Without Any Results?

Politics, the media, and the scientific community were divided as to the benefits of these costly large-scale events, which, in the frequency of their occurrence, may in some ways have resembled traveling circuses, burdening both the host countries and the participating states, NGOs and media corporations with not insubstantial costs. The headlines tended to read: "Despite the costs, nothing new on the conference front?" Notwithstanding all criticism of the disproportion between input and output, the most recent world conferences have entailed the following *functions* and *impacts*:

First, they constitute *fora of international communications*, for exchanges of views on problems, the exploration of chances for compromise and cooperation, and the search for joint solutions to pressing problems. As opposed to consultations in the UN General Assembly (→ General Assembly), world conferences are meeting places for experts from sectoral ministries with other experts from international organizations, trade associations, and specialized NGOs.

Second, the search for compromises constitutes an important *learning process*. The developing countries learned from the North-South conferences of the 1970s that majorities and maximum demands contribute very little to changing the power structures in world politics and the world economy (→ International Economic Relations and New International Economic Order (NIEO)). The industrialized countries were forced to learn that a power-backed refusal to accept compromises only blocks the way to joint solutions to problems that lie in their own interest. Yet conflicts of interest between industrialized and developing countries have overshadowed negotiations, be they on reduction targets for CO_2 emissions, on the use of tropical rainforests, on the universality of human rights and the "right to development", on the legitimization of political conditionalities in the provision of development assistance, on the terms of debt management, or on new methods of development finance. This resulting North-South conflict ($\to$ North-South-Relations and the UN) has also made it difficult for NGOs to come up with joint positions. Here the organizational and financial preeminence of the "North NGOs" has also proven to be a factor giving rise to conflict.

Third, the world conferences, accompanied as they are by an impressive media presence, have an important *educational and information function* on the state of world problems. Aside from their *"meeting function"*, they also have a *"focusing function"* which involves pinpointing the world's attention, at least for the short term, on the specific problems under negotiation, though media interest has tended to be short-lived, especially in view of the fact that the frequency at which world conferences have been convened has often meant abrupt changes of scene and subject matter.

Fourth, the history of the world conferences shows that initially non-binding declarations have gradually assumed normative force. While the *Agenda 21* adopted by the Rio Conference is not binding under international law, it has spurred on international efforts aimed at working out international regimes and conventions. The "Local Agenda 21" has stimulated, throughout the world, initiatives aimed at encouraging a more sustainable approach to the environment and adding concrete guidelines to the formula "Think global – act local". A number of countries have worked out national agendas for sustainable development geared to the aims of *"Agenda 21"*. It is thanks to the Copenhagen World Social Summit that the OECD in 1996 presented a strategy for halving the number of the world's poor by the year 2015.

Fifth, individual governments have undertaken steps toward putting into practice at least some of the voluntary commitments contained in the programs of actions they signed. As an example:

the recommendations of the Rio Conference, the Cairo World Population Conference, and the Beijing World Women's Conference nudged the German Development Ministry (*BMZ*) in the direction of upgrading environmental protection and the promotion of women to the level of development priorities. At the same time, these voluntary commitments serve as a *normative orientation* for criticism. Parliamentary opposition and NGOs alike can now use these reference documents of good international conduct to put governments under pressure to act.

Balance: World Conferences as the Dramaturgy of Globalism

The world conferences have been accused of having brought about no more than masterpieces of *"paper diplomacy"*, consisting of non-binding declarations of intent. This blanket criticism overlooks the fact that some of these conferences adopted landmark problem analyses and action programs, and in some areas promoted new initiatives aimed at coming up with joint solutions to world problems. Even hegemonic states have been forced to recognize that there is no way out of the constraint to cooperate necessitated by intensifying global interdependencies.

The action programs adopted by the world conferences have made it plain that what international community and world society in like manner lack are not knowledge and material resources, but the political will to seek joint solutions to various world problems. If the countries concerned were to translate only part of their insights and commitments into action, they could change the world. To this extent the world conferences have left behind a mixture of hope that world problems can be solved and disappointment over existing contradictions between insights, declarations of intent, and concrete action. (cf. *Haas* 2002, 75)

New Type of World Conferences: High-level Summits

Despite the ongoing series of "classical" world conferences in the new millennium trying to keep the conference impact effective in the UN system and despite the follow-up meetings on different levels (GA special sessions, ECOSOC meetings, CSD and CSW meetings), world conferences in their traditional form proved to be not any longer politically effective: not further world conferences, but two high-level meetings within the framework of the General Assembly – the *Millennium Summit 2000* and the *World Summit 2005*, were surprisingly able to attract the attention of the world public again and to generate a considerable political impact in the form of defining political goals and of establishing new UN institutions.

While the Millennium Summit established the politically most effective *Millennium Development Goals (MDGs)* through its *Millennium Declaration* (UN Doc. A/RES/55/2 of 8 September 2000), defining new universally accepted benchmarks for sustainable and human development, the World Summit 2005 started with its "World Summit Outcome Document (UN Doc. A/RES/60/1 of 16 September 2005) the process for the establishment of the *Peacebuilding Commission* and of the *Human Rights Council*, replacing the heavily criticized *Commission on Human Rights*.

Both summits – like the world conferences in the 1990s – were able to set effectively the political agenda, to raise the political awareness of the world public, to popularize the issues at stake, to make the heads of states and of governments of the UN member states set new standards and to establish new institutions.

This format of high-level meetings at the UN premises and according to the rules of procedure of the GA finds – in contrast to the world conferences – the support of the large payers in the UN, as the high-level meetings are cheaper, can be prepared by panel reports and reports of the Secretary-General instead of by time-consuming and expensive preparatory conferences and – to the frustration of the NGOs, but to the delight of a number of UN member states – the access of NGOs to the high-level meetings is determined according to the rules applied for special sessions of the GA, being much more restrictive than the rules for NGO access to world conferences.

Only a few NGO representatives were for example invited by the GA to speak at the very end of the 2005 World Summit – after everything had been decided. The majority of NGOs was offered only the chance to talk to the representatives of the member states early in the preparatory stages of the World Summit at an interactive hearing three months before the summit.

Thus the two high-level summits can be considered likewise as political success in UN summitry with regard to institutional UN reform and as step back with regard to the participation of the NGOs as important element of UN politics. Apparently the actors of the larger powers seem to be of the opinion that they could decide on the global problems largely without the NGOs – a questionable development for world summitry. Summitry is part of the dramaturgy of globalism (→ Globalization), the latter an element of the future of world politics. And the forum is the United Nations.

Franz Nuscheler

Lit.: *Friedman, E.J./Hochstetter, K./Clark, A.M.:* Sovereignty, Democracy and Global Civil Society: State-Society Relations at UN World Conferences, Albany/USA 2005; *Fues, T./Hamm, B. (eds.):* Die Weltkonferenzen der 90er Jahre: Baustellen für Global Governance? Bonn 2001; *Haas, P.M.:* UN Conferences and Constructivist Governance of the Environment, in: Global Governance 8 (2002), 73-91; *Messner, D./Nuscheler, F. (ed.):* Weltkonferenzen und Weltberichte, Bonn 1996; *Nye, J.S./Donahue, J.D. (eds.):* Governance in a Globalizing World, Cambridge 2000; *Schechter, M.G. (ed.):* United Nations-sponsored World Conferences: Focus on Impact and Follow-up, Tokyo 2001.

Internet: Information on world conferences and high-level meetings: www.un.org/events/conferences.htm.

World Reports

Since the 1980s, the United Nations and its → specialized agencies have published a growing number of reports focusing on the global situation in a certain field of world politics, reports which are called *"World Reports"* by their authors. It should be noted that there is no clear line of demarcation between these *World Reports* and the *annual reports* of the *UN organizations*. If an annual report includes comprehensive analysis and interpretation of an issue of world politics by using statistical data, it seems justified to classify it as "world report" as well. (Accordingly, the following list of World Reports includes also reports which are not officially labelled as "World Reports").

Furthermore, the World Reports of the UN are distinct from the *reports* of the *Independent Commissions* (→ Independent Commissions, Reports of), for instance the report "North-South: A Programme for Survival" of the *Independent Commission on International Development Issues ("Brandt Commission")* which was submitted to the UN Secretary-General and published in 1980, the report "Common Security" of the *Independent Commission on Disarmament and Security Issues ("Palme Commission")* which was submitted and published in 1982, or the report "Our Common Future" of the *World Commission on Environment and Development ("Brundtland Commission")* which was presented in 1987 to the UN General Assembly. These reports were submitted by independent groups of outstanding personalities belonging to the policy or the business sector of the Western industrial countries and of the least developed countries (LDCs). Different organs of the UN have requested these personalities to give the UN system "external" advice on a number of subjects – → development cooperation

of the UN system, → disarmament and security, environment and development (→ Environmental Protection) and to make suggestions for reforms (→ Reform of the UN).

Functions of the World Reports

The World Reports of the UN, on the contrary, are to fulfill the following three functions:

- they are to function as *progress reports*, released by the respective UN organs in order to inform the governments of the member states;
- they are to serve as a *basis for the discussions* in the Economic and Social Council (→ ECOSOC) and in the → General Assembly of the UN;
- they are to *inform* an increasingly interested *public*, especially the *nongovernmental organizations* (→ NGOs) in the member states which are conducting activities in the respective issue areas (for instance, world food supply, environmental protection).

At the beginning, the World Reports mostly served as *progress reports* and *basis for* internal *discussions* only. But the third function, *informing the public*, has gained more and more importance in the course of time, since the mass media in the member states introduce and comment on the reports to the public. This tendency has given rise to a hope that the understanding of and support for the work of UN organizations will increase, and that this will in turn result in stronger financial support by the member states.

Divergent Theoretical Concepts

However, the high number of reports, the greatly varying methodological concepts and the different political intentions of the respective editors present a growing problem which is likely to neutralize in part the useful effects hoped for. The authors have different theoretical concepts and use dissimilar techniques for statistics and forecasting. Under these circumstances, their evaluations of actual economic, social and cultural problems vary noticeably with regard to their significance for the economic and social life quality, as well as their assessments of upcoming chances and dangers. This in turn leads to diverse political recommendations, which can be influenced and changed by the superior interests and long term strategies of the publishers, for instance the World Bank (→ World Bank, World Bank Group) or the United Nations Development Programme (→ UNDP).

It would be helpful to compare and to point to the differences between World Reports which target the same issue areas, and to discuss these differences and viewpoints overtly within the UN and in the member states in order to contribute to solving actual problems.

Multidimensional Approach

The majority of the World Reports are limited to the detailed, empirically-based situation analysis of an issue area, but some are providing a more sophisticated approach, since they combine the analysis of economic data with the examination of the social and cultural dimensions of living. This is valid especially for the *"Reports on the World Social Situation"*, which are published by the Department of Economic and Social Affairs (DESA) of the → Secretariat and for the → *"Human Development Reports"* published by the → UNDP.

Due to their comprehensive *multidimensional concept of development*, which is based on the assessment of economic, social and cultural conditions of living instead of being limited to the collection and evaluation of economic data, the *Human Development Reports* have contributed to a modified understanding of development and have gained world-wide public and political attention.

The "Human Development Reports" exemplify the functions of the World Reports: to inform about the current activities of UN organs in a large number of global issue areas, and, most importantly, to discuss concepts which can contribute to a better understanding and which can help to solve the interde-

pendent economic, social and cultural problems of mankind.

Helmut Volger

A selection of the most important world reports:

Children:

UNICEF: The State of the World's Children, annually, since 1980;

Development:

BRD (World Bank): World Development Report, annually, since 1978;

UNDP: Human Development Report, annually, since 1990;

Education:

UNESCO: *World Education Report*, annually, since 1991;

Environment:

UNEP: *The State of the Environment*, annually, since 1974;

UNEP: *Global Environment Outlook*, since 1997, published in irregular intervals (1997, 2000, 2002, 2007);

WMO/UNEP – Intergovernmental Panel on Climate Change (IPCC): *IPCC Assessment Report: Climate Change*, since 1990, roughly every five years;

UNEP et al. – Millennium Ecosystem Assessment (MA): Ecosystems and Human Well-being, Report in 6 vols., published in 2005;

UNESCO – World Water Forum: UN World Water Development Report, every three years since 2003;

Food:

FAO: The State of Food and Agriculture, annually, since 1947;

FAO: The State of Food Insecurity in the World, annually, since 1999;

Health:

WHO: World Health Report; annually, since 1995;

UNODC: *World Drug Report*, annually since 2004;

Industry:

UNIDO: Industry and Development Global Report, annually, since 1985;

Labour:

ILO: World Labour Report, annually, since 1984;

ILO: *World Employment Report*, annually, since 1995;

Population:

UNFPA: *UNFPA Annual Report*, annually, since 1997;

UNFPA: *State of World Population*, annually, since 1996;

Public Administration:

UN – DESA: *World Public Sector Report*, roughly every three years since 2001;

Settlement:

UN Centre for Human Settlements /HABITAT: Global Report on Human Settlements, annually, since 1986;

Social Situation:

UN: Report on the World Social Situation, since 1952, from 1952-2001 published in a four-year cycle, since 2002 published bi-annually;

Trade/World Economy:

GATT/WTO: *International Trade*, annually, since 1952; until 1994 edited by the GATT, since 1995 edited by the WTO;

UNCTAD: *Trade and Development Report*, annually, since 1981;

UNCTAD: World Investment Report, annually, since 1991;

Women:

UN – DPI: World Survey on the Role of Women in Development; roughly every five years, since 1985;

World Economy:

IMF: *World Economic Outlook*, annually since 1980, semi-annually since 1984;

UN: *World Economic and Social Survey*, annually, 1949-1954 published as: World Economic Report; 1955-1993; published as: World Economic Survey;

Youth:

UN – DESA: *World Youth Report*, every two years since 2003.

Lit.: *Hüfner, K.:* World Reports, in: Wolfrum, R. (ed.): United Nations: Law, Policies and Practice, Vol. 2, Munich/Dordrecht 1995, 1493-1500; *Messner, D./Nuscheler, F. (eds.):* Weltkonferenzen und Weltberichte. Ein Wegweiser durch die internationale Diskussion, Bonn 1996.

WTO – World Trade Organization, GATT – General Agreement on Tariffs and Trade

I. History and Development

The experience of the global economic crisis played an important role in the development of the international system after World War II. Within the United Nations, a special principal organ, the Economic and Social Council ($\rightarrow$ ECOSOC), was created in order to do justice to economic and social questions and their implications for world peace. At the *Bretton Woods Conference*, two special institutions, the *World Bank* ($\rightarrow$ World Bank, World Bank Group) and the *International Monetary Fund* ($\rightarrow$ IMF), were created. ECOSOC wanted to create a similar organization in the area of trade, and therefore convened a UN Conference on Trade and Employment which passed the so-called *"Havana Charter"* for an International Trade Organization in 1948.

The *Havana Charter* established a comprehensive institutional and substantial order for international economic relations, which is of unparalleled density and almost prophetic foresight. In addition to tariffs and trade barriers, it addressed questions of economic development, trade in natural resources and even questions of anti-trust relations. These turned out to be central, and highly susceptible to frictions in the further development of the international economic order.

The obligations of states to lower custom duties constituted an important preliminary result of the conference. In order to give these obligations immediate effect, a special agreement, which was intended to be a provisional instrument, was concluded. Beside the lists of customs concessions, this also included some of the provisions of the draft agreement – the *General Agreement on Tariffs and Trade* (GATT).

As it became clear quite early on that the Havana Charter would not enter into force, the world trade order developed on the basis of GATT. An interim commission – later called *GATT Secretariat* – assumed the functions of the secretariat. It had been created by the Conference on Trade and Employment for a completely different purpose, namely to supervise the entry into force of the Havana Charter.

Rounds of negotiations – so-called *GATT Rounds* – took place regularly. At these, the further lowering of taxes and sometimes even new rules – mostly as separate agreements because of the different majorities – were agreed on.

In the 1960s and 1970s, the questions which had been discussed in the Havana Charter but had not found entry into GATT resurfaced and became even more pressing. They found their stage in the United Nations Conference on Trade and Development (UNCTAD)– , which later declared a *"New International Economic Order"* (→ International Economic Relations and New International Economic Order (NIEO)), which was greatly dominated by the interests of developing countries. Except for one formality, the exemption from the most-favored nation clause for beneficial treatment granted to developing countries, GATT played hardly any part in this development and was at times in derogatory terms called a "rich men's club".

In the mid-1980s, GATT's limited scope and provisional status led to a crisis which was meant to be overcome by means of a new *GATT Round*, the *Uruguay Round*. It led to a remarkable consolidation and broadening in scope of the world trade order.

This was to a great extent also made possible because in the meantime, the prospects for the objectives and mechanisms of the *New International Economic Order* had become less favorable. The different economic and social successes of the various developing countries which had become visible, the shifting of interests which accompanied this development, but also a shift in the power structure led to a new setting of priorities: together with the many smaller states of the North they fought in changing alliances with and against the major industrialized countries for free trade, and a strong multilateral international trade order based on the rule of law.

The centerpieces were the creation of a new organization – the *World Trade Organization (WTO)* – in 1994 by the "Agreement Establishing the World Trade Organization" (UNTS Vol. 1867, No. 31874) – and a significant strengthening of the legal foundations and their enforceability by means of dispute settlement. Moreover, new rules concerning services – *General Agreement on Trade in Services (GATS)* – and intellectual property – Agreement on Trade-related Aspects of Intellectual Property Rights (TRIPs) – were adopted (both agreements: UNTS, Vol. 1869, No. 31874).

The WTO has developed well. Its dispute settlement mechanism has seen and settled more than 350 cases and a new round of negotiations was initiated in 2001, the so-called Doha Round, which, however, has subsequently experienced a stalemate. Also, it has to be noted that the WTO has been the subject of quite some criticism, which in substance points out that the system has importantly promoted trade liberalization and globalization, but is allegedly incapable of addressing its important developmental, social and environmental consequences.

II. The Institutional and Legal Framework

The *principal organs* of the WTO are the *Ministerial Conference* which meets every two years, the *General Council* as permanent body which takes the role of the Ministerial Conference between its meetings, and the *Secretariat* which is led by a *Director-General*. Further organs of the Council, Committees and Working Groups, complete the institutional tableau. Three organs of the Council which are subordinated to the General Council are especially noteworthy: the Council for Trade in Goods, the Council for Trade in Services, and the Council for Trade-Related Aspects of Intellectual Property.

By contrast, the so-called *Dispute Settlement Body (DSB)*, which administers the system of dispute settlement mechanisms, is not really a separate organ in its own right. Its functions are exercised by the General Council, which in this case, however, has separate sessions with a special set of procedural rules and can elect its own chairperson (Art. IV (3) of the Agreement). The same holds true for the *Trade Policy Review Body* (Art. IV (4)). The special construction of these two bodies can be viewed as a first step towards institutional autonomy. The WTO copied the GATT tradition of passing consensual decisions. Voting is only admissible under special circumstances.

At present, the WTO has 153 members (as of July 2008). China joined the WTO in 2001 and Saudi Arabia in 2005. The only major state, which so far remained outside the organization is Russia. New members can be admitted by means of a two-thirds majority vote in the Ministerial Conference. As membership of the WTO not only obligates states to abide by WTO law, but also obligates all states to make concessions in view of market access – a state which seeks membership must first enter into negotiations about liberalization and make the pertinent concessions. At pre-sent, such negotiations are under way with 30 states, including Russia.

The WTO has forged numerous relationships with other international organizations. As the GATT did previously, it has the place of a *de facto* UN specialized agency (→ Specialized Agencies) within the → UN system. As it was felt that no formal links were needed, the relationship between the WTO and the United Nations is governed by the "Arrangements for Effective Cooperation with other Intergovernmental Organizations" (WTO Doc. WT/GC/W/10 of November 1995), which are based on an exchange of letters between the United Nations Secretary-General and the Director-General of the World Trade Organization (reproduced in the abovementioned document). The arrangements basically envisage that the practice of consultation and cooperation, which had evolved at the time of the GATT shall continue.

There are also close ties to the International Monetary Fund (→ IMF). Furthermore, the "Agreement on the Establishment of the World Trade Organization" expressly states that the WTO should cooperate with non-governmental organizations (→ NGOs). The Council has recently passed the necessary guidelines. These provide that the public should have a better access to more detailed information, but do not give NGOs a right to take part in meetings. NGOs cannot directly participate in controversial cases, either. But they can and sometimes do deliver statements, so-called *amicus curiae* briefs, which may be taken into account by Panels or the Appellate Body. It is not uncommon for states to adopt the arguments put forward by NGOs and to append them to their own written pleadings.

The GATT rules, which developed in different treaties and grew exceedingly difficult to survey, have been made more uniform under the WTO because of the sheer numbers of member states – all states had to commit themselves to adopt in their entirety both the old treaties, which were often substantially revised, and the newly negotiated treaties. Nonetheless, there are still almost 40 relevant treaties, among them a modified form of the old GATT. Also, many decisions and resolutions of the GATT were adopted.

1. Principles and Mechanisms

It is often stated that the objective and purpose of the WTO is free trade. In a general manner, this correctly repeats the programs and successes of the organization and the order of global trade on which it is based. The statement is also a sensible characterization of the WTO's place in the complete system of global economic relations and their institutional structures.

A closer look, however, reveals that this characterization must be considerably revised regarding the objectives and functions of the WTO. Concerning the objectives, the WTO takes a much broader approach. The Preamble of the WTO Agreement lists higher economic goals, such as: raising standards of living, full employment, effective demand, expansion of the production of and trade in goods and services, optimal use of the world's resources in accordance with the objective of sustainable development, protection and preservation of the environment, and economic development.

Concerning the mechanisms, the design of the WTO is more humble – which explains their success. Generally, the WTO does not obligate states themselves to liberalize trade unconditionally, but accepts the economic policy guidelines of the states; moreover, the WTO leaves it to the states themselves to agree on steps to further liberalize trade on the basis of mutual concessions. The WTO does, however, stipulate a framework within which global economic relations and state actions must take place.

Legal "Binding Force" and Dispute Settlement

First and foremost, the validity of law and the possibilities of enforcing it are part of its legally binding character. The WTO rules, including the concessions concerning liberalization, are legally binding. This binding force is ensured by dispute settlement. But in various ways the WTO rules also demand that states follow WTO instructions and create regulations within their own domestic jurisdiction, that they guard the principles of predictability and transparency, and that they provide participation of those concerned and sufficient legal protection.

As for enforcement, the dispute settlement mechanism of the WTO must be mentioned, since it is considered "a central element in providing security and predictability to the multilateral trading system" in the words of Article 3.8 of the Understanding on Rules and Procedures Governing the Settlement of Disputes – the core legal instrument of the WTO in this regard. The system envisages a two-tiered procedure of interstate judicial settlement. Complaints by members can be put before a Panel of Experts. Its decision can be appealed by the parties to the dispute before a standing Appellate Body. In the case where a member's measure is found not to be consistent with the rules of the WTO the DSB will supervise the implementation of the decision by such member. In the case of a failure of the party to bring its measures in conformity with the rules, the complaining party may resort eventually to retaliatory measures, mainly a suspension of its obligations vis-à-vis the non-compliant member.

Non-Discrimination

Based on what has just been described, there is also a strict rule of non-discrimination. Advantages granted to goods and services from one state must also be granted without further distinctions to all other foreign goods and services (most-favored nation status). Except for those trade barriers still valid and bound by concessions, foreign goods may no longer be discriminated against on the internal markets, but must instead be treated in the same manner as domestic goods (national treatment).

Proportionality and Efficiency of Trade Policy Measures

A further principle of the WTO is that of proportionality and efficiency of measures concerning trade policy. A number of different rules request the states to pursue their trade policy goals – also the protectionist ones – with means that must be as effective as possible. As a result, import restrictions in terms of quantity, for example, are mostly prohibited, because a state's market can usually be protected more effectively by means of tariffs.

Liberalization by Means of Mutual Concessions

The system of market access based on mutual negotiations is founded on these principles. States negotiate about liberalization of the trade in goods – usually about tariff concessions – under special rules in regular, fixed periods. In these negotiations, very complicated factors of market access must be defined and negotiated. These concessions, which are often negotiated between few member states only, nonetheless benefit all member states because of the most-favored nation clause – there are very limited exceptions to this rule in the field of services. The WTO protects these mutual concessions and their value, *inter alia*, through rules concerning the definition of the origin of goods, the calculation of the value of tariffs with the help of procedures to modify according to changed circumstances, and when well-founded expectations are disappointed.

Protection of Fair Trade

Finally, the WTO contains rules which should protect trade against unfair measures by states (subventions), and sale under market price by private actors (anti-dumping). In both cases, these rules allow states to levy punitive tariffs, albeit under very strict conditions and procedures.

The System of Exceptions

In the WTO, the rigid obligations and "binding force" are offset by different exceptions which provide exact rules about reasons, procedures and, when necessary, compensation. The first group of exceptions relates to measures concerning international security and domestic public order. Among the latter the protection of health and the environment – Article XX *lit.* b and g of the GATT agreement – are especially relevant. They have been subject to a number of pertinent disputes, such as, for instance, the Shrimp-Turtle case (WTO Doc. DS58/AB/R). The second group of exceptions concerns crisis situations in national economies. When there are crises concerning the balance of payments, measures, including quantitative import limitations, may be taken after consultations with a WTO committee which has been created to deal with exactly these cases. Insofar as they endanger a domestic branch of industry, tariff concessions may be amended or revoked, but only after negotiations to adapt the concessions to the present situation have taken place. Further exceptions concern trade with developing countries: special beneficial treatment of developing countries is, under these rules, not subject to the most-favored nation clause and therefore need not be extended to all other states. Finally, the most-favored nation status does not cover benefits accorded by states to other states when founding a regional free trade area.

Enforceability and Dispute Settlement

By comparison with other mechanisms for enforcing legal rules in international regimes, the WTO dispute settlement system is viewed as being extremely effective. By means of it, states may rebuke breaches of law by other states and can, as a last resort, impose sanctions against lawbreakers. Unlike under GATT, this system is strongly oriented towards court concepts. Although the system is still administered by an organ which is essentially political, the DSB, this organ is bound by a strict time limits and may deny the setting up of a dispute settlement panel, the adoption of its final report or the report of the appellate body, or its permission to impose trade sanctions only if a consensus has been reached. All that has remained of the more political orientation under GATT, especially in view of the diametrically opposite requirements for decision-making, is the obligation to attempt dispute settlement through consultations at the beginning of the procedure, as well as the possibility of granting other compensations to prevent the imposition of sanctions.

In addition to the dispute settlement system, there also exists a Trade Policy Review Mechanism as an instance of preventive political control and enforcement which regularly, at the exact time agreed upon, reviews the trade policy of every state and publishes the reports and findings.

Innovation

The WTO has different and far-reaching instruments with which to develop its policies and rules, adopt them to changed circumstances and achieve further liberalization. The treaties themselves contain a number of orders to monitor and negotiate – the so-called built-in agenda of the WTO. Also, crucial impulses often come from the Ministerial Conference. Finally, next to the special and regular negotiations on liberalization, additional "major" WTO Rounds in the style of former GATT Rounds are provided for. Currently, as mentioned above, the so-called Doha Round of Trade Negotiations is taking place, aiming particularly at serving the needs and interests of developing states. In detail, the negotiations focus on improving the access to markets of industrialized countries for developing countries and their exports, which mainly include agricultural goods, foods and textiles. Also, changed perceptions can be taken into account by interpreting or changing existing treaties, adopting new treaties, or by passing resolutions or decisions. By contrast, the dispute settle-

ment system has consciously and expressly been fashioned to carefully clarify and nurture existing rules of law and expressly lacks any powers to actively develop them.

2. Trade in Goods

Due to their long development under GATT, the rules concerning trade in goods, which were largely taken over into the WTO and further expanded are vast and detailed. Here, all the above-mentioned mechanisms and principles are fully developed and regulated. Note must be especially taken of rules concerning technical trade barriers, which should ensure that well-founded protection interests and political settings of member states are not disproportionately hampered. In this context, the Agreement on the Application of Sanitary and Phytosanitary Measures (SPS-Agreement) is of special importance. It allows such measures, but requires that the states using them are able to justify their use by means of a rational assessment of risks. Finally, the Agreement on Technical Barriers to Trade (TBT-Agreement) regulates the validity, recognition and harmonization of technical standards.

3. Intellectual Property

So far, protecting intellectual property has only been dealt with by the *World Intellectual Property Organization* (→ WIPO), but in the view of technologically developed countries this regulation has not met the needs of global trade. The Uruguay Round countered tendencies to unilaterally enforce protection interests through trade sanctions by adopting a new regulation, the TRIPs Agreement. While this agreement was originally drafted to combat trademark piracy and copying, in its present form it contains comprehensive protection standards for copyrights, trademarks, statements of origin, patented designs, patents, the design of computer chips and for company secrets. To a large extent, they are valid alongside existing conventions in this area which were negotiated under the auspices of and are administered by WIPO. In addition, extremely detailed rules concerning the legal protection which states should accord to the owner of the intellectual property right so that he may enforce it, and which go so far as to contain rules about interim measures, are of major significance.

4. Trade in Services

Though the GATT only concerned the trade in goods, the increasing importance of services made it necessary to regulate this area. Due to some differences, this was done in a completely new and separate agreement which has the same structure as the GATT. It rightly follows an extremely demanding approach in that it includes not only cases of transboundary provision of services, but also cases in which a service is provided to a foreigner in the home country of the service provider, or in opposite cases, in which foreigners provide services in the home country of the customer. But at the same time, this approach gives rise to new and complex problems, such as questions concerning immigration law and the right to abode in a foreign country. Also, it is more difficult to negotiate further liberalization in this field. The opening of markets cannot simply be achieved by lowering tariffs, but depends instead on various factors whose value is not easily assessable for the purposes of concessions and consideration. Despite these difficulties, far-reaching and binding liberalization has been achieved in some sectors, including telecommunications and financial services. These have been prescribed in special additional protocols to GATS.

III. New Aspects and Problems

1. From a Trade Order to an Economic Order

It is not infrequent that liberalization and the growing international interdependency of trade lead to new problems which require states to cooperate. The WTO has a voluminous "built-in agen-

da". But it can already be foreseen that additional topics will have to be addressed within the WTO. Working groups are discussing questions of competition policy and investments. Like the TRIPs Agreement and parts of the GATT, these issues lead beyond mere questions of trade. They contain approaches which may broaden the scope of the WTO to include general questions of a global economic order.

2. Environment and Social Standards

The growing interdependency of international trade also raises questions concerning the link between the global economic order and other political areas, especially environmental and social issues. The liberalization of the world's markets needs to be accompanied by international cooperation in order to cope with the environmental consequences of economic growth and the decline in the effectiveness of national policies of protection. The latter results from the fact that, under conditions of open markets, strict environmental policies may threaten domestic industries by import competition from places with less strict standards and might even prompt businesses to shift their activities to other countries. These issues and the role that the WTO plays or should play in this regard have been debated at length and critically. Such discussion has *inter alia* taken place within the WTO Committee on Trade and Environment (CTE). Indeed, while taking on board the principle of sustainable development in the preambular language of its establishing Agreement, the WTO is first and foremost a trade organization. It is very unlikely that it might experience a development similar to the EU, whose mandate has been enlarged over time to cover environment protection and other issues of common concern taking into account the need for common policy-making in view of the development of the single European market. → Environmental protection at international level is – and for the foreseeable future will be – taken care of by the distinct and manifold international agencies and multilateral environmental agreements (MEAs). While, in general, trade regulation and environmental protection can and do co-exist and even may be mutually supportive at international level, conflicts may arise in a small number of cases, where environmental protection seeks to employ trade measures as for instance import bans. As an example, the Cartagena Protocol on Biological Safety – a MEA – may be mentioned, which allows for quite some discretion by states to consider, evaluate and possibly refuse the import of genetically modified organisms. As most experts tend to consider these standards to be more "environmentalist" than relevant WTO standards would allow, a clash may possibly arise in this sensitive area. Unfortunately, to date, in spite of considerable efforts, no lasting and effective links and mechanisms of coordination have been established. Thus possible clashes are very likely to be submitted to WTO dispute settlement, although a purely judicial settlement of this matter appears to be inappropriate. On the other hand, dispute settlement has been helpful in other cases in defining the proper scope of environmental policies under WTO rules. It has been made clear that states have the power to protect people and the environment against the negative impact resulting from the properties of a certain product. On the other hand, the use of trade bans to force other states to agree to certain standards of environmentally sound production methods have been largely considered unlawful, where the products as such are safe.

Low labor costs are a legitimate competitive benefit in the global economic order. But problems arise when these low labor costs are achieved by denying human beings their social rights. At present, the WTO only allows action when prisoners are forced to work. So far, demands to incorporate further social standards into the WTO, such as minimum age, the right to organize in trade unions and collective representation of interests, have not been successful.

3. Outlook

The concept of a world trade order has been impressively strengthened and developed towards a world economic order by the WTO. With its institutional structure and many regulations and issues, the WTO has after almost 50 years taken up many of the ideas of the Havana Charter. Its long-term success will depend on whether it manages to fully acknowledge concerns and needs relating to economic and social development. In this regard, the recent stalemate of the Doha Round must be noted with concern, as is also true for a recent tendency to conclude bilateral and regional agreements on trade or investment, which might put into question the relevance of the WTO. Also, while acknowledging the limited role that the trade system can play in this regard, the WTO certainly needs further to improve its responsiveness in view of developmental, social and environmental concerns.

Peter Tobias Stoll

Lit.: *I. General: Barton, J.R.:* The Evolution of the Trade Regime, Princeton 2006; *Bhala, R.:* World Trade Law, Charlottesville 1998; *Evenett, S.:* Can the WTO rise to the Challenge of Economic Development? In: Aussenwirtschaft 60 (2005), 257-276; *Goldstein, J.L. et al.:* Institutions in international relations: Understanding the Effects of the GATT and the WTO on World Trade, in: IO 61 (2007), 37-67; *Hamel, H.H.R. van (ed.):* The World Trade Organization, The Hague 1997; *Jackson, J.H.:* The World Trading System: Law and Policy of International Economic Relations, 2nd edn., Cambridge, Mass. 1997; *Janow, M.E. (ed.):* The WTO, New York 2008; *Marcrory, P.F. J. (ed.):* The World Trade Organization, Berlin/Heidelberg 2005; *Sampson, G.P.:* The WTO and sustainable development, Tokyo 2005; *Stoll, P.T./Schorkopf F.:* WTO – World Economic Order, World Trade Law, Leiden 2006; *Sutherland, P. et al.:* The Future of the WTO. Addressing institutional challenges in the new millennium. Report by the Consultative Board to the Director-General Su-

pachai Panitchpakdi by Peter Sutherland et al., WTO, Geneva 2004;
II. Particular questions: Berman, J.A.: WTO Law and Developing Countries, New York 2007; *Bernasconi-Osterwalder, N.:* Environment and Trade, London 2006; *Charnovitz, S.:* The WTO's Environmental Progress, in: Journal of International Economic Law 10 (2007) 685-706; *Correa, C.M.:* Trade Related Aspects of Intellectual Property Rights, Oxford 2007; *Gehring, M.W. (ed.):* Sustainable Development in World Trade Law, The Hague 2005; *Grammling, S.:* WTO at a crossroad: the importance of the Doha „development" round, in: Dialogue and Cooperation, No. 1/2007, 33-46; *Hohmann, H. (ed.):* Agreeing and Implementing the Doha Round of the WTO, Cambridge 2007; *Jansen M./Lee E.:* Trade and Employment – Challenges for Policy Research, a Joint Study of the International Labour Office and the Secretariat of the World Trade Organization, Geneva 2007; *Leary, V.A. (ed.):* Social Issues, Globalisation and International Institutions – Labour Rights in the EU, ILO, OECD and WTO, Leiden 2006; *Moore, M.:* Ten Years of the WTO: A Success Story of Global Governance, in: IPG 60 (2005), 12-20; *Petersmann, E.U. (ed.):* International trade law and the GATT/WTO dispute settlement system, London 1997; *Sevilla, C.R.:* 'The WTO Doha Development Agenda', in: Berkeley Journal of International Law 25 (2007), 425-433; *Stoll, P.T.:* How to Overcome the Dichotomy between WTO Rules and MEAs?, in: ZaöRV 62 (2003), 439-458; *Werksman, J.:* The WTO and Sustainable Development, in: Berkeley Journal of International Law 25 (2007), 459-484; *Wolfrum, R./Stoll, T./Kaiser, K. (eds):* Max Planck Commentaries on World Trade Law, Vol. 2: Institutions and Dispute Settlement, Leiden 2006; *Zhao, Y.:* Trade and Environment, in: Columbia Journal of International Law 23 (2007) 41-97; *Zimmermann, G.A.:* WTO dispute settlement at ten. Evolution, experiences and evaluation, in: Aussenwirtschaft 60 (2005), 27-61.

Internet: *WTO Homepage:* www.wto.org; *Legal texts:* www.wto.org/english/docs_e/legal_e/legal_e.htm; *Documents:* www.wto.org/english/docs_e/docs_e.htm

Charter of the United Nations

of June 26, 1945, (Text: UNCIO XV, 335)

as amended by General Assembly Resolution 1991 (XVIII) of 17 December 1963 – in force since 31 August 1965 (UNTS 557, 143), 2101 (XX) of 20 December 1965 – in force since 12 June 1968 (UNTS 638, 308), and 2847 (XXVI) of 20 December 1971 – in force since 24 September 1973 (UNTS 892, 119).

WE THE PEOPLES OF THE UNITED NATIONS DETERMINED

to save succeeding generations from the scourge of war, which twice in our lifetime has brought untold sorrow to mankind, and

to reaffirm faith in fundamental human rights, in the dignity and worth of the human person, in the equal rights of men and women and of nations large and small, and

to establish conditions under which justice and respect for the obligations arising from treaties and other sources of international law can be maintained, and

to promote social progress and better standards of life in larger freedom,

AND FOR THESE ENDS

to practice tolerance and live together in peace with one another as good neighbors, and

to unite our strength to maintain international peace and security, and

to ensure, by the acceptance of principles and the institution of methods, that armed force shall not be used, save in the common interest, and

to employ international machinery for the promotion of the economic and social advancement of all peoples,

HAVE RESOLVED TO COMBINE OUR EFFORTS TO ACCOMPLISH THESE AIMS.

Accordingly, our respective Governments, through representatives assembled in the city of San Francisco, who have exhibited their full powers found to be in good and due form, have agreed to the present Charter of the United Nations and do hereby establish an international organization to be known as the United Nations.

Chapter I
Purposes and Principles

Article 1

The Purposes of the United Nations are:
1. To maintain international peace and security, and to that end: to take effective collective measures for the prevention and removal of threats to the peace, and for the suppression of acts of aggression or other breaches of the peace, and to bring about by peaceful means, and in conformity with the principles of justice and international law, adjustment or settlement of international disputes or situations which might lead to a breach of the peace;
2. To develop friendly relations among nations based on respect for the principle of equal rights and self-determination of peoples, and to take other appropriate measures to strengthen universal peace;
3. To achieve international co-operation in solving international problems of an economic, social, cultural, or humanitarian character, and in promoting and encouraging respect for human rights and for fundamental freedoms for all without distinction as to race, sex, language, or religion; and
4. To be a centre for harmonizing the actions of nations in the attainment of these common ends.

Article 2

The Organization and its Members, in pursuit of the Purposes stated in Article 1, shall act in accordance with the following Principles.
1. The Organization is based on the principle of the sovereign equality of all its Members.
2. All Members, in order to ensure to all of them the rights and benefits resulting from membership, shall fulfil in good faith the obligations assumed by them in accordance with the present Charter.
3. All Members shall settle their international disputes by peaceful means in such a manner that international peace and security, and justice, are not endangered.
4. All Members shall refrain in their international relations from the threat or use of force against the territorial integrity or political independence of any state, or in any other manner inconsistent with the Purposes of the United Nations.
5. All Members shall give the United Nations every assistance in any action it takes in accordance with the present Charter, and

shall refrain from giving assistance to any state against which the United Nations is taking preventive or enforcement action.

6. The Organization shall ensure that states which are not Members of the United Nations act in accordance with these Principles so far as may be necessary for the maintenance of international peace and security.

7. Nothing contained in the present Charter shall authorize the United Nations to intervene in matters which are essentially within the domestic jurisdiction of any state or shall require the Members to submit such matters to settlement under the present Charter; but this principle shall not prejudice the application of enforcement measures under Chapter VII.

Chapter II
Membership

Article 3

The original Members of the United Nations shall be the states which, having participated in the United Nations Conference on International Organization at San Francisco, or having previously signed the Declaration by United Nations of January 1, 1942, sign the present Charter and ratify it in accordance with Article 110.

Article 4

1. Membership in the United Nations is open to all other peace-loving states which accept the obligations contained in the present Charter and, in the judgment of the Organization, are able and willing to carry out these obligations.

2. The admission of any such state to membership in the United Nations will be effected by a decision of the General Assembly upon the recommendation of the Security Council.

Article 5

A Member of the United Nations against which preventive or enforcement action has been taken by the Security Council may be suspended from the exercise of the rights and privileges of membership by the General Assembly upon the recommendation of the Security Council. The exercise of these rights and privileges may be restored by the Security Council.

Article 6

A Member of the United Nations which has persistently violated the Principles contained in the present Charter may be expelled from the Organization by the General Assembly upon the recommendation of the Security Council.

Chapter III
Organs

Article 7

1. There are established as the principal organs of the United Nations: a General Assembly, a Security Council, an Economic and Social Council, a Trusteeship Council, an International Court of Justice, and a Secretariat.

2. Such subsidiary organs as may be found necessary may be established in accordance with the present Charter.

Article 8

The United Nations shall place no restrictions on the eligibility of men and women to participate in any capacity and under conditions of equality in its principal and subsidiary organs.

Chapter IV
The General Assembly

Composition

Article 9

1. The General Assembly shall consist of all the Members of the United Nations.

2. Each Member shall have not more than five representatives in the General Assembly.

Functions and Powers

Article 10

The General Assembly may discuss any questions or any matters within the scope of the present Charter or relating to the powers and functions of any organs provided for in the present Charter, and, except as provided in Article 12, may make recommendations to the Members of the United Nations or to the Security Council or to both on any such questions or matters.

Article 11

1. The General Assembly may consider the general principles of co-operation in the maintenance of international peace and security, including the principles governing disarmament and the regulation of armaments, and may make recommendations with regard to such principles to the Members or to the Security Council or to both.

2. The General Assembly may discuss any questions relating to the maintenance of international peace and security brought before it by any Member of the United Nations, or by the Security Council, or by a state which is not a Member of the United Nations in accordance with Article 35, paragraph 2, and, except as provided in Article 12, may make recommendations with regard to any such questions to the state or states concerned or to the Security Council or to both. Any such question on which action is necessary shall be referred to the Security Council by the General Assembly either before or after discussion.

3. The General Assembly may call the attention of the Security Council to situations which are likely to endanger international peace and security.

4. The powers of the General Assembly set forth in this Article shall not limit the general scope of Article 10.

Article 12

1. While the Security Council is exercising in respect of any dispute or situation the functions assigned to it in the present Charter, the General Assembly shall not make any recommendation with regard to that dispute or situation unless the Security Council so requests.

2. The Secretary-General, with the consent of the Security Council, shall notify the General Assembly at each session of any matters relative to the maintenance of international peace and security which are being dealt with by the Security Council and shall similarly notify the General Assembly, or the Members of the United Nations if the General Assembly is not in session, immediately the Security Council ceases to deal with such matters.

Article 13

1. The General Assembly shall initiate studies and make recommendations for the purpose of:
(a) promoting international co-operation in the political field and encouraging the pro-

gressive development of international law and its codification;
(b) promoting international co-operation in the economic, social, cultural, educational, and health fields, and assisting in the realization of human rights and fundamental freedoms for all without distinction as to race, sex, language, or religion.

2. The further responsibilities, functions and powers of the General Assembly with respect to matters mentioned in paragraph 1 (b) above are set forth in Chapters IX and X.

Article 14

Subject to the provisions of Article 12, the General Assembly may recommend measures for the peaceful adjustment of any situation, regardless of origin, which it deems likely to impair the general welfare or friendly relations among nations, including situations resulting from a violation of the provisions of the present Charter setting forth the Purposes and Principles of the United Nations.

Article 15

1. The General Assembly shall receive and consider annual and special reports from the Security Council; these reports shall include an account of the measures that the Security Council has decided upon or taken to maintain international peace and security.

2. The General Assembly shall receive and consider reports from the other organs of the United Nations.

Article 16

The General Assembly shall perform such functions with respect to the international trusteeship system as are assigned to it under Chapters XII and XIII, including the approval of the trusteeship agreements for areas not designated as strategic.

Article 17

1. The General Assembly shall consider and approve the budget of the Organization.

2. The expenses of the Organization shall be borne by the Members as apportioned by the General Assembly.

3. The General Assembly shall consider and approve any financial and budgetary arrangements with specialized agencies referred to in Article 57 and shall examine the administrative budgets of such specialized agencies with a view to making recommendations to the agencies concerned.

Voting

Article 18

1. Each member of the General Assembly shall have one vote.

2. Decisions of the General Assembly on important questions shall be made by a two-thirds majority of the members present and voting. These questions shall include: recommendations with respect to the maintenance of international peace and security, the election of the non-permanent members of the Security Council, the election of the members of the Economic and Social Council, the election of members of the Trusteeship Council in accordance with paragraph 1 (c) of Article 86, the admission of new Members to the United Nations, the suspension of the rights and privileges of membership, the expulsion of Members, questions relating to the operation of the trusteeship system, and budgetary questions.

3. Decisions on other questions, including the determination of additional categories of questions to be decided by a two-thirds majority, shall be made by a majority of the members present and voting.

Article 19

A Member of the United Nations which is in arrears in the payment of its financial contributions to the Organization shall have no vote in the General Assembly if the amount of its arrears equals or exceeds the amount of the contributions due from it for the preceding two full years. The General Assembly may, nevertheless, permit such a Member to vote if it is satisfied that the failure to pay is due to conditions beyond the control of the Member.

Procedure

Article 20

The General Assembly shall meet in regular annual sessions and in such special sessions as occasion may require. Special sessions shall be convoked by the Secretary-General at the request of the Security Council or of a majority of the Members of the United Nations.

Article 21

The General Assembly shall adopt its own rules of procedure. It shall elect its President for each session.

Article 22

The General Assembly may establish such subsidiary organs as it deems necessary for the performance of its functions.

Chapter V
The Security Council

Composition

Article 23

1. The Security Council shall consist of fifteen Members of the United Nations. The Republic of China, France, the Union of Soviet Socialist Republics, the United Kingdom of Great Britain and Northern Ireland, and the United States of America shall be permanent members of the Security Council. The General Assembly shall elect ten other Members of the United Nations to be non-permanent members of the Security Council, due regard being specially paid, in the first instance to the contribution of Members of the United Nations to the maintenance of international peace and security and to the other purposes of the Organization, and also to equitable geographical distribution.

2. The non-permanent members of the Security Council shall be elected for a term of two years. In the first election of the non-permanent members after the increase of the membership of the Security Council from eleven to fifteen, two of the four additional members shall be chosen for a term of one year. A retiring member shall not be eligible for immediate re-election.

3. Each member of the Security Council shall have one representative.

Functions and Powers

Article 24

1. In order to ensure prompt and effective action by the United Nations, its Members confer on the Security Council primary responsibility for the maintenance of international peace and security, and agree that in carrying out its duties under this responsibility the Security Council acts on their behalf.

2. In discharging these duties the Security Council shall act in accordance with the Purposes and Principles of the United Nations. The specific powers granted to the Security Council for the discharge of these duties are laid down in Chapters VI, VII, VIII, and XII.

3. The Security Council shall submit annual and, when necessary, special reports to the General Assembly for its consideration.

Article 25

The Members of the United Nations agree to accept and carry out the decisions of the Security Council in accordance with the present Charter.

Article 26

In order to promote the establishment and maintenance of international peace and security with the least diversion for armaments of the world's human and economic resources, the Security Council shall be responsible for formulating, with the assistance of the Military Staff Committee referred to in Article 47, plans to be submitted to the Members of the United Nations for the establishment of a system for the regulation of armaments.

Voting

Article 27

1. Each member of the Security Council shall have one vote.

2. Decisions of the Security Council on procedural matters shall be made by an affirmative vote of nine members.

3. Decisions of the Security Council on all other matters shall be made by an affirmative vote of nine members including the concurring votes of the permanent members; provided that, in decisions under Chapter VI, and under paragraph 3 of Article 52, a party to a dispute shall abstain from voting.

Procedure

Article 28

1. The Security Council shall be so organized as to be able to function continuously. Each member of the Security Council shall for this purpose be represented at all times at the seat of the Organization.

2. The Security Council shall hold periodic meetings at which each of its members may, if it so desires, be represented by a member of the government or by some other specially designated representative.

3. The Security Council may hold meetings at such places other than the seat of the Organization as in its judgment will best facilitate its work.

Article 29

The Security Council may establish such subsidiary organs as it deems necessary for the performance of its functions.

Article 30

The Security Council shall adopt its own rules of procedure, including the method of selecting its President.

Article 31

Any Member of the United Nations which is not a member of the Security Council may participate, without vote, in the discussion of any question brought before the Security Council whenever the latter considers that the interests of that Member are specially affected.

Article 32

Any Member of the United Nations which is not a member of the Security Council or any state which is not a Member of the United Nations, if it is a party to a dispute under consideration by the Security Council, shall be invited to participate, without vote, in the discussion relating to the dispute. The Security Council shall lay down such conditions as it deems just for the participation of a state which is not a Member of the United Nations.

Chapter VI
Pacific Settlement of Disputes

Article 33

1. The parties to any dispute, the continuance of which is likely to endanger the maintenance of international peace and security, shall, first of all, seek a solution by negotiation, enquiry, mediation, conciliation, arbitration, judicial settlement, resort to regional agencies or arrangements, or other peaceful means of their own choice.

2. The Security Council shall, when it deems necessary, call upon the parties to settle their dispute by such means.

Article 34

The Security Council may investigate any dispute, or any situation which might lead to international friction or give rise to a dispute, in order to determine whether the continuance of the dispute or situation is likely to endanger the maintenance of international peace and security.

Article 35

1. Any Member of the United Nations may bring any dispute, or any situation of the nature referred to in Article 34, to the attention of the Security Council or of the General Assembly.
2. A state which is not a Member of the United Nations may bring to the attention of the Security Council or of the General Assembly any dispute to which it is a party if it accepts in advance, for the purposes of the dispute, the obligations of pacific settlement provided in the present Charter.
3. The proceedings of the General Assembly in respect of matters brought to its attention under this Article will be subject to the provisions of Articles 11 and 12.

Article 36

1. The Security Council may, at any stage of a dispute of the nature referred to in Article 33 or of a situation of like nature, recommend appropriate procedures or methods of adjustment.
2. The Security Council should take into consideration any procedures for the settlement of the dispute which have already been adopted by the parties.
3. In making recommendations under this Article the Security Council should also take into consideration that legal disputes should as a general rule be referred by the parties to the International Court of Justice in accordance with the provisions of the Statute of the Court.

Article 37

1. Should the parties to a dispute of the nature referred to in Article 33 fail to settle it by the means indicated in that Article, they shall refer it to the Security Council.
2. If the Security Council deems that the continuance of the dispute is in fact likely to endanger the maintenance of international peace and security, it shall decide whether to take action under Article 36 or to recommend such terms of settlement as it may consider appropriate.

Article 38

Without prejudice to the provisions of Articles 33 to 37, the Security Council may, if all the parties to any dispute so request, make recommendations to the parties with a view to a pacific settlement of the dispute.

Chapter VII
Action with the Respect to Threats to the Peace, Breaches of the Peace, and Acts of Aggression

Article 39

The Security Council shall determine the existence of any threat to the peace, breach of the peace, or act of aggression and shall make recommendations, or decide what measures shall be taken in accordance with Articles 41 and 42, to maintain or restore international peace and security.

Article 40

In order to prevent an aggravation of the situation, the Security Council may, before making the recommendations or deciding upon the measures provided for in Article 39, call upon the parties concerned to comply with such provisional measures as it deems necessary or desirable. Such provisional measures shall be without prejudice to the rights, claims, or position of the parties concerned. The Security Council shall duly take account of failure to comply with such provisional measures.

Article 41

The Security Council may decide what measures not involving the use of armed force are to be employed to give effect to its decisions, and it may call upon the Members of the United Nations to apply such measures. These may include complete or partial interruption of economic relations and of rail, sea, air, postal, telegraphic, radio, and other means of communication, and the severance of diplomatic relations.

Article 42

Should the Security Council consider that measures provided for in Article 41 would be inadequate or have proved to be inadequate, it may take such action by air, sea, or land forces as may be necessary to maintain or restore international peace and security. Such action may include demonstrations, blockade, and other operations by air, sea, or land forces of Members of the United Nations.

Article 43

1. All Members of the United Nations, in order to contribute to the maintenance of international peace and security, undertake to make available to the Security Council, on its call and in accordance with a special agreement or agreements, armed forces, assistance, and facilities, including rights of passage, necessary for the purpose of maintaining international peace and security.
2. Such agreement or agreements shall govern the numbers and types of forces, their degree of readiness and general location, and the nature of the facilities and assistance to be provided.
3. The agreement or agreements shall be negotiated as soon as possible on the initiative of the Security Council. They shall be concluded between the Security Council and Members or between the Security Council and groups of Members and shall be subject to ratification by the signatory states in accordance with their respective constitutional processes.

Article 44

When the Security Council has decided to use force it shall, before calling upon a Member not represented on it to provide armed forces in fulfillment of the obligations assumed under Article 43, invite that Member, if the Member so desires, to participate in the decisions of the Security Council concerning the employment of contingents of that Member's armed forces.

Article 45

In order to enable the United Nations to take urgent military measures, Members shall hold immediately available national air-force contingents for combined international enforcement action. The strength and degree of readiness of these contingents and plans for their combined action shall be determined within the limits laid down in the special agreement or agreements referred to in Article 43, by the Security Council with the assistance of the Military Staff Committee.

Article 46

Plans for the application of armed force shall be made by the Security Council with the assistance of the Military Staff Committee.

Article 47

1. There shall be established a Military Staff Committee to advise and assist the Security Council on all questions relating to the Security Council's military requirements for the maintenance of international peace and security, the employment and command of forces placed at its disposal, the regulation of armaments, and possible disarmament.
2. The Military Staff Committee shall consist of the Chiefs of Staff of the permanent members of the Security Council or their representatives. Any Member of the United Nations not permanently represented on the Committee shall be invited by the Committee to be associated with it when the efficient discharge of the Committee's responsibilities requires the participation of that Member in its work.
3. The Military Staff Committee shall be responsible under the Security Council for the strategic direction of any armed forces placed at the disposal of the Security Council. Questions relating to the command of such forces shall be worked out subsequently.
4. The Military Staff Committee, with the authorization of the Security Council and after consultation with appropriate regional agencies, may establish regional sub-committees.

Article 48

1. The action required to carry out the decisions of the Security Council for the maintenance of international peace and security shall be taken by all the Members of the United Nations or by some of them, as the Security Council may determine.
2. Such decisions shall be carried out by the Members of the United Nations directly and through their action in the appropriate international agencies of which they are members.

Article 49

The Members of the United Nations shall join in affording mutual assistance in carrying out the measures decided upon by the Security Council.

Article 50

If preventive or enforcement measures against any state are taken by the Security Council, any other state, whether a Member of the United Nations or not, which finds itself confronted with special economic problems arising from the carrying out of those measures shall have the right to consult the Security Council with regard to a solution of those problems.

Article 51

Nothing in the present Charter shall impair the inherent right of individual or collective self-defense if an armed attack occurs against a Member of the United Nations, until the Security Council has taken measures necessary to maintain international peace and security. Measures taken by Members in the exercise of this right of self-defense shall be immediately reported to the Security Council and shall not in any way affect the authority and responsibility of the Security Council under the present Charter to take at any time such action as it deems necessary in order to maintain or restore international peace and security.

Chapter VIII
Regional Arrangements

Article 52

1. Nothing in the present Charter precludes the existence of regional arrangements or agencies for dealing with such matters relating to the maintenance of international peace and security as are appropriate for regional action provided that such arrangements or agencies and their activities are consistent with the Purposes and Principles of the United Nations.
2. The Members of the United Nations entering into such arrangements or constituting such agencies shall make every effort to achieve pacific settlement of local disputes through such regional arrangements or by such regional agencies before referring them to the Security Council.
3. The Security Council shall encourage the development of pacific settlement of local disputes through such regional arrangements or by such regional agencies either on the initiative of the states concerned or by reference from the Security Council.
4. This Article in no way impairs the application of Articles 34 and 35.

Article 53

1. The Security Council shall, where appropriate, utilize such regional arrangements or agencies for enforcement action under its authority. But no enforcement action shall be taken under regional arrangements or by regional agencies without the authorization of the Security Council, with the exception of measures against any enemy state, as defined in paragraph 2 of this Article, provided for pursuant to Article 107 or in regional arrangements directed against renewal of aggressive policy on the part of any such state, until such time as the Organization may, on request of the Governments concerned, be charged with the responsibility for preventing further aggression by such a state.
2. The term enemy state as used in paragraph 1 of this Article applies to any state which during the Second World War has been an enemy of any signatory of the present Charter.

Article 54

The Security Council shall at all times be kept fully informed of activities undertaken or in contemplation under regional arrangements or by regional agencies for the maintenance of international peace and security.

Chapter IX
International economic and social co-operation

Article 55

With a view to the creation of conditions of stability and well-being which are necessary for peaceful and friendly relations among nations based on respect for the principle of equal rights and self-determination of peoples, the United Nations shall promote:
a) higher standards of living, full employment, and conditions of economic and social progress and development;
b) solutions of international economic, social, health, and related problems; and international cultural and educational cooperation; and
c) universal respect for, and observance of, human rights and fundamental freedoms for all without distinction as to race, sex, language, or religion.

Article 56

All Members pledge themselves to take joint and separate action in co-operation with the

Organization for the achievement of the purposes set forth in Article 55.

Article 57

1. The various specialized agencies, established by intergovernmental agreement and having wide international responsibilities, as defined in their basic instruments, in economic, social, cultural, educational, health, and related fields, shall be brought into relationship with the United Nations in accordance with the provisions of Article 63.

2. Such agencies thus brought into relationship with the United Nations are hereinafter referred to as specialized agencies.

Article 58

The Organization shall make recommendations for the co-ordination of the policies and activities of the specialized agencies.

Article 59

The Organization shall, where appropriate, initiate negotiations among the states concerned for the creation of any new specialized agencies required for the accomplishment of the purposes set forth in Article 55.

Article 60

Responsibility for the discharge of the functions of the Organization set forth in this Chapter shall be vested in the General Assembly and, under the authority of the General Assembly, in the Economic and Social Council, which shall have for this purpose the powers set forth in Chapter X.

**Chapter X
The Economic and Social Council**

Composition

Article 61

1. The Economic and Social Council shall consist of fifty-four Members of the United Nations elected by the General Assembly.

2. Subject to the provisions of paragraph 3, eighteen members of the Economic and Social Council shall be elected each year for a term of three years. A retiring member shall be eligible for immediate re-election.

3. At the first election after the increase in the membership of the Economic and Social Council from twenty-seven to fifty-four members, in addition to the members elected in place of the nine members whose term of office expires at the end of that year, twenty-seven additional members shall be elected. Of these twenty-seven additional members, the term of office of nine members so elected shall expire at the end of one year, and of nine other members at the end of two years, in accordance with arrangements made by the General Assembly.

4. Each member of the Economic and Social Council shall have one representative.

Functions and Powers

Article 62

1. The Economic and Social Council may make or initiate studies and reports with respect to international economic, social, cultural, educational, health, and related matters and may make recommendations with respect to any such matters to the General Assembly to the Members of the United Nations, and to the specialized agencies concerned.

2. It may make recommendations for the purpose of promoting respect for, and observance of, human rights and fundamental freedoms for all.

3. It may prepare draft conventions for submission to the General Assembly, with respect to matters falling within its competence.

4. It may call, in accordance with the rules prescribed by the United Nations, international conferences on matters falling within its competence.

Article 63

1. The Economic and Social Council may enter into agreements with any of the agencies referred to in Article 57, defining the terms on which the agency concerned shall be brought into relationship with the United Nations. Such agreements shall be subject to approval by the General Assembly.

2. It may co-ordinate the activities of the specialized agencies through consultation with and recommendations to such agencies and through recommendations to the General Assembly and to the Members of the United Nations.

Article 64

1. The Economic and Social Council may take appropriate steps to obtain regular reports from the specialized agencies. It may make arrangements with the Members of the United Nations and with the specialized agencies to obtain reports on the steps taken to give effect to its own recommendations and to recommendations on matters falling within its competence made by the General Assembly.
2. It may communicate its observations on these reports to the General Assembly.

Article 65

The Economic and Social Council may furnish information to the Security Council and shall assist the Security Council upon its request.

Article 66

1. The Economic and Social Council shall perform such functions as fall within its competence in connection with the carrying out of the recommendations of the General Assembly.
2. It may, with the approval of the General Assembly, perform services at the request of Members of the United Nations and at the request of specialized agencies.
3. It shall perform such other functions as are specified elsewhere in the present Charter or as may be assigned to it by the General Assembly.

Voting

Article 67

1. Each member of the Economic and Social Council shall have one vote.
2. Decisions of the Economic and Social Council shall be made by a majority of the members present and voting.

Procedure

Article 68

The Economic and Social Council shall set up commissions in economic and social fields and for the promotion of human rights, and such other commissions as may be required for the performance of its functions.

Article 69

The Economic and Social Council shall invite any Member of the United Nations to participate, without vote, in its deliberations on any matter of particular concern to that Member.

Article 70

The Economic and Social Council may make arrangements for representatives of the specialized agencies to participate, without vote, in its deliberations and in those of the commissions established by it, and for its representatives to participate in the deliberations of the specialized agencies.

Article 71

The Economic and Social Council may make suitable arrangements for consultation with non-governmental organizations which are concerned with matters within its competence. Such arrangements may be made with international organizations and, where appropriate, with national organizations after consultation with the Member of the United Nations concerned.

Article 72

1. The Economic and Social Council shall adopt its own rules of procedure, including the method of selecting its President.
2. The Economic and Social Council shall meet as required in accordance with its rules, which shall include provision for the convening of meetings on the request of a majority of its members.

Chapter XI
Declaration Regarding Non-self-governing Territories

Article 73

Members of the United Nations which have or assume responsibilities for the administration of territories whose peoples have not yet attained a full measure of self-government recognize the principle that the interests of the inhabitants of these territories are paramount, and accept as a sacred trust the obligation to promote to the utmost, within the system of international peace and security established by the present Charter, the well-being of the inhabitants of these territories, and, to this end:

a) to ensure, with due respect for the culture of the peoples concerned, their political, economic, social, and educational advancement, their just treatment, and their protection against abuses;
b) to develop self-government, to take due account of the political aspirations of the peoples, and to assist them in the progressive development of their free political institutions, according to the particular circumstances of each territory and its peoples and their varying stages of advancement;
c) to further international peace and security;
d) to promote constructive measures of development, to encourage research, and to cooperate with one another and, when and where appropriate, with specialized international bodies with a view to the practical achievement of the social, economic, and scientific purposes set forth in this Article; and
e) to transmit regularly to the Secretary-General for information purposes, subject to such limitation as security and constitutional considerations may require, statistical and other information of a technical nature relating to economic, social, and educational conditions in the territories for which they are respectively responsible other than those territories to which Chapters XII and XIII apply.

Article 74

Members of the United Nations also agree that their policy in respect of the territories to which this Chapter applies, no less than in respect of their metropolitan areas, must be based on the general principle of good-neighborliness, due account being taken of the interests and well-being of the rest of the world, in social, economic, and commercial matters.

Chapter XII
International Trusteeship System

Article 75

The United Nations shall establish under its authority an international trusteeship system for the administration and supervision of such territories as may be placed thereunder by subsequent individual agreements. These territories are hereinafter referred to as trust territories.

Article 76

The basic objectives of the trusteeship system, in accordance with the Purposes of the United Nations laid down in Article 1 of the present Charter, shall be:
a) to further international peace and security;
b) to promote the political, economic, social, and educational advancement of the inhabitants of the trust territories, and their progressive development towards self-government or independence as may be appropriate to the particular circumstances of each territory and its peoples and the freely expressed wishes of the peoples concerned, and as may be provided by the terms of each trusteeship agreement;
c) to encourage respect for human rights and for fundamental freedoms for all without distinction as to race, sex, language, or religion, and to encourage recognition of the interdependence of the peoples of the world; and
d) to ensure equal treatment in social, economic, and commercial matters for all Members of the United Nations and their nationals, and also equal treatment for the latter in the administration of justice, without prejudice to the attainment of the foregoing objectives and subject to the provisions of Article 80.

Article 77

1. The trusteeship system shall apply to such territories in the following categories as may be placed thereunder by means of trusteeship agreements:
a) territories now held under mandate;
b) territories which may be detached from enemy states as a result of the Second World War; and
c) territories voluntarily placed under the system by states responsible for their administration.
2. It will be a matter for subsequent agreement as to which territories in the foregoing categories will be brought under the trusteeship system and upon what terms.

Article 78

The trusteeship system shall not apply to territories which have become Members of the United Nations, relationship among which shall be based on respect for the principle of sovereign equality.

Article 79

The terms of trusteeship for each territory to be placed under the trusteeship system, including any alteration or amendment, shall be agreed upon by the states directly concerned, including the mandatory power in the case of territories held under mandate by a Member of the United Nations, and shall be approved as provided for in Articles 83 and 85.

Article 80

1. Except as may be agreed upon in individual trusteeship agreements, made under Articles 77, 79, and 81, placing each territory under the trusteeship system, and until such agreements have been concluded, nothing in this Chapter shall be construed in or of itself to alter in any manner the rights whatsoever of any states or any peoples or the terms of existing international instruments to which Members of the United Nations may respectively be parties.

2. Paragraph 1 of this Article shall not be interpreted as giving grounds for delay or postponement of the negotiation and conclusion of agreements for placing mandated and other territories under the trusteeship system as provided for in Article 77.

Article 81

The trusteeship agreement shall in each case include the terms under which the trust territory will be administered and designate the authority which will exercise the administration of the trust territory. Such authority, hereinafter called the administering authority, may be one or more states or the Organization itself.

Article 82

There may be designated, in any trusteeship agreement, a strategic area or areas which may include part or all of the trust territory to which the agreement applies, without prejudice to any special agreement or agreements made under Article 43.

Article 83

1. All functions of the United Nations relating to strategic areas, including the approval of the terms of the trusteeship agreements and of their alteration or amendment shall be exercised by the Security Council.

2. The basic objectives set forth in Article 76 shall be applicable to the people of each strategic area.

3. The Security Council shall, subject to the provisions of the trusteeship agreements and

without prejudice to security considerations, avail itself of the assistance of the Trusteeship Council to perform those functions of the United Nations under the trusteeship system relating to political, economic, social, and educational matters in the strategic areas.

Article 84

It shall be the duty of the administering authority to ensure that the trust territory shall play its part in the maintenance of international peace and security. To this end the administering authority may make use of volunteer forces, facilities, and assistance from the trust territory in carrying out the obligations towards the Security Council undertaken in this regard by the administering authority, as well as for local defense and the maintenance of law and order within the trust territory.

Article 85

1. The functions of the United Nations with regard to trusteeship agreements for all areas not designated as strategic, including the approval of the terms of the trusteeship agreements and of their alteration or amendment, shall be exercised by the General Assembly.

2. The Trusteeship Council, operating under the authority of the General Assembly shall assist the General Assembly in carrying out these functions.

**Chapter XIII
The Trusteeship Council**

Composition

Article 86

1. The Trusteeship Council shall consist of the following Members of the United Nations:

a) those Members administering trust territories;

b) such of those Members mentioned by name in Article 23 as are not administering trust territories; and

c) as many other Members elected for three-year terms by the General Assembly as may be necessary to ensure that the total number of members of the Trusteeship Council is equally divided between those Members of the United Nations which administer trust territories and those which do not.

2. Each member of the Trusteeship Council shall designate one specially qualified person to represent it therein.

Functions and Powers

Article 87

The General Assembly and, under its authority, the Trusteeship Council, in carrying out their functions, may:
a) consider reports submitted by the administering authority;
b) accept petitions and examine them in consultation with the administering authority;
c) provide for periodic visits to the respective trust territories at times agreed upon with the administering authority; and
d) take these and other actions in conformity with the terms of the trusteeship agreements.

Article 88

The Trusteeship Council shall formulate a questionnaire on the political, economic, social, and educational advancement of the inhabitants of each trust territory, and the administering authority for each trust territory within the competence of the General Assembly shall make an annual report to the General Assembly upon the basis of such questionnaire.

Voting

Article 89

1. Each member of the Trusteeship Council shall have one vote.
2. Decisions of the Trusteeship Council shall be made by a majority of the members present and voting.

Procedure

Article 90

1. The Trusteeship Council shall adopt its own rules of procedure, including the method of selecting its President.
2. The Trusteeship Council shall meet as required in accordance with its rules, which shall include provision for the convening of meetings on the request of a majority of its members.

Article 91

The Trusteeship Council shall, when appropriate, avail itself of the assistance of the Economic and Social Council and of the specialized agencies in regard to matters with which they are respectively concerned.

Chapter XIV
The International Court of Justice

Article 92

The International Court of Justice shall be the principal judicial organ of the United Nations. It shall function in accordance with the annexed Statute, which is based upon the Statute of the Permanent Court of International Justice and forms an integral part of the present Charter.

Article 93

1. All Members of the United Nations are *ipso facto* parties to the Statute of the International Court of Justice.
2. A state which is not a Member of the United Nations may become a party to the Statute of the International Court of Justice on conditions to be determined in each case by the General Assembly upon the recommendation of the Security Council.

Article 94

1. Each Member of the United Nations undertakes to comply with the decision of the International Court of Justice in any case to which it is a party.
2. If any party to a case fails to perform the obligations incumbent upon it under a judgment rendered by the Court, the other party may have recourse to the Security Council, which may, if it deems necessary, make recommendations or decide upon measures to be taken to give effect to the judgment.

Article 95

Nothing in the present Charter shall prevent Members of the United Nations from entrusting the solution of their differences to other tribunals by virtue of agreements already in existence or which may be concluded in the future.

Article 96

1. The General Assembly or the Security Council may request the International Court of Justice to give an advisory opinion on any legal question.

2. Other organs of the United Nations and specialized agencies, which may at any time be so authorized by the General Assembly, may also request advisory opinions of the Court on legal questions arising within the scope of their activities.

Chapter XV
The Secretariat

Article 97

The Secretariat shall comprise a Secretary-General and such staff as the Organization may require. The Secretary-General shall be appointed by the General Assembly upon the recommendation of the Security Council. He shall be the chief administrative officer of the Organization.

Article 98

The Secretary-General shall act in that capacity in all meetings of the General Assembly, of the Security Council, of the Economic and Social Council, and of the Trusteeship Council, and shall perform such other functions as are entrusted to him by these organs. The Secretary-General shall make an annual report to the General Assembly on the work of the Organization.

Article 99

The Secretary-General may bring to the attention of the Security Council any matter which in his opinion may threaten the maintenance of international peace and security.

Article 100

1. In the performance of their duties the Secretary-General and the staff shall not seek or receive instructions from any government or from any other authority external to the Organization. They shall refrain from any action which might reflect on their position as international officials responsible only to the Organization.
2. Each Member of the United Nations undertakes to respect the exclusively international character of the responsibilities of the Secretary-General and the staff and not to seek to influence them in the discharge of their responsibilities.

Article 101

1. The staff shall be appointed by the Secretary-General under regulations established by the General Assembly.

2. Appropriate staffs shall be permanently assigned to the Economic and Social Council, the Trusteeship Council, and, as required, to other organs of the United Nations. These staffs shall form a part of the Secretariat.
3. The paramount consideration in the employment of the staff and in the determination of the conditions of service shall be the necessity of securing the highest standards of efficiency, competence, and integrity. Due regard shall be paid to the importance of recruiting the staff on as wide a geographical basis as possible.

Chapter XVI
Miscellaneous Provisions

Article 102

1. Every treaty and every international agreement entered into by any Member of the United Nations after the present Charter comes into force shall as soon as possible be registered with the Secretariat and published by it.
2. No party to any such treaty or international agreement which has not been registered in accordance with the provisions of paragraph 1 of this Article may invoke that treaty or agreement before any organ of the United Nations.

Article 103

In the event of a conflict between the obligations of the Members of the United Nations under the present Charter and their obligations under any other international agreement, their obligations under the present Charter shall prevail.

Article 104

The Organization shall enjoy in the territory of each of its Members such legal capacity as may be necessary for the exercise of its functions and the fulfillment of its purposes.

Article 105

1. The Organization shall enjoy in the territory of each of its Members such privileges and immunities as are necessary for the fulfillment of its purposes.

2. Representatives of the Members of the United Nations and officials of the Organization shall similarly enjoy such privileges and immunities as are necessary for the independent exercise of their functions in connection with the Organization.

3. The General Assembly may make recommendations with a view to determining the details of the application of paragraphs 1 and 2 of this Article or may propose conventions to the Members of the United Nations for this purpose.

Chapter XVII
Transitional Security Arrangements

Article 106

Pending the coming into force of such special agreements referred to in Article 43 as in the opinion of the Security Council enable it to begin the exercise of its responsibilities under Article 42, the parties to the Four-Nation Declaration, signed at Moscow, 30 October 1943, and France, shall, in accordance with the provisions of paragraph 5 of that Declaration, consult with one another and as occasion requires with other Members of the United Nations with a view to such joint action on behalf of the Organization as may be necessary for the purpose of maintaining international peace and security.

Article 107

Nothing in the present Charter shall invalidate or preclude action, in relation to any state which during the Second World War has been an enemy of any signatory to the present Charter, taken or authorized as a result of that war by the Governments having responsibility for such action.

Chapter XVIII
Amendments

Article 108

Amendments to the present Charter shall come into force for all Members of the United Nations when they have been adopted by a vote of two thirds of the members of the General Assembly and ratified in accordance with their respective constitutional processes by two thirds of the Members of

the United Nations, including all the permanent members of the Security Council.

Article 109

1. A General Conference of the Members of the United Nations for the purpose of reviewing the present Charter may be held at a date and place to be fixed by a two-thirds vote of the members of the General Assembly and by a vote of any nine members of the Security Council. Each Member of the United Nations shall have one vote in the conference.

2. Any alteration of the present Charter recommended by a two-thirds vote of the conference shall take effect when ratified in accordance with their respective constitutional processes by two thirds of the Members of the United Nations including all the permanent members of the Security Council.

3. If such a conference has not been held before the tenth annual session of the General Assembly following the coming into force of the present Charter, the proposal to call such a conference shall be placed on the agenda of that session of the General Assembly, and the conference shall be held if so decided by a majority vote of the members of the General Assembly and by a vote of any seven members of the Security Council.

Chapter XIX
Ratification and Signature

Article 110

1. The present Charter shall be ratified by the signatory states in accordance with their respective constitutional processes.

2. The ratifications shall be deposited with the Government of the United States of America, which shall notify all the signatory states of each deposit as well as the Secretary-General of the Organization when he has been appointed.

3. The present Charter shall come into force upon the deposit of ratifications by the Republic of China, France, the Union of Soviet Socialist Republics, the United Kingdom of Great Britain and Northern Ireland, and the United States of America, and by a majority of the other signatory states. A protocol of the ratifications deposited shall thereupon be drawn up by the Government of the United States of America which shall communicate copies thereof to all the signatory states.

4. The states signatory to the present Charter which ratify it after it has come into force will become original Members of the United Nations on the date of the deposit of their respective ratifications.

Article 111
The present Charter, of which the Chinese, French, Russian, English, and Spanish texts are equally authentic, shall remain deposited in the archives of the Government of the United States of America. Duly certified copies thereof shall be transmitted by that Government to the Governments of the other signatory states.

IN FAITH WHEREOF the representatives of the Governments of the United Nations have signed the present Charter.

DONE at the city of San Francisco the twenty-sixth day of June, one thousand nine hundred and forty-five.

membership of the Economic and Social Council from eighteen to twenty-seven. The subsequent amendment to that Article, which entered into force on 24 September 1973, further increased the membership of the Council from twenty-seven to fifty-four.

The amendment to Article 109, which relates to the first paragraph of that Article, provides that a General Conference of Member States for the purpose of reviewing the Charter may be held at a date and place to be fixed by a two-thirds vote of the members of the General Assembly and by a vote of any nine members (formerly seven) of the Security Council. Paragraph 3 of Article 109, which deals with the consideration of a possible review conference during the tenth regular session of the General Assembly, has been retained in its original form in its reference to a "vote of any seven members of the Security Council", the paragraph having been acted upon in 1955 by the General Assembly, at its tenth regular session, and by the Security Council.

NOTE

The Charter of the United Nations was signed on 26 June 1945, in San Francisco, at the conclusion of the United Nations Conference on International Organization, and came into force on 24 October 1945.

Amendments to Articles 23, 27 and 61 of the Charter were adopted by the General Assembly on 17 December 1963 and came into force on 31 August 1965. A further amendment to Article 61 was adopted by the General Assembly on 20 December 1971, and came into force on 24 September 1973. An amendment to Article 109, adopted by the General Assembly on 20 December 1965, came into force on 12 June 1968.

The amendment to Article 23 enlarges the membership of the Security Council from eleven to fifteen. The amended Article 27 provides that decisions of the Security Council on procedural matters shall be made by an affirmative vote of nine members (formerly seven) and on all other matters by an affirmative vote of nine members (formerly seven), including the concurring votes of the five permanent members of the Security Council.

The amendment to Article 61, which entered into force on 31 August 1965, enlarged the

926

List of the Member States of the United Nations
(with dates on which they joined the Organization)

Member States (in alphabetical order)	Date of Admission
Afghanistan	19 November 1946
Albania	14 December 1955
Algeria	8 October 1962
Andorra	28 July 1993
Angola	1 December 1976
Antigua and Barbuda	11 November 1981
Argentina	24 October 1945
Armenia	2 March 1992
Australia	1 November 1945
Austria	14 December 1955
Azerbaijan	9 March 1992
Bahamas	18 September 1973
Bahrain	21 September 1971
Bangladesh	17 September 1974
Barbados	9 December 1966
Belarus[1]	24 October 1945
Belgium	27 December 1945
Belize	25 September 1981
Benin	20 September 1960
Bhutan	21 September 1971
Bolivia	14 November 1945
Bosnia and Herzegovina[2]	22 May 1992
Botswana	17 October 1966
Brazil	24 October 1945
Brunei Darussalam	21 September 1984
Bulgaria	14 December 1955
Burkina Faso[3]	20 September 1960
Burundi	18 September 1962
Cambodia	14 December 1955
Cameroon	20 September 1960
Canada	9 November 1945
Cape Verde	16 September 1975
Central African Republic	20 September 1960
Chad	20 September 1960
Chile	24 October 1945
China[4]	24 October 1945
Colombia	5 November 1945
Comoros	12 November 1975
Congo	20 September 1960

---

[1] On 19 September 1991, Byelorussia informed the United Nations that it had changed its name to Belarus.

[2] The Socialist Federal Republic of Yugoslavia was an original member of the United Nations, the Charter having been signed on its behalf on 26 June 1945 and ratified 19 October 1945, until its dissolution following the establishment and subsequent admission as new members of Bosnia and Herzegovina, the Republic of Croatia, the Republic of Slovenia, The former Yugoslav Republic of Macedonia, and the Federal Republic of Yugoslavia. The Republic of Bosnia and Herzegovina was admitted as a member of the United Nations on 22 May 1992.

[3] Until 1984 Upper Volta.

[4] From the date of the foundation of the United Nations (24 October 1945) until 25 October 1971 the Republic of China (Taiwan) represented China in the United Nations. On 25 October 1971 by A/RES/2758 (XXVI) (1971) the General Assembly decided "to restore all its rights to the People's Republic of China and to recognize the representatives of its Government as the only legitimate representatives of China in the UN".

927

List of the Member States of the United Nations

Member States (in alphabetical order)	Date of Admission
Costa Rica	2 November 1945
Cote D'Ivoire[5]	20 September 1960
Croatia[6]	22 May 1992
Cuba	24 October 1945
Cyprus	20 September 1960
Czech Republic[7]	19 January 1993
Democratic People's Republic of Korea	17 September 1991
Democratic Republic of the Congo[8]	20 September 1960
Denmark	24 October 1945
Djibouti	20 September 1977
Dominica	18 December 1978
Dominican Republic	24 October 1945
Ecuador	21 December 1945
Egypt[9]	24 October 1945
El Salvador	24 October 1945
Equatorial Guinea	12 November 1968
Eritrea[10]	28 May 1993
Estonia	17 September 1991
Ethiopia	13 November 1945
Fiji	13 October 1970
Finland	14 December 1955
France	24 October 1945
Gabon	20 September 1960
Gambia	21 September 1965
Georgia	31 July 1992
Germany[11]	18 September 1973
Ghana	8 March 1957
Greece	25 October 1945
Grenada	17 September 1974

[5] Formerly (until 1986): Ivory Coast.

[6] The Socialist Federal Republic of Yugoslavia was an original member of the United Nations, the Charter having been signed on its behalf on 26 June 1945 and ratified 19 October 1945, until its dissolution following the establishment and subsequent admission as new members of Bosnia and Herzegovina, the Republic of Croatia, the Republic of Slovenia, The former Yugoslav Republic of Macedonia, and the Federal Republic of Yugoslavia. The Republic of Croatia was admitted as a member of the United Nations on 22 May 1992.

[7] Czechoslovakia was an original member of the United Nations from 24 October 1945. In a letter dated 10 December 1992, its Permanent Representative informed the Secretary-General that the Czech and Slovak Federal Republic would cease to exist on 31 December 1992 and that the Czech Republic and the Slovak Republic, as successor states, would apply for membership in the United Nations. Following the receipt of its application, the Security Council, on 8 January 1993, recommended to the General Assembly that the Czech Republic be admitted to United Nations membership. The Czech Republic was thus admitted on 19 January of that year as a member state.

[8] On 17 May 1997 Zaire informed the UN that it had changed its name to the Democratic Republic of the Congo.

[9] Egypt and Syria were original members of the United Nations from 24 October 1945. Following a plebiscite on 21 February 1958, the United Arab Republic was established by a union of Egypt and Syria and continued as a single member on 1 March 1958. On 13 October 1961, Syria, having resumed its status as an independent state after leaving the UAR, resumed its separate membership in the United Nations, while Egypt remained member under the name United Arab Republic. On 2 September 1971, the United Arab Republic changed its name to the Arab Republic of Egypt.

[10] On 24 May 1993 the former Ethiopian province Eritrea established itself as the independent state Eritrea and was admitted as member of the United Nations on 28 May 1993.

[11] The Federal Republic of Germany and the German Democratic Republic were admitted as two sovereign states to membership in the United Nations on 18 September 1973. Through the accession of the German Democratic Republic to the Federal Republic of Germany, effective from 3 October 1990, the two German states have united to form one sovereign state. As from the date of reunification the Federal Republic of Germany acts in the UN under the designation 'Germany'.

Member States (in alphabetical order)	Date of Admission
Guatemala	21 November 1945
Guinea	12 December 1958
Guinea-Bissau	17 September 1974
Guyana	20 September 1966
Haiti	24 October 1945
Honduras	17 December 1945
Hungary	14 December 1955
Iceland	19 November 1946
India	30 October 1945
Indonesia[12]	28 September 1950
Iran (Islamic Republic of)	24 October 1945
Iraq	21 December 1945
Ireland	14 December 1955
Israel	11 May 1949
Italy	14 December 1955
Jamaica	18 September 1962
Japan	18 December 1956
Jordan	14 December 1955
Kazakhstan	2 March 1992
Kenya	16 December 1963
Kiribati	14 September 1999
Kuwait	14 May 1963
Kyrgyzstan	2 March 1992
Lao People's Democratic Republic	14 December 1955
Latvia	17 September 1991
Lebanon	24 October 1945
Lesotho	17 October 1966
Liberia	2 November 1945
Libyan Arab Jamahiriya	14 December 1955
Liechtenstein	18 September 1990
Lithuania	17 September 1991
Luxembourg	24 October 1945
Madagascar	20 September 1960
Malawi	1 December 1964
Malaysia[13]	17 September 1957
Maldives	21 September 1965
Mali	28 September 1960
Malta	1 December 1964
Marshall Islands	17 September 1991
Mauritania	7 October 1961
Mauritius	24 April 1968
Mexico	7 November 1945
Micronesia (Federated States of)	17 September 1991
Monaco	28 May 1993
Mongolia	27 October 1961
Montenegro[14]	28 June 2006

[12] By letter of 20 January 1965, Indonesia announced its decision to withdraw from the United Nations "at this stage and under the present circumstances". By telegram of 19 September 1966, it announced its decision "to resume full cooperation with the United Nations and to resume participation in its activities". On 28 September 1966, the General Assembly took note of this decision and the President invited representatives of Indonesia to take seats in the Assembly.

[13] The Federation of Malaya joined the United Nations on 17 September 1957. On 16 September 1963, its name was changed to Malaysia, following the admission to the new federation of Singapore, Sabah (North Borneo) and Sarawak. After the separation from the Federation of Malaysia Singapore became an independent state on 9 August 1965 and a member of the United Nations on 21 September 1965.

[14] The Socialist Federal Republic of Yugoslavia was an original member of the United Nations, the Charter having been signed on its behalf on 26 June 1945 and ratified 19 October 1945, until its dissolution following the establishment and subsequent admission as new members of Bosnia and Herze-

List of the Member States of the United Nations

Member States (in alphabetical order)	Date of Admission
Morocco	12 November 1956
Mozambique	16 September 1975
Myanmar[15]	19 April 1948
Namibia	23 April 1990
Nauru	14 September 1999
Nepal	14 December 1955
Netherlands	10 December 1945
New Zealand	24 October 1945
Nicaragua	24 October 1945
Niger	20 September 1960
Nigeria	7 October 1960
Norway	27 November 1945
Oman	7 October 1971
Pakistan	30 September 1947
Palau	15 December 1994
Panama	13 November 1945
Papua New Guinea	10 October 1975
Paraguay	24 October 1945
Peru	31 October 1945
Philippines	24 October 1945
Poland[16]	24 October 1945
Portugal	14 December 1955
Qatar	21 September 1971
Republic of Korea	17 September 1991
Republic of Moldova	2 March 1992
Romania	14 December 1955
Russian Federation[17]	24 October 1945
Rwanda	18 September 1962
Saint Kitts and Nevis	23 September 1983
Saint Lucia	18 September 1979
Saint Vincent and the Grenadines	16 September 1980
Samoa	15 December 1976
San Marino	2 March 1992
Sao Tome and Principe	16 September 1975
Saudi Arabia	24 October 1945
Senegal	28 September 1960
Serbia[18]	1 November 2000

govina, the Republic of Croatia, the Republic of Slovenia, The former Yugoslav Republic of Macedonia, and the Federal Republic of Yugoslavia. In resolution A/RES/47/1 of 22 September 1992 the General Assembly decided that the Federal Republic of Yugoslavia (Serbia and Montenegro) could not automatically continue the membership of the former Socialist Federal Republic of Yugoslavia in the United Nations but should apply for membership in the UN and should not participate in the work of the General Assembly. As the UN Legal Counsel stated in a letter of 29 September 1992 the decision of the General Assembly did not terminate or suspend the member ship of Yugoslavia in the Organization nor did it take away the right of Yugoslavia to participate in the work of organs other than Assembly bodies. On 1 November 2000 the Federal Republic of Yugoslavia was admitted with resolution A/RES/55/12 to membership in the United Nations. On 4 February 2003 the Federal Republic of Yugoslavia informed the UN that it had changed its name to "Serbia and Montenegro". On 3 June 2006 the National Assembly of Montenegro declared the independence of Montenegro. The Republic of Montenegro was admitted as member to the UN on 28 June 2006 with resolution A/RES/60/264.

[15] Formerly: Burma.

[16] Although Poland was not represented at San Francisco, it was agreed that it should sign the Charter subsequently as an original member.

[17] The Union of Soviet Socialist Republics was an original member of the United Nations from 24 October 1945. In a letter dated 24 December 1991, Boris Yeltsin, the President of the Russian Federation, informed the Secretary-General that the membership of the Soviet Union in the Security Council and all other United Nations organs was being continued by the Russian Federation with the support of the 11 member countries of the Commonwealth of Independent States.

Member States (in alphabetical order)	Date of Admission
Seychelles	21 September 1976
Sierra Leone	27 September 1961
Singapore[19]	21 September 1965
Slovakia[20]	19 January 1993
Slovenia[21]	22 May 1992
Solomon Islands	19 September 1978
Somalia	20 September 1960
South Africa	7 November 1945
Spain	14 December 1955
Sri Lanka	14 December 1955
Sudan	12 November 1956
Suriname	4 December 1975
Swaziland	24 September 1968
Sweden	19 November 1946
Switzerland	10 September 2002
Syrian Arab Republic[22]	24 October 1945
Tajikistan	2 March 1992

[18] The Socialist Federal Republic of Yugoslavia was an original member of the United Nations, the Charter having been signed on its behalf on 26 June 1945 and ratified 19 October 1945, until its dissolution following the establishment and subsequent admission as new members of Bosnia and Herzegovina, the Republic of Croatia, the Republic of Slovenia, The former Yugoslav Republic of Macedonia, and the Federal Republic of Yugoslavia. In resolution A/RES/47/1 of 22 September 1992 the General Assembly decided that the Federal Republic of Yugoslavia (Serbia and Montenegro) could not automatically continue the membership of the former Socialist Federal Republic of Yugoslavia in the United Nations but should apply for membership in the UN and should not participate in the work of the General Assembly. As the UN Legal Counsel stated in a letter of 29 September 1992 the decision of the General Assembly did not terminate or suspend the member ship of Yugoslavia in the Organization nor did it take away the right of Yugoslavia to participate in the work of organs other than Assembly bodies. On 1 November 2000 the Federal Republic of Yugoslavia was admitted with resolution A/RES/55/12 to membership in the United Nations. On 4 February 2003 the Federal Republic of Yugoslavia informed the UN that it had changed its name to "Serbia and Montenegro". On 3 June the Republic of Serbia notified the UN that the membership of the State Union of Serbia and Montenegro in the UN, including all organs and organizations of the UN system, was continued by the Republic of Serbia on the basis of Article 60 of the Constitutional Charter of Serbia and Montenegro, activated by the Declaration of Independence adopted by the National Assembly of Montenegro on 3 June 2006.

[19] The Federation of Malaya joined the United Nations on 17 September 1957. On 16 September 1963, its name was changed to Malaysia, following the admission to the new federation of Singapore, Sabah (North Borneo) and Sarawak. After the separation from the Federation of Malaysia Singapore became an independent state on 9 August 1965 and a member of the United Nations on 21 September 1965.

[20] Czechoslovakia was an original member of the United Nations from 24 October 1945. In a letter dated 10 December 1992, its Permanent Representative informed the Secretary-General that the Czech and Slovak Federal Republic would cease to exist on 31 December 1992 and that the Czech Republic and the Slovak Republic, as successor states, would apply for membership in the United Nations. Following the receipt of its application, the Security Council, on 8 January 1993, recommended to the General Assembly that the Slovak Republic be admitted to United Nations membership. The Slovak Republic was thus admitted on 19 January of that year as a member state.

[21] The Socialist Federal Republic of Yugoslavia was an original member of the United Nations, the Charter having been signed on its behalf on 26 June 1945 and ratified 19 October 1945, until its dissolution following the establishment and subsequent admission as new members of Bosnia and Herzegovina, the Republic of Croatia, the Republic of Slovenia, The former Yugoslav Republic of Macedonia, and the Federal Republic of Yugoslavia. The Republic of Slovenia was admitted as a member of the United Nations on 22 May 1992.

[22] Egypt and Syria were original members of the United Nations from 24 October 1945. Following a plebiscite on 21 February 1958, the United Arab Republic was established by a union of Egypt and Syria and continued as a single member on 1 March 1958. On 13 October 1961, Syria, having resumed its status as an independent state after leaving the UAR, resumed its separate membership in the United Nations.

List of the Member States of the United Nations

Member States (in alphabetical order)	Date of Admission
Thailand	16 December 1946
The former Yugoslav Republic of Macedonia[23]	8 April 1993
Timor-Leste	27 September 2002
Togo	20 September 1960
Tonga	14 September 1999
Trinidad and Tobago	18 September 1962
Tunisia	12 November 1956
Turkey	24 October 1945
Turkmenistan	2 March 1992
Tuvalu	5 September 2000
Uganda	25 October 1962
Ukraine	24 October 1945
United Arab Emirates	9 December 1971
United Kingdom of Great Britain and Northern Ireland	24 October 1945
United Republic of Tanzania[24]	14 December 1961
United States of America	24 October 1945
Uruguay	18 December 1945
Uzbekistan	2 March 1992
Vanuatu	15 September 1981
Venezuela	15 November 1945
Viet Nam	20 September 1977

[23] The Socialist Federal Republic of Yugoslavia was an original member of the United Nations, the Charter having been signed on its behalf on 26 June 1945 and ratified 19 October 1945, until its dissolution following the establishment and subsequent admission as new members of Bosnia and Herzegovina, the Republic of Croatia, the Republic of Slovenia, The former Yugoslav Republic of Macedonia, and the Federal Republic of Yugoslavia. By resolution A/RES/47/225 of 8 April 1993, the General Assembly decided to admit as a member of the United Nations the state being provisionally referred to for all purposes within the United Nations as "The former Yugoslav Republic of Macedonia" pending settlement of the difference that had arisen over its name.

[24] Tanganyika was a member of the United Nations from 14 December 1961 and Zanzibar was a member from 16 December 1963. Following the ratification on 26 April 1964 of Articles of Union between Tanganyika and Zanzibar, the United Republic of Tanganyika and Zanzibar continued as a single member, changing its name to the United Republic of Tanzania on 1 November 1964.

Member States (in alphabetical order)	**Date of Admission**
Yemen[25]	30 September 1947
Zambia	1 December 1964
Zimbabwe	25 August 1980

---

[25] On 22 May 1990 Democratic Yemen and the Arab Republic of Yemen became a single sovereign state called the Republic of Yemen. Both had previously been members of the UN, Democratic Yemen since 14 December 1967 and the Arab Republic of Yemen since 30 September 1947. The Republic of Yemen acts in the United Nations under the designation 'Yemen'.

Information Facilities of the United Nations

I. General Enquiries

1. UN Headquarters

UN Dag Hammarskjöld Library:

United Nations Library
at Daily News Building
Room DN-2425
220 East 42nd Street
New York, N.Y. 10017
USA
Reference Services Unit:
Reference Desk
Phone: (212) 963-7412
Fax: (212) 963-8861

Directory of Services:
www.un.org/Depts/dhl/direct.htm

2. UN Libraries Central Gateway:

www.un.org/unlibraries/unlibe/index.html

3. United Nations Information Centres

Internet: http://unic.un.org

a) link to UN Information Centres (UNICs) on the web

b) link to UNIC directory

II. Inquiries concerning UN Terminology:

UNTERM is a multilingual terminology database which provides United Nations nomenclature and special terms in all six official UN languages – English, French, Spanish, Russian, Chinese and Arabic.
The database can be accessed at:
http://unterm.un.org/

III. Inquiries concerning German Translations and the German UN Terminology

Inquiries concerning German Translations and German Terminology can be addressed directly to the Germans Translation Section:
United Nations
German Translation Section
(Deutscher Übersetzungsdienst)
Room DC2-0702

New York, N.Y. 10017
USA
Fax: (1-212) 963-2577
E-mail: deutsch@un.org
Phone: (1-212) 963-2097
Internet:
www.un.org/Depts/german/e_index.html

There is also a terminology database maintained by the German Translation Section, called DETERM, which is equally accessible to the public on the Internet. This database (in English, German, French, and Spanish) contains organizational names, acronyms, conventions, declarations and other terms frequently used in the United Nations system:
DETERM: http://unhq-appspub-01.un.org/dgaacs/gts_term.nsf/

IV. Internship Programmes at the United Nations

There are internship programmes for the United Nations Secretariat as well as for other UN offices, funds and programmes.

Those interested in internship programmes at United Nations Headquarters should access the website: www.un.org/Depts/OHRM/sds/internsh/index.htm to get further information.

Students interested in interning at organizations or offices other than the UN Headquarters Secretariat should contact the respective offices directly. Information on the Internships Programmes of the different organizations and Internet links: www.un.org/esa/socdev/unyin/internships.htm

V. Information about job opportunities and job advertisements at the United Nations

On the website of the Office for Human Resources Management in the UN Secretariat in New York you can find under www.un.org/Depts/OHRM:

a) link to job vacancies of the United Nations Secretariat: http://jobs.un.org
(UN Human Resources "Galaxy" e-Staffing System)
b) link to other vacancies in the UN system: www.un.org/Depts/OHRM/indexpo.htm

c) Information about the "National Competitive Recruitment Examination" and other competitive examinations: www.un.org/Depts/OHRM/examin/exam.htm

VI. UN Documents and other UN Publications

1. Inquiries and Lending:

Inquiries about UN Documents and other UN Publications should be addressed best to the → Depositary Libraries of the United Nations. The UN texts may there be viewed by the users or borrowed or photocopied.
Further information about the UN Depositary Libraries and their addresses etc. can be found at www.un.org/Depts/dhl/deplib/index.html.

2. How to Order UN Documents and Publications:

UN Documents and Publications of the United Nations may be purchased at the UN Bookshops in New York and Geneva:

a) in New York:

United Nations Bookshop
Visitors Lobby GA-32
1st Avenue and 46th Street
New York, NY 10017
USA
Phone: 1-212-963-7680
Fax: 1-212-963-4910
Internet: https://unp.un.org/bookshop/
E-Mail: bookshop@un.org

b) in Geneva:

United Nations Bookshop
Door 40
Palais des Nations
CH-1211 Geneva 10
Phone: (41-22) 917-4872
Fax: (41-22) 917-0610
E-mail: unogbookshop@unog.ch

VII. Information through the Internet

Information about the United Nations and the organizations of the UN system in the Internet:

1. Homepage of the United Nations (www.un.org) provides access to all the Internet-Websites of the United Nations:

Topical information from the United Nations (decisions of the Un principal organs, speeches of the UN Secretary-General, press releases, press conferences, press briefings: www.un.org/News/

a) Information from UN Principal Organs:
General Assembly: www.un.org/ga/

Security Council: www.un.org/Docs/sc/

ECOSOC: www.un.org/ecosoc/

Trusteeship Council:
www.un.org/en/mainbodies/trusteeship/

Secretariat: www.un.org/en/mainbodies/secretariat/index.hmtl

Department and Offices of the Secretariat: www.un.org/Depts/

International Court of Justice (ICJ):
www.icj-cij.org/

Secretary-General: www.un.org/sg/

b) Information about UN issues:
UN reform: www.un.org/reform/

UN and international law (UN Treaties, ICJ, ICC etc.): www.un.org/en/law/index.shmtl

UN and human rights: www.un.org/en/rights/index.shmtl

UN and peace and security:
www.un.org/en/peace/

UN and humanitarian affairs:
www.un.org/en/humanitarian/

UN and economic and social development:
www.un.org/en/development/index.shmtl

Global Issues on the United Nations Agenda: alphabetical index of links to UN issues: www.un.org/en/globalissues/

UN membership: information on UN members, their permanent missions etc.:
www.un.org/en/members/index.shmtl

Global Search Engine for the UN (documents, press releases etc.):
www.un.org/en/search/index.shmtl

2. Search for UN Documents:

Helpful background information for the UN document search is provided on the website "United Nations Documentation: Research Guide" of the UN Dag Hammarskjöld Library (www.un.org/Depts/dhl/resguide/) with regard to the different types of UN texts, the respective document numbering systems

a) A useful gate way to the texts of the UN principal organs (Security Council, General Assembly, ECOSOC, Secretariat, International Court of Justice and Trusteeship Council is provided on the website *"Documents"*, available at www.un.org/en/documents/index. shmtl. Links are provided to the different types of documents of the organs (resolutions, meeting records, reports). Links to the resolutions of General Assembly and Security Council are provided for resolutions from 1946 onward, for resolutions of the ECOSOC from 2001 onward.

b) The *UN Bibliographic Information* System (UNBISNET), available at http://unbisnet. un.org, can be used as search engine to find

- *Resolutions* passed by the Security Council, the General Assembly and the ECOSOC (1946 onward);
- *Voting records* for all resolutions adopted by the General Assembly (1983 onward) and the Security Council;
- *Speeches* made in the General Assembly (1983 onward), the Security Council (1983 onward), the ECOSOC (1983 onward) and the Trusteeship Council (1982 onward.

c) The *Official Document System of the United Nations (ODS)*, available at http://documents.un.org, can be used to search for General Assembly and Security Council resolutions from 1946 onwards, for other UN documents from 1993 onwards.

3. Homepage of the UN System:

www.unsystem.org

It provides access to the Internet websites of all the organizations of the UN system:

a) Alphabetical Index of Websites of the UN System of Organizations

b) Thematic Index of Websites of the UN System of Organizations

Further information about other Internet addresses concerning the United Nations may be found in the contribution "Internet-Access/Homepage of the UN" in this encyclopedia.

VIII. Important Reference Books about the United Nations

1. topical reference literature:

United Nations Handbook, published by the New Zealand Ministry of Foreign Affairs and Trade, contains in concise form the most important topical information about the United Nations, its organs and specialized agencies, such as history, structure, membership, addresses and Internet addresses; copies may be purchased from: Ministry of Foreign Affairs and Trade, Private Bag 18-901 Wellington, New Zealand, Phone: (64 4) 439-8000, Fax: (64 4) 439-8511, E-mail: enquiries@mft.govt.nz, and New Zealand Embassies overseas; Internet website: www.mfat.govt.nz (link "publications").

2. historical:

Yearbook of the United Nations, ed. Office of Public Information, United Nations, New York. This yearly publication provides a comprehensive survey on the activities of the United Nations in the respective year.
It can be accessed via Internet:
http://unyearbook.un.org

3. for basic issues:

a) The Charter of the United Nations. A Commentary, 2nd edn., 2 Vols., ed. Bruno Simma, Oxford 2002 (renowned Charter commentary)

b) United Nations: Law, Policies and Practice. 2 Vols., ed. Rüdiger Wolfrum, (New, rev. English edn.), Munich and Dordrecht 1995 (comprehensive basic publication on the United Nations)

c) The Oxford Handbook on the United Nations, eds. Thomas G. Weiss/Sam Daws, Oxford 2007 (in-depth essays on a number of important aspects of the United Nations)

UN Documentation System

UN Document Symbols or Document Numbers: Each UN document has a document symbol or document number at the top of the title page. If issued jointly by two UN bodies, the document may have two numbers, one in the sequence of documents issued by each body, e.g. A/55/305-S/2000/809.

If reprinted as a part of the Official Records of the issuing body, the document keeps the document number.

Structure of UN Document Symbols

UN document symbols are a combination of capital letters and numbers which serve to identify the issuing body, the document type, the modifications of the original document, and the distribution category.
The different elements of the document symbol are separated by forward slashes (/).
All language versions of a document carry the same symbol.

1. The *first element* of the UN document number usually identifies the *major organizational unit* issuing the document or to which the document is being submitted:

A/-	General Assembly
S/-	Security Council
E/-	Economic and Social Council
ST/-	Secretariat
T/-	Trusteeship Council

The exception to this rule are bodies for which a *special series symbol* has been created not reflecting the parent organ. For example:

DP	United Nations Development Programme (UNDP)
CCPR	International Covenant on Civil and Political Rights
TD	United Nations Conference on Trade and Development (UNCTAD)
UNEP	United Nations Environment Programme

For example: UNEP/GC/24/INF/23; UNEP is a subsidiary organ of the General Assembly, but has its own special series symbol, not indicating the fact that UNEP has the General Assembly as parent organ.

2. Elements denoting *subsidiary organs*:

Symbols of documents from committees, commissions, or other subsidiary bodies of the five principal organs usually have an element identifying the *subsidiary body* after the symbol of the parent body, as follows:

-/AC. .../-	Ad hoc committee
-/C. .../-	Standing/permanent/main committee
-/CN. .../-	Commission

937

-/CONF. .../-	Conference
-/GC. .../-	Governing council
-/PC/. .../-	Preparatory committee
-/SC. .../-	Subcommittee
-/Sub. .../-	Subcommission
-/WG. .../-	Working group

For example: "A/CONF.157/" refers to all documents issued by the 157th conference organized by the General Assembly, the Vienna Conference on Human Rights.

3. *Type of Document*

The *type of document* may be indicated by a symbol before the sequential document number:

-/RES/-	Text of adopted resolution
-/DEC/-	Text of adopted decision
-INF/-	Information series (e.g., lists of participants)
-/NGO/-	Statement by non-governmental organizations
-/PET/-	Petition
-/PRST/-	Statement by the President of the Security Council
-/PV. ...	Verbatim record of meeting (i.e. procès-verbaux)
-/SR. ...	Summary record of meeting
-/WP. ...	Working paper
-/CRP.	Conference room paper

4. Symbol element denoting *modification of the document*:

Other symbol elements show that the original document has been changed:

-/Add. ...	Addendum
-/Amend. ...	Alteration, by decision of a competent authority, of a portion of an adopted formal text
-/Corr. ...	Corrigendum (which may not apply to all language versions)
-/Rev. ...	Revision (replacing texts previously issued)
-/Summary	Summarized version
-/-*	Reissuance of a document for technical reasons

5. Symbol elements denoting *distribution category*:

These letters indicate how widely the documents were distributed:

-/L.	Limited (limited distribution, for example draft texts); thought for distribution at UN headquarters or at meetings and not considered to be of general interest
-/R.	Restricted (confidential papers, only restricted distribution)

6. Symbol elements denoting *session* or *year*:

a) *General Assembly documents*:
Since 1976 (31st session) the second major element of a General Assembly document number indicates the session. Individual documents are then numbered chronologically within the session (e.g. A/59/2000).
Prior to 1976, General Assembly documents were numbered continuously from the first session (e.g. A/PV.3).

Since 1978 (8th special session), *General Assembly special session documents* carry an "S-" and the number of the special session (e.g. A/S-8/5). Since 1980 *General Assembly emergency special session documents* carry an "ES-" and the number of the emergency special session (e.g. A/ES-6/1).

Resolutions of the General Assembly have the element "RES" after the first element "A", the resolutions prior to 1976 followed directly by the sequential number of the resolution and the number of the session in roman numbers in brackets, e.g. A/RES/2847 (XXVI), the resolutions since 1976 carry after the element "RES" first the number of the session and then the sequential number, e.g. A/RES/60/1.

b) *Security Council documents:* Prior to 1994 Security Council documents had the structure "S/(sequential number)", e.g. S/4573.
Since 1994 the second major element of a Security Council document indicates the year, e.g. S/1994/308, with the exception of the Security Council resolutions:
resolutions of the Security Council have the element "RES" after the first element "S", followed directly by the sequential number of the resolution and the year of adoption in brackets, e.g. S/RES/157 (1960).

c) *Economic and Social Council (ECOSOC) documents:* Since 1978 the second major element of an ECOSOC document number indicates the year of a meeting, followed by a sequential number for the year, e.g. E/1980/1.
Resolutions of the ECOSOC have the element "RES" after the first element "E", followed by the year of the adoption and the sequential number of the resolution, e.g. E/RES/1996/31.

Examples:
A/C.2./48/SR.5 = Summary Record of the 5th meeting of the Second Committee of the General Assembly during the 48th session of the GA
A/34/355 = General Assembly, 34th session, 355th document issued in the session
A/RES/60/1 = General Assembly, 60th session, first resolution
E/1980/SR.34 = Economic and Social Council, Summary Record of the 34th meeting of the Council in the 1980 annual session
A/59/PV.114 = Verbatim record of the 114th meeting of the 59th session of the General Assembly

Contributing Authors

Altenburg, Günther, Dr., Ambassador (ret.), 2001-2005 Assistant Secretary-General for Political Affairs and Security Policy at NATO, Brussels; in his diplomatic career he served, *inter alia*, in the following functions: 1983-1984 Deputy Head of the Division for Disarmament and Arms Control in the United Nations in the Federal Foreign Office; 1988-1992 Deputy Head of the Delegation of the FRG at the CSCE-Conferences in Vienna and Helsinki; 1992-1997 Head of the UN Policy Division in the Federal Foreign Office; 1998-2001 Head of the Department for Global Issues, the United Nations, Human Rights and Humanitarian Aid in the Federal Foreign Office of Germany in Berlin.

Arnold, Hans, Dr., Ambassador (ret.), Lecturer at the College for Politics, Munich.

Betz, Joachim, Professor Dr. rer. soc., Principal Research Fellow, German Institute of Global and Area Studies, University of Hamburg.

Beyerlin, Ulrich, Professor Dr. jur., Professor of Law at the Max Planck Institute for Comparative Public Law and International Law, and at the University of Heidelberg.

Blätte, Andreas, Professor Dr., 1996-2001 study of political science, European law and economics from 1996-2001 in Munich and at the University of Wales, Aberystwyth; 2001-2009 research and teaching assistant at the Chair for Comparative Government, Faculty for Law, Economics and Sociology of the University of Erfurt; since 2009 junior professor for political science at the Institute for Political Sciences of the University Duisburg-Essen.

Boor, Felix, Assessor iur., study of law of the universities of Göttingen and Geneva; legal clerkship at the District Court (Landgericht) in Kassel; employment at an internationally active law firm in Göttingen; since December 2007 teaching and research assistant at the Department of Public Law, Ruhr University Bochum (Germany) in the fields of European law, international public law and international economic law (Chair Professor Dr. Adelheid Puttler, LL.M.); fields of research: international economic law, in particular the international arbitration procedure, and international humanitarian law.

Bottigelli, Daniela, M.A. in political science and international law, Faculty of Political Sciences, University of Milan, Italy; Training Associate, International Law Programme, Peace, Security and Diplomacy Unit, United Nations Institute for Training and Research (UNITAR).

Boven, Theo van, Professor Dr. iur., M.L., Dr. h. c. mult., Professor of International Law, Faculty of Law at University of Maastricht; Representative of the Netherlands on the UN Commission on Human Rights 1970-1975; Director of the UN Division of Human Rights 1977-1982; Special Rapporteur on the Right of Reparation for Victims of Gross Violations of Human Rights 1989-1993; Registrar of the Ad Hoc International Criminal Tribunal for the Former Yugoslavia 1994; Member of the Committee on the Elimination of Racial Discrimination 1992-2000; Special Rapporteur on torture and other cruel, inhuman or degrading treatment or punishment 2001-2004.

Brauch, Hans Günter, Dr. phil. habil., PD (Adjunct Professor), Otto Suhr Institute for Political Science, Free University Berlin; Chairman, Peace Research and European Security Studies (AFES-PRESS) e.V.; Senior Academic Consultant & CASA Fellow, UNU-EHS, Bonn; Editor of the Hexagon Book Series; 1989-1998 Guest Professor at the universities of Frankfurt, Leipzig and Greifswald, and at the Teachers Training College in Erfurt.

Brecht, Eberhard, Dr. rer. nat., Quedlinburg, 1990 - July 2001 Member of the German Federal Parliament (Deutscher Bundestag); September 1991 - July 2001 Chairman of the Subcommittee on United Nations/International Organizations of the Committee on Foreign Relations of the German Federal Parliament; Deputy Spokesman of Foreign Relations of the SPD Parliamentary Group; since July 2001 Mayor of the town Quedlinburg.

Dicke, Klaus, Professor Dr., Institute for Political Science, Friedrich Schiller University of Jena; Chairman of the Deutsche Gesellschaft für die Vereinten Nationen (German Association for the United Nations); numerous publications on political theories and the history of ideas, international relations, in particular on the organization and activities of the UN.

Dippel, Anne Kathrin, M.A., study of political science, law and economics in Munich and Edinburgh. After attending the German School for Journalism in Munich she works as a journalist in Hamburg.

Dülffer, Jost, Professor Dr., Professor of Modern History, Historisches Seminar, Universität zu Köln (Historical Institute of the University of Cologne).

Ehrhart, Wolfgang, Expert on the United Nations of the SPD-Parliamentary Group in the Deutsche Bundestag (German Federal Parliament), Berlin.

Eisele, Manfred, Assistant Secretary-General for Planning and Support (ret.) Department of Peacekeeping Operations, United Nations, New York; General (Ret.); Freelance Lecturer, *inter alia* at the NATO Defence College Rome, the Staff Academy of the Bundeswehr (German Federal Army), Hamburg, universities, political academies and endowments, counsellor for the fields international politics, strategy, logistics, holder of the Dag Hammarskjöld Honorary Medal of the Deutsche Gesellschaft für die Vereinten Nationen.

Fassbender, Bardo, Dr. jur. (Berlin), LL.M. (Yale), Professor of International Law, Institute of Public and International Law, Universität der Bundeswehr München (University of the Federal Armed Forces Munich).

Fastenrath, Ulrich, Professor of Constitutional, European Community and Public International Law, Law School, University of Dresden.

Ferdowsi, Mir A., Professor Dr., Professor for Political Science, Ludwig Maximilians University of Munich.

Fröhlich, Manuel, Professor Dr. phil., Professor for International Organization and Globalization, Department of Political Science, Friedrich-Schiller-University, Jena.

Fues, Thomas, Dr., since 2004 Senior Fellow at German Development Institute (DIE), Bonn; main research interests: global governance, emerging powers, United Nations and international development cooperation; his recent publications include articles on G8 reform, the role of China and India in the global system, the UN development sector as well as on human rights and global governance. In addition to his research tasks, Dr. Fues is responsible for the Global Governance School at the German Development Institute as part of the training and dialogue programme "Managing Global Governance" with young professionals from governments and think-tanks of emerging economies.

Gastaut, Thérèse, holds a diploma from the Institute of Political Sciences from Paris and a Masters Degree from the School of International Affairs at Columbia University, New York. Thérèse Gastaut joined the Secretariat of the United Nations in 1967. In the course of her 37-year career with the United Nations, she served in a number of senior positions: from 1984 to 1989, she headed the UN Information Service at Geneva. Prior to this, she held posts in New York and Brussels. From 1990 to1992, she served as Chief of Information of the World Health Organization (WHO). From 1993 to 1996, Ms. Gastaut was spokeswoman for the Secretary-General of the United Nations, Dr. Boutros Boutros-Ghali, based in Geneva. She was also the Director of the Information Service of the United Nations Office at Geneva. In addition to her regular duties, she served as spokeswoman for the World Conference on Human Rights in Vienna in 1993 and the Fourth World Conference on Women in Beijing in 1995. From 1999 to 2004, she was Director of the Strategic Communications Division of the Department of Public Information (DPI) at the United Nations in New York. During this period, Ms. Gastaut was in charge of the promotional campaign for the Millennium Summit (2000), for which she was the spokeswoman, as well as of information programmes for United Nations conferences and such initiatives as the Special Session of the General Assembly on HIV/AIDS (2001), the World Summit on Sustainable Development (2002), and the World Summit on the Information Society (2003-2005). Thérèse Gastaut is currently giving post-graduate and PhD courses on multilateral diplomacy, global governance and communications in international organisations at public and private universities in Paris.

Göthel, Dieter, Assistant Secretary-General and President of the Staff-Management Coordination Committee in the UN Secretariat; more than 35 years' experience in the UN System, mostly in management positions including Director of Human Resources at the IAEA, Vienna, Chief of Personnel in ICAO, Montreal, moderator and spokesperson of the UN System Human Resources Network (a subsidiary of the CEB), chairman of the UN Joint Staff Pension Fund and others.

Grote, Jenny, LL.M., Maître en Droit, Research Fellow at the Max Planck Institute for Comparative Public Law and International Law, Heidelberg.

Haedrich, Martina, Professor Dr., Professor of Public and International Law at the Friedrich Schiller University of Jena.

Heideking, Jürgen, †, Professor Dr., Anglo-American Department of the Historical Seminar of the University of Cologne.

Heintze, Hans-Joachim, Dr. iur. habil., Institute for International Law of Peace and Armed Conflict, Ruhr University of Bochum.

Henn, Heike, Dr., Dipl.-Sozialwiss., German Federal Ministry for Economic Cooperation and Development, Bonn.

Hennings, Antje, Ass. Iur., 1999-2004: legal studies at the law schools of the Universities of Göttingen and Aarhus, Denmark; 2004 First State Law Exam; 2005-2006

Ph.D.-candidate, Institute of International Law, chair of Professor Dr. Peter-Tobias Stoll, University of Göttingen; 2006-2008 legal clerk in the district of the Court of Appeals Braunschweig (OLG), as such deputized i.a. to the Deutsche Hochschule für Verwaltungswissenschaften in Speyer (DHV) and to the Bundesministrium des Innern, Berlin; 2008 Second State Law Exam (Assessor Iuris); since 2008 graduate assistant at the Institute of International Law, University of Göttingen.

Hildebrand, Marius, Student, study of geography, political science and Romance languages and literatures at the Albert-Ludwigs-University Freiburg/Breisgau.

Hoffmann, Friederike, Dipl.-Pol., project manager, Stiftung Charité, Berlin. She studied in Berlin and Istanbul and worked at the Herbert Quandt Endowment and the Gesellschaft für Technische Zusammenarbeit (GTZ) in Berlin, the San Francisco State University, as well as for the Office of the High Representative and the Council of Europe in Sarajevo.

Hoffmeister, Frank, Professor Dr., studied law in Frankfurt (Main), Geneva and Heidelberg (1989-1994). He was a researcher at the Max Planck Institute for Foreign Public Law and International Law in Heidelberg (1994-1996), writing a PhD dissertation on "Human Rights and Democracy Clauses in the external relations of the European Community". He obtained admission to the bar ("second state examen") in Berlin (1998) and worked as a scientific assistant at the Chair for European and International Law at the Humboldt-University (1999-2001). In 2001, he joined the European Commission, serving as an official in the Directorates General for Enlargement and of the Legal Service. Since 2006 he also teaches international economic law at the Free University of Brussels.

Hofner, Barbara, M.A. (International Relations).

Holbrook, Sherry, Legal Officer, Treaty Section, Office of Legal Affairs, United Nations, New York.

Hüfner, Klaus, former Professor at the Free University Berlin; Honorary President of the World Federation of the United Nations Associations – WFUNA (Geneva/New York); former President of the German Commission for UNESCO (Bonn); Senior Research Fellow of the Global Policy Forum (New York).

Jetzlsperger, Christian, German diplomat; he served at the German Embassy in Tirana (Albania) and the Federal Foreign Office in Berlin and is currently posted to the German Embassy in Kabul (Afghanistan); a graduate in history and political sciences, he has published various books and articles on European integration, international relations, and contemporary German history.

Junker, Denise, Student, study of political science (herein main subject: international relations and UN and international law) at the University of Potsdam; work as student staff member at the Herbert Quandt Endowment, Berlin.

Kaltenbach, Egbert C., lawyer by education (legal studies in Cologne, Geneva and Saarbrücken); he has been in government audit, both external and internal, for more than 20 years. Prior to his current function as Director of the Office of Audit and Investigations of the United Nations Development Programme (UNDP), he was the Executive Secretary of the Geneva based Joint Inspection Unit (JIU). From 1995-2005 he served in various functions at the United Nations Office of Internal Oversight Services (OIOS), both in Geneva and in New York. Prior to joining the United Nations, Mr. Kaltenbach was a member of the German Federal Court of Audit, serving in various positions, *inter alia* as Head of the Court's International Relations Department.

Kämmerer, Jörn Axel, Professor Dr. iur., Maître en droit, holder of the Chair for Public Law, Public International Law and European Law at Bucerius Law School, Hamburg.

Kaul, Inge, Dr., Adjunct Professor, Hertie School of Governance, Berlin.

Klein, Eckart, Professor (emeritus), Dr. iur., Faculty of Law and Director of Human Rights Centre of the University of Potsdam; Member of the United Nations Human Rights Committee 1995-2002.

Klingebiel, Stephan, Dr., political scientist, working as head of department at the German Development Institute (GDI) in Bonn. He is currently on leave and leading an office of a development organization in Kigali, Rwanda. In his research work he has taken a particular interest in the debate on possible contributions of development cooperation to crisis prevention and conflict management, and on the effectiveness and reform of the United Nations development cooperation.

Knapp, Manfred, Dr., Professor (emeritus), Institute for International Politics, Helmut-Schmidt-Universität (University of the Bundeswehr (Federal Armed Forces) Hamburg.

Kohrs, Ramona, Librarian (MLS), has been working at the Dag Hammarskjöld Library at United Nations Headquarters in New York in various capacities since 1989.

Kolk, Gregor, M.A., Munich.

Koppe, Karlheinz, Professor Dr. h.c., senior lecturer (ret.) at the University of Münster (peace research).

Kotthaus, Hans Peter, retired United Nations official; 1991-1998 Chief External Relations Office of the United Nations Relief and Works Agency for Palestine Refugees in the Near East (UNRWA) Vienna/Gaza 1991–1998; 1982-1991 Secretary General of the Parliamentary Association for Euro-Arab Cooperation, Paris/Brussels.

Körppen, Daniela, works as a researcher for the Berghof Foundation for Peace Support (BFPS). She is coordinating an action research project on systemic conflict transformation, which explores the potential of systemic thinking for conflict transformation strategies. The main idea of this project is to further develop the framework of a systemic approach to conflict transformation. She takes special interest in practice-oriented research and in developing methodologies for conflict analysis and evaluation. In her PhD project she is working on the development of a systemic-constructivistic framework for the analysis and transformation of political conflicts. Daniela Körppen joined the BFPS in 2005. She graduated in sociology and Latin American studies (M.A.) and in peace and conflict studies (M.A.). She has several years of work experience as a journalist.

Kreisel, Wilfried, Dr., Former Exececutive Director, World Health Organization, Geneva, Switzerland.

Kulessa, Manfred, Dr.iur., author and consultant to UN, governments, churches and and NGOs; Managing Director of German Volunteer Service (1969-74), director in UNDP (1974-88), UN coordinator in China; Honorary Consul of Bhutan in Bonn (2000-2008).

Lassen, Hans J., 1969-1974 Press Section of the Federal Ministry for Economic Cooperation and Development in Bonn; 1974-1985 establishment of a German-speaking information unit in Geneva; 1985-1996 Spokesman of the UN Economic Commission for Europe (ECE), 1997 temporarily with the Information

Staff of the UN Transitional Administration for East Slavonia UNTAES; since April 1999 work as freelance journalist and organizational counsellor in Geneva.

Lodgaard, Sverre, 1971 M.A. (political science), University of Oslo; 1980-1986 Head of European Security and Disarmament Studies at the Stockholm International Peace Research Institute (SIPRI); 1987-1992 Director of the International Peace Research Institute, Oslo (PRIO); 1992-1996 Director of the United Nations Institute for Disarmament Research (UNIDIR); 1997-2007 Director of the Norwegian Institute of International Affairs (NUPI) Oslo; 1992-1999 Member of the UN Secretary General's Advisory Board on Disarmament; latest book: Nuclear proliferation and International Security, New York 2007.

Löwe, Volker, Dr., Senate Chancellery of Berlin, Head of the Bureau of the Bundesland (Federal State) Berlin at the European Union, Brussels.

Maier, Jürgen, Director of the German NGO Forum Environment & Development (Forum Umwelt & Entwicklung; www.forumue.de) in Berlin. This network has been coordinating the participation of German NGOs in international negotiations relevant to sustainable development since 1992.

Melchers, Konrad, Dr. rer. pol., Member of the Executive Board of the Third World Journalists Network, Berlin.

Metzger, Martina, Dr., is with the Berlin Institute of Financial Market Research (BIF). Before joining BIF, she was Assistant Professor for Macroeconomics at the University of Applied Science in Berlin. She previously served as a research fellow and lecturer at the Department of Economics of the Free University of Berlin, of which she holds a PhD, and the Berlin School of Economics. She was also with UNCTAD (Geneva) and worked as a consultant for several governmental and non-governmental institutions. She has widely published on exchange rate regimes, regional monetary and financial integration in Africa and Asia and development theory.

Mittermaier, Jana, study of political science, public international law and communication science at the Ludwig Maximilians University of Munich; Head of the Transparency International Brussels Office at the European Union.

Morphet, Sally, was educated in the Middle East, the United States and the United Kingdom. She worked as a research analyst in the United Kingdom Foreign and Commonwealth from the mid-60s until her retirement in 2000. Within the FCO, she first specialized in South and South-East Asia, and from 1974, in general international and UN questions besides becoming a Board member of ACUNS (Academic Council on the UN System). She has since worked on a freelance basis and for two three-year terms as a Visiting Professor of the University of Kent. She has published articles and chapters on human rights, the environment, NGOs, the non-aligned, peacekeeping and the Security Council. She is co-author of a book on The South in World Politics, due to come out in 2009.

Naumann, Jens, Professor Dr., former Professor at the Department of Education and Social Sciences, University of Münster, Germany, active member of the Deutsche Gesellschaft für die Vereinten Nationen (German United Nations Association) since 1960.

Neugebauer, Bernhard Robert, Dr. rer. pol., Dipl.-Pol., Berlin; Diplomatic Service of the GDR 1953 –1990, *inter alia*: Representative of the GDR at the United Nations, president of diverse UN organs; Chairman of the UNESCO Commission of the GDR; Deputy Foreign Minister of the GDR.

Neutz, Sabrina, student at Free University of Berlin; study of geography (main subject: development research) and of contemporary German literature for M.A. degree, Berlin.

Nuscheler, Franz Dr., Professor Emeritus, Senior Fellow at the Institute for Development and Peace (INEF) of the University of Duisburg-Essen; Senior Fellow of the Johannes Kepler University, Linz, Austria.

Oellers-Frahm, Karin, Dr. iur., Max-Planck-Institute for Comparative Public Law and International Law, Heidelberg.

Opitz, Peter J., Dr. phil., Professor (emeritus), 1966 Doctor of Philosophy in Political Science, Sinology and Philosophy; 1966/67 Research Fellow at the University of California, Berkeley; 1971 Habilitation (appointment as University lecturer) in the Faculty of Political Economy, Ludwig Maximilians University of Munich, Venia Legendi for Political Science; 1977 Professorship in Political Science at the Geschwister Scholl Institute of Political Science, Ludwig Maximilians University of Munich; Lecturer at the College of Political Science/Munich; Member of the Scientific Directorate of the Federal Institute for International and East European Studies/Cologne from 1984 until 1992; Member of the Advisory Board on UN Affairs of the German Federal Foreign Office and of the Federal Ministry for Economic Cooperation Affairs in Bonn; numerous publications on the United Nations, Asian issues (foreign policy, economics, culture) and development problems.

Ott, Patrick Oliver, M.A., M.P.A.; former member of State Parliament in Saxony (1990-1994), degrees from Ludwig Maximilians University of Munich (Master of Arts in political sciences), Harvard Law School (International Tax Programme, Class of 2000), Harvard John F. Kennedy School (Master of Public Administration); fields of expertise: international trade, international taxation, strategic negotiation and mediation.

Pallek, Markus, is a legal officer with the Office of the Under-Secretary-General (OUSG) in the Office of Legal Affairs (OLA) of the United Nations Secretariat in New York. In this capacity he assists the Legal Counsel of the United Nations, Ms. Patricia O'Brien, in the discharge of her responsibilities as Head of the Office of Legal Affairs and member of the Secretary-General's senior management team. Mr. Pallek is a member of the New York and District of Columbia Bars and is also qualified to practice law in his home country Germany. He is Ancien Elève de l'Ecole Nationale d'Administration (*Promotion René Cassin*) in Paris and Strasbourg/France and holds a Master of Public Administration (MPA) from that school. Moreover, he earned a Master of Laws (LL.M.) from New York University - School of Law and a Doctorate in Law from the Faculty of Law of the University of Würzburg/Germany.

Paqué, Ruprecht, Dr. phil., Düsseldorf; Founding Chief of the German Translation Section at the United Nations Secretariat, New York 1975-1985.

Prantl, Jochen, Dr., Acting Director of the Centre for International Studies, Senior Research Fellow in International Relations and Fellow of Nuffield College, University of Oxford.

Reichenstein, Birgit, economist, Deutsche Bundesbank (German Federal Bank), International Relations Department, Frankfurt (Main).

Reinery, Isabelle, M.A., study of political science, international law and international communication at the Ludwig Maximilians University of Munich.

Reschke, Brigitte, Editor Law, Springer-Verlag, Heidelberg.

Ropers, Norbert, Dr. phil., Director of the Sri Lanka Office of the Berghof Foundation for Conflict Studies, Sri Lanka.

Roth, Andrea, M.A. (Master of Arts) in political science of the Ludwig Maximilians University of Munich; journalist working for the Bavarian Television Programme (Bayerisches Fernsehen), Munich.

Schattenmann, Marc, Dr., M.A., Junior Professor for Public Policy at the University of Erfurt until autumn 2008; since then work in the administration of the Deutsche Bundestag (German Federal Parliament).

Schmidl, Erwin A., Dr. phil. habil., Head of the Department of Contemporary History at the Austrian National Defence Academy in Vienna, lecturer at the universities of Innsbruck, Graz and Vienna; previously served in various capacities in the Austrian Ministry of Defence. 1995-96 Senior Fellow at the U.S. Institute of Peace in Washington D.C.; 1994 UN Observer Mission in South Africa, 1991-92 seconded to Austrian Ministry of Foreign Affairs, UN Department. Since 1990 research on peace operations.

Schorlemer, Sabine von, Professor Dr. Dr., Professor for International Law, Law of the European Union and International Relations; Director of the Research Center "United Nations" of the Faculty of Law, Technical University of Dresden.

Schöpp-Schilling, Hanna Beate, Dr. phil., Consultant/Lecturer in Human Rights, Wohltorf, Germany; Member (Expert) in the Committee on the Elimination of Discrimination Against Women (CEDAW) 1989-2008.

Schulze, Peter M., Dr. paed., M.A. (Notre Dame), Grammar School Teacher, Zeuthen near Berlin.

Schwanitz, Simone, Dr. phil., Head of the Staff Bureau for Supraregional Coordination in the Ministry for Education, Science, Youth and Culture of the State Government of Rheinland-Pfalz (Rhineland-Palatinate), Mainz.

Simma, Bruno, Professor Dr. iur. (Doctorate of Law, University of Innsbruck, Austria 1966); Judge at the International Court of Justice in The Hague since 2003; Professor of International Law and European Community Law, Director of the Institute of International Law, University of Munich (1973-2003); Member of the United Nations Committee on Economic, Social and Cultural Rights (1987-1996); Member of the United Nations International Law Commission (1996-2003).

Spröte, Wolfgang, Dr. sc. pol., Potsdam; Professor (emeritus) for International Economic Organizations; participation in sessions of the UN General Assembly and other UN organs; Vice-Chairman, *inter alia*, of the Special Sessions of the Commission for Transnational Corporations 1983-1990; Vice-President of the Liga der Vereinten Nationen (League of the United Nations) of the GDR.

Stiel, Ursula, M.A. (political science), Munich.

Stoll, Peter-Tobias, Professor Dr. iur., Institute for International Law and European Law of the University of Göttingen.

Strauss, Ekkehard, Dr. iur., Human Rights Officer, Office of the High Commissioner for Human Rights, United Nations, New York.

Sultan-Khan, Athar, a graduate in international affairs (law and diplomacy) from Columbia University in New York, is the Chef de Cabinet of UNHCR since June 2002. Before this appointment, he held various positions in UNHCR, since joining in 1979 in New York, including, Representative in Algeria; Coordinator for the Western Sahara; Head of Desk for the Middle East and North Africa; Deputy Regional Representative and Coordinator for South-East Asia in Malaysia; Head of Recruitment in the Division of Human Resources Management; and Field Officer posts in Sudan, the Democratic Republic of Congo, Cameroon and Somalia.

Swamy Meier-Ewert, Gita, political scientist (Dipl. Pol), United Nations Development Programme, Geneva.

Talmon, Stefan, D.Phil., LL.M, M.A., Professor of Public International Law, University of Oxford; Barrister, 20 Essex Street Chambers, London.

Tams, Christian J., Dr. LL.M. (Cambridge); Lecturer, Walter Schücking Institute for International Law, University of Kiel.

Theodoridis, Alexander, M.A., M.Sc. (University of Munich).

Unser, Günther, Dr. rer. pol., Senior Lecturer on Political Science, Institute of Political Science, University of Technology of Aachen.

Urquhart, Sir Brian, Scholar-in-Residence at the International Affairs Programme of the Ford Foundation, New York; Member of the Secretariat of the United Nations 1945-1986, Under-Secretary-General for Special Political Affairs 1974-1986.

Volger, Helmut, Dr. phil., Falkensee near Berlin; Coordinator of the Forschungskreis Vereinte Nationen (Research Group United Nations); scientific author since 1987; numerous publications on the United Nations.

Walter, Marina, M.A. of Vanderbilt University, Nashville/USA; Diploma in Political Science, Otto Suhr Institute for Political Science, Free University of Berlin; previously (or former) Programme Officer at the United Nations Institute for Training and Research (UNITAR).

Weggel, Oskar, Dr. iur., Institut für Asienkunde (Institute for Asian Studies), University of Hamburg; expert for China and Indochina.

Weinz, Irene, Dipl.-Pol., 1999-2005: studies of political science at Freie Universität Berlin and Charles University Prague, 2005-2007: research assistant at the Law Faculty of Freie Universität Berlin, since 2007 working at the program area International Relations Western Europe, America, Turkey, Japan, India at Robert Bosch Stiftung, Stuttgart.

Weiß, Norman, Dr. iur. habil., Human Rights Centre of the University of Potsdam.

Weisser, Claudia Shirin, Rechtsreferendarin (legal clerk), Deisenhofen.

Wesel, Reinhard, M.A., Dr. phil. (political science); since 1983 research assistant at the Ludwig-Maximilians-Universität München; since 1996 Assistant Professor at the University of Magdeburg; research areas and publications: political theory, political symbolism and symbolic politics (political metaphors, political rituals), development policy, United Nations/Model United Nations.

Winkelmann, Ingo, J.D. (Freiburg i.Br.); Head of the Law of the Sea Division, German Federal Foreign Office, Berlin; 1995-1998 Counsellor at the Permanent Mission of the Federal Republic of Germany at the United Nations in New York.

Wölte, Sonja, Dr., freelance author, researcher and consultant for women's and gender issues, human rights and gender and development.

Wüstenhagen, Axel, Dr. jur., 1966-72 Secretary-General of the Austrian United Nations Association; joined UN service in 1972 and served in various information capacities with the UN Industrial Development Organization (UNIDO) and the UN in Vienna;1990-93 Director, UN Information Centre Athens (serving Greece,

Israel and Cyprus; Spokesman for UN humanitarian relief operations in Amman, Jordan, during the Gulf War; 1993-96, Director, UN Information Service Vienna (serving Austria, Germany and Hungary); 1996-2003 Director, United Nations Information Centre Bonn.

Zayas, Alfred de, J.D. (Harvard), Dr. phil. (Göttingen), member New York Bar, Florida Bar. 1980-2003 lawyer with the Division/Centre/Office of the UN High Commissioner for Human Rights, Geneva, Chief of the Petitions Section and Secretary of the UN Human Rights Committee; Visiting Professor for International Law at DePaul (Chicago), University of British Columbia (Vancouver), Institut Universitaire des Hautes Etudes Internationales (Geneva); since 2005 Professor at the Geneva School of Diplomacy; Member of the Advisory Board of the Académie Internationale de Droit Constitutionnel; President, P.E.N: International, Centre Suisse Romande.

Zitka, Frank, Dr., Spokesman, Deutscher Beamten-Bund (German Civil Service Federation), Berlin.

Index

The names of the keywords (entries) of the encyclopedia are printed in bold type as well as the corresponding page numbers.